THE PAPERS OF
THOMAS JEFFERSON

THE PAPERS OF
Thomas Jefferson

Volume 1 · 1760-1776

JULIAN P. BOYD, EDITOR

LYMAN H. BUTTERFIELD AND MINA R. BRYAN,

ASSOCIATE EDITORS

PRINCETON, NEW JERSEY

PRINCETON UNIVERSITY PRESS

1950

Printed in the United States of America by
Princeton University Press, Princeton, New Jersey

DEDICATED TO THE MEMORY OF

ADOLPH S. OCHS

PUBLISHER OF THE NEW YORK TIMES

1896-1935

WHO BY THE EXAMPLE OF A RESPONSIBLE

PRESS ENLARGED AND FORTIFIED

THE JEFFERSONIAN CONCEPT

OF A FREE PRESS

A GENERAL VIEW OF
THE WORK

THE PURPOSE OF THIS WORK is to present the writings and recorded actions of Thomas Jefferson as accurately and as completely as possible. Completeness in such a task, even for one who transmitted to posterity so full a record as Jefferson did, is only theoretically possible. "A great deal of the knolege of things," Jefferson once wrote Joel Barlow in an effort to persuade him to write a history of the American Revolution, "is not on paper but only within ourselves, for verbal communication."[1] He might have added that, so far as posterity was concerned, much was not communicable at all, verbally or otherwise. But few if any of Jefferson's contemporaries recognized an obligation to history so clearly as he did, and none exceeded him in his effort to discharge the debt. His aid to historians such as Girardin, Hazard, Ramsay, Wirt, and others; his indefatigable labors as a young lawyer in transcribing the ancient manuscript laws of Virginia; his answers to the queries of Marbois which resulted in one of the notable books of the eighteenth century; his compilation of vocabularies of Indian dialects; his meticulous care in recording the fullest and most exact account of the debates on the Declaration of Independence; his making available the best private library in America as the foundation of our national library; his copying, indexing, and organizing the vast number of letters, memoranda, accounts, and records in his personal files—these and countless other acts, performed throughout his career and at the cost of an untold amount of time and energy, reveal the consciousness of his effort to preserve for posterity a full account of the major events through which the country passed in its formative years and of his own part in those events.

Because of this conscious effort and because of his complete identity with the national purpose as it was pursued during his day, this and succeeding volumes take on significant meaning. They are, first of all, the record of a man's career—a record which, in the accepted opinion of a competent scholar, constitutes "the richest treasure house of historical information ever left by a single man."[2] But also, since the achievements of Jefferson's long career were

[1] To Joel Barlow, 3 May 1802.
[2] Chinard, *Thomas Jefferson*, Boston, 1929, p. xvi.

extraordinarily fruitful, these volumes may be regarded as being, in part, a record of the origin, formation, and early growth of the Republic. More, they may be taken as being the best single gateway to the eighteenth century in America and to the manifold hopes then stirring the minds of men that reason and justice could be substituted for authority and superstition in guiding human affairs.

Yet, above all, these volumes should be regarded as the embodiment of an idea. They need to be viewed so if only because Jefferson's remarkable versatility and the very mass of evidence tend to obscure the nature of the idea. The generally accepted opinion of Jefferson as a versatile genius whose all-embracing mind explored every avenue of science and culture, much of which he enriched and all of which he gathered within the orbit of his lofty purpose, is indubitably correct and is amply set forth in these volumes. Parton's description of him as "a gentleman of thirty-two who could calculate an eclipse, survey an estate, tie an artery, plan an edifice, try a cause, break a horse, dance a minuet, and play the violin" is, for all its incongruity, only a partial picture. Among all Jefferson's contemporaries in America, if not among all who preceded and followed him, only Franklin could be said to approach him in the extent and variety of his inquiry. To catalogue the areas of his explorations is to list most of the principal categories of knowledge —law, government, history, mathematics, architecture, medicine, agriculture, languages and literature, education, music, philosophy, religion, and almost every branch of the natural sciences from astronomy through meteorology to zoology. Yet, in the twentieth century when the vast accumulation of knowledge has made universal inquiry impossible and specialization inevitable, versatility is too likely to be regarded either as an accomplishment reserved to the geniuses of the earth, and therefore inaccessible to the generality of human beings, or as a fruitless dispersal of energy through meaningless inquiry, and therefore not to be emulated.

To view Jefferson's versatile and endless inquiries from either point of view would be to run the risk of unduly magnifying his genius or, worse, to miss its central meaning. That he possessed many of the qualities of a genius is plain; the drafting of the Declaration of Independence and the invention of a cryptographic device more than a century in advance of his time[3]—to take two wholly

[3] "Jefferson's invention of the *Wheel Cypher* represents a contribution to cryptographic science so far in advance of his time that at least a century had to elapse before a similar invention was independently made by a second inventor in the field" (extracted from a communication to the editors, 17 Nov. 1949, from William F. Friedman, Chief of the Technical Division, Armed Forces Security Agency).

unrelated examples—are surely evidences of an elevated and even inspired intellect. But his natural genius was supported by indefatigable industry, an industry exhibited with such unremitting application as to be almost without parallel. In this varied and ceaseless pursuit of knowledge, ramifying in all directions, Jefferson nevertheless rarely if ever revealed the defects of his virtues. Omnivorous of knowledge, he was the least pedantic of men and scornful of ostentatious learning; a prodigious transcriber of statutes, he was never an unimaginative drudge; a zealous traveler who delighted in new scenes and took countless notes on his journeys, he was far removed from the mere gazers at new sights; an unrivaled collector of books about his own country and about every subject of human thought, he never descended to bibliolatry; a legislator and therefore a politician, he was recognized and respected as one who consistently acted upon principle. The inescapable conclusion—a conclusion that has forced itself insistently upon those who are editing these volumes—is that Jefferson's compulsion to investigate all avenues of human knowledge was purposeful.

This purpose aimed beyond his own time or his own country. "Jefferson aspired beyond the ambition of a nationality and embraced in his view the whole future of man," wrote Henry Adams. This, to Jefferson, was the meaning of the American Revolution. "A just and solid republican government maintained here," he wrote to John Dickinson, "will be a standing monument and example for the aim and imitation of the people of other countries; and I join with you in the hope and belief that they will see from our example that a free government is of all others the most energetic; that the enquiry which has been excited among the mass of mankind by our revolution and it's consequences, will ameliorate the condition of man over a great portion of the globe. What a satisfaction have we in the contemplation of the benevolent effects of our efforts, compared with those of the leaders on the other side, who have discountenanced all advances in science as dangerous innovations, have endeavored to render philosophy and republicanism terms of reproach, to persuade us that man cannot be governed but by the rod, &c. I shall have the happiness of living and dying in the contrary hope."[4] But this hope and this satisfaction would disappear if the standing monument fell. Its strength and virtue lay in its character as an example to be emulated, a beacon to be followed. Its force would be a moral force, and this meant that all of the citizens of the free government—every citizen—faced a re-

4 To John Dickinson, 6 Mch. 1801.

sponsibility to sustain the example and to keep it from failure. The urgency that permeated all of Jefferson's versatile activity betrayed, perhaps, a fear that the great experiment might fail; that the mass of the people here might not be, as he knew they were not in some parts of the world, ready for the trial; and if he exhibited a missionary zeal in what he called the "holy republican gospel," it was no doubt because he felt it necessary to set an example to his fellow citizens as they in turn were obligated to set it for other peoples. When, therefore, as ambassador, he sat in an Italian dairy from dawn until dusk to learn the process by which Parmesan cheese was made, or when, in the same capacity, he smuggled a few grains of rice from the valley of the Po to send to South Carolina; when, as traveler, he jotted down data about "designs for machines and furniture and landscape details; recipes for macaroni and other dishes; . . . and notes and memoranda on an incredible variety of subjects, from the use of Archimedes' screw at Kew to snuff, Sophocles, and specific gravity";[5] when, as governor, he interrupted his activities in behalf of the defense of the Commonwealth to answer questions about ancient records; when, as president, he investigated the possibilities of vaccination against smallpox and, against the preponderance of conservative medical opinion, successfully carried out the first mass vaccination in America; when, in retirement, he studied new methods of improving agriculture or projected an institution of higher learning or explored the languages of the Anglo-Saxons and of the American Indians— when he engaged in these and countless other activities, his investigations were guided by a central and controlling purpose, unifying all and elevating the lowliest to a majestic dignity.

That purpose is to be found stated and restated, explicitly and implicitly, in this and in the volumes that are to follow. It was far from being a new concept. But what caused it to seize upon Jefferson with the power of religious conviction and to dominate his entire life was the fact that here in America, for the first time in history, the philosophical concept seemed ready to march hand in hand with actuality. Here was to be tried the grand experiment of self-government, on whose success or failure would hang the future course of human improvement. It was reserved to Jefferson to join actuality with philosophy for himself, for his countrymen, and for all humanity when he wrote: "We hold these truths to be self-evident; that all men are created equal, that they are endowed

[5] Lyman H. Butterfield, "The Papers of Thomas Jefferson: Progress and Procedures in the Enterprise at Princeton," *American Archivist*, XII (1949), 132-3.

by their creator with certain inalienable rights; that among these are life, liberty, & the pursuit of happiness; that to secure these rights, governments are instituted among men, deriving their just powers from the consent of the governed; that whenever any form of government becomes destructive of these ends, it is the right of the people to alter or to abolish it, & to institute new government, laying it's foundation on such principles & organising it's powers in such form, as to them shall seem most likely to effect their safety & happiness."[6]

This, perhaps the most potent idea of modern history, as valid for the twentieth century as for the eighteenth, was the idea that gave meaning to Jefferson's versatile inquiry and selfless industry. It is the idea that dominated and guided his entire life, the idea to which he yielded an allegiance warmed by a passionate faith, clarified by a brilliant intellect, and expressed by an eloquent and felicitous pen. These volumes, like his own public life, will begin and end with the same affirmation; the principles set forth in the Declaration of Independence were reaffirmed half a century later in a final testament of faith: "May it be to the world what I believe it will be (to some parts sooner, to others later, but finally to all) the Signal of arousing men to burst the chains, under which Monkish ignorance and superstition had persuaded them to bind themselves, and to assume the blessings and security of self-government. The form which we have substituted restores the free right to the unbounded exercise of reason and freedom of opinion. All eyes are opened, or opening to the rights of man. The general spread of the light of science has already laid open to every view the palpable truth that the mass of mankind has not been born, with saddles on their backs, nor a favored few booted and spurred, ready to ride them legitimately, by the grace of god."[7]

"THE letters of a person, especially of one whose business has been chiefly transacted by letters," wrote Jefferson late in life, "form the only full and genuine journal of his life."[8] The observation is as sound as it is comprehensive, for it views "the letters of a person" not merely as those written by him but also as embracing letters received and other correspondence involved in the transaction

6 Quoted from Jefferson's "original Rough draught" of the Declaration of Independence.
7 To Roger C. Weightman, 24 June 1826.
8 To Robert Walsh, 5 Apr. 1823.

of business. It is an observation particularly applicable to the man who made it. For Thomas Jefferson ranks high among the great letter writers of his own or of any other age, and the Jefferson canon, though it includes also public addresses, statutes, state papers, pamphlets, and many other types of documents, is to be found primarily in his voluminous correspondence. The extent of this correspondence is as remarkable as its content. Beginning in 1760 when its author was a youthful subject of the monarch of Great Britain and ending in 1826 when he was already revered as one of the great citizens of the vigorous young Republic, this correspondence, carried on with thousands of persons of every station of life—scientists, statesmen, explorers, merchants, scholars, philosophers, planters, overseers, soldiers, family, and friends, at home and abroad—is estimated to number upwards of fifty thousand separate items.

Though the special quality which makes this correspondence still significant was the lofty purpose and the felicitous style which characterized even its most trivial part, its sheer volume and the energy required to produce it were as impressive to Jefferson's contemporaries as they are to us. "I wonder how Mr. Jefferson made out to answer everybody who wrote to him even while the labours of the Department of State and then of the Presidency were on his hands?" wrote William Wirt in 1827.[9] Knowing that Jefferson's lifelong habit was to spend several hours daily at his desk, Wirt placed a discerning finger on one of the chief means by which Jefferson accomplished so much when he exclaimed, in answer to his own question, "O! System!" As none of Jefferson's contemporaries equaled him in the volume and richness of his correspondence, so none equaled him in the systematic organization of his personal archives. Though he was felicitous in phrasing, Jefferson was not facile in composition, and it was not merely his interest in technical improvements that drove him to the use of the letterpress, the polygraph, the stylograph, and other devices for making multiple copies of letters and documents. These devices were means by which his hours at the desk were employed creatively rather than in the drudgery of copying. Among the prodigious letter writers of his generation, for example Washington and Franklin, Jefferson was alone also in the production of an exact, laboriously compiled, and precisely indexed record of his correspondence—the so-called "Epistolary Record," extending from 1783 to 1826, in which he recorded in parallel columns virtually

[9] William Wirt to Dabney Carr, 27 Oct. 1827, MS, Virginia State Library.

every letter that he wrote or received. Important as this remarkable 656-page document may have been in enabling its compiler to transact his extensive business and in what it reveals to us of his love of system and order, it became equally important as a legacy to his editors, providing as it does an almost complete census of his letters and also an authoritative device for establishing the dates of undated or mutilated letters, for ascertaining the author's whereabouts, and for unlocking some of the mysteries of postal communication during his time. Nor was this all. Dispersed and confused as Jefferson's personal archives have become since 1826, they must have presented at his death an exemplary picture of systematic arrangement. A single fragment of what was probably a comprehensive catalogue of his records shows in part what that arrangement was. This fragment includes such rubrics as "Law cases, opinions and tracts"; "State Revolutionary proceedings"; "Draughts, Notes &c. relating to Revised Code"; "documents for Notes on Virginia"; "Rough draughts, notes &c. while Member of Congress & Minister Plenipo. at Paris."; "Bank Accounts"; "Acct books, to wit. P. Jefferson. J. Harvey. N. Lewis. Th: J's"; and "family letters, plantation papers," &c.[10]

Even if the editors had been granted the inestimable privilege of examining this vast corpus of manuscripts as it was in all of its systematic completeness at the time of Jefferson's death, these volumes would yet include many records that, for one reason or another, were never gathered into his private archives and some, indeed, which he did not even see. They include, of course, those of his own private letters for which he retained no file copies. They include legislative, diplomatic, and executive documents which by their nature ultimately came to rest in government archives. They include, naturally, those letters signed by others when it is known that the true author was Jefferson—as, for example, the letter written by James Madison as Secretary of State to the American Minister in Madrid in March 1801, a letter which Jefferson declared was "written by myself, tho' in the name of, and signed by the Secretary of state."[11] They include some letters of other persons not addressed to Jefferson which, because of their importance or because of their allusion to him or because they passed through his hands, deserve to be printed or at least recorded among his papers. They include many public documents

[10] Memorandum in Jefferson's hand, in the possession of Roger W. Barrett, Chicago.
[11] To Thomas McKean, 26 Mch. 1801.

of which he was not the author or with which his only known connection was that of a signatory or about which he expressed his views or took some course of action; among these are the draft of a Declaration of Rights prepared for the Virginia Convention of August 1774; Franklin's Proposed Articles of Confederation, annotated by Jefferson; the various texts showing the evolution of the Virginia Constitution of 1776, adopted by a convention at which Jefferson was not present; the testimony of Major Sherburne and others before a congressional investigating committee of which Jefferson was merely the amanuensis, &c. Conversely, these volumes do *not* include certain documents that were present among Jefferson's manuscripts at Monticello, even though some of these were in his own handwriting—for example, the voluminous copies of manuscript statutes that he made or copies of seventeenth-century documents which he caused to be made for his own or others' researches.

In short, "completeness" as applied to this or any other attempt at an exhaustive edition is a relative term, theoretically possible but practically unattainable and in some respects undesirable. The editors have aimed at the inclusion of everything legitimately Jeffersonian by reason of authorship or of relationship, and at the exclusion of great masses of materials that have only a technical claim to being regarded as Jefferson documents. Some of the latter are indeed authentic Jefferson documents of high importance, signed by him as governor or president, such as statutes enacted by the Congress, land warrants, commissions, ships' clearance papers, &c. To have included these in such an edition as this would have so enormously increased the mass of records as to make publication impracticable and would have magnified the already-present danger of inundating the central core of Jefferson's papers with a flood of sometimes important though irrelevant archives. Thus, in defining a Jefferson document, the editors have endeavored to be liberal but also realistic.

So defined, *The Papers of Thomas Jefferson* will proceed on the following plan. The estimated minimum of fifty volumes that will be required to present the Jefferson papers in full will be divided into two series. The first series will be organized chronologically and the second topically. The first will consist primarily of letters written by or addressed to Jefferson. All such letters will be presented in this edition in one or the other of three forms—in full, in a summarization, or in a record entry. All available texts of letters by Jefferson will be printed in full with the exception of letters that substantially duplicate one another, such as letters of introduction, and letters of a merely routine or trivial nature. Even these, however, will be noted in conjunction with the text that is printed or will be briefly summarized under their proper dates. Other documents that will normally be summarized include applications for office, letters of neurotic persons, and other letters addressed to Jefferson that are not of special importance or that are readily available in print elsewhere. In general, more documents will be summarized during the periods of Jefferson's service as governor, as secretary of state, and as president than for other periods of his life. Whenever possible, references will be given to printed texts of documents here summarized.

The chronological series, of which this volume is the first, will thus include in one form or another every available letter known to have been written by or to Thomas Jefferson. Both in-letters and out-letters are embraced in the editorial plan for the simple reason that Jefferson's own letters can scarcely achieve the fullest degree of meaning unless it is known what points in his correspondents' letters he chose to comment upon and what he chose to ignore. Indeed it is quite possible that some of the most significant additions to historical knowledge will be found in the letters addressed to Jefferson, for, while it has been conjectured that about a third of the estimated nineteen thousand letters written by him have been published in one form or another, it is thought that less than a fifteenth of the much larger number of letters written to him have ever appeared in print.

The chronological series, however, will include much besides correspondence. It will include messages, speeches, reports, legislative bills, state papers, memoranda, travel journals, resolutions, petitions, advertisements, minutes of proceedings, and other non-epistolary documents that were written by Jefferson or had a direct relationship with him. It is estimated that four-fifths of the volumes of this edition will be required to embrace those materials which by their nature fall most logically and readily into a chronological plan of arrangement.

The second series, numbering an estimated one fifth of the volumes, will be devoted to those materials which seem most naturally to permit a classified arrangement. These volumes will include: (1) the Autobiography, *Notes on the State of Virginia*, the *Manual of Parliamentary Practice*, "The Life and Morals of Jesus of Nazareth"; (2) the legal papers—a very significant group of documents which will require perhaps three volumes and will include briefs, dockets, case and fee books, writings on law, the legal commonplace books, &c.; (3) architectural and other drawings; (4) maps, surveys, and land papers; (5) account books, miscellaneous accounts, itineraries; (6) the Farm Book, the Garden Book, meteorological data, recipes; (7) literary and linguistic papers, documents pertaining to the founding of the University of Virginia, &c.; (8) unclassified and supplementary documents.

It is intended that a separate supplementary volume may be added to the chronological and topical series, to consist of an essential aid in the use and understanding of the whole. This would be a biographical register containing concise sketches of all of Jefferson's correspondents and of other persons mentioned in the work who had significant or continuing relations with him. In this register the treatment of well-known figures like Washington, Madison, or Vergennes, for whom easily accessible biographies in full scale are available, would place emphasis upon their relationship with Jefferson. For obscurer figures such as Jefferson's French cook or the Brazilian adventurer José da Maia, the sketches would attempt to give a general though very concise biographical account. It is obvious that it would be an advantage to readers to have in a single source such data about the thousands of persons whose names occur and re-occur in these volumes, rather than to be thrown back upon the usual device of having such biographical information scattered in footnotes throughout the whole series of volumes. It is also obvious that such a consolidation of biographical data would relieve the editorial notes of a great deal of matter, much of it repetitive.

One other editorial aid is contemplated, in the form of a full chronology and itinerary of Jefferson's life and travels. This compilation will gather in one place, in greatly amplified form, the brief chronologies printed at the beginning of each volume.

The index to these volumes will be issued in one or more volumes at the conclusion of the enterprise, and every effort will be made to present in it an accurate and exhaustive key to the names of persons, places, events, and subjects mentioned in the work. *The individual volumes will contain no indexes since, upon the issuance of the final index, these separate indexes would represent a needless encroachment upon space required for documents. Nevertheless, since unindexed volumes could not be satisfactorily used while the work is in progress, temporary indexes for groups of volumes will be issued periodically.*

IT was only five months after Jefferson had retired as President that the first proposal was brought forth to publish "a complete edition" of his writings. To this Jefferson gave a depreciative response: the *Notes on the State of Virginia*, he wrote, was to be revised and enlarged; messages to Congress, interesting at the moment, would scarcely be read a second time, "and answers to addresses are hardly read a first time." In short, only those who were in the habit of preserving state papers would be interested in such a publication and, Jefferson added, they "are not many."[12]

Historians and the general public have differed with this over-modest appraisal. Aside from numerous publications of Jefferson documents in newspapers, periodicals, biographies, monographs, and selected volumes, there have been four collected editions of his letters and writings. The first was that edited by his grandson, Thomas Jefferson Randolph, *Memoirs, Correspondence, and Miscellanies from the Papers of Thomas Jefferson*, in four volumes, which first appeared at Charlottesville in 1829 and was promptly brought out in other editions printed in London (1829), Boston (1830), and Paris (1833). The second was edited by Henry A. Washington, *The Writings of Thomas Jefferson*, published in nine volumes at Washington in 1853-1854. The third was *The Writings of Thomas Jefferson*, edited by Paul Leicester Ford and published at New York in ten volumes between the years 1892 and 1899; it was reissued in twelve volumes as the "Federal Edition," 1904-1905. The fourth, with the same title, was edited by A. A. Lipscomb and A. E. Bergh in twenty volumes, Washington, 1903-1904, and was several times reissued.

The first of these four collected editions was issued in 6,000 copies, all of which were subscribed for within the year in which they were published.[13] Each succeeding edition, exerting an incalculable influence in establishing Jefferson as one of the great figures of world history, brought about an increasing demand for a complete and more dependable text of his utterances. The reason for this demand lay not alone in the quality of Jefferson's mind and in the warmth of his faith, but also in the character of the editions themselves, all of which are long since out of print. The most accurate and useful edition—that edited by Ford—suffered from a severe limitation of space and from a disproportionate emphasis upon the purely political aspects of Jefferson's career. The most

---

[12] To John W. Campbell, 3 Sep. 1809.
[13] *The Virginia Literary Museum*, I (1829), 432.

recent, the most extensive, and the most widely used edition—that edited by Lipscomb and Bergh and usually referred to as the Memorial Edition—was in large part a mere reprinting of the text of the Henry A. Washington edition of 1853-1854. Though Washington's edition of *The Writings of Thomas Jefferson* was a noteworthy accomplishment in its day and added greatly to the public knowledge of Jefferson in the mid-nineteenth century, it was characterized by the sort of editorial liberties with the text which reflected the inexact scholarly standards of that day. Thus the only edition originating in the twentieth century and the one most widely used is one that includes such distortions as the willful suppression of names, the silent omission of passages, and the substitution of the editors' choice of words for Jefferson's.

The inaccuracies, incompleteness, and unavailability of all previous editions led to an increasing demand on the part of historians for an edition of Jefferson's writings so comprehensive in scope and so accurate in presentation that the work would never need to be done again. This demand, though advanced and supported by a very large segment of the professional historians of the country, met with no effective response until the establishment of a commission to celebrate the 200th anniversary of Jefferson's birth. From its inception, the Thomas Jefferson Bicentennial Commission, created by Act of Congress, included several members who labored diligently to achieve the object that had long been in the minds of American historians. Among those members of the Commission who took a leading part in this effort were the late Stuart G. Gibboney and Dr. Fiske Kimball. Mr. Gibboney, described by *The New York Times* in a well-deserved editorial tribute as "a great Jeffersonian," was the founder of the Thomas Jefferson Memorial Foundation which insured the preservation of Monticello as a national shrine, and in 1940 he became one of the original members of The Thomas Jefferson Bicentennial Commission. His long labors in these and other capacities undoubtedly had much influence in bringing the Commission as well as the public to recognize the importance of a new and comprehensive edition of Jefferson's writings. Dr. Kimball, a lifelong student of Jefferson who, early in life, produced a scholarly work on Jefferson as an architect—still the standard authority in its field—supported with characteristic vigor and enthusiasm the plan for a new edition. To these men, therefore, is due a large part of the praise for the inauguration of the movement which led to the present enterprise.

The Thomas Jefferson Bicentennial Commission was authorized

and directed by an Act of Congress of 1943 "to prepare as a congressional memorial to Thomas Jefferson a new edition of the writings of Thomas Jefferson, including additional material and unpublished manuscripts preserved in the Library of Congress and elsewhere, at a cost not to exceed $15,000 for the preparation of the manuscript." The same Act authorized the Commission to employ a Historian, and at its meeting on 12 March 1943 the Commission appointed the editor of the present work to that office. The Commission at the same time directed the Historian to make a study which would analyze the scope, probable cost, and length of time required for the preparation of such an edition. In pursuance of this directive, the Historian made an extended investigation and on 25 September 1943 submitted his findings.[14] This report led to a proposal to the Commission by Princeton University, whereby the latter institution would sponsor the edition, aided by a subvention of $200,000 from The New York Times Company. The Commission, at its meeting on 20 October 1943, took this proposal into consideration and adopted the following resolution: "Resolved, that the Commission gives its approval, in principle, as the realization of its task and effort, to the publication by Princeton University of this edition of the writings of Thomas Jefferson, subject to submission by the University of a memorandum covering all details of the proposed undertaking, and to approval of such a memorandum by the President of the United States, and by a subcommittee of three members of the Commission to be appointed by the chair. Subject to such approval, the Commission invokes the cooperation of the Library of Congress and other governmental and private agencies in making available for this edition all of the Jefferson manuscripts in their possession."

The required memorandum outlining in detail the plans of the edition was submitted by Dr. Harold W. Dodds, President of Princeton University, to the subcommittee of the Commission and by them to President Roosevelt. The proposed plan met with approval, the agreement between The New York Times Company and Princeton University became effective, and in the spring of 1944 the editorial office was established in the Princeton University Library. Thus was begun the arduous task of accumulating photoduplicates of Jefferson documents from all quarters of the world.

[14] Julian P. Boyd, *Report to the Thomas Jefferson Bicentennial Commission on the Need, Scope, Proposed Method of Preparation, Probable Cost, and Possible Means of Publishing a Comprehensive Edition of the Writings of Thomas Jefferson*, 1943. This report was a 32-page mimeographed document with printed charts and suggested specimen pages.

INTRODUCTION

The inception of the present edition, then, was immediately due to the stimulus and activity of The Thomas Jefferson Bicentennial Commission. Out of its own funds the Commission prepared what appeared to be the first serious study of the scope and cost of such an enterprise. Consequently, the present publication resulted in large part from the firm conviction of members of the Commission that the writings of Jefferson should be collected, edited, and presented in complete form to the American people, and the members of the Commission who provided this stimulus should be as gratefully remembered as those who provided the means of executing their plan.

ACKNOWLEDGMENTS

THE subvention of The New York Times Company of $200,-000 was both generous and, quite literally, indispensable. It is especially fitting that the publication of the papers of the American statesman who believed that the press "is the best instrument for enlightening the mind of man, and improving him as a rational, moral, and social being"[15] should be made possible by a great metropolitan newspaper. For the same reason it is appropriate that this edition of Jefferson's writings should be dedicated to Adolph S. Ochs, publisher of *The New York Times* from 1896 to his death in 1935, a period during which he exhibited in the pages of that paper ample evidence that he shared Jefferson's belief in the importance of a free press and in the concept of the responsible role of journalism in a republic. Without the support of The New York Times Company, the previous efforts of historians and of the Thomas Jefferson Bicentennial Commission might well have ended in frustration. It is therefore with profound gratitude that the editors express their appreciation for this timely and indispensable support.

The acknowledgments of the editors, as well as the gratitude of the public, are due also to the Director and Trustees of the Princeton University Press. The magnitude of their support of the enterprise can be understood only when viewed in perspective. In 1943, though only the publication of Jefferson's correspondence was contemplated and though costs were estimated to be far less than at present, the Princeton University Press, in common with other similar institutions, felt that it could not underwrite manufacturing and publishing costs for so large an enterprise. Yet six years later the Trustees of the Press, in order to provide the editors with every assistance possible, agreed to bear without subsidy from any source the entire expenses of manufacture and distribution. For this magnanimous action the editors wish to express both their appreciation and their admiration. Such a courageous act on the part of the Trustees is also a well-deserved expression of confidence in the Director of the Press who suggested it, Mr. Datus C. Smith, Jr. To him and to his colleagues, who have on every occasion manifested a cordiality and a courtesy towards the editorial staff that have been equaled only by their efficiency as printers and publishers, the editors wish to express their sense of grateful obligation.

[15] To Adamantios Coray, 31 Oct. 1823.

The more than fifty thousand documents that have been assembled in facsimile form by the editors have been drawn from more than four hundred and twenty-five different sources, including libraries, archives, governmental agencies, historical societies, schools, clubs, banks, commercial firms, dealers, and nearly two hundred and fifty private owners of Jefferson documents. These documents have come from thirty-eight states and the District of Columbia and from many foreign countries, including Australia, France, Great Britain, Holland, Italy, and Switzerland. The editors' debt of gratitude is not limited to those institutions and individuals who possess Jefferson manuscripts, for the problem of locating documents in obscure places is one whose solution is difficult and haphazard, and the measure of success that has been made toward its solution has depended upon a wide circle of interested friends of the enterprise, including representatives of the public press and the radio. Both those who have custody of documents and those who have supplied valuable information are gratefully recognized by the editors as colleagues engaged in a common cause, and in due course a full expression of appreciation will be made to them. Yet, at this stage, specific acknowledgment must be accorded to the conspicuous services of some. First among these is the distinguished Librarian of Congress, Dr. Luther H. Evans, and the great national library over which he presides. The Library of Congress is not merely the repository of what is by far the largest single aggregation of Jefferson manuscripts, but the Librarian and his staff have graciously and efficiently rendered a service to this enterprise without which it would have been literally impossible to carry it forward. Other institutions that have rendered significant services and continue to respond with generous cooperation to the appeals of the editors include the following: the Alderman Library of the University of Virginia, the Massachusetts Historical Society, the Missouri Historical Society at St. Louis, the Virginia State Archives, the Virginia Historical Society, Colonial Williamsburg, Inc., the Library of the College of William and Mary, the State Historical Society of Wisconsin, the Historical Society of Pennsylvania, the New York Public Library, the New-York Historical Society, the American Philosophical Society, the American Antiquarian Society, the National Archives, the Huntington Library, the Clements Library, the Pierpont Morgan Library, and Yale University Library. Among the officers of these and other institutions who have unfailingly and freely given aid to the editors in exploring the manuscript collections in their custody or in sharing their expert historical and bibliographical knowledge are Dr. St. George L. Sioussat, former Chief of the Division of Manuscripts of the Library of Congress, and his successor, Dr. Solon J. Buck; Mrs. Vincent L. Eaton, a member of the staff of that Division, and Mrs. Helen D. Bullock, a former member; Mr. Donald C. Holmes, present, and Mr. George A. Schwegmann, former, Chief of Photo-duplication Service, Library of Congress; Mr. Harry Clemons, Librarian, Mr. Francis L. Berkeley, Jr., Curator of Manuscripts, Miss Louise Savage, Acquisitions Librarian, and Mr. John C. Wyllie, Curator of Rare Books, of the Alderman Library of the University of Virginia; Mr. William J. Van Schreeven, Head Archivist of the Virginia State Library; Mr. R. Norris Williams, 2nd, Director of the Historical Society of Pennsylvania; Mr. R. W. G. Vail, Director, and Miss Dorothy C. Barck, Librarian, of the New-York Historical Society; Dr. William E. Lingelbach, Librarian, and Mrs. Gertrude D. Hess, Assistant Librarian, of the American Philosophical Society; Miss Norma Cuthbert, Curator of Manuscripts at the Huntington Library; Dr. Clarence S. Brigham, Director of the American Antiquarian Society; the late Allyn B. Forbes, formerly Director, and Mr. Stephen T. Riley, Librarian, of the Massachusetts Historical Society; Mr. Lawrence Heyl, Associate Librarian, and Mr. Malcolm O. Young, Reference Librarian, of the Princeton University Library; Mr. John M. Jennings, Librarian of the Virginia Historical Society; Dr. Lester J. Cappon, Archivist, Institute of Early American History and Culture, Williamsburg; Dr. Douglass Adair, Editor of the *William and Mary Quarterly*; Professor John V. A. Fine, Department of Classics, Princeton University; and Dr. Howard C. Rice, Jr., formerly the representative of this enterprise in France, and now Chief of the Department of Rare Books and Special Collections, Princeton University Library. Finally to the Advisory Committee, composed of Jefferson specialists and others who have generously shared their knowledge and who have at all stages rendered helpful and frequently indispensable assistance, the editors wish to express a deep sense of gratitude.

This edition would be lacking in much of its value were it not for the industry, devotion, scholarly competence, and cooperative effort of those who have been associated with the editor as members of the editorial staff. Mr. Butterfield and Mrs. Bryan, Associate Editors, sharing full editorial responsibility under a division of labor that has been evolved from experience, and Miss Dorothy Demko, editorial secretary, who has the duty of transcribing docu-

INTRODUCTION

ments and performing many other services, discharge their responsibilities with high competence and an enthusiasm born of the stimulus of close association with the spirit and mind of Thomas Jefferson.

EDITORIAL METHOD

THE present editors of the writings of Thomas Jefferson have enjoyed one immense advantage over those who have preceded them. This is the existence of a technological device that Jefferson would have been among the first to appreciate—the microfilm camera. Whereas Lyman C. Draper had traveled by ox-cart and stage up and down the Appalachian frontier to collect the records of the first American West, and previous editors of Jefferson had laboriously transcribed manuscripts by hand in whatever remote place they might be found, we were in the fortunate position of being able to assemble in one place exact photoduplicates of documents drawn from many sources in many distant places. Aside from the fact that the camera all but abolished barriers of time and space, it presented other editorial advantages. In transcribing, arranging, and annotating, one could not deal so freely with any original manuscript, to say nothing of one so precious to the American people as Jefferson's draft of the Declaration of Independence, as with a photographic reproduction. The latter could be stamped or marked for classification purposes, marginal notes or decipherings could be placed upon it, and, if necessary, as in the case of letter books or a single piece of writing paper used for several documents, could be cut apart and distributed by date through the files.

Nor was the advantage presented by the camera one that benefited the editors exclusively. Our decision to carry through the whole editorial process by the use of photofacsimiles was conceived in the interest of future historians as well. By agreement with the Library of Congress the entire file of photoduplicates will, at the conclusion of the enterprise, be deposited in the Library of Congress, together with notes, indexes, and all other data accumulated during the course of the work. Thus it will be possible for future scholars to resort to one central depository to verify transcriptions or obtain full texts of summarized documents. Though every effort is being made in these volumes to insure complete accuracy, such an opportunity for verification or amplification is often of great importance.

Yet scientific devices that produce such efficiency and such accuracy exact their price, generally a twofold levy. The first is esthetic and has never been so well stated as by Nathaniel Hawthorne in his essay on "A Book of Autographs": "To give them their full effect, we should imagine that these letters have this moment been brought to town by the splashed and wayworn post rider, or perhaps by an orderly dragoon, who has ridden in a perilous hurry to deliver his despatches. They are magic scrolls, if read in the right spirit. The roll of the drum and the fanfare of the trumpet is latent in some of them; and in others, an echo of the oratory that resounded in the old halls of the Continental Congress, at Philadelphia; or the words may come to us as with the living utterance of one of those illustrious men, speaking face to face, in friendly communion. Strange, that the mere identity of paper and ink should be so powerful. The same thoughts might look cold and ineffectual, in a printed book. Human nature craves a certain materialism, and clings pertinaciously to what is tangible, as if that were of more importance than the spirit accidentally involved in it. And, in truth, the original manuscript has always something which print itself must inevitably lose. An erasure, even a blot, a casual irregularity of hand, and all such little imperfections of mechanical execution, bring us close to the writer, and perhaps convey some of those subtle intimations for which language has no shape." Photographs, as well as cold type, lose some of those subtle intimations for which language has no shape. The intricate problem presented by the first page of Jefferson's first draft of a constitution for Virginia in 1776 probably could not have been solved if its solution had depended in every stage upon the use of the precious original, but the satisfaction of achieving such a result is altogether different from the satisfaction that few have been privileged to experience of holding the manuscript which Jefferson had before him as he drew up the memorable indictment against George III of England.

The other limitation of photoduplicates belongs to a category of intimations neither subtle nor beyond the shape of language to compass. In any large quantity of photographs made from mounted or loose manuscripts, one may invariably depend upon a few accidental omissions. If blank pages are not photographed, endorsements and docketed memoranda of consequence are sometimes overlooked. "Reading from poor prints, or prints made from defective originals, can be among the most exasperating experiences of editorial life. One is forever straining to discover what was in the inner margin into which the camera did not reach, or in the outer margin obscured by the mounting sheet."[16] But daily experience induces in the editors a lively sense of caution about such limitations, and there goes forth from the editorial office a stream of appeals to patient and obliging librarians and archivists for verification, for the recti-

[16] Butterfield, "The Papers of Thomas Jefferson," p. 134.

fication of error, and for the examination of watermarks and other evidence which the camera cannot reveal.

Another basic decision made by the editors early in the work and closely related to that concerning the use of photoduplication was the determination to gather for purposes of comparison and legibility every known copy of every Jefferson document. The editorial files are thus sprinkled with variant texts, often numbering two and sometimes three, four, or even more copies or versions of a single document. These may consist of a rough draft with its scored-out passages and the blots, erasures, and alterations which give evidence of Jefferson's attention to style; of a letterpress or polygraph copy of the fair draft; and of the recipient's copy, bearing perhaps an address, postal markings, and endorsements. Letterpress copies, which were offset impressions made by putting a moist, transparently thin sheet of paper under pressure against the face of the original manuscript, are often blurred to the point of illegibility; polygraph copies, which in 1804 replaced those made by the letterpress, were such perfect duplications as to defy differentiation, and therefore the file copies that Jefferson retained after that year present few of the problems posed by those made earlier. Clerks' copies of Jefferson's letters present their own problems. Though much has been said, often without justice, about the inefficiency of Jefferson's administration as Governor, the present editors feel qualified from painful experience to pass judgment, which they do without hesitation, upon the inefficiency of the clerks who assisted him in making copies of his voluminous executive correspondence. Only those thoroughly familiar with the distinctive style and orthography of Jefferson can penetrate the veil thrown over his original letters by these often careless, probably overworked, and certainly inaccurate clerks.

Thus the effort to accumulate photoduplicates of all variant copies is intended to offset and so far as possible to eliminate the errors that might result from dependence upon a single perhaps incomplete or otherwise imperfect text. Even duplicates such as those made by the polygraph sometimes differ because of additions made by Jefferson after using the polygraph and before dispatching the letter. In some instances it is manifestly impossible to transcribe a letterpress copy until the text that actually went through the post has been found and photographed. A spectacular example is Jefferson's letter to Robert R. Livingston of 18 April 1802, instructing him, as minister to France, to acquire New Orleans for the United States. The text of this momentous document has often been printed, though never fully, because the press copy in the Library of Congress is not completely legible. The recent acquisition by the Museum of the City of New York of the copy that Livingston received now enables the editors to present the complete text of one of the most significant letters in American history.

But the bringing to light of the letters that Jefferson sent through the mails is a far more difficult process than that of locating his file copies. Many of the former have been irretrievably lost. Others have come to the surface momentarily, leaving a trace in the catalogues of autograph dealers or auction houses, and have fallen back into obscurity. Still others yet repose in the papers of obscure or famous Americans hidden away in unknown attics or barns. The search for such documents continues and will continue throughout the course of this enterprise; a supplementary volume will no doubt be required to publish those that come to the editors' attention too late to be inserted in their proper chronological order. The editorial files record at present a substantial number of such documents that are known to have been written but have not come to light. Letters known to be missing because acknowledged in other letters are mentioned as missing in the notes to the letters acknowledging them. Other missing letters and documents, information about which derives from such unimpeachable sources as Jefferson's Epistolary Record, will be given "record entries," which will provide the data available concerning them in their proper chronological order in these volumes.

Though the accumulation of photoduplicates of texts in a single, manageable editorial file was fundamentally important, the decisions respecting the method of presenting these texts in type were of even greater significance. The mid-nineteenth century editor who preceded those who have the responsibility for these volumes also had access to Jefferson's original texts; but the era in which he lived was one in which the amenities and a respect for the privacy and feelings of individuals took precedence over the exacting claims of history. With different motives and with a loftier aim than the clerks who served under Governor Jefferson, he nevertheless did greater violence to the letters which he, as well as they, had the duty of transcribing accurately. The present editors, though they endeavor rigidly to adhere to scrupulous exactness in the presentation of the texts as Jefferson wrote them, are aware, first, that complete exactitude is impossible in transmuting handwriting into print and, second, that this process inevitably loses "those subtle intimations for which language has no shape." Yet over a period of years they have evolved through tedious experience and through an earnest effort to anticipate all problems a standard methodology which, though sometimes consciously inconsistent, is nevertheless precise. Their manual of procedures in the handling of the Jeffersonian texts, which underwent revision after revision, could not hope to anticipate every problem that will be encountered, but the serious reader of these volumes is entitled to know precisely what the editorial standards are, wherein they vary from established practices, and with what degree of consistency they have been applied.

IN GENERAL the editorial policy follows a middle course between those editors of historical documents who believe, on the one hand, that nothing short of facsimile reproduction can be faithful to the originals and those who, on the other hand, believe in complete modernization of the text. Within certain limits, there is much to be said for each of these extreme views. Facsimile reproduction is indubitably capable of greater fidelity than printing from type; modernization of the text of an eighteenth-century writer under many circumstances is a justifiable procedure. But to adopt either course in an enterprise of this size would erect serious barriers to the effective use of the work. Facsimile reproduction would make it intolerably difficult for the reader to follow Jefferson's text readily, as in the case of many letterpress copies or in the case of such a letter as that written to Governor Patrick Henry on 27 March 1779, for which no text survives except an all-but-indecipherable rough draft. Nevertheless, on occasion in these volumes, facsimile reproduction will be employed, as for example in the presentation of architectural and other drawings, tabular documents, account books, &c. Modernization of the text would sacrifice many of Jefferson's peculiarities of orthography and style. The standards of editorial procedure described below are intended, then, to present as accurate a text as possible and to preserve as many of Jefferson's distinctive mannerisms of writing as can be done.

However, the various devices of conventionalization that have been necessarily adopted, though they will be applied to all correspondence and to the greater part of other ordinary documents, will not be applied to: (1) business papers (accounts and invoices) and tabular documents of all kinds, which will be presented literally except for the lowering of superior letters; and (2) certain documents of great textual importance and complexity, such as the Declaration of Independence, likewise to be presented literally. The place and date-line, the salutation, and the complimentary close in letters will also be retained in literal form. However, the date-line is uniformly placed at the head of a letter regardless of where it occurs in the manuscript.

Spelling and grammar will be preserved as they stand in the original manuscripts. Even with respect to proper names, Jefferson's orthography was far from conventional. Though he sat on committees with Elbridge Gerry in the Continental Congress, knew him well, and on occasion saw his name in print, Jefferson persisted in addressing him as "Mr. Gherry." Mathew Carey signed his letters with beautiful clarity, but Jefferson invariably addressed him as "Matthew Cary"; and Thomas Leiper was always to him "Thomas Lieper." Such vagaries will be respected in the text, though in the captions, the annotation, and elsewhere in the editorial apparatus the correct forms will be observed. In the matter of capitalization Jefferson differed from his contemporaries in two important respects—he used capitals with extreme economy and he began each sentence with a lower-case letter. The editors will follow his style of capitalization in the text, but they have felt warranted in departing from his norm in respect to the beginning letter of each sentence, which will be capitalized in these volumes except in the treatment of highly important documents where literalness seems essential. Such exceptions will be noted at the appropriate place. As for capitalization in letters written to Jefferson and even in clerks' copies of his own letters, as well as in most other documents not written by Jefferson, the style of the original manuscripts will be followed, though the editors frankly acknowledge that it is at times impossible to determine whether the writer intended to capitalize or not. In the case of such ambiguities, modern practice will be followed. Punctuation will also be preserved as it is in the original manuscript, but for the sake of clarity this literal policy will be less rigorously applied than in the matters of spelling, grammar, and capitalization. Periods will be supplied at the end of sentences. Superfluous dashes, for example those occurring after periods, will be eliminated. Passages in documents not in Jefferson's handwriting that are seriously misleading or obscure because of missing or incorrect punctuation will be corrected silently in preference to the use of brackets or footnotes. If, however, such a passage admits of more than one meaning, its punctuation will be allowed to stand and a clarifying note will be subjoined.

As for contractions and abbreviations, these will normally be expanded in ordinary documents, and raised letters at the close of such contractions or abbreviations will in all cases be lowered. In many instances, however, particularly in such a document as Jefferson's notes and outlines of his argument in behalf of religious freedom in 1776, the text will be presented quite literally even though many of the contractions present a difficult problem of decipherment. A single example of the kind of expansion that the editors have in mind in adopting this conventionalized practice will suffice. If presented literally, what Jefferson wrote as he took down hasty notes in a congressional investigating committee in the busy summer of 1776 would read as follows: "Carleton havg hrd yt we were returning with considble reinfmt, so terrifd, yt wd hve retird immedly hd h. nt bn infmd by spies of deplorble condn to wch sm pox hd redd us." Such a passage, by the conventionalization to be followed in these volumes, will read: "Carleton having heard that we were returning with considerable reinforcement, [was] so terrified, that [he] would have retired immediately had he not been informed by spies of [the] deplorable conditions to which small pox had reduced us." This expanded text represents the kind of clear and readable form that Jefferson himself would have used for a document intended for formal presentation in print. It makes for clarity and readability and yet sacrifices nothing of Jefferson's words or meaning. Among the typical forms to be expanded, except in those outstanding documents in which a literal presentation is adopted, are the ampersand and the thorn, though the ampersand will be retained in the names of firms, the form "&c." will be employed since it was widely used in eighteenth-century printing, and the thorn, much as the editors object to the attempt to represent it by the letter "y," will be employed in the case of a few highly important documents which are given with literal exactness. Among other typical forms to be expanded are the following: *agst* (against), *cos* (companies), *commee* (committee), *dft* (defendant), *exors* (executors), *plt* (plaintiff), and *pr* (per; though the symbol ℔ will be retained when employed for per, pre, and pro).

However, all money designations, such as *lb.*, *℔*, *lib.*, *stg.*, *sterl.*; all units of measure and weight, as *hhd.*, *i.* and *f.* (inches and feet); and such forms as *brot* (brought), *cou'd, shou'd, wou'd, do.* (ditto), *pr.* (pair), *pray'd*, &c., will be retained as written. Abbreviations and contractions for proper names will be retained, but they will be uniformly capitalized; superscript letters will be lowered; contraction signs will be omitted; and a period will be inserted if no other punctuation appears. Abbreviated geographical names, such as *Wmsbg* or *Wmsbgh* for Williamsburg, will be retained, though when a contraction is confusing or not clear from the context, the expanded form will be added in square brackets. Thus "C.town" will be given as "C.town [Charleston]," and "B————s Ferry" will become "B————s [Burwell's] Ferry."

When gaps occur in the text, the following procedure will be followed: (1) if one or two words or parts thereof are missing because of mutilation or fading of the manuscript (when these words are not conjecturable), that fact will be indicated by three suspension points inside square brackets (thus: "[. . .]," though "[. . . .]" will be employed at the end of a sentence); (2) if the missing matter consists of more than two or of an indeterminate number of words, a note to this effect will be subjoined; (3) numbers or parts of numbers missing will, however, be indicated by a blank space inside square brackets, the amount of space to vary with the number of digits believed missing; (4) whenever possible, missing words or numerals will be supplied by conjecture, this conjectural reading to be printed in roman type inside square brackets (thus: "My eyes still continue [as red a]s ever"), and if the reading is doubtful a question mark will be inserted. When a word or passage is too illegible to be deciphered with certainty, it will be followed by a question mark and enclosed in square brackets, and if more than one reading is plausible, the alternative or alternatives will be given in a subjoined note.

Editorial insertions and corrections will be indicated as follows: (1) directive words inserted editorially will be italicized and enclosed in square brackets (thus: "[*In the margin*]"); (2) expanded forms of proper names and dates supplied at the head of undated letters and documents will be printed in roman type and enclosed in square brackets (thus: "Brand. [Brandon]" and "[ca. 24 September 1804]"); (3) corrections of "slips of the pen" and copyists' obvious errors will be treated differently according to whether they are found in documents written by Jefferson or by others. In Jefferson documents the correct form will normally be given in the text, but the original reading will be subjoined in a note; in other documents such errors will normally be corrected silently, though if an error has psychological significance it will be allowed to stand, with a note when required. Variant readings occurring in two or more copies of a given document will not be recorded in the text but in notes keyed to the text by superscript numerals. In ordinary documents only those variants deemed to be especially significant will be noted, whereas in documents of major importance all variants will be recorded.

In the comparison of texts involving rough drafts and occasionally in other texts as well, scored-out passages will be treated in the following manner. In ordinary documents words or passages lined or scored out by the writer will, if significant, be recorded in notes keyed to the text by superscript numerals. In all major documents such deleted passages will, so far as possible, be printed *in the text* inside angle brackets and in italic type. Normally the words or passages that have been supplanted will be placed *before* the matter substituted; but in the case of a series of changes made by the author at one place, each change, if clearly separable, will be enclosed with its own set of angle brackets in the order in which the changes were made, as nearly as this can be determined; in cases where a long passage has been struck out, any parts of such passages deleted before the whole was struck out, will, if determinable, be recorded in textual notes; so far as possible Jefferson's own drafts of resolutions, reports, &c., will be rendered as he wrote them before modification by collaborators, and the deletions and substitutions made later will be recorded in footnotes.

Enclosures will be accounted for so far as possible. Those that are letters from and to Jefferson will of course be printed in full or summarized in their appropriate chronological places, with cross references between them and their respective covering letters. Letters not by or to Jefferson will also, if of capital importance, be printed in full in their chronological places, also with cross references, but more often they will be summarized or listed in the notes appended to the covering letter. Papers other than letters will be printed in full, summarized, or listed (according to their degree of importance) with the covering letter. The listing of an enclosure not printed in full will always include both the location of the manuscript and, if possible, the designation of a printed text.

After considerable experimentation, the editors have been forced to the conclusion that exhaustive annotation of such a large mass of documents is not practicable and perhaps not desirable. However tempting it is to any editor of Jefferson's papers to explore the multitudinous bypaths that his letters invariably point to; to attempt to assay the historical significance of each document in relation to its context; to identify or explain all persons, events, and places; to separate fact from rumor; to explain obsolete, technical, and regional terms; to trace literary quotations to their sources; or to furnish references to pertinent literature, &c.—such a procedure would prolong the editorial task indefinitely, if not postpone its completion altogether. The editors construe their primary task as that of placing the whole body of Jefferson's writings in the hands of historians and of the public as expeditiously as can be done in view of the size and complexity of the undertaking and of the need for completeness and for scrupulous accuracy. Nevertheless, the policy decided upon with respect to annotation is that of providing a certain minimum basis of information essential to the understanding of each document. Though such a policy, ideally, admits a very wide latitude for interpretation, the editors in applying it will lay emphasis upon the words "minimum" and "essential." Even so, it is important to note that two general exceptions to this policy have been adopted. First, in the chronological series the early volumes will receive a greater degree of annotation than those that will come later. This seemingly disproportionate emphasis is to be accounted for partly by the fact that the total number of documents in the early years is relatively insignificant compared with later years, their context is therefore less fully explained by the documentation itself, and the need for explanation greater; and partly by the fact that in the early volumes, particularly the first, some of the most important and most complex documents—for example, the Constitution of Virginia of 1776 and the Declaration of Independence—require for proper presentation a full degree of annotation. Second, it has been thought of more value to annotate important and complex documents thoroughly and to restrict ordinary or routine documents to a minimum than to provide what would inevitably become an artificial equality of treatment. Our disproportionate emphasis is perhaps arbitrary, but it recognizes that there is a wide variation in the value, character, and historical importance of the documents presented in these volumes. In respect to certain highly important documents for which several texts exist, or in the case of series of documents closely related to each other, the annotation for the whole has been so liberally interpreted as to permit not merely the usual note for each separate part but also a general introductory comment to the whole. Examples of the former are the Declaration of the Causes and Necessity for Taking Up Arms, Notes of Proceedings in the Continental Congress, the Constitution of Virginia of 1776, and the Declaration of Independence. Examples of the latter are the Notes and Proceedings on Discontinuing the Establishment of the

Church of England and the Drafts of Bills Establishing Courts of Justice within the Commonwealth.

In respect to the form of annotation, the editors have decided that a single note appended to each document would be preferable to the usual form of annotation by means of superscript numerals keyed to the text. This subjoined note is considered, therefore, as an editorial introduction to the document to which it pertains. It will normally consist of two and frequently three complementary parts: (1) a descriptive note; (2) an explanatory note; and (3), where necessary, a textual note or notes.

(1) *The descriptive note*. This will contain a physical description of the document and a record of all known versions. These data will be given briefly, and usually by symbols, as follows: (a) the character of the document—that is, whether it is a recipient's copy, a polygraph copy, a letterpress copy, a duplicate, &c. (see list of Descriptive Symbols, p. xxxix, below); and (b) the location of the document, whether in public or private possession (see list of Location Symbols, p. xl, below). The location of original documents will be carried further than the bare symbol in the case of three institutions which have a large number of Jefferson documents in more than one collection, namely the Library of Congress, the Massachusetts Historical Society, and the National Archives. The symbols DLC and MHi by themselves will stand for the collections of Jefferson Papers proper in the first two of these repositories; when texts are drawn from other collections held by these two institutions, the names of the particular collections will be added. In the case of the National Archives the symbol DNA will always be followed by the Archives' own record group number (thus, RG59), together, when necessary, with the name of the particular file within the record group in which the original is to be found. *When more than one version of a document is recorded in the descriptive note, the first symbol to be listed always represents the version used for the printed text.* Thus in the series of designations "RC (MHi); Dft (DLC); Tr in hand of Jared Sparks (MH)," the basis of our text is the recipient's copy in the Massachusetts Historical Society, not the draft in the Library of Congress or the transcript by Sparks in the Harvard College Library. When only a printed text is available, it will of course be used and the descriptive note will so indicate. The descriptive note will also include, as required, such data as the condition of the manuscript, if incomplete, mutilated, or in other respects unusual; the address, including bearer, ship, frank, and the like; the docketing, endorsement, or other memo-

randa on the manuscript in other hands, together with notes on any unusual provenance; notice of lack of signature; watermark and measurements when required, though this will be seldom; comment on the handwriting if this is in any respect unusual; and cross references to enclosures or covering letters. Postmarks will be given only when important in establishing the date. For summarized documents the descriptive note also indicates the number of pages in the original manuscript; this number always represents the number of pages *on which writing occurs,* including address and endorsement when they occur, but not blanks. This method has been adopted in order to show how many exposures a photoduplicate of the original will require at the rate of one page for each exposure.

(2) *The explanatory note.* This will be rigorously restricted within the terms of the general editorial policy governing annotation as set forth above. The explanatory note is invariably the second paragraph of the annotation. Since this note is a short commentary on the document to which it pertains, and is meant to be readable by itself, considerable flexibility in form and order of treatment is to be allowed, in order to permit, if desirable, generalization regarding the document and a logical rather than serial grouping of the topics annotated. Since reference numbers are not used for the topics annotated, the key words of these topics will be printed in the note in small capitals, allowing the eye to travel easily from the text to the annotation. Among the items that will normally be annotated under this procedure are the following: the names of correspondents whose identity is subject to doubt; nicknames, pseudonyms, initials; misspelled names; official titles employed in the text instead of personal names; the names of persons who had the same names as others and are likely to be confused with them; the names of places when these are ambiguous, obscure in form, or otherwise confusing; unfamiliar technical terms and linguistic forms, &c.

(3) *The textual note.* This, when necessary, will form a third section of the annotation and will be keyed by superscript numerals to the text. The editorial policy does not call for full collation of every document extant in more than one version or for recording minor corrections or variations in ordinary documents. Thus textual notes will be largely confined to those documents of major importance in which all deletions and variations between drafts are noted. However, in ordinary documents, such notes will also be employed to record corrections or to indicate differences between

variant copies when these are significant; to indicate insertions in the text in a different hand from that of the principal author; to indicate the presence of square brackets in the manuscript; to indicate how many words are missing in a gap in the text; to interpret badly expressed, ill-punctuated, or illegible passages; to record marginalia that cannot be easily incorporated in the text proper; to confirm an obviously mistaken or otherwise unexpected reading in the manuscript; and to indicate an editorial correction.

All works referred to repeatedly throughout the edition or any part of it will be cited by short titles. Most of the short titles (e.g., Burnett, *Letters of Members*; Kimball, *Jefferson, Architect*) are self-explanatory; but others, cited with great frequency, are drastically abbreviated (e.g., PMHB for *Pennsylvania Magazine of History and Biography*). A preliminary list of the very abbreviated short titles is given in the Guide to Editorial Apparatus at page xlii in this volume.

From the foregoing it may be observed that the editors have endeavored to simplify the technical apparatus as much as possible so that it could be grasped quickly by the specialist or by the general reader. Our descriptive and location symbols, explained in the Guide to Editorial Apparatus, are intended to accord with logic rather than caprice; we have not taken as a model the editor of Benjamin Franklin's *Political, Miscellaneous, and Philosophical Pieces*, who used the symbols "A.B.T." and "A.D.T." to stand respectively for "American Politics *before* the Troubles" and "American Politics *during* the Troubles." Our moderate degree of conventionalization of the text is also intended to make for ready use of the volumes. If even this degree of conventionalization, however, should be disturbing to those who prefer a high literal fidelity to the text, there is much to be said for the method we have chosen. First, though Jefferson made extensive use of abbreviations and contractions in informal memoranda and in rough drafts of letters, he himself expanded such words in fair copies of letters and in documents intended for public view; he often wrote "Xn" in a rough draft, but "Christian" in the fair copy of it. Since professional historians, editors of historical documents, and specialists are the ones who are most likely to be interested in exact literalness, our editorial files and photoduplicates will be permanently deposited in the Library of Congress, where the accuracy of the editors' expansions of abbreviations and contractions can easily be verified.

Finally, to express a hope rather than a conviction, the editors wish to avoid adding one particular item to the editorial apparatus.

INTRODUCTION

They will do all that is possible to eliminate the need for it, but they fear that a part of the final volume of this series will be obliged to bear the rubric *errata et corrigenda*. Recognizing the impossibility of full success, the editors will nevertheless exert every effort to reduce this section of the work to the smallest dimensions possible. The editors will be grateful to all who discover and report errors of any sort—typographical, editorial, factual, or otherwise. They will also appreciate any information about any Jefferson letters or documents or variant copies thereof which may be discovered during the progress of the work.

JULIAN P. BOYD

1 February 1950

GUIDE TO EDITORIAL APPARATUS

1. *TEXTUAL DEVICES*

The following devices are employed throughout the work to clarify the presentation of the text.

[. . .], [. . . .]   One or two words missing and not conjecturable.

[. . .]¹, [. . . .]¹   More than two words missing and not conjectur-able; subjoined footnote estimates number of words missing.

[   ]   Number or part of a number missing or illegible.

[roman]   Conjectural reading for missing or illegible matter. A question mark follows when the reading is doubtful.

[*italic*]   Editorial comment inserted in the text.

⟨*italic*⟩   Matter deleted in the MS but restored in our text.

2. *DESCRIPTIVE SYMBOLS*

The following symbols are employed throughout the work to describe the various kinds of manuscript originals. When a series of versions is recorded, *the first to be recorded is the version used for the printed text.*

Dft   draft (Usually a composition or rough draft; later drafts, when identifiable as such, are des-ignated "2d Dft," &c.)

Dupl   duplicate

MS   manuscript (arbitrarily applied to most docu-ments other than letters)

N   note, notes (memoranda, fragments, &c.)

PoC   polygraph copy

PrC   press copy

RC   recipient's copy

SC   stylograph copy

Tripl   triplicate

All manuscripts of the above types are assumed to be in the hand of the author of the document to which the descriptive symbol pertains. If not, that fact is stated. On the other hand, the follow-

ing types of manuscripts are assumed *not* to be in the hand of the author, and exceptions will be noted:

FC   file copy (Applied to all forms of retained copies, such as letter-book copies, clerks' copies, &c.)

Tr   transcript (Applied to both contemporary and later copies; period of transcription, unless clear by implication, will be given when known.)

3. LOCATION SYMBOLS

The locations of documents printed in this edition from originals in public institutions in the United States are indicated by means of the symbols used in the National Union Catalog in the Library of Congress. The locations of documents printed from originals in institutions not in the United States, or from originals in private hands, or from printed sources, are given in fuller, self-explanatory form. The following list specifies only the symbols for institutions in the United States which are represented in Volume 1; a similar list, appropriately revised and augmented, will appear in each succeeding volume. The list for Volume 1 illustrates fairly adequately the principles on which these symbols are made. A typical symbol consists of three units joined together, proceeding from the largest to the smallest geographical unit: (1) an abbreviation for the state, followed by (2) an abbreviation for the city or town, followed and completed by (3) an abbreviation for the institution in question. Hence MWA stands for Massachusetts, Worcester, American Antiquarian Society. To obtain further compression, all state libraries are represented by the abbreviation for the state alone (thus Ct for Connecticut State Library); the symbols for state universities and statewide historical societies omit the city or town (thus ViU for University of Virginia, MHi for Massachusetts Historical Society); and the symbols for certain large and readily identifiable libraries likewise omit the second (city or town) unit (thus CtY for Yale University, DLC for Library of Congress).

CSmH   Henry E. Huntington Library, San Marino, California
Ct   Connecticut State Library
CtSoP   Pequot Library, Southport, Connecticut
CtY   Yale University
DLC   Library of Congress

MB	Boston Public Library
MHi	Massachusetts Historical Society
MWA	American Antiquarian Society, Worcester, Massachusetts
MeHi	Maine Historical Society
NHi	New-York Historical Society
NN	New York Public Library
NNP	Pierpont Morgan Library, New York City
NcDAH	North Carolina Department of Archives and History
NcU	University of North Carolina
NjP	Princeton University
PHi	Historical Society of Pennsylvania
PPAP	American Philosophical Society, Philadelphia, Pennsylvania
RHi	Rhode Island Historical Society
Vi	Virginia State Library
ViHi	Virginia Historical Society
ViU	University of Virginia
ViWC	Colonial Williamsburg, Inc., Williamsburg, Virginia
WHi	State Historical Society of Wisconsin

4. OTHER ABBREVIATIONS

The following abbreviations are commonly employed in the annotation throughout the work.

TJ   Thomas Jefferson

TJ Editorial Files   Photoduplicates and other editorial materials in the office of *The Papers of Thomas Jefferson*, Princeton University Library

TJ Papers   Jefferson Papers (Applied to a collection of manuscripts when the precise location of a given document must be furnished, and always preceded by the symbol for the institutional repository; thus "DLC: TJ Papers, 4:628-9" represents a document in the Library of Congress, Jefferson Papers, volume 4, pages 628 and 629.)

PCC   Papers of the Continental Congress, in the Library of Congress

RG   Record Group (Used in designating the location of documents in the National Archives.)

5. SHORT TITLES

The following list includes only those short titles of works cited with great frequency, and therefore in very abbreviated form, throughout this edition. Their expanded forms are given here only in the degree of fullness needed for unmistakable identification. Since it is impossible to anticipate all the works to be cited in such very abbreviated form, the list will be revised, as necessary, from volume to volume.

Biog. Dir. Cong.   *Biographical Directory of Congress, 1774-1927*

B.M. Cat.   British Museum, *General Catalogue of Printed Books,* London, 1931—. Also *The British Museum Catalogue of Printed Books, 1881-1900,* Ann Arbor, 1946.

B.N. Cat.   *Catalogue général des livres imprimés de la Bibliothèque Nationale. Auteurs.*

C & D   See *Va. Gaz.*

Clayton-Torrence   William Clayton-Torrence, *A Trial Bibliography of Colonial Virginia (1754-1776)*; printed as part of Virginia State Library, *Sixth Report,* 1909

CVSP   *Calendar of Virginia State Papers . . . Preserved in the Capitol at Richmond*

Conv. Jour.   See *Va. Conv. Jour.*

D & H   See *Va. Gaz.*

D & N   See *Va. Gaz.*

DAB   *Dictionary of American Biography*

DAE   *Dictionary of American English*

DAH   *Dictionary of American History*

DNB   *Dictionary of National Biography*

Evans   Charles Evans, *American Bibliography*

Ford   Paul Leicester Ford, ed., *The Writings of Thomas Jefferson,* "Letterpress Edition," N.Y., 1892-1899

HAW   Henry A. Washington, ed., *The Writings of Thomas Jefferson,* Washington, 1853-1854

Heitman   Francis B. Heitman, *Historical Register of Officers of the Continental Army,* new edn., Washington, 1914; also the same compiler's *Historical Register and Dictionary of the United States Army* [1789-1903], Washington, 1903

Hening   William W. Hening, *The Statutes at Large; Being a Collection of All the Laws of Virginia*

JCC   *Journals of the Continental Congress, 1774-1789,* ed. W. C. Ford and others, Washington, 1904-1937

JHB *Journals of the House of Burgesses of Virginia, 1619-1776*, Richmond, 1905-1915

JHD *Journal of the House of Delegates of the Commonwealth of Virginia* (cited by session and date of publication)

Johnston, "Jefferson Bibliography" Richard H. Johnston, "A Contribution to a Bibliography of Thomas Jefferson," *Writings of Thomas Jefferson*, ed. Lipscomb and Bergh, xx, separately paged following the Index

L & B Andrew A. Lipscomb and Albert E. Bergh, eds., *The Writings of Thomas Jefferson*, "Memorial Edition," Washington, 1903-1904

L.C. Cat. *A Catalogue of Books Represented by Library of Congress Printed Cards*, Ann Arbor, 1942-1946; also *Supplement*, 1948.

Library Catalogue, 1783 Jefferson's MS list of books owned and wanted in 1783 (original in Massachusetts Historical Society)

Library Catalogue, 1815 *Catalogue of the Library of the United States*, Washington, 1815

Library Catalogue, 1829 *Catalogue. President Jefferson's Library*, Washington, 1829

OED *A New English Dictionary on Historical Principles*, Oxford, 1888-1933

Official Letters *Official Letters of the Governors of the State of Virginia*, ed. H. R. McIlwaine

P & D See *Va. Gaz.*

PMHB *The Pennsylvania Magazine of History and Biography*

Randall, *Life* Henry S. Randall, *The Life of Thomas Jefferson*

Randolph, *Domestic Life* Sarah N. Randolph, *The Domestic Life of Thomas Jefferson*

Sabin Joseph Sabin and others, *Bibliotheca Americana. A Dictionary of Books Relating to America*

Swem, "Va. Bibliog." Earl G. Swem, "A Bibliography of Virginia," Virginia State Library, *Bulletin*, VIII, X, XII (1915-1919)

TJR Thomas Jefferson Randolph, ed., *Memoir, Correspondence, and Miscellanies, from the Papers of Thomas Jefferson*, Charlottesville, 1829

Tucker, *Life* George Tucker, *The Life of Thomas Jefferson*, Philadelphia, 1837

Tyler, *Va. Biog.* Lyon G. Tyler, *Encyclopedia of Virginia Biography*

Va. Conv. Jour. *Proceedings of the Convention of Delegates . . . in the Colony of Virginia* (cited by session and date of publication)

Va. Gaz. *Virginia Gazette* (Williamsburg, 1751-1780, and Richmond, 1780-1781). Abbreviations for publishers of the several newspapers of this name, frequently published concurrently, include the following: C & D (Clarkson & Davis), D & H (Dixon & Hunter), D & N (Dixon & Nicolson), P & D (Purdie & Dixon). In all other cases the publisher's name is not abbreviated.

VMHB *Virginia Magazine of History and Biography*
WMQ *William and Mary Quarterly*

CONTENTS

·◁§ 1768 §▷·

·◁§ 1769 §▷·

▷§ 1770 §▷·

·◁§ 1771 §▷·

CONTENTS · 1773

1774

1775

CONTENTS · 1775

CONTENTS · 1776

1776

[l]

CONTENTS · 1776

CONTENTS · 1776

CONTENTS · 1776

CONTENTS ·1776

APPENDICES

ILLUSTRATIONS

ILLUSTRATIONS

VOLUME 1

1760 · 1776

JEFFERSON CHRONOLOGY

VOLUME 1

(Only major dates are entered here. A full Jefferson Chronology is planned as one of the editorial aids at the end of this edition.)

1743 April 13 (new style). Born at Shadwell, Goochland (now Albemarle) County, Virginia.

1757 August 17. His father, Peter Jefferson, died.

1760-1762. Attended College of William and Mary.

1762. Began to study law with George Wythe at Williamsburg.

1766 May. Journeyed to Philadelphia and New York.

1767. Admitted to the bar. Began planting at Monticello.

1769. Began building at Monticello.

1769-1776. Member of House of Burgesses for Albemarle County.

1770 February. His home at Shadwell burned.

1770 November 26. Moved to Monticello.

1772 January 1. Married Martha Wayles Skelton.

1772 September 27. His daughter Martha born.

1774 August. His *Summary View of the Rights of British America* published.

1775 March. Attended Virginia Convention at Richmond.

1775 June 21 to July 31. Attended Continental Congress at Philadelphia.

1775 August. Attended Virginia Convention at Richmond.

1775 October 2 to December 28. Attended Continental Congress at Philadelphia.

1776 March 31. His mother, Jane Randolph Jefferson, died.

1776 May 15 to September 2. Attended Continental Congress at Philadelphia.

1776 June. Drafted Declaration of Independence.

1776 September 26. Appointed Commissioner to France. October 11, declined to serve.

1776 October 11 to December 14. Attended Virginia General Assembly at Williamsburg as a member of House of Delegates.

1776 November 5. Appointed to a Committee to Revise the Laws of the Commonwealth.

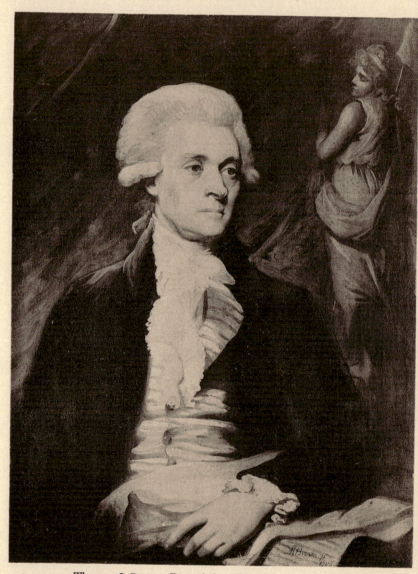

Thomas Jefferson. Portrait by Mather Brown, 1786.

THE PAPERS OF
· THOMAS JEFFERSON

To John Harvie

SIR   Shadwell, Jan. 14, 1760.

I was at Colo. Peter Randolph's about a Fortnight ago, and my Schooling falling into Discourse, he said he thought it would be to my Advantage to go to the College, and was desirous I should go, as indeed I am myself for several Reasons. In the first place as long as I stay at the Mountains the Loss of one fourth of my Time is inevitable, by Company's coming here and detaining me from School. And likewise my Absence will in a great Measure put a Stop to so much Company, and by that Means lessen the Expences of the Estate in House-Keeping. And on the other Hand by going to the College I shall get a more universal Acquaintance, which may hereafter be serviceable to me; and I suppose I can pursue my Studies in the Greek and Latin as well there as here, and likewise learn something of the Mathematics. I shall be glad of your opinion.

MS not located. Text from Ford, I, 340, where it was printed, without signature, from a copy furnished by Dr. J. S. H. Fogg of Boston. Printed earlier in Randall, *Life*, I, 19, from a copy furnished by TJ's grandson, George Wythe Randolph, of Richmond. Search of the Fogg Autograph Collection in MeHi and of auction records has not located the original.

This earliest surviving letter of TJ's, written at the age of sixteen from the home of his birth, is addressed to one of his guardians and reports a discussion of his education with another guardian—Col. PETER RANDOLPH, 1708-1767, of Chatsworth on the James, cousin of TJ's mother Jane Randolph (Randall, *Life*, I, 19; Randolph, *The Randolphs*, p. 11).

To John Page

DEAR PAGE   Fairfeilds Dec: 25. 1762.

This very day, to others the day of greatest mirth and jollity, sees me overwhelmed with more and greater misfortunes than have befallen a descendant of Adam for these thousand years past I am sure; and perhaps, after excepting Job, since the creation of the world. I think his misfortunes were somewhat greater than mine: for although we may be pretty nearly on a level in other respects, yet I thank my God I have the advantage of brother Job in this, that Satan has not as yet put forth his hand to load me with bodily afflictions. You must know, dear Page, that I am now in a house surrounded with enemies, who take counsel together against my soul and when I lay me down to rest they say among themselves Come let us destroy him. I am sure if there is such a thing as a devil in this world, he must have been here last night and have had some hand in contriving what happened to me. Do you think the cursed rats (at his instigation I suppose) did not eat up my pocket-book which was in my pocket within a foot of my head? And not contented with plenty for the present they carried away my Jemmy worked silk garters and half a dozen new minuets I had just got, to serve I suppose as provision for the winter. But of this I should not have accused the devil (because you know rats will be rats, and hunger without the addition of his instigations might have urged them to do this) if something worse and from a different quarter had not happened. You know it rained last night, or if you do not know it I am sure I do. When I went to bed I laid my watch in the usual place, and going to take her up after I arose this morning I found her, in the same place it's true but! Quantum mutatus ab illo! all afloat in water let in at a leak in the roof of the house, and as silent and still as the rats that had eat my pocket-book. Now you know if Chance had had any thing to do in this matter, there were a thousand other spots where it might have chanced to leak as well as at this one which was perpendicularly over my watch. But I'll tell you: It's my opinion that the Devil came and bored the hole over it on purpose. Well as I was saying, my poor watch had lost her speech: I should not have cared much for this, but something worse attended it: the subtle particles of the water with which the case was filled had by their penetration so overcome the cohesion of the particles of the paper of which my dear picture and watch paper were composed that in attempting to take them out to dry them Good God! mens horret referre! my cursed fingers gave them such a rent as I fear I never shall get over. This, cried I, was the last stroke Satan had in reserve for me: he knew I cared not for any thing else he could do to me, and was determined to try this last most fatal expedient. 'Multis fortunæ vulneribus percussus, huic uni me imparem sensi, et penitus succubui'! I would have cryed bitterly, but I thought it beneath the dignity of a man, and a man too who had read των οντων τα μεν εστιν εφ' ημιν τα δ'ουκ εφ'ημιν.

However whatever misfortunes may attend the picture or lover, my hearty prayers shall be that all the health and happiness which heaven can send may be the portion of the original, and that so much goodness may ever meet with what may be most agreeable in this world, as I am sure it must in the next. And now although the picture be defaced there is so lively an image of her imprinted in my mind that I shall think of her too often I fear for my peace of mind, and too often I am sure to get through Old Cooke [Coke] this winter: for God knows I have not seen him since I packed him up in my trunk in Williamsburgh.

Well, Page, I do wish the Devil had old Cooke, for I am sure I never was so tired of an old dull scoundrel in my life. What! are there so few inquietudes tacked to this momentary life of ours that we must need be loading ourselves with a thousand more? Or as brother Job sais (who by the bye I think began to whine a little under his afflictions) 'Are not my days few? Cease then that I may take comfort a little before I go whence I shall not return, even to the land of darkness and the shadow of death.' But the old-fellows say we must read to gain knowledge; and gain knowledge to make us happy and be admired. Mere jargon! Is there any such thing as happiness in this world? No: And as for admiration I am sure the man who powders most, parfumes most, embroiders most, and talks most nonsense, is most admired. Though to be candid, there are some who have too much good sense to esteem such monkey-like animals as these, in whose formation, as the saying is, the taylors and barbers go halves with God almighty: and since these are the only persons whose esteem is worth a wish, I do not know but that upon the whole the advice of these old fellows may be worth following.

You cannot conceive the satisfaction it would give me to have a letter from you: Write me very circumstantially everything which happened at the wedding. Was SHE there? Because if she was I ought to have been at the devil for not being there too. If there is any news stirring in town or country, such as deaths, courtships and marriages in the circle of my acquaintance let me know it. Remember me affectionately to all the young ladies of my acquaintance, particularly the Miss Burwells and Miss Potters, and tell them that though that heavy earthly part of me, my body, be absent, the better half of me, my soul, is ever with them, and that my best wishes shall ever attend them. Tell Miss Alice Corbin that I verily believe the rats knew I was to win a pair of garters from her, or they never would have been so cruel as to carry mine away. This

[5]

very consideration makes me so sure of the bet that I shall ask every body I see from that part of the world what pretty gentleman is making his addresses to her. I would fain ask the favor of Miss Becca Burwell to give me another watch paper, of her own cutting which I should esteem much more though it were a plain round one, than the nicest in the world cut by other hands: however I am afraid she would think this presumption after my suffering the other to get spoiled. If you think you can excuse me to her for this I should be glad if you would ask her. Tell Miss Suckey Potter that I heard just before I came out of town that she was offended with me about something: what it is I know not: but this I know, that I never was guilty of the least disrespect to her in my life either in word or deed: as far from it as it has been possible for me to be: I suppose when we meet next she will be endeavoring to repay an imaginary affront with a real one: but she may save herself the trouble, for nothing that she can say or do to me shall ever lessen her in my esteem. And I am determined allways to look upon her as the same honest-hearted good-humored agreeable lady I ever did. Tell—tell—In short tell them all ten thousand things more than either you or I can now or ever shall think of as long as we live.

My mind has been so taken up with thinking of my acquaintances that till this moment I almost imagined myself in Williamsburgh talking to you in our old unreserved way, and never observed till I turned over this leaf to what an immoderate size I had swelled my letter: however that I may not tire your patience by further additions I will make but this one more that I am sincerely and affectionately Dr Page your friend and servant, T: JEFFERSON

P. S. I am now within an easy day's ride of Shadwell whither I shall proceed in two or three days.

MS not located. Text printed from Tucker, *Life*, I, 29-33, and collated with a photostat (DLC) of the original.

TJ here first alludes to his checkered and perhaps scarcely wholehearted courtship of Rebecca Burwell, sister of a college mate, Lewis Burwell, Jr., of Gloucester co. She is the "R. B.," "Belinda," "Adnileb," and "Campana in die" of the following letters. The Burwells' Gloucester residence was named FAIRFIELD, and it has been supposed that TJ's letter was written from there, but Rebecca lived at York, and from the postscript ("I am now within an easy day's ride of Shadwell"), TJ must have been staying at a different Fairfield(s), most likely Col. John Bolling's place in Chesterfield co.; Bolling married TJ's sister Mary, 24 June 1760 (Randolph, *The Randolphs*, p. 114), and TJ's official papers were stored at Bolling's Fairfield during the British invasion in 1781 (Bolling Stark to TJ, 30 Apr. 1781).

To John Page

Dr. Page   Shadwell Jan. 20th. 1763.

I have been thinking this half hour how to begin my letter and cannot for my soul make it out. I wish to the Lord one could write a letter without any beginning for I am sure it allways puzzles me more than all the rest of it. And to tell you the plain truth I have not a syllable to write to you about. For I do not conceive that any thing can happen in my world which you would give a curse to know, or I either. All things here appear to me to trudge on in one and the same round: we rise in the morning that we may eat breakfast, dinner and supper and go to bed again that we may get up the next morning and do the same: so that you never saw two peas more alike than our yesterday and to-day. Under these circumstances what would you have me say? Would you that I should write nothing but truth? I tell you I know nothing that is true. Or would you rather that I should write you a pack of lies? Why unless they were more ingenious than I am able to invent they would furnish you with little amusement. What can I do then? Nothing, but ask you the news in your world. How have you done since I saw you? How did Nancy look at you when you danced with her at Southal's? Have you any glimmering of hope? How does R. B. do? What do you think of my affair, or what would you advise me to do? Had I better stay here and do nothing, or go down and do less? Or in other words had I better stay here while I am here, or go down that I may have the pleasure of sailing up the river again in a full-rigged flat? Inclination tells me to go, receive my sentence, and be no longer in suspence: but, reason says if you go and your attempt proves unsuccesful you will be ten times more wretched than ever. In my last to you dated Fairfeilds Dec: 25th I wrote to you of the losses I had sustained; in the present I may mention one more which is the loss of the whites of my eyes, in the room of which I have got reds, which give me such exquisite pain that I have not attempted to read any thing since a few days after Jack Walker went down, and God knows when I shall be able to do it. I have some thoughts of going to Petersburg if the actors go there in May. If I do, I do not know but I may keep on to Williamsburg as the birthnight will be near. I hear that Ben: Harrison has been to Wilton: let me know his success. Have you an inclination to travel, Page? Because if you have I shall be glad of your company. For you must know that as soon [as t]he Rebecca (the name [I] intend to give the vessel above mentioned) is completely finished I intend to hoist sail and away. I shall visit particularly England Holland France Spain Italy (where I would buy me a good fiddle) and Egypt and return through the British provinces to the northward home. This, to be sure, would take us two or three years and if we should not both be cured of love in that time I think the devil would be in it. After desiring you to remember me to acquaintances below, male and female I subscribe myself Dr Page Your friend and servant   T: JEFFERSON

P. S. Feb: 12th. As I was disappointed in sending the above at the time I expected I think I have a right to add a postscript half as long as the letter at least. In a letter from Jack Walker received since writing the above he assures me the small pox is in town, so you may scratch out that sentence of my letter wherein I mentioned coming to ·Williamsburgh so soon. I have heard that poor Nancy wandered from home not long since in the night, and that it was supposed to be occasioned by a fit of the Hystericks, however if she did, and if what you told me about the West-Indian and her was true, I ascribe it to a different cause, and would not draw my bet with J: Edmunds for a bottle of claret. [My] eyes still continue [as red a]s ever, and if they were to begin to mend now I should not expect to be [. . .] any thing this month. The small-pox being in town will open an inexhaustible fund of news for you to write me. Miss Willis is to be married next week to Dangerfield. Why cannot you and I be married too, Page, when and to whom we would chuse? Do you think it would cause any such mighty disorders among the planets? Or do you imagine it would be attended with such very bad consequences in this bit of a world, this clod of dirt, which I insist is the vilest of the whole system? No body knows how much I wish to be with you, 'sed non ita facto datum.' Remember me to Brown, to Willis, to W: Armistead, and to every body else. When is Brown to be married? Is there no probability of either you or Willis's paying the infant of arrack we betted? I shall begin to curse you very soon if you do not write to me. You can not complain that you want opportunities since you need only put a letter in the post-office at any time and I shall soon get it. I verily beleive Page that I shall die soon, and yet I can give no other reason for it but that I am tired with living. At this moment when I am writing I am scarcely sensible that I exist. Adieu Dear Page.

T: JEFFERSON

P. S.   March 11th.   Being again disappointed and too indolent to transcribe the letter I add another postscript. Since writing [. . .]

I have heard the w[hole] story of Nancy's misfortune, as also of her [recov]ery. If you are in Williamsburg write to me by the bearer who stays in town a day. I am Dr. Page yours &c.,

T: JEFFERSON

RC (CtY). Printed frequently but defectively since its first appearance in Tucker, *Life*, I, 33-4; the postscript of 12 Feb. was first printed by Kimball, *Road to Glory*, p. 68-9. Customarily read as the 20th, the date may be Jan. 28th.

This letter mentions a number of the correspondents' friends and haunts that are not identifiable with certainty. Those that can be identified are: NANCY, probably Anne Randolph (called Nancy Wilton from her father's place on the James), who married TJ's friend BENJAMIN HARRISON (1743-1807) of Brandon (VMHB, XXXIV [1926], 386); SOUTHAL'S, presumably the home of James Barrett Southal or Southall in Williamsburg (Tyler, *Williamsburg*, frontispiece map; XLV [1937], 282); R[EBECCA] B[UR-WELL]; JACK WALKER of Castle Hill, Albemarle co., John EDMUNDS, and Westwood ARMISTEAD, three of TJ's and Page's college mates (WMQ, 2d ser., I [1921], 29, 32, 41); Mary WIL-LIS and Col. William DANGERFIELD, of Coventry, Spotsylvania co., who were married 10 Mch. 1763 (VMHB, XXXII [1924], 135); and Francis WILLIS of White Hall, Gloucester co., a fellow student in law at Williamsburg (Tyler, *The Tylers*, I, 55). The expression FULL-RIGGED FLAT alludes to the flat-boats used in transporting tobacco on the Virginia rivers (see DAE, *flat*, noun 4); TJ doubtless means he would return empty-handed. INFANT OF AR-RACK: "Infant" is perhaps a playful term for a large container (see OED, *infant*, noun 4); the phrase suggests the famous agreement between Peter Jefferson and William Randolph, whereby TJ's father in 1736 acquired the Shadwell property "for and in consideration of Henry Wetherburn's biggest bowl of Arrack punch" (WMQ, 1st ser., V [1896-1897], 112).

To John Page

DEAR PAGE   Shadwell July 15'th 1763

Your's of May 30'th came safe to hand. The rival you mentioned I know not whether to think formidable or not as there has been so great an opening for him during my absence. I say 'has been' because I expect there is one no longer since you have undertaken to act as my attorney. You advise me to 'go immediately and lay siege in form.' You certainly did not think at the time you wrote this of that paragraph in my letter wherein I mentioned to you my resolution of going to Britain. And to begin an affair of that kind now, and carry it on so long a time in form is by no means a proper plan. No, no, Page, whatever assurances I may give her in private of my esteem for her, or whatever assurances I may ask in return from her, depend on it they must be kept in private. Necessity will oblige me to proceed in a method which is not generally thought fair, that of treating with a ward before obtaining the approbation of her guardian. I say necessity will oblige me to it, because I never can bear to remain in suspence so long a time. If I am to succeed the sooner I know it the less uneasiness I shall have to go through: if I am to meet with a disappointment the sooner I know it the more of life I shall have to wear it off: and if I do meet with one, I hope in god and verily beleive it will be the last. I assure you that I almost envy you your present freedom; and if Belinda will not accept of my service it shall never be offered to another. That she may I pray most sincerely, but that she will, she never gave me reason to hope. With regard to my not proceeding in form I do not know how she may like it: I am afraid not much: that her guardians would not if they should know of it is very certain. But I should think that if they were consulted after my return, it would be sufficient. The greatest inconvenience would be my not having the liberty of visiting so freely. This is a subject worth your talking over with her; and I wish you would and would transmit me your whole confab at length. I should be scared to death at making her so unreasonable a proposal as that of waiting untill I returned from Britain, unless she could be first prepared for it. I am afraid it will make my chance of succeeding considerably worse. But the event at last must be this, that if she consents, I shall be happy; if she does not, I must endeavor to be as much so as possible. I have thought a good deal on your case, and as mine may perhaps be similar, I must endeavor to look on it in the same light in which I have often advised you to look on yours. Perfect happiness I beleive was never intended by the deity to be the lot of any one of his creatures in this world; but that he has very much put in our power the nearness of our approaches to it, is what I as stedfastly beleive. The most fortunate of us all in our journey through life frequently meet with calamities and misfortunes which may greatly afflict us: and to fortify our minds against the attacks of these calamities and misfortunes should be one of the principal studies and endeavors of our lives. The only method of doing this is to assume a perfect resignation to the divine will, to consider that whatever does happen, must happen, and that by our uneasiness we cannot prevent the blow before it does fall, but we may add to it's force after it has fallen. These considerations and others such as these may enable us in some measure to surmount the difficulties thrown in our way, to bear up with a tolerable degree of patience under this burthen of life, and to proceed with a pious and unshaken resignation till we arrive at our journey's end, where we may deliver up our trust into the hands of him who gave it, and receive such reward as to him shall seem proportioned to our merit. Such dear Page, will be the language of the man who considers his situation in this life, and such should be the language of every man who would wish to render that situation as easy as the nature of it will admit. Few things will disturb him at all; nothing will disturb him much.

If this letter was to fall into the hands of some of our gay acquaintance, your correspondent and his solemn notions would probably be the subjects of a great deal of mirth and raillery, but to you I think I can venture to send it. It is in effect but a continuation of the many conversations we have had on subjects of this kind; and I heartily wish we could now continue these conversations face to face. The time will not be very long now before we may do it, as I expect to be in Williamsburg by the first of October if not sooner. I do not know that I shall have occasion to return if I can rent rooms in town to lodge in; and to prevent the inconveniency of moving my lodgings for the future, I think to build. No castle though I assure you, only a small house which shall contain a room for myself and another for you, and no more, unless Belinda should think proper to favor us with her company, in which case I will enlarge the plan as much as she pleases. Make my compliments to her particularly, as also to Suckey Potter, Judey Burwell and such others of my acquaintances as enquire after me. I am Dear Page your sincere friend,　　　　　　　　　　　　T: JEFFERSON

RC (George A. Ball, Muncie, Indiana, 1944).

Page's letter of 30 May is missing. THE RIVAL was Jacquelin Ambler of Yorktown, who married Rebecca Burwell 24 May 1764 (VMHB, X [1902-1903], 177).

To John Page

DEAR PAGE　　　　　　　　Williamsburg, October 7, 1763.

In the most melancholy fit that ever any poor soul was, I sit down to write to you. Last night, as merry as agreeable company and dancing with Belinda in the Apollo could make me, I never could have thought the succeeding sun would have seen me so wretched as I now am! I was prepared to say a great deal: I had dressed up in my own mind, such thoughts as occurred to me, in as moving language as I knew how, and expected to have performed in a tolerably creditable manner. But, good God! When I had an opportunity of venting them, a few broken sentences, uttered in great disorder, and interrupted with pauses of uncommon length, were the too visible marks of my strange confusion! The whole confab I will tell you, word for word, if I can, when I see you, which God send may be soon. Affairs at W. and M. are in the greatest confusion. Walker, M'Clurg and Wat Jones are expelled *pro tempore,* or, as Horrox softens it, rusticated for a month. Lewis Burwell, Warner Lewis, and one Thompson have fled to escape flagellation. I should have excepted Warner Lewis, who came off of his own accord. Jack Walker leaves town on Monday. The court is now at hand, which I must attend constantly, so that unless you come to town, there is little probability of my meeting with you any where else. For God's sake come. I am, dear Page, Your sincere friend,   T. JEFFERSON

MS not located. Text from Tucker, *Life,* I, 37, where the letter was printed from a copy furnished by a son of John Page.

In the list of disciplined students those not already identified are James MC CLURG, Walter JONES, WARNER LEWIS, and John or William THOMPSON, all of the class of 1763 (Wm. & Mary Coll., *Prov. List of Alumni,* 1941); the first two became well-known physicians. The Rev. James HORROX (i.e., Horrocks) was master of the grammar school at the College; in the following year he became president of the College and may at this time have been acting president (Tyler, *College of William and Mary,* p. 48). The order of rustication to Walker, McClurg, and Jones, on account of "injurious Behavior on Tuesday Night last to a family in Town," will be found in WMQ, 1st ser., IV (1895-1896), 44-5.

To William Fleming

DEAR WILL   Ri[chmond, ca. October 1763]

From a croud of disagreeable [companions] among whom I have spent three or four of the most tedious hours of my life, I retire into Gunn's bedchamber to converse in black and white with an absent friend. I heartily wish you were here that I might converse with a Christian once more before I die: for die I must this night unless I should be releived by the arrival of some sociable fellow. But I will now endeavor to forget my present sufferings and think of what is more agreeable to both of us. Last Saturday I left Ned Carter's where I had been happy in other good company, but particularly that of Miss Jenny Taliaferro: and though I can view the beauties of this world with the most philosophical indifference, I could not but be sensible of the justice of the character you had given me of her. She has in my opinion a great resemblance of Nancy Wilton, but prettier. I was vastly pleased with her playing on the spinnette and singing, and could not help calling to mind those sublime verses of the Cumberland genius

Oh! how I was charmed to see
Orpheus' music all in thee.

When you see Patsy Dandridge, tell her 'god bless her.' I do not like the ups and downs of a country life: to day you are frolicking with a fine girl and tomorrow you are moping by yourself. Thank god! I shall shortly be where my happiness will be less interrupted. I shall salute all the girls below in your name, particularly S——y P——r. Dear Will I have thought of the cleverest plan of life that can be imagined. You exchange your land for Edgehill, or I mine for Fairfeilds, you marry S——y P——r, I marry R————a B————l, [join] and get a pole chair and a pair of keen horses, practise the law in the same courts, and drive about to all the dances in the country together. How do you like it? Well I am sorry you are at such a distance I cannot hear your answer, however you must let me know it by the first opportunity, and all the other news in the world which you imagine will affect me. I am dear Will yours affectionately, TH: JEFFERSON

RC (The Rosenbach Company, Philadelphia, 1946). The MS is mutilated; the place and date line are almost wholly missing; and one word has been supplied from the text in the *Southern Literary Messenger*, III (1837), 305, where it was printed with four other letters to William Fleming "from the papers of a deceased revolutionary patriot, once a Judge of the Supreme Court of Appeals of Virginia"—presumably Fleming.

Probably written from the home of James Gunn (see Dumbauld, *Jefferson American Tourist*, p. 36). S——Y P——R: Suckey (Suzanna) Potter, daughter of Dr. Henry Potter of Middlesex co. (VMHB, XXVI [1919], 408). EDGEHILL . . . FAIRFEILDS: Edgehill was a plantation owned by Thomas Mann Randolph in Albemarle co. (VMHB, XXXII [1924], 39), but of the numerous estates named Fairfields or Fairfield, it is only possible to say that TJ proposed to reside at one that was near Fleming's home.

To John Page

DEAR PAGE   Devilsburgh Jan: 19. 1764.

The contents of your letter have not a little alarmed me: and really upon seriously weighing them with what has formerly passed between αδνιλεβ and myself I am somewhat at a loss what to conclude. Your 'semper saltat, semper ridet, semper loquitur, semper solicitat' &c. appear a little suspicious, but good god! it is impossible! I told you our confab in the Apollo: but I beleive I never told you that we had on another occasion. I then opened my mind more freely and more fully. I mentioned the necessity of my going to England, and the delays which would consequently be occasioned by that. I said in what manner I should conduct myself till then and explained my reasons, which appeared to give that satisfaction

I could have wished. In short I managed in such a manner that I was tolerably easy myself without doing anything which could give αδνιλεβ's friends the least umbrage, were the whole that passed to be related to them. I asked no question which would admit of a categorical answer, but assured αδνιλεβ that such questions would one day be asked. In short were I to have another interview with him I could say nothing now which I did not say then: and were I, with a view of obtaining one, licentiam solicitandi ab iis quibus degit postulare, it would be previously necessary to go the rounds cum custodibus: and after all this he could be in no other situation than he is at present. After the proofs I have given of my sincerity he can be under no apprehensions of a change in my sentiments: and were I to do as my friends advise me, I could give him no better security than he has at present. He is satisfied that I shall make him an offer, and if he intends to accept of it he will disregard those made by others. My fate depends on αδνιλεβ's present resolutions: by them I must stand or fall: if they are not favorable to me, it is out of my power to say anything to make them so which I have not said already: so that a visit could not possibly be of the least weight, and it is I am sure what he does not in the least expect. I hear you are courting F——y B————l but shall not listen to it till I hear from you. When I was up the country I wrote a letter to you dated Fairfeilds December 25. 1763. Let me know if you have received such a one. As I suppose you do not use your Statutes of Britain if you can lend them to me till I can provide myself with a copy it will infinitely oblige me. Adieu dear Page.

RC (CtY). Unsigned.

DEVILSBURGH is Williamsburg at this unhappy moment. Page's letter is lost. Αδνιλεβ is an anagram, slightly disguised by Greek characters, for Belinda (Rebecca Burwell); TJ has attempted, somewhat ineffectually, to reinforce the disguise by using masculine pronouns. F——Y B————L: Frances Burwell, daughter of Robert Carter Burwell of Isle of Wight co., who soon afterwards married John Page (VMHB, X [1902-1903], 177; DAB, under Page). TJ's letter from "up the country" of 25 Dec. 1763 has not been found.

To John Page

DEAR PAGE   Devilsburg, January 23d, 1764.

I received your letter of Wednesday the 18th instant; in that, of this day, you mention one which you wrote last Friday, and sent by the Secretary's boy; but I have neither seen nor heard of such a one. God send, mine of Jan. 19 to you may not have shared the same fate; for, by your letter, I am uncertain whether you have received it or not; you therein say, 'you hope to have received an answer from me by this time,' by which I judge it has miscarried; but you mention mine of Dec. 25, which puts me in spirits again, as I do not know how you should have got intelligence that I had wrote such a one, unless you had seen my letter of Jan. 19, in which it was mentioned—yes, there is one other way by which you might have received such intelligence. My letter of Jan. 19, may have been opened, and the person who did it may have been further incited by curiosity, to ask you if you had received such a letter as they saw mentioned therein; but God send, and I hope this is not the case. Sukey Potter, to whom I sent it, told me yesterday she delivered it to Mr. T. Nelson, the younger, who had delivered it to you—I hope with his own hand. I wish I had followed your example, and wrote it in Latin, and that I had called my dear *campana in die*, instead of αδνιλεβ.

We must fall on some scheme of communicating our thoughts to each other, which shall be totally unintelligible to every one but to ourselves. I will send you some of these days Shelton's Tachygraphical Alphabet, and directions. Jack Walker is engaged to Betsy Moore, and desired all his brethren might be made acquainted with his happiness. But I hear he will not be married this year or two. Put *campana in die* in mind of me; tell him I think as I always did. I have sent my horses up the country, so that it is out of my power to take even an airing on horseback at any time. My paper holds out no longer, so Must bid you adieu.

MS not located. Text from Tucker, *Life*, I, 37-8, where it was printed, without signature, from a copy furnished by the son of John Page.

Page's letters of 18 and 20 ("last Friday") Jan., and TJ's letter of 25 Dec. are missing. THE SECRETARY is Thomas Nelson, Sr. (1716-1782); and T. NELSON, THE YOUNGER is his nephew (1738-1789), the "Signer" and TJ's successor as governor. SHELTON'S . . .

ALPHABET: Thomas Shelton's *Tachy-Graphy. The Most Exact and Compendious Methode of Short and Swift Writing That Hath Ever Yet Been Published*. . . . London, 1646. BETSY MOORE: Elizabeth Moore, daughter of Bernard Moore of Chelsea, King William co.; she was married to John Walker in June 1764 (WMQ, 1st ser., XIX [1910-1911], 178; Walker's statement to Henry Lee, 28 Mch. 1805, in DLC: TJ Papers, 155:27117).

To William Fleming

DEAR WILL   Wmsburgh. March. 20. 1764. 11. o'clock at night.

As the messenger who delivered me your letter, informs me that your boy is to leave town tomorrow morning I will endeavor to answer it as circumstantially as the hour of the night, and a violent head ach, with which I have been afflicted these two days, will permit. With regard to the scheme which I proposed to you some time since, I am sorry to tell you it is totally frustrated by Miss R. B's marriage with Jacquelin Ambler which the people here tell me they daily expect: I say, the people here tell me so, for (can you beleive it?) I have been so abominably indolent as not to have seen her since last October, wherefore I cannot affirm that I know it from herself, though am as well satisfied that it is true as if she had told me. Well the lord bless her I say! But S——y P——r is still left for you. I have given her a description of the gentleman who, as I told her, intended to make her an offer of his hand, and asked whether or not he might expect it would be accepted. She would not determine till she saw him or his picture. Now Will, as you are a piece of a limner I desire that you will seat yourself immediately before your lookingglass and draw such a picture of yourself as you think proper: and if it should be defective, blame yourself. (Mind that I mentioned no name to her.) You say you are determined to be married as soon as possible: and advise me to do the same. No, thank ye; I will consider of it first. Many and great are the comforts of a single state, and neither of the reasons you urge can have any influence with an inhabitant and a young inhabitant too of Wmsburgh. For St. Paul only says that it is better to be married than to burn. Now I presume that if that apostle had known that providence would at an after day be so kind to any particular set of people as to furnish them with other means of extinguishing their fire than those of matrimony, he would have earnestly recommended them to their practice. Who told you that I reported you was courting Miss Dandridge and Miss Dangerfeild? It might be worth your while to ask whether they were in earnest or not. So far was I from it that I frequently bantered Miss J——y T——o about you, and told her how feelingly you spoke of her. There is scarcely any thing new going on here. You have heard I suppose that J. Page is courting Fanny Burwell. W. Bland, and Betsy Yates are to be married thursday se'nnight. The Secretary's son is expected in shortly. Willis has left town intirely so that your commands to him cannot be executed immediately, but those to the ladies I shall do myself the pleasure of delivering tomorrow night at the ball. Tom: Randolph of Tuckahoe has a suit of Mecklenburgh Silk which he offered me for a suit of broadcloth. Tell him that if they can be altered to fit me, I will be glad to take them on them terms, and if they cannot, I make no doubt but I can dispose of them here to his advantage. Perhaps you will have room to bring them in your portmanteau, or can contrive them down by some other opportunity. Let him know this immediately. My head achs, my candle is just going out, and my boy asleep, so must bid you adieu.

RC (The Rosenbach Company, Philadelphia, 1946). Unsigned. Endorsed: "Tom Jefferson's Letter 20th. March, 1764." First printed in *Southern Literary Messenger*, III (1837), 305, which omits two sentences, beginning "For St. Paul only says. . . ."

TJ'S VIOLENT HEAD ACH is the earliest recorded reference to a lifelong affliction. S——Y P——R: Sukey Potter; TJ is of course bantering Fleming about a portrait for her, since they knew one another. J——Y T——O: Jenny Taliaferro, of a far-flung Virginia family, has not been precisely identified.

To John Page

DEAR PAGE   Devilsburgh April 9th 1764.

This letter will be conveied to you by the assistance of our friend Warner Lewis. Poor fellow! never did I see one more sincerely captivated in my life. He walked to the Indian camp with her yesterday, by which means he had an opportunity of giving her two or three love squeezes by the hand, and like a true Arcadian swain, has been so enraptured ever since that he is company for no one. Betsy Yates has at last bestowed her hand on B——d and whether it was for money, beauty, or principle, will bear so nice a dispute that no one will venture to pronounce. Two days before the wedding I was not a little surprised on going to the door at my house to see him alight from his horse. He stepped up to me and desired the favor of me to come to Mr. Yates's at such a time. It was so unexpected that for some time I could make no reply; at last I said "yes" and turned about and walked back into my room. I accordingly attended, and to crown the joke, when I got there, was dubbed a bridesman. There were many other curious circumstances too tedious to mention here. Jack Walker is expected in town tomorrow. How does your pulse beat after your trip to the Isle of White? What a high figure I should have cut had I gone! When I heard who visited you there I thought I had met with the narrowest escape in the world. I wonder how I should have behaved? I am sure I should have been at a great loss. If your mistress can spare you a little time, your friends here would be very glad to see you, particularly Small, and myself, as everything is now ready for taking the height of this place above the water of the creeks. Fleming's relapse will justly afford you great matter of triumph after rallying you so much on being in love. Adieu dear Page.

[17]

P. S. Walker is just arrived: he goes out of town on Wednesday and will return again in about three weeks.

RC (CtY). Unsigned.

B——D: William Bland; his bride's father was Rev. William YATES, who until his death later this year was president of the College of William and

Mary (Meade, *Old Churches and Families*, I, 113; Tyler, *College of William and Mary*, p. 48). Page's bride-to-be, Frances Burwell, lived in ISLE OF WHITE (i.e., Wight) co.

George Gilmer to John Morgan

DEAR SIR   Virginia 11 May 1766

Give me leave to introduce the bearer my particular friend Mr. Thomas Jefferson. I need say nothing to recommend him to your esteem, your penetrating genius will discover him to be a Gentleman emminently worthy your accquaintance. Since your departure from Edinburgh there has no incident occurd worth relating. In Medecine not one article. Our friend Cocks died of a fever in London about six months past. Miss Knelly Kinaird made a run away match with Mr. Dana a Gentleman from New England; Mr. Thos: Warton married a Daughter of Sr: Robt. McKinzie [and] is appointed sole Solicitor to the Excise. Blair had not in Sepr: last put on the Toga. All the Professors I left in good health except Dr. Whyte who had been long ill of a Diabetes and was fully satisfied within himself that there was no remedy. Excuse Dear Sir this scrole. If in your memory I yet have a place, pray honour me with a line by Mr. Thos: Jefferson and you'll oblige one who ever esteemd you and shall be pleasd to have some rank in your favour. From your friend & Servant,   GEO: GILMER

RC (PHi). Addressed: "To Doctor John Morgan Professor of Medecine in Philadelphia By the particular favour of Mr Thos: Jefferson." Endorsed: "from Doctr. Geo: Gillmer Virginia May 11. 1766."

This is the single surviving letter of introduction TJ carried with him on his first trip north, reported in the following letters to Page and Willis. One

of TJ's purposes in going to Philadelphia was to be inoculated, and it is possible that Morgan performed this service for him, though according to family tradition Dr. William Shippen, Jr., did so (Malone, *Jefferson*, I, 99-100). For Gilmer, see the same, also Blanton, *Medicine in Va. in the 18th Cent.*, p. 23, 34, &c.; for Morgan see DAB.

To John Page

DEAR PAGE   Annapolis May. 25. 1766.

I received your last by T. Nelson whom I luckily met on my road hither. Surely never did small hero experience greater misadventures than I did on the first two or three days of my travelling. Twice did my horse run away with me and greatly endanger the breaking my neck on the first day. On the second I drove two hours through as copious a rain as ever I have seen, without meeting with a single house to which I could repair for shelter. On the third in going through Pamunkey, being unacquainted with the ford, I passed through water so deep as to run over the cushion as I sat on it, and to add to the danger, at that instant one wheel mounted a rock which I am confident was as high as the axle, and rendered it necessary for me to exercise all my skill in the doctrine of gravity, in order to prevent the center of gravity from being left unsupported the consequence of which would according to Bob. Carter's opinion have been the corruition of myself, chair and all into the water. Whether that would have been the case or not, let the learned determine: it was not convenient for me to try the experiment at that time, and I therefore threw my whole weight on the mounted wheel and escaped the danger. I confess that on this occasion I was seised with a violent hydrophobia. I had the pleasure of passing two or three days on my way hither at the two Will. Fitzhugh's and Colo. Harrison's where were S. Potter, P. Stith, and Ben Harrison, since which time I have seen no face known to me before, except Capt. Mitchell's who is here. But I will now give you some account of what I have seen in this Metropolis. The assembly happens to be sitting at this time. Their upper and lower house, as they call them, sit in different houses. I went into the lower, sitting in an old court-house, which, judging from it's form and appearance, was built in the year one. I was surprised on approaching it to hear as great a noise and hubbub as you will usually observe at a publick meeting of the planters in Virginia. The first object which struck me after my entrance was the figure of a little old man dressed but indifferently, with a yellow queüe wig on, and mounted in the judge's chair. This the gentleman who walked with me informed me was the speaker, a man of a very fair character, but who by the bye has very little the air of a speaker. At one end of the justices' bench stood a man whom in another place I should from his dress and phis have taken for Goodall the lawyer in Williamsburgh, reading a bill then before the house with a schoolboy tone and an abrupt pause at every half dozen words. This I found to be the clerk of the assembly. The mob (for such was their appearance) sat covered on the justices' and lawyers' benches, and were divided into little clubs amusing themselves in the common chit chat way. I was surprised to see them address the speaker without rising from their seats, and three, four, and five at a time without being checked. When [a motion was] made, the speaker instead of putting the question in the usual form only asked the gentlemen whether they chose that such or such a thing should be done, and was answered by a yes sir, or no sir: and tho' the voices appeared frequently to be divided, they never would go to the trouble of dividing the house, but the clerk entered the resolutions, I supposed, as he thought proper. In short every thing seems to be carried without the house in general's knowing what was proposed. The situation of this place is extremely beautiful, and very commodious for trade having a most secure port capable of receiving the largest vessels, those of 400 hh'ds being able to brush against the sides of the dock. The houses are in general better than those in Williamsburgh, but the gardens more indifferent. The two towns seem much of a size. They have no publick buildings worth mentioning except a governor's house, the hull of which after being nearly finished, they have suffered to go to ruin. I would give you an account of the rejoicings here on the repeal of the stamp act but this you will probably see in print before my letter can reach you. I shall proceed tomorrow to Philadelphia where I shall make the stay necessary for inoculation, thence going on to New York. I shall return by water to Williamsburgh, about the middle of July, till which time you have the prayers of Dear Page your affectionate friend,   TH: JEFFERSON

P. S. I should be glad if you could in some indirect manner, without discovering that it was my desire, let J. Randolph know when I propose to be in the city of Williamsburgh.

RC (NN). Addressed: "Mr John Page jun'r in York Virginia."

Since TJ's surviving Account Books begin in 1767, it is not possible to trace his route north with perfect accuracy. His accident occurred while fording the PAMUNKEY River, the principal tributary of the York, though since this was not on the route from Albemarle to Annapolis, TJ perhaps started from Williamsburg. CORRUTION: Apparently coined by TJ from Lat. *corruo*, to collapse or tumble down. The following commentary on TJ's account of the Maryland Assembly was furnished by Mr. Morris L. Radoff, Archivist, Hall of Records, Annapolis: "The Assembly to which Jefferson referred had been elected in 1764. This was its third meeting: it opened on May 9 and was prorogued on May 27, 1766. The 'courthouse' in which the Lower House met was the State House constructed over the ruins of the first Capitol, which burned in 1704. The new building was used for the first time in 1706 and was therefore 60 years old at this time. The detached building in which the Upper House met is presumed to have been the old Armory. Other observers recorded equally bad impressions of the building, and it was shortly thereafter torn down to make way for the beautiful structure now standing on the same site. The Speaker of the Lower House at this session was Colonel Robert Lloyd of Queen Anne's County; the clerk, Michael Macnemara. It cannot be certain, of course, that these are the gentlemen to whom Jefferson referred with so little admiration. The behavior of the members of the Lower House and its careless manner of conducting business are traditional. The port which Jefferson admired has long since become part of the U.S. Naval Academy grounds. The Governor's house was begun for Governor Bladen; it remained unfinished until it was occupied by St. John's College after the Revolution. It is now called McDowell Hall."

To Francis Willis

DEAR WILLIS   Wmsburgh July 23. 1766.

I am at length arrived here, after a long, but agreeable trip along the continent as far as New York; which however was less agreeable for want of a companion, whose equal curiosity might have kept one in countenance in rambling over the different places which lie on the road. This I expected from you, and wrote to you upon that subject early in the spring; and nothing could equal my vexation at finding you had taken the same trip a few weeks before me; without giving me previous notice; but when I learned in Philadelphia the importance of the business you went on, it cooperated with a secret partiality with which I judge of all your actions in exculpating a step which had given me such discontent. I wrote up the country a few days ago for my horses, which I shall expect from the 29'th of this month till the 8'th of the next. Between these two days I think they will certainly be here. I shall go to Colo. Moore's tomorrow where I propose to stay with J. Walker till their arrival and from thence I shall come immediately to Gloucester. Make my compliments to Warner Lewis, and, if you should see him, to Jack Page, and acquaint them with the near prospect I have of being happy in their company. I have many things to say to you but as I shall see you soon, I will not trust them to black and white; in the mean time be assured that I am Dr. Willis Your friend and servt.,   TH: JEFFERSON

P. S. My compliments to Mr. and Mrs. Willis and the family.

RC (Mrs. Ellen Barbour Glines, Puerto Rico; deposited in Ct, 1946).
TJ's earlier letter to Willis has not been found, nor is the nature of Willis' pressing business in New York known.

Notice of a Land Lottery

Pittsylvania, April 8, 1768.

A SCHEME

For disposing of (by way of Lottery) the several valuable tracts of LAND *that are below mentioned, belonging to the subscriber.*

CONTENTS OF THE PRIZES.

	No.	Val. £
A TRACT of 100 acres of land, 40 acres of which are good low grounds, on *Roanoke* river, in *Mecklenburg* county, with an established ferry belonging to it; and also 700 acres on *Neuse* river, *North Carolina*; about 200 acres thereof very good low grounds, and the high land very good.	—1—	500
A tract of 950 acres in *Amherst* county on *Stoval's* creek, being fine tobacco land, and within 3 or four miles of *Stoval's* ferry, on *James* river, from whence tobacco, &c. are transported to market down by water.	—1—	250
A tract of 300 acres on the said Stoval's creek, adjoining the last-mentioned tract, being also extraordinary good tobacco land.	—1—	120
A tract of 361 acres of *Stoval's* creek aforesaid, being also good tobacco land.	—1—	80
A tract of 357 acres on the south side of *Roanoke*, in *Mecklenburg*, being kind free land and tolerable good for tobacco.	—1—	80
An entry of 640 acres of good land, on *Fall* creek, near the *Neuse* tract.	—1—	50
A tract of 400 acres on *Stoval's* creek, adjoining the other tracts on the said creek.	—1—	20
A prize to be paid in cash, out of the produce of the lottery.	—1—	75
Twenty-five at £.5, to be paid as aforesaid.	—25—	125

	£.1300
33 Prizes, - - -	
227 Blanks, - - -	

	£.1300
260 Tickets at £.5.	

Those that purchase tickets are only required to give their bonds for the money, payable when the lottery is drawn, which is to be on *Monday* the 24th day of *October* next, at the *Rocky Ridge*, under the management of *Clement Read, Isaac Read, Paul Carrington, Matthew Marable, Robert Munford* of Mecklenburg, *Henry Delony, David Garland, William Taylor, John Winn, David Mason, Gray Briggs, John Bolling, William Cabell, Joseph Cabell, Alexander Trent, Peterfield Trent, Thomas Jefferson* of *Albemarle*, and *George Robertson* of *Chesterfield*, Gentlemen, who will be impowered to execute conveyances for the prizes drawn by the fortunate adventurers, and of whom tickets may be had, also at both the Printing-Offices, and of the subscriber.

GEORGE JEFFERSON.

Printed from *Virginia Gazette* (Rind), 28 Apr. 1768.

To William Preston

DEAR SIR   Staunton Aug. 18. 1768.

I sit down to petition your suffrage in favor of a friend, whose virtues and abilities have made him such to me, and will give him equal place in your esteem whenever you have an opportunity of becoming acquainted with them. The gentleman I speak of is the Revd. James Fontaine, who offers himself as a candidate for the place of chaplain to the house of burgesses. I do not wish to derogate from the merit of the gentleman who possessed that office last, but I can not help hoping that every friend to genius, where the other qualities of the competitors are equal, will give a preference to superior abilities. Integrity of heart and purity of manners recommend Messrs. Price and Fontaine equally to our esteem; but in acuteness of penetration, accuracy of judgment, elegance of composition, propriety of performing the divine service, and in every work of genius, the former is left a great distance behind the latter. I do not ask your favor on a bare assurance of this from me, but from that knowledge of Mr. Fontaine's superiority which you will obtain on enquiring of others. I have heard as yet no argument against the preference of Fontaine, but that the other has been possessed of the office, an argument which with you will need no confutation. These small preferments should be reserved to reward and encorage genius, and not be strowed with an indiscriminating hand among the common herd of competitors. I am Dear Sir Your friend and servt,   TH: JEFFERSON

RC (NN). The name of the addressee, apparently cut from the address, has been attached at the lower left front of the MS. The half of the sheet which should bear the address is not present.

To Thomas Turpin

DEAR SIR   Shadwell Feb. 5. 1769.

I am truly concerned that it is not in my power to undertake the superintendance of your son in his studies; but my situation both present and future render it utterly impossible. I do not expect to be here more than two months in the whole between this and November next, at which time I propose to remove to another habitation which I am about to erect, and on a plan so contracted as that I shall have but one spare bedchamber for whatever visitants I may have. Nor have I reason to expect at any future day to pass a greater proportion of my time at home. Thus situated it would even have been injustice to Phill to have undertaken to give him an assistance which will not be within my power; a task which I otherwise should with the greatest pleasure have taken on me, and would have desired no higher satisfaction than to see him hold that rank in the profession to which his genius and application must surely advance him. These however encourage me to hope that the presence of an assistant will be little necessary. I always was of opinion that the placing a youth to study with an attorney was rather a prejudice than a help. We are all too apt by shifting on them our business, to incroach on that time which should be devoted to their studies. The only help a youth wants is to be directed what books to read, and in what order to read them. I have accordingly recommended strongly to Phill to put himself into apprenticeship with no one, but to employ his time for himself alone. To enable him to do this to advantage I have laid down a plan of study which will afford him all the assistance a tutor could, without subjecting him to the inconvenience of expending his own time for the emolument of another. One difficulty only occurs, that is, the want of books. But this I am in hopes you will think less of remedying when it is considered that had he been placed under the care of another, a proper collection of books must have been provided for him before he engaged in the practice of his profession; for a lawyer without books would be like a workman without tools. The only difference then is that they must now be procured something earlier. Should you think it necessary, it would be better to consider the money laid out in books as a part of the provision made for him, and to deduct it from what you intended to give him, than that he should be without them. I have given him a catalogue of such as will be necessary, amounting in the whole to about £100. sterling, but divided into four invoices. Should Phill enter on the plan of study recommended, I shall endeavor as often as possible to take your house in my way to and from Williamsburgh as it will afford me the double satisfaction of observing his progress in science and of seeing yourself, my aunt, and the family. I am Dear Sir with great respect your most humble servant,   TH: JEFFERSON

RC (Members of the Turpin family, Cincinnati, 1946).

A letter remarkable for its sweeping and penetrating criticism of the apprentice system of legal training, in which TJ was himself schooled and which was universal in eighteenth-century America. Richard B. Morris, of Columbia University, cites other criticisms, as follows: Theodore Sedgwick, *Memoirs of the Life of William Livingston*, N.Y., 1833, p. 57-8; John Adams, *Works*, II, 52; see also John Macpherson (a student in John Dickinson's office) to William Paterson, 9 Apr. 1769, in Glenn, *Some Colonial Mansions*, 2d ser., p. 456-7. PHILL, i.e., Philip Turpin, TJ's first cousin, later

studied medicine at Edinburgh; see TJ's letter to him, 29 July 1783. The PLAN OF STUDY drawn up by TJ is missing, but some idea of it can be obtained from a reading list TJ sent about this time to Bernard Moore, another young man beginning the study of law (original missing; revised copy enclosed in TJ to John Minor, 30 Aug. 1814). ANOTHER HABITATION: This is the earliest reference in TJ's surviving correspondence to Monticello, though an entry in the Garden Book, 3 Aug. 1767, records inoculating "common cherry buds into stocks of large kind at Monticello." For the progress of plans and work on the new home, see Kimball, *Road to Glory*, p. 147ff.

To Alexander White

[Dea]r Sir   Williamsburgh April 19. 1769.

Your messenger being about to return before I have an opportunity of conferring with Mr. Blair on the subject of your caveats, I must undertake an answer to your letter tho' deprived of his assistance.

As to the small survey of 220 acres, we need be at no other trouble or expence about it, Mrs. Wood and James Wood not proposing to defend it, and Harrison (as I understand) laying no claim to that. Yet for fear he should officiously defend it for them by proving the works were returned and fees paid, it might not be improper to procure from Mrs. Wood and James Wood in writing a declaration of their assent to a confirmation of your Caveat against them. This would effectually prevent an injury from any defence which Harrison should set up on their behalf either in this or the other Caveat.

As to the larger tract of 400 acres which Harrison has entered, Mrs. Wood and James, as I understand you, will be passive: and opposition can only come from Harrison who may interplead to support his own right. Here then it will be necessary to prove the prior entry and survey made by Colo. Wood, by a copy of the entry under the surveior's hand and also of the platt if it is to be had. This backed by the testimony of either Green or Sevear will in my opinion be sufficient to set aside Harrison's claim. It may not be amiss, when we dispute with him, to be furnished with written proof that Colo. Wood's title has come to the defendants, in case we should want it. As Harrison and Sevear could only prove the same facts I shall summon one of them alone, to save expence: since besides the charges of attendance there is a dollar to be paid for every summons and we sometimes issue two or three before the sheriffs will serve them.

Benson's entering for lands already patented affords sufficient ground for a caveat before he obtains a patent for them and this is the only method of preventing his obtaining a patent. But in this each party must bear his own costs, as the council have no power of giving costs, unless when they give them against a plaintiff by annexing it as a condition before they will give him an order of council. I shall have the Secretary's office searched for the works in the above caveats. I am Dr. Sir Your friend and servt.,

TH: JEFFERSON

RC (ViU). Endorsed: "Jefferson Apl 1769."

The recipient's name is here first assigned, on the basis of evidence in TJ's Case Book. In the present letter TJ is advising his client, plaintiff in Cases 140 and 141, dated 18 Aug. 1768. These are both suits by Alexander White against Mary WOOD and JAMES WOOD involving properties on the Shenandoah River in Augusta co. The suits were strictly family affairs, for Mary Wood was the widow of Col. James WOOD, founder of Winchester, Va.; James (colonel in the Revolution and governor of Virginia, 1799-1802) was her son; and Alexander White (later a congressman), of Frederick co., was her son-in-law. Mathew HARRISON, of Augusta co., mentioned in the second paragraph, was another son-in-law; TJ acted for White in a suit against Harrison a little later; see TJ's Case Book, No. 305, 22 June 1769. On the Wood family, see T. K. Cartmell, *Shenandoah Valley Pioneers*, Winchester, Va., 1909, p. 288-90; on WHITE, see *Biog. Dir. Cong.* SEVEAR must be John Sevier, the well-known Tennessee pioneer, at this time resident in the Shenandoah Valley (DAB).

Resolutions for an Answer to Governor Botetourt's Speech

[8 May 1769]

Resolved, Nemine contradicente, That a most humble and dutiful Address be presented to his Excellency the Governor, returning Thanks for his very affectionate Speech at the Opening of this Session;

Expressing our firm Attachment to his Majesty's sacred Person and Government, and a lively Sense of his Royal Favour, manifested by frequent Approbations of our former Conduct; by extending his Paternal Regard to all his Subjects however remote; and, by his gracious Purpose, that our Chief Governor shall, in future, reside among us;

Declaring, that we esteem, as a peculiar Mark of Attention to our Happiness, the Appointment of his Lordship to preside over this Colony; and, that his Virtues and Abilities, manifested ever since his Arrival here, are to us the firmest Assurance, that Wisdom and Benevolence will distinguish his Administration;

Joining, in Congratulations on the Birth of another Princess, and the happy Restoration of her Majesty's Health;

Assuring his Excellency, that we shall, with Candour, proceed to the important Business on which we are met in General Assembly; and that, if in the Course of our Deliberations, any Matters shall arise, which may in any way affect the Interests of *Great-Britain*, these shall ever be discussed on this ruling Principle, that her Interests, and Ours, are inseparably the same: And, finally, offering our Prayers, that Providence, and the Royal Pleasure, may long continue his Lordship the happy Ruler of a free and an happy People.

MS not located. Text from *Journals of the House of Burgesses, 1766-1769*, Richmond, 1906, p. 189.

This, the first of TJ's state papers, is purely ceremonial in nature and was prepared by him on the first day of the first session of the House of Burgesses in which he sat as a member for Albemarle co. For his own account of the circumstances, see TJ to William Wirt, 5 Aug. 1815. He prepared a draft address (now missing) which was objected to by Robert Carter Nicholas. The amplified version by Nicholas, which was accepted, is printed in JHB, 1766-1769, p. 199-200.

Virginia Nonimportation Resolutions, 1769

WILLIAMSBURG.

WEDNESDAY, THE 17TH MAY, 1769.

ABOUT 12 o'Clock his Excellency the Governor was pleased, by his Messenger, to command the Attendance of the House of Burgesses in the Council Chamber, whereupon, in Obedience to his Lordship's Command, the House, with their Speaker, immediately waited upon his Excellency, when he thought fit to dissolve the General Assembly.

The late Representatives of the People then judging it necessary that some Measures should be taken in their distressed Situation, for preserving the true and essential Interests of the Colony, resolved upon a Meeting for that very salutary Purpose, and therefore immediately, with the greatest Order and Decorum, repaired to the House of Mr. *Anthony Hay* in this City, where being assembled, it was first proposed, for the more decent and regular Discussion of such Matters as might be taken into Consideration, that a **Moderator** should be appointed, and, on the Question being put, *Peyton Randolph*, Esq; late Speaker of the House of Burgesses, was unanimously elected.

The true State of the Colony being then opened and fully explained, and it being proposed that a regular Association should be formed, a Committee was appointed to prepare the necessary and most proper Regulations for that Purpose, and they were ordered to make their Report to the General Meeting the next Day at 10 o'Clock.

THURSDAY, MAY 18.

A T A farther Meeting, according to Adjournment, the Committee appointed Yesterday, made their Report, which being read, seriously considered, and approved, was signed by a great Number of the principal Gentlemen of the Colony then present, and is as follows:

W E his Majesty's most dutiful Subjects, the late Representatives of all the Freeholders of the Colony of *Virginia*, avowing our inviolable and unshaken Fidelity and Loyalty to our most gracious Sovereign, our Affection for all our Fellow Subjects of *Great-Britain*; protesting against every Act or Thing, which may have the most distant Tendency to interrupt, or in any wise disturb his Majesty's Peace, and the good Order of his Government in this Colony, which we are resolved, at the Risque of our Lives and Fortune, to maintain and defend; but, at the same Time, being deeply affected with the Grievances and Distresses, with which his Majesty's *American* Subjects are oppressed, and dreading the Evils which threaten the Ruin of ourselves and our Posterity, by reducing us from a free and happy People to a wretched and miserable State of Slavery; and having taken into our most serious Consideration the present State of the Trade of this Colony, and of the *American* Commerce in general, observe with Anxiety, that the Debt due to *Great-Britain* for Goods imported from thence is very great, and that the Means of paying this Debt, in the present Situation of Affairs, are likely to become more and more precarious; that the Difficulties, under which we now labour, are owing to the Restrictions, Prohibitions, and ill advised Regulations, in several late Acts of Parliament of *Great-Britain*, in particular, that the late unconstitutional Act, imposing Duties on Tea, Paper, Glass, &c. for the sole Purpose of raising a Revenue in *America*, is injurious to Property, and destructive to Liberty, hath a necessary Tendency to prevent the Payment of the Debt due from this Colony to *Great-Britain*, and is, of Consequence, ruinous to Trade; that, notwithstanding the many earnest Applications already made, there is little Reason to expect a Redress of those Grievances; Therefore, in Justice to ourselves and our Posterity, as well as to the Traders of *Great-Britain* concerned in the *American* Commerce, we, the Subscribers, have voluntarily and unanimously entered into the following Resolutions, in Hopes that our Example will induce the good People of this Colony to be frugal in the Use and Consumption of *British* Manufactures, and that the Merchants and Manufacturers of *Great-Britain* may, from Motives of Interest, Friendship, and Justice, be engaged to exert themselves to obtain for us a Redress of those Grievances, under which the Trade and Inhabitants of *America* at present labour; We do therefore most earnestly recommend this our Association to the serious Attention of all Gentlemen, Merchants, Traders, and other Inhabitants of this Colony, in Hopes, that they will very readily and cordially accede thereto.

First, It is UNANIMOUSLY agreed on and resolved this 18th Day of *May*, 1769, that the Subscribers, as well by their own Example, as all other legal Ways and Means in their Power, will promote and encourage Industry and Frugality, and discourage all Manner of Luxury and Extravagance.

Secondly, That they will not at any Time hereafter, directly or indirectly import, or cause to be imported, any Manner of Goods, Merchandize, or Manufactures, which are, or shall hereafter be taxed by Act of Parliament, for the Purpose of raising a Revenue in *America* (except Paper, not exceeding Eight Shillings Sterling per Ream, and except such Articles only, as Orders have been already sent for) nor purchase any such after the First Day of *September* next, of any Person whatsoever, but that they will always consider such Taxation, in every Respect, as an absolute Prohibition, and in all future Orders, direct their Correspondents to ship them no Goods whatever, taxed as aforesaid, except as is above excepted.

Thirdly, That the Subscribers will not hereafter, directly or indirectly, import or cause to be imported from *Great-Britain*, or any Part of *Europe* (except such Articles of the Produce or Manufacture of *Ireland* as may be immediately and legally brought from thence, and except also all such Goods as Orders have been already sent for) any of the Goods herein after enumerated, viz. Spirits, Wine, Cyder, Perry, Beer, Ale, Malt, Barley, Pease, Beef, Pork, Fish, Butter, Cheese, Tallow, Candles, Oil, Fruit, Sugar, Pickles, Confectionary, Pewter, Hoes, Axes, Watches, Clocks, Tables, Chairs, Looking Glasses, Carriages, Joiner's and Cabinet Work of all Sorts, Upholstery of all Sorts, Trinkets and Jewellery, Plate and Gold, and Silversmith's Work of all Sorts, Ribbon and Millinery of all Sorts, Lace of all Sorts, *India* Goods of all Sorts, except Spices, Silks of all Sorts, except Sewing Silk, Cambrick, Lawn, Muslin, Gauze, except Boulting Cloths, Callico or Cotton Stuffs of more than Two Shillings per Yard, Linens of more than Two Shillings per Yard, Woollens, Worsted Stuffs of all Sorts of more than One Shilling and Six Pence per Yard, Broad Cloths of all Kinds at more than Eight Shillings per Yard, Narrow Cloths of all Kinds at more than Three Shillings per Yard, Hats, Stockings (Plaid and *Irish* Hose excepted) Shoes and Boots, Saddles, and all Manufactures of Leather and Skins of all Kinds, until the late Acts of Parliament imposing Duties on Tea, Paper, Glass, &c. for the Purpose of raising a Revenue in *America*, are repealed, and that they will not, after the First of *September* next, purchase any of the above enumerated Goods of any Person whatsoever, unless the above mentioned Acts of Parliament are repealed.

Fourthly, That in all Orders, which any of the Subscribers may hereafter send to *Great-Britain*, they shall, and will expressly direct their Correspondents not to ship them any of the before enumerated Goods, until the before mentioned Acts of Parliament are repealed; and if any Goods are shipped to them contrary to the Tenor of this Agreement, they will refuse to take the same, or make themselves chargeable therewith.

Fifthly, That they will not import any Slaves, or purchase any imported, after the First Day of *November* next, until the said Acts of Parliament are repealed.

Sixthly, That they will not import any Wines of any Kind whatever, or purchase the same from any Person whatever, after the First Day of *September* next, except such Wines as are already ordered, until the Acts of Parliament imposing Duties thereon are repealed.

Seventhly, For the better Preservation of the Breed of Sheep, That they will not kill, or suffer to be killed, any Lambs, that shall be yeaned before the First Day of *May*, in any Year, nor dispose of such to any Butcher or other Person, whom they may have Reason to expect, intends to kill the same.

Eighthly and Lastly, That these Resolves shall be binding on all and each of the Subscribers, who do hereby each and every Person for himself, upon his Word and Honour, agree that he will strictly and firmly adhere to and abide by every Article in this Agreement, from the Time of his signing the same, for and during the Continuance of the before mentioned Acts of Parliament, or until a general Meeting of the Subscribers, after one Month's public Notice, shall determine otherwise, the second Article of this Agreement still and for ever continuing in full Power and Force.

Peyton Randolph,	*Thomson Mason,*	*David Mason,*
Robert Carter	*Josias Payne,* jun.	*William Macon,* jun.
Nicholas,	*Burwell Basset,*	*Hugh Innes,*
Richard Bland,	*Richard Anderson,*	*Bolling Stark,*
Archibald Cary,	*James Scott,* jun.	*Robert Bolling,*
Richard Henry Lee,	*John Green,*	*Paul Carrington,*
Charles Carter,	*Wilson Miles Cary,*	*Thomas Walker,*
Lancaster.	*Gabriel Jones,*	*William Cabell,* jun.
George Washington,	*Willis Riddick,*	*Nathaniel Edwards,*
Carter Braxton,	*Thomas Glascock,*	jun.
Severn Eyre,	*John Woodson,*	*Robert Rutherford,*
Richard Randolph,	*Benjamin Howard,*	*Thomas Barbour,*
Patrick Henry, jun.	*Isaac Read,*	*Charles Lynch,*
Peter Johnston,	*Foushee Tebbs,*	*James Hamilton,*
Henry Lee,	*Edward Osborne,*	*John Wilson,* Augusta.
Nathaniel Terry,	*Francis Peyton,*	*William Clayton,*
Thomas Whiting,	*Abraham Hite,*	*Robert Munford,*
Thomas Jefferson,	*James Wood,*	Mecklenburg.
Thomas Nelson, jun.	*Richard Baker,*	*Thomas Bailey,*
James Walker,	*Edwin Gray,*	*Thomas Scott,*
John Alexander,	*Robert Munford,*	*Lewis Burwell,*
Champion Travis,	Amelia.	*John Harmanson,*
George Ball,	*Henry Taylor,*	*Thomas Parramore,*
Thomas Harrison,	*Joseph Cabell,*	*John Donelson,*
Thomas Claiborne,	*Alexander Tren[t],*	*Cornelius Thomas,*
John Blair, jun.	*John Mayo,*	*Thomas Johnson,*

John Lewis, jun.	*Edward Hack Moseley*,	*Philip Ludwell*
William Roane,	jun.	*Grymes,*
William A[crill]	*John Ackiss,*	*Charles Carter*, King
Hartwell Cocke,	*James Bridger,*	George.
John Talbot,	*David Meade,*	*Richard Starke*, Clerk
Richard Lee,	*Southy Simpson,*	to the Association.
Joseph Hutchings,	*Peter Poythress,*	

The Business being finished, the following TOASTS were drank, and the Gentlemen retired.

The KING.

The QUEEN and ROYAL FAMILY.

His Excellency Lord BOTETOURT, and Prosperity to *VIRGINIA.*

A speedy and lasting Union between *Great-Britain* and her Colonies.

The constitutional *British* Liberty in *America*, and all true Patriots, the Supporters thereof.

DUKE of RICHMOND.	The late SPEAKER.
EARL of SHELBURNE.	The TREASURER of the Colony.
Col. BARRE.	The FARMER and MONITOR.

IN compliance with the foregoing Invitation, we do most cordially accede and agree to the Association so laudably proposed; and in Testimony thereof have subscribed our Names this　　　　Day of　　　 1769.

William Matthis	Samuel Tatem	Richard Melton
Jas. Lane	N: Ellzey	Wm. Stanhope
Tho. Gist.	Travers Nash	Wm. Walrond
Wm. George	Isaac Davis	Samuel Baker
George Headon	Daniel Kincheloe	J. Gwatkin
Amos Davis	John Terry	Rd. Milton
	Thos. Bird	

Printed document (Vi). Evans 11513; Sabin 100504; Clayton-Torrence 354. The names of the members of the late House of Burgesses are printed; the names of the subscribers to the Association are in autograph.

The present document was prepared by George Mason of Gunston Hall, Fairfax co.; it is said to have been introduced by George Washington, among whose papers the MS remains. Printed copies of the Resolutions, such as the one from which the present text is taken, were carried by the members of the late House to their constituents for signatures, and there is evidence that many did sign; see Rowland, *Mason*, I, 136-42, 389-93. THE FARMER AND MONITOR: Pen names for John Dickinson, author of *Letters from a Farmer in Pennsylvania to the Inhabitants of the British Colonies*, published in the *Penna. Chronicle*, widely reprinted, and collected, 1768; and Arthur Lee, author of a series of letters in Rind's *Va. Gaz.* in the spring of the same year (DAB, under Dickinson and Lee). Glenn C. Smith, "An Era of Non-Importation Associations," WMQ, 2d ser., XX (1940), 84-98, shows that Lee's "Monitor" letters anticipated at many points Mason's Non-importation Resolutions.

To John Walker

GALFRIDI-FILIUS AMBULATORI S.   Sep. 3. 1769.

Ero apud Society spring on Tuesday per quatuor. Fortasse et I. Lepus-æmula veniet. Apis ibi et tu quoque. Ferto sequelam tuam Septentrionalem. Ferto etiam, ut ante tibi præcepi, tabulam scaccariam. Oculus feram viros. Si possemus gignere tabulam pro hac vice expressè factam, lignum apis puteus. Sed de hoc postea confabulemur. Suntne bubulæ terræ patris tui in Augusta salvæ? Id est nonne sint lapsabiles pro defectu cultûs vel quitrentorum? Non dubito quin salvæ sint, tamen vide dum potes. Verbum sat sapienti. Magna clades mox erit iis qui aliter sunt. Vale.

P. S. Celeberrimus ille Ferguson, qui scripsit de astronomia, venturus est, ut fertur, ad Coll. Gul. et Mar. successor dignus dignissimi Parvi!

TRANSLATION

JEFFREY'S-SON TO WALKER, GREETINGS   Sep. 3. 1769.

I shall be at Society spring on Tuesday at four. Perhaps J[ohn] Har(e)-vie will also come. And bee you there too. Bring your northern following [friend?]. Bring also, as I asked you before, a chess board. Eye shall bring the men. If we could get a board made expressly for this use it wood bee well. But we will speak of that later. Are your father's grazing lands in Augusta safe? That is, may they not be subject to lapse through lack of cultivation or quitrents? I have no doubt but that they are safe, but see to it while you can. A word to the wise. A great loss will soon come to those who are otherwise. Good-bye.

P. S. That most famous Ferguson, who wrote on astronomy, will come, it is said, to the College of William and Mary, an excellent successor to the most excellent Small!

RC (CtY). Addressed: "To John Walker esq. Belvoir." English translation by Dr. Torsten Petersson, formerly Bibliographer of the Princeton University Library.

TJ's bilingual puns—a time-honored form of verbal play among students—scarcely need explanation. SOCIETY SPRING: Probably an allusion to the Flat Hat Club, the earliest secret college society in America, of which TJ wrote many years later, "When I was a student . . . there existed a society called the F. H. C. society, confined to the number of six students only, of which I was a member, but it had no useful object, nor do I know whether it now exists" (to Thomas McAuley, 14 June 1819).

Advertisement for a Runaway Slave

[7 September 1769]

RUN away from the subscriber in *Albemarle*, a Mulatto slave called *Sandy*, about 35 years of age, his stature is rather low, inclining to corpulence, and his complexion light; he is a shoemaker by trade, in which he uses his left hand principally, can do coarse carpenters work, and is something of a horse jockey; he is greatly addicted to drink, and when drunk is insolent and disorderly, in his conversation he swears much, and his behaviour is artful and knavish. He took with him a white horse, much scarred with traces, of which it is expected he will endeavour to dispose; he also carried his shoemakers tools, and will probably endeavour to get employment that way. Whoever conveys the said slave to me in *Albemarle*, shall have 40 s. reward, if taken up within the county, 4 l. if elsewhere within the colony, and 10 l. if in any other colony, from   THOMAS JEFFERSON.

Printed from *Virginia Gazette* (Purdie & Dixon), 14 Sep. 1769. (The advertisement first appeared in the preceding issue, 7 Sep., but the text is not available there because of mutilation.)

SANDY is twice mentioned in TJ's Accounts with the Jefferson Family,

1764-1775: first, in an undated entry, "To hire for Sandy from my father's death 1757 to Dec. 31, 1762 5½ years @ £18"; second, under 29 Jan. 1773, "To negro Sandy sold to Colo. Charles Lewis £100."

From Perkins, Buchanan & Brown

SIR   London 2d. Octr. 1769

Having entered into some engagements with our worthy Friend Mr: Thos. Adams for Mr: Jordan by which we are to have a Ship in James River in March next we take the Liberty through his Recommendation to Solicit the favour of your Assistance in the dispatch of the said ship by the Consignment of some part of your Tobacco and be assured you shall not suffer by putt[ing] it into our hands as we will Answer for the Account Sale being at least equal to any sent from this place for Tobacco of the same quality. You may likewise depend on our utmost care in the purchase of any Goods you may have Occasion for or that we will answer your Bills to the full Amount of your Consignment and that upon every other Occasion we shall Regard your Interest as our own. We beg leave to Refer you to Mr. Adams, for any further Information you may Require relative to our house. We are Sir Your most humble Servants,   PERKINS, BUCHANAN & BROWN

P. S. Inclosed you have Invoice &c. for the Books, you order'd of

Mr. Adams, which we send by Capt: Lowes and Debit you for the amount £14.15. and heartily wish you a happy meeting with our Friend.

INVOICE

Messrs. Perkins Buchanan & Brown

Bot. of T. Cadell Successor to Mr. Millar

Sept. 19	J. M. Jordan	£ s d
Petits Jus Parliamentum C Gilt marble		
Leaves extra very elegant		1. 4.0
Gordons History of Parliaments 2 vol do. & do.		0.12.0
Modus tenendi Parliamentum very scarce		
and could not be got otherwise bound		0. 4.0
Determinations of the House of Commons extra		0. 7.0
Locke on Government do. & do.		0. 6.0
Burlamaque Le Droit Natural do. & do.		0.18.0
Ellis's Tracts on Liberty do. & do.		1. 1.0
Warners History of Ireland do. & do.		1. 4.0
———— History of Civil Wars do. & do.		1. 4.0
Pettys Survey of Ireland do. & do.		0. 5.0
Ouvres de Montesqieu 3 Vol do. & do.		2.12.6
Fergusons Civil Society do. & do.		0.17.0
Stewarts Political Oeconomy do. & do.		2.12.6
Paid for a Box.		0. 3.0
		£13:10:0

Pettys Survey of Ireland could only be got in Octavo. I sent Montesqieus Works and the Spirit of Laws &c. could not be got separate in Quarto.

RC (ViHi). The books ordered by TJ are highly significant in view of his having entered the House of Burgesses this year.

To John Page

DEAR PAGE Charlottesville Feb. 21. 1770.

I am to acquaint Mrs. Page of the loss of my favorite pullet; the consequence of which will readily occur to her. I promised also to give her some Virginia silk which I had expected, and I begin to wish my expectations may not prove vain. I fear she will think me but an ungainly acquaintance. My late loss may perhaps have reac[hed y]ou by this time, I mean the loss of my mother's house by fire, and in it, of every pa[per I] had in the world, and almost every book. On a reasonable estimate I calculate th[e cost o]f t[he b]ooks burned to have been £200. sterling. Would to god it had been the money [;then] had it never cost me a sigh! To make the loss more sensible it fell principally on m[y books] of common law, of which I have but one left, at that time lent out. Of papers too of every kind I am utterly destitute. All of these, whether public or private, of business or of amusement have perished in the flames. I had made some progress in preparing for the succeeding general court, and having, as was my custom, thrown my thoughts into the form of notes, I troubled my head no more with them. These are gone, and 'like the baseless fabric of a vision, Leave not a trace behind.' The records also and other papers, which furnished me with states of the several cases, having shared the same fate, I have no foundation whereon to set out anew. I have in vain attempted to recollect some of them, the defect sometimes of one, sometimes of more circumstances, rendering them so imperfect that I can make nothing of them. What am I to do then in April? The resolutions which the court have declared of admitting no continuances of causes seemed to be unalterable. Yet it might surely be urged that my case is too singular to admit of their being often troubled with the like excuse. Should it be asked what are the misfortunes of an individual to a court? The answer of a court, as well as of an individual, if left to me, should be in the words of Terence, 'homo sum; humani nîl a me alienum puto.'—but a truce with this disagreeable subject.

Am I never more to have a letter from you? Why the devil don't you write? But I suppose you are always in the moon, or some of the planetary regions. I mean you are there in idea, and unless you mend, you shall have my consent to be there de facto; at least during the vacations of the court and assembly. If your spirit is too elevated to advert to sublunary subjects, depute my friend Mrs. Page to support your correspondencies. Methinks I should with wonderful pleasure open and peruse a letter written by so fair, and (what is better) so friendly hands. If thinking much of you would entitle me to the civility of a letter, I assure you I merit a very long one. If this conflagration, by which I am burned out of a home, had come before I had advanced so far in preparing another, I do not know but I might have cherished some treasonable thoughts of leaving [thes]e my native hills. Indeed I should be much happier were I nearer to Rosewell and Sever[n] hall. However the gods I fancy were apprehensive that if we were placed together we s[houl]d pull down the moon or play some such devilish prank with their works. [I r]efl[ect oft]en with pleasure on the philosophical evenings I passed at Rosewell in my last [visit]s there. I was always fond of philosophy even in it's dryer forms, but from a ruby [lip] it comes with charms irresistible. Such a feast of sentiment must exhilarate and lengthen life at least as much as the feast of the sensualist shortens it. In a word I prize it so highly that if you will at any time collect the same Belle assemblèe on giving me three days previous notice, I shall certainly repair to my place as a member of it. Should it not happen before I come down I will carry Sally Nicholas in the green chair to Newquarter, where your perry-auger (how the devil should I spell that word?) will meet us, automaton like, of it's own accord. You know I had a waggon which moved itself; cannot we construct a boat then which shall row itself? Amicus noster, Fons, quo modo agit, et quid agit? You may be all dead for anything we can tell here. I expect he will follow the good old rule of driving one passion out by letting another in. Clavum clavo pangere was your advice to me on a similar occasion. I hope you will watch his immersion as narrowly as if he were one of Jupiter's satellites, and give me immediate notice, that I may prepare a dish of advice. I do not mean, madam, to advise him against it. On the contrary I am become an advocate for the passion: for I too am cœlo tactus. Currus bene se habet. He speaks, thinks, and dreams of nothing but his young son. This friend of ours, Page, in a very small house, with a table, half a dozen chairs, and one or two servants, is the happiest man in the universe. He possesses truly the art of extracting comfort from things the most trivial. Every incident in life he so takes as to render it a source of pleasure. With as much benevolence as the heart of man will hold, but with an utter neglect of the costly apparatus of life, he exhibits to the world a new phaenomenon in philosophy, the Samian sage in the tub of the Cynic. Name me sometimes Homunculo tuo, not forgetting little Dic-mendacium. I am determined not to enter on the next page lest I should extend this nonsense to the bottom of that also. A-dieu je vous commis, not doubting his care of you both.

TH: JEFFERSON

RC (CtY). MS mutilated.

MY LATE LOSS: The destruction by fire of the Jefferson home at Shadwell, 1 Feb. 1770, while TJ and his mother were on a visit to a neighbor (see TJ's Fee Book and Misc. Accounts, under this date in the account with Mrs. Jane Jefferson; Tucker, *Life*, I, 47). ROSE-WELL was the Pages' home near White-marsh, Gloucester co., and SEVERN HALL the home of Warner Lewis on the Severn River nearby (Waterman, *Mansions of Va.*, p. 110-23; VMHB, XXIV [1916], 95). NEWQUARTER: There was a New Quarter Branch in Glouces-ter co. (Polly C. Mason, comp., *Records of Colonial Gloucester Co., Va.*, I, New-port News, 1946, p. 20). PERRYAUGER: Variously spelled (periaugua, petty-auger, &c.), this is the Carib-Spanish term for a dugout canoe (DAE). CUR-RUS: Dabney Carr, TJ's brother-in-law.

HOMUNCULO TUO . . . DIC-MENDACIUM: Punning compliments "to your little Man" and "little Say-lie," i.e., Page's children, Mann and Sally.

From Thomas Nelson, Sr.

DR. SIR York March 6th. 1770.

I was extremely concerned to hear of your Loss the account of which had reached us some time ago. As I have a pretty good collection of Books, it will give me pleasure to have it in my power to furnish you with any you may want. The bearer carries 4 pr. dove-tail-hinges for doors, 2 Mortise locks, 20 Pullies, and 20 pr. of Shutter-hinges. I have none of the sort proper for the Leaves, which may be either the common small dovetail or H hinges. I am Sir Yr. most obedt. hble Servt., THOS. NELSON

RC (MHi). Addressed: "To Thos. Jefferson Esqr. in Albemarle." Endorsed: "T. Nelson senr. to T. J."

Thomas Nelson, Sr., lawyer, burgess for York co., was known as "the Secretary" from his long tenure (1743-1776) as secretary for the Virginia council of state (Tyler, *Va. Biog.*, I, 157-8).

From Thomas Nelson, Jr.

DEAR JEFFERSON York March 6th 1770

I just received your melancholy account of the Loss you have sustaind, and have only time, (the messenger that brought the Wheat being in a great hurry to return) to assure you that nothing can give me so much pleasure as to render you every service that is in my power. You may depend on your Letter to your Bookseller being sent by the first opportunity; it would be prudent to send a Copy of the Letter for fear the original should miscarry.

If by "the Door that might be opend to relieve your distress" you mean the Court's indulging you with a Continuance of your Causes; My Father says you may be certain of that, as the Court has frequently done it where there have been good reasons for it.

Page desires I will inclose you a few lines that he has scribled in as great hurry as I have.

I am Your hle Sert., THOS. NELSON JUN.

RC (MHi). Addressed: "To Thomas Jefferson Esqr in Albemarle." Endorsed: "T. Nelson junr to T: J." Enclosure: John Page to TJ, same date.

The writer is Thomas Nelson the "Signer" and governor (1738-1789), son of William Nelson ("President Nelson") and nephew of Thomas Nelson ("Secretary Nelson"), writer of the preceding letter, who also had a son styled Thomas Nelson, Jr. (R. C. M. Page, *Genealogy of the Page Family in Virginia*, N.Y., 1883, p. 169).

From John Page

Dear Jefferson   York March 6th. 70.

I have heard of your Loss [and] heartily condole with you, but am much pleased with the Philosop[hy] you manifest in your Letter which I this Moment received. I will very soon convince you that I had not forgot you, for I have a Letter at Home which I wrote some Month[s] since, and will send you in[close]d in another as soon as I [. . . .] I snatched up my Pen [. . .] these few Lines not wi[thstanding] the hurry and Confusion we are in. Poor Mrs. Burwell died about an hour ago. I have only time to wish you all Happiness and Carr and long Continuance of his.   John Page Jr.

RC (MHi). MS mutilated. Endorsed: "J. Page to Th: J." Enclosed in Thomas Nelson, Jr., to TJ, same date.

From George Wythe

G. W. to T. Jefferson   9. Mar. 1770.

I send you some nectarine and apricot graffs and grapevines, the best I had; and have directed your messenger to call upon Major Taliaferro for some of his. You will also receive two of Foulis's catalogues. Mrs. Wythe will send you some garden peas.

You bear your misfortune so becomingly, that, as I am convinced you will surmount the difficulties it has plunged you into, so I foresee you will hereafter reap advantages from it several ways. Durate, et vosmet rebus servate secundis.

RC (MHi). Addressed: "To Thomas Jefferson esq. Charlottesville."

From James Ogilvie

Dear Sir   London March 28th. 1770

I am disappointed hitherto in every attempt to get ordained. The Commissary wrote against me in these words. Colo. Mercer saw the letter. "Mr. Ogilvie applied to me last spring for a recommendation to your Lordship for holy Orders. For reasons which then existed I refused him. He has now applied to me a second time, as these reasons are not removed I have denied him again, but he goes home in opposition." Nothing could have been more artfully couched to do me a prejudice. The Bishop observed to Colo. Mercer that had Mr. Horrocks mentioned what his objections were it would have left him to judge whether they were such as he might have overlooked or not, but that so general a charge laid my whole character open to censure so as to be out of my power to vindicate it. I have one chance still but whether it will succeed or not I am uncertain.

I must therefore apply again for your freindly offices as well as those of my other freinds in Virginia.

If by means of Mr. Blair you can get the Commissary to acquaint the Bishop that his objections were owing to my deficiency in the Greek it will remove every obstacle. If he still refuses, will you be so obliging as through Mr. Jones of Augusta to procure a letter from Ld. Fairfax requesting my ordination. Could you likewise procure another certificate signed by as many gentlemen of fortune and credit as you can conveniently? Your freind Mr. Walker and the Revd. Mr. White will be both very active, I do not doubt. A letter from the Attorney Genl. to Mr. Jennings here, or a letter from one or more of the Council to Mr. Abercromby their Agent in London may be of special service. But particularly could Mr. Horrocks be prevailed with it will make me easy. Perhaps an application from Colo. Byrd and Mr. Balfour would have effect with him.

I have here prescribed you a severe trial of your freindship, but let my necessity plead an excuse. You are to judge what part of it you can best execute. The warmth with which you have already interested yourself in my favour encourages me to write in this stile, and I think I can venture to flatter myself that from your regard to Mr. Walker, (for merit of my own with you, Sir, I can plead none) that you will not spare a little trouble to execute that on which the success of my future life depends. Shall I mention a happiness of a still dearer nature which is also dependant upon this? But should I enter on so tender a subject it will melt down my resolution, which is so necessary at present.

My life has been a continued scene of misfortune and disappointment. I am naturally endowed with keen passions, and in the early part of my life they took a byass which has softened and rendered them most sensible of every accident that has befallen me. Yet among the few lucky circumstances of my life I reckon those first which occasioned my acquaintance with Mr. Walker and yourself. In whatever situation my future life may be spent, though fortune may place me at a distance from you, I shall ever think of you with respect and affection, my warmest wishes will ever accompany you. I shall flatter myself that you are happy and successful, and spite of misfortune I shall find an hour to rejoice in that hope.

I have purchased a few of your Commissions, the others I delayed till the measures of Parliament were known. My private circumstances have taken up so much room that I have not had an opportunity to insert any public news. We are in hopes the duties upon Tea will be taken off before the end of the Sessions. The disappointment in respect to my obtaining Orders, has not come alone. I am sorry to observe that the freinds I have mett with in Virga. have been more sincerely and warmly attached to me than many of my relations.

Adieu my Dear Sir. I will not detain your attention longer by attempting an apology for the length or matter of this but subscribe myself with every affectionate desire for your prosperity Your much obliged and very obedient servt,   JAS. OGILVIE

A letter to Mr. Walker accompanies this. Direct for me att Mrs. Ballard's Hungerford Street in the Strand London.

RC (MHi). Endorsed: "James Ogilvie to T. J."

THE COMMISSARY: James Horrocks, president of the College of William and Mary, was then commissary to the Bishop of London, Richard Terrick (Goodwin, *Colonial Church in Va.*, p. 279); an ambitious and unpopular cleric, he was involved in the controversy over the establishment of colonial bishoprics, and this may have been the cause of his unfriendliness to Ogilvie. THE ATTORNEY GENERAL: John Randolph (1727-1784).

From Mary Walker Lewis

SIR   Albemarle 14th. [April?] 1770.

It is with pleasure I inform you that Mr. Lewis is much recoverd; he has been over your Plantations the other side the River but not withstanding he finds him self not able to write you; and desires me to send you a line, and to assure you that he will write very fully as soon as he can and as often as you would wish. We send you with this a hhd. of Hams containing 64 of Bacon and 6 Venison which your friend Colonel Bell desiers me to send you a Compliment. We intend to keep some for your use when you should return. We should have sent you more Bacon but the Waggon carry's a hhd. of Tobaco and cant take more at this time. Should you wish a farther Supply we will send it imediately after hearing from you. Your Negros have been sickly sence you left us no deaths have hapned and they are now in better helth. I fear you have sufferd by Mr. Lewiss illness particularly at Shadwell as he finds things out of sorts. We have had intelegance from Bedford by a litter from Clark and allso from Mr. Meriwether who informs us that they are in great fowardness and every necessary preparition for a Crop and the Overcears are manageing uncomonly well. The Weat there commands 5/6 now at Richmond 7/ and the rise which terms Mr. Lewis has directed Clark to sel for he has refus'd 28/ for his Shear of Tobaco at Linchburge. Mr. Lewis hopes to go to Bedford to the Next Court. We have never been to Montello; inten'd our selves that pleasure yesterday, but was prevented by the weather which is yet wet with us. George has been frequently hear and reports that all is well. We have been sickly genraly and now have the Measels and hooping cough in the Neibourhod. The Measels is a moung your Negros at Bedford but thay have lost none. Hope you will excues this ill writen scroll as Mr. Lewis attemt'd and could not finish his litter. I am much hurry'd with this. Mr. Lewis desiers me to tender his most respectfull Compliments. I am Sir with very Great Esteem Your Sincear Friend,   M. LEWIS

RC (ViU). Endorsed: "Lewis Mary recd May 12."

TJ was in Williamsburg attending the general court and the Assembly at this time; unless the date of either the letter or the endorsement is wrong, it took a surprisingly long time to come to hand. GEORGE was presumably one of the slaves at Monticello.

From John Page, Jr.

April. 1770

When you were at Col. Lewis's my Heart was with you, but something more than a Punctillio, for it was a Coach Load of Hospitality, kept my Body from you. When I reflect on the Restraint I was under during this Seperation of Heart and Body, and as I am still in the same divided state tho' now from a different Cause; I can hardly refrain from describing it. There is a great and secret Satisfaction in disclosing our Griefs to a Friend. But as it is impossible to give a true Description of them when great, we had better not attempt it. Therefore I am resolved not to attempt to describe mine. And as the Time is not very Distant, but when viewed through the Object Glass of Friendship'[s] Perspective, when I shall be heartily and Bodi[ly] with you, let Grief give way to a feeling tho' not more delicate more welcome. I shall not detain you longer from persuing the Plan you have with so much Judgement drawn, and so indefatigably followed, not even to tell you which of your Friends wrote this. Adieu.

RC (MHi). Unsigned. Endorsed: "J. Page to T. J. April. 1770."

No explanation of the circumstances prompting this letter, nor of TJ's "Plan" alluded to at the end, can be given.

Commission as Lieutenant of Albemarle

[9 June 1770]

HIS EXCELLENCY

The Right Honourable NORBORNE Baron de BOTETOURT, his Majesty's Lieutenant and Governor General of the Colony and Dominion of Virginia, and Vice Admiral of the same.

To Thomas Jefferson Esquire

BY Virtue of the Power and Authority to me given as his Majesty's Lieutenant and Governor General of this his Colony and Dominion, I, reposing special Trust and Confidence in your Loyalty, Courage and Conduct, do hereby constitute and appoint you the said *Thomas Jefferson* to be Lieutenant of the County of *Albemarle* and Chief Commander of all his Majesty's Militia, Horse and Foot, in the said County of *Albemarle*. And I do give unto you full Power and Authority to command, levy, arm and muster, all Persons which are or shall be liable to be levied and listed in the said County. You are therefore carefully and diligently to discharge the Duty of Lieutenant and Chief Commander of the Militia, by doing and performing all, and all Manner of Things thereunto belonging, particularly by taking care that the said Militia be well provided with Arms and Ammunition as the Law of this Colony directs; and that all Officers and Soldiers be duly exercised, and kept in good Order and Discipline. And in Case of any sudden Disturbance or Invasion, I do likewise empower you to raise, order, and march all or such part of the said Militia, as to you shall seem meet, for resisting and subduing the Enemy: And I do hereby command all the Officers and Soldiers of his Majesty's Militia, in the said County, to obey you as their Lieutenant, or Chief Commander; and you are to observe and follow such Orders and Directions, from Time to Time, as you shall receive from me, or the Commander in Chief of this Colony for the Time being, or from any other your superior Officer, according to the Rules and Discipline of War.

GIVEN under my Hand, and the Seal of the Colony, at WILLIAMSBURG, the *Ninth* Day of *June* in the *Tenth* Year of his Majesty's Reign, ANNOQUE DOMINI 17 70. *Botetourt*

Printed form, filled in and signed (DLC).

By this commission TJ succeeded to an office his father had held (Malone, *Jefferson*, I, 26). The county lieutenant was the commander of the county militia and was entitled to be called colonel; "he was in every respect as much the representative of the power resident at the seat of the Colonial government as the latter was of the Crown itself" (CVSP, I, xxii). The Militia Act of 1757, under the terms of which TJ performed his duties, will be found in Hening, VII, 93-106; see also an Act of the same session "for reducing the several acts for making a provision against invasions and insurrections into one act," which is still more detailed in its terms (same, p. 106-16). Another commission to TJ as lieutenant of Albemarle, dated 15 Dec. 1770 and identical in form except that it was issued and signed by William Nelson, President of the Council, is in DLC: TJ Papers, 1:53.

Virginia Nonimportation Resolutions, 1770

[22 June 1770]

The ASSOCIATION *entered into last* Friday, *the 22d instant, by the Gentlemen of the House of Burgesses, and the Body of Merchants, assembled in this city.*

WE his Majesty's most dutiful and loyal subjects of *Virginia*, declaring our inviolable and unshaken fidelity and attachment to our gracious sovereign, our affection for all our fellow subjects of *Great Britain*, and our firm determination to support, at the hazard of our lives and fortunes, the laws, the peace, and good order of government in this colony; but at the same time affected with great and just apprehensions of the fatal consequences certainly to follow from the arbitrary imposition of taxes on the people of *America*, for the purpose of raising a revenue from them, without the consent of their representatives; and as we consider it to be the indispensable duty of every virtuous member of society to prevent the ruin, and promote the happiness, of his country, by every lawful means, although in the prosecution of such a laudable and necessary design some unhappy consequences may be derived to many innocent fellow subjects, whom we wish not to injure, and who we hope will impute our conduct to the real necessity of our affairs: Influenced by these reasons, we do most earnestly recommend this our association to the serious attention of all Gentlemen merchants, traders, and other inhabitants of this colony, not doubting but they will readily and cordially accede thereto. And at the same time we, and every of us, do most solemnly oblige ourselves, upon our word and honour, to promote the welfare and commercial interests of all those truly worthy merchants, traders, and others, inhabitants of this colony, who shall hereafter conform to the spirit of this association; but that we will upon all occasions, and at all times hereafter, avoid purchasing any commodit[y o]r article of goods whatsoever from any importer or seller of *British* merchandise or *European* goods, whom we may know or believe, in violation of the essential interests of this colony, to have preferred their own private emolument, by importing or selling articles prohibited by this association, to the destruction of the dearest rights of the people of this colony. And for the more effectual discovery of such defaulters, it is resolved,

That a committee of five be chosen in every county, by the majority of associators in each county, who, or any three of them, are hereby authorized to publish the names of such signers of the association as shall violate their agreement; and when there shall be an importation of goods into any county, such committee, or any three of them, are empowered to convene themselves, and in a civil manner apply to the merchant or importers concerned and desire to see the invoices and papers respecting such importation, and if they find any goods therein contrary to the association to let the importers know that it is the opinion and request of the county that such goods shall not be opened or stored, but reshipped to the place from whence they came: And in case of refusal, without any manner of violence, inform them of the consequences, and proceed to publish an account of their conduct.

Secondly. That we the subscribers, as well by our own example as all other legal ways and means in our power, will promote and encourage industry and frugality, and discourage all manner of luxury and extravagance.

Thirdly. That we will not hereafter, directly or indirectly, import, or cause to be imported, from *Great Britain*, any of the goods hereafter enumerated, either for sale or for our own use; to wit, spirits, cider, perry, beer, ale, porter, malt, pease, beef, fish, butter, cheese, tallow, candles, fruit, pickles, confectionary, chairs, tables, looking glasses, carriages, joiners work, and cabinet work of all sorts, riband, *India* goods of all sorts (except spices) calico of more than 3s. sterling per yard, upholstery (by which is meant paper hangings, beds ready made, furniture for beds, and carpetting) watches, clocks, silversmiths work of all sorts, silks of all sorts (except womens bonnets and hats, sewing silk, and netting silk) cotton stuffs of more than 3s. sterling per yard, linens of more than 2s. sterling per yard (except *Irish* linens) gauze, lawns, cambrick of more than 6s. sterling per yard, woollen and worsted stuffs of all sorts of more than 2s. sterling per yard, broadcloths of more than 8s. sterling per yard, narrow cloths of all kinds of more than 4s. sterling per yard, not less than 7-8ths yard wide, hats of greater value than 10s. sterling, stockings of more than 36s. sterling per dozen, shoes of more than 5s. sterling per pair, boots, saddles, mens exceeding 25s. and womens exceeding 40s. sterling, exclusive of bridles, which are allowed, portmanteaus, saddle bags, and all other manufactured leather, neither oil or painters colours, if both, or either of them, be subject to any duty after the 1st of *December* next. And that we will not import, or cause to be imported, any horses, nor purchase those which may be imported by others after the 1st of *November* next.

Fourthly. That we will not import or bring into the colony, or cause to be imported or brought into the colony, either by sea or land, any slaves, or make sale of any upon commission, or purchase any slave or slaves that may be imported by others after the 1st day of *November* next, unless the same have been twelve months upon the continent.

Fifthly. That we will not import any wines, on which a duty is laid by act of Parliament for the purpose of raising a revenue in *America*, or purchase such as may be imported by others, after the 1st day of *September* next.

Sixthly. That no wine be imported by any of the subscribers, or other person, from any of the colonies on this continent, or any other place, from the time of signing this association, contrary to the terms thereof.

Seventhly. That all such goods as may or shall be imported into this colony, in consequence of their having been rejected by the association committees in any of our sister colonies, shall not be purchased by any associator; but that we will exert every lawful means in our power absolutely to prevent the sale of all such goods, and to cause the same to be exported as quickly as possible.

Eighthly. That we will not receive from *Great Britain*, or make sale of, upon commission, any of the articles above excepted to, after the first day of *September* next, nor any of those articles which may have been really and *bona fide* ordered by us, after the 25th of *December* next.

Ninthly. That we will not receive into our custody, make sale of, or become chargeable with, any of the articles aforementioned, that may be ordered after the 15th of *June* instant, nor give orders for any from this time; and that in all orders which any of us may hereafter send to *Great Britain* we will expressly direct and request our correspondents not to ship us any of the articles before excepted, and if any such goods are shipped contrary to the tenour of this agreement we will refuse to take the same, or make ourselves chargeable therewith.

Provided nevertheless, that such goods as are already on hand, or may be imported according to the true intent and meaning of this association, may be continued for sale.

Tenthly. That a committee of merchants, to be named by their own body, when called together by their chairman, be appointed to take under their consideration the general state of the trade in this colony, and report to the association, at their next meeting, a list of such other manufactures of *Great Britain*, or commodities of any kind whatever, now imported, as may reasonably, and with benefit to the colony, be excepted to.

Eleventhly. That we do hereby engage ourselves, by those most sacred ties of honour and love to our country, that we will not, either upon the goods which we have already upon hand or may hereafter import within the true meaning of this association, make any advance in price, with a view to profit by the restrictions hereby laid on the trade of this colony.

Twelfthly. That we will not at any time hereafter, directly or indirectly, import, or cause to be imported, or purchase from any person who shall import, any merchandise or manufactures exported from *Great Britain*, which are, or hereafter shall be, taxed by act of Parliament for the purposes of raising a revenue in America.

Resolved, that a meeting of the associators shall be called at the discretion of the Moderator, or at the request of twenty members of the association, signified to him in writing; and in case of the death of the present Moderator, the next person subscribing hereto be considered as Moderator, and act as such until the next general meeting.

Lastly. That these resolves shall be binding on all and each of the subscribers, who do hereby, each and every person for himself, agree that he will strictly and firmly adhere to and abide by every article of this association from the time of his signing the same until the act of Parliament which imposes a duty on tea, paper, glass, and painters colours, be totally repealed, or until a general meeting of one hundred associators, after one month's publick notice, shall determine otherwise, the twelfth article of this agreement still and for ever continuing in force, until the contrary be declared by a general meeting of the members of this association.

Signed in *Williamsburg*, this 22d of *June*, 1770.

Peyton Randolph, Moderator.
Andrew Sprowle, Chairman of the Trade.
Ro. C. Nicholas.
Richard Bland.
Edmund Pendleton.
Archibald Cary.
Richard Henry Lee.
Henry Lee.
Charles Carter, Corotoman.
Thomas Jefferson.
Severn Eyre.
Thomas Whiting.
Edward Hack Moseley, jun.
George Washington.
Burwell Bassett.
Spencer M. Ball.
James Walker.
Edward Osborn.
Southy Simpson.
Richard Lee.
John Alexander.
John Burton.
William Clayton.
Richard Randolph.
Benjamin Harrison.
P. Carrington.
James Pride.
William Acrill.
Peter Poythress.
James Mercer.
N. Edwards, jun.
Richard Adams.
Thomas Newton, jun.
Francis Peyton.
Thomas Barber.

Lewis Burwell.
James Cocke.
Richard Baker.
Benjamin Howard.
R. Rutherford.
Archibald Campbell.
James Balfour.
W. Cabell, jun.
Daniel Barraud.
James Mills.
David Jameson.
Charles Duncan.
John Wayles.
John Bell.
Thomas Adams.
Henry Taylor.
Alexander Shaw.
John Banister.
Thomas Bailey.
William Robinson.
James Wood.
Bolling Stark.
Thomas Pettus.
John Woodson.
Henry Feild, jun.
William Roane.
Wilson Miles Cary.
John Blair.
James Wallace.
Richard Mitchell.
Cornelius Thomas.
James Dennistone.
William Snodgrass.
Benjamin Baker.
Patrick Coutts.
Neill Campbell.
John Donelson.
Neil M'Coull.
Thomas Jett.
Samuel Kerr.

James Robinson.
Archibald Ritchie.
Samuel Eskredge.
Thomas Stith.
James Edmondson.
Anthony Walke.
John Wilson, of Augusta.
George Logan.
John Hutchings.
W. Lyne.
Edward Ker.
Alexander Trent.
John Talbott.
Joseph Cabell.
Gardner Fleming.
Samuel Harwood.
Humphrey Roberts.
Thomas M. Randolph.
Robert Wormeley Carter.
Jerman Baker.
John Gilchrist.
James Archdeacon.
Robert Donald.
James M'Dowall.
Alexander Baine.
John Smith.
Purdie & Dixon.
James Buchanan.
Thomas Scott.
Alexander Banks.
John Johnson.
Archibald Govan.
Hugh M'Mekin.
Foushee Tebbs.
Archibald M'Call.
Daniel Hutchings.
Henry Morse.
Nathaniel Terry.

Isaac Read.
William Rind.
Benjamin Harrison, jun.
Josiah Granbery.
James Robb.
Neil Jamieson.
Walter Peter.
Robert Crooks.
John Winn.
John Esdale.
Nathaniel Lyttleton Savage.
Jacob Wray.
John Fisher.
Hartwell Cocke.
Edwin Gray.
Daniel M'Callum.
James Donald.

Thomas Nelson, jun.
Robert Gilmour.
George Riddell.
John Bland.
Robert Miller.
Francis Lightfoot Lee.
Meriwether Smith.
Ro. Munford, Mecklenburg.
Roger Atkinson.
J. H. Norton.
Lewis Burwell, of Gloucester.
Abraham Hite.
James Parker.
Edward Brisbane.
James Baird.
Neill Buchanan.

Archibald Buchanan.
Andrew Mackie.
Thomas Everard.
George Purdie.
Patrick Ramsay.
Walter Boyd.
John Tabb.
Richard Booker.
John Page, jun.
Robert Andrews.
John Tayloe Corbin.
John Tazewell.
John Prentis.
William Holt.
John Greenhow.
Haldenby Dixon.
William Russell.
Thomas Hornsby.

The subscribers inhabitants of the County of Fairfax in the Colony of Virginia having duly considered the above agreement and Association, and being well convinc'd of the Utility and real necessity of the Measures therein recomended do sincerely and cordialy Accede thereto. And do hereby voluntarily and faithfully each and every person for himself, upon his word and honour, Agree and promise, that he will Strictly and firmly adhere and abide by every Article and resolution therein contain'd, according to the true intent and meaning of the same.

Wm. Adams
David Davies
Wm. Ballendine
Shapleigh Neale
Thomas Pearson
Nelson Reid
Jacob Gooding
George Minor
Henry Darne
John Fruzel
Owen Williams
William Forgurson
Joseph Moxley
Benja. Boswell
William Steel
James Baker
John Bowling
Thomas Darne
James Hurst
Mathey Carp
Francis Summers

James Thomas
Chas. Currey
John Boucher
Philip Adams
John Ball
William Vollin
George Bryan
William Carp
John Stewart
John Flint
Charles Chrage
Thomas Vinnard
James Gray
James Roberson
William Cook
Mark Mallenly
William Darne
Edwd. Harden
William Eliott
John Forgurson
John Elott

Daniel Summers
Shadrach Hill
Ambrus Nelson
Jacob Payne
Moses Ball
Jonothin Thomas
George Thrift
William Garnor
Moses Ball jr.
Annias Payne
John Payne
John Rollings
Joseph Thompson
Wm. Thomas
Edwd. Davis
Francis Backster
Alexander Williams
Richd. Hollinsbeary
William Green
Samuel Johnson
John Ratcliff

Broadside (DLC: Broadside Collection). Evans 11911; Sabin 100503; Clayton-Torrence 365. Beginning at the point "The subscribers inhabitants of the County of Fairfax," the remainder, including the list of names, is in the hand of an unidentified copyist. The handwritten names seem to have been at times spelled phonetically.

This Association, the authorship of which is undetermined, replaced that of 18 May 1769, q.v. The chief addition in the 1770 Association was the establishment of county committees to enforce the nonimportation measures. See JHB, 1770-1772, p. xxvi-xxxi; Rowland, *Mason*, I, 144-5; Glenn C. Smith, "An Era of Non-Importation Associations," WMQ, 2d ser., XX (1940), 84-98.

To Thomas Adams

DEAR SIR   Charlottesville July 11: 1770.

I take the liberty of interceding for your friendly aid to Mr. James Ogilvie a gentleman of my acquaintance now in London. Purposing last fall to go to Britain for orders he made the usual application to the commissary for his recommendatory letter to the bishop. This man, partly from an evil disposition to defeat the wishes of some gentlemen, no favorites of his, who bore a warm friendship to Mr. Ogilvie, and partly from that elation of mind which usually attends preferment without merit and which has no other object in view but to hang out to the world it's own importance, peremptorily refused his recommendation. The cause of refusal which he assigned unfortunately gave the lie to his own conduct of a few weeks before. He thought Ogilvie not qualified for the sacred function because he did not possess a critical knowlege of the Greek; tho' but a very few weeks before he had thought his sadler properly qualified who was not only a stranger to the characters, but perhaps even to the present existence of that language. He did however condescend to promise Ogilvie that he would not oppose his ordination with the bishop; a promise which seems to have been made with no other than the wanton purpose of sporting with truth: for tho' Ogilvie sailed within a few days after receiving this promise the commissary's letter found means to be before him, and to lodge with the bishop a caveat against his ordination. Here then the matter rests, till his friends can take proper measures for counteracting the designs of this worthy representative of episcopal faith; and as he is obliged to remain in London in the mean time and probably went unprovided for so long a stay, I would ask the favor of you, and I shall deem it a very great one, to procure him credit with your mercantile friends in London for any monies of which he may be in need, for the repaiment of which I enter myself security. I do not know that I can proffer you any reward for this favor, other than the sublime pleasure of relieving distressed merit, a pleasure which can be properly felt by the virtuous alone. I would hope at the same time that the receipt of interest might prevent any pecuniary injury from such advancements. Should you find it convenient to lend such assistance you will be pleased to give Mr. Ogilvie notice of it by a letter directed to him at Mrs. Ballard's Hungerford street in the Strand. I would also beg in that case that you would embrace the first opportunity of doing it, as we are totally in the dark what may be the necessities of his situation. You will be pleased to excuse the freedom and perhaps impropriety of this application. My feelings are warm in the cause of this gentleman, and having no connections or correspondence on that side the water I apply to the single friendship from which I could hope effectual aid to any person there in whose welfare I am interested. Nevertheless if this aid should be attended with inconvenience I expect and insist that you shall decline it with the same freedom with which I ask it. And be assured that I am with much sincerity Your friend & humble sert.

Dft (MHi). Endorsed: "To Mr. Thomas Adams. Richmond."

For Ogilvie's predicament, see his letter to TJ of 28 Mch. 1770, above. The Commissary's (i.e., Rev. James Horrocks') SADLER who was ordained without Greek appears to be James Stephenson (or Stevenson); see the following letter.

To Peyton Randolph

HONORABLE SIR   Albemarle July 23. 1770.

I am to beg the favor of your friendly interposition in the following case, which I hope you will think sufficient to excuse the freedom of the application. Sometime last fall Mr. Jas. Ogilvie proposing to go to Britain for orders made the usual application to the commissary for his recommendatory letter to the bishop. The commissary finding him somewhat deficient in his Greek expressed some doubts whether he could recommend him. Ogilvie to remove them did without thought to be sure make use of a very unfortunate argument; mentioning to the commissary the case of Stevenson who without understanding a word of greek had been lately recommended. The commissary took flame at the hint and peremptorily refused his recommendation. In several subsequent visits Ogilvie attempted to soften him and did at length prevail so far as to obtain a promise that he would not oppose his ordination with the bishop. With this assurance, and with an actual nomination to a parish in his pocket he took his departure. But whether the commissary's frame is such as that he does not feel the obligations of an engagement, or whether he really thought he had done wrong in entering into it I cannot say, but before Ogilvie reached London he had lodged a letter with the bishop in which were these words 'Mr. Ogilvie applied to me last spring for a recommendation to your Lordship for holy orders. *For reasons which then existed* I refused him. He has now applied to me a second time, as these reasons are not removed I have denied him again, but he goes home in opposition.' Nothing could have been more artfully couched to do him a prejudice. The bishop observed to Colo. Mercer, who had espoused Ogilvie's interest with some warmth, that had Mr. Horrocks mentioned his objections, it would have left him to judge whether they were such as he might have overlooked; but that a charge so general laid his whole character open to censure in such a manner as to put it out of his power to vindicate it. This young gentleman seems to have been guided thro' life by the hand of misfortune itself. Some hard fatality which presides over all his measures has rendered abortive every scheme which either his prudence or the anxiety of his friends have ever proposed for his advancement. His present undertaking was peculiarly unfortunate. Before he went to London he paid a visit to his father a presbyterian minister in Aberdeen, who received him with all the joy with which an absence of many years could inspire a parent. Yet, so wonderful is the dominion of bigotry over her votaries that on the first information of his purpose to receive episcopal ordination he shut him from his doors and abjured every parental duty. Thus rejected by that hand from which he had expected some assistance necessary even for the short residence on that side the water which he had then in contemplation he hastened to London, and there received the last stroke which fortune had in reserve for him. The distresses of his situation operating on a mind uncommonly sensible to the pains as well as to the pleasures of life may be conceived even by those to whom fortune has been kinder. There he still remains then, and there he must remain (for it is his last stake) till the commissary can be prevailed on either to withdraw his opposition or to explain the ground of it, or till we can take such other measures as may counteract it's malignity. The former is the easier and shorter relief to Ogilvie's distress, and it is not impossible but that the commissary may by this time be disposed to assist him. For this purpose I have ventured to ask your interposition with him on behalf of this gentleman in whose cause I have warm feelings. This liberty I have taken with you not on any assumed rights of friendship or acquaintance, but merely on the principles of common humanity to which his situation seems to recommend him, and on the hope that you will think with the good man in the play 'homo sum: humani nîl a me alienum puto.' I have no interest at our episcopal palace, and indeed any application if known to come from me would rather be of disservice. I flatter myself your interposition there would have certain effect, and assure you it would lay me under lasting obligations. I suppose the most certain assistance would be a letter from the commissary to the bishop. But one thing I must conjure you to do; to see the letter yourself, that you may judge whether it be really friendly or not. I confess to you Mr. Speaker that I put not the least confidence in the most solemn promises of this reverend gentleman. And unless yourself can be assured of the sincerity of his endeavors I had rather proceed at once in such measures as may answer our purpose tho' 'in opposition.' After your application I have one further favor to ask of you, that if it is unsuccessful you will give me notice by a line lodged in the post office, if succesful (as I doubt not but it will be) you would be so kind as to inclose his letter under cover to Ogilvie, and direct to him at Mrs. Ballard's Hungerford street in the Strand London; as this would be a more speedy communication of relief to him than sending the letter viâ Albemarle. I have no proffers to make you in return for all this trouble; fortune seems to have reserved your obligations for herself. You have nothing to ask, I nothing to give. I can only assure you then that I sincerely rejoice in the independance of your situation; I mean an independan[ce] on all but your own merit, than which I am sure you cannot have a more permanent dependance. I am Sir with much truth Your very humble servt.

Dft (MHi). Endorsed: "To Peyton Randolph esq. Wmsburgh." (This endorsement is on the face of the first page; another is found on a blank leaf accompanying the letter.)

STEVENSON must be the person desig-nated by TJ in his letter to Thomas Adams of 11 July as Horrocks' saddler; according to Goodwin, *Colonial Church in Va.*, p. 309, James Stevenson or Stephenson (d. 1809) was licensed for Va. 29 Sep. 1768, and served as minister in various parishes, 1769-1805.

From Alexander McCaul

Dr. Sir   Glasgow Augt. the 26. 1770.

The last time I had the pleasure of writting you accompanied an Account of some Books you ordered which were unfortunately lost,

I received the order from London but they are not to come to hand time enough to be sent by this Opportunity. They will be sent you soon and if they come too late for you you'll be so good as dispose off them to the best advantage. This will be delivered you by the bearer Mr. William Mitchell whom I beg leave to recommend to your Civilitys. He goes out employed by our Company to Collect their long Winded outstanding debts. Since the begining of our Concern two of our principall partners are dead and their Sons, want to know the true value of their Subject in Virginia which they cannot do without such a Measure as this. We do not mean by this to give up our trade, on the Contrary we mean still to carry it on and to have it more in our power to do it to purpose by having less of our Money in the hands of Negligent Slothfull planters. I have desired Mr. Mitchell in all his General Court business soley to employ you, And I must further beg the favour of you at some leisure time to instruct him in some ordinary Matters that he may not be at a loss. A Collector should certainly understand as much of the law as relates to the Recovery of debts.

It would give me pleasure to hear from you, and if I could render you any service in this part of the World your commands would Oblige me. I have sent out a Nephew to live some time with Richd. Harvie. He is Young and auward being always used to the Country. If youll take some notice of him it would much Oblige me. I am with much esteem Dr Sir your very hl Servt. ALEXR. McCAUL

RC (MHi). Addressed: "To Mr. Thomas Jefferson Attorney at Law Albemarle County Virginia ✠. fav. of Mr Wm. Mitchell." Endorsed: "Alx. McCaul to T. J."

Thomas Burke to Neil Jamieson

DR. SIR   Augst 28th 1770

I yesterday received a Letter from Mr. Jefferson relative to the Suit Intended against Coll. Tucker's Executors wherein he has Judiciously considered the several points upon which our Inquiry can properly turn in Chancery and an Abstract of his reasoning follows.

"The Question whether Mr. Hunt is to be considered as a Bill of Exchange or Simple Contract Creditor is properly triable at Law and will be finally determined upon the Suit Hunts vs Tuckers Executors on which the Hunts have appealed. The Subjecting Coll. Tucker's Lands to American as well as British Debts under the act of parliament 6 Ge: 2d is foreign to the Jurisdiction of Chancery.

I should rather advise that Executions be levied on the Lands by American Creditors. It would be fair, as the point is undetermined, to Indemnify the Sheriff, and Should he not withstanding this to levy the Executions I should think him liable. The next Object is, if this cannot be done, to oblige the Hunts and Creditors by Specialties to levy their Executions on the Lands and to leave the personal Assets to American Creditors by Simple Contract or if already leavied to let the Latter come in their place on the Lands. The 4th to prove a devastavit (or Waste) in the Executors and Subject them to make it good out of thier own Estates. The 5th to compel Mrs. Tucker to restore the Goods She purchased collusively or to restore to the Creditors their real value and lastly to prevent Taylor from recovering a greater proportion of the money due to him on Marriage Promise than other Creditors.[1] This last point Mr. Jefferson thinks will be determined by the Suit now before the Court of Hustings or by appeal removed to the General Court. Now as Mr. Jefferson is of Opinion the most matterial Question will more properly be determined at Law we are next to consider how Such determination will Affect the original design of the Inquiry. If Executions are levied as Mr. Jefferson Advises they must be in the names of the particular plaintiffs in the Judgements, and perhaps no one or two plaintiffs would Chuse to run the Hazard of an Appeal. But I should apprehend all those who were determined to prosecute the Suit in Chancery even to an Appeal might more chearfully engage in this last design on Such Terms as the following Vizt. That all the money to be levied upon the Lands (tho levied in the names of particular Creditors) should be applied for the Satisfaction of the Joining Creditors, and all Expences of Law Suits and Appeals be born by them all in proportion and again the same Creditors to have a proportional Advantage of the money that might be recovered on the Questions brought before the Court of Chancery. The reason why I recommend Such a proceeding as this is because I am exceeding clear in my own Opinion that the Question on the 6 of Geor: 2d, altho' it may go against us here, yet will Indubitably be for us on an Appeal home. Herein I am Strengthened by the uniform Construction of the Neighbouring Colonies upon that act and the clear and conclusive Oppinion of Mr. Dulany and also because I think it the most Speedy and Eligiable Way of determing this, by far the most Important Question, Since all were agreed to prosecute to all length the most tedious Way, I see no reason why they should not prosecute Jointly in this most Speedy Way. Thus then I would advise—Let Executions be Immediately levied on the Lands at Suit of the Joining Creditors or so many of them as the Lands will Satisfy. Let them Join in Indemnifying the Sheriff let the money levied by the Executions be applied to the Satisfaction of their Several claims So far as it will go on an Average and let them Jointly bear the Expence of Law Suits and Appeals then let those who are not Satisfied Join nominally in the Bill in Chancery which is to Litigate the other Questions, and let the monies recovered be averaged among the Joining Creditors, or the Expences proportionally born by them. By this Means in my humble Opinion will the Matters of greatest Importance be tried in the most Speedy Manner, and perhaps more to the advantage of the Creditors Joining against Mr. Hunt than it would otherwise be for a reason Obvious enough when it is considered that the Lands are not Sufficient to Satisfy Mr. Hunts Claim and that the personal Assets are already consumed in paying Debts of Superior Dignity. If Mr. Hunt has no preference (which I am convinced of) then the Executions are legally levied and the money will be left where the Law places it: on the other Hand if he has a preference the money must be refunded to him and the Creditors remain where they were. Now if Hunt has or has not A preference will be determined when Hunt Sues the Persons who will receive the money for the Lands and Charges them as having received money to his Use. Upon this they will defend them selves under the act of Parliament and whether the Act Subjects Lands to one Debt as well as an other will be the Question. This as I have already Observed will very probably go against us here because the general Court have a Standing Rule that the Question is never to be agitated again unless the Matter be sufficient for an Appeal and then they are resolved upon having it finally determined at home. I must now Submit whether the above method will not be most desireable and Should be glad to be informed whether it is approved of by the gentlemen Concerned and whether they will Indemnify the Sheriff. I must also observe that no time should be lost because it may be fatal. I must beg the favor of you to communicate this to them, and also Inform them that I am ready in behalf of Messrs. Cortlandt & Cuyler to come into the above Scheme. I should also wish that Mr. Thomas Stabler might be consulted on behalf of Mr. Reese Meredith. I shall Impatiently wait the Answer, and beg it may be Speedy that I may have time enough to prosecute the Suit before the October Court. I am Sir &c.

FC, autograph (NcDAH). The earliest recorded connection between Burke and TJ is in a letter from TJ to Burke, 15 July 1770, now lost but mentioned in the present letter and acknowledged in Burke's letter to TJ of 3 Sep., below. TJ's letter dealt with "the Suit of Tuckers Creditors vs. his Executors" and its antecedents, as did most of the subsequent correspondence between the two lawyers in 1770-1771; the present note applies generally to this early series of legal letters. Respecting the Tucker case, TJ's Account Book has this entry under 29 Aug. 1769: "Committed my opinion to writing in the case of Henry Tucker (Norfolk) charge 20/." In his Case Book, same date, No. 325, TJ says the same thing, adding only the date for receipt of fee (30 Aug. 1770). No further record of TJ's action in this

case has been found in his legal papers, but Burke's further letters indicate that TJ continued to serve as consultant in the case. In his letter book (whence all these letters are taken) Burke appended a summary of the case, as it then stood, to his letter of 10 July 1771, q.v., below. MR. HUNT was a London creditor of Tucker's estate; TJ's Case Book, No. 465 (31 Oct. 1771), records TJ's employment by the heirs of a Robert Tucker of Norfolk in a suit brought by the Hunts, merchants of London.

1 Closing quotation marks should probably be inserted here.

From Thomas Burke

DR. SIR   Sepr. 3d 1770

I received yours of July 15th a few days past, and Immediately communicated your Sentiments and my own relative to the Suit of Tuckers Creditors vs his Executors to the persons concerned and endeavoured to enforce what you recommended which was Intirely agreeable to my own Opinion. I also recommended the Joining Creditors to undertake all the Enquiries at their common Expence and to average all that may be recovered amongst them. This I recommended lest any one or two Creditors might not chuse to risque an Appeal which I apprehend will be Inevitable. But when I came to consider in what manner Executions were to be levied I found myself altogether at a loss how to proceed probably owing to my Ignorance of the Proceedings on the Act of Parliament or Indeed of any methods of levying Executions except what are pointed out by the Common Law, the older Statutes, or our own acts of Assembly. In whatever View I turn these I cannot discover that Execution can be levied in Hands of Executors without A Sc: fac: when the Judgements have been obtained against the Testator or against the Executors, when Assets, the Latter of these is our Case, all our Judgements are in that predicament; and unless the act of Parliament makes Lands Assets in their Hands I cannot See what use even a Sc: fac: against them will be of, and if the Lands are only Assets in the Hands of the Heir, I presume he must be in Court Before any Execution can go against his Inheritance. The same reasoning will hold good with regard to the Hæres factus mutatis mutandis. But on the other Hand if the Act makes them

Assets, and it has been adjudged that no Sc: fac: is Necessary, I should be glad to have your direction and Opinion relative thereto. I have Just read an Abstract of the Law in these Words. "All real Estates shall be chargeable with all Just Debts Whatsoever as they are by the Law of England liable to Satisfaction of Debts due by Bond or other Specialties, and Subject to like remedies and proceedings in any Court in any of the Plantations in the same manner as personal Estates are there." Now Sir if this Law Extends to charging Lands in the Colonies with provincial Debts (which I am very clear in) The only Question, I think will be what would be our remedy against personal Estates under our Circumstances? Can we take Execution against the personal Estate without bringing A Sc: fac: against the Executors? If we can, I make no Question but we also can against the Lands Since they are subject to the Same remedies. I shall leave these Things Sir to your determination; fairly confessing my Ideas are not clear enough to enable me to act or Judge Effectually. Upon reconsidering this Matter, I incline Strongly to conclude No Sc: fac: is Necessary because I find the Rule laid down in many Books, but clearly in Ld. Raymond, that a Sc: fac: is only Necessary when persons who are not parties to the Judgement are to be charged therewith, or have the Execution. This then cannot be the Case, because the Executor is party to the Judgement altho they are Conditional. I suppose then the way is to Issue the Execution and let the Sheriff Nulla Bona or devastavit as he finds the Case. In our Case then if we Indemnify him and Shew him Assets I must agree with you that if those Assets Should Afterwards be found Chargeable, the Officer would be liable. I know it is an Idea amongst us, that a Sc: fac: must Issue against the Executors on Such Conditional Judgements before Execution. But I can find no Precedent and know no Statute or rule of Law on which it can be founded. If I am wrong I doubt not your giving me Such Instructions as will Intirely remove my difficulties. Altho I have fatigued you so long on this Subject, I must beg your Patience while I offer a few Considerations on the other Points. You will recollect that Coll. Tucker in the begining of his Will, previous to any particular dispositions, directs his Just Debts to be paid; also that he has left certain Lands to be Sold for performing his Will. Now Sir I will premise that if by Virtue of 5th: G: 2d all his Estates were Assets for the payment of Debts of what kindsoever, then his Will need not be Considered, because it must be postponed to the payment of Debts which is all we are to Consider: I need not repeat Sir that this is my Opinion Nor my Reasons for thinking so, because I have before declared them to you, and they will Occur to you, but if it should not be the case, let us enquire how far his Will makes those Lands Assets. And here let me also premise that he could not make any disposition by his Will which could Operate against Law. Therefore the Bond Creditors could not be prevented from recovering from the Executors, or the personal Estate, or be compelled by his Will in Case of a Deficiency of Assets to take an Average of their Claims when they have a prior Right to be fully Satisfied. We must Set it down then, that the Creditors by Specialty must be paid, and all that remains for Consideration is how far his Will Subjects his [heirs?] to the payment of his Simple Contract Debts. Had he died Intestate Chancery would Subject them as far as personal Estate had been Applied in paying Spec. Therefore the Spec. being paid, It is not matterial what Estate they were paid from, if the Will Subjects all his Lands to pay his Debts, and that it does I stronly Incline for the Reasons, and Authorities which follow. His first direction in his Will, Seems clearly to me to Intend a Charge upon his Estate for payment of his Debts in preference to all other Dispositions, and that his Succeeding Dispositions were only to take place in case of his Estate being fully Sufficient for them after his Debts paid, and when he made his Will he had Expectations that his Estate would have been Sufficient for all his purposes, and what prevented it were Subsequent Accidents. Still the Charge remains on what is left, and Indeed no man has any Estate until his Debts are paid, the rest is Æs alienum. But if that general Charge can make that Estate Assets which was not so before, or by Law, Seems to be our grand Question, and this I will endeavour to discuss. (here are Inserted Paragraphs from 2d Bac: Abr: [Bacon's Abridgment] 65 and Vern: [Vernon] 225 & 690 Quoted). Not to tire you with any more Cases, I shall only refer you to that of Harris vs Ingledew 3d P: W: [Peere Williams] 91 which is as Strong in our Favor as any Words could make it, the Words being "as to all my Worldly Estate, my Debts being first Satisfied I devise the Same as follows" And clearly held that the Lands both Freehold and Copyhold were Subject because nothing is devised until the Debts are paid. In this Case the Subject is so elegantly and Judiciously treated I think I can not better Support my Opinion than by refering to the perusal of it. Taking it for granted then that the Will Subjects the Lands, the next Question arising is are they legal or Equitable Assets? In Walker vs Meager. 2d P: W:552 it is laid down by Lord Chancellor King that Equitable Assets in the Hands of the Executors, must be applied as legal Assets are, and in Frumould vs: Dedire 1st: P:W: 430, 431 the Distinction is taken between Lands devised for payment of Debts and Lands charged with the Debts and descending charged, which I apprehend to be our Case, and in which Case the Ld. Chancellor said the Specialties Should be first Satisfied. The reason why I have Investigated the last Question is because I Apprehend if the Lands are now Subjected under the Will, the Judgements must be paid in their legal Order Since Each has now the Same Superority one over the other that one Specialty can have over another Vizt priority of time. And again if Mr. Hunt has any preference, which is most Extraordinary and unaccountable, the Enquiry may as well cease Since the Lands will not be Sufficient to pay him. Indeed I should apprehend the very Will would prevent Such a Claim, for surely it will not be denied that a man *may* pay his American Debts with his Lands, tho he must pay his British with them. If then they are Subject to one as well as the other what gives him any preference? Real Estates can be no exclusive fund for British Debts; and Supposing a Man had no real Estate, is his Executor Obliged to give his British Creditors the Preference? I think a man would be deservedly laughed at who would advance such a possition, and surely when real and personal assets are made Assets alike he can have no claim to A Privilege; and an American Creditor having first Intitled himself would most assuredly be first Satisfied. We are come at length then to Conclude on this Head, If Lands in Virginia are Subject by Act of Parliament to every Species of Just Debt without Distinction, then the Lands are liable to our Recovery. If they are not Subject by Statute yet they may be so by the Will. If so By the Will They are Assets, and must be Applied in legal Order In which Order Mr. Hunt only can come in Turn (for his Debt has no Dignity, and the utmost they can claim is a right to take the Lands in Execution, when provincial Creditors might Not, and if they have not taken them, surely they cannot prevent an other man who has as good a right, which I suppose we have by the Will). I must own I have thought Mr. Waller's prohibitting the Sale of Coll. Tucker's Lands when advertised by the Executors a most unwarrantable proceeding, for tho' my Lands may be Subject to the payment of a British Debt, or rather to an Execution for a British Debt when recovered, has the person who Sues me any kind of right to prevent my Selling those Lands before he recovers his Judgement, because he may chuse to levy his Execution, when he gets one, on that part of my property? This indeed would be to bind the Property of the Lands from the time of contracting the Debt, a Length which I believe the Notion was never carried. Surely there can be no reason to prevent Coll. Tucker or even his Executor from giving the preference to any Creditor in equal Degree, and if he was authorised by his Testator to Sell all his Lands and pay off other Creditors before Mr. Hunt could get a Judgement has he not a right to do So? This reasoning must hold Just unless it be contended that the British Debt is a specific Lien upon the Lands, a position hard to be maintained. As to Marshalling the Assets I believe it would answer little purpose since the personal Estate is already Exhausted in paying Specialties, and there are not Lands Sufficient even to pay Mr. Hunt. You have the Copy of the account Sales and Appraisement, you will see the Iniquity appearing in them, and Covin I believe may be proved. The Purpose you mention for making Mrs. Tucker a party is certainly a good one, And Mr. Taylors claim will depend upon whether Coll. Tucker's Promise was a Voluntary one or for valuable Consideration. Mr. Taylor made no Settlement. Q: is the Promise not Voluntary. It is a Settled Point that even Voluntary Bonds must be postponed to Simple Contract Debts afortiori A Promise. I am at length come to an End of this Tedious Letter, during the writing of which I have suffered many Interuptions, and have turned over many Volumes. But as I can do nothing Conclusively until I hear from you again I must beg of you to write as soon as possible. Mr. Coles will be coming Down in a Little time. I shall write again as soon as I hear from the gentlemen on James River. I remain Sir with much Esteem &c.

FC, autograph (NcDAH).
See note on preceding letter. TJ's letter of 15 July is missing. The several legal compilations mentioned and quoted by Burke were all owned by TJ; see Library Catalogue, 1815, p. 72 (twice), 74, 82.

Notice of Sale of Bernard Moore's Property

[10 January 1771]

To be SOLD *to the highest Bidders, on* Thursday *the 31st of this Instant* (January) *at the House of Colonel* Bernard Moore, *in* King William,

EIGHTEEN Hundred Acres of LAND for the Life of Colonel *Moore,* lying on *Mattapony* River, in the said County, being the Land whereon Colonel *Moore* now lives. Also the Fee Simple Estate in eleven Hundred and twenty five Acres of exceeding fine well timbered Land, lying in the said County, on *Pamunkey* River, below *Ruffin's* Ferry, where Colonel *Moore* formerly lived. The above Lands are subject to Mrs. *Moore's* Dower. At the same Time will be sold all the personal Estate of Colonel *Moore*; consisting of Plate, Household and Kitchen Furniture, Horses, Hogs, Sheep, Cattle, Corn, Fodder, Plantation Utensils, and sixteen House Servants.-----And on *Tuesday* the 5th of *February*, being the Day after *Henrico* Court, will be sold to the highest Bidders, at *Richmond* Town, the Remainder of Colonel *Moore's* Slaves, being near one Hundred, amongst which are Tradesmen of several Sorts.-----All the above Estate hath been conveyed to the Subscribers, as Trustees, for the Purpose of paying Colonel *Moore's* Debts. As it is the Desire of the Trustees to make the most of the Estate, for the Benefit of the Creditors, they request that all Persons who have Mortgages on, or Demands against, the Estate, may attend the Sale to assist them, and see that every Thing is conducted to their Satisfaction. Twelve Months Credit will be allowed for the above Estate, the Purchasers giving Bond, with approved Security, to

> CARTER BRAXTON,
> GEORGE WEBB,
> THOMAS WALKER, } Trustees.
> THOMAS JEFFERSON,
> JACK POWER,

Printed from *Virginia Gazette* (Purdie & Dixon), 10 Jan. 1771.

In a notice dated 3 Nov. 1770, BERNARD MOORE declared that he was about "to deliver up, upon oath, [his] whole estate, of every kind whatever," to the five trustees who subscribed the present notice, "to dispose of it for the benefit of [his] creditors, in such order as the law directs" (*Va. Gaz.* [Rind], 8 Nov. 1770).

Notice of Bidding
for the Erection of a Prison

[31 January 1771]

To be LET to the lowest bidder, on Thursday *the 14th of* March, *at* Charlottesville, *in* Albemarle,

THE building of a PRISON of brick, with two rooms below, and two above stairs. Plans, prepared for the inspection of those disposed to undertake the same, may be seen on application to

> JOHN HENDERSON,
> THOMAS JEFFERSON,
> JOHN WALKER.

Printed from *Virginia Gazette* (Rind), 31 Jan. 1771. The notice continued to appear through the issue of 7 Mch.

It does not appear whether the contemplated PRISON at Charlottesville was built (see Woods, *Albemarle County*, p. 80-1). The earliest jail whose date is known, according to Miss Mary Rawlings, historian of Charlottesville, was erected in 1785. The PLANS, which would be interesting in the light of TJ's later prison plans, have not been found.

To Thomas Adams

Not expecting to have the pleasure of seeing you again before you leave the country I inclose you an order on the inspectors at Shockoe for two hhds. of tobacco which I consign to you, and give you also the trouble of shipping as I am too far from the spot to do it myself. They are to be laid out in the purchase of the articles on the back hereof. You will observe that part of these articles (such as are licensed by the association) are to be sent at any event. Another part (being prohibited) are only to be sent if the tea act should be repealed before you get home. If it is not you will observe a third class to be sent instead of those which are prohibited. I am not without expectation that the repeal may take place. I beleive the parliament want nothing but a colorable motive to adopt this measure. The conduct of our brethren of New York affords them this. You will observe by my invoice that I have supposed my tobacco to clear me £10 sterl. per hhd. Should it be less, dock the invoice of such articles as you think I may get in the country.

In consequence of your recommendation I wrote to Waller last June for 45£ sterl. [worth of books inclosing him] a bill of exchange [to that] amount. [Having written] to Benson [Fearon] for another parcel [of nearly] the same amount I [directed] him to purchase them also of Waller. I acquainted both of the necessity of my situation brought on by the unlucky loss of my library, and pressed them most earnestly to lose not a day in sending them. The vessel which carried my letters sailed the first day of July and is returned long since. Yet I have heard not a tittle from either gentleman.

I mentioned to you that I had become one of several securities for a gentleman of my acquaintance lately engaged in trade. I hope and indeed hear he is doing very well. I would not therefore take any step to wound his credit. But as far as it can possibly be done without affecting that I must beg you to have me secured. It can surely do no mischeif to see that his remittances are placed to the credit of the money for which we stand engaged, and not of any new importations of goods made afterwards. I must rely entirely on your friendly assistance in this matter, which I assure you gives me concern, as should my friend prove unsuccesful (and ill fortune may render any person unsuccesful) it might sweep away the whole of my little fortune. I must once more trouble you for my friend Ogilvie. The Commissary promised to write in his favor to the bishop by Necks. I did not see his letter, and with this gentleman I beleive no farther than I see. I wrote by the same opportunity to Ogilvie and apprised him of the Commissary's engagement. Should your route to the ship be thro' Wmsburgh I would trouble you to know whether he has in truth written or not. The inclosed letter to Ogilvie you will please to deliver with our most earnest advice that he lose not a day in coming over.

One farther favor and I am done, to search the Herald's office for the arms of my family. I have what I have been told were the family arms, but on what authority I know not. It is possible there may be none. If so I would with your assistance become a purchaser, having Sterne's word for it that a coat of arms may be purchased as cheap as any other coat.

The things I have desired you to purchase for me I would beg you to hasten, particularly the Clavichord which I have directed to be purchased in Hamburgh because they are better made there, and much cheaper. Leave me a line before you go away with instructions how to direct to you. I am Dr. Sir Your [affectionate Friend,]   Th: Jefferson

RC (ViHi). Below the signature the following memorandum appears: "Credit for £13.16.2 by Mr. Maury. Feby. 20th 1771. No. 26." Enclosures missing. The MS is badly worn, and some words in our text have been supplied in brackets from a printed text in *Harper's New Monthly Magazine*, LXXXI (1890), 205-6.

The letter illustrates TJ's difficulties in building and furnishing Monticello while the Nonimportation Association, to which he was himself a subscriber, was still in effect (see 22 June 1770, above). By this time, however, it had been rendered of little effect by the defection of the New York merchants (here sarcastically referred to as "our brethren in New York"), who had agreed just at that time to import everything except tea, the sole article on which the duty had not been repealed (A. M. Schlesinger, *The Colonial Merchants and the American Revolution*, New York, 1918, p. 134-8, 197-9; Stokes, *Iconography of Manhattan Island*, IV, 811-14; TJ to Thomas Adams, 1 June 1771). The list of articles TJ ordered is missing, and no entries for them have been found in his Accounts.

To James Ogilvie

Dear Ogilvie   Monticello Feb. 20. 1771

I wrote you a line from Wmsburgh last October; but lest that may have miscarried I take this opportunity of repeating what was material in that. On receipt of your letter (and, oh shame! of your only letter) of March 28. 1770. which came not to hand till August we took proper measures for prevailing on the commissary to withdraw his opposition. But lest you should be uneasy in your situation in the mean time I directed Mr. T. Adams by the means of

his partners Perkins and Brown to let you know they would answer
any calls from you. In this your friend Mr. Walker insisted on
joining me. In October I transmitted to the commissary a certificate
of your conduct in life, on which he promised to write in your favor
by Necks, and tho I did not see the letter I expect he did. By the
same opportunity I wrote to you inclosing a duplicate of the certificate of which you might avail yourself if the commissary should
fail us again. About the same time I wrote from Wmsburgh to a
gentleman of the vestry in Orange to secure for you a vacancy
which had happened in that parish by the death of Martin. I have
had no answer, but the parish is still vacant which gives me hopes
it is kept for you. Mr. Maury incumbent in Fredericksville parish
(of which I was when you were here) has a tempting offer from
another quarter. I know not whether he will accept of it. If he
should we shall do for you all that can be done in your absence.
But for god's sake let not that be a moment longer than is of absolute
necessity. Your settlement here would make your friends happy,
and I think would be agreeable to yourself. Your Dulcinea is in
health. Her brother T. Strachan is settled with J. Walker for lif[e,]
another inducement for her and you to wish for a residence with us.
He is wishing to take to himself a wife; and nothing obstructs it
but the unfeeling temper of a parent who delays, perhaps refuses
to approve her daughter's choice. I too am in that way; and have
still greater difficulties to encounter not from the frowardness of
parents, nor perhaps want of feeling in the fair one, but from other
causes as unpliable to my wishes as these. Since you left us I was
unlucky enough to lose the house in which we lived, and in which
all it's contents were consumed. A very few books, two or three
beds &c. were with difficulty saved from the flames. I have lately
removed to the mountain from whence this is dated, and with which
you are not unacquainted. I have here but one room, which, like the
cobler's, serves me for parlour for kitchen and hall. I may add, for
bed chamber and study too. My friends sometimes take a temperate
dinner with me and then retire to look for beds elsewhere. I have
hopes however of getting more elbow room this summer. But be
this as may happen, whether my tenements be great or small
homely or elegant they will always receive you with a hearty welcome. If any thing should obstruct your setting out immediately
for Virginia I would beg the favor of you to send the things I asked of
you to purchase by some careful captain coming to James river:
such of them as were for my buildings, or for house-keeping I am
in particular want of. Nothing material occurs relative to the health

or fortunes of your friends here. They are well in both as far as I can recollect them. I conclude my epistle with every wish for your felicity which friendship can inspire. Adieu and beleive me to be Your's sincerely,   TH: JEFFERSON

Dft (MHi). Endorsed: "To James Ogilvie London." TJ's letter of Oct. 1770 is missing. The present letter contains TJ's first reference to his courtship of Martha, daughter of John and Martha Eppes Wayles of The Forest, Charles City co., and widow of Bathurst Skelton (1744-1768); TJ married Martha Wayles Skelton on 1 Jan. 1772.

Advertisement of Sale of Other Property and Effects of Bernard Moore

[21 February 1771]

To be SOLD to the highest Bidders, on the second Wednesday in March, being the Day before Caroline Court, at Colonel Bernard Moore's Plantation in Caroline,

THE Stocks of CATTLE, HOGS, CORN, and FODDER. Twelve Months Credit will be allowed, the Purchasers giving Bond, with Security, to Colonel Moore's Trustees. Mr. Samuel Redd will attend the Sale, in Behalf of the Trustees.

Also, on the second Thursday in March, being Caroline Court Day, at Caroline Courthouse, will be sold, to the highest Bidder, three Hundred and seventy Acres of well timbered LAND, with a good Dwellinghouse, and all convenient Outhouses, a good Garden, and an Orchard. Those inclinable to purchase the Land may be shown the same by Mr. Samuel Redd, who lives in the Neighbourhood of it. Twelve Months Credit will be allowed, the Purchasers giving Bond and Security to

CARTER BRAXTON,
GEORGE WEBB,
THOMAS WALKER,   } Trustees.
THOMAS JEFFERSON,
JACK POWER,

Printed from Virginia Gazette (Purdie & Dixon), 21 Feb. 1771.

Further Advertisement of Sale of Bernard Moore's Property

[28 February 1771]

To be SOLD to the highest Bidders, on the third Thursday in March, at King William Courthouse, being Court Day,

ELEVEN Hundred and twenty five Acres of exceeding fine well timbered LAND lying on Pamunkey, below Ruffin's Ferry, on the main Road from the Courthouse to *West Point*, being the Land whereon Colonel *Bernard Moore* formerly lived. In the last Advertisement of this Land it was, by Mistake, said to be subject to Mrs. *Moore*'s Dower; but Mrs. *Moore* has already been satisfied for her Dower, by the late Speaker's Administrators, so that the Subscribers can now undertake to convey the Land discharged from all Encumbrances. At the same Time and Place will be sold several SLAVES, which could not be carried to the Sale at *Richmond*. Twelve Months Credit will be allowed, the Purchasers giving Bond, with Security, to

CARTER BRAXTON,
GEORGE WEBB,
THOMAS WALKER, } Trustees.
THOMAS JEFFERSON,
JACK POWER,

Printed from *Virginia Gazette* (Purdie & Dixon), 28 Feb. 1771.

From Mrs. Drummond

Wmsburgh. March 12th. [1771]

I am sorry to say, by this Man, who is come down so late that all the valluable fruite, and flower roots, cannot be medled with, and I can procure nothing [w]orthy of the Acceptance of my Amiable freind, except four Apricot Trees, one Medler [. . .]¹ and some pumgranuts. I am promis't but every thing, of the flower roots in Octbr. all freinds that I've applied too, declairing the roots now, wou'd perish if dug Up, and spoil those, they were taken from. I was vext, and tho't my Self like the Hair, with many friends, but the fall wil' determine. I hope You've not only reciv'd some hunderds, of Grafts, by Mr. Coles, of the choicest Englis fruite Green Spring afforded, but that you have grafted them too. He promist to take perticuler care of them, and You Sr. may depend their all, from the best English Trees. Mr. Wilkinson, cut, and label'd them him Self, as I told him they were for You. With these few things you wil' recive, two Bundls of Grafts, from Majr. Taliaferro. I sent to aske the favour, of a few grafted Trees—and loe—the Majr. sent Grafts.—But hang this long preamble, about nothing. Let me recolect Your discription, which bars all the Romantic, Poetical, ones I ever read. Poor Coles, falls flat on the Ground behind it. No pen but Yrs., cou'd, (surely so butiful discribe) espeshally, those few lines, in the Miltonic Stile. Thou wonderful Young Man, so piously entertaining, thro out that, exalted Letter. Indeed I shal' think, Spirits of an higher order, inhabits Yr. Aerey Mountains,— or rather Mountain, which I may contemplate, but never can aspire too. Oh! this dirty pudle, but all places in this World wil' soon be alike to Me, so many warnings, and so many dificultys. (Old Age, —Old Maid-Servant Old Horse, and Old Chair. Such a retinue of Momentos.—No! it never wil' be,—because, for all the Above reasons,—it cannot be.—I wil just mention,—what needs no explanation, in Yr. Letter, and Say, persever thou, good Young Man, persevere.—She has good Sence, and good Nature, and I hope wil not refuse (the Blessing shal' I say) why not as I think it,—of Yr. hand, if her Hearts, not ingagd allready. I've only now[2] to tel' you, how happy I shu'd think my Self, if you woud throw away, a few leasure hours, in talking to Me. As to a corispondance, how insipid, frome Me to You. Oh! fie upon it, belive me this, shal, as it is the first, be the last.—Now be sincear, and say thank Ye.—And belive me, that I most sincearly wish You, the full completion, of all Yr. wishes, both as to the Lady and every thing else—

A wit's a feather, and a cheifs a rod:
An Honest Mans, the Noblest work of God.
So says Pope, and so thinks, of Jefferson, his friend & humb. Servt.,
S.[3] DRUMMOND

RC (MHi). Addressed: "To Jefferson Esqur. on Monticello." Endorsed: "Mrs. Drummond to T. J."

The date is established from the fact that TJ had moved this winter to Monticello and was courting Martha Wayles Skelton, to whom the ROMANTIC, POETICAL DISCRIPTION, mentioned here but unhappily lost, must have appertained. Almost nothing certain is known of Mrs. DRUMMOND, though it is apparent that this obviously charming lady had married into the family descended from Nathaniel Bacon's fellow-rebel William Drummond (hanged by Governor Berkeley in 1676), for these Drummonds were established at GREEN SPRING, a few miles southwest of Williamsburg (VMHB, XVIII [1910], 2-5; WMQ, 2d ser., XX [1940], 484, and map facing p. 476). She had a place in Williamsburg and was friendly with the Wythes; on 7 Dec. 1776 TJ, who had been using George Wythe's house briefly, "left with Mrs. Drummond for Mr. Wythe 30/" (Account Book under date).

1 Illegible: apparently "Bufitism."
2 Perhaps "rom" (i.e., room).
3 The initial is uncertain, being written in monogram fashion with the following initial.

Agreement with John Randolph

October [i.e., April?] 11th, 1771.

It is agreed between John Randolph, Esq., of the City of Williamsburg, and Thomas Jefferson, of the County of Albemarle, that in case the said John shall survive the said Thomas, that the Executors or Administrators of the said Thomas shall deliver to the said John 100 pounds sterling of the books of the said Thomas, to be chosen by the said John, or if not books sufficient, the deficiency to be made up in money: And in case the said Thomas should survive the said John, that the Executors of the said John shall deliver to the said Thomas the violin which the said John brought with him into Virginia, together with all his music composed for the violin, or in lieu thereof, if destroyed by any accident, 60 pounds sterling worth of books of the said John, to be chosen by the said Thomas. In witness whereof the said John and Thomas have hereunto subscribed their names and affixed their seals the day and year above written.   JOHN RANDOLPH (L.S.)

                                                                TH. JEFFERSON (L.S.)

Sealed and delivered in presence of:

G. WYTHE,   P. HENRY, JR.   WM. JOHNSON,

THO'S EVERARD,   WILL. DREW,   JA. STEPTOE.

                         RICHARD STARKE,

Virginia, ss.

At a general court held at the capitol on the 12th day of April, 1771, this agreement was acknowledged by John Randolph and Thomas Jefferson, parties thereto, and ordered to be recorded.

Teste,

BEN. WALLER, C. C. CUR.

MS not located. Text from Randall, *Life*, I, 131, from a copy said to have been furnished by Richard Randolph from the records of the General Court.

The MS copy furnished to Randall must have been very defective, and he not only failed to correct it but perhaps added other errors. The dates are inconsistent: an agreement recorded on 12 April could not have been made in the following October; we have followed Ford in arbitrarily fixing on the April date. Randall's text gives the value of the books TJ is to deliver to Randolph as £800, an absurdly large sum; this has been corrected to £100 on the authority of TJ's Account Book entry for 17 Aug. 1775, which notes that this agreement has been canceled; see also TJ to Randolph, 25 Aug. 1775. Thomas EVERARD, not "Everand" as printed by Randall, was clerk of the committee of the courts of justice (JHB, 1770-1772, p. 101, 158).

From James Ogilvie

MY DEAR SIR   Berwick upon Tweed April 26th. 1771.

Though I have wrote you and Mr. Walker twice, yet I am at a loss to know whether any of my letters have come to hand or not as I have never heard from Virginia, but once since I left it which was a letter dated last Novr. from my young freind at Belvidere. I have the pleasure however to inform you that I have got into deacon's Orders by the Bishop of Durham, independant of Horrocks by means of a reccommendation from the Magistrates and Ministers of Aberdeen, but as I was ordained to a living in England and not

America, I was obliged to accept a Curacy in Berwick and to wait till next September before I can obtain the Order of Preist. This plan I pursued by the advice of the Archbishop of York who has showed me great freindship and who would have ordained me but that the Bp. of London had signified that as he had refused me ordination he expected he would not interfere. The Archbishop however saw Horrocks's letter and told me had he been his Commissary he would have paid no regard to so general an accusation.

Though (as I have informed Mr. Walker) I might to great advantage settle in England, yet my heart and thoughts are all eagerly bent upon Virginia. The connections I formed in your Colony were at that early time of life when the affections expand themselves with a sympathy too generous to admitt any selfish or interested views. I loved because I found an object every way qualifyed to yeild that happiness to which the gratifications of Ambition appear as an empty dream; I have had that love most generously returned. Every scheme therefore of life which I have ever planned has so enterwoven with it a communication of happiness to the person beloved, that I find myself unable to partake of enjoyment in any other way. Allow me to add that the continuance of your freindship is more than a secondary inducement for my returning among you. Permit me Dear Sir to flatter myself that Mr. Walker and you will still preserve whatever share of esteem and regard you supposed my merit might draw from you while I was with you. Enclosed you have the Bristol and London prices of Masonry a copy of which I sent you before. You are perhaps surprised at my not answering your commissions before now, but my continualy expecting to see America myself prevented me, and the remoteness of Berwick from any place of trade with Virga. makes my opportunities of even writing but seldom. As I cannot take shipping at any rate before October, I shall esteem it as a particular mark of freindship if you'll favour me with a line either by London or Glasgow under cover to my Father at Aberdeen. My very respectful Compliments wait upon your Mother. I am with much esteem Dear Sir your much obliged & very affect. servant,   JAS. OGILVIE

RC (MHi). Addressed: "To Thomas Jefferson Esqr. Albemarle County Virginia."

BELVIDERE was the ancient seat of the Byrd family and later of the Harvies near the Falls of the James, now in the city of Richmond (Glenn, *Some Colonial Mansions*, p. 20; Mary N. Stanard, *Richmond*, Phila. and London, 1923, p. 39).

From Thomas Burke

[ca. April 1771]

I have been labouring to prevail on Tuckers Executors to come to a Speedy trial of the Cause, but without Success. Mr. Taylor seems determined to remove it by   if possible, and even Mr. Wallers advice to the Contrary Seems to have no Effect on him. I fear we must have recourse to an Injunction unless It may be your Opinion that if ever Mr. Hunt Subjects the lands we shall be able to recover their amount from the Executors upon making it appear that they are Assets in their Hands and ought to be administered legally. This I own is my Opinion; for if the   in the Will Subjecting them to pay Debts, and directing the Executors to pay those Debts Impowers the Executors to Administer, they must surely administer legally, or submit to the legal penalty for breach or Neglect of Duty, at all events I apprehend there is sufficient reason demanding an Injunction. Great part of the Subject which at least it is probable the Executor is obliged to administer otherwise is in danger by legal Judgement being taken out of his power, and Injury must follow either to him or the Creditors. Again it is Certain the Testator has subjected his Estate Generally, and here a particular Creditor endeavours to engrove [engross?] the whole benefit and without giving the Executor an Opportunity of defending if he claims any advantage from the 5 G:2 the 3d and 4W: & M is expressly for the Creditors when it directs that all   or appointments for payment of Debts shall be in force. If Mr. Hunt prevails at Law this is Impossible, and he must prevail without the Interposition of Chancery. I have ventured upon these few Hints on which I am satisfied you will Improve if they deserve it. If not your own Judgement will better and I shall submit entirely to your Council.

I am next to inform you that the Revd. Mr. Agnew Incumbent of Nansemond, or Suffolk Parish has lately appealed from a Judgement of Nd. Court and I must beg your appearing and Conducting it for him. Has in it nothing   : want of a Declaration will save you all trouble. Among the Causes on Mr. Blairs Docket which I directed him to put under your Case is one Reid vs. Snaip & al. in Chancery to Stay Effects &c. I must beg of you to attend particularly to it, and if the Effects can be Obtain'd on security next April, I will procure it. I shall furnish you with Documents. In April Sir I will point out to you the other   and Inform you as much as I can of their Circumstances.

We must watch Attentively in the affair of Tuckers Creditors. Can we procure a Sale of the Lands and leave to Contend for the Money? Would it not become a Court of Equity to make some such Order and prevent Waste that happens every day in in so valuable a subject?

FC (NcDAH). The blanks are in the MS, attesting the clerk's difficulty in reading Burke's legal style and hand.

The letter may be dated with some confidence in Apr. 1771, for TJ stated in his Case Book, 9 Apr. 1771, that he

had received a letter from Burke asking him to act for the Rev. John AGNEW of Nansemond co. in a suit there summarized (No. 530); REID vs. SNAIP is not listed in the index to TJ's Case Book. On the Tucker case, see note on Burke to TJ, 28 Aug. 1770.

From Thomas Mann Randolph

DEAR SIR   Lortons May 10. 1771

I omitted giving the Treasurer my Bond for things purchas'd at the Palace Amount £8:18:6. Indeed it ought to have been Cash, but as I hope it will make little difference I shall take it as a favor if you would do it for me, and this shall indemnify you. I am Your hum Servt,

THOMAS M. RANDOLPH

RC (NjP). Addressed: "To Thomas Jefferson Esqr in Williamsburg. Favr. Mr Barrett." Endorsed: "T. M. Randolph" (not in TJ's hand). The cover bears arithmetical calculations by TJ and also a brief, undated message: "C[arter] H[enry] Harrison compls. Mr.

Jefferson and begs he will call on Walt: Lenox for a pr. Curles for his Aunt."

LORTONS was perhaps a lodging house, but the initial letter is uncertain in the MS, and the place has not been identified.

To Messrs. Inglis and Long

GENTLEMEN   Williamsburgh, May 11, 1771.

Yours of the eighth of April I have received, and since that your favour of five pounds as counsel for Messrs. Cunningham & Nisbett at the suit of Jamieson & Taylor. Before we can regularly proceed to take any proofs in the cause it will be necessary for Messrs. Cunningham & Nisbett to send us their answer denying or admitting the several charges in the bill as far as their own knowledge enables them. For this purpose a copy of the bill should be transmitted them. The answer must be sworn to before some justice of the peace, and that he is such must be certified under the seal of their province. As soon as I shall receive the answer immediate care shall be taken to send a commission for the examination of any witnesses Messrs. Cunningham & Nisbett may choose to call on, with directions what matters it will most avail them to prove. This I shall be the better enabled to do when their answer shall have apprised me of the nature of their defence.

With respect to the part yourselves are to act, it will be very plain, as you are not concerned in interest. You must declare what effects of Cunningham & Nisbett you have in your hands, and submit them to the direction of the Court. If you will be pleased by way of letter to state these matters to me I will put them into the usual form of answers and return them to be sworn to. Any further instructions you may think proper to give in this matter shall be diligently attended to by Gent., your very hble servt.

MS not located. Text from Ford, I, 393-4, where it is printed, without signature, from a copy then owned by Mrs. J. W. Drexel. The MS was later sold at the Parke-Bernet Galleries, N.Y., in the Gribbel Sale, Part I, 30 Oct. to 1 Nov. 1940, lot 668.

On the case as a whole, see Case Book, No. 546, "Neill Jamieson & Jas. Taylor (Norfolk) v. Reese Meredith, Cuningham & Nisbett merchts & partners (Philadelphia) and Inglis & Long merchts & partn. (Portsmouth)." YOURS OF THE EIGHTH OF APRIL is missing.

To Thomas Adams

DEAR SIR   Monticello. June 1. 1771.

As it was somewhat doubtful when you left the country how far my little invoice delivered you might be complied with till we should know the fate of the association, I desired you to withhold purchasing the things till you should hear further from me. The day appointed for the meeting of the associates is not yet arrived, however from the universal sense of those who are likely to attend it seems reduced to a certainty that the restrictions will be taken off everything but the dutied articles. I will therefore venture to desire that branch of my invoice may be complied with in which were some shoes and other prohibited articles; since if contrary to our expectations the restrictions should be continued I can store, or otherwise dispose of them as our committees please. I must alter one article in the invoice. I wrote therein for a Clavichord. I have since seen a Forte-piano and am charmed with it. Send me this instrument then instead of the Clavichord. Let the case be of fine mahogany, solid, not vineered. The compass from Double G. to F. in alt. a plenty of spare strings; and the workmanship of the whole very handsome, and worthy the acceptance of a lady for whom I intend it. I must add also ½ doz. pr. India cotton stockings for myself

@ 10/ sterl. per pair. ½ doz. pr. best white silk do.; and a large **Umbrella** with brass ribs covered with green silk, and neatly finished. By this change of the Clavichord into a Forte-piano and addition of the other things I shall be brought in debt to you, to discharge which I will ship you of the first tobaccos I get to the warehouse in the fall. I expect by that time, and also from year to year afterwards I must send you an invoice, with tobaccos, somewhat enlarged, as I have it in prospect to become more regularly a paterfamilias.

I desired the favor of you to procure me an architect. I must repeat the request earnestly and that you would send him in as soon as you can.

I shall conclude with one petition; that you send me the articles contained in my invoice and written for above as soon as you receive this, as I suppose they may be bought ready made; and particularly the Forte-piano for which I shall be very impatient. By this means I may get them in Octob., which will prevent my being obliged to purchase, as I must do if they do not come in time. I am Dr Sir Your affectionate friend,   Th: Jefferson

RC (ViHi). Addressed: "To Mr. Thomas Adams to be left at Nando's Coffee house Fleet-street, London." Endorsed: "T. Jefferson Esq June 1st. 1771." The date may be read as either 1 or 4 June, but the recipient's reading of it has been followed.

To Thomas Burke

Dear Sir   Albemarle June 30. 177[1].

The case of Plume v. Portlock now lies at the Rules in danger of a dismission for want of a declaration. Mr. Blair directed me to apply to you for instructions in this matter. Your favor herein will oblige Dr. Sir Your friend and servt.,   Th: Jefferson

P. S. On looking further into the Rule docket I find myself referred to you also for instructions to draw the bill in McVee v. Wilson. I have Wilson's bond to McVee.

RC (NcU: Southern Historical Collection). Addressed: "To Dr. Thomas Burke Norfolk." Endorsed: "Mr. Jefferson."

TJ omitted the last digit of the date, which is ascertainable from Burke's acknowledgement, dated 19 Aug. 1771. The action of PLUME v. PORTLOCK is entered in TJ's Case Book, No. 509, under 14 Feb. 1771; Burke in his reply of 19 Aug. discusses at length this suit growing out of a false imprisonment (as he believed). The suit of Matthew MC-VEE (whose name is variously spelled) of Norfolk v. James WILSON of Jamaica is entered in TJ's Case Book under the same date, No. 508; see also Burke's reply, and TJ to Burke?, 6 Dec. 1771.

To —— ——

                              Albemarle June 30. 1771.

Among the Treasurer's causes which I have undertaken to finish is a suit brought against you by Martar. As I am an utter stranger to the nature of the demand of the plaintiff, and of your defence I must trouble you to give me timely notice of both. If you would chuse subpoenas to summon any evidences be pleased to write a line to Mr. James Steptoe my agent at the Secretary's office who will take care to forward them to you. A letter directed to me and sent to the care of the same gentleman or of Mr. Neill Campbell merchant Richmond will probably get safe to Sir Your humble servt.,   TH: JEFFERSON

Dft (DLC).
The addressee was being sued by one MARTAR, but no record of a suit in which Martar was plaintiff is to be found in TJ's Case Book, and Martar himself has not been identified. The case was one among those turned over to TJ by Robert Carter Nicholas (THE TREASURER) when Nicholas retired from practice in the spring of 1771. TJ did not continue Nicholas' practice after the fall of 1771; see Case Book, No. 612, entry for 31 Oct. 1771.

From Thomas Burke

                            Norfolk July 10th. 1771.

I have at length prevailed on Mr. Taylor to answer a Bill in our Court spedily, and I here inclose you a Draught of what I purpose filing which you will please return with your remarks and Improvements. We purpose not Coming into Court untill all our papers are ready and then to set it for hearing immediately. If the Decree here be in our Favor we are to give him Security for performing it and if against us we Immediately appeal, 'tis also purposed that the Heir and Devisee (who are not Parties to our Bill) pray an Injunction whereon the Question respecting our claims shall be discussed before the General Court, Viz. whether the Decree here taking from them the Assets which they have Confessed and vesting them in the Executor for Payment of Debts is agreable to Equity and a Sufficient reason to excuse them from their Plea. Hereby we Involve Hunts Judgments with the Determination of our Question and all must Depend on the appeal at Home. The reason for not making the Heir or Devisee party to our Bill is to prevent the Delay they would occasion, and the Influence of Mr. Hunt over them Operating to our Disadvantage, I believe we could Support the Position that the making them parties is not Necessary. Vid: Harris & Ingledew 3 Pr. Will: [Peere Williams] also the rule that none should be parties but such against whom we can have a Decree. I shall be Glad to have Your Answer as soon as your Leizure will permit. I am &c.

BURKE'S STATEMENT OF THE TUCKER CASE

The late Henry Tucker delivered Bonds to Thomas Burke and Directed him to apply for the money due on them. By a written order he directed the money when recieved to be paid to Thomas Roberts to whom he was Indebted. Thomas Burke applied for the money before Henry Tuckers Death and the Obligor promised payment but it was not then Convenient, whereupon Thomas Burke Informing Captain Roberts of this Circumstance promised to pay the money to him as soon as it should be recieved. Henry Tucker dying and Mr. Jameison taking Administration, Thomas Burke on the one hand is forbidden to recieve or pay According to Henry Tuckers Directions by the Administrator and on the other he is commanded and required to apply for the money and pay it agreeable thereto. The Bonds are for Large sums but only a Ballance of £34 remains due on them. When the Ballance was £100 or more Henry Tucker drew an order for it in favor of Messrs. Gilchrist & Taylor or James Gilchrist, it was accepted and by Payments reduced to the £34 when Henry Tucker took up the order and put that and the Bonds in the Hands of Thomas Burke as aforesaid.

Mr. Jameison Submits to Mr. Wythe whether he as Administrator is Intitled to the Ballance due on those Bonds? And Whether he can Lawfully forbid the recieving and paying agreeable to Henry Tucker's Order?

See Mr. Wythe's opinion at the End of this Book.

FC (NcDAH). The statement of the case follows the copy of Burke's letter in his letter book; there is no evidence that the statement was sent to TJ.

WYTHE'S OPINION is unfortunately missing from Burke's letter book, which lacks the pages at the end.

From Robert Skipwith

DEAR SIR   17th July 1771.

This I have left at the Forest to remind you of your obliging promise and withal to guide you in your choice of books for me, both as to the number and matter of them. I would have them suited to the capacity of a common reader who understands but little of the classicks and who has not leisure for any intricate or tedious study. Let them be improving as well as amusing and among the rest let there be Hume's history of England, the new edition of Shakespear, the short Roman history you mentioned and all Sterne's works. I am very fond of Bumgarden's manner of binding but can't afford it unless Fingal or some of those new works be bound up only after that manner; that one, Belisarius, and some others of the kind I would have if bound in gold. Let them amount to about five and twenty pounds sterling, or, if you think proper, to thirty pounds.

With the list please to send me particular directions for importing them, including the bookseller's place of residence. Your very hble servant, ROBT. SKIPWITH

RC (MHi). Addressed: "To Thomas Jefferson Esquire. To the care of Miss Wayles." Endorsed: "Rob. Skipwith to T. J."

Robert Skipwith married about this time Tabitha Wayles, the "Tibby" of the following letters, half-sister of TJ's bride-to-be (Kimball, *Road to Glory*, p. 324; Malone, *Jefferson*, I, 433). This is the first of many similar requests for a CHOICE OF BOOKS that survive among TJ's papers, and the ready and full response to it (see TJ to Skipwith, 3 Aug. 1771) was of the kind TJ unfailingly made. (Except in striking or important cases, the editors have not attempted to identify titles, authors, and editions in these requests and lists.) BUMGARDEN, i.e., Baumgarten, one of a group of German bookbinders at work in London in the eighteenth century, was distinguished for his use of marbled papers and marbled edges (information supplied by Mr. Ellic Howe, of London, whose forthcoming monograph, *A List of London Bookbinders, 1650-1815*, to be published by The Bibliographical Society, contains a detailed note on Baumgarten.)

From John Ogilvie

SIR   Aberdeen July, 19. 1771.

Though the distance at which we are removed deprives me of the benefit of personal acquaintance with a Gentleman whose character I so highly esteem, yet I cannot omitt this opportunity of expressing that esteem, and of making my acknowledgments for the generous friendship you have shown to a Brother whom I love as my own heart. From me, any encomium on him would lye open to an imputation so obvious that I shall say only upon this occasion: that as I know his opinion of your capacity, his confidence in your integrity, and his gratitude for your good offices to render You at present high in his estimation, so from what I believe of You both I am apt to think that a friendship from these motives may be established betwixt You upon a solid and unalterable basis. This highest of human pleasures the mind in proportion to the degree of it's sensibility and comprehension commonly relisheth with the highest satisfaction and gives up with the greatest reluctance. You will accept of the little complement which my Brother will give You along with this as a triffling, but very sincere expression of that real esteem with which I have the honour to be Sir Your most obedt. & affectionate, hum: serv[t.,]   J: OGILVIE

RC (MHi).

Signed "J: Ogilvie," this letter is assigned to John Ogilvie through circumstantial evidence. He was an older brother of James, TJ's friend, and the subject of his letter is TJ's kindness to James.

John (1733-1813), Presbyterian minister of the parish of Midmar, Aberdeen, was also a poet, hymn-writer, and acquaintance of Boswell (DNB). Very likely the COMPLEMENT he sent TJ was one of his own publications.

To Robert Skipwith,

with a List of Books for a Private Library

TH: JEFFERSON TO R. SHIPWITH   Monticello. Aug. 3. 1771.

I sat down with a design of executing your request to form a catalogue of books amounting to about 30. lib. sterl. but could by no means satisfy myself with any partial choice I could make. Thinking therefore it might be as agreeable to you, I have framed such a general collection as I think you would wish, and might in time find convenient, to procure. Out of this you will chuse for yourself to the amount you mentioned for the present year, and may hereafter as shall be convenient proceed in completing the whole. A view of the second column in this catalogue would I suppose extort a smile from the face of gravity. Peace to it's wisdom! Let me not awaken it. A little attention however to the nature of the human mind evinces that the entertainments of fiction are useful as well as pleasant. That they are pleasant when well written, every person feels who reads. But wherein is it's utility, asks the reverend sage, big with the notion that nothing can be useful but the learned lumber of Greek and Roman reading with which his head is stored? I answer, every thing is useful which contributes to fix us in the principles and practice of virtue. When any signal act of charity or of gratitude, for instance, is presented either to our sight or imagination, we are deeply impressed with it's beauty and feel a strong desire in ourselves of doing charitable and grateful acts also. On the contrary when we see or read of any atrocious deed, we are disgusted with it's deformity and conceive an abhorrence of vice. Now every emotion of this kind is an exercise of our virtuous dispositions; and dispositions of the mind, like limbs of the body, acquire strength by exercise. But exercise produces habit; and in the instance of which we speak, the exercise being of the moral feelings, produces a habit of thinking and acting virtuously. We never reflect whether the story we read be truth or fiction. If the painting be lively, and a tolerable picture of nature, we are thrown into a reverie, from which if we awaken it is the fault of the writer. I appeal to every reader of feeling and sentiment whether the fictitious murther of Duncan by Macbeth in Shakespeare does not excite in him as great horror of villainy, as the real one of Henry IV by Ravaillac as related by Davila? And whether the fidelity of Nelson, and generosity of Blandford in Marmontel do not dilate his breast, and elevate his sentiments as much as any similar incident which real history can furnish? Does he not in fact feel himself a better man while reading them, and privately covenant to copy the fair example? We neither know nor care whether Lawrence Sterne really went to France, whether he was there accosted by the poor Franciscan, at first rebuked him unkindly, and then gave him a peace offering; or whether the whole be not a fiction. In either case we are equally sorrowful at the rebuke, and secretly resolve *we* will never do so: we are pleased with the subsequent atonement, and view with emulation a soul candidly acknowleging it's fault, and making a just reparation. Considering history as a moral exercise, her lessons would be too unfrequent if confined to real life. Of those recorded by historians few incidents have been attended with such circumstances as to excite in any high degree this sympathetic emotion of virtue. We are therefore wisely framed to be as warmly interested for a fictitious as for a real personage. The spacious field of imagination is thus laid open to our use, and lessons may be formed to illustrate and carry home to the mind every moral rule of life. Thus a lively and lasting sense of filial duty is more effectually impressed on the mind of a son or daughter by reading King Lear, than by all the dry volumes of ethics and divinity that ever were written. This is my idea of well-written Romance, of Tragedy, Comedy, and Epic Poetry.—If you are fond of speculation, the books under the head of Criticism, will afford you much pleasure. Of Politicks and Trade I have given you a few only of the best books, as you would probably chuse to be not unacquainted with those commercial principles which bring wealth into our country, and the constitutional security we have for the enjoiment of that wealth. In Law I mention a few systematical books, as a knowlege of the minutiae of that science is not necessary for a private gentleman. In Religion, History, Natural philosophy, I have followed the same plan in general.—But whence the necessity of this collection? Come to the new Rowanty, from which you may reach your hand to a library formed on a more extensive plan. Separated from each other but a few paces, the possessions of each would be open to the other. A spring, centrically situated, might be the scene of every evening's joy. There we should talk over the lessons of the day, or lose them in Musick, Chess, or the merriments of our family companions. The heart thus lightened, our pillows would be soft, and health and long life would attend the happy scene. Come then and bring our dear Tibby with you; the first in your affections, and second in mine. Offer prayers for me too at that shrine to which, tho' absent, I pay continual devotion. In every scheme of happiness she is placed in the fore-ground of the picture, as the principal figure. Take that away, and it is no picture for me. Bear my affections to Wintipock, cloathed in the warmest expressions of sincerity; and to yourself be every human felicity. Adieu.

ENCLOSURE

FINE ARTS[1]

Observations on gardening. Payne. 5/

Webb's essay on painting. 12mo 3/

Pope's Iliad. 18/

————Odyssey. 15/

Dryden's Virgil. 12mo. 12/

Milton's works. 2 v. 8vo. Donaldson. Edinburgh 1762. 10/

Hoole's Tasso. 12mo. 5/

Ossian with Blair's criticisms. 2 v. 8vo. 10/

Telemachus by Dodsley. 6/

Capell's Shakespear. 12mo. 30/

Dryden's plays. 6 v. 12mo. 18/

Addison's plays. 12mo. 3/

Otway's plays. 3 v. 12mo. 9/

Rowe's works. 2 v. 12mo. 6/

Thompson's works. 4 v. 12mo. 12/

Young's works. 4 v. 12mo. 12/

Home's plays. 12mo. 3/

Mallet's works. 3 v. 12mo. 9/

Mason's poetical works. 5/

Terence. Eng. 3/

Moliere. Eng. 15/

Farquhar's plays. 2 v. 12mo. 6/

Vanbrugh's plays. 2 v. 12mo. 6/[2]

Steele's plays. 3/

Congreve's works. 3 v. 12mo. 9/

Garric's dramatic works. 2 v. 8vo. 10/

Foote's dramatic works. 2 v. 8vo. 10/

Rousseau's Eloisa. Eng. 4 v. 12-mo. 12/

———— Emilius and Sophia. Eng. 4 v. 12mo. 12/

Marmontel's moral tales. Eng. 2 v. 12mo. 9/

Gil Blas. by Smollett. 6/

Don Quixot. by Smollett 4 v. 12 mo. 12/[3]

David Simple. 2 v. 12mo. 6/

Roderic Random. 2 v. 12mo. 6/

Peregrine Pickle. 4 v. 12mo. 12/

Launcelot Graves. 6/

Adventures of a guinea. 2 v. 12mo. 6/

these are written by Smollett.

Pamela. 4 v. 12mo. ⎫
12/   ⎪
Clarissa. 8 v. 12mo. ⎪
24/   *these are by*
Grandison. 7 v.   ⎬*Richardson.*
12mo. 21/   ⎪
Fool of quality. 3 v. ⎪
12mo. 9/   ⎭
Feilding's works. 12 v. 12mo.
£1.16
Constantia. 2 v.   ⎫
12mo. 6/   ⎪
Solyman and   ⎬*by Langhorne.*
Almena 12 mo.   ⎪
3/   ⎭
Belle assemblee. 4 v. 12mo. 12/
Vicar of Wakefeild. 2 v. 12mo.
6/. by Dr. Goldsmith
Sidney Bidulph. 5 v. 12mo. 15/
Lady Julia Mandeville. 2 v. 12mo.
6/
Almoran and Hamet. 2 v. 12mo.
6/
Tristam Shandy. 9 v. 12mo. £1.7
Sentimental journey. 2 v. 12mo.
6/
Fragments of antient poetry. Edin-
burgh. 2/
Percy's Runic poems. 3/
Percy's reliques of antient Eng-
lish poetry. 3 v. 12mo. 9/
Percy's Han Kiou Chouan. 4 v.
12mo. 12/
Percy's Miscellaneous Chinese
peices. 2 v. 12mo. 6/
Chaucer. 10/
Spencer. 6 v. 12mo. 15/
Waller's poems. 12mo. 3/
Dodsley's collection of poems. 6 v.
12mo. 18/
Pearch's collection of poems. 4 v.
12mo. 12/
Gray's works. 5/
Ogilvie's poems. 5/
Prior's poems. 2 v. 12mo. Foulis.
6/
Gay's works. 12mo. Foulis. 3/
Shenstone's works. 2 v. 12mo. 6/

Dryden's works. 4 v. 12mo.
Foulis. 12/
Pope's works. by Warburton. 12-
mo. £1.4
Churchill's poems. 4 v. 12mo. 12/
Hudibrass. 3/
Swift's works. 21 v. small 8vo.
£3.3
Swift's literary correspondence. 3
v. 9/
Spectator. 9 v. 12mo. £1.7
Tatler. 5 v. 12mo. 15/
Guardian. 2 v. 12mo. 6/
Freeholder. 12mo. 3/
Ld. Lyttleton's Persian letters. 12-
mo. 3/

CRITICISM ON THE FINE ARTS

Ld. Kaim's elements of criticism.
2 v. 8vo. 10/
Burke on the sublime and beauti-
ful. 8 vo. 5/
Hogarth's analysis of beauty. 4to.
£1.1
Reid on the human mind. 8vo. 5/
Smith's theory of moral senti-
ments. 8vo. 5/
Johnson's dictionary. 2 v. fol. £3
Capell's prolusions. 12mo. 3/

POLITICKS, TRADE.

Montesquieu's spirit of laws. 2 v.
12mo. 6/
Locke on government. 8vo. 5/
Sidney on government. 4to. 15/
Marmontel's Belisarius. 12mo.
Eng. 3/
Ld. Bolingbroke's political works.
5 v. 8vo. £1.5
Montesquieu's rise & fall of the
Roman governmt. 12mo. 3/
Steuart's Political oeconomy. 2 v.
4to. £1.10
Petty's Political arithmetic. 8vo.
5/

RELIGION.

Locke's conduct of the mind in
search of truth. 12mo. 3/

Xenophon's memoirs of Socrates. by Feilding. 8vo. 5/

Epictetus. by Mrs. Carter. 2 v. 12mo. 6/

Antoninus by Collins. 3/

Seneca. by L'Estrange. 8vo. 5/⁴

Cicero's Offices. by Guthrie. 8vo. 5/

Cicero's Tusculan questions. Eng. 3/

Ld. Bolingbroke's Philosophical works. 5 v. 8vo. £1.5

Hume's essays. 4 v. 12mo. 12/

Ld. Kaim's Natural religion. 8vo. 6/

Philosophical survey of Nature. 3/

Oeconomy of human life. 2/

Sterne's sermons. 7 v. 12mo. £1.1

Sherlock on death. 8vo. 5/

Sherlock on a future state. 5/

LAW

Ld. Kaim's Principles of equity. fol. £1.1

Blackstone's Commentaries. 4 v. 4to. £4.4

Cuningham's Law dictionary. 2 v. fol. £3

HISTORY. ANTIENT.

Bible. 6/

Rollin's Antient history. Eng. 13 v. 12mo. £1.19

Stanyan's Graecian history. 2 v. 8vo. 10/

Livy. (the late translation). 12/

Sallust by Gordon. 12mo. 12/

Tacitus by Gordon. 12mo. 15/

Caesar by Bladen. 8vo. 5/

Josephus. Eng. 1.0²

Vertot's Revolutions of Rome. Eng. 9/

Plutarch's lives. by Langhorne. 6 v. 8vo. £1.10

Bayle's Dictionary. 5 v. fol. £7.10.

Jeffery's Historical & Chronological chart. 15/

HISTORY. MODERN.

Robertson's History of Charles the Vth. 3 v. 4to. £3.3

Bossuet's history of France. 4 v. 12mo. 12/

Davila. by Farneworth. 2 v. 4to. £1.10.

Hume's history of England. 8 v. 8vo. £2.8.

Clarendon's history of the rebellion. 6 v. 8vo. £1.10.

Robertson's history of Scotland. 2 v. 8vo. 12/

Keith's history of Virginia. 4to. 12/

Stith's history of Virginia. 6/

NATURAL PHILOSOPHY.
NATURAL HISTORY &C.

Nature displayed. Eng. 7 v. 12mo.

Franklin on Electricity. 4to. 10/

Macqueer's elements of Chemistry. 2 v. 8vo. 10/⁴

Home's principles of agriculture. 8vo. 4/

Tull's horse-hoeing husbandry. 8vo. 5/

Duhamel's husbandry. 4to. 15/

Millar's Gardener's dict. fol. £2.10.

Buffon's natural history. Eng. £2.10.

A compendium of Physic & Surgery. Nourse. 12mo. 1765. 3/

Addison's travels. 12mo. 3/

Anson's voiage. 8vo. 6/

Thompson's travels. 2 v. 12mo. 6/

Lady M. W. Montague's letters. 3 v. 12mo. 9/

MISCELLANEOUS

Ld. Lyttleton's dialogues of the dead. 8vo. 5/

Fenelon's dialogues of the dead. Eng. 12mo. 3/

Voltaire's works. Eng. £4.

Locke on Education. 12mo. 3/

Owen's Dict. of arts & sciences. 4 v. 8vo. £2.

These books if bound quite plain will cost the prices affixed in this catalogue. If bound elegantly, gilt, lettered, and marbled on the leaves, they will cost 20. p. cent more. If bound by Bumgarden in fine Marbled bindings, they will cost 50. p. cent more.

Apply to Thomas Waller, bookseller, Fleet-street London.

This whole catalogue as rated here comes to £107.10.

RC (ViU); Dft (DLC). Enclosure: RC (NN); Dft (MHi). The recipient's copy of the letter is unsigned. The draft letter is docketed: "To Mr. Robert Skipwith." The recipient's copy of the enclosure bears this memorandum: "The within is a catalogue made by Thos. Jefferson for my grandfather. R. Skipwith." An occasional figure that is obscure in the text of the list is supplied from the draft.

TJ's use of the form SHIPWITH here and "Skipwith" elsewhere indicates that the spelling was interchangeable. The defense of fiction in his letter is perhaps less noteworthy (since it represents the views of English critics from Sir Philip Sidney to Addison and Johnson) than the up-to-the-minute character of the list: some of the titles in the section headed "Fine Arts" had been very recently published. TJ's alterations between the draft and revised list, pointed out in the notes, furnish further evidence of his bibliographical scrupulousness. In the course of his argument TJ alludes to the *History of the Civil Wars of France* by Enrico Caterino DAVILA (recommended in the book list in the translation by Ellis Farneworth, London, 1758); to "L'Amitié à l'Epreuve,"

a story in *Les Contes Moraux* by J. F. MARMONTEL, The Hague and Paris, 1761; and to Laurence STERNE'S *Sentimental Journey through France and England*, London, 1768. NEW ROWANTY: TJ evidently associates Monticello with " 'The mountain of the world,' or Rowandiz, the Accadian Olympos, [which] was believed to be the pivot on which the heaven rested" (Sayce, *Ancient Monuments*, cited in *Century Cyclo. of Names* under "Rowandiz"). WINTIPOCK: Probably Winterpock, a plantation of the Eppes family in Chesterfield co. (VMHB, XXXIII [1925], 26); the mother of TJ's bride-to-be was an Eppes. It is more likely that TJ's hand than his mind erred in assigning *Chrysal, or The Adventures of a Guinea*, by Charles Johnston, to Smollett, and *The Fool of Quality*, by Henry Brooke, to Richardson.

[1] Caption inadvertently omitted in recipient's copy; supplied from draft.

[2] Price not in recipient's copy; supplied from draft.

[3] The "second column," mentioned by TJ in the letter, begins with this entry and continues through "Gray's works."

[4] This entry not in draft.

From Thomas Burke

DR SIR   Norfolk August 19th. 1771.

I have your Favours of June and July 20th the first dated from Albermale the last from Williamsburg. I wish I had the Pleasure of Conferring with you when you were down but my business so Interposed it was not in my Power. The case of Plume vs. Portlock was thus, A Warrent of the Peace was Obtained vs. Plume, upon hearing the Court Continued the Recognizance. Costs Consequently accrued. Plume went to the Office enquired the amount and offered Payment. Mr. Boush the Clerk told him it was then Inconvenient to Inform him, but Assured him no Execution should Issue and that as soon as Convenient he would Send him a Copy of the Costs.

The time of the Imprisonment of the Sailors Plume went to the Prison to give them some Norishment which being disagreable to J. Calvert and Portlock his Instrument Portlock being Sherriff Arrested Plume as on an Execution and detained him some little time in Prison. I happened to come by and was called by Plume to give him some advice. Upon his Relating the Circumstances I assured him Mr. Boush would not have decieved him so Ungenteely and advised him to pay the money and demand the Execution. Upon this Demand no Execution could be produced, and Mr. Portlock finding he was likely to be Detected discharged him out of Custody. Upon Enquiry at the Office it appeared Mr. Boush had kept his Word and that no Execution ever had Issued. It was very Evident that this was a Mallicious Arrest and Imprisonment and I hope Officers may be taught better. The case of McVaa & Wilson is Simple. Wilson entered into Bond to McVaa (the Condition will Inform you for what) and removed to Jamaica. Major William Orange was his Attorney here and had Effects. The Suit is to Subject those Effects. I think I recollect something about Indemnification and Security. I will send for McVaa and subjoin any more Partcular Account he gives me.

I am exceedingly at a Loss how to Proceed against Tuckers Executors. There are many Cases which seem to Authorise leaving out the Heir at Law and even Devisee. The rule laid down by Jekill is that such only to be parties against whom a Decree can be obtained. We can obtain no Decree except against the Executors. It also laid down that there must be a Demurer for want of Parties or Exceptions at hearing. In Either case our Bill will only lie over for Parties but the Gentlemen have Promisd me not to Demur and only to Submit to the Court whether the Lands are Assets in their Hands and what kind of Assets. Now if upon appeal we may be admitted to add Parties if once we get Hunts Claim and ours Involved together we gain our Point, and should we prevail here I suppose the Injunction for the Heirs may be so framed as to bring all Parties before the General Court. Consider then it will be from the Decree there we appeal and there will be no want of Parties Either if we are allowed to add them above or the Injunction Necessarily makes them so. Now whether we can add them above or not I am not clear. What think you of a Supplimental Bill above for that purpose? One thing is Certain if we Join Heir or Devisee here we are again Inevitably tied up by a Certiorari and we may as well Desist all together. In short Sir the Heir [does] not favor us, and we Expect as little Favor from the Devisee. At worst we can but Add

Parties afterwards and it may not be amiss to make the Experiment in hope of Entangling Mr. Hunts affair with ours. I think the principle Reason given in the reporters for making the Heir a Party is that thereby the Will is Established as proved. Now Sir if you will Consider the Different ways of proving Wills here and at home I think it will appear to You there can be no Necessity for making him a party for that Purpose. And as to Devisee I am Inclined to think the Executors Answer which will set forth that all will fall short of payment of Debts will Sufficiently take off the force of any Objection on that account: were there any probability of a residue there would be a resulting Trust but as it is very clear there will not, I imagine an objection on that Account will be overuled. To you Sir I Submit the whole, and must Inform you that I have Just learned that Mr. Wyth is Informed of our purpose and have given Directions to the Clerk to furnish him with Copies as soon as filed nor will Mr. Taylor Agree to come to Trial untill Mr. Waller has Notice. He will however agree that in his Name a Motion be made to Change the Plea put in by the Devisee, or any other Step which in the General Court can prevent Mr. Hunt from getting an advantage. Upon the whole I am Inclined to think we must at length proceed [as] above by some means or Other. If you resolve on it you will be Pleased to let me know by the first Opportunity. Meantime If I can by any Means prevail on Mr. Taylor to proceed here it shall be done. I shall add nothing at present but I am &c.

FC (NcDAH).
Burke acknowledges TJ's letter of 30 June, above, and a missing letter of 20 July. When TJ was at Norfolk does not appear. On the Tucker case, see note on Burke, 28 Aug. 1770.

From Robert Skipwith

DEAR SIR   The Forest, September 20th, 1771.

Agreeable to my general fate I could not get here until some time after your departure. It is hard indeed that I should be continually disappointed of the company I delight in and which one would suppose I had the best opportunities of enjoying. Your obliging letter I have received and am much pleased with your deviation from the plan I proposed in the formation of a catalogue of books and am sorry your endeavours strictly to comply with my request should have given you so much trouble when a contrary conduct would have been so much more convenient to you and beneficial to myself. Your arguments in favour of well written romance, tragedy, comedy and epic-poetry are I think unanswerable by the wisest and gravest of it's enemies. They were unnecessary for the purpose you intended them, of inducing me to approve of your choice, for books of that stamp I have always been fond of but why I could not give any satisfactory reason. This subject you have handled in a new and pleasing manner: new, because it is, to me, demonstrative; and pleasing because it has flattered my own feelings, and confirmed me in that taste which heretofore I have always thought corrupt. Very sorry am I when I reflect how much time I have laboured to throw away in studying the minutiæ of the law and some other sciences which I might have more agreeably and beneficially employed in a different pursuit. The only comfort I have in my ignorance is that the pleasure of acquiring knowledge is still to come; for I believe the human mind is often more pleased with it's first acquaintance with some subjects than it is with any subsequent reflections upon them. Your invitation to the New Rowanty with the pleasing plan for a happy life but above all the affectionate manner in which you speak of my dearest Tibby are so flattering that were it not ruinous to my small fortune I would at all events be neighbours to a couple so well calculated and disposed to communicate knowledge and pleasure. My sister Skelton, Jefferson I wish it were, with the greatest fund of good nature has all that sprightliness and sensibility which promises to ensure you the greatest happiness mortals are capable of enjoying. May business and play musick and the merriments of your family companions lighten your hearts, soften your pillows and procure you health long life and every human felicity! Adieu!   R. SKIPWITH

RC (MHi).   See Skipwith to TJ, 17 July, and TJ to Skipwith, 3 Aug. 1771.

From Thomas Burke

DR SIR   Norfolk Septr: 24th. 1771.

I have long laboured to do something with Mr. Taylor but almost in vain. Altho the Question is undoubtly of greatest Importance to him Viz. whether Colo. Tuckers Assets shall be legally or Illegally administered there is no Possibility of awakeing him to his Danger. All I have been able to do is to get a faint Consent from him to use his Name in Obtaining the Injunction or Interpleader. I have written to him for his final answer, and every moment expect it.

To morrow I set off on a long Jorney and therefore give you these few Hints lest any time should be lost. If any Scire facias is brought against the Executors here they will pray a Certiorari. If any Suit in Chancery be Commenced above Will not the Question of Mr. Hunt's preference be favored? Will that not occasion great delay and expence for appeals &c.? In fine what think you of an action in the General Court on the Executors bond for not duly administering the Goods and Chattles according as the Law Charges? Will this bring the Question before a Jury, and can we Trust the Question with a Jury? I am putting these Queries on Supposition that Mr. Taylor will not agree to be party to a Bill of Injunction and I submit entirely to you and the Gentlemen you will Consult what Proceedings we shall next Commence. I will write to you Immediately on my return which I hope will be in three Weeks at farthest, and I hope by that time some Effectual Course may be fallen upon which may facilitate the Recovery of the Monies we are in pursuit of. I shall subjoin whatever Mr. Taylor says if I get his Answer before my Departure and if I do not I Suppose he will not answer at all. I am &c.

P:S: Inclosed is a Copy of Mr. Taylors answer and I waited both on him and Mr. Holt. The result is Mr. Taylor will become Interpleader, or if not obliged to give Security will pray the Injunction. Of this matter I shall write fully on my return. Mean time I know you will not [omit?]¹ any thing Necessary.

FC (NcDAH).   See note on Burke to TJ, 28 Aug. 1770.   ¹ Left blank in MS.

To Thomas Burke?

Dear Sir   Monticello Dec. 6. 1771.

I must again trouble you in the case of MacVee v. Wilson &c. Oranges, since on a second attempt to draw the bill I find my instructions deficient. The condition of the bond of Wilson to McVee is 'that Wilson shall indemnify McVee from all costs of suits writs or disturbances that shall arise against the said McVee on the said James Wilson's account by Mr. Paul Loyall or his assigns, and if any suits by bill bond or book debts should be brought against the said McVee then the said Wilson to pay the said McVee all such costs and charges whatsoever he shall expend touching the same.'

On sight of this condition you will percieve it necessary that Mr. McVee should set forth in his bill circumstantially how and in what cases he became answerable for Wilson; that the above bond was given to indemnify him therein; and in what cases he has sustained any and what injury. Without giving you so much trouble in this matter (for I have already given you too much) Mr. McVee I doubt not could send me in writing a circumstantial account of his connections with and sufferings for Wilson. He would also do well to inform me of what nature the effects are which Orange has in his hands. I should be glad of this information as soon as possible, since I am a little apprehensive we may not be much longer indulged. A letter directed to me and sent to the care of Ninian Minzies Richmond will probably get safe to Dr. Sir Your friend and servt.,   TH: JEFFERSON

P. S. Brown v. Tucker. I shall be obliged to Mr. Brown for a copy of his account with Tucker as I thought it necessary in the bill to refer to such an account as annext. In the mean time I file the bill without it, if they will receive it. Also the name of the slave, the rate of hire, the time at which Tucker attached the vessel, and the balance then due to Tucker. The costs also of that litigation in Bermud as incurred by Brown. I fear the making Davenport a party may have been wrong as neither person nor effects of his are within our jurisdiction. I therefore omit charging him in the bill.

RC (ViU). Burke was the probable recipient, since he collaborated with TJ in both the cases discussed, namely, MC VEE v. WILSON, on which see above, TJ to Burke, 30 June, and Burke to TJ, 19 Aug.; and BROWN v. TUCKER, which is entered in TJ's Case Book, No. 548, 25 Apr. 1771, as a suit in chancery by Henry Brown of Portsmouth against William Tucker and Robert DAVENPORT of Bermuda and William Goodrich, place not given, to stay the effects of Tucker in the hands of Goodrich.

Bond for Marriage License

[23 December 1771]

Know all men by these presents that we Thomas Jefferson and Francis Eppes are held and firmly bound to our sovereign lord the king his heirs and successors in the sum of fifty pounds current money of Virginia, to the paiment of which, well and truly to be made we bind ourselves jointly and severally, our joint and several heirs executors and administrators in witness whereof we have hereto set our hands and seals this twenty third day of December in the year of our lord one thousand seven hundred and seventy one.

The condition of the above obligation is such that if there be no lawful cause to obstruct a marriage intended to be had and solemnized between the abovebound Thomas Jefferson and Martha Skelton of the county of Charles city, Widow,[1] for which a license is desired, then this obligation is to be null and void; otherwise to remain in full force.　　　　　　　　　　TH: JEFFERSON

　　　　　　　　　　　　　　　　　　　　　FRANCIS EPPES

MS in TJ's hand (Vi). Endorsed in a clerk's hand: "Jefferson to the King Bond for. Marr: License 1771." A small seal is affixed to each signature.

FRANCIS EPPES, of Eppington, Chesterfield co.; he had married Elizabeth Wayles, a half-sister of the prospective Mrs. Jefferson, and the Jeffersons' daughter Maria was eventually to marry Francis Eppes' son John Wayles (VMHB,

III [1895-1896], 396). On 30 Dec. 1771 TJ paid forty shillings for the license proper, and on 1 Jan. 1772 he and Martha Wayles were married at The Forest (Account Book entries under those dates; Randall, *Life*, I, 64).

[1] "Widow," inserted above "spinster," lined out, is not in TJ's hand.

Project for Making the Rivanna River Navigable

[1771?]

Trustees. Thos. Walker, Edwd. Carter, Chas. Lewis, Nich. Lewis, Thos. Jefferson, Nich. Meriwether, John Walker, Valentine Wood, James Adams, Richd. Harvie, Roger Thompson.

Trustees shall give them the benefit of a moiety of subscriptions till [they] shall have made thereout sum of £　 and another moiety till &c.

Shall empower them to use their names in petitions and suits, but not to be chargeable themselves.

Undertaker to clear passage from Rook's ford to mouth of river.
Shall be 15.f. wide in all falls and　 f. wide in other places.
The passages thro' falls and for　 feet above them shall be strait, and elsewhere reasonably so as well respecting the convenience of the waterman as the labor of the undertaker.
There shall be no rock, gravel or other obstruction left within 21.I. of surface of water at Winter tide.
Winter tide to be accounted the lowest tide between 1. Jan. and 30. April.
Adams's falls to be cleared by 30th. Octob. 1772.
The rest by 30th. Octob. 1773.
To be examined and received by Wm. Cabell, Jos. Cabell, James Neville, Cornelius Thomas, Bennet Henderson, Martin Key or any three, whose to be first.[1]

MS (DLC). At foot of page are rough notes on Emblements in the Case of A. B. and R. B., omitted here.

This is a rough memorandum, to which we have assigned an arbitrary but plausible date, on the earliest public cause in which TJ interested himself. In a statement made long afterwards summarizing the acts for clearing the Rivanna, or North Branch of the James, TJ wrote:

"In 1763 (I was not then quite of age) learning that a canoe, with a family in it, had passed and repassed several times between Buck island creek in Albemarle and the Byrd creek in Goochland, and that there were no serious obstacles below Adams's falls (now Magruder's) I went in a canoe from Mountain falls (now Milton falls) to Adams's and found that that section of the river could be made navigable for loaded boats by removing loose rock only. I set on foot a subscription and obtained £200. Dr. Walker our representative, got inserted, in the act here cited, a nomination of 11 trustees, with authority to do what was necessary for effecting the navigation of this river, from the mouth upwards. Roger and George Thompson, then living on the river, undertook and executed the work, and on what was then done the river was navigated habitually for 35. years before any thing more was done to it" ("Notes on

the several acts of assembly for clearing the Rivanna river," DLC: TJ Papers, 211: 37587).

This is a somewhat simplified account, for though an act was passed in the 1765 session of the Assembly "for clearing the great falls of James River, the Chickahominy, and the north branch [i.e., the Rivanna] of James river" (Hening, VIII, 148-50), the work was still to be done some years later. The present statement is in part a summary of the act of 1765, but changes in the list of trustees (e.g., the substitution of Richard Harvie for John Harvie, who died in 1767) show that it was later. In 1800 TJ listed this successful project first in order among the services he had rendered (second in the list is the Declaration of Independence); see DLC: TJ Papers, 219: 39161. From 1791, and especially from 1811 on, he was to be much concerned with enlargements of the early navigation scheme and the litigation that grew out of them. The documents relating to this litigation will be printed in the Legal Papers under the Rivanna Canal case. See Malone, *Jefferson*, I, 115-16; Woods, *Albemarle County*, p. 83-5.

[1] Thus in MS. There may have been a continuation that would have clarified the passage.

Amendments to a Bill concerning the Keeping of Roads and Bridges

[April 1772?]

Whereas[1] it is sometimes requisite for the public convenience that roads should be opened thro' the lands and plantations of others, whereby the proprietors not only lose the use of the lands occupied by such road but also are often obliged to make and keep up fences on each side thereof, and it is just that they should receive compensation for the same Be it therefore enacted by[2] the Governor Council and Burgesses of this present General Assembly and it is hereby enacted by authority of the same that upon the return of the persons appointed to view and report the conveniences and inconveniences of any public road proposed, if the court shall be of opinion that such road may be convenient, they shall if required by the proprietor or proprietors of the lands thro' which such road is proposed to be opened, order a writ to be issued in the nature of an Ad quod damnum to the sheriff of their county commanding him to enquire by the oath of good and lawful men of his said county to what damage or prejudice of such proprietor or proprietors so requesting such writ it will be if the said road shall be established: and upon return of the inquisition if the court shall be of opinion that such road ought to be established, then it shall and may be lawful for the justices of the said court, and they are hereby required, at the next laying of their county levy, to levy and pay to the proprietor or proprietors at whose instance such writ of Ad quod damnum was issued the damages found for him or them in such inquisition: and where the lands of any person or persons are so situated that convenient ways from them may not be had to Courthouse, churches and mills without passing thro' the lands of others it shall and may be lawful on the petition of such person or persons for the court of the county wherein such private way is proposed to order a view thereof; and on the return of the viewers, if the court in their discretion shall be of opinion that such private way ought to be allowed they shall direct of what breadth the same shall be, and, where it is to pass thro' any inclosed grounds, whether the proprietor of such inclosed grounds shall keep gates or lanes through the same, and also shall order a writ or writs of Ad quod damnum to issue and such other proceedings to be had as is before directed in the case of public roads, which writ or writs and other proceedings shall be at the proper cost and charges of the petitioner or petitioners. And if on the return of the inquisition or inquisitions or at any time within   months after, the petitioner or petitioners shall pay to the person or persons thro whose lands the said private way shall be allowed, the damages found for them respectively in the inquisition or inquisitions together with his and their lawful costs the said private way shall be established. Provided alwais that where any way private or public shall be petitioned for, one month's notice thereof shall be given to the several proprietors of the land thro' which it is proposed to pass if they be resident within this colony, or if they be not resident therein, then to their attorney or agent if any be to be found.

And be it further enacted by the authority aforesaid that where it shall be necessary to make any causeway in [. . .] within the body of a county which would be too great a burthen for the overseer and his assistants, the court of that county wherein such causeway shall be wanting is hereby empowered and required to contract and agree for the making and repairing thereof and to levy the charge in their county levy.

And whereas one[3] [act of the general assembly, made in the third year of his present majesty's reign, intituled An act for the more effectual keeping the public roads and bridges in repair, which was continued and amended by another act, made in the seventh year of his said majesty's reign, expired on the sixteenth day of December, in the year one thousand seven hundred and seventy one, and it is necessary and expedient that the same should be revived: Be it therefore enacted][4] by the authority aforesaid, [That the said recited acts, of the third and seventh years of his present majesty's reign,] together with this act, [shall be revived, and shall continue and be in force, from and after the passing hereof, for and during the term of two years, and from thence to the end of the next session of assembly.]

MS (Vi). This, perhaps the earliest Bill drawn by TJ, was originally put in the form of amendments. For the sake of clarity, these amendments have been merged with the bill to which they refer (printed as an Act in Hening, VIII, 542-3), the terms drawn from the latter being supplied in square brackets.

These Amendments refer clearly to the general Road Act of 1766 which was revived by the Act of April 1772. TJ originally wrote these as amendments, but, since he did not arrive in Williamsburg for the session of Assembly until 9 or 10 Apr. 1772 and since the Act reviving the Road Act of 1766 passed the House on 8 Apr. and was then laid before the Council on that day, he evidently changed his Amendments to read as a new bill, incorporating therein the reviving clauses of the bill that had just been passed and reenacting them "together with this act." The fact that his Amendments, or new bill, refer to the 1772 reviving bill is proved by the various phrases, noted below, that were employed in referring his Amendments to the bill; no other general Road Act between 1766 and 1776 fills all these requirements. It is possible, of course, that TJ merely wrote out his Amendments and did not introduce them, for there is no mention of his name in connection with any activity at this 1772 session. It is probable that TJ revived his road bill in the session of 1774, for he was certainly interested in the subject at that time (see Notes on the Progress of Certain Bills, 9-25 May 1774); it is also possible that what he had intended as amendments in 1772 were recast in the form of a new bill in 1774.

[1] At the beginning of this paragraph TJ wrote: "Strike out 'Whereas the' in the beginning of the bill and insert." The Road Act of 1772 began with the words "Whereas the."

[2] TJ first wrote: "the authority aforesaid" and then changed it to read as given in the text. This, and other similar changes, show that he first considered merely amending another bill; then, perhaps because he found that bill already passed, he changed his Amendments to the form of a new bill.

[3] The 1772 Road Act began "Whereas the"; this was struck out by TJ as noted above; then, at this point in the MS he wrote: "and whereas one." The MS does not quote remainder of enacting clause of 1772 bill, but the part in brackets is taken from the Act.

[4] At this point the 1772 Road Act reads: "Governor, Council, and Burgesses of this present General Assembly, and it is hereby enacted by the authority of the same." The MS reads: "Line 10 and 11 strike out 'Governor, Council and Burgesses of this present General Assembly and it is hereby enacted by the authority of the same' and insert 'by the authority aforesaid.'"

To Messrs. Inglis and Long

Gent.   Williamsburgh June 11. 1772.

I have just received notice from Mr. Wythe that in the case of Jamieson and Taylor v. Meredith and others he will move at the next court to have the effects delivered into the plaintiff's hands. I have not yet had time to enquire whether such steps have been yet taken as will entitle him to do this. However it is better that your correspondents prevent it which cannot be done with certainty but by their sending in their answers in proper form before the next court. I am this moment leaving town having just taken time to inform you of this measure & am Gent Your very humble servt.,

Th: Jefferson

P. S. Be pleased to send your own answers immediately to Mr. Everard inclosed.

RC (MHi: Washburn Papers). Addressed: "To Messrs Ingles and Long Merchts Portsmouth." Endorsed: "Thomas Jefferson Esq Williamsbg June 11th 1772 Answd June 21st 1772, Not Copd."

See Case No. 546 in TJ's Case Book; also TJ's letters of 11 May 1771 and 4 July, 13 Oct. 1772. Reese MEREDITH was a co-defendant in the case.

To Messrs. Inglis and Long

Messrs. Inglis and Long

Gentlemen   Albemarle July 4. [1772]

In the suit in Chancery brought by Jamieson and Taylor against Meredith, Cuningham and Nisbett, Macall Stedman and company underwriters to the policy of insurance which is the foundation of the suit, and yourselves as having effects of some of the underwriters in your hands, I find the only interrogatory of the bill you are concerned to answer is this 'whether you or either of you have in your hands any and what money, goods or effects of the said underwriters, or any, and which of them?' This question refers to the time at which the subpoena was served on you: so that you will be pleased to inform me by letter what you had in your hands at that time. If money, the sum must be named; if other effects, they must be enumerated. If you had any demand of your own against the same person it will be proper to state that also, since the balance only in your hands after stopping your own demand, would be condemned. On recieving information of these matters I shall immediately prepare your answer and transmit it to you to be sworn to.

Any letter sent to the care of Mr. James Steptoe my agent at the Secretary's office, or of Mr. Neill Campbell merchant Richmond will probably get safe to Gent. Your very humble servt.,

TH: JEFFERSON

RC (Gilbert S. McClintock, Wilkes-Barré, Penna., 1947).
See Case No. 546 in TJ's Case Book; also TJ's letters of 11 May 1771, 11 June and 13 Oct. 1772.

From Alexander McCaul

DR. SIR   Glasgow July 8 1772

I received yours of the 7th of Septr. last only the 10th of June last, and where it had been wandering all that time I am at a loss to know, but no doubt you would think me negligent not to answer you in course.

I have not yet been able to procure for you a Gardiner, but have made application to a friend in the East Country and have little doubt of getting one for you to send you in our own Ship. I Assure you it will always give me pleasure to do you any service, and I am sorry the Misscarriage of a letter should give you the least room to doubt of my readiness to do it.

I am extreamly much Obliged to you for your kind expressions for my happiness. I am Contented with my present lot, tho in some Measure neglected the proper Season to secure it in one respect, I mean by chusing a proper Partner to sweeten the Cares and anxietys in life that every body more or less have to Struggle with. A Man come to my years and who slaved and toiled twenty long Years in a Virginia Climate had better not meddle with the Matrimonial state, tho I own to you an Old Batchellor makes but an indifferent figure and especially in Scotland where the fair Sex abound in such Plenty. However to drop the Subject with regard to myself it is a state I wish every friend I have may enter into and by a Virginia Paper I see you are among the Number, in which I wish you All the happiness Your best friends Wish you.

I Spent two Months of this Spring and Summer in our Neighbour Kingdom where I never was before and was much pleased and delighted with my Jaunt. It is Certainly the finest Country in the known World. You see their fields Cultivated with the utmost care, Covered with a rich Verdure, and abounding with everything to make Glad the heart of Man, the Towns and Villages crowded with Inhabitants, and Industry and it's attendant Plenty to be seen every where I past through. Indeed we have hitherto had the finest

Season that has been known these many Years. Your Acquaintance Neill Jamieson and I were together on the whole trip. We Spent a Month in the great City, and a Great City it is—that indeed exhibit'd to us a greater Variety, Trade and Commerce carried to its greatest extent, also every refinement in Luxury, every kind of Apetite may there be satiated. We did not stay there long enough to be tired of it, but I imagine a constant repetition of these things would tire any Man. I saw several of our old Virginia friends and on the Change of London you would meet with many faces you had seen before.

There has been in the course of this last Month a sad revolution among many of the Merchants in both Kingdoms. It has it seems been long a practise with Many to support their Credit, or rather to stretch it further than their Capitals would admitt off by drawing and redrawing Bills. This the Bank of England saw (for they have every thing in their power) and were resolved to crush it. This they Effectually did by refusing to discount Bills. The Consequence was that many Houses in London esteem'd eminent and Wealthy failed and they brot along with them many in Edh. [Edinburgh] and some in this City. We however have escaped pretty well, as there is only one House of any Note failed. However it has thrown a damp on Publick Credit, and it will be some time before it is perfectly restored. Every body of property rejoices that the iniquitous practice of drawing fictitious Bills for the purpose of raising Money is now at an end—tho many innocent and Knowing will be much injured. The Publick papers however will give you a distincter Account of this then I can by a letter. It is happy for the Natives of Brittain, they have such a resource as No. America for there, if they happen to be reduced, they may always have bread with Industry. The Virga. Planters may thank their Starrs they have so good a Country to Cultivate, tho many of them are not sensible of the happiness they enjoy.

It will give me pleasure now and then to hear from you. I beg you'll offer my Compliments to all my old friends who enquire for me and believe me to be with sincere regard Dr sir Your Obliged huml servt,   Alexr. McCaul

RC (MHi).

TJ's letter to McCaul of 7 Sep. 1771, requesting that a gardener be sent out, has not been found. BY A VIRGINIA PAPER . . . : In the *Va. Gaz.* (P & D), 2 Jan. 1772, TJ's marriage was announced as follows: "*Thomas Jefferson*, Esquire, one of the Representatives for Albemarle, to Mrs. *Martha Skelton*, Relict of Mr. *Bathurst Skelton.*" On the practice of DRAWING AND REDRAWING BILLS, we are indebted to Professor Jacob Viner for references to Sir John Clapham, *The Bank of England, A History*, Cambridge, 1945, I, 244ff., and Adam Smith, *Wealth of Nations*, ed. G. Cannan, London, 1904, I, 292ff.

To William Wood

SIR   July 17. 1772.

I obtained for you last June an order of council against Price for the 234. acres of land caveated by you. You must therefore before the 10th. day of December return to the Secretary's office a copy of the order of council which will cost you 10/9, a copy of the survey, 5. rights 29/2, the governor's fee 21/6, and Secretary's fee 10/6 or the lands will be liable to a caveat. I observe Price had entered 4 caveats himself for lands I fancy in the same neighborhood which were all dismissed for want of his having emploied some attorney. I suppose it is by such sham proceedings he covers so many tracts of land in that part of the country.—The Summons against Kincaid was not executed so you have no order there yet. I am Sir Your humble sert.,   TH: JEFFERSON

RC (CtSoP). Addressed: "To Capt. William Wood Albemarle." Endorsed: "Mr. Jeffersons Letter informing Wm. Wood that he had obtain'd an Order of Council for 237 Acres Land Survey'd for John Price & John McAnally on wch.

I delivered him the Original Surveys." Two entries in TJ's Case Book give the facts relating to these transactions: No. 591, Wood v. Kincaid, and No. 592, Wood v. Price, both dated 24 Sep. 1771.

To William Cabell

SIR   Monticello Sep. 3. 1772.

Inclosed is a copy of Dickie's bill against you. You will be pleased to send me a state of the case as it is to be set forth in your answer. In this you should take care to answer every allegation and interrogatory. As soon as I recieve this I shall put it into the form of an answer and return it to you to be sworn to. I am Sir Your humble sert.,   TH: JEFFERSON

RC (ViU: Cabell Deposit). On the back are notes, doubtless in Cabell's hand and apparently bearing on this case; since portions are missing and the hand is only semi-legible, these notes are here omitted.
On this case, TJ has this entry (No.

535) in his Case Book under date of 13 Apr. 1771: "James Dickey (   ) v. Wm. Cabell senr. (Amherst) a suit in Canc. at the Rules. Appear for def.— 1774 Apr. abated by def's death." (Cabell died 12 Apr. 1774.)

To Samuel Inglis

DEAR SIR   Wmsbgh. Oct. 13. 1772.

Your scruples on that part of the answer which denies your having in your hands effects of any the defendants except Messrs.

Conyngham and Nesbitt, are just. The circumstance of your holding any thing of Mr. McCaul's was unknown to me. I now send you two answers. The one admits effects of Conyngham and Nesbitt and also of McCaul, and denies it as to the others. The other answer admits as to Conyngham and Nesbitt and is silent as to the others. Yet I must inform you that the latter is for that very reason insufficient. It may perhaps be looked over; but if excepted to, you must hereafter answer as to the other defendants and pay costs of the exceptions. You will use whichever you think proper. As to the answer of Messrs. Conyngham and Nesbitt I shall prepare such an one as can be drawn on the papers in my possession. This I will send you either during or immediately after the court: so that it cannot be sworn to and returned to me till the April court. In the mean time you know a motion is to be made during the present court to have the attached effects delivered up to the plaintiffs. Thus therefore I shall conduct myself unless you advise to the contrary. I shall first endeavor to get further time till the April court to file our answers. If that is granted it will stay all further proceeding till that time. If it is refused I will then plead to the jurisdiction of the court. The plea I know will be overruled, because our act of assembly gives express jurisdiction but it will give me an opportunity of urging the objections of Messrs. Conyngham and Nesbitt; and will answer the purpose of a dilatory so as to give us time for the return of the answers. The overruling the plea will be attended with an expence of £5. to Messrs. Conyngh. & Nesb. but that I expect is preferable to a delivery of the attached effects. Your particular answer you will be pleased to return by the earliest opportunity as I know not the day on which the motion will be made, and the want of it might involve you in the same difficulties which arise from a want of the answers of the other gentlemen. Your attendance in person I suppose would be inconvenient, and is not necessary. I am Dear Sir Your friend and sert.,   TH: JEFFERSON

RC (CtY). Enclosures missing. The addressee has been identified from internal evidence; see Case No.

546 in TJ's Case Book; also TJ's letters of 11 May 1771 and 11 June, 4 July 1772.

From John Wayles

SIR   Octr. 20. 1772.

I received your favour by [. . .]st and thank you for the various intellig[ence. The?] Genl. Courts determination concern[ing] the

devise of slaves must be attended w[ith] Mischievious consequences. I have hea[rd] nothing about dear Patty since you left this
place. Our sale of Slaves go[es] on Slowly so 'tis uncertain when we
shall be down but I suppose before the Rebel party leaves town.
I am Your afft. Svt.,   J. WAYLES

RC (MHi). Mutilated. Addressed: "To
Thomas Jefferson Esqr. Wmsburgh."
  John Wayles, of The Forest, Charles
City co., Jefferson's father-in-law, died
in the following May (Kimball, *Road to
Glory*, p. 178-80; Malone, *Jefferson*, I,
432). His reference to the GENERAL
COURTS DETERMINATION is probably to
the decision in the case of Herndon v.
Carr, reported in full detail by TJ him-
self in *Reports of Cases Determined in
the General Court of Virginia*, Char-
lottesville, 1829, p. 132-6, q.v. OUR SALE
OF SLAVES: An advertisement in the *Va.*

Gaz. (P & D) for 8 Oct. 1772 (repeated
15 and 22 Oct.) reads as follows:
  "Just arrived from *Africa*, the Ship
Prince of Wales, *James Bivins* Commander, with about four Hundred five
healthy *Slaves*; the Sale of which will
begin at *Bermuda Hundred* on *Thursday*
the 8th of *October*, and continue until
all are sold.   *John Wayles.
                      Richard Randolph.*"
PATTY: The familiar name for Martha
Wayles Jefferson used by TJ and her
family.

To Charles McPherson

DEAR SIR   Albemarle in Virga. Feb. 25. 1773.

Encouraged by the small acquaintance which I had the pleasure
of having contracted with you during your residence in this country, I take the liberty of making the present application to you. I
understood you were related to the gentleman of your name Mr.
James Macpherson to whom the world is so much indebted for the
collection, arrangement and elegant translation, of Ossian's poems.
These peices have been, and will I think during my life continue to
be to me, the source of daily and exalted pleasure. The tender, and
the sublime emotions of the mind were never before so finely
wrought up by[1] human hand. I am not ashamed to own that I think
this rude bard[2] of the North the greatest Poet that has ever existed.
Merely for the pleasure of reading his works I am become desirous
of learning the language in which he sung and of possessing his
songs in their original form. Mr. Macpherson I think informs us
he is possessed of the originals. Indeed a gentleman has lately told
me he had seen them in print; but I am afraid he has mistaken the
specimen from Temora annexed to some of the editions of the translation, for the whole works. If they are printed, it will abridge[3] my
request and your trouble to the sending me a printed copy. But if
there be none such, my petition is that you would be so good as to
use your interest with Mr. Mcpherson to obtain leave to take a
manuscript copy of them; and procure it to be done.[4] I would chuse
it in a fair, round, hand, on fine paper, with a good margin, bound

in parchment as elegantly as possible, lettered on the back and marbled or gilt on the edges of the leaves. I should not regard expence in doing this. I would further beg the favor of you to give me a catalogue of books written in that language, and to send me such of them as may be necessary for learning it.[5] These will of course include a grammar and dictionary. The cost of these as well as of[6] the copy of Ossian will be answered for me on demand by Mr. Alexr. McCaul sometime of Virga. merchant but now of Glasgow, or by your friend Mr. Ninian Minzies of Richmond in Virga. to whose care the books may be sent. You can perhaps tell me whether we may ever hope to see any more of those Celtic peices published. Manuscript copies of any which are not in print it would at any time give me the greatest happiness to receive. The glow of one warm thought is to me worth more than money. I hear with pleasure from your friends that your path through life is likely to be smoothed by success. I wish the business and the pleasures of your situation could admit leisure now and then to scribble a line to one who wishes you every felicity and would willingly merit the appellation of Dr. Sir Your friend and humble servt.

Dft (DLC). Memorandum of address at end of text: "To Mr. Charles Macpherson Merchant in Edinburgh." The principal alterations in the draft are indicated in the textual notes below.

Charles McPherson (this being the form he himself used) is a shadowy figure. An advertisement in the *Va. Gaz.* (P & D), 6 Nov. 1766, announces the dissolution of his partnership in the mercantile firm of M'Pherson and Minzies (presumably the NINIAN MINZIES mentioned in the letter). TJ's profound regard for Ossian is attested not only by the present letter but by other evidence, e.g., the account by Chastellux in his *Travels in North America in the Years 1780, 1781, and 1782* (London, 1787, II, 45-6) of an Ossianic evening at Monticello in 1782. Gilbert Chinard, in printing the Jefferson-McPherson correspondence for the first time (*Modern Language Notes*, XXXVIII [1923], 201-5),

notes the extreme pains TJ took in drafting an appeal which might be placed before the celebrated "translator" himself. For the interesting consequences of TJ's appeal, see below, James Macpherson to Charles McPherson, 7 Aug., and Charles McPherson to TJ, 12 Aug. 1773.

[1] For this phrase TJ first wrote: "so happily hit upon," then: "so finely touched by the."
[2] TJ first wrote: "that uncultivated bard."
[3] TJ first wrote: "shorten."
[4] TJ first wrote: "and employ the best scribe for that purpose."
[5] TJ first added at the end of this sentence: "such as a dictionary, grammar and a few others to begin with."
[6] TJ first wrote after this word and then struck out without substitution: "taking."

To William Fleming

DEAR FLEMING   May 19. 1773. Mrs. Carr's

You have before this heard and lamented the death of our good friend Carr. Some steps are necessary to be immediately taken on behalf of his clients. You practised in all his courts except Chesterfeild and Albemarle. I shall think I cannot better serve them than by putting their papers into your hands if you will be so good as to take them. I once mentioned to you the court of Albemarle as worthy your attention. If you chuse now to go there I would get you to take his papers for that court also. They would put you in possession of a valuable business. The king's attorney's place is vacant there, and might be worth your solliciting. If you think so you should dispatch an express for the commission. Otherwise you may be prevented. Write me a line in answer to this and lodge it here within a week, as I shall about that time call here to take the law papers and put them into some channel. Your assistance in these matters will much oblige Dear Fleming Your friend and humble servt.,

Th: Jefferson

RC (The Rosenbach Co., Philadelphia, 1946). Addressed: "To Mr. William Fleming at Mount-pleasant." Endorsed: "Thos. Jefferson."

THE DEATH OF . . . CARR: Dabney Carr, TJ's brother-in-law, had died on 16 May; TJ wrote an epitaph for his tombstone at Monticello and subscribed it as from "Thomas Jefferson, who of all men living, loved him most"; Carr's widow and children later came to live

with TJ (Garden Book, 22 May 1773, and p. 41-2, 44; Randall, Life, I, 83-4; Randolph, Domestic Life, p. 47; Malone, Jefferson, I, 161-2, 431, note). MRS. CARR'S: The home of Carr's widow, i.e., TJ's sister Martha, has not been precisely located, though it is believed to have been a place named Spring Forest in Goochland co. (Communication from Mr. Francis L. Berkeley, Jr., University of Virginia Library.)

Notice concerning Legal Fees

[20 May 1773]

ON serious Consideration of the present State of our Practice in the General Court, we find it can no longer be continued on the same Terms. The Fees allowed by Law, if regularly paid, would barely compensate our incessant Labours, reimburse our Expenses, and the Losses incurred by Neglect of our private Affairs; yet even these Rewards, confessedly moderate, are withheld from us, in a great Proportion, by the unworthy Part of our Clients. Some Regulation, therefore, is become absolutely requisite to establish Terms more equal between the Client and his Counsel. To effect this, we have come to the following Resolution, for the invariable Observance of which we mutually plight our Honour to each other: "That after the 10th Day of *October* next we will not give an Opinion on any Case stated to us but on Payment of the whole Fee, nor prosecute or defend any Suit or Motion unless the Tax, and one Half the Fee, be previously advanced, excepting those Cases only where we choose to act *gratis*;" and we hope no Person whatever will think of applying to us in any other Way. To prevent Disappointment, however, in Case this should be done, we think it proper to give this farther Warning, that no such Application, either verbal or by Way of Letter, will be answered or attended to in the smallest Degree. We should feel much Concern if a Thought could be entertained that the worthy Part of our Clients could disapprove this Measure. Their Conduct has been such as calls for our Acknowledgments, and might merit Exemption from this Strictness, were such Exemption practicable; but they will readily perceive this would defeat the Purpose, and that no Distinction of Persons can by any Means be attempted. We hope, therefore, from their Friendship, a cheerful Concurrence in this our Plan, since the Requisition is such only as their Punctuality would of itself prevent.   JOHN RANDOLPH.   THOMAS JEFFERSON.

EDMUND PENDLETON.   PATRICK HENRY, Junior.

JAMES MERCER.   GUSTAVUS SCOTT.

The Subscriber by no Means disapproves of the above Resolution; but as he has long determined to quit his Practice as an Attorney, and practise only as a Counsel in such Causes as are ready for Trial, he has declined signing the above, as he shall not engage in any Cause for the future but such in which he shall previously receive an adequate Satisfaction for his Trouble, which they may be assured will not be less than the legal Fees.   THOMPSON MASON.

Printed from *Virginia Gazette* (Purdie & Dixon), 20 May 1773.

For the background of this announcement, and a general statement on TJ's income as a lawyer and difficulty in collecting legal fees, see Malone, *Jefferson*, I, 122-3. THE FEES ALLOWED BY LAW were fixed by a statute of 1765, which permitted a charge of five pounds for a case in the general court, thirty shillings for a case in a county or other inferior court, "and in all other actions, except by petition, fifteen shillings" (Hening, VIII, 184-5).

Commission as Surveyor of Albemarle County

[6 June 1773]

To all to whom these Presents shall come, Greeting: Know ye, that we the President and Masters of the College of William and Mary in Virginia, by Virtue of a royal Grant from their late Majesties King William and Queen Mary, of the Office of Surveyor General of the Colony of Virginia to the said College, have constituted and appointed, and by these Presents do constitute and appoint *Thomas Jefferson* Surveyor of *Albemarle County* during Pleasure, in the Place and Stead of

In Witness whereof we have hereunto set our Hands, and caused the Seal of the said College to be affixed, this *sixth Day of June* in the *fourteenth* Year of the Reign of our Sovereign Lord *George*, King of *Great Britain, France,* and *Ireland, &c.* And in the Year of our Lord God one thousand seven hundred and seventy three.

John Camm Pr.
T. Gwatkin
James Madison

Printed form, filled in and signed (DLC). Seal of the College of William and Mary in lower left corner. The space for the previous incumbent's name is blank.

An identical form, with the same date, empowering TJ to appoint his own assistant, is in DLC. By Article XVI of the charter of the College of William and Mary, 1693, the surveyor-generalship of Virginia was vested in the trustees of the College (Henry Hartwell, et al., *The Present State of Virginia, and the College*, ed. H. D. Farish, Williamsburg, 1940, p. 90-2). In coming to this office TJ was again following in the footsteps of his father, who had been surveyor for Goochland and Albemarle (Malone, *Jefferson*, I, 26).

Notice of Sale of Wayles Properties

[15 July 1773]

TO BE SOLD

TWO Thousand five Hundred and twenty Acres of LAND in *Cumberland*, commonly known by the Name of SAINT JAMES'S; one Thousand four Hundred and twenty Acres in the Counties of *Goochland* and *Cumberland*, on both Sides of *James* River, opposite to *Elk* Island; and one Thousand four Hundred and eighty Acres on *Herring* Creek, in *Charles City* County. The above Tracts of Land were of the Estate of the late *John Wayles*, deceased, devised to the Subscribers, and are now offered for Sale. Persons disposed to purchase may be informed of the Terms, on Application to any one of the Subscribers; and the Times of Payment will be made easy, on giving Bond and Security to

THOMAS JEFFERSON.
FRANCIS EPPES.
HENRY SKIPWITH.

Printed from *Virginia Gazette* (Purdie & Dixon), 15 July 1773.
John Wayles, TJ's father-in-law, had died on 28 May 1773; his will is printed in *Tyler's Quart.*, VI (1924-1925), 268-70. The co-signers with TJ were also sons-in-law of Wayles (Malone, *Jefferson*, I, 432-3).

James Macpherson to Charles McPherson

MY DEAR SIR   London August 7th 1773

I received your letter. I should be glad to accommodate any friend of yours; especially one of Mr. Jefferson's taste and character. But I cannot, having [re]fused them to so many, give a copy of the Gaëlic poems with any decency [o]ut of my hands. The labour, besides, would be great. I know of none, that could copy them. My manner and my spelling differ from others: And I have the vanity [to] think, that I am in the right. Make my humble respects to your American friend. Excuse me as you can to him; and pray excuse me yourself. I seldom hear from you; the truth is I am so negligent in writing myself, that I cannot, with any justice, blame any other, on that head. I have heard from your friend William once. I suppose he has, now, dived behind his hills. He has his comfortable things there also; though, I suppose he recollects London with some pleasure. I am My dear Sir Yours most affectionately,

JAMES MACPHERSON

RC (DLC). Enclosed in Charles Mc-Pherson's letter to TJ of 12 Aug., following. Fading has rendered some portions of the MS nearly illegible.

For the background of this letter and the Ossian affair, see TJ's letter to Charles McPherson, 25 Feb. 1773; see also McPherson to TJ, following.

From Charles McPherson

DEAR SIR   Edinburgh 12th. August 1773.

I regret, exceedingly, that I have at this distance of time to answer your very polite letter of the 20th February. I only received it about the end of last month. It came under cover of a letter from Mr. Ninian Minzies, dated the 20th. May. I recollect, with pleasure, the acquaintance which I had with you in Virginia. I enjoy the thoughts of renewing that acquaintance; and I am much indebted to you, Sir, for favouring me with the opportunity.

Excepting the specimen of Temora, Ossians Poems, in the original, never were in print. Sorry I am that a copy of the Gaelic manuscript, of these poems, cannot be procured. I take the liberty of transmitting you Mr. Macphersons letter to me upon the subject. Every thing, allow me to assure you, that depended upon me, was, with alacrity, done towards the indulging of your request. This much was due, setting my acquaintance with Mr. Jefferson aside, to the elegant, the feeling admirer of the *Voice of Cona*. Ossian himself, from his Cloud, might bend, and listen, with pleasure, to such praise. And the praise is due. For, if to melt, to transport the soul be an excellence, as sure it is, our venerable Bard possesses it in an eminent, a superlative degree. Elegant, however, and pleasant as these poems, in their present form, may appear; they, in common with other translations, have lost, considerably, of their native beauty and fire. This naturally creates a desire of becoming acquainted with the original. I do not at all wonder that *you* should be "desirous of learning the language in which Ossian thought, in which he sung." But, alas, I am afraid that this will be attended with insuperable difficultys. A few religious Books excepted, we have no publication in the Gaelic Language, no dictionary, no grammar. I have sent you, to the care of Mr. Minzies, to whom this letter goes inclosed, a Gaelic New Testament, which has a few rules, affixed, for learning the language. This, with a vocabulary, which is also sent, is all the assistance that, at this distance, I can give you to learn my mother tongue. Had this been thought of when I had the pleasure of being with you, at your sweet retreat, at the mountains, I woud have, cheerfully, become your instructor. Should any Celtic pieces, hereafter, be ushered into light, I shall do myself the pleasure of sending them to you. I hear of no intended publication; few, or none indeed, are equal to the task. In the remote Highlands there are still to be found a number of Ossians Poems, abounding equally in the tender and sublime with those with which Mr. Macpherson has favored the public, and these are chanted away, with a wildness a sweetness of enthusiasm, in the true spirit of Song. I rejoice to hear of your success in life. If I can render you any acceptable service here, I beg you may command me, with a freindly freedom. For, I can, with truth, assure you, that, I am, with the utmost sincerity and regard, Dear Sir Your most obedient most humble Servant,

CHARLES McPHERSON

RC (DLC). Enclosure: James Macpherson to Charles McPherson, 7 Aug. 1773.

See TJ to Charles McPherson, 25 Feb. 1773, and the enclosure printed immediately above. The GAELIC NEW TESTAMENT sent by McPherson must have been *Tiomnadh Nuadh*, Edinburgh: Balfour, Auld, and Smellie, 1767, which had an appendix containing "Rules for Reading the Galic Lan-guage" (British and Foreign Bible Society, *Historical Catalogue*, ed. T. H. Darlow and H. F. Moule, London, 1903-1911, No. 4081; see TJ's Library Catalogue, 1815, p. 167). The VOCABULARY accompanying it was *A Galick and English Vocabulary . . . Written for the Use of Charity Schools . . . in the Highlands*, Edinburgh: R. Fleming, 1761 (information from Miss E. M. Sowerby; see Library Catalogue, 1815, p. 165).

From James Taylor

SIR   Orange Augt. 20th. 1773

There is no Such Will as Joseph Smiths Recorded in the County of Orange.

I am Sr. Yr. Hble Servt.,   JAMES TAYLOR

RC (MHi). Addressed: "To Thomas Jefferson Esqr. In Albemarle." James Taylor was clerk of Orange co., 1772-1798 (Frederick Johnston, *Memorials of Old Virginia Clerks*, Lynchburg, 1888, p. 271).

Further Notice of Sale
of Wayles Properties

[9 September 1773]

TO BE SOLD,

FIVE Hundred and fifty Acres of LAND in the County of *Charles City*, with a convenient Dwellinghouse and other Improvements, Two Hundred and twenty Acres, in the same County, pleasantly situated on *James* River.

Two Thousand five Hundred and twenty Acres in the County of *Cumberland*, commonly known by the Name of *Saint James's*.

And one Thousand four Hundred and twenty one Acres in the Counties of *Goochland* and *Cumberland*, on both Sides of *James* River, opposite to *Elk* Island.

The above TRACTS of LAND were of the Estate of the late *John Wayles*, deceased, devised to the Subscribers, and are now offered for Sale. Persons disposed to purchase may be informed of the Terms, on Application to any one of the Subscribers; and the Times of Payment will be made easy, on giving Bond and Security to

THOMAS JEFFERSON.
FRANCIS EPPES.
HENRY SKIPWITH.

Printed from *Virginia Gazette* (Purdie & Dixon), 9 Sep. 1773.
See note on the earlier Notice of Sale, 15 July 1773.

From John Blair

DEAR SIR   Williamsburg. March 2d. 1774.

I have noted the Time of your Petitions coming into the Office, which will give them Priority when the Land Office is open. There is an Order of Council (but seldom I think complied with) that every Order for Land shall be entered in the Auditor's Office, and he is to indorse on it that it is so. This was to be done previous to the surveying; I conceive, therefore, that if the Land be already surveyed (which often is the Case without the Auditor's knowing any Thing of the Matter) it can answer no End now to enter it in that Office. I have delivered to Mr. Brown, who entered 2 Caveats, a Summons in each.

I have spoke to one or two Gentlemen of the Council about the Order made on Scott's Petition, but they did not remember the Affair sufficiently to instruct me what Entry ought to have been made. That which was made (as I before informed you) was confined to that particular Case, which was agreeable to my own Sense of the Order. For otherwise, I conceive the Clerk would be made a sort of a Judge, to determine on the Evidence of the Title of the deceased, and of his having died without Heir.

The 21st. ult' about 2 in the Afternoon (some say ½ Hour later) we had a very moderate Trembling of the Earth, so moderate that not many perceived it, but Dr. Gilmer informs me it was a pretty smart Shock with You; and by all accounts it was more and more severe as You advance to the West.

Lady Dunmore, and 6 of her Children (the youngest being left in Scotland) arrived at the Palace the 27th ult' and is I understand well pleased with every Thing hitherto; every Mark of Respect having been shewn her, and To-morrow the Governor is to receive an Address from this Corporation on the Event. My respectful Compts. to Mrs. Jefferson. And I am Dr. Sir Your Friend & Servant, JOHN BLAIR

RC (MHi). Addressed: "To Thomas Jefferson Esqr. Monticello in Albemarle." Endorsed: "John Blair's Lre. relative to my orders of council."

Of the several applications for grants of land made by TJ in 1773 and 1774, it is not possible to tell with certainty to which Blair refers. TREMBLING OF THE EARTH: TJ recorded two violent earthquake shocks at Monticello on the afternoon of 21 Feb. 1774, and another on the afternoon of the 22d (Account Book, under dates); see also *Va. Gaz.* (P & D), 24 Feb. 1774.

Notes on the Progress of Certain Bills

[9-25 May 1774]

Entail bill (my own)

May 9. 1774. leave to bring in the bill

    10.   bill read first time & ordd. to be read 2d time

    13.   Committed

    19.   reported & ingrossed

    20.   read 3d time and passed.

General Entail bill

May 25. leave to bring in bill to empower certain persons to convey away their lands.

    26. presented, read, & to be read 2d time

Road bill

    presentd. by Commee Cts. justce. read 1st. time & ordd. to be Committd.

Ferry bill Fluvanna.

May 21st. report made by Commee. for insertg. clauses in general
      bill
    25. instruction to discontinue other ferries.

N (DLC).

The first of these Bills pertained to TJ personally and the others to Albemarle co.; he was not on any of the committees to bring them in. Though his own entail bill was passed by the House, it did not become a law because on 26 May the House was dissolved before any bills for this session received the assent of the governor and council. The other three bills got no further than TJ records; for their full titles, see JHB, 1773-1776, p. 129, 89, and 118, respectively. TJ's own bill is of special interest in the light of his responsibility for the abolition of entails by the statute of 14 Oct. 1776 (TJ's Autobiography, Ford, I, 49-50). Under 9 May 1774 the Journal records his and his wife's joint petition as follows:

"A *Petition* of *Thomas Jefferson* and *Martha* his Wife was presented to the House, and read; setting forth that *Fran-cis Eppes*, grandfather of the Petitioner *Martha*, by his last Will and Testament in writing devised to her Mother, in fee tail general, one Moiety of two thousand and four hundred Acres of land, now in the County of *Cumberland*; that the Petitioner *Martha* is the sole heir of the Body of her said Mother; that the Petitioners have contracted to make sale of their Moiety of the said lands; and that it will be greatly to their Interest and that of their Families to have the said contract carried into effect, by docking the Intail and settling lands, in the County of *Goochland*, of equal value, in lieu of the said Moiety; and therefore praying that leave may be given to bring in a Bill for that purpose.

"*Ordered*, that leave, be given to bring in a Bill pursuant to the prayer of the said Petition; and that Mr. *Bland* do prepare and bring in the same."

Resolution of the House of Burgesses Designating a Day of Fasting and Prayer

TUESDAY, THE 24TH OF MAY, 14 GEO. III. 1774.

THIS House being deeply impressed with Apprehension of the great Dangers to be derived to *British America*, from the hostile Invasion of the City of *Boston*, in our Sister Colony of *Massachusetts Bay*, whose Commerce and Harbour are on the 1st Day of *June* next to be stopped by an armed Force, deem it highly necessary that the said first Day of *June* be set apart by the Members of this House as a Day of Fasting, Humiliation, and Prayer, devoutly to implore the divine Interposition for averting the heavy Calamity, which threatens Destruction to our civil Rights, and the Evils of civil War; to give us one Heart and one Mind firmly to oppose, by all just and proper Means, every Injury to *American* Rights, and that the Minds of his Majesty and his Parliament may be inspired from above with Wisdom, Moderation, and Justice, to remove from the loyal People of *America* all Cause of Danger from a continued Pursuit of Measures pregnant with their Ruin.

Ordered, therefore, that the Members of this House do attend in their Places at the Hour of ten in the Forenoon, on the said 1st Day of *June* next, in Order to proceed with the Speaker and the Mace to the Church in this City for the Purposes aforesaid; and that the Reverend Mr. *Price* be appointed to read Prayers, and the Reverend Mr. *Gwatkin* to preach a Sermon suitable to the Occasion.

Ordered, that this Order be forthwith printed and published.

By the HOUSE *of* BURGESSES.

GEORGE WYTHE, C. H. B.

Broadside (MHi: Washburn Papers.) Docketed at foot of text: "This Occasioned the dissolution. E. P. [Edmund Pendleton]." A copy now in NN, identical in text, was sent to Connecticut in a letter of 28 May (also NN) signed by Randolph, Nicholas, and Digges (the Committee of Correspondence). The entries for this broadside in the standard bibliographies are confusing, to say the least. Evans' entry, No. 13746, is correct but gives no location and adds, in brackets, the imprint "Williamsburg: Printed by Clementina Rind, 1774." There is no clear evidence that Mrs. Rind, rather than her competitors, Purdie & Dixon, printed this broadside. Clayton-Torrence, No. 416, copies Evans' entry, omitting the brackets around the assigned imprint, and then subjoins *another* entry, No. 417, which is correct, adding the Rind imprint in brackets. Sabin, No. 99926, condenses Clayton-Torrence's two entries but gives the imprint without brackets. The Fast-Day Proclamation was also printed in Rind's and in Purdie & Dixon's *Virginia Gazette* in their issues dated 26 May 1774; but since there is unquestionable evidence that neither paper was printed before the 27th or 28th, there can be no doubt that Governor Dunmore referred to the broadside printing when, on 26 May, he summoned the burgesses to the council room and thus addressed them: "I have in my hand a Paper published by Order of your House, conceived in such Terms as reflect highly upon his Majesty and the Parliament of *Great Britain*; which makes it necessary for me to dissolve you; and you are dissolved accordingly" (JHB, 1773-1776, p. 132).

The news of the passage of the Boston Port Act had reached Williamsburg before 19 May (see both *Virginia Gazettes* for that date). In his Autobiography, TJ tells of his part in drafting the Fast-Day Resolution:

"The lead in the house on these subjects being no longer left to the old members, Mr. Henry, R. H. Lee, Fr. L. Lee, 3. or 4. other members, whom I do not recollect, and myself, agreeing that we must boldly take an unequivocal stand in the line with Massachusetts, determined to meet and consult on the proper measures in the council chamber, for the benefit of the library in that room. We were under conviction of the necessity of arousing our people from the lethargy into which they had fallen as to passing events; and thought that the appointment of a day of general fasting and prayer would be most likely to call up and alarm their attention. No example of such a solemnity had existed since the days of our distresses in the war of 55. since which a new generation had grown up. With the help therefore of Rushworth, whom we rummaged over for the revolutionary precedents and forms of the Puritans of that day, preserved by him, we cooked up a resolution, somewhat modernizing their phrases, for appointing the 1st day of June, on which the Port bill was to commence, for a day of fasting, humiliation and prayer, to implore heaven to avert from us the evils of civil war, to inspire us with firmness in support of our rights, and to turn the hearts of the King and parliament to moderation and justice. To give greater emphasis to our proposition, we agreed to wait the next morning on Mr. Nicholas, whose grave and religious character was more in unison with the tone of our resolution and to solicit him to move it. We accordingly went to him in the morning. He moved it the same day; the 1st of June was proposed and it passed without opposition" (Ford, I, 9-11).

For the probable model of the Fast-Day Resolution "cooked up" by the radical clique, see John Rushworth, *Historical Collections*, London, 1659-1701, I, pt. iii, p. 494 (a proclamation by Charles I in 1642); and also p. 29. The Burgesses' Resolution, which signified an open break with royal authority, also precipitated a battle of pamphlets in Virginia. *Considerations on the Present State of Virginia*, 1774, without place or publisher's name but doubtless the work of Attorney General John Randolph, is a persuasive statement of loyalist views. It was answered in *Considerations on the Present State of Virginia Examined*, 1774, also without place or publisher's name but known to be the work of the Treasurer, Robert Carter Nicholas, who had introduced the Resolution. The Fast Sermon at Bruton Church was delivered by Thomas Price, since, according to Lord Dunmore, Mr. Gwatkin "civilly but with firmness declined being employed for such a purpose" (Dunmore to Lord Dartmouth, 6 June 1774; Hansard, *Parl. Hist.*, XVIII, 137-8). Under the title of *The Doctrine of a Providence Considered*, it was advertised as to be published (*Va. Gaz.* [P & D], 16 June 1774), but no copies are recorded. Attention should be called, finally, to a point omitted in TJ's Autobiography. In sending a copy of the Fast-Day Resolution to George William Fairfax, 10 June 1774, George Washington said that "this Dissolution was as sudden as unexpected for there were other resolves of a much more spirited nature ready to be offered to the House wch. would have been unani-mously adopted respecting the Boston Port Bill as it is calld but were withheld till the Important business of the Country could be gone through" (*Writings*, ed. Fitzpatrick, III, 223). R. H. Lee, in a letter of 23 June to Samuel Adams, stated that the "more spirited" resolves included a denunciation of the Port Act as "a most violent and dangerous attempt to destroy the constitutional liberty of and rights of all North America" and a proposal that deputies be appointed to meet in an intercolonial congress (*Letters*, I, 111; see also R. H. Lee to Arthur Lee, 26 June, same, p. 114-18). The Fast-Day Resolution of 24 May 1774 is the first in a series of closely related printed and MS documents climaxed by TJ's *Summary View* and illustrating the rapid course of the Revolutionary movement in Virginia in the summer of 1774. These have never before been brought together in sequence. Somewhat fuller annotation than usual has been given them in order to show their relations and to provide a background for the *Summary View*.

Association of Members of the Late House of Burgesses

[27 May 1774]

AN ASSOCIATION, SIGNED BY 89 MEMBERS OF THE LATE HOUSE OF BURGESSES.

WE his Majesty's most dutiful and loyal subjects, the late representatives of the good people of this country, having been deprived by the sudden interposition of the executive part of this government from giving our countrymen the advice we wished to convey to them in a legislative capacity, find ourselves under the hard necessity of adopting this, the only method we have left, of pointing out to our countrymen such measures as in our opinion are best fitted to secure our dearest rights and liberty from destruction, by the heavy hand of power now lifted against North America: With much grief we find that our dutiful applications to Great Britain for security of our just, antient, and constitutional rights, have been not only disregarded, but that a determined system is formed and pressed for reducing the inhabitants of British America to slavery, by subjecting them to the payment of taxes, imposed without the consent of the people or their representatives; and that in pursuit of this system, we find an act of the British parliament, lately passed, for stopping the harbour and commerce of the town of Boston, in our sister colony of Massachusetts Bay, until the people there submit to the payment of such unconstitutional taxes, and which act most violently and arbitrarily deprives them of their property, in wharfs erected by private persons, at their own great and proper expence, which act is, in our opinion, a most dangerous attempt to destroy the constitutional liberty and rights of all North America. It is further our opinion, that as TEA, on its importation into America, is charged with a duty, imposed by parliament for the purpose of raising a revenue, without the consent of the people, it ought not to be used by any person who wishes well to the constitutional rights and liberty of British America. And whereas the India company have ungenerously attempted the ruin of America, by sending many ships loaded with tea into the colonies, thereby intending to fix a precedent in favour of arbitrary taxation, we deem it highly proper and do accordingly recommend it strongly to our countrymen, not to purchase or use any kind of East India commodity whatsoever, except saltpetre and spices, until the grievances of America are redressed. We are further clearly of opinion, that an attack, made on one of our sister colonies, to compel submission to arbitrary taxes, is an attack made on all British America, and threatens ruin to the rights of all, unless the united wisdom of the whole be applied. And for this purpose it is recommended to the committee of correspondence, that they communicate, with their several corresponding committees, on the expediency of appointing deputies from the several colonies of British America, to meet in general congress, at such place annually as shall be thought most convenient; there to deliberate on those general measures which the united interests of America may from time to time require.

A tender regard for the interest of our fellow subjects, the merchants, and manufacturers of Great Britain, prevents us from going further at this time; most earnestly hoping, that the unconstitutional principle of taxing the colonies without their consent will not be persisted in, thereby to compel us against our will, to avoid all commercial intercourse with Britain. Wishing them and our people free and happy, we are their affectionate friends, the late representatives of Virginia.

The 27th day of May, 1774.

Peyton Randolph, Ro. C. Nicholas, Richard Bland, Edmund Pendleton, Richard Henry Lee, Archibald Cary, Benjamin Harrison, George Washington, William Harwood, Robert Wormeley Carter, Robert Munford, Thomas Jefferson, John West, Mann Page, junior, *John Syme, Peter Le Grand, Joseph Hutchings, Francis Peyton, Richard Adams, B. Dandridge, Henry Pendleton, Patrick Henry,* junior, *Richard Mitchell, James Holt, Charles Carter, James Scott, Burwell Bassett, Henry Lee, John Burton, Thomas Whiting, Peter Poythress, John Winn, James Wood, William Cabell, David Mason, Joseph Cabell, John Bowyer, Charles Linch, William Aylett, Isaac Zane, Francis Slaughter, William Langhorne, Henry Taylor, James Montague, William Fleming, Rodham Kenner, William Acril, Charles Carter,* of *Stafford, John Woodson, Nathaniel Terry, Richard Lee, Henry Field, Matthew Marable, Thomas Pettus, Robert Rutherford, Samuel M'Dowell, John Bowdoin, James Edmondson, Southy Simpson, John Walker, Hugh Innes,*

Henry Bell, Nicholas Faulcon, junior, James Taylor, junior, Lewis Burwell, of Gloucester, W. Roane, Joseph Nevil, Richard Hardy, Edwin Gray, H. King, Samuel Du Val, John Hite, junior, John Banister, Worlich Westwood, John Donelson, Thomas Newton, junior, P. Carrington, James Speed, James Henry, Champion Travis, Isaac Coles, Edmund Berkeley, Charles May, Thomas Johnson, Benjamin Watkins, Francis Lightfoot Lee, John Talbot, Thomas Nelson, junior, Lewis Burwell.

W E the subscribers, clergymen and other inhabitants of the colony and dominion of Virginia, having maturely considered the contents of the above association, do most cordially approve and accede thereto.

William Harrison, William Hubard, Benjamin Blagrove, William Bland, H. J. Burges, Samuel Smith M'Croskey, Joseph Davenport, Thomas Price, David Griffith, William Leigh, Robert Andrews, Samuel Klug, Ichabod Camp, William Clayton, Richard Cary, Thomas Adams, Hinde Russell, William Holt, Arthur Dickenson, Thomas Stuart, James Innes.

Broadside (DLC: Broadside Collection). Another copy (NN) was enclosed in the letter of 28 May from the Virginia Committee of Safety to the Connecticut committee, and bears an endorsement identical with that on the Fast-Day Resolution of 24 May, above. Evans 13747; Clayton-Torrence 407; Sabin 100007.

As TJ stated in his Autobiography, after Dunmore had "dissolved us as usual," the burgesses "retired to the Apollo . . . , agreed to an association, and instructed the committee of correspondence to propose to the corresponding committees of the other colonies to appoint deputies to meet in Congress at such place, *annually*, as should be convenient to direct, from time to time, the measures required by the general interest: and we declared that an attack on one colony should be considered as an attack on the whole" (Ford, I, 11). Peyton Randolph, who was both speaker of the House of Burgesses and chairman of the committee of correspondence, acted as "moderator" of the meeting; the eighty-nine members who signed the declaration issued by the meeting constituted all but fourteen of the membership known to have attended the recent session of the House. It is not known who prepared the text of the declaration; it was probably, though not certainly, printed by Clementina Rind. Though it was among the earlier calls for a general congress, the Virginia proposal was not the very first; see E. I. Miller, "The Virginia Committee of Correspondence of 1773-1775," WMQ, 1st ser., XXII (1913-1914), 109, and note. On the following day (28 May) the committee of correspondence met, TJ being present, and ordered letters to be sent to all the colonies transmitting the Resolves of the meeting of the 27th; for the form of the letters of transmittal, see JHB, 1773-1776, p. 138.

Proceedings of a Meeting
of Representatives in Williamsburg

30th May 1774

At a Meeting of 25 of the late Representatives legally assembled by the Moderator, it was agreed

That Letters be wrote to all our Sister Colonies, acknowledging the Receipt of the Letters and Resolves from Boston &c. informing them, that before the same came to hand, the Virginia Assembly had been unexpectedly dissolved, and most of the Members returned to their respective Counties.

That it is the Opinion of all the late House of Burgesses who could be convened on the present Occasion, that the Colony of Virginia will concur with the other Colonies in such Measures as shall be judged most effectual for the Preservation of the Common Rights and Liberty of British America; that they are of Opinion particularly that an Association against Importations will probably be entered into, as soon as the late Representatives can be collected, and perhaps against Exportations also after a certain Time. But that this must not be considered as an Engagement on the part of this Colony, which it would be presumption in us to enter into, and that we are sending Dispatches to call together the late Representatives to meet at Williamsburg on the first Day of August next to conclude finally on these important Questions.

Peyton Randolph, Moderator.	Th: Jefferson	John Walker
Ro. C. Nicholas	Mann Page Junr.	James Wood.
Edmd Pendleton	Chars. Carter Senr:	Wm Langhorne
Will: Harwood	Js. Mercer	T Blackburn
Richd Adams	R Wormeley Carter.	Edmd Berkeley
Thom Whiting	G: Washington	Jno. Donelson
Henry Lee	Francis Lightfoot Lee	P. Carrington
Lemuel Riddick	Thos Nelson jr.	Lewis Burwell
	R Rutherford	(Gloster)

MS in an unidentified hand (Vi). Autograph signatures.

The dispatches emanating from the Boston town meeting of 13 May, convened upon the arrival of a copy of the Port Act (see Force, *Archives*, 4th ser., I, 331), reached Williamsburg on 29 May, having been relayed by the committees at Philadelphia and Annapolis. The Bostonians appealed for a strict nonimportation, nonexportation agreement among all the colonies in their support—a measure that the Williamsburg meeting of 27 May had explicitly stopped short of. What followed is related in *Va. Gaz.* (P & D), 2 June:

"Immediately upon receiving the Letters, the Honourable Peyton Randolph, Esq; Moderator of the Committee of the late House of Representatives, thought it proper to convene all the Members that were then in Town; who, on considering those important Papers, came to a Resolution to call together the several other Members near this City, to whom Notice could be given. Twenty five of them accordingly met next Day at ten o'Clock, when it was unanimously agreed to refer the farther Consideration of this Matter to the first Day of August next; at which Time it is expected there will be a very general Attendance of the late Members of the House of Burgesses, and that a Non-Importation Agreement will be then entered into, as well as Resolutions to suspend, at some future Day, exporting any of our Commodities to Britain, should the present odious Measures, so inimical to the just Rights and Liberty of America, be pursued."

Copies of the present document, the authorship of which is unknown, were forwarded on 31 May to the Maryland Committee with the request "that it may be immediately transmitted through the Hands of our Friends in *Philadelphia* to our Friends in *Boston*, in the same Manner as their Sentiments and Resolutions have been conveyed to us" (JHB, 1773-1776, p. 139-40; see also Washington to George Fairfax, 10 June 1774, *Writings*, ed. Fitzpatrick, III, 223-4).

From Peyton Randolph and Others
to Members of the Late House of Burgesses

GENTLEMEN   WILLIAMSBURG, *May* 31, 1774.

LAST *Sunday* Morning several Letters were received from *Boston*, *Philadelphia*, and *Maryland*, on the most interesting and important Subject of *American* Grievances. The Inhabitants of *Boston* seem to be in a most piteous and melancholy Situation, and are doubtful whether they will be able to sustain the impending Blow without the Assistance and Co-operation of the other Colonies. By the Resolutions of their Town Meeting, it appears to be their Opinion that the most effectual Assistance which can be given them by their Sister Colonies will arise from a general Association against Exports and Imports, of every Kind, to or from *Great Britain*. Upon Receipt of this important Intelligence, the Moderator judged it most prudent immediately to convene as many of the late Representatives as could be got together, and yesterday, at a Meeting of twenty five of the late Members, we took the Business under our most serious Consideration. Most Gentlemen present seemed to think it absolutely necessary for us to enlarge our late Association, and that we ought to adopt the Scheme of Nonimportation to a very large Extent; but we were divided in our Opinions as to stopping our Exports. We could not, however, being so small a Proportion of the late Associates, presume to make any Alteration in the Terms of the general Association, and therefore resolved to invite all the Members of the late House of Burgesses to a general Meeting in this City on the first Day of *August* next. We fixed this distant Day in Hopes of accommodating the Meeting to every Gentleman's private Affairs, and that they might, in the mean Time, have an Opportunity of collecting the Sense of their respective Counties. The Inhabitants of this City were convened yesterday in the Afternoon, and most chearfully acceded to the Measures we had adopted.

We flatter ourselves it is unnecessary to multiply Words to induce your Compliance with this Invitation, upon an Occasion which is, confessedly, of the most lasting Importance to all *America*. Things seem to be hurrying to an alarming Crisis, and demand the speedy, united Councils of all those who have a Regard for the common Cause. We are, Gentlemen, your most affectionate Friends, and obedient humble Servants,

PEYTON RANDOLPH, MODERATOR; *Robert C. Nicholas, Edmund Pendleton, William Harwood, Richard Adams, Thomas Whiting, Henry Lee, Lemuel Riddick, Thomas Jefferson, Mann Page*, junior, *Charles Carter*, Lancaster, *James Mercer, Robert Wormeley Carter, George*

Washington, Francis Lightfoot Lee, Thomas Nelson, junior, Robert Rutherford, John Walker, James Wood, William Langhorne, Thomas Blackburne, Edmund Berkeley, John Donelson, Paul Carrington, Lewis Burwell.

Printed letter (DLC: Washington Papers). Addressed: "To George Washington Esqr. Fairfax." Endorsed by Washington: "From The Virginia Convenn 31st. May 1774. V." Not entered in the standard bibliographies, though mentioned under Sabin 100008.

This is one of the "Despatches to call together the late Representatives" on 1 Aug. referred to in the preceding document. TJ, who left Williamsburg on the 31st (see Account Book under that date), must, like Washington, have received a copy of this summons from the body of which he had himself been a member, but no copy survives in his papers. Besides the copy in the Washington Papers, printed in S. M. Hamilton, ed., *Letters to Washington*, Boston and N.Y., 1901, III, 354-6, a second copy, that sent to Edmund Berkeley, member for Middlesex co., is now in ViU.

Petition of George Mason
for Warrants for Lands in Fincastle County

[June 1774]

To his Excellency the Governor and the Council of Virginia. The Memorial & Petition of George Mason of the County of Fairfax.

That in[1] the Charter granted by King James the first to the Virginia Company in the year 1609 is Among Others a Clause declaring "That it is his Royal will and Pleasure, and Charging, comanding warranting and authorising the Treasurer and the said Company, and their Successors, to Convey asign and sett Over, Such particular portions of lands, Tenaments and Heriditaments, unto such his Majestys loving Subjects, Naturally born, Denizens, or Others, as well adventurers as planters, as by the said Company shall be nominated, appointed and Allowed, where in Respect to be had as well of the proportion of the adventure, as of the speciale Service, Hazard, Exploit, or Meritt of any person, so to be recompenc[ed,] Advanced or rewarded." Pursuant to which, within a few years after, fifty Acres of Land were ordered to be asigned and granted to every person importing himself into this Collony; and to every person who should import others, fifty Acres for each person so imported. This, as your Memorialist Conceives, was the Original, or first Rise of the Antient Custom of granting Lands in Virginia, Upon Importation-Rights; which is[2] now more than an hundred and fifty years Old, and appears to have been interwoven with the Constitution of the Colony, from its first settlement, That the same was Constantly practised during the said Company's Government here. And after the Government was taken into the Hands of the Croun, upon the Dissolution of the Virginia Company, the same Custom and Right was always Allowed and Continued, as Appears by the Patents, and Records in the Secretarys Office; the Titles to great part of the Lands in this Colony being founded upon importation-Rights; and the Constant Stile of the Old Patents is "the said Lands being due by and for the transportation, or by and for the Importation of . . . . . . Persons into this Colony." That in the Year 1662, an Act of Genral Assembly was made, prescribing the Manner of proving Rights to Lands due for the Importation of Servants, and obtaining Certificates thereon, to intitle the Importers to Surveys and Patents; and giving such proofs and Certificates the preference to Actual Surveys without them. And in the same Year, another Act of Assembly was made, reciting that the former laws[2] concerning deserted Lands, reserved to the first Taker-up his Rights to take up Land in Another Place, and enacting that for the future, in Care of deserted Lands, the Rights as well as the Lands shall be forfeited, and the grantee made incapable of useing any of them afterwards: from which Law it is Clear, that Importation-Rights are Always good, Until they have been Applyed to Patents for Land, and the Said Land forfeited, by Want of Seating and Planting. That in the Year 1676, the said custom and Right to Lands was solemnly confirmed and continued, by Charter and Letters patent from King Charles the Second, to the[1] Colony of Virginia, under the Great Seal of England "*As According as hath been used and Allowed from the first plantation*; to be[1] held of his Majesty his Heirs and Successors, as of their Manor of East Greenwich in their County of Kent, in free and common Soccage" and declaring "That all and Every Clause, Article and Sentence, in the said Letters patent contained, shall be from time to time for ever hereafter, as often as any Ambiguity, Doubt or Question, Sha[ll] or may happen to Arise thereupon, expounded, construed, deemed and taken to be meant and intended, and Shall enure and take Effect, in the *most beneficial and available Sense*, to All intents and purposes, for *the proffit and Advantage of the Subjects of Virginia*, as well against *his Majesty his Heirs and Successors*, as against all and Every other Person or Persons whatsoever" which Charter was recognised by an Act of Assembly in the year 1677, prescribing[3] a perticular form of *all Patents* for the future; in which form is recited "That his Majesty had been graciously pleased, by his said Letters Patent, to Continue and Confirm the Ancient Right and priviledge of granting fifty Acres of Land *for every Person imported* into his Majesty's Colony of Virginia" and it Appears from the Patent Record books, that all Lands in this Colony, except escheat Lands, Were Granted upon importation-Rights Only; until in or about the year 1710, when Treasury-Rights, or paying a certain Consideration in Money to the[1] Croun for Lands, Was first Introduced here; but that the same nevr affected Lands claimed under the Royal Charter; for the Ancient Rights to Lands due for the importation of people Still Continued upon the same footing as before, and hath ever been held Sacred and inviolable and Subject to no[1] new Charge or Imposition whatever; and great Quantitys[4] of Land, from time to time granted Acordingly. That from the Earliest times of this Colony, there hath been alowed to the secretary, and the[1] Clerks of Countys by Law, a certain fee for Certificates of Rights to Land; and upon the Last Regulation of the Fee-Bill in Virginia, Within thess few years, the Legislature Alowed to the County Court Clerks "For proving Rights for Land, produced at one time, belonging to one person, and Certificates thereof, a Fee of thirteen Pounds of Tobacco" and to the Secretary "for recording[1] a Certificate of rights[5] fifteen Pounds of Tobacco" and by An Act of Assembly made in the year 1710, when Treasury Rights were first introduced, it was (among other things) enacted "That upon the passing of any patent for Land thereafter, the Secretary of this Colony and Dominion, for the time being, should cause such patent to be truly Entred upon the Records of his office, together With the[1] Certificate of Rights, *either by importation*, or by Money paid the receiver-General of this Colony" which Your Memorialist is well informed hath Continued to be the practice ever Since; and that thess two modes of granting Lands, Since the year 1710, as before mentiond have never in the[1] Least interfered with Each Other; as the Croun Could only Alter the Terms, or fix a New price upon the Lands, to which there was no Legal Right. So that Mr. Stith, in his History of Virginia (which is Chiefly extracted from Records) mentioning the Custom of[6] granting lands for the importation of People, had good reason for his remark; that "this is the Antient, Legal, and a most indubitable Method of granting Lands in Virginia." And your Memorialist, with All due submission, begs Leave to Observe, that the King being as much bound by the Act of his Royal Predecessors, as any Private Subject, holding an Estate from his Ancestor is bound by the Act of that[1] Ancestor; and the before mentioned Antient Right to Any vacant or ungranted Lands in this Colony, having been Solemnly continued and Confirmed, by the Said Charter from King Charles the Second, in Manner herein before mentioned, the same was thereby made part of the Law and Constitution of this Country, and hath remained so ever since; and therefore can not be Avoided, injured, invalidated, or in any manner affected, by any proclamation, Instruction, or other Act of Goverment; nor[7] subjected to any new Charge, Expence, Burthen, or Imposition whatsoever. For which reasons, your Memorialist most Humbly Conceives that Any instruction,[8] or Late Regulations, respecting the ungranted Lands in this Colony, from our[1] present most gracious Sovering, ever observant of the Laws, and atentive to the just Rights of his People, were never meant, or intended to affect Lands due as aforesaid, under the Royal Charter. That your Petitioner confiding in, and upon the faith of the before mentioned Royal Charter, Laws and Custom hath been at great trouble and Expence, and hath Laid out Considerable Sums of Money, in purchasing from the Importers, Legal Certificates of Rights to Large Quantity's of Land, due for the Importation of People from Great Britain and Irland into this Colony. And prays that he may be admited to Entrys for the said Lands, upon the Western Waters, in the County of Fincastle; upon his producing the usual Certificates and Assignments, or that his Excellency the Governor, will be Pleased to Grant your petitioner his Warrants for Surveying the same, which Ever his Excellency and this[1] Honorable board Shall Judge most proper.

And Your petitioner will Ever pray.   G. Mason

MS (DLC). Signature as well as text in a copyist's hand. Docketed in the same hand: "Copy of the petition presented to the [*this word is interlined in TJ's hand*] Governor & Council June 1774 by George Mason, praying Entrys, or Warrants, for Lands Due for the importation of People, According to the Royal Charter." The text contains frequent corrections in TJ's hand, noted below.

By an order of 7 Apr. 1773 the Privy Council stopped further grants of land by the colonial governors, and by an order of 3 Feb. 1774 the same body set forth a plan for subsequent disposition of lands—namely, by auction—and abrogated the previous methods, such as the long-standing importation or headright system by which fifty acres of land were assigned to an individual for each person imported and settled by that individual in America. See St. George L.

Sioussat, "The Breakdown of the Royal Management of Lands in the Southern Provinces, 1773-1775," *Agricultural History*, III (1929), 67-98, for a fully documented discussion which is drawn on throughout this note; the Privy Council's Instructions to the Governors of Feb. 1774 are printed in *Sources and Documents Illustrating the American Revolution*, ed. S. E. Morison, 2d edn., Oxford, 1929, p. 97-100. Governor Dunmore informed the colonial secretary, Lord Dartmouth, in May 1774, that the new plan was highly repugnant to the Virginians, and for a time Dunmore did not proclaim it in force. When he was obliged to do so, his action provoked steps toward resistance by the Virginia Convention of Mch. 1775; see below, TJ's Resolution appointing a committee on land grants, 27 Mch. 1775. Meanwhile, George Mason, of Gunston Hall, Fairfax co., decided to make a test case. Mason came to Williamsburg late in

May 1774 to present his petition, but the dissolution of the Assembly and subsequent events apparently prevented action upon it; see Mason to Martin Cockburn, 26 May 1774, Rowland, *Mason*, I, 168-9. However, on 23 Nov. 1778, Mason presented to the Virginia General Assembly a memorial requesting confirmation of his claim to western lands due him on "charter importation rights, which hath been recognized by the governor and council during the British government as legal and valid" (JHD, Oct. 1778, 1827 edn., p. 80). No action was taken on Mason's claim until the Act (drawn by Mason and TJ) for Adjusting and Settling the Titles of Claimers to Unpatented Lands was passed in 1779 (q.v., printed under 14 Jan. 1778). Whether TJ acquired and corrected Mason's Petition in June 1774 or at some later time cannot be ascertained. TJ worked with Mason on the western land claims from 1776 to 1779, when the question was finally settled by law. Though

TJ did not touch on Mason's particular grievance in the *Summary View*, he did do so in his proposed Constitution for Virginia and in the Declaration of Independence, where "raising the conditions of new appropriations of lands" is listed among the injuries sustained by the colonists at the hands of George III; the Convention of 1776 deleted the charge when it adopted TJ's preamble.

1 This word interlined by TJ.
2 This word substituted by TJ for "Lands," crossed out.
3 This word substituted by TJ for "presenting," crossed out.
4 Corrected by TJ from "Quantys."
5 Two preceding words interlined by TJ.
6 This word substituted by TJ for "for," crossed out.
7 This word substituted by TJ for "not," crossed out.
8 This word substituted by TJ for "Construction," crossed out.

Thomas Jefferson and John Walker
to the Inhabitants of the Parish of St. Anne

[Before 23 July 1774]

To the Inhabitants of the parish of Saint Anne.

The members of the late house of Burgesses having taken into their consideration the dangers impending over British America from the hostile invasion of a sister colony, thought proper that it should be recommended to the several parishes in this colony that they set apart some convenient day for fasting, humiliation and prayer devoutly to implore the divine interposition in behalf of an injured and oppressed people; and that the minds of his majesty, his ministers, and parliament, might be inspired with wisdom from above, to avert from us the dangers which threaten our civil rights, and all the evils of civil war. We do therefore recommend to the inhabitants of the parish of Saint Anne that Saturday the 23d instant be by them set apart for the purpose aforesaid, on which day will be prayers and a sermon suited to the occasion by the reverend Mr. Clay at the new church on Hardware river, which place is thought the most centrical to the parishioners in General.

JOHN WALKER

THOMAS JEFFERSON

MS not located. Text from Ford, I, 418, who gives no source.

John Walker was TJ's fellow member from Albemarle in the House of Burgesses. The Parish of St. Anne embraced the southern portion of Albemarle co., and TJ was a vestryman of the parish, "though it does not appear that he ever acted" (Meade, *Old Churches and Families*, II, 48-9). TJ's Autobiography gives this general account of the proceedings in the counties:

"We returned home, and in our several counties invited the clergy to meet assemblies of the people on the 1st of June [actually at various times in June and July], to perform the ceremonies of the day, and to address to them discourses suited to the occasion. The people met generally, with anxiety and alarm in their countenances, and the effect of the day thro' the whole colony was like a shock of electricity, arousing every man and placing him erect and solidly on his centre."

Though the document is conjecturally dated in June by Ford, the Albemarle fast day was evidently fixed by TJ and Walker for 23 July, which was a Saturday. The delay was probably more expedient than necessary, for though TJ did not return to Albemarle very promptly after the Williamsburg proceedings, the fixing of the fast on 23 July was very likely owing to a desire to make a strong impression on the popular mind just before the county election on the 26th. Rev. Charles CLAY was minister of St. Anne's parish, 1769-1785; a zealous patriot, he was a lifelong friend of TJ; see Meade, *Old Churches and Families*, II, 48-50; Subscription of Feb. 1777, and Testimonial to Clay, 15 Aug. 1779, qq.v.

Resolutions of the Freeholders of Albemarle County

[26 July 1774]

At a meeting of the freeholders of the county of Albemarle, assembled in their collective body, at the courthouse of the said county, on the 26th day of July, 1774,

RESOLVED, that the inhabitants of the several states of British America are subject to the laws which they adopted at their first settlement, and to such others as have been since made by their respective legislatures, duly constituted and appointed with their own consent; that no other legislature whatever may rightfully exercise authority over them, and that these privileges they hold as the common rights of mankind, confirmed by the political constitutions they have respectively assumed, and also by several charters of compact from the crown.

Resolved, that these their natural and legal rights have in frequent instances been invaded by the parliament of Great Britain, and particularly that they were so by an act lately passed to take away the trade of the inhabitants of the town of Boston, in the province of Massachusetts Bay, that all such assumptions of unlawful power are dangerous to the rights of the British empire in general, and should be considered as its common cause, and that we will ever be ready to join with our fellow subjects, in every part of the same, in exerting all those rightful powers, which God has given us, for the re-establishing and guaranteeing such their constitutional rights, when, where, and by whomsoever invaded.

It is the opinion of this meeting, that the most eligible means of effecting these purposes will be to put an immediate stop to all imports from Great Britain (cotton, oznabrigs, striped duffil, medicines, gunpowder, lead, books and printed papers, the necessary tools and implements for the handycraft arts and manufactures excepted for a limited time) and to all exports thereto after the 1st day of October, which shall be in the year of our Lord, 1775; and immediately to discontinue all commercial intercourse with every part of the British empire which shall not in like manner break off their commerce with Great Britain.

It is the opinion of this meeting, that we immediately cease to import all commodities from every part of the world which are subjected by the British parliament to the payment of duties in America.

It is the opinion of this meeting that these measures should be pursued until a repeal be obtained of the act for blocking up the harbour of Boston, of the acts prohibiting or restraining internal manufactures in America, of the acts imposing on any commodities duties to be paid in America, and of the acts laying restrictions on the American trade; and that on such repeal it will be reasonable to grant to our brethren of Great Britain such privileges in commerce as may amply compensate their fraternal assistance, past and future.

Resolved, however, that this meeting do submit these their opinions to the convention of deputies from the several counties of this colony, appointed to be held at Williamsburg on the 1st day of August next, and also to the general congress of deputies from the several American states, when and wheresoever held; and that they will concur in these or any other measures which such convention or such congress shall adopt as most expedient for the American good. And we do appoint THOMAS JEFFERSON and JOHN WALKER our deputies to act for this county at the said convention, and instruct them to conform themselves to these our resolutions and opinions.

Printed from Rind's *Virginia Gazette*, 4 Aug. 1774.

The proposal of the meeting of twenty-five members on 30 May was to reassemble the members of the late House in order to answer the Bostonians' appeal for an embargo. The letter of 31 May therefore simply invited "all the Members of the late House of Burgesses to a general Meeting in this City on the first day of *August* next." Such a meeting of a dissolved body would have been extra-legal, but meanwhile the Governor was under pressure to authorize the election of a new assembly, which he did sometime in June, fixing the date of meeting for 11 Aug. (R. H. Lee to Samuel Adams, 23 June 1774; R. H. Lee, *Letters*, I, 112). In the counties, during June and July, the freeholders held meetings at which they elected and instructed their delegates, but in the earlier elections it is a question whether the deputies were being elected for a new assembly or for the revolutionary convention. The answer seems to be—

for either or both. Thus the Westmoreland co. resolutions, which are for the most part typical of the numerous papers of this kind printed in the *Gazettes*, have this paragraph at the end:

"And as it may happen that the assembly now called to meet on the 11th day of August, may be prorogued to a future day, and many of the deputies appointed to meet on the 1st of August, trusting to the certainty of meeting in assembly on the 11th, may fail to attend on the first, by which means decisive injury may arise to the common cause of liberty, by the general sense of the country not being early known at this dangerous crisis of American freedom, we do therefore direct, that our deputies chosen fail not to attend at Williamsburg on the said first day of August; and it is our earnest wish, that the deputies from the other counties be directed to do the same for the reasons above assigned" (*Va. Gaz.* [Rind], 30 June 1774; see also "Moderator" Ran-

View of the College of William and Mary.

John Page. Portrait as a boy, by John Wollaston.

dolph's notice to the same effect in the same issue).

As expected, Dunmore did, on 8 July, prorogue the House before it met, and continued to do so until 1 June 1775 (Lingley, *Transition in Virginia*, p. 83). Elections held thereafter were for the convention exclusively. Concerning TJ's authorship of the Albemarle Resolu-

tions, there has always been agreement. As Ford (I, 418, note) observes, from their similarity to the *Summary View* (which was being written at the same time), "it is evident that they proceeded from the same pen." For an instructive comparison of the Albemarle Resolves with those of other Virginia counties, see Randall, *Life*, I, 86-8.

Draft of a Declaration of Rights
Prepared for the Virginia Convention of August 1774

[ca. 26 July 1774]

A Declaration of rights and League for their support by the inhabitants of Virginia.

We the subscribers inhabitants of the colony of Virginia do declare that the people of the several states of British America are subject to the laws which they adopted at their first settlement and to such others as have been since made by their respective Legislatures duly constituted and appointed with their own consent. That no other Legislature whatever may rightfully exercise authority over them, and that these privileges they hold as the common rights of mankind, confirmed by the political constitutions they have respectively assumed, and also by several charters of compact from the crown.

We do declare that these their natural and legal rights have in frequent instances been invaded by the parliament of Great Britain and particularly that they were so by an act lately passed to take away the trade of the inhabitants of the town of Boston in the province of Massachusetts bay; that all such assumptions of unlawful power are dangerous to the rights of the British empire in general and should be considered as it's common cause; and that we will ever be ready to join with our fellow subjects in every part of the same in exerting all these rightful powers which god has given us for the re-establishing and guaranteeing such their constitutional rights, when, where, and by whom, soever invaded.

We do declare that we will not henceforth directly or indirectly import nor purchase when imported from the island of Great Britain any article or thing whatsoever excepting only Cotton, Oznabrigs, striped Duffel, Gunpowder, lead, Medicines, the necessary tools and implements for the handicraft arts and manufactures, books and printed papers, and that after the   day of
which shall be in the year of our lord   we will not import

[119]

nor purchase when imported thence any of the said excepted articles save only Medicines, Books and printed papers, and that after the 1st. day of October which shall be in the year of our lord 1775. we will not directly or indirectly export to the said island of Great Britain any article or thing whatsoever.

We do declare that we will immediately discontinue all commercial intercourse with every part of the British empire which shall not in like manner break of their commerce with Great Britain.

We do declare that we will immediately cease to import all commodities from every part of the world which are subjected by the British parliament to the paiment of duties in America.

We do declare that we will pursue and adhere to these measures until a repeal be obtained of the act for blocking up the harbor of Boston, of the acts prohibiting or restraining internal manufactures in America, of the acts imposing on any commodities duties to be paid in America, and of the acts laying restrictions on the American trade: and that on such repeal we shall be ready to grant to our brethren of Great Britain, such reasonable privileges in commerce as may amply compensate their fraternal assistance past and future. Saving alwais to our selves the liberty of relinquishing such of these measures as may be disapproved by any General Congress of deputies from the several American states, and of adopting any others which such Congress may think more expedient for the American good.

MS copy in an unidentified hand (DLC).

This document appears to be a draft of a declaration of rights drawn up in order to give effect to the Albemarle Resolutions of 26 July 1774. The phraseology of the two is almost identical, but there is an important difference. The Albemarle Resolves merely asserted, "It is the opinion of this meeting that these measures should be pursued," &c.; the Declaration of Rights was a forthright pronouncement: "We do declare that we will pursue and adhere to these measures," &c. The former instructed the Albemarle deputies; the latter was intended to be an official proclamation by the Convention that this course would be followed. Of TJ's authorship of the Albemarle Resolves, despite the lack of a MS, there has never been any question. Though the Declaration is in the hand of a copyist (probably the copyist of *A Summary View*, printed immediately below), the evidence for TJ's authorship is conclusive, quite aside from its distinctive style, its near identity with the Resolves, and the similarity of its ideas with those of the *Summary View*. For the use of lower-case letters at the beginning of sentences, the avoidance of capitalization for "god," and the use of "it's" for "its," "paiment" for "payment," and "alwais" for "always" stamp it as a literal copy of a paper in TJ's autograph. But having established these points, it is still difficult to determine where the present document fits into the sequence of events. The most likely explanation is that TJ drafted the Declaration after the meeting and election of 26 July and sent it to Williamsburg with the proposed Instructions to the Virginia delegates to Congress (the *Summary View*) for the Convention to issue as a statement of its position. The Convention issued a much more elaborate statement, which TJ duly received and which is printed below under 1-6 Aug. 1774.

Draft of Instructions
to the Virginia Delegates in the
Continental Congress
(MS Text of *A Summary View*, &c.)

[July 1774]

Resolved that it be an instruction to the said deputies when assembled in General Congress with the deputies from the other states
of British America to propose to the said Congress that an humble
and dutiful address be presented to his majesty begging leave to
lay before him as chief magistrate of the British empire the united
complaints of his majesty's subjects in America; complaints which
are excited by many unwarrantable incroachments and usurpations,
attempted to be made by the legislature of one part of the empire,
upon those rights which god and the laws have given equally and
independently to all. To represent to his majesty that these his
states have often individually made humble application to his imperial throne, to obtain thro' it's intervention some redress of their
injured rights; to none of which was ever even an answer condescended. Humbly to hope that this their joint address, penned in the
language of truth, and divested of those expressions of servility
which would persuade his majesty that we are asking favors and
not rights, shall obtain from his majesty a more respectful acceptance. And this his majesty will think we have reason to expect when
he reflects that he is no more than the chief officer of the people,
appointed by the laws, and circumscribed with definite powers, to
assist in working the great machine of government erected for their
use, and consequently subject to their superintendance. And in
order that these our rights, as well as the invasions of them, may be
laid more fully before his majesty, to take a view of them from the
origin and first settlement of these countries.

To remind him that our ancestors, before their emigration to
America, were the free inhabitants of the British dominions in
Europe, and possessed a right, which nature has given to all men,
of departing from the country in which chance, not choice has
placed them, of going in quest of new habitations, and of there
establishing new societies, under such laws and regulations as to
them shall seem most likely to promote public happiness. That
their Saxon ancestors had under this universal law, in like manner,
left their native wilds and woods in the North of Europe, had pos-

sessed themselves of the island of Britain then less charged with inhabitants, and had established there that system of laws which has so long been the glory and protection of that country. Nor was ever any claim of superiority or dependance asserted over them by that mother country from which they had migrated: and were such a claim made it is beleived[1] his majesty's subjects in Great Britain have too firm a feeling of the rights derived to them from their ancestors to bow down the sovereignty of their state before such visionary pretensions. And it is thought that no circumstance has occurred to distinguish materially the British from the Saxon emigration. America was conquered, and her settlements made and firmly established, at the expence of individuals, and not of the British public. Their own blood was spilt in acquiring lands for their settlement, their own fortunes expended in making that settlement effectual. For themselves they fought, for themselves they conquered, and for themselves alone they have right to hold. No shilling[2] was ever issued from the public treasures of his majesty or his ancestors for their assistance, till of very late times, after the colonies had become established on a firm and permanent footing. That then indeed, having become valuable to Great Britain for her commercial purposes, his parliament was pleased to lend them assistance against an enemy who would fain have drawn to herself the benefits of their commerce to the great aggrandisement of herself and danger of Great Britain. Such assistance, and in such circumstances, they had often before given to Portugal and[3] other allied states, with whom they carry on a commercial intercourse. Yet these states never supposed that, by calling in her aid, they thereby submitted themselves to her sovereignty. Had such terms been proposed, they would have rejected them with disdain, and trusted for better to the moderation of their enemies, or to a vigorous exertion of their own force. We do not however mean to underrate those aids, which to us were doubtless valuable, on whatever principles granted: but we would shew that they cannot give a title to that authority which the British parliament would arrogate over us; and that they may amply be repaid, by our giving to the inhabitants of Great Britain such exclusive privileges in trade as may be advantageous to them, and at the same time not too restrictive to ourselves. That settlements having been thus effected in the wilds of America, the emigrants thought proper to adopt that system of laws under which they had hitherto lived in the mother country, and to continue their union with her by submitting themselves to the same common sovereign, who was thereby made the central

link connecting the several parts of the empire thus newly multiplied.

But that not long were they permitted, however far they thought
themselves removed from the hand of oppression, to hold undisturbed the rights thus acquired at the hazard of their lives and loss
of their fortunes. A family of princes was then on the British
throne, whose treasonable crimes against their people brought on
them afterwards the exertion of those sacred and sovereign rights
of punishment, reserved in the hands of the people for cases of
extreme necessity, and judged by the constitution unsafe to be
delegated to any other judicature. While every day brought forth
some new and unjustifiable exertion of power over their subjects
on that side the water, it was not to be expected that those here,
much less able at that time to oppose the designs of despotism,
should be exempted from injury. Accordingly that country which _Division of_
had been acquired by the lives, the labors and the fortunes of in- _colonies._
dividual adventurers, was by these princes at several times parted
out⁴ and distributed among the favorites and *followers of their *1632. Mary-
fortunes; and by an assumed right of the crown alone were⁶ erected land was
into distinct and independent governments; a measure which it is Ld. Balti-
beleived his majesty's prudence and understanding would prevent more.
him from imitating at this day; as no exercise of such a power of 14. C. 2.
dividing and dismembering a country has ever occurred in his to Penn.
majesty's realm of England, tho' now of very antient standing; 15. C. 2.
nor could it be justified or acquiesced under there or in any other 1732. the
part of his majesty's empire. Jersey's⁵

That the exercise of a free trade with all parts of the world, pos- _Restrictions_
sessed by the American colonists as of natural right, and which _on our trade._
no law of their own had taken away or abridged, was next the
object of unjust incroachment. Some of the colonies having thought
proper to continue the administration of their government in the
name and under the authority of his majesty king Charles the first,
whom notwithstanding his late deposition by the Common-wealth
of England, they continued in the sovereignty of their state, the
Parliament for the Common-wealth took the same in high offence,
and assumed upon themselves the power of prohibiting their trade
with all other parts of the world except the island of Great Britain.
This arbitrary act however they soon recalled, and by solemn treaty
entered into on the 12th. day of March 1651, between the said
Commonwealth by their Commissioners and the colony of Virginia
by their house of Burgesses, it was expressly stipulated by the 8th.
article of the said treaty that they should have 'free trade as the

people of England do enjoy to all places and with all nations according to the laws of that Commonwealth.' But that, upon the restoration of his majesty King Charles the second, their rights of free commerce fell once more a victim to arbitrary power: and by several 12. C. 2. c. 18. acts of his reign as well as of some of his successors the trade of 14. C. 2. c. 11. the colonies was laid under such restrictions as shew what hopes 25. C. 2. c. 7. 7. 8. W. M. c. 22. they might form from the justice of a British parliament were its 11. W. uncontrouled power admitted over these states. History has in- 3. 4. Anne. formed us that bodies of men as well as individuals are susceptible 6. G. 2. c. 13. of the spirit of tyranny. A view of these acts of parliament for regulation, as it has been affectedly called, of the American trade, if all other evidence were removed out of the case, would undeniably evince the truth of this observation. Besides the duties they impose on our articles of export and import, they prohibit our going to any Markets Northward of cape Finesterra in the kingdom of Spain for the sale of commodities which Great Britain will not take from us, and for the purchase of others with which she cannot supply us; and that for no other than the arbitrary purpose of purchasing for themselves by a sacrifice of our rights and interests, certain privileges in their commerce with an allied state, who, in confidence that their exclusive trade with America will be continued while the principles and power of the British parliament be the same, have induldged themselves in every exorbitance which their avarice could dictate, or our necessities extort: have raised their commodities called for in America to the double and treble of what they sold for before such exclusive privileges were given them, and of what better commodities of the same kind would cost us elsewhere; and at the same time give us much less for what we carry thither, than might be had at more convenient ports. That these acts prohibit us from carrying in quest of other purchasers the surplus of our tobaccoes remaining after the consumption of Great Britain is supplied: so that we must leave them with the British merchant for whatever he will please to allow us, to be by him reshipped to foreign markets, where he will reap the benefits of making sale of them for full value. That to heighten still the idea of parliamentary justice, and to shew with what moderation they are like to exercise power, where themselves are to feel no part of it's weight, we take leave to mention to his majesty certain other acts of British parliament, by which they would prohibit us from manufacturing for our own use the articles we raise on our own lands with our own 5. G. 2. labor. By an act passed in the 5th. year of the reign of his late majesty king George the second an American subject is forbidden to make a hat for himself of the fur which he has taken perhaps on his own soil. An instance of despotism to which no parallel can be produced in the most arbitrary ages of British history. By one other act passed in the 23d. year of the same reign, the iron which we make we are forbidden to manufacture; and, heavy as that article is, and necessary in every branch of husbandry, besides commission and insurance, we are to pay freight for it to Great Britain, and freight for it back again, for the purpose of supporting, not men, but machines, in the island of Great Britain. In the same spirit of equal and impartial legislation is to be viewed the act of parliament passed in the 5th. year of the same reign, by which American lands are made subject to the demands of British creditors, while their own lands were still continued unanswerable for their debts; from which one of these conclusions must necessarily follow, either that justice is not the same thing in[8] America as in Britain, or else that the British parliament pay less regard to it here than there. But that we do not point out to his majesty the injustice of these acts with intent to rest on that principle the cause of their nullity, but to shew that experience confirms the propriety of those political principles which exempt us from the jurisdiction of the British parliament. The true ground on which we declare these acts void is that the British parliament has no right to exercise authority over us.

That these exercises of usurped power have not been confined to instances alone in which themselves were interested; but they have also intermeddled with the regulation of the internal affairs of the colonies. The act of the 9th. of Anne for establishing a post office in America seems to have had little connection with British convenience, except that of accomodating his majesty's ministers and favorites with the sale of a lucrative and easy office.

That thus have we hastened thro' the reigns which preceded his majesty's, during which the violation of our rights[9] were less alarming, because repeated at more distant intervals, than that rapid and bold succession of injuries which is likely to distinguish the present from all other periods of American story. Scarcely have our minds been able to emerge from the astonishment into which one stroke of parliamentary thunder has involved us, before another more heavy and more alarming is fallen on us. Single acts of tyranny may be ascribed to the accidental opinion of a day; but a series of oppressions, begun at a distinguished period, and pursued unalterably thro' every change of ministers, too plainly prove a deliberate, systematical[10] plan of reducing us to slavery.

23. G. 2. c. 29.

5. G. 2. c. 7.[7]

9. Anne.

Act for [levy]ing cert[ain] That the act passed in the 4th. year of his majesty's
duties. 4. G. 3. c. 15. reign intitled 'an act[11]

Stamp act. 5. G. 3. c. 12. one other act passed in the 5th. year of his reign intitled
'an act[12]

Act declaring the right of one other act passed in the 6th. year of his reign intitled
parliament over the 'an act[13]
colonies. 6. G. 3. c. 12.

Act for granting duties on and one other act passed in the 7th. year of his reign in-
paper, tea &c. 7. G. 3. titled 'an act[14]

form that connected chain of parliamentary usurpation which has
already been the subject of frequent applications to his majesty
and the houses of Lords and Commons of Great Britain; and, no
answers having yet been condescended to any of these, we shall
not trouble his majesty with a repetition of the matters they contained.

Act suspend- But that one other act passed in the same 7th. year of his reign,[15]
ing legisla- having been a peculiar attempt, must ever require peculiar men-
ture of New tion. It is intitled 'an act[16]
York.
7. G. 3. c. 59. One free and independent legislature hereby takes upon itself
to suspend the powers of another, free and independent as itself,
thus exhibiting a phaenomenon, unknown in nature, the creator
and creature of it's own power. Not only the principles of common sense, but the common[17] feelings of human nature must
be surrendered up, before his majesty's subjects here can be
persuaded to beleive that they hold[18] their political existence
at the will of a British parliament Shall these governments be
dissolved, their property annihilated, and their people reduced to
a state of nature, at the imperious breath of a body of men whom
they never saw, in whom they never confided, and over whom they
have no powers of punishment or removal, let their crimes against
the American public be ever so great? Can any one reason be assigned why 160,000 electors in the island of Great Britain should
give law to four millions in the states of America, every individual
of whom is equal to every individual of them in virtue, in understanding, and in bodily strength? Were this to be admitted, instead
of being a free people, as we have hitherto supposed, and mean to
continue, ourselves, we should suddenly be found the slaves, not
of one, but of 160,000 tyrants, distinguished too from all others
by this singular circumstance that they are removed from the reach
of fear, the only restraining motive which may hold the hand of
a tyrant.

14. G. 3. That by 'an act to discontinue in such manner and for such time

as are therein mentioned the landing and discharging lading or shipping of goods wares and merchandize at the town and within the harbor of Boston in the province of Massachusett's bay in North America' which was passed at the last session of British parliament, a large and populous town, whose trade was their sole subsistence, was deprived of that trade, and involved in utter ruin. Let us for a while suppose the question of right suspended, in order to examine this act on[19] principles of justice. An act of parliament had been passed imposing duties on teas to be paid in America, against which act the Americans had protested as inauthoritative. The East India company, who till that time had never sent a pound of tea to America on their own account, step forth on that occasion the asserters of parliamentary right, and send hither many ship loads of that obnoxious commodity. The masters of their several vessels however, on their arrival in America, wisely attended to admonition, and returned with their cargoes. In the province of New England[20] alone the remonstrances of the people were disregarded, and a compliance, after being many days waited for, was flatly refused. Whether in this the master of the vessel was governed by his obstinacy or his instructions, let those who know, say. There are extraordinary situations which require extraordinary interposition. An exasperated people, who feel that they possess power, are not easily restrained within limits strictly regular. A number of them assembled in the town of Boston, threw the tea into the ocean and dispersed without doing any other act of violence. If in this they did wrong, they were known, and were amenable to the laws of the land, against which it could not be objected that they had ever in any instance been obstructed or diverted from their regular course in favor of popular offenders. They should therefore not have been distrusted on this occasion. But that ill-fated colony had formerly been bold in their enmities against the house of Stuart, and were now devoted to ruin by that unseen hand which governs the momentous affairs of this great empire. On the partial representations of a few worthless ministerial dependants, whose constant office it has been to keep that government embroiled, and who by their treacheries hope to obtain the dignity of the British knighthood,[21] without calling for a party accused, without asking a proof, without attempting a distinction between the guilty and the innocent, the whole of that antient and wealthy town is in a moment reduced from opulence to beggary. Men who had spent their lives in extending the British commerce, who had invested in that place the wealth their honest endeavors had merited, found themselves and their families thrown at once on the world for subsistence by it's charities. Not the hundredth part of the inhabitants of that town had been concerned in the act complained of; many of them were in Great Britain and in other parts beyond sea; yet all were involved in one indiscriminate ruin, by a new executive power unheard of till then, that of a British parliament. A property of the value of many millions of money was sacrifised to revenge, not repay, the loss of a few thousands. This is administering justice with a heavy hand indeed! And when is this tempest to be arrested in it's course? Two wharfs are to be opened again when his majesty shall think proper: the residue which lined the extensive shores of the bay of Boston are forever interdicted the exercise of commerce. This little exception seems to have been thrown in for no other purpose[22] than that of setting a precedent for investing his majesty with legislative powers. If the pulse of his people shall beat calmly under this experiment, another and another will be tried till the measure of despotism be filled up. It would be an insult on common sense to pretend that this exception was made in order to restore it's commerce to that great town. The trade which cannot be received at two wharfs alone, must of necessity be transferred to some other place; to which it will soon[23] be followed by that of the two wharfs. Considered in this light it would be an insolent and cruel mockery at the annihilation of the town of Boston.

14. G. 3. By the act for the suppression of riots and tumults in the town of Boston, passed also in the last session of parliament, a murder committed there is, if the governor pleases, to be tried in the court of King's bench in the island of Great Britain, by a jury of Middlesex. The witnesses too, on receipt of such a sum as the Governor shall think it reasonable for them to expend, are to enter into recognisance to appear at the trial. This is in other words taxing them to the amount of their recognisance; and that amount may be whatever a Governor pleases. For who does his majesty think can be prevailed on to cross the Atlantick for the sole purpose of bearing evidence to a fact? His expences are to be borne indeed as they shall be estimated by a Governor; but who are to feed the wife and children whom he leaves behind, and who have had no other subsistence but his daily labor? Those epidemical disorders too, so terrible in a foreign climate, is the cure of them to be estimated among the articles of expence, and their danger to be warded off by the almighty power of a parliament? And the wretched criminal, if he happen to have offended on the American side, stripped of his

privilege of trial by peers, of his vicinage, removed from the place where alone full evidence could be obtained, without money, without counsel, without friends, without exculpatory proof, is tried before judges predetermined to condemn. The cowards who would suffer a countryman to be torn from the bowels of their society in order to be thus offered a sacrifice to parliamentary tyranny, would merit that everlasting infamy now fixed on the authors of the act! A clause for a similar purpose had been introduced into an act passed in the 12th. year of his majesty's reign entitled 'an act for the better securing and preserving his majesty's dock-yards, magazines, ships, ammunition and stores,' against which as meriting the same censures the several colonies have already protested.

12. G. 3. c. 24.

That these are the acts of power assumed by a body of men foreign to our constitutions, and unacknowleged by our laws; against which we do, on behalf of the inhabitants of British America, enter this our solemn and determined protest. And we do earnestly intreat his majesty, as yet the only mediatory power between the several states of the British empire, to recommend to his parliament of Great Britain the total revocation of these acts, which however nugatory they be, may yet prove the cause of further discontents and jealousies among us.

That we next proceed to consider the conduct of his majesty, as holding the executive powers of the laws of these states, and mark out his deviations from the line of duty. By the constitution of Great Britain as well as of the several American states, his majesty possesses the power of refusing to pass into a law any bill which has already passed the other two branches of legislature. His majesty however and his ancestors, conscious of the impropriety of opposing their single opinion to the united wisdom of two houses of parliament, while their proceedings were unbiassed by interested principles, for several ages past have modestly declined the exercise of this power in that part of his empire called Great Britain. But by change of circumstances, other principles than those of justice simply have obtained an influence on their determinations. The addition of new states to the British empire has produced an addition of new, and sometimes opposite interests. It is now therefore the great office of his majesty to resume the exercise of his negative power, and to prevent the passage of laws by any one legislature of the empire which might bear injuriously on the rights and interests of another. Yet this will not excuse the wanton exercise of this power which we have seen his majesty practice on the laws of the American legislatures. For the most

Refusing assent to laws for trifling reasons.

trifling reasons, and sometimes for no conceivable reason at all, his majesty has rejected laws of the most salutary tendency. The abolition of domestic slavery is the great object of desire in those colonies where it was unhappily introduced in their infant state. But previous to the infranchisement of the slaves we have, it is necessary to exclude all further importations from Africa. Yet our repeated attempts to effect this by prohibitions, and by imposing duties which might amount to a prohibition, have been hitherto defeated by his majesty's negative: thus preferring the immediate advantages of a few British corsairs[24] to the lasting interests of the American states, and to the rights of human nature deeply wounded by this infamous practice. Nay the single interposition of an interested individual against a law was scarcely ever known to fail of success, tho' in the opposite scale were placed the interests of a whole country. That this is so shameful an abuse of a power trusted with his majesty for other purposes, as if not reformed would call for some legal restrictions.

Delaying the consideration of our laws. With equal inattention to the necessities of his people here, has his majesty permitted our laws to lie neglected in England for years, neither confirming them by his assent, nor annulling them by his negative: so that such of them as have no suspending clause, we hold on the most precarious of all tenures, his majesty's will, and such of them as suspend themselves till his majesty's assent be obtained we have feared might be called into existence at some future and distant period, when time and change of circumstances shall have rendered them destructive to his people here. And to *Requiring suspending clause to almost every act.* render this grievance still more oppressive, his majesty by his instructions has laid his governors under such restrictions that they can pass no law of any moment unless it have such suspending clause: so that, however immediate may be the call for legislative interposition, the law cannot be executed till it has twice crossed the Atlantic, by which time the evil may have spent it's whole force.

Endeavoring to take from the people the right of representation. But in what terms reconcileable to majesty and at the same time to truth, shall we speak of a late instruction to his majesty's[25] governor of the colony of Virginia, by which he is forbidden to assent to any law for the division of a county, unless the new county will consent to have no representative in assembly? That colony has as yet affixed[26] no boundary to the Westward. Their Western counties therefore are of indefinite extent. Some of them are actually seated many hundred miles from their Eastern limits. Is it possible then that his majesty can have bestowed a single thought on the situation of those people, who, in order to obtain justice for injuries however great or small, must, by the laws of that colony, attend their county court at such a distance, with all their witnesses, monthly, till their litigation be determined? Or does his majesty seriously wish, and publish it to the world, that his subjects should give up the glorious right of representation, with all the benefits derived from that, and submit themselves the absolute slaves of his sovereign will? Or is it rather meant to confine the legislative body to their present numbers, that they may be the cheaper bargain whenever they shall become worth a purchase?

One of the articles of impeachment against Tresilian and the other judges of Westminster Hall in the reign of Richard the second, for which they suffered death as traitors to their country, was that they had advised the king that he might dissolve his parliament at any time: and succeeding kings have adopted the opinion of these unjust judges. Since the establishment[27] however of the British constitution[28] at the glorious* Revolution on it's free and antient principles, neither his majesty nor his ancestors have exercised such a power of dissolution in the island of Great Britain; and when his majesty was petitioned by the united voice of his people there to dissolve the present parliament, who had become obnoxious to[30] them, his ministers were heard to declare in open parliament that his majesty possessed no such power by the constitution.[31] But how different their language and his practice here! To declare as their duty required the known rights of their country, to oppose the usurpation[32] of every foreign judicature, to disregard the imperious mandates of a minister or governor, have been the avowed causes of dissolving houses of representatives in America. But if such powers be really vested in his majesty, can he suppose they are there placed to awe the members from such purposes as these? When the representative body have lost the confidence of their constituents, when they have notoriously made sale of their most valuable rights, when they have assumed to themselves powers which the people never put into their hands, then indeed their continuing in office becomes dangerous to the state, and calls for an exercise of the power of dissolution. Such being the causes for which the representative body should and should not be dissolved, will it not appear strange to an unbiassed observer that that of Great Britain was not dissolved, while those of the colonies have repeatedly incurred that sentence?

But your majesty or your Governors have carried this power beyond every limit known or provided for by the laws. After dissolving one house of representatives, they have refused to call

Dissolution of representative bodies for doing their duty.

*On further enquiry I find two instances of dissolutions before the parl. would of itself have been at an end, viz. the parl. called to meet Aug. 24. 1698. was dissolved by K. Wm. Dec. 19. 1700. & a new one called to meet Feb. 6. 1701. which was also dissolved Nov. 11. 1701. & a new one met Dec. 30. 1701.[29]

Delaying to issue writs for choice of new representatives.

another, so that for a great length of time the legislature provided by the laws has been out of existence. From the nature of things, every society must at all times possess within itself the sovereign powers of legislation. The feelings of human nature revolt against the supposition of a state so situated as that it may not in any emergency provide against dangers which perhaps threaten immediate ruin. While those bodies are in existence to whom the people have delegated the powers of legislation, they alone possess and may exercise those powers. But when they are dissolved by the lopping off one or more of their branches, the power reverts to the people, who may use it[33] to unlimited extent, either assembling together in person, sending deputies, or in any other way they may think proper.[34] We forbear to trace consequences further; the dangers are conspicuous with which this practice is replete.

Undertaking to grant lands on advanced terms. That we shall at this time also take notice of an error in the nature of our landholdings, which crept in at a very early period of our settlement. The introduction of the Feudal tenures into the kingdom of England, though antient, is well enough understood to set this matter in a proper light. In the earlier ages of the Saxon settlement feudal holdings were certainly altogether unknown, and very few, if any, had been introduced at the time of the Norman conquest. Our Saxon ancestors held their lands, as they did their personal property, in absolute dominion, disencumbered with any superior, answering nearly to the nature of those possessions which the Feudalists term Allodial: William the Norman first introduced that system generally. The lands which had belonged to those who fell in the battle of Hastings, and in the subsequent insurrections of his reign, formed a considerable proportion of the lands of the whole kingdom. These he granted out, subject to feudal duties, as did he also those of a great number of his new subjects, who by persuasions or threats were induced to surrender them for that purpose. But still much was left in the hands of his Saxon subjects, held of no superior, and not subject to feudal conditions. These therefore by express laws, enacted to render uniform the system of military defence, were made liable to the same military duties as if they had been feuds: and the Norman lawyers soon found means to saddle them also with all the other feudal burthens. But still they had not been surrendered to the king, they were not derived from his grant, and therefore they were not holden of him. A general principle indeed was introduced that 'all lands in England were held either mediately or immediately of the crown': but this was borrowed from those holdings which were truly feudal, and only applied to others for the purposes of illustration. Feudal holdings were therefore but exceptions out of the Saxon laws of possession, under which all lands were held in absolute right. These therefore still form the basis or groundwork of the Common law, to prevail wheresoever the exceptions have not taken place. America was not conquered by William the Norman, nor it's lands surrendered to him or any of his successors. Possessions there are undoubtedly of the Allodial nature. Our ancestors however, who migrated hither, were laborers,[35] not lawyers. The fictitious principle that all lands belong originally to the king, they were early persuaded to beleive real, and accordingly took grants of their own lands from the crown. And while the crown continued to grant for small sums and on reasonable rents, there was no inducement to arrest the error and lay it open to public view. But his majesty has lately taken on him to advance the terms of purchase and of holding to the double of what they were, by which means the acquisition of lands being rendered difficult, the population of our country is likely to be checked. It is time therefore for us to lay this matter before his majesty, and to declare that he has no right to grant lands of himself. From the nature and purpose of civil institutions, all the lands within the limits which any particular society has circumscribed around itself, are assumed by that society, and subject to their allotment only. This may be done by themselves assembled collectively, or by their legislature to whom they may have delegated sovereign authority: and, if they are allotted in neither of these ways, each individual of the society may appropriate to himself such lands as he finds vacant, and occupancy will give him title.

That, in order to inforce the arbitrary measures before complained of, his majesty has from time to time sent among us large bodies of armed forces, not made up of the people here, nor raised by the authority of our laws. Did his majesty possess such a right as this, it might swallow up all our other rights whenever he should think proper. But his majesty has no right to land a single armed man on our shores; and those whom he sends here are liable to our laws for[36] the suppression and punishment of Riots, Routs, and unlawful assemblies, or are hostile bodies invading us in defiance of law. When in the course of the late war it became expedient that a body of Hanoverian troops should be brought over for the defence of Great Britain, his majesty's grandfather, our late sovereign, did not pretend to introduce them under any authority he possessed. Such a measure would have given just alarm to his subjects in

Sending armed troops among us.

Great Britain, whose liberties would not be safe if armed men of another country, and of another spirit, might be brought into the realm at any time without the consent of their legislature. He therefore applied to parliament who passed an act for that purpose, limiting the number to be brought in and the time they were to continue. In like manner is his majesty restrained in every part of the empire. He possesses indeed the executive power of the laws in every state; but they are the laws of the particular state which he is to administer within that state, and not those of any one within the limits of another. Every state must judge for itself the number of armed men which they may safely trust among them, of whom they are to consist, and under what restrictions they are to be laid.[37] To render these proceedings still more criminal against our laws, instead of subjecting the military to the civil power,[38] his majesty has expressly made the civil subordinate to the military. But can his majesty thus put down all law under his feet? Can he erect a power superior to that which erected himself? He has done it indeed by force; but let him remember that force cannot give right.

Making military superior to civil power.

That these are our grievances which we have thus laid before his majesty with that freedom of language and sentiment which becomes a free people, claiming their rights as derived from the laws of nature, and not as the gift of their chief magistrate. Let those flatter, who fear: it is not an American art. To give praise where it is not due,[39] might be well from the venal, but would ill beseem those who are asserting the rights of human nature. They know, and will therefore say, that kings are the servants, not the proprietors of the people. Open your breast Sire, to liberal and expanded thought. Let not the name of George the third be a blot in the page of history. You are surrounded by British counsellors, but remember that they are parties. You have no ministers for American affairs, because you have none taken from among us, nor amenable to the laws on which they are to give you advice. It behoves you therefore to think and to act for yourself and your people. The great principles of right and wrong are legible to every reader: to pursue them requires not the aid of many counsellors. The whole art of government consists in the art of being honest. Only aim to do your duty, and mankind will give you credit where you fail. No longer persevere in sacrificing the rights of one part of the empire to the inordinate desires of another: but deal out to all equal and impartial right. Let no act be passed by any one legislature which may infringe on the rights and liberties of another. This is the important post in which fortune has placed you,

(2)

A
SUMMARY VIEW
OF THE
RIGHTS
OF
BRITISH AMERICA.
SET FORTH IN SOME
RESOLUTIONS
INTENDED FOR THE
INSPECTION
OF THE PRESENT
DELEGATES
OF THE
PEOPLE OF VIRGINIA.
NOW IN
CONVENTION.

By a NATIVE, and MEMBER of the
HOUSE of BURGESSES.

by Thomas Jefferson.

WILLIAMSBURG:
PRINTED BY CLEMENTINA RIND.

Titlepage of Jefferson's copy of *A Summary View
of the Rights of British America.*

"The Alternative of Williams-Burg." A British comment
on the colonial Associations of 1774.

holding the balance of a great, if a well poised empire. This, Sire, is the advice of your great American council, on the observance of which may perhaps depend your felicity and future fame, and the preservation of that harmony which alone can continue both to Great Britain and America the reciprocal advantages of their connection. It is neither our wish nor our interest to separate from her. We are willing on our part to sacrifice every thing which reason can ask to the restoration of that tranquility for which all must wish. On their part let them be ready to establish union on a generous plan.[40] Let them name their terms, but let them be just. Accept of every commercial preference it is in our power to give for such things as we can raise for their use, or they make for ours. But let them not think to exclude us from going to other markets, to dispose of those commodities which they cannot use, nor[41] to supply those wants which they cannot supply. Still less let it be proposed that our properties within our own territories shall be taxed or regulated by any power on earth but our own. The god who gave us life, gave us liberty at the same time: the hand of force may destroy, but cannot disjoin them. This, Sire, is our last, our determined resolution: and that you will be pleased to interpose with that efficacy which your earnest endeavors may insure to procure redress of these our great grievances, to quiet the minds of your subjects in British America against any apprehensions of future incroachment, to establish fraternal love and harmony thro' the whole empire, and that that[42] may continue to the latest ages of time, is the fervent prayer of all British America.

MS in hand of Anderson Bryan, with additions and corrections by TJ (DLC).

This draft of resolutions to be presented to the Virginia Convention of Aug. 1774, and intended by TJ to serve as instructions for the guidance of the Virginia delegates to the first Continental Congress in preparing an address to the King, is best known to the world as *A Summary View of the Rights of British America*—the title given this paper by TJ's friends who printed it without his knowledge when he, because of illness, could not attend the Convention. The MS from which the present text is derived is a copy of a missing earlier draft, and contains both less and more than the pamphlet edited by members of the Convention: for example, some of the marginal glosses are merely outlined in the MS though completed in the pamphlet, and some glosses appear in the MS that are not in the pamphlet. A few revisions were evidently also made in the MS after the two copies (see Appendix I) were sent off by TJ to Peyton Randolph and Patrick Henry. Appendix I in the present volume gathers in one place the available data on the transmission, publication, and consequences of this notable paper. In the textual notes below are recorded all variations between the MS (designated as such), the Williamsburg pamphlet (designated as "A"), and TJ's own corrected copy of the Williamsburg pamphlet (now in the Library of Congress and designated as "B"). However, it is to be assumed that those marginal glosses printed here in *italic type* appear only in the MS, and that differences in spelling, punctuation, and capitalization are disregarded.

[1] A: "believed that."
[2] A: "Not a shilling." B was altered

by TJ to read "No shilling" as in MS.

3 In B the words "Portugal, and" were deleted by TJ.

4 B was altered by TJ to read: "parcelled out."

5 In A this note reads as follows: "1632 Maryland was granted to lord Baltimore, 14. c. 2. [*an error; see TJ's correction in B, below*] Pennsylvania to Penn, and the province of Carolina was in the year 1663 granted by letters patent of majesty, king Charles II. in the 15th year of his reign, in propriety, unto the right honourable Edward earl of Clarendon, George duke of Albemarle, William earl of Craven, John lord Berkeley, Anthony lord Ashley, sir George Carteret, sir John Coleton, knight and boronet, and sir William Berkley, knight; by which letters patent the laws of England were to be in force in Carolina: But the lords proprietors had power, *with the consent of the inhabitants*, to make bye-laws for the better government of the said province; so that no money could be received, or law made, without the consent of the inhabitants, or their representatives." In B this footnote was rewritten to read: "In 1621. Nova Scotia was granted by James I. to Sir Wm. Alexander. In 1632. Maryland was granted by Charles I. to Lord Baltimore. In 1664. New York was granted by Charles II. to D. of York: so also was New Jersey, which the D. of York conveied again to Ld. Berkeley & Sr. Geo. Carteret. So also were the Delaware counties, which the same Duke conveied again to Wm. Penn. In 1665. the country including North & South Carolina, Georgia & the Floridas was granted by Charles II. to the E. of Clarendon, D. of Albemarle, E. of Craven, Ld. Berkeley, Ld. Ashley, Sr. George Carteret, Sr. John Coleton, & Sr. Wm. Berkely. In 1681. Pennsylvania was granted by Charles II. to Wm. Penn."

6 B was altered to read: "alone, was erected."

7 A reads, quite erroneously: "5. G. .27c."

8 A: "not the same in."

9 A: "violations of our right."

10 A: "deliberate and systematical." Note that the phraseology of this sentence closely parallels the text of the Declaration of Independence as phrased in the Rough Draft, which reads: "But when a long train of abuses & usurpations, begun at a distinguished period, & pursuing invariably the same object,

evinces a design to subject them to arbitrary power," &c.

11 A gives the full title of the Act: "An act for granting certain duties in the British colonies and plantations in America, &c."

12 A gives full title: "An act for granting and applying certain stamp duties and other duties in the British colonies and plantations in America, &c."

13 A gives full title: "An act for the better securing the dependency of his majesty's dominions in America upon the crown and parliament of Great Britain."

14 A gives full title: "An act for granting duties on paper, tea, &c."

15 A: "of the reign." B was corrected by TJ to agree with MS.

16 A gives the full title: "An act for suspending the legislature of New York."

17 B was altered by TJ to read: "but the feelings of human nature."

18 B, strangely, was altered to read: "that they withhold their political existence," thus changing the meaning or at least confusing the pronouns. Perhaps TJ intended to make a further change in the sentence but omitted doing so.

19 MS repeats the word "on."

20 B was altered by TJ to read: "province of Massachusetts alone."

21 In B, TJ added the following note at this point: "alluding to the knighting of Sir Francis Bernard."

22 In the MS the word "purpose" is interlined in TJ's hand.

23 In the MS the word "soon" is interlined in TJ's hand.

24 In the MS a word appears to have been erased here and "British" written over it. A reads: "a few African corsairs," but TJ altered B to read: "British corsairs" as in the MS. The apparent erasure in the MS may indicate that the copyist originally wrote, perhaps by force of habit, "African corsairs" and that this was the form used in the two copies sent to Randolph and Henry.

25 B was altered to read: "to the majesty's," &c.

26 A: "has as yet fixed no boundary."

27 B was altered to read: "since the reign of the second William."

28 B was altered to read: "however under which the British constitution."

29 This note is in TJ's hand and appears only in the MS.

30 In the MS the word "to" is interlined in TJ's hand.

³¹ In B, TJ added this note: "Since this period the King has several times dissolved the parliament a few weeks before its expiration, merely as an assertion of right."

³² A: "usurpations."

³³ A: "exercise it."

³⁴ In B, TJ added the following thinly veiled threat: "and the frame of government thus dissolved, should the people take upon them to lay the throne of your majesty prostrate, or to discontinue their connection with the British empire, none will be so bold as to decide against the right or the efficacy of such avulsion."

³⁵ In the MS this was originally written "farmers," then apparently erased and "laborers" superimposed. In B "farmers" was deleted by TJ and "laborers" inserted. These changes seem to indicate clearly that they were made after the two copies were sent to the Convention.

³⁶ A: "made for."

³⁷ A: "they shall be laid."

³⁸ A: "powers."

³⁹ A: "which is not due."

⁴⁰ A: "union and a generous plan." B was altered to agree with MS.

⁴¹ A: "or."

⁴² A: "that these."

Resolutions and Association of the Virginia Convention of 1774

[1-6 August 1774]

At a very full Meeting of DELEGATES *from the different Counties in the Colony and Dominion of Virginia, begun in Williamsburg the first Day of August, in the Year of our Lord 1774, and continued by several Adjournments to Saturday the 6th of the same Month, the following* ASSOCIATION *was unanimously resolved upon and agreed to.*

WE his Majesty's dutiful and loyal Subjects, the Delegates of the Freeholders of VIRGINIA, deputed to represent them at a general Meeting in the City of Williamsburg, avowing our inviolable and unshaken Fidelity and Attachment to our most gracious Sovereign, our Regard and Affection for all our Friends and Fellow Subjects in Great Britain and elsewhere, protesting against every Act or Thing which may have the most distant Tendency to interrupt, or in any Wise disturb, his Majesty's Peace, and the good Order of Government within this his ancient Colony, which we are resolved to maintain and defend at the Risk of our Lives and Fortunes; but, at the same Time, affected with the deepest Anxiety, and most alarming Apprehensions, of those Grievances and Distresses by which his Majesty's American Subjects are oppressed; and having taken under our most serious Deliberation the State of the whole Continent; find, that the present unhappy Situation of our Affairs is chiefly occasioned by certain ill advised Regulations, as well of our Trade as internal Polity, introduced by several unconstitutional Acts of the British Parliament, and, at length, attempted to be enforced by the Hand of Power. Solely influenced by these important and weighty Considerations, we think it an indispensable Duty which we owe to our Country, ourselves, and latest Posterity, to guard against such dangerous and extensive Mischiefs, by every just and proper Means.

If, by the Measures adopted, some unhappy Consequences and Inconveniencies should be derived to our Fellow Subjects, whom we wish not to injure in the smallest Degree, we hope, and flatter ourselves, that they will impute them to their real Cause, the hard Necessity to which we are driven.

That the good People of this Colony may, on so trying an Occasion, continue stedfastly directed to their most essential Interests, in Hopes that they will be influenced and stimulated by our Example to the greatest Industry, the strictest Economy and Frugality, and the Exertion of every publick Virtue; persuaded that the Merchants, Manufacturers, and other Inhabitants of Great Britain, and, above all, that the British Parliament will be convinced how much the true Interest of that Kingdom must depend on the Restoration and Continuance of that mutual Friendship and Cordiality which so happily subsisted between us; we have, unanimously, and with one Voice, entered into the following Resolutions and Association, which we do oblige ourselves, by those sacred Ties of Honour and Love to our Country, strictly to observe: And farther declare, before God and the World, that we will religiously adhere to and keep the same inviolate in every Particular, until Redress of all such American Grievances as may be defined and settled at the General Congress of Delegates from the different Colonies shall be fully obtained, or until this Association shall be abrogated or altered by a general Meeting of the Deputies of this Colony, to be convened as is herein after directed. And we do, with the greatest Earnestness, recommend this our Association to all Gentlemen, Merchants, Traders, and other Inhabitants of this Colony, hoping that they will cheerfully and cordially accede thereto.

1st. We do hereby resolve and declare, that we will not, either directly or indirectly, after the 1st Day of November next, import from Great Britain any Goods, Wares, or Merchandises whatever, Medicines excepted; nor will we, after that Day, import any British Manufactures, either from the West Indies or any other Place, nor any Article whatever which we shall know, or have Reason to believe, was brought into such Countries from Great Britain; nor will we purchase any such Articles so imported of any Person or Persons whatsoever, except such as are now in the Country, or such as may arrive on or before the said 1st Day of November, in Consequence of Orders already given, and which cannot now be countermanded in Time.

2dly. We will neither ourselves import, nor purchase, any Slave, or Slaves, imported by any Person, after the 1st Day of November next, either from Africa, the West Indies, or any other Place.

3dly. Considering the Article of Tea as the detestable Instrument which laid the Foundation of the present Sufferings of our distressed Friends in the Town of Boston; we view it with Horrour; and therefore resolve, that we will not, from this Day, either import Tea of any Kind whatever, nor will we use, or suffer even such of it as is now on Hand to be used, in any of our Families.

4thly. If the Inhabitants of the Town of Boston, or any other Colony, should, by Violence or dire Necessity, be compelled to pay the East India Company for destroying any Tea, which they have lately by their

Agents unjustly attempted to force into the Colonies, we will not, directly or indirectly, import or purchase any British East India Commodity whatever, till the Company, or some other Person on their Behalf, shall refund and fully restore to the Owners all such Sum or Sums of Money as may be so extorted.

5thly. We do resolve, that unless American Grievances are redressed before the 10th Day of August, 1775, we will not, after that Day, directly or indirectly, export Tobacco, or any other Article whatever, to Great Britain; nor will we sell any such Articles as we think can be exported to Great Britain with a Prospect of Gain to any Person or Persons whatever, with a Design of putting it into his or their Power to export the same to Great Britain, either on our own, his, or their, Account. And that this Resolution may be the more effectually carried into Execution, we do hereby recommend it to the Inhabitants of this Colony to refrain from the Cultivation of Tobacco, as much as conveniently may be; and, in Lieu thereof, that they will, as we resolve to do, apply their Attention and Industry to the Cultivation of all such Articles as may form a proper Basis for Manufactures of all Sorts, which we will endeavour to encourage throughout this Colony to the utmost of our Abilities.

6thly. We will endeavour to improve our Breed of Sheep, and increase their Number to the utmost Extent, and to this End we will be as sparing as we conveniently can in killing of Sheep, especially those of the most profitable Kind; and if we should at any Time be overstocked, or can conveniently spare any, we will dispose of them to our Neighbours, especially the poorer Sort of People, upon moderate Terms.

7thly. Resolved, that the Merchants, and other Venders of Goods and Merchandises within this Colony, ought not to take Advantage of the Scarcity of Goods that may be occasioned by this Association, but that they ought to sell the same at the Rates they have been accustomed to for twelve Months last past; and if they shall sell any such Goods on higher Terms, or shall in any Manner, or by any Device whatever, violate or depart from this Resolution, we will not, and are of Opinion that no Inhabitant of this Colony ought, at any Time thereafter, to deal with any such Persons, their Factors or Agents, for any Commodity whatever. And it is recommended to the Deputies of the several Counties, that Committees be chosen in each County, by such Persons as accede to this Association, to take effectual Care that these Resolves be properly observed, and for corresponding occasionally with the general Committee of Correspondence in the City of Williamsburg. Provided, that if Exchange should rise, such Advance may be made in the Prices of Goods as shall be approved by the Committee of each County.

8thly. In Order the better to distinguish such worthy Merchants and Traders who are Well-wishers to this Colony, from those who may attempt, through Motives of Self-Interest, to obstruct our Views, we do hereby resolve, that we will not, after the first Day of November next, deal with any Merchant or Trader who will not sign this Association, nor until he hath obtained a Certificate of his having done so from the County Committee, or any three Members thereof. And if any Merchant, Trader, or other Person, shall import any Goods or Merchandise after the said first Day of November, contrary to this Association, we give it as our Opinion that such Goods and Merchandise should be either forthwith re-shipped or delivered up to the County Committee, to be stored at the Risk of the Importer, unless such Importer shall give a proper Assurance to the said Committee that such Goods or Merchandises shall not be sold within this Colony during the Continuance of this Association; and if such Importer shall refuse to comply with one or the other of these Terms, upon Application and due Caution given to him, or her, by the said Committee, or any three Members thereof, such Committee is required to publish the Truth of the Case in the Gazettes, and in the County where he or she resides, and we will thereafter consider such Person or Persons as inimical to this Country, and break off every Connection and all Dealings with them.

9thly. Resolved, that if any Person or Persons shall export Tobacco, or any other Commodity, to Great Britain, after the 10th Day of August 1775, contrary to this Association, we shall hold ourselves obliged to consider such Person or Persons as inimical to the Community, *and as an Approver of American Grievances*; and give it as our Opinion, that the Publick should be advertised of his Conduct, as in the 8th Article is desired.

10thly. Being fully persuaded that the united Wisdom of the General Congress may improve these our Endeavours to preserve the Rights and Liberties in British America, we decline enlarging at present; but do hereby resolve, that we will conform to, and strictly observe, all such Alterations or Additions, assented to by the Delegates for this Colony, as they may judge it necessary to adopt, after the same shall be published and made known to us.

11thly. Resolved, that we think ourselves called upon, by every Principle of Humanity and brotherly Affection, to extend the utmost and speediest Relief to our distressed Fellow Subjects in the Town of Boston; and therefore most earnestly recommend it to all the Inhabitants of this Colony to make such liberal Contributions as they can afford, to be collected and remitted to Boston in such Manner as may best answer so desirable a Purpose.

12thly. and lastly. Resolved, that the Moderator of this Meeting, and, in Case of his Death, ROBERT CARTER NICHOLAS, Esquire, be empowered, on any future Occasion, that may in his Opinion require it, to convene the several Delegates of this Colony, at such Time and Place as he may judge proper; and, in Case of the Death or Absence of any Delegate, it is recommended that another be chosen in his Place.

Text from Purdie and Dixon's *Virginia Gazette*, 11 Aug. 1774.

This paper, which was the Virginia Association proper as agreed upon by the Convention, was presumably separately printed for circulation in the colony, but no copy has been recorded or located. The evidence for its separate publication is an entry of 6 Aug. 1774 in Washington's "Ledger B," cited by Fitzpatrick in his edition of Washington's *Diaries*, II, 159, note 5, reading as follows: "By the Printers for the Association Papers 12s." Furthermore, TJ seems to refer to this document in saying that he had received a copy of the "new association" about 11 Aug. (letter to Cary and Harrison, 9 Dec. 1774). It

is possible, however, that both Washington and TJ referred to the Convention's
Instructions to the Virginia Delegates
(the following document). The terms of
the official Association should be compared with those in the draft probably
prepared by TJ for the same purpose,
assigned to 26 July 1774, above.

Instructions by the Virginia Convention to Their Delegates in Congress, 1774

[1-6] Aug. 1774

Instructions for the DEPUTIES *appointed to meet in* GENERAL CON-
GRESS *on the Part of this Colony.*

THE unhappy Disputes between Great Britain and her American
Colonies, which began about the third Year of the Reign of his
present Majesty, and since, continually increasing, have proceeded to
Lengths so dangerous and alarming as to excite just Apprehensions in
the Minds of his Majesty's faithful Subjects of this Colony that they are
in Danger of being deprived of their natural, ancient, constitutional, and
chartered Rights, have compelled them to take the same into their most
serious Consideration; and, being deprived of their usual and accustomed Mode of making known their Grievances, have appointed us
their Representatives to consider what is proper to be done in this
dangerous Crisis of American Affairs. It being our Opinion that the
united Wisdom of North America should be collected in a General
Congress of all the Colonies, we have appointed the Honourable PEYTON
RANDOLPH, Esquire, RICHARD HENRY LEE, GEORGE WASHINGTON,
PATRICK HENRY, RICHARD BLAND, BENJAMIN HARRISON, and ED-
MUND PENDLETON, Esquires, Deputies to represent this Colony in the
said Congress, to be held at Philadelphia on the first Monday in September next.

And that they may be the better informed of our Sentiments touching
the Conduct we wish them to observe on this important Occasion, we
desire that they will express, in the first Place, our Faith and true Allegiance to his Majesty King George the Third, our lawful and rightful
Sovereign; and that we are determined, with our Lives and Fortunes,
to support him in the legal Exercise of all his just Rights and Prerogatives. And however misrepresented, we sincerely approve of a constitutional Connexion with Great Britain, and wish most ardently a Return
of that Intercourse of Affection and commercial Connexion that formerly
united both Countries, which can only be effected by a Removal of those
Causes of Discontent which have of late unhappily divided us.

It cannot admit of a Doubt but that British Subjects in America are
entitled to the same Rights and Privileges as their Fellow Subjects
possess in Britain; and therefore, that the Power assumed by the British
Parliament to bind America by their Statutes, in all Cases whatsoever,
is unconstitutional, and the Source of these unhappy Differences.

The End of Government would be defeated by the British Parliament exercising a Power over the Lives, the Property, and the Liberty of the American Subject; who are not, and, from their local Circumstances, cannot, be there represented. Of this Nature we consider the several Acts of Parliament for raising a Revenue in America, for extending the Jurisdiction of the Courts of Admiralty, for seizing American Subjects and transporting them to Britain to be tried for Crimes committed in America, and the several late oppressive Acts respecting the Town of Boston and Province of the Massachusetts Bay.

The original Constitution of the American Colonies possessing their Assemblies with the sole Right of directing their internal Polity, it is absolutely destructive of the End of their Institution that their Legislatures should be suspended, or prevented, by hasty Dissolutions, from exercising their legislative Powers.

Wanting the Protection of Britain, we have long acquiesced in their Acts of Navigation restrictive of our Commerce, which we consider as an ample Recompense for such Protection; but as those Acts derive their Efficacy from that Foundation alone, we have Reason to expect they will be restrained so as to produce the reasonable Purposes of Britain, and not injurious to us.

To obtain Redress of these Grievances, without which the People of America can neither be safe, free, nor happy, they are willing to undergo the great Inconvenience that will be derived to them from stopping all Imports whatsoever from Great Britain after the first Day of November next, and also to cease exporting any Commodity whatsoever to the same Place after the tenth Day of August 1775. The earnest Desire we have to make as quick and full Payment as possible of our Debts to Great Britain, and to avoid the heavy Injury that would arise to this Country from an earlier Adoption of the Non-exportation Plan, after the People have already applied so much of their Labour to the perfecting of the present Crop, by which Means they have been prevented from pursuing other Methods of clothing and supporting their Families, have rendered it necessary to restrain you in this Article of Non-exportation; but it is our Desire that you cordially co-operate with our Sister Colonies in General Congress in such other just and proper Methods as they, or the Majority, shall deem necessary for the Accomplishment of these valuable Ends.

The Proclamation issued by General Gage, in the Government of the Province of the Massachusetts Bay, declaring it Treason for the Inhabitants of that Province to assemble themselves to consider of their Grievances and form Associations for their common Conduct on the Occasion, and requiring the Civil Magistrates and Officers to apprehend all such Persons to be tried for their supposed Offences, is the most alarming Process that ever appeared in a British Government; that the said General Gage hath thereby assumed and taken upon himself Powers denied by the Constitution to our legal Sovereign; that he, not having condescended to disclose by what Authority he exercises such extensive and unheard of Powers, we are at a Loss to determine whether he intends to justify himself as the Representative of the King or as the Commander in Chief of his Majesty's Forces in America. If he considers himself as acting in the Character of his Majesty's Representative, we would remind him that the Statute 25th Edward III. has expressed and defined all treasonable Offences, and that the Legislature of Great Britain hath declared that no Offence shall be construed to be Treason but such as is pointed out by that Statute, and that this was done to take out of the Hands of tyrannical Kings, and of weak and wicked Ministers, that deadly Weapon which constructive Treason had furnished them with, and which had drawn the Blood of the best and honestest Men in the Kingdom; and that the King of Great Britain hath no Right by his Proclamation to subject his People to Imprisonment, Pains, and Penalties.

That if the said General Gage conceives he is empowered to act in this Manner, as the Commander in Chief of his Majesty's Forces in America, this odious and illegal Proclamation must be considered as a plain and full Declaration that this despotick Viceroy will be bound by no Law, nor regard the constitutional Rights of his Majesty's Subjects, whenever they interfere with the Plan he has formed for oppressing the good People of the Massachusetts Bay; and therefore, that the executing, or attempting to execute, such Proclamation, will justify Resistance and Reprisal.

OBSERVATIONS BY JEFFERSON ON THE FOREGOING

Defects in the association.

—We are permitted to buy any goods imported before Nov. 1. 1774.

+We are not allowed to import the implements of manufacturing, nor books.

—We may still import wines, Coffee &c. tho' dutied articles.

—We are allowed to continue commerce with the other parts of the British empire, tho' they should refuse to join us.

* The American grievances are not defined.

* We are to conform to such resolutions only of the Congress as our deputies assent to: which totally destroys that union of conduct in the several colonies which was the very purpose of calling a Congress.

Upon the whole we may truly say

We have left undone those things which we ought to have done. And we have done those things which we ought not to have done.

Printed document (DLC). The date ("Aug. 1774") at the head and the list of "Defects in the association" at the end are added in TJ's hand. Sabin, No. 100008, locates three copies, not including that found in TJ's own papers, and corrects the entries for this document in Evans and Clayton-Torrence.

These are the "instructions very temperately and properly expressed, both as to style and matter" (as TJ described them in his Autobiography), substituted by the Convention for his own proposed Instructions subsequently printed as *A Summary View*. TJ's criticisms of the Instructions (erroneously supposed by Ford, I, 448, to apply to the Continental Association of 20 Oct. 1774) should be considered in the light of, first, his philosophical justification of colonial resistance as set forth in *A Summary View*; second, the more stringent nonimportation and nonexportation provisions of the Albemarle Resolutions and the draft Declaration of Rights, printed under the date 26 July 1774, above; and, finally, the explicit subordination, in the two TJ documents just mentioned, of Virginia's interests to those of the colonies generally as represented in the coming Congress. As things worked out, a preponderance of attention was given in the Instructions to THE PROCLAMATION ISSUED BY GENERAL GAGE at Salem, Mass., on 29 June 1774, ordering the arrest of persons circulating the "Solemn League and Covenant" (i.e., the Massachusetts Association) as an "unlawful instrument"; Gage's Proclamation is printed in Force, *Archives*, 4th ser., I, 491-2.

From Ebenezer Hazard, with Jefferson's MS Memoranda

SIR   NEW-YORK, August 23, 1774.

As the Collection, mentioned in the Proposals annexed, is a Matter of Importance to the Colonies in general, and may answer valuable Purposes, I flatter myself you will think it not unworthy of your Patronage;—and therefore take the Liberty of soliciting your kind Assistance by favouring me with the Use of such suitable Papers, relating to your Colony, as it may be convenient for you to procure.

SIR, Your most obedient, And very humble Servant,

EBEN. HAZARD

WHEN the Conduct of Individuals in a Community is such as to attract public Attention, others are very naturally led to many Inquiries about them; so when civil States rise into Importance, even their earliest History becomes the object of Speculation. From a Principle of Curiosity, many who have but little, or no Connection with the British Colonies in America, are now prying into the Story of their rise and progress, while others wish for a farther Acquaintance with them, from better, though perhaps more interested Motives. The Means of obtaining this Information are not accessible by every Person, and if they were, are so scattered, that more Time would be necessary for collecting them, than would be requisite for reading them after they were collected.

To remove this Obstruction from the path of Science, and at the same Time to lay the Foundation of a good American History, by preserving from oblivion valuable Materials for that Purpose,

IT IS PROPOSED

To form a complete Collection of what may be with Propriety stiled,

AMERICAN STATE PAPERS.

This Collection will begin with the Grant from *Henry* 7th, to *John Cabot*, and his Sons for making Discoveries; and will include every important public Paper (such as Royal Grants, Charters, Acts of Parliament, &c. &c.) relating to America, of which either the original, or authentic Copies can be procured, down to the present Time. The History of the STAMP-ACT, and other Acts of the British Parliament for raising a Revenue among us by internal Taxation;—Resolves of the American Assemblies;—Votes of Town Meetings;—and such political Pamphlets and other fugitive Pieces as are properly connected with the general Design, and are worthy of Preservation, will also be included; and to the Whole will be added an INTRODUCTION, containing an Account of the Constitution of the different British American Colonies, and a very copious INDEX.

It is supposed that the Whole may be comprised in five Volumes Octavo, and that the Price of each Volume, well bound and lettered, will not exceed One Dollar and an Half.

The Compilation is already begun, and shall be sent to the Press as soon as it can be got ready, and a sufficient Number of Subscribers can be procured. Every Person must see that this Undertaking is attended with many and great Difficulties; and that the Compiler needs, what the Work if well executed will merit, the friendly Assistance of others. He therefore solicits the public Patronage; and as the Work will not only serve to gratify the Curiosity of the inquisitive, but be eminently useful in much more important Points of View, he begs that Gentlemen who are possessed of proper Materials for the Purpose, will be kind enough to favour him with the Use of them, and they shall be carefully returned.——They will be safely forwarded to him, if deposited in the Hands of either of the following Gentlemen, who will also take in Subscriptions, viz.

Peter Timothy, Charles Town, — South-Carolina.
William Davis, Printer, Newbern, — North-Carolina.
John Dixon, Post-Master, in — Williamsburg.
Catherine Green, and Son, — Annapolis.
William and Thomas Bradford, } John Sparhawk, — in Philadelphia.
Noel and Hazard, } John Holt, — in New-York.
James Lockwood, Bookseller, New-Haven; E. Watson, Printer, Hartford; Timothy Green, Printer, New-London; Robertson and Trumbull, Norwich, } Connecticut.
John Carter, Printer, Providence; Solomon Southwick, Newport, } Rhode-Island.
Isaiah Thomas, Edes and Gill, Boston; Samuel Hall, Printer, Salem, } Massachusetts-Bay.
Daniel Fowle, Printer, Portsmouth, — New-Hampshire.

SUBSCRIBERS FOR THE BOOK[1]

John Walker	Philip Mazzei	Jerman Baker.
George Gilmer	Thos. Jefferson	Chesterfield
John Harvie	Charles Bellini	Thos. Fleming.
Thos. Millar	Wm. Fleming	Cumberland
(Cumberld.)	Cumd.	Thomas M. Randolph

Rolfe Eldridge	Henry Skipwith	Jas. Jones
Benj. Harrison	James P. Cocke	Thos. Nelson, jr.
Brand.[*Brandon*]	Edm: Randolph	Chas. Lewis

LIST OF PAPERS FOR HAZARD'S
PROPOSED COLLECTION[2]

1650	'A declaration of Lord Willoughby governor of Barbadoes and of his council against an act of parliament of 3d Octob. 1650.' [The act had forbidden commerce with the Barbadoes Virginia, Bermudas, & Antigua.][3] 4th. vol. Polit. Regist. pa. 2. cited from 4th. vol. Neale's hist. of the Puritans, Appendix No. 12.
1769. May. 17.	the petn. of H. B. of Virga. to k.
1772. Apr. 12.	do. see 3d. Salmon's Modern hist. the substance of the Grant of Virginia to Sr. Walter Raleigh
	Treaty of Aix la Chapelle
1713. Apr. 28.	Treaty of Utrecht
	Treaty of Paris
	Capitulation at the taking Quebec.
1763. Oct.	the King's proclamn. confirming the same.
1764. Dec. 18.	the petn. of Council and H. B. of Virga. to k.
	Grants to Ld. Fairfx
1764. Dec. 18.	Memorial of Council & H. B. to Lds.
	Remonstrance of H. B. to Commons.
	Treaties with Indians.
	Deeds of purchase of Indians
1765. Oct. 7.	Proceedings of the Congress held at New York
1765. May. 29.	Resolns. of the house of burgesses of Virga.
1765. Oct. 1.	Representn. of the Lds. Commissnrs. for trade & plantns. touching proceedgs. of Representves. Mass. bay
1765. Sep. 21.	Resolns. of Assembly of Pennsylva.
1768. Jan. 20.	Petn. of the Representves. of Mass. bay to King.
1768. Apr. 8.	the petn., memorial & remonstr. of Council & H. B. Virga.
[1607] Mar. 9.	4 Jac. 1. an ordinance & Constitn. enlarging the Council of the 2. colonies in Virga. & America and augmenting their authority. M.S. No. 1.
[1624] Sep. 18	22. Jac. 1. a Commn. to Sr. Fr. Wyatt to be governor & to Fras. West & others to be the council of Virga. M.S.
[1634] June 19	10. Car. 1. a Commn. concerning tobacco. M.S.
[1682] Nov. 27	34 Car. 2. a Commn. to Thos. Ld. Culpepper to be Lieutt. & Govr. Genl. of Virga. M.S.
[1674] Feb. 25	25. Car. 2 a demise of the colony of Virga. to the Earl of Arlington & Ld. Culpeper for 31 years M.S.
[1683] Sep. 28.	35. Car. 2 a Commn. to Ld. Howard of Effingham to be Lieutt. & Govr. Genl. of Virga. M.S.

1606. Apr. 10.	Jac. 1. a grant to Sr. Thos. Gates & others of Virga.
1609 May. 23.	Jac. 1. a charter.
1611/12 Mar. 12	Jac. 1. a charter
1617.	Jac. [1] a commn. to Sr. Walter Ralegh
1621. July. 24.	An ordinance & constitution of the Treasurer council & company in England for a council of state & General Assembly. Stith.
1634.	A Commn. to the Archbp. of Cant. & 11 others for governing the American colonies.
1651. Mar. 17.	A Treaty
1621.	Jac. 1. a grant of Nova Scotia to Sr. Wm. Alexander.
1632.	Car. 1. a grant of Maryld. to Ld. Baltimore.
1664. Mar. 12.	Car. 2 a grant of New York to the D. of York a grant of New Jersey to do. a Conveiance of New Jersey by D. of York to Ld. Berkley & Sr. Geo. Carteret. a grant of Delaware counties to D. of Y. a conveiance of Delaware counties to Wm. Penn
1665.	Car. 2. a grant of the country including N. & S. Caroln. Georga. & the Floridas to the E. of Clarendon & al.
1681 Mar. 4.	Car. 2. a grant of Pennsylva. to Wm. Penn.
1620. Nov. 3.	a grant of New England to the Council of Plymouth.
1627. Mar. 19.	a grant of Massachusets bay by the Council of Plymouth to Sr. Henry Roswell & others
1628. Mar. 4.	Car. 1. a confirmn. of the grant of Mass. bay
1630.	Car. 1. a grant of Connecticut by Council of Plymouth to the E. of Warwick.
1630.	Car. 1. a confirmn. of the same [sd. to be in the petty bag office in Engld.][3]
1631. Mar. 19.	a conveiance of Connecticut by the E. of Warwick to Ld. Say & Seal & others. Smith's Examn. of the [Connecticut Claim.]
1643	Articles of Union & Confederacy entd. into by Massachusets, Plymouth, Connecticut & New Haven. 1 Neale
1650	a final settlemt. of boundaries the Dutch New Netherlands & Connecticut.
1662. Apr. 23.	Charter of the Colony of Conn. Sm's examn. App. 6.
1635. July. 18.	A Commn. from Ld. Say & Seal & others to John Winthrop to be governor of Connecticut. Smith vo. 2
1644.	Deed from George Fenwick to old Conn. jurisdiction.
1661.	Petn. of the Gen. Ct. at Hartford upon Connecticut for a charter. Smith's examn. &c. App. 4
1635.	Car. 1. a grant to Duke Hamilton.
1664. Apr. 26.	Car. 2. a commn. to Colo. Nicholas & others to

	settle disputes in N. England. Hutch's hist. Mass. bay. App. pa. 537
1664. Dec. 1.	determn. of sd. Commrs. of boundary betw. D. of York & Conn. Sm's. Exmn. App. 9.
[ ]⁴	a Confirmn. of that boundary by the crown
1633. July 3.	a petn. of the planters of Virga. agt. the grant to Ld. Baltimore
1623.	a grant to Sr. Edmond Ployden of New Albion. mentd. Smith's examn. 82.
1732.	Deed of Release by govmt. of Conn. to Govmt. of N.Y.
1664.	New Haven case. Sm's. exmn. App. 20.
1688 [abt]³	papers relating to taking away appeals to H. Burg. of Virga.
1674 (or thereabouts.)	Beverley [. . . re]monstrances agt. Charles 2 [. . .] Southern Virga. sent to England by Ludwell which thou[gh . . .] kept dormant till now.⁵
1651/2 Mar. 12.	The treaty betw. the h. of bu[. . . .]⁶
1763.	The k's proclamn. against settling on any lands on the waters westward of the Alleghany.⁷
1680.	Public papers on the Separation of Co[. . . .]⁸ Removal of App [. . . .]⁹
1765. May 29.	The Resolns. of H. B. and [. . . re]monstrances & Memorials to K. L. & [. . .] time except the Petn. Meml. [. . .] the Petn. of 1769. May. 17. & the Petn. [. . . .]¹⁰

Printed document (DLC). Hazard's letter is signed in autograph. Addressed: "To Thomas Jefferson Esqr. Virginia." The list of subscribers appears below Hazard's letter, and TJ's rough list of colonial records appears on blank portions of three different pages of the four-page leaflet.

The pioneer efforts of Ebenezer Hazard (1744-1817), of New York and Philadelphia, in collecting the archival records of the United States resulted in a two-volume compilation entitled *Historical Collections; Consisting of State Papers . . . Intended as Materials for an History of the United States*, Philadelphia, 1792-1794. Though officially supported by the Continental Congress, the work suffered a long interruption from Hazard's appointment in 1782 as postmaster general, and after the publication of two volumes (containing documents through the year 1664) it was dropped for want of patronage (DAB; JCC, XI, 682, 705-6; Hazard's Preface to vol. I). As one who had a lifelong interest in American history and in the preservation of historical records, TJ responded cordially; see TJ to Hazard, 30 Apr. 1775, and also 18 Feb. 1791; and for a documented discussion of TJ's important collection of Virginia archival records, acquired not long after he compiled this list, see Kingsbury, *Records of the Virginia Company of London*, I, 41-54. TJ's list of papers to be brought to Hazard's attention is actually a set of rough notes of which a portion, without much doubt, is now missing. That he later copied the list in more finished form is evident from his having numbered the items chronologically and then run a line from top to bottom through the entire list. No fair copy has been found, though many of the same entries appear in a list appended to the answer to Query XXIII in *Notes on Virginia* (Ford, III, 283-95). No attempt has been made to annotate the documents listed, but the principal printed collections consulted by TJ should be given fuller titles. They were: Daniel Neal, *The History of the Puritans or Protestant Non-Conformists, from the Reformation to the Death of Queen Elizabeth*, London, 1732, 4 vol.; William Stith, *The*

History of the First Discovery and Settlement of Virginia, Williamsburg, 1747; William Smith, *An Examination of the Connecticut Claim to Lands in Pennsylvania*, Philadelphia, 1774; Thomas Hutchinson, *The History of the Colony of Massachusets-Bay* [1628-1691], Boston, 1764 (completed in 3 vol., 1828); and [Robert Beverley] *The History and Present State of Virginia*, London, 1705. PETTY BAG: "An office formerly belonging to the Common Law jurisdiction of the Court of Chancery, for suits for and against solicitors of that court" (OED).

1 The first six names are in TJ's hand; the others are autograph signatures.

2 Caption supplied. TJ ran a line from top to bottom through the entire list after he had copied it. To facilitate his copying the items in chronological order, he numbered each item in the left-hand margin, but many of the numbers having faded or disappeared in the margin, they are all omitted in the present text. In a few cases where portions of the text are missing, they have been supplied from the list in *Notes on Virginia*. When the year is missing from a date, it has been supplied by the editors, but TJ's other omissions are not filled in.

3 Brackets in MS.

4 Illegible date.

5 In the *Notes on Virginia* list, the entry corresponding to this paragraph reads: "Remonstrance against the two grants of Charles II. of Northern and Southern Virginia. Mentd. Beverley 65."

6 Undetermined number of words missing. The articles for the surrender of Virginia to the Commonwealth of England at this time were printed in full from a MS, in *Notes on Virginia*, q.v. (Ford, III, 218-19).

7 The last several words, missing in the MS, are supplied from the list in *Notes on Virginia*.

8 Undetermined number of words missing. Presumably the entry refers to the "Extracts of proceedings of the committee of trade and plantations; copies of letters, reports, &c." pertaining to the settlement of the Pennsylvania-New York boundary, 1680-1681, entered in the *Notes on Virginia* list under date of 14 June 1680.

9 Undetermined number of words missing.

10 Undetermined number of words missing in the gaps. The Resolutions of 29 May 1765 were those offered by Patrick Henry at the time of his celebrated speech against the Stamp Act; see JHB, 1761-1765, p. lxiv-lxv, and TJ's Autobiography (Ford, I, 6).

Continental Association of 20 October 1774

The ASSOCIATION *entered into by the* AMERICAN [CONTI]NENTAL CONGRESS *in Behalf of all the Colo[nies]*

WE his Majesty's most dutiful and loyal Subjects, the Delegates of the several Colonies of New Hampshire, Massachusetts Bay, Rhode Island, Connecticut, New York, New Jersey, Pennsylvania, the Three Lower Counties of Newcastle, Kent, and Sussex, on Delaware, Maryland, Virginia, North Carolina, and South Carolina, deputed to represent them in a Continental Congress, held in the City of Philadelphia on the 5th Day of September 1774, avowing our Allegiance to his Majesty, our Affection and Regard for our Fellow Subjects in Great Britain and elsewhere, affected with the deepest Anxiety, and most alarming Apprehensions at those Grievances and Distresses with which his Majesty's American Subjects are oppressed, and having taken under our most serious Deliberation the State of the whole Continent, find that the present unhappy Situation of our Affairs is occasioned by a ruinous System of Colony Administration, adopted by the British Ministry about the Year 1763, evidently calculated for enslaving these Colonies, and, with them, the British Empire: In Prosecution of which System, various Acts of Parliament have been passed for raising a Revenue in America, for depriving the American Subjects, in many Instances, of the constitutional Trial by Jury, exposing their Lives to Danger, by directing a new and illegal Trial beyond the Seas, for Crimes alledged to have been committed in America; and, in Prosecution of the same System, several late, cruel, and oppressive Acts, have been passed respecting the Town of Boston and the Massachusetts Bay, and also an Act for extending the Province of Quebeck, so as to border on the western Frontiers of these Colonies, establishing an arbitrary Government therein, and discouraging the Settlement of British Subjects in that wide-extended Country; thus, by the Influence of civil Principles, and ancient Prejudices, to dispose the Inhabitants to act with Hostility against the free Protestant Colonies, whenever a wicked Ministry shall choose so to direct them.

To obtain Redress of these Grievances, which threaten Destruction to the Lives, Liberty, and Property, of his Majesty's Subjects in North America, we are of Opinion that a Non-importation, Non-consumption, and Non-exportation Agreement, faithfully adhered to, will prove the most speedy, effectual, and peaceable Measure; and therefore we do, for ourselves and the Inhabitants of the several Colonies whom we represent, firmly agree and associate, under the sacred Ties of Virtue, Honour, and Love of our Country, as follows:

First. That from and after the first Day of December next we will not import into British America, from Great Britain or Ireland, any Goods, Wares, or Merchandise whatsoever, or from any other Place, any such Goods, Wares, or Merchandise, as shall have been exported from Great Britain or Ireland; nor will we, after that Day, import any East India Tea from any Part of the World, nor any Molosses, Syrups, Paneles, Coffee, or Pimenta, from the British Plantations, or from Dominica, nor Wines from Madeira, or the Western Islands, nor foreign Indigo.

Second. That we will neither import nor purchase any Slave imported after the first Day of December next, after which Time we will wholly discontinue the Slave Trade, and will neither be concerned in it ourselves, nor will we hire our Vessels, nor sell our Commodities or Manufactures, to those who are concerned in it.

Third. As a Non-consumption Agreement, strictly adhered to, will be an effectual Security for the Observation of the Non-importation, we, as above, solemnly agree and associate, that, from this Day, we will not purchase or use any Tea imported on Account of the East India Company, or any on which a Duty hath been or shall be paid; and, from and after the first Day of March next, we will not purchase or use any East India Tea whatever: Nor will we, nor shall any Person for or under us, purchase or use any of those Goods, Wares, or Merchandise, we have agreed not to import, which we shall know, or have Cause to suspect, were imported after the first Day of December, except such as come under the Rules and Directions of the tenth Article, hereafter mentioned.

Fourth. The earnest Desire we have not to injure our Fellow Subjects in Great Britain, Ireland, or the West Indies, induces us to suspend a Non-exportation until the tenth Day of September 1775; at which Time, if the said Acts, and Parts of Acts of the British Parliament herein after mentioned, are not repealed, we will not, directly or indirectly, export any Merchandise, or Commodity whatsoever, to Great Britain, Ireland, or the West Indies, except Rice, to Europe.

Fifth. Such as are Merchants, and use the British and Irish Trade, will give Orders, as soon as possible, to their Factors, Agents, and Correspondents, in Great Britain and Ireland, not to ship any Goods to them, on any Pretence whatsoever, as they cannot be received in America; and if any Merchant residing in Great Britain or Ireland shall, directly or indirectly, ship any Goods, Wares, or Merchandise, for America, in Order to break the said Non-importation Agreement, or in any Manner contravene the same, on such unworthy Conduct being well attested, it ought to be made publick; and, on the same being so done, we will not, from thenceforth, have any commercial Connexion with such Merchant.

Sixth. That such as are Ow[ners] of Vessels will give positive Orders to their Captains, or Masters, n[ot to] receive on Board their Vessels any Goods prohibited by the said Non-importation Agreement, on Pain of immediate Dismission from their Service.

Seventh. We will use our utmost Endeavours to improve the Breed of Sheep, and increase their Number to the greatest Extent; and to that End we will kill them as sparingly as may be, especially those of the most profitable Kind: Nor will we export any to the West Indies, or elsewhere. And those of us who are or may become overstocked with, or can conveniently spare any Sheep, will dispose of them to our Neighbours, especially to the poorer Sort, on moderate Terms.

Eighth. That we will, in our several Stations, encourage Frugality Economy, and Industry; and promote Agriculture, Arts, and the Manufactures of this Country, especially that of Wool; and will discountenance and discourage every Species of Extravagance and Dissipation, especially all Horse-racing, and all Kinds of Gaming, Cock-fighting, Exhibitions of Shows, Plays, and other expensive Diversions and Entertainments; and on the Death of any Relation, or Friend, none of us, or any of our Families, will go into any farther Mourning Dress than a black Crape or Riband on the Arm or Hat for Gentlemen, and a black Riband and Necklace for Ladies, and we will discontinue the giving of Gloves and Scarfs at Funerals.

Ninth. That such as are Venders of Goods or Merchandise will not take Advantage of the Scarcity of Goods that may be occasioned by this Associacion, but will sell the same at the Rates we have been respectively accustomed to do for twelve Months last past; and if any Venders of Goods or Merchandise shall sell any such Goods on higher Terms, or shall in any Manner, or by any Device whatsoever, violate or depart from this Agreement, no Person ought, nor will any of us deal with any such Person, or his or her Factor or Agent, at any Time thereafter, for any Commodity whatever.

Tenth. In Case any Merchant, Trader, or other Persons, shall import any Goods or Merchandise after the first Day of December, and before the first Day of February next, the same ought forthwith, at the Election of the Owner, to be either reshipped or delivered up to the Committee of the County or Town wherein they shall be imported, to be stored at the Risk of the Importer, until the Non-importation Agreement shall cease, or be sold under the Direction of the Committee aforesaid: And, in the last mentioned Case, the Owne[r or owners of such goods shall be reim]bursed (out of the Sales) the [first cost and charges, the profit, if any,] to be applied towards relievi[ng and employing such poor inhabitants of] the Town of Boston as are im[mediate sufferers by the Boston Port Bill,] and a particular Account of all [goods so returned, stored, or sold, to be] inserted in the publick Papers. A[nd if any goods or merchandizes shall be] imported after the said first Day [of February the same ought forthwith] to be sent back again, without br[eaking any of the packages thereof.]

Eleventh. That a Committee b[e chosen in every County, City, and] Town, by those who are qualifi[ed to vote for representatives in the] Legislature, whose Business it shall [be attentively to observe the conduct] of all Persons touching this Assoc[iation; and when it shall be made to] appear, to the Satisfaction of a Maj[ority of any such Committee that any] Person within the Limits of their Ap[pointment has violated this associa]tion, that such Majority do forthwith [cause the truth of the case to be] published in the Gazette, to the End [that all such foes to the rights of] British America may be publickly known [and universally contemned as] the Enemies of American Liberty; and th[ence forth we respectively will] break off all Dealings with him, or her.

Twelfth. That the Committee of Corre[spondence, in the respective] Colonies do frequently inspect the Entries [of their Custom Houses, and] inform each other, from Time to Time, of t[he true state thereof and of] every other material Circumstance that ma[y occur relative to this asso]ciation.

Thirteenth. That all Manufactures of [this country be sold at reason]able Prices, so that no undue Advantage [be taken of a future scarcity of] Goods.

Fourteenth. And we do farther agr[ee and resolve, that we will have] no Trade, Commerce, Dealings, o[r intercourse whatsoever, with any] Colony or Province in North Ame[rica, which shall not accede to, or] which shall hereafter violate, thi[s association, but will hold them as] unworthy of the Rights of Free[men, and as inimical to the liberties of] their Country.

And we do solemnly bind [ourselves and our Constituents under the] Ties aforesaid, to adhere to th[is Association until such parts of the several] Acts of Parliament, passed sin[ce the Close of the last War as impose or] continue Duties on Tea, Wine, [Molosses, Syrups, paneles], Coffee, Sugar, Pimenta, Indigo, foreign Pap[er, glass] and Painters Colours, imported into America, and extend the Powers of the Admiralty Courts beyond their ancient Limits, deprive the American Subject of

Trial by Jury, authorise the Judge's Certificate to indemnify the Prosecutor from Damages that he might otherwise be liable to from a Trial by his Peers, require oppressive Security from a Claimant of Ships or Goods seized before he shall be allowed to defend his Property, are repealed; and until that Part of the Act of the 12th of George III. Chapter 24th, entitled "An Act for the better securing his Majesty's Dockyards, Magazines, Ships, Ammunition, and Stores," by which any Persons charged with committing any of the Offences therein described in America may be tried in any Shire or County within the Realm, is repealed; and until the four Acts passed in the last Session of Parliament, viz. that for stopping the Port and blocking up the Harbour of Boston, that for altering the Charter and Government of Massachusetts Bay; and that which is entitled "An Act for the better Administration of Justice, &c." and that "For extending the Limits of Quebeck, &c." are repealed. And we recommend it to the Provincial Conventions, and to the Committees in the respective Colonies, to establish such farther Regulations as they may think proper, for carrying into Execution this Association.

The foregoing Association being determined upon by the Congress, was ordered to be subscribed by the several Members thereof; and thereupon, we have hereunto set our respective Names accordingly.

IN CONGRESS, PHILADELPHIA, OCTOBER 20, 1774.

Signed, PEYTON RANDOLPH, *President.*

John Sullivan,
Nathaniel Folsom,
} of New Hampshire.

Thomas Cushing,
Samuel Adams,
John Adams,
Robert Treat Paine,
} of Massachusetts Bay.

Stephen Hopkins,
Samuel Ward,
} of Rhode Island

Eliphalet Dyer,
Roger Sherman,
Silas Deane,
} of Connecticutt.

Isaac Low,
John Alsop,
John Jay,
James Duane,
William Floyd,
Henry Weisner,
S. Boerum,
} of New York.

James Kinsey,
William Livingston,
Stephen Crane,
Richard Smith,
} of New Jersey.

Joseph Galloway,
John Dickinson,
Charles Humphreys,
Thomas Mifflin,
Edward Biddle,
John Morton,
George Ross,
} of Pennsylvania.

Caesar Rodney,
Thomas M'Kean,
George Read,
} of Newcastle, &c.

Matthew Tilghman,
Thomas Johnson,
William Paca,
Samuel Chase,
} of Maryland.

Richard Henry Lee,
George Washington,
Patrick Henry,
JUNIOR,
Richard Bland,
Benjamin Harrison,
Edmund Pendleton,
} of Virginia.

William Hooper,			Henry Middleton,		
Joseph Hewes,	of North		Thomas Lynch,		
R. Caswell,	Carolina.		Christopher Gadsden,	of South	
			John Rutledge,	Carolina.	
			Edward Rutledge,		

Th: Jefferson
Randolph Jefferson
Val: Wood

Francis Alberte
A. Bryan[1]
Francis Eppes

Broadside (DLC), with six written signatures at end. This single-page printing of the Association appears to be unrecorded and was presumably a Williamsburg imprint. For other pamphlet and broadside printings, see Evans 13703-5, and JCC, I, 127-8, Nos. 2-6. A large fragment of text has been torn away from TJ's copy; the missing matter has here been supplied from the facsimile of the original Association (DLC: PCC) in the pocket at the back of JCC, I. For the circumstances under which the Continental Association was prepared and adopted, see JCC, I, 53, 57, 62-3, 74-81; Burnett, *Continental Congress*, ch. III. Burnett (p. 55) points out that "Both the name and the form ap-pear to have been derived from the Virginia Association of August 1774" (printed above under 1-6 Aug. 1774). It appears from news items in the *Virginia Gazette* that meetings were held in the various counties during November and December, at which the Continental Association was read and approved, and local committees were elected to enforce observance of it (*Va. Gaz.* [Pinkney], 1 Dec., 22 Dec. 1774). See, further, TJ to Cary and Harrison, 9 Dec. 1774.

[1] From other evidence this name is known to be that of Anderson Bryan, but the fanciful form in which the first name or initials are written cannot be deciphered.

To Archibald Cary and Benjamin Harrison

[DEA]R SIR   Monticello Dec. 9. 1774.

As I mean to be a conscientious observer of the measures generally thought requisite for the preservation of our independent rights, so I think myself bound to account to my country for any act of mine which might wear an appearance of contravening them. I therefore take the liberty of stating to you the following matter that thro' your friendly intervention it may be communicated to the committee of your county.

You may remember it was about the last of May that the house of Burgesses after it's dissolution met in the Raleigh and formed our first Association against the future use of *tea only*. Tho' the proceedings of the ministry against the town of Boston were then well known to us, I believe nobody thought at that time of extending our Association further to the total interruption of our commerce with Britain: or if it was proposed by any (which I do not recollect) it was condemned by the general sense of the members who formed that Association. Two or three days therefore after this

I wrote to Cary & co. of London for 14. pair of sash windows to be sent me ready made and glazed with a small parcel of spare glass to mend with. This letter went by a ship which sailed about the third of June just before Capt. Power arrived here, and I did not suppose they would send them till Power should come in again in the spring of 1775. About the middle of June, as nearly as I can recollect, a few of the late members were again convened (in consequence of fresh advices from Boston) and then it was suggested a more extensive Association might be necessary. A Convention met for that purpose the first of August and formed a new Association of which I received a copy about the 11th. of the month: but as a General Congress was appointed to be held within four weeks of that time to reconsider the same matters, and it was agreed that our Association should be subject to any alterations that might recommend I did not write to countermand my order, thinking I should have sufficient time, after the final determinations of the congress should be known, to countermand it before Power should sail in the spring. Accordingly within a few days after receiving a copy of the General association I wrote to Cary & co. not to send the sashes, glass &c. which I had ordered and gave my letter to the care of a gentleman (Mr. Evans) just then going downwards who promised to send it out speedily. But three or four days after I received a letter from those gentlemen dated Aug. 29, in which they inform me my window frames and glass are ready, but that, it being necessary to detain them about a month to harden the puttying, they were not sent by that, but might be expected by the first ship afterwards. From this I conclude they may be near arriving at this time, in which case they will come under the 1st. and 10th. articles of the association. In order therefore that no proceedings of mine might give a handle for traducing our measures I thought it better previously to lay before your committee (within whose ward they will probably be landed) a full state of the matter by which it might be seen under what expectations I had failed to give an earlier countermand and to shew that as they come within the prohibitions of the Continental Association (which without the spirit of prophecy could not have been foretold when I ordered them) so I mean they shall be subject to it's condemnation. To your committee therefore if landed within their county I submit the disposal of them, which shall be obeyed as soon as made known to their and your most humble servt.,   TH: JEFFERSON

2d Dft (DLC); 1st Dft (DLC). The first draft has been docketed: "Dec. 9. 1774. A copy of this sent by Mr. Mazzei to Col. A. Cary & another to Col. B.

Harrison." The first draft contains numerous false starts and interlineations, but, as corrected, its text is virtually identical with the second draft, which is a retained fair copy.

Archibald Cary and Benjamin Harrison (ca. 1726-1791), of Berkeley, were both members of the Virginia committee of correspondence and represented counties on the James (Chesterfield and Charles City, respectively) where the sash might have been landed. THE 1ST AND 10TH ARTICLES OF ... THE CONTINENTAL ASSOCIATION, issued by the Congress at Philadelphia on 20 Oct. 1774 and printed above under that date, prohibited importation of all goods from Great Britain, and provided that goods arriving between 1 Dec. 1774 and 1 Feb. 1775 were, at the election of the owner, to be reshipped, delivered over to the committee of the town or county where landed and held until the Association ceased, or sold for the benefit of the Bostonians suffering under the Port Act (JCC, I, 75-81). TJ's recollection of the date of the meeting of A FEW OF THE LATE MEMBERS who summoned the convention was surprisingly far off; this had occurred on 31 May (see under that date), and TJ had presumably attended that meeting. It is not in accord with either his character or his known views on the subject of an embargo for him to have tried to deceive anyone on this point, and he could not have hoped to deceive two members of the committee of correspondence. He had clearly planned and hoped to receive the window sash for Monticello before stringent measures were adopted. His two letters to CARY & CO. are unfortunately missing.

Plan of Philip Mazzei's Agricultural Company

[1774]

PROPOSALS for forming a Company or Partnership, for the Purpose of raising and making Wine, Oil, agruminous Plants and Silk

1. So much money as may be procured, shall be subscribed in shares of fifty Pounds Sterling each, and in all Proceedings of the Company a Vote shall be allowed for every share; the Subscribers of smaller sums than fifty Pounds, being at liberty to associate in shares, and appoint any one of their Number to vote for such share.

2. Such shares shall not be subject to the Rights of Survivorship; and if any Proprietor shall at any time be disposed to sell out his Part, the Company shall have the Refusal of it, giving for the same, as much as any other person will give: but none to be at liberty to withdraw their Part, until the thirty first day of December 1784.

3. The Monies subscribed shall be paid by the Subscribers, at the City of Williamsburg, to Philip Mazzei Esquire, or any other person to be appointed, as hereafter directed, or in their absence to Robert Carter Nicholas Esquire, in manner following; that is to say, one fourth part shall be paid on or before the first day of November 1774, and one other fourth part at the end of every six Months after, 'til the whole be paid, which Payments shall be made, either in Sterling, or in other money, at the rate of Exchange then

current: and where any Subscribers shall come in after one or more Payments shall have been made, they shall make present Payment of such Proportion of their subscription, as the former Subscribers shall have already paid, and shall pay the residue at the same Times it is payable by the said former Subscribers: and if at any time it shall happen, that any payment shall be one Month in arrear, and unpaid, such Subscriber, so in arrear, shall forfeit his former Payments, and all Interest in the said Partnership, which shall thereon become vested in the residue of the Partners.

4. The said Philip Mazzei is to invest or employ the Monies to be received, as he shall think best for the Purposes aforesaid, and to superintend the said Business, as Factor for the said Company, for which he is to draw from the Proffits, or principal Money paid, five per centum per annum, on the capital sum subscribed, besides being at liberty to use for his Table or Houshold, such necessaries, as may be raised on the Lands of the Company.

5. That any Lands, or other Possessions of the said Philip Mazzei, which he may at this time have, and which are proper for the purposes of the said Partnership, after being valued by three men indifferently chosen by the said Philip Mazzei, and any five of the Partners, shall be taken at such valuation as part of the said Philip Mazzei's subscription, and together with the Lands, Slaves, Servants, Utensils and other things to be purchased with the monies of the Company, shall become vested in the Subscribers, their Heirs, Executors, Administrators, or assigns, in proportion to the several sums they shall have subscribed.

6. That the expences of carrying on the said Business be defrayed out of the Monies subscribed, so that there be no future calls on the Partners, for any other sums of money.

7. That the said Philip Mazzei shall on the last day of December in every year, during the Partnership, make up an Account of all his Buyings, Sellings, Receipts and disbursements whatsoever, made on account of the said Partnership, of which Accounts a Copy shall be lodged in the Hands of Robert Carter Nicholas Esqr. for the free perusal of the Parties interested.

8. That a standing Committee shall be appointed to consist of his Excellency Earl Dunmore, the Honble. John Page of Rosewell Esqr. the Honble. Peyton Randolph Esqr., Robert C. Nicholas, Thomas Nelson Junr., John Blair, Wilson Miles Cary and James McClurg Esqrs. any three of whom may proceed to business. Whose Business it shall be from time to time to give advice to the said Philip Mazzei, or other Factor for the time being, on all mat-

ters, relating to the Affairs of the Company, and, whenever they shall think requisite, to call a meeting of the Subscribers, fifteen of whom, possessing or representing not less than fifteen whole shares, may proceed to Business: and such meeting may if a Majority concur in Opinion have power to fill up any Vacancies, which may happen in the standing Committee, to regulate the Salary of the Factor for the time being, to appoint such other person, as they shall think proper, to be Factor, in case of the death, or removal of the said Philip Mazzei, to appoint any other person to be Holder of the Monies belonging to the Company, and to make Dividends of the annual Proffits, if they shall think that more beneficial to the Company, than adding the same to the Capital would be.

N. B. Subscribers to the Original, or other papers are marked *

*Dunmore, four shares.
*Peyton Randolph, £50. Stel:
*R. C. Nicholas, two shares.
*Thos. Adams, one share.
*James Donald, one share.
*G Mason, one share.
*Go: Washington, one share.
*John Page, one share
*John Page of Rosewell one share
*Th: Jefferson one share,
*Benja. Harrison, Brandon, one share.
*Thomas M. Randolph, one share.
*James McClurg one share.
*Peter Randolph, one share.
*Thos. Nelson jr., one share.
*Richd. & Everard Meade one share
*John Tabb one share
Chars. Carter Junr. one Share
*Richard Randolph one share
*Daniel L. Hilton one share

*John Banister one share
*John Blair one share
*Theo: Bland Jr. one share
*John Tayloe one share
*Archbald Cary one share
*Wilson Miles Cary one share
*Jams. Parke Farley one share
John Parke Custis.
*{ Joseph Scott, & } one share
{ Ths. Pleasants }
*Robert Pleasants, one share, on condition that he may withdraw his subscription in case, that any slaves should be purchased on account of the Company.
*William Murray one share
*Rayland Randolph one share
*Allen Cocke one share
*Philip Mazzei four shares
*{ Mann Page Junr., & } one
{ Hugh Nelson } share

N. B. It is requested as a favour of those Gentlemen who are Kind enough to procure Subscribers, that when any new Subscribers are added to the list, they will transmit their names to Robt. C. Nicholas Esqr., or the Factor.

MS (DLC: Virginia Miscellany). Another MS (ViHi). Both MSS (including the subscribers' names) are copies of a missing original and are in different, unidentified hands. The MS in DLC is endorsed: "Proposals for forming a Compy for raising Wine Oyl Silk &c." It is evidently the earlier of the two copies, since it contains a few interlineations (in a hand other than that of the copyist) that are incorporated in the MS in ViHi. However, it also adds the names of seven subscribers not in the other MS.

This interesting scheme was produced

by the fertile brain of Philip Mazzei, who had arrived at Williamsburg from Leghorn, in Nov. 1773, under the sponsorship of TJ's merchant friend Thomas Adams. He was warmly received in Virginia and was induced by TJ to undertake his experiments in viniculture on a plantation near Monticello which Mazzei named Colle. He appears to have begun them early in 1774, for TJ's Fee Book and Miscellaneous Accounts (CSmH) contain two pages of entries for TJ's account with "The Wine company" for the period 6 Apr. 1774 to 11 Feb. 1778. This was the beginning of a long association between the two men. The coming of the Revolution prevented the present scheme from materializing despite its promising beginnings. In 1779 Mazzei returned to Europe on a mission to borrow money for Virginia; Colle was rented to the Riedesels; and Mazzei's imported laborers drifted off, as TJ relates in a letter to Albert Gallatin, 25 Jan. 1793. (See also Mazzei, *Memoirs*, p. 188ff.; Garlick, *Mazzei*, IV.)

Draft of Resolution
concerning Adherence of New York to Articles of Association

[24 March 1775]

Ordered that certain paragraphs in the public papers, said to have been the votes of the house of representatives of New York be read.

The house of Convention taking into their consideration that the said province of New York did by their delegates in General Congress solemnly accede to the compact of Association there formed for the preservation of American rights, that a defection from such their compact would be a perfidy too atrocious to be charged on a sister colony but on the most authentic information, and also doubting whether from some radical defect in the constitution of that government the sense of their house of representatives on questions of this nature should be considered as the sense of the people in general, come to the following resolution.

Resolved, that it be an instruction to the Committee of correspondence for this colony that they procure authentic information from the Committee of Correspondence for the province of New York or otherwise Whether their house of representatives by any vote or votes whatsoever have deserted the Union[1] with the other American Colonies[2] formed in General Congress for the preservation of their just rights; Whether the other Colonies[3] are to consider such vote or votes as declaring truly the sense of the people of their province in general, and as forming a rule for their future conduct; And if they are not so to be considered that then they inform us by their names and other sufficient descriptions, of the individuals who may have concurred in such vote, or votes: and that the said Committee lay such their information before the next Convention or Assembly.

Dft (Vi). Changes in nomenclature made by TJ as he wrote have been noted. THE VOTES OF THE HOUSE OF REPRESENTATIVES OF NEW YORK refers to the refusal, on 23 Feb., of the New York Assembly to elect delegates to the Second Continental Congress, appointed to

convene in May; see Martha J. Lamb, *History of the City of New York*, N.Y. and Chicago, 1877, II, 18-19.

1 Altered from "their confederacy."
2 Altered from "states."
3 Altered from "American states."

Report of Committee to Prepare a Plan for a Militia

[25 March 1775]

The Committee appointed to prepare a plan for embodying arming and disciplining a militia for the purpose of putting this colony into an immediate posture of defence have had the same under their consideration and agreed to a report as follows.

The Committee propose that it be strongly recommended to the colony diligently to put in execution the Militia law passed in the year 1738 entitled 'An Act &c.

which act has become in force by the expiration of all subsequent Militia laws.

The Committee are further of opinion that, as from the expiration of the abovementioned latter laws, and various other causes, the legal and necessary disciplining of the militia has been much neglected and a proper provision of arms and ammunition has not been made, to the evident danger of the community in case of invasion or insurrection, that it be recommended to the inhabitants of the several counties of this colony that they form one or more Voluntier companies of infantry and troops of horse in each county and be in constant training and readiness to act on any emergency.

That it be recommended particularly to the counties of Brunswick, Dinwiddie, Chesterfeild, Henrico, Hanover, Spotsylvania, King George and Stafford and to all counties below these that out of such their Voluntiers they form each of them one or more troops of horse: and to all the counties above these it is recommended that they pay a more particular attention to the forming a good infantry.

That each company of infantry consist of sixty eight rank and file to be commanded by one captain, two lieutenants, one ensign, four serjeants, four corporals and that they have a[1] drummer and be furnished with a drum and colors: that every man be provided with a good Rifle if to be had, or otherwise with a common firelock, bayonet and cartouch box; and also with a tomahawk, one pound of gunpowder, and four pounds of ball at least fitted to the bore of his gun; that he be cloathed in a hunting shirt by way of uniform; and that all endeavor as soon as possible to become acquainted with the military exercise for infantry appointed to be used by his majesty in the year 1764.

That each troop of horse consist of thirty exclusive of officers: that every horseman be provided with a good horse, bridle, saddle with pistols and Holsters,[2] a carbine or other short firelock with a bucket, a cutting Sword or[3] tomahawk, one pound of gunpowder and four pound of ball at the least, and use the utmost diligence in training and accustoming his horse to stand the discharge of fire-arms, and in making himself acquainted with the military exercise for Cavalry.

That in order to make a further and more ample provision of ammunition it be recommended to the Committees of the several counties that they collect from their constituents in such manner as shall be most agreeable to them, so much money as will be suffi-cient to purchase half a pound of gun-powder, one pound of lead, necessary flints and cartridge paper for every titheable person in their county, that they immediately take effectual measures for the procuring such gunpowder, lead, flints and cartridge paper, and dispose thereof when procured in such place or places of safety as they may think best. And it is earnestly recommended to each in-dividual to pay such proportion of the money necessary for these purposes as by the respective committees shall be judged requisite.

That as it may happen that some counties from their situation may not be apprised of the most certain and speedy method of pro-curing the articles beforementioned, one general committee should be appointed whose business it should be to procure for such coun-ties as may make application to them such articles and so much thereof as the monies wherewith they shall furnish the said com-mittee will purchase after deducting the charges of transportation and other necessary expences.

Dft (Vi). Endorsed: "agd. [agreed] to."

On 23 Mch. the Convention resolved "That a well regulated militia, composed of Gentlemen and Yeomen, is the natural strength, and only security, of a free government," and appointed a commit-tee to prepare a plan for embodying a militia to put the colony "into a posture of defence." TJ was a member of the committee, which reported the next day, but the Report was postponed. On 25 Mch. the Report, "being read, and amended, was unanimously agreed to" (*Conv. Jour.*, Mch. 1775, 1816 edn., p. 5-6). The MILITARY EXERCISE FOR IN-

FANTRY established in 1764 refers to *The Manual Exercise, as Ordered by His Majesty, in the Year 1764, Together with Plans and Explanations of the Method Generally Practised at Reviews and Field-Days, . . . with Copperplates,* Boston, 1774 (Sabin 30771). This had been printed in pursuance of a resolve of the Provincial Congress of Massachusetts, and George Washington ordered six copies at this time (A. P. C. Griffin, *Catalogue of the Washington Collection in the Boston Athenaeum,* Boston, 1897, p. 135-6).

[1] Preceding four words interlined in the hand of John Tazewell, clerk of this Convention. This and the two following alterations were doubtless made by the Convention before adopting the report.
[2] Corrected by Tazewell from "holsters and pistols."
[3] Preceding three words interlined in Tazewell's hand.

Resolution on Land Grants

[27 March 1775]

His Excellency the Governor having by proclamation bearing date the 21st. day of March in the present year declared that his majesty hath given orders that all vacant lands within this colony shall be put up in lots to public sale and that the highest bidder for such lot shall be the purchaser thereof, and shall hold the same subject to a reservation of one half-penny sterling per acre by way of annual quit rent and of all mines of gold, silver, and precious stones; which terms are an innovation on the established usage of granting lands within this colony;

Resolved, that a Committee be appointed to enquire whether his majesty may of right advance the terms of granting lands in this colony, and make report thereof to the next General assembly or Convention. And that in the mean time it be recommended to all persons whatever to forbear purchasing or[1] accepting grants of lands on the conditions beforementioned; and that

be appointed to be of the said Committee.

Dft (Vi). Written by TJ on a fragment of paper bearing, at the top, the notation "Passd." and, on the back, a draft of the same Resolution which is probably the earliest draft, since it contains a correction by TJ that was incorporated in the draft adopted; unfortunately the hand in the first draft is not certainly identifiable.

For the background of Dunmore's PROCLAMATION of 21 Mch., see note on George Mason's Petition for Lands in Fincastle County, June 1774, above; the Proclamation itself is printed in Force, *Archives,* 4th ser., II, 174. On 27 Mch. the Convention adopted the Resolution as framed by TJ and his unidentified collaborator (*Conv. Jour.,* Mch. 1775, 1816 edn., p. 8). W. W. Henry (*Life of Henry,* I, 274-5) says that Patrick Henry drafted the Resolution, and the draft mentioned above may possibly be in his hand. The committee appointed to investigate the right of granting lands consisted of Patrick Henry, Richard Bland, TJ, R. C. Nicholas, and Edmund Pendleton. TJ began assembling documents at once (see letters from Wythe of 5 and 6 Apr.), but the committee never reported. On 15 Aug. the new Convention resolved that, until the committee did report, "all persons should forbear to purchase or accept grants of land under the late instructions from the governor," and that "all surveyors be, and they are hereby directed, to make no surveys under the said instructions, nor pay any regard to the said proclamation" (*Conv. Jour.*, Mch. 1775, 1816 edn., p. 17). See further, C. H. Lamb, "British Regulation of Crown Lands in the West . . . , 1773-1775," WMQ, 2d ser., X (1930), 52-5.

1 Two preceding words interlined in John Tazewell's hand.

From George Wythe

DEAR SIR   Williamsburg, 5 April, 1775.

I do not know that the terms on which the crown engaged to grant the lands in Virginia are contained in any other charter than that by Car. ii. the 10. of Oct. 28 of his reign. The original, I believe although the seal is not now to it, I found in my office; and I understand it is recorded in the Secretary's office. A copy of it I now inclose to be sent by the first opportunity. In the mean time I will look over some other charters transmitted some years ago by agent Montagu to the committee of correspondence and send you a list of them with copies of those if there be any which relate to the subject you are investigating and will procure you copies of such others as you shall signify a desire to have. I am, dear sir, Your friend and servant,   G. WYTHE

RC (DLC); only the date line, complimentary close, and signature are in Wythe's hand. Enclosure: clerk's copy of letters patent of 28 Charles II, 10 Oct. 1676; see explanatory note.

TJ had evidently asked Wythe's assistance in gathering materials for the investigation of land-granting practices;

see Resolution of 27 Mch. 1775, above. The document of which Wythe enclosed a copy, from the original in the office of the clerk of the House of Burgesses, confirmed, among other things, the right to fifty acres of unappropriated land on the part of "every person . . . comeing to dwell" in Virginia; it is printed in Hening, II, 532-3.

From George Wythe

DEAR SIR   6 Apr. 177[5]

Since my letter of yesterday, I have looked cursorily over all the charters in my office. Of those sent by Mr. Montagu the three which seem to concern the matter you are considering are the same that are in the appendix to Mr. Stith's history and the other which is all that I have of them besides is an ordinance relating to the appointment of a council in England for the affairs of the colony. Among these I find several commissions by James the first and his son appointing commissioners to consider of the state of the colony and of the proper means to advance it &c. Shall I send you copies

of them? Is there any thing else in which I can assist you? I am,
dear sir, your   G. WYTHE

RC (DLC). MS worn and date partly torn away.

The CHARTERS and ORDINANCE to which Wythe refers are in all probability the four documents printed in William Stith's *History of Virginia*, Williamsburg, 1747, *Appendix*; see Stith's preface to the *Appendix*.

To Ebenezer Hazard

SIR   Virginia April 30. 1775.

Your letter of Aug. 23. 1774 and Proposals for collecting and publishing the American state papers I have received. It is an undertaking of great utility to the continent in general, as it will not only contribute to the information of all those concerned in the administration of government, but will furnish to any historical genius which may happen to arise those materials which he would otherwise acquire with great difficulty and perhaps not acquire at all. Any thing in my power I will most gladly contribute to the compilation. I will direct office copies of our charters, resolutions of assembly &c. and of our treaty with the commonwealth of England to be immediately made out, and will forward them by the best means I can. I had before began a perusal of our antient records, which however I can only carry on when my attendance in assembly calls me to our capital from which my ordinary residence is remote. My progress in this will of course be slow. But it is probable it will enable me to bring into light some other valuable papers which do not come within any description I can at present make out to the clerk. As fast as any such occur I will forward them to you. But in the mean time I would recommend to your particular application Colo. Richard Bland one of our delegates in congress, a great antiquarian, and possessed of many valuable public papers which are not in our office, and which it is beleived are not in existence any where but in his collection. It is in his power to furnish every thing which this colony possesses proper for your purpose. If any thing further should occur in which I can be useful, be pleased to impart it to me with freedom, and my best endeavors shall be exerted to shew you how much I wish to see such a work forwarded. As the article of subscriptions has also it's importance I shall hope to render service in procuring them at least. I am Sir Your very humble servt.,   TH: JEFFERSON

RC (PPAP). Addressed: "To Ebenezer Hazard esq. at New-York." Endorsed: "Letter Thos. Jefferson Esqr. April 30th. 1775."

See Hazard's printed letter and Prospectus of 23 Aug. 1774, with TJ's memoranda thereon, and the accompanying note. Col. RICHARD BLAND, lawyer, politician, and antiquarian of Jordan's Point, Prince George co., was a delegate to the first and second Continental Congresses and was considered by TJ and others the most learned authority on constitutional history in the colony; TJ purchased Bland's library after the latter's death in 1776, and in consequence some of the Bland MSS relating to the Virginia Company are now in the Library of Congress (DAB; E. G. Swem, introduction to reprint of Bland's *Inquiry into the Rights of the British Colonies*, Richmond, 1922, p. v-viii; Kingsbury, *Records of the Virginia Company*, I, 41-8).

To William Small

DEAR SIR   Virginia May 7. 1775.

I had the pleasure by a gentleman who saw you at Birmingham to hear of your welfare. By Capt. Aselby of the True-patriot belonging to Messrs. Farrell & Jones of Bristol I send you three dozen bottles of Madeira, being the half of a present which I had laid by for you. The captain was afraid to take more on board lest it should draw upon him the officers of the customs. The remaining three dozen therefore I propose to send by Capt. Drew belonging to the same mercantile house, who is just arrived here. That which goes by Aselby will be delivered by him to your order; the residue by Drew, or by Farrell & Jones, I know not which as yet. I hope you will find it fine as it came to me genuine from the island and has been kept in my own cellar eight years.

Within this week we have received the unhappy news of an action of considerable magnitude between the king's troops and our brethren of Boston, in which it is said 500. of the former with Earl Piercy are slain. That such an action has happened is undoubted, tho' perhaps the circumstances may not yet have reached us with truth. This accident has cut off our last hopes of reconciliation, and a phrenzy of revenge seems to have seized all ranks of people.[1] It is a lamentable circumstance that the only mediatory power acknoleged by both parties, instead of leading to a reconciliation his divided people, should pursue the incendiary purpose of still blowing up the flames as we find him constantly doing in every speech and public declaration. This may perhaps be intended to intimidate into acquiescence, but the effect has been most unfortunately otherwise. A little knolege of human nature and attention to it's ordinary workings might have foreseen that the spirits of the people here were in a state in which they were more likely to be provoked than frightened by haughty deportment. And, to fill up the measure of irritation, proscription of individuals has been substituted in the room of just trial. Can it be beleived that a grateful people will suffer those to be consigned to execution whose sole crime has been the developing and asserting their rights? Had the parliament possessed the liberty of reflection they would have avoided a measure as impotent as it was inflammatory.[2] When I saw Lord Chatham's bill I entertained high hope that a reconciliation could have been brought about. The difference between his terms and those offered by our congress might have been accomodated if entered on by both parties with a disposition to accomodate. But the dignity of parliament it seems can brook no opposition to it's power. Strange that a set of men who have made sale of their virtue to the minister should yet talk of retaining dignity!—But I am getting into politics tho' I sat down only to ask your acceptance of the wine, and express my constant wishes for your happiness. This however seems secured by your philosophy and peaceful vocation. I shall still hope that amidst public dissension private friendship may be preserved inviolate, and among the warmest you can ever possess is that of Your obliged humble servt.,

TH. JEFFERSON

RC (Assay Office, Birmingham, England). Dft (DLC). The recipient's copy is addressed to William Small "in Birmingham by the true patriot," but the address is not in TJ's hand and is partly obscured by a stain. Endorsed by the unknown recipient: "T. Jefferson to Dr Small 1775." Two significant variations between the two copies are given in the textual notes.

Small, TJ's former teacher and close friend, had returned to England in the fall of 1764; he died 18 Feb. 1775, at the age of forty, some months before TJ's letter was written (Herbert L. Ganter, "William Small, Jefferson's Beloved Teacher," WMQ, 3d ser., IV [1947], 505-11; Mr. Ganter prints and thoroughly annotates the present letter in his article). Composed with extreme care, and bringing in political issues in a studiously casual way, the letter to Small should be compared with TJ's letter to John Randolph of 25 Aug. 1775. LORD CHATHAM'S BILL, presented in the House of Lords on 1 Feb. 1775 after consultation with Benjamin Franklin, was a plan for an imperial union: he proposed that the Continental Congress be made official and permanent, that it be asked to make a voluntary grant for imperial purposes, and that Parliament suspend the punitive acts; this plan, after warm debate, was voted down by the ministerial majority (Hansard, *Parl. Hist.*, XVIII, 198-215; Van Doren, *Franklin*, p. 508-13).

[1] In the Dft there follows a long passage which has been struck out: "It is a lamentable thing that the persons entrusted by the king with the administration of government should have kept their emploiers under such constant delusion. It appears now by their letters laid before the parliament that from the beginning they have labored to make the ministry beleive that the whole ferment has been raised and constantly kept up by a few ⟨hot headed demagogues⟩ principal men in every colony, and that it might be expected to subside in a short time either of itself, or by the assistance of a coercive power. The reverse of this is most assuredly the truth: the utmost efforts of the more intelligent people having been requisite and exerted to moderate the almost ungovernable fury of the people. That the abler part has been pushed forward to support

their rights in the feild of reason is true; and it was there alone they wished to decide the contest. To these men those very governors who have so much traduced them are indebted that there is this day one man of them left in existence. Within this week past there have been at least 10,000 men in arms in this colony, from whom Ld. Dunmore was in the last danger. Some of them had got within 16. miles of the capitol before the intercessions of the principal people could prevail on them to return to their habitations. This however was at length done and at present we appear to possess internal quiet."

2 Lined out in Dft: "But for god's sake where am I got to? For ever absorbed in the distresses of my country I cannot for three sentences keep clear of it's political struggles." TJ then added at the foot of the page the following sentences on Chatham's Bill for insertion at this point.

From St. George Tucker

SIR   Williamsburg June 8th: 1775.

I must apologize to you for the Liberty I take in addressing you as a Member of the General Congress, but the Importance of the Occasion I hope will excuse it. I shall therefore without further prelude proceed to the Occasion of this Letter.

The Island of Bermuda, by it's detached Situation, by the Number of it's Inhabitants, by its inconsiderable produce, and by the small progress made there in Manufactures, must be reduced to the most dreadful Calamities by the present Contest between Great Britain and the Colonies, should both parties demand a Complyance with their respective Measures. Utterly destitute of the Means of obtaining Provisions for their Support, except from the Continent; and altogether unable to procure Cloathing from any other Source than Great Britain, since the Island affords neither Materials, nor Manufacturers, it is altogether impossible for them to exist without the Assistance of both. Their Commerce with Great Britain, I apprehend does not amount to more than £20,000, Stg. per An: if so much. Their Remittances, having no produce of their own, are made either in Cash, Bills of Exchange, or Logwood and Mahogany which they procure at the Bay of Honduras; so that no Revenue arises to Great Britain from any Exports from thence. Their Commerce, therefore, is so trifling as to be utterly incapable of affecting the Trade of Great Britain in any Respect. Again, from America they are supplied with provisions, for their shipping, and, indeed, for the support of the whole Island for at least ten Months in the Year. These are procured, either in Exchange for Cash, or Salt, or else purchased by the hire of their Vessels, which have been Carriers for America and the West Indies from the first Settlement of the Island. The Inhabitants are a people, who, from their immediate Connection and frequent Intercourse with the Continent, have contracted an affection for this Country. They consider the Americans as Brethren, and their Souls are animated with the same generous Ardor for Liberty that prevails on the Continent; they are most Zealous Friends to the Cause of America, and would readily join with it, in any Measures to secure those inestimable privileges now contending for; in short, they consider the Cause as their own, and with pleasure behold every step that has been taken in support of it. Their Conduct, on a former occasion, by refusing to admit the Stamps in 1765, and obliging the Stamp Master to resign his office, I think must be considered as a proof of what I have here advanced. But so incapable are they of *acting* in Conjunction with America, on this Occasion, however ardently they might wish to do so, that a single Ship of War might cut off all Communication whatsoever with the Continent, and reduce the Island to the most horrid state of Distress, if once obnoxious to Great Britain. It is from this apprehension that they have not declared their most cordial Concurrence in the Measures of the Congress, and adopted them for their own Government; since such a step might involve above 12,000. people in the most irretrievable Distress. Such are the Motives which have restrained their Conduct hitherto. By Letters from some of the principal Gentlemen of the Island I think myself authorised to make this Declaration of their Sentiments, and, further to add, that if the Congress will agree to supply them with provisions, they will with Chearfulness accede to any Restrictions they may think proper to impose. They will enter into the most solemn Engagements that no Commodities shall be reshipped from thence to any other place which the Congress may think proper to have no Commerce with. They will enter into an association against all sumptuary Articles, if it is demanded of them, and will agree to import nothing from Great Britain except the *absolute* Necessaries of Life. They will further engage to supply the Colonies with Salt from Turk's Island, Tortuga's, &c. in Exchange for those Commodities they shall recieve from them. And, finally, will readily adopt any Measures which may be judged necessary for the Benefit of America, and will strenuously oppose whatsoever may make against it's Interest. If, therefore, the Congress will agree to supply them with provisions, I think I may venture to engage, that an Association, agreeable to what I have above stated, if required, will be entered into by the first of September, the Day when all Commerce with the rest of the British Dominions is to cease.

Perhaps, Sir, such a Measure may be attended with mutual advantages to Bermuda and the Colonies. Of this I cannot pretend to determine, but beg leave to submit the following Queries to your Consideration.

Do any of the Acts of Trade and Navigation prohibit the reshipping and Exportation of any of the produce of the Colonies from those British American Islands into which they were imported, to those parts of Europe, or other foreign Markets to which they might be exported immediately from the Colonies? *Qu: 1st.*

If there is no such prohibition contained in any former Acts of parliament, does the restraining Bill, by Construction, amount to such prohibition? *Qu: 2d:*

May not those Commodities which are permitted to be exported to the Mediterranean, and other parts of Europe, except Great Britain and Ireland, by the Congress, be exported by the way of Bermuda, notwithstanding the restraining Bill, if, upon their entering into proper Engagements, the Congress should think proper to continue their Exports to that Island. *Qu: 3d:*

Would not such a Continuation of the Grain Trade be attended with the most happy and salutary Effects, and be the Means of enabling America to make a more lasting Resistance to parliamentary Measures? *Qu: 4th:*

I have ventured [to] throw together these few Hints, with a design of offering them to your Consideration as I understand you intend to join the American Congress soon. And if any thing I have here said should be the Means of prevailing on you to offer your Interest with that august Body, in behalf of my wretched Country, I shall esteem it a peculiar Happiness of my Life to have taken this opportunity of subscribing myself, with the most unfeigned Esteem, Sir, Your most humble Servant, St. George Tucker

RC (DLC).

In addressing the present appeal to TJ, Tucker was following the instructions of his father, Henry Tucker, Sr. (1713-1787), Bermuda merchant, who was attempting to find for Bermuda some *modus vivendi* with the continental colonies short of outright resistance to the mother country, which would have promptly destroyed the economic life of the island (Wilfred B. Kerr, *Bermuda and the American Revolution*, Princeton, 1936, p. 14, 40, and ch. III, *passim*).

AS A MEMBER OF THE GENERAL CONGRESS: On 27 Mch. TJ had been elected to the second Continental Congress in the room of Peyton Randolph, "in case of the non-attendance of the said Peyton Randolph" (*Conv. Jour.*, Mch. 1775, 1816 edn., p. 8). Randolph had returned to Williamsburg to preside over the newly convened House of Burgesses. TJ left Williamsburg on 11 June and arrived in Philadelphia on 20 June (Account Book, under dates).

To St. George Tucker

DEAR SIR   Wmsburgh June 10. 1774 [i.e., 1775]

I am to acknoledge the receipt of your letter, and to scribble a line in answer, being just in the moment of setting out on my journey. The situation of your island is truly hard, and I should think deserves a relaxation of our terms if I may trust my first thoughts on the subject. I also think it probable it might be mutually beneficial to us. Should I continue of that opinion I will certainly do any little offices in my power to bring it about. But I refer it to yourself whether there should not be some body with some kind of public authority as well to give information of facts, as to satisfy the Congress that the inhabitants of Bermuda will enter into such engagements as may secure them against any infraction of the American Association. I have time to add nothing more than that I am Dr. Sir Your friend & servt.,   TH: JEFFERSON

RC (ViWC). Addressed: "To Mr. Saint George Tucker." Endorsed: "Original draught of a Letter to Peyton Randolph & Thomas Jefferson Esquires with the respective Answers of those Gentlemen. June 9th: 1775." The probable explanation of the endorsement is that Tucker filed in one packet the following documents: (1) a draft of his letter to TJ of 8 June (preceding document), a copy of which was also sent to Peyton Randolph; (2) TJ's reply of 10 June (the present document); (3) Randolph's reply of 9 June. The letters to and from Randolph have not been found.

The error in the date is manifest from the fact that TJ is replying to Tucker's letter of 8 June 1775, q.v. See also Tucker to TJ, 12 Aug. 1775.

Virginia Resolutions
on Lord North's Conciliatory Proposal

[10 June 1775]

Resolved, that it is the Opinion of this Committee that an Address be presented to his Excellency, the Governor, to inform him that we have taken into our Consideration the joint Address of the two Houses of Parliament, his Majesty's Answer, and the Resolution of the Commons which his Lordship has been pleased to lay before us. That wishing nothing so sincerely as the perpetual continuance of that brotherly love which we bear to our fellow subjects of *Great Britain* and still continuing to hope and believe that they do not approve the measures which have so long oppressed their brethren in *America*, we were pleased to receive his *Lordship's* notification that a benevolent tender had at length been made by the british House of Commons towards bringing to a good end our unhappy disputes with the Mother Country: that next to the possession of liberty, we should consider such Reconciliation the greatest of all human blessings. With these dispositions we entered into consideration of that Resolution: we examined it minutely; we viewed it in every point of light in which we were able to place it; and with pain and disappointment we must ultimately declare it only changes the form of oppression, without lightening its burthen. That we cannot close with the terms of that Resolution for these Reasons.

Because the British Parliament has no right to intermeddle with the support of civil government in the Colonies. For us, not for them, has government been instituted here; agreeable to our Ideas provision has been made for such Officers as we think necessary for the administration of public affairs; and we cannot conceive that any other legislature has a right to prescribe either the number or pecuniary appointments of our Offices. As a proof that the Claim of Parliament to interfere in the necessary Provisions for support of civil Government is novel and of a late Date we take leave to refer to an Act of our Assembly passed so long since as the thirty second Year of the Reign of King *Charles* the second intituled *An Act for raising a public Revenue and for the better support of the Government of this his Majesty's Colony of Virginia*. This Act was brought over by Lord *Culpeper* then Governor under the great Seal of *England* and was enacted in the name of the "King's most excellent Majesty by and with the Consent of the General Assembly."

Because to render perpetual our exemption from an unjust taxation, we must saddle ourselves with a perpetual tax adequate to the expectations and subject to the disposal of Parliament alone. Whereas, we have right to give our money, as the Parliament does theirs, without coercion, from time to time, as public exigencies may require, we conceive that we alone are the judges of the condition, circumstances, and situation of our people, as the Parliament are of theirs. It is not merely the mode of raising, but the freedom of granting our Money for which we have contended. Without this we possess no check on the royal prerogative, and what must be much lamented by dutiful and loyal subjects, we should be stript of the only means, as well of recommending this Country to the favour of our most gracious Sovereign as of strengthening those bands of Amity with our fellow subjects which we would wish to remain indissoluble.

Because on our undertaking to grant money as is proposed, the Commons only resolve to forbear levying pecuniary taxes on us;

still leaving unrepealed their several Acts passed for the purposes of restraining the trade and altering the form of Government of the Eastern Colonies; extending the boundaries and changing the Government and Religion of *Quebec*; enlarging the jurisdiction of the Courts of Admiralty, and taking from us the right of trial by jury; and transporting us into other Countries to be tried for criminal Offences. Standing armies too are still to be kept among us, and the other numerous grievancies of which ourselves and sister Colonies separately and by our representatives in General Congress have so often complained, are still to continue without redress.

Because at the very time of requiring from us grants of Money they are making disposition to invade us with large Armaments by Sea and land, which is a stile of asking gifts not reconcileable to our freedom. They are also proceeding to a Repetition of injury by passing acts for restraining the commerce and fisheries of the Provinces of *New England*, and for prohibiting the Trade of the other Colonies with all parts of the world except the Islands of *Great Britain*, *Ireland*, and the *West Indies*. This seems to bespeak no intention to discontinue the exercise of this usurped Power over us in future.

Because on our agreeing to contribute our proportion towards the common defence, they do not propose to lay open to us a free trade with all the world: whereas to us it appears just that those who bear equally the burthens of Government, should equally participate of it's benefits. Either be content with the monopoly of our trade, which brings greater loss to us and benefit to them than the amount of our proportional contributions to the common defence; or, if the latter be preferred, relinquish the former, and do not propose, by holding both, to exact from us double contributions. Yet we would remind Government that on former emergencies when called upon as a free People, however cramped by this monopoly in our resources of wealth, we have liberally contributed to the common defence. Be assured then that we shall be generous in future as in past times, disdaining the shackles of proportion when called to our free station in the general system of the Empire.

Because the proposition now made to us involves the interest of all the other Colonies. We are now represented in General Congress, by members approved by this House where our former Union it is hoped will be so strongly cemented that no partial Application can produce the slightest departure from the common Cause. We consider ourselves as bound in Honor as well as Interest to share one general Fate with our Sister Colonies, and should hold ourselves base Deserters of that Union, to which we have acceded, were we to agree on any Measures distinct and apart from them.

To *observe* that there was indeed a plan of accomodation offered in Parliament, which tho' not entirely equal to the terms we had a right to ask, yet differed but in few Points from what the General Congress had held out. Had Parliament been disposed sincerely as we are to bring about a reconciliation, reasonable men had hoped that by meeting us on this ground something might have been done. Lord *Chatham's* bill on the one part and the terms of the Congress on the other would have formed a basis for negotiation which a spirit of accomodation on both sides might perhaps have reconciled. It came recommended too from one whose successful experience in the art of Government should have ensured to it some attention from those to whom it was tendered. He had shown to the world that *Great Britain* with her Colonies, united firmly under a just and honest government, formed a power which might bid defiance to the most potent enemies. With a change of Ministers however a total change of measures took place; the component parts of the empire have from that moment been falling asunder, and a total annihilation of its weight in the political scale of the World seems justly to be apprehended.

To *declare* that these are our sentiments on this important subject, which we offer only as an individual part of the whole empire. Final determination we leave to the General Congress now sitting, before whom we shall lay the Papers his Lordship has communicated to us. To their Wisdom we commit the improvement of this important advance; if it can be wrought into any good, we are assured they will do it. To them also we refer the discovery of that proper method of representing our well founded grievancies which his Lordship assures us will meet with the attention and regard so justly due to them. For ourselves, we have exhausted every mode of application which our invention could suggest as proper and promising. We have decently remonstrated with Parliament; they have added new injuries to the old: we have wearied our King with supplication, he has not deigned to answer us: We have appealed to the native honour and justice of the British nation; their efforts in our favour have been hitherto ineffectual.[1] What then remains to be done? That we commit our injuries to the even-handed justice of that being who doth no wrong, earnestly beseeching him to illuminate the Councils and prosper the endeavors of those to whom America hath confided her hopes; that thro' their wise direction we may again see reunited the blessings of Liberty, Property, and Union with *Great Britain.*

Printed from *Journals of the House of Burgesses, 1773-1776,* Richmond, 1905, p. 212-14.

On 20 Feb. 1775 Lord North laid before the House of Commons a resolution proposing that whenever any colonial assembly agreed to make a grant for the common defense and the support of civil government in the colony (such grants to be "disposable by Parliament"), the British government would forbear to impose on that colony any other tax or assessment for these purposes (Force, *Archives,* 4th ser., I, 1598; text of the proposal also printed in Resolutions of Congress on Lord North's Conciliatory Proposals, 25-31 July 1775, below). The resolution was passed a week later and sent to the colonial governors for presentation to the several assemblies. In Virginia Gov. Dunmore summoned the House of Burgesses for 1 June and communicated to that body what has always been called North's conciliatory proposal (JHB, 1773-1776, p. 174-6). TJ was one of a committee chosen to answer the address, but in the answer presented by Treasurer Nicholas and adopted on 5 June, TJ's hand is not apparent. Touching on several other critical matters, that answer merely promised further study of the North proposal (same, p. 177, 187-9). On 7, 9, and 10 June the House considered North's proposal in a committee of the whole, of which Archibald Cary was chairman, and on the final day Cary presented the Resolutions here printed, which were unanimously agreed to by the House (same, p. 212-14). TJ's authorship is stated in his Autobiography. He there says that Peyton Randolph, who had returned from Congress in order to preside over the House of Bur-

gesses, "was anxious that the answer [to North's proposal] of our assembly, likely to be the first, should harmonize with what he knew to be the sentiments and wishes of the body he had recently left. He feared that Mr. Nicholas, whose mind was not yet up to the mark of the times, would undertake the answer, and therefore pressed me to prepare an answer. I did so, and with his aid carried it through the house with long and doubtful scruples from Mr. Nicholas and James Mercer, and a dash of cold water on it here and there, enfeebling it somewhat, but finally with unanimity or a vote approaching it. This being passed, I repaired immediately to Philadelphia, and conveyed to Congress the first notice they had of it" (Ford, I, 15). In one respect TJ's account is slightly misleading: what he drafted was the Resolutions agreed upon in the committee of the whole; these, upon being accepted by the House, were put into the form of an address and communicated on 12 June to Dunmore as the definitive answer to his address on the opening day of the session (JHB, 1773-1776, p. 219-21). TJ having left for Congress on 11 June, the Burgesses' formal address was presented by Archibald Cary, but inasmuch as the changes between the Resolutions and the address are nearly imperceptible, TJ may be credited with the authorship of the latter as well as the former. When the Continental Congress came to prepare an answer to North's proposal, it was TJ who drew up the answer; see 25 July 1775, below.

[1] Preceding four words omitted (by a printer's error?) from the text of the Resolutions; they are supplied from the Address of 12 June (see note, above).

To Francis Eppes

[DE]AR SIR   Philadelphia June 26. 1775.

You will before this have heard that the war is now heartily entered into, without a prospect of accomodation but thro' the effectual interposition of arms. General Gage has received considerable reinforcements, tho' not to the [wh]ole amount of what was expected. There has lately been an action at the outlet of the town of Boston. The particulars we have not yet been able to get with certainty. The event however was considerably in our favor as to the numbers killed. Our account sais we had between 40 and 70 killed and 140. wounded. The enemy had certainly 500. wounded and the same account supposes that number killed; but judging from the proportion of wounded and slain on our part, they should not have perhaps above [200 killed. This] happened on Saturd[ay, and] on Monday when the express came away the provincials had began to make another attack. Washington set out from here on Friday last as Generalissimo of all the Provincial troops in North-America. Ward and Lee are appointed major Generals, and Gates Adjutant. We are exceedingly anxious till we hear of their arrival at Boston, as it is evident to every one that the provincial encampment is the most injudicious that can possibly be conceived. For the sole purpose of covering two small towns near Boston they have encamped so near the line of the ministerial army that the centries may converse. Gage too being well fortified is in little danger of an attack from them, while their situation is such that he may attack them when he pleases, and if he is unsuccesful they cannot pursue him a foot scarcely, on account of the ships and floating batteries bearing on the neck of Boston. If no evil arises from this till General Washington arrives we may expect to hear of his withdrawing the provincial troops to a greater distance. The Congress have directed 20,000 men to be ra[ised] and hope by a vigorous campaign to dispose our enemies to treaty. Governor Carleton has been spiriting up the Canadian Indians to fall on our back settlements but this we hope will be prevented. Governor Skeene appointed [to] take charge of the fortresses on [the] lakes was intercepted here, and as we had already taken poses[sion] of those fortifications and provided a governor there was no occasion for him to proceed. He is now therefore our prisoner. My best affections attend Mrs. Eppes and family, and am Dr. Sir Your friend & servt,   TH: JEFFERSON

RC (Lloyd W. Smith, Madison, N.J., 1946). MS worn. A few letters and words, enclosed in brackets, have been supplied from the text in Randall, *Life*, III, 567-8, which also provides an address, as follows: "Francis Eppes, Esq., At the Forest, Charles City."

From Ebenezer Hazard

SIR New York June 30th. 1775

Your very obliging Letter of 30th. April did not come to hand before a few Days ago, or it should have been answered sooner.

I am happy that you coincide with me in Sentiment respecting the Utility of my Undertaking, and, judging of the whole from the Materials I am already possessed of, I cannot help thinking the Collection will be vastly more important than I at first imagined.

The polite Manner in which you offer your Assistance lays me under great Obligations, and I beg you will be assured I shall chearfully embrace Opportunities of rendering you any Service in my Power here.

To prevent your having unnecessary Trouble respecting my Collection I take the Liberty of sending you the following List of the Papers I have relating to Virginia; vizt.

Queen Elizabeth's Patent to Sir W. Ralegh for making Discoveries.

The Names of the Persons who composed the 1st. and 2d Colonies which settled in Virginia.

First, Second, and Third Charters, from Stith's History.

King James's Commission to Sir Walter Ralegh in 1617.

An Ordinance and Constitution of the Treasurer, Council and Company in England for a Council of State and General Assembly. July 24th. 1621. This last is from Stith.

A Commission to the Archbishop of Canterbury and eleven others for governing the American Colonies 1634;—and

The Commonwealth's Instructions to Capt. Dennis &c. "appointed Commissioners for the reducing of Virginia, and the Inhabitants thereof to their due Obedience to the Commonwealth of England."—1651.

These are all I have yet been able to procure.

Though I had not the Honor of an Acquaintance with Colo. Bland I took the Liberty of troubling him with a Letter and my Proposals while the former Congress was sitting, but have not been favored with any Thing in Answer. I beg you will be kind enough to remind him of this, and oblige me with his Reply.

I am Sir, Your very humble Servt., EBEN: HAZARD

RC (DLC). See Hazard to TJ, 23 Aug. 1774; TJ to Hazard, 30 Apr. 1775.

Jefferson's Annotated Copy of Franklin's Proposed Articles of Confederation

[June-July 1775]

Articles of confederation and perpetual Union proposed by[1] the delegates of the several colonies of New Hampshire &c. in General Congress met at Philadelphia May. 10. 1775.

The name of this confederacy shall henceforth be 'The united ⟨*colonies*⟩[2] states of North[3] America.' Art. I.

The said united colonies hereby severally enter into a firm league of friendship with each other binding on themselves and their posterity for their common defence against their enemies for the security of their liberties and properties, the safety of their persons and families[4] and their[5] mutual and general welfare. Art. II.

That each colony shall enjoy and retain as much as it may think fit of it's o[wn] present[6] laws, customs,[6] rights, privileges and peculiar[7] jurisdictions within it's own limits; and may amend it's own constitution as shall seem best to it's own assembly or convention. Art. III.

That for the more convenient management of general interests, delegates shall be annually elected in each colony to meet in General congress at such time and place[8] as shall be agreed on in the next preceding Congress. Only where particular circumstances do not make a deviation necessary, it is understood to be a rule that each succeeding Congress be held in a different colony till the whole number be gone through and so in perpetual rotation; and that accordingly the next Congress after the present shall be held at [Annapolis in Maryland].[9] Art. IV.

That the power and duty of the Congress shall extend to the determining on war and peace,[10] the entring into alliances, the reconciliation with Great-Britain;[11] the settling all disputes and differences between colony and colony[12] if such should arise; and the planting of new colonies when proper. The Congress shall also make such general ordinances as, tho' necessary to the general welfare, particular assemblies cannot be competent to viz. those that may relate to our general commerce, or general currency, to the establishment of posts, the regulation of our common forces. The Congress shall also have the appointment of all officers civil and military appurtaining to the General confederacy, such as General Treasurer, Secretary &c. Art. V.

Art. VI.   All charges of wars and all other general expences to be incurred for the common welfare, shall be defrayed out of a common treasury, which is to be supplyed by each colony in proportion to it's number of male polls between 16. and 60. years of age; the taxes for paying that proportion are to be laid and levied by the laws of each colony.

Art. VII.   The number of Delegates to be elected and sent to the Congress by each colony shall be regulated from time to time by the number of such polls returned; so as that one Delegate be allowed for every [5000.] polls,[13] and the Delegates are to bring with them to every Congress, an authenticated return of the number of polls in their respective provinces which is to be triennially taken for the purposes abovementioned.

Art. VII[I.] Each Delegate at the Congress shall have a vote in all cases, and if necessarily absent shall be allowed to appoint any other Delegate from the same colony to be his proxy who may vote for him. At every meeting of the Congress a majority one half[14] of the members returned exclusive of proxies shall be necessary to make a Quorum.

Art. IX.   An executive council shall be appointed by the Congress out of their own body, consisting of [12.][15] persons; one person from each colony;[16] of whom in the first appointment one third viz. [4.] shall be for one year, [4] for two years, and [4] for three years; and as the said terms expire the vacancies shall be filled by appointments for three years, whereby one third of the members will be changed annually, and each person who has served the said term of three years as counsellor shall have a respite of three years before he can be elected again.[17] This council (of whom two thirds shall be a Quorum) in the Recess of the Congress is to execute what shall have been enjoined thereby, to manage the general Continental business and interests, to receive applications from foreign countries, to prepare matters for the consideration of the Congress; to fill up pro tempore Continental offices that fall vacant; and to draw on the general Treasurer for such monies as may be necessary for general services and appropriated by the congress to such services.

Art. X.   No colony shall engage in an offensive war with any nation of Indians without the consent of the Congress or great council abovementioned who are first to consider the justice and necessity of such war.

Art. XI.   A perpetual alliance offensive and defensive is to be entered into as soon as may be with the Indian six[18] nations; their limits to be[19] secured to them; their lands not to be encroached on, nor any private or colony purchases made of them hereafter to be held good; nor

any contract for lands to be made but between the great council of
the Indians at Onondaga[20] and the General congress. The boundaries and lands of all the other Indians shall also be ascertained
and secured to them in the same manner; and persons appointed to
reside among them in proper districts who shall take care to prevent injustice in the trade with them, and be enabled at our general
expence by occasional small supplies to relieve their personal wants
and distresses, and all purchases from them shall be by the Congress for the General advantage and benefit of the United colonies.[21]

As all new institutions may have imperfections which only time   Art. XII.
and experience can discover, it is agreed, that the General Congress
from time to time shall propose such amendments of this constitution as may be found necessary; which being approved by a
majority of the colony assemblies, shall be equally binding with the
rest of the articles of this Confederation.

Any and every colony from Great Britain upon the continent of   Art. XIII.
North America not at present engaged in our association may upon
application and joining the said association be received into this
Confederation, viz. Quebec, Canada, St. John's, Nova Scotia, Bermudas, and the East and West Floridas:[22] and shall thereupon be
entitled to all the advantages and obligations[23] of our union, mutual
assistance and commerce.

These articles shall be proposed to the several provincial conventions or assemblies to be by them considered and if approved
they are advised to empower their delegates to agree to and ratify
the same in the ensuing Congress: after which the union thereby
established is to continue firm till[24] the terms of reconciliation proposed in the petition of the last Congress to the king are agreed to,
till the acts since made restraining the American commerce and
fisheries are repealed, till reparation is made for the injury done to
Boston by shutting up it's port; for the burning of Charlestown, and
for the expence of this unjust war; and till all the British troops are
withdrawn from America. On the arrival of these events, the colonies are to return to their former connection and friendship with
Britain: but on failure thereof this Confederation is to be perpetual.[25]

Tr (DLC); copy in TJ's hand, with "additions" and comments by him.

This is the plan of union as drawn by Benjamin Franklin and read in Congress on 21 July 1775, though not acted upon at that time. TJ's observations upon it are of the first importance;

an amendment offered by him to the 1776 revision of the Franklin plan by Dickinson and the committee of which he was a member is equally important. While there is no evidence to show that TJ made this copy in 1775, there is both his own statement and internal evidence indicating that he

probably transcribed and almost certainly made use of it when the matter came officially before Congress in 1776. Of this plan of union TJ wrote in 1786: "I was absent from Congress from the beginning of January, 1776, to the middle of May. Either just before I left Congress, or immediately on my return to it (I rather think it was the former) Doctor Franklin put into my hands the draught of a plan of confederation, desiring me to read it and tell him what I thought of it. I approved it highly" (TJ to François Soulès, 13 Sep. 1786). The notes below indicate that TJ's copy was not transcribed from the MS in Franklin's handwriting that was read before Congress; that MS (DLC: PCC, No. 47:1-7; printed in JCC, II, 195) was probably not the only one made by Franklin, but it is the only one known to be extant. Numerous other copies of Franklin's plan were made by members of Congress, and there is evidence that some of these were intended for circulation to legislatures or conventions of the several colonies, though Congress took no official action on Franklin's plan. For example, "A Draught of Articles of Confederacy, proposed for the Consideration of the several Colonies in North America was brought into [the Provincial] Congress" of North Carolina on 24 Aug. 1775, and the secretary was ordered to "furnish the delegates for each County with a Copy thereof" (*Colonial Records of N. Car.*, x, 174-9). This draft was prefaced by a statement, evidently prepared by the North Carolina delegates in Congress, that the plan should "be considered not as having had the sanction of the Continental Congress, or Recommended by them, or as expressing the Sentiments of the Delegates who Represented this province in the last Continental Congress," but "as a Subject which will be proposed to the Continental Congress at their next session" and as Articles to be "dispassionately Debated and approved or Condemned upon their own Intrinsick merits." This proliferation of copies in North Carolina resulted in publication in England, though the title and first Article were lacking in all cases (*Gent. Mag.*, XLV [1775], 572-3; *Scot's Magazine*, XXXVII [1775], 665-7). Publication in the *Annual Register* for 1775 ("Chronicle," p. 252-3), however, proceeded evidently from another source, for its title was not only present but given

as "Articles of Confederation and Perpetual Union *entered into* by the several colonies of New Hampshire, &c." (italics supplied). A variation of the Franklin Plan also appeared in the *Pennsylvania Evening Post*, 5 Mch. 1776. Other copies of the Franklin Plan are: (1) copy (Ct), which varies in important respects from the Franklin MS; (2) copy in John Hancock's hand (MHi: Miscellany), which agrees most closely with the Franklin MS and was very probably copied from it; (3) copy in an unidentified hand (MHi: Miscellany); (4) copy (NHi: Duane Papers); (5) copy in a hand attributed to George Wythe and with some "Remarks by G:W" (DLC: PCC, Miscellany; JCC, II, 199).

The Franklin plan was unquestionably before the committee appointed 12 June 1776 "to prepare and digest the form of a confederation to be entered into between these colonies" (JCC, v, 433). The draft reported on 12 July 1776 is in John Dickinson's handwriting and follows the Franklin Plan in many particulars, though with important additions and variations (DLC: PCC, No. 47: 9-18; JCC, v, 546-54). This draft contains an amendment in TJ's hand (see note 21, below). The draft reported by the committee was ordered to be printed under strict injunctions of secrecy (JCC, v, 555-6; Evans 15148); a copy of this printing of the committee report is in DLC: TJ Papers, 1:5; 1:140-1; it contains annotations by TJ, though these are principally indications of amendments made in the course of debates (JCC, v, 674-89; see Notes of Proceedings in the Continental Congress, below). The revision of this committee report by Congress was also printed (JCC, v, 689; Evans 15149), and a copy of it is in DLC: TJ Papers, 2: 292-4, but contains no marginalia or notes by TJ, since the subject did not come before Congress again during his period of service in 1776. Thereafter his connection with the progress of the Articles of Confederation was indirect, being confined to the suggestion made to John Adams concerning a compromise solution to the vexed problem of methods of voting (TJ to John Adams, 16 May 1777), and to his comments to J. N. Démeunier (see TJ's Observations on the Article Etats-Unis, 22 June 1786).

[1] Franklin MS reads "proposed ⟨*agre*⟩"

with the words "entred into" interlined above.

2 All copies of the Franklin MS listed above read "colonies"; TJ must have added the word "states" during 1776, perhaps during the debates of July and August, since the report of the Committee of 12 July 1776 in Dickinson's hand employed the word "colonies" (except in the title).

3 The word "North" is enclosed by rectangular lines; the significance of this and other similar markings noted below is not always clear.

4 The words "for the security . . . persons & families" are enclosed in rectangular lines; the copy in Ct omits this phrase in Franklin MS: "the Safety of their Persons and Families."

5 Above "their" TJ inserted "(a)" and, on the last page of his copy, wrote this significant comment: "(a) qu. what 'their mutual and general welfare' means. There should be no vague terms in an instrument of this kind. It's objects should be precisely and determinately fixed."

6 This word is enclosed in rectangular lines.

7 The words "privileges and peculiar" are enclosed in rectangular lines.

8 The words "and place" are enclosed in rectangular lines.

9 Brackets in MS.

10 The Franklin MS has the following interlined at this point: "sending and receiving ambassadors and." Neither TJ's copy nor any of those listed above includes this interlineation, indicating that the addition must have been made after the Franklin Plan was read 21 July 1775, or that TJ and the other copyists employed a different prototype. See note 12, below.

11 The phrase "the reconciliation with Great-Britain" is enclosed in rectangular lines in TJ's copy and bracketed in Franklin MS.

12 The Franklin MS has the following interlined at this point: "about Limits or any other cause." Neither the copy by TJ nor any of the others listed above includes this addition; see note 10 above.

13 Above "[5000.]" (brackets in MS) TJ interlined "(b) 10,000" and, on the last page of his copy, wrote the following: "(b) a vote for every 10,000 male polls will make 75. members in the whole, supposing we have 3. millions. But this clause should go further and have some such clause as this 'provided

that when by the increase of male polls the whole number of delegates shall be likely to amount to more than one hundred the Congress shall so ⟨adjust⟩ al⟨lot⟩ter and adjust the number of male polls entitled to send a delegate as that there shall be not more than 100. ⟨in the⟩ nor less than 50. in the whole: and so from time to time as the increase or decrease of male polls may require, the members shall be so adjusted as to keep the whole number of delegates within those limits.' " TJ's Draft of a Constitution for Virginia included a similar provision for maximum and minimum representation, with the right of adjustment according to fluctuation in voting population vested in the legislature.

14 The words "one half" are enclosed in rectangular lines and the words "a majority" are interlined above. In the Franklin MS the words "At every meeting . . . to make a Quorum, and" are written in the margin and a caret inserted at the beginning of the words "Each Delegate at the Congress. . . ." The copy by Hancock, the copy in the Duane Papers, and the North Carolina copy follow the arrangement indicated by Franklin; the fact that copies by TJ and others depart from this sequence is an indication that they were using a different prototype.

15 The brackets around "12" and the numbers that follow in this paragraph are in both Franklin's MS and in TJ's copy of it.

16 The words "[12.] persons" are enclosed in rectangular lines, and the words "one person from each colony" are interlined.

17 It is to be noted that TJ's Draft of a Constitution for Virginia provided for a somewhat similar method of overlapping of terms of service in the Senate.

18 The word "six" is enclosed in rectangular lines and the word "Indian" interlined above.

19 Franklin MS has the words "ascertain'd and" interlined at this point.

20 The words "at Onondaga" and, following this, the words "the boundaries . . . in the same manner" are enclosed in rectangular lines.

21 Opposite Article XIV of the MS of the Dickinson draft of 12 July 1776 (corresponding to the subject matter of Article XI of the Franklin plan) there is a slip of paper in TJ's hand, with the following words in Charles Thomson's hand written on it: "Amendment pro-

posed." This highly significant amendment offered by TJ reads as follows: "Art. XIV. No purchases *hereafter* to be made by individual states or persons of lands on this continent not within the boundaries of any of the United states, shall be valid: but all purchases of such lands shall be made by contract between the United states assembled or persons authorized by them, and the great Councils of the Indians; *and when purchased shall be given freely to those who may be permitted to seat them.*" The italicized words have lines drawn through them, probably because this part of the proposed amendment was struck out before the whole was rejected (JCC, V, 680). Abernethy, *Western Lands*, p. 170-1, citing E. S. Corwin, *French Policy and the American Alliance of 1778*, and W. H. Mohr, *Federal Indian Relations, 1774-1788*, asserts that a determined effort was made by Franklin, Dickinson, and others to secure for Congress the right to fix boundaries "of the States claiming Western lands" and to make all purchases of territory from the Indians and that the Virginia delegates opposed this. As to the former (right to fix state boundaries), TJ opposed it; but as to the latter (right to control purchases of lands lying outside state boundaries),

TJ's amendment, which he offered on 25 July 1776, proves that the Virginia delegation was not unanimously opposed (JCC, VI, 1076-7, 1083).

22 The word "Quebec" is enclosed in rectangular lines and the word "Canada" interlined above; Franklin MS reads: "[Ireland], the West India Islands, Quebec, St. Johns, Nova Scotia, Bermudas, and the East and West-Floridas."

23 The words "and obligations" do not appear in Franklin MS or in any of the copies listed above and are interlined in TJ's copy. They were perhaps inserted by TJ as a suggested alteration.

24 All of the remainder of this paragraph was enclosed in rectangular lines. The copy of the Franklin plan in Ct ends at this point with the words: "the union thereby established is to continue firm and inviolate."

25 Following this TJ wrote: "Read before Congress July. 21. 1775." and, on the next page three paragraphs headed "Additions." The first of these reads: "No colony shall keep any standing forces without consent of General Congress or the colonies bordering on it." The second and third paragraphs are given above in notes 5 and 13 respectively.

Financial and Military Estimates for Continental Defense

[June-July 1775]

Apportionment of $2,000,000 in bills of credit according to population

		souls	dollars
	New Hampshire	100,000	82,713
2	Massachusets	350,000	289,496
	Rhode island	58,000	47,973
	Connecticut	200,000	165,426
	New York	200,000	165,426
	New Jersey	130,000	107,527
3	Pennsylvania	300,000	248,139
	Delaware counties	30,000	24,813
4	Maryland	250,000	206,783
1	Virginia	400,000	330,852
	North Carolina	200,000	165,426
	South Carolina	200,000	165,426
		2,418,000	2,000,000

An estimate of the charge and expence of an army composed of 27,000 private men with the general & staff officers necessary for such a body of infantry.

		dollars
1.	General & commander in chief per month	500.
4.	Major generals [. . .]@166. dollars per month	664.
	allowance for th[e major gen]eral in separate department	166.
8.	Brigadier gener[als . . . a]t 125. pr. m.	1000.
1.	Adjutant gene[eral]	125.
1.	Deputy Adjutan[t gener]al or Brigade major suppose	60.
1.	Commissary General	80.
1.	Deputy Commissary General	60.
1.	Quarter master General	80.
1.	Deputy Quarter master General	40.
1.	Paymaster General	100.
1.	Deputy paymaster	50.
1.	Cheif Engineer	60.
2.	Assistant do.@20. dollrs. each	40.
1.	Chief Engineer in a separate department	60.
2.	Assistants do.@20. dollrs. each	40.
3.	Aid de Camps@33. doll. each	99.
1.	Secretary to the General	66.
1.	Secretary to the Major General in separate department	33.
	Commissary of the musters	20.
	Deputy muster master for New York department suppose	20.
[8.]	Aid de camps to the Major Generals@33. doll. pr. month each	264.
[8].	Brigade majors@30 doll. pr. M. each	240.
1.	Commissary of the Artillery suppose	50.
46.	battalions of 554. privates@£1551-18 pr. M.	237,956
24.	companies of riflemen or light infantry@£181-2 pr. M.	14,[480]
10.	companies of Artillery consisting of 57. men each, officers included at £142-7 each company pr. M.	[4,733]
	36,000 rations of provisions@6d pr. day each, for one month	90,[000]

Transportation of them, stores &c. will at a gross calculation amount to one half the expence of the provisions but
this must be governed by circumstances, so cannot at
present be more exactly calculated   45,[000]

                                                    _____

                                                       396,[086]

                                                    _____

[Total for six months]   2,376,5[16]

2000 barrels of Gunpowder
140 tons of lead
shot & shells with the necessary [. . .] and repairs to be made to the
artillery for the two armies
tents, drums & colours for the whole of the troops

Entrenching & Pioneers tools

Hospital, medicines, Physician, Chirurgeon [apoth]ecary &
attendants

Unavoidable & Contingent expences which [cannot be] foreseen
the above articles for 15,000 [men amount to] the
sum of £105011 by the former es[timate] £105011
the like articles for 27,000 men will
[. . .] be   70006
                                                          ———————
                                                               175017

which in dollars amounts to   583,39[0]

                                                          ———————
                                                            2,959,90[6]

N (DLC). Portions of the text worn and faded; certain figures or parts thereof have been supplied, in brackets, by simple calculation. The caption for the table of bills of credit has also been supplied.

These tabular notes may have been originally compiled by TJ, or he may have merely copied them from papers drawn up during the sittings of the Congress as a committee of the whole "on the state of America" from 11 May until 22 July 1775. Whichever is the case, the notes display at the outset of TJ's national career his habit of making and keeping records of current transactions for later reference that marked his whole public life. Apparently not available elsewhere in print (with the exception noted below), they are well worth study as records of the earliest steps taken by Congress after the outbreak of hostilities. For this first emission of Continental bills of credit, the Journals have only the brief entry, under 22 June, that bills of credit to the value of 2,000,000 Spanish milled dollars were to be emitted "for the defence of America," and that the "twelve confederated colonies" were pledged to redeem them (JCC, II, 103). In 1786 TJ turned over the table showing the apportionment of the bills of credit to J. N. Démeunier for use in the *Encyclopédie methodique: Economie politique et diplomatique*, Paris, 1784-1788, where it is printed in the article "Etats-Unis" (II, 415) as an official estimate of American population at the outbreak of the Revolution; see TJ's Observations on the Article Etats-Unis, 22 June 1786. Concerning the numbers and staff of the Continental army when first organized, there were protracted discussions by the Congress that are impossible to follow because conducted in a committee of the whole, though see the resolutions of 26 May (JCC, II, 65), 14 June (p. 89-90), 15 June (p. 91), 16 June (p. 93-4), 22 June (p. 103-4), and 21 July (p. 201-2).

To Francis Eppes

DEAR SIR   Philadelphia, July 4th, 1775.

Since my last, nothing new has happened. Our accounts of the battle of Charleston have become clear, and greatly to our satisfaction. Contrary to what usually happens, the first accounts were below truth; it is now certain that the regulars have had between 1200 and 1400 killed and wounded in that engagement, and that of these 500 are killed. Major Pitcairn is among the slain, at which everybody rejoices, as he was the commanding officer at Lexington, was the first who fired his own piece there and gave the command to fire. On our part were killed between 60 and 70, and about 150 wounded. Among those killed was a Dr. Warren, a man who seems to have been immensely valued in the North. The New Englanders are fitting out light vessels of war, by which it is hoped we shall not only clear the seas and bays here of everything below the size of a ship of war, but that they will visit the coasts of Europe and distress the British trade in every part of the world. The adventurous genius and intrepidity of those people is amazing. They are now intent on burning Boston as a hive which gives cover to regulars; and none are more bent on it than the very people who come out of it and whose whole prosperity lies there. This however, if done at all, it is thought better to defer till the cold season is coming on, as it would then lay them under irremediable distress. Powder seems now to be our only difficulty, and towards getting plenty of that nothing is wanting but saltpetre. If we can weather out this campaign, I hope that we shall be able to have a plenty made for another. Nothing is requisite but to set about it, as every colony has materials, but more especially Virginia and Maryland. My compliments most affectionately to Mrs. Eppes. Mr. and Mrs. Skipwith, I expect, have left you. Adieu. TH. JEFFERSON

MS not located. Text from Randall, *Life*, III, 568, where the letter was printed from a copy furnished by Fran- cis Eppes of Tallahassee, Florida, grandson of TJ. Addressed: "Francis Eppes, Esq., In Charles City County, Virginia."

To George Gilmer

[5 July 1775]

The battle of Charlestown I expect you have heard, but perhaps not so as you may depend on. The provincials sustained two attacks in their trenches, and twice repulsed the ministerial forces, with immense slaughter. The third attack, however, being made with fixed bayonets, the provincials gave ground, retired a little way, and rallied ready for their enemy; but they, having been pretty roughly handled, did not choose to pursue. We lost between 60 and 70 killed, and about 150 wounded. The enemy had 1400 killed and wounded, of whom were about 500 killed. Major Pitcairn was among the slain; an event at which every one rejoices, as he was the commanding-officer at Lexington, first fired his own piece, and gave command to fire. On our side doctor Warren fell, a man immensely valued to the north. The New Englanders are fitting out privateers, with which they expect to be able to scour the seas and bays of every thing below ships of war; and may probably go to the

European coasts, to distress the British trade there. The enterprising genius and intrepidity of these people are amazing. They are now intent on burning Boston, in order to oust the regulars; and none are more eager for it than those who have escaped out, and who have left their whole property in it: So that, their rage has got the better of every interested principle.

Nobody now entertains a doubt but that we are able to cope with the whole force of Great Britain, if we are but willing to exert ourselves. It will indeed be expensive, extremely expensive; but people must lay aside views of building up fortunes during these troubles, and set apart a good proportion of their income to secure the rest. As our enemies have found we can reason like men, so now let us show them we can fight like men also. The government of Pennsylvania have raised 35,000l. to put their country in a posture of defence. There appear to be as many soldiers here as men. Powder is the great want, and towards having plenty of that nothing is wanting but salt-petre.

The Congress have directed 20,000 men to be raised immediately, the greater part of which is already raised. Two millions of dollars also are voted. This is all I am at liberty to tell of their proceedings. As to the time of their rising, it is totally beyond conjecture, expresses after expresses daily coming from the northward; and the machinations of the *people in office*, on other parts of the continent, keep us from making any progress in the main business. At the same time, such an impatience for home seems to possess us all, that nothing keeps the Congress together but the visible certainty that, till our military proceedings are got into a good train, their separation would endanger the common cause greatly. If things cannot be got into such a state soon as they may be left, we must petition to be exchanged, for fresh hands, that we may return to our families.

P. S. After folding up my letter, we received an account, from an undoubted hand, that the mortality among the wounded regulars has been so great, that the killed on the spot, and those who have died of their wounds, make up 1000. The reason of this is, that they have been long confined to salt provisions, having not so much as a vegetable, a drop of milk, or even any fresh meat.

MS not located. Text from *Virginia Gazette* (Purdie), 28 July 1775, where the letter (presumably complete except for personal compliments) appeared under the caption "*Extract of a letter from one of the* Virginia *delegates, dated* Philadelphia, *July* 5." There can be no question of its having been written by TJ and addressed to George Gilmer, for Gilmer's reply, printed below under the assigned date of 26 or 27 July, deals seriatim with the topics in the present letter. Compare also TJ's letter to Francis Eppes, 4 July 1775.

Declaration of the Causes and Necessity for Taking Up Arms

I. JEFFERSON'S COMPOSITION DRAFT
II. JEFFERSON'S FAIR COPY FOR THE COMMITTEE
III. JOHN DICKINSON'S COMPOSITION DRAFT
IV. THE DECLARATION AS ADOPTED BY CONGRESS

[26 June to 6 July 1775]

EDITORIAL NOTE

THE Declaration of the Causes and Necessity for Taking Up Arms was one of several addresses issued by Congress in the summer of 1775 with the object of justifying to the American people and to the world the necessity for armed resistance. The authorship of this Declaration was the subject of a needless and largely fruitless controversy throughout the nineteenth century. These facts make it necessary to present all known texts of the Declaration and to provide particular comment on the question of authorship.

On 23 June, two days after Jefferson's arrival in Philadelphia, Congress resolved "That a Committee of five be appointed to draw up a declaration, to be published by General Washington, upon his arrival at the camp before Boston. That the committee consist of the following members, viz: Mr. J[ohn] Rutledge, Mr. W[illiam] Livingston, Mr. [Benjamin] Franklin, Mr. [John] Jay, and Mr. [Thomas] Johnson." On the following day, 24 June, the committee reported the draft of a declaration, said to have been written by John Rutledge. No copy of this draft is known to be in existence. After some debate, this draft was postponed for further consideration to Monday, 26 June. On that day it was recommitted, and John Dickinson and Thomas Jefferson were added to the committee. Then followed a delay of about two weeks, caused by Dickinson's unwillingness to accept Jefferson's draft. With that draft before him, however, Dickinson produced a draft which the committee reported to Congress on 6 July, and on the same day it was approved with slight modification. (JCC, II, 101-2, 105-8, 127; see also note on Document IV, below.)

Apparently the first public statement made respecting the authorship of the Declaration was that of John Dickinson in 1801 in a prefatory statement to the two-volume edition of his works published in that year, in which the Declaration and several other addresses and petitions are alluded to as having "always been ascribed to the pen of Mr. Dickinson" (*Political Writings of John Dickinson*, Wilmington, 1801, II, 1; this work was supervised by Dickinson himself). In a letter to John Marshall concerning another address in these volumes, Dickinson made a general statement applicable to the Declaration of Causes and other pieces therein: "I must be guilty of the greatest baseness if, for my

[187]

credit, I knowingly permitted writings which I had not composed to be publicly imputed to me, without a positive and public contradiction of the imputation. This contradiction I never have made, and never shall make, conscious as I am, that every one of those writings was composed by me" (G. H. Moore, *Suum Cuique: John Dickinson, the Author of the Declaration on Taking Up Arms in 1775*, N.Y., 1890, p. 23). Curiously, John Dickinson did not engage in correspondence with Jefferson until the year Dickinson's *Political Writings* was published, but thereafter there was a cordial if somewhat reserved exchange between the two. Nevertheless, despite the fact that Jefferson and every member of his cabinet subscribed to Dickinson's volumes, the subject of his writings was never referred to in the letters that are extant. It is difficult to imagine that Jefferson did not notice Dickinson's claim to authorship of the Declaration on the first page of the second volume.

Jefferson himself made two statements about the authorship of the Declaration. The first of these was written on the verso of the last leaf of what is here referred to as Jefferson's Fair Copy for the Committee (Document II, below; see descriptive note thereon). There can be little room for doubt that this is the earlier of his two statements, as it is certainly the more accurate. The date at which Jefferson wrote that the committee desired Dickinson "to retouch" his own draft cannot be established, but it is very unlikely that it was written in 1775. It was probably written before Dickinson's *Political Writings* appeared in 1801 and was certainly written many years before Jefferson's second statement about the authorship of the Declaration. A plausible guess is that it was written in 1783, for in that year Jefferson had his first approximation of leisure, during which time he went over many of his early Revolutionary documents, including the Declaration of Independence and his Notes of Proceedings in Congress, 7 June to 1 Aug. 1776, making copies of some, endorsing others, jotting down brief commentaries on still others. Whatever the date of composition, the important fact about this statement is that it remained unpublished until 1892, when P. L. Ford included it in his edition (Ford, I, 463). Because of this, Jefferson's second statement, made in his Autobiography begun in 1821, has been more widely quoted and accepted by historians. This statement, made from memory when Jefferson was about 78 years of age, was first published by Randolph in 1829. It was first employed by a biographer in 1837, when George Tucker made use of it in his *Life of Thomas Jefferson*. From that time until the present it has been accepted by a long line of historians, including Parton, Randall, Bancroft, and others. Unfortunately, Jefferson's second statement is so demonstrably erroneous as to raise interesting questions concerning the origins of the claim in his own mind.

This second statement reads in part: "I prepared a Draught of the Declaration committed to us. It was too strong for Mr. Dickinson. He still retained the hope of reconciliation with the mother country, and was unwilling it should be lessened by offensive statements. He was so honest a man, and so able a one that he was greatly indulged even by those who could not feel his scruples. We therefore requested him to take the paper and put it into a form he could approve. He did so, preparing an entire new statement, and preserving of the former one only the last 4. paragraphs and half of the preceding one. We approved and reported it to Congress who accepted it" (Ford, i, 463-4).

It was this statement about the last four and a half paragraphs that historians throughout the nineteenth century accepted in preference to the claims of Dickinson. However, in 1882 G. H. Moore read a paper before the New-York Historical Society in which he announced the discovery of the original composition draft by Dickinson of the Declaration of Causes. Moore expanded this paper and published it privately in 1890 under the title already cited, including in this publication an excellent facsimile of the draft (see Document III, below). The fact that this manuscript bore all the customary evidences of original composition led Moore and others to deny that Jefferson's draft had any influence over it; certainly the erasures, interlineations, and marginalia gave every appearance of being an original rather than a collaborative composition. George Bancroft, forsaking the error into which Jefferson's errant memory had led him, was only the most prominent of those to embrace the new error advanced by Moore. In the final revision of his *History of the United States* he declared: "Of this paper, the author from the first word to the last was Dickinson" (Author's Last Revision, 1891, IV, 237-8; see Stillé, *Life and Times of John Dickinson*, p. 161).

As is readily to be seen by a comparison of the following drafts of the Declaration, both Jefferson's autobiographical statement about the last four and a half paragraphs and Dickinson's claim of 1801, together with the more extreme claims of Moore, Bancroft, Stillé, and others, are erroneous. From these drafts it is possible to reconstruct, with some degree of plausibility, the course of the Declaration in committee and to assess the conflicting claims to authorship. In the absence of the Rutledge draft we can only conjecture what influence it may have had over Jefferson's draft. At least one member of the committee, William Livingston, regarded both as having the same qualities: "Both had the faults common to our Southern gentlemen. Much fault-finding and declamation, with little sense or dignity. They seem to think a reiteration of tyranny, despotism, bloody, &c., all that is needed to unite us at home and convince the bribed voters of North of the justice of our cause" (to William Alexander, 4 July 1775; JCC, II, 128). Jefferson's composition draft, like that by Dickinson, is marked up, crossed out, and interlined. Yet, despite this fact, and despite Livingston's comparison of the two drafts, it is probable that Jefferson made a fresh start.

The statement endorsed by Jefferson on the Fair Copy of his draft (see note on Document II) indicates that "on a meeting of the committee" Dickinson made objections. It seems more likely, however, that Jefferson submitted his Fair Copy to Dickinson before submitting it to the committee; at least it is certain that Dickinson in his own handwriting made some corrections in the phraseology of the text and appended several queries as to the advisability of adding other points to the report. Jefferson then took these suggestions under advisement, rejecting all of the suggested additions and accepting one or two of Dickinson's minor changes of phrasing.

It is quite likely that Jefferson then prepared another fair copy for the committee. His disinclination to incorporate any of the suggested additions or to accept all of the minor changes in phraseology made by Dickinson may have led him to make another draft, and this draft, if one was in fact made, may have been that used by Dickinson in his revision. At any rate, the committee reached some sort of impasse, and Dickinson was called upon to prepare another text. Jefferson's first comment asserted less and his second comment asserted more than Dickinson actually did: the Dickinson draft was more than a "retouching" of the Jefferson text and it was less than "an entire new statement." It can best be described as a revision of the Jefferson draft. The final text of the Declaration as adopted by Congress was, therefore, the result of a collaboration on the part of the two men, however unwilling each was to accept the work of the other. How Jefferson ever came to think that Dickinson had tacked four and a half paragraphs of his draft onto an entirely new statement must remain inexplicable except in terms of an errant memory.

The general conclusion reached by Jefferson himself and by most historians is one that reflects a common appraisal of the two men rather than an exact comparison of their respective contributions to the text of the Declaration. Jefferson's radicalism and Dickinson's conservatism, as generally understood, have been the touchstones by which the Declaration has been judged. The result has been less than justice to either in respect to the authorship of one of the most popular of all state papers of the early days of the Revolution. Their respective contributions can best be judged, both stylistically and in substance, by considering what Dickinson rejected, what he added, and in what manner he altered Jefferson's words.

It is apparent at a glance that Dickinson followed the outline and structure of Jefferson's draft, occasionally copying long passages almost verbatim in the beginning, middle, and end of the text. It is apparent, too, that, far from softening Jefferson's words, Dickinson actually went further in severity. Stylistically, Dickinson both harmed and improved upon Jefferson. Jefferson's preamble, stating the fact of usurpation of power by Parliament and an attempt to enforce by arms what could not be done by right or law, is simple, straightforward, and direct. Dickinson's opening sentence is extraordinarily complex and involved, and his whole prefatory statement requires much more than twice the number of words that Jefferson used to say the same thing. The author of *The Rights of Great Britain Asserted* (4th edn., London, 1776, p. 2-3) made his initial attack on this "involved period, which either contains no meaning, or a meaning not founded on the principles of reason." In respect to substance, this criticism applies equally to the drafts by Jefferson and Dickinson, but in respect to style there can be no doubt that Dickinson's opening is much more of an "involved period" than Jefferson's. Yet it was Dickinson who contributed the bold and quotable words toward the close of the document: "Our cause is just. Our union is perfect. Our internal resources are great, and, if necessary, foreign assistance is attainable." This is not the language of one who is intent upon watering down a statement; it is daring and threatening, and its rhythm and terseness admirably suited it to the purpose at hand.

In the development of the Declaration, devoted to an explanation of the origin of the colonies, their establishment of "a residence for civil & religious freedom," their growth, and their contribution to the wealth and power of the British Empire, Jefferson conceded that in the past the colonies had occasionally, from warmth of affection, acquiesced in some assumptions of power by Parliament in legislating for the colonies. The concession is a tribute to his historical accuracy and to his sense of justice, but forensically it was a serious admission. Dickinson followed the maxim of the hustings: attack everything and admit nothing. He therefore omitted the concession that Jefferson had made. In the same part of the Declaration Dickinson gave an apparent indication of his unwillingness to accept Jefferson's theory of imperial relations: that is, colonies arranged "by charters of compact under the same common king, who thus completed their powers of full and perfect legislation and became the link of union between the several parts of the empire." Dickinson changed this to read: "Societies or governments, vested with perfect Legislatures, were formed under Charters from the Crown, and an harmonious Intercourse was established between the Colonies and the Kingdom from which they derived their Origin." Jefferson's statement is a more forthright assertion of the doctrine he had set forth in the *Summary View* and one that was rapidly coming to be accepted in America. Dickinson's revision of Jefferson's statement was, to say the least, ambiguous. The term "perfect Legislatures" implied agreement in substance with Jefferson. The term "Charters from the Crown," however, was rather inconsistent with a later revision of Jefferson's text. At another point Jefferson had used the phrase "secured by charters on the part of the crown and confirmed by acts of it's own legislature." Dickinson altered this to read: charters "secured by Acts of its own Legislature solemnly confirmed by the Crown." Both statements inferentially were inconsistent with Jefferson's interpretation of the imperial constitution, though technically Jefferson was more correct. In conceding Parliament an authority to participate in the granting of charters, both made some concession to Jefferson's theory, with Jefferson placing more emphasis upon the crown and Dickinson placing more upon the Parliament. In short, it would seem to be too much to say that Dickinson categorically rejected Jefferson's theory of imperial relations; it appears to be closer to the truth to say that he softened the blunt expression of it, partially obscuring the meaning in doing so.

Dickinson's chief departures from the Jefferson text are the following: (1) his tribute to Pitt, who publicly declared that the colonies had materially assisted in winning the late war with France; (2) his elaboration of Jefferson's list of the "new legislation" (which in Dickinson's more severe phrase becomes "the pernicious Project"); for example, Dickinson added to Jefferson's list the charges of exempting "murderers of colonists" from legal trial and of quartering soldiers on the colonists in time of peace; (3) the account of the treatment of the Petition to the Crown of 1774; (4) the mention of the Address of the

Lords and Commons declaring Massachusetts in a state of rebellion; (5) the proposal of Lord North "to extort from us, at the point of the Bayonet, the unknown sums that should be sufficient to gratify, if possible to gratify, ministerial Rapacity. . ."; (6) the charge that Governor Carleton was engaged in instigating Canadians and Indians to attack the colonists. These are all additions to Jefferson's text; nothing of importance in the corresponding parts of Jefferson's draft is omitted by Dickinson. It will be readily seen that the most significant of these additions are precisely those that Dickinson had suggested to Jefferson (see queries written by Dickinson on the last page of Document II).

From the foregoing it is apparent that the impasse reached in committee between 26 June and 6 July cannot be ascribed, as has generally been done by historians and was, indeed, done by Jefferson himself, to the fact that Jefferson proposed a radical declaration that seemed to close the door to conciliation and that Dickinson weakened and modified this bold proclamation in order to promote harmony and attempts at reconciliation. Such an interpretation no doubt coincides with the general opinion of the characters of the two men, but it does not coincide with the facts respecting the text of the Declaration. Both expressed hope for a restoration of harmony. Both declared merely the aim of resisting violence and not of intending something else. But whereas Jefferson employed a circumlocution ("we mean not in any wise to affect that union with them" and "we did not embody a soldiery to commit aggression on them"), Dickinson was blunt ("we mean not to dissolve that union" and "we have not raised armies with ambitious designs of separating from Great-Britain, and of establishing independent States . . ."). When Jefferson unveiled the implicit threat in these words, he was also less blunt than Dickinson: "That necessity must be hard indeed which may force upon us this desperate measure." Dickinson's comparable words were more suited to his bold mention of independence: "Necessity has not yet driven us into that desperate measure," the words "not yet" carrying an ominous warning. In his appeal to pro-American Whigs in England, in his elaboration of Jefferson's arguments, in his detailed account of the suffering of Americans in Massachusetts ("wives separated from husbands, children from parents . . ."), and in his closing affirmation of the justice of the American cause and the strength of its union, Dickinson helped make it both a more suitable and a more inflammatory Declaration. Jefferson's refusal to accept Dickinson's suggestions resulted in a stronger, not a weaker text. In the final analysis the differences in the Committee, instead of revolving around polarities of radicalism and conservatism, are reduced to issues of style and method of presentation between two of the great penmen of the Revolution. (For a more extended analysis, see Julian P. Boyd, "The Disputed Authorship of the Declaration on the Causes and Necessity for Taking Up Arms, 1775," PMHB, LXXIV [1950], 51-73.)

This series of documents is presented with literal fidelity, and all deletions and alterations are indicated so far as they can be discerned. In such heavily revised texts as Documents I and III, particularly the latter, it is not possible, however, to render all the successive stages of revision satisfactorily in print.

I. Jefferson's Composition Draft

The large strides ⟨advances⟩ of late taken by the legislature of
Great Britain towards establishing ⟨in⟩ over[1] the colonies their
absolute rule, and the hardiness of their present attempt to effect
by force of arms what by law or right they could never effect
render⟨s⟩ it necessary for us also to change ⟨shift⟩ the ground of
opposition and to close with their last[2] appeal from reason to arms.
And as it behoves those who are called to this great decision to be
assured that their cause is approved before supreme reason so is it
of great avail that it's justice be made known to the world whose
⟨prayers cannot be wanting intercessions⟩ affections will ever ⟨be
favorable to a people⟩ take part with those encountring oppression.
our forefathers, inhabitants of the island of Gr. Britn. ⟨harrassed⟩
having ⟨vainly⟩ ⟨there⟩ long endeavored to bear up against the evils
of misrule, left their native land to seek on these shores a residence
for civil & religious freedom. at the expence of their blood ⟨with⟩
to the ⟨loss⟩ ruin of their fortunes, with the relinquishment of every
thing quiet & comfortable in life, they effected settlements in the
inhospitable wilds of America; they there established civil societies ⟨under⟩ with various forms of constitution but possessing all,
what is inherent in all, the full & perfect powers of legislation. to
continue their connection with ⟨those⟩ the friends whom they had
left ⟨& loved⟩ ⟨but⟩ they arranged themselves by charters of compact under ⟨the same⟩ one common king ⟨who became the⟩ ⟨thro
whom a union was ensured to the now multiplied⟩ who thus became
the link ⟨uniting⟩ of union between the several parts of the empire.
some occasional assumptions of power by the parl. of Gr. Brit.
however ⟨unknown to⟩ ⟨foreign to⟩ unacknoleged by the constitu-
tion⟨s we had formed⟩ of our governments, were finally acquiesced
[. . .] in ⟨in⟩ thro' ⟨the⟩ warmth of affectn. proceeding thus in the
fulness of harmony & confidence both parts of the empire encreased
in population and in wealth with a rapidity unknown in the history
of m[an]. the ⟨various soils⟩ political institutions of America, it's
various ⟨climes⟩ soils & climates open[ed] ⟨certain⟩ ⟨sure⟩ certain
resource to the unfortunate & to the enterprising of ⟨all⟩ every
countr⟨ies⟩y ⟨where⟩ and ensured to them the acquisition & free
possession of property. Great Britain too acquired a lustre & a
weight ⟨in the political [sys]tem⟩ among the powers of the ⟨world⟩
earth which ⟨it is thought⟩ her internal resources could never have
given her. to ⟨the⟩ a communication of the wealth & the power of
⟨the several parts of the⟩ ⟨whole⟩ every part of the empire we may

surely ascribe in some measure ⟨*surely ascribe*⟩ [the illu]strious character she sustained ⟨*in*⟩ thro'[3] [her la]st European war [& it's succes]sful event. At the close of that war however ⟨*Gr. Britain*⟩ having subdued all her foes, she took up the unfortunate idea of subduing her friends also. her parliament then for the first time asserted a right of unbounded legislation ⟨*for*⟩ over the colonies of America ⟨*by several acts*[4] *passed in the*[5] *5th*[6] *the 6th the 7th &* *the 8th years of the reign of her present majesty several duties were imposed for the purpose of raising a revenue on the American colonists, the powers of courts of admiralty were extended beyond their antient limits and the inestimable right*[7] [*of*] *trial by twelve peers of our vicinage was taken away in cases affecting both life & property. by part of an act passed in the 12th year of the present reign an American colonist charged with the offences described in that act may be transported beyond sea for trial*[8] *by the very persons against whose pretended sovereignty the*[9] *offence is supposed to be committed*⟩ and pursuing with eagerness the newly assumed thought ⟨*have*⟩ in the space of 10 years during which they have exercised ys. right have ⟨*made*⟩ given such ⟨*strides towards the establishment of absolute government over us*⟩ ⟨*severe*⟩ decisive specimens of the spirit ⟨*in which*⟩ of this new legislation ⟨*would be exercised*⟩ ⟨*conducted*⟩ as leaves no room to [doubt the] consequence of ⟨*our further*⟩ acquiescence under it. ⟨*by*[10] *two acts passed in the 14th y. of his present majesty they have assumed a right of alter- ing the form of our governments altogether, and of thereby taking away every security for the possession of life or of property.*⟩ by several acts of parliament passed ⟨*in the reign of his present maj- esty*⟩ within ⟨*since*⟩ that ⟨*period*⟩ space of time they have ⟨*imposed upon us duties for the purpose of raising a revenue*⟩ attempted to take from us our money without our consent, they have ⟨*taken away the*⟩ interdicted all commerce ⟨*first of*⟩ to one of our principal ⟨*trading*⟩ towns thereby annihilating it's property in the hands of the holders, ⟨*& more lately*⟩ they have cut off ⟨*our*⟩ the commercial intercourse ⟨*with all of several of these*⟩ of whole ⟨*whole*⟩ colonies with ⟨*all*⟩ foreign countries ⟨*whatsoever*⟩; they have extended the jurisdiction of ⟨*the*⟩ courts of admiralty beyond their antient limits, thereby depriving us of the inestimable right of trial by jur⟨*ies*⟩y in cases affecting both life & property ⟨*& subjecting both to the*[11] *arbitrary decision of a single & dependent judge*⟩; they have de- clared that American subjects ⟨*committing*⟩ charged with certain ⟨*pretended*⟩ offences shall be transported beyond sea ⟨*for trial*⟩ to be tried before the very persons against whose pretended sovereignty offence is supposed to be committed; they have attempted fundamentally to alter the form of government in one of these colonies, a form established by acts of it's own legislature, and further secured ⟨to them⟩ by charters ⟨of compact with⟩ ⟨& grants from⟩ on the part of the crown; they have erected ⟨a tyranny⟩ in a neighboring province, acquired by the joint arms of Great Britain & America, a tyranny dangerous to the very existence [of all] these colonies. but why should we enumerate their injuries in the detail? by one act they have suspended the powers of one American legislature & by another ⟨they⟩ have declared they may legislate for us themselves in all cases whatsoever. these two acts alone form a basis broad enough whereon to erect a despotism of unlimited extent, ⟨when it is considered that the persons by whom these acts are passed are not with us subject to their evil⟩ and what is to ⟨prevent⟩ secure us against ⟨the demolition of our present & establishment of new & despotic forms of government?⟩ this dreaded evil? the persons ⟨who⟩ assuming these powers ⟨of doing this⟩ are not chosen by ⟨ourselves⟩ us, are not subject to ⟨us⟩ our controul ⟨from us⟩, are ⟨themselves freed⟩ exempted by their situation from the operation of these laws ⟨they thus pass⟩, and ⟨remove from themselves as much burthen as they impose upon us⟩ lighten their own burthens in proportion as they increase ours. these ⟨are⟩ temptations might put to trial the severest characters of antient virtue: with what new armour then shall a British parliament then encounter the rude assault? toward these deadly injuries from the tender plant of liberty which we have brought over & with so much affection ⟨we have planted⟩ and have fostered on these our own shores we have pursued every lawful & every respectful measure. we have sup[plicat]ed our king at various times in terms almost disgraceful to freedom; we have reasoned, we have remonstrated with parliament in the most mild & decent language; we have even proceeded to ⟨break off our commercial intercourse with them altogether, as to⟩ ⟨the last peaceable admonition of our determination to be free by breaking off altogether our commercial intercourse with them⟩ break off our commercial intercourse with ⟨them⟩ our fellow subjects, as the last peaceable admonition that our attachment to no nation on earth should supplant our attachment to liberty: and here we had well hoped was the ultimate step of the controversy. but subsequent events have shewn how vain was even this last remain of confidence in the moderation of the British ministry. during the course of the last year ⟨they⟩ their troops in a hostile manner invested the town of Boston in the province of

Massachuset's bay, ⟨wh⟩ and from that time have held the same
beleaguered by sea & land. on the 19th day of April ⟨last⟩ in the
present year they made an unprovoked ⟨attack⟩ assault on the inhabitants of the sd province at the town of Lexington, ⟨killed⟩
murdered eight of them on the spot and wound⟨ing⟩ed many others.
from thence they proceeded in ⟨warlike⟩ ⟨the same⟩ all the array
of war to the town of Concord where they ⟨attacked⟩ set upon another party of the inhabitants of the ⟨sd⟩ same province killing many
of them also burning ⟨their⟩ houses ⟨&⟩ laying waste ⟨their⟩ property ⟨& continuing these depredations⟩ until repressed by the arms
of the people assembled to oppose this ⟨hostile invasion on their
lives & properties⟩ ⟨unprovoked⟩ cruel aggression. hostilities ⟨being
thus⟩ thus commenced on the part of the ⟨British⟩ Ministerial
⟨troops they⟩ army have been since ⟨without respite⟩ by them pursued ⟨the same⟩ ⟨by them⟩ without regard to faith or to fame. the
inhabitants of the ⟨said⟩ town of Boston having entered into treaty
with a certain Thomas Gage, ⟨said to be commander in chief of
the adverse[12] troops, & who has actually been a principal actor in
the seige of the town of Boston, proffered to the inhabitants of the
sd town a liberty to depart from the same on⟩ principal ⟨actor⟩ &
instigator of these ⟨enormities⟩ ⟨violences⟩ enormities, it was stipulated that the sd inhabitants having first deposited ⟨their arms and
mili⟩ with their own magistrates their arms & military stores should
have free liberty to depart ⟨out of the same⟩ ⟨from⟩ the sd town
taking with them their other goods and ⟨other⟩ effects. their arms
& military stores ⟨were⟩ they accordingly delivered in ⟨to their
magistrates⟩, & claimed the stipulated license of departing with
their effects. but in open violation of plighted faith & honor, in
defiance of ⟨those⟩ th⟨at⟩e sacred ⟨laws of nations⟩ obligations of
treaty which even ⟨the⟩ savage nations observe⟨s⟩, their arms &
warlike stores deposited with their own magistrates to be ⟨kept⟩
preserved as their property were immediately seised by a body of
armed men under orders from the sd Thomas Gage, the greater
part of the inhabitants were detained in the town & the few permitted to depart were compelled to leave their most valuable ⟨goods⟩
effects behind. we leave ⟨to⟩ the world ⟨to their⟩ to it's own reflections on this atrocious perfidy. ⟨the same Thos Gage on the 12th
day of June⟩ that we might no longer ⟨be in⟩ doubt the ultimate
⟨purpose⟩ ⟨object⟩ aim of these Ministerial manoeuvres, the same
Thos. Gage ⟨on⟩ by proclamn bearing date the 12th day of June
⟨by⟩ after reciting the ⟨most abandoned⟩ grossest falshoods &
calumnies against the⟨s⟩ good people of ⟨America⟩ these colonies

proceeds to declare them all either by name or description to be rebels & traitors, to supersede by his own authority the exercise of the common law ⟨of the land⟩ of the sd province and to proclaim & order instead thereof the use & exercise of the law martial ⟨throughout the sd province⟩. this bloody edict issued, he has proceeded to commit further ravages & murders in the same province burning the town of Charlestown ⟨&⟩ attacking & killing great numbers of the people residing or assembled therein; and is now going on in an avowed course of murder & devastation, taking every occasion to destroy⟨ing⟩ the lives & properties of the inhabitants ⟨whenever he can⟩ ⟨continue to⟩ ⟨find occasion⟩ ⟨get them within his power⟩ of the sd province. to oppose ⟨their⟩ his arms we also have taken ⟨up⟩ arms. we should be wanting to ourselves, we should be ⟨wanting⟩ perfidious to ⟨our⟩ posterity, we should be unworthy that free ancestry from ⟨which both they & we[13] derived[14] our common birth were we to suffer ourselves to be butchered & our properties to be laid waste⟩ whom we derive our ⟨birth⟩ descent should we submit with folded arms to military butchery & depredation to gratify the lordly ambition ⟨of any nation on earth and⟩ or sate the avarice of a British ministry. We do then, most solemnly ⟨in the presence of⟩ ⟨befo⟩ before God & the world declare that, regardless of every consequence, at the risk of every distress, ⟨that⟩ the arms we have been compelled to assume we will wage with ⟨bitter⟩ perseverance, exerting to their utmost energies all those powers ⟨with⟩ which our creator hath ⟨given⟩ ⟨invested⟩ given us to ⟨guard⟩ preserve that ⟨sacred⟩ Liberty which he committed to us in sacred deposit & to protect from every hostile hand our lives & our properties. But that this our declaration ⟨& our determined resolution⟩ may ⟨give no disquietude to⟩[15] not disquiet the minds of our good fellow subjects in all parts of the empire, we do further ⟨declare⟩ ⟨add⟩ assure them that we mean not in any wise to affect that union with them in which we have so long & so happily lived & which we wish so much to see again restored. that necessity must be hard indeed which ⟨could⟩ may force upon us this desperate measure, or induce us to avail ourselves of any aid ⟨which⟩ their[16] enemies ⟨of Great Britain⟩ might proffer. we took ⟨up⟩ arms ⟨to defend⟩ in defence of our persons & properties under actual⟨ly⟩ violat⟨ed⟩ion: ⟨when the ministerial party therefore⟩ ⟨hostilities shall cease⟩ ⟨on the ministerial⟩ when that viol[ation?] shall be removed, when hostilities shall ⟨be suspended⟩ ⟨hostilities⟩ cease on the⟨ir⟩ ⟨ministerial⟩ part of the aggressors, ⟨they⟩ hostilities shall ⟨be suspended⟩ cease on our part also; ⟨when⟩ the moment they withdraw their armies we will disband ours. ⟨*next to a vigorous exertion of our own internal force, we throw ourselves for*⟩ we did not embody ⟨*men*⟩ a soldiery to commit aggression on them; we did not raise armies for[17] ⟨*march to*⟩ glory or for[17] conquest ⟨*or to glory*⟩; we did not invade their island ⟨*proffering*⟩ carrying death or slavery to [it's inhab]itants. towards the atchievement of this happy event we call ⟨*on*⟩ ⟨*in*⟩ for & confide in the good offices of our fellow subjects beyond the Atlantic. ⟨*of*⟩ of their friendly dispositions we ⟨*confide*⟩ ⟨*hope with justice*⟩ ⟨*reason*⟩ can not yet cease to hope, ⟨*& assure them they are*⟩ aware as they must be that they have nothing more to expect from the same common enemy than the humble favor of being last devoured.

Dft (DLC); this four-page manuscript in TJ's hand lacks title, date, and endorsement. A good example tending to prove the present document an original composition as opposed to the kind of rough draft of a revision produced by Dickinson is to be found in the last ten lines of the first page of the manuscript, where TJ first provided a brief summary of the various offensive acts of Parliament. As a summary it was effective, but if it served merely as an introduction to a more detailed account of these acts, then it was needlessly repetitive. It was struck out, and in the next page TJ proceeded for more than forty lines to restate the same subject matter, only to conclude with the words: "But why should we enumerate their injuries in the detail?" He had, in short, struck out the summary, provided the detail, and then rhetorically asked why it was necessary. This device, for an address intended to win popular support, was indubitably effective, and it would scarcely have resulted if TJ had merely been revising Rutledge's draft as Dickinson later revised TJ's. He was actually engaged in a fresh composition, and a close study of the labored text reveals something of the effort that TJ devoted to the style of his first major state paper. The two significant textual differences between the Composition Draft (the present document) and the Fair Copy (Document II, below) are: (1) the former lacks a title, the one included in the Fair Copy bearing evidence of having been composed rather than copied; (2) a final sentence was added to the Fair Copy: "And we do devoutly implore the assistance of Almighty god to conduct us happily thro' this great conflict. . . ." Either or both of these additions may have been suggested by Dickinson or by the committee.

[1] TJ originally wrote "to establish in these colonies."

[2] "Last" is interlined.

[3] The change here illustrates the impossibility of following all minute alterations except perhaps by facsimile reproduction. TJ originally wrote "in her"; then struck out "in," interlined "t" before "her"; and superimposed "hro'" on "her."

[4] TJ first wrote "an act."

[5] The word "years" has here been earlier deleted.

[6] "&" has here been earlier deleted.

[7] The words "of being tried in all cases civil" have here been earlier deleted.

[8] The words "of such offence" have here been earlier deleted.

[9] The word "supposed" has here been earlier deleted.

[10] Here TJ first wrote "two other acts," then struck out "two" and wrote "three," then struck out "three" and "other."

[11] The word "decision" has here been earlier deleted.

[12] TJ first wrote "sd."

[13] The word "are" has here been interlined and then deleted.

[14] The word "our" has here been earlier deleted; "one" was substituted for it and in turn deleted.

[15] Dft does not delete "give"; TJ first wrote the phrase as given in brackets, then added "t" to "no," deleted "disquietude to" and interlined "disquiet." The presence of "in" interlined and de-

leted above the first syllable of "disquietude" suggests that TJ may first have
altered the phrase to make it read "may
give no inquietude to" but that, in further changing it, he neglected to strike
out "give."

16 TJ first wrote "the enemies of
Great Britain," then struck out "of
Great Britain" and added "ir" to "the."
17 In both places TJ first wrote "to"
and then, after changing the subsequent phrase, wrote "for" over "to."

II. Jefferson's Fair Copy for the Committee

⟨We⟩ A Declaration ⟨of⟩ by the representatives of the United
colonies of America now sitting in General Congress, ⟨to all nations
send greeting⟩ ⟨of⟩ setting forth the causes & necessity of their
tak[ing up arms].

The large strides of late taken by the *legislature of Great Britain*
towards establishing over these colonies their absolute rule, and
the hardiness of the[1] present attempt to effect by force of arms what
by law or right they could never effect, *render* it necessary for us
also to change the ground of opposition, and to close with their last
appeal from reason to arms. and as it behoves those, *who are called
to this great decision*, to be assured that their cause is approved
before supreme reason; so is it of great avail that it's justice be
made known to the world, whose affections will ever take part with
those encountering oppression. Our forefathers, inhabitants of the
island of Great Britain ⟨*having long endeavored to bear up against
the evils of misrule*⟩, left their native land⟨*s*⟩[2] to seek on these shores
a residence for civil & religious freedom. at the expence of their
blood, ⟨*with*⟩[3] to the ruin of their fortunes, with the relinquishment
of every thing quiet & comfortable in life, they effected settlements
in the inhospitable wilds of America; ⟨*they*⟩ and there established
civil societies with various forms of constitution⟨*s*⟩ ⟨*but possessing
all what is inherent in all, the full and perfect powers of legislation*⟩.
to continue their connection with the friends whom they had left
they arranged themselves by charters of compact under ⟨*one*⟩ the
same common king, who thus completed their powers of full and
perfect legislation and became the link of union between the several
parts of the empire. some occasional assumptions of power by the
parliament of Great Britain, however unacknowledged by the constitution of our governments, were finally acquiesced in thro'
warmth of affection. proceeding thus in the fulness of mutual[4]
harmony and confidence, both parts of the empire increased in population & in wealth with a rapidity unknown in the history of man.
the political institutions of America, it's various [soils and climates
opened a] certain resource to the unfortunate & to the enterprising of

every country, and ensured to them the acquisition & free possession of property. Great Britain too acquired a lustre and a weight among the powers of the earth, which her internal resources could never have given her. to a communication of the wealth and the power of ⟨*the whole*⟩[5] every part of the empire we may surely ascribe in some measure the illustrious character she sustained through her last European war, & it's successful event. at the close of that war ⟨*however having subdued all her foes, she*⟩ ⟨*her successful & glorious Minister was discarded & successive*[6]⟩ it pleased our sovereign to make a change.[7] the new ministry finding all the foes of Britain subdued took up the unfortunate idea of subduing her friends also. ⟨*by their Influence*[8]⟩ her parliament then for the first time ⟨*asserted a right*⟩ ⟨*were persuaded to assume & assert*[6]⟩ assumed a power of unbounded legislation over the Colonies of America; and[9] in the ⟨*space*⟩ course of ten years ⟨*during which they have*⟩ ⟨*proceeded to exercise*⟩⟨*d*⟩ ⟨*this right*⟩ have given such decisive specimen[10] of the spirit of this new legislation as leaves no room to doubt the consequence of acquiescence under it. by several acts of parliament passed within that spa[ce of time] they have ⟨*attempted to take from us*⟩ undertaken to give and grant our money without our consent, a right of which we have ever had the exclusive exercise; they have interdicted all commerce to one of our principal towns, thereby annihilating it's property in the hands of the holders; they have cut off the commercial intercourse of whole colonies with foreign countries; they have extended the jurisdiction of courts of admiralty beyond their antient limits; the⟨*reb*⟩y have depriv⟨*ing*⟩ed us of the inestimable ⟨*right*⟩ privilege of trial by a jury of the vicinage in cases affecting both*[11] life & property; they have declared that American subjects charged with certain offences shall be transported beyond sea to be tried before the very persons against whose pretended sovereignty the[12] offence is supposed to be committed; they have attempted fundamentally to alter the form of government in one of these colonies, a form ⟨*established*⟩ secured by charters on the part of the crown and confirmed by acts of it's own legislature ⟨*and further secured by charters on the part of the crown*⟩; they have erected in a neighboring province, acquired by the joint arms of Great Britain & America a tyranny dangerous to the very existence of all these colonies. But why should we enumerate their injuries in the detail? by one act they have suspended the powers of one American legislature, & by another have declared they may legislate for us themselves in all cases whatsoever. these two acts alone form a basis broad enough whereon to erect a despotism of unlimited extent. and what is to secure us against this dreaded evil? the persons assuming these powers are not chosen by us, are not subject to our controul or influ[ence][13] are exempted by their situation from the operation of these laws, and lighten their own burthens in proportion as they increase ours. these temptations might put to trial the severest characters of antient virtue: with what new armour then shall a British parliament encounter the rude assault? toward these deadly injuries from the tender plant of liberty which we have brought over, & with so much affection fostered on these our own shores we have pursued every temperate, every respectful measure. we have supplicated our king at various times, in terms almost disgraceful to freedom; we have reasoned, we have remonstrated with parliament in the most mild & decent language; we have even proceeded to break off our commercial intercourse with our fellow subjects, as the last peaceable admonition that our attachment to no nation on earth should supplant our attachment to liberty. and here we had well hoped was the ultimate step of the controversy. but subsequent events have shewn how vain was even this last remain of confidence in the moderation of the British ministry.*[14] during the course of the last year their troops in a hostile manner invested the town of Boston in the province of Massachuset's bay, and from that time have held the same beleaguered by sea & land. on the 19th day of April in the present year they made an unprovoked ⟨attack⟩[5] assault on the inhabitants of the said province at the town of Lexington, murdered eight of them on the spot and wounded many others. from thence they proceeded in ⟨the⟩ all the array of war to the town of Concord where they set upon another party of the inhabitants of the same province, killing many of them also burning houses, & laying waste property until repressed by ⟨the arms of⟩ the ⟨Country⟩[8] people ⟨who⟩[8] suddenly assembled to oppose this cruel aggression. hostilities thus commenced on the part of the ministerial army have been since by them pursued without regard to faith or to fame. the inhabitants of the town of Boston in order to procure their enlargement having entered into treaty with ⟨a certain Thomas Gage, principal instigator of these enormities⟩ General Gage their Governor ⟨to procure their Enlargement⟩,[15] it was stipulated that the said inhabitants, ⟨after⟩[8] having first deposited their arms with their own magistrates ⟨their arms & military stores⟩ should have free liberty to depart out of the said town, taking with them their other ⟨goods &⟩ effects. their arms ⟨and military stores⟩ they accordingly delivered in, and claimed the stipulated license of departing with their effects. but in open violation of plighted faith & honor, in defiance of the sacred obligations of treaty which even savage nations observe, their arms ⟨and warlike stores⟩, deposited with their own magistrates to be preserved as their property, were immediately seised by a body of armed men under orders from the said ⟨Thomas⟩ General [Gage,] the greater part of the inhabitants were detained in the town, and the few permitted to depart were compelled to leave their most valuable effects behind. we leave the world to ⟨their⟩ it's own reflections on this atrocious perfidy. that we might no longer doubt the ultimate aim of these ministerial manoeuvres, ⟨the same Thomas⟩ General Gage, by proclamation bearing date the 12th day of June, after reciting the grossest falsehoods and calumnies against the good people of these colonies, proceeds to declare them all, either by name or description, to be rebels & traitors, to supersede ⟨by his own authority⟩ the exercise of the common law of the said province, and to proclaim and order instead thereof the use and exercise of the law martial. this bloody edict issued, he has proceeded to commit further ravages & murders in the same province, burning the town of Charlestown, attacking & killing great numbers of the people residing or assembled therein; and is now going on in an avowed course of murder & devastation, taking every occasion to destroy the lives & properties of the inhabitants ⟨of the said province⟩. to oppose his arms, we also have taken arms. we should be wanting to ourselves, we should be perfidious to posterity, we should be unworthy that free ancestry from ⟨whom⟩ ⟨which⟩ ⟨whom⟩ which we derive our descent, should we submit with folded arms to military butchery & depredation, to gratify the lordly ambition, or sate the avarice of a British ministry. We do then most solemnly, before god and the world declare, that, regardless of every consequence, at the risk of every distress, the arms we have been compelled to assume we will ⟨wage⟩ use with perseverance, exerting to the utmost energies all those powers which our creator hath given us, to ⟨guard⟩[5] preserve that liberty which he committed to us in sacred deposit, & to protect from every hostile hand our lives & our properties. But that this ⟨our⟩ declaration may not disquiet the minds of our ⟨good⟩ Friends &[16] fellow subjects ⟨in Britain or other⟩ in any part⟨s⟩[17] of the empire, we do further assure them that we mean not in any wise to affect that union with them in which we have so long & so happily lived, and which we wish so much to see again restored. that necessity must be hard indeed which may force upon us this desperate measure, or induce us to avail ourselves of any aid ⟨which⟩[5] their enemies might proffer. we did not embody a soldiery to commit aggression on them; we did not raise armies for glory or for conquest. we did not invade their island carrying death or slavery to it's inhabitants.[18] ⟨we took arms⟩ in defence of our persons and properties under actual violation we ⟨have taken⟩ took up arms. when that violence shall be removed, when hostilities shall cease on the part of the aggressors, hostilities shall cease on our part also. ⟨the moment they withdraw their armies we will disband ours.⟩ for the atchievement[19] of this happy event, we call for & confide in the good offices of our fellow subjects beyond the Atlantic. of their friendly dispositions we do not yet cease to hope; aware, as they must be, that they have nothing more to expect from the same common enemy than the humble favor of being last devoured. and we devoutly implore the assistance of Almighty god to conduct us happily thro' this great conflict to dispose ⟨the minds of⟩ his majesty, his ministers, & parliament to ⟨reasonable terms⟩ reconciliation with us on reasonable terms & to deliver[20] us from the evils of a civil war.[21]

2d Dft (DLC); a fair copy endorsed by TJ on verso of second leaf: "1775. June 23. Congress appointed a commee. to prepare a Declaration to be published by Genl. Washington on his arrival at the camp before Boston, to wit, J. Rutledge, W. Livingston, Dr. Franklin, Mr. Jay, & Mr. Johnson. June 24. a draught was reported. June 26. being disliked, it was recommitted & ⟨T. Jeff⟩ Mr. Dickinson & T. Jefferson added to the committee. the latter being desired by the commee. to draw up a new one, he prepared this paper. on a meeting of the commee., J. Dickinson objected that it was too harsh, wanted softening &c. whereupon the commee. desired him to retouch it, which he did in the form which they reported July 6. which was adopted by Congress." Neither the 2d Dft nor its endorsement bears a date; the latter may have been written about 1783 (see Editorial Note preceding this series of documents). 2d Dft also has some corrections and queries in the hand of Dickinson (see notes below).

Inasmuch as TJ failed to adopt most of Dickinson's suggestions, it is quite probable that he made still another fair copy from the 2d Dft for presentation to the committee. Dickinson certainly had before him a text of TJ's 2d Dft when he made his own rough draft revision of it. The fact that this one is still among TJ's papers would seem to indicate that Dickinson must have employed some other copy; if so, it is not known to be in existence and is not to be found among the Dickinson manuscripts. 2d Dft, referred to in the notes below as Fair Copy, follows the Composition Draft except for the minor changes noted below.

[1] Composition Draft reads "their."
[2] Composition Draft reads "land"; copied as "lands" and then changed back to original form.
[3] Composition Draft reads "with"; both were changed to "to" in the course of copying.
[4] Fair Copy departs from Composition Draft by addition of "mutual."
[5] This correction made in both drafts in the course of copying.
[6] The second deletion is interlined in a different hand, apparently that of John Dickinson; then deleted.
[7] Both Ford (I, 466) and JCC (II, 131) present this reading: "to make a change in his counsels." But the word "change" is at the end of a line and no further words can be discerned after it. The phrase "change in his counsels" does, however, occur in the Dickinson draft.
[8] This word or passage, believed to be in Dickinson's hand, was interlined and then in turn deleted.
[9] Fair Copy omits the following phrase found in Composition Draft: "pursuing with eagerness the newly assumed thought."
[10] Composition Draft: "specimens."

11 The asterisk here and another in the margin were probably inserted by Dickinson, but no words follow the marginal asterisk.

12 The word interlined seems to be in another hand, probably that of Dickinson.

13 Preceding two words not in Composition Draft.

14 This asterisk, similar in characteristics and in being repeated in the margin to that described in note 11, was inserted by Dickinson. Following the asterisk in the margin are the following words in Dickinson's hand: "Here insert the substance of the Address declaring a Rebellion to exist in Massachusetts Bay."

15 The words in brackets were interlined by Dickinson; TJ then struck out the phrase and interlined it in the first part of the sentence, prefixing the words "in order"; in short, he accepted Dickinson's addition, but rearranged the sentence making it slightly less awkward. However, TJ did accept Dickinson's modification of the undignified reference to "a certain Thomas Gage" and interlined in his own hand the words "General Gage their Governor."

16 The words "Friends &" interlined in Dickinson's hand.

17 The words "in Britain or other" were interlined in Dickinson's hand and

"s" added to "part." This change was then deleted and the words "in any" underscored.

18 The two preceding sentences were written at the bottom of the last page of the Composition Draft, apparently after the Fair Copy was drawn off, since these two sentences are interlined in the Fair Copy at this point.

19 Composition Draft reads: "towards the achievement."

20 Written originally as "relieve" and then changed to "deliver" by overwriting.

21 This final sentence is not in the Composition Draft. It was probably composed by TJ, though perhaps at the suggestion of Dickinson or of the committee; the deleted words are not interlined. Following this sentence, at the bottom of the page, is the following in the hand of Dickinson: "Q. if it might not be proper to take notice of Ld. Chathams Plan & its being rej[ected,] mentioning his great abilities? Q. if it might not be proper to take Notice how many great men in Parlt. & how many considerable Cities & towns in England have acknowledg'd [the] justice of our Cause? Q. Ld. North's ℗posal." These suggestions were not followed; their incorporation in the Dickinson draft constitutes one of its chief differences from the draft by TJ.

III. John Dickinson's Composition Draft

A Declaration by the Representatives of the United Colonies of North America now ⟨sitting⟩ met in General Congress at Philadelphia, setting forth the Causes and Necessity of their taking up Arms.

If it was possible for ⟨Beings endued with Reason to believe, that the Divine Author of their Existence⟩ ⟨who⟩ ⟨entert⟩⟨feel a proper Reverence for⟩ Men who exercise their Reason in contemplating the works of Creation, to believe, that the Divine Author of our Existence, intended a Part of the human Race to hold an absolute property in & an unbounded Power over others mark'd out by his infinite ⟨Mercy⟩ Goodness & Wisdom, as the legal Objects of a Domination never rightfully ⟨to be⟩ resistable, however severe & oppressive, the Inhabitants of these Colonies ⟨would⟩ might ⟨at least with propriety⟩ ⟨with⟩ at least require from the Parliament of Great

Britain some Evidence, that this dreadful ⟨*Authority was vested in that Body*⟩ authority over them has been granted to that Body. But since ⟨*Reflecti*⟩⟨*Considerations drawn a due Reverence*⟩ a Reverence for our great Creator, ⟨*sentiments*⟩ Principles of Humanity, ⟨*and the Dictates of Reason have convinc'd the wise and good*⟩ and the Dictates of Common Sense, ⟨*have con*⟩ must convince all those who will reflect upon the subject, that Government was instituted to promote the Wellfare of Mankind, ⟨*since these generous & noble Principles have on no Part of the Earth been so well*⟩⟨*vindicated*⟩ ⟨*asserted & enforced as in Great Britain, the Legislature of that Kingdom, hurried on by an inordinate Passion for Power of ambition for a Power, which their own most admired Writers & their very Constitution demonstrate to be unjust, and which they know to*⟩⟨*be inconsistent with*⟩⟨*be reprobated by the very*⟩⟨*their own political Constitution*⟩ and ought to be administred for the attainment of that End. The legislature of Great Britain, stimulated by an inordinate ⟨*Passion for a Power manifestly unjust and which*⟩ Passion for a Power not only ⟨*generally*⟩⟨*pronounced to be*⟩⟨*held*⟩ unjust, but unjustifiable, but which they know to be peculiarly reprobated by the very Constitution of that Kingdom, and desperate of success ⟨*in a*⟩⟨*in a Mode of Contest*⟩ in any Mode of Contest where a⟨*ny*⟩ Regard should be had to Truth ⟨*Justice or Reason have at*⟩⟨*last appeal'd length*⟩ Law or Right, have at length attempted to effect their cruel & impolitic Purpose by violence, and have thereby rendered it necessary for Us to ⟨*change*⟩ close with their last appeal from Reason to Arms. Yet, However blinded ⟨*they*⟩ that assembly may be by their intemperate Rage, ⟨*yet*⟩ we esteem ourselves bound by Obligations of Respect to the rest of the World, to make known the Justice of our Cause.

Our forefathers, inhabitants of the Island of GB. left their native Land, to seek ⟨*in the distant & inhospitable wilds of America*⟩ on these shores a Residence for civil & religious ⟨*Liberty*⟩ Freedom. To describe the Dangers, Difficulties & Distresses ⟨*the Expence of Blood &*⟩⟨*Fortun*⟩⟨*Treasure*⟩ they were obliged to encounter in executing their generous Resolutions, would require volumes. It may suffice to observe, that, at the Expence of their Blood, to the Ruin of their Fortunes, ⟨*& every Prospect of advantage in their native Country*⟩ without the least Charge to the Country from which they removed, ⟨*with*⟩ by unceasing Labor and an unconquerable Spirit, they effected Settlements in the distant & inhospitable wilds of America, then fill'd with numerous & warlike Nations of Barbarians. Societies or Governments vested with perfect legislatures

⟨*within them*⟩ were formed under Charters from the Crown, and ⟨*such*⟩ an harmonious Intercourse ⟨*and Union*⟩ was established between the colonies & the Kingdom from which they derived their origin. ⟨*The mutual Benefits of this Union that some occasional Assumptions of*⟩ The mutual Benefits of this Union became in a short Time so extraordinary as to excite the Astonishment of other Nations. Every British writer of Eminence who has treated of ⟨*the subject*⟩ Politics for near a Century past, has uniformly asserted that the amazing⟨*ly*⟩ Increase of the Wealth Strength & Navigation of ⟨*that Kingdom*⟩ the Realm arose from this Source: and The Minister who so ⟨*gloriously succeeded*⟩ ⟨*ably*⟩ wisely & successfully directed the ⟨*Councils*⟩ ⟨*affairs*⟩ Measures of Great Britain ⟨*during*⟩ in the last War, publickly declared, that these Colonies ⟨*had enabled*⟩ enabled her to triumph over her Enemies.

⟨*At*⟩ Towards the Conclusion of that War, it pleased our Sovereign to make a Change in his Counsels. From that fatal Moment, the Affairs of the British Empire began to ⟨*slide*⟩ fall into ⟨*a*⟩ Confusion, ⟨*that since has been continually encreasing and now has produced the most alarming Effects*⟩ & gradually ⟨*declining*⟩ sliding from that splendid summit of glorious Prosperity to which they had been ⟨*carried*⟩ advanced by the Virtues & abilities of one Man, are at Length distracted by the ⟨*most alarming*⟩ ⟨*present most*⟩ Convulsions, that now shake it to its ⟨*lowest*⟩ deepest Foundations. The new Ministry finding the ⟨*brave*⟩ brave Foes of Britain ⟨*subdued, took up the unfortunate Ideas of*⟩ ⟨*defeated yet*⟩ ⟨*bravely*⟩ ⟨*struggli*⟩ ⟨*contending tho after repeated defeats*⟩ tho frequently defeated yet ⟨*bravely*⟩ still contending took up the unfortunate Ideas of granting ⟨*them*⟩ a hasty Peace ⟨*and then*⟩ to them & of then ⟨*of*⟩ subduing her ⟨*ever*⟩ Faithful Friends.

⟨*They judg'd*⟩ ⟨*These devoted Colonies were judg'd to be in such a state as*[1] *to present to them a Prospect of Victories without Bloodshed,*[2] *Battles and all*⟩ ⟨*the cheap bought*⟩ ⟨*the easy profit of*⟩ ⟨*statutable Plunder*⟩ ⟨*Emoluments . . . though*⟩ ⟨*Parliament was*⟩ ⟨. . .⟩ ⟨*taught for the first time to assume an unbounded Legislation over them, and in the Course of*⟩ ⟨*to adopt . . .*⟩ ⟨*influenced to adopt the scheme by . . . & facilitate its Execution by assuming a new Power over them, and*⟩ ⟨*in*⟩ ⟨*during the course of*⟩ ⟨*eleven*⟩ ⟨*ten years have given such decisive specimens of the spirit and Consequences of this new Power as to*⟩ ⟨*remove*⟩ ⟨*Leave no Doubt concerning the Effects of acquiescence under it.*⟩[3]

These devoted Colonies were judg'd to be in such a state, as to present ⟨*a Prospect*⟩ Victories without Bloodshed, and all the easy

Emoluments of statutable Plunder. The uninterrupted Tenor of their peaceable & respectful Behaviour from the Beginning of Colonization, their ⟨old⟩ dutiful, ⟨use⟩ zealous & useful services during the War that has been mentioned, tho so recently & amply acknowledged in the most honorable Manner by his Majesty, by the late King, and by Parliament,[4] could not ⟨avail to⟩ save them from the meditated Innovations. Parliament was influenced to adopt the pernicious project, and ⟨to facilitate its Execution⟩ by assuming a new Power over them, have in the Course of eleven Years, given such decisive specimens of the Spirit & Consequences attending this Power, as to leave no Doubt concerning the Effects of Acquiescence under it.

Statutes have been passed for taking our Money from us without our ⟨own⟩ Consent, tho ⟨every Colony on this Continent has from its Beginning always ex⟩ we have ever exercised an exclusive Right to dispose of our own Property; for extending the Jurisdiction of Courts of Admiralty & Viceadmiralty beyond their antient Limits; for depriving us of the accustomed & inestimable Privilege of Trial by Jury in Cases affecting both Life & Property; ⟨for interdicting all Commerce to one of our Principal Towns the Capital of another & of;⟩ ⟨for exempting the Murderers of Colonists from legal Punishment;⟩ for suspending the ⟨Powers of⟩ Legislat⟨ion⟩ure ⟨in⟩ of one of the Colonies; for interdicting all Commerce of another, and for altering fundamentally the Form of Government ⟨in one of the Colonies, a Form secured⟩ established by Charter, and ⟨confirmed⟩ secured by Acts of its own Legislature solemnly ⟨and assented to⟩ confirmed by the Crown; ⟨for erecting in a neighbouring⟩ for exempting the "Murderers" of Colonists from legal Punishment; for erecting in a neighbouring Province, ⟨conquered⟩ acquired by the joint Arms of Great Britain & America, a ⟨Tyranno⟩ Despotism dangerous to ⟨the⟩ our very Existence ⟨of the Colonies⟩; and for quartering Officers & soldiers upon the Colonists in Time of profound Peace. It has also been ⟨declared⟩ resolved in Parliament that Colonists charged with committing certain offences, shall ⟨by Virtue of a Statute made before any of th⟩ ⟨then⟩ be transported to England to be tried.

But why should we enumerate our Injuries in Detail? By one ⟨Act of Parl⟩ Statute it is declared, that Parliament can "of right make Laws to bind us IN ALL CASES WHATSOEVER." What is to defend us against ⟨so enormous a Power⟩ ⟨such⟩ ⟨so⟩ ⟨& such⟩ ⟨so unlimited a⟩ so enormous, so unlimited a Power? ⟨The Persons assuming these⟩ Not ⟨one of⟩ a single man of those who assume it, is chosen by Us; or is subject to our Controul or Influence; but on the contrary, ⟨is⟩ they are all of them exempt from the Operations of such Laws, and actually lighten⟨s his⟩ their own Burdens, in exact proportion to ⟨those⟩ the Burdens ⟨he⟩ they impose⟨s⟩ on us. ⟨These Temptations⟩ ⟨might put⟩ ⟨are⟩ ⟨scarce⟩ ⟨too great to be offered to characters of the severest⟩ Administration sensible that we should regard these oppressive Measures as Freemen ought to do, sent over Fleets & Armies to enforce them. The Indignation of the ⟨Colonies was rouz'd: by their Virtue⟩ Americans was rouz'd, it is true: but it was the Indignation of a virtuous, ⟨peaceable,⟩ loyal, ⟨subjects,⟩ and affectionate People. A Congress of Delegates from the United Colonies was assembled at Philadelphia on the fifth Day of last September. We ⟨felt⟩ saw the weapons levell'd at our ⟨Brea⟩ Bosoms, but We perceiv'd them at the same Time ⟨held in⟩ grasp'd by a Parent's Hands. We cast ourselves upon our Knees prostrate at the Feet of ⟨the Throne⟩ our Sovereign. Tho for ten years we had ⟨fatigued the Ears of Authority with ineffectual and despis'd Petitions, Supplications, yet the⟩ ⟨beseig'd the Throne⟩ ineffectually besieged the Throne as Supplicants, yet we resolved again to offer an humble & dutiful Petition to the King, and ⟨agreed⟩ ⟨sent⟩ also to send an Address to our Fellow subjects in Great Britain, informing them of our agree⟨ing⟩ment at ⟨a⟩ certain Days to break off all our Commercial Intercourse with ⟨our Fellow subjects in Great Britain, as the last peaceable⟩ them as a⟨n⟩ peaceable admonition, that our Attachment to no Nation upon ⟨the⟩ Earth should supplant our Attachment to Liberty. This, we flattered ourselves, was the ultimate step of the Controversy: But subsequent Events have shewn, how vain was this ⟨last⟩ Hope of Moderation in ⟨the Ministry⟩ our Enemies.

Our Petition was treated with Contempt ⟨&⟩. Without the least Mention of ⟨its⟩ our application, several threatening Expressions against the Colonies were inserted in his Majesty's speech to ⟨both⟩ the two Houses of Parliament; and afterwards the Petition was huddled into the House of Commons, the last amongst a neglected Bundle of American Papers. The Lords & Commons in their Address ⟨to his Majesty⟩, in the Month of February, said, that "a Rebellion at that Time actually existed within the Province of Massachusetts Bay; ⟨and⟩ that those concern'd in it, had been countenanc'd & encouraged by unlawful Combinations & Engagements entered into by his Majesty's subjects in several of the other Colonies; and therefore they besought his Majesty, that he would take the most effectual Measures to enforce due obedience to the

Laws ⟨of⟩ & Authority of the Supreme Legislature." Soon after the commercial Intercourse of whole Colonies with foreign Countries was cutt off by an Act of Parliament ⟨and⟩; by another, several of them were entirely prohibited from the Fisheries in the ⟨neighbouring⟩ Seas near their Coasts, on which they always depended for their sustenance; and large Reinforcements of Ships & Troops were immediately sent over to General Gage.

⟨With such a⟩ ⟨headlon⟩ ⟨heedless⟩ ⟨Rage⟩ ⟨fury were these outrageous proceedings of⟩ ⟨accumulated & unexampled outrages hurried on, that all the Prayers⟩ ⟨Vain⟩ ⟨Fruitless were⟩ Fruitless were all the Entreaties, Arguments & Eloquence of ⟨these⟩ ⟨a very considerable⟩ an illustrious Band of the most distinguished Peers & Commoners, who nobly confest & strenuously asserted the Justice of our Cause, to stay or even to mitigate the heedless Fury ⟨of⟩ with which these accumulated & unexampled outrages were ⟨rapidly⟩ hurried on. Equally Fruitless was the interference of ⟨that⟩ the august City of London, ⟨supplicating⟩ of Bristol, and many other respectable Towns in our Favor. A Plan of Reconciliation digested by the patriotic cares of that great & good Man before mentioned, & which might easily have been improved to produce every Effect his generous Heart desired, was contemptuously rejected, to give way to an insidious ⟨Ministerial⟩ Maneuvre, calculated to divide us, ⟨and⟩ to establish a perpetual Auction of Taxation, where Colony should bid against Colony, all of them uninform'd what Ransom would redeem their Lives, and thus to extort from us at the Point of the Bayonet ⟨sums⟩ the unknown sums that should be sufficient to gratify, if possible to gratify, ministerial Rapacity, with the miserable Indulgence left to us of raising in our own Modes the prescribed Tribute.

⟨When the Intelligence of these proceedings arriv'd on this Continent, we perceiv'd it appeared evident, that our Destruction was . . . determined upon, and that we had⟩ ⟨no Alternative to⟩ ⟨Choice to make but of⟩ ⟨our choice must be, either an "unconditional submission," as one of the Ministry express'd himself, or⟩ ⟨of⟩ ⟨Resistance.⟩

Soon after the Intelligence of these Proceedings arrived on this Continent, ⟨where⟩ General Gage, who in the course of the last Year, had taken Possession of the Town of Boston, in the Province of Massachusetts Bay, and still occupied it as a Garrison ⟨Place⟩, on the 19th Day of ⟨last⟩ April ⟨last⟩, sent out ⟨of⟩ from that Place a large Detachment of his Army, who made an unprovoked Assault on the Inhabitants of the said Province, at the Town of Lexington, as appears by the Affidavits of a great number of persons, some of whom were officers & soldiers of that Detachment, murdered eight of the Inhabitants, and wounded many others. From thence the Troop proceeded in warlike array to the Town of Concord, where they set upon another party of the Inhabitants of the same Province, killing several, & wounding ⟨others⟩ more untill compell'd to retreat by the People suddenly assembled to repell this cruel Aggression. Hostilities thus commenc'd by the British Troops, have been since prosecuted by them without Regard to Faith or Reputation. The Inhabitants of Boston being confined within that Town by the General their Governor & having in order to procure their Dismission entered into a Treaty with him, it was stipulated ⟨between the⟩ that the said Inhabitants having deposited their Arms with their own Magistrates, should have ⟨free⟩ Liberty to depart ⟨out of the said Town⟩, taking with them their other Effects. They accordingly delivered up their Arms, but in open violation of Honor, in Defiance of the Obligations of ⟨a⟩ Treat⟨y⟩ies, which even savage Nations esteem sacred, ⟨General Gage⟩ the Governor ordered the Arms deposited as aforesaid that they might be preserved for their owners, to be seized by a Body of ⟨armed Men⟩ soldiers, detained the greater Part of the Inhabitants in the Town, and compell'd the few who were permitted to retire, to leave their most valuable Effects behind. By this perfidy, Wives are separated from their Husbands, Children from their Parents, the aged & sick from their Relatives & Friends who wish to attend & ⟨reliev⟩ take care of them; and those who have been used to live ⟨with Elegan⟩ in Plenty & even in Elegance, are reduced to deplorable Distress.

The General further emulating ⟨the⟩ his ministerial Masters, by a Proclamation bearing Date on the 12th Day of June, after venting the grossest Falsehoods and Calumnies against the good People of these Colonies, proceeds to "declare them all either by name or Description to be Rebels & Traitors, to supercede the Course of the Common Law, and instead thereof to publish & order the use & Exercise of the Law Martial." His Troops have butchered our Countrymen; have burnt Charlestown, besides a considerable number of Houses in other Places; our ships & Vessels are seized; ⟨and⟩ ⟨and⟩ the necessary supplies of Provisions are ⟨stopp'd, and he is now spreading Destruction & Devastation around him as far as he can, all the complicated Cal⟩ intercepted and he is exerting his utmost Power to spread Destruction & Devastation around him. We have receiv'd certain Intelligence that ⟨Governor⟩ General Carleton the Governor of Canada, ⟨under⟩ by orders from the Ministry is instigating the People of that Province and the Indians to fall upon us; and that schemes have been form'd to excite domestic Enemies against Us. In brief, a Part of these Colonies now feels, & all of them are ⟨sure of⟩ sure of feeling, as far as ⟨the Vengeance of⟩ the Vengeance of Administration can inflict them, ⟨all⟩ the complicated Calamities of Fire, Sword & Famine. ⟨By our⟩ ⟨The suggestions of Duty & Affection can no longer lull us into a lethargic Notion, too lately relinquished, that⟩ ⟨Armies &⟩ ⟨Fleets & Armies are only de- sign'd to intimidate us.⟩ We are reduced to the Alternative of chus- ing an unconditional submission to the ⟨Tyrannic Vengeance of irri- tated,⟩ Tyranny of irritated Ministers, ⟨who know⟩ ⟨who knowing that we despise them, & that they deserve to be thus despised, are therefore implacable⟩ or Resistance by Force. The latter is our Choice.

⟨We know, that by an infamous Surrender of the Freedom & Happiness of Ourselves & our Posterity, we might obtain that wretched Honor, Justice & Humanity forbid us⟩ ⟨surre⟩ ⟨basely to surrender that Freedom, Liberty & Happiness which we receiv'd from our gallant Ancestors, and which it is our Duty to transmit undiminished to our Posterity. Called upon by the Law of Self pres- ervation implanted in our Nature by our allwise Creator, with pre- pared Hands and resolved Hearts, we will⟩ We have counted the Cost of this Contest, & ⟨being perfectly convinced, that it is infinety[5]⟩ find nothing so dreadful in our Computation, as ⟨Infamy &⟩ volun- tary slavery ⟨united⟩. Honor, Justice & Humanity forbid us tamely to surrender that Freedom which We receiv'd from our gallant An- cestors, and which our innocent Posterity have a Right to receive from us. We cannot endure the Infamy & Guilt of resigning suc- ceeding Generations to that Wretchedness which inevitably Awaits them, if we basely entail hereditary Bondage upon them.

Our Cause is just. Our Union is perfect. ⟨Our Hearts are re- solved. Our Hands are prepared.⟩ Our preparations are nearly com- pleted. Our internal Resources ⟨within our own Country⟩ are ⟨many⟩ great; and our Assurance of foreign Assistance is certain. We grate- fully acknowledge as a singular Instance of the Divine ⟨Goodness⟩ Favor towards us, ⟨& consider it as a singular mark of his Favor, in not permitting us to be⟩ that his Providence would not permit us to be ⟨called⟩ called into ⟨so⟩ this severe ⟨a⟩ Controversy, untill ⟨our⟩ we were grown up to our present strength, ⟨was so⟩ ⟨and⟩ had been prelusively exercis'd in warlike operations, ⟨to which some Years ago we were almost entire strangers⟩ and ⟨that we⟩ were possest of the Means for defending ourselves ⟨, of which till lately we were in *want*). With Hearts fortified by these animating Reflections, we do most solemnly before God and the World declare, that, exerting the utmost Energies of those Powers which our beneficent Creator hath graciously bestowed upon us, the Arms we have been ⟨*thus*⟩ compell'd by our Enemies to assume ⟨*for our just Defence,*⟩ we will, in defiance of every Hazard with unabating Firmness & perseverance, ⟨*in Defiance of every Hazard, use*⟩ ⟨*we will*⟩ employ for the preservation of our Liberties, ⟨*deeming it infinitely preferable*⟩ being with one mind resolved, to dye free men rather than to live slaves.

⟨*B*⟩ Least this Declaration should disquiet the Minds of our Friends & fellow subjects in any part of the ⟨*World*⟩ Empire, we assure them, that we mean not ⟨*in any manner*⟩ to dissolve that Union with them ⟨*in*⟩ which ⟨*we have*⟩ has so long & so happily ⟨*lived*⟩ subsisted between us, and which we ⟨*so*⟩ ⟨*ardently*⟩ ⟨*much*⟩ ⟨*sincere*⟩ sincerely wish to see restored. ⟨*The*⟩ Necessity ⟨*must be hard indeed*⟩ has not yet driven us into that desperate Measure, or to excite ⟨*their*⟩ other Nations to War against them. We have not rais'd armies ⟨*from*⟩ with ambitious Designs of separating from Great Britain & establishing independant states. We ⟨*have not invaded that Island proffering to its Inhabitants Death or Slavery*⟩ fight not for Glory or for Conquest. We exhibit to Mankind the remarkable spectacle of a People ⟨*charg'd till . . .*⟩ attack'd without any Imputation or even Suspicion of Offence by unprovoked Enemies, who ⟨*audaciously proffer to them the not milder*⟩ ⟨*Terms*⟩ ⟨*Conditions than Death or Slavery*⟩ boast of their ⟨*Freedom*⟩ Priviledges & Civilization, and yet proffer no milder Conditions than ⟨*Death or Slave*⟩ Servitude or Death. In our Native Land—in Defence of ⟨*Liberties*⟩ the ⟨*Liberty*⟩ Freedom that is our Birthright, and which we ever enjoyed till the late Violations of it—for the protection of our property acquired solely by the honest Industry of our Forefathers & ourselves ⟨*we have taken up arms solely to oppose & repell against . . . of the Violence actually offered to us*⟩, against Violence actually offered, we have taken up Arms. ⟨*We shall*⟩ We shall lay them down, When Hostilities shall cease on the Part of the Aggressors, and all Danger of their being renewed, shall be removed, and not before.

With an humble Confidence in the ⟨*divine*⟩ Mercies of the supreme & impartial Judge & Ruler of the Universe, we most devoutly implore ⟨*Almighty God*⟩ his divine Goodness to conduct us happily thro this great Conflict, to dispose our Adversaries to Reconciliation on reasonable Terms, & thereby to relieve the Empire from the ⟨*Evils*⟩ Calamities of Civil War.

Dft (NHi). Entirely in Dickinson's handwriting, this draft consists of eight numbered pages. It was first identified by George H. Moore, who described it in a paper read before the New-York Historical Society in 1882, later expanded and privately printed in New York in 1890 as *Suum Cuique: John Dickinson, the Author of the Declaration on Taking Up Arms in 1775*. Moore's pamphlet includes a splendid reproduction of the MS, the discovery of which was the chief contribution made to the study of the text of the Declaration during the nineteenth century; but his extreme conclusions are no longer tenable. There can be no doubt that Dickinson had before him a copy of TJ's text when he executed this revision.

1 The phrase "to be in such a state as"

is repeated; it occurs once interlined and once in the margin, both being deleted with the remainder of the paragraph.

2 The phrase "Victories without Bloodshed" is repeated.

3 A part of this heavily scored-out passage is illegible; some words and phrases (represented by dots of elision) have therefore had to be omitted, and the order of the successive revisions has not been satisfactorily established.

4 This paragraph is written in two columns in the margin. The second part is headed by a deleted clause which seems to belong properly to the context at this point, though there is no asterisk or other indication in the MS itself: "& their constantly favourable statements from their whole [press?]."

5 Thus in MS.

IV. The Declaration as Adopted by Congress

[6 July 1775]

A Declaration *by the* Representatives *of the United Colonies of North-America, now met in Congress at Philadelphia, setting forth the Causes and Necessity of their taking up Arms.*

IF IT was possible for Men, who exercise their Reason to believe, that the Divine Author of our Existence intended a Part of the human Race to hold an absolute Property in, and an unbounded Power over others, marked out by his infinite Goodness and Wisdom, as the Objects of a legal Domination never rightfully resistible, however severe and oppressive, the Inhabitants of these Colonies might at least require from the Parliament of Great-Britain some Evidence, that this dreadful Authority over them has been granted to that Body. But a Reverence for our great Creator, Principles of Humanity, and the Dictates of Common Sense, must convince all those who reflect upon the Subject, that Government was instituted to promote the Welfare of Mankind, and ought to be administered for the Attainment of that End. The Legislature of Great-Britain, however, stimulated by an inordinate Passion for a Power not only unjustifiable, but which they know to be peculiarly reprobated by the very Constitution of that Kingdom, and desperate of Success in any Mode of Contest, where Regard should be had to Truth, Law, or Right, have at Length, deserting those, attempted to effect their cruel and impolitic Purpose of enslaving these Colonies by Violence, and have thereby *rendered it necessary for us to close with their last Appeal from Reason to Arms.* Yet, however blinded that Assembly may be, by their intemperate Rage for unlimited Domination, so to Slight Justice and the Opinion of Mankind, we esteem ourselves bound by Obligations of

Respect to the Rest of the World, to make known the Justice of our Cause.

Our Forefathers, Inhabitants of the Island of Great-Britain, left their Native Land, to seek on these Shores a Residence for civil and religious Freedom. At the Expence of their Blood, at the Hazard of their Fortunes, without the least Charge to the Country from which they removed, by unceasing Labour and an unconquerable Spirit, *they effected Settlements in the distant and inhospitable Wilds of America,* then filled with numerous and warlike Nations of Barbarians. Societies or Governments, vested with perfect Legislatures, were formed under Charters from the Crown, and an harmonious Intercourse was established between the Colonies and the Kingdom from which they derived their Origin. The mutual Benefits of this Union became in a short Time so extraordinary, as to excite Astonishment. It is universally confessed, that the amazing Increase of the Wealth, Strength, and Navigation of the Realm, arose from this Source; and the Minister, who so wisely and successfully directed the Measures of Great-Britain in the late War, publicly declared, that these Colonies enabled her to triumph over her Enemies. Towards the Conclusion of that War, *it pleased our Sovereign to make a Change in his Counsels.* From that fatal Moment, the Affairs of the British Empire began to fall into Confusion, and gradually sliding from the Summit of glorious Prosperity to which they had been advanced by the Virtues and Abilities of one Man, are at length distracted by the Convulsions, that now shake it to its deepest Foundations. *The new Ministry finding the brave Foes of Britain, though frequently defeated, yet still contending, took up the unfortunate Idea of granting them a hasty Peace, and of then subduing her faithful Friends.*

These devoted Colonies were judged to be in such a State, as to present Victories without Bloodshed, and all the easy Emoluments of statuteable Plunder. The uninterrupted Tenor of their peaceable and respectful Behaviour from the Beginning of Colonization, their dutiful, zealous, and useful Services during the War, though so recently and amply acknowledged in the most honourable Manner by his Majesty, by the late King, and by Parliament, could not save them from the meditated Innovations. *Parliament was influenced to adopt the pernicious Project, and assuming a new Power over them, have in the Course of eleven Years given such decisive Specimens of the Spirit and Consequences attending this Power, as to leave no Doubt concerning the Effects of Acquiescence under it. They have undertaken to give and grant our Money without our Consent, though we have ever exercised an exclusive Right to dispose of our own Property; Statutes have been passed for extending the Jurisdiction of Courts of Admiralty and Vice-Admiralty beyond their ancient Limits; for depriving us of the accustomed and inestimable Privilege of Trial by Jury in Cases affecting both Life and Property;* for suspending the Legislature of one of the Colonies; *for interdicting all Commerce to the Capital of another; and for altering fundamentally the Form of Government established by Charter, and secured by Acts of its own Legislature solemnly confirmed by the Crown;* for exempting the "Murderers" of Colonists from legal Trial, and in

Effect, from Punishment; *for erecting in a neighbouring Province, acquired by the joint Arms of Great-Britain and America, a Despotism dangerous to our very Existence*; and for quartering Soldiers upon the Colonists in Time of profound Peace. It has also been resolved in Parliament, that *Colonists charged with committing certain Offences, shall be transported to England to be tried.*

But why should we enumerate our Injuries in detail? By one Statute it is declared, that Parliament can "of right make Laws to bind us in all Cases whatsoever." What is to defend us against so enormous, so unlimited a Power? Not a single Man of those who assume it, is chosen by us; or is subject to our Controul or Influence; but on the Contrary, they are all of them exempt from the Operation of such Laws, and an American Revenue, if not diverted from the ostensible Purposes for which it is raised, *would actually lighten their own Burdens in Proportion, as they increase ours.*[1] We saw the Misery to which such Despotism would reduce us. *We for ten Years incessantly and ineffectually besieged the Throne as Supplicants; we reasoned, we remonstrated with Parliament in the most mild and decent Language.*[2]

Administration sensible that we should regard these oppressive Measures as Freemen ought to do, sent over Fleets and Armies to enforce them. The Indignation of the Americans was roused, it is true; but it was the Indignation of a virtuous, loyal, and affectionate People. A Congress of Delegates from the United Colonies was assembled at Philadelphia, on the fifth Day of last September.[3] We resolved again to offer an humble and dutiful Petition to the King, and also addressed our Fellow Subjects of Great-Britain. *We have pursued every temperate, every respectful Measure; we have even proceeded to break off our commercial Intercourse with our Fellow Subjects, as the last peaceable Admonition, that our Attachment to no Nation upon Earth should supplant our Attachment to Liberty. This, we flattered ourselves, was the ultimate Step of the Controversy: But subsequent Events have shewn, how vain was this Hope of finding Moderation in our Enemies.*

Several threatening Expressions against the Colonies were inserted in His Majesty's Speech; our Petition, tho' we were told it was a Decent one, and that his Majesty had been pleased to receive it graciously, and to promise laying it before his Parliament, was huddled into both Houses among a Bundle of American Papers, and there neglected. The Lords and Commons in their Address, in the Month of February, said, that "a Rebellion at that Time actually existed within the Province of Massachusetts-Bay; and that those concerned in it, had been countenanced and encouraged by unlawful Combinations and Engagements, entered into by his Majesty's Subjects in several of the other Colonies; and therefore they besought his Majesty, that he would take the most effectual Measures to inforce due Obedience to the Laws and Authority of the Supreme Legislature." Soon after, the commercial Intercourse of whole Colonies, with foreign Countries, and with each other, was cut off by an Act of Parliament; by another, several of them were intirely prohibited from the Fisheries in the Seas near their Coasts, on which they always depended for their Sustenance; and large Re-inforcements of Ships and Troops were immediately sent over to General Gage.

Fruitless were all the entreaties, arguments, and eloquence of an Illustrious Band of the most distinguished Peers, and Commoners, who nobly and strenuously asserted the Justice of our Cause, to stay, or even to mitigate the heedless fury with which these accumulated and unexampled Outrages were hurried on. Equally fruitless was the interference of the City of London, of Bristol, and many other respectable Towns in our Favour.[4] Parliament adopted an insidious Manoeuvre calculated to divide us, to establish a perpetual Auction of Taxations where Colony should bid against Colony, all of them uninformed what Ransom would redeem their Lives; and thus to extort from us, at the Point of the Bayonet, the unknown sums that should be sufficient to gratify, if possible to gratify, ministerial Rapacity, with the miserable indulgence left to us of raising, in our own Mode, the prescribed Tribute. What Terms more rigid and humiliating could have been dictated by remorseless Victors to conquered Enemies? In our circumstances to accept them, would be to deserve them.[5]

Soon after the Intelligence of these proceedings arrived on this Continent, General Gage, who in the course of the last Year had taken Possession of the Town of Boston, in the Province of Massachusetts-Bay, and still occupied it as a Garrison, on the 19th day of April, sent out from that Place a large detachment of his Army, who made an unprovoked Assault on the Inhabitants of the said Province, at the Town of Lexington, as appears by the Affidavits of a great Number of Persons, some of whom were Officers and Soldiers of that detachment, murdered eight of the Inhabitants, and wounded many others. From thence the Troops proceeded in warlike Array to the Town of Concord, where they set upon another Party of the Inhabitants of the same Province, killing several and wounding more, until compelled to retreat by the country People suddenly assembled to repel this cruel Aggression. Hostilities, thus commenced by the British Troops, have been since prosecuted by them without regard to Faith or Reputation. The Inhabitants of Boston being confined within that Town by the General their Governor, and having, in order to procure their dismission, entered into a Treaty with him, it was stipulated that the said Inhabitants having deposited their Arms with their own Magistrates, should have liberty to depart, taking with them their other Effects. They accordingly delivered up their Arms, but in open violation of Honour, in defiance of the obligation of Treaties, which even savage Nations esteemed sacred, the Governor ordered the Arms deposited as aforesaid, that they might be preserved for their owners, to be seized by a Body of Soldiers; detained the greatest part of the Inhabitants in the Town, and compelled the few who were permitted to retire, to leave their most valuable Effects behind.

By this perfidy Wives are separated from their Husbands, Children from their Parents, the aged and the sick from their Relations and Friends, who wish to attend and comfort them; and those who have been used to live in Plenty and even Elegance, are reduced to deplorable Distress.

*The General, further emulating his ministerial Masters, by a Procla-
mation bearing date on the 12th day of June, after venting the grossest
Falsehoods and Calumnies against the good People of these Colonies,
proceeds to "declare them all, either by Name or Description, to be
Rebels and Traitors, to supersede the course of the Common Law, and
instead thereof to publish and order the use and exercise of the Law
Martial." His Troops have butchered our Countrymen, have wantonly
burnt Charlestown, besides a considerable number of Houses in other
Places; our Ships and Vessels are seized; the necessary supplies of Provisions are intercepted, and he is exerting his utmost Power to spread
destruction and devastation around him.*

We have **received certain Intelligence**, that General Carleton, the
Governor of Canada,[6] is instigating the People of that Province and the
Indians to fall upon us; and we have but too much reason to apprehend,
that Schemes have been formed to excite domestic Enemies against us.
In brief, a part of these Colonies now feel, and all of them are sure of
feeling, as far as the Vengeance of Administration can inflict them, the
complicated Calamities of Fire, Sword, and Famine. We are reduced to
the alternative of chusing an unconditional Submission to the tyranny
of irritated Ministers, or resistance by Force. The latter is our choice.
We have counted the cost of this contest, and find nothing so dreadful
as voluntary Slavery. Honour, Justice, and Humanity, forbid us tamely
to surrender that Freedom which we received from our gallant Ancestors, and which our innocent Posterity have a right to receive from
us. We cannot endure the infamy and guilt of resigning succeeding Generations to that wretchedness which inevitably awaits them, if we basely
entail hereditary Bondage upon them.

Our cause is just. Our union is perfect.[7] Our internal Resources are
great, and, if necessary, foreign Assistance is undoubtedly attainable.
We gratefully acknowledge, as signal Instances of the Divine Favour
towards us, that his Providence would not permit us to be called into this
severe Controversy, until we were grown up to our present strength, had
been previously exercised in warlike Operation, and possessed of the
means of defending ourselves. With hearts fortified with these animating Reflections, *we most solemnly, before God and the World, declare,
that, exerting the utmost Energy of those Powers, which our beneficent
Creator hath graciously bestowed upon us, the Arms we have been compelled by our Enemies to assume, we will, in defiance of every Hazard,
with unabating Firmness and Perseverence, employ for the preservation
of our Liberties*; being with one Mind resolved to die Freemen rather
than to live Slaves.

*Lest this Declaration should disquiet the Minds of our Friends and
Fellow-Subjects in any part of the Empire, we assure them that we mean
not to dissolve that Union which has so long and so happily subsisted
between us, and which we sincerely wish to see restored. Necessity has
not yet driven us into that desperate Measure, or induced us to excite any
other Nation to War against them. We have not raised Armies with ambitious Designs* of separating from Great-Britain, and establishing Independent States. *We fight not for Glory or for Conquest. We exhibit to*

Mankind the remarkable Spectacle of a People attacked by unprovoked Enemies, without any imputation or even suspicion of Offence. They boast of their Privileges and Civilization, and yet proffer no milder Conditions than Servitude or Death.

In our own native Land, in defence of the Freedom that is our Birthright, and which we ever enjoyed till the late Violation of it—for the protection of our Property, acquired solely by the honest Industry of our fore-fathers and ourselves,[8] *against Violence actually offered, we have taken up Arms. We shall lay them down when Hostilities shall cease on the part of the Aggressors, and all danger of their being renewed shall be removed, and not before.*

With an humble Confidence in the Mercies of the supreme and impartial Judge and Ruler of the Universe, *we most devoutly implore his Divine Goodness to protect us happily through this great Conflict, to dispose our Adversaries to reconciliation on reasonable Terms, and thereby to relieve the Empire from the Calamities of civil War.*

Journals of Congress, I, Philadelphia: R. Aitken, 1777 (Evans 15683), p. 143-8. The text of the Declaration as adopted does not occur in the so-called "Rough Journal" of the Continental Congress, nor is it in the "Secret Journal Domestic," which was the only other form of Journal then being kept by Charles Thomson. While the original resolution had directed that the Declaration was to be "published" by General Washington on his arrival at Boston, the first printing occurred in the *Pennsylvania Packet* of 10 July; it was also published in the *Pennsylvania Journal* of 12 July and in a Postscript to the *Pennsylvania Gazette* of the same day. Almost immediately William and Thomas Bradford in Philadelphia brought out a pamphlet edition under the title *A Declaration by the Representatives of the United Colonies of North-America, Now Met in General Congress, Seting Forth the Causes and Necessity of their Taking Up Arms.* Other printers in New York, Newport, Providence, Watertown, and Portsmouth brought out editions during the year (Evans 14544-14450).

In the present text, in order to facilitate comparison of the various texts and to show at a glance the extent to which Dickinson followed TJ's draft, those parts which are either exact transcriptions of TJ's words or so closely paraphrased as to make it clear that Dickinson was merely rewriting are italicized. (Italicized words in the printed source have necessarily been disregarded.) In DLC: TJ Papers, 1: 150-7, will also be found a manuscript of the

Declaration in Italian, with marginal comments in an unknown hand. The most important of the marginal comments explains the nature of Lord North's proposal and the attitude of the colonists toward it. A comparison of Dickinson's Draft with the final text adopted by Congress reveals at least thirty-four changes, most of them minor variations in phraseology. Dickinson obviously must have prepared a fair copy of his draft for the committee, but in the absence of such a text we cannot be certain whether these changes were made by Dickinson himself, by the committee, or by Congress. A few of the more important of these are noted below.

[1] The alteration of the phraseology at the close of this passage made it conform more closely to TJ's text than it had when revised by Dickinson.

[2] This sentence, drawn from TJ's draft, does not appear in Dickinson's draft.

[3] Three sentences from Dickinson's draft are omitted at this point, the last reading "We cast ourselves upon our Knees prostrate at the Feet of our sovereign." This passage is one usually taken to illustrate Dickinson's conciliatory attitude, but it should be interpreted in the light of the opening sentence of the following paragraph of his draft: "Our Petition was treated with Contempt," a sentence also deleted in the final text. Read in this context, the language emphasizes the enormity of the treatment received rather than the servility of the colonists.

4 Dickinson's adulatory tribute to Pitt's Plan of Reconciliation was deleted at this point.

5 The two preceding sentences are not in Dickinson's draft.

6 Dickinson's draft reads "By orders of the ministry."

7 The text at this point is strengthened by the omission of the following from Dickinson's draft: "Our preparations are nearly completed."

8 It is noteworthy that the point Dickinson makes here ("acquired solely by the honest Industry of our fore-fathers and ourselves"), and repeated earlier in the Declaration ("without the least charge to the Country from which they removed"), both inserted in passages in which Dickinson was copying TJ almost literally, anticipates an argument to which TJ devoted some attention in the ensuing months (see Refutation of the Argument that the Colonies were Established at the Expense of the British Nation, printed below under the date 19 Jan. 1776).

Second Petition from Congress to the King

[8 July 1775]

TO THE KINGS MOST EXCELLENT MAJESTY

Most gracious Sovereign

We your Majesty's faithful subjects of the colonies of New-hampshire, Massachusetts-bay, Rhode island and Providence plantations, Connecticut, New-York, New-Jersey, Pennsylvania, the counties of New Castle Kent and Sussex on Delaware, Maryland, Virginia, North Carolina and South Carolina, in behalf of ourselves and the inhabitants of these colonies, who have deputed us to represent them in general Congress, entreat your Majestys gracious attention to this our humble petition.

The union between our Mother Country and these colonies, and the energy of mild and just government, produced benefits so remarkably important, and afforded such an assurance of their permanency and increase, that the wonder and envy of other Nations were excited, while they beheld Great Britain riseing to a power the most extraordinary the world had ever known.

Her rivals observing, that there was no probability of this happy connection being broken by civil dissentions, and apprehending its future effects, if left any longer undisturbed, resolved to prevent her receiving such continual and formidable accessions of wealth and strength, by checking the growth of these settlements from which they were to be derived.

In the prosecution of this attempt events so unfavourable to the design took place, that every friend to the interests of Great Britain and these colonies entertained pleasing and reasonable expectations of seeing an additional force and extention immediately given to the operations of the union hitherto experienced, by an enlargement of the dominions of the Crown, and the removal of ancient and warlike enemies to a greater distance.

At the conclusion therefore of the late war, the most glorious and advantagious that ever had been carried on by British arms, your loyal colonists having contributed to its success, by such repeated and strenuous exertions, as frequently procured them the distinguished approbation of your Majesty, of the late king, and of Parliament, doubted not but that they should be permitted with the rest of the empire, to share in the blessings of peace and the emoluments of victory and conquest. While these recent and honorable acknowledgments of their merits remained on record in the journals and acts of that august legislature the Parliament, undefaced by the imputation or even the suspicion of any offence, they were alarmed by a new system of Statutes and regulations adopted for the administration of the colonies, that filled their minds with the most painful fears and jealousies; and to their inexpressible astonishment perceived the dangers of a foreign quarrel quickly succeeded by domestic dangers, in their judgment of a more dreadful kind.

Nor were their anxieties alleviated by any tendency in this system to promote the welfare of the Mother Country. For 'tho its effects were more immediately felt by them, yet its influence appeared to be injurious to the commerce and prosperity of Great Britain.

We shall decline the ungrateful task of describing the irksome variety of artifices practised by many of your Majestys ministers, the delusive pretences, fruitless terrors, and unavailing severities, that have from time to time been dealt out by them, in their attempts to execute this impolitic plan, or of traceing thro' a series of years past the progress of the unhappy differences between Great Britain and these colonies which have flowed from this fatal source.

Your Majestys ministers persevering in their measures and proceeding to open hostilities for enforcing them, have compelled us to arm in our own defence, and have engaged us in a controversy so peculiarly abhorrent to the affections of your still faithful colonists, that when we consider whom we must oppose in this contest, and if it continues, what may be the consequences, our own particular misfortunes are accounted by us, only as parts of our distress.

Knowing, to what violent resentments and incurable animosities, civil discords are apt to exasperate and inflame the contending parties, we think ourselves required by indispensable obligations to Almighty God, to your Majesty, to our fellow subjects, and to ourselves, immediately to use all the means in our power not incompatible with our safety, for stopping the further effusion of blood, and for averting the impending calamities that threaten the British Empire.

Thus called upon to address your Majesty on affairs of such moment to America, and probably to all your dominions, we are earnestly desirous of performing this office with the utmost deference for your Majesty; and we therefore pray, that your royal magnanimity and benevolence may make the most favourable construction of our expressions on so uncommon an occasion. Could we represent in their full force the sentiments that agitate the minds of us your dutiful subjects, we are persuaded, your Majesty would ascribe any seeming deviation from reverence, in our language, and even in our conduct, not to any reprehensible intention but to the impossibility of reconciling the usual appearances of respect with a just attention to our own preservation against those artful and cruel enemies, who abuse your royal confidence and authority for the purpose of effecting our destruction.

Attached to your Majestys person, family and government with all the devotion that principle and affection can inspire, connected with Great Britain by the strongest ties that can unite societies, and deploring every event that tends in any degree to weaken them, we solemnly assure your Majesty, that we not only most ardently desire the former harmony between her and these colonies may be restored but that a concord may be established between them upon so firm a basis, as to perpetuate its blessings uninterrupted by any future dissentions to succeeding generations in both countries, and to transmit your Majestys name to posterity adorned with that signal and lasting glory that has attended the memory of those illustrious personages, whose virtues and abilities have extricated states from dangerous convulsions, and by securing happiness to others, have erected the most noble and durable monuments to their own fame.

We beg leave further to assure your Majesty that notwithstanding the sufferings of your loyal colonists during the course of the present controversy, our breasts retain too tender a regard for the kingdom from which we derive our origin to request such a reconciliation as might in any manner be inconsistent with her dignity or her welfare. These, related as we are to her, honor and duty, as well as inclination induce us to support and advance; and the apprehensions that now oppress our hearts with unspeakable grief, being once removed, your Majesty will find your faithful subjects on this continent ready and willing at all times, as they ever have been with their lives and fortunes to assert and maintain the rights and interests of your Majesty and of our Mother Country.

We therefore beseech your Majesty, that your royal authority and influence may be graciously interposed to procure us releif from our afflicting fears and jealousies occasioned by the system before mentioned, and to settle peace through every part of your dominions, with all humility submitting to your Majesty's wise consideration, whether it may not be expedient for facilitating those important purposes, that your Majesty be pleased to direct some mode by which the united applications of your faithful colonists to the throne, in pursuance of their common councils, may be improved into a happy and permanent reconciliation; and that in the meantime measures be taken for preventing the further destruction of the lives of your Majesty's subjects; and that such statutes as more immediately distress any of your Majestys colonies be repealed: For by such arrangements as your Majestys wisdom can form for collecting the united sense of your American people, we are convinced, your Majesty would receive such satisfactory proofs of the disposition of the colonists towards their sovereign and the parent state, that the wished for opportunity would soon be restored to them, of evincing the sincerity of their professions by every testimony of devotion becoming the most dutiful subjects and the most affectionate colonists.

That your Majesty may enjoy a long and prosperous reign, and that your descendants may govern your dominions with honor to themselves and happiness to their subjects is our sincere and fervent prayer.   JOHN HANCOCK

COLONY OF NEW HAMPSHIRE
   John Langdon
COLONY OF MASSACHUSETTS-BAY
   Thomas Cushing
   Saml. Adams
   John Adams
   Rob. Treat Paine
COLONY OF RHODE-ISLAND AND
PROVIDENCE PLANTATIONS
   Step. Hopkins
   Sam: Ward
COLONY OF CONNECTICUT
   Elipht. Dyer
   Roger Sherman
   Silas Deane
COLONY OF NEW YORK
   Phil. Livingston

Jas. Duane
John Alsop
Frans. Lewis
John Jay
Robt. R. Livingston junr.
Lewis Morris
Wm. Floyd
Henry Wisner
NEW JERSEY
   Wil. Livingston
   John DeHart
   Richd. Smith
PENNSYLVANIA
   John Dickinson
   B. Franklin
   Geo: Ross
   James Wilson

Cha. Humphreys
Edwd. Biddle
COUNTIES OF NEW CASTLE
KENT & SUSSEX ON DELAWARE
Cæsar Rodney
Tho. M: Kean
Geo: Read
MARYLAND
Mat. Tilghman
Ths. Johnson Junr.
Wm. Paca
Samuel Chase
Thos: Stone

COLONY OF VIRGINIA
P. Henry Jr.
Richard Henry Lee
Edmund Pendleton
Benja. Harrison
Th: Jefferson
NORTH CAROLINA
Will. Hooper
Joseph Hewes
SOUTH CAROLINA
Henry Middleton
Tho. Lynch
Christ. Gadsden
J. Rutledge
Edward Rutledge

Text from *Facsimile of the Olive Branch Petition, 8 July 1775. From the Original in H. M. Public Record Office, London.* London: His Majesty's Stationery Office, 1934. The engrossed original contains autograph signatures of the delegates to Congress, and is endorsed: "Petition of the Congress to The King. Septr: 1st. 1775—Delivered to the Earl of Dartmouth by Messrs. Penn & Lee." A second engrossed and signed copy of this document was acquired by the New York Public Library in 1948. This document was written by John Dickinson with much satisfaction, and was signed by Thomas Jefferson and some of the other delegates with considerably less satisfaction. See TJ, Autobiography, Ford, I, 17-18; Adams, "Diary" (*Works*, II, 409-11); *Charles Thomson Papers,* NYHS, *Colls.,* 1878, p. 284-5; Burnett, *Letters of Members,* I, Nos. 217, 218, 265. The Petition was met with royal disregard in England; see Richard Penn and Arthur Lee to the President of Congress, 2 Sep. 1775, Force, *Archives,* 4th ser., III, 627.

To the President of the Virginia Convention

SIR   Philadelphia July 11. 1775.

The continued sitting of Congress prevents us from attending our colony Convention: but, directed by a sense of duty, we transmit to the Convention such determinations of the Congress as they have directed to be made public. The papers speak for themselves, and require no comment from us. A petition to the king is already sent away, earnestly entreating the royal interposition to prevent the further progress of civil contention by redressing American grievances; but we are prevented from transmitting a copy of it, because a public communication, before it has been presented, may be improper.—The Convention, we hope, will pardon us for venturing our sentiments on the following subjects, which we submit to their superior wisdom. The continuance and the extent of this conflict we consider as among the secrets of providence; but we also reflect on the propriety of being prepared for the worst events, and, so far as human foresight can provide, to be guarded against probable evils at least. Military skill we are certainly not so well provided with as military violence opposed to us may render necessary. Will not this deficiency be supplied by sending at the publick expence a few gentlemen of genius and spirit to the military school before Boston to learn that necessary art, which in these days of rapine can only be relied upon for public safety.

The present crisis is so full of danger and incertainty that opinions here are various. Some think a continued sitting of Congress necessary, whilst others are of opinion that an adjournment to the Fall will answer as well. We conclude that our powers go not to the latter, but that a Fall Congress will be indispensible, with adjourning powers given to your delegates that they may be prepared to meet contingencies. The Convention will therefore see the propriety of proceeding to a new choice of delegates and being explicit about the time to which they chuse to limit the continuance of their delegation. It is expected that at the next Congress the delegates from the respective colonies come provided with an exact account of the number of people of all ages and sexes, including slaves. The Convention will provide for this.

It is with singular pleasure that we can congratulate you on the success with which providence has been pleased to favor our righteous cause by giving success to the operations in defence of American liberty. We are Sir Your most humble servants,

P. HENRY, JR.

RICHARD HENRY LEE

EDMD. PENDLETON

BENJA. HARRISON

TH: JEFFERSON

RC (PHi). An official letter in TJ's hand and signed by all the Virginia delegates in Congress. The Virginia Convention did not meet until 17 July, but it was doubtless understood by everyone that Peyton Randolph would be elected president, as he was on the first day of the session. He is therefore the addressee of this letter, which was referred to the committee of the whole on 27 July. (*Conv. Jour.*, July 1775, p. 4, 7).

THE MILITARY SCHOOL BEFORE BOSTON was apparently only a matter of discussion, not of action, though it went far enough for the *Virginia Gazette* (Purdie)

to report on 28 July 1775 that "At the recommendation of the General Congress, we hear that 60 young gentlemen are to be immediately sent from this colony to the camp near Boston, to serve as cadets in the army under general Washington." As for the ADJOURNMENT of Congress and the NEW CHOICE OF DELEGATES, Congress adjourned on 31 July; all of the delegates except R. H. Lee returned to take seats in the Convention on 9 Aug.; and two days later Lee, TJ, Harrison, and four new delegates were elected for a year's term in Congress (*Conv. Jour.*, July 1775, p. 12, 14).

Resolutions of Congress on Lord North's Conciliatory Proposal

I. JEFFERSON'S DRAFT RESOLUTIONS

[25 July 1775]

The Congress proceeding to take into their consideration a resolution of the House of Commons of Gr. Br. referred to them by the several assemblies of New Jersey, Pennsylva. and Virga., which resolution is in these words 'that it is the opinion &c.' are of Opinion

That the colonies of America possess ⟨an⟩ the exclusive ⟨right⟩ privilege of giving and granting their own money; that this involves a right of deliberating whether they will ⟨give any sums⟩ make any gift, for what purposes ⟨they will give them⟩ it shall be made, and what shall be ⟨the⟩ it's amount ⟨of the gift⟩ and that it is a high breach of this privilege for any body of men, extraneous to their constitution, to prescribe the purposes for which money shall be levied on them, ⟨and⟩ to take to themselves the authority of judging ⟨what shall be a sufficient levy⟩ of their conditions circumstances, and situation and of determining the ⟨sufficiency or insufficiency of any the levy proposed⟩ amount of the contribution to be levied.

That as they possess a right of appropriating their gifts, so are they entitled at all times to enquire into ⟨it's⟩ their application; to see that ⟨it⟩ they be not ⟨distributed⟩ wasted among the venal and corrupt ⟨to sap⟩ for the purpose of ⟨sapping⟩ undermining the⟨ir⟩ civil rights of the givers, ⟨of overbearing them with military force⟩ ⟨power⟩ ⟨by diverting them⟩ nor yet ⟨applied⟩ be diverted to the support of standing armies ⟨for the purpose of overbearing these rights by military⟩ inconsistent with ⟨domestic quiet . . .⟩ their freedom and subversive of ⟨our⟩ their quiet. to propose therefore as this resolution does that the monies given by the colonies shall be subject to the dispos⟨ition⟩al of parliament alone, is to propose that they shall ⟨surrender up⟩ ⟨give away⟩ relinquish this right of enquiry, and ⟨to⟩ put it in the power of others to render their gifts ruinous in proportion as they are liberal.

That this privilege of giving or of witholding our monies is an important barrier against ⟨an⟩ the undue exertion of prerogative, which if left altogether without controul ⟨might⟩ may be exercised to our great oppression; ⟨and that is also⟩ and all history shews ⟨it's⟩ how efficacious is it's intercession for redress of grievances and reestablishment of rights and how improvident would be the surrender of so powerful a mediator.

⟨*We are farther of opinion*⟩ We are ⟨*farther*⟩ of opinion That the proposition contained in this resolution is ⟨*uncandid*⟩ unreasonable ⟨*unequal*⟩ and insidious: ⟨*uncandid*⟩ unreasonable ⟨*unequal*⟩, because if we declare we accede to it, we declare ⟨*in absolute terms*⟩ without reservation we will purchase the favor of parliament ⟨*and leave the price of that purchase to be fixed by the sellers alone*⟩ ⟨*without*⟩ not knowing at the same time at what price they will please to estimate their favor; it is insidious, because ⟨*a colony*⟩ ⟨*any*⟩ individual colonies ⟨*on refusal of any proferred sum*⟩ having bid and bidden again till ⟨*it*⟩ they find⟨*s*⟩ the ⟨*height of parliamentary*⟩ avidity of the seller unattainable by all ⟨*it's*⟩ their powers, ⟨*are*⟩ are then to return into opposition ⟨*single and unsupported*⟩ divided from ⟨*its*⟩ their sister colonies ⟨*having*⟩ ⟨*being*⟩ ⟨*in the mean time been taken*⟩ ⟨*being artfully*⟩ whom the minister ⟨*shall*⟩ will have previously detached ⟨*from the Union*⟩ by ⟨*acceptance*⟩ a grant of easier terms, ⟨*or deluded into inactivity by keeping up*⟩ ⟨*into*⟩ ⟨*a definitive answer*⟩ ⟨*by delaying of the definitive answer*⟩ or by an artful procrastination of a definitive answer.

That the suspension of the exercise of their pretended power ⟨*to*⟩ ⟨*tax*⟩ ⟨*levy taxes*⟩ of taxation being expressly made commensurate with the ⟨*duration*⟩ continuance of our gifts, ⟨*in order*⟩ these must be perpetual to make that so: ⟨*and experience has invariably proved that to render a governing power perpetually independent it is not the best method of preserving the friendship and good offices of any part of government to render it independent by vesting it with perpetual revenue and*⟩ whereas no experience has shewn that a gift of perpetual revenue secures a perpetual return of duty or of ⟨*good*⟩ kind dispositions. on the contrary the parliament itself, ⟨*with a wisdom we mean to imitate*⟩ ⟨*worthy imitation*⟩ ⟨*prudently*⟩ ⟨*cautiously*⟩ wisely attentive to this ⟨*circumstance*⟩ observation are in the established practice of granting their own money ⟨*but*⟩ from year to year only.

⟨*We are of opinion that even fair terms could hardly be accepted by freemen, when attended with circumstances so insultive*⟩ ⟨*cirstances*⟩

Tho desirous and determined to consider in the most dispassionate ⟨*light*⟩ view every advance towards reconciliation made by the British parliament, let our brethren of Britain reflect what ⟨*must*⟩ would have been the sacrifice to men of free spirits, ⟨*to accept*⟩ had even fair terms ⟨*been*⟩ been proferred as these were with ⟨*the most irritating*⟩ circumstances of insult and defiance. a proposition to give our money, ⟨*when*⟩ accompanied with large fleets and armies seems addressed to our fears rather than to our freedom. ⟨let⟩ ⟨Britons⟩ ⟨our brethren of Britain⟩ ⟨reflect⟩ with what patience ⟨they⟩ would they have received articles of treaty from any power on earth when ⟨sent by such messengers⟩ ⟨plenipotentiaries⟩ borne ⟨by⟩ on the point of a bayonet by ⟨the hands of⟩ military plenipotentiaries? ⟨on the point of a bayonet.⟩

We think ⟨that⟩ the attempt⟨s⟩ ⟨alike unaccountable and⟩ unnecessary and unaccountable to raise upon us by force or by threats our proportional contributions to the common defence, when all know, and themselves acknoledge⟨d⟩ we have ⟨ever freely and⟩ fully ⟨given those⟩ contribut⟨ions⟩ed whenever called ⟨upon as⟩ to contribute in the character [of]¹ freemen ⟨is one among⟩ ⟨should be⟩ ⟨a plain proof, among many others, that not the obtaining this but the reducing us to their absolute dominion was⟩ ⟨not⟩ ⟨the ultimate end of Parliamentary⟩ ⟨object of parliament.⟩

We are of opinion it is not just that the colonies should ⟨make any⟩ ⟨oblige themselves to stipulate⟩ be required to oblige themselves to other contributions while Great Britain possesses a monopoly of their trade. this ⟨is of⟩ does of itself lay them under ⟨a⟩ heavy contribution ⟨levied on them⟩. to demand therefore an⟨other⟩ additional Contribution ⟨by way⟩ in the form of a tax is to demand the double of their equal proportion. ⟨we conceive no reason⟩ if we are to contribute ⟨proportionably⟩ equally with the other parts of the empire, let us equally with them enjoy ⟨with them equal rights of⟩ free commerce with the whole world. but while the restrictions on our trade shut ⟨up⟩ to us the resources of wealth ⟨we cannot bear⟩ ⟨it⟩ is it ⟨un⟩just we should ⟨be expected to⟩ bear all other burthens equally with those ⟨who⟩ to whom ⟨are under no restrictions⟩ ⟨have⟩ every resource is open?

We conceive that the Brit. parliament has no right to intermeddle with our provision⟨s⟩ for the support of civil government, or administration of justice. ⟨that⟩ th⟨at⟩e provisions ⟨have been made in such manner as to⟩ ⟨we have already⟩ we have made are such as please ourselves, they answer the substantial purposes of government and of justice, and other purposes than these should not be answered. we do not mean ⟨to burthen⟩ that our people ⟨should⟩ shall be burthened with ⟨heavy and⟩ oppressive taxes to provide sinecures for the ⟨drones of creation⟩ ⟨ministerial partisans⟩ the idle or wicked under color of providing for a civil list. ⟨but⟩ while parliament pursue ⟨their unmolested⟩ their plan of civil government within their own jurisdiction we also hope to pursue ours ⟨also⟩ without molestation.

We are of opinion the proposition is altogether unsatisfactory, because ⟨*the parliament*⟩ it imports only a suspension, not a renunciation of the right to tax us; because as it ⟨*is*⟩ does not propose⟨*d*⟩ to repeal the several acts of parliament passed for the purposes of restraining the trade and altering the form of government of the Eastern colonies; extending the boundaries, and changing the government and religion of Quebec; enlarging the jurisdiction of the courts of admiralty and viceadmiralty; taking from us the rights of trial by jury of the vicinage in cases affecting both life and property; ⟨*exempting the murderers of colonists from legal trial*⟩ transporting us into other countries to be tried for criminal offences; exempting by mock-trial the murderers of colonists from punishment; and ⟨*for*⟩ quartering soldiers on us in times of profound peace. nor do they renounce the power of suspending our own legislatures and of legislating for us themselves in all cases whatsoever. ⟨*So far indeed from repealing the injurious acts of parliament beforementioned they pass others at the same time equally injurious,*⟩ On the contrary to shew they mean no⟨*t to*⟩ discontinu⟨*e*⟩ance ⟨*of their exercise*⟩ of injur⟨*ies*⟩y ⟨*at the very time of making their proposition*⟩ they ⟨*are*⟩ pass⟨*ing*⟩ acts at the very time of ⟨*making*⟩ holding out this proposition, for restraining the commerce and fisheries of the provinces of New England and for interdicting ⟨*in general*⟩ the trade of other colonies with all foreign nations. this ⟨*proof is*⟩ proves unequivocaly ⟨*of what we may expect in future*⟩ they mean not ⟨*no discontinuance of*⟩ to relinquish ⟨*this usurpation*⟩ the exercise of indiscriminate legislation over us.

Upon the whole

This proposition seems to have been held up to the world to deceive ⟨*them*⟩ it into a belieif that ⟨*the colonies are unreasonable;*⟩ that there was no matter in dispute between us but the single circumstance of the mode of levying taxes, which mode as they are so good as to give up to us of course that the colonies are unreasonable if they are not thereby perfectly satisfied: whereas in truth our adversaries not only still claim a right of demanding ad libitum and of taxing us themselves to the full amount of their demands if we do not fulfill their pleasure, which leaves us without any thing we can call property, but what is of more importance and what they keep in this proposal out of sight as if no such point was in contest, they claim a right of altering all our charters and established laws which leaves us without the least security for our lives or liberties. the proposition seems also calculated[2] more particularly to lull into fatal security our well affected fellow subjects on ⟨*that*⟩

the other side the water ⟨*into a fatal security*⟩ till time should be given for the operation of those arms which a British minister pronounced would instantaneously reduce the "*cowardly*" sons of America to unreserved submission. but when the world reflects how inadequate to justice are the⟨se⟩ vaunted term*s* ⟨*offered*⟩, when it attends to the rapid and bold succession of injuries which ⟨*for the space*⟩ during a course of 11. years have been aimed at these colonies ⟨*by a wicked administration*⟩, when it reviews the pacific and respectful ⟨*applications*⟩ ⟨*complaints*⟩ expostulations which during that whole time have been ⟨*made*⟩ the sole arms we opposed to ⟨*their usurpations*⟩ them, when it ⟨*considers*⟩ observes that our complaints were either not heard at all, or were answered with new and accumulated injury, when it ⟨*considers*⟩ recollects that the minister himself declared ⟨*from the beginning*⟩ on an ⟨*former*⟩ early occasion he would never cease[3]   till America was at his feet, and that an avowed partisan of ministry ⟨*has*⟩ has more lately ⟨. . .⟩ denounced against America the dreadful sentence 'Delenda est Carthago,' that this was done in the presence of a British senate and being unreproved by them ⟨*we*⟩ must be ⟨*considered*⟩ taken to be ⟨*as approved*⟩ their own sentiment; when it considers the great armaments ⟨*by sea and land*⟩ with which they have invaded us ⟨*by sea and land*⟩, and the circumstances of cruelty with which the⟨se⟩y have commenced and prosecuted hostilities; when these things we say are laid together and attentively considered, can the world be deceived ⟨*by the artifices of a ministry*⟩ into an opinion that we are unreasonable, or can it hesitate to beleive with us that nothing but our own exertions ⟨*can*⟩ may defeat the ministerial sentence of ⟨. . .⟩ death or submission ⟨*to*⟩.

Dft (DLC). This document being the composition draft of an important state paper, it is presented literally, and an attempt has been made to indicate all of the deletions and corrections made by TJ as he wrote and revised. This has proved difficult, because not only are scored-out passages and interlineations numerous and written in a fine hand, but the MS is in places worn and blurred. A few readings have therefore necessarily been taken from Ford, i, 476-82, and JCC, ii, 225-34; these texts were carefully prepared from the MS some decades ago, but differ from one another and from our text in many small details. Since TJ here, as frequently elsewhere, went back over his draft report (it being the only copy of the paper he retained)

and inserted amendments made by the committee, it is probably impossible to furnish a printed text that will show not only all the alterations but the order in which they were made. The further changes made by Congress, which are relatively minor, may be seen by comparing the present document with the following one, the official version released to the newspapers.

For Lord North's conciliatory proposal and its rejection by the House of Burgesses, see the Virginia Resolutions of 10 June 1775. Both the Pennsylvania and New Jersey assemblies had earlier rejected the proposal, the former on 4 May, the latter on 20 May. Both, like Virginia, had insisted that they could not act individually now that a union had been formed among the colonies as represented in the Congress (*Penna. Archives*, 8th ser., VIII, 7224-30; *Minutes of the Provincial Congress and the Council of Safety of New Jersey*, Trenton, 1879, p. 119-42). The New Jersey delegates laid North's plan before Congress on 26 May, but though it was referred to the committee of the whole, no action was taken until 22 July, when Franklin, TJ, John Adams, and R. H. Lee were appointed a committee to report thereon (JCC, II, 61-3, 202; see also TJ's Autobiography, Ford, I, 18). On the 25th the committee reported; on the 31st the Report was "debated by paragraphs" and adopted as printed in the following document (JCC, II, 203, 224). See TJ's letter to William Wirt, 5 Aug. 1815. Franklin's early and acute judgment on North's motion is in a letter to Joseph Galloway, 25 Feb. 1775 (*Writings*, VI, 313-14).

¹ Inadvertently omitted by TJ.
² The preceding passage beginning "that there was no matter . . ." was inserted by TJ at the end of the text. It derived from an amendment by Franklin, the draft of which was written on a fragment of paper formerly in the Jefferson Papers, now in the Franklin Papers, Miscellany (DLC). Franklin's draft, in his hand but with caption by TJ, "amendment by Dr. Franklin," reads as follows: "that there was no Matter in Dispute between us but the single Circumstance of the *Mode* of Levying Taxes, which *Mode* as [*this word supplied in pencil*] they are so good as to give up to us; ⟨and⟩ of course that the Colonies are unreasonable if they are not perfectly satisfied: Whereas in truth ⟨they⟩ our Adversaries not only still claim a Right of demanding *ad libitum*, and of taxing us themselves to the full Amount of their Demands [*preceding three words interlined by John Adams(?)*] if we do not fulfill their Pleasure, which leaves us without any thing we can call Property; but what is of more Importance, and what they keep in this Proposal out of sight, as if no such Point was in Contest, they claim a Right [*several illegible words are here interlined and struck out*] of altering all our Charters and establish'd Laws, which ⟨would⟩ leave⟨s⟩s us ⟨not the Shadow of Liberty⟩ without the least Security ⟨for our Lives or Liber⟩ ⟨of Life or⟩ for our Lives or Libert⟨ies⟩y. The Proposition seems also calculated more particularly &c."
³ Blank in MS; see, however, the Resolutions as adopted, below.

II. THE RESOLUTIONS AS ADOPTED BY CONGRESS

Philadelphia, July 31, 1775.

IN CONGRESS.

THE several Assemblies of NEW JERSEY, PENNSYLVANIA and VIRGINIA, having refered to the Congress a resolution of the House of Commons of GREAT BRITAIN, which resolution is in these words, viz.

Lunae, 20° die Feb. 1775.

The House in a Committee on the American papers. Motion made, and question proposed.

THAT *it is the opinion of this Committee, that when the General Council and Assembly, or General Court of any of his Majesty's provinces, or colonies in America, shall propose to make provision, according to the condition, circumstance, or situation of such province or colony, for contributing their proportion to the common defence (such proportion to be raised under the authority of the General Court, or General Assembly of such province or colony, and disposable by Parliament) and shall engage to make provision also, for the support of the civil government, and the Administration of justice in such province or colony, it will be proper if such proposal shall be approved by his Majesty and the two Houses of Parliament; and for so long as such provision shall be made accordingly, to forbear in respect of such province or colony, to lay any duty, tax, or assessment, or to impose any further duty, tax or assessment, except only such duties as it may be expedient to continue to levy or impose, for the regulation of commerce, the net produce of the duties last mentioned, to be carried to the account of such province or colony respectively.*

The Congress took the said resolution into consideration, and are thereupon of opinion:

That the colonies of America are entitled to the sole and exclusive privilege of giving and granting their own money; that this involves a right of deliberating whether they will make any gift, for what purposes it shall be made, and what shall be it's amount; and that it is a high breach of this privilege for any body of men, extraneous to their constitutions, to prescribe the purposes for which money shall be levied on them, to take to themselves the authority of judging of their conditions, circumstances and situations; and of determining the amount of the contribution to be levied.

That as the colonies possess a right of appropriating their gifts, so are they entitled at all times to enquire into their application, to see that they be not wasted among the venal and corrupt for the purpose of undermining the civil rights of the givers, nor yet be diverted to the support of standing armies, inconsistent with their freedom and subversive of their quiet. To propose therefore, as this resolution does, that the monies given by the colonies shall be subject to the disposal of parliament alone, is to propose that they shall relinquish this right of enquiry, and put it in the power of others to render their gifts, ruinous, in proportion as they are liberal.

That this privilege of giving or of witholding our monies is an important barrier against the undue exertion of prerogative, which if left altogether without controul may be exercised to our great oppression; and all history shews how efficacious is its intercession for redress of grievances and re-establishment of rights, and how improvident it would be to part with so powerful a mediator.

We are of opinion that the proposition contained in this resolution is unreasonable and insidious: unreasonable, because, if we declare we accede to it, we declare without reservation, we will purchase the favour of Parliament, not knowing at the same time at what price they will please to estimate their favor: It is insidious, because, individual colonies, having bid and bidden again, till they find the avidity of the seller too great for all their powers to satisfy; are then to return into opposition, divided from their sister colonies whom the minister will have previously detached by a grant of easier terms, or by an artful procrastination of a definitive answer.

That the suspension of the exercise of their pretended power of taxation being expressly made commensurate with the continuance of our gifts, these must be perpetual to make that so. Whereas no experience has shewn that a gift of perpetual revenue secures a perpetual return of duty or of kind disposition. On the contrary, the Parliament itself, wisely attentive to this observation, are in the established practice of granting their supplies from year to year only.

Desirous and determined as we are to consider in the most dispassionate view every seeming advance towards a reconciliation made by the British Parliament, let our brethren of Britain reflect what would have been the sacrifice to men of free spirits had even fair terms been proffered, as these insidious proposals were with circumstances of insult and defiance. A proposition to give our money, accompanied with large fleets and armies, seems addressed to our fears rather than to our freedom. With what patience would Britons have received articles of treaty from any power on earth when borne on the point of a bayonet by military plenipotentiaries?

We think the attempt unnecessary to raise upon us by force or by threats our proportional contributions to the common defence, when all know, and themselves acknowledge we have fully contributed, whenever called upon to do so in the character of freemen.

We are of opinion it is not just that the colonies should be required to oblige themselves to other contributions, while Great Britain possesses a monopoly of their trade. This of itself lays them under heavy contribution. To demand therefore, additional aids in the form of a tax, is to demand the double of their equal proportion, if we are to contribute equally with the other parts of the empire, let us equally with them enjoy free commerce with the whole world. But while the restrictions on our trade shut to us the resources of wealth, is it just we should bear all other burthens equally with those to whom every resource is open.

We conceive that the British Parliament has no right to intermeddle with our provisions for the support of civil government, or administration of justice. The provisions we have made are such as please ourselves, and are agreeable to our own circumstances; they answer the substantial purposes of government and of justice, and other purposes than these should not be answered. We do not mean that our people shall be burthened with oppressive taxes to provide sinecures for the idle or the wicked, under colour of providing for a civil list. While Parliament pursue their plan of civil government within their own jurisdiction, we also hope to pursue ours without molestation.

We are of opinion the proposition is altogether unsatisfactory because it imports only a suspension of the mode, not a renunciation of the pretended right to tax us: Because too it does not propose to repeal the several Acts of Parliament passed for the purposes of restraining the trade and altering the form of government of one of our Colonies; extending the boundaries and changing the government of Quebec; enlarging the jurisdiction of the Courts of Admiralty and Vice Admiralty; taking from us the rights of trial by a Jury of the vicinage in cases affecting both life and property; transporting us into other countries to be tried for criminal offences; exempting by mock-trial the murderers of Colonists from punishment; and quartering soldiers on us in times of profound peace. Nor do they renounce the power of suspending our own Legislatures, and of legislating for us themselves in all cases whatsoever. On the contrary, to shew they mean no discontinuance of injury, they pass acts, at the very time of holding out this proposition, for restraining the commerce and fisheries of the Provinces of New-England, and for interdicting the trade of other Colonies with all foreign nations and with each other. This proves unequivocally they mean not to relinquish the exercise of indiscriminate legislation over us.

Upon the whole, this proposition seems to have been held up to the world, to deceive it into a belief that there was nothing in dispute between us but the *mode* of levying taxes; and that the Parliament having now been so good as to give up this, the Colonies are unreasonable if not perfectly satisfied: Whereas in truth, our adversaries still claim a right of demanding *ad libitum*, and of taxing us themselves to the full amount of their demand, if we do not comply with it. This leaves us without any thing we can call property. But, what is of more importance, and what in this proposal they keep out of sight, as if no such point was now in contest between us, they claim a right to alter our Charters and established laws, and leave us without any security for our Lives or Liberties. The proposition seems also to have been calculated more particularly to lull into fatal security our well-affected fellow subjects on the other side the water, till time should be given for the operation of those arms, which a British Minister pronounced would instantaneously reduce the "cowardly" sons of America to unreserved submission. But when the world reflects, how inadequate to justice are these vaunted terms; when it attends to the rapid and bold succession of injuries, which, during a course of eleven years, have been aimed at these Colonies; when it reviews the pacific and respectful expostulations, which, during that whole time, were the sole arms we opposed to them; when it observes that our complaints were either not heard at all, or were answered with new and accumulated injury; when it recollects that the Minister himself on an early occasion declared, "that he would never treat with America, till he had brought her to his feet," and that an avowed partisan of Ministry has more lately denounced against us the dreadful sentence "*delenda est Carthago*," that this was done in presence of a British Senate, and being unreproved by them, must be taken to be their own sentiment, (especially as the purpose has already in part been carried into execution by their treatment of Boston, and burning of Charlestown) when it considers the great armaments with which they have invaded us, and the circumstances of cruelty with which these have commenced and prosecuted hostilities; when these things, we say, are laid together, and attentively considered, can the world be deceived into an opinion that we are unreasonable, or can it hesitate to believe with us, that nothing but our own exertions may defeat the ministerial sentence of death or abject submission.

By Order of the Congress,

JOHN HANCOCK, *President.*

Printed from the *Pennsylvania Packet*, 7 Aug. 1775.

This is the version adopted by Congress of TJ's Draft (submitted 25 July) for the committee on Lord North's conciliatory plan of 20 Feb. 1775. See the preceding document and note thereon.

Virginia and Pennsylvania Delegates in Congress to the Inhabitants West of Laurel Hill

FRIENDS AND COUNTRYMEN   Philadelphia 25 July 1775

It gives us much concern to find that disturbances have arisen and still continue among you concerning the boundaries of our colonies. In the character in which we now address you, it is unnecessary to enquire into the origin of those unhappy disputes, and it would be improper for us to express our approbation or censure on either side: But as representatives of two of the colonies united, among many others, for the defence of the liberties of America, we think it our duty to remove, as far as lies in our power, every obstacle that may prevent her sons from co-operating as vigorously as they would wish to do towards the attainment of this great and important end. Influenced solely by this motive, our joint and our earnest request to you is, that all animosities, which have heretofore subsisted among you as inhabitants of distinct colonies may now give place to generous and concurring efforts for the preservation of every thing that can make our common country dear to us.

We are fully persuaded that you, as well as we, wish to see your differences terminate in this happy issue. For this desireable purpose, we recommend it to you, that all bodies of armed men kept up under either province be dismissed; that all those, who, on either side, are in confinement or under bail for taking a part in the contest be discharged; and that until the dispute be decided every person be permitted to retain his possessions unmolested. By observing these directions the public tranquility will be secured without injury to the titles on either side. The period we flatter ourselves, will soon arrive when this unfortunate dispute, which has produced much mischief, and, as far as we can learn, no good, will be peaceably and constitutionally determined.

We are Your Friends & Countrymen

P. HENRY JR.	JOHN DICKINSON
RICHARD HENRY LEE	GEO: ROSS
BENJA. HARRISON	B. FRANKLIN
TH: JEFFERSON	JAMES WILSON
	CHA. HUMPHREYS

MS in an unidentified hand (DLC: Pennsylvania Papers). This is the original or official copy, with autograph signatures. Docketed: "An Address from

Penna. & Vigina. Delegates in Congress to the Inhabitants West of Laurel Hill 1775."

TJ was to be concerned with the protracted dispute over the boundary between Virginia and Pennsylvania in turn as colonial and state legislator, as delegate to Congress, and as governor, but (unlike many of his friends and colleagues) not as a speculator in western lands. He acquired and grouped together a number of papers relating to this dispute; the cover for this packet, docketed "Pensylvania & Virginia. papers relating to their boundary," is still among his papers in DLC. The dispute arose out of ambiguities in the 1609 and 1681 charters of Virginia and Pennsylvania, respectively, summarized in Boyd Crumrine, "The Boundary Controversy between Pennsylvania and Virginia; 1748-1785," *Annals of the Carnegie Museum*, I (1901-1902), 505-24, the standard older account, now superseded by Solon J. and Elizabeth H. Buck, *The Planting of Civilization in Western Pennsylvania*, Pittsburgh, 1939, ch. VIII, see also Paullin and Wright, *Atlas*, p. 77, and pl. 97G. The crux of the argument was whether Virginia or Pennsylvania should possess the Forks of the Ohio, the site of modern Pittsburgh. The progress of the struggle, from before the French and Indian War until after the Revolution, brought into conflict not only colony against colony (later state against state), but colonial against imperial interests, the great land magnates against the small settlers and against each other, Indian tribes against other tribes, whigs against tories, and, ultimately, state against federal authority. The phase of the struggle to which the present document pertains began in 1773 with the erection of rival jurisdictions over the territory west of the Laurel Hill or Ridge (the penultimate range of the Alleghenies in western Pennsylvania). Pennsylvania established Westmoreland co., with its seat of justice at Hanna's Town near present Greensburg; and Virginia created the District of West Augusta, with a court periodically adjourned from Staunton to Pittsburgh (Crumrine, p. 514; Buck, p. 158, 167; Abernethy, *Western Lands*, p. 93-4). The early months of 1774 brought on local warfare between the partisans of Virginia under Dr. John Connolly (who held a commission from Gov. Dunmore as "Captain, Commandant of the Militia

of Pittsburgh and its Dependencies") and the partisans of Pennsylvania under Arthur St. Clair, prothonotary of Westmoreland co. (*Penna. Archives*, 1st ser., IV, 476-93; Jos. A. Waddell, *Annals of Augusta County, Virginia*, Staunton, 1902, p. 225-6). A serious attempt to reach an agreement on a line was made in May 1774 when Gov. John Penn sent two commissioners to Williamsburg for this purpose; proposals and counter-proposals were made, but negotiations broke down when Dunmore refused to yield Pittsburgh (*Penna. Colonial Records*, X, 181-91; Buck, p. 166-7; Paullin and Wright, *Atlas*, p. 77 and pl. 97G). It is quite possible that TJ was consulted during these negotiations; see his Memoranda on the Virginia, Pennsylvania, and Maryland Boundaries, printed under the date of 5 Nov. 1776, below. The two governors continued to issue proclamations and counter-proclamations claiming jurisdiction of the upper Ohio, and in the autumn of 1774 Dunmore established a garrison at Fort Pitt, newly renamed for himself (Force, *Archives*, 4th ser., I, 790, 856; Thwaites and Kellogg, *Doc. Hist. of Dunmore's War*, p. 380). The coming of the Revolution, however, divided the Virginians in that region, for Capt. Connolly was a zealous loyalist; see his "Narrative," serialized in PMHB, XII-XIII (1888-1889). In May 1775 the West Augusta patriots organized a committee of safety, which promptly addressed an appeal to Congress. The text of the appeal is missing, but the action of Congress is recorded as follows:

"A petition from 'the Committee representing the people in that part of Augusta county, in the colony of Virginia, on the west side of the Allegeny Mountain,' being laid before Congress and read, intimating fears of a rupture with the Indians on Accot of Ld. Dunmore's conduct, and desiring 'commissioners from the colony of Virginia, and province of Pensylvania, to attend a meeting of the Indians at Pittsburgh, on behalf of these colonies.' Also a resolve of the sd. committee in these words, viz. 'That the unsettled boundary between this colony and the province of Pensylvania is the occasion of many disputes' [*the last sentence was lined out in the Journal*].

"Ordered, That the above be referred to the delegates of the colonies of Virginia and Pensylvania" (JCC, II, 76).

The present joint address probably

resulted from this appeal. It is not known how it was circulated. Meanwhile other steps were being taken, by both Virginia and Congress, to be mentioned later; see Thomas Walker and others to TJ, 13 Sep. 1775; Virginia Committee of Safety to Virginia Delegates in Congress, 17 June 1776.

From the Virginia Delegates in Congress to George Washington

DEAR SIR   Philadelphia 26 July 1775

With the most cordial warmth we recommend our Countryman Mr. Edmund Randolph to your patronage and favor.

This young Gentlemans abilities, natural and acquired, his extensive connections, and above all, his desire to serve his Country in this arduous struggle, are circumstances that cannot fail to gain him your countenance and protection.

You will readily discern Sir, how important a consideration it is, that our Country should be furnished with the security and strength derived from our young Gentry being possessed of military knowledge, so necessary in these times of turbulence and danger.

Encouraged by your friendship, and instructed by your example, we hope Mr. Randolph will become useful to his Country and profitable to himself.

We most heartily wish you health and success, with a happy return to your family and Country, being with grea[t] sincerity dear Sir Your affectionate frien[ds] and obedient servants,

RICHARD HENRY LEE

P. HENRY

TH: JEFFERSON

RC (DLC: Washington Papers). In R. H. Lee's hand, with autograph signatures. Endorsed by Washington.

From George Gilmer

DR. SIR   [26 or 27 July 1775]

Your favour of the 5th Inst. this instant came to my hands in our encampment in Wallers Grove, the account of the battle at Charles town is pleasing, I wish it is true. It appears astonishing to me that some armed Vessel has not attempted to bring in powder &c. it certainly is practicable and wants proper encouragement only to put it in execution. Do order some of those Privateers to all the Islands to Holland Spain [&c.?] Give them positive instructions to bring powder. A high premium must ensure this matter. I could wish our little insignificant Town were in ashes, something could be done, but we dread the bombardment of York, &c. As to myself I have buried every view of Interest that does not center in the general cause and to proceed according to military order on an Application of the Mayor Recorder and Treasurer for assistance as 1st Lieutenant to the 1st Company of Ind[ependen]ts I have Marched to Wmsbg. with 28 Chosen Riffle men, old Isaac Davis at the head and a very respectable set of Volunteers, who do give our County credit. The number of men required from different Counties amounted to [250?] which number have been some time placed in the grove, totally inactive: no order. Capt. Scott our commander in chief, whos goodness and merit is great, fear[1] to offend, and by that many members are rather disorderly. We appear rather invited to feast than fight. Anderson and Southall's entertain elegantly the first in the best manner by far. Indeed I began to think we should have a campaingn[1] without action, but proposed laying hands on all his Majesties money immediately which proposal was readily agreed to on which the officers waited on the proper officers in some Cases swore the officer most solemnly not to disburse what might be on hand on pain of Confiscation of their whole Estate and being treated as a Traitor to the Cause. Unhappy that this tho all along necessary should [have] been posponed till almost all the money was shiped to Boston by order of the board there. 1200 Dollars went from Jaquelin Ambler this month, large sums from other Collectors In bills, &c. We collected 900£ from L. Burwell, have sent detatchments to wait on Corbin &c. with positive orders for him to deliver up all his Majesties Cash or bind his whole estate as security for his not disbursing, remitting or otherwise using one Copper, and [on?] refusing to comply he is ordered to appear in our encampment. We have sent an Express to the Convention to Sanctify our proceedings.

You alarm me greatly with your account of the scar[cit]y of powder. We were informed here that it was made in abundance in Philadelphia. It is astonishing When the materials are so easily obtained, that no person should think it worth while. Salt petre may be had in large quantities from the [Stores?] why not buy it up? It may be collected [spontaneously?] in many places. It is to be collected by an easy and cheap process from all putrid subs[tances]. I will try and send you a small specimen soon. I have made Gun powder full strong, but can not grain it tho we have tried every plan proposed by Chambers Posthlwait &c. &c. The news from the

Convention you'l receive by the Delegate who may be appointed in place of Genl. Washington. We shall have an inexperienced[2] Commander it is supposed. The confusion in our country daily increases. At the last Committee I proposed appointing a Delegate in your Room. The same day I was ordered to March My detatchment to Wmsbg. and Continue there till the 20th Inst. This put it out of my power offering as intended and as desired by Numbers. Therefore insisted on Chs. Lewis's declaring himself. On the day of Election Mr. or Capt. John Ware, also Declared, a poll was taken and some say Lewis had four votes for one. He was 90 odd before and is now in Convention. Dunmore goes on shore at Norfolk but appears no where beside. Tis said there [are] a number of people in that place who will not swear alegiance to the American States, being informed of it the officers here sent a letter to the Committee requesting an account of the matter but they denied the fact and say there are some suspected persons there.

I am just returned from York but could Collect none of his Majesties money. Emanuel Jones has ordered a hunting shirt, keeps three guns high charged by him. Capt. Frs. Epps is order'd with a detatchment to Portobello to enquire the business of a Cutter that appears in those quarters. Every rank and denomination of people full of marshal notions, I wish the Plan of the Convention may give General Satisfaction. I am determined to die in the cause if necessary on any of thier Establishments but shall I believe stick to the Volunteer list. Poor Bob. Bolling has run his race, adieu to Burgundy, died suddenly at Richmond. You must not think of returning. We must Escort your wives and families to you or get a General license for moderate indulgences from them. Wishing you all the Joys that heaven can send I remain with great respect your friend and St.,   GEO. GILMER

FC, autograph, in Gilmer's Diary (ViHi). At foot of text: "To Thos. Jefferson at the Congress." The copy is undated, but it may be precisely dated from allusions in the text; see below.

Gilmer's acknowledgment of a letter OF THE 5TH INST. identifies the extract printed above under 5 July 1775 as a letter from TJ to Gilmer. Gilmer did not receive that letter until his return to WALLERS GROVE, at the east end of the town of Williamsburg, where the independent company of Albemarle volunteers, commanded by Capt. Charles SCOTT, was encamped with volunteer companies from other counties. This must have been before 28 July, when TJ's letter of the 5th was printed anonymously in Purdie's Gazette, but not before 26 July, when the officers of the several companies sent AN EXPRESS TO THE CONVENTION then sitting at Richmond; hence the date of 26 or 27 July for the present letter may be fixed with certainty. The text of the officers' message and of numerous documents relating to the formation and movements of the independent companies will be found in "The Gilmer Papers," Va. Hist. Colls., new ser., VI (1887), 69–140. No delegate to Congress was AP-

POINTED IN PLACE OF GENL. WASHINGTON until the election of a new delegation on 11 Aug.; in the meantime Congress had adjourned, 1 Aug., and TJ and other members of the old delegation had taken their places in the Virginia Convention, 9 Aug. (*Conv. Jour.*, July 1775, 1816 edn., p. 14, 12); therefore TJ could not have received this letter in Philadelphia. Col. CHARLES LEWIS, of Belvoir, had been serving as TJ's substitute in the Convention. PORTOBELLO (or Porto Bello) was the name of Gov. Dunmore's estate in York co. (WMQ, 1st ser., XVI [1907-1908], 54). Col. Robert BOLLING, of Buckingham co., died 21 July (*Va. Gaz.* [Purdie], 28 July 1775).

1 Thus in MS.
2 This word is crowded at the end of a line and is not perfectly legible.

From St. George Tucker

DEAR SIR   Bermuda Augst: 12th: 1775.

Were I certain that a Letter I addressed to you a few Weeks ago, by way of Virginia had been delivered to you, I should not have intruded on Business of greater Importance in which you may be at present engaged, a second Time. But lest any Accident should have happened thereto, I take the Liberty of enclosing you the Plan for continuing the Exports from America to foreign Markets, which I hinted at in the Letter I took the Liberty of troubling you with in Williamsburg. Doctor Franklin has been addressed by my Father on this Subject, and he has enclosed a Plan for supplying this Island without Danger of infringing the continental Association. Should you think proper to communicate the enclosed to Doctor Franklin, it may possibly serve as a Foundation for some more eligible superstructure.

I am with the greatest Esteem for yourself and the most ardent Wishes in favor of that glorious Cause in which you are at present engaged, Dear Sir Your most obedient humble servant,

ST. GEORGE TUCKER

PROPOSAL CONCERNING BERMUDA

In order to continue the Exports from America to foreign Markets, it is proposed that all non-enumerated Goods be permitted to be imported into Bermuda from the Continent upon proper and sufficient Assurances from the Inhabitants of that Island that they will not infringe that part of the Continental Association which relates to Exports.

For this purpose the Cargoes must be discharged in Bermuda in order to obtain a certificate to cancel the Bond given at the Custom Houses in America in obedience to the restraining Bill.

In order to give a Colour to the Trade being carried on by the

Inhabitants of Bermuda (since it might possibly endanger the success should it be carried on in the name of the Americans, as Hostilities have commenced between Great Britain and the Continent,) the Invoices, Bills of Lading &c. should be made out there and executed in the Name of the Inhabitants of that Island.

Perhaps it might not be amiss to appoint Committees of Inspection, whose Business it should be to see that no Vessel should sail from any port on the Continent untill Charter Parties, or other Engagements be entered into for the landing such Commodities as should be taken on board, in Bermuda without Fraud or Covin.

A Committee should likewise be appointed in Bermuda to prevent the re-exportation of any Commodities imported from the Continent, to any place except what the Congress shall allow. And the same Precautions should there be taken as on the Continent.

For the same Reasons that the Invoices and Bills of Lading should be made out in the name of the Agents in Bermuda, the Charter parties should also be executed in the same Manner.

Mediterranean passes should be procured on the Continent as there may be some Difficulty in getting them in Bermuda.

The above is respectfully submitted to the Consideration of Thomas Jefferson Esquire of Virginia, by, His most humble Servant,

ST: GEORGE TUCKER

Bermuda Aug: 12th: 1775

RC (DLC). Enclosure in Tucker's hand; printed herewith, with caption supplied.

For background, see note on Tucker to TJ, 8 June. Tucker's LETTER . . . BY WAY OF VIRGINIA is missing. The letter from Henry Tucker to FRANKLIN, dated 12 Aug. 1775, is in Amer. Philos. Soc., Franklin Papers, (*Cal. Franklin Pap.*, I, 174). The PLAN sent to Franklin by Henry Tucker with this letter is an undated document entitled "Proposals offered to the general Con[gress by] the Inhabitants of Bermuda," &c., entered in the same, IV, 391.

To John Randolph

DEAR SIR   Monticello. Aug. 25. 1775.

I received your message by Mr. Braxton and immediately gave him an order on the Treasurer for the money, which the Treasurer assured me should be answered on his return. I now send the bearer for the violin and such musick appurtaining to her as may be of no use to the young ladies. I beleive you had no case to her. If so, be so good as to direct Watt Lenox to get from Prentis's some bays or other coarse woollen to wrap her in, and then to pack her securely in a wooden box.

I am sorry the situation of our country should render it not eligible to you to remain longer in it. I hope the returning wisdom of Great Britain will e'er long put an end to this unnatural contest. There may be people to whose tempers and dispositions Contention may be pleasing, and who may therefore wish a continuance of confusion. But to me it is of all states, but one, the most horrid. My first wish is a restoration of our just rights; my second a return of the happy period when, consistently with duty, I may withdraw myself totally from the public stage and pass the rest of my days in domestic ease and tranquillity, banishing every desire of afterwards even hearing what passes in the world. Perhaps ardour for the latter may add considerably to the warmth of the former wish. Looking with fondness towards a reconciliation with Great Britain, I cannot help hoping you may be able to contribute towards expediting this good work. I think it must be evident to yourself that the ministry have been deceived by their officers on this side the water, who (for what purposes I cannot tell) have constantly represented the American opposition as that of a small faction, in which the body of the people took little part. This you can inform them of your own knolege to be untrue. They have taken it into their heads too that we are cowards and shall surrender at discretion to an armed force. The past and future operations of the war must confirm or undeceive them on that head. I wish they were thoroughly and minutely acquainted with every circumstance relative to America as it exists in truth. I am persuaded this would go far towards disposing them to reconciliation. Even those in parliament who are called friends to America seem to know nothing of our real determinations. I observe they pronounced in the last parliament that the Congress of 1774 did not mean to insist rigorously on the terms they held out, but kept something in reserve to give up; and in fact that they would give up everything but the article of taxation. Now the truth is far from this, as I can affirm, and put my honor to the assertion; and their continuance in this error may perhaps have very ill consequences. The Congress stated the lowest terms they thought possible to be accepted in order to convince the world they were not unreasonable. They gave up the monopoly and regulation of trade, and all the acts of parliament prior to 1764. leaving to British generosity to render these at some future time as easy to America as the interest of Britain would admit. But this was before blood was spilt. I cannot affirm, but have reason to think, these terms would not now be accepted. I wish no false sense of honor, no ignorance of our real intentions, no vain hope that partial concessions of right will be accepted may induce the ministry to trifle with accomodation till it shall be put even out of our own power ever to accomodate. If indeed Great Britain, disjoined from her colonies, be a match for the most potent nations of Europe with the colonies thrown into their scale, they may go on securely.[1] But if they are not assured of this, it would be certainly unwise, by trying the event of another campaign, to risque our accepting a foreign aid which perhaps may not be obtainable but on a condition of everlasting avulsion from Great Britain. This would be thought a hard condition to those who still wish for reunion with their parent country. I am sincerely one of those, and would rather be in dependance on Great Britain, properly limited, than on any nation upon earth, or than on no nation. But I am one of those too who rather than submit to the right of legislating for us assumed by the British parliament, and which late experience has shewn they will so cruelly exercise, would lend my hand to sink the whole island in the ocean.

If undeceiving the minister as to matters of fact may change his dispositions, it will perhaps be in your power by assisting to do this, to render service to the whole empire, at the most critical time certainly that it has ever seen. Whether Britain shall continue the head of the greatest empire on earth, or shall return to her original station in the political scale of Europe depends perhaps on the resolutions of the succeeding winter. God send they may be wise and salutary for us all!

I shall be glad to hear from you as often as you may be disposed to think of things here. You may be at liberty I expect to communicate some things consistently with your honor and the duties you will owe to a protecting nation. Such a communication among individuals may be mutually beneficial to the contending parties. On this or any future occasion if I affirm to you any facts, your knolege of me will enable you to decide on their credibility; if I hazard opinions on the dispositions of men, or other speculative points, you can only know they are my opinions. My best wishes for your felicity attend you wherever you go, and beleive me to be assuredly Your friend & servt.,   Th: Jefferson

P.S. My collection of classics and of books of parliamentary learning particularly is not so complete as I could wish. As you are going to the land of literature and of books you may be willing to dispose of some of yours here and replace them there in better editions. I should be willing to treat on this head with any body you may think proper to empower for that purpose.

RC (Earl of Dartmouth's MSS, Patshull House, Wolverhampton; facsimile in Stevens' *Facsimiles*, XXIV, no. 2038). Dft (DLC). Dft docketed by TJ: "Randolph, John (Atty. Gen.) An exact copy." The Dft contains numerous deletions, but only one particularly significant example has been recorded in the textual note below.

This letter, which begins with a violin, like the letter of 7 May 1775 to William Small, which begins with madeira wine, was designed to open the eyes of Englishmen to the true state of affairs in America. John Randolph, to whom it was directed, had in the previous summer stated his feelings on the dispute with admirable force and clarity in *Considerations on the Present State of Virginia* (see the Heartman reprint, N.Y., 1919, especially p. 36-8). The fact that TJ's letter came into the hands of the second Earl of Dartmouth, secretary of state for colonies, 1772-1775, indicates that Randolph brought it to the atten-

tion of government authorities. Randolph's MESSAGE BY MR. BRAXTON has not survived. THE VIOLIN was the instrument concerning which TJ and Randolph had entered into a remarkable agreement; see 11 Apr. 1771, above. On 17 Aug. 1775 TJ recorded in his Account Book:

"Delivered to Carter Braxton an order on the Treasurer [Robert Carter Nicholas] in favor of J. Randolph Atty. General for £13. the purchase money for his violin. This dissolves our bargain recorded in the Gen. ct. & revokes a legacy of £100. sterling to him now standing in my will which was made in consequence of that bargain."

1 Deleted in Dft: "But even in that event I verily beleive that her successes would produce an effect she has little thought of a measure which as yet has been hardly suggested. I mean the dereliction of our lower Country and establishment beyond the mountains."

From Edmund Randolph

DEAR SIR   Headquarters August 31. 1775.

No new Occurrence at Cambridge can justify an Intrusion on the well-employ'd Moments of a Delegate. I must, however, urge you, to assign a Reason for the Supineness of Virginia, amidst the Robberies, and other Violations of private Property, said to have been committed by Lord Dunmore. He plunders Custom-Houses, and reviews his Body-Guard at Gosport, unarrested. What is the Conclusion from hence? That Virginia has become eminent in her Forgiveness of former Injuries, and fearful of revenging new. But such an Inference is surely uncharitable, unless, what I cannot believe, she has ceased to be virtuous. His Lordship's Demands upon me on the Score of Gratitude I can never satisfy, but by acknowledging the Justness of them: yet a Demand from a higher Feeling must be first answered. Therefore I impeach him.

Since our Possession of Plowed Hill, distant about ½ Mile from the Enemy, Balls, and Shells are no Rarities. It is an Approach towards them certainly; but, as I am not oracular in military matters, my conjectures that it is not tenable in our present *craving*

Circumstances, will not dishearten you. For your own Sakes, be expeditious in enabling us to burn the Traitors out of their Hole.

Desertions have been lately undertaken with the utmost Audacity. An enterprizing Genius, who was one of 30 Regulars on Board a floating Battery, in the Absence of the commanding Officer opened his Intentions of quitting them to the whole Crew, without Reserve or Sounding them individually. The Rhetoric, which an appetite for fresh Meat, ever suggests, prevailed with three others to join him in his Escape—with the remaining 26 to connive at it.

My Brother Aid de Camp has just now set off for Providence, to purchase 8 Tons of Powder lately arrived.

Yr. Friend & Servt., EDM: RANDOLPH

RC (DLC).

From John Randolph

DR. SR. August 31. 1775

I have recieved ten Guineas of the Treasurer and have left the Violin with Mr. Cocke of Wmsburg. I wish I had had a Case for it. Tho we *may politically* differ in Sentiments, yet I see no Reason why *privately* we may not cherish the same Esteem for each other which formerly I believe Subsisted between us. Should any Coolness happen between us, I'll take Care not to be the first mover of it. We both of us seem to be steering opposite Courses; the Success of either lies in the Womb of Time. But whether it falls to my share or not, be assured that I wish you all Health and Happiness. I am Dr Sr Your most obedt Servant, JOHN RANDOLPH

RC (DLC). See TJ's letter of 25 Aug. to Randolph.

From Thomas Walker and Others

DEAR SIR Fort Pitt 13th. Sept. 1775.

After a very disagreeable, wet and fateagueing Journey, we got here on the 10th Inst. the day appointed for opening the Treaty, but found scarcely any Indians here. We have dispatched runners to meet them and hope they will be in soon. We are told that the Shawnese and Delawares are on their way, but can not hear a tittle of the Wiandotts, from which circumstance 'tis feared that they have acceded to the terms proposed to them by Carlton and Johnson. The few Indians here seem perfectly well disposed toward us,

and all things would go on well, were it not for the unhappy terri-
torial dispute between the two Colonies which has proceeded to an
inconceiviable length, and we are sorry to say, that a certain eminent
Gentleman who we conceive was sent here for very difrent purposes,
appears to us to have greatly interested himself in this affair. Application has been made to us, to join in a letter to Congress praying their Interposition, but we thought it out of our province. In
case the Pensylvanians should petition to this purpose, we hope
the Congress will not go precipitately into it, or if they should, that
you and the other Virginians will object to the giving up any of the
Teritory west of the Laurel hill. This is only intended as a hint for
our Friends. We are Dr. Sir Your obedt. Servts.,

THOMAS WALKER   ADAM STEPHEN

ANDW. LEWIS   JN. WALKER

RC (MHi). In John(?) Walker's hand; autograph signatures. Endorsed by TJ: "Walker Jno." A paper in DLC: TJ Papers, 1: 167-8, may be assumed to be an enclosure. It is docketed "Information rec'd at Fort Pitt Sepr. 13th 1775" and begins: "The following intelligence I have just recieved from a man who lately returned from the Indian Country, where I sent him as a Spy." The writer was without much doubt Thomas Walker, and the information of his agent relates to disaffection towards the Americans among the Tribes of the upper Ohio, the arrival of 300 French to aid the British at Detroit, and the temporary neutrality of the Six Nations.

In response to appeals from the Virginia settlers in the Pittsburgh area (see the Virginia and Pennsylvania Delegates' letter of 25 July 1775), the Virginia House of Burgesses on 24 June 1775 appointed George Washington, Thomas Walker, James Wood, Andrew Lewis, John Walker, and Adam Stephen commissioners to meet with the Ohio Indians (JHB, 1773-1776, p. 282). In July Congress established three Indian departments; Benjamin Franklin, James Wilson, and Patrick Henry were chosen commissioners of the middle department; Henry and Franklin declining, Thomas Walker and Lewis Morris were chosen in their stead and joined Wilson and the

Virginia commissioners at Pittsburgh in September (JCC, II, 174-7, 183, 251; Force, Archives, 4th ser., III, 717). The speeches and proceedings on this occasion, which confirmed the Ohio River as the boundary between white men's and red men's territory, are printed in full in R. G. Thwaites and L. P. Kellogg, Revolution on the Upper Ohio, Madison, 1908, p. 25-127; see also Abernethy, Western Lands, p. 141-2, and R. C. Downes, Council Fires on the Upper Ohio, Pittsburgh, 1940, p. 184-6. The CERTAIN EMINENT GENTLEMAN was unquestionably James Wilson, who, like other Pennsylvanians, resented the occupation of Fort Pitt just before the proceedings began by a force of militia commanded by Capt. John Neville under orders from the Virginia Convention; see letters cited by Burnett, Letters of Members, I, 279, note. On the subject of the Virginia garrison and the conduct of Wilson, see, further, Pendleton's letter to the Virginia Delegates in Congress, 15 July 1776. ADAM STEPHEN and ANDREW LEWIS, well-known Virginia frontiersmen and old companions-in-arms of George Washington, both served as brigadier generals in the Continental Army; MS memoirs of both by Lyman C. Draper are quoted in R. G. Thwaites and L. P. Kellogg, Documentary History of Dunmore's War, p. 191, 426-8.

Commission as Lieutenant of Albemarle

THE COMMITTEE OF SAFETY
FOR THE COLONY OF VIRGINIA

To *Thomas Jefferson Esquire*

By Virtue of the Power and Authority invested in us, by the Delegates and Representatives of the several Counties and Corporations in General Convention assembled, we, reposing especial Trust and Confidence in your Patriotism, Fidelity, Courage, and good Conduct, do, by these Presents, constitute and appoint you to be *Lieutenant and Commander in Chief* of the Militia of the County of *Albemarle*; and you are therefore carefully and diligently to discharge the Trust reposed in you, by disciplining all Officers and Soldiers under your Command. And we do hereby require them to obey you as their *Commander in Chief*. And you are to observe and follow all such Orders and Directions as you shall from Time to Time receive from the Convention, the Committee of Safety for the Time being, or any superiour Officers, according to the Rules and Regulations established by the Convention.

GIVEN *under our Hands, at Williamsburg this*

26th. Day of *September* ANNO DOMINI 177*5.*

Edmd. Pendleton
Thos. Lud: Lee
P. Carrington
Dudley Digges
Carter Braxton
[*James*] *Mercer*[1]
John Tabb

Printed form, filled in and signed (DLC). The words filled in are in the hand of Edmund Pendleton.

TJ had been appointed lieutenant of Albemarle 9 June 1770; see his commission of that date. He was now reappointed by the authority of the Committee of Safety, the executive agency of the revolutionary Convention.

[1] A name following Mercer's had faded beyond legibility.

To Francis Eppes

DEAR SIR   Philadelphia, Oct. 10th, 1775.

I wrote to Patty on my arrival here, and there being then nothing new in the political way I inclosed her letter under a blank cover to you. Since that we have received from England news of much importance, which coming thro' many channels we beleive may be confidently relied on. Both the ministerial and provincial accounts of the battle of Bunker's hill had got to England. The ministry were determined to push the war with vigor, a measure in which they were fixed by the defeat of the Spaniards by the Moors. 90. brass cannon were embarked from the tower and may be hourly expected either at N. York or Boston. 2000 troops were to sail from Ireland about the 25th. Sep. These we have reason to beleive are destined for N. York. Commodore Shuldam was to sail about the same time with a great number of frigates and small vessels of war to be distributed among the middle colonies. He comes at the express and earnest intercessions of Ld. Dunmore, and the plan is to lay waste all the plantations on our river sides. Of this we gave immediate notice to our committee of safety by an express whom we dispatched hence last Friday, that if any defence could be provided on the rivers by fortifications or small vessels it might be done immediately. In the spring 10,000 men more are to come over. They are to be procured by taking away two thirds of the Garrison at Gibralter (who are to be replaced by some Hessians) by 2000 Highlanders and 5000 Roman Catholics whom they propose to raise in Ireland. Instead of the Roman Catholics however some of our accounts say foreigners are to be sent. Their plan is this. They are to take possession of New York and Albany, keeping up a communication between them by means of their vessels. Between Albany and St. John's they propose also to keep open the communication; and again between St. John's, Quebec, and Boston. By this means they expect Gage, Tryon and Carleton may distress us on every side acting in concert with one another. By means of Hudson's river they expect to cut off all correspondence between the Northern and Southern rivers. Gage was appointed Governor General of all America; but Sir Jeffery Amherst consented afterwards to come over, so that Gage is to be recalled. But it [is] beleived Amherst will not come till the Spring. In the mean time Howe will have the command. The co-operation of the Canadians is taken for granted in all the ministerial schemes. We hope therefore they will all be dislocated by the events in that quarter. For an account of these I must refer you to Patty. My warmest affection to Mrs. Eppes. Adieu.

RC (ViU). Unsigned. MS mutilated. Salutation and date have been supplied from the text in Randall, *Life*, III, 568-9. TJ had arrived in Philadelphia and taken his seat in Congress on 30 Sep.; see his Account of Expenses as Delegate to Congress, submitted 17 Mch. 1776 (MHi, to be printed with TJ's Accounts). His letter to PATTY (Mrs. Jefferson) is missing.

Memoranda
on the Connecticut-Pennsylvania Boundary Dispute

[17 October 1775?]

Connecticut is bounded Westward

1. by the N. W. line of Virginia.
2. by the Proviso in the Plymouth grant in favr. of the Southern colony.
3. by the decision of Nicholson & al. pa. 14. declard *Western boundary*, to which Connecticut assented.
4. by the grant of Pensylvania.

N (DLC).

These notes on the protracted dispute between Pennsylvania and Connecticut over the Wyoming Valley are arbitrarily assigned to this date because they appear to be TJ's first rough jottings on a controversy with which he was first concerned when appointed on this day to a committee "to take into consideration the disputes between the people of Connecticut and Pensylvania, and report what in their opinion is proper to be done by Congress" (JCC, III, 297). On 4 Nov. the committee brought in its report, which was debated and on 27 Nov. was recommitted, with instructions to the committee to hear evidence on the dispute (same, p. 321, 377). This having been done, Congress on 20 Dec. adopted and later published a somewhat innocuous resolution urging both parties to "cease all hostilities, and avoid every appearance of force, until the dispute can be legally decided" (same, p. 439-40; see also p. 435). Since no MS of the committee's reports survives, it is impossible to tell what part TJ may have had in it. For a summary of the Wyoming dispute, see J. P. Boyd, "The Susquehannah Company," *Jour. of Economic and Business Hist.*, IV [1931], 38-69.

To Francis Eppes

DEAR SIR   Philadelphia, Oct. 24, 1775.

Since my last, we have nothing new from England or from the camps at either Cambridge or St. John's. Our eyes are turned to the latter place with no little anxiety, the weather having been uncommonly bad for troops in that quarter, exposed to the inclemencies of the sky without any protection. Carleton is retired to Quebec, and though it does not appear he has any intimation of Arnold's expedition, yet we hear he has embodied 1,100 men to be on his guard. A small vessel was the other day cast away on the Jersey shore (she was one of the transports which had some time ago brought over troops to Boston), on board of which were a captain, with his subordinate officers and marines, amounting to 23 in all, and also a Duncan Campbell, who was going to recruit men at New York for General Gage, he having some time before undertaken the same business in the same place, and actually carried off

60 men. The marines and their officers were all taken immediately, except their captain and the recruiting gentleman; these pushed off in a little boat, and coasted it to Long Island, where they got on board a sloop which was to have sailed in an hour, when the party sent after them came upon them. They were brought to this city this morning, the marines having been here some time. Our good old Speaker died the night before last. For the particulars of that melancholy event I must refer you to Patty. My affections attend Mrs. Eppes. Adieu.   TH. JEFFERSON.

MS not located. Text from Randall, *Life*, III, 569, where the letter was published from a copy furnished by Francis Eppes of Tallahassee, Fla., grandson of

TJ. Addressed: "To Mr. Francis Eppes, At the Forest, in Charles City County, Virginia."

From Archibald Cary

DEAR SIR   Ampthill October, 31st. 1775.

I had the Pleasure of yours of the 17th Instant last night by Post, am much obliged to you for it. As well as yourself I am much at a loss why Gage &c. should be sent for, and cannot judge whether it Augurs Good or Evel; but my Fears are that no Good Can Happen to America from any Orders of Those in Power on the other side the Atlantick. I think very much depends on the Success of the Expedition against Quebeck, for should the Munition of War in that Garrison fall into our Hands, I realy think we shall be able to defeat all the Troops they Can Send against us.

This Week past hostilitys Commenc'd in this Colony, by An Attack from the Navy on Hampton. Our Young Treasurer Aided by Capt. Lyn behaved Like Heroes of Old, but the Papers will Give you the Affair at Large.

I have been Honord with the Command of the Battalion in this district, it is not Yet Compleat. The three Companys in Chesterfield are Full. Only one in Amelia and one in Cumberland Compleat but I learn all are nigh full. I received orders Yesterday to Send down Two Companys from this County. They shall March on Thursday. I fear but few Battalions of Minute Men will be rais'd. The reasons assign'd are the Improper Appointment of Officers, in some districts I think it is realy so but fear in others it proceeds from another Cause. However I hope this Brush at Hampton, will Spur the People up a little, and the Honorable Manner in which our Young Officers and Men are Spoken of, will Give a little more Fire to Such as Wanted it.

I returnd from the Western Waters on Satturday Sevennight, but am Sorry to tell you I was Sent for two days After to my Brother in Law, John Randolph, and found Him on his death Bed, last Sunday we paid him our last Office. He got Cold by rideing in the Night to See Thos. M. Randolph who was expected to die, and a very narrow chance he had, thank God he is now Well but very Week. My Chariot went up Yesterday to assist in bringing his Famaly down to day.

I have not heard of your Famaly Since I Came down, for I have been but two days at Home, and when abroad Confin'd by My Friends bedside.

As to News the Papers will Give you all I know, Except a very disagreable one in this Neighbourhood. A dispute arose at Dinner at Chatsworth between Payton Randolph and his Brother Lewis Burwell, who Gave the other the Lye, on which Payton Struck him, Burwell Snatch'd a knife and struck him in the side, but fortunately a Rib prevented it's proving Mortal. He was prevented by the Ladys from making a Second Stroke. You'l judge what Poor Mrs. Randolph must suffer on this Unhappy Affair, but she is become Familiar with Misfortune. Payton is Well and no Notice is Taken of the Affair As I can see by Either. They Dined at my House the day After I got Home. If the Speaker and his Lady have not been Acquainted with this Matter say nothing of it to them. Be so Good as Give my Complyments to all your Assosiats in Office I mean from Virginia. Tell Mr. Wyth I Expect a letter from Him, I have been Favourd with one from Col: R. H. Lee, which I Answer by this Oppartunity. I shall Write the Speaker next Week, I hope he will find A little time to let me hear from him. I Am Sir With Great regard Your Friend and Hble Servt.,   ARCHIBALD CARY

RC (DLC).

TJ's letter to Cary of 17 Oct. is missing. OUR YOUNG TREASURER is a playful name for George, son of Treasurer Robert C. Nicholas, who had been commissioned captain in the Virginia Line earlier this month. CAPT. LYN was George Lyne, at this time captain in the state forces (Heitman). The grim affair at CHATSWORTH on the James, home of POOR MRS. RANDOLPH (the former Lucy Bolling, widow of Peter Randolph), involved her nephew PAYTON (i.e., Peyton) RANDOLPH (1738-1794) and LEWIS BURWELL, who had married Peyton's sister Lucy (Randolph, *The Randolphs*, p. 11, 21, 27).

To John Page

DEAR PAGE   Philadelphia Oct. 31. 1775.

We have nothing new from England or the camp before Boston. By a private letter this day to a gentleman of Congress from

General Montgomery we learn that our forces before St. John's are 4000. in number besides 500. Canadians the latter of whom have repelled with great intrepidity three different attacks from the fort. We apprehend it will not hold out much longer as Monsr. St. Luc de la Corne and several other principal inhabitants of Montreal who have been our great enemies have offered to make terms. This St. Luc is a great Seigneur among the Canadians, and almost absolute with the Indians. He has been our most bitter enemy. He is acknowleged to be the greatest of all scoundrels. To be assured of this I need only mention to you that he is the ruffian who when during the last war Fort William Henry was surrendered to the French and Indians on condition of saving the lives of the garrison, had every soul murdered in cold blood. The check which the Canadians received at first is now wearing off. They were made to beleive we had an army of 15,000 men going there. This put them in high spirits. But when they saw Montgomery with but 2700 they were thunderstruck at the situation they had brought themselves into. However when they found even this small armament march boldly to invest St. John's and put a good face on the matter they revived, and the recruits since have contributed to inspirit them more.

I have set apart nearly one day in every week since I came here to write letters. Notwithstanding this I have never received the scrip of a pen from any mortal breathing. I should have excepted two lines from Mr. Pendleton to desire me to buy him 24. ℔ of wire from which I concluded he was alive. I speak not this for you from whom I would not wish to receive a letter till I know you can write one without injury to your health. But in future as I must be satisfied with information from my collegues that my country still exists, so I am determined to be satisfied also with their epistolary communications of what passes within our knowlege. Adieu Dear Page.

DELENDA EST NORFOLK.

RC (NN). Addressed: "To The honorable John Page esq. at Williamsburgh." On the address sheet Page has written what are apparently memoranda for his next letter to TJ: "Ld. D. Forces . . . our plan," &c.

Not even the TWO LINES FROM MR. PENDLETON survive. DELENDA EST NORFOLK alludes to Dunmore's more or less effective use of the town and its vicinity as a base for his naval depredations; he had many collaborators among the Scottish merchants and factors in that region. See Page to TJ, 11 Nov. 1775, and Wertenbaker, *Norfolk*, p. 56ff.

To Francis Eppes

DEAR SIR   Philadelphia Nov. 7. 1775

We have no late intelligence here except of the surrender of Chambly, with 90. prisoners of war, 6½ tons of powder, 150 stands of arms and some other small matters. The acquisition of this powder we hope has before this made us masters of St. John's, on which Montreal and the upper parts of St. Laurence will of course be ours. The fate of Arnold's expedition we know not as yet. We have had some disagreeable accounts of internal commotions in South Carolina.

I have never received the scrip of a pen from any mortal in Virginia since I left it, nor been able by any enquiries I could make to hear of my family. I had hoped that when Mrs. Byrd came I should have heard something of them, but she could tell me nothing about them. The suspense under which I am is too terrible to be endured. If any thing has happened, for god's sake let me know it. My best affections to Mrs. Eppes. Adieu.

RC (J. H. Elliott, Atlanta Museum, Inc., Atlanta, Ga., 1946). Unsigned. Addressed: "To Mr. Francis Eppes at the Forest Charles-city."

MRS. BYRD was the former Mary Willing of Philadelphia; she was the second wife of William Byrd, III, of Westover (VMHB, XXXVIII [1930], 53).

Continental Congress: Agreement of Secrecy

In Congress Novr. 9th: 17 [75]

Resolved That every member of this Congress considers himself under the ties of virtue, honor and love of his Country not to divulge directly or indirectly any matter or thing agitated or debated in Congress before the same shall have been determined, without leave of the Congress; nor any matter or thing determined in Congress which a majority of the Congress shall order to be kept secret, and that if any member shall violate this agreement he shall be expelled this Congress and deemed an enemy to the liberties of America and liable to be treated as such, and that every member signify his consent to this agreement by signing the same.

John Hancock

Jas. Duane	Wm. Floyd
Lewis Morris	Robt R Livingston junr
Frans. Lewis	Henry Wisner

Stepn. Crane
Wil: Livingston
Thos. Willing
Andw. Allen
C: Humphreys
James Wilson
Robt Morris
B Franklin
John Dickinson
E Biddle
Josiah Bartlett
John Langdon
Thomas Cushing
Saml Adams
John Adams
Robt Treat Paine
Step. Hopkins
Sam. Ward
Elipht Dyer
Roger Sherman
Silas Deane
Th [Johnson Ju]nr
Wm Paca
Samuel Chase

Richard Henry Lee
Th: Jefferson
Benja Harrison
Thos Nelson jr
G. Wythe
Francis Lightfoot Lee
John Penn
Will Hooper
Joseph Hewes Nov. 10th.

Tho Lynch
Christ Gadsden
Edward Rutledge
Archd: Bulloch
John Houstoun
Thomas Lynch Junr.
Arthur Middleton
Fras. Hopkinson 28 June

Thos M:Kean
Geo: Read
Cæsar Rodney
John Jay
Richd: Smith (Jersey)

Philada. 18 Jany. 1776

Saml. Huntington
Robt. Alexander
Oliver Wolcott
J Rogers
Elbridge Gerry

T: Stone
Jona D Sergeant
Geo: Clinton
Wm: Whipple
Mat. Tilghman
Carter Braxton
Thos. Heyward Junr:
Lyman Hall   May 20th
Button Gwinnett   20th
William Ellery
Jno Witherspoon
Abra: Clark
Geo Walton
John Hart
B Rush. 22 July 1776
Wm. Williams, 30 July 1776
Geo. Clymer
Chas. Carroll
Jonathn. Elmer
Mann Page Junr.
Nathan Brownson Feb. 3d 1777
Matthew Thornton
James Lovell
Tho. Burke
W: Smith
Wm: Duer June 5th: 1777
Nichs. VanDyke
Hy Marchant
Geo: Frost

MS (DLC: PCC, Safe). Text in Charles Thomson's hand, with autograph signatures. Endorsed by Thomson: "Engagement of the Members to Secresy." There is also another similar endorsement in a presumably later hand. MS worn at edges and folds.

On 11 May 1775, the second day of the session, Congress had resolved "that the members consider themselves under the strongest obligations of honor to keep the proceedings secret, until the majority shall direct them to be made public" (JCC, II, 22). The stringent terms of the new agreement of 9 Nov. suggest that there had been violations of the earlier one. See Burnett, *Letters of Members*, I, No. 363, note, with references there. The significance of the dates, some of which are in Thomson's hand and some in the signers', can be worked out only from a study of the MS (facsimile available in Force, *Archives*, 4th ser., III, between col. 1916-17). Thus Hopkinson apparently inserted his name at the foot of a left-hand column on 28 June [1776] (date added by Thomson) *ahead* of the Delaware delegates in the following right-hand column, who had signed in Nov. 1775. Burnett discusses these points in his prefatory summaries of the delegates' periods of service; it is his opinion that the last four signatures were all added on 5 June 1777.

From Robert Carter Nicholas

DEAR SIR   Virginia 10th. Novr. 1775.

I was favour'd with your Letter the other Day by Mrs. Randolph. We had before her Arrival heard of the death of our worthy Friend. The great Load of Business I have had on Hand ever since the Convention obliged me to confine my Correspondence to him, knowing that he would communicate my Letters to the rest of the Associates. The infamous Practice of opening all Letters passing thro' the Government Post Office made it prudent to write with a confined Pen, contenting myself with Hints and Allusions, instead of aiming at Perspicuity. I had wrote to the late Speaker before he left Virginia desiring that he would take the earliest Opportunity of procuring Paper &c. for the small Notes, viz' 50,000 @ 2/6 and 50m. @ 1/3 as our Ordinance directs. The Design of the Convention was that the Paper with proper Plates should be sent, that the Money might be struck here, which Gentlemen supposed would give us an additional Security against Counterfeits. By his Letter to me I understood that the Business was in great forwardness and I am in Daily Expectation of receiving the Bills, which are much wanted for small Change. This was not all; we hoped from Mr. Tabb's Account that there would have been Paper enough of the James River Bank kind to make the full Emission; but he was exceedingly mistaken. When I came to examine it I found it short at least £200,000 allowing many of the Bills to be larger than I would chuse or than will be convenient. I am by the Ordinance restricted to the Use of certain kinds of Paper, so that no other can be issued without the Sanction of a future Convention. Under this Difficulty I consulted with our Committee of Safety, who thought with me that it would be most adviseable to endeavour to procure a sufficient Quantity of proper Paper &c. at Philadelphia, as this Country will not furnish it. This was in part the Subject of my last Letters to the Speaker. I did not confine him to particular Denominations, as I wish'd him to consult with the best Judges and supposed he would, being on the Spot, be best able to fix the Matter with them in the most proper Manner. I desired that a Proportion of Bills might be small and now see a greater Necessity for this, than when I wrote. Large Bills will be of no Use to the Soldiers. To have a great Number of small ones will make the Paper come dearer, but this will be nothing compared to the Advantage of having the Money made most convenient to the Holders. I have thought of the following Denominations, viz' 100,000 @ 10s/, 100,000 @ 5s/, 20,000 @ £5., and 25,000 @ 20s/. The sooner this Paper can be had the better, as it will be *speedily* wanted. Indeed, if our Disturbances continue over the Year I do not know what further Quantity may be necessary. Perhaps it might be better to engage more, but I have no Authority to do it. Excuse me for distinguishing, but I must again tell you that the Paper for the 100,000 small Bills is *immediately* wanted; the rest as soon as *possible*. One great Difficulty I labour under is to procure proper Money to defray Expences in other Provinces. It is to be wish'd that the Congress could do something to give our Paper a general Currency and this I should think might be done by establishing an Exchange for the continental Money, a considerable part of which, I understand, is issued upon our Credit, and surely this must be equally good for our own. Besides it is expected, and I think with the greatest Reason, that a just Proportion of the Expences incurr'd for the necessary Defence of this Country will be made a *continental* Charge. I presume that Many Merchants of Philadelphia must have Money Matters to transact here; it would be most convenient to us if Money could be had there by Drafts upon me to be *paid* in Virga. Currency; I mean *Paper*, as Specie is grown so scarce that I can't undertake Payments in that. If the Paper desired for emitting our Money cannot be had on other Terms I will give my Bills for it; tho' this I would wish to avoid, *if possible*.

You must have seen in the Papers an Account of the different Occurrences here since your Departure. I could say much were it not for fear of inquisitive Peepers. Our People are likely to be much distress'd for want of Salt. This is an Article so necessary to Life that I think it may be fairly submitted whether it would not be adviseable to give the same Encouragement for it's Importation as was done for another *certain Article*. You may have wonder'd that the Lists of Tithables &c. have not been forwarded to our Delegates and perhaps may be more surprized when I tell you of a general Disinclination in People to furnish their Lists. I have not received them from more than three Districts in the whole Colony. It's a Pity the Business of the Congress would not permit our Delegates to return home, as I am persuaded they are much wanted in their several Counties. We are all Impatience to hear from Canada. God grant us Success and an happy Issue to your Deliberations. I am constantly interrupted and can only add that I am Yr. Affte. Friend & Servt.,

Ro. C. NICHOLAS

RC (DLC). TJ's letter sent by MRS. RANDOLPH (the former Elizabeth, or Bettie, Harrison, widow of Speaker Peyton Randolph) is missing. AS OUR ORDINANCE DIRECTS: This refers to an ordinance of the Convention of July 1775 authorizing Nicholas to emit treasury notes to pay the Virginia militia and other forces; see Conv. Jour., July 1775, 1816 edn., p. 51;

see also below, Nicholas to TJ, 25 Nov. 1775, and to the Virginia Delegates, 12 Dec., on the same subject, and Benjamin Harrison to R. C. Nicholas, 17 Jan. 1776 (NNP), which states that all the letters relative to the Virginia notes were in TJ's hands. (The latter letter is in part printed in Burnett, *Letters of Members*, I, No. 498, with the addressee wrongly identified as TJ.)

From John Page

MY DEAR JEFFERSON   Wmsburg Novr. the 11th. [1775]

I thank God I am now so well that I could venture to write you a long Letter if a Multiplicity of Business did not render it impossible. But I will make the best Use of my Time and scribble you some fugitive Sentences.

I wrote to Col. Nelson and you by the Post before the last, giving some Account of the Norfolk and Hampton Affairs. I can assure that our young Soldiers behaved extremely well, and Col. Woodford shewed a great deal of Coolness of Courage Presence of Mind and Judgement in the Engagement at Hampton. I have often wished that the Convention had empowered us to raise a Company of Horse. The Necessity of having one was evident in the late Affair at Hampton. For as soon as an Express arrived here, which was at 8 P.M. giving an Account of the Skirmish of Thursday and praying for Assistance the Committee met and agreed to equip 50 Rifle men with Horses and send them immediately down. Col. Woodford offered to go and take the Command of all the Forces which were there or might be called in. With the Assistance of waggon Horses and such as were lent by the Gentlemen of the Town the Col., Captn. Bluford and his Rifle Company were enabled to reach Hampton about 7 O'Clock A.M. They rode through an incessant and heavy Rain. When the Col. entered the Town, having left the Rifle Men in the Church to dry themselves he rode down to the River took A view of the Town, and then seeing the Six Tenders at Anchor in the

River went to Col. Cary's to dry himself and eat his Breakfast. But before he could do either the Tenders had cut their Way through the Vessel's Boltsprit which was sunk to impede their Passage and having a very fresh and fair Gale had anchored in the Creek and abreast of the Town. The People were so astonished at their unexpe[cted] and sudden Arrival that they stood staring at them and omitt[ed] to give the Col. the least Notice of their approach. The first Intelligence he had of this Affair was from the Discharge of a 4 Pounder. He mounted his Horse and riding down to the Warf found that the Peop[le] of the Town had abandoned their Houses and the Militia had left the Breast Work which had been thrown up across the Wharf and Street. He returned to order down Captn. Nicholas's Company and Bluford's and meeting Nicholas's, which had been encamped near Col. Car[y's] he lead them pulling down the Garden Pails through Jones's Garden under Cover of his House, and lodged them in the House directing them to fire from the Window which they did with great Spirit. He then returned and lead Bluford's Company in the same manner under Cover of Houses on the other Side of the Street placing some in a House and others at a Breast Work on the Shore. Here he found the Militia had crowded in, and incommoded the Rifle me[n.] He therefore ordered them off and stationed them with Captn. Lynes on the back of the Town to prevent a surprise, by an Attack of Regulars who it was said had landed at Back water. Captn. Barron with the Town Militia and Part of Nicholas's Company were stationed at the Breast Work on the Wharf and across the Street. The Fire was now general and constant on both Sides. Cannon Balls Grape Shot and Musket Balls whistled over the Heads of our Men, Whilst our Muskets and Rifles poured Showers of Balls into their Vessels and they were so well directed that the Men on Board the Schooner in which Captn. Squires himself commanded, were unable to stand to their 4 Pounders which were not sheltered by a Netting, and gave but one Round of them but kept up an incessant firing of smaller Guns and swivels, as did 2 Sloops and 3 Boats for more than an Hour and ¼, when they slipt their Cables and towed out except the Hawk Tender a Pilot Boat they had taken some Time before from a Man of Hampton, which was taken. In her they found 3 wounded Men 6 Sailors and 2 Negros. Liutent. Wright who commanded her had been forced to jump over Board and was attended to the Shore by 2 Negros and a white Man, one of the Negros was shot by a Rifle Man across the Creek at 400 yds. distance. If Col. Woodford's Men whom he had ordered rou[nd] to the Creeks Mouth could have got there soon enough they would undoubtedly have taken the little Squadron, for the Sailors could not possibly have towed them through their Fire. Although the nearest of the Tenders was 3 Hundred Yds. and the farthest about 450 from our Me[n,] yet our Fire was [so] well directed that the Sailor[s] were not able to stand to their Guns and serve them pr[operly] but fir[ed] them at Random at an Unaccountable Degree of Elevation. The same Squadron came up Jas. River some Days after and attempted to land at Jas. Town but were prevented by about [　] Rifle men and as many Country People who happened to be there. A few Rifle Balls con[. . .] the 34 Four Pounders with which our Ea[rs] were saluted. Our Men brought up a 4 ℔ Ba[ll.] And yesterday the King Fisher and 3 Large Tenders (which had come up to B———s [Burwell's] Ferry to prevent the Passage of our 2d. Regiment and the Culpep[er] Batalion which were ordered down to Norfo[lk] fired on a Vessel at the Ferry Landing order[ing] her to come along side, but our Rifle men stationed there ordered the Skipper to stay where he was. The Vessel lay about 3 Hundred Yds. from our Men and about ¾ Mile from the Man of War, which began to fire on her, and finding that her Shot had no Effect sent off a Barge full of Men to take her, but as soon as the Barge had got within a small Distance of the Vessel the Riflemen fired and say they killed three Men. However it be, the Barge put back and then made a 2d Attempt which was defeated in the same Manner except that the Rifle[men] say they killed but one man the 2d. Time. The Man of War fired many 6 Pounders at our Men—however but 2 of them struck near them. One went through a Stone House and the other lodged in the Bank over the Heads of our Men which they dug out and sent by Captn. Green to Col. Henry. I can assure you that about 20 Rifle Men have disputed with the Man of War and her Tenders for this Vessel 2 Days and they have hitherto kept her and the Ferry Boats safe, which it is supposed they wish to burn. It is incredible how much they dread a Rifle. Before the Man of War had come up the River, 250 of our Men had crossed over with their Baggage. The Remainder are to join them as soon as possible either by venturing over before the Enemies [Faces?] or by passing over higher up.

The People at Norfolk are under dreadful Apprehensions of having their Town burnt by this Detachment. They know they deserve it, but we seem to be at a Loss what to do with them. Many of them deserve to be ruined and hanged but others again have acted dastardly for Want of Protection. But at all Events rather than the Town should be garrisoned by our Enemies and a Trade opened for all the Scoundrels in the Country, we must be prepared to destroy it. If we had but Salt enough to satisfy our Country Men who begin to complain for want of it, and Arms and Amunition, we should be able to make a very good Stand against all the Forces that can be sent to Virginia, for I can assure you notwithstanding the Affair of Norfolk and Kemps Landing, Your Country Men are brave and hearty in the Cause.

We care not for our Towns, and the Destruction of our Houses would not cost us a Sigh. I have long since given up mine as lost. I have not moved many of my Things away—indeed nothing but my Papers a few Books and some necessaries for Housekeeping. I can declare without boasting that I feel such Indignation against the Authors of our Grievances and the Scoundrel Pirates in our Rivers and such Concern for the Public at large that I have not and can not think of my own puny Person and insignificant Affairs. The Committee has met and want my Attendance. I must therefore bid you Adieu. Give my Love to Col. Nelson and his Lady and my Compliments and best Wishes to our Delegates. I am Yrs.,

JOHN PAGE

P.S. I have just seen the K———s Proclamation. I forgot to mention that Yesterday a Man came to the Camp and said that Captn. Montag[ue] desired to speak with one of our Officers, and sa[id] he would come ashore, or receive our Officer on Board. Upon this Col. Bullet was permitted by Col. H——y to go down to the River and enquire into this Matter. The Co[l.] dressed himself in Red, rode down to the Sh[ore] at a Distance from every Person, bowed to the Ship and waved his Hat, but they immediately run out all their Guns primed them and discharged one at him. The Col. however paraded it for some ti[me] to shew he was not afraid and then came ba[ck] satisfied that he had been misinformed or that it was intended as an insult altogether.   J. P.

RC (DLC).

Page gives a fuller account of the action at NORFOLK AND HAMPTON on 26-7 Oct. than is perhaps available anywhere else. BLUFORD is an error for Abraham Buford, who rose to a colonelcy in the Continental Line (Heitman). BOLTSPRIT is an archaic variant for bowsprit; and a NETTING was a coarse network of small ropes used for various protective pur-

poses on naval vessels (OED). The attempted British landing at JAS. TOWN occurred on 9 Nov.; see Pendleton to TJ, 16 Nov., and Va. Gaz. (Purdie), 17 Nov. THE K[IN]G'S PROCLAMATION of 23 Aug. 1775, declaring America to be in a state of "open and avowed rebellion," was paraphrased in Va. Gaz. (Purdie) on 10 Nov.; it is also in Force, Archives, 4th ser., III, 240-1.

From Edmund Pendleton

Virga. Caroline
Novr. 16th. 1775.

E. PENDLETON TO THOMAS JEFFERSON, ESQR.

Former labours in Various Public emploiements now appear as recreations compared with the present, which affords a scanty allowance for food and sleep; I mention this as an Appology to you and my other freinds for not having wrote more frequently. The Committee having now Adjourned for a fortnight, I am at home and mean to write for Next Post as I set out on a small mountain excursion tomorrow, in pursuit of health and a little bracing up. We have at last Fixed three Posts with men well armed. Woodford is gone to the neighbourhood of Norfolk with 6 Companies of his Regiment, (the Berkley Riflemen not come yet) and 5 Companies of minutemen from Culpeper Batallion, making in the whole 660. 5 Companies of Minute men stationed at Hampton, who have effectually stop'd up the Channel and thrown up a breast work, so as to think themselves perfectly safe against a landing there, unless a very considerable reinforcement should arrive. Colo. Henry remains at Wmsburg with 6 Companies of his Regiment and 4 Companys of Minute men; his two Companies from West Auga. and Pitsa. are not yet come down. The life and Soul of this Corps is Capt. Green's Company of Riflemen from Culpeper, who in three Reliefs of about 22 at a time, scour the Rivers, and have in various Attempts, prevented a landing of the enemy. Last week the King Fisher and four tenders full of men came up to Burwells Ferry and made several attempts to land during three days stay, but never came nearer than to receive a discharge of the Rifles, when they retired with great pricipitation, and 'tis Supposed the loss of some men. They had in [the?] time a droll contest for a small Cyder boat with one man, who lay between them about 200 yds. from shore. He attempted to come on Shore, when a Cannon Ball from the Navy passed just over his head and deter'd him. He then set sail for them, when a Rifle brought him too; he gave a Signal to the Man of War, who sent a Boat full of men for him, but When near, a Volly of Rifle bullets hurried them back without their prize. This was several times repeated 'til the Fleet moved up to James Town, when the Rifflemen seised the Boa⁺, but the Man and Cyder were gone. At James Town they have Attempted to Land two or three times, but flie off as soon as a gun is fired at them. It is Supposed their errand up was to destroy the Boats at those Ferrys, to prevent the

Passage of the Troops to Norfolk, whose destination disturbs them much. Mighty threats and Cajolings have by turns been thrown out to stop it. Our last Accounts from Ld. Dunmore are that he daily expects to be recalled. May the Intelligence be speedy. I think the papers seem to give a gleam of hope that our Petition may yet produce peace; A happy period to the Campaign in Canada, should we be lucky enough to obtain it, may go a great way in hastening peace. Nor do I think Ld. Dunmore will be so sanguine about his Piratical War, as he was, since he finds that small Arms in the hands of a few men will keep numbers from landing. His slave scheme is also at an end, since it is now Public that he has sent off a sloop load to the West Indies, which has made others use every endeavor to escape from him, and will stop his further increase of that Crew. [I hope] the taking Chambley has enabled Montgomery to compleat his work at St. Johns. I had only [to] mention our friend Wythe to the Town. It met their Warmest Wishes and he will be Chosen, and I fancy Jos. Prentis will be his Substitute, unless Mr. Everard will accept it. Greet him and his good Lady, Colo. Lee's, Colo. Harrison, Colo. Nelson and Lady, Mr. Willing, Mr. Mease and all my worthy acquaintance in the City. I can write but one Letter now. May wisdom and Felicity overshadow you all. Farewell.

RC (DLC). Tr in nineteenth century hand (PPAP). A fragment in the margin of RC has been torn away; the missing words are supplied from Tr.

Lord DUNMORE, who did not leave Virginia waters until the following June, had on 7 Nov. issued a proclamation freeing all slaves and indented servants "appertaining to Rebels" and inviting them into the British service. The broadside was printed on the press of John Holt, lately seized at Norfolk, on board one of Dunmore's vessels (Evans 14592; text in Force, *Archives*, 4th ser., III, 1385; facsimile in *Dunmore's Proclamation of Emancipation* [Charlottesville, Va.], 1941, where will be found an admirably full and authoritative account by Francis L. Berkeley of the whole episode). Dunmore's action aroused bitter indignation (see the letters to TJ that follow), and it was to be included in the schedule of royal crimes in the Declaration of Independence.

From Charles Lynch

DEAR SIR   Bedford County Virginia Novr. the 20th. 1775.

I receiv'd your favour dated Philadelphia Oct. 26th by the Express. In answer thereto I assure you I have not the least doubt but we shall be able to procure that Necessary article of Salt Petre if Attended to. I find Gentlemen here loath to risk as much cash as wou'd Make the Necessary preperations. I have been kept back my self by sickness in my famely, and have been much indispos'd my self.

I was first determind to se the mineral Salt Petre before I fix'd on a plan. I have describ'd the Place, the Mineral, and my intentions in answer to the Joint letter of our worthy Delegates. I gave three Negroes a part pay for the Place as cash was scarce with me. I have hands to hire, workmen to imploy, Provisions to buy, boilers &c. to purchase, that it will be attended with a good deal of Expence at first setting Out, Especially at the distance of one hundred Miles from me, but I am firmly of Opinion if I can carry it on with spirit as I beleive can be done with two or three hundred Pounds, I shall make great quantitys of Salt Petre. As there are several Other places works may be carryed on and when it is known that it may be done to advantage I doubt not but it will be done, and we shall be supply'd with that necessary article. I could set several Places cleverly a going with five hundred Pounds. I wou'd by no means have the country neglect their floors and to have trash. As to sulpher there is abundance in many Places, but no one that I know of has attemt'd to refine it. For my own part I have not had time, but make no doubt but I cou'd do it. You Will be the best judges after this information and trying the mineral what will be best to be done for the good of the country. For my part I intend to push it as far and as fast as I am Able. I receiv'd by Express from the committee of Safety not long since, their letter informing Me of their kind intentions of giveing Me every reasonable incouragement in manufacturing the article of gun Powder, lending me money if Wanted &c. In answer I let them know Salt Petre was the Principle thing Wanted, and Possably I might apply With proper Security for Money on that Occation. I had not then determin'd on the place or plan. I have not yet Apply'd for any Nor heard farther from them. I am Sir With great regard your freind & Humbl. Servt,

CHARS. LYNCH

RC (DLC). The following letter was doubtless enclosed in this one.

TJ's letter to Lynch of 26 Oct., not found, was written in consequence of instructions by Congress to the Virginia delegation to ascertain the truth of a report that saltpeter deposits had been found in Virginia, and to obtain specimens thereof (JCC, III, 307).

From Charles Lynch
to the Virginia Delegates in Congress

GENT   Bedford county Virginia Novr. the 20th 1775.

The express Messenger has been long detain'd, by my not being at home. It so hapend I was out in serch of the Mineral Salt Petre when he came to my house. I have at sundry times had small parcels of Salt Petre made from that mineral to manufacture into gun powder and find it to be very good, when properly refin'd. But no one attemting to carry on the business so as to be of Use to the Country I resolv'd to Exert My self that way as far as my small fortune woud admit. I have purchas'd a place on New River Where a small river cal'd Reed Iseland emtys in about Eight Miles below the Led mines. The Mineral lies on the south West side of Reed Iseland river facing the North East. It is three or four hundred yds. long from one to two hundred feet high. It aperars White, yellow, Purple and blue in places Promiscuously, on the south west it is cover'd With a large hill of earth. In some parts this Mineral produced Nitre in Others a Salt I take to be that of the Glober Kind. I have not any of the Mineral Salt Petre in its refin'd state by me, but have sent you samples of the Mineral. I only broke into the rock about Eighteen inches deep. The Salt Petre appear'd, betwen the diferent Stratums of Mineral. You will observe the thickness of each layer by the rock sent you. I have sent a small matter of the Salt Petre as it appears betwen Each layer of rock, also sample of the other salts Just as it is found there. I am told by the Man I purchasd of that the cold north East winds and freezing rains, moulter the Rocks and bring it down in great quantitys. On the north East Side of Reed Iseland River, almost Opposite the rocks, on a piece of clear'd ground about half an acre The Salt Petre appears on the surface of the Earth and small Stones rather first on a soft redish stone a Sample of Which you have. It is on decending ground and When rain Washes all off, Which Appears again in twenty four howers fair weather, and so shoots out till wash'd of [off] again. This hapen'd Twice in four days that I was there. This place I intend to cover for Sweepings and of the Moulter'd and pounded rock With dirt to Erect Pillars under Shelters like those describ'd at Hanover. If I can be able to compleat these I doubt not of Success. I intend immediately to set about it, but what quantity I can Make in a year you Will be as good Judges as My Self As I have fairly represent'd the Whole. I am inform'd there are Several places in those Parts Where the Mineral is preferable to that I have describ'd. I made choice of it for two reasons to Wit—that of the Salt Petre Appearing Spontaneously on the Surface of the Earth and small stones, and for an Exceeding good Spot of ground Adjoining to Rayse bred. I have Sent a sample of Salt Petre Made from dirt. A number of People in those parts Make Salt Petre from floors of Old Houses, Although in small quantitys and Many Make it into gunpowder. Pardon Me if I have been short in anything, While I assure you I am with the greatest Esteem Gent. your most Obet. most Humb. Servt., CHAS. LYNCH

RC (DLC). Presumably enclosed in the preceding letter.

The location of the deposits of MINERAL SALT PETRE was in present Wythe co., southwestern Virginia. THE LE[A]D

MINES, "Chiswell's Mines," important in Virginia's war effort, were in the vicinity of present Austinville, see account in *Virginia: A Guide to the Old Dominion* (Amer. Guide Ser.), N.Y., 1946, p. 477-8.

To Francis Eppes

DEAR SIR   Philadelphia Nov. 21. 1775.

After sealing my last letter to you we received an account of the capture of St. John's which I wrote on the letter. What I there gave you was a true account of that matter. We consider this as having determined the fate of Canada. A Committee of Congress is gone to improve circumstances so as to bring the Canadians into our Union. We have accounts of Arnold as late as Octob. 13. All well and in fine spirits. We cannot help hoping him in possession of Quebec as we know Carleton to be absent in the neighborhood of Montreal. Our armed vessels to the northward have taken some of the ships coming with provisions from Ireland to Boston. By the intercepted letters we have a confirmation that they will have an army of four or five and twenty thousand there by the spring. But they will be raw teagues. 3000. are lately arrived there. I have written to Patty a proposition to keep yourselves at a distance from the alarms of Ld. Dunmore. To her therefore for want of time I must refer you and shall hope to meet you as proposed. I am Dr. Sir with my best affections to Mrs. Eppes Your friend & servt.,

TH: JEFFERSON

RC (Stanley Neyhart, Brooklyn, 1948). Addressed and franked: "To Francis Eppes esq. at the Forest Charles City free

Th: Jefferson."
    TJ'S LAST LETTER, probably written about 14 Nov., is missing.

From John Page

MY DEAR JEFFERSON   Wmsburg the 24th. [November 177]5

I was not a little disappointed to find that you still complain of my not writing to you, when I have written twice since the Norfolk and Hampton Affairs. Your not mentioning those Letters greatly discourages me—not that I care who sees what I write, but that

I stil should write and write again
And you of my Neglect complain.

The Affair of Princess Ann mentioned in your joint Letter to our Committee, which I took the Liberty of assuring you was altogether a Fiction, but which I told you had Since been almost veryfied, was I have since found, when it really happened, almost as disgraceful and cowardly as the prophetic Fiction represented. Two hundred of the Militia of Pr. Ann were as judiciously disposed of in Ambush as could be, and the Ministerial Tools fell into it very compleatly, but were so faintly attacked, that although the advanced Guards were thrown into Confusion, They with little or no Loss gained a compleat Victory. Not a tenth Part of the Militia fired. They fled in a most dastardly manner. Col. Hutchings, who served in the Ranks as a common Soldier, and several others stood bravely, but being shamefully deserted were taken Prisoners. Our late Governor, as we now call him, was so ela[ted] with this Victory, that he erected the Standard, pub[lished] the Proclamation you will see in our Papers, which he had before printed in the Press he had taken from Norfolk, and marched about making Prisoners of a Number of People, and administering an Oath of his own Framing, by which the Cong[ress] Conventions and Committees are utterly disclaimed and all obedience and Submission, I suppose promised to Acts of Parliament. In short he has made a compleat Conquest of Princess Ann and Norfolk and Numbers of Negros, and Cowardly Scoundrels flock to his Standard. But we hope soon to put a stop to his Career and recover all we have lost, for Col. Woodford after innumerable Delays for want of Arms &c. &c. is by this Time very near him with his Regiment and 250 Minute Men of the Culpeper Batalion, and a Number of Voluntiers. Last Monday Night Col. Woodford received an Express from Sufolk desiring Assistance, but I need not mention this as you will see it related in Purdies Paper. I must also refer you to Purd[ie] for the News respecting the Men of War and Ten[ders]. We are so used to hear Cannon now that we think nothing of it, and I can assure you that 50 Men kept the King Fisher and 3 Tenders at a Distance at Jas. Town where they might have come within 250 Yds. of them. I think if we had but Powder enough some good Cannon and a few Privateers we might do very well. We have 3—18 Pounders some 12s 9s and 4s but We have not Powder even to prove them, and I know not who will venture to import more since Gatrick and his Sons are Prisoners. For God's Sake endeavour to procure us Arms and Amunitions and if our King is so determined a Tyrant as not to listen to your Petition crave Assistance from any and every Power that can afford it. Our Committee had adjourned before the News of Ld. D———s Success reached Wmsburg which may be an unlucky Circumstance, if Woodford should be defeated, or should there be an Insurrection of the Negros, since Col. Henry is not empowered to call in any Assistance but such as the neighbouring Minute and Militia Companies may afford, which is at present in Fact none at all. I have long wished to see a sufficient Number of Men drawn out to crush him and his whole Party at once. I think myself, it would have been an easy Matter some Time ago to have destroyed the Ships Tenders and his Soldiers, but they are now so much on their Guard and are so much reinforced that he is become not only very secure but formidable. You will see by the Proclamation that he has only spoken out and avowed what he has hitherto concealed. I hope the Convention will publish a Counter Proclamation, raise at least another Regiment, and instead of Minute Men, unless they can be put on a better footing, have the Militia compleatly armed as well trained as the Time they can spare will admit of, and make Draughts from it when Men are wanted. I am delighted with the News of the Taking of St. Johns, and hope by your next to hear of Montreal and Quebec being in our Possession. I have been writing too much before and it is now late, so that I must bid you Adieu. I am yrs, JOHN PAGE

P.S. Pray enquire for the Letter[s] I wrote by the 2 last Posts.

RC (DLC).
One of the two letters that Page says he wrote is missing; the other is that of 11 Nov. 1775. The JOINT LETTER from the Virginia delegates to the Virginia Committee of Safety is also missing. GATRICK: John Goodrich, Sr. (whose name is variously spelled), a trader and planter of Isle of Wight and Nansemond, went over to the loyalist side and was in turn imprisoned by the patriots; see VMHB, XV (1907-1908), 160-5, and Goodrich to TJ, 20 Jan. 1777.

From Robert Carter Nicholas
to the Virginia Delegates in Congress

GENTLEMEN   Williamsburg 25th. Novr. 1775.

As the Committee of Safety is not sitting, I take the Liberty of addressing you on the Subject of the unhappy Situation of our Country. Former Occurrances you are unquestionably acquainted with. A few Days since was handed to us from Norfolk Ld. D's infamous Proclamation, declaring the Law martial in force throughout this Colony and offering Freedom to such of our Slaves, as would join him. This contains the first Fruits of his Plunder from Norfolk and to you can need no Comment. It will surely be considered as an Object worthy the most serious Attention of the Congress, since all the Colonies are more or less likely to be materially affected by it. You will see an Account of the Engagement with the Militia of Princess Anne; the particulars we are not yet fully acquainted with, so totally is our Communication with that part of the Country cut off. Colo. Woodford is gone down with about 800 Men and we are in hopes he will open it again and support our Friends in that Quarter. Report says that great Number's have flocked to L. D's Standard. The Tories of Norfolk are said to be the Ringleaders; many of our Natives it is said have been intimidated and compeld to join them and great Numbers of Slaves from different Quarters have graced their Corps. The Tenders are plying up the Rivers, plundering Plantations and using every Art to seduce the Negroes. The Person of no Man in the Colony is safe, when marked out as an Object of their Vengeance; unless he is immediately under the Protection of our little Army. They have many Prisoners of different Classes; Colo. Jo. Hutchings and Colo. Lawson of Princess Anne are of the Number. These two Gentlemen were in the Engagement; Hutchings was taken on the Spot; Lawson escaped with a few friends to the Borders of Carolina, where they were taken by Surprize in their Beds. The Party we are told was headed by a Colo. Courtland of So. Carolina, who lately fled and join'd L. D. Old Capt. Jno. Gutridge and his Son William have been likewise seised. They have given mortal Offence in securing and bringing into us a little Gun Powder. Are these things to be born? Engaged, as we are, in one general Cause, I submit to your Consideration whether it will not be prudent and necessary to make it a Point with General Washington to retain proper Hostages for the Security of any Persons that may be seised on any *part* of the Continent. I fear no time is to be *lost*, as we understand the Gentlemen and others taken here are to be sent to Boston to undergo what is infamously call'd a Trial.

I beg leave to refer you to my Letters to the Speaker and Mr. Jefferson respecting the Paper for our Treasury Notes. That for 2/6 and 1/3 Bills I am exceedingly in want of; my Office is almost drain'd of Silver and it is most *essential* to the Credit of our Money that People should be accommodated with small Notes for the Convenience of Change. The rest of the Paper, wanted to supply the Deficiency of the Quantity I Expected from Mr. Tabb, There will very *soon* be Occasion for; the *earlier* I can get it the better. Indeed, if our Troubles continue, I don't see how we can do without still a larger Quantity. I wish, with all my Soul, the Congress could hit on some happy Expedient to render a future Emission unnecessary. I am so troubled and jaded with the present that it is my hearty wish to see no more of it. I fancy my Opinion that a greater Number of Regulars was necessary for the tolerable Security of this Country will be found right. Neither Militia or Minutemen will do, except for sudden and expeditious Service. I can not doubt but that the Congress will see the *Justice* and Necessity of puting a sufficient Number of Men for our Defence upon Continental Pay; this will be a great Ease to us, tho' we ultimately redeem our Quota; it will also greatly facilitate our Intercourse and Negociations with the other Colonies. How I shall remit young Mr. Byrd's Allowance, I do not know, and should be obliged by your Advice. The General has kindly promised me that he shall not want; but then he ought to be regularly reimbursed.

The Committee of Safety judging it absolutely necessary that a general Convention should be speedily held, I have summon'd it to meet the first of Decr. at Richmond, but it is generally supposed, for many cogent Reasons, that the Members will immediately adjourn to this Place. I need not tell you how necessary your Presence will be. No Country ever required greater Exertions of Wisdom than ours does at present. If you should be prevented from leaving the Congress by Matters of greater Consequence, tho' I scarce think greater can arise, will it not be necessary to communicate to the Convention any material Occurrences, which it may be necessary for them to know for their better Guidance? I am very respectfully, Gentlemen, Yr. mo. obt. Servt., ROBT. CARTER NICHOLAS

RC (DLC). On a blank page at the end are several lines of notes by TJ, partly illegible, beginning "200 men @ 40/ a month 400. subsistence @ 8d 200," &c.

GUTRIDGE is the "Gatrick," actually Goodrich, mentioned in Page's letter to TJ, 24 Nov. PAPER FOR OUR TREASURY NOTES: See Nicholas to TJ, 10 Nov. and 12 Dec. 1775.

To John Randolph

DEAR SIR   Philadelphia Nov. 29. 1775.

I am to give you the melancholy intelligence of the death of our most worthy Speaker which happened here on the 22d of the last month. He was struck with an Apoplexy, and expired within five hours.

I have it in my power to acquaint you that the successes of our arms have corresponded with the justice of our cause. Chambly and St. John's have been taken some weeks ago, and in them the whole regular army in Canada except about 40. or 50. men. This day we receive certain intelligence that our General Montgomery is received into Montreal: and expect every hour to be informed that Quebec has opened it's arms to Colo. Arnold who with 1100 men was sent from Boston up the Kennebec and down the Chaudiere river to that place. He expected to be there early this month. Montreal acceded to us on the 13th. and Carleton set out with the shattered remain[s] of his little army for Quebec where we hope he will be taken up by Arnold. In a short time we have reason to hope the delegates of Canada will join us in Congress and complete the American Union as far as we wish to have it completed. We hear that one of the British transports is arrived at Boston, the rest are beating off the coast in very bad weather. You will have heard before this reaches you that Ld. Dunmore has commenced hostilities in Virginia. That people bore with every thing till he attempted to burn the town of Hampton. They opposed and repelled him with considerable loss on his side and none on ours. It has raised our country into perfect phrensy. It is an immense misfortune to the whole empire to have a king of such a disposition at such a time. We are told and every thing proves it true that he is the bitterest enemy we have. His minister is able, and that satisfies me that ignorance or wickedness somewhere controuls him. In an earlier part of this contest our petitions told him that from our king there was but one appeal. The admonition was despised and that appeal forced on us. To undo his empire he has but one truth more to learn, that after colonies have drawn the sword there is but one step more they can take. That step is now pressed upon us by the measures adopted as if they were afraid we would not take it. Beleive me Dear Sir there is not in the British empire a man who more cordially loves a Union with Gr. Britain than I do. But by the god that made me I will cease to exist before I yeild to a connection on such terms as the British parliament propose and in this I think I speak the sentiments of America. We want neither inducement nor power to declare and assert a separation. It is will alone which is wanting and that is growing apace under the fostering hand of our king. One bloody campaign will probably decide everlastingly our future course; I am sorry to find a bloody campaign is decided on. If our winds and waters should not combine to rescue their shores from slavery, and General Howe's reinforcement should arrive in safety we have hopes he will be inspirited to come out of Boston and take

another drubbing: and we must drub you soundly before the scep-
tered tyrant will know we are not mere brutes, to crouch under his
hand and kiss the rod with which he deigns to scourge us.

Edmund passed thro' this city on his way to Williamsburgh to
see whether his presence might be of service in settling his uncle's
affairs. He was in perfect health, and will return again to the camp
at Cambridge. My compliments to Mrs. Randolph and the young
ladies and beleive me to be Dear Sir Your's &c.

Dft (DLC). Endorsed: "John Randolph."

To John Page

Th: J. to J. Page   [Philadelphia, ca. 10 December 1775]

De rebus novis, ita est. One of our armed vessels has taken an
English storeship coming with all the implements of war (except
powder) to Boston. She is worth about £30,000 sterling as General
Washington informs us, and the stores are adapted to his wants
as perfectly as if he had sent the invoice. They have also taken two
small provision vessels from Ireland to Boston; a forty gun ship
blew up the other day by accident in the harbor of Boston. Of a
certainty the hand of god is upon them. Our last intelligence from
Arnold to be relied on is by letter from him: he was then at Point
Levy opposite Quebec and had a great number of Cannoes ready
to cross the river. The Canadians received him with cordiality and
the regular force in Quebec was too inconsiderable to give him any
inquietude. A later report makes him in possession of Quebec, but
this is not authenticated. Montgomery had proceeded in quest of
Carleton and his small fleet of 11. pickeroons then on Lake St.
Francis. He had got below him and had batteries so planted as to
prevent his passing. It is thought he cannot escape their vigilance.
I hope Ld. Chatham may live till the fortune of war puts his son
into our hands, and enables us by returning him safe to his father,
to pay a debt of gratitude. I wish you would get into Convention
and come here. Think of it. Accomplish it. Adieu.

The Congress have promoted Brigadier Genl. Montgomery to be
a Major General, and on being assured that Arnold is in possession
of Quebec it is probable he will be made a Brigadier General, one
of those offices being vacant by Montgomery's promotion. This
march of Arnold's is equal to Xenophon's retreat. Be so good as to
enquire for the box of books you lodged for me at Nelson's and get

them to a place of safety. Perhaps some opportunity may offer of sending it to Richmond.

RC (MWA). Addressed and franked: "To the Honble. John Page esq. Williamsburgh Free Th: Jefferson." Concerning the date: The letter was written soon after 6 Dec. 1775, when a letter from Gen. Washington, of 30 Nov., announcing the capture of the British store ship, was read in Congress (JCC, III, 413; Washington, *Writings*, ed. Fitzpatrick, IV, 132).

From Robert Carter Nicholas
to the Virginia Delegates in Congress

GENTLEMEN   Virginia 12th. Decr. 1775.

Referring you to a former Letter, in which amongst other Things, I mentioned the Necessity we should be under of having a large Quantity of Paper to make up the Sum of Money voted by the last Convention, besides the 2/6 and 1/3 penny Bills, which I have immediate Occasion for, I must repeat my request that the whole may be provided and forwarded with all Expedition. The Committee of Safety writes also upon this Subject. I sent Mr. Jefferson a List of Denominations, which appear'd to me most proper; having no Copy, I have endeavour'd to recollect it in the inclosed Memo. You can hardly conceive how people are distress'd for want of small change. I have no doubt but every Care will be taken to guard the Money against Forgeries. You have an Opportunity of consulting superior Judges and there I do not presume to prescribe.

I fear your long Session will make a Supply of Money necessary and have therefore inclosed you my Bills for £500 stg.; the blanks to be fill'd up with either or all your Names, as may be requisite and I think you may be assured that the Bills will meet with due Honor. The Money which these Bills will produce I am hopeful will be sufficient to pay for the paper &c. and answer your present *immediate* Occasions. I shall want to know the Exchange they are sold at, valued in Virga. Money.

By many intercepted Letters to and from Gt. Britain we have discover'd the greatest Scenes of villainy. Some Rascals, all *foreigners*, are already looking out for Places and handsome Seats, from their infernal Hopes that our Notes are to be forfeited. Pray forward the Letter of Advice by a safe Hand. I write with the utmost Precipitation and therefore can only add that I am Gent, Yr. respectful hble Servt.,   Ro. C. NICHOLAS

If the Paper does not arrive soon, I must shut up Shop.

RC (Vi). Endorsed by TJ: "Nicholas, Rob. Carter. Dec. 12. 1775. desiring paper to be sent. inclosg. bills of excha: 500.£ sterl." The "inclosed Memo." is missing, but see Nicholas to TJ, 10 Nov. 1775.

A FORMER LETTER: I.e., Nicholas to the Virginia Delegates, 25 Nov. 1775.

Draft of Report
on the Powers of a Committee of Congress
to Sit During Recess

[15 December 1775]

The Committee appointed to consider and prepare instructions for a committee who are to sit during the recess of Congress have agreed to the following Resolutions:

Resolved that it is the opinion of this committee that the said Committee during the Recess of Congress should be authorized and instructed

To receive and open all letters directed to the Congress.[1]

To correspond with the several Conventions, Assemblies, or Committees of safety, with the Committee of Congress sent to Canada, the Commissioners for Indian affairs; and the Commanding officers of the Continental forces in the several departments.

To give counsel to the said commanding officers whenever applied to by them.

To supply the Continental forces by sea and land with all necessaries from time to time.

To expedite the striking monies ordered by the Congress to be struck.

To transmit to the several Commanding officers, Paymasters and Commissaries from time to time such sums of money as may be necessary for the pay and subsistence of the Continental forces, and to order paiment by the Treasurer for such contracts as the said committee may make in pursuance of the authorities and instructions given them.

To take charge of all Military stores belonging to the United colonies, to procure such further quantities as may probably be wanted, and to order any part thereof wheresoever it may be most requisite for the Common service.

To direct the safe keeping and comfortable accomodation of all Prisoners of war.

To contribute their counsel and authority towards raising recruits ordered by Congress.

To procure intelligence of the condition and designs of the enemy.

To direct military operations by sea and land; not changing any objects or expeditions determined on by Congress.

To attend to the defence and preservation of forts and strong posts and to prevent the enemy from acquiring new holds.

To apply to such officers in the several colonies as are entrusted with the executive powers of government for the occasional aid of Minute-men and militia whenever and wherever necessary.

In case of the death of any officer within the appointment of Congress, to employ a person to fulfil his duties, until the meeting of Congress, unless the office be of such a nature as to admit a delay of appointment until such meeting.

To examine public claims and accounts and report the same to the next Congress.

To publish and disperse authentic accounts of military operations.

To expedite the printing of the Journals of Congress as by them directed to be published.

To summon a meeting of Congress at an earlier day than that to which it may stand adjourned, if any great and unexpected emergency shall render it necessary for the safety or good of the United colonies.

And to lay before the Congress at their meeting all letters received by them with a report of their proceedings.

Resolved that the said Committee be authorised to appoint their own clerk who shall take an oath of secrecy before he enters on the exercise of his office.

Resolved that in case of the death of any member of the said Committee, they immediately apply to his surviving colleagues to appoint some [one] of themselves to be a member of the said Committee.

Resolved that the Treasurers be directed to pay out of the Continental Monies in their hands all Draughts made on them by the said Committee.[2]

Dft (DLC: PCC, No. 23); in TJ's hand; endorsed by Thomson: "Report made 15 Decr. 1775. . . . No. 2. Report of the Comee. app. to prepare instructions to the Comee. in Recess. . . ." Written on the back of the top half of a broadside proclamation appointing a fast day: "In Congress, June 12, 1775 . . ." (Evans 14563; JCC, III, 507, No. 47).

TJ was appointed to this committee on 13 Dec., and its report was submitted and read on 15 Dec. (JCC, III, 426-7, 430-1). But no action was taken on the report. TJ was later concerned with the powers to be invested in a "committee of the states"; see Report dated 30 Jan. 1784.

[1] Deleted (in committee or in Congress): "and to give such answers to the same as they shall be authorized to give."

[2] This paragraph is in an unidentified hand.

Report of Committee

to Ascertain Unfinished Business before Congress

[23 December 1775]

The Committee appointed to examine the journals and state what business remains still before Congress unfinished, have agreed to the following report.

Report of the Proposed Articles of Confederation (adjourned from August last).[1]

The Report of the Committee appointed to draw instructions for a Committee during Recess of Congress is on the table.

The Committee appointed to draw an answer to some ministerial proclamations have reported an answer to one of them only.

The Committee appointed to draw instructions to Colo. Irwin [James Irvine] have not yet reported.

Part of the report of the Committee appointed to take into their consideration the [state o]f [the co]lony of Virginia is on the table.

A report of the committee appointed to consider the information against persons refusing Continental currency is on the table.

A report from the same committee who were also instructed to consider an application from the Convention of N. York.[2]

The Committee appointed to consider a petition for supplying the island of Grenada with lumber have made no report.

The Committee of the whole on the trade of the United colonies have not closed their report.

The report of a Committee appointed Nov. 23. to consider certain letters from General Schuyler is on the table.

The Committee appointed to consider the petition of [Peter][3] Berton have made no report.[4]

The report of the Committee appointed to confer with the Indians now in this city is on the table.

The report of the committee appointed Dec. 18. to consider certain other letters from General Schuyler is on the table.

A report from the Committee appointed to prepare a plan for establishing expresses is on the table.[5]

Part of a report from the Committee appointed to confer with Mr. Kirkland is still on the table.

A Committee appointed Nov. 23. to enquire into certain frauds have not yet made a final report.

The report of the Committee appointed to consider Dow's [Douw's] letter and the Indian treaty is still on the table.

Two Brigadier-generals remain to be appointed.

An Information against persons selling tea is yet to be considered.

The report of the Commissioners for Indian affairs in Middle Department is on the table.[6]

The report of the Commissioners for Indian affairs in Southern department is on the table.

The report of the Committee on Lord Sterlings letter is on the table.

The report of the Committee on the vessel taken in New Hampshire is on the table.

The report of the Committee appointed to repair to Ticonderoga to confer with Gen. Schuyler is on the table.

In addition to the above there is the following Business unfinished.[7]

Report of the proposed Articles of Confederation (Reported before the last Adjournment).

Report of Secret Committee of Articles Necessary for supplying the Army (lies on the Table).

Committee for devising Ways and Means for supplying the Indian Nations with Goods (not yet reported).

Committee for inquiring after Virgin Lead, and Leaden Oar also after the cheapest method of making Salt (appointed before the Adjournment not yet reported).

Dft (DLC: PCC, No. 23). Endorsed by Charles Thomson: "No. 1. Report of the Comee appointed to examine the Journal. Decr. 23. 1775." The paper underwent several stages of amendment, which could not be fully represented except by a facsimile. These are: TJ's own verbal corrections as he wrote (not noted in the present text); alterations by the committee or by Congress when the Report was submitted (indicated here by footnotes); Secretary Thomson's checking off of a number of the items of business after their completion (not noted here).

TJ was appointed on 22 Dec. to this committee, which reported next day. Congress thereupon "Ordered, That the several committees to whom any matters are referred, conclude their business with all dispatch, and report to Congress" (JCC, III, 445, 454-6). It is evident that TJ had Secretary Thomson's aid in compiling the schedule of unfinished business.

[1] This paragraph, begun in TJ's hand and completed in another, was scored out, probably by the committee.

[2] This paragraph deleted by Congress.

[3] Blank in MS.

[4] Altered in Thomson's hand to read "have laid in their report." (This committee reported on 23 Dec.; JCC, III, 454).

[5] In margin in Thomson's hand: "Postponed till Dr. F: can make Enquiry."

[6] This and each of the four following paragraphs are partly in TJ's hand and partly in Thomson's, Thomson supplying the name of the committee in each case.

[7] This and the remaining paragraphs are in an unidentified hand.

Draft of a Declaration
on the British Treatment of Ethan Allen

To Majr. Genl. Howe &c.   [2 January 1776]

A Declaration by the Representatives of the United colonies in Congress.

When necessity compelled us to take arms against Great Britain in defence of our just rights, we thought it a circumstance of comfort that our enemy was brave and civilized. It is the happiness of modern times that the evils of necessary war are softened by refinement of manners and sentiment, and that an enemy is an object of vengeance, in arms and in the feild only. It is with pain we hear that Mr. Allen and others taken with him while fighting bravely in their country's cause, are sent to Britain in *irons*, to be *punished* for pretended treasons; treasons created by one of those very laws whose obligation we deny, and mean to contest by the sword. This question will not be decided by reeking vengeance on a few helpless captives, but by atchieving success in the fields of war, and gathering there those laurels which grow for the superior brave. In this light we view the object between us; in this line we have hitherto conducted ourselves for it's attainment. To those who, bearing your arms, have fallen into our hands, we have afforded every comfort for which captivity and misfortune called. Enlargement and comfortable subsistence have been extended to officers and men; and their restraint is a restraint of honor only. Should you think proper in these days to revive antient barbarism, and again disgrace our nature with the practice of human sacrifice, the fortune of war has put into our power subjects for multiplied retaliation. To them, to you, and to the world we declare they shall not be wretched, unless their imprudence or your example shall oblige us to make them so; but we declare also that their lives shall teach our enemies to respect the rights of nations. We have ordered Brigadier General Prescot to be bound in irons, and confined in close jail, there to experience corresponding miseries with those which shall be inflicted on Mr. Allen. His life shall answer for that of Allen, and the lives of as many others for those of the brave men captivated with him. We deplore the event which shall oblige us to shed blood for blood, and shall resort to retaliation but as the means of stopping the progress of butchery. It is a duty we owe to those engaged in the cause of their country, to assure them that if any unlucky circumstance, baffling the efforts of their bravery, shall put them in the power of

their enemies, we will use the pledges in our hands to warrant their
lives from sacrifice.

MS (DLC: PCC, No. 58); Dft (DLC).
The MS, a fair copy, is endorsed by
Thomson: "Motion of Col Harrison Jany
2. 1776: posponed." The Dft has the
following caption: "A Declaration [or a
letter to Howe] on Allen's case," and
has on the back a list by TJ of the
permanent committees of Congress (here
omitted). Since this is a case where TJ
went back over his rough draft to bring
it into conformity with the fair copy he
submitted to Congress, the texts of the
two MSS are almost identical. The Dft,
with its deletions and alterations, has
been printed both by Ford (I, 494-5)
and in JCC (IV, 22-3).

Congress on 2 Dec. 1775, having received word that Ethan Allen had been
taken prisoner near Montreal and "confined in irons on board a vessel in the
river St. Lawrence," ordered that Gen.
Washington "be directed to apply to
General Howe on this matter, and desire
he may be exchanged" (JCC, III, 402).
A motion was also made for a public
protest by Congress, and TJ was appointed to draft it, but on 2 Jan. 1776
action on the protest was postponed and
was not resumed. Nothing concerning
this motion appears in the original Journals. Evidently Congress preferred to
leave the matter in Washington's hands.
See Washington to Howe, 18 Dec. 1775
(*Writings*, ed. Fitzpatrick, IV, 170-1),
and Burnett, *Letters of Members*, I, No.
415, with references there.

Refutation of the Argument
that the Colonies Were Established at the Expense
of the British Nation

[After 19 January 1776]

Queen Elizabeth by letters patent bearing date the 11th. of
June 1578. granted to Sr. Humphrey Gilbert license to search for
uninhabited countries, and to hold the same to him and his heirs,
with all jurisdiction and royalties by sea and land, reserving to the
crown of England his allegiance and the fifth part of all the oar of
gold and silver which should be gotten there. He had moreover
liberty to wage war with any persons who should annoy him by sea
or land, or who should settle without his leave within 200 leagues
of any place or places where he or his associates should within six
years make their dwellings and abidings. He had also power to
govern and rule the subjects who should settle in such new countries or within 200. leagues as aforesaid according to such statutes,
laws and ordinances as he or his heirs should devise or establish,
so as they were as nearly as convenient agreeable to the form of
the laws and policy of England, and were not against the Christian
faith then professed in the church of England: Provided that if he
or his heirs, or any other by their license should commit unjust
hostility against the subjects of the queen or her successors or of
any other state in amity with them, it should[1] for her and her successors to put Sir Humphrey and his heirs and the inhabitants of

such new countries out of their allegiance and protection, from which time Sr. Humphrey and his heirs and the said inhabitants, and the places within their possession and rule, should be out of her protection and allegiance, and free for all princes and others to pursue with hostilities as being not her subjects, nor by her to be advowed, nor to her protection or allegiance belonging.

Sir Humphrey set out the 11th. of June 1583. with five ships and 260. men equipped at his own expence, and that of his brother in law Sr. Walter Ralegh. One of these however soon put back in distress. Sr. Humphrey with the others passed by Penguin island into St. John's where he came to anchor Aug. 3. He found there a great number of fishing vessels from England, Spain, Portugal, France, &c. To these he declared his intentions of taking possession of the island of New-found-land in the behalf of the crown of England. He landed on the 4th. of Aug. On the 5th. he summoned the people both English and strangers to attend. He read before them his commission and by virtue thereof took possession of the harbour of St. John and 200. leagues every way, by taking livery of a twig and turf. He ordained three laws, for the conformity of religion to the English church, for punishing treason, and against disrespectful speaking of the Queen. He then had the English arms engraven in lead, and erected on a pillar, and granted to sundry of the fishermen in fee-farm divers parcels of land by the water side in the harbor of St. John's and elsewhere, for the purpose of dressing and drying their fish; reserving a yearly rent to him and his heirs.

Aug. the 20th. Sr. Humphrey and his people with the ships they had left, which were only three, sailed from St. John's for the Southern parts of America, which he wished also to bring within the compass of his patent. But one of the vessels being lost off Newfoundland, he concluded to return with the other two to England; in which return he himself perished with the vessel he was in and all his crew: so that one only got back of the four which had gone out.

Sr. George Peckham in his relation 2.[2] Hakl. 167. tells us 'he understands that the adherents, associates and friends of Sr. Humphrey Gilbert mean to pursue the American settlement.' Accordingly, Sr. Humphrey's patent being expired, we find Sr. Walter Ralegh taking up the matter in his own right, and obtaining from the crown letters patent bearing date the 25th. of March 1584. copied almost verbally from those given to Sr. Humphrey Gilbert. They are in these words.[3]

1584. In consequence of this compact with the crown Sr. Walter

Ralegh fitted out two barks under the command of Capt. Philip Amadas and Capt. Arthur Barlowe who left England Apr. 27. 1584. They touched at the West Indian islands, from whence they sailed up the coast, intending to put into the first river they should find. On the 13th. of July a river appeared into which they put. They landed immediately and took possession of the country in right of the queen and afterwards delivered it over to the use of Sr. Walter Ralegh and his heirs, according to the queen's grant. This proved to be the island of Wokokon, 20. miles long and 6. wide. From hence they visited an island about 16. miles long, and some other of the islands which stretch along the Carolinian coast. Capt. Barlowe, who writes the account in Hakluyt, describes this as a tract of islands 200. miles in length, and about six miles wide in general, having only two or three entrances into the sea. The sound between the islands and the main from 20. to 50. miles over and in this above 100. islands interspersed. Having thus examined the country and taken possession they returned to England where they arrived about the middle of September, carrying with them two of the American natives. On the 18th. of December a[4] bill in confirmation of Sr. Walter's patent passed the house of Commons: but what became of it afterwards we know not.

1585.

In the spring following, Sr. Walter fitted out 7. sail of vessels under the command of Sr. Richard Greenvile. They sailed from Plymouth Apr. 9. 1585. touched at the West Indies, and arrived at Wococon the 26'th of June. On the 11th. of July they visited the main land for the first time, and on the 25th. of August, such of the vessels as remained weighed anchor for England, leaving 107. men under the charge of Mr. Ralph Lane, to settle the country. They chose for their habitation the island of[5] Roanoke. From hence they extended their discoveries to Secotan, 80 miles Southward of Roanoke; to the Chesepians, 130. miles Northward; and to Chawanook 130. miles Northwestward, of the same island. In the spring of 1586. they put into the ground seeds sufficient to produce them a plentiful subsistence for two years. Okisko, king of Weopomeiok, in a full council of the natives, acknoleged himself servant and homager to the queen of England and after her to Sr. Walter Ralegh. Soon after this the colony became greatly distressed for provisions, and despairing at so late a season of the supplies which Sr. Richard Greenvill had promised should certainly come before Easter, and Sr. Francis Drake touching there to visit his friend's colony on his return from the expedition against Cartagena, St. Augustine, and St. Domingo, they took their passage on board his fleet the 19'th of June, 1586, and arrived at Portsmouth July 27. following.

1586.

In the mean time a vessel, fitted out by Sr. Walter Ralegh, had sailed with supplies for the colony. It arrived immediately after the departure of the colonists, and, having in vain sought for them, returned. About 14. or 15. days after her departure, Sir Richard Greenvill arrived with three other vessels under his command. Being unable after great search to find or hear any thing either of the colony, or of the ship which had been sent before him, and unwilling to lose possession of the country, he left 15. or as[6] some say 50. men in the island of Roanoke, with plentiful provisions for two years, and departed for England.

1587.

In 1587. Sr. Walter Ralegh sent out a new colony of 150. men under the charge of John White as governor. He appointed him 12 assistants, gave them a charter, and incorporated them by the name of the Governor and Assistants of the city of Ralegh in Virginia. He instructed them particularly, on their arrival in Virginia, to remove the settlement to the bay of Chesepiok, and there to make their seat and fort. They sailed in three vessels from Portsmouth Apr. 26. 1587. and arrived at Hatorask the 22d. of July following. They immediately sent a party of men to the island of Roanoake to search for those whom Sr. Richard Greenvill had left there the year before, but none of them were to be found, nor any signs of them, except the bones of one: and they afterwards learned that part of them had been cut off by the savages and the rest driven out to sea in a boat in which they must have perished. On the 18th. of August Mrs. Dare was delivered of the first child born in Virginia, who was christianed Virginia. August the 27th. the governor at the entreaty, and almost by compulsion of the planters returned to England for supplies. Upon his arrival in England Sr. Walter Ralegh immediately appointed a pinnace to be sent thither with such provisions as were wanted, and wrote letters to the planters assuring them he would send a plentiful supply of shipping, men, and necessaries the next summer.

1588.

He accordingly prepared a fleet to go under the command of Sr. Richard Greenvill; and it waited only a fair wind when Sr.

Richard received orders from the state not to depart the kingdom, the Spanish Armada being then daily expected. Governor White upon this procured two pinnaces to be sent with fifteen planters, and provisions for the colony. They left Biddeford Apr. 22. 1588. But being more intent on gain than on supplying the colony they went in quest of prizes, and after being shattered in some unsuccesful encounters with the enemy they put back to England.

1589.

Ralegh, having received[7] no assistance from the crown in any of these enterprizes, and having now expended 40,000. pounds in them, made an assignment to divers gentlemen and merchants of London 'for continuing the action of inhabiting and planting his people in Virginia.' The particulars of that assignment, says Oldys, we may gather from an indenture made the 7'th of March. 31st. Eliz. between 'Sr. Walter Ralegh of Coliton in Devonshire, as he is therein distinguished, chief governor of Virginia and Thomas Smith with other merchants of London and adventurers to Virginia, and John White and other gentlemen, reciting that Sr. Walter Ralegh (by her majesty's letters patents beforementioned) had granted on the 7th. of January 1587. to John White and the rest free liberty to carry into Virginia and inhabit there such of her majesty's subjects as should willingly accompany them. And that the said Thomas Smith and others the said adventurers purposing to be made free of the corporation and company late constituted by Sr. Walter in the city of Ralegh, by this indenture grants to the said Thomas Smith and others, and to the said John White and the rest their several heirs and assigns free trade and traffick for all manner of merchandize to and from Virginia or any other parts of America where the said Sr. Walter his heirs or assigns did or might claim any interest title or privilege; free from all rents customs and other charges except the fifth part of the oar of gold and silver which he reserves to himself and his heirs. And further the said Sr. Walter Ralegh as well for and in especial regard and zeal of planting the Christian religion in and among the said barbarous and heathen countries and for the advancement and preferment of the same and the common utility and profit of the inhabitants therein as also for the encouragement of the said adventurers and other assistants in Virginia does freely and liberally give them the sum of one hundred pounds.'[8]

1590.

About the end of February 1590. Mr. John Wattes a merchant of

London, at his own special charge had prepared three ships to go to Virginia when an embargo was laid on all the shipping of England. By the interest however of Sr. Walter Ralegh Mr. John White obtained leave for them to depart with men and necessaries for the colony. But the commanders of the vessels, who seem to have had other views, found means to obstruct and prevent the governor from putting any thing on board, and from carrying even a boy to attend on himself. After cruising in the West Indies and taking some Spanish prizes they landed in Roanoke island Aug. 20. On going to the place where the colony had been left in the year 1587. they found it deserted and on a tree the Roman characters CRO. carved. On a post of a fort also, which they had built they found the letters CROATOAN. This, according to an agreement between Mr. White and them, intimated that they were removed to Croatoan, and moreover that they were in no distress, as in that case a note of distress was to have been added. They then returned on board their ships, and weighed anchor for Croatoan; but the weather coming on very foul, and being destitute of fresh water, they concluded to run down to the islands of St. John, Hispaniola, or Trinidad to winter there and return to Virginia in the spring. However the weather still continuing bad and the wind driving them off to the Eastward greatly, they determined to go to the Azores, from whence they sailed for England. What was the fate of the colony whom they thus deserted, was never known, as no search was made for them afterwards. Oldys indeed, in his life of Sr. Walter Ralegh, tells us that tho' he[9] had made an assignment of his patent to others, yet they making no succesful progress, he was so regardful of the English he had planted there, that he continued to send to them almost every other year. Insomuch that besides the five first voiages made chiefly at his expence we are well[10] informed of five voiages more, the last of which was in the last year of the queen's reign under the command of Samuel Mace. But it is beleived Sr. Walter was deceived by the persons he employed to go there, and that no one of them ever performed the voiage except Mace, who undertook it in the year 1602. and as is[11] said, was killed by the natives on his going on shore. His crew who attended him, escaped with difficulty. In 1602. Captain Gosnold with 32. men sailed in a small vessel for Virginia, and in 1603. Mr. Richard Hakluyt (compiler of the Voiages) having prevailed on some merchants of Bristol to join with him in raising a stock of £1000. for the adventure, and obtaining leave from Sr. Walter Ralegh, sent out two small vessels under the command of Martin Pringe.

But both Gosnold and Pringe confined their discoveries to that part of the American coast which lies between 41. and 43°. North Latitude. The Northern parts of the continent seem after this to have attracted all the adventurers until the year 1606; when several gentlemen and merchants, supposing that by the attainder of Sr. Walter Ralegh his patent was wholly forfeited, petitioned king James the first for new letters patent to authorize them to raise a joint stock and to settle colonies in Virginia. This he accordingly did, dividing them into two companies, the Northern and Southern. A colony was sent out by the latter under the command of Captain Newport, who effected a settlement on the river Powhatan, now James river which has been ever since maintained. In 1624. James the first by proclamation suspended the proceedings of the Virginia company: and in 1626. Charles the first took the government of the country into his own hands. A Quo warranto indeed is said to have issued against the company, in order to draw over these arbitrary proceedings the veil of legal form. But it is[12] doubted whether any judgment was ever obtained. The company in establishing this colony had expended an hundred thousand pounds.

This short narration of facts, extracted principally from Hakluyt's voiages, may enable us to judge of the effect which the charter to Sr. Walter Ralegh may have on our own constitution and also on those of the other colonies within it's limits, to which it is of equal concernment. It serves also to expose the distress of those ministerial writers, who, in order to prove that the British parliament may of right legislate for the colonies, are driven to the necessity of advancing this palpable untruth that 'the colonies were planted and nursed at the expence of the British nation': an untruth which even majesty itself, descending from it's dignity, has lately been induced to utter from the throne. Kings are much to be pitied, who, misled by weak ministers, and deceived by wicked favourites, run into political errors, which involve their families in ruin: and it might prove some solace to his present majesty, when, fallen from the head of the greatest empire the world has seen, he shall again exhibit in the political system of Europe the original character of a petty king of Britain, could he impute his fall to error alone. Error is to be pitied and pardoned: it is the weakness of human nature. But vice is a foul blemish, not pardonable in any character. A king who can adopt[13] falshood, and solemnize it from the throne, justifies the revolution of fortune which reduces him to a private station. When the accident of situation is to give us a place in history, for which nature has not prepared us by corresponding endowments, it is the duty of those about us carefully to veil from the public eye the weaknesses, and still more, the vices of our character. A minister who can prompt his sovereign publicly to betray either, will merit the perpetual execrations of those who, in the future page of history, shall see consecrated to infamy the names of their nearest relations. Such was the sovereign, and such the minister, of October the 28th. 1775.

MS (DLC). Written in a bound note-book, with binder's title "Historical Notes of Virginia." Only the first seven-ty-five pages in the notebook contain writing. The first portion (on p. 1-20, numbered in a later hand) comprises a narrative drawn largely from Hakluyt's *Voyages*, with one long quotation in-serted in a clerk's hand, and a conclud-ing paragraph by TJ denouncing the King's Speech. The much longer re-maining portion (unpaged) consists of copies of seven royal ordinances, com-missions, and grants relating to Vir-ginia, 1607-1683, copied from MSS in government offices in Williamsburg. The latter are in the same amanuensis' hand, with a few interlineations by TJ, and are omitted in the present text.

This specimen of TJ's researches in American colonial beginnings was in-spired by the King's Speech upon the convening of Parliament in Oct. 1775. Declaring that the colonists were aiming at independence, the King said:

"The object is too important, the spirit of the British nation too high, the resources with which God hath blessed her too numerous, to give up so many colonies which she has planted with great industry, nursed with great ten-derness, encouraged with many commer-cial advantages, and protected and de-fended at much expence and treasure" (Hansard, *Parl. Hist.*, XVIII, 696).

As is shown by his misquoting the date of its delivery (28th for 26th Oct. 1775), TJ read this speech in the *Va. Gaz.* (Purdie) for 19 Jan. 1776 and promptly turned to his library for evi-dence to refute the assertion in the para-graph quoted. It is quite possible that he had in mind publication of the ma-terial thus assembled; but, if so, domes-tic events interfered and public events moved too fast. The paper seems to have been hitherto published for the first and only time in *Americana*, XXXIV (1940), 447-57, by W. F. Keller, who provides

useful notes and points out that TJ's argument was to be embodied in the Declaration of Independence, though much more fully in the drafts than in the version adopted; see TJ's rough draft, penultimate paragraph: "We have reminded them of the circumstances of our emigration and settlement here . . . : that these were effected at the expence of our own blood and treasure, unas-sisted by the wealth or the strength of Great Britain." TJ's view of this matter had been anticipated both in his *Sum-mary View* and his draft of the Declara-tion on Taking Up Arms. The present paper ought also to be compared with Paine's *Common Sense*, issued at just this time: the two writers agreed about George III, but arrived at their conclu-sions by very different means. It is pos-sible that the publication of *Common Sense* (a copy of which was sent him with a letter from Thomas Nelson, 4 Feb. 1776) obviated in TJ's mind the need for publishing his own statement.

1 Thus in MS; one or more words missing.

2 Error for "3." TJ here cites the three-volume edition of Hakluyt's *Voy-ages*, London, 1599-1600.

3 At this point is inserted in a clerk's hand a full text of Letters Patent issued by Queen Elizabeth to Sir Walter Ra-leigh, 25 Mch. 1584 (p. 3-12 in MS), followed by the statement: "The above is copied litterally from 3. Hackluyt's voiages. 243." The narrative is then resumed in TJ's hand.

4 Note by TJ: "Dewes's [i.e., D'Ewes'] journ. fol. 341."

5 Note by TJ: "About Latitude 35.° 50.′ "

6 Note by TJ: "Smith's hist. of Vir-ginia."

7 Note by TJ: "Hakluyt's dedication of his translation of Bassanier's history of the first discovery of Florida."

8 Note by TJ: "This assignment may

be seen at large in the first edition of Hakluyt's voyages. fol. 1589. pa. 815."

⁹ Note in margin by TJ: "He never did assign it."

¹⁰ Note by TJ: "4. Purchas's Pilgrims. Virginia's Verger."

¹¹ Note by TJ: "3. Salm. [i.e., Salmon] Mod. hist. 429."

¹² Note by TJ: "Stith's history of Virginia. 330."

¹³ Here TJ inserted an asterisk but did not subjoin a note.

From Thomas Nelson, Jr.

DEAR JEFFERSON   Philadelphia. [Fe]by 4th. 1776.

I had written to you soon after the repulse of our Troops at Quebec, giving you, as I thought, a true state of that unfortunate affair; but upon comparing it, (altho I had my information from a person who pretended to know a good deal of the matter) with one that I saw afterwards, I found they differ'd so materially that I burnt my Letter and determin'd to leave you to the News papers for your intelligence.

We have late advices from England, which you will see in the inclos'd papers. I had rather send you a dozen Ledgers and Evening Posts, than transcribe three paragraphs out of them. But I have good News for you, which neither of these papers contains. A Vessel arriv'd two nights ago with 60 Tons of Salt Petre, 13 Tons of Gunpowder and 2000 Stands of Arms and we are in daily expectation of 25 Tons more of Gun powder.

Troops are marching every day from hence to support the remains of our Army before Quebec. The Eastern Governments are raising Men for the same purpose. One Battallion has already march[ed] from Connecticut, so that We are still in hopes of reducing the Garrison before it can be reliev'd in the Spring.

General Washington has sent Major General Lee [to] New York at the head of 1200 Volunteers from Connecticut to defend that Province against a detachment sent from Boston, which the General was informed by a deserter, was certainly intended for that place. The Deserter, I fancy, was mistaken, sufficient time having elaps'd since they sail'd for their arriving there, and we have no account of them. The Committee of safety of New York however sent a remonstra[nce] to Lee setting forth the extreme danger the City would be in from the Men of War, should he ente[r] it, and especially as they were apprehensive he intended to make an attack upon the Ships. Lee sent the remonstrance to Congress and wrote the President that he thought it his Duty to carry his Orders into execution, which he was preparing to do with the first division, the rest of the Troops being ready to support him. The Letter and remonstrance being read, a violent debate arose on one side as to the propriety of an armed force from one province, entering another without permission of the civil power of that province, or without express orders of Congress. It was alledged that this was setting up the Military above the Civil. On the other side was urged the absolute necessity of securing that province, the loss of which would cut off all communication between the Northern and Southern Colonies and which if effected would ruin America. The debate ended in the appointment of a Committee of Congress to confer with Lee and the Committee of Safety. Harrison, Lynch and Allen were the Committee and they sat out the next day upon their Ambassy, but what the result has been we are not inform'd, not having heard from them since they went.

You would be surpriz'd to see with how much dispatch we have done business since Dyer and Gaddesden left us. The former you know was superseeded and the latter was order'd home to take command of his Regiment.

I have much more to say to you but the person who carrys this to you is impatient to set out on his journey. He is one of your County Men by the name of Blane.

You must certainly bring Mrs. Jefferson with you. Mrs. Nelson shall nurse her in the small pox and take all possible care of her. We expect Braxton every day and then I shall beat a march for a few Weeks. I have not time to add more than to desire my Compliments to Mrs. Jefferson and to beg that you will believe me Your sincere friend & hb Sert.,   THOS. NELSON JR

P: S: I send you a present of 2/ worth of Common Sense. I had like to have omitted to send you a present from the Quakers also.

RC (DLC). Endorsed: "Nelson Thos." GADDESDEN: Christopher Gadsden, late delegate from South Carolina, had left Congress on 18 Jan. (Burnett, *Letters of Members*, I, lxii). BLANE: Perhaps "Blare." Paine's COMMON SENSE had been published on 9 Jan. A PRESENT FROM THE QUAKERS alludes to *The Ancient Testimony and Principles of the People Called Quakers, Renewed, with Respect to the King and Government*, a flysheet issued by representatives of the Philadelphia Monthly Meeting, 20 Jan. (Sabin 59614).

From James McClurg

DEAR SIR   Wmsburg April 6th. 76.

If this should find you at Congress, when the business it relates to is undetermined, I hope you will use your Influence in favor of your humble Servant. It is believ'd here that a Physician will be appointed to the Continental Troops in this Colony; an office that I desire Exceedingly, as it would gratify at the same time my passion for Improvement in the profession I am destined to, and my zeal to do my Country some Service. In this time of general activity, I do not like to be an idle Spectator; and I know not any post which would suit me so well. Genl. Lee has found us worse prepared for defence than he expected. He broke ground to day in intrenching; but there are not tools for that business to employ half the Number of Men we could spare. The Indolence or Ignorance of Majority of our Committee, and their former General, seem to be too glaring for concealment. I congratulate you on our recovery of Boston. It will be a day of solemn festival, I reckon, in Massachus[etts.] The Notion of Indepency seems to spread fast in this Colony, and will be adopted, I dare say, by Majority of next Convention. The Ele[ctors] of James-City, it is said, are preparing Instructions for the Treasurer to vote in it's favor. I am, Dear Sir Yours sincerely,

JAS. McCLURG

RC (DLC). The PHYSICIAN TO THE CONTINENTAL TROOPS in Virginia appointed by Congress, 18 May 1776, was Dr. William Rickman; McClurg did, however, enter the hospital service, becoming surgeon general of Virginia state troops, 1777 (JCC, IV, 364; Heitman; Blanton, *Medicine in Va. in the 18th Century*, 331-2).

From John Page

DEAR JEFFERSON   Wmsburg April the 6th. 1776.

I wish you would use your Interest in behalf of Dr. McClurg. He offers his Service as Physician to the Continental Forces in Virginia. Such a Person is much wanted. Col. Grayson who behaved admirably well at Hampton and who has taken great Pains to improve himself in the Military Science intends to offer his Service to the Congress. He is highly deserving of Encouragement. Do introduce him and recommend him to your Friends. He will make a Figure at the Head of a Regiment. He displayed Spirit and Conduct at Hampton. For God's sake declare the Colonies independant at once, and save us from ruin. Adieu—written in haste by yrs,   JOHN PAGE

RC (DLC). William GRAYSON was appointed assistant secretary to Washington, 21 June 1776 (Heitman; see also DAB).

From John Page

My Dear Jefferson   Wmsburg April the 26th. 1776.

I have snatched a few Moments to scribble you a few loose Thoughts on our present critical Situation. I think our Countrymen have exhibited an uncommon Degree of Virtue, not only in submiting to all the hard Restrictions and exposing themselves to all the Dangers which are the Consequence of the Disputes they are involved in with Great Britain, but in behaving so peaceably and honestly as they have when they were free from the Restraint of Laws. But how long this may be the Case who can tell? When to their Want of Salt there shall be added a Want of Clothes and Blankets and when to this there may be added the Terrors of a desolating War raging unchecked for Want of Arms and Ammunition, who can say what the People might not do in such a Situation, and tempted with the Prospect of Peace Security and a Trade equal to their wishes? Might they not be induced to give up the Authors of their Misfortunes, their Leaders, who had lead them into such a Scrape, and be willing to sacrifice them to a Reconciliation? I think therefore it behoves the Congress and Conventions to prevent this as much as possible. Every Method that can be devised for the manufacturing of Salt, Salt-petre, Sulphur, Gun-powder, Arms Wollens and Linens should be immediately adopted; and because these Articles can not in several Colonies be made quick enough for their demand, some sure Means of importing them should be instantly fallen upon, and as no Means can be so certain and can so fully answer our Purpose, as forming a commercial Alliance with France, no Time should be lost in doing so. And to prevent Disorders in each Colony a Constitution should be formed as nearly resembling the old one as Circumstances, and the Merit of that Constitution will admit of. And it is undoubtedly high Time that a Plan of a Confederation should be drawn and indeed compleatly executed. These Things should be done without loseing a Moment.

Would you believe it, that we have not yet erected one Powder Mill at the public Expence, and that the only one which has received any Encouragement from the Public has made but about 700 ℔., and that I have not been able to procure the least Assistance from the Committee for Bucktrout's hand-Mill, except their selling him about 400 ℔. of Salt-petre of the Shops half dirt and common Salt for which they demand 3/ per ℔., although his Mill is an elegant Machine and 2 Men can work it with ease, beating with 6 Pestles weighing 60 ℔s. each in Mortars containing 20 ℔s. of Paste, and he has actually beat 120 ℔. of Powder in them and grained 40 ℔. which has been used in proving Cannon &c. and which was found to be strong and good under every disadvantage of want of Sieves and being made with bad Sulphur and Nitre. And he has been at great Pains in erecting his Mill and Apparatus for it, and for a Salt-petre work with it, yet the Committee of Safety refused any Motion to allow him 30 or 40 Pounds as a Reward for his public Spirit and Ingenuity and to enable him to go on with his Plan. They insist on it that the premium of 6/ per ℔. is sufficient Encouragement for making Gun powder, and are deaf to my Argument that Works of this Sort can not be erected and set a going without a good Stock of Money and that Premiums will do very well to keep up any Art once introduced, but are by no Means sufficient to introduce it into ready and general Use. This Powder Mill is so simple that if it were once cleverly at work it would please every one who saw it, and would lead numbers of ingenious People to erect such in different Parts of the Country. There might be one in every Coun[ty] which in my Opinion might work up the Salt-petre which ought to be made in each County, and in this Manner Powder enough might be made for all America. And could you believe it, the Salt petre Works are but little attended to. Some Money it is true has been advanced to different People but I kn[ow] of no grand Work at the public Expence. Sulphur Mines have been discovered but not a Pound extracted nor do I know of any Order about them, and Salt is little thought of. Tate was refused any more Money and referred to the Convention. A valuable Sulphur Mine has been discovered in Spotsylvania by a Man who sold it to one Daniel of Middlesex who is an ingenious Smith and has extracted some from its Ore, which he says is exceedingly rich—5/7 of it Sulphur. Since scribbling the above I have been called off by Business, and upon reading it over find it such a confused Piece of Stuff that I almost determined not to trouble you with it, but bad as it is I shall charge you with a Letter for it, and will therefore send it without Ceremony. Our Friend Innes resigned very handsomely in favour of Captn. Arundel, for which General Lee has recommended him to the Congress to be Major in the 9th. Regiment. You know his Spirit, Abilities, and Deserts, I mean his active Opposition to Ld. D., and his bold attack on him, Foy, Corbin, Byrd, and Wormeley in the Papers for which he lost his Place at College. But was it not a little extraordinary that you should appoint a Captain to the Artillery when we had actually appointed one Who had raised his

Company and was training it, or did you (as I suppose) intend that there should be 2 Companies of Artillery, for I observe your Resolve was that General Lee should direct one to be raised for the southern Department. I wish you would appoint Dr. McClurg Physician to the Army in Virginia and Superintendant of the Public Hospital, and Pope Chief Surgeon. Our sold[iers] would have many more chances for Life and Limbs than they now have. I must refer you to Majr. Innes for News &c. and conclude I am yours sincerely,

JOHN PAGE

RC (DLC).
For James INNES' dismissal as head usher of the William and Mary grammar school in 1775, on account of his patriotic activities, see WMQ, 1st ser., XV (1906-1907), 134-5; VMHB, XIII (1905-1906), 48-50.

Resolutions of the Virginia Convention Calling for Independence

IN CONVENTION MAY THE 15TH 1776.
PRESENT ONE HUNDRED AND TWELVE MEMBERS.

FORASMUCH as all the endeavours of the United Colonies by the most decent representations and petitions to the king and parliament of Great Britain to restore peace and security to America under the British government and a re-union with that people upon just and liberal terms instead of a redress of grievances have produced from an imperious and vindictive administration increased insult oppression and a vigorous attempt to effect our total destruction. By a late act, all these colonies are declared to be in rebellion, and out of the protection of the British crown our properties subjected to confiscation, our people, when captivated, compelled to join in the murder and plunder of their relations and countrymen, and all former rapine and oppression of Americans declared legal and just. Fleets and armies are raised, and the aid of foreign troops engaged to assist these destructive purposes: The king's representative in this colony hath not only withheld all the powers of government from operating for our safety, but, having retired on board an armed ship, is carrying on a piratical and savage war against us tempting our slaves by every artifice to resort to him, and training and employing them against their masters. In this state of extreme danger, we have no alternative left but an abject submission to the will of those over-bearing tyrants, or a total separation from the crown and government of Great Britain, uniting and exerting the strength of all America for defence, and forming alliances with foreign powers for commerce and aid in war: Wherefore, appealing to the SEARCHER OF HEARTS for the sincerity of former declarations, expressing our desire to preserve the connection with that nation, and that we are driven from that inclination by their wicked councils, and the eternal laws of self-preservation.

RESOLVED unanimously, that the delegates appointed to represent this colony in General Congress be instructed to propose to that respectable body to declare the United Colonies free and independent states, absolved from all allegiance to, or dependence upon, the crown or parliament of Great Britain; and that they give the assent of this colony to such declaration, and to whatever measures may be thought proper and necessary by the Congress for forming foreign alliances and a confederation of the colonies, at such time, and in the manner, as to them shall seem best: Provided, that the power of forming government for, and the regulations of the internal concerns of each colony, be left to the respective colonial legislatures.

RESOLVED unanimously, that a committee be appointed to prepare a DECLARATION OF RIGHTS, and such a plan of government as will be most likely to maintain peace and order in this colony, and secure substantial and equal liberty to the people.

a Copy   EDMD. PENDLETON P.

    JOHN TAZEWELL
    Clerk of the Convention

Engrossed copy (DLC: PCC, portfolio 104); with autograph signatures of Pendleton and Tazewell. Endorsed by Charles Thomson: "Instructions given by the Convention of Virginia to their delegates. read 27. May 1776. May 15th. 1776." Also: printed broadside (MB), which varies only in punctuation from the MS (Swem, "Bibliog. of Va. Conventions," No. 147; Evans 15200; Sabin 100023).

For the proceedings in the Convention on the subject of independence, and the adoption of the present Resolutions (which were composed by Pendleton), see *Conv. Jour.*, May 1776, 1816 edn., p. 7, 11, 13-16; Henry, *Henry*, I, 390-400; Hazelton, *Declaration of Independence*, p. 76-80; Hilldrup, *Pendleton*, p. 160-4. The Resolutions are believed to have been brought to Philadelphia by Thomas Nelson, Jr., though this is open to dispute on account of Nelson's attendance record; see Henry, *Henry*, I, 400; Hazelton, *Declaration of Independence*, p. 80, 401; Burnett, *Letters of Members*, I, lxv). They were read in Congress on 27 May, and the result was the Resolution of 7 June, q.v., below.

To Thomas Nelson

DEAR NELSON   Philadelphia May. 16. 1776.

I arrived here last Tuesday after being detained hence six weeks longer than I intended by a malady of which Gilmer can inform you. I have nothing new to inform you of as the last post carried you an account of the naval engagement in Delaware. I inclose a vote of yesterday on the subject of government as the ensuing campaign is likely to require greater exertion than our unorganized powers may at present effect. Should our Convention propose to establish now a form of government perhaps it might be agreeable to recall for a short time their delegates. It is a work of the most interesting nature and such as every individual would wish to have his voice in. In truth it is the whole object of the present controversy; for should a bad government be instituted for us in future it had been as well to have accepted at first the bad one offered to us from beyond the water without the risk and expence of contest. But this I mention to you in confidence, as in our situation, a hint to any other is too delicate however anxiously interesting the subject is to our feelings. In future you shall hear from me weekly while you stay, and I shall be glad to receive Conventional as well as publick intelligence from you. I am at present in our old lodgings tho' I think, as the excessive heats of the city are coming on fast, to endeavor to get lodgings in the skirts of the town where I may have the benefit of a freely circulating air. Tell Page and Mc.lurgh that I received their letters this morning and shall devote myself to their contents. I am here in the same uneasy anxious state in which I was the last fall without Mrs. Jefferson who could not come with me. I wish much to see you here, yet hope you will contrive to bring on as early as you can in convention the great questions of the session. I suppose they will tell us what to say on the subject of independence, but hope respect will be expressed to the right of opinion in other colonies who may happen to differ from them. When at home I took great pains to enquire into the sentiments of the people on that head. In the upper counties I think I may safely say nine out of ten are for it. Adieu. My compliments to Mrs. Nelson.

P.S. In the other colonies who have instituted government they recalled their delegates leaving only one or two to give information to Congress of matters which might relate to their country particularly, and giving them a vote during the interval of absence.

May 19. Yesterday we received the disagreeable news of a second defeat at Quebec. Two men of war, two frigates and a tender arrived there early on the 6th. instant. About 11. o'clock the same day the enemy sallied out to the number of a thousand. Our forces were so dispersed at different posts that not more than 200 could be collected at Headquarter's. This small force could not resist the enemy. All our cannon, 500 muskets and 200 sick men fell into their hands. Besides this one of their frigates got possession of a batteau with 30. barrels of powder and an armed vessel which our crew was forced to abandon. Our army was to retreat to the mouth of the Sorel. Genl. Arnold was to set off from Montreal to join them immediately, upon whose rejoining them it was hoped they might return as far as Dechambeau. General Wooster has the credit of this misadventure, and if he cannot give a better account of it than has yet been heard I hope he will be made an example of. Generals Thomas and Sullivan were on their way with reinforcements. Arnold had gone up to Montreal on business, or as some say, disgusted by Wooster.

The congress having ordered a new battalion of riflemen to be raised in Virginia Innis wishes much to be translated to it from the Eastern shore which was so disagreeable to him that he had determined to have resigned.

RC (MWA). Unsigned. Addressed: "Thomas Nelson esq. in Williamsburgh." Enclosure missing.

TJ had arrived in Philadelphia on 14 May (Account Book, under date). On the MALADY that delayed his return to Congress, see Pendleton to TJ, 24 May 1776. The enclosed VOTE OF YESTERDAY was actually a resolve of 10 May, with a preamble by John Adams agreed to on the 15th, instructing the colonies to adopt new governments; it was printed as a broadside by order of Congress (JCC, IV, 342, 357-8; VI, 1120, No. 106; see also John Adams' "Autobiography,"

Works, III, 44-6). TJ's OLD LODGINGS with Nelson were in the house of Benjamin Randolph, cabinetmaker, on Chestnut Street between Third and Fourth; on 23 May he moved to the second floor of the newly built house of Jacob Graff, Jr. (spelled "Graaf" by TJ) on the southwest corner of Seventh and High (now Market) Streets (Account Book, 23, 27 May; TJ to James Mease, 16 Sep. 1825; Mease to TJ, 4 Nov. 1825; Thomas Donaldson, *The House in Which Jefferson Wrote the Declaration of Independence*, Philadelphia, 1898, p. 83-6).

To John Page

DEAR PAGE   Philadelphia May. 17. 1776.

Having arrived here but lately I have little to communicate. I have been so long out of the political world that I am almost a new man in it. You will have heard before this reaches you of the naval engagement in the Delaware. There are letters in town it is said from General Sullivan which inform that the lower town of Quebec is taken and a breach made in the wall of the upper; but I do not know myself that there are such letters; and if there be, whether Sullivan mentions his intelligence as authentic, as he could not then have reached Quebec himself. As to the articles of salt, blankets &c. every colony I beleive will be to shift for itself, as I see nothing but the measure of a foreign alliance which can promise a prospect of importing either, and for that measure several colonies, and some of them weighty, are not yet quite ripe. I hope ours is and that they will tell us so. But as to salt it is a shame we should say a word about it; the means of supplying the world with it is so much in our power, that nothing but the indolence of Southern constitutions could suffer themselves to be in danger of want. Mr. Innis tells me Gwatkin's books are left with Molly Digges for sale. I should be much obliged to you if you could procure and send me here a catalogue of them; and in the mean time purchase two of them which I recollect he had and have long wished to get; Histoire des Celtes de Pelloutier. 2. vols. 12mo. and Observations on Gardening printed by Payne, London. 8vo. For their cost I will get you to apply to Colo. Nelson to whom I can refund it here. This office will perhaps remind you of a box of books you have of mine which I am in hopes some of the military or commissary's waggons will furnish you with an opportunity of sending to Albemarle, to Richmond, or to Mr. Eppes's in Charles City. Adieu.

May. 19. 1776. For the melancholy reverse of the Quebec news received yesterday I must refer you to Nelson. For our disappointment in the office of director to the hospital, to Innis who will be with you soon, and will give yourself and Mc.lurgh a full account in what manner we were surprised out of it.

RC (NN). Unsigned. Addressed: "To The honble John Page esq. Williamsburgh."

TJ either at this time or later acquired both the books mentioned, namely, Simon Pelloutier, HISTOIRE DES CELTES, The Hague, 1750, and [Thomas Whately] OBSERVATIONS ON [MODERN] GARDENING, London, 1770 (Library Catalogue, 1815, p. 13, 132).

Virginia Delegates in Congress to the Virginia Convention

GENTLEMEN   Philadelphia, 18 April, [i.e., May] 1776.

The inclosed resolutions were reported by a committee appointed to consider of a letter from general Lee to the president. We have nothing to observe upon them unless it be, that the surgeons whom the director general of the hospital is empowered to appoint, and the regimental surgeons to be nominated by the convention, according to a resolution lately forwarded to you, are different officers. Upon the arrival of two ships of war, two frigates and one tender at Quebeck, the 6th instant, the [. . .][1] with the forces the vessels brought, of no more than about a thousand men, made a sally upon our army there, and routed it. The resolution of the 15th of May we send a printed copy of, lest the manuscript, which we desired the secretary to furnish us with, should not come time enough to go by this opportunity. We are, Gentlemen, Your most obedient servants.

Dft in Wythe's hand (DLC). Enclosures missing. TJ retained this paper and used blank portions of it for a table of values of coins; see his Report of 2 Sep. 1776.

Drafted by Wythe for all the Virginia delegates to sign, this letter was presumably revised before it was dispatched. It is probably the letter received and read in Convention on 27

May (*Conv. Jour.*, May, 1776, 1816 edn., p. 25). The error in the date is manifest from the fact that the INCLOSED RESOLUTIONS on Gen. Lee's letter were passed on 18 May (JCC, IV, 363-5). For THE RESOLUTION OF THE 15TH OF MAY, see TJ to Nelson, 16 May 1776.

[1] Two or three words faded or worn beyond legibility.

Amendment to Report

of Committee on Letters from Washington, Schuyler, and the Commissioners in Canada

[21 May 1776]

Strike out 3d. 4th. and 5th.

Instead of 11th. substitute 'that General Schuyler be informed that Congress have in view these two great objects, the Protection and assistance of our Canadian friends, and the Securing[1] so much of that country as may prevent any communication between our enemies and the Indians. The means of effecting these purposes by fortifying proper posts, building armed vessels where most expedient, opening roads of communication or otherwise, are left to the determination of a council or councils of war governing themselv[es] by events and their knowlege of the country.'

Dft (DLC: PCC, No. 19, VI). This is a separate slip inserted in a much longer committee report drafted by other hands; the full report, as revised by members of the committee and in turn by Congress, is printed in JCC, IV, 375-8. TJ's substitution for the eleventh par-

agraph, struck out, is the third paragraph of the report as adopted.

On 14 May 1776 a letter from Washington of 11 May, one from Schuyler of 3 May, and one from Capt. Daniel Robertson (a captured British officer) of 9 May, were read in Congress and referred to a committee composed of TJ, William Livingston, and John Adams; on 16 May a letter from the Commissioners in Canada of 1 May, one from Schuyler of 10 May, and one from Washington of 15 May were read and referred to the same committee; on 18 May a letter from Washington of 17 May and three letters from the Commissioners in Canada of 6, 8, and 10 May, respectively, were read and referred to the same committee, which was then enlarged by the appointment of Robert Morris, Duane, R. H. Lee, Edward Rutledge, and R. R. Livingston (JCC, IV, 352, 358-9, 362-3). On 21 May the committee reported, but only on the letters received on 16 and 18 May; Congress debated its recommendations that day and passed them, with omissions and alterations, on the next (same, p. 374, 375-8). TJ did not contribute to the later report of this committee, which was submitted and partly adopted 25 May, on the earlier letters of Washington, Schuyler, and Capt. Robertson; see JCC, V, 392. He was, however, to review the whole report, for most of its recommendations were referred to the "committee of conference," appointed 23 May and augmented 25 May, to confer with Generals Washington, Gates, and Mifflin "upon the most speedy and effectual means for supporting the American cause in Canada" (JCC, IV, 383-4, 391, 394-5). For the results, see TJ's Reports of 17 June, below.

[1] Substituted in another hand for "Retaining."

From Edmund Pendleton

Wmsburg May 24th. 1776.

EDMD. PENDLETON TO THOS. JEFFERSON, ESQE.

I am conscious of a large Arrears of debt to you for favor received before you left Congress in the Winter, but your return to Virga. and my continued hopes of the pleasure of seing you, postponed my writing 'til I heard you had resumed your charge in Congress and I will now endeavor to pay some of the debt. I am sorry to hear your pleasure at home was interrupted by an inveterate head ach, (I don't remember the hard name for it) which I hope you travelled off. You'l have seen your Instructions to propose Independance and our resolutions to form a Government. The Political Cooks are busy in preparing the dish, and as Colo. Mason seems to have the Ascendancy in the great work, I have Sanguine hopes it will be framed so as to Answer it's end, Prosperity to the Community and Security to Individuals, but I am yet a stranger to the Plan. I find Our Session will be a long one, and indeed the importance of our business requires it and we must sweat it out with Fortitude. Genl. Lee is in North Carolina, where it is uncertain what number of the Enemy's Troops are arrived. The Genl. is of Opinion they will not stay there longer than to take an Airing, and to go to So. Carolina or Virginia. He means to stay at Newburn to Watch the determination and meet them at either place. He thinks rage and revenge may prompt them to Attack Wilmington, but hopes Brigr. Moore is sufficiently prepared for them. We have had repeated Accounts lately from Norfolk by deserters that Dunmore and his Fleet were reduced to half allowance and were preparing to depart. A Letter from Colo. Woodford at Norfolk informs Us they were all Sailed on Wednesday and had got below Crainy Island, except four which were under Way below the New Distillery; they had taken on board the Shattered remains of the Ethiopn. regiment and abandoned the Intrenchments which our Troops are destroying. A deserter from the 14th. Regiment and 5 Sailors, who left them at their departure said they were going to Cape Fear and had the Small Pox on board. By Letter from Hampton yesterday we are informed they were Collecting just below the Mouth of James River and they expected an Attack. Brigr. Lewis sent off a reinforcement last night and is gone himself this morning. If they land, I think you'l have a good Account of them.

We have heard much of the Arrival of Russians, Hessians and Commrs. to the Eastward, but nothing we can rely on. Perhaps the post to day may give us something conclusive, and relieve us from Anxiety about Quebec. Greet my friend Wythe and all your Companions. I shall write to some of them tomorrow. Farewell.

Pray tell me the cost of the Wire that I may remit you the money.

RC (DLC).

From the opening sentence it is clear that several letters from TJ to Pendleton, written in the fall of 1775, are missing. For Pendleton's WIRE, see TJ to Page, 31 Oct. 1775. COMMRS. (Commissioners), i.e., the Howe brothers who, when they took command in America, were also commissioned to negotiate for peace (Troyer S. Anderson, *The Command of the Howe Brothers*, N.Y. and London, 1936, p. 43, 51, 150ff.; see also Francis Lightfoot Lee to TJ, 17 Sep. 1776).

From Edmund Pendleton

Wmsburg June 1. 1776.

I am much obliged by the intelligence inclosed in your favor of the 21st. All the circumstances which have occurred in America, seem to confirm the Account, as Cornwallis is said to be arrived at Cape Fear, and his troops from 3 to 4000. We must defend our selves as well as we can. I am concerned to find there is danger of disunion at such a crisis, as that only can give Success to our Enemies. Maryland has behaved badly. We shall reprove them severely; We build our Government slowly, I hope it will be founded on a Rock. Dunmore with 400 half starved motly soldiers on Gwyns Island, and 2000 of Our men on the Main are looking at each other as two Tenders are in the thoroughfare between Milford Haven and Piankatank to stop the Passage and the Fleet in the River to Protect the Island. Adieu my freind and lets have no more of your "Honble Sirs." Your Affecte.

EDMD. PENDLETON

Tel Mrs. Wythe all are well. I am to dine with the Major tomorrow.

RC (DLC). TJ's FAVOR OF THE 21ST of May is missing. THE MAJOR: Richard Taliaferro, Mrs. Wythe's father.

Resolution of Independence
Moved by R. H. Lee for the Virginia Delegation

[7 June 1776]

Resolved

That[1] these United Colonies are, and of right ought to be, free and independent States, that they are absolved from all allegiance to the British Crown, and that all political connection between them and the State of Great Britain is, and ought to be, totally dissolved.

That it is expedient forthwith to take the most effectual measures for forming foreign Alliances.

That a plan of confederation be prepared and transmitted to the respective Colonies for their consideration and approbation.

[*On verso in several hands as indicated:*]

Resolved that it is the opinion of this Committee tha[t] the first Resolution[2] be postponed to this day three weeks and that in the mean time[3] least any time should be lost in case the Congress agree to this resolution[4] a committee be appointed to prepare a Declaration to the effect of the said first resolution.[5]

MS (DLC: PCC, No. 23); in R. H. Lee's hand; slightly worn and torn at the lateral edges. Endorsed by Charles Thomson: "[J]une 7. 1776. No. 4. Resolutions moved June 7th. 1776. referred for consideration till to morrow respecting Independanc[e *or* y] of the U.S."

The present Resolution was introduced in accordance with the instructions sent to the Virginia delegation by the Convention of that colony, 15 May 1776, q.v. Written and introduced by R. H. Lee and seconded by John Adams, it was considered by TJ to be a motion by the Virginia delegation (John Adams, "Autobiography," *Works*, III, 51; Adams to Richard H. Lee, 24 Feb. 1821, same, X, 396; also, James Madi-

son to Thomas Ritchie, 13 Aug. 1822, in *Writings*, ed. Hunt, IX, 110-11). Discussion of the Resolution was deferred until the following day (a Saturday), when it was debated in a committee of the whole, as it was again on Monday, 10 June; on the latter day the committee of the whole reported and Congress adopted the additional (fourth) resolution above (JCC, V, 426-9). The purpose of the postponement for three weeks (i.e., until 1 July) was "in order to give the Assemblies of the Middle Colonies an opportunity to take off their restrictions and let their Delegates unite in the measure" (Elbridge Gerry to James Warren, 11 June 1776, Burnett, *Letters of Members*, I, No. 699); TJ in his Notes on Debates lists the colonies requiring the postponement as New York, New Jersey, Pennsylvania, Delaware, Maryland, and South Carolina.

1 Here an insertion, apparently "the good people of," was made and crossed out.
2 Up to this point this paragraph is

in the hand of Benjamin Harrison, chairman of the committee of the whole.
3 Preceding words in Thomson's hand.
4 Preceding words are written below, with a mark of insertion, in R. R. Livingston's hand.
5 The Resolution is completed in Thomson's hand.

Notes of Proceedings in the Continental Congress

[7 June to 1 August 1776]

EDITORIAL NOTE

JEFFERSON'S extraordinarily graphic account of the debates and proceedings in Congress during two critical months in the summer of 1776 is perhaps the best single source of information concerning the movement toward independence and the formation of the Articles of Confederation, not even excepting the similar notes made by John Adams (*Works*, II, 485-502; also JCC, VI, 1071-83). Nevertheless, its claim to contemporaneity and even to accuracy in respect to the account of the signing of the Declaration of Independence has been challenged by Ford, Hazelton, and other careful scholars. For this reason it is essential that the manuscript and the facts surrounding it be examined in some detail.

The text of the Notes of Proceedings (hereafter referred to as Notes) as here presented was inserted by Jefferson in the manuscript of his Autobiography; all previous editors of Jefferson's papers have printed it with the Autobiography at the place where Jefferson inserted it (TJR, I, 10-29; HAW, I, 12-35; Ford, I, 18-47; L & B, I, 17-53). However, it now seems clear that Jefferson's insertion was an afterthought, and it is felt that the Notes would not only serve to illuminate the events of 1776 better but would also be more accurately understood if presented independently.

Jefferson's Autobiography, begun 6 Jan. 1821 and closed, or rather suspended, 29 July 1821, is a MS of 90 leaves, all versos being blank save three; however, Jefferson numbered only the alternate leaves and counted blank versos in his pagination. After he had written the MS and numbered its pages, he inserted the 20-page MS of the Notes. At present this insertion lies between leaves [19-20] and 21-[22], but Jefferson probably placed it between leaves 21-[22] and [23-24]. For page [23], which is only half-filled, is not a continuation of page 21 but of the last page of the Notes, and it contains no mention of the Declaration of Independence. It is, therefore, a substitute for a cancelled leaf which must have briefly summarized the proceedings on both the Declaration and the Articles of Confederation, a summarization rendered superfluous by the much more detailed account supplied with the insertion of the

Notes. This supposition is further supported by the evident fact that Jefferson made an effort to keep the various events of his Autobiography in proportion (see his statement at the conclusion of the account of the French Revolution, Ford, i, 147). A one- or two-page account of the Declaration would have conformed to the plan of the whole, but the 20-page insertion of the Notes threw it greatly out of scale. Jefferson did not explain this disproportionate amount of detail as he did in the case of his account of the French Revolution; nevertheless, there must have been some compelling cause for his action in deleting a brief account and in substituting therefor an extended one, particularly since it was done after the Autobiography had already covered the events of 1776.

That compulsion would be better understood, perhaps, if it were known at what date the insertion of the Notes was made. The most that can be said, however, is that the insertion followed the completion of the Autobiography. It is a plausible assumption that the insertion took place at the time of the renewed discussions of the authorship and signing of the Declaration of Independence between 1822 and 1825 and that it was caused by the rather partisan efforts to depreciate Jefferson's claim to sole authorship. Obviously Jefferson was not moved to insert the Notes in the Autobiography because of the differences of opinion over the question of the signing of the Declaration on 4 July 1776, for that question had been publicly agitated since 1817 and Jefferson had in 1819 given a detailed account of the matter, basing this account on the Notes (TJ to Samuel A. Wells, 12 May 1819). The same subject came up again when he purchased a copy of the newly published *Secret Journals of Congress* (see postscript to letter to Wells, added 6 Aug. 1822). If the agitation of the question of the signing on 4 July had not been sufficient cause to induce Jefferson to make the insertion in 1821, when it had been brought to his attention four years earlier, it seems unlikely that the revival of the question in 1822 would have caused him to do it.

But the question of Jefferson's authorship of the Declaration was something that touched his sensitive feelings more deeply. In 1822 at least two Federalist newspapers, the *Philadelphia Union* and the *Federal Republican*, sought "to deprive Mr. Jefferson of all credit for originality in drawing up the Declaration of Independence" (Hazelton, *Declaration of Independence*, p. 350-1). This Jefferson could probably have accepted with equanimity, for he had been subjected to much worse from Federalist newspapers. But the following year at Salem, Mass., Timothy Pickering delivered a Fourth of July oration in which he endeavored to depreciate Jefferson's role as author, employing for that purpose a letter written by John Adams which seemed to support Pickering's views. This brought the matter into public view in a manner which Jefferson could not ignore. He wrote soon afterwards to James Madison, expressing some skepticism concerning the accuracy of Pickering's use of statements by Adams and giving Madison an account of the drafting of the Declaration, basing this account upon "written notes, taken by myself at the moment and on the spot" (TJ to Madison, 30

Aug. 1823). It seems plausible to assume, in the absence of exact evidence, that this discussion of the question of Jefferson's part in the drafting of the Declaration may have provided the stimulus that caused him to insert the Notes in the Autobiography. The insertion may possibly have occurred then or later, for the question continued to be discussed down to 1825; but there appears no valid reason for assuming that it took place earlier.

The manuscript of the Notes is not the same as "written notes, taken . . . at the moment and on the spot"; Jefferson may actually have had such original notes when he wrote to Madison. If so, they are not now known to be extant. The difference between these original memoranda and the Notes is explained by a slip of paper pasted onto page 12 of the Notes and bearing five lines on the recto and four on the verso in Jefferson's hand:

"the Declaration thus signed on the 4th. on paper was engrossed on parchment, & signed again on the 2d. of Aug. Some erroneous statements of the proceedings on the declaration of independance having got before the public in latter times, Mr. Samuel A. Wells asked explanations of me, which are given in my letter to him of May 12. 19. before and now again referred to. I took notes in my place while these things were going on, and at their close wrote them out in form and with correctness and ⟨this and⟩ from 1. to 7. of the two preceding sheets are the originals then written; as the two following are of the earlier debates on the Confederation, which I took in like manner."

This statement is of first importance for establishing the date and dependability of the Notes, but before its value as evidence can be properly assessed, it becomes necessary to clarify the character of this insertion within an insertion. Obviously the slip was written after 1819. Hazelton (p. 594) is of the opinion that it "was penned at, or soon after, the time of writing the letter to Wells" (TJ to Wells, 12 May 1819). This is possible, but Jefferson's allusion to that letter ("*before and now again referred to*") indicates that some interval had elapsed. The allusion is not clear, but it is certain that, at the time of writing the slip, Jefferson had made some earlier reference to the letter to Wells. At any rate, there is evidence in the slip itself that it was inserted in the Notes before the Notes were inserted in the Autobiography. This is to be found in the middle part of the final sentence, which originally read "this and the two preceding sheets are the originals" (the reference to sheets is made clear by the fact that the Notes consisted of five sheets or signatures of four pages each; the slip was attached to page 12 of the middle sheet; hence the correctness of the reference to the two preceding and the two following sheets). However, Jefferson struck out the words "this and" and interlined the words "from 1. to 7. of." It seems plausible to assume from this that the Notes were not paged until this correction was made and that the pagination was inserted to avoid confusion, a confusion which could have been created only by the intermingling of the sheets of the Notes with some other group of sheets such as those of the Autobiography; hence the likelihood that the pagination was made at the time of the insertion and that the slip, therefore, was written originally at some time before the insertion. Another point needs to be noted about the slip: the first sentence, penned in a smaller hand, was obviously added after the slip had been written with the beginning words "Some erroneous statements . . ."; Hazelton is of the opinion that this addition was made 6 Aug. 1822 (p. 594), for the very plausible reason that the reference to the signing of the paper copy of the Declaration is to the same effect as the postscript that Jefferson added on that date to his file copy of the letter to Wells of 12 May 1819.

The real significance of the slip, however, lies in Jefferson's categorical statement that "I took notes in my place while these things were going on, and at their close wrote them out in form and with correctness and from 1. to 7. of the two proceeding sheets are the originals then written." Ford has thrown grave doubt upon the accuracy of this assertion (I, 47); Hazelton and others have agreed with Ford's opinion in more or less degree. At the conclusion of the Notes in his edition, Ford (I, 47) makes this statement: "Here end the notes which Jefferson states were taken 'while these things were going on, and at their close' were 'written out in form and with correctness.' Much of their value depends on the date of their writing, but there is nothing to show this, except negative evidence. The sheets were all written at the same time, which makes the writing after Aug. 1, 1776; while the misstatements as to the signing, and as to Dickinson's presence, would seem almost impossible unless greater time even than this had elapsed between the occurrence and the notes. The MS. is, moreover, considerably corrected and interlined, which would hardly be the case if merely a transcript of rough notes." Hazelton agrees with the implication here that in a critical passage Jefferson relied upon memory and with the statement that there is no evidence to show when the Notes were written "in form and with correctness" (p. 204-5, 422, 594). Both agree that the misstatements are in fact misstatements. If this is correct, then Jefferson's assertions in the Notes are indeed open to question. Hence the necessity for examining (1) the opinion that there is no evidence of date attached to the Notes and (2) the "misstatements" that caused doubt to arise in the first place.

First, as to the question of evidences of date, there is no room for doubt that the Notes were written before 1 June 1783. It is true, as Ford observes, that the MS of the Notes is "considerably corrected and interlined." But this fact, far from casting doubt on the contemporary nature of the Notes as Ford implies, is the essential evidence for establishing the terminal date after which the Notes could not possibly have been written. Ford was led to this erroneous inference, no doubt, by a misreading of Jefferson's statement on the slip. That statement does not assert, as Ford seemed to think, that the Notes were "merely a transcript of rough notes." On the contrary, Jefferson seems rather explicit in his explanation that the notes taken during the debates were, at the close of the proceedings, employed as the basis for writing "them out in form and with correctness," not for the purpose of transcription.

Many of the corrections and interlineations were made before 1 June 1783, when Jefferson sent a copy of the Notes to Madison (see notes following this document); some bear evidence of having been made at the time of the transcription; others indubitably were made much later, perhaps during the years 1819-1825. In short, we are dealing here with an overlay of corrections and additions precisely similar to that which occurred in the first page of Jefferson's First Draft of the Virginia Constitution and in the "Rough draught" of the Declaration of Independence. Just as the Third Draft of the former and Adams' Copy of the latter provided the dividing line for separating the earlier and the later additions in each case, so the presence of the Madison copy of the Notes provides a dividing line for separating the corrections and additions made prior to 1 June 1783 from the overlay made subsequent to that date. The textual notes given below will point out every example of corrections made after the Madison copy was drawn off; the italicized words in angle brackets in the text of the Notes, representing deletions, will show at a glance what corrections were made prior to 1 June 1783. It may be safely assumed that the Madison copy suffered no such sophistication subsequent to 1783 as did the Notes from which it was taken and which remained in Jefferson's hands.

This terminal date of 1 June 1783 definitely removes the Notes from the suspicion of having been, at least in part, dependent upon an older man's memory. But may we accept Jefferson's statement that the Notes were written "in form and with correctness" at the close of debates, meaning thereby soon after 1 Aug. 1776? Ford and Hazelton think not, chiefly because of inability to reconcile with accepted views Jefferson's categorical assertion about the signing of the Declaration of Independence on 4 July 1776, an assertion which the general consensus of historical opinion has rejected. Ford expresses no opinion as to the date at which the Notes may have been written. Hazelton thinks that the writing took place after Jefferson retired from Congress, but he does not specify whether this means after he retired in 1776 or in 1784 or indeed at what period after retirement the rewriting of the original notes took place. Though both knew of the existence of the Madison copy and made use of it, neither recognized its importance in establishing a terminal date. Each concluded that Jefferson had written the Notes at a later period than he asserted because of his "misstatement" about the signing of the Declaration on 4 July. It is noteworthy that, except for this and the implied assertion by Jefferson as to Dickinson's presence in Congress on 4 July, neither impugns Jefferson's testimony as given in the Notes in respect to any other single important statement of fact or opinion. Before examining the criteria by which they measure Jefferson's accuracy on this point, it is worth noting that the Notes, taken as a whole, are so explicit, so detailed, so capable of being checked and verified by other reliable sources, that we must inescapably conclude (as indeed Hazelton does) that the MS was written from notes taken "while these things were going on." In view of this, it is evident that the standards by which any part of Jefferson's generally unimpeachable contemporary account are to be challenged must be of equal if not superior validity.

But just how contemporary were the Notes? There is no evidence other than Jefferson's statement on the slip written after 1819 to show that the original notes were put in form at the close of the debates on the Declaration and the Articles of Confederation. But since it is possible to narrow the dates of the Notes to the period from 1 Aug. 1776 to 1 June 1783, the task of attempting to ascertain the accuracy of Jefferson's statement is relatively simplified. The first and most important fact to be observed is that Jefferson fully realized the historic significance of the act of separation from the British Empire and of drafting the justification for that separation as well as stating the political ideals of the new nation. If proof of this were needed it is to be found not only in his entire career, guided as it was by constant reference to the leading principles then stated, but also in the numbers of copies of the Declaration "as originally written" that he found time to make and send to distant friends during the busy days of July; in the fact that he found time during June and July—two of his busiest months in Congress—to make such detailed notes of proceedings and debates; in his incorporating the text of his draft of the Declaration in the Notes—all evidences of his pride in the authorship of this statement of national ideals; finally, in the care that he took in putting the Notes "in form and with correctness," a style which, whether intended for publication or not, could easily have been put to press without further alteration. In 1787 Jefferson wrote of the nine-hour debate on 1 July "during which all the powers of the soul had been distended with the magnitude of the object" (TJ to the Editor of the *Journal de Paris*, 29 Aug. 1787). If the magnitude of the object made such an impression on him and if he had intended from the beginning to make full and exact notes of these momentous transactions, what motive could explain his deferring the putting these notes in form? The pressure of business in Congress might have deprived him of the time necessary to make these copies, but he was fully as preoccupied with the affairs of Virginia from Oct. 1776 to the summer of 1781 as he was during July of the former year. During the early part of July 1776 he was arduously engaged in the affairs of the army in Canada and with the debates on the Articles of Confederation—far more so than in the following months when he was preparing to return to Virginia—yet this preoccupation did not prevent him from making at least six copies of the Declaration to send to friends during the busy days of early July. Jefferson, as Adams said, was always "prompt and explicit" in the Congress and throughout life he conducted business, especially paper work, with dispatch and efficiency. It seems plausible to assume, therefore, that, especially during Aug. 1776, Jefferson had as full an opportunity to put his rough notes in form as he had at any other time prior to 1781. In the absence of evidence to the contrary, it would seem reasonable to conclude that Jefferson's statement as to the Notes being put in form at the close of debate should be given much weight, particularly in view of the high degree of trustworthiness of the document as a whole.

But, according to the general view, there is evidence to the contrary: the evidence lies in Jefferson's statement in the Notes that "The declaration was reported by the commee., agreed to by the house, and signed by every member present except Mr. Dickinson." This statement, Ford and Hazelton agree, could scarcely have been written except from memory and after a greater interval than Jefferson claimed for the writing of the Notes, since (1) the Declaration of Independence was not signed on 4 July and since (2) Dickinson was not present.

To take up the second item first, it is necessary only to point out the fact (with which Hazelton agrees) that the word "present" in Jefferson's statement was not in the Madison copy of the Notes, was not in the letter of 1787 to the Editor of the *Journal de Paris* (which was certainly based on the Notes), and was interlined in the letter to Wells in 1819 and therefore presumably interlined in the Notes at the same time. Up to 1819, then, what Jefferson had said in the Notes was that the Declaration was signed on 4 July by every member except Mr. Dickinson; this is very different from an assertion that Dickinson was or was not present. The fact of Dickinson's presence or absence, then, cannot be regarded as valid evidence for discrediting Jefferson's statement about the date of the Notes. By 1819 Jefferson's interlineation of the word "present" indubitably caused him to make from memory what Ford called a "misstatement"; but we are concerned here with plausible or provable misstatements in the Notes as the text stood prior to 1 June 1783, not thereafter.

Yet there remain two most troublesome items in Jefferson's statement; first, that the Declaration was signed 4 July; second, that it was signed by "every member." Again to consider the second point first, did Jefferson mean every member who was duly elected and actually serving in Congress at the time? Did he mean the same members who signed the engrossed parchment copy of the Declaration on 2 Aug.? Hazelton has accumulated a vast amount of information from many sources tending to show where each member was on 4 July, what his status was, whether or not it was possible for him to have signed on that day, and indicating which of those who signed the engrossed copy on 2 Aug. might have or could not have signed on the earlier date (Hazelton, *Declaration of Independence*, p. 193-219, 495-543). The result is inconclusive. It only establishes, with some doubtful exceptions, a list of members who could have signed a copy of the Declaration on 4 July. In the absence of such a copy dated or datable on 4 July we cannot know precisely what members Jefferson had in mind, whether those legally qualified or those actually present. The question is a baffling one in any case and is made more so by the situation of the New York delegates, who were so bound by instructions that they could not vote on the question on 2 July and who, though present, could not have voted for or signed the Declaration on 4 July. Jefferson in 1819 got around this major difficulty by saying that, when the New York instructions were changed, the New York delegates signed on 15 July. This statement has the appearance of being based on the transactions reported in the Journals of Congress on that day, where, of course, no mention is made of signing though the authorization of the New York Convention for their delegates to concert in the act of independence was presented

(JCC, V, 560; TJ to Wells, 12 May 1819). Nevertheless, a copy of the *Journals of Congress* (Philadelphia: Aitken, 1777) in the New York Public Library contains a marginal note in the handwriting of Charles Thomson listing the names of four New York delegates, and opposite these names is the following: "signed July 15." This marginal note was obviously written late in Thomson's life (Hazelton, p. 207-8), but it was the considered statement of the usually reliable Secretary of Congress.

Finally, was the Declaration signed on 4 July? The question appears rhetorical in view of the general consensus of historical opinion that a negative answer is the only valid one. That opinion is supported by impressive reasons, which may be summarized as follows: (1) neither the Rough Journal, the Corrected Journal, nor the Secret Journal of Congress, which were the only ones kept by Thomson at that time, contains any mention of a signing; (2) the printed broadside of the Declaration wafered into the Rough Journal contains no names except those of Hancock and Thomson, both printed; (3) no signed copy dated or datable on 4 July is known to be in existence; (4) on 9 July 1776 John Adams wrote that "As soon as an American Seal is prepared, I conjecture the Declaration will be subscribed by all the members"; (5) Elbridge Gerry wrote on 21 July 1776: "Pray subscribe for me the Declaration of Independence if the same is to be signed as proposed"; (6) the New York delegates were not authorized to sign on 4 July and could not have done so; (7) no contemporary letters are known to be extant by members of Congress stating categorically that a copy of the Declaration was signed on that date; (8) had such a signing taken place, it is difficult to conceive of the neglect and disappearance of such a cherished document, particularly in view of such expressions as those in the letters of Adams and Gerry indicating a desire to transmit to posterity signal evidence of assent to the great decision; (9) the Journals of Congress for 4 July merely require that the Declaration "be authenticated and printed," whereas the entry for 19 July requires that the Declaration "be fairly engrossed on parchment . . . and . . . signed by every member of Congress" (Hazelton, *Declaration of Independence*, p. 193-219, 495-543; Burnett, *Letters of Members*, I, p. 528-32; Charles Warren, "Fourth of July Myths," WMQ, 3d ser., II [1945], 242-8).

These impressive reasons are all but overwhelming proof that Jefferson was mistaken. Yet it must be observed that every single one of these proofs is merely negative. No member of Congress ever stated in so many words that a Declaration was *not* signed on 4 July, except for the statement of Thomas McKean in 1813. But McKean's account was made from memory, is charged with a number of glaring errors in other respects, and cannot be compared with the general accuracy of Jefferson's Notes.

Opposed to these negative reasons there is only Jefferson's statement in the Notes, though in later years both Franklin and Adams (the latter repeatedly; see Burnett, *Letters of Members*, I, p. 531) did casually refer to the signing of the Declaration on 4 July, references which must not be regarded, however, as considered comments addressed to the specific question. Hazelton, recognizing the high degree of accuracy of the Notes considered as a whole, resolved the difficulty by assuming that the words "signed by every member" may not have been intended by Jefferson to be controlled by the words "in the evening of the last" (4 July) and that, putting his rough notes in form at a later date and certainly after the signing on 2 Aug., Jefferson may merely have intended his brief summary of these proceedings to apply to the whole process from the adoption on 4 July to the signing on 2 Aug. This seems a valid and plausible interpretation.

But is it the only one? We now know that the Report of the Committee of Five of 28 June, submitting the text of the Declaration to Congress, has disappeared (Boyd, *Declaration of Independence*, 1945, p. 40-1). It is at least possible to suppose that this copy may have borne the signatures of those who were in Congress on 4 July and even of those delegates from New York on or after 15 July. The fact of the disappearance of this copy of the Declaration of Independence certainly invalidates one of the strongest of the negative reasons given above, namely, that if a copy had been signed on 4 July "great care would no doubt have been taken to preserve it" (Burnett, *Letters of Members*, I, p. 531). On the contrary, it may be that the strong desire among members of Congress to sign the document, the very formal engrossing and signing on 2 Aug., and the existence of the official parchment copy bearing signatures may be advanced as reasons for both an informal signing on 4 July and for the disposal of a copy which, in respect to the number of signatures, was at variance with the engrossed and authorized copy. It is also possible to interpret the statements of Adams and Gerry as meaning that there had been an informal signing on 4 July; that some, perhaps for legal reasons or because of absence, had not signed; that it was therefore proposed to do the thing with more formality and hence the Declaration, by order of Congress, was to be engrossed and signed; and that Adams believed "all the members" would sign such a copy and Gerry, being absent, hoped someone would do it for him. For similar reasons the difference between the entries in the Journal of Congress of 4 July and 19 July can be plausibly explained, the former omitting any mention of signing perhaps because some had not, for one reason or another, desired such a personal record of treason; and the latter, by action of Congress, requiring members to sign. A significant fact which has been overlooked in previous discussions of this matter is that the final paragraph of the Declaration makes signing almost obligatory: "We, therefore . . . mutually pledge to each other our lives, our fortunes, and our sacred honour" was a solemn pledge which almost by definition required the formality of individual signatures. When these words were approved on 4 July the "several members" must have understood this to be so. The fact that the order to sign an engrossed copy was delayed until 19 July may be explained by the situation of the New York delegation and does not exclude the possibility of the signing of a paper copy on 4 July. It is also important to observe that, in at least one notable instance, a formal document was signed in more than one form by the members; the engrossed Association of 1774 was signed by the several members and ordered to be printed; after which at least two and perhaps more of the printed copies were signed. These two copies are in NN and PHi; the copy in NN reveals the fact that the signing of the engrossed copy and of the printed copy resembled in certain respects the confused signing of the Declaration of Independence—Henry and Pendleton signed the engrossed copy but not the printed; six members signed the latter but not the former; and Rodney was absent at the original signing of the engrossed copy but his "name was written in by his order" (JCC, I, 80-1). It is, therefore, plausible to assume that a similar procedure may have resulted in July 1776—that is, the signing of a paper copy on 4 July and the signing of an engrossed copy later.

Finally, it should be pointed out that Jefferson's Notes were written at a much earlier date than has been generally supposed; neither Ford, Hazelton, nor Burnett points out that the Notes were written before 1783 or admits the probability that Jefferson may have been correct in stating that they were put "in form and with correctness" at the end of the debates. If, as is highly probable, Jefferson wrote the Notes in the late summer or early autumn of 1776, greater weight than has hitherto been accorded must be attached to his statement that "in the evening of the last . . . the declaration was . . . signed by every member." Even so, the interpretation placed by Hazelton on these words would still be plausible and may indeed be the correct answer to the vexed question.

Nevertheless, on the basis of evidence thus far advanced—all of it negative and some of it demonstrably untenable—the question cannot be regarded as closed. On this great issue of independence, in which "all the powers of the soul had been distended with the magnitude of the object," and on the precise details of its final resolution, no one was more acutely interested than Jefferson, and none recorded the procedure with such fullness and exactness. His testimony should not be discarded except on the basis of irrefragable proof of a positive nature. This has not yet been brought forth.

The text of this document has been reproduced with literal fidelity. All square brackets in the printed text are in the MS.

BIBLIOGRAPHICAL NOTE

The principal discussions of the question of the signing on 4 July 1776 are the following, arranged chronologically: Mellen Chamberlain, "The Alleged Signing of the Declaration of Independence, July 4, 1776," Mass. Hist. Soc., *Procs.*, 2d ser., I (1884-1885), 272-98; P. L. Ford, *Writings of Thomas Jefferson*, I (1892), 28-9; Herbert Friedenwald, *The Declaration of Independence* (1904), ch. VI; John H. Hazelton, *The Declaration of Independence* (1906), *passim*; E. C. Burnett, *Letters of Members of the Continental Congress*, I (1921), p. 528-38; Charles Warren, "Fourth of July Myths," WMQ, 3d ser., II (1945), 242-8.

Notes of Proceedings
in the Continental Congress

[7 June to 1 August 1776]

Friday June 7. 1776. the Delegates from Virginia moved in obedience to instructions from their constituents that the Congress should declare that these United colonies are & of right ought to be free & independant states, that they are absolved from all allegiance[1] to the British crown, and that all political connection between them and the state of Great Britain is & ought to be totally dissolved; that measures should be immediately taken for procuring the assistance of foreign powers, and a Confederation be formed to bind the colonies more closely together.

The house being obliged to attend at that time to some other business, the ⟨resolution⟩ proposition was referred to the next day when the members were ordered to attend punctually at ten o'clock.

Saturday June 8. they ⟨resolution proposed was⟩ ⟨house⟩[2] proceeded to take it into consideration and referred it to a committee of the whole, into which ⟨it⟩ they immediately resolved themselves, and passed that day & Monday the 10th. in debating on the subject.

It was argued by Wilson, Robert R. Livingston, ⟨the two⟩ E.[3] Rutlege⟨s⟩, Dickinson and others.

That tho' they were friends to the measures themselves, and saw the impossibility that we should ever again be united with Gr. Britain, yet they were against adopting them at th⟨at⟩is time:

That the conduct we had formerly observed was wise & proper now, of deferring to take any capital step till the voice of the people drove us into it:

That they were our power, & without them our declarations could not be carried into effect:

That the people of the middle colonies (⟨Pennsylvania⟩ Maryland, ⟨Dela⟩ Delaware, Pennsylva., the Jersies & N. York) were not yet ripe for bidding adieu to British connection but that they were fast ripening & in a short time would join in the general voice of America:

That the resolution entered into by this house on the 15th. of May for suppressing the exercise of all powers derived from the crown, had shewn, by the ferment into which it had thrown these middle colonies, that they had not yet accomodated their minds to a separation from the mother country:

That some of them had expressly forbidden their delegates to consent to such a declaration, and others had given no instructions, & consequently no powers to give such consent:

That if the delegates of any particular colony had no power to declare such colony independant, certain they were the others could not declare it for them; the colonies being as yet perfectly independant of each other:

That the assembly of Pennsylvania was now sitting above stairs, their convention would sit within a few days, the convention of New York was now sitting, & those of the Jersies & Delaware counties would meet on the Monday following & it was probable these bodies would take up the question of Independance & would declare to their delegates the voice of their state:

That if such a declaration should now be agreed to, these delegates must ⟨now⟩ retire & possibly their colonies might secede from the Union:

That such a secession would weaken us more than could be compensated by any foreign alliance:

That in the event of such a division, foreign powers would either refuse to join themselves to our fortunes, or having us so much in their power as that desperate declaration would place us, they would insist on terms proportionably more hard & prejudicial:

That we had little reason to expect an alliance with those to whom alone as yet we had cast our eyes:

That France & Spain had reason to be jealous of that rising power which would one day certainly strip them of all their American possessions:

That it was more likely they should form a connection with the British court, who, if they should find themselves unable otherwise to extricate themselves from their difficulties, would agree to a partition of our territories, restoring Canada to France, & the Floridas to Spain, to accomplish for themselves a recovery of these colonies:

That it would not be long before we should receive certain information of the disposition of the French court, from the agent whom we had sent to Paris for that purpose:

That if this disposition should be favourable, by waiting the event of ⟨another⟩ the present campaign, which we all hoped would be ⟨favourable⟩ succesful, we should have reason to expect an alliance on better terms:

That this would in fact work no delay of any effectual aid from such ally, as, from the advance of the season & distance of our situation, it was impossible we could receive any assistance during this campaign:

That it was prudent to fix among ourselves the terms on which we would form alliance, before we declared we would form one at all events:

And that if these were agreed on & our Declaration of Independance ready by the time our Ambassadour should be prepared[4] to sail, it would be as well, as to go into that Declaration at this day.

On the other side it was urged by J. Adams, Lee, Wythe and others

That no gentleman had argued against the policy or the right of separation from Britain, nor had supposed it possible we should ever renew our connection: that they had only opposed it's being now declared:

That the question was not whether, by a declaration of independance, we should make ourselves what we are not; but whether we should declare a fact which already exists:

That as to the people or parliament of England, we had alwais been independant of them, their restraints on our trade deriving efficacy from our acquiescence only & not from any rights they possessed of imposing them, & that so far our connection had been federal only, & was now dissolved by the commencement of hostilities:

That as to the king, we had been bound to him by allegiance, but that this bond was now dissolved by his assent to the late act of parliament, by which he declares us out of his protection, and by his levying war on us, a fact which had long ago proved us out of his protection; it being a certain position in law that allegiance & protection are reciprocal, the one ceasing when the other is withdrawn:

That James the IId. never declared the people of England out of his protection yet his actions proved it & the parliament declared it:

No delegates then can be denied, or ever want, a power of declaring an existent truth:

That the delegates from the Delaware counties having declared their constituents ready to join, there are only two colonies Pennsylvania & Maryland whose delegates are absolutely tied up, and that these had by their instructions only reserved a right of confirming or rejecting the measure:

That the instructions from Pennsylvania might be accounted for from the times in which they were drawn, near a twelvemonth ago, since which the face of affairs has totally changed:

That ⟨sin⟩ within that time it had become apparent that Britain was determined to accept nothing less than a carte blanche, and that the king's answer to the Lord Mayor Aldermen & common council of London, which had come to hand four days ago, must have satisfied every one of this point:

That the people wait for us to lead the way ⟨in this step⟩:

That *they* are in favour of the measure, tho' the instructions given by some of their *representatives* are not:

That the voice of the representatives is not alwais consonant ⟨to⟩ with the voice of the people, and that this is remarkeably the case in these[5] middle colonies:

That the effect of the resolution of the 15th. of May has proved this, which, raising the murmurs of some in the colonies of Pennsylvania & Maryland, called forth the opposing voice of the freer part of the people, & proved them to be the majority, even in these colonies: ·

That the backwardness of these two colonies might be ascribed partly to the influence of proprietary power & connections, & partly to their having not yet been attacked by the enemy:

That these causes were not likely to be soon removed, as there seemed no probability that the enemy would make either of these the seat of this summer's war:

That it would be vain to wait either weeks or months for perfect unanimity, since it was impossible that all men should ever become of one sentiment on any question:

That the conduct of some colonies from the beginning of this contest, had given reason to suspect it was their settled policy to keep in the rear of the confederacy, that their particular prospect might be better even in the worst event:

That therefore it was necessary for those colonies who had thrown themselves forward & hazarded all from the beginning, to come forward now also, and put all again to their own hazard:

That the history of the Dutch revolution, of whom three states only confederated at first proved that a secession of some colonies would not be so dangerous as some apprehended:

That a declaration of Independance alone could render it consistent with European delicacy for European powers to treat with us, or even to receive an Ambassador from us:

That till this they would not receive our vessels into their ports, nor acknowlege the adjudications of our courts of Admiralty to be legitimate, in cases of capture of British vessels:

That tho' France & Spain may be jealous of our rising power, they must think it will be much more formidable with the addition of Great Britain; and will therefore see it their interest to prevent a coalition; but should they refuse, we shall be but where we are; whereas without trying we shall never know whether they will aid us or not:

That the present campaign may be unsuccessful, & therefore we had better propose an alliance while our affairs wear a hopeful aspect:

That to wait the event of this campaign will certainly work delay, because during this summer France may assist us effectually by cutting off those supplies of provisions from England & Ireland on which the enemy's armies here are to depend; or by setting in motion the great power they have collected in the West Indies, & calling our enemy to the defence of the possessions they have there:

That it would be idle to lose time in settling the terms of alliance, till we had first determined we would enter into alliance:

That it is necessary to lose no time in opening a trade for our people, who will want clothes, and will want money too for the paiment of taxes:

And that the only misfortune is that we did not enter into alliance with France six months sooner, as besides opening their ports for the vent of our last year's produce, they might have marched an army into Germany and prevented the petty princes there from selling their unhappy subjects to subdue us.

It appearing in the course of these debates that the colonies of N. York, New Jersey, Pennsylvania, Delaware ⟨&⟩ Maryland ⟨*had not yet advanced to*⟩ & South Carolina[6] were not yet matured for falling ⟨*off*⟩ from the parent stem, but that they were fast advancing to that state, it was thought most prudent to wait a while for them, and to postpone the final decision to July 1. but that this might occasion as little delay as possible, a committee was appointed to prepare a declaration of independance. the Commee. were J. Adams, Dr. Franklin, Roger Sherman, Robert R. Livingston & myself. committees were also appointed at the same time to prepare a plan of confederation for the colonies, and to state the terms proper to be proposed for foreign alliance. the committee for drawing the declaration of Independence desired me to ⟨*prepare*⟩ do it. ⟨*I did so*⟩ it was accordingly done and being approved by them, I reported it to the house on Friday the 28th. of June when it was read and   June 28.[7]

July 1. ordered to lie on the table. on Monday the 1st. of July the house resolved itself into a commee. of the whole & resumed the consideration of the original motion made by the delegates of Virginia, which being again debated through the day, was carried in the affirmative by the votes of N. Hampshire, Connecticut, Massachusets, Rhode island, N. Jersey, Maryland, Virginia, N. Carolina, & Georgia. S. Carolina and Pennsylvania voted against it. Delaware having but two members present, they were divided: the delegates for New York declared they were for it themselves, & were assured their constituents were for it, but that their instructions having been drawn near a twelvemonth before, when reconciliation was still the general object, they were enjoined by them to do nothing which should impede that object. they therefore thought themselves not justifiable in voting on either side, and asked leave to withdraw from the question, which ⟨they had⟩ was given them. the Commee. rose & reported their resolution to the house. Mr.[8] Rutlege of S. Carolina then ⟨desired⟩ requested the determination might be put off to the next day, as he beleived his collegues, tho' they disapproved of the resolution, would then join in it for the sake of unanimity. ⟨this was done⟩ the ultimate question whether the house would agree to the resolution of the committee was accordingly

July 2. postponed to the next day, when it was again moved and[9] S. Carolina concurred in voting for it. in the mean time a third member had come post from the Delaware counties and turned the vote of that colony in favour of the resolution. members of a different sentiment attending that morning from Pennsylvania also, their vote was changed, so that the whole 12. colonies, who were authorized to

*July 9. vote at all, gave their voices for it; and within a few days[10] the convention of N. York approved of it ⟨by their votes to⟩ and thus supplied[11] the void occasioned by the withdrawing of their delegates from the vote.

July 2. Congress proceeded the same day to consider the declaration of Independance, which had been reported & laid on the table the Friday preceding, and on Monday referred to a commee. of the whole.[12] the pusillanimous idea that we had friends in England worth keeping terms with, still haunted the minds of many. for this reason those passages which conveyed censures on the people of England were struck out, lest they should give them offence. the clause too, reprobating the enslaving the inhabitants of Africa, was struck out in complaisance to[13] South Carolina & Georgia, who had never attempted to restrain the importation of slaves, and who on the contrary still wished to continue it. our Northern brethren also

I believe felt a little tender ⟨on that⟩ under those censures; for tho'
their people have very few slaves themselves yet they had been
pretty considerable carriers of them to others. the debates having
taken up the greater parts of the 2d. 3d. & 4th. days of July were, July 3. 4.
in the evening of the last closed. the declaration was reported by
the commee., agreed to by the house, and signed by every member
present[14] except Mr. Dickinson. As the sentiments of men are
known not only by what they receive, but what they reject also, I
will state the form of the[15] declaration as originally reported ⟨is here
subjoined⟩. the parts ⟨omitted and⟩ struck out by Congress ⟨are⟩
shall be distinguished by a black line drawn under them;[16] & those
inserted ⟨are⟩ by them shall be placed in the margin or in a concurrent column⟨s⟩.

A Declaration by the representatives of the United states of
America, in General Congress assembled
When in the course of human events it becomes necessary for
one people to dissolve the political bands which have connected
them with another, and to assume among the powers of the earth
the separate & equal station to which the laws of nature and of
nature's god entitle them, a decent respect to the opinions of mankind requires that they should declare the causes which impel them
to the separation.
We hold these truths to be self evident: that all men are created
equal; that they are endowed by their creator with ∧ inherent and   ∧certain
inalienable rights; that among these are life, liberty & the pursuit
of happiness: that to secure these rights, governments are instituted among men, deriving their just powers from the consent of
the governed; that whenever any form of government becomes
destructive of these ends, it is the right of the people to alter or to
abolish it, & to institute new government, laying it's foundation on
such principles, & organising it's powers in such form, as to them
shall seem most likely to effect their safety & happiness. prudence
indeed will dictate that governments long established should not be
changed for light & transient causes; and accordingly all experience
hath shewn that mankind are more disposed to suffer while evils
are sufferable than to right themselves by abolishing the forms to
which they are accustomed. but when a long train of abuses &
usurpations [begun at a distinguished period and] pursuing invariably the same object, evinces a design to reduce them under absolute despotism it is their right, it is their duty to throw off such

government, & to provide new guards for their future security. such has been the patient sufferance of these colonies; & such is now ∧ alter the necessity which constrains them to ∧ [expunge] their former systems of government. the history of the present king of Great ∧ repeated Britain is a history of ∧ [unremitting] injuries & usurpations, [among which appears no solitary fact to contradict the uniform ∧ all having tenor of the rest but all have] ∧ in direct object the establishment of an absolute tyranny over these states. to prove this let facts be submitted to a candid world [for the truth of which we pledge a faith yet unsullied by falsehood.]

he has refused his assent to laws the most wholsome & necessary for the public good.

he has forbidden his governors to pass laws of immediate & pressing importance, unless suspended in their operation till his assent should be obtained; & when so suspended, he has utterly neglected to attend to them.

he has refused to pass other laws for the accomodation of large districts of people, unless those people would relinquish the right of representation in the legislature, a right inestimable to them, & formidable to tyrants only.

he has called together legislative bodies at places unusual, uncomfortable, and distant from the depository of their public records, for the sole purpose of fatiguing them into compliance with his measures.

he has dissolved representative houses repeatedly [& continually] for opposing with manly firmness his invasions on the rights of the people.

he has refused for a long time after such dissolutions to cause others to be elected, whereby the legislative powers, incapable of annihilation, have returned to the people at large for their exercise, the state remaining in the mean time exposed to all the dangers of invasion from without & convulsions within.

he has endeavored to prevent the population of these states; for that purpose obstructing the laws for naturalization of foreigners, refusing to pass others to encourage their migrations hither, & raising the conditions of new appropriations of lands.

∧ obstructed he has ∧ [suffered] the administration of justice [totally to cease ∧ by in some of these states] ∧ refusing his assent to laws for establishing judiciary powers.

he has made [our] judges dependant on his will alone, for the tenure of their offices, & the amount & paiment of their salaries.

he has erected a multitude of new offices [by a self assumed power] and sent hither swarms of new officers to harrass our people and eat out their substance.

he has kept among us in times of peace standing armies [and ships of war] without the consent of our legislatures.

he has affected to render the military independant of, & superior to the civil power.

he has combined with others to subject us to a jurisdiction foreign to our constitutions & unacknoleged by our laws, giving his assent to their acts of pretended legislation for quartering large bodies of armed troops among us; for protecting them by a mock-trial from punishment for any murders which they should commit on the inhabitants of these states; for cutting off our trade with all parts of the world; for imposing taxes on us without our consent; for depriving us ∧ of the benefits of trial by jury; for transporting us beyond seas to be tried for pretended offences; for abolishing the free system of English laws in a neighboring province, establishing therein an arbitrary government, and enlarging it's boundaries, so as to render it at once an example and fit instrument for introducing the same absolute rule into these ∧ [states]; for taking away our charters, abolishing our most valuable laws, and altering fundamentally the forms of our governments; for suspending our own legislatures, & declaring themselves invested with power to legislate for us in all cases whatsoever.   ∧ in many cases   ∧ colonies

he has abdicated government here ∧ [withdrawing his governors, and declaring us out of his allegiance & protection]   ∧ by declaring us out of his protection & waging war against us.

he has plundered our seas, ravaged our coasts, burnt our towns, & destroyed the lives of our people.

he is at this time transporting large armies of[17] foreign mercenaries to compleat the works of death, desolation & tyranny already begun with circumstances of cruelty and perfidy ∧ unworthy the head of a civilized nation.   ∧ scarcely paralleled in the most barbarous ages, & totally

he has constrained our fellow citizens taken captive on the high seas to bear arms against their country, to become the executioners of their friends & brethren, or to fall themselves by their hands.

he has ∧ endeavored to bring on the inhabitants of our frontiers the merciless Indian savages, whose known rule of warfare is an undistinguished destruction of all ages, sexes, & conditions [of existence.]   ∧ excited domestic insurrections amongst us, & has

[he has incited treasonable insurrections of our fellow-citizens, with the allurements of forfeiture & confiscation of our property.

he has waged cruel war against human nature itself, violating it's most sacred rights of life and liberty in the persons of a distant people who never offended him, captivating & carrying them into slavery in another hemisphere or to incur miserable death in their transportation thither. this piratical warfare, the opprobrium of *infidel* powers, is the warfare of the *Christian* king of Great Britain. determined to keep open a market where *Men* should be bought & sold, he has prostituted his negative for suppressing every legislative attempt to prohibit or to restrain this execrable commerce. and that this assemblage of horrors might want no fact of distinguished die, he is now exciting those very people to rise in arms among us, and to purchase that liberty of which he has deprived them, by murdering the people on whom he also obtruded them: thus paying off former crimes committed against the *Liberties* of one people, with crimes which he urges them to commit against the *lives* of another.]

In every stage of these oppressions we have petitioned for redress in the most humble terms: our repeated petitions have been answered only by repeated injuries. a prince whose character is thus marked by every act which may define a tyrant is unfit to be the ruler of a ‸ people [who mean to be free. future ages will scarcely ‸free believe that the hardiness of one man adventured, within the short compass of twelve years only, to lay a foundation so broad & so undisguised for tyranny over a people fostered & fixed in principles of freedom.]

Nor have we been wanting in attentions to our British brethren. we have warned them from time to time of attempts by their legis-
‸an un-
warrantable lature to extend ‸ [a] jurisdiction over ‸ [these our states.] we have
‸us reminded them of the circumstances of our emigration & settlement here, [no one of which could warrant so strange a pretension: that these were effected at the expence of our own blood & treasure, unassisted by the wealth or the strength of Great Britain: that in constituting indeed our several forms of government, we had adopted one common king, thereby laying a foundation for perpetual league & amity with them: but that submission to their
‸have parliament was no part of our constitution, nor ever in idea, if
‸and we history may be credited: and,] we ‸ appealed to their native justice
have conjured them and magnanimity ‸ [as well as to] the ties of our common kindred
by to disavow these usurpations which ‸ [were likely to] interrupt our
‸would connection and correspondence. they too have been deaf to the
inevitably voice of justice & of consanguinity, [and when occasions have been given them, by the regular course of their laws, of removing from their councils the disturbers of our harmony, they have, by their free election, re-established them in power. at this very time too they are permitting their chief magistrate to send over not only

souldiers of our common blood, but Scotch &[18] foreign mercenaries to invade & destroy us. these facts have given the last stab to agonizing affection, and manly spirit bids us to renounce for ever these unfeeling brethren. we must endeavor to forget our former love for them, and to hold them as we hold the rest of mankind enemies in war, in peace friends. we might have been a free and a great people together; but a communication of grandeur & of freedom it seems is below their dignity. be it so, since they will have it. the road to happiness & to glory is open to us too. we will tread[19] it apart from them, and]ʌ acquiesce in the necessity which denounces our [eternal] separation ʌ !

ʌwe must
therefore

ʌand hold
them as we
hold the rest
of mankind,
enemies in
war, in peace
friends.

We therefore the representatives of the United states of America in General Congress assembled do in the name, & by the authority of the good people of these [states reject & renounce all allegiance & subjection to the kings of Great Britain & all others who may hereafter claim by, through or under them: we utterly dissolve all political connection which may heretofore have subsisted between us & the people or parliament of Great Britain: & finally we do assert & declare these colonies to be free & independant states,] & that as free & independant states, they have full power to levy war, conclude peace, contract alliances, establish commerce, & to do all other acts & things which independant states may of right do. and for the support of this declaration we mutually pledge to each other our lives, our fortunes & our sacred honour.

We therefore the representatives of the United states of America in General Congress assembled, appealing to the supreme judge of the world for the rectitude of our intentions, do in the name, & by the authority of the good people of these colonies, solemnly publish & declare that these United colonies are & of right ought to be free & independant states; that they are absolved from all allegiance to the British crown, and that all political connection between them & the state of Great Britain is, & ought to be, totally dissolved; & that as free & independant states they have full power to levy war, conclude peace, contract alliances, establish commerce & to do all other acts & things which independant states may of right do.
and for the support of this declaration, with a firm reliance on the protection of divine providence we mutually pledge to each other our lives, our fortunes & our sacred honour.[20]

On Friday July 12. the Committee appointed to draw the articles of confederation reported them and on the 22d. the house resolved themselves into a committee to take them into consideration. on the 30th. and 31st. of that month & 1st. of the ensuing, those articles were debated which determined the ⟨*manner of voting in Congress, & that of fixing the*⟩[21] proportion or quota⟨*s*⟩ of money which each state should furnish to the common treasury, and the manner of voting in Congress. The first of these articles was expressed in the original draught in these words. '*Art.* XI. All charges of war & all other expences that shall be incurred for the common defence, or general welfare, and allowed by the United states assembled, shall be defrayed out of a common treasury, which shall be supplied by the several colonies in proportion to the number of inhabitants of every age, sex & quality, except Indians not paying taxes, in each colony, a true account of which, distinguishing the white inhabitants, shall be triennially taken & transmitted to the assembly of the United states.'

Mr. Chase moved that the quotas should be fixed, not by the number of inhabitants of every condition, but by that of the 'white inhabitants.' He admitted that taxation should be alwais in proportion to property; that this was in theory the true rule, but that from a variety of difficulties it was a rule which could never be adopted in practice. ⟨*that therefore it*⟩ the value of the property in every state could never be estimated justly & equally. Some other ⟨*barometer for*⟩ measur⟨*ing*⟩e for the wealth of the state must therefore be devised, some ⟨*measure of wealth must be*⟩ standard referred to which would be more simple. he considered the number of inhabitants as a tolerably good criterion of property, and that this[22] might alwais be obtained. ⟨*yet numbers simply would not*⟩ he therefore thought it the best mode which we could adopt, with ⟨*some*⟩ one exception⟨*s*⟩ only. he observed that negroes are property, and as such cannot be distinguished from the lands or personalties held in those states where there are few slaves. that the surplus of profit which a Northern farmer is able to lay by, he invests in ⟨*lands*⟩ cattle, horses &c. whereas a Southern farmer lays out that same surplus in slaves. there is no more reason therefore for taxing the Southern states on the farmer's head, & on his slave's head, than the Northern ones on their farmer's heads & the heads of their cattle. that the method proposed would therefore tax the Southern states according to their numbers & their wealth conjunctly, while the Northern would be taxed on numbers only: ⟨*and*⟩ that Negroes in fact should not be considered as members of the state more than cattle & that they have no more interest in it.

Mr. John Adams observed that the numbers of people were taken by this article as an index of the wealth of the state & not as subjects of taxation. that as to this matter it was of no consequence by what name you called your people, whether by that of freemen or of slaves. that in some countries the labouring poor were called freemen, in others they were called slaves; but that the difference as to the state was imaginary only. what matters it whether a landlord employing ten labourers in his farm, gives them annually as much money as will buy them the necessaries of life, or gives them those necessaries at short hand. the ten labourers add as much wealth annually to the state, increase it's exports as much in the one case as the other. certainly 500 freemen produce no more profits, no greater surplus for the paiment of taxes than 500 slaves. therefore the state in which are the labourers called freemen should be taxed no more than that in which are those called slaves. suppose by any extraordinary operation ⟨of law or⟩ of nature or of law one half the labourers of a state could in the course of one night be transformed into slaves: would the state be made the poorer or the less able to pay taxes?[23] that the condition of the labouring poor in most countries, that of the fishermen particularly of the Northern states is as ⟨painful⟩ abject as that of slaves. it is the number of labourers which produce the surplus for taxation, and numbers therefore indiscriminately are the fair index of wealth. that it is the use of the word 'property' here, & it's application to some of the people of the state, which produces the fallacy. how does the Southern farmer procure slaves? either by importation or by purchase from his neighbor. if he imports a slave, he adds one to the number of labourers in his country, and proportionably to it's profits & abilities to pay taxes. if he buys from his neighbor, it is only a transfer of a labourer from one farm to another, which does not change the annual produce of the state, & therefore should not change it's tax. that if a Northern farmer works ten labourers on his farm, he can, it is true, invest the surplus of ten men's labour in cattle: but so may the Southern farmer working ten slaves. that a state of 100,000 freemen can maintain no more cattle than one of 100,000 slaves. therefore they have no more of that kind of property. that a slave may indeed from the custom of speech be more properly called the wealth of his master, than the free labourer might be called the wealth of his employer: but ⟨both⟩ as to the state both were equally it's wealth, and should therefore equally add to the quota of it's tax.

Mr. Harrison proposed a compromise, that two slaves should be counted as one freeman. he affirmed that slaves did not do so much work as freemen, and doubted if two effected more than one. that this was proved by the price of labor, the hire of a labourer in the Southern colonies being from 8. to £12, while in the Northern it was generally £24.[24]

Mr. Wilson said that if this amendment should take place the Southern colonies would have all the benefit⟨s⟩ of slaves, whilst the Northern ones would bear the burthen⟨s⟩. that slaves increase the profits of a state, which the Southern states mean to take to themselves; that they also increase the burthen of defence, which would of course fall so much the heavier on the Northern. that slaves occupy the places of freemen and eat their food. dismiss your slaves & freemen will take their places. it is our duty to lay every discouragement on the importation of slaves; but this amendment would ⟨be⟩ giv⟨ing⟩e the *jus trium liberorum* to him who would import ⟨them⟩ slaves. that other kinds of property were pretty equally distributed thro' all the colonies: there were as many cattle, horses, & sheep in the North as the South, & South as the North: but not so as to slaves. that experience has shewn that those colonies have been alwais able to pay most which have the most ⟨males⟩ inhabitants, whether they be black or white. and the practice of the Southern colonies has alwais been to make every farmer pay poll taxes upon all his labourers whether they be black or white. he acknoleges indeed that freemen work the most; but they consume the most also. they do not produce a greater surplus for taxation. the slave is neither fed nor clothed so expensively as a freeman. again white women are exempted from labour generally, which negro women are not. in this then the Southern states have an advantage as the article now stands. it has sometimes been said that slavery is necessary because the commodities they raise would be too dear for market if cultivated by freemen; but now it is said that the labor of the slave is the dearest.

Mr. Payne ⟨desired⟩ urged the original resolution of Congress, to proportion the quotas of the states to the number of souls.[23]

Dr. Witherspoon was of opinion that the value of lands & houses was the best estimate of the wealth of a nation, and that it was practicable to obtain such a valuation. this is the true barometer of wealth. the one now proposed is imperfect in itself, and unequal between the states. it has been objected that negroes eat the food of freemen

& therefore should be taxed. horses also eat the food of freemen; therefore they also should be taxed. it has been said too that in ⟨making⟩ carrying slaves ⟨enter⟩ into the estimate of the taxes the state is to pay, we do no more than those states themselves do, who alwais ⟨m⟩take slaves ⟨enter⟩ into the estimate of the taxes the individual is to pay. but the cases are not parallel. in the Southern colonies slaves pervade the whole colony; but they do not pervade the whole continent. that as to the original resolution of Congress to proportion the quotas according to the souls,[25] it was temporary only, & related to the monies heretofore emitted: whereas we are now entering into a new compact and therefore stand on original ground.

Aug. 1. the question being put the amendment proposed was rejected by the votes of N. Hampshire, Massachusets, Rhodeisland, Connecticut, N. York, N. Jersey, & Pennsylvania, against those of Delaware, Maryland, Virginia, North & South Carolina. Georgia was divided.

The other article was in these words. 'Art. XVII. In determining questions each colony shall have one vote.'

July 30. 31. Aug. 1. present 41. members. Mr. Chase observed that this article was the most likely to divide us of any one proposed in the draught then under consideration. that the larger colonies had threatened they would not confederate at all if their weight in congress should not be equal to the numbers of people they added to the confederacy; while the smaller ones declared against an union if they did not retain an equal vote for the protection of their rights. that it was of the utmost consequence to bring the parties together, as should we sever from each other, either no foreign power will ally with us at all, or ⟨that⟩ the different states ⟨would⟩ will form different alliances, and thus increase the horrors of those scenes of civil war and bloodshed which in such a state of separation & independance would render us a miserable people. that our importance, our interests, our peace required that we should confederate, and that mutual sacrifices should be made to effect a compromise of this difficult question. he was of opinion the smaller colonies would lose their rights, if they were not in some instances allowed an ⟨single⟩[26] equal vote; and therefore that a discrimination should take place among the questions which would come before Congress. ⟨he therefore proposed⟩ that the smaller states should be secured in all questions concerning life or liberty & the greater ones in all respecting property. he therefore proposed that in ⟨all⟩ votes relating to money, the voice of each colony should be proportioned to the number of it's inhabitants.

Dr. Franklin ⟨*seconded the proposition*⟩ thought that the votes should be so proportioned in all cases. he took notice that the Delaware counties had bound up their Delegates to disagree to this article. he thought it a very extraordinary language to be held by any state, that they would not confederate with us unless we would let them dispose of our money. certainly if we vote equally we ought to pay equally: but the smaller states will hardly purchase the privilege at this price. that had he lived in a state where the representation, originally equal, had become unequal by time & accident he might have submitted rather than disturb government: but that we should be very wrong to set out in this practice when it is in our power to establish what is right. that at the time of the Union between England and Scotland the latter had made the objection which the smaller states now do. but experience had ⟨*shewn*⟩ proved that no unfairness had ever been shewn them. that their advocates had prognosticated that it would again happen as in times of old that the whale would swallow Jonas, but he thought the prediction reversed in event and that Jonas had swallowed the whale, for the Scotch had in fact got possession of the government and gave laws to the English. he reprobated the original agreement of Congress to vote by colonies, and therefore was for their voting in all cases according to the number of taxables ⟨, *so far going beyond Mr. Chase's proposition*⟩.

Dr. Witherspoon opposed every alteration of the article. all men admit that a confederacy is necessary. should the idea get abroad that there is likely to be no union among us, it will damp the minds of the people, diminish the glory of our struggle, & lessen it's importance, because it will open to our view future prospects of war & dissension among ourselves. ⟨*that*⟩ if an equal vote be refused, the smaller states will become vassals to the larger; & all experience has shewn that the vassals & subjects of free states ⟨*were*⟩ are the ⟨*greatest of all slaves*⟩ most enslaved. he instanced the Helots of Sparta & the provinces of Rome. he observed that foreign powers discovering this blemish would make it a handle for disengaging the smaller states from so unequal a confederacy. that the colonies should in fact be considered as individuals; and that as such in all disputes they should have an equal vote. that they are now collected as individuals making a bargain with each other, & of course had a right to vote as individuals.[23] that ⟨*thus*⟩ in the East India company they voted by persons, & not by their proportion of stock.

that the Belgic confederacy voted by provinces. that in questions of war the smaller states were as much interested as the larger, & therefore should vote equally; and indeed that the larger states were more likely to bring ⟨on⟩ war on the ⟨whole⟩ confederacy, in proportion as their frontier was more extensive ⟨,and⟩. he admitted that equality of representation was an excellent principle, but then it must be of things which are co-ordinate; that is, of things similar & of the same nature: that nothing relating to individuals could ever come before Congress; nothing but what would respect colonies. he distinguished between an incorporating & a federal union. the union of England was an incorporating one; yet Scotland had suffered by that union: for that[27] it's inhabitants were drawn from it by the hopes of places & employments. nor was it an instance of equality of representation; because while Scotland was allowed nearly a thirteenth of representation, they were to pay only one fortieth of the land tax. he expressed his hopes that in the present enlightened state of men's minds we might expect a lasting confederacy, if it was founded on fair principles.

John Adams advocated the voting in proportion to numbers. he said that we stand here as the representatives of the people. that in some states the people are many, in others they are few; that therefore their vote here should be proportioned to the numbers from whom it comes. reason, justice, & equity never had weight enough on the face of the earth to govern the councils of men. it is interest alone which does it, and it is interest alone which can be trusted. that therefore the interests within doors should be the mathematical representatives of the interests without doors. ⟨if A has £50. B⟩ that the individuality of the colonies is a mere sound. does the individuality of a colony increase it's wealth or numbers? if it does; pay equally. if it does not add weight in the scale of the confederacy, it cannot add to their rights, nor weight in argument. A. has £50. B. £500. C. £1000 in partnership. is it just they should equally dispose of the monies of the partnership? it has been said we are independant individuals making a bargain together. the question is not what we are now, but what we ought to be when our bargain shall be made. the confederacy is to make us one individual only; it is to form us, like separate parcels of metal, into one common mass. we shall no longer retain our separate individuality, but become a single individual as to all questions submitted to the Confederacy. therefore all those reasons which prove the justice & expediency of equal representation in other assemblies, hold good here. it has been objected that a proportional vote will endanger the smaller states. we answer that an equal vote will endanger the larger. Virginia, Pennsylvania, & Massachusets are the three greater colonies. consider their distance, their difference of produce, of interests, & of manners, & it is apparent they can never have an interest or inclination to combine for the oppression of the smaller. that the smaller will naturally divide on all questions with the larger. Rhodeisld. ⟨will⟩ from ⟨their⟩ it's relation, similarity & intercourse will generally pursue the same objects with Massachusets; Jersey, Delaware & Maryland with Pennsylvania.

Dr. Rush took notice that the decay of the liberties of the Dutch republic proceeded from three causes. 1. the perfect unanimity requisite on all occasions. 2. their obligation to consult their constituents. 3. their voting by provinces. this last destroyed the equality of representation, and the liberties of Great Britain also are sinking from the same defect. that a part of our rights ⟨are⟩ is deposited in the hands of our legislatures. there it was admitted there should be an equality of representation. another part of our rights is deposited in the hands of Congress: why is it not equally necessary there should be an equal representation there? were it possible to collect the whole body of the people together, they would determine the questions submitted to them by their majority. why should not the same majority decide when ⟨collected⟩ voting here by their representatives? the larger colonies are so providentially divided in situation as to render every fear of their combining visionary. their interests are different, & their circumstances dissimilar. it is more probable they will become rivals & leave it in the power of the smaller states to give preponderance to any scale they please. the voting by the number of free inhabitants will have one excellent effect, that of inducing the colonies to discourage slavery & to encourage the increase of their free inhabitants.

Mr. Hopkins observed there were 4 larger, 4 smaller & 4 middlesized colonies. that the 4. largest would contain more than half the inhabitants of the Confederating states, & therefore would govern the others as they should please. that history affords no instance of such a thing as equal representation. the Germanic body votes by states. the Helvetic body does the same; & so does the Belgic confederacy. that too little is known of the antient confederations to say what was their practice.

Mr. Wilson thought that taxation should be in proportion to wealth, but that representation should accord with the number of freemen. that government is a collection or result of the wills of all. that if any government could speak the will of all it would be perfect; and that so far as it departs from this it becomes imperfect. it has been said that Congress is a representation of states; not of individuals. I say that the objects of it's care are all the ⟨representatives⟩ individuals of the states. it is strange that annexing the name of 'State' to ten thousand men, should give them an equal right with forty thousand. this must be the effect of magic, not of reason. as to those matters which are referred to Congress, we are not so many states; we are one large ⟨one⟩ state. we lay aside our individuality whenever we come here. the Germanic body is a burlesque on government: and their practice on any point is a sufficient authority & proof that it is wrong. the greatest imperfection in the constitution of the Belgic confederacy is their voting by provinces. the interest of the whole is constantly sacrificed to that of the small states. the history of the war in the reign of Q. Anne sufficiently proves this. it is asked Shall nine colonies put it into the power of four to govern them as they please? I invert the question and ask Shall ⟨a⟩ two millions of people put it in the power of one million to govern them as they please? it is pretended too that the smaller colonies will be in danger from the greater. speak in honest language & say the minority will be in danger from the majority. and is there an assembly on earth where this danger may not be equally pretended? the truth is that our proceedings will then be consentaneous with the interests of the majority, and so they ought to be. the probability is much greater that the larger states will disagree than that they will combine. I defy the wit of man to invent a possible case ⟨where⟩ or to suggest any one thing on earth which shall be for the interests of Virginia, Pennsylvania & Massachusets, and which will not also be for the interest of the other states.

MS (DLC); 20 numbered pages in TJ's hand. Another MS (DLC); in TJ's hand, consisting of 49 pages; this copy was transmitted to Madison by TJ on 1 June 1783 (but has now been placed with the Jefferson Papers in the Library of Congress) and was probably made on or shortly before that date. In the letter of transmittal TJ wrote: "I send you inclosed the debates in Congress on the subjects of Independance, Voting in Congress, and the Quotas of money to be required from the states. I found on looking that I had taken no others save only in one trifling case. As you were desirous of having a copy of the original of the declaration of Independance I have inserted it at full length distinguishing the alterations it underwent."

This would seem to indicate that the Notes, as originally copied "in form and with correctness," did not contain a text of the Declaration. This is to be doubted (see note 15 below). For convenience the fair copy of Notes made for Madison is referred to below as MFC; its text is printed in JCC, VI, 1087-1106 and in *Madison Papers*, ed. Gilpin, I, 9-39; that part of it containing the Declaration of Independence is reproduced in Boyd, *Declaration of Independence*, 1945, pl. VIII. The original notes or memoranda of debates from which the Notes were written are not known to be extant.

For a discussion of the significance of this document as a whole and of its date and certain other controversial features, see the Editorial Note preceding it. The text of the Declaration of Independence as copied by TJ in the Notes of Proceedings, though printed here in its rightful place, is also considered as Document IV in the sequence of Declaration of Independence documents, below; see the Editorial Notes on that sequence.

1 MFC reads "obedience."

2 TJ added "y" to "the" after making the two deletions; Hazelton reads "howev" for "house," thus confusing the manner of making the deletion. TJ first struck out "resolution proposed was"; then added "house" on the same line (proving incidentally that this is the draft of the Notes put "in form and with correctness"); then struck out "house" and added "y" to "the," causing the sentence to read as it was subsequently copied in the Madison copy.

3 "E" is interlined.

4 MFC reads "ready."

5 TJ originally wrote "the."

6 MFC reads "N. York, N. Jersey, Pennsylvania, Delaware & Maryland were not yet matured. . ."; the deletion of "&" before "Maryland" and the interlineation of "& South Carolina" must therefore have been made after 1783.

7 The marginal dates are not in MFC. They appear to have been added much later.

8 "Edward" is interlined; it does not appear in MFC and was obviously added much later.

9 The words "it was again moved and" are interlined.

10 An asterisk is inserted at this point, referring to the date in the margin, obviously an addition made at a later date.

11 The words "and thus" are interlined. The word "supplied" was originally written "supply" and overwritten after the deletion.

12 The words after "preceding" are interlined.

13 The word "to" was struck out; "with" interlined and then struck out; and then "to" restored.

14 The word "present" is interlined; it is not in MFC nor in TJ's letter to the Editor of the *Journal de Paris* in 1787; it is, however, in the letter to Samuel A. Wells, 12 May 1819, and is there also interlined. Hence it is almost certain that the interlining of "present" in the Notes took place at the time of writing the letter to Wells.

15 The preceding part of this sentence is written in a minuscule hand and inter-lined. The alterations in this paragraph are significant. The word "declaration" was written over an erasure, clearly being done after the preceding interlineation. The erasure was of the words "it's form." These changes present strong presumptive evidence that they were made at the time TJ copied off MFC. If so, then the passage as originally written must have read: ". . . signed by every member except Mr. Dickinson. it's form as originally reported is here subjoined." This, together with the character of the Notes and the orderly sequence of the first seven pages of debates, the Declaration, and the subsequent debates on the Articles of Confederation, is conclusive evidence that the text of the Declaration was from the beginning an integral part of the Notes and not "inserted" as Jefferson said in his letter to Madison of 1 June 1783.

16 All but the first two were also enclosed by TJ in square brackets; in MFC these two are bracketed. The first of these (the word "General" in the title) is one of three alterations apparently contemplated during the debates of 2-4 July that were either not made or were eliminated by larger excisions which included them (Boyd, *Declaration of Independence*, 1945, p. 34-5). For the other two proposed alterations, see notes 17, 18, and 19 below.

17 At this point in TJ's "Rough Draught," but in no other copy made by him, the words "Scotch and other" were interlined. This was obviously an alteration proposed in Congress after the change discussed in note 18 below had been made (same, p. 35).

18 In the copies of the Declaration made by TJ for R. H. Lee and George Wythe, but in no other copy, the words "Scotch and" were bracketed for deletion. Probably after the whole passage had been struck out by Congress, the insertion of the words "Scotch and other" in an earlier passage was proposed but not adopted (same, p. 35; see note 17 above).

19 MFC also reads "tread." In the Wythe and Lee copies, as in the "Rough Draught" originally, the text read "climb." This was struck out in the "Rough Draught" and "tread" interlined, a change no doubt proposed in Congress before the whole passage was eliminated (same, p. 35).

20 At this point TJ inserted on a separate slip his controversial statement on

the signing of the Declaration which is quoted and discussed in the Editorial Note above.

21 The words "in Congress" were interlined and then struck out with the remainder of the passage.

22 Originally written "these."

23 This sentence is written in a minuscule hand and interlined.

24 This paragraph is written in the margin.

25 The words "to proportion the quotas

according to the souls" are not in MFC. TJ may have overlooked the passage or, what is more probable, he may have decided it was not necessary to copy it; it is certain, however, that the words were in the Notes when MFC was made, for they are not a correction, addition, or interlineation.

26 The word "a" was changed to "an" after the deletion was made.

27 MFC omits "that."

The Virginia Constitution

I. FIRST DRAFT BY JEFFERSON

II. SECOND DRAFT BY JEFFERSON

III. THIRD DRAFT BY JEFFERSON

IV. THE PLAN OF GOVERNMENT AS ORIGINALLY DRAWN
BY GEORGE MASON

V. THE MASON PLAN AS REVISED BY THE COMMITTEE

VI. THE DRAFT REPORTED BY THE COMMITTEE (AMENDMENTS
THERETO OFFERED IN CONVENTION)

VII. THE CONSTITUTION AS ADOPTED BY THE CONVENTION

[June 1776]

EDITORIAL NOTE

THE three drafts of Jefferson's proposed bill outlining the "fundamental constitutions of Virginia," here brought together for the first time, are so important in the light they cast upon Jefferson's early ideas of government and upon the drafting of the Declaration of Independence that they require special comment and a particular form of presentation. Each of the three drafts printed below differs from the others. Only a meticulous collation of the numerous deletions, additions, variations, interlineations, and substitutions will establish the basis for a full understanding of the nature of the documents and of Jefferson's constitutional thinking at this period. Each of the drafts is accompanied by detailed notes, descriptive and textual, but a general commentary on the chronology, relationships, and nature of these documents and their background is required.

This necessity is reinforced by the apparent fact that Jefferson regarded the drafting of fundamental plans or constitutions as "the whole object" at this period. All of his other major state papers up to this point—the *Summary View*, the Declaration of the Causes and Necessity for Taking Up Arms, even the Declaration of Independence—were topical or forensic in nature. Though each of these contained statements of his political theories, the drafting of a fundamental law was Jefferson's first effort to make a concrete application of these theories and ideals.

On 10 May 1776, four days before Jefferson arrived in Philadelphia,

Congress adopted John Adams' resolution recommending that the colonies assume all the powers of government. On 15 May the Virginia Convention adopted its famous resolution calling for independence and appointed a committee to draft a plan of government. Jefferson, who had already given much thought to this urgent problem, wrote on 16 May to Thomas Nelson, delicately suggesting that the delegates in Congress be recalled to Virginia to assist in the work of framing a new government, which he described as "the whole object of the present controversy; for should a bad government be instituted for us in future it had been as well to have accepted at first the bad one offered to us from beyond the water without the risk and expence of contest." It is difficult to overestimate the importance of this statement about "the whole object" and its relation to Jefferson's drafting of the proposed constitution. The feeling and purpose expressed here must be the basis for an understanding of Jefferson's legal reforms in Virginia by which he sought to alter the aristocratic structure of society; of his misunderstood administration as governor; of his disappointment over the frame of government adopted by the Convention; of his efforts to reform the constitution of 1776 (see *Notes on the State of Virginia*, Query XIII; his "Fundamental Constitution" of 1783, and "Notes for a Constitution" in 1794). Jefferson, quite properly, always regarded the Constitution of 1776 as merely an act of legislature "subject to be changed by subsequent legislatures, possessing equal powers with themselves" and as an act which should be superseded and "rendered permanent by a power superior to that of the ordinary legislature"; that is, by the sovereign people.

When two of these three drafts were discovered about 1890, an effort was made to show that the constitutional ideas advanced in them were at variance with Jefferson's later views, exhibiting in general a conservative position (W. C. Ford, "Jefferson's Constitution for Virginia," *Nation*, LI [1890], 107; Ford, II, 7-9). This interpretation has been subsequently but only partially refuted (D. R. Anderson, "Jefferson and the Va. Const.," *Amer. Hist. Rev.*, XXI [1915-1916], 750-4; Malone, *Jefferson*, I, 235-40). The documents here drawn up contain, indeed, most if not all of the leading principles to which Jefferson's entire career was dedicated: the people as the source of authority; the protection of "public liberty" and of individual rights against authoritarian control; the widening of suffrage and an equalization of the distribution of representation in the legislative branch; the use of unappropriated lands for the establishment of a society of independent farmers who would hold their lands "in full and absolute dominion of no superior whatever"; the just and equitable treatment of the Indians; the use of the western lands so as to remove friction with neighboring states and promote the cause of nationality; the encouragement of immigration and the lowering of barriers to naturalization; the elevation of the civil over the military authority; the abolition of privilege and prerogative; and so on. Indeed, Jefferson's constitution foreshadowed much of his legislative reforms of 1776-1777: the provision for the regulation of descents went even further than his later bill for abolishing primogeniture—a provision much more radical in the First Draft than in the Second and Third Drafts. The adoption of his constitution would also have eliminated the need for his Bill for Religious Freedom and would have avoided years of discussion and debate on that subject. And the provisions against capital punishment and the denial of the pardoning power anticipated the views expressed in his later Bill for Proportioning Crimes and Punishments.

These fundamental topics form the subject of a notable exchange of letters between Jefferson and Edmund Pendleton, president of the Virginia Convention, between 24 May and 26 Aug. (the last is particularly notable). Therein Jefferson explained clearly what he had in mind in drafting various provisions in his proposed constitution—why he had long favored an allodial system of land tenure, why he proposed an extension of the suffrage, what he intended by his treatment of crimes and punishments, &c. Pendleton, an able and intelligent product of the eighteenth century Enlightenment, could not, however, go all the way with Jefferson. This correspondence is only a fragment—what must have been one of its best examples, Jefferson's letter of 29 July, is missing—but enough remains to show with remarkable clarity how two intelligent, responsible statesmen of Virginia discussed dispassionately the principal issues of their day. Each presented his arguments cogently, each respected the other's integrity and point of view. But their differences serve only to emphasize the strength and extent of Jefferson's early convictions and to explain in large measure some of the events of the ensuing months. Certainly these differences over land tenure help to explain the remarkable vigor of Jefferson's legislative reforms in the autumn of 1776, as they do Pendleton's opposition at that time to Jefferson's attack upon the holding of lands in fee-tail. Bitterly disappointed over the Convention's failure to remold Virginia society in accord with republican principles, Jefferson then set about, as he declared later, to reframe the whole body of law, to achieve by legislation what he had not been able to accomplish in the framing of a constitution.

The text of the Constitution adopted by the Convention is included here in order to provide a basis of comparison with these leading Jeffersonian principles: on the essential questions of extension of the suffrage and equalization of the basis of representation the contrast is greatest. Here the Convention's plan of government tended to support the status quo. But there is another reason for including this Constitution: it is, in part, a Jefferson document and, as the notes below indicate, more of Jefferson's constitution was incorporated in it than he remembered or most historians have discerned. Whereas Jefferson's catalogue of the misdeeds of "George   Guelph" prefaced a constitution that sought to establish a polity where such misdeeds and the authority under which they were committed would be forever abolished, making preamble and text a complementary whole, this catalogue of the results of privilege and prerogative became rather incongruous in a constitution that sought to substitute one kind of privilege and prerogative for another. Yet the Convention did incorporate several other provisions from Jefferson's draft.

Quite aside from these fundamental points, it is necessary to present all of Jefferson's drafts because the first of the three must now assume a stature greater than has hitherto been accorded it. As a result of a minute comparison of the three texts, the First Draft must now be regarded as a single document adapted to two purposes. Its first page, bearing the list of charges against the king, served as the rough draft for that portion of the Third Draft of the Virginia Constitution. Having served this purpose, it was then altered, added to, and its paragraphs numbered in a different order so as to adapt it to a similar purpose in the Declaration of Independence. Even after Jefferson had drawn up the Declaration of Independence and had permitted John Adams to make a copy of it, at least one change was made in both the Declaration and in this first page of the First Draft. To be sure, the similarities between this part of the First Draft and the Declaration had been noted even during Jefferson's lifetime: in 1825 he declared that "both having the same object, of justifying our separation from Great Britain, they used necessarily the same materials of justification: hence their similitude" (TJ to Augustus B. Woodward, 3 Apr. 1825). In the discussions of the drafting of the Declaration of Independence that occurred a few years before his death, Jefferson declared that he had "turned to neither book nor pamphlet while writing" the Declaration and that it was not copied "from any particular and previous writing" (TJ to Madison, 30 Aug. 1823; to Henry Lee, 8 May 1825). Nevertheless, the evidence is conclusive that Jefferson did use the first page of the First Draft of his Virginia Constitution in drawing up the corresponding part of the Declaration. We are now justified in elevating this remarkable document to the status of a part of the composition draft of the Declaration of Independence.

Moreover, there can scarcely be any doubt that the Virginia Resolutions of 15 May provided at least some of the additional charges against the king inserted on page 1 of the First Draft when Jefferson revised it to meet the purposes of the Declaration of Independence. "I expected," Edmund Pendleton wrote to Jefferson on 22 July, "you had in the Preamble to our form of Government, exhausted the Subject of complaint against Geo. 3d. and was at a loss to discover what the Congress would do for one to their Declaration of Independance without copying, but find you have acquitted yourselves very well on that score." The answer is that Jefferson not only copied from the First Draft of his constitution but also, in part, utilized the Resolutions adopted by the Virginia Convention of 15 May (see notes under Declaration of Independence).

It is not enough, however, merely to present the three Jefferson drafts and the text of the Constitution as finally adopted by the Convention. The extent of Jefferson's contribution to that document cannot be fully gauged without an examination of some of the other texts that formed the antecedents of the Virginia Constitution. From the autumn of 1775 down through the final days of the Convention, various leaders in and out of Virginia contributed to the momentous discussion: John Adams, Richard Henry Lee, Meriwether Smith, George Mason, Carter Braxton, Patrick Henry, and others besides Jefferson are among those who wrote or are reputed to have written plans of government that may have been considered by the Convention of 1776. As Edmund Randolph, a member of the Convention, wrote in his MS History of Virginia: "A very large committee was nominated to prepare the proper instruments, and many projects of a bill of rights and constitution discovered the ardor for political notice, rather than a ripeness in political wisdom. That proposed by George Mason swallowed up all the rest, by fixing the grounds and plan, which after great discussion and correction, were finally ratified" (Randolph, "Essay," VMHB, XLIV [1936], 44). This welter of proposed drafts of constitutions, together with remembered statements of political leaders of that day and investigations of historians, makes the question of authorship of the Virginia Constitution a complex and difficult one. K. M. Rowland (*Mason*, I, 250ff.) makes the most extensive claim in support of Randolph's statement that the plan proposed by Mason "swallowed up all the rest." But C. R. Lingley (*Transition in Virginia*, 158-71) presents the best summary of the question of authorship and concludes: "The brevity of the records in regard to the plan has left the authorship of the document in obscurity and so has given rise to a controversy which in most respects is not useful. The truth probably is that Mason's draft was more influential than the others."

The fact is, however, that those documents still in existence, admittedly few in number, have never been precisely analyzed textually and chronologically. An analysis of them, involving a presentation of all of the texts and an examination of their various stages of emendation and amendment, cannot be undertaken here. Nevertheless, in order to fix as exactly as possible the extent of Jefferson's contribution, it is necessary to describe briefly and to attempt to identify chronologically the salient plans other than his that are known to have been used or were available to the Convention. Those that antedated the final Constitution will be referred to in the notes by the designation here given each:

THE ADAMS PLAN. John Adams, who had also advised John Penn of North Carolina and Jonathan Dickinson Sergeant of New Jersey about the framing of constitutions for those states, really drew up two plans for Virginia, the second an amplification of the first.

The first was set down in brief form in a letter to Richard Henry Lee, 15 Nov. 1775 (Adams, *Works*, IV, 185-7).

The second resulted from a conversation between Wythe and Adams in Philadelphia in Jan. 1776. Wythe requested Adams to reduce his ideas to writing, and Adams complied the following day. Wythe communicated the result to his colleague Richard Henry Lee, who asked for and received Adams' permission to publish (same, 191). The printed version was entitled *Thoughts on Government: Applicable to the Present State of the American Colonies. In a Letter from a Gentleman to his Friend*, Philadelphia: Dunlap, 1776 (same, 189-202). At one time, according to C. F. Adams (same, 191), this pamphlet was attributed to Jefferson, but the authorship by Adams is indisputable. It is an elaboration of the plan outlined for Richard Henry Lee in the preceding November. Lee sent copies of *Thoughts on Government* to Patrick Henry, Charles Lee, Robert Carter Nicholas, and perhaps to others (R. H. Lee,

Letters, I, 179, 183, 184) and said that Adams' "plan, with some variation, would in fact be nearly the form we have been used to."

THE GAZETTE PLAN. On 10 May, 1776, shortly after the Convention had assembled, a brief outline of a plan of government for the colony was published in Purdie's *Virginia Gazette*. This may have been written by Richard Henry Lee, who sent a copy of Adams' *Thoughts on Government* to Patrick Henry on 20 Apr. 1776, and added this comment: "The small scheme printed in hand bill I had written before I saw this work of Mr. Adams, and he agrees that the Council of State had better be a distinct body from the Upper House" (Henry, *Henry*, I, 381). The *Gazette* Plan makes the council separate, but in most other respects it follows the Adams Plan closely; indeed, it is probable that Lee's "small scheme" was merely a rephrasing of the plan that Adams had given to him on 15 Nov. 1775, for both are alike in substance and in distinctive phraseology. It was the Adams letter of 15 Nov. that first employed, for each of the provisions, the distinctive beginning: "Let the House choose . . . ," "Let the governor . . . ," &c., a form employed in the *Gazette* Plan and in both the Braxton Plan and the Mason Plan discussed below. It is most likely, as William Wirt Henry suggests, that Richard Henry Lee modified the Adams Plan and that Patrick Henry was responsible for placing this in the *Virginia Gazette* of 10 May (Henry, *Henry*, I, 418-20), though there is evidence, noted below, that Mason used it and may indeed have been responsible for it. No copy of the handbill enclosed in Lee's letter of 20 Apr. has been found. It is important to note that Lee left Philadelphia on 13 June with Wythe in order to take part in the framing of the Constitution. "The desire of being here at the formation of our new Government brought me from Philadelphia. . . . I have been in this City a week [he presumably arrived, as did Wythe, June 23] where I had the pleasure to see our new plan of Government go on well. This day will put a finishing hand to it. 'Tis very much of the democratic kind" (R. H. Lee, *Letters*, I, 203, 207). The last statement may throw some light on Lee's preference for the Adams Plan to that of Jefferson, since the Adams Plan was essentially what the colony had been used to and Jefferson's was a radical departure. It suggests also that Lee may have been responsible for the inclusion of some features of the Adams Plan (see below) among amendments offered after the Committee Plan was submitted to the Convention. At any rate, though not a member of the Convention, Lee unquestionably had influence in and out of doors: "A fortnights stay here," he wrote Samuel Adams on 6 July, "has enabled me to assist my Countrymen in finishing our form of Government" (R. H. Lee, *Letters*, I, 207).

THE BRAXTON PLAN. In the spring of 1776 there appeared in Philadelphia, written in answer to Adams' *Thoughts on Government*, a pamphlet entitled *Address to the Convention of the Colony and Ancient Dominion of Virginia, on the Subject of Government in General, and Recommending a Particular Form to Their Consideration. By a Native of the Colony* (Philadelphia: Dunlap, 1776; Force, *Archives*, 4th ser., VI, 748-54). This has been generally attributed to Carter Braxton. Its point of view was so aristocratic that Patrick Henry declared it "a silly thing . . . an affront and disgrace to this country" (Adams, *Works*, IV, 201-2). Braxton's position is opposed to the republicanism of the Adams Plan and is reflected by the query as to whether, "if the [British] Constitution was brought back to its original state, and its present imperfections remedied, it would not afford more happiness than any other." The *Address to the Convention* was printed in Dixon & Hunter's *Virginia Gazette* of 8 and 15 June. Aside from the fact that it arrived late, its extreme conservatism was enough to prevent its having any influence on the Convention. The Braxton Plan arrived in Williamsburg around 20 May (Adams, *Works*, IV, 201-2; Henry, *Henry*, I, 411, 413). John Adams reported to Patrick Henry that it was "whispered to have been the joint production of one native of Virginia, and two natives of New York" and was "too absurd to be considered twice" (Henry, *Henry*, I, 415). Richard Henry Lee, agreeing with Patrick Henry's appraisal, said: "This Contemptible little Tract, betrays the little Knot or Junto from whence it proceeded" (R. H. Lee, *Letters*, I, 190).

THE MASON PLAN (Document IV below). William Fleming's letter of 22 June to Jefferson sets at rest the question of the extent of George Mason's authorship of the Constitution: "The inclosed printed plan was drawn by Colo. G. Mason and by him laid before the committee." Fleming's letter also seems to establish the fact that this plan was laid before the committee about 8-10 June. Mason, delayed by illness, arrived in Williamsburg on 18 May and was immediately appointed to the committee charged with the duty of drawing up a constitution. It is probable, therefore, that his MS draft (not now known to be extant) was drawn up late in May or early in June. As the notes indicate, he almost certainly made use of the Adams and *Gazette* Plans, but the provisions for a senatorial electoral college and for suffrage qualifications bear strong evidence of being original and the product of Mason's distinguished mind.

THE MASON PLAN AS REVISED BY THE COMMITTEE (Document V below). This Plan is the most important for the present purpose. The letter of William Fleming to Jefferson, 22 June, enclosed the printed Mason Plan as revised by the Committee up to 22 June, representing the approximate final form of the Constitution as it stood in the committee just prior to the arrival of Jefferson's Draft. But the Mason Plan had undergone much change. Fleming's copy of it bears numerous marginal comments indicating what changes had been made in the progress of the Plan through the committee. This Plan included fifteen numbered paragraphs; opposite paragraphs 1, 2, and 6 Fleming wrote the word "Agreed," all other paragraphs having been altered or wholly deleted. A comparison of the Mason Plan as thus amended with the Constitution as adopted and with Jefferson's Third Draft provides the basis for determining the extent of Jefferson's contribution (see notes on Document VII, below).

THE DRAFT REPORTED BY THE COMMITTEE (Document VI below).

The final and complete Report of the Committee would be even more important for textual comparisons than the incomplete list of amendments and alterations of the Mason Plan as given by Fleming to Jefferson. Unfortunately, the full text of the Report of the Committee is not known to be in existence. But that there was such a complete Report, embracing some alterations made subsequent to those detailed by Fleming, is proved by the presence of a three-page MS in the Virginia State Archives bearing the caption "Amendments to the Plan of Government Continued." These amendments, which were offered in Convention during 26-28 June, are unhappily incomplete, but enough are included to prove (1) that the Report of the Committee was not the printed Mason Plan with alterations written thereon, as in Fleming's copy, but a new draft, now missing; (2) that it may have contained the preamble but probably no other parts from Jefferson's proposed constitution; and (3) that, before reporting to the Convention, the Committee made alterations in the Mason Plan in addition to those reported by Fleming. The partial MS is printed in the following series (Document VI) in order to show, as far as possible, the progress of the drafting of the Constitution between 22 and 28 June. The notes to this MS indicate some of the reasons for the conclusions here stated.

But by far the most important contribution made by this list of amendments is that revealing the manner in which Jefferson's Draft was employed by the Convention. Though this process cannot be followed in full, since the amendments are incomplete, it is possible now to state that the Convention at least considered the inclusion of that part of Jefferson's constitution limiting the powers of the governor. One of the amendments embraces several sentences, copied word for word from Jefferson's Draft; but his words were struck from the amendment before it was adopted. Another noteworthy contribution of this list of amendments is that revealing Wythe's presence in the Convention and his offering an amendment drawn from Jefferson's Draft.

The *Virginia Literary Museum* for 23 Sep. 1829 (I, 225-7) published what was described as "Original Draught of the Constitution of Virginia" with the statement that "the printed report of the constitution from which the subjoined draught is taken, is, perhaps, the only copy extant. The report is dated June 24, 1776." This statement, taken in connection with the date given, would seem to indicate that the "Original Draught" was the printed Report of the Committee made on 24 June. An examination of the text given in the *Virginia Literary Museum*, however, reveals that the document printed is merely the original printing of the Mason Plan (there are two variations in section 6 and section 8 but these were obviously printer's errors; the same text was printed in *Richmond Enquirer* for 6 Oct. 1829).

THE CONSTITUTION AS ADOPTED BY THE CONVENTION (Document VII below). This is obviously the MS copy of the Constitution that the Convention on 28 June ordered "to be fairly transcribed." A few amendments and changes, some of them quite significant, were made in this text even after this complete fair copy of the Constitution was made; these are indicated in the notes to Document VII.

In view of the foregoing, it is obvious that no single person can be advanced as the "author" of the Virginia Constitution. That Adams' *Thoughts on Government* had a direct influence on the Mason Plan and the Constitution can be demonstrated by a comparison of phraseology (e.g., Adams' remarks on commissions, writs, and indictments, *Works*, IV, 199, are followed almost verbatim in the Mason Plan and in the Constitution). That Richard Henry Lee modified the Adams Plan is probable, as it is equally probable that Patrick Henry introduced one or the other or a modification thereof in the *Virginia Gazette*. Second, the Constitution, deriving from various plans and discussions of preceding months, was fought over, as Jefferson said, "inch by inch." Many modifications were made and many persons had a hand in these modifications.

The contributions of Jefferson to the Virginia Constitution can be unmistakably identified by comparing his texts with the Committee revision, with the amendments offered in Convention, and with the final Constitution; certain parts are indisputably Jefferson's in phraseology and substance. Of all the plans that are known, only Jefferson's can be regarded as a complete, finished, detailed form of government: all others that are known were outlines, some merely describing and distributing the major powers of government. His was a carefully and thoroughly wrought document, exact in detail, harmonious in structure, consistent in purpose, and instinct with the leading principles that guided his entire life. Different as his constitution was in its preciseness and in its magnificent vision from that under contemplation by the Convention, it received its greatest tribute when the Convention, worn out with its own struggles over constitution-making and many other problems, reopened an almost closed chapter and incorporated as much as it dared of Jefferson's Draft. The remarkable thing under the circumstances is not that Jefferson's advanced ideas were rejected but that, at the last moment, the Convention was willing even to consider his constitution. The fact that use was made of considerable part of it is a tribute to its excellence and to the influence of its author.

The notes to the Virginia Constitution (Document VII) identify those parts of the Constitution that are here, for the first time, identified as certainly or probably Jefferson's. All the texts in this sequence are reproduced with literal fidelity. Square brackets in printed texts are in the MSS.

I. First Draft by Jefferson

[Before 13 June 1776]

Whereas George   Guelph King of Great Britain & Ireland and Elector of Hanover, heretofore entrusted with the exercise of the kingly office in this government, hath endeavored to pervert the same into a detestable & insupportable tyranny by ⟨neg⟩ putting his negative on laws the most wholesome & necessary for the public good

by denying to his governors permission to pass laws of ⟨the most⟩ immediate & pressing importance, unless suspended in their operation for his ⟨con⟩ assent &, when so suspended, neglecting ⟨for m⟩ to attend to them for many years:

by refusing to pass certain other laws, unless the persons to be benefited by them would relinquish the inestimable right⟨s⟩ of representation in the legislature:

by dissolving legislative assemblies repeatedly & continually for opposing with manly firmness his invasions on the rights of the people:

when dissolved, by refusing to call others for a long space of time, thereby leaving the political system ⟨[in a state of dissolution]⟩ without any legislative ⟨body⟩ head.

by endeavoring to prevent the population of our country ⟨by⟩ & for that purpose obstructing the laws for the naturalization of foreigners & raising the conditions of new appropriati⟨ng⟩ons ⟨new⟩ of lands:

by keeping among us in times of peace standing armies & ships of war:

by affecting to render the military independant of & superior to the civil power:

by combining with others to subject us to a foreign jurisdiction giving his ⟨con⟩ assent to their pretended acts of legislation ⟨for imposing taxes on us without our consent.⟩

for quartering large bodies of armed troops among us:

for cutting off our trade with all parts of the world:

for ⟨depriving us of⟩ imposing taxes on us without our consent:

for depriving us of the benefits of trial by jury:

for transporting us beyond seas to be tried for pretended offences:

for suspending our own legislatures & declaring themselves invested with power to legislate for us in all cases whatsoever

by plundering our seas, ravaging our coasts, burning our towns, ⟨des⟩ & destroying the lives of our people:

by inciting insurrections of our fellow subjects with the allurements of forfeiture & confiscation

by prompting our negroes to rise in arms among us; those very negroes whom by an inhuman use of his negative he hath ⟨from time to time⟩ refused us permission to exclude by law:[1]

by endeavoring to bring on the inhabitants of our frontiers the merciless Indian savages whose known rule of warfare is an undistinguished destruction of all ages, sexes, & conditions ⟨of life⟩ of existence.

by transporting at this time a large army of foreign mercenaries to compleat the works of death, desolation, & tyranny already begun ⟨in a stile⟩ with circumstances of cruelty & perfidy so unworthy ⟨a⟩ the head of a civilized ⟨people⟩ nation

by answering our repeated petitions ⟨against this repeated⟩ for redress with a repetition of injur⟨y⟩ies: ⟨with an accumulation of new injury⟩[2]

and finally by abandoning the helm of government ⟨&⟩ & declaring us out of his allegiance & protection.[3]

⟨[and by various other acts of tyranny too often enumerated to need repetition, and too cruel for the reflection of those who have felt them.]⟩

⟨Whereby it has become absolutely necessary⟩ by which several acts of misrule the sd. George   Guelf has forfeited the kingly office, and has rendered it necessary for the preservation of the people ⟨that the said George   Guelp⟩ ⟨it is become absolutely necessary⟩ that he should be immediately deposed from the ⟨kingly office⟩ same & divested of all it's privileges, powers, & prerogatives

And forasmuch as the public liberty may be more ⟨effectually⟩ certainly secured by abolishing an office which all experience hath shewn to be inveterately inimical thereto, ⟨in which case it⟩ and it will thereupon become⟨s⟩ further necessary to re-establish such antient principles as are friendly to the rights of the people & to declare certain others which may ⟨fortify &⟩ co-operate with & fortify the same in future.[4]

And whereas by an act of [. . .][5] of the present parliament of Great Britain passed for the purpose of prohibiting all trade & intercourse with the colonies of New Hampshire, Massachusets bay, Rhode Island, Connecticut, New York, New Jersey, Pennsylvania, the three lower counties on Delaware, Maryland, Virginia, North Carolina, South Carolina, & Georgia it is declared that the said colonies are in a state of open Rebellion & hostility against the king & his parliament of Great Britain, that they are out of their allegiance to him & are thereby also put [out][6] of his protection: and ⟨in one⟩ it is further declared ⟨in the said act⟩ that as divers persons within the sd. colonies may have been destroyed for the publick service in withstanding or suppressing the said rebellion, it is therefore enacted 'that all such acts shall be deemed just & legal to all intents ⟨& purposes⟩ constructions & purposes' to which act the sd. George   Guelp hath given his assent & thereby put us out of his allegiance & protection; in which case it is provided by the original charter of compact granted to Sr. Walter Ralegh on behalf of himself & the settlers of this colony & bearing date the 25th day of March 1584. 'that if the said Walter Ralegh his heirs or assigns or any of them or any other by their licence or appointment should at any time thereafter do any act of unjust or unlawful hostility, to any of the subjects of the sd. queen her heirs or successors it should be lawful to the said queen her heirs & successors to put the sd Walter Ralegh his heirs and assigns and adherents & all the inhabitants of the said places to be discovered as is therein described, or any of them out of her allegiance & protection, and that from & after such time of putting out of protection of the said Walter Ralegh his heirs assigns & adherents & others so to be put out, & the sd. places within their habitation possession & rule, should be out of her allegiance & protection & free for all princes & others to pursue with hostility as being not her subjects, nor by her any way to be avouched maintained or defended, nor to be holden as any of hers, nor to her protection or dominion or allegiance any way belonging' so that the sd. George   Guelp having by the said act of parliament declared us in a state of Rebellion & hostility & put us out of his allegiance & protection, it follows by the sd. charter that, from & after the time of such putting out, ourselves, and the places within our habitation, possession & rule are not subject to him, & are not to be holden as any of his, nor to his dominion any way belonging.

From all which premisses it appears that the sd. George   Guelp, not only for his criminal abuses of the high duties of the kingly office, but also by his own free & voluntary act of abandoning & putting us from his allegiance subjection & dominion, may now lawfully, rightfully, & by consent of both parties be divested of the kingly powers:

Legislative Executive & Judicial Powers shall be for ever separate

I.

1. Legislative shall be exercised by two separate houses to be called the General assembly to wit, a house of Representves ⟨which⟩ and a house of Senators shall be chosen ⟨on one certain day yearly through the whole colony by⟩ annually ⟨fresh without bribe⟩, the sd. house of Representves shall have power to meet on

a certain day & on their own adjournments, on call of the executive power ⟨or of their Speaker⟩ & to continue sitting so long as they please.

qualifications of electors shall be such as prove a fixed purpose of residence [— as ld.⁷ or being inhabt. payg. scot & lot.

qualification of elected, an oath to govmt., ⟨&⟩ that shall not have bribed & to hold no place of profit

⟨one representative for every⟩

representatives in propn. to number of qualifd. electors so as not to ⟨exceed⟩ be fewer than [125] nor more than [300] in the whole & in order to keep the proportion within these numbers the first in every [10] years shall be set apart for changing the number.

when met shall be free to act according to own judgmt. that business may not be delayed or obstructed

two third parts a quorum

2. the house of Senators shall ⟨be appointed by the house of⟩ consist of not less than [15] ⟨nor more than [   ]⟩ members who shall be appointed by the house of Representatives & when appointed shall be in for life, their numbers to be regulated within the limits aforsd. every [10th.] year by the house of Representatives according to the circumstances of the colony

with whom shall sit the judges of Gl. ct. & Chy. with right of deliberation but not of suffrage.

their qualification an oath ⟨to⟩ of fidelity to govmt. & no bribery, no place prof.

to meet with house of representatives

these houses shall each have power to originate amend & negative, except that money bills shall originate with representatives

no power of ordaining capital punmts but for
        not of inflicting torture in any cause

no laws ⟨for the continuing⟩ ⟨bodie⟩ ⟨armed men embodied, or⟩ for the levying money shall have force for any longer term than [   ] years ⟨nor shall⟩ the

II.

the Executive powers shall be exercised by an [Admr.] to be annually chosen on certain day but not to be invested with powers of Adm. till one year after by the house of representatives who after serving [one] year shall be incapable of serving again till interval of [five] years

he shall possess the powers formerly held by king save only that he
   shall be bound by acts of legislature tho' not named
   shall have no negative on bills
   shall not have prerogative of ⟨his own⟩
      Dissolving house of Representatives or prorogg. or adjg. ym.
         ⟨within 30 days⟩
      Declaring war or peace
      issuing letters of marque or reprisal
      raising or introducing armed forces ⟨or⟩ building armed ves-
         sels ⟨without⟩ forts or strong holds
      coining monies or regulating ⟨money⟩ their value
      regulating weights & measures
      erecting courts, offices, boroughs, corporations, fairs, mar-
         kets, ports, beacons, light houses, seamarks
      laying embargoes or prohibiting exportn. for more than 40
         days
      retaining or recalling a member of state but by legal process
         ⟨& for law⟩ pro delicto vel contractu.
      making denizens
      pardoning crimes or remitting fines or punishmts
      ⟨granting rights⟩ creating dignities or granting rights of prec-
         edence
      but these ⟨prerogatives⟩ powers to be exercised by legislature
         alone.
⟨Lieutenant⟩
⟨Admr. elect to be apptd. one year before⟩ ⟨who shall have power to
   act⟩ ⟨to assist & to act as principal in case of death or absence⟩
a privy council to be annually appd. by   to
   consist of ⟨not less than [   ] nor more than [   ]⟩ such number
      as Representatives may from time to time appoint.
⟨Judges of Genl. Ct.⟩ all officers civil, & military to be appd. by
   Admr ⟨with advice of council, during good behavr.⟩ subject to
   negative of council ⟨except sherif⟩
⟨A Supreme court to consist of not less than [5] nor more than
   [   ] members to be appd. by Representatives durg. good behavior whose office to determine appeals finally & try impeachmts
   by Representatives.⟩
Sheriffs and coroners, ⟨and County justices⟩ to be chosen annually
   by persons qualified to chuse represves.
Treasurer to be appd. by H. R. but to issue no money nor removble
   without joint authority of ⟨H. & Admr.⟩ both houses ⟨to have

session, but not suffrage in the house of representatives ⟨*shall not be member of H. of R.*⟩

III.

The Judicial powers shall be exercised

1st. by ⟨*General*⟩ County or borough courts ⟨*or as*⟩ or other jurisdictions inferior to these as already established or hereafter to be established by Legislature

2dly. by a General court & a court of Chancery with powers to receive appeals from inferior courts & take cognisance of such original causes as the laws have already given to the General court or may hereafter give to the same court or court of Chancery now to be separated.

3dly. by a Court of Appeals whose office shall be to hear & determine appeals from the Genl. ct. or Ct. of Chy. and to try impeachments entd. by H. of Representatives and inflict such punishmts as ⟨*the*⟩ future laws shall direct

the justices of the County or borough courts shall be appd. by admr. subject to negative of Council ⟨*and*⟩ shall not be fewer than five in number, and shall be removble for misbehavior by Ct. of Appeals

the justices of the General court and judges of Ct. of Chancery shall be appointed by the admr and council ⟨*&*⟩ shall consist of 5 members each, at the least, who shall have been of the faculty of the law & shall have actually practised the same in this colony seven years, shall hold their commissions during good behavior ⟨*and*⟩ which shall be tried by court of appeals only

the Court of Appeals shall consist of not less than [7] nor more than [ ] members to be ⟨*annually*⟩ chosen by Representatives to hold their commns. ⟨*for life*⟩ during good behavior and removeable only by act of legislature in which the judges of the Genl. ct. & Ct. of Chy. shall have session & deliberative[s] voice bt. no suffrage

all facts ⟨*whether arising in the courts of*⟩ in causes whether of Chancery ⟨*or*⟩ Admiralty, Ecclesiastical or Common law shall be tried by jury upon evidence viva voce unless in those cases where the courts of Common law now permit the use of deposns or of witnesses out of the colony

all fines & amercemts shall be fixed by juries

all judicial process shall issue in the name of the court ⟨*of*⟩ from which it issues

Unappropriated or forfeited lands shall be appropriated by the Admr.

[50]⁹ acres of land shall be ⟨granted⟩ appropriated without ⟨fee⟩ purchase money to every person not owning nor having ever owned that quantity ⟨of lands.⟩ & no other person shall be capable of taking an appropriation.

Lands heretofore holden of the crown, and those hereafter to be appropriated shall be holden of none. but this shall ⟨prejudice⟩ extend to the rights of subinfeudation

no lands shall be appropriated until purchased of the Indian natives nor shall any purchases be made from them ⟨within the limits of latitude but by an⟩ but on behalf of public under acts of legislation to be specially past for that purpose.

⟨all lands⟩ ⟨shall⟩ ⟨held in fee simple shall descend in future⟩

⟨lands which by the laws heretofore in force would have descended to one heir at law shall now⟩

⟨Descents shall be to all the children of the decedent or to all⟩ ⟨the⟩ ⟨his brothers & sisters of the whole blood, or to all⟩ ⟨the⟩ ⟨his other cousins⟩

Descents, instead of being to the eldest son, brother, or other male cousin of the ancestor, ⟨shall be to all his⟩ as directed by the laws heretofore shall be to all the brothers & sisters of the sd. heir at law who shall be of the whole blood of the ancestor, each of whom shall have an equal portion with the heir at law. but where lands shall have been given by such ancestor to any one of the sd. co-heirs it shall be brought into hotchpot or such ⟨heir⟩ coheir not entitled to any further share of the inheritance.

⟨Residence⟩ All persons who by their own oath, or affirmation or by other testimony shall ⟨satisfy⟩ give satisfactory proof to any court of record that he purposes to reside in this country for [7] years at least and who shall subscribe to the fundamental laws shall be declared by such court invested with the rights of a member natural born.

⟨No person⟩

All persons shall have full & free liberty of religious opinion, nor shall any be compelled to frequent or maintain any religious service or institution [but seditious behavior to be punble ⟨by⟩ by civil magistrate accdg to the laws already made or hereafter to be made.]¹⁰

No freeman shall ever be debarred the use of arms.

⟨No souldier shall be capable of continuing in⟩

there shall be no standing army but in time of ⟨peace⟩ actual war

Printing presses shall be free, except ⟨so far as they or their managers shall be subject themselves to the private action of any indi-

vidual⟩ where by commission of private injury they shall give cause of private action

All forfeitures formerly going to king shall go to ⟨*publick*⟩ the State ⟨*Wrecks, waifs, & strays*⟩

the Royal ⟨*right*⟩ ⟨*usurpations on*⟩ right⟨*s*⟩ to Wrecks, waifs, strays, treasure trove, royal mines, royal fish, royal birds & such fooleries ⟨*shall be*⟩ are declared usurpations

No salaries or perquisites shall be given to any officer but by act of legislature, ⟨*nor shall any*⟩ no salaries shall be given to the Admr, principal or elect, the houses of legislature, judges of the court of appeals, justices of the peace, privy council or delegates of Congress; ⟨*their*⟩ tho their reasonable ⟨*expences*⟩ subsistence only ⟨*of*⟩ while acting in their office to be borne, but the house of Senators not to have their expences

the qualifications of all officers, Execve, judicial, ⟨*and*⟩ military & eccles: oath of fidelity & no bribery

None of these fundamental constitutions to be ⟨*alter*⟩ repealed but by unanimous consent of both legislative houses.

The laws heretofore in force in this colony shall be still in force save only so far as they may be changed by the foregoing fundamental laws or by future acts of the legislature.

Dft (DLC). This six-page document, not included in any previous edition, was first identified about 1920 by John C. Fitzpatrick and described in *D. A. R. Magazine*, LV (1921), 363ff., and in his *Spirit of the Revolution*, Boston and N.Y., 1924, p. 1-7. The first two pages were reproduced in facsimile in Boyd, *Declaration of Independence*, 1945, pl. II, and its relation to the Declaration of Independence is discussed at p. 12-15. The document has the following endorsement by TJ in the margin of the first page: "Constitution of Virginia first ideas of Th: J. communicated to a member of the Convention." It bears no date, but TJ stated an obvious fact when he declared it to be "prior in composition to the Declaration" (TJ to Augustus B. Woodward, 3 Apr. 1825). It was certainly drawn up, as were the Second and Third Drafts, before 13 June 1776, when George Wythe left Philadelphia bearing the Third Draft. Internal evidence indicates that the First Draft was drawn up before 27 May, when the Virginia Resolutions of 15 May were read in Congress. For example, the important provision respecting western territories in the Second and Third Drafts was not

in the First, possibly indicating that this was added after the Virginia Resolutions arrived in Philadelphia around 26-27 May. As noted above in the foreword to this series of documents, the subject of constitution-making was one of the foremost topics of discussion during the spring of 1776, and TJ, who regarded this as "the whole object" of the Revolutionary movement, may well have formulated the rough notes in the First Draft even before he arrived in Philadelphia on 14 May (TJ to Nelson, 16 May 1776). In view of the general situation and of the internal evidence in these documents, it seems unlikely that all three drafts were composed between 27 May and 13 June as Ford, Fitzpatrick, Marie Kimball, and others have supposed. It is even possible that the Second and Third Drafts were completed before the Virginia Resolutions arrived; evidence of this is the fact that after TJ had completed the Third Draft, he added to the list of charges against the king some that evidently were drawn from or suggested by the Virginia Resolutions (see notes on Declaration of Independence).

It is important to note that page 1 of the First Draft, although greatly altered by interlining, crossing out, &c., actually became the final form of this part of the document from which TJ copied the corresponding part of the Third Draft. Page 2, containing an elaboration of the justification "by consent of both parties," was not employed at all in the Third Draft; and pages 3 to 6 are mere headings or outlines of a fundamental law. The Second Draft contains no preamble or justification corresponding to pages 1 and 2 of the First Draft, a fact which has led previous writers to suppose it missing. The probability is that there never was such a preamble or justification attached to the Second Draft. For, as the textual notes and a comparison of the texts amply prove, TJ used page 1 of the First Draft for copying that portion of the Third Draft, while the remainder of the Third Draft (i.e., the Constitution proper, pages 3 to 6) was copied from another text, possibly the Second Draft but more likely another copy of it not now known to be extant.

This, however, is not the end of complication in the First Draft. As noted above, after his Virginia Constitution had been sent to the Convention, TJ altered the first page of the First Draft by making interlined additions; he also numbered the charges against the king, adding some that do not appear in the Third Draft and causing the new list of charges to coincide exactly with that in the Declaration of Independence. The accompanying facsimiles of page 1 of the First Draft and page 1 of the Third Draft will show this at a glance: items 1 to 9 in this list on the First Draft coincide exactly with the corresponding unnumbered charges in the Third Draft, but between items 6 and 7 are three interlined items—

"refused judiciary establmts . . .
judges dependant
erected swarms of offices."

These particular subjects do not occur in the Third Draft at any point; they do occur precisely at this point and in this order in the Declaration of Independence. It is obvious, then, that the text of this part of the Third Draft, since it was copied (as noted in textual notes below) from the First Draft, shows the state of the First Draft before TJ added the subject headings and numbered the paragraphs so as to put them in the order they were to follow in the Declaration of Independence. This comparison provides

the means of isolating and identifying those items that were added in the course of adapting the First Draft to its second purpose. Hence the text as given here is the one that conforms to the fair copy (or Third Draft) made from it; the paragraphs thus isolated as having been added after the Third Draft was completed are discussed in the notes on the Declaration of Independence.

[1] This passage proves that TJ used the first page of the First Draft as the text from which he copied the Third Draft. This particular passage read in the First Draft: "those very negroes whom he hath from time to time refused us permission to exclude by law." It was so copied in the Third Draft. TJ then made corrections and interlineations in both texts to cause the passage to read: "those very negroes whom by an inhuman use of his negative he hath refused us permission to exclude by law." See text of this part of Third Draft for two other examples of changes made in both drafts in the process of copying the Third from the First Draft (i.e., "⟨con⟩ assent" and "⟨in which⟩"). However, the conclusive fact is that the text of this part of the First Draft, disregarding the scored-out portions and the subject headings interlined later, coincides wholly with the corresponding portion of the Third Draft.

[2] Before being changed this passage read: "by answering our repeated petitions against this repeated injury with an accumulation of new injury."

[3] This passage is interlined in the First Draft, but this fact does not warrant its being included in those interlined passages which TJ added when he used the First Draft in composing the Declaration of Independence, for the passage appears in the Third Draft, not interlined. It was copied precisely at this point in the Third Draft, but later TJ gave it the number "16" on the First Draft and then inserted another "16" between "9" and "10"; in the Declaration of Independence the passage occurs precisely between the points corresponding to the paragraphs numbered 9 and 10.

[4] At this point, in the lower right-hand corner of the first page, TJ had written and then crossed out the words "turn over." The verso of the first page contains the long passage consisting of the two paragraphs that follow in the present text; these were not, of course, copied in the Third Draft. It is apparent that

originally page 1 of the First Draft ended with the preceding paragraph (". . . divested of all it's privileges, powers, & prerogatives"). When, however, TJ discarded the argument contained in the two paragraphs on the verso of page 1, he added, at the bottom of that page, the four lines beginning "and forasmuch as. . . ." It is at this point in the text of the First Draft that TJ ceased employing it as a copy for the Third Draft.

5 MS torn. The citation of the act may have been omitted and a blank space left at this point.

6 This word inadvertently omitted in MS.

7 I.e., "—acres of land." The words,

numerals, or blank spaces in square brackets here and below were so written by TJ. In the present instance the bracket was not closed.

8 MS faded; this word supplied from Second and Third Drafts.

9 The numeral is blotted out in MS except "0." The Second and Third Drafts read "50," and this reading has been conjectured here.

10 This highly interesting passage about seditious behavior was bracketed by TJ in the First Draft, indicating that he regarded it as optional or possibly open to question; he copied it in the Second Draft, then struck it out; it was omitted entirely from the Third Draft.

II. Second Draft by Jefferson

[Before 13 June 1776]

A Bill for new modelling the form of government and for establishing the Fundamental principles of our future Constitution

Whereas George   king of Great Britain & Ireland and Elector of Hanover[1]

Be it therefore enacted by the authority of the people that the said George the third king of Great Britain ⟨formerly holding & exercising the kingly⟩ ⟨power⟩ ⟨office within this colony be, & he is⟩ and elector of Hanover be & he is hereby, ⟨absolutely divested of⟩ deposed from the kingly office ⟨& powers within this colony⟩ within ys. governmt. & absolutely divested of all it's rights & powers, & that he & his descendants & all persons claimg. by or through him & all other persons whatsoever ⟨are hereby declared⟩ shall be & for ever remain incapable of ⟨being again appointed to⟩ ⟨holding⟩ the same; & ⟨further⟩ that the sd. office shall henceforth cease & be never more erected within this ⟨government⟩ colony.

And be it further enacted by the authority aforesaid that ⟨the⟩ ⟨in lieu of those which have heretofore taken place,⟩ the following fundamental laws & principles of government shall henceforth be established.

The Legislative, Executive, & Judicial offices shall be kept for ever separate, & no person exercising the one shall be capable of appointment to the others or to either of them.

Legislation shall be exercised by two separate houses ⟨who shall   LEGISLATIVE.

be called the General assembly of Virginia⟩ to wit a house of Representatives and a house of Senators which shall be called the General assembly of Virginia.

Representatives The sd. house of representatives shall be composed of persons chosen by the people annually on the [day of ⟨*December*⟩][2] and shall have power to meet in General assembly on the [day of ⟨*January*⟩] following & so from time to time on their own adjournments, or at any other time when summoned by the Administrator & to continue sitting so long as they shall think the publick service requires.

Vacancies in the sd house by death or disqualification shall be filled up by the electors under a warrant from the Speaker of the house.

⟨*All persons holding*⟩ All male persons of full age & sane mind having a freehold estate in [⟨*half*⟩ ¼ of an acre] of land in any town, or in [⟨*50*⟩25] acres of land in the country, & all persons resident in ⟨*this country*⟩ the colony who shall have paid scot & lot to government the last [⟨*three*⟩ two] years shall have right to ⟨*vote*⟩ give their vote in the election of their respective representatives. and ⟨*all*⟩ every person⟨*s*⟩ so qualified to ⟨*vote*⟩ elect, shall be capable of being elected, provided he shall have given no bribe either directly or indirectly to any elector ⟨*voting for &*⟩ and shall take an oath of fidelity to the ⟨*government, and shall*⟩ state & of duty in his office before he enters on the exercise thereof ⟨*his office*⟩; and ⟨*shall hold*⟩ during his continuance ⟨*therein*⟩ in the said office he shall hold no ⟨*pl*⟩[3] public post of profit either himself or by another for his use.

The number of Representatives for each county or borough shall be so proportioned to the number of it's qualified electors: ⟨*but*⟩ ⟨*save*⟩ that the whole number of representatives shall not exceed [300] nor be less than [150].[4] for the present there shall be one representative for every [400] qualified electors in each county or borough; but whenever this or any future proportion shall be likely to exceed or fall short of the limits beforementioned, the proportion shall be again adjusted by the house of representatives.[5]

The house of representatives when met shall be free to act according to their own judgments.

Senate. The Senate shall consist of ⟨[*15*]⟩ not less than [15] nor more than [50] members ⟨*at the least*⟩, who shall be appointed by the house of representatives[6] ⟨, *and, when appointed, shall hold their offices for life*⟩. one third of them shall be removed out of office by lot at the end of the first three years & their places be supplied by a

[348]

new appointment; one other third shall be removed by lot in like manner at the end of the second three years & their places be supplied by a new appointment; after which one third shall be removed annually at the end of every three years according to seniority. when once removed they shall be for ever incapable of being reappointed to that house. their qualifications shall be an oath of fidelity to ⟨*government*⟩ the state and of duty in their office, the being of [31] years of age at the least, and the having given no bribe⟨*s*⟩ directly or indirectly to obtain their appointment: while in the Senatorial office they shall be incapable of holding any public post⟨*s*⟩ of profit either themselves or by others for their use.

⟨*with the house of Senators*⟩

The judges of the General court & of the High court of Chancery shall have session & deliberative voice but not suffrage in the house of Senators.

The Senate & the house of representatives shall each of them have power to originate & amend bills, save only that money bills shall be originated & amended by the Representatives only: ⟨*, and*⟩ the assent of both houses shall be requisite to pass a law.

The General assembly shall have no power to pass any law inflicting death for any crime except⟨*for*⟩ing murder ⟨*nor for inflicting*⟩ & excepting also those offences in the military service for which they shall think punishment of death absolutely necessary; ⟨*nor shall they have power to prescribe torture*⟩ ⟨*for*⟩ ⟨*in any case what*⟩[7] and all capital punishments in other cases are hereby abolished: nor shall they have power to prescribe torture in any case whatever; nor shall any law for levying money be in force longer than [ten] years from the time of it's commencement.

Two thirds of the members of either house shall be a quorum to proceed to business.[8]

⟨*For*⟩ The ⟨*exercise of the*⟩ executive powers shall be exercised ⟨*by*⟩ in manner following one person to be called the [Administrator] ⟨*who*⟩ shall be ⟨*ap*⟩ annually appointed by the [house of representatives   ] on the second day of their first session, ⟨*&*⟩ who after having acted [one] year shall be incapable of being again appointed ⟨*till*⟩ to that office until he shall have been out of the ⟨*said office*⟩ same [three] years. Executive
Administrator

Under him shall be appointed by the same house & at the same time a Deputy Administrator to assist his principal in the discharge of his office, & to succeed ⟨*to the whole powers thereof*⟩ in case of his death before the year shall have expired, to the whole powers thereof during the residue of the year. Deputy Admr.

The Administrator shall possess the powers formerly held by the king save only that

he shall be bound by acts of legislature tho' not expressly named.

he shall have no negative on the bills of the Legislature

he shall be liable to action tho' not to personal restraint for private duties or wrongs.

he shall not possess ⟨no⟩ the prerogatives ⟨of⟩

of Dissolving, proroguing, or adjourning either house of assembly

of ⟨issuing⟩ Declaring war or ⟨making⟩ concluding peace.

of issuing letters of marque or reprisal.

of raising or introducing armed forces, building armed vessels, forts or strong holds.

of coining monies or regulating their value.

of regulating weights & measures.

of erecting courts, offices, boroughs, corporations, fairs, markets, ports, beacons, lighthouses, seamarks.

of laying embargoes or prohibiting the exportation of any commodity for a longer space than [40] days.

of retaining or recalling a member of the state but by legal process pro delicto vel contractu.

of making denizens

of pardoning crimes or remitting fines or punishmts.

of creating dignities or granting rights of precedence.

but these powers shall be exercised by the legislature alone.

Privy council. A privy Council shall be annually appointed by the house of Representatives ⟨to consist of such number as they shall⟩ whose duty it shall be to give advice to the Administrator when called on by him. with them the Deputy Admr. shall have session & suffrage.

Delegates. insert here[9] ⟨Delegates⟩

Treasurer. A Treasurer &c. see below[10]

Sheriffs &c. High Sheriffs and coroners of counties shall be annually elected by those qualified to vote for representatives: ⟨but officers of the courts of general jurisdiction⟩ ⟨by their respective courts⟩ and ⟨every⟩ no person who shall have served as high sheriff [one] year shall be ⟨in⟩capable of being re-elected to the said office in the same county till he shall have[11] been out of office[11] [five] years.

Other officers All other officers civil & military shall be appointed by the Administrator but such appointment shall be subject to the negative of the privy council, saving however to the legislature a ⟨right⟩ power of transferring ⟨the right of⟩ ⟨from the Administrator the⟩ to any other persons ye. appointment ⟨*of such officers*⟩ of such officers ⟨*to any persons they may think fit*⟩ or of any of them.

⟨*The*⟩ A Treasurer shall be appointed by the house of Representatives, who shall issue no money but by ⟨*warrant from*⟩ authority of both houses.

Delegates ⟨*appointed*⟩ ⟨*shall be*⟩ to represent this colony in the American Congress ⟨*shall not be e*⟩ shall be appointed when necessary by the H. of Represves. ⟨*who*⟩ after serving [two] years in that office they shall not be capable of being re-appointed to the same during an interval of [two] years. **Delegates.**

The Judicial powers shall be exercised **III. JUDICIAL**

First by County courts & other inferior jurisdictions.

Secondly by a General court & a High Court of Chancery.

Thirdly by a Court of Appeals.

The ⟨*justices*⟩ judges of the County courts & other inferior jurisdictions shall be appointed by the Administrator, subject to the negative of the privy council. they shall not be fewer than [five] in number. their jurisdiction shall be defined from time to time by the Legislature: & they shall be removeable for misbehavior by the court of Appeals. **County courts**

The judges of the General court & of the High court of Chancery shall be appointed by the Administrator and Privy council. if kept united they shall be [5] in number, if separate there shall be [5] for the General Court[11] & [3] for the High court of Chancery. the appointment shall be made from the faculty of the law and of such persons of that faculty as shall have actually exercised the same at ⟨*some*⟩ the bar ⟨*or bars*⟩ of some court or courts of record within this colony for [seven] years. they shall hold their commissions during good behavior, for breach of which they shall be removeable by the court of Appeals. their jurisdiction shall be defined from time to time by the Legislature. **Genl. Court & Chancery**

The court of Appeals shall consist of not less than [7] nor more than [11] members to be ⟨*chosen . . .*⟩ appointed by the house of Representves; they shall hold their offices during good behavior, for breach of which they shall be removeable by an act of the legislature only. their jurisdiction shall be to determine finally all causes removed before them from the General court or High court of Chancery on suggestion of error: to remove judges of the General court or High court of Chancery or of the County courts or other inferior jurisdictions for misbehavior: [to try impeachments ⟨*of*⟩ against high offenders ⟨*to be*⟩ lodged before them by the House of representatives for such crimes as ⟨*shall be hereafter defined*⟩ shall **Court of Appeals**

[351]

hereafter be precisely defined by the Legislature ⟨*shall hereafter define with precision and*⟩ ⟨*pres to which th*⟩ and for the punishment of which the sd. Legislature shall have previously prescribed certain & determinate pains.] in this court the judges of the Genl. Ct. & High Ct. of Chan'y shall have session and deliberative voice but no suffrage.

Juries   All facts, in causes, whether of Chancery, Common, Ecclesiastical or Marine law shall be tried by a jury upon evidence given viva voce in open court; ⟨*unless*⟩ but where witnesses are out of the colony ⟨*in which case their depositions may be used*⟩ or unable to attend ⟨*through*⟩ ⟨*by*⟩ through sickness or other invincible necessity, their depositions may be ⟨*proposed*⟩ submitted to the credit of the jury.

Fines.   All Fines & Amercements shall be ⟨*fixed by juries and pains determined*⟩ assessed and terms of imprisonment for Contempts ⟨*shall*⟩ or misdemeanors shall be fixed by the verdict of a jury.

Process   All process, original & judicial ⟨*process*⟩ shall ⟨*issue*⟩ run in the name of the court from[11] which it issues.

Quorum.   Two thirds of the members of the General court, High court of Chancery, or Court of Appeals shall be a Quorum to proceed to business.

IV. LANDS.   Unappropriated or Forfeited lands shall be appropriated by the Administrator ⟨*and*⟩ with the consent of the privy council

  ⟨[*Fifty*] *acres of la*⟩

Every ⟨*male*⟩ person of full age neither owning nor having owned [50] acres of land shall be entitled to an appropriation of [50] acres or to so much as shall make up what he owns or has owned [50] acres in full and absolute dominion. and no other person shall be capable of taking an appropriation.

Lands heretofore holden of the crown in fee simple and those hereafter to be appropriated shall be holden ⟨*of no superior by him*⟩ in full & absolute dominion of no superior whatever.

No lands shall be appropriated until purchased of the Indian native⟨*s*⟩ proprietors, nor shall any purchases be made of them but on behalf of the public by authority of acts of the General assembly to be ⟨*made*⟩ passed for every purchase[11] specially.

The territories[11] ⟨*describe*⟩ contained within the charters erecting the colonies of Maryland Pennsylvania, North & South Carolina are hereby ⟨*f*⟩ ceded ⟨*&*⟩ released and for ever confirmed to the people of those ⟨*pro*⟩ colonies respectively with all the rights of ⟨*jurisdiction and*⟩ property, jurisdiction ⟨*&*⟩ and government, and all other rights whatsoever ⟨*claimed . . .*⟩ which might at any time heretofore have been claimed by this colony. The Western and Northern extent of this country shall in all other respects stand as ⟨described⟩ fixed by[11] the Charter of

until by act of the Legislature ⟨any new⟩ ⟨a territory or⟩ one or more territories shall be laid off Westward of the Alleganey mountains for ⟨any⟩ ⟨the establishment of⟩ new ⟨colony or⟩ colonies, which ⟨colony or⟩ colonies ⟨when established shall be free & independent of this & shall⟩ shall be established on the same fundamental laws contained in this instrument & shall be free & independent of this colony and of all the world.

Descents shall go according to the laws of Gavelkind, save only that females shall have equal rights with males.

No person hereafter coming into this country shall be held in slavery under any pretext whatever.[12] **Slaves.**

All persons who by their own oath or affirmation or by other testimony shall give satisfactory proof to any court of record in this colony that they purpose to reside in the same [7] years at the least and who shall subscribe the fundamental laws shall be considered as ⟨a⟩ residents & entitled to all the rights of ⟨a⟩ persons natural born. **Naturalization**

All persons shall have full & free liberty of religious opinion: nor shall any be compelled to frequent or maintain any religious institution. ⟨but this shall not be held to justify any seditious preaching or conversation against the authority of the civil government.⟩ **Religion**

No freeman shall be debarred the use of arms [within his own lands or tenements]. **Arms**

There shall be no standing army but in time of actual war. **Standing army**

Printing presses shall be free, except so far as by commission[11] of private injury they may give cause of private action. **Free Presses**

All forfeitures heretofore going to the king shall go to the state, save only such as the legislature may hereafter abolish. **Forfeitures**

The royal claim to Wrecks, Waifs, Strays, Treasure-trove, royal mines, royal fish, royal birds, are declared to have been usurpations on common right.[13] **Wrecks &c.**

No salaries or perquisites shall be given to any officer but by act of the legislature. no salaries shall be given to the Administrator, members of the ⟨house of Representatives⟩ Legislative houses, judges of the court of appeals, ⟨justices of the peace, members of the privy council,⟩ judges of the County courts or other inferior jurisdictions, Privy counsellors, or delegates to the American Congress. but the reasonable expences of the Administrator, **Salaries &c.**

members of the house of Representatives, judges of the court of Appeals, ⟨members of⟩ Privy counsellors & Delegates for subsistence while acting in the duties of their office ⟨shall⟩ may be borne by the public if the Legislature shall so direct.

Qualificns. of Officers   The Qualifications of all officers ⟨Civil, military, Executi Judicial,⟩ Civil, military & Ecclesiastical shall be an oath of fidelity to the ⟨governm⟩ state and the having given no bribe to obtain their office.

None of these fundamental laws & principles of government shall be repealed ⟨or alt⟩ or altered but by the personal consent of the people ⟨to be⟩ on summon⟨ed⟩s to meet in their respective counties on one & the same day by an act of Legislature to be passed for every special occasion: and if in such county meetings the people of two thirds of the counties shall give their suffrage for any particular alteration or repeal referred to them by the said act, the same shall be accordingly repealed or altered ⟨or repealed⟩ and such repeal or alteration shall take it's place among these fundamentals, and stand on[11] the same footing with them in lieu of the article repealed or altered.

The laws heretofore in force in this colony shall remain still in force except so far as they are altered by the foregoing fundamental laws, or so far as they may be hereafter altered by acts of the legislature.

It is proposed that the above bill, after correction by the Convention, shall be referred by them to the people to be assembled in their respective counties: and that the suffrages of two thirds of the counties shall be requisite to establish it.

Dft (DLC). This MS, which Ford labels "First Draft," was acquired by the Library of Congress in 1930, being donated by W. E. Benjamin of New York (*Report of the Librarian of Congress*, 1930, p. 64), who obtained it from Cassius F. Lee, Jr., of Alexandria, Va. The MS of the Third Draft, described below, and the Wythe copy of the Declaration of Independence were also at one time in the possession of Lee, (Boyd, *Declaration of Independence*, 1945, p. 39, 42, 43-5), from whom Ford obtained facsimiles of both the Second and Third Drafts (Ford, II, 7). However, some parts of the Second Draft became separated from the MS before it was acquired by the Library of Congress. These missing portions are noted below and the text is from Ford, II, 7. That part of the MS in DLC consists of eight pages and one tipped-in slip of paper. The present location of these missing parts is unknown. It is possible that Lee obtained the Second Draft, as he certainly did the Third, directly or indirectly from the papers of George Wythe. It is also most likely, as indicated in the notes to the Third Draft, that TJ sent more than one copy to the Virginia Convention. If so, this might explain the fact that the Second Draft became separated from the main corpus of Jefferson's papers. Ford (II, 7) noted that the Second Draft lacked the introductory part containing the justification for abolishing the "kingly office" and setting up new forms of government. As suggested above, in the

II. JEFFERSON'S SECOND DRAFT

notes to First Draft, it is very unlikely that such a preamble to the Second Draft ever existed (see footnote 1, below).

The supposition that TJ sent more than one copy of his proposed constitution to Virginia is possibly confirmed by the statements of William Wirt and B. W. Leigh. These statements have every appearance of being reliable: they were made independently, separated widely in time, and uttered by men of recognized probity, one of whom supported and the other of whom opposed Jeffersonian principles. Each flatly asserted that he had seen in the State archives at Richmond a draft of a proposed constitution of Virginia, in TJ's handwriting, that he had submitted to the Convention in 1776 (Wirt, *Henry*, I, 196; B. W. Leigh, *Procs. and Debates of the Va. State Conv. of 1829-1830*, Richmond, 1830, p. 160). Leigh added, in the statement he made in 1830, that the MS had "long since" disappeared from the council chamber. It is known that the Third Draft of TJ's proposed constitution was found among George Wythe's papers at his death in 1806 (see notes to Third Draft). Wythe must, therefore, have retained this text, even though it was the fair copy, correctly docketed by TJ as a bill ready to be introduced. In view of this and of the clear indications that the Third Draft was copied from another text than our Second Draft, Wirt and Leigh must have seen some other copy in the council chamber. If so, that copy, having disappeared before 1830, is not known to be in existence. It could not have been our Second Draft (see above and note 1, below).

1 The foregoing title and beginning of preamble are not in MS in DLC. Text is supplied from Ford, II, 7, where it is asserted that "This heading is written on a separate sheet, the remainder of the page being left blank." He adds: "The rough draft [i.e., our Second Draft] has no preamble, though space was left for it." If space was left for it and if, as shown above, this part of the text was copied from the first page of the First Draft when TJ made his fair copy or copies, there not only was no need to include the preamble in the Second Draft, but the indication is that none was intended to be placed there. The Ford fac-similes of the Second Draft in NN do not include such a page as he describes.

2 The square brackets are in MS here and elsewhere in Second Draft.

3 Doubtful reading.

4 TJ apparently wrote "[125]" first, the number found at this point in the Third Draft.

5 TJ inserted square brackets before and after the phrase "house of representatives" and then struck them out.

6 The two following sentences beginning "one third of them . . ." are written on a slip of paper containing nine lines, intended to be inserted at this point. Ford (II, 16) inserts these sentences at a different place. Two reasons justify the insertion at this point in our Second Draft: (1) the context is suitable and the sentences coincide with the order in the Third Draft; (2) the slip of paper has at its beginning part of a cue word—"tatives"—and this cue word occurs only at the beginning of the line at the point indicated, the remainder of the line ⟨, *and, when . . . life*⟩ being struck out as indicated.

7 This sentence was altered and interlined to read "torture in any case whatever," but TJ neglected to strike out these words when the phrase was repeated below.

8 At this point in the margin TJ wrote "Delegates," but struck out the word and then added "see post." Several other instances of the same sort occur elsewhere in the margin of Dft, but have been disregarded.

9 The paragraph below beginning "Delegates to represent . . ." was written at the bottom of the page and TJ indicated that the paragraph on delegates was to be inserted at this point, as in Third Draft.

10 Comment in note 9 applies, save that the paragraph on the Treasurer precedes that on Delegates at the bottom of the page in MS.

11 Illegible; supplied from Third Draft.

12 The MS of the Second Draft in DLC ends at this point; the remainder of the text is supplied from the facsimile made by Ford about 1890.

13 As may be noted in the First Draft, TJ had employed the phrase "& such fooleries" in the First Draft. The Second Draft gained in dignity by the excision of these words, but their presence in the First Draft serves nevertheless to reveal the warmth of TJ's antipathy to royal privilege and prerogative.

III. Third Draft by Jefferson

[Before 13 June 1776]

A Bill[1] for new-modelling the form of Government and for establishing[1] the Fundamental principles thereof in future.

Whereas George   Guelf king of Great Britain and Ireland and Elector of Hanover, heretofore entrusted with the exercise of the kingly office in this government hath endeavored to pervert the same into a detestable and insupportable tyranny;

by putting his negative on laws the most wholesome & necessary for ye. public good;

by denying to his governors permission to pass laws of immediate & pressing importance, unless suspended in their operation for his ⟨con⟩ assent, and, when so suspended, neglecting to attend to them for many years;

by refusing to pass certain other laws, unless the persons to be benefited by them would relinquish the inestimable right of representation in the legislature

by dissolving legislative assemblies repeatedly and continually for opposing with manly firmness his invasions on the rights of the people;

when dissolved, by refusing to call others for a long space of time, thereby leaving the political system without any legislative head;

by endeavoring to prevent the population of our country, & for that purpose obstructing[1] the laws for the naturalization of foreigners & raising the conditions of new appropriations[1] of lands;

by keeping among us,[1] in times of peace, standing armies & ships of war;

by affecting[1] to render the military independent of & superior to the civil power;

by combining with others to subject us to a foreign jurisdiction, giving his assent to their pretended acts of legislation

for quartering large bodies of troops among us;

for cutting off our trade with all parts of the world;

for imposing taxes on us without our consent;

for depriving us of the benefits of trial by jury;

for transporting us beyond seas to be tried for pretended offences; and

for suspending our own legislatures & declaring themselves invested with power to legislate for us in all cases whatsoever;

by plundering our seas, ravaging our coasts, burning our towns
and destroying the lives of our people;

by inciting insurrections of our fellow subjects with the allurements of forfeiture & confiscation

by prompting our negroes to rise in arms among us; those very
negroes whom ⟨he hath from time to time⟩ by an inhuman use
of his negative he hath refused us permission to exclude by law

by endeavoring to bring on the inhabitants of our frontiers the
merciless Indian savages, whose known rule of warfare is an
undistinguished destruction of all ages, sexes, & conditions of
existence;

by transporting at this time a large army of foreign mercenaries
to compleat[1] the works of death, desolation, & tyranny already
begun with circumstances[1] of cruelty & perfidy so unworthy the
head of a civilized nation;

by answering our repeated petitions for redress with a repetition
of injuries;

and finally by abandoning the helm of government and declaring
us out of his allegiance & protection;

by which several acts of misrule the said George
Guelf has forfeited the kingly office and has rendered it necessary
for the preservation of the people that he should be immediately
deposed from the same, and divested of all it's privileges, powers,
& prerogatives:

And forasmuch as the public liberty may be more certainly
secured by abolishing an office which all experience hath shewn
to be inveterately inimical thereto ⟨in which⟩ and it will thereupon
become further necessary to re-establish such antient principles as
are friendly to the rights of the people and to declare certain others
which may co-operate with and fortify the same in future.

Be it therefore enacted by the authority of the people that the
said George   Guelf be, and he hereby is deposed
from the kingly office within this government and absolutely divested of all it's rights, powers and prerogatives; and that he and
his descendants and all persons claiming[1] by or through him, and
all other persons whatsoever shall be & for ever remain[1] incapable
of[2] the same; and that the said office shall henceforth cease[1] and
never more either in name or substance be re-established within this
colony.[1]

And be it further enacted by the authority aforesaid that the
following fundamental laws and principles of government shall
henceforth be established.

The Legislative, Executive and Judiciary offices shall be kept for ever separate, & no person exercising the one shall be capable of appointment to the others, or to either of them.

I. LEGISLATIVE.

Legislation shall be exercised by two separate houses, to wit a house of Representatives and a house of Senators, which shall be called the General Assembly of Virginia.

H. of Representatives. The sd. house of Representatives shall be composed of persons chosen by the people annually on the [1'st day of October]³ and shall meet in General assembly on the [15'th day of November] following, and so from time to time on their own adjournments, or at any other time when summoned by the Administrator and ⟨to⟩ shall continue sitting so long as they shall think the publick service requires.

Vacancies in the said house by death or disqualification shall be filled by the electors under a warrant from the Speaker of the said house.

Electors. All male persons of full age and sane mind having a freehold estate in [one fourth of an acre] of land in any town, or in [25] acres of land in the country, and all persons resident in the colony who shall have paid *scot* and *lot* to government the last [two years] shall have right to give their vote in the election of their respective repre-

Elected. sentatives. and every person so qualified to elect shall be capable of being elected, provided he shall have given no bribe either directly or indirectly to any elector, and shall take an oath of fidelity to the state and of duty in his office, before he enters on the exercise thereof. during his continuance in the said office he shall hold no public pension nor post of profit, either himself, or by another for his use.

The number of representatives for each county or borough shall be so proportioned to the number of it's qualified electors that the whole number of representatives shall not exceed [300] nor be less than [125.] for the present there shall be one representative for every [   ] qualified electors in each county or borough: but whenever this or any future proportion shall be likely to exceed or fall short of the limits beforementioned, it shall be again adjusted by the house of representatives.

The house of Representatives when met shall be free to act according to their own judgment⟨s⟩ and conscience.

Senate. The Senate shall consist of not less than [15] nor more than [50] members who shall be appointed by the house of Representatives.

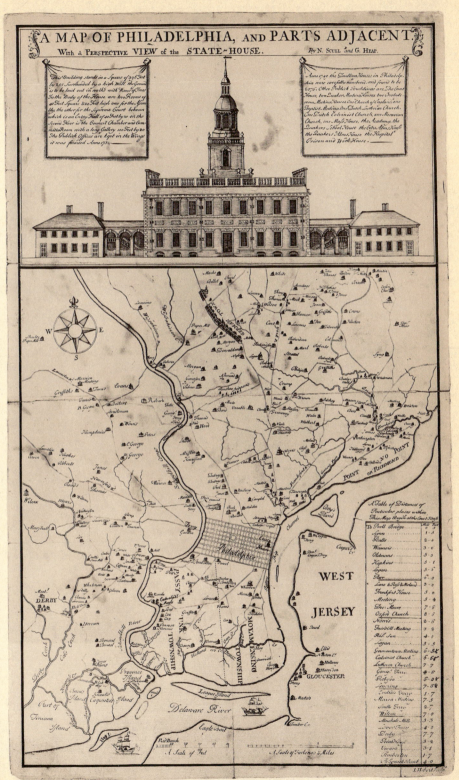

Map of Philadelphia and view of the State House. By Nicholas Scull and George Heap.

one third of them shall be removed out of office by lot at the end of the first [three] years and their places be supplied by a new appointment; one other third shall be removed by lot in like manner at the end of the second [three] years and their places be supplied by a new appointment; after which one third shall be removed annually at the end of every [three] years according to seniority. when once removed, they shall be for ever incapable of being re-appointed to that house. their qualifications shall be an oath of fidelity to the state, and of duty in their office, the being [31] years of age at the least, and the having given no bribe directly or indirectly to obtain their appointment. while in the Senatorial office they shall be incapable of holding any public pension or post of profit either themselves, or by others for their use.

The judges of the General court and of the High court of Chancery shall have session and deliberative voice, but not suffrage in the house of Senators.

The Senate and the house of representatives shall each of them have power to originate and amend bills; save only that bills for levying money ⟨bills⟩ shall be originated and amended by the representatives only: the assent of both houses shall be requisite to pass a law.

The General assembly shall have no power to pass any law inflicting death for any crime, excepting murder, & ⟨such⟩ those offences in the military service for which they shall think punishment by death absolutely necessary: and all capital punishments in other cases are hereby abolished. nor shall they have power to prescribe torture in any case whatever: nor shall there be power any where to pardon crimes or to remit fines or punishments: nor shall any law for levying money be in force longer than [ten years.] from the time of it's commencement.

[Two thirds] of the members of either house shall be a *Quorum* to proceed to business.

II. EXECUTIVE.

The executive powers shall be exercised in manner following.

One person to be called the [Administrator] shall be annually appointed by the house of Representatives on the second day of their first session, who after having acted [one] year shall be incapable of being again appointed to that office until he shall have been out of the same [three] years. _{Administrator}

Under him shall be appointed by the same house and at the same time a Deputy Administrator to assist his principal in the discharge _{Deputy Admr.}

of his office, and to succeed, in case of his death before the year shall have expired, to the whole powers thereof during the residue of the year.

The Administrator shall possess the powers formerly held by the king: save only that, he shall be bound by acts of legislature tho' not expressly named;

he shall have no negative on the bills of the Legislature;

he shall be liable to action, tho' not to personal restraint for private duties or wrongs;

he shall not possess the prerogatives

of dissolving, proroguing or adjourning either house of Assembly;

of declaring war or concluding peace;

of issuing letters of marque or reprisal;

of raising or introducing armed forces, building armed vessels, forts, or strong holds;

of coining monies or regulating their value;

of regulating weights and measures;

of erecting courts, offices, boroughs, corporations, fairs, markets, ports, beacons, lighthouses, seamarks.

of laying embargoes, or prohibiting the exportation of any commodity for a longer space than [40] days.

of retaining or recalling a member of the state but by legal process pro delicto vel contractu.

of making denizens;

⟨of pardoning crimes, or remitting fines or punishments;⟩[4]

of creating dignities or granting rights of precedence.

but these powers shall be exercised by the legislature alone. and excepting also those powers which by these fundamentals are given to others, or abolished.

Privy council A Privy council shall be annually appointed by the house of representatives, whose duty it shall be to give advice to the Administrator when called on by him. with them the Deputy Administrator shall have session and suffrage.

Delegates. Delegates to represent this colony in the American Congress shall be appointed when necessary by the house of Representatives. after serving [one] year in that office they shall not be capable of being re-appointed to the same during an interval of [one] year.

Treasurer. a Treasurer shall be appointed by the house of Representatives who shall issue no money but by authority of both houses.

Attorney Genl. an Attorney general shall be appointed by the house of Representatives.

High-sheriffs and Coroners of counties shall be annually elected by those qualified to vote for representatives: and no person who shall have served as highsheriff [one] year shall be capable of being re-elected to the said office in the same county till he shall have been out of office [five] years. High sheriffs &c.

All other Officers civil and military shall be appointed by the Administrator; but such appointment shall be subject to the negative of the Privy council, saving however to the Legislature a power of transferring to any other persons the appointment of such officers or of any of them. other Officers.

III. JUDICIARY.

The Judiciary powers shall be exercised

First by County courts and other inferior jurisdictions:

Secondly by a General court & a High court of Chancery:

Thirdly by a Court of Appeals.

The judges of the County courts and other inferior jurisdictions shall be appointed by the Administrator, subject to the negative of the privy council. they shall not be fewer than [five] in number. their jurisdiction shall be defined from time to time by the legislature: and they shall be removeable for misbehavior by the court of Appeals. County Courts &c.

The Judges of the General court and of the High court of Chancery shall be appointed by the Administrator and Privy council. if kept united they shall be [5] in number, if separate, there shall be [5] for the General court & [3] for the High court of Chancery. the appointment shall be made from the faculty of the law, and of such persons of that faculty as shall have actually exercised the same at the bar of some court or courts of record within this colony for [seven] years. they shall hold their commissions during good behavior, for breach of which they shall be removeable by the court of Appeals. their jurisdiction shall be defined from time to time by the Legislature. Genl. Court and High Ct. of Chancery.

The Court of Appeals shall consist of not less than [7] nor more than [11] members, to be appointed by the house of Representatives: they shall hold their offices during good behavior, for breach of which they shall be removeable[5] by an act of the legislature only. their jurisdiction shall be to determine finally all causes removed before them from the General court or High court of Chancery on suggestion of error: to remove judges of the General court or High court of Chancery, or of the County courts or other inferior jurisdictions for misbehavior: [to try impeachments against high of- Court of Appeals.

fenders lodged before them by the house of representatives for such crimes as shall hereafter be precisely defined by the Legislature, and for the punishment of which the said legislature shall have previously prescribed certain and determinate pains.] in this court the judges of the General court and High court of Chancery shall have session and deliberative voice, but no suffrage.

Juries. All facts in causes, whether of Chancery, Common, Ecclesiastical, or Marine law, shall be tried by a jury upon evidence given vivâ voce, in open court: but where witnesses are out of the colony or unable to attend through sickness or other invincible necessity, their depositions may be submitted to the credit of the jury.

Fines &c. All Fines and Amercements shall be assessed, & Terms of imprisonment for Contempts & Misdemeanors shall be fixed by the verdict of a jury.

Process. All Process Original & Judicial shall run in the name of the court from which it issues.

Quorum. Two thirds of the members of the General court, High court of Chancery, or Court of Appeals shall be a Quorum to proceed to business.

IV. RIGHTS PRIVATE AND PUBLIC.

Lands. Unappropriated or Forfeited lands shall be appropriated by the Administrator with the consent of the Privy council.

Every person of full age neither owning nor having owned [50] acres of land, shall be entitled to an appropriation of [50] acres or to so much as shall make up what he owns or has owned [50] acres in full and absolute dominion, and no other person shall be capable of taking an appropriation.

Lands heretofore holden ⟨in fee⟩ of the crown in feesimple, and those hereafter to be appropriated shall be holden in full and absolute dominion, of no superior whatever.

No lands shall be appropriated until purchased of the Indian native proprietors; nor shall any purchases be made of them but on behalf of the public, by authority of acts of the General assembly to be passed for every purchase specially.

The territories contained within the charters erecting the colonies of Maryland Pennsylvania, North and South Carolina, are hereby ceded, released, & for ever confirmed to the people of those colonies respectively, with all the rights of property, jurisdiction and government and all other rights whatsoever which might at any time heretofore have been claimed by this colony. the Western and

Northern extent of this country shall in all other respects stand as fixed by the charter of

until by act of the Legislature one or more territories shall be laid off Westward of the Alleghaney mountains for new colonies, which colonies shall be established on the same fundamental laws contained in this instrument, and shall be free and independant of this colony and of all the world.

Descents shall go according to the laws of Gavelkind, save only that females shall have equal rights with males.

No person hereafter coming into this country shall be held within the same in slavery under any pretext whatever. — Slaves.

All persons who by their own oath or affirmation, or by other testimony shall give satisfactory proof to any court of record in this colony that they purpose to reside in the same [7] years at the least and who shall subscribe the fundamental laws, shall be considered as residents and entitled to all the rights of persons natural born. — Naturalization.

All persons shall have full and free liberty of religious opinion; nor shall any be compelled to frequent or maintain any religious institution. — Religion.

No freeman shall be debarred the use of arms [within his own lands or tenements] — Arms.

There shall be no standing army but in time of actual war. — Standing army.

Printing presses shall be free, except so far as by commission of private injury cause may be given of private action. — Free press.

All Forfeitures heretofore going to the king, shall go to the state; save only such as the legislature may hereafter abolish. — Forfeitures.

The royal claim to Wrecks, waifs, strays, treasure-trove, royal mines, royal fish, royal birds, are declared to have been usurpations on common right. — Wrecks.

No Salaries or Perquisites shall be given to any officer but by some future act of the legislature. no salaries shall be given to the Administrator, members of the Legislative houses, judges of the court of Appeals, judges of the County courts, or other inferior jurisdictions, Privy counsellors, or Delegates to the American Congress: but the reasonable expences of the Administrator, members of the house of representatives, judges of the court of Appeals, Privy counsellors, & Delegates, for subsistence while acting in the duties of their office, may be borne by the public, if the Legislature shall so direct. — Salaries.

⟨*The Qualifications of all officers not otherwise hereby directed, shall be an oath of fidelity to the state, and the having given no bribe* — Qualifications.

to obtain their office⟩ No person shall be capable of acting in any office, Civil, Military [or Ecclesiastical] who shall have given any bribe to obtain such office, or who shall not previously take an oath of fidelity to the state.

None of these fundamental laws and principles of government shall be repealed or altered, but by the personal consent of the people on summons to meet in their respective counties on one and the same day by an act of Legislature to be passed for every special occasion: and if in such county meetings the people of two thirds of the counties shall give their suffrage for any particular alteration or repeal referred to them by the said act, the same shall be accordingly repealed or altered, and such repeal or alteration shall take it's place among these fundamentals & stand on the same footing with them, in lieu of the article repealed or altered.

The laws heretofore in force in this colony shall remain ⟨*still*⟩ in force, except so far as they are altered by the foregoing fundamental laws, or so far as they may be hereafter altered by acts of the Legislature.

Dft (NN). This copy of TJ's constitution was folded and docketed in correct legislative form. At the top of the two sheets, after it was folded, TJ endorsed this title on his substantive law: "A *Bill* for new modelling the form of government, & for establishing the fundamental principles thereof in future." Below this, he added: "It is proposed that this bill, after correction by the Convention, shall be referred by them to the people to be assembled in their respective counties and that the suffrages of two thirds of the counties shall be requisite to establish it."

The provenance of this text is given in a memorandum of Victor H. Paltsits (Ford Papers, NN, 1 Feb. 1916): the document was acquired from Cassius F. Lee, Jr., of Alexandria, by "William Evarts Benjamin, then a well-known dealer of New York City who acted in the matter for some woman whose name is not revealed." Alexander Maitland purchased it of Benjamin for the Lenox Library. Shortly after this text was brought to light in 1890, efforts were made to identify it as the copy that TJ had given to George Wythe to convey to the Virginia Convention (D. R. Anderson, "Jefferson and the Va. Const.," *Amer. Hist. Rev.*, XXI [1915-1916], 751). A close comparison of the copy found among Wythe's

papers at his death in 1806 and printed with meticulous accuracy in the *Richmond Enquirer*, 20 June 1806, clearly establishes the identity of that copy and the one now in the New York Public Library, here designated as the Third Draft (Boyd, *Declaration of Independence*, 1945, p. 44-5). In 1825 TJ wrote: "I . . . drew a sketch or outline of a Constitution, with a preamble, which I sent to Mr. Pendleton, president of the convention. . . . He informed me afterwards by letter, that he received it on the day on which the Committee of the whole had reported to the House the plan they had agreed to . . ." (TJ to Augustus B. Woodward, 3 Apr. 1825). It has been assumed that this was a mistake of memory on TJ's part and that he confused Pendleton with Wythe (Hazelton, p. 451). Wythe reported to TJ that "the one you put into my hands was *shewn* [italics supplied]" to those chiefly engaged in framing the Constitution (Wythe to TJ, 27 July 1776). This, together with the significant fact that Wythe's copy remained among his papers, indicates that TJ was correct in saying he had sent a copy to Pendleton. If so, this would tend to confirm the supposition advanced in the notes to the Second Draft that two copies were sent. Wirt indicates that the copy he saw in the State archives was the one "forwarded . . . to Mr. Wythe";

however, he also describes it as "an original rough draught," a description which scarcely fits the Wythe copy or Third Draft (Wirt, *Henry*, I, 196). Moreover, if Wythe's copy had been used by the Convention as the text from which several parts were taken for incorporation in the Constitution adopted by that body, it seems very likely that some corrections or markings on the MS of the text would have been made to indicate what parts had been selected, how they had been altered, &c. (see *Conv. Jour.*, May 1776, 1816 edn., p. 78, for 28 June, when it was ordered that "the said plan of government, together with the amendments, be *fairly transcribed*" [italics supplied]). No such alterations or markings appear on the Third Draft.

¹ MS torn; text supplied from the precisely correct and literal text printed in the *Richmond Enquirer*, 20 June 1806.

² A word must have been omitted by TJ at this point; elsewhere in the document the comparable phrase is employed: e.g., "incapable of holding any public pension . . . ," not "incapable of any pension." The fact is that at this point in the Second Draft TJ wrote: "incapable of being again appointed to the same"; then struck out the words "being again appointed to"; then interlined "holding," making the phrase read as he usually wrote it "incapable of holding the same." However, the word "holding" appears also to have had a line drawn through it, though it also bears evidence of the slight smudge that TJ occasionally made in his rough drafts, as if he had run his finger over a freshly drawn line or word to expunge it. At all events, it is certain that "incapable of *holding*" is what he normally would have written and it is equally certain that "holding" was interlined though perhaps lined out. The point is worth noting since both the text of the Third Draft and the text of the *Enquirer* omit the word "holding" at this point, thus adding to the preponderant evidence that they are identical.

³ The square brackets here and below in the text are in the MS.

⁴ The words in italics were struck out, and then TJ interlined the following words at the top of the same page of MS: "nor shall there be power any where to pardon or to remit fines or punishments." This clause was finally inserted in the next to the last paragraph under "I. Legislative," above.

⁵ The six lines in the MS beginning with the words "by an act of the legislature" down to and including "defined by the legislature, and for" are written on a slip of paper pasted on the MS at this point. This represents a curious omission made by TJ in copying, an omission that seems inexplicable except on the ground that the Third Draft (Wythe's copy in NN) was copied not from the Second Draft (DLC) but from another text. As originally copied in the Third Draft, TJ caused this passage to read in part, without a break in the lines, "for breach of which they shall be removeable [end of line] the punishment of which the said legislature shall have previously prescribed certain and determinate pains. . . ." The First Draft includes in rough, interlined form the six lines thus omitted at the end of the line "they shall be removeable," but in the Second Draft this passage comprises four and a half lines at the bottom of page 7 and two and a half lines at the top of page 8. It is conceivable that TJ could have accidentally skipped such a passage if it had ended at the bottom of a page or if its beginning and end coincided with the beginning and end of a line. But it is difficult to believe that he could have made this error if he had been copying from a text where the passage began in the middle of the line near the bottom of one page and ended in the middle of the line near the top of another, particularly in a case where the omission involved such a sharp break in the continuity and sense. The evidence in this instance alone is not conclusive, but taken in connection with TJ's remarks in 1825, with the statements of Wirt and Leigh as cited in notes to the Second Draft, and other evidences given in these notes, it seems certain that the Third Draft was copied from another fair copy made from the Second Draft. At all events, the omission of this passage conclusively proves that the Third Draft is the copy that George Wythe carried to Virginia, for the *Richmond Enquirer* printed the six lines written on the slip of paper, but neglected to include the lines written underneath. This typographical error obviously could have occurred only in the use of the copy now in NN, which, therefore, is the copy transmitted by Wythe.

IV. The Plan of Government
as Originally Drawn by George Mason

[8-10 June 1776]

A PLAN OF GOVERNMENT

Laid before the committee of the House, which they have
ordered to be printed for the perusal of
the members.

1. LET the legislative, executive, and judicative departments, be separate and distinct, so that neither exercise the powers properly belonging to the other.

2. Let the legislative be formed of two distinct branches, who, together, shall be a complete legislature. They shall meet once, or oftener, every year, and shall be called the GENERAL ASSEMBLY of VIRGINIA.[1]

3. Let one of these be called the Lower House of Assembly, and consist of two delegates, or representatives, chosen for each county, annually; of such men as have resided in the same for one year last past, are freeholders of the county, possess an estate of inheritance of land, in *Virginia*, of at least one thousand pounds value, and are upwards of twenty four years of age.[2]

4. Let the other be called the Upper House of Assembly, and consist of twenty four members; for whose election, let the different counties be divided into twenty four districts, and each county of the respective district, at the time of the election of its delegates for the Lower House, choose twelve deputies, or sub-electors, being freeholders residing therein, and having an estate of inheritance of lands within the district of at least five hundred pounds value. In case of dispute, the qualifications to be determined by the majority of the said deputies. Let these deputies choose, by ballot, one member for the Upper House of Assembly, who is a freeholder of the district, hath been a resident therein for one year last past, possesses an estate of inheritance of lands in *Virginia* of at least two thousand pounds value, and is upwards of twenty eight years of age. To keep up this assembly, by rotation, let the districts be equally divided into four classes, and numbered, at the end of one year after the general election. Let the six members elected by the first division be displaced, rendered ineligible for four years, and the vacancies be supplied in the manner aforesaid. Let this rotation be applied to each division according to its number, and continued in due order annually.[3]

5. Let each House settle its own rules of proceeding direct writs of election for supplying intermediate vacancies; and let the right of suffrage, both in the election of members for the Lower House, and of deputies for the districts, be extended to those having leases for land, in which there is an unexpired term of seven years, and to every housekeeper who hath resided for one year last past in the county, and hath been the father of three children in this country.[4]

6. Let all laws originate in the Lower House, to be approved, or re-

jected, by the Upper House, or to be amended with the consent of the Lower House, except money bills, which in no instance shall be altered by the Upper House, but wholly approved or rejected.

7. Let a Governour, or chief magistrate, be chosen annually, by joint ballot of both Houses; who shall not continue in that office longer than three years successively, and then be ineligible for the next three years. Let an adequate, but moderate salary, be settled on him, during his continuance in office; and let him, with the advice of a Council of State, exercise the executive powers of government, and the power of proroguing or adjourning the General Assembly, or of calling it upon emergencies, and of granting reprieves or pardons, except in cases where the prosecution shall have been carried on by the Lower House of Assembly.

8. Let a Privy Council, or Council of State, consisting of eight members, be chosen by joint ballot of both Houses of Assembly, promiscuously[5] from their members, or the people at large, to assist in the administration of government. Let the Governour be President of this Council; but let them annually choose one of their own members, as Vice-President, who, in case of the death or absence of the Governour, shall act as Lieutenant-Governour. Let three members be sufficient to act, and their advice be entered of record in their proceedings. Let them appoint their own clerk, who shall have a salary settled by law, and take an oath of secrecy, in such matters as he shall be directed by the Board to conceal, unless called upon by the Lower House of Assembly for information. Let a sum of money, appropriated to that purpose, be divided annually among the members, in proportion to their attendance; and let them be incapable, during their continuance of office, of sitting in either House of Assembly. Let two members be removed, by ballot of their own Board, at the end of every three years, and be ineligible for the three next years. Let this be regularly continued, by rotation, so as that no member be removed before he hath been three years in the Council; and let these vacancies, as well as those occasioned by death or incapacity, be supplied by new elections, in the same manner as the first.

9. Let the Governour, with the advice of the Privy Council, have the appointment of the militia officers, and the government of the militia, under the laws of the country.

10. Let the two Houses of Assembly, by joint ballot, appoint judges of the supreme court, judges in chancery, judges of admiralty, and the attorney-general, to be commissioned by the Governour, and continue in office during good behaviour. In case of death or incapacity, let the Governour, with the advice of the Privy Council, appoint persons to succeed in office *pro tempore*, to be approved or displaced by both Houses. Let these officers have fixed and adequate salaries, and be incapable of having a seat in either House of Assembly, or in the Privy Council, except the attorney-general and the treasurer, who may be permitted to a seat in the Lower House of Assembly.

11. Let the Governour, and Privy Council, appoint justices of the peace for the counties. Let the clerks of all the courts, the sheriffs, and coroners, be nominated by the respective courts, approved by the Governour and Privy Council, and commissioned by the Governour. Let the

clerks be continued during good behaviour, and all fees be regulated by law. Let the justices appoint constables.

12. Let the Governour, any of the Privy Counsellors, judges of the supreme court, and all other officers of government, for mal-administration, or corruption, be prosecuted by the Lower House of Assembly (to be carried on by the attorney-general, or such other person as the House may appoint) in the supreme court of common law. If found guilty, let him, or them, be either removed from office, or for ever disabled to hold any office under the government, or subjected to such pains or penalties as the laws shall direct.

13. Let all commissions run in the name of the *Commonwealth of Virginia*, and be tested by the Governour, with the seal of the commonwealth annexed. Let writs run in the same manner, and be tested by the clerks of the several courts. Let indictments conclude, *Against the peace and dignity of the commonwealth.*[6]

14. Let a treasurer be appointed annually, by joint ballot of both Houses.

15. In order to introduce this government, let the representatives of the people, now met in Convention, choose twenty four members to be an upper House; and let both Houses, by joint ballot, choose a Governour and Privy Council; the Upper House to continue until the last day of *March* next, and the other officers until the end of the succeeding session of Assembly. In case of vacancies, the President to issue writs for new elections.

Two-page printed leaflet (DLC); Sabin 100027. Another copy is in DLC, Madison Papers; this copy appears to have been a four-page leaflet containing both the Declaration of Rights and the Plan of Government, but the two leaves were apparently separated when the Madison Papers were bound. The copy in the TJ Papers was sent to TJ by William Fleming with his letter of 22 June 1776, which settles the question of Mason's authorship of this Plan. The text given here is the text as originally put in type, without the numerous MS emendations recorded by Fleming (for which see Document v, following). No copy of George Mason's MS from which this text was printed is known to be extant; according to Fleming's letter, Mason's Plan was laid before the Committee about 8-10 June. The subtitle of Madison's copy has been altered in his handwriting to read: "Laid before the committee appointed for that purpose, which they have ordered to be printed for the perusal of the members of the House." In explanation of this change, see a note in a MS copy of the Mason Plan and of the Constitution as adopted (in parallel columns) made by James Madison late in life, which reads: "From this correc-

tion it appears that what was laid before the Committee was printed by its order not by that of the Convention . . . nor is there in the Journal any order for printing any plan of Government reported to the Convention from a Committee" (DLC, Madison Papers, I; Madison, *Writings*, ed. Hunt, I, 35-40; see also Madison to Augustus B. Woodward, 11 Sep. 1824, same, IX, 207-8; and Rives, *Madison*, I, 151, note; Brant, *Madison*, I, 256-7). For a different alteration in the subtitle, recorded by Fleming, see the Committee Revision (Document v, following).

[1] All of the plans discussed, even that of Carter Braxton, agreed upon a bicameral legislature and the principle of separation of powers.

[2] The basis of representation was one of the two major issues—the other being suffrage qualifications—discussed in the constitutional debates of 1776 and in succeeding years. The plan of representation proposed by Mason and in substance adopted by the Convention was in marked contrast to that of TJ, which aimed at an equalization of representation among the counties according to population and at redressing the balance

as between Tidewater and Piedmont Virginia.

3 This interesting proposal for a sort of electoral college has the appearance of being an original scheme, probably one that Mason conceived.

4 This restrictive and highly novel provision for the basis of suffrage, including the rather ambiguous parenthood qualification (were the children to be living, legitimate, white, actually born "in this country," &c.?) certainly has the stamp of originality. The suffrage as then exercised in Virginia, which the Convention preferred to Mason's more restrictive basis, was limited to males over twenty-one possessing property; women, minors, recusants, convicts, free Negroes, mulattoes, and Indians, even though freeholders, were incapable of voting or being elected to

the House of Burgesses (Act of 1769, Hening, VIII, 305-17; J. F. Prufer, "The Franchise in Virginia from Jefferson through the Convention of 1829," WMQ, 2d ser., VII [1927], 256-9).

5 The word "promiscuously" suggests that Mason may have employed the *Gazette* Plan, in which the word is used and the provisions are substantially in agreement.

6 This provision for commissions, writs, and indictments seems clearly to reflect, both in substance and phraseology, the Adams Plan, indicating that Mason had read it carefully. Indeed, except for the apparently original provisions noted above (notes 3 and 4) and the separation of the privy council from the upper house, the Mason and Adams Plans substantially agree (Adams, *Works*, IV, 199).

V. The Mason Plan as Revised by the Committee

[22 June 1776]

A PLAN

Laid before [a] committee of the House, [appointed to prepare a form of Government] which they have ordered to be printed for the perusal of the members.

1. LET the legislative, executive, and judicative departments, be separate and distinct, so that neither exercise the powers properly belonging to the other.

2. Let the legislative be formed of two distinct branches, who, together, shall be a complete legislature. They shall meet once, or oftener, every year, and shall be called the GENERAL ASSEMBLY of VIRGINIA.[1]

3. Let one of these be called the Lower House of Assembly, and consist of two delegates, or representatives, [for each county, one for the Town of Jas. City, one for the city of Wmsbg. one for the W & Mary college, & one for the borough of Norfolk, to be chosen annually of such men as are freeholders and in other respects qualified according to law and ancient usage.]

4. Let the other be called the Upper House of Assembly, and consist of twenty four members; [of whom 12 shall constitute a house to proceed on business] for whose election, let the different counties be divided into twenty four districts, and each county of the respective district, at the time of the election of its delegates for the Lower House, choose twelve deputies, or sub-electors, being freeholders residing therein, [And not be a delegate or representative of the lower house] and having an

estate of inheritance of lands within the district of at least five hundred pounds value. In case of dispute, the qualifications to be determined by the majority of the said deputies. Let these deputies [or any nine from each and every county] choose [annually], by ballot, one member for the Upper House of Assembly, who is a freeholder [residing in] the district.[2]

5. Let the right of suffrage, both in the election of members for the Lower House, and of deputies for the districts, [remain as exercised at present and let each house settle its own rules of proceding, & direct writs of election for supplying intermediate vacancies.]

6. Let all laws originate in the Lower House, to be approved, or rejected, by the Upper House, or to be amended with the consent of the Lower House, except money bills, which in no instance shall be altered by the Upper House, but wholly approved or rejected.

7. Let a Governour, or chief magistrate, be chosen annually, by joint ballot of both Houses; who shall not continue in that office longer than three years successively, and then be ineligible for the next [four] years. Let an adequate, but moderate salary, be settled on him, during his continuance in office; and let him, with the advice of a Council of State, exercise the executive powers of government, and of granting reprieves or pardons, except in cases [hereinafter mentioned] where the prosecution shall have been carried on by the Lower House of Assembly, [or where the laws shall otherwise particularly direct, unless the lower house of assembly shall address the Govr. or commr. for such reprieve or pardon.]

[Let each house of the general assembly adjourn themselves respectively. Let not the governor, or commander in chief adjourn, prorogue, or dissolve them: but let him, if necessary, by advice of the council of state, or on application of the majority of the lower house call them before the time to which they shall stand adjourn'd.][3]

8. Let a Privy Council, or Council of State, consisting of eight members, be chosen by joint ballot of both Houses of Assembly, [taken in the lower house, either] from their own members, or the people at large, to assist in the administration of government. Let the Governour be President of this Council; but let them annually choose one of their own members, as Vice-President, who, in case of the death [inability or necessary] absence of the Governour, shall act as Lieutenant-Governour. Let [four] members be sufficient to act, and their advice be entered of record, [and sign'd by the members giving such advice, to be laid before the general assembly when called for by them, but let not this be done, but on extraordinary occasions.] Let them appoint their own clerk, who shall have a salary settled by law, and take an oath of secrecy, in such matters as he shall be directed by the Board to conceal. Let a sum of money, appropriated to that purpose, be divided annually among the members, in proportion to their attendance; and let them be incapable, during their continuance of office, of sitting in either House of Assembly. Let two members be removed, by ballot of their own Board, at the end of every three years, and be ineligible for the three next years. Let this be regularly continued, by rotation, so as that no member be removed before he hath been three years in the Council; and let these

vacancies, as well as those occasioned by death or incapacity, be supplied by new elections, in the same manner as the first.

[9. Let the delegates for Virginia to the Continental congress be chosen annually or superseded in the mean time by joint ballot of both houses of assembly. Let the present militia officers be continued and vacancies supplyed by appointmt. of the governour or commander in chief, with advice of the privy council, on recommendation of the county courts of double the number of officers immediately necessary, but let the govr. & council have a power of displacing any officer, on complaint for misbehaviour or inability, or to supply vacancies of officers happening when in actual service. Let the govr. embody the militia with the advice of the privy council, and when embodied, let the govr. alone have the direction of the militia, under the laws of the country.][4]

10. Let the two Houses of Assembly, by joint ballot, appoint judges of the supreme court, [superior courts,] judges in chancery, judges of admiralty, [secretary,] and the attorney-general, to be commissioned by the Governour, and continue in office during good behaviour. In case of death [resignation,] or incapacity, let the Governour, with the advice of the Privy Council, appoint persons to succeed in office *pro tempore*, to be approved or displaced by both Houses. Let these officers have fixed and adequate salaries, and [together with all others holding lucrative offices] be incapable of having a seat in either House of Assembly, or in the Privy Council, except the treasurer, who may be permitted to a seat in the Lower House of Assembly.

11. [12. Let the govr. or comr. in chief, with the advice of the privy council appoint justices of the peace for the counties, and, in case of Vancies, or a necessity of increasing the number, let double the number of magistrates requisite be recommended by the courts, & such as may be necessary appointed by the govr. or commr. in chief with the advice of the privy council. Let the present acting secretary in Virga. & clerks of all the courts continue in office. In case of vacancies, either by death, incapacity or resignation, let a secretary be appointed as before directed, & all the clerks by the respective courts. Let the present & future clerks hold their offices during good behaviour to be judged & determined in the supreme court. Let the sherifs & coroners be nominated by the respective courts, approv'd by the Govr. or commr. in chief, with the advice of the privy council, & commissioned by the govr. Let the justices appoint constables, and all fees of the aforesd. officers be regulated by Law.][5]

12. [11. Let the Govr. when he is out of office, and all other offenders agt. the State, either by mal-administration, corruption or other means, by which the safety of the state may be endangered, be impeached by the lower house of assembly, such impeachmt. to be prosecuted by the attny. genl. or such other person or persons as the house may appoint, in the supreme court of common law, according to the laws of the land, if found guilty.[6] Let him or them be either forever disabled to hold any office under government, or remov'd from such office pro tempore, or subjected to such pains & penalties as the law shall direct. If all or any of the judges of the supreme court of common law shall on good grounds

to be judged of by the lower house of assembly, be accused of any of the crimes or offences before mentioned, let such lower house impeach the judge or judges so accused before the upper house of assembly, & thereupon let such upper house appoint commissioners for the trial of the accused in such manner as the law shall direct.][7]

13. Let commissions [& grants] run in the name of the *Commonwealth of Virginia*, and be [at]tested by the Governour, with the seal of the commonwealth annexed. Let writs run in the same manner, and be [at]tested by the clerks of the several courts. Let indictments conclude, *Against the peace and dignity of the commonwealth.*

14. Let a treasurer be appointed annually, by joint ballot of both Houses.

15. In order to introduce this government, let the representatives of the people, met in Convention, choose twenty four members to be an upper House; and let both Houses, by joint ballot, choose a Governour and Privy Council; the Upper House to continue until the last day of *March* next, and the other officers until the end of the succeeding session of Assembly. In case of vacancies, the President to issue writs for new elections.[8]

Two-page printed leaflet (DLC), Sabin 100027 (same copy as in Document IV), bearing numerous cancellations and marginalia by William Fleming, together with a MS on a separate page (also DLC: TJ Papers, 235: 42207) containing four paragraphs, in Fleming's hand, to be substituted for those deleted in the Mason Plan by the Committee. These were enclosed in Fleming's letter to TJ, 22 June 1776. That letter enables us to assign to this revision an exact date, indeed an exact hour: at the time the bell rang for the Convention to meet on 22 June, the status of revision of the Mason Plan by the Committee was as here printed. At this time the Committee had been engaged in discussing and amending the Mason Plan for "about a fortnights time." Some additional amendments were subsequently made by the Committee, by the Committee of the Whole, or by the Convention. Nevertheless, this precisely dated revision, made toward the close of the Committee's labors and just a day prior to the arrival of George Wythe carrying TJ's Third Draft, provides a fortuitous base line for identifying the amendments and additions drawn by the Convention from TJ's Draft. The marginalia or interlineations in the leaflet in the handwriting of Fleming are identified here by supplied square brackets; those on the separate page are also enclosed in brackets and noted in footnotes 3, 4, 5, and 7.

[1] Opposite paragraphs 1, 2, and 6 Fleming drew a bracket and added the word "Agreed." It is almost certain that he did this for paragraph 14 also: the bracket is present, but the writing in the margin is illegible. Paragraph 14, as this indicates, remained substantially unchanged and was adopted by the Convention.

[2] The remainder of this paragraph in the printed Plan, struck out by the Committee, was restored in large part by subsequent amendment in Committee of the Whole or in Convention.

[3] This amendment was written on the separate sheet which Fleming sent along with the printed Plan, opposite which he wrote: "Between the 7th & 8th article add this clause or article."

[4] Paragraph 9 in the Mason Plan (appointment of militia officers) was struck out by the Committee. On the separate sheet Fleming transcribed this paragraph which the Committee substituted for paragraph 9 in the Mason Plan.

[5] Following the first sentence in the Mason Plan as printed, a sentence concerning vacancies was at one point inserted in the margin, with the following comment: "(Once agreed to by the committee, & afterwards rejected.)" The whole paragraph was then struck out

and a new paragraph substituted on the separate sheet. This paragraph was then renumbered "12" by Fleming, and paragraph 12 in the Mason Plan was renumbered "11."

6 Thus in MS. The passage obviously should read: "according to the laws of the land. If found guilty, let him," &c.

7 Paragraph 12 of the Mason Plan was at one point amended by the insertion of the words "when he is out of office" after "Let the Governour"; then Fleming crossed out the whole and on the separate sheet rewrote and renumbered the paragraph as given here.

8 Only one change in this paragraph was indicated by Fleming, since this section was being discussed by the Committee as he was writing to TJ on 22 June. This change was the elimination of the word "now" before "met in Convention," an alteration indicating that some members of the Convention may have shared TJ's view that the Convention itself lacked the power to promulgate a substantive law; also, as amended, Mason's proviso that the Convention itself should choose the first members of the Senate was dropped. Both the Declaration of Rights and the Virginia Constitution as adopted had the status of ordinances. TJ drafted his constitution as a legislative bill, but he included the proviso that it should be submitted to the electors for approval, whereas the Constitution of Virginia, as adopted by the Convention, remained merely an ordinance until revised in 1829-1830. This was the cause of much of TJ's long-continued opposition to it.

VI. The Draft Reported by the Committee

(Amendments Thereto Offered in Convention)

[24 June 1776]

Amendments to the plan of Government continued[1]

Page 3 line 23.[2] leave out from the word *successively* to the word *an* in the next line & insert *nor be eligible until the expiration of four years after he shall have been out of that office.*

24. after the word *salary* insert *shall.*

25. strike out the words *let him* and insert *he shall*

26. strike out from the word Government to the end of the Clause & insert according to the laws of this common Wealth and shall not under any pretence exercise any power or prerogative by virtue of any law statute or custom of England. ⟨*He shall be bound by the Acts of the legislature tho' not expressly named; he shall have no negative on the Bills of the legislature; he shall be liable to action tho' not to personal restraint for private duties or wrongs; he shall not possess the prerogatives of declaring War or concluding Peace or issuing letters of Marque or Reprisal, of raising or introducing arm'd forces building armed Vessels forts or strong holds,*⟩[3] but he shall with the advice of the Council of State have the power of granting reprieves or pardons except where the prosecution shall have been carried on by the House of Delegates, or the law shall otherwise particularly direct, in which

Cases no reprieve or pardon shall be granted but by resolve of the House of Delegates

Page 5. line 1. Strike out the words *let each* & insert *either*
same line after the Word *assembly* insert *may*
Strike out from the word respectively in the same line to the word prorogue in the next line and insert "the Governor shall not"

3. Strike out the words "*let him*" and insert "he shall"

6. Strike out the word *let*
same line after the word Members insert shall

7. strike out from the word Assembly to the Word either in the same line

8. strike out from the Word Government to the Word President in the tenth line & insert they shall annually choose out of their own Members a

11. after the word Governor insert "from the Government"
Same line strike out *Let* & insert shall after the word *Members*

12. after the word Advice insert and proceedings
same line strike out from the word Members to the word to in the same line and insert present to any part whereof any Member may enter his dissent

13. Strike out from the Word them to the Word appoint in the next line and insert "this Council may"

15. Strike out the Word let

16. After the word purpose insert "shall be"

17. Strike out the words *let them* & insert *they shall*

18. Strike out the Word let

Line 18. After the Word Members insert shall

19. Strike out the word let
same line after the Word this insert shall

21. Strike out the word let
same line after the word incapacity insert shall

23. Strike out the word let

24. same line after the word Congress insert shall

25. Strike out the word let
same line after the word officers insert shall

26. Strike out the words "or commander in chief

27. Strike out from the word *from*[4] to the Word *in* in the next line and insert the respective County Courts but the Governor & Council shall have a power of suspending any officer & ordering Martial

29. Strike out from the word Service to the word embody in the next line & insert the Governor may
31. Strike out the word Let
   same line after the word *alone* insert *shall*

Page 7. line 1. Strike out the word *let*
   same line after the word Assembly insert shall
   same line strike out or Superior Courts & insert of appeals & Genl. Court.

Line the 3d. strike out *Let* & after *Council* in the next line insert *shall*.

4. Strike out the words Pro tempore
5. Strike out the word *let*
   same line after the word *officers* insert *shall*
6. Strike out the words *having a seat in* & insert being elected Members of
   same line after the Word or strike out the word in
   same line strike out from the Word Council to the end of the Clause
8. Strike out the word *let* & the words *commander in chief*
   same line after the word Council insert *shall*
9. Strike out from the Word number to the Word *the* in the eleventh line & insert *hereafter* such appointments to be made upon the Recommendation of the respective County Courts
12. After the word *Courts* insert *shall*.
14. Strike out the word *Let*
   same line after the word Clerks insert *shall*
15. Strike out the word supreme & insert *General* strike out *let*
   same line after the word Coroners insert *shall*
16. Strike out the words *or Commander in chief*
17. Strike out the word *Let*
   same line after the word Justices insert *shall*
18. Strike out the word Let
   same line strike out *all other offenders* & insert others offending
20. Strike out the word *impeached* & insert *impeachable*

Page 7. line 21. Strike out the words *supreme Court of common law* & insert *Genl. Court.*

22. Strike out the Words *let him or them* & insert *he or they shall*
25. Strike out the Words *supreme Court of common Law* & insert *Genl. Court.*
26. Strike out the Word *Let*[5]

30. Strike out the Word *Let*

same line after the word *Grants* insert *shall*

same line Strike out the Words *be attested* & insert *bear teste*

31. Strike out the Word *Let*

same line after the word *Writs* insert *shall*

same line strike out the Words *be attested* & insert *bear teste*

32. Strike out the Word *Let*

same line after the Word *indictments* insert *shall*

34. Strike out the word *Let*

same line after the Word *Treasurer* insert *shall*

MS (Vi); in an unidentified clerk's hand, with corrections by others, one of whom is Edmund Pendleton.

1 While these amendments are "continued," this does not necessarily mean that some parts of the MS are missing; the amendments to the first part of the Constitution may have been made directly on page 1 of the Report of the Committee itself. It is in the first and last parts of the Constitution that most of the borrowings from TJ's Draft were made, and the amendments to these parts may, therefore, have been made on his MS, since it was obviously not a part of the Report of the Committee and could not be cited with the same precision that that Report is cited in this MS list of amendments.

The Report of the Committee of 24 June, to which these amendments refer, is missing. That the amendments do refer to that Report is proved by the fact, among others, that the missing draft employed, as the Mason Plan did, the subjunctive rather than the imperative form ("Let a Privy Council . . . be chosen" instead of "A Privy Council . . . shall be chosen"). From these amendments it is possible to reconstruct and to conjecture some of the characteristics of the missing Report of the Committee: it was an eight-page document; its text was only on rectos 1, 3, 5, 7; the verso pages (2, 4, 6, 8) were possibly left blank as space for the inclusion of amendments. It was almost certainly printed; the Mason Plan had been printed "for the perusal of the members" and the missing Report, which was obviously a fair copy and not the printed Mason Plan with marginal amendments, as in Fleming's copy of it, was equally if not more necessary to be printed. Moreover, the assumption that there were blank pages

would seem more clearly to indicate a printed than a written text; printed on one side the report would have required only one instead of two impressions by the slow hand-presses of the day—and time was important to the Convention. Finally, by using these amendments in reference to the Committee Revision on 22 June (Document v), the enlarged and missing Report of the Committee of 24 June can be substantially reconstructed to fit pages 3, 5, and 7 in lines of precise and provable length. This reconstruction of the missing Report establishes with certainty 34 lines on page 7, 31 lines on page 5, and 8 lines on page 3. Since the length of lines may be regarded as constant, the remainder of page 3 and page 1 can be established by extrapolation. This procedure, however, reveals the surprising fact that only two lines of the text are left over for page 1. Now the preamble to TJ's Draft is of the right length to fill the remainder of page 1. Consequently, it seems a plausible conjecture that the Committee may have added TJ's preamble to its own text before reporting (but see Document VII, explanatory note). The conjectured opinion that the missing Report of the Committee was printed is further supported by the alteration made in the subtitle of the printed Mason Plan by Madison (see Document IV, descriptive note).

2 This amendment refers to the paragraph corresponding to section 7 in the Committee's Revision of the Mason Plan, q.v. The first entry was deleted: "line 22. After the Word *Magistrates* insert *shall*." This seems to be a further indication that preceding amendments were made directly on the Report of the Committee. Other deletions appear in the list of amendments, but are not noted in all cases, being unimportant or repetitive.

³ The preceding sentence had been drawn directly from TJ's Draft. The remainder of the amendment, preceding and following this, was retained and became part of the Constitution.

⁴ This amendment (referring to paragraph 9 of the Committee Report, concerning militia officers) indicates that the Committee made further changes in the text after Fleming wrote on 22 June, for his copy of the Committee's Revision of the Mason Plan does not contain the word "from" in paragraph 9; it is, of course, possible that such an amendment was made in Convention, prior to these amendments.

⁵ At this point the following are struck out: "27. After the word *House* insert *shall*. 28. Strike out the word *Let*. Same line after the word *House* insert *shall*."

Opposite these deleted lines is written, in an unidentified hand: "see Mr. Wythe's amt." This amendment refers to paragraph 12 of the Committee's Revision of the Mason Plan; there it was provided that judges of the "supreme court of common law" could be impeached by the lower house before the upper house and tried before commissioners appointed by the latter. Wythe's amendment provided that judges of the General Court could be impeached by the House of Delegates and tried before the Court of Appeals, which is precisely what TJ's Draft provided for. This marginal note establishes Wythe's presence in the Convention and also is evidence that he himself offered an amendment based on TJ's Draft (see note 17 to Document VII).

VII. The Constitution as Adopted by the Convention

[29 June 1776]

In a General Convention.

Begun and holden at the Capitol, in the City of Williamsburg, on Monday the sixth day of May, one thousand seven hundred and seventy six, and continued, by adjournments to the   day of June following:

A CONSTITUTION, OR FORM OF GOVERNMENT,

agreed to and resolved upon by the Delegates and Representatives of the several Counties and Corporations of Virginia.

Whereas George the Third, King of Great Britain and Ireland, and Elector of Hanover, heretofore intrusted with the exercise of the Kingly Office in this Government, hath endeavoured to pervert the same into a detestable and insupportable Tyranny; by putting his negative on laws the most wholesome and necessary for the publick good;

by denying his Governours permission to pass Laws of immediate and pressing importance, unless suspended in their operation for his assent, and, when so suspended, neglecting to attend to them for many Years;

by refusing to pass certain other laws, unless the persons to be benefited by them would relinquish the inestimable right of representation in the legislature;

[377]

by dissolving legislative assemblies repeatedly and continually, for opposing with manly firmness his invasions of the rights of the people;

when dissolved, by refusing to call others for a long space of time, thereby leaving the political system without any legislative head;

by endeavouring to prevent the population of our Country, and, for that purpose, obstructing the laws for the naturalization of foreigners;[1]

by keeping among us, in times of peace, standing Armies and Ships of War;

by affecting to render the Military independent of, and superiour to, the civil power;

by combining with others to subject us to a foreign Jurisdiction, giving his assent to their pretended Acts of Legislation;

for quartering large bodies of armed troops among us;

for cutting off our Trade with all parts of the World;

for imposing Taxes on us without our Consent;

for depriving us of the Benefits of Trial by Jury;

for transporting us beyond Seas, to be tried for pretended Offences;

for suspending our own Legislatures, and declaring themselves invested with power to legislate for us in all Cases whatsoever;

by plundering our Seas, ravaging our Coasts, burning our Towns, and destroying the lives of our People;

by inciting insurrections of our fellow Subjects, with the allurements of forfeiture and confiscation;

by prompting our Negroes to rise in Arms among us, those very negroes whom, by an inhuman use of his negative, he hath refused us permission to exclude by Law;

by endeavouring to bring on the inhabitants of our Frontiers the merciless Indian savages, whose known rule of Warfare is an undistinguished Destruction of all Ages, Sexes, and Conditions of Existance;

by transporting, at this time, a large Army of foreign Mercenaries, to compleat the Works of Death, desolation, and Tyranny, already begun with circumstances of Cruelty and Perfidy unworthy the head of a civilized Nation;

by answering our repeated Petitions for Redress with a Repetition of Injuries;

and finally, by abandoning the Helm of Government, and declaring us out of his Allegiance and Protection;

By which several Acts of Misrule,[2] the Government of this Country, as formerly exercised under the Crown of Great Britain, is totally dissolved; We therefore, the Delegates and Representatives of the good People of Virginia, having maturely considered the Premises, and viewing with great concern the deplorable condition to which this once happy Country must be reduced, unless some regular adequate Mode of civil Polity is speedily adopted, and in Compliance with a Recommendation of the General Congress, do ordain and declare the future Form of Government of Virginia to be as followeth:

The legislative, executive, and judiciary departments, shall be separate and distinct, so that neither exercise the Powers properly belonging to the other; nor shall any person exercise the powers of more than one of them at the same time, except that the Justices of the County Courts shall be eligible to either House of Assembly.[3]

The legislative shall be formed of two distinct branches, who, together, shall be a complete Legislature. They shall meet once, or oftener, every Year, and shall be called the General Assembly of Virginia.

One of these shall be called the House of Delegates, and consist of two[4] Representatives to be chosen for each County, and for the District of West Augusta, annually, of such Men as actually reside in and are freeholders of the same, or duly qualified according to Law, and also of one Delegate or Representative to be chosen annually for the city of Williamsburg, and one for the Borough of Norfolk, and a Representative for each of such other Cities and Boroughs, as many hereafter be allowed particular Representation by the legislature; but when any City or Borough shall so decrease as that the number of persons having right of Suffrage therein shall have been for the space of seven Years successively less than half the number of Voters in some one County in Virginia, such City or Borough thenceforward shall cease to send a Delegate or Representative to the Assembly.

The other shall be called the Senate,[5] and consist of twenty four Members, of whom thirteen shall constitute a House to proceed on Business for whose election the different Counties shall be divided into twenty four districts, and each County of the respective District, at the time of the election of its Delegates, shall vote for one[6] Senator, who is actually a resident and freeholder within the District, or duly qualified according to Law, and is upwards of twenty five Years of Age; And the sheriff of each County, within five days at farthest after the last County election in the District, shall meet at some convenient place, and from the Poll so taken in their respective Counties return as a[6] Senator to the House of Senators the Man who shall have the greatest number of Votes in the whole District. To keep up this Assembly by rotation, the Districts shall be equally divided into four Classes, and numbered by Lot. At the end of one Year after the General Election, the six Members elected by the first division shall be displaced, and the vacancies thereby occasioned supplied from such Class or division, by new Election, in the manner aforesaid. This Rotation shall be applied to each division, according to its number, and continued in due order annually.

The right of Suffrage in the Election of Members for both Houses shall remain as exercised at present, and each House shall choose its own Speaker, appoint its own Officers, settle its own rules of proceding, and direct Writs of Election for supplying intermediate vacancies.[7]

All Laws shall originate in the House of Delegates, to be approved or rejected by the[5] Senate or to be amended with the Consent of the House of Delegates; except Money Bills, which in no instance shall be altered by the[5] Senate but wholly approved or rejected[8]

A Governour,[9] or chief Magistrate, shall be chosen annually, by joint Ballot of both Houses, (to be taken in each House respectively, deposited in the Conference room, the Boxes examined jointly by a Committee of each House, and the numbers severally reported to them, that the appointments may be entered, which shall be the mode of taking the joint Ballot of both Houses in all Cases)[10] who shall not continue in that office longer than three Years successively, nor be eligible until the expiration of four Years after he shall have been out of that office: An adequate, but moderate Salary, shall be settled on him during his Continuance in Office; and he shall, with the advice of a Council of State, exercise the Executive powers of Government according to the laws of this Commonwealth; and shall not, under any pretence, exercise any power or prerogative by virtue of any Law, statute, or Custom, of England; But he shall, with the advice of the Council of State, have the power of granting reprieves or pardons, except where the prosecution shall have been carried on by the House of Delegates, or the Law shall otherwise particularly direct; in which Cases, no reprieve or Pardon shall be granted but by resolve of the House of Delegates.

Either House of the General Assembly may adjourn themselves respectively: The Governour shall not prorogue or adjourn the Assembly during their setting, nor dissolve them at any Time; but he shall, if necessary, either by advice of the Council of State, or on application of a Majority of the House of Delegates, call them before the time to which they shall stand prorogued or adjourned.

A Privy Council, or Council of State, consisting of eight Members, shall be chosen by joint Ballot of both Houses of Assembly, either from their own Members or the People at large, to assist in the Administration of Government. They shall annually choose out of their own Members, a President, who, in case of the death, inability, or necessary absence of the Governour from the Government, shall act as lieutenant Governour. Four Members shall be sufficient to act, and their Advice and proceedings shall be entered of Record, and signed by the Members present (to any part whereof any Member may enter his dissent) to be laid before the General Assembly, when called for by them. This Council may appoint their own Clerk, who shall have a Salary settled by Law, and take an Oath of Secrecy in such matters as he shall be directed by the Board to conceal. A sum of Money[11] appropriated to that purpose shall be divided annually among the Members, in proportion to their attendance; and they shall be incapable, during their continuance in Office, of sitting in either House of Assembly. Two Members shall be removed, by joint[12] Ballot of both houses of Assembly[13] at the end of every three Years, and be ineligible for the three next years.[14] These Vacancies, as well as those occasioned by death or incapacity, shall be supplied by new Elections, in the same manner.[15]

The Delegates for Virginia to the Continental Congress shall be chosen annually, or superseded in the mean time by joint Ballot of both Houses of Assembly.

The present Militia Officers shall be continued, and Vacancies supplied by appointment of the Governour, with the advice of the privy Council, or recommendations from the respective County Courts; but the Governour and Council shall have a power of suspending any Officer, and ordering a Court-Martial on Complaint for misbehaviour or inability, or to supply Vacancies of Officers happening when in actual Service. The Governour may embody the Militia, with the advice of the privy Council; and, when embodied, shall alone have the direction of the Militia under the laws of the Country.

The two Houses of Assembly shall, by joint Ballot, appoint judges of the supreme Court of Appeals, and General Court, Judges in Chancery, Judges of Admiralty, Secretary, and the Attorney-General, to be commissioned by the Governour, and continue in Office during good behaviour. In case of death, incapacity, or resignation, the Governour, with the advice of the privy Council, shall appoint Persons to succeed in Office, to be approved or displaced by both Houses. These Officers shall have fixed and adequate Salaries, and, together with all others holding lucrative Offices, and all Ministers of the Gospel of every Denomination,[16] be incapable of being elected Members of either House of Assembly, or the privy Council.

The Governour, with the Advice of the privy Council, shall appoint Justices of the Peace for the Counties; and in case of Vacancies, or a necessity of increasing the number hereafter, such appointments to be made upon the recommendation of the respective County Courts. The present acting Secretary in Virginia, and Clerks of all the County Courts, shall continue in Office. In case of Vacancies, either by death, incapacity, or resignation, a Secretary shall be appointed as before directed, and the Clerks by the respective Courts. The present and future Clerks shall hold their Offices during good behaviour, to be judged of and determined in the General Court. The Sheriffs and Coroners shall be nominated by the respective Courts, approved by the Governor with the advice of the privy Council, and commissioned by the Governour. The Justices shall appoint Constables, and all fees of the aforesaid Officers be regulated by law.

The Governor, when he is out of Office, and others offending against the State, either by Mal-administration, Corruption, or other Means, by which the safety of the State may be endangered, shall be impeachable by the House of Delegates. Such impeachment to be prosecuted by the Attorney General, or such other Person or Persons as the House may appoint in the General Court, according to the laws of the Land. If found guilty, he or they shall be either for ever disabled to hold any Office under Government, or removed from such Office *Pro tempore*, or subjected to such Pains or Penalties as the laws shall direct.

If all, or any of the Judges of the General Court, should, on good grounds (to be judged of by the House of Delegates) be accused of any of the Crimes or Offences before-mentioned, such House of Delegates may, in like manner, impeach the Judge or Judges so accused, to be prosecuted in the Court of Appeals; and he or they, if found guilty, shall be punished in the same manner as is prescribed in the preceding Clause.[17]

Commissions and Grants shall run, *In the Name of the Common Wealth of* Virginia, and bear teste by the Governour, with the Seal of the Common wealth annexed. Writs shall run in the same manner, and bear teste by the Clerks of the several Courts. Indictments shall conclude, *Against the Peace and Dignity of the Common-Wealth.*

A Treasurer shall be appointed annually, by joint Ballot of both Houses.

All escheats, penalties, and forfeitures, heretofore going to the King, shall go to the Common Wealth, save only such, as the Legislature may abolish, or otherwise provide for.[18]

The territories contained within the Charters erecting the Colonies of Maryland, Pennsylvania, North and South Carolina, are hereby ceded, released, and forever confirmed to the People of those Colonies respectively, with all the rights of property, jurisdiction, and Government, and all other rights whatsoever which might at any time heretofore have been claimed by Virginia, except the free Navigation and use of the Rivers Potowmack and Pohomoke, with the property of the Virginia Shores or strands bordering on either of the said Rivers, and all improvements which have been or shall be made thereon. The western and northern extent of Virginia shall in all other respects stand as fixed by the Charter of King James the first, in the Year one thousand six hundred and nine, and by the publick Treaty of Peace between the Courts of Great Britain and France in the year one thousand seven hundred and sixty three; Unless by act of this legislature, one or more Territories shall hereafter be laid off, and Governments established Westward of the *Allegheny* Mountains.[19] And no purchases of Land shall be made of the *Indian* Natives but on behalf of the Publick, by authority of the General Assembly.[20]

In order to introduce this Government, the Representatives of the People met in Convention shall choose a Governour and privy Council, also[21] such other Officers directed to be chosen by both Houses as may be judged necessary to be immediately appointed. The Senate,[22] to be first chosen by the people, to continue until the last day of March next, and the other Officers until the end of the succeeding Session of Assembly. In case of Vacancies, the Speaker of either House shall issue Writs for new Elections.

MS (Vi); in clerk's hand and obviously the copy ordered by the Convention on 28 June 1776 to "be fairly transcribed"; alterations and interlineations in the hand of John Tazewell. This is the identical copy sent to the printer of Purdie's *Virginia Gazette*, where it was published in a Supplement to 5 July 1776; this fact is proved by symbols giving direction to the printer for capitals, lower-case letters, and italics. The first are indicated (e.g., "TOTALLY DISSOLVED") by three short, horizontal lines under the middle of each word; the second by a single short line similarly placed; the third by a single line underscoring all the words to be italicized. Capitalization here follows the MS rather than the printed version. Editors of historical documents who follow the general rule of attempting to print a document "as it would have been printed at the time" will, however, find this MS and its printer's directions quite disconcerting.

This document is included here not only because it must be regarded as in part a TJ document, but also because it is essential in establishing a significant fact: that TJ's contribution to the Virginia Constitution is greater than has been generally supposed. Wythe wrote TJ on 27 July: "To those who had the chief hand in forming it the one you put into my hands was shewn. *Two or three parts of this* [italics supplied] were, with little alteration, inserted in that." Despite this reference to the inclusion of "two or three parts" of TJ's Draft, most historians have accepted the view that the Virginia Constitution included only the preamble (though Wirt, *Henry*, I, 196 and K. M. Rowland, "A Lost Paper of Thomas Jefferson," WMQ, 1st ser., I [1892-1893], 37, incidentally refer to but do not otherwise identify "the modifications introduced into the body" of the Constitution from TJ's Draft). Indeed, TJ himself in 1825 agreed with this view: he asserted that Pendleton had informed him by letter that the members had been so long in debate upon a plan of government—"disputed inch by inch, and the subject of so much altercation and debate"—that they "could not, from mere lassitude, have been induced to open the instrument again; but that, being pleased with the Preamble to mine, they adopted it in the House, by way of Amendment to the Report of the Committee; and thus my Preamble became tacked to the work of George Mason" (TJ to Augustus B. Woodward, 3 Apr. 1825).

The fact is, however, that the Convention did "open the instrument again" and for the purpose of doing more than tacking on TJ's preamble. When Wythe and Lee arrived in Williamsburg on Sunday, 23 June, the Committee on the Plan of Government had, presumably, finished its labors (Fleming to TJ, 22 June). On Monday the 24th Archibald Cary for the Committee "reported a plan of government for this colony"; on Wednesday to Friday, 26 to 28 June, the Convention resolved itself into a Committee of the Whole to discuss this plan; the amendments were agreed to on the last date and the Constitution as amended ordered to be "fairly transcribed"; thus amended, it was unanimously adopted on the third reading, 29 June (*Conv. Jour.*, May

1776, 1816 edn., p. 64, 66, 76, 78). From this it seems clear that some parts from TJ's Draft were added by the Committee of the Whole; but see Document VII, explanatory note, where it is conjectured that the Committee may have incorporated TJ's preamble in the missing Report. Hence by comparing the Committee Revision (Document V) and TJ's Third Draft (Document III) with the present document it is possible to identify with more or less certainty the passages from the Third Draft that were incorporated in the Constitution. The results of such a comparison are presented in the notes below. From this it appears that there were four distinct parts of TJ's Draft, not "two or three," embodied in the Constitution "with little alteration" (notes 2, 18, 19, and 20); three parts that very probably had direct influence on the revisions made 26-28 June (notes 3, 16, and 17); and one part that was copied from TJ's Draft during the amending process and later struck out (see note 3 Document VI).

[1] The phrase "& raising the conditions of new appropriations of lands" which appeared in the First and Third Drafts was not adopted by the Virginia Convention, though it was retained by the Continental Congress as a permanent part of the Declaration of Independence. On 15 Aug. 1775 the Virginia Convention directed surveyors to make no surveys under "the late instructions" to the governor (see petition of George Mason, June 1774); now, faced by pressures from the Transylvania Company and other land companies, it is possible, as St. George L. Sioussat plausibly suggests (private communication to editor, 1 Mch. 1949), that the Convention may have thought it would conceivably be necessary further to alter, if not "raise" the "conditions of new appropriations of lands." Dr. Sioussat first called attention to the omission of this phrase in the Virginia Constitution ("The Breakdown of the Royal Management of Lands in the Southern Provinces, 1773-1775," *Agricultural History*, III [1929], 67-98).

[2] The TJ preamble ends at this point. Whereas TJ's Draft had divested George III of all authority and deposed him for abuse of the "kingly office"; had abolished an office "which all experience hath shewn to be inveterately inimical to the public liberty"; and had forever prohibited the reestablishment of the

royal authority in Virginia, the more conservative Convention merely dissolved the government formerly exercised under the crown in Virginia. However, it is to be noted that the Mason Plan included no preamble whatever; the one adopted from TJ's Draft required the insertion of these transitional sentences, even though their terms are very different from those used by TJ. The remainder of this paragraph may, therefore, be properly regarded as an amendment or revision of this part of TJ's Draft.

3 It is probable, though not conclusively demonstrable, that part of the second half of this paragraph was drawn from TJ's Draft. The distinctive provision that *no person* exercising one power should be capable of appointment to the others does not occur in the Mason Plan or the Committee's Revision, but does occur, differently phrased, in TJ's Draft. The fact that this amendment was not brought forth in the two weeks' prior debate, yet was included after the arrival of the one draft that incorporated such a provision, would seem to indicate the direct influence of TJ's Draft. However, the provision that justices of the peace should be allowed to sit in the Assembly is so foreign to the ideas incorporated in TJ's Draft that it may have been inserted by way of reaction to his more strict adherence to separation of powers; even judges of the High Court of Chancery and of the General Court, under his constitution, would only have "session and deliberative voice, but not suffrage" in the Senate.

4 MS deletes: "Delegates or," though "Delegates or Representatives" is used elsewhere in this paragraph. This and other amendments noted below were probably made on 29 June, after this "fairly transcribed" copy was presented for the third reading.

5 MS deletes: "House of Senators."

6 MS deletes: "Member for the House of Senators."

7 The important matter of suffrage was retained by the Convention precisely as amended in the Committee.

8 This and the paragraph respecting the appointment of a treasurer are the only parts of the Mason Plan passed without revision beyond necessary changes in phraseology.

9 MS originally had the spelling "Governor" throughout, but in every case it was changed—possibly by the printer—to "Governour."

10 The printer of the *Virginia Gazette* erred in beginning the parentheses before "which"; MS had originally closed the parenthetic part at that point, but then deleted the closing parenthesis and inserted it as given here.

11 MS deletes: "shall be."

12 The word "joint" is interlined in hand of John Tazewell, clerk of the Convention.

13 MS deletes: "their own Board."

14 MS deletes the following: "This shall be regularly continued by rotation, so as that no Member be removed before he hath been three Years in the Council, and."

15 MS deletes: "as the first."

16 The words "and all Ministers of the Gospel of every Denomination" are interlined in the hand of John Tazewell. This paragraph seems clearly to have been amended by the Convention to conform to the judicial structure set forth in TJ's Draft, since his was the only plan to specify a court of appeals and a general court.

17 This paragraph was amended by Wythe to accord with that provision in TJ's Draft giving the court of appeals jurisdiction over impeachments of "high offenders" and empowering the court of appeals to remove judges of the general court for misbehavior.

18 This paragraph was obviously copied from TJ's Draft, with the addition of the words "escheats, penalties" at one place and the phrase "or otherwise provide for" at another; the substitution of "commonwealth" for "state"; and the deletion of the word "hereafter."

19 This paragraph was copied from TJ's Draft, almost literally, except for the following major differences: (1) the addition of the reservation of free navigation of the Potomac and Pohomoke; and (2) the elimination of the requirement that western territories should be established on "the same fundamental laws contained in this instrument, and ... be free and independent of this colony and of all the world." This, stated T. P. Abernethy, who does not identify it as TJ's contribution to the Constitution, "was the first sweeping assertion by Virginia of her right to jurisdiction over all the land remaining within the boundaries fixed by the charter of 1609" (Abernethy, *Western Lands*, p. 148, where its effect on the strategy of the Indiana Company and the Articles of Confederation are also indicated).

20 Copied from another part of TJ's Draft, though included in the same paragraph with the foregoing. However, TJ's Draft provided that (1) no lands should be appropriated until purchased of the Indians and (2) every Indian purchase should have the authority of an act of legislature for each transaction. These two important provisos were not included in the Constitution as adopted. However, though the language is TJ's, such a provision probably would have been included in the Constitution anyway. For on 24 June, probably as a result of what Wythe and Richard Henry Lee had learned in Philadelphia of the plans of the Indiana Company as well as for the reasons stated (that is, in response to petitions from inhabitants on the western frontiers), the Convention passed a resolution which declared "That no purchases of lands within the Chartered limits of Virginia shall be made, under any pretence whatever, from any Indian tribe or nation, without the approbation of the Virginia legislature" (*Conv. Jour.*, May 1776, 1816 edn., p.63; Abernethy, *Western Lands*, p. 147-8).

21 MS deletes: "twenty four members to be the House of Senators and."

22 MS deletes: "House of Senators which shall continue," and the words "to be first chosen by the people" are interlined.

From William Fleming

DEAR SIR   Wmsburg. 15th. June, 1776.

I thank you for your favor by the post, and beg you will be so obliging as to repeat it, whenever you have leisure. The news from Canada which I fear is too true, is very discouraging, tho' I am not without hope that things will take a favourable turn in that quarter. A letter I have seen from general Washington seems to cherish it. Military operations in the southern department seem for the present near at a stand. We have great reason to apprehend an immediate war with the overhill Cherokees, Creeks, and other Southern tribes of Indians, and have ordered 6 companies of rangers, under the command of Lieutenant Colo. W. Russel to be stationed on the Southwestern frontier to protect the inhabitants from their inroads. Mr. Walker is return'd having concluded a treaty with the lower Cherokees &c., the particulars of which have not yet transpired. Will not the disaster at the Cedars, probably, bring some of the northern tribes of Indians on us? We have not yet been able to learn any thing of Clinton's destination since he left Cape Fear, tho' a report prevailed here a few days ago, that he was arriv'd at Sandy Hook. Yesterday was finished the appointment of officers to the 6 Troops of horse, to be raised for the defence of this colony. The Captains are Dr. Bland, Ben Temple, John Jameson of Culpeper, Lewellen Jones of Amelia, Harry Lee, jr., and John Nelson of York. On the ballot for a cornet, to the fifth troop, the numbers stood as follows—for John Watts 37—for *Richard Lee esqr.* 19—for Henry Clements 19—for Colo. Digges 16—for By.[Beverley] Whiting 7—

&c. The previous question was then put whether the question should be put between Mr. Watts and the Squire or Mr. Clements, when it was determined in favor of the latter, of which opinion I was myself, principally because the Squire expressed his desire to relinquish the office and cannot well be spared from the chair of the committee of claims.

The progress of the business in convention is, according to custom, but slow. The declaration of rights which is to serve as the basis of a new government, you will see in the news papers; the form or constitution of which is yet in embryo, but from the conversation I have heard on the subject among gentlemen who have turned their thoughts that way, the legislature will probably consist of three branches, a governour, a council and a house of representatives; all of whom are to be annually elected. The executive power to be lodged with the governour, who is to have the assistance of a council of state distinct from the legislative council. The Judges to hold their offices during good behaviour.

An express is just arrivd from Hampton, who says a ship is gone up James river but what she is or from whence no body knows.

I shall do as you desire with your books in the College. I am Dr. Sr. Your friend & servt., WM. FLEMING

P.S. Pray give yourself no further trouble about the mahogany; but get me a case of good lancets, if to be had in Philadelphia.

The palace, by resolution of Convention, was this day appropriated to the purpose of a public hospital; and commissioners are appointed to make sale of Dunmore's slaves and personal estate.

RC (DLC). Tr (PPAP).
TJ's letter of uncertain date acknowledged by Fleming is missing. For the balloting on officers for the six troops of horse, see *Conv. Jour.*, May 1776, 1816 edn., p. 45-8, where the names of the candidates are given in their full and correct forms.

From the Virginia Committee of Safety
to the Virginia Delegates in Congress

GENTLEMEN   Williamsburg June 17. 1776.

The confusion which hath for some time happened amongst the People in the disputed Lands between Pennsylvania and this Colony, and a Representation to the Convention, that a Civil War, was like to be the consequence if something was not done to prevent it, Induced that Body to take the Subject into consideration, who were sorry to discover that a Jealousy seemed to prevail in the Governing Powers of Pennsylvania, of our intending the Garrisons on the Ohio to influence that dispute, and to overawe their people, whereas we only mean by them to protect our people, and those in the contested Settlement from the danger they are exposed to of Indian ravages, without the most distant view to offer any Injury to our friends and neighbours; with whom it is our Inclination as well as Interest to unite, a Temporary boundary appeared to the Convention the only means of quieting the people, until we have liesure to refer the final decision to some Arbitrating Power between us; and in fixing that they judged, that to point out a line, which would most nearly leave the Inhabitants in the countrey they respectively settled under, would be most likely to give general Satisfaction. And having examined several Gentlemen well acquainted with that country, who were of opinion that end would be answered by the line described in the enclosed Resolution, they have Resolved to propose that line to the Pennsylvania Assembly, and have Commanded us to transmit it to you, requesting you would negotiate the matter in such manner as you shall think most effectual. They will probably say that having fixed the boundary with Maryland they have a right to continue their line there begun to its utmost Western Extent, Whereas we shall contend in the Ultimate Settlement, that we are not bound by any determination or compromise to which we were not parties; that their bounds are to come no further than to the 40th. degree of Latitude, to which we have a right to confine them after the termination of the Maryland Boundary, the Meridian of the head Spring of Potowmack: However by allowing them to come to Braddocks road, we leave them a considerable tract which if we are right will belong to us, but which for the sake of our principle, we suffer to rest with them for the present. You'l please to inform us the success of your application.

We Inclose you our Declaration of Rights now agreed to. The Plan of Government is forming but not complete. We have no Arrivals here, nor have we any further Intelligence of Clinton and his Troops. We are with great regard, Gentlemen Your obedt humble Servts.

EDMD. PENDLETON	THOS. LUD: LEE
DUDLEY DIGGES	W: CABELL
P. CARRINGTON	JOS: JONES

RC (DLC); in a clerk's hand, with autograph signatures and a notation at foot of text reading: "The honble. the Virga. Delegates at Congress." Enclosure: Resolution of Virginia Convention of 15 June 1776 (DLC, copy attested by John Tazewell, clerk of Convention), on which see the explanatory note below.

For the background of the Virginia-

Pennsylvania boundary dispute, see the Virginia and Pennsylvania Delegates' address to settlers west of Laurel Hill, 25 July 1775, and Thomas Walker and Others to TJ, 13 Sep. 1775. Since the date of the latter, the danger of a loyalist-Indian combination had been allayed at least temporarily by the seizure of John Connolly at Hagerstown, Md., on his way to Pittsburgh (R. G. Thwaites and L. P. Kellogg, *Revolution on the Upper Ohio*, Madison, 1908, p. 136-42). This merely encouraged the rivalry between the two groups of settlers and, as Dorsey Pentecost wrote from West Augusta on 2 June 1776, their "unhappy difference . . . hath lately been Productive of more disturbances than ever," both governments exercising their jurisdiction "in one and the same place" and neither being able to enforce its authority (to the President of the Virginia Committee of Safety, VMHB, XVI [1908], p. 48-9). Responding to this and similar appeals, the Virginia Convention resolved on 15 June 1776 to propose A TEMPORARY BOUNDARY LINE for the reasons and on the terms stated herewith (*Conv. Jour.*, May 1776, 1816 edn., p. 53-4). The line proposed was as follows:

"From that part of the meridian of the head fountain of Potomac, where it is intersected by Braddocks road, along the said road to the great crossing of the Youghagany, thence down the meanders of that River, to the chesnut ridge, thence along that ridge, to the easterly branch of Jacobs creek, otherways called Green lick run; thence down the said run, to Braddocks old road, thence along the same, and the new road leading to Pittsburgh, to a place called the Bullock Pens, now in the tenure of William Elliott, & from thence a direct course to the mouth of plumb run on the Alleghany River above Col. Croghan's" (text from copy of Resolution enclosed in the present letter).

This line is shown in Paullin and Wright's *Atlas*, pl. 97G, but may be traced in more detail on the historical map of southwestern Pennsylvania in *Report of the Commission to Locate the Site of the Frontier Forts of Pennsylvania*, n.p., 1896, II, between p. 64-5. The details are essential in connection with TJ's Memoranda on the Virginia, Pennsylvania, and Maryland Boundaries, printed below under the date of 5 Nov. 1776. For the Virginia delegates' action on the present instructions, see their letter to the Speaker of the Pennsylvania Convention, 15 July 1776.

First Report of the Committee

to Digest the Resolutions of the Committee of the
Whole respecting Canada, &c.

[17 June 1776]

Resolved that the Commissioners for Indian affairs in the Northern department be directed to use their utmost endeavors to procure the assistance of the Indians within their department to act against the enemies of these colonies, that they particularly endeavor to engage them to undertake the reduction of Niagara, engaging on behalf of Congress to pay them 133 1/3 dollars[3] for every prisoner they shall take and bring to head quarters, or to the said Commissioners.

R. 1.[1]
pospon'd[2]

Resolved that the Commissioners for Indian affairs in the Middle department be directed to use their utmost endeavors to procure the assistance of the Indians within their department: that they particularly endeavor to engage them to undertake the reduction of

R. 2.
pospon'd

Detroit upon the same terms offered the Indians who shall go against Niagara.

R. 3. pospon'd

Resolved that the Commissioners in each of the said departments be directed to employ one or more able partisans whom the Congress will liberally reward for their exertions in the business to be committed to them.

R. 4. referred to NJ and P for the mode

Resolved that it is the opinion of this Committee that there be raised for the service of the United colonies one battalion of Germans.[4]

R. 5.

Resolved that the companies of rifle men from Virginia and Maryland be regimented, and that the regiment be compleated to the original number of the Pennsylvania battalion.

R. 6. a.

Resolved that the Pennsylvania battalion of rifle men be compleated to their original establishment.

R. 6. b.

Resolved that two companies of the forces now in the Delaware counties be ordered to Cape May.

R. 7.

Resolved that the committee appointed to Contract for[5] cannon be directed to procure a number of brass or iron, field peices to be made or purchased immediately.

R. 8. Committee already appointed to provide medicines.

Resolved that a proper assortment of medicines be sent to Canada.

R. 9.

Resolved that Mr. James Mease be directed to purchase and forward to the Quarter master general in New York as much cloth for tents as he can procure.

R. 10. Committed to the Committee of which Mr. Shearman is Chairman.

Resolved that proper persons be appointed by Congress to purchase such articles as may be wanted for the use of the soldiers in Canada and send the same to Albany, that they may be forwarded to the army in Canada: and that they be particularly attentive to provide in time a sufficient number of leathern breeches and underwaistcoats, and such other winter cloathing as may be necessary for them.

R. 11.

Resolved that the Committee appointed to contract for the making of shoes for the army, be directed to forward with all expedition to the Quarter master in Canada such as are already provided.

R. 12.

Resolved that Prisoners taken by continental arms be not exchanged by any authority but the Continental Congress.

R. 13.

Resolved that it is the opinion of this Committee that all vessels which sailed from the port or harbor of Boston whilst the town of Boston was in possession of the enemy having on board effects belonging to the enemies of America and which have been or may be seized, be liable, together with the said effects, to confiscation;

in the same manner and proportions as have been heretofore resolved by Congress.

Resolved that the Continental agents in the respective colonies R. 14.
where no courts have been established for the trial of captures have
power and be directed to dispose at public sale of such articles of a
perishable nature as shall be taken from the enemies of America,
and that the money arising from such sale be liable to the decree
of such court whenever established.

Resolved that the inventory of the Ordinance stores taken by
Capt. Manly be sent to General Washington, and that he be requested to appoint a person on the part of the colonies to join one
on the part of Captain Manly and his crew, who, having first taken
an oath for that purpose, shall proceed to value the same, and if
they cannot agree in the value they shall call in a third person to
determine the same: that the report of such persons be returned
to Congress so soon as may be, and the value of the stores belonging to Captn. Manly and his crew be thereupon transmitted them.

Dft (DLC: PCC, No. 19, VI). Without date or endorsement.

On 30 May Congress resolved itself into a committee of the whole, Benjamin Harrison chairman, "to take into consideration the report of the committee appointed to confer with the generals" (JCC, IV, 406); see above, Report of Committee on Letters from Washington, Schuyler, and the Commissioners in Canada, 21 May 1776. On 16 June the committee of the whole resolved "That a committee of four be appointed to digest and arrange the several resolutions reported"; TJ, Braxton, Middleton, and Robert Treat Paine were appointed, and they reported next day (JCC, V, 446). The present document was evidently one form or part of their report; the lack of the usual formal introductory paragraph or of an endorsement by Charles Thomson suggests that it was not presented to Congress but to the committee of the whole. Ford (II, 4-6) prints it under an assigned date of 21 May as the report of a mythical "Committee on Canadian Affairs," but it embraces a wide range of topics that engaged the attention of Congress over a period of several weeks. Thus Resolutions 1, 2, and 3 are identical with the third to fifth resolutions in the report of the committee to confer with the generals drawn by Edward Rutledge and submitted 25 May (JCC, IV, 394-5). Resolution 4, originally voted on 25 May as one of the recommendations of the committee reporting on the letters from Washington, Schuyler, and Robertson, was struck out of the present report and referred to a committee of delegates from the middle states and was subsequently passed on 27 June (JCC, IV, 392; V, 454, 487-8). Resolutions 5-14, together with the last (unnumbered) resolution, appear in TJ's draft in the same form in which they were adopted by Congress and copied into the Journal (JCC, V, 452-4). For the committee "of which Mr. Shearman is Chairman," to which Resolution 10 was referred, see JCC, V, 420-1. Resolutions 6b, 13, and 14 had appeared first in a much earlier report, of 10 May (JCC, IV, 343-4). From this it appears that the committee of the whole reviewed the work of several special committees, some of whose recommendations had already been agreed upon.

1 The numbering of the resolutions is in TJ's hand. In the draft reports of the earlier special committees whose work the committee of the whole reviewed, TJ has written corresponding marginal numbers beside the resolutions drawn from the several reports.
2 This and the following marginal notations (except the numbers) are assigned to Benjamin Harrison in JCC.
3 In the Rutledge draft report this figure is £50 Pennsylvania currency.

4 This paragraph deleted in committee of the whole; see explanatory note, above.   5 Preceding three words in another hand; the blank space after the word "cannon" is in the MS.

Additional Report of the Committee

to Digest the Resolutions of the Committee of the Whole respecting Canada

[17 June 1776]

The Committee to whom the reports from the Committee of the whole house was recommitted, have had the same under their consideration and agreed to the following resolutions.

G. 1. Resolved that it is the opinion of this Committee that an experienced general be immediately sent into Canada, with power to appoint a deputy adjutant general, a Deputy Quarter master general, and such other officers as he shall find necessary for the good of the service, and to fill up vacancies in the army in Canada, and

G. 2. notify the same to Congress for their approbation. That he also have power to suspend any officer there till the pleasure of Congress be known, he[1] transmitting to Congress as soon as possible the charge against such officer.[2]

G. 3. Resolved that no officer suttle or sell to the soldiers, on penalty of being fined one months pay and dismissed the service with infamy on conviction before a court martial.

G. 4. Resolved that the baggage of Officers and soldiers be regulated conformably to the rules in the British armies.

G. 4. b. Resolved that all sales of arms, ammunition, cloathing and accoutrements made by soldiers be void.

G. 5. Resolved that no troops employed in Canada, be disbanded there: that all soldiers in Canada ordered to be disbanded, or whose times of enlistment being expired shall refuse to re-enlist, shall be sent under proper officers to Ticonderoga or such other post on the lakes as the General shall direct, where they shall be mustered, and the arms, accoutrements, blankets, and utensils, which they may have belonging to the public shall be delivered up and deposited in the public store.

G. 6. Resolved that Doctor Potts be employed in the Continental service in the Canadian department or at Lake George as the General shall think best; and that his pay be   dollars per month. But this appointment is not intended to interfere with the office of Doctr. Stringer.[3]

Resolved that a Deputy Muster Master General be immediately G. 7.
sent into Canada.

Resolved that the local Commissaries and Quartermasters ap- G. 8.
pointed at the different garrisons or posts shall make weekly returns to the General of the provisions and stores in the places at
which they may happen to be stationed.

Resolved that the General to be sent to Canada be directed to G. 10.
view Point au fer, and to order a fortress to be erected there if he
should think proper.

Resolved that the General officers, Deputy Quarter master gen- C. 1.
eral, Local commissaries, Paymaster in Canada, and all other persons there who have received public monies be ordered without
delay to render and settle their accounts; on which settlement no
Brigadier not keeping a table shall receive the allowance for one,
nor shall any Brigadier[4] receive pay as colonel of a regiment.[5]

Resolved that Commissioners be appointed to settle in Canada C. 2.
the debts due on Certificates given by officers to the Canadians for
carriages and other services: and to settle also the accounts for such
goods as may have been seized through necessity for the use of the
army. That it be given in instruction to them to attend particularly
to the case of Mr. Bernard: and also that in settling the Certified C. 3.
debts they state carefully the names of all those who have given
Certificates, the nature of the service and the time when performed;
and to return the whole when settled and stated to the board of
treasury to be by them finally examined and discharged.[3]

Resolved that the Deputy Paymaster General be directed to C. 4.
transmit to Congress copies of the particulars beforementioned on
the original certificates, with the report and remarks of the Commissioners thereon.[3]

Resolved that General Schuyler be directed to make a good S. 1.
waggon road from Fort Edward to Cheshire's; to clear Wood creek
and to construct a Lock at Skenesborough, so as to have a continued navigation for batteaus from Cheshire's into lake Champlain;
to erect a grand magazine at Cheshire's and to secure it by a
stockaded fort; to erect a saw mill on Schoon creek; to order skilful
persons to survey and take the level of the waters falling into
Hudson's river near Fort Edward and those which fall into Wood
creek and interlock with the former, particularly Jones's run and
Half-way brook, the latter of which is said to discharge itself into
Wood creek at Cheshire's. That he be directed to have a greater S. 2.
number of boats and hands kept on Hudson's river, at the different
stations between Albany and Fort Edward, in order to save the

S. 3. expence of waggonage. That he be empowered to appoint proper officers to superintend the carriage by land and transportation by water of provisions, military stores and other things into Canada,

S. 4. that neither waste nor delay may arise therein. That he build with all expedition as many gallies and armed vessels as in the opinion of himself and the General officer to be sent into Canada shall be sufficient to make us indisputably masters of the lakes Champlain and George: for which purpose it is the opinion of this Committee there should be sent to him a master carpenter acquainted with the construction of the gallies used on the Delaware, who should take

S. 5. with him other carpenters, and models also if requisite. And that it be submitted to General Schuyler whether a temporary fortification or entrenched camp either at Crown point or opposite to Ticonderoga may be necessary.

W. 1. Resolved that the Commissary general be directed to supply the army in Canada with provisions, and to appoint proper officers under him to receive and issue the same at the several posts taking

W. 2. the directions of the General: that he be impowered to contract with proper persons in Canada for supplying the army there with fresh provisions; that he be directed to purchase for them a quantity of Albany peas, and to furnish as much biscuit as may be neces-

W. 3. a. sary; and that his pay be raised to[6]   dollars per month.

W. 3. b. Resolved that the Quarter-master General be directed to provide and forward such tents cloathing and utensils as are wanted for the army in Canada, subject to the direction of the commander in chief.

W. 4. Resolved that General Washington be directed to send into
W. 5. Canada such small brass or iron field peices as he can spare: that he be instructed to issue orders that no certificates be given in future by any but Brigadiers, Quarter-masters and their deputies, or a feild officer on a march or officer commanding at a detached post.

W. 7. Resolved that General Washington be directed to order an
Referr'd to enquiry to be made into the causes of the miscarriages in Canada
18 June and into[7] the conduct of the officers heretofore employed in that[8] department; and that the said enquiry be made at such times and places as in his judgment shall be most likely to do justice as well to the public as to the individuals; and that the result of the said enquiry together with the testimonies upon the subject be trans-

W. 6. mitted to Congress. That moreover all officers accused of cowardice, plundering, embezzlement of public monies and other misde-

meanors be immediately brought to trial. And whereas Congress is W. 8.
informed that an opinion has prevailed that officers resigning their
commissions are not subject to trial by a court martial for offences
committed previous to such resignation, whereby some have evaded
the punishments to which they were liable, it is hereby declared
that such opinion is not just.

Resolved that it is the opinion of this Committee that Lieutt. W. 9.
Colonel Burbeck be dismissed from the Continental service for
disobedience of orders.[3]

Resolved that it is the opinion of this Committee that General W. 10.
Washington be authorized to fill up vacancies in the army by issuing commissions to such officers under the rank of feild officers as
he shall think proper to supply such vacancy; he making a monthly
return to Congress of such appointments which unless disapproved
of by Congress on such return, shall stand confirmed: and that
blank commissions be sent to the General for that purpose.[3]

Resolved that the pay of such of the soldiers at New York as have W. 11.
been enlisted at five dollars per month be raised to six dollars and
two thirds per month.[3]

Resolved that a bounty of[10]   dollars be given to every W. 12.
Non-commissioned officer and soldier who will enlist to serve dur- Agre[e]d[9]
ing the war.[11]

Resolved that letters be written to the Conventions of New Jer- W. 13. b.
sey and New York, and to the Assembly of Connecticut recommending to them to authorize the Commander in chief in the colony of W. 13. a.
New York, to call to the assistance of that colony (when necessity
shall require it) such of the militia of those colonies as may be
necessary; and to afford him such other assistance as the situation
of affairs may require. And that it be further recommended to the W. 14.
Convention of New York to empower the said Commander in chief
to impress carriages and water craft when necessary for the public
service, and also to remove ships and other vessels in Hudson's and
the East rivers for the purpose of securing them from the enemy.

Resolved that General Washington be permitted to employ the W. 15.
Indians that[12] he may take into the service of the United colonies
pursuant to a resolution of Congress of the[13]
in any place where he shall judge they will be most useful, and that
he be authorized to offer them a reward of[14]   dollars
for every Commissioned officer, and of[15]   dollars for every
private soldier of the king's troops that they shall take prisoners in
the Indian country or on the frontiers of these colonies.

Dft (DLC: PCC, No. 19, VI). Without date or endorsement. The text given here represents TJ's composition draft; deletions and insertions made in committee or in Congress are given in the textual notes.

This Report is printed in JCC, V, 448-52, as part of the resolutions adopted by Congress on 17 June (see preceding document and notes thereon), though the resolutions as reported in the MS that were introduced or adopted at other times are printed in JCC under earlier or later dates. Thus G.6, struck out here, appears in a report submitted 10 May (IV, 344); C.2-4, also struck out, are printed under 18 June (V, 463); W.6-8 under 21 June (V, 472); W.9 under 25 May (IV, 392); and W.12 under 26 June (V, 483). Concerning the marginal symbols, the editor of JCC states a belief "that G. refers to such paragraphs as were suggested by Gates; C. to those of Congress or its committees; S. to those of Schuyler, and W. to those of Washington." It seems more likely that they indicate the resolutions upon which those persons or Congress, respectively, were to *act*. But the whole story of these proceedings is as complicated and confused as the Canadian campaign itself.

1 Inserted in another hand: "giving his reasons for so doing in the orders of suspension and."

2 Added in another hand: "provided that this power of suspending officers and filling up vacancies shall not be continued beyond the first day of October next."

3 This paragraph deleted in committee or in Congress.

4 The words from the preceding semi-colon to this point were struck out and the following substituted in another hand: "on which settlement no General officer."

5 Added in another hand: "nor Field officer as Captain of a Company."

6 Inserted in another hand: "One hundred and fifty."

7 Preceding nine words struck out in committee; the marginal notation was added in Harrison's(?) hand.

8 This word altered in another hand to: "the Canadn."

9 In Harrison's(?) hand.

10 Inserted in another hand: "Ten."

11 Preceding three words altered in another hand to: "for the term of three years."

12 Altered in Thomson's(?) hand to: "whom."

13 Inserted in Thomson's(?) hand is the date "25 May last."

14 Inserted in Thomson's(?) hand is "One hundred."

15 Inserted in Thomson's hand is "Thirty."

Major Sherburne's Testimony on the Affair at the Cedars

MAJOR SHERBURNE   [17 June 1776]

The place called the Cedars is on the river St. Lawrence, about 43 miles above Montreal. At this place Colo. Bedel was posted with 390 men. He had here laid off some works of defence inclosed the greater part of them with picquets and the rest with lines of earth and had two canons mounted. Colo. Bedel having received intelligence on Wednesday the 15th. of May that the enemy were approaching and were within 9. miles immediately set out to Montreal for a reinforcement whereby the command devolved on major Butterfield. In consequence of Bedel's application Major Sherburne with 140 men marched from Montreal the next day to their assistance and a greater detachment under General Arnold was getting ready for the same purpose. On Friday the 17th. of May the enemy invested the fort. They consisted of about 150, or 200 regulars Canadians and Indians commanded by Capt. Forster. They increased however in their numbers hourly. Friday, Saturday and Sunday they kept up loose scattering fire, and frequently sent in flags to demand a surrender. Major Butterfield would fain have accepted of the very first of these, shewing the greatest marks of terror, during the whole investment. The men from time to time sollicited leave to sally on the enemy, but he not only refused it, but restrained them from firing even from within the lines as much as possible. A flag being sent in on Sunday afternoon with an offer of terms, he determined to accept of them. Capt. Stevens and Capt. Easterbrook with their companies insisted for permission to sally out and fight their way through the enemy, preferring that chance for escape to the being put into their hands and their men provided themselves for that purpose. But this also was refused by major Butterfield who alleged that it might induce the enemy to rush on the rest and tomahawk them or to retract from them the benefit of the terms offered. There were at this time provisions belonging to the garrison and live stock at a priest's house within the lines sufficient to have lasted the garrison [. . .]¹ barrels of pork, 1½ barrels [. . .]² and contrary to the faith of the capitulation the garrison were delivered over into the custody of the savages who plundered them of thei[r clothes?] leaving many of them naked in most inclement weather. He [*i.e., Sherburne*] immediately proceeded towards that place with one hundred men only, the rest being left as guards with the ba[ggage]. When he had advanced 5. miles he was attacked by the enemy. He fought them about an hour when finding that they had now increased to about 500, of whom 100. were Canadians and the rest Indians, and that they were endeavoring to cut off his retreat, he made a proper disposition and then ordered a retreat. His men retired in extreme good order for 40. minutes, no one quitting his line, except when occasionally ordered to rush on the enemy in order to dislodge them from barns and other houses in which they placed themselves, which they alwais effected and did good execution. After retiring about 3. miles along the edge of the lake an advanced party of the enemy found means to intercept and take off the first of the three divisions. The second division then rushed forwards with their bayonets, forced their way through that party of the enemy, but then found themselves in the hands of another party still farther advanced and were made prisoners also. The third and last division with major Sherburne were then encompassed by the main body of the enemy and forced to surrender. In this rencounter 12 were killed and wounded on the part of major Sherburne and 22 on that of the enemy. They were then carried to where Butterfield and his party were, and submitted to the custody and plunder of the savages who stripped them of their clothes and baggage. The officers were then carried to Conesadago, and the privates to St. Anne's and a small island above that. Capt. Forster obliged the officers to sign a written parole engaging that they would remain quiet and keep within the precincts they should be ordered to and would hold no correspondence [. . .][3] notwithstanding which he still kept them in custody of [savages?]. The evening after major Sherburne was taken the Indians killed and scalped 2 of his men. Afterwards at different times they killed 4. or 5 others, one of whom was of those who had surrendered on capitulation at the cedars and was killed the 8th. day after that surrender. One other (as was affirmed by his companion now in possession of the savages and who saw the act) was first shot so however as not to kill him and then roasted. Others were left exposed on an island, naked and perishing with cold and famine, in which state they were found by Genl. Arnold's detachment. On Sunday the 26th. Capt. Forster (having heard as is supposed of the approach of General Arnold) required majors Sherburne and Butterfield and the other officers to sign what he called a Cartel for the exchange of prisoners, whereby they were to agree [not only to an] exchange of prisoners equal in number and rank but that those given up by Capt. Forster should thereafter not bear arms against the British government. They accordingly signed at [. . .][4] defend also their father the king; that he must consider it as a mercy never before shewn in their wars that they had put to death so few of the prisoners, and that he must expect and so inform General Arnold that all who should hereafter fall into their hands should certainly be put to death. Captain Forster joined in desiring that this bloody message should be delivered to General Arnold. The flag was then sent accompanied by Major Sherburne with the cartel to Genl. Arnold and he was informed from Capt. Forster that if he rejected it and should attack him, the prisoners then in his hands would be every man of them put to death. The cartel was rejected by Genl. Arnold and his reasons assigned. It was then made in some measure more conformable, and sent back to him a second time and a second time rejected. It was then further altered, returned and finally accepted and signed by him on the 27th of May. The substance was that the prisoners should be delivered within 6 days on the South shore of the St. Lawrence within one league of Coughnowaga; and that as many of equal rank of the British troops in our possession should be returned within 2. months, allowing a moderate time also for casualties, which might prevent the delivery within that time, and that four captains should be sent to Quebec as hostages and remain there till the exchange should be made. Four hostages were accordingly delivered, to wit Capts. Sullivan, Bliss, Green and Stevens. [. . .]⁵ delivered to Capt. James Osgood 1 major 4 captains, 16. subalterns and 355 privates, and others to [. . .]⁵ other persons, but the [. . .]⁵ the last of whom were delivered on the 31st. of May but of these [. . .]⁵ during the whole time of their captivity not half food was allowed them and they were continually insulted, buffeted, and ill-treated by the savages. When the first parties were brought off from the shore to be delivered to general Arnold the savages fired mud balls at them, and at the last parties they fired with musket bullets. The hostages were plundered and stripped after they were delivered as hostages. Twelve Canadians were retained by Captn. Forster who alledged in excuse that living under a military government they were to be considered as deserters from his majesty's armies and that his orders expressly forbid his exchanging these. These were carried off by him in irons but afterwards released. Several also of the other prisoners natives of the United colonies were detained and sent into the Indian countries in custody of the savages. Capt. Forster's behavior personally was polite; nor is it believed he could have prevented the ill treatment the prisoners received from the savages; but [. . .] of this [. . .] that before they left their country and in order to induce them to engage in the enterprize he promised them free plunder. This fact he was charged with by the Indians through their interpreter, in presence of Capt. Easterbrook and other officers and did not deny it. Before the Indians engaged with him they were 7. days in council debating whether they should take arms against the colonies: during the first 6. days they seemed [to] be on a balance or rather inclined in favor of the colonies. On the [7]th they were brought over by excessive high offers which the British officers were enabled to make by merchants in Montreal who not only had supplied them with goods for that purpose, but offered to advance for them £20,000 in specie and what other goods they should want. Particularly a certain Monsr. De Rochèt. A Canadian told major Sherburne that he was in Montreal when major Sherburne marched from it, and did not leave it till the next day when having obtained from the Commissioners a pass to carry a boat load of goods on pretence of trading with the friendly Indians, he had carried them to those very Indians who invested the Cedars and was himself in the engagement against major Sherburne. The Indians who engaged in this expedition were principally Senecas, there were some Conasedagas, some Oneidas, about 60. Mohawks and some others.

N (DLC), entirely in TJ's hand. Mutilated and worn.

These notes were taken down by TJ in an interview with Maj. Henry Sherburne, a Rhode Island officer who had been captured in May at the Cedars, an American strong point on the St. Lawrence above Montreal. For the several actions at and near the Cedars, see Justin H. Smith, *Our Struggle for the Fourteenth Colony*, II, ch. XXXII. The text of the Cartel for the exchange of prisoners, signed by Capt. George Forster on the part of the British and by Brig. Gen. Arnold on the part of the Americans, 27

May 1776, is in Force, 4th ser., VI, 597. TJ had been appointed on 15 June to a committee to report on the Cartel. For the Report he drew up, see the following document; for an unofficial narrative of the Cedars episode, see his letter to Eppes, 15 July 1776.

[1] Four or five words missing.
[2] A line or more missing at foot of page.
[3] Five or six words missing.
[4] A line and a half missing.
[5] Indeterminate number of words missing.

Report of the Committee on the Cedars Cartel

[17 June 1776]

The Committee to whom were re-committed the Cartel between Brigadier General Arnold and Captain Forster for the exchange of prisoners and the several papers relating thereto have had the same under their consideration and agreed to the following report.

Your committee having proceeded to make enquiry into the facts relating to the agreement entered into at St. Anne's between Brigadier General Arnold and Capt. Forster find a part of them well authenticated, and others n[ot,] yet being apprehensive that silence on the part of Congress may be construed by some into a ratification of the said agreement they have thought it best to state the same as they appear at present, with such resolutions as they will justify if found true, reserving final decision till the whole truth shall be accurately enquired into and transmitted to Congress.

Your Committee on the best information they have been able to obtain, find

That on the 24th:[1] day of May last a party of the enemy consisting as is said of about 600. men under the command of Capt. Forster attacked a post at the Cedars held by a garrison of 350.

Con[tinental for]ces, then under the command of Major Butterfeild.

That the said post was secured by a Sto[ckade of picquets?] to cover the garrison from the enemy's musquetry, that there were mounted therein two feild peices, and that the enemy had no cannon.

That the said garrison had ammunition and provisions sufficient to have lasted them ten days. That they had reason to expect a reinforcement in a few days which on a requisition from themselves, was actually on it's way from Montreal, and moreover were so near the main body of the army that they could not doubt being joined by detachments from thence sufficient to oblige the enemy to retire.

That the enemy for two days kept up only a scattering fire, by which not a single man of the garrison was killed or wounded, and that on the third day the garrison surrendered themselves prisoners of war having capitulated for the preservation of their own baggage from plunder,[2] and that their persons should not be deliver'd into the hands of the Savages.

That the enemy broke the capitulation utterly and immediately on their part, plundering the garrison of their baggage and stripping the cloathes from their backs,[2] and Delivering the Prisoners into the hands of the Savages.

That they then proceeded against the reinforcement which was on it's way consisting of about 150. men under the command of Major Sherburne. That Major Sherburne and his party engaged and fought them with bravery: but being at length surrounded by numbers greatly superior, and informed that the fort and garrison were already in the hands of the enemy, they were obliged to surrender themselves prisoners of war also: but whether on capitulation or not your committee are not informed.

That after they had put themselves into the hands of the enemy, the said enemy murdered two of them, butchering the one with tomahawks and drowning the other; and left divers others exposed in an island naked and perishing with cold and famine.

That by this time Brigadier General Arnold, who had been detached by Major General Thomas to relieve the fort at the Cedars, approached and was making dispositions to attack the enemy.

That Captn. Forster thereupon sent a flag to General Arnold, notifying that if he attacked him, the prisoners, then 500 in number, would every man of them be put to death; and proposing at the same time an exchange of [prisoners.]

[That General] Arnold was ext[reme]ly averse to entering on any agreement of that kind, and was at length induced to do it by no other motive than that of saving the prisoners from cruel and inhuman death, threatened in such terms as left no doubt it was to be perpetrated.

That an agreement was thereupon entered into between Brigadr. Genl. Arnold and Capt. Forster, bearing date at St. Anne's on the 27th. day of May, whereby the said Forster stipulated that he would deliver up all the said prisoners, except such as were[3] Canadians, to Genl. Arnold; who agreed on the other part that so many of equal rank and condition should be returned to the enemy of those taken by our arms on former occasions: that the prisoners so stipulated to be given up to the enemy were not in the possession of Genl. Arnold, nor under his direction, but were at that time distributed through various parts of the continent under the orders of this house.

That Capt. Forster in violation of this agreement also detained a considerable number of the prisoners he had thus stipulated to deliver and sent them into the Indian countries for purposes unknown.

Whereupon your Committee have come to the following resolutions

Resolved[4] that it is the opinion of this Committee that plundering the baggage of the garrison at the Cedars, stripping them of their clothes and delivering the Prisoners into the hands of the Savages,[5] was a breach of the capitulation on the part of the enemy, for which satisfaction ought to be demanded.

Resolved[4] that the murder of two of the prisoners of war was a gross and barbarous violation of the laws of nature and nations, for which satisfaction should be made by the enemy by delivering into our hands either Captain Forster, or the individuals concerned in committing the murder.

Resolved[4] that the agreement entered into at St. Anne's was a mere sponsion on the part of Brigadr. Genl. Arnold, he not being invested with powers for the absolute disposal of the Continental prisoners in general; and that therefore it is subject to be ratified or annulled at the discretion of this house, the sole representative of the United states of America.[6]

Resolved that it is the opinion of this Committee that Major Sherburne and his party having fought as men should do, so much of the said sponsion as relates to their exchange should be ratified and confirmed by this house; and that an equal number of captives from the enemy, of the same rank and condition should be restored to them as stipulated by the said sponsion.

Resolved that [it is the o]pinion of this com[mittee that so much of] the said sponsion as relates to the exchange of Major Butterfeild [and the] garrison surrendering with him, ought not to be ratified: because we should redeem none but those who will fight; and because too the said sponsion excepted the Canadian prisoners, and we will in no case admit a distinction of countries among men fighting in the same cause.

Resolved therefore that the said Major Butterfeild and garrison should still be considered as prisoners of war, appurtaining to the enemy; but as by the actual murder of two of the prisoners, and the threats at St. Anne's to put the others to death, the enemy are found capable of destroying their captives, the said prisoners ought not to be put into their hands, but should be permitted to remain in their own country: that in the mean time they shall not bear arms, nor otherwise act against the enemy, but are bound to demean themselves in all things in the manner of prisoners of war enlarged on their parole, and to hold themselves subject to be recalled by the enemy whenever proper security shall have been given that their lives shall be safe.

Resolved that previous to the delivery of the prisoners to be returned in lieu of Majr. Sherburne and those captivated with him, satisfaction be required from the enemy for the murder of the two prisoners by delivering into our hands Capt. Forster, or the individuals concerned in perpetrating that horrid act; and likewise restitution for the plunder at the Cedars taken contrary to the faith of the capitulation: and that till such satisfaction and restitution be made, the said prisoners be not delivered.

Resolved that it is the opinion of this committee that if the enemy shall put to death, torture, or otherwise ill-treat any of the hostages in their hands, or of the Canadian or other prisoners captivated by them in the service of the United colonies, recourse must be had to retaliation as the sole means of stopping the progress of human butchery, and that for that purpose punishments of the same kind and degree be inflicted on an equal number of their subjects taken by us, till they shall be taught due respect to the violated rights of nations.

Resolved that it is the opinion of this Committee that a copy of this report be transmitted to the Commander in chief of the Continental forces in Canada to be by him sent to the British commander there: and that he moreover make further and diligent [inquiry] into the facts therein stated and such others as may [appertain to the ?] same subject and [report th]e same duly authentic[ated with all po]ssible despatch [to Congress] for their final decis[ion,] and that in the mean time the prisoners delivered up by the enemy abstain from bearing arms or otherwise acting against them.

MS (DLC: PCC, No. 29). Mutilated. Endorsed by Charles Thomson: "Report of the Comee. on the capitulation entered into between genl. Arnold & Captn. Forster.—No 1. brot. in June 17. 1776 read & ordered to lie on the table. recommitted June 24. 1776. [*In a different hand:*] passed July 10." Of a number of alterations and additions, presumably made in Congress, only the most significant have been noted; these changes are attributed in JCC to John Hancock. There also survives a partial draft of this report in DLC: TJ Papers, 4: 647 verso, on the back of a page of TJ's proposed Resolution on the Case of General Sullivan, printed under 29 July, below.

On 15 June TJ was appointed with Braxton, Paine, and Middleton to a committee part of whose business was to report on the Cedars Cartel (JCC, V, 446; see also the preceding document). The present paper may or may not be the Report the committee submitted on the 17th. From the "No 1." of the endorsement it would seem to be, and it is so printed by Ford and in the modern edition of the Journals. According to this view, TJ's use of the word "re-committed" in the

first line must be a slip. The first Report was debated on 20 and 24 June and recommitted (JCC, V, 468, 475). A revised Report, for which no MS has been found, was brought in and adopted on 10 July, and on 23 July it was ordered published; though expanded, it does not differ materially from the provisions of TJ's Report (same, V, 533-9, 601). The events following Congress' rejection of the Cartel may be traced in Washington's *Writings*, ed. Fitzpatrick; see the Index under "Cedars."

[1] This date, an error, was inserted by another hand in a blank space left by TJ. The date should be 18 May.
[2] Remainder of sentence added in another hand.
[3] Preceding three words substituted in another hand for an illegible number deleted.
[4] Opposite this resolution appears "Agreed" in another hand.
[5] "and delivering . . . Savages" inserted in another hand.
[6] For "states of America" there is substituted in another hand the word "Colonies."

To Benjamin Franklin

TH: J. TO DOCTR. FRANKLYN   Friday morn. [21 June 1776?]

The inclosed paper has been read and with some small alterations approved of by the committee. Will Doctr. Franklyn be so good as to peruse it and suggest such alterations as his more enlarged view of the subject will dictate? The paper having been returned to me to change a particular sentiment or two, I propose laying it again before the committee tomorrow morning, if Doctr. Franklyn can think of it before that time.

RC (PPAP); addressed in TJ's hand "To Doctor Franklyn." Watermark LVG. Respecting the enclosure, see the explanatory note below.

I. Minis Hays thought it possible the enclosure referred to was the Declaration of Independence (*Cal. Franklin*

Pap., I, 181). This is plausible, though other possibilities are not to be ruled out. The letter was obviously written during the years 1775-1776, for Franklin and TJ were associated together in Congress only between the following dates: 21 June to 31 July 1775; 2 Nov. to 31 Dec. 1775; and 31 May to 2 Sep. 1776. During this period TJ served on at least thirty-four committees. It seems clear that the document enclosed must have been of some importance; this is indicated both by the fact that TJ had been asked "to change a particular sentiment or two" and by the fact that he appealed to Franklin for advice. There were eleven committees on which TJ and Franklin served together in 1775-1776, several of which can be eliminated because TJ did not write the committee report, or because the time elapsed between the appointment and report of the committee did not cover a "Friday morn." But we cannot be certain that this matter involved a committee on which *both* sat. All we know definitely is that TJ was a member; that at least two meetings of the committee were held; that he wrote the draft which it considered; that he consulted Franklin; that the work of the committee extended over a Friday and a Saturday; and that the committee was not wholly satisfied with his draft. To these criteria we should add the assumption that the matter involved was one of importance. The editors, applying these criteria as rigorously as possible, have reached the conclusion that the "Friday morn." note could with some plausibility refer to the committees concerned with the Declaration of Independence, the Declaration of the Causes and Necessity for Taking Up Arms, the Appeal to the Hessians, Lord North's Proposal, and the Seal of the United States. It is conceivable that it might apply to the work of one of the other 29 committees on which TJ served during 1775-1776, but these have been eliminated for what have seemed valid reasons. Even the last two of the five listed above seem improbable. The committee concerned with the Seal of the United States did not depend so much upon a draft by a single member as upon a genuine collaborative effort. The committee on Lord North's Proposal was appointed on Saturday, 22 July 1775, and reported on the following Tuesday, when the report was laid on the table to be taken up Monday, 31 July. To admit this document as a possibility would involve the improbable assumption that the committee continued to meet and revise its draft after submitting its report. As for the appeal to the Hessians, the note could possibly refer to the earlier of the two reports, 14 Aug. 1776 (see note to Report of 27 Aug.). But for this there is no MS and no proof positive of TJ's authorship. Then too, this committee was appointed on Friday, 9 Aug., and reported on Wednesday, 14 Aug.; it is possible, of course, that TJ could have written the report, that he wrote it the day of the committee's appointment, and that the committee planned to meet again the next day. TJ was always prompt and attentive to business, but such urgency in this case seems unlikely. (If the committee seemed under such necessity for haste and if it met on Friday and Saturday, why should it have delayed until the following Wednesday to report when all that needed changing was "a particular sentiment or two"?) As for the Declaration of the Causes and Necessity for Taking Up Arms, we know that TJ wrote one draft, but the person whom he consulted individually was John Dickinson, who made alterations on TJ's fair copy. We do not know that TJ consulted Franklin privately on this occasion. It is also certain that Dickinson objected to more than "a particular sentiment or two" in the draft by TJ; he wanted to change the phraseology considerably and in particular to insert certain sentiments which TJ must have been unwilling to accept. Nevertheless, it is possible that the "Friday morn." note is really an appeal to Franklin for support as against the changes TJ was disinclined to make. Yet, of all the possibilities to be considered, the Declaration of Independence is the only one concerning which we know indisputably that TJ consulted Franklin privately (Boyd, *Declaration of Independence*, 1945, p. 24). We also know that Franklin was ill some of the time during which the Declaration was before the Committee of Five, thus making a communication by letter seem plausible. On 21 June, Franklin wrote to Washington, "I am just recovering a severe fit of the Gout, which has kept me from Congress and Company almost ever since you left us, so that I know little of what has pass'd there, except that a Declaration of Independence is preparing. . . " (Burnett, *Letters of Members*, I, No. 722). This was ten days after the Committee of Five had been appointed and only a week before the draft was reported on 28 June. It is quite possible, therefore, that after TJ had first consulted Adams about the Declaration, he then consulted the Committee of Five and, after that, Franklin, though this is contrary to TJ's later recollection (Boyd, *Declaration of Independence*, 1945, p. 11, 26).

Though the evidence is far from conclusive, the editors feel that Dr. Hays' conjecture probably has more plausibility than a similar claim that might be advanced for any of the other papers drawn up by TJ for Congress in 1775-1776.

From William Fleming

Dear Sir   Wmsburg, 22d. June, 1776. 3 o'clock, P.M.

I, being inform'd that the post is to set out in an hour, have just left the committee appointed to prepare a form of government to give you a summary of their proceeding. The inclosed printed plan was drawn by Colo. G. Mason and by him laid before the committee. They proceeded to examine it clause by clause, and have made such alterations as you will observe by examining the printed copy and the manuscript together; tho' I am fearful you will not readily understand them, having made my notes in a hurry at the table, as the alterations were made. I left the committee debating on some amendments proposed to the last clause, which they have probably finished, as the bell, for the meeting of the house, is now ringing. This business has already taken up about a fortnights time, I mean in committee.

As some of your friends have, no doubt, given you a history of our late election of delegates to serve in congress, and of the spirit (evil spirit I had almost said) and general proceedings of our convention, I shall, for the present, forbear any animadversions thereon: indeed, were I ever so much inclined to it the time would not allow me.

There were found on board the transport brought up by the two Barons [Barrons], 200 matrasses, 100 tents, 3 hhds. rum, and 2 barrels of Gun Powder.

Purdie has promised to pack up your books, and Colo. Tom to carry them to Tuckahoe. He this day told me you desired him to enquire, of me, something about Vatels law of nations. You did not mention it in your letter to me. I can lend you a copy for a few months which [when?] you return to Virginia. I am Dr. Sr. yr. friend & serv.,   Wm. Fleming

N.B. Mr. Wythe was at Port royal Thursday night, and will be in town tomorrow.

RC (DLC). Enclosure: "A Plan of Government Laid before the committee of the House, which they have ordered to be printed for perusal of the members"; broadside, Sabin 100027, annotated and with a MS addendum in William Fleming's hand (DLC); the enclosure is printed as Document No. v under the Virginia Constitution, above.

colo. tom: Though nicknames were

unusual among the Virginia gentry, this seems clearly to be the reading and presumably refers to Thomas Mann Randolph, Sr. (1741-1793), of Tuckahoe, delegate from Goochland co. to the Convention of May 1776 (*Conv. Jour.*, May 1776, 1816 edn., List of Delegates).

From Edmund Randolph

DEAR SIR   Wmsburg June 23. 1776.

Gilmer, not being able to attend the Convention the other Day, when the Delegates were chosen, sent a Memo. to me, to press your Non-election. I urged it in decent Terms: but stirred up a Swarm of Wasps about my Ears, who seemed suspicious, that I designed to prejudice you. However, fortunately for my Credit, your Letter to the President was yesterday read to the House, confirming, What I had asserted. Your Excuse was rejected, as made by me. Whether they will admit it, as now made by yourself, I know not. If they do, for God's Sake, be with us quickly. Our Counsels want every Thing, to stamp Value on them.

I should have made the Attempt, recommended to me in your Favour. But the Veterans to a Man exclaimed vs. it. This however would not have intimidated me, had it not been for the vast affection, which the present Body have for being the Manufacturers of the new Government.

Barron has brought in the Transport, taken by Capt. Biddle off the Banks of Newfoundland, and separated from him by a Storm. Her Cargo, consisting of 217 Scotch Highland Regulars, came up to this Town yesterday. Among them, we are told, are many valuable Artificers. Measures are in Agitation to reconcile them to prosecute their different Occupations in this Country. Some of them are violent vs. America, others tolerably moderate, and many from contending Passions curse the Parliament and Congress in the same Breath.

Colo. Harrison and Braxton are omitted in the Delegation for the next Year. Before the Day of ballotting arrived, no small Pains were taken to effectuate this Business: and I am in doubt, whether the Reduction of your Number to five proceeded more from a Desire of saving the Wages of the other two, than excluding Harrison.

The ½ Joh: loses a Grain every Time it is mentioned. It is sweated as low as thirty Shillings, according to the prevailing opinion out of Doors. An Ordinance comes in today, to amend that, which gave it. I wish you may survive this Attack with even 20/ per Day. Yr. friend & Servt.,   E. R.

RC (DLC).

George Gilmer's MEMO. (memorandum? memorial?) has not been found. TJ had suggested that the Virginia delegates be recalled for the purpose of taking part in the framing of the Virginia constitution (see TJ to Thomas Nelson, 16 May 1776). His present plea may, however, have been based on domestic grounds, presumably Mrs. Jefferson's illness, but unfortunately his LETTER TO THE PRESIDENT (Pendleton), said by Randolph to have been read to the Convention, is missing, and it is not mentioned in the Journal. On 20 June TJ had been reelected for another year's service from 11 Aug. 1776 (*Conv. Jour.*, May 1776, 1816 edn., p. 58). For political and personal aspects of that election, see TJ to Fleming, 1-2 July, and Fleming to TJ, 27 July 1776. ½ JOH: Half Johannes, usually "half joe," a Portuguese gold coin. A year earlier the Convention had fixed the daily wage of delegates to Congress at forty-five shillings; an ordinance passed on 24 June 1776 reduced this to thirty shillings (*Conv. Jour.*, July 1775, 1816 edn., p. 53; same for May 1776, 1816 edn., p. 64, *Ordinances*, p. 12).

To Edmund Pendleton

HONBLE. SIR   [ca. 30 June 1776]

I this day received information that the Convention had been pleased to reappoint me to the office in which I have now the honor to be serving them and through you must beg leave to return them my sincere thanks for this mark of their continued confidence. I am sorry the situation of my domestic affairs renders it indispensably necessary that I should sollicit the substitution of some other person here in my room. The delicacy of the house will not require me to enter minutely into the private causes which render this necessary: I trust they will be satisfied I would not have urged it again were it not necessary. I shall with chearfulness continue in duty here till the expiration of our year by which time I hope it will be convenient for my successor to attend.

Dft (DLC). The addressee's name is derived from internal evidence: the letter was clearly written to Pendleton in his official status as president of the Virginia Convention.

The date may be satisfactorily fixed within narrow limits: on 20 June TJ had been reelected to Congress, and his notification would have taken from eight to ten days to reach Philadelphia; in the letter to Fleming, dated 1-2 July, TJ mentions having received that notification. Pendleton could not have received the present letter before the Convention adjourned on 5 July, so TJ's wish could not be gratified. On 10 Oct., however, Benjamin Harrison was elected "in the room of" TJ (JHD, Oct. 1776, 1828 edn., p. 6).

To William Randolph

DEAR SIR   Philadelphia [ca. June] 1776

Your's of August I received in this place, that of Nov. 24th. is just now come to hand; the one of October I imagine has miscarried.

On receiving the first of these, I proposed to have spoken to the gentleman you mention, as I was then about to return to my own country and had expectations of seeing him. I knew him to be just and good; but I knew at the same time that for some cause or other he was somewhat displeased. I therefore thought it better not to trust to the cold intercession of a letter, but to defer doing any thing till I could see him, and personally press on him those considerations which I was assured would have weight with him. However when I returned home, which was in January, I heard he was very ill, and so he continued till March, at which time I was taken sick myself and detained by that till my duty again called me to this place. As it will now be some time before I can see him I have written to him on the subject. Whether he will be able to procure any channel of remittance is what I cannot say, as I know not at this moment by what possible means I shall convey this letter to you. I am extremely concerned at the difficulties under which you are thrown by the stoppage of trade. I know not the particular situation of Maryland where your mercantile connections were; but if it be the same with that of Virginia, I can easily conceive their remittances to have been inconsiderable. With us they have been so of necessity; for the crops of those who make tobacco, still lie in their warehouses, and the wheat of the farmers is rotting in their barns. It is my hope however that a day of justice will come to suffering individuals on both sides the water.

I heartily join with you in wishing you had chosen a residence among us. I should have found myself happy in your neighborhood. Our interior situation is to me most agreeable, as withdrawing me in a great measure from the noise and bustle of the world. It's remoteness from the seat of war, which you mention as conferring security, we do not however consider in that point of view. Our idea is that every place is secure except those which lie immediately on the water edge; and these we are prepared to give up. But I can easily conceive the situation of a farmer, depending on none but the soil and seasons, preferable to the precarious tho' more enlarged prospects of trade.

The death of my mother you have probably not heard of. This happened on the last day of March after an illness of not more than an hour. We suppose it to have been apoplectic. Be pleased to tender my affectionate wishes to Mrs. Randolph and my unknown cousins, of whom some I suppose must now have nearly attained years of maturity. I hope no dissentions between the bodies politic of which we happen to be members will ever interfere with the ties of relation. Tho' most heartily engaged in the quarrel on my part from a sense of the most unprovoked injuries, I retain the same affection for individuals which nature or knowledge of their merit calls for.

Dft or perhaps RC not sent (MHi). Without signature. Name of addressee and approximate date supplied from internal evidence.

Numerous bits of evidence make it clear that this letter was written not long after TJ's arrival in Philadelphia in the middle of May 1776; the precise date was apparently left to be filled in when TJ found a means of sending the letter. (It is possible that he never found a means to do so.) With little doubt it was addressed to William Randolph, brother of TJ's mother. William had gone years earlier to England and settled as a merchant in Bristol. By the will of Jane Randolph, TJ's grandmother, her estate of Dungeness was bequeathed to her eldest son, Isham, and was to pass from him, if he proved childless, to her second son, William. By the time this letter was written Isham had probably died child-

less, and it is a very plausible supposition that William had asked his nephew TJ to secure the Dungeness rentals rightfully due to him (William). This would require TJ's going to the third son, his uncle Thomas Randolph, who resided at Dungeness and who is without much doubt the GENTLEMAN alluded to throughout the first paragraph. In 1779 Dungeness was confiscated, under the act pertaining to British property in Virginia, and passed to Thomas, who, much later, deeded the estate to his nephew Thomas Eston Randolph, eldest son of William. Failure to locate the several letters to and from TJ relative to the transaction mentioned in the present letter makes it impossible to confirm this explanation. See, however, Randolph, *The Randolphs*, p. 107, 109; and two articles by the same writer in VMHB, XLV (1937), 383-6; XLIX (1941), 78-80.

To George Wythe

[June? 1776]

The dignity and stability of government in all its branches, the morals of the people, and every blessing of society, depend so much upon an upright and skilful administration of justice, that the judicial power ought to be distinct from both the legislative and executive, and *independent* upon both, that so it may be a *check* upon both, as both should be checks upon that. The judges, therefore, should always be men of learning and experience in the laws, of exemplary morals, great patience, calmness, coolness and attention; their minds should not be *distracted with jarring interests*; they should not be *dependent upon any man, or body of men*. To these ends they should hold *estates for life* in their offices, or, in other words, their commissions should be *during good behaviour*, and their salaries ascertained and established by law.

For *misbehaviour*, the grand inquest of the colony, the house of representatives, should impeach them before the governor and council, when they should have time and opportunity to make their defence; but *if convicted*, should be *removed* from their offices, and subjected to such other punishment as shall be thought proper.

TH: JEFFERSON

MS not located. Text from an extract in Charleston (S.C.) *Courier*, 6 April 1803, where it is stated that the letter was written by TJ to Wythe in 1776.

The text of this letter is highly suspect and the date uncertain. Wythe had left Congress on 13 June, and soon afterward (as we know from John Page's letter of 6 July) TJ wrote him a letter that dealt with personal matters and that may have dealt with the Virginia Constitution. The present extract *may* have been taken from this missing letter, but both its substance and the circumstances under which the only version known came to light throw grave doubts upon its authenticity. The provisions for the Virginia judiciary stated in the extract do not wholly conform to any known plan proposed by TJ; for example, he advocated in his authentic proposals of this period that state officers be paid only expenses, not salaries. The extract was printed in the *Courier* as part of a violent Federalist attack upon the national administration during the controversy over the federal judiciary in 1803. How a personal letter written in 1776 by TJ to Wythe (who was still alive in 1803) could have come into a Charleston newspaper editor's hands is not accounted for.

Proposed Resolution

for Rotation of Membership in the Continental Congress

[Before 2 July 1776]

To prevent every danger which might arise to American freedom by continuing too long in office the members of the Continental Congress, to preserve to that body the confidence of their friends, and to disarm the malignant imputations of their enemies It is earnestly recommended to the several Provincial Assemblies or Conventions of the United colonies that in their future elections of delegates to the Continental Congress one half at least of the persons chosen be such as were not of the delegation next preceeding, and the residue be of such as shall not have served in that office longer than two years. And that their deputies be chosen for one year, with powers to adjourn themselves from time to time and from place to place as occasions may require, and also to fix the time and place at which their Successors shall meet.

Dft (DLC).
There is nothing in the Journals of Congress to indicate when, or even if, this Resolution was proposed. From the terms "Provincial Assemblies" and "United colonies," it is probable, however, that TJ drafted it before 2 July 1776. Congress was much concerned with its own rules and procedures at this time; see TJ's Memorandum printed under 10 July, below.

To William Fleming

DEAR FLEMING   Philadelphia. July 1. 1776.

Your's of 22d June came to hand this morning and gratified me much as this with your former contains interesting intelligence.

Our affairs in Canada go still retrograde, but I hope they are now nearly at their worst. The fatal sources of these misfortunes have been want of hard money with which to procure provisions, the ravages of the small pox with which one half of our army is still down, and an unlucky choice of some officers. By our last letters, Genl. Sullivan was retired as far as Isle au noix with his dispirited army and Burgoyne pursuing him with one of double or treble his numbers. It gives much concern that he had determined to make a stand there as it exposes to great danger of losing him and his army; and it was the universal sense of his officers that he ought to retire. Genl. Schuyler has sent him positive orders to retire to Crown point but whether they will reach him time enough to withdraw him from danger is questionable. Here it seems to be the opinion of all the General officers that an effectual stand may be made and the enemy not only prevented access into New York, but by preserving a superiority on the lakes we may renew our attacks on them to advantage as soon as our army is recovered from the small pox and recruited. But recruits, tho long ordered, are very difficult to be procured on account of that dreadful disorder.

The Conspiracy at New York is not yet thoroughly developed, nor has any thing transpired, the whole being kept secret till the whole is got through. One fact is known of necessity, that one of the General's lifeguard being thoroughly convicted was to be shot last Saturday. General Howe with some ships (we know not how many) is arrived at the Hook, and, as is said, has landed some horse on the Jersey shore. The famous Major Rogers is in custody on violent suspicion of being concerned in the conspiracy.

I am glad to hear of the Highlanders carried into Virginia. It does not appear certainly how many of these people we have but I imagine at least six or eight hundred. Great efforts should be made to keep up the spirits of the people the succeeding three months: which in the universal opinion will be the only ones in which our trial can be severe.

I wish you had depended on yourself rather than others for giving me an account of the late nomination of delegates. I have no other state of it but the number of votes for each person. The omission of Harrison and Braxton and my being next to the lag give me some alarm. It is a painful situation to be 300. miles from one's country, and thereby open to secret assassination without a possibility of self-defence. I am willing to hope nothing of this kind has been done in my case, and yet I cannot be easy. If any doubt has arisen as to me, my country will have my political creed in the form of a 'Declaration &c.' which I was lately directed to draw. This will give decisive proof that my own sentiment concurred with the vote they instructed us to give. Had the post been to go a day later we might have been at liberty to communicate this whole matter.

July. 2. I have kept open my letter till this morning but nothing more new. Adieu.   TH: JEFFERSON

RC (The Rosenbach Co., New York, 1946). Addressed and franked: "To Mr. William Fleming Williamsburgh. free Th: Jefferson."

THE CONSPIRACY AT NEW YORK: The so-called Hickey Plot; see Washington, *Writings*, ed. Fitzpatrick, v, 182, and note. NEXT TO THE LAG: Next to the last;

according to OED, "lag" as a noun in the sense of hindmost is now rare except in schoolboy use. See Fleming's explanation of the election, 27 July, below. DECLARATION &c.: On 1 July Congress had referred the Declaration of Independence to a committee of the whole "to take into consideration the resolution of independence" (JCC, V, 504).

The Declaration of Independence

[11 June to 4 July 1776]

I. COMPOSITION DRAFT OF THAT PART OF THE DECLARATION OF IN-
DEPENDENCE CONTAINING THE CHARGES AGAINST THE CROWN

II. FRAGMENT OF THE COMPOSITION DRAFT OF THE DECLARATION OF
INDEPENDENCE

III. JEFFERSON'S "ORIGINAL ROUGH DRAUGHT" OF THE DECLARATION
OF INDEPENDENCE

IV. THE DECLARATION OF INDEPENDENCE AS AMENDED BY THE COM-
MITTEE AND BY CONGRESS

V. THE DECLARATION OF INDEPENDENCE AS ADOPTED BY CONGRESS

EDITORIAL NOTE

A FULL analysis of the many textual changes made in the Declaration of Independence from the time it was drafted by Jefferson to the time of its final adoption by Congress has been made in the following: John H. Hazelton, *The Declaration of Independence: Its History*, N.Y., 1906; Carl Becker, *The Declaration of Independence. A Study in the History of Political Ideas*, N.Y., 1922 and 1942; and Julian P. Boyd, *The Declaration of Independence: The Evolution of the Text*, Princeton, 1945. Nevertheless, the transcendent importance of this charter of national liberties and the recent discovery of additional information respecting Jefferson's drafting of it require special presentation, though this cannot be as detailed and as comprehensive as the studies of Hazelton and others.

On 15 May 1776 the Virginia Convention unanimously adopted the Resolutions (q.v. under date) instructing its delegates in Congress to propose independence; and the consequence was Richard Henry Lee's Resolution of Independence, 7 June 1776 (q.v. under its date). On 8 and 10 June Congress considered this Resolution, and on the latter date postponed action on it to 1 July. Since this delay was apparently caused by the desire for unanimity and since the act of independence was a foregone conclusion, Congress decided to avoid further delay by appointing a Committee of Five to draft a declaration that would announce to the world and at the same time justify the act. On 11 June this Committee of Five was appointed, consisting of Thomas Jefferson, John Adams, Benjamin Franklin, Roger Sherman, and Robert R. Livingston. The draft of the Declaration agreed upon by the Committee was reported to Congress on 28 June. Congress, sitting as a committee of the whole on 1 July, debated the Lee Resolution for nine hours without interruption; this was the decisive debate but the Resolution was not put to vote by Congress until the following day, when it was adopted. This, however, was not a unanimous vote, since the delegates of New York were bound by their instructions and abstained from voting (they were released by the New York Convention on 9 July). It was for this reason, doubtless, that the Declaration as adopted on 4 July bore the title "A Declaration by the Representatives of the United States of America, in General Congress Assembled," whereas the engrossed parchment copy of the Declaration was entitled "The Unanimous Declaration of the Thirteen United States of America."

Jefferson's Declaration was debated on 2-4 July and was, after considerable revision, adopted on the last day. The question as to whether it was signed on 4 July is discussed in the notes to Jefferson's Notes of Proceedings in the Continental Congress, 7 June to 1 Aug. 1776. On 19 July Congress ordered the Declaration to be engrossed and signed. The signing of the engrossed parchment copy took place on 2 Aug.

The procedure of the Committee of Five between 11 and 28 June became the subject of some difference of opinion between Adams and Jefferson in 1823. Yet the main outlines are clear and indisputable. The Committee selected Jefferson to prepare a draft. He did so, submitting it first to Adams and then to Franklin. Some of their suggested alterations, if not all, were made in their own handwriting on the draft that Jefferson later endorsed "original Rough draught." The Committee itself apparently made few changes, but Congress excised about a fourth of the text, including the famous passage concerning Negro slavery. In all there were eighty-six alterations, made at various stages by Jefferson, by Adams and Franklin, by the Committee of Five, and by Congress. Almost all of these were indicated on the "Rough draught," and one minor change was made even after Congress had adopted the final text (Boyd, *Declaration of Independence*, 1945, p. 17). It would be difficult if not impossible to say at what stage or by whom these various changes had been made if it were not for the fact that several contemporary copies of Jefferson's text were made. The earliest and most important of these is the copy in John Adams' handwriting, probably made before Jefferson had shown the text to Franklin but after a few minor changes had been effected (this copy is reproduced in Boyd, *Declaration of Independence*,

Whereas George ―――― Guelph king of Great Britain & Ireland and
Elector of Hanover, heretofore entrusted with the exercise of the kingly office in this government
hath endeavored to pervert the same into a detestable & insupportable tyranny

by putting his negative on laws the most wholesome & necessary for the public good
by denying to his governors permission to pass laws of ―――― immediate & pressing importance, unless suspended in their operation for his assent, & when so suspended
neglecting to attend to them for many years:
by refusing to pass certain other laws, unless the persons to be benefited by them would
relinquish the inestimable right of representation in the legislature
by dissolving legislative assemblies repeatedly & continually for opposing with manly firmness his invasions on the rights of the people:
when dissolved, by refusing to call others for a long space of time, thereby leaving the poli-
-tical system without any legislative head.
by endeavoring to prevent the population of our country & obstructing the laws for
naturalization of foreigners & raising the conditions of appropriations of lands:
by keeping among us in times of peace standing armies & ships of war:
by affecting to render the military independent of & superior to the civil power:
by combining with others to subject us to a foreign jurisdiction, giving his assent
to their pretended acts of legislation
a. for quartering large bodies of armed troops among us & protecting them &c.

c. for imposing taxes on us without our consent:
d. for depriving us of the benefits of trial by jury:
e. for transporting us beyond seas to be tried for pretended offences:
f. for suspending our own legislatures & declaring themselves invested with power
to legislate for us in all cases whatsoever
by plundering our seas, ravaging our coasts, burning our towns, & destroying the lives
of our people:
by inciting insurrections of our fellow subjects with the allurements of forfeiture & confiscation
by prompting our negroes to rise in arms among us; those very negroes whom he hath
refused us permission to exclude by law:
by endeavoring to bring on the inhabitants of our frontiers the merciless Indian savages
whose known rule of warfare is an undistinguished destruction of all ages, sexes, & conditions
by transporting at this time a large army of foreign mercenaries to compleat the works of
death, desolation, & tyranny already begun so unworthy the head of a civilized nation
by answering our repeated petitions for redress with a repetition of injuries
and by taking the helm of government, & declaring us out of his allegiance & protection
and by various other acts of tyranny too often enumerated to need repetition
by which several acts of misrule the said George hath forfeited the kingly office, and has rendered it necessary
for the preservation of the people that he
should be immediately deposed from the kingly
office & divested of all its privileges, powers, & prerogatives:
And forasmuch as the public liberty may be more certainly secured by abolishing our office
which all experience hath shewn to be inveterately inimical thereto
necessary to re-establish such ancient principles as are friendly to the rights of the people & to declare
certain others which may co-operate with & fortify the same in future

& for new-modelling the form of Government and for _____lishing the Fundamental principles thereof in future.

Whereas George _____ Guelf king of Great Britain and Ireland and Elector of Hanover, heretofore entrusted with the exercise of the kingly office in this government hath endeavored to pervert the same into a detestable and insupportable tyranny;

by putting his negative on laws the most wholesome & necessary for ỹ public good;

by denying to his governors permission to pass laws of immediate & pressing importance, unless suspended in their operation for his assent, and, when so suspended, neglecting to attend to them for many years;

by refusing to pass certain other laws, unless the persons to be benefited by them would relinquish the inestimable right of representation in the legislature

by dissolving legislative assemblies repeatedly and continually for opposing with manly firmness his invasions on the rights of the people;

when dissolved, by refusing to call others for a long space of time, thereby leaving the political system without any legislative head;

by endeavoring to prevent the population of our country, & for that purpose ob- ____ the laws for the naturalization of foreigners & raising the condition

_____ riations of lands;

_____ in times of peace, standing armies & ships of war;

_____ g to render the military independent of & superior to the civil power;

by combining with others to subject us to a foreign jurisdiction. giving his as- ____sent to their pretended acts of legislation

for quartering large bodies of troops among us;

for cutting off our trade with all parts of the world;

for imposing taxes on us without our consent;

for depriving us of the benefits of trial by jury;

for transporting us beyond seas to be tried for pretended offences; and

for suspending our own legislatures & declaring themselves invested with power to legislate for us in all cases whatsoever;

by plundering our seas, ravaging our coasts, burning our towns and destroy- ing the lives of our people;

by inciting insurrections of our fellow subjects with the allurements of forfeiture & confiscation.

by prompting our negroes to rise in arms among us; those very negroes whom ~~by the~~ ~~from time to time~~ by an inhuman use of his negative he hath refused us permission to exclude by law

by endeavoring to bring on the inhabitants of our frontiers the merciless Indian sa- vages, whose known rule of warfare is an undistinguished destruction of all ages, sexes, & conditions of existence;

Page one of Jefferson's Third Draft of the
Virginia Constitution.

Fragment of the earliest draft of the Declaration of Independence, discovered in 1947. (The writing upside-down on this page is part of a Resolution on General Sullivan.)

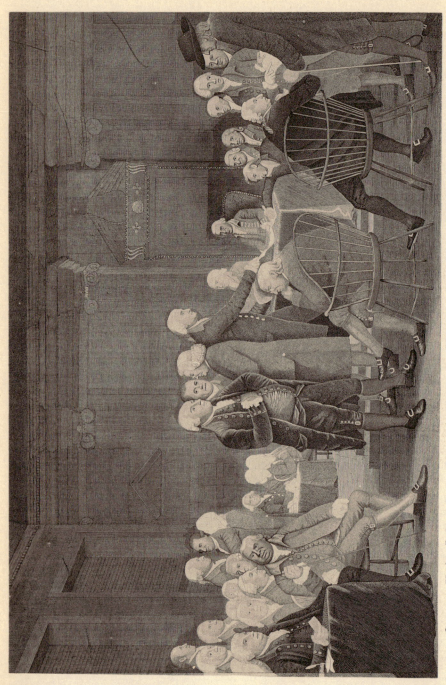

Congress Voting Independence. Copperplate engraving by Edward Savage after a painting by Pine and Savage.

together with all known texts in Jefferson's handwriting). Shortly after the adoption of the Declaration, Jefferson made copies of the "Rough draught" and sent them to distant friends, including Richard Henry Lee, Edmund Pendleton, George Wythe, Philip Mazzei, and probably John Page. With the aid of these copies, the one at an early stage and the others at a later, it has been possible to determine the evolution of the text with more or less precision. Such a detailed analysis will not be attempted here except insofar as it becomes necessary to establish the character and relationships of the first three documents in the present series.

When Jefferson wrote to Richard Henry Lee on 8 July, enclosing a copy of the Declaration, he described it as conforming to the text "as originally framed." The copy that he enclosed, however, was a copy of the "Rough draught." In 1823 Jefferson also declared that he had "turned to neither book or pamphlet while writing" the Declaration (TJ to Madison, 30 Aug. 1823), and that it was not "copied from any particular and previous writing" (TJ to Henry Lee, 8 May 1825). Despite these statements, Jefferson was misled when he endorsed the most famous and most interesting copy of the Declaration as the "original Rough draught." It is small wonder that, nearly half a century after the event, he should have thought it was the original rough draft, for its interlineations, additions, deletions, and marginalia certainly gave it the appearance of being a composition draft. Yet, as Documents I and II in this series prove, the "original Rough draught" is a fair copy of an earlier text. It would be technically correct to refer to it as the Committee Draft or as the Fair Copy prepared for the Committee; but historians have long since become accustomed to designating it as the Rough Draft and so this time-honored label has been retained, though with the difference that Jefferson's original spelling has been preserved in this series.

Document I is here referred to as a Composition Draft for a part of the Declaration. It is, of course, the first page of the First Draft of Jefferson's Constitution for Virginia, and it served as a rough draft for that document before being employed in the same capacity for the Declaration of Independence. The notes to Document I of the Virginia Constitution, q.v., and the notes to Document I in this series show that, after Jefferson had copied off the Third Draft of the Virginia Constitution, he returned to the first page of the First Draft and made several additions to the "black Catalogue of unprovoked injuries"; he also numbered the various paragraphs and rearranged them in such a sequence as he desired them to have in the Declaration of Independence. Not only this, but one alteration was made in both after the latter had been copied. It has long been noticed, of course, that the preamble to the Virginia Constitution and the charges against the crown in the Declaration were very similar and in many cases identical in phraseology; Jefferson himself explained this similarity in 1825 by saying that "both having the same object, of justifying our separation from Great Britain, they used necessarily the same materials of justification: and hence their similitude" (TJ to Augustus B. Woodward, 3 Apr. 1825). But the identity between the two is closer than this implies. The rearrangement of the list of charges was the result of a conscious effort to adapt them to the purposes of the Declaration, not the accidental similarity resulting from a use of the same materials. While it is not correct to say that the "Rough draught" is an exact copy of this part of the revised first page of the Virginia Constitution, since some verbal discrepancies between the two exist despite the additions and rearrangement, the adaptation of it to the purposes of the Declaration is so clearly indicated, and the two were brought thereby into such close identity, as to justify its designation as a Composition Draft for this particular part of the Declaration (see notes to Document I).

Document II is only a fragment, but it presents conclusive proof that the "Rough draught" was copied from an earlier text—copied with exact verbal fidelity, at least in the part here presented, and not merely with close identity as in the case of Document I. In the process of making the "Rough draught," however, Jefferson continued to alter his selection of words, effecting changes in both the copy and in the text copied, as he frequently did with writings far less important than the Declaration of Independence.

Since Document II is a fragment, the only method of ascertaining the text of the Declaration "as originally framed" is to employ the Adams copy as a means of separating the overlay of corrections, additions, and deletions made by the Committee of Five and by Congress. Some sixteen alterations had been made in the text by the time Adams copied it; these are all indicated in the notes to Document III. Document III, therefore, is the "Rough draught" of the Declaration approximately as it was when Jefferson had copied it off and was ready to submit it to the Committee of Five.

The next two stages of the evolution of the text of the Declaration, including both those alterations made by the Committee of Five and those made by Congress (though Jefferson does not differentiate between the two stages), are indicated in Document IV, the text that Jefferson copied for James Madison in 1783 from his Notes of Proceedings in Congress, 7 June to 1 Aug. 1776. This text, given only a brief entry in the present sequence, is printed in its proper place in the Notes of Proceedings (q.v., p. 315). In those Notes Jefferson referred to the text "as originally reported" (which is incorrect either as referring to his report of a draft to the Committee or as referring to a draft reported by the Committee to Congress) and wrote: "the parts struck out by Congress shall be distinguished by a black line drawn under them; & those inserted by them shall be placed in the margin or in a concurrent column." By referring to this text it is possible to see approximately what alterations were made by the Committee of Five and by Congress; but Jefferson's notations were not exact or comprehensive (see Boyd, *Declaration of Independence*, 1945, p. 34-6).

Document V is an official text of the Declaration of Independence. Even this, however, requires explanation. Actually there are three texts of the famous document that can properly be referred to as the official text "as adopted by Congress." The first of these is the broadside printed by John Dunlap, probably on the night of 4-5 July, and wafered into a blank space left for it in the Rough Journal of Congress (same, pl. x), being preceded by the words: "The Declaration being again read was agreed to as follows." This printed copy was signed by John Hancock "by Order and in Behalf of the Congress" and attested by Charles Thomson (M. J. Walsh, "Contemporary Broadside Editions of the Declaration of Independence," *Harvard Library Bulletin*, III [1949], 31-43). The second official text of the Declaration is that in the Corrected Journal of Congress (Hazelton, *Declaration of Independence*, p. 306-42). The third is the famous engrossed copy on parchment, signed by the delegates in Congress. These three copies have minute and unimportant variations, and concerning the last Carl Becker wrote that "The capitalization and punctuation, following neither previous copies, nor reason, nor the custom of any age known to man, is one of the irremediable evils of life to be accepted with becoming resignation." The present text follows the engrossed and signed parchment copy, though, as with almost all other copies made in the past century, it is derived not directly from the parchment itself but from the copperplate engraving made from it at the direction of Secretary of State John Quincy Adams in 1823 (see note on Document v).

I. Composition Draft of that Part of the Declaration of Independence Containing the Charges against the Crown

Whereas George   Guelph King of Great Britain & Ireland and Elector of Hanover, heretofore entrusted with the exercise of the Kingly office in this government, hath endeavored to pervert the same into a detestable & insupportable tyranny

1. by ⟨neg⟩ putting his negative on laws the most wholesome & necessary for the public good
   ⟨has kept some colonies without judiciary establmts⟩[1]
2. by denying to his governors permission to pass laws of ⟨the most⟩ immediate & pressing importance, unless suspended in their operation for his ⟨con⟩assent &, when so suspended, neglecting ⟨for m⟩ to attend to them for many years:
3. by refusing to pass certain other laws, unless the persons to be benefited by them would relinquish the inestimable right⟨s⟩ of representation in the legislature:
   ⟨judges dependant⟩[2]
4. by dissolving legislative assemblies repeatedly & continually for

opposing with manly firmness his invasions on the rights of the people:

5. when dissolved, by refusing to call others for a long space of time, thereby leaving the political system ⟨[*in a state of dissolution*]⟩[3] without any legislative ⟨*body*⟩ head.

6. by endeavoring to prevent the population of our country ⟨*by*⟩ & for that purpose obstructing the laws [for the naturalization] encouraging the importn[4] of foreigners & raising the conditions of new appropriati⟨*ng*⟩ons ⟨*new*⟩ of lands:
   refused judiciary establmts to some without unjust & partial[5] judges dependant
   erected swarms of offices[6]

7. by keeping among us in times of peace standing armies & ships of war:

8. by affecting to render the military independant of & superior to the civil power:

9. by combining with others to subject us to a foreign jurisdiction giving his ⟨*con*⟩assent to their pretended acts of legislation ⟨*for imposing taxes on us without our consent.*⟩
   a. for quartering large bodies of armed troops among us: & protectg them &c.—murders[7]
   b. for cutting off our trade with all parts of the world:
   c. for ⟨*depriving us of*⟩ imposing taxes on us without our consent:
   d. for depriving us of the benefits of trial by jury:
   e. for transporting us beyond seas to be tried for pretended offences:
      for taking away our charters & altering fundamentally the forms of our governments[8]
   f. for suspending our own legislatures & declaring themselves invested with power to legislate for us in all cases whatsoever

16.

10. by plundering our seas, ravaging our coasts, burning our towns, ⟨*des*⟩ & destroying the lives of our people:

14.13.

11. by inciting insurrections of our fellow ⟨*subjects*⟩ citizens[9] with the allurements of forfeiture & confiscation

12. by prompting our negroes to rise in arms among us; those very negroes whom by an inhuman use of his negative he hath ⟨*from time to time*⟩ refused us permission to exclude by law:[10]

13. by endeavoring to bring on the inhabitants of our frontiers the

merciless Indian savages whose known rule of warfare is an undistinguished destruction of all ages, sexes, & conditions ⟨of life⟩ of existence.¹¹

14. by transporting at this time a large army of foreign mercenaries to compleat the works of death, desolation, & tyranny already begun ⟨in a stile⟩ with circumstances of cruelty & perfidy so unworthy ⟨a⟩ the head of a civilized ⟨people⟩ nation¹²

15. by answering our repeated petitions ⟨against this repeated⟩ for redress with a repetition of injur⟨y⟩ies: ⟨with an accumulation of new injury⟩¹³

16. and finally by abandoning the helm of government ⟨&⟩ & declaring us out of his allegiance & protection.¹⁴
⟨[and by various other acts of tyranny too often enumerated to need repetition, and too cruel for the reflection of those who have felt them.]⟩¹⁵

Dft (DLC). Endorsed in margin: "Constitution of Virginia first ideas of Th: J. communicated to a member of the convention." For a full description of this document, see the Virginia Constitution, June 1776, notes to Document I, where a close comparison is made between the First and Third Drafts in order to establish the text of the first page of the former as it existed prior to the additions and rearrangement made by TJ when he employed it as the composition draft of that part of the Declaration of Independence containing the list of charges against the crown. The notes below indicate the extent of TJ's additions and rearrangement for this purpose. The terms First Draft and Third Draft, as employed in the following notes, refer respectively to these drafts of the Virginia Constitution, q.v.

The extent of TJ's additions shows how carefully and continually he endeavored to lengthen "this black Catalogue of unprovoked injuries," as it was termed in the Address to the Inhabitants of Great Britain in 1775 (JCC, II, 164); TJ's *Summary View* and Declaration of Causes and Necessity for Taking Up Arms included briefer lists of this nature, and the First Draft of the Virginia Constitution was a further elaboration. Even that, however, did not exhaust the possibilities, nor, indeed, did these additions to the First Draft complete the catalogue, for when the "Rough draught" of the Declaration was finished TJ was still able to add to the list. The Virginia Res-

olutions of 15 May 1776, which contained a brief list of charges against the crown, may possibly have furnished inspiration for a part of TJ's initial bill of particulars as expressed in the First Draft.

¹ This sentence interlined and struck out after the Third Draft was made; see note 4. The paragraphs were numbered by TJ for convenience in rearranging them; see notes 9, 10, and 12.

² Interlined and struck out after Third Draft was made; see note 4.

³ Bracketed in MS and deleted before Third Draft was made.

⁴ The words "for the naturalization" were bracketed in the MS, and the words "encouraging the importn" were interlined after the Third Draft was made. The corresponding passage in the "Rough draught" of the Declaration of Independence incorporates both phrases.

⁵ Text only partly legible, and intended sense doubtful.

⁶ The three subject-headings between paragraphs 6 and 7 were added after the Third Draft was made. The first (see note 1) and the second (see note 2) were interlined at other places and then struck out. These subject-headings appear in expanded form and in this particular sequence at the corresponding point of the "Rough draught." Being unnumbered, these subject-headings were obviously interlined at this point after TJ had finished numbering the paragraphs on the first page of the First Draft.

7 The phrase "& protectg them &c.—murders" was added after the Third Draft was made; this addition was raised to the status of a separate item on the list of charges in the "Rough draught." These subheadings were alphabetized after the Third Draft was made.

8 This sentence was interlined after the Third Draft was made and indeed after the subheadings in this section were alphabetized; it occurs at this point, and in precisely the same phraseology, in the "Rough draught" of the Declaration.

9 This change is important as indicating that TJ used this part of the First Draft as a composition draft for the Declaration. Both the First Draft and the Third Draft read "fellow subjects"; so did the "Rough draught" as originally written. However, TJ erased the word "subjects" and wrote "citizens" over it; this was perhaps done as he was making the "Rough draught," for the Adams copy of the Declaration reads "fellow citizens." But the important point to be noted is that, in making the correction in the "Rough draught," he also made it in the First Draft. He would scarcely have done so if he had not been using the First Draft as the composition text for the "Rough draught."

10 This passage was greatly expanded in the Declaration of Independence, differing markedly in this respect from all other paragraphs in this part of the First Draft, some of which were copied verbatim in the "Rough draught" and all others with slight modification. By his rearrangement TJ caused paragraph 12 to fall at the end of his list of charges; this being so, he may very well have rewritten it in the composition text of which Document II in this series was a part. It is difficult to imagine so oratorical a passage (the phrase is John Adams') being written as it appears in the "Rough draught" without having been preceded by some other composition text aside from the corresponding part in the First Draft.

11 This paragraph is bracketed in the margin of the First Draft, obviously because TJ decided to place it between paragraphs 10 and 11, where he had inserted the figures "14.13." (see note 12).

12 This paragraph is also bracketed in the margin of the First Draft for insertion between paragraphs 10 and 11. The "Rough draught" includes paragraphs 14 and 13, in this order, so as to coincide precisely with the arrangement indicated by TJ when he inserted "14.13." between paragraphs 10 and 11.

13 This paragraph, though bracketed in the margin of the First Draft, is repeated in the "Rough draught" not as a separate charge but as a part of the summation: "in every stage of these oppressions we have petitioned for redress in the most humble terms; our repeated petitions have been answered by repeated injuries. . . ."

14 This paragraph is bracketed in the margin of the First Draft. It occurs in the "Rough draught" precisely at the point indicated by TJ in placing the figure 16 between paragraphs 9 and 10 of the First Draft.

15 Brackets in MS. This passage was not included in the Third Draft and must therefore have been deleted before that Draft was made.

II. Fragment of the Composition Draft of the Declaration of Independence

re-established them in po[wer . . .]¹ ⟨*this conduct and*⟩ at this very time too, they are permitting their ⟨*sovereign*⟩ chief magistrate to send over not only soldiers of our ⟨*own*⟩ common blood but Scotch & foreign mercenaries to ⟨*destroy us*⟩ invade and deluge us in blood.² ⟨*this is too much to be borne even by relations. enough then be it to say, we are now done with them.*⟩ these facts have given

the last stab to agonizing affection, & manly spirit bids us to renounce for ever these unfeeling brethren![3] we must endeavor to
forget our former love for them and to hold them, as we hold the
rest of mankind, enemies in war, in peace friends. we might have
been a ⟨great⟩ free & a ⟨happy⟩ great people together, but a com-
municat⟨ed⟩ion of ⟨happiness⟩ [g]randeur & of ⟨grandeur⟩ freedom
it seems is be⟨neath⟩low their dignity. ⟨we will climb then the roads
to glory & happiness apart⟩ be it so, since they will have it: the
road to ⟨glory &⟩ ⟨to⟩ happiness & to glory[4] is open to us too, we
will climb it ⟨in a separate state⟩ apart from them[5] & acquiesce in
the necessity which ⟨pro⟩ denounces[6] our ⟨everlasting Adieu⟩ eternal
separation.[7]
⟨these facts have given the last stab to agonizing affection, & manly
spirit bids us to renounce for ever these unjust⟩ ⟨unfeeling⟩ ⟨breth-
ren.⟩

Dft. (DLC). This fragment appears on
one of three half-leaves (TJ Papers, 4:
647-9) which embrace all or part of several documents: (1) rough draft of Resolution on the Case of General Sullivan,
29 July 1776, q.v. (recto of p. 647 and
half of recto of p. 649); (2) fair copy of
same (beginning on verso and concluding on recto of p. 648); (3) part of rough
draft of Report of the Committee on the
Cedars Cartel, 17 June 1776, q.v. (verso
of p. 647); (4) Fragment of the Composition Draft of the Declaration of Independence (half of recto of p. 649); and
(5) pencil notes of the dimensions and
characteristics of a horse stall (verso of
p. 649). The last, which will be printed
in the volume containing TJ's architectural papers and drawings, pertains to
the stable of Governor John Penn (see
Kimball, Jefferson, Architect, pl. 60, for
a drawing and memorandum based on
these pencil notes). None of these bears a
date, though all were written after 11
June 1776 and all save the last were certainly penned before 29 July 1776; the
last was very probably done before 29
July, since, otherwise, TJ would no
doubt have written the concluding part
of the Resolution on Sullivan on the
verso of p. 649 instead of upside down
on the recto. See Julian P. Boyd, "New
Light on Jefferson and His Great Task,"
New York Times Magazine, 13 Apr.
1947, p. 17+.

This recently discovered fragment, containing part of the earliest known text of
the Declaration of Independence, bears

internal evidence (1) that it was earlier
than the copy that TJ, late in life, endorsed as the "original Rough draught";
(2) that what TJ called the "Rough
draught" was in fact copied from the
text of which this fragment was a part;
(3) that this fragment was indeed a part
of the original composition draft; and
(4) that the original composition draft
was not, as in all other copies of the Declaration made by TJ, a single consecu-
tive text occupying four pages of a whole
sheet folded once, but was made up of
at least two and possibly more parts.

The fact that the Fragment is earlier than TJ's so-called "original Rough
draught" and that the latter was copied
from its text is easily demonstrable. The
Fragment contains several words and
passages that are crossed out; none of
these was copied in the "Rough draught"
(or true fair copy). The Fragment also
contains, in its undeleted 148 words that
were copied in the "Rough draught," 43
words caretted and interlined; none of
these was so treated in the "Rough
draught." Such deletions and interlineations in themselves do not prove the
Fragment to have been part of a composition draft, but the unusual treatment
of one important deletion and interlineation does support this conclusion. After
he had completed the whole passage, TJ
began a new line ("these facts have
given the last stab . . .") in order to rephrase the awkward transitional sentence between the statement of facts
justifying separation and the statement
of the conclusion that "eternal separa-

tion" was the result of these facts. This new attempt to rephrase the sentence was only a slight improvement over the one it was intended to supplant, and Congress later deleted it. But, satisfied with the new phrasing, TJ then crossed out the sentence "this is too much to be borne even by relations . . . ," and interlined the second above it and also crossed out the "composition draft" of the new sentence at the bottom of the Fragment. To be sure, there are numerous instances in TJ's papers of a word or passage being crossed out in a rough draft and then being transferred and interlined at some other place for the sake of clarity, rhythm, or force. But the fact that the sentence "these facts have given the last stab . . ." was written on a new line and at the conclusion of the whole passage, where it obviously could not follow in sequence, shows that it was a trial phrasing for something else already stated. When TJ was satisfied that this tentative phrasing was an improvement, he made the necessary interlineation at the only point where the initial words "these facts" could be appropriately applied. If he had been copying rather than composing, he would merely have struck out the awkward sentence and interlined the substitute. Other indications in the MS support the conclusion that the Fragment is part of a composition draft; for example, the sentence "we will climb the roads to glory & happiness apart" was struck out, and TJ then proceeded to rephrase the same thought not by interlineation but by continuing on the same line.

But perhaps the most conclusive evidence that the Fragment is a part of the earliest composition text derives from its position on the page. All other contemporary copies of the text of the Declaration in TJ's hand occupy four full pages; a rough, composition draft presumably would have occupied even more space because of deletions and additions (the fragmentary text here presented occupies fully thirteen lines, and the corresponding passage in the "Rough draught" occupies slightly more than ten). Yet the text of the Fragment ends in the middle of the half-leaf, the remainder being blank until, late in July, TJ used it for the concluding part of the Sullivan Resolution. Its verso was completely blank until TJ jotted down the penciled dimensions of Governor Penn's stable. In short, if we assume that TJ began composing the Declaration on a whole sheet folded once to make four pages, as was the case in every other known copy of the Declaration made by him in 1776, the text of the Fragment would occur on the third page and would occupy the third quarter of that page, the final quarter being blank and all of page four being blank. The question at once arises as to how this could be so, since the full text of the Declaration as copied by TJ occupies four full pages. The answer, it seems obvious, is that the long list of charges in the indictment of the crown was not present in this composition draft of which we have a fragment. There was no need for it to be included in this composition draft since TJ had employed the first page of his First Draft of a Constitution for Virginia for such a purpose. Allowing for the absence from the Fragment of the concluding paragraph of the Declaration giving effect to the Resolution of Independence of 7 June, and allowing also for the omission from this composition text of the indictment against the crown we are presented with plausible evidence for the supposition that the Fragment ends on the third quarter of the third page. This supposition that TJ omitted the list of charges against the crown from this composition draft is made all but conclusive by the fact that in both the first page of the First Draft of the Virginia Constitution and in the text of the Fragment, deletions and interlineations were made *after* the "Rough draught" had been copied off (see notes to Document I and textual notes below). If the list of charges had been included in the text of which the Fragment is a part, TJ would scarcely have gone back to the first page of the First Draft of the Virginia Constitution to make an alteration that had been made in the "Rough draught." Hence, both because of its position on the page and also because of these corrections, we conclude that the text of the Fragment did not include the list of charges and that it was, therefore, an incomplete composition draft in respect to this and also in respect to its omission of the final paragraph of the Declaration. Whether this final paragraph was composed during the process of copying the "Rough draught," or whether a tentative draft of it was written on another sheet of paper before being copied, cannot be determined.

1 Half a line of text missing along the torn top edge of the MS.

2 The phrase "deluge us in blood" is deleted in the "Rough draught" and the words "destroy us" are interlined in the handwriting of Benjamin Franklin. In making this correction, Franklin chose precisely the words that TJ had originally written and rejected for the more oratorical phrase.

3 This sentence was interlined at this point after it was written and deleted below.

4 TJ copied the phrase "to glory & happiness" in the "Rough draught" and then corrected both that and the text of the Fragment by striking out "glory &" and interlining "& to glory" in each. This change was made before John Adams copied off his text of the "Rough draught."

5 TJ copied the phrase "in a separate state" in the "Rough draught" and then, by appropriate changes, reduced it to the word "separately." This was not satisfactory, and so he struck out "separately" in the "Rough draught" and interlined "apart from them," doing the same in the text of the Fragment. Adams' copy was made after the interlineation of "apart from them." This correction is important in showing that TJ indulged in an occasional bit of composition even while copying the "Rought draught" from the text of the Fragment.

6 TJ altered "pronounces" to "denounces" in the process of copying the "Rough draught," making the alteration in both that and the text of the Fragment. This change also was made before Adams took his copy.

7 TJ struck out "everlasting Adieu" in the "Rough draught" and also in the text of the Fragment and then added "eternal separation" in each. He had omitted the exclamation point after "unfeeling brethren" in the "Rough draught" and then placed one after "eternal separation," though none occurs at this point in the text of the Fragment. This change was made before the Adams copy was taken.

III. Jefferson's "original Rough draught" of the Declaration of Independence

A Declaration of[1] the Representatives of the UNITED STATES OF AMERICA, in General Congress assembled.

When in the course of human events it becomes necessary for a people to advance from that subordination in which they have hitherto remained, & to assume among the powers of the earth the equal & independant station to which the laws of nature & of nature's god entitle them, a decent respect to the opinions of mankind requires that they should declare the causes which impel them to the change.

We hold these truths to be sacred & undeniable;[2] that all men are created equal & independant, that from that equal creation they derive rights[3] inherent & inalienable, among which are the preservation of life, & liberty, & the pursuit of happiness; that to secure these ends, governments are instituted among men, deriving their just powers from the consent of the governed; that whenever any form of government shall become destructive of these ends, it is the right of the people to alter or to abolish it, & to institute new government, laying it's foundation on such principles & organising it's powers in such form, as to them shall seem most likely to effect their safety & happiness. prudence indeed will dictate that governments long established should not be changed for light & transient causes: and accordingly all experience hath shewn that mankind are more disposed to suffer while evils are sufferable, than to right themselves by abolishing the forms to which they are accustomed. but when a long train of abuses & usurpations, begun at a distinguished period, & pursuing invariably the same object, evinces a design to subject[4] them to arbitrary power,[5] it is their right, it is their duty, to throw off such government & to provide new guards for their future security. such has been the patient sufferance of these colonies; & such is now the necessity which constrains them to expunge their former systems of government. the history of his present majesty, is a history of unremitting injuries and usurpations, among which no one fact stands single or solitary to contradict the uniform tenor of the rest, all of which have in direct object the establishment of an absolute tyranny over these states. to prove this, let facts be submitted to a candid world, for the truth of which we pledge a faith yet unsullied by falsehood.

he has refused his assent to laws the most wholesome and necessary for the public good:

he has forbidden his governors to pass laws of immediate & pressing importance, unless suspended in their operation till his assent should be obtained; and when so suspended, he has neglected utterly to attend to them.

he has refused to pass other laws for the accomodation of large districts of people unless those people would relinquish the right of representation,[6] a right inestimable to them, & formidable to tyrants alone:[7]

he has dissolved Representative houses repeatedly & continually, for opposing with manly firmness his invasions on the rights of the people:

he has refused[8] for a long space of time[9] to cause others to be elected, whereby the legislative powers, incapable of annihilation, have returned to the people at large for their exercise, the state remaining in the mean time exposed to all the dangers of invasion from without, & convulsions within:

he has endeavored to prevent the population of these states; for that purpose obstructing the laws for naturalization of foreigners; refusing to pass others to encourage their migrations hither; & raising the conditions of new appropriations of lands:

he has suffered the administration of justice totally to cease in some of these colonies, refusing his assent to laws for establishing judiciary powers:

he has made our judges dependant on his will alone, for the tenure of their offices, and amount of their salaries:

he has erected a multitude of new offices by a self-assumed power, & sent hither swarms of officers to harrass our people & eat out their substance:

he has kept among us in times of peace standing armies & ships of war:

he has affected to render the military, independant of & superior to the civil power:

he has combined with others to subject us to a jurisdiction foreign to our constitutions and unacknoleged by our laws; giving his assent to their pretended acts of legislation, for quartering large bodies of armed troops among us;

> for protecting them by a mock-trial from punishment for any murders they should commit on the inhabitants of these states;

> for cutting off our trade with all parts of the world;

> for imposing taxes on us without our consent;

> for depriving us of the benefits of trial by jury;

> for transporting us beyond seas to be tried for pretended offences:

> for taking away our charters, & altering fundamentally the forms of our governments;

> for suspending our own legislatures & declaring themselves invested with power to legislate for us in all cases whatsoever:

he has abdicated government here, withdrawing his governors, & declaring us out of his allegiance & protection:

he has plundered our seas, ravaged our coasts, burnt our towns & destroyed the lives of our people:

he is at this time transporting large armies of foreign mercenaries to compleat the works of death, desolation & tyranny, already begun with circumstances of cruelty & perfidy unworthy the head of a civilized nation:

he has endeavored to bring on the inhabitants of our frontiers the merciless Indian savages, whose known rule of warfare is an undistinguished destruction of all ages, sexes, & conditions of existence:

he has incited treasonable insurrections in our fellow-subjects,[10] with the allurements of forfeiture & confiscation of our property:

he has waged cruel war against human nature itself, violating it's most sacred rights of life & liberty in the persons of a distant people who never offended him, captivating & carrying them into slavery in another hemisphere, or to incur miserable death in their transportation thither. this piratical warfare, the opprobrium of *infidel* powers, is the warfare of the CHRISTIAN king of Great Britain. determined to keep open a market where MEN should be bought & sold, he has prostituted his negative for suppressing every legislative attempt to prohibit or to restrain this execrable commerce:[11] and that this assemblage of horrors might want no fact of distinguished die, he is now exciting those very people to rise in arms among us, and to purchase that liberty of which *he* has deprived them, by murdering the people upon whom *he* also obtruded them; thus paying off former crimes committed against the *liberties* of one people, with crimes which he urges them to commit against the *lives* of another.

in every stage of these oppressions we have petitioned for redress in the most humble terms; our repeated petitions have been answered by repeated injury. a prince whose character is thus marked by every act which may define a tyrant, is unfit to be the ruler of a people who mean to be free. future ages will scarce believe that the hardiness of one man, adventured within the short compass of 12[12] years only, on so many acts of tyranny without a mask, over a people fostered & fixed in principles of liberty.

Nor have we been wanting in attentions to our British brethren. we have warned them from time to time of attempts by their legislature to extend a jurisdiction over these our states. we have reminded them of the circumstances of our emigration & settlement here, no one of which could warrant so strange a pretension: that these were effected at the expence of our own blood & treasure, unassisted by the wealth or the strength of Great Britain: that in constituting indeed our several forms of government, we had adopted one common king, thereby laying a foundation for perpetual league & amity with them: but that submission to their parliament was no part of our constitution, nor ever in idea, if history may be credited: and we appealed to their native justice & magnanimity, as well as to the ties of our common kindred to disavow these usurpations which were likely to interrupt our correspondence & connection. they too have been deaf to the voice of justice & of consanguinity, & when occasions have been given them, by the regular course of their laws, of removing from their councils the disturbers of our harmony, they have by their free election re-established them in power. at this very time too they are permitting their chief magistrate to send over not only soldiers of our common blood, but Scotch & foreign mercenaries to invade & deluge us in blood. these facts have given the last stab to agonizing affection, and manly spirit bids us to renounce for ever these unfeeling brethren. we must endeavor to forget our former love for them, and to hold them as we hold the rest of mankind, enemies in war, in peace friends. we might have been a free & a great people together; but a communication of grandeur & of freedom it seems is below their dignity. be it so, since they will have it: the road to glory & happiness[13] is open to us too; we will climb it in a separate state,[14] and acquiesce in the necessity which pronounces[15] our everlasting Adieu![16]

We therefore the representatives of the United States of America in General Congress assembled do, in the name & by authority of the good people of these states, reject and renounce all allegiance & subjection to the kings of Great Britain & all others who may hereafter claim by, through, or under them; we utterly dissolve & break off all political connection which may have heretofore subsisted between us & the people or parliament of Great Britain; and finally we do assert and declare these colonies to be free and independant states, and that as free & independant states they shall hereafter have power to levy war, conclude peace, contract alliances, establish commerce, & to do all other acts and things which independant states may of right do. And for the support of this declaration we mutually pledge to each other our lives, our fortunes, & our sacred honour.

Dft (DLC). Endorsed by TJ, late in life, "Independance. Declaration of original Rough draught."

The text here presented approximates its state at the time TJ transcribed it from the manuscript of which the Fragment was a part (Document II; Boyd, *Declaration of Independence*, 1945, p. 18-22) and before John Adams took off the copy in his own handwriting (MS in Adams Manuscript Trust, Boston; facsimile in Boyd, pl. IV). The "Rough draught" includes changes made in the text in the various stages of its evolution —changes made by TJ himself, by Adams and Franklin, who were consulted separately, by the Committee or by Congress. The separation of the alterations made in these various stages has been traced in Hazelton, p. 306-42;

Becker, ch. IV; and Boyd, p. 28-33. TJ's indication of the changes made during the progress of the text at its various stages may be seen in Document IV in the present sequence of texts (printed above with TJ's Notes of Proceedings in the Continental Congress, 7 June to 1 Aug. 1776). The alterations made in the text as here presented, with the possible exception of that indicated in note 9, were probably made by TJ in the course of making the "Rough draught"; this was certainly true of those indicated in notes 13-16.

[1] TJ first wrote "of" and then changed it to "by."
[2] The phrase "sacred & undeniable" was changed to "self-evident" before Adams made his copy. This change has been attributed to Franklin, but the opin-

ion rests on no conclusive evidence, and there seems to be even stronger evidence that the change was made by TJ or at least that it is in his handwriting (Boyd, *Declaration of Independence*, 1945, p. 22-3).

3 The word "in" was deleted before "rights"; TJ may have started to write "inherent."

4 The word "subject" was changed to "reduce"; this, however, was not an interlineation but was a correction made on the same line, a clear evidence that the alteration was made at the time TJ wrote out the "Rough draught."

5 The phrase "to arbitrary power" was changed, in a sequence of two alterations, to "under absolute Despotism," the first alteration being made by TJ so that, when Adams made his copy, the phrase read "under absolute power." Franklin made the second change, substituting "Despotism" for "power."

6 The phrase "in the legislature" was interlined after the word "representation"; this change was probably made in the course of copying the "Rough draught," for "in the legislature" occurs at the same point in Document I.

7 The word "alone" was changed to read "only." This change, like that indicated in notes 1, 10, and 12, was made by expunging or erasing one word while the ink was still wet and overwriting the substituted word; thus all three of these changes were probably made by TJ in the course of copying the "Rough draught."

8 The phrase "he has dissolved" was struck out at the beginning of this line; it is obvious that TJ had started to repeat the preceding sentence—a clear evidence that he was copying from an earlier draft (Boyd, *Declaration of Independence*, 1945, p. 26).

9 Here an alteration was made by John Adams. After Adams had interlined, with a caret, the words "after such Dissolutions" and had transcribed the document as it stood with these alterations, TJ then crossed out the words "space of time" and prefixed "time" to Adams' interlineation.

10 TJ originally wrote "fellow-subjects," copying the term from the corresponding passage in the first page of the First Draft of the Virginia Constitution; then, while the ink was still wet on the "Rough draught" he expunged or erased "subjects" and wrote "citizens" over it. The fact that he made the same change in Document I is evidence that he was using that document as the composition text for this part of the Declaration.

11 The words "determined to keep open a market where MEN should be bought & sold" were bracketed in the "Rough draught" and then interlined at the point indicated; Adams copied the clause at the same point. TJ subsequently deleted the brackets, crossed out the interlined repetition of the words after "commerce," and thus restored the original reading. While, therefore, the text at this point does not reflect its state at the time the Adams copy was written, it does give the text in the order in which TJ first copied it in the "Rough draught." Congress, of course, struck out the entire passage.

12 TJ first wrote the figure "12" and then, as in the changes indicated in notes 1, 7, and 10, wrote the word "twelve" over it, the correction being made in the course of copying.

13 TJ deleted "glory &" before, and interlined "& to glory" after "happiness"; this alteration was made in the course of copying, since the same change was made in Document II.

14 TJ changed "in a separate state" to "separately" in the "Rough draught"; then altered both that and the passage in Document II to read "apart from them"; this was the form which Adams copied. Thus we are able to follow TJ here in turning to two alternative readings in the "Rough draught" before going back to the text of Document II to record the one that finally satisfied him.

15 This word was changed to "denounces" in both the "Rough draught" and in Document II; the Adams copy reads "denounces."

16 TJ struck out "everlasting Adieu" in both the "Rough draught" and the text of Document II, and substituted "eternal separation," which is the reading of the Adams copy.

IV. The Declaration of Independence
as Amended by the
Committee and by Congress

[*Ed. Note*: This document is TJ's text of the Declaration as copied into his Notes of Proceedings in the Continental Congress, 7 June to 1 Aug. 1776 (which was eventually incorporated in his Autobiography) and is printed above as part of these Notes (q.v., p. 315), above; a facsimile text is available in Boyd, *Declaration of Independence*, 1945, pl. VIII. This copy (actually there are two, varying in minor particulars; see notes to TJ's Notes of Proceedings) carefully records the deletions and insertions made by Congress. The changes made by the Committee of Five and by TJ himself in the second stage of his composition (listed in Boyd, p. 29-31) can be discerned by comparing this text with that of the "Rough draught" and excluding the changes made by Congress.]

V. The Declaration of Independence
as Adopted by Congress

IN CONGRESS, JULY 4, 1776.

THE UNANIMOUS DECLARATION
OF THE THIRTEEN UNITED STATES
OF AMERICA,

WHEN in the Course of human events, it becomes necessary for one people to dissolve the political bands which have connected them with another, and to assume among the powers of the earth, the separate and equal station to which the Laws of Nature and of Nature's God entitle them, a decent respect to the opinions of mankind requires that they should declare the causes which impel them to the separation. We hold these truths to be self-evident, that all men are created equal, that they are endowed by their Creator with certain unalienable Rights, that among these are Life, Liberty and the pursuit of Happiness. That to secure these rights, Governments are instituted among Men, deriving their just powers from the consent of the governed, That whenever any Form of Government becomes destructive of these ends, it is the Right of the People to alter or to abolish it, and to institute new Government, laying its foundation on such principles and organizing its powers in such form, as to them shall seem most likely to effect their Safety and Happiness. Prudence, indeed, will dictate that Governments long established should not be changed for light and transient causes; and accordingly all experience hath shewn, that mankind are more disposed to suffer, while evils are sufferable, than to right themselves by abolishing the forms to which they are accustomed. But when a long train of abuses and usurpations, pursuing invariably the same Object evinces a design to reduce them under absolute Despotism, it is their right, it is their duty, to throw off such Government, and to provide new Guards for their future security. Such has been the patient sufferance of these Colonies; and such is now the necessity which constrains them to alter their former Systems of Government. The history of the present King of Great Britain is a history of repeated injuries and usurpations, all having in direct object the establishment of an absolute Tyranny over these States. To prove this, let Facts be submitted to a candid world. He has refused his Assent to Laws, the most wholesome and necessary for the public good. He has forbidden his Governors to pass Laws of immediate and pressing importance, unless suspended in their operation till his Assent should be obtained; and when so suspended, he has utterly neglected to attend to them. He has refused to pass other Laws for the accommodation of large districts of people, unless those people would relinquish the right of Representation in the Legislature, a right inestimable to them and formidable to tyrants only. He has called together legislative bodies at places unusual, uncomfortable, and distant from the depository of their public Records, for the sole purpose of fatiguing them into compliance with his measures. He has dissolved Representative Houses repeatedly, for opposing with manly firmness his invasions on the rights of the people. He has refused for a long time, after such dissolutions, to cause others to be elected; whereby the Legislative powers, incapable of Annihilation, have returned to the People at large for their exercise; the State remaining in the mean time exposed to all the dangers of invasion from without, and convulsions within. He has endeavoured to prevent the population of these States; for that purpose obstructing the Laws for Naturalization of Foreigners; refusing to pass others to encourage their migrations hither, and raising the conditions of new Appropriations of Lands. He has obstructed the Administration of Justice, by refusing his Assent to Laws for establishing Judiciary powers. He has made Judges dependent on his Will alone, for the tenure of their offices, and the amount and payment of their salaries. He has erected a multitude of New Offices, and sent hither swarms of Officers to harrass our people, and eat out their substance. He has kept among us, in times of peace, standing Armies without the Consent of our legislatures. He has affected to render the Military independent of and superior to the Civil power. He has combined with others to subject us to a jurisdiction foreign to our constitution, and unacknowledged by our laws; giving his Assent to their Acts of pretended Legislation: For Quartering large bodies of armed troops among us: For protecting them, by a mock Trial, from punishment for any Murders which they should commit on the Inhabitants of these States: For cutting off our Trade with all parts of the world: For imposing Taxes on us without our Consent: For depriving us in many cases of the benefits of Trial by Jury: For transporting us beyond Seas to be tried for pretended offences: For abolishing the free System of English Laws in a neighbouring Province, establishing therein an Arbitrary government, and enlarging its Boundaries so as to render it at once an example and fit instrument for introducing the same absolute rule into these Colonies: For taking away our Charters, abolishing our most valuable Laws, and altering fundamentally the Forms of our Governments: For suspending our own Legislatures, and declaring themselves invested with power to legislate for us in all cases whatsoever. He has abdicated Government here, by declaring us out of his Protection and waging War against us. He has plundered our seas, ravaged our Coasts, burnt our towns, and destroyed the Lives of our people. He is at this time transporting large Armies of foreign Mercenaries to compleat the works of death, desolation and tyranny, already begun with circumstances of Cruelty & perfidy scarcely paralleled in the most barbarous ages, and totally unworthy the Head of a civilized nation. He has constrained our fellow Citizens taken Captive on the high Seas to bear Arms against their Country, to become the executioners of their friends and Brethren, or to fall themselves by their Hands. He has excited domestic insurrections amongst us, and has endeavoured to bring on the inhabitants of our frontiers, the merciless Indian Savages, whose known rule of warfare, is an undistinguished destruction of all ages, sexes and conditions. In every stage of these Oppressions We have Petitioned for Redress in the most humble terms: Our repeated Petitions have been answered only by repeated injury. A Prince, whose character is thus marked by every act which may define a Tyrant, is unfit to be the ruler of a free people. Nor have We been wanting in attentions to our Brittish brethren. We have warned them from time to time of attempts by their legislature to extend an unwarrantable jurisdiction over us. We have reminded them of the circumstances of our emigration and settlement here. We have appealed to their native justice and magnanimity, and we have conjured them by the ties of our common kindred to disavow these usurpations, which, would inevitably interrupt our connections and correspondence. They too have been deaf to the voice of justice and of consanguinity. We must, therefore, acquiesce in the necessity, which denounces our Separation, and hold them, as we hold the rest of mankind, Enemies in War, in Peace Friends.

We, therefore, the Representatives of the united States of America, in General Congress, Assembled, appealing to the Supreme Judge of the world for the rectitude of our intentions, do, in the Name, and by Authority of the good People of these Colonies, solemnly publish and declare, That these United Colonies are, and of Right ought to be Free and Independent States; that they are Absolved from all Allegiance to the British Crown, and that all political connection between them and the State of Great Britain, is and ought to be totally dissolved; and that as Free and Independent States, they have full Power to levy War, conclude Peace, contract Alliances, establish Commerce, and to do all other Acts and Things which Independent States may of right do. And for the support of this Declaration, with a firm reliance on the protection of divine Providence, we mutually pledge to each other our Lives, our Fortunes and our sacred Honor.

John Hancock

Button Gwinnett	Thos. Nelson jr.	Richd. Stockton
Lyman Hall	Francis Lightfoot Lee	Jno Witherspoon
Geo Walton.	Carter Braxton	Fras. Hopkinson
Wm. Hooper	Robt. Morris	John Hart
Joseph Hewes,	Benjamin Rush	Abra Clark
John Penn	Benja. Franklin	Josiah Bartlett
Edward Rutledge.	John Morton	Wm: Whipple
Thos. Heyward Junr.	Geo Clymer	Saml. Adams
Thomas Lynch Junr.	Jas. Smith.	John Adams
Arthur Middleton	Geo. Taylor	Robt. Treat Paine
Samuel Chase	James Wilson	Elbridge Gerry
Wm. Paca	Geo. Ross	Step. Hopkins
Thos. Stone	Cæsar Rodney	William Ellery
Charles Carroll of	Geo Read	Roger Sherman
Carrollton	Tho M:Kean	Saml. Huntington
George Wythe	Wm. Floyd	Wm. Williams
Richard Henry Lee	Phil. Livingston	Oliver Wolcott
Th: Jefferson	Frans. Lewis	Matthew Thornton
Benja. Harrison	Lewis Morris	

Engrossed and signed parchment copy (DLC: Shrine) as engraved by W. J. Stone in 1823 and reproduced in Force, *Archives*, 5th ser., I, facing col. 1597-8.

Among the three official texts of the Declaration of Independence, the parchment copy, believed to have been engrossed by Timothy Matlack (DAB, art. on Matlack) and known to have been signed on 2 Aug. 1776 (JCC, V, 626), generally takes precedence. On the signing, see Editorial Note to TJ's Notes of Proceedings in the Continental Congress, 7 June to 1 Aug. 1776. Respecting the capitalization and punctuation of this text, see a comment by Carl Becker, quoted at the end of the general Editorial Note, above. The parchment copy was, by law, in the custody of the Department of State from 1789. In 1823 a lithographed facsimile in an edition of 200 copies was made by W. J. Stone, and the copies were distributed in accordance with a joint resolution of Congress of 26 May 1824. (As a surviving signer, TJ received two copies; see Secretary of State J. Q. Adams to TJ, 24 June 1824, and TJ's acknowledgment of 18 July 1824.) From 1841 to 1877 the parchment copy was exhibited in the Patent Office, and from then until 1894 in the Department of State. In the latter year, because the text had been seriously damaged both by the wet-press process Stone had used in making his facsimile and by many years' exposure to light (see photograph in Michael, cited below, between p. 14-15), it was put away in a steel case in the Department, and a facsimile was exhibited instead. By executive order in 1921 the custody of the engrossed and signed copies of both the Declaration and the Constitution was transferred to the Librarian of Congress, and on 28 Feb. 1924 these two documents were placed in a bronze and marble shrine on the second floor of the Library, where they remain on perpetual exhibit under proper guard. (William H. Michael, *The Declaration of Independence: Illustrated Story of Its Adoption*, Washington, 1904; Hazelton, *Declaration of Independence*, ch. IX and notes; Gaillard Hunt, *The Department of State of the United States*, New Haven, 1914, p. 295-313; Librarian of Congress, *Annual Report* for 1949, p. 36ff.).

Notes of Witnesses' Testimony concerning the Canadian Campaign

[1-27 July 1776]

Mr. John Blake. July. 1. 1776.

He lives at Montreal. A merchant. Has lived there almost from the year 1760.

Was a great scarcity hard cash, could not supply troops with clothes or food, wood.

He lent 471-18-9 and 394-15-3 in January. If had been cash in Canada, provisions might have been had.

He has lent individuals of army 130. half Joes.

Continental bills would not have passed in Canada. A few particulars received them but charged higher, some of them he has heard double, when to be paid in Cont. bills.

He has heard that the army before Quebec sometimes were short of provisions during the winter.

He left Montreal Apr. 13. 1776.

Mar. 1. was said a body of Indians were to come down the St. Lawrence.

[433]

The Indian traders very few of them were friendly to the colonies.

He does not think the failing to supply Indians was cause of their coming down because in the usual course of trade supplies were not to go till May.

Canadians in general well disposed. The merchants in general against us. Priests rather against us, and some have been active against us.

The Canadians would not willingly be under French government. They liked the former Eng. government but not the present.

Canadians would chuse to lie neuter. Does not think they will enlist voluntarily with enemy.

Nothing but taking Canada will keep Indians off.

Complaints against Mr. Nicholson town major for confining a man against orders. Genl. Wooster broke him for it.

Capt. Hector McNeal. July 2.

Lived last year in Quebec. He came out of it on 24th. Nov. on Carleton's proclamation for all to go out who would not take arms. He staid at point au Tremble (6. leagues from headquarters) till 6th. May. When he came out of Quebec, the army had been before it but had retired to be recruited, Montgomery being expected. The army then in a dreadful situation for want of clothes, shoes &c. Had this blockade been kept up the place must soon have fallen. He might have prevented the enemy from getting a single cord of wood carried in. They would also soon have wanted provisions. But on the retreat from before, great stores of Wood and provisions were carried in. Arnold arrived at Point levi the 9th. Novemb. crossed a week after. The men Arnold had were sufficient to have kept up the blockade had they had ammunition and clothes. After the 2d approach to Quebeck the army was well supplied with provisions till about beginning of April. When clothes came (with Genl. Montgomery) they were tolerably clad, tho' not well, and especially not for that country. When Montgomery came, he brought but a very small supply of ammunition: so that he was unable to use his cannon till he sent for a supply of powder from St. John's. He brought but about 5. barrels of powder at first and no cartridge paper. Montgomery had intended to attack the upper town with the wind and snow in his back. But he changed his mind and attacked the lower town with the wind in his face. The army was dissatisfied with being kept after the time of their enlistment was out, and were in some measure constrained by Montgom. Some of the men, 3. companies particularly were against storming. He thinks the short enlistments have been of infinite prejudice, and occasioned great confusions. That no service can succeed while that is the case. When matters went in the least ill, the soldiers were very difficult to govern. As soon as Montgomery was killed, the troops being dispirited and dissatisfied went away in droves. He thinks Wooster's going was lucky, as he kept the men there, which he thinks Arnold could not have done: that the New York troops particularly were dissatisfied with Arnold because he wrote some letter which appeared in the newspapers, reflecting on them. The fact was true that they did retreat, but it was by order of Colo. Campbell who commanded them on the death of Montgomery. It appears that the guard who fired on him immediately abandoned their post (for which the capt. of the guard was afterwards broke). If Campbell had gone on he would have taken the lower town and formed a junction with Arnold's party. The firing of that guard had ceased before Campbell retreated. After that defeat their distresses grew, very cold, few men and hard duty. The snow 5. f. deep. The small pox was sent out of Quebeck by Carleton, inoculating the poor people at government expence for the purpose of giving it to our army. It had just begun to appear in the army before Montgom's death, after which it spread fast. Orders were given against inoculation, but they would inoculate. Of those who took it in the natural way 1. in 4. died. Of those who inoculated themselves and had no assistance of Doctors 1. in 20.

When Genl. Wooster arrived which was Apr. 1st. there were something upwards 2700. men in all of whom 800. were sick. Of these there were 1653. whose times were out the 15th. of April. Provisions were then scarce and Genl. Wooster told them he would not give them provisions if they went away. They threatened to plunder the inhabitants, upon which he refused to let them go at all. There was a mutiny by 15 which was quelled by Colo. Clinton. From 1st. Jan. to 1st. March never had more than 700 and sometimes not more than 500. fit to do duty and 26. miles of lines to occupy. Does not think it appeared adviseable to retreat from Quebec sooner because a reinforcement was expected. But a fleet of 13. vessels appearing in the river, there being but 6. days provisions left a council of war determined to retreat. A sudden change of the wind brought up 3. of the ships sooner than was expected which occasioned a more precipitate retreat. He thinks it was a blunder, since a retreat had been concluded on, that the men were not called from their several posts. Genl. Thomas arrived the 2d of May. The retreat was the 6th. Genl. Wooster left it the morning of the retreat.

The blame of provisions not going to Quebec he supposes lay on this side the lakes. He never saw any embezzlement of provisions. At the time of the retreat he does not think there was a barrel of pork between lake George and Quebec for the army. Provisions were dealt out by a Commissary and with great care and regularity. He has never seen any thing in Genl. Wooster but the greatest care. Things were carried on more harmoniously under him than would have been under Arnold after the discontent against him. If the troops had had provisions they might have stopped at Dechambeau, and maintained themselves till reinforcements would have reached them. But he thinks those troops would not have staid there whose time was out the 15th. April. He thinks 1000. men might have been kept there, which would have done. 12. days before the retreat Genl. Wooster had sent an engineer with 36. men and 4. carpenters and 2 blacksmiths to fortify Dechambeau. Genl. Thomas staid there with 500 men, after the retreat, till want of provisions forced him to leave it. The deponent then came out of the country. He met no provisions going down till he came to point au fer, the 18th. May.   5. battea¹ loads. flour was sent by some of our friends to Dechambaud before the army left it. He found them building one gally at Chambly. They were building a house for their black-smith to work in. There were about 1. doz. carpenters there. The Schooner on lake Champlain wanted a foresail, and running rigging and was not armed. But he met 2. waggonloads of cordage near Albany going up. Besides the Schooner, there is a sloop taken in the spring, and a row galley taken at St. John's. The row gallies had no sails. They were carried down in the winter to Point au tremble to cover powder. The sloop wanted rigging but her sails would do. She had no guns aboard.

Another material want before Quebec was medicines. Another the Indian traders going from Montreal and carrying goods &c. to the Indians. One Goddard, Richd. Walker and one Larimy went with 2000. half Joes to the Indians to invite them come down. This was known a month before the Commissioners went out there, and some person on suspicion of being concerned with them had absconded from Montreal before the Commissioners went there. 32. slays with merchandize had also gone up to them. Genl. Wooster had 7. of them brought back.

Doctor Coates. July 2.

Accompanied Genl. Arnold up the Kennebeck. Arrived at Point Levi with about 600. effective men he thinks, while before Quebec provision plenty but want of clothes. Genl. Montgomery alwais to attack in bad weather and bad weather only. The attack was before day light: Colo. Campbell (who succeeded on Montgom's death) ordered retreat as soon as was known that he was killed. Campbell was with Genl. Montgomery. They had past the first picquets. The fire from which Campbell retreated was trifling. Never heard that the men with Campbell were reluctant to go on. Has heard that the men could not get their guns off the storm was so bad. There was a difference of opinion, some thinking if Campbell had gone on he would have joined Arnold's party, others that they would have been all taken. The time of the greatest part of the New Englanders was out the very day of the attack. He thinks this might urge Montgomery to attack at that time. The defeat was the 31st. Decemb. Duty then became hard on the men. Small pox had made considerable appearance in army before the defeat. Was supposed Carlton sent out people with it. Orders against inoculation, but they did inoculate. Suffered for want of medicine. Colo. Enos brought back one of the medicine ches[ts] and the other was left in the woods. The first recruits after the defeat came in about 6. weeks. These were 25 men. after which they kept dropping in by companies. As fast as they came they were laid up with the small pox. Might be about 27. or 2800 just before Wooster arrived. Of these might be not more 800 or 900 effective. Duty fell cheifly on Pennsylvanians and New Jersey men. The soldiers had sometimes salt, sometimes fresh meat till latterly. [1057 in all marched from Cambridge. Enos carried back one third. Supposes had he gone on they might have stormed the town. When Enos quitted them it would take about as long to get to Quebeck as to get back, so the same provisions would have lasted. Arnold's party had but 5. pints of flour a man to the last 120. miles from Canadian settlement which was 90 leagues from Quebec. They were 4. or 5. days going it. 1½ day of that time they were lost, there being no path, and no man having ever before gone that way. Lost about a dozen men on the way by sickness as he has heard.][2]

When Wooster arrived the Yorkers time was to expire the 15th. April the New Englanders also. Most of them Genl. Wooster prevailed on then to stay. Does not think there was any waste of provision. The sick allowed but half rations. The want of hard money was the cause of wanting provisions. There was enough in country if could been bought. Flour and fresh provisions had alwais been bought in country, and was their principal food in first part of winter; what salt provisions they used came across lakes. Does not know that Genl. Schuyler was warned that provisions would be wanting. He met great quantities of provisions as he came over the lakes about the 13th. of May.

July 3. General Wooster.

>Letters. Octob. 4. 1775. Tyonderoga. Schuyler to Wooster. Orders to go by Wood creek

Octob. 9. S. to W. Tyonderoga. Orders to go by Lake George

>19. S. to W. Tyonderoga. To know if will give place to Montgom. according to Continental rank

>19. W. to S. Tyonderoga. That he will take rank according to Continental commission.

Dec. 31. S. to W. Albany. Has not yet sent paymaster up because has not yet received hard money from Congress.

1776. Jan. 4. W. to S. Montreal. Informs of death of Montgom. That situation will be bad till relief from colonies

>Few men. More immediately necessary. No confidence in Canadians

>Hard money wanting. Price has hitherto supplied us.

>Has hitherto advanced about 20,000£. Could not have subsisted without him.

>Clergy are against us.

>Has ordered that no men shall leave Canada, time out, or not No men to spare from Montreal.

>14. S. to W. Albany. At such distance cannot order him what measures

>Sends money as per invoice (does not say how much). Wooster sais it was about £7000. Pennsylvania or N. York money.

>Has pressed G. Washington to detach 3000. men to his assistance.

>Has furnished Colo. Warner with money to get men.

>Tories in Tryon in arms. He is marching against them.

>Must not let men come away though time out.

>Directs him to secure retreat for Arnold at Montreal.

>14. W. to S. Montreal. Has drained freinds here of all their cash.

>Has sent 120 men to Quebec, all that could be spared.

>Has sent to Onion river for Green Mountain boys, and to Warner.

>The river at Quebec not yet frozen, but will soon.

>Wants cannon, shells, shot, cartridges &c.

>Recommends to employ suttlers to bring sugar, rum &c. across the lakes, which may be paid for in Continental.

19. W. to S. Montreal. Sends him prisoners from Montreal.
Is sending 70 men more to Quebec.
Every thing going to ruin for want of money and paymaster.
Every thing should be here by Mar. 1. in the ammunition way.
Palisier will cast shells and shot.

26. S. to W. Albany. Acknoleges receipt of Letter of 14th.
(Some little incivility in the expressions)
Orders him to send hither all prisoners.
Also a return of the army in Canada.
Incloses bill on Jordan for 500. Dollars.
Colo. Warner has sent some men.
Other troops on their way and raising.

27. W. to S. Montreal. Acknoleges receipt of Letter of 14th.
and money.
Some of the reinforcements are come in.
Provisions in Quebec sufficient to last them till can be relieved
in sp[ring.]
Therefore large supply of military stores necessary.
Again recommends bringing necessaries over lakes.
Palisier cannot cast shells till May. 1.
Has appointed Rantseleer [Van Rensselaer] Deputy Muster
Master General.
Will shortly want more hard money.

27. W. to Congress. Montreal. Will soon go to Quebec.
Want men money mortars shot shells, heavy cannon and large
supply of cannon, not being more than 4 tons in province

Jan. 29. S. to W. Albany. Desires return of officers in Canada and
to recommend others.
Sends orders for Commissaries.
Deputy pay master General will come immediately.
Desires to send names of Commissaries now in Canada and to
advise him how the army is supplied with provisions.
How much salt may be wanting for a year.
Send also rolls and accounts which had ordered from Mont-
gomery.
Make return also of killed at the [Lakes?]

29. W. to S. Montreal. Has received inventory from Arnold of
what is at Quebec and what may be wanting.
Will immediately send inventory of all stores in the province.
Some of the new recruits have bad arms and obliged to stop
here to repair

Feb. 2. S. to W. Albany. Troops daily coming on. Ad[vise] to send best from Montreal.

    Desires list of all stores at St. John's, Montreal, Quebec, and in the province in general.

    Heavy cannon is sent to Cambridge. No artillery here. If Quebec cannot be taken without, fears it will fail.

    Suttlers are gone off and more will go in a few days.

6. W. to S. Montreal. Receipt of Jan. 26.

    Expresses sense of incivil orders in it.

    (It is a quarelling letter. Sais he will send all the letters to Congress who may judge.)

    Alleges the commanding officer in Canada is the only competent and proper judge what orders to give army, and will therefore do it.

9. S. to W. Albany. Directs to muster Warner's men.

11. W. to Congress. Montreal. Will be delivered by Walker and Price who have been serviceable friends.

    Has permitted merchants trading to upper country to chuse commi[ttee?] to petition Congress for opening trade.

    Prays a committee of Congress may be sent.

    Arnold so well reinforced, that no danger from a Sortie.

    Proposes soon to join him: but artillery greatly wanting.

    Complains of Schuyler's ill treatment.

13. W. to Congress. Montreal. Thinks ministry will send great force here in spring.

    In that case more men will be wanting. Wishes for 10,000 by the first of May.

    Refers to Walker and Price.

    Quebec ought to be taken before May 1. but has neither proper artillery nor ammunitions.

    However hopes a sufficient number of men of resolution will affect it.

13. W. to S. Montreal. Receipt of letter of 2d. Inst.

    Great plenty of salt. More than enough for a year.

    Gallies will be wanting in St. Lawrence.

    Will be better built here, but no pitch, tar, turpentine.

    Good workmen for them will be wanting.

    A return of ordnance has been already sent him Van Renselear gone to Quebec to muster troops there.

    Few of the troops here will re-enlist.

Feb. 19. W. to S. Montreal. Paymaster came and no hard money.

    Cannot buy provision or wood with Continental.

If not bought before middle March, after which will be no passing for 3 or 4. weeks, so that the expedition may fail for want of supplies.

Desires pork may be sent over the lakes.

Not £1000. left of money formerly sent.

A gunner (Mr. Brazier) wanting particular articles of military stores.

21. S. to W. Albany. Receipt of 11th. and 13th. by Mr. Price.

Has sent Congress a return of Artillery and stores in this department: they are small and has urged for more.

Has sent to New York for tar, pitch, and turpentine and to Philadelphia for ship carpenters.

Has directed the Deputy Commissary General to send deputies to Canada to superintend his department there.

Has accordingly sent two.

Wishes for return of provisions in Canada.

Fears will be in distress before that from lakes can be sent.

Desires to know if beef or pork can be had in Canada and for how long.

Wants nails to build batteaux. Wishes would send from merchants there.

Troops came here half cloathed and half armed from Green Mountains &c.

21. W. to Congress. Montreal. Fatal consequences apprehended from want of cash.

Has therefore sent Cole for some.

Cannot get provisions or wood, or pay transportation of any [. . . .]

Not half money in hand to answer pressing demands.

Flour and all other provisions will be gone immediately.

Credit sunk.

Considerable supply must be sent immediately.

21. W. to S. Montreal. Paymaster come, nothing but paper money.

But one week's flour left.

Cannot pay half debts to country people. Credit su[nk.]

Cannot pay for transportation.

Cole sent for money to Genl. Schuyl. and Congress.

(Note after middle March roads impassable because then the rains come and soften the snow, so that cannot draw any thing a mile)

24. S. to W. Albany. Receipt of 19th.

Is sensible if hard money not sent will suffer.

Has not 6d. Has employed persons to procure on own credit

Has got sleds to carry 400. barrles pork.

Will forward cannon[3] and shot from posts above.

Must have been great waste of provisions in Canada.

Will send Brazier if such person or any other fit.

Does not think Canadian traders will be suffered to go into Canada.

Feb. 26. S. to W. A Postscript. Albany. Recommends to get bills on him from Merchants in Montreal. Paiable in 30. days sight.

(700 barrels pork and 700 barr. flour were taken at Sorel from Carleton's fleet about middle November)

25. W. to S. Montreal. Refers him to Flemng for state of things.

25. W. to Washington. Montreal. Receipt 27th. of last.

Wishes a large army in Spring as Ministry will send large army.

Wants cannon, mortars, shots and shells.

Assault must be attempted if no other way.

Troops coming in. Will soon join Genl. Arnold.

28. Lee to Wooster. N. York. Notifies his appointment to Can-[ada]

Directs him to contract for and grind 20,000 bush. Wheat.

Has ordered 13 12lbrs. from Crown point to Sorel.

Appears to him ought to be post established at falls of Richlieu.

28. S. to W. Albany. Has raised £2139-18-10 N. York money which sends by Benson. Will get more if possible.

Mar. 1. W. to S. Montreal. Receipt of 21st. ult.

Return of provisions in Montreal and Quebec.

None of Chamblee and St. Johns.

Has engaged several thousand bushels wheat and sent to mills.

Desires pork from lakes.

Beef is @ 4. coppers if had money.

Want medicine.

Proposes to build gallies at Chambli.

Return of provisions Quebec. 10,000 ℔. beef. 62. barr. pork. 51. firkins butt[er] 60. B. flour 200 ℔ each.

Montreal 6864. ℔. beef. 458 B. pork and 14 do. damaged. 71. firkins butter. 28,500 ℔. flour for 12 or 14. days baking. 2000 bread. 16¼ bush. rice. 70. gals. rum. large quantity salt. 105 ℔. soap.

4. S. to W. Albany. (About a prisoner)

6. S. to W. Albany. Has sent Winslow further directions for paying troops in Canada.

Could not get so many sleds to send provisions as intended .

As soon as ice open will send supply.

5. W. to S. Montreal. Receipt of cash by Benson.

Merchants not disposed to assist us.

Glad of arrival of Commissioners.

Critical situation prevents thorough enquiry into conduct of Commissaries.

Thinks consumption has been greater than should been.

Hopes the 400. bar. pork with what have on hand and what can be procured here will do till lakes open. [There came but 350. B. for want of slays ut supra].[2]

But 417. in Warner's regiment [there came a few afterwards][2]

Reason to apprehend something from above, Oswegatchy &c.

Mar. 13. W. to S. Montreal. Apprehends mischeif from Upper country, that they will make descent on Montreal while men are gone to Quebec.

Not 1500. men yet come in from the colonies.

14. S. to W. Albany. Heavy cannon yet at Pakipsy. Powder not come, nor money.

General Lee is ordered to Virginia.

16. W. to S. Montreal. Draws on him in favor of Blake for £394-15-3 and 471-18-9.

Blake has been very friendly.

Mischeif contriving from Detroit.

Have not more than 60. rounds powder for 6000. men in the country even if have no cannon.

Money in a manner gone.

Deputy pay master has sent 15000 Dollars paper to Quebec to pay army.

Troops come in so slow that has not gone to Quebec yet.

Will be of greatest importance of our affairs if you can be spared from New York and can be at Albany to furnish army.

26. W. to S. Montreal. Receipt of 14th.

Shall set off to Quebeck tomorrow.

April 10. W. to Congress. Before Quebec. Arrived here, and Genl. Arnold to go to Montreal.

Between 2 and 3000, not half to do duty with Small pox. Most to go 15th. April.

13. S. to W. Fort George. Refers him for particulars to Colo. Hazel [Hazen], left in command at Montreal.

Mentions evacuation of Boston

Cole is here with some hard cash and 25,000 D. Continental, with which he will proceed to Canada with Genl. Thomas.

May. 15. Genl. Thoms. to Commissioners. Three rivers. Called at Jacques Cartier and Dechambeau on return from Quebec.

Staid there 6. days in hopes of receiving supply provisions, entrenching tools &c.

Want of these compelled to quit

Had only 3 ℔. meal a man and not an ounce of meat when left it.

Arrived here this morning with 800 men.

Shall proceed to Sorel and if possible will return to Decham[beau.]

20. Genl. Thoms. to Commissioners. Sorel. Army been for 2 days without meat.

No money to buy, no contractors to purchase.

Want of provisions oblige men to leave Three rivers.

A retreating army, disheartened, sick, without necessaries, and as they think wholly neglected.

Unless something done army cannot be kept together.

[Wooster sais the lakes opened about the 23d of April. Genl. Thomas went in 1st. boat. Commissioners next.]² From Fort George to Dechambeau provisions may be carried generally in 10 days, tho' winds in the lakes may retard or expedite. Army left Quebeck May 6. Genl. Thomas left Dechambeau May 13 The first provisions (by McNeal) were 5. batteaus which he met May 18. at Point au fer.

July 4. Genl. Wooster.

When he went into Canada there were about 2200 men in the upper country, viz. Montreal, the Sorel &c. This was about the 20th. of October. St. John's surrendered the 3d of Novemb. Montreal about the 10th. Nov. Genl. Montgom. proceeded about the 23d or 24th. of Nov. down the river to join Genl. Arnold. He carried with him between 4 and 500 men. Arnold had then between 6 and 700 men of whom about 550. were effective. Many of the troops went off from Montreal, their time being not quite out, under a former promise from Genl. Montgomery to encourage them to go on to take Montreal. But one feild officer of Connecticut would stay, so that Genl. Montgomery to induce the men to stay appointed Genl. Wooster to the regiment, who enlisted about 500. He never knew that this was contrary to the resolutions of Congress, till this last winter heard so. He called on paymaster for money which he mea[nt] to charge himself with as Colonel. He recd. £52 in that character. He meant at the time that the Congress should as they please allow this or not. The want of powder obliged Arnold to retreat from Quebeck he having but 5. rounds a man. This prevented the place falling into his hands. The small pox broke out in Montgomery's army a few days before the assault. The unfortunate determination to attack the lower instead of the upper town, was a main cause of the failure. He doubts whether, if Campbell had not retreated, he could have carried the lower town, and if he had carried it, they must notwithstanding have been made prisoners by the upper town. After they had been out a while it is said their guns were so wet, not one in 10. would go off. These men had been obliged to make a circuit of 4. miles before they could get at the place of attack. After this about 3 weeks the small pox became pretty general in the army and with their want of ammunition prevented any subsequent attack. They began to suffer about May 1st. Genl. Wooster went to Quebec 1st. April. Found army in small pox. Some whole regiments down. Were between 1900. men. and 2000. Of these about 900. fit for duty. These were dispersed at different posts to keep up blockade, as it appeared they were short of wood, by their burning their old houses, the garden pickets &c. Expected reinforcements of men, ammunition, provisions &c. as soon as ice should be broke. Did not give up this hope till Genl. Thos. came, when council of war hearing of none near, and the enemy's reinforcement being coming up the river they determined Sunday the 5th. to retreat. Orders were next morning sent to the out-posts to inform them of determination of council of war, and to make ready for retreat. Those from Beauport and island of Orleans were to proceed to Augustine to join main body 10. mi. from Quebec. Those at Point Levi were to go to Celery or point au tremble. The rest about 400 were to repair by the Head Quarters by 2. o'clock. They were doing this. Genl. Wooster was sent by Genl. Thomas to Jacques Cartier and set off about 9. o'clock, and the attack was at 10. oclock. There were then but 200. got together. The enemy were between 1200 and 1500 with 6. peices of cannon. About half a dozen of the sick only fell into enemy's hands. All the cannon was lost, an armed schooner also and 3500 ℔. of powder being part of

4 tons sent down to them, and 3 or 400. arms. These arms had belonged to the souldiers who had gone away on the expiration of the time of their enlistment. The retreating army met Lt. Colo. Allen 8 miles from Quebec with 261 men. They had all about 2 or 3 days provisions. Falls of Richlieu are about 3 miles. The channel is but about 60 f. wide for a mile and ½, crooked and confined between rocks. There must be a gale of 6 knots an hour to pass up it. It passes within ½ a mile of Point Dechambeau where the land is 50. f. high. Jacques Cartier is 36 miles below this. But Point Dechambeau may still be taken by superior land army, there being a small descent on the back part of about ¼ of a mile and then the ground rises gently so as to give command over Dechambeau. Jacques Cartier is an excellent land post, inaccessible, and prohibiting absolutely the pass of an army. But it does not command the water, so that vessels may pass it. 50. men may prevent 1000. from passing it by land. Does not know nor ever heard Genl. Woedlke drinks. He is very active, vigilant, and contriving, and a great disciplinarian. Genl. Thomas was taken with the small pox at Sorel.

1776. July 6. Major Saml. Blackden.

Went into Canada Mar. 4. 1776. Acted as major of brigade: was with Wooster. Major Grey. and St. George Dupris had commissions under Carleton which they would not resign, were busy among people with improper conversation, refused to give parole that they would not act against us, wherefore Wooster sent them prisoners to Chambli; the Commissioners released them without consulting him. He went to Quebec with Genl. Wooter [Wooster] Apr. 1. Were about 900. fit for duty at different posts; a vast number sick. Had then provision enough. Provision began to grow scant about Apr. 20. They never did suffer very greatly while there for want of provision. They would be sometimes on half allowance for two or three days, and sometimes 2 or 3 days without bread. They never had vegetables: but they bore it tolerably patiently. The General seldom dined with less than 18, 20, or 25 gentlemen: he had the best provisions the country afforded. Two chaplains (one a Frenchman) alwais dined with him. Regular discipline was observed, as far as they could be made to observe discipline. The men were out of duty only one night in 48. hours, being on gard the other night, and by day alwais doing duty. From the time Genl. Wooster went there till he came away, there never came out one deserter; so could not know certainly their state. About a dozen deserted from us into the town in that time. It appeared they were in want of wood by their burning their houses. The times of the four N. York battalion was[1] out 15th. April. About one third of them agreed on the 14th. to stay till recruits arrived. The others refused. However all went off (about 600) April 28th. before the attack, except about 80 or 90. who had enlisted in a new regiment. Genl. Thomas arrived 1st. May at Quebeck. The 2d May an attempt was made with a fire ship. Had 720 men collected from the posts (being all except those from Pt. Levi and Orleans) and paraded on the heights of Abraham to take advantage of any confusion the ship might produce. The whole men then were 1975. Of these 1025 were fit for duty. Supposed the enemy had 1500. who did duty within town. The fire ship was disappointed by a boom chain fixed across the Cul de sac; a deserter having given them notice. Council was Apr. 5th. Determined to retreat. Orders given to posts in morning of May 6. to assemble at head quarters with baggage and sick (except those from out posts who were to go different rout). They were doing it when attack was made about 10. or 11 oclock. A woman the night before had carried into the town intelligence that we intended to retreat. The enemy were within 80 rods before we retreated. Some of the men appeared in panic. However they were drawn up and retreated slowly to let the sick keep before. Snow knee deep. The enemy followed about 2 miles. About 1200 of enemy. Campbell kept with the army to Jacques Cartier, there he and many other officers (who had no particular command) left the army and went up to Montreal without orders from the general. He has heard that Colo. Nicholson left his command at Point Levi, and went quite up to Montreal. Very few sick were lost. He continued at Dechambeau with Genl. Thomas, and 932 men till May 13. Part of these tho' were two new regiments who had not been to Quebec. When they got to Dechambeau provisions were quite gone. There they found 180. bushels wheat and 4 little oxen, on which they lived. Of this about 2 or 3 ℔. a man of flour remained when they left Dechambeau. They had but 15 rounds of powder a man. There was not a pr. of shoes to 3 men. The snow and mud most of the way half leg deep.

Major Lockwood.

Went into Canada latter part of Octob. as secretary to Genl. Wooster. Then was appointed Brigade major, and then to a regiment. He went to Quebec a few days after Montgomery went there, and came away a few days before his death. Were about 7 or 800 of Arnold's men sick and well and 4 or 500 of those who went with

Montgomery, on the whole not quite 1100. Of these 2 or 300 were sick. Was said but no proof that Carleton had sent it into the suburbs of St. Roc where some of our men were quartered. Hence it spread. Began to appear in army about middle of Decemb. or earlier. He has heard that when Montgom. made the attack there were 2 or 300 sick. Genl. Montgom's inducements to storm town were 1. the troops began to be uneasy to get home. 2. the great stores of artillery stores in the town. 3. hoped a speedy reduction of Quebec during session of parliament would have effect in parliament. 4. appeared practicable from accounts he had that greater part of inhabitants would lay down arms. Has heard it supposed these were the reasons of attacking lower town. A deserter went over to enemy and told plan of attacking upper town. This was testified by a deserter from enemy who came over the day after our deserter went in. Snow in general about 2½ f. deep at time of attack, but much drifted. Cause of failure was fire arms wet, the very injudicious attack in the lower town, and some think Campbell's ordering a retreat, and most think if he had gone on he might have relieved Arnold's party and all got out together. No cause appeared for Campbell's retreating which did not exist against attacking, unless he might perceive any dispiritedness in [. . . .] Many suppose if had taken lower town, upper would have given up [. . . .] Merchants lived there, treasure was there, ships might been burnt; and [at any] rate it might have been maintained some time. Deponent returned to Quebec beginning of Mar. More than half the [. . .] provisions enough till retreat only sometimes on half allowance a [. . .] while. Had no vegetables. Colo. Nicholson left his post and past Dechambeau knowing the army to be there. Colo. Campbell left the army at Jacques Cartier he beleives, without orders. Dechambeau would not have been tenable without an equal army. Vessels must pass within 200 yards of guns on the point, but he is certain not more than 300 yards.

July 10. 1776. Mr. Price

Genl. Montgomy. carried about 230 men to Quebec, and about 220 followed him. They were cloathed. They carried clothes for Arnold's men, tho' not quite enough. Price went with Montgom. They found Arnold's army almost naked, without ammunition. The time of some of them was then out and they insisted on going away, but were prevailed on to stay. The impatience of the troops to come away when their time was out he thinks urged the Genl. to make his attack so soon. The Genl. was made to beleive after taking great

pains to discover it that the towns people would deliver it up as soon
as he opened his batteries. The attack was made in a terrible snow
storm. The snow 4½ f. deep, about 6. o'clock in the morning, Montgom. had to go 4 miles [ar]ound to make his attack. The men could
only go in Indian file. They made a line of 2 or 3 miles (having
between 4 and 500 men) Montgom., McPherson and Cheeseman
were at the head. Never more than 10 came to the place of action
before these three were shot. Their peices would not go off. Colo.
Campbell immediately ordered a retreat. He was induced to attack
at the place he did because he was informed the enemy trusting to
the difficulty of access there, kept no guard in that quarter. We had
about 400. taken and killed in the whol. About 30 of them were
killed. Doubtful whether Campbell could have got throug to Arnold's party. If they had got possession of lower town, could not
have kept, could only have destroyed property. Montgom's whole
number was 1250 of whom 200 were Canadians. A few of the army
had the small pox then. The Genl. had taken great care to keep it
out. It did not attack them generally till towards spring. Price had
left Quebec the 23d Decemb. He returned to the army the 12th. of
Jan. He left it again the 20th. Jan. to get cash and necessaries. The
7th. of Feb. he [le]ft Montreal to come to Philadelphia and returned
13th. May. He met the army on the lake, and at St. John's &c. retreating. The failure of the expedition was owing to short enlistments, small pox, want of hard money, and want of Commissary to
provide necessaries. After the defeat they were reinforced to about
11. or 1200 men, Price met part of this reinforcement the 20th.
Jan. at Trois rivieres. Some necessaries Price sent down by them,
others soon after. The Canadians are disposed favorably to us, notwithstanding the endeavors of the priests. They will now do nothing
but what they are forced to by the enemy, unless it be a few. They
would rather we should be there than the enemy, that is the peas-
antry. The priests, the lawyers, the Seigneurs, the merchants and
the petite noblesse are against us. They liked the former English
government much. After this martial law was proclaimed, which
the inhabitants took and take now to be the Quebec bill. The Quebec
bill is in favor of priests and lawyers, the Noblesse are bribed by
pensions. The merchants have been led into it by fashion, and connection with these people and hopes of having their trade to Britain
opened. About 110,000 thousand[1] inhabitants. About ¾ of these
are above Dechambeau. There is no proportion of English inhabitants. Their militia do well for a coup de main, but not for regulars.
Our troops have so little discipline so little subordination that it is

impossible they should ever make head against regulars. Guards neglect their duty utterly. Do not keep guard. Officers gave them no orders. Would leave same men on guard 48. hours. No difference when officers there and not there. Genl. Arnold is vigilant and careful, but not attentive to discipline. Genl. Wooster no disciplinarian. They give good orders, but take no care to have them obeyed. Would sometimes have courts of enquiry but would let the men down. St. John's utterly neglected. Price got in there in the night so little care was taken. The savages might have gone in and cut off the retreat of the army. He thinks Isle aux noix the key to Canada. It commands the passage of the lake so that it is impossible for an army to pass it if properly fortified. Every thing depends on keeping possession of lake Champlain. If they get over that Crown point is not easily tenable, Tyonderoga is incapable of being made defensible. He thinks the guns belonging to the sloop and Schooner must be at Tyonderoga. Besides this there are 60 at Crown point, but they are not all good.

July 11. Mr. Palisier. He is the owner of iron works at Trois rivieres.

The water on each side Isle [aux] noix is from ½ to ¾ mile wide. Batteaus may pass on both sides. The channel for large vessels is on the East side. They must pass within 300 yds. of the island. A fortification there will certainly prevent passage. The French extended picquets chevaux de frise from shore to shore so that it was impossible to pass. No battery can be erected on the opposite shore it is so marshy. No part of the channel opposite the island is above 10 f. deep. Nothing but an entrenchment all round the island with some chevaux de frise on the outside extending into the water, is requisite; with covered ways to prevent the effect of shells. The island is not ¾ mile long and ¼ wide. 3500 men are sufficient to hold it against 50,000. The enemy cannot come by land so far as isle aux noix without making a road with fascines through a morass for 30 miles. 1500 men at isle aux noix last war deterred Genl. Amherst from attempting to pass with 20,000. Genl. Burlamaqui with 1500 men compleated the necessary works in less than [a] month last war. But should the enemy get possession of isle aux noix and we keep the lake we may yet pass into Canada by the rivers Chasuè and Chatoguy, between which is a passage of 3 miles. Chatoguy empties into St. Lawrence about 18 miles above Montreal.

Crown point is a pentagon with 5. bastions. It is all rock entirely. Cannot make an entrenchment. Neither trees nor earth. If ever we regain Canada we must act as Conquerors, and take down their Seigneurs, Lawyers and higher people. This will please the people. To require an oath of fidelity, and arrest those who refuse.

John Hamtranck. He is a Canadian and lived at Quebeck till 4 years ago, since which he has lived at Chamblee. Engaged in Continental service Sep. 15. 1775. as a commissary, appointed by Colo. Livingston. He staid in that part till Feb. 5. He then went recruiting and raised 26 men. Was appointed a Lieutenant. He was sent to the Cedars with Colo. Beadel and stationed at the Cedars. He had then but 10. Canadians with him. They were employed in erecting works of defence. Some of the men (about 20 or 30) had the small pox when attacked. Colo. Beadle had it there also but was recovered. They had heard the enemy were coming, before Beadle left the fort. He left it 4 or 6 days before the attack, and said he would send reinforcements and provisions. He appeared to be well and able to go about business. 15 regulars, privates, 3 officers, 350 Indians and Canadians. There came some more regulars next day. Butterfeild had 350 men. There were in the fort 3. barrels of pork, 700 ℔. meat, 1000 bushels wheat 3 cows, 2 horses, and 5 hogs, and about 200. bushels of peas. 20 rounds of cartridges a man, 13 rounds for cannon, 13 grape shot and 10 or 15 balls, ½ barrel powder, and a box of musket ball. Only a few guns were fired to let the enemy know they were in the fort. No body killed or wounded. Capt. Wilkens, and Stephens, all the subalterns and all the men were desirious of fighting, many of them cried with vexation. The enemy kept a loose fire. Flags of truce came in three times, to demand a surrender. Butterfeild held a council of war of the captains on Saturday and Sunday. At the last it was determined to Surrender by all the captains except Wilkins and Stephens. There were 5 captains in all. They sent out a flag of truce to surrender. There was a capitulation in writing that the clothes and baggage of the officers should be free from plunder, as Butterfeild and Stephens told him. The Indians immediately took all their clothes, money, and baggage. Sherburne and his party were brought there. Then they were sent to Quinze chenes. Did not see the Indians kill any of the people, but heard they killed three. Larimier was in some command over the Indians and Canadians. They put the Canadians (except the deponent who was an officer) in irons. On this the deponent went to Forster and reminded him that by the capitulation the Canadians were to have the same treatment with the others, whereon Forster permitted the deponent to go and stay with the Continental officers, but left the men in irons. This was done to terrify the other Canadians. They were kept in irons 12 days, that is 3 days after the exchange; Forster having placed the common men at Quinze chenes and the officers on their parole at Canesadgo under Canadian guards, went with his regulars and Indians to take Montreal. He was joined by a great number of people who fled from Montreal. He proceeded however no further than La Chene. There he discovered Arnold on the other side with 1000 men, on which he returned [to] Quinze chenes. There the exchange was made of prisoners, except [. . . Can]adians. Forster then proceeded up the river 72 miles to the point of the lake. He had there but three or 4. batteaux to carry his men, the refugees from Montreal, the cannon baggage the hostages and Canadian prisoners. He therefore left the Canadian prisoners on the bank without saying a word. As soon as they saw the boats go off they run. They had no provisions and only a few old blanket coats on them. The men went to their families, and the deponent to Chambli to his colonel. The hostages were stripped and very ill used. The Indians carried away about 20 of our people besides the hostages. These were well used and permitted to go at large. The Canadians who were in Forster's service (many of whom were compelled) told the deponent they heard the Indians remind Forster that at Oswagatchy he had promised them all the prisoners, and now he would not let them kill any. Capt. Green, Easterbrook and Down were not willing to fight. Easterbrook is since dead of the small pox. Colo. Hazen gave leave to his men (Canadians) to go home to their houses.

July 18. Francois Guillot dit La Rose. A captain of Canadian militia under commissions from Wooster and Sullivan.

He was a friend to the American cause. When our troops retreated from Canada he was obliged to remove. He had hired and paid for four waggons to remove his effects. When they got to Chamblee Colo. Hazen stopped them, insulted and beat the deponent, and took the waggons. In the fray one of the guard by order of Colo. Hazen discharged his peice at the deponent, and he was put into the guard house where he staid an hour and a half when Genl. Sullivan came up, had him relieved, and his effects forwarded. He also endeavored to arrest Hardoin Merlet, a Continental major in the Canadian militia for no other cause but remonstrating with him on his treatment of Guillot, but Merlet escaped.

Hardoin Merlet, a Continental major in the Canadian Militia.

The deponent and Charles Robert dit La Fontaine a Canadian friend were removing their effects out of Canada in Batteaux. They remonstrated with Hazen on his treatment of Guillot, whereupon Hazen had Robert arrested, and would have taken Merlet, but he got off. They both had passports from Baron Woedlke.

William Haywood. An inhabitant of Montreal.

No body is allowed, or was ever, to carry goods into upper co[untr]y without permit. Mr. Bernard and Mr. Wadden had goods stolen out of town in [. . .] and loaded a number of slays out of town with the goods and were carrying them into the upper country. Genl. Wooster sent after them and overtook 6 or 7. which were brought back by major Nicholson and Capt. Scott. Colo. Hazen generally suspected of being unfriendly. He h[ad] alwais exerted his interest to get our enemies released. A priest conf[ined] by Baron Woedlke Colo. Hazen became security for.

July 19. Mr. Mason sais there was an officer (whose name he has forgotten) put under arrest by Colo. Fleming for having taken some wine of Genl. Prescot's. He has heard Genl. Prescot had one hogshead of bottled wine taken which was sold to one Pharis a tavern keeper in Montreal. The stores taken by Colo. Easton on board the fleet were 658. Barr' pork, 480 Barr' flour, 38. Barr' peas, 23 Barr' rice, 294 firkins of butter 42. barr biscuit. There were 13 Barr' pork besides and sundry other stores sent by Genl. Montgom' to Quebec of which deponent had no account.

July 27. Mr. Bonfeild.

A Mr. Halstead acted at Quebeck as commissary by appointment of Genl. Montgomery. He continued to act till the retreat from Quebec. The deponent lived at Scillery 4 miles above Quebec. The provisions which came down were lodged in his store. There came down in the month of March, April and the beginning of May pork enough to have lasted till June. [This came down in batteaux but *Price.* seems to have been the same which Genl. Schuyler had sent off in slays.][2] There were 100 barrels of pork in his store at the time of Genl. Thomas's retreat from Quebeck. He does not suppose the Commander knew any thing of it. He thinks the Commissaries made no regular returns. This fell into the hands of the enemy, the deponent saw them take it away.

Levingston the Deputy Commissary was Commissary of that *Blackburne.* department. He appointed Schwartz and Benson assistant Deputy *Wooster.* Commissar[ies] Genl. and they again appointed sub-commissaries.

Blackburne.

They went down to Quebec in March and tho' their appointment superseded Halstead, yet as they could not speak French and were not acquainted with the people or country, Halstead continued to act. A hundred barr[els][1] of pork would have lasted the retreating army 11. days. Had they known of the pork at Scilleri at the time of the retreat they could not[3] have got it, and if they had ordered it up in batteaux it would have fallen into the enemy's hands.

N (DLC). MS slightly mutilated.

On 24 June TJ was appointed to a committee to inquire into the miscarriages in Canada; the committee was enlarged on 6 July; it brought in a report on 19 July, which was debated, recommitted, and on 30 July in part adopted (JCC, V, 474, 524, 592, 617-18). It is not possible to tell what part TJ had in the report, since no MS has been found. Further reports were brought in from time to time, and on 7 Oct., five weeks after TJ had left Congress, a new committee was appointed to continue the investigation (same, p. 623, 629, 633, 644-5, 741, 852). The present notes of testimony by participants represent TJ's known contribution to this pioneer congressional investigation and illustrate his methods of work. They contain facts not elsewhere available, though most of the correspondence abstracted by TJ is printed from the Papers of the Continental Congress by Force, *Archives*, 4th ser., IV.

[1] Thus in MS.
[2] Brackets in MS.
[3] MS: "cannot."

From John Page

MY DEAR JEFFERSON   Wmsburg July the 6th. 1776.

When I wrote last week to Col. Nelson I promised to write to both of you by this Post, a circumstantial Account of the State of Things here, but the whole Week has slipt away in the Hurry of Business, without my being able to spare a single Minute for that Purpose and I am now as much in Want of Time as ever, the Post being about to set out in a few Hours, in which Time I am to wait on our new Governour to administer to him the Oaths, to be qualified by him to act in my new Department, and to dispatch some public Business of Importance. So what can I do? Why you will say, make no more long winded Complaints of want of Time, but begin at once to tell us what has happened with you, and make a better Use of the little Time you have to spare. I must refer you to the Papers for what has been done in Convention. I believe I mentioned in my last the Manner in which the Barrons took the Transport with 217 Scotch Highlanders on Board. Did Captn. Biddle get in safe with his other Prize? Every one here looks upon the wonderfull Manner in which the great Number of Highlanders have fallen into our Hands as truly providential. Our Batteries at Gwyns Island are not yet finished, but I hope in a few Days to hear that they are. We have sent down 2, 18 Pounders, 4, 9 lbers., 3, 6 lbers. and 2 field

Pieces and 2, 12's and another 9 Pounder are ordered down, which I think will be sufficient to drive the Fleet from their Station, silence the Batteries, and break up the Enemies Camp. If they do not receive a Reinforcement before our Batteries are opened, I think we may easily drive them out of the Island. But it is doubted by some People whether it is worth while to run any risque to do this since they will easily get Possession of some other Island, or perhaps some Place of more Consequence. Col. Stephen is fortifying Portsmouth but we are in great Want of Cannon to mount on the Works necessary to command the whole Harbour of Norfolk. Our Cruizers and Gallies have taken up all the good Cannon we had except 1 at Jas. Town and those at Gwyn's Island. We want 6 or 8 24s or 18s for our Fort at Jas. Town, as many more for a floating Battery to be anchored opposite the Fort, the like Number for every other River, and 3 or 4 more for the Works at Burwells Ferry. I have mislaid your Letter in which you desired me to buy some of Johnsons or Gwatkin's Books. Ld. Dunmores Instruments &c. were all sold before I saw your Letter to Mr. Wyth.

Washington's Behaviour has eclipsed Cicero's. His Conduct was really like himself truly great. My Love to Nelson. I am broke in upon again as I have been 15 Times Since I began this scrawl. I must immediately attend the Governour who is very ill. If he should die before we have qualified and chosen a President the Country will be without any head—every Thing must be in Confusion. But four of our Board are in Town, who cannot chuse a President. Adieu. I am yrs. sincerely, JOHN PAGE

RC (DLC).

OUR NEW GOVERNOUR . . . MY NEW DEPARTMENT: On 29 June 1776 Patrick Henry had been elected first governor of the State of Virginia, and Page had been elected to the governor's council (*Conv. Jour.*, May 1776, 1816 edn., p. 78-9). GWYN'S ISLAND: I.e., Gwynn's Island in Chesapeake Bay, off the mouth of the Piankatank; see, further, Pendleton to TJ, 1 June; Page to TJ, 15, 20 July; *Va. Gaz.* (D & H), 13 July, 31 Aug.; and especially TJ's sketch map of Gwynn's Island, reproduced in this volume. TJ's letter to Wythe mentioning DUNMORES INSTRUMENTS is missing, unless it be the same as that from which only a doubtful extract survives, printed above under the assigned date of June? 1776. On 15 June the Convention had arranged for the disposal of Dunmore's property by auction; see *Conv. Jour.*, (as above), p. 51.

To Richard Henry Lee

DR SIR   Philadelphia July 8th. 1776

For news I refer you to your brother who writes on that head. I enclose you a copy of the declaration of independence as agreed to by the House, and also, as originally framed. You will judge whether it is the better or worse for the Critics. I shall return to Virginia after the 11th of August. I wish my successor may be certain to Come before that time, in that case, I shall hope to see you and Mr. Wythe in Convention, that the business of Government, which is of everlasting Concern, may receive your aid. Adieu, and beleive me to be Your friend & Servant,

THOMAS JEFFERSON

Original missing. Text from Tr (Vi-Hi); endorsed "True Copy Francis Barclay" and with address leaf reading: "To Richard Henry Lee Esqr. at Chantilly Virginia to be left at Fredericksburg for the Westmoreland rider." Also endorsed on address leaf in hand of Henry Lee: "Copy of Jefferson's draft of Independence & letter." This was perhaps the earliest copy made of TJ's letter and draft of the Declaration, being made early in the nineteenth century. For an account of this and other copies, see Boyd, *Declaration of Independence*, 1945, p. 42-3. Accompanying this transcript is a transcript, also in Barclay's handwriting, of the copy of the Declaration that TJ sent to R. H. Lee; both are in the Lee-Ludwell papers given to the Virginia Historical Society by Cassius F. Lee, Jr., who had also, at one time, owned the copies of the Declaration and of TJ's draft of a constitution for Virginia that were sent to George Wythe. Several other transcripts are extant, the letter having acquired accidental notoriety through Timothy Pickering's interest in the text of the Declaration of Independence that accompanied it and that was later presented to the American Philosophical Society; see Boyd, *Declaration of Independence*, 1945, p. 41-3.

Report of the Committee
to Draw Up Rules of Procedure in Congress

[Before 10 July 1776]

The Committee appointed to draw up Rules and Orders for the Government of this House have agreed to the following report.[1]

III. No Member shall read any printed Paper in the House during the sitting thereof without Leave of the Congress.

VII. No Member shall speak more than twice in any one Debate without Leave of the House.

IX. No Motion shall be debated until the same be seconded.

X. When a Motion shall be made and seconded it shall be reduced to writing if Desir'd by the President or any Member[2] delivered in at the Table and read by the President before the same shall be allowed to be debated.

XI. When a Motion is made and seconded the Matter of the Motion shall receive a Determination by the Question or be[3] laid aside by general Consent or postponed by the previous Question before any other Motion be *received*.

XIV. When the Question is put by the Chair every colony present[4] shall be counted on one side[5] or the other unless it's delegates be divided.[6]

IV. No Member in coming into the House or in removing from his Place shall pass between the President and the Member then speaking.

V. When the House is sitting no Member shall speak [or whisper][7] to another so as to interrupt any Member who may be speaking in the Debate.

[V]III. When two Members rise together the President shall name the Person to speak.

II. No Member shall depart from the service of[8] the House without Permission of the Congress or order from his constituents.[9]

XVI. No Person shall be appointed to any office of Profit unless he shall have the Consent of Seven Colonies. Nor shall any Ballot be counted unless the Person for whom the Ballot shall be given be first named to the House before the balloting be gone into.

VI. Every Person shall speak from his seat, and when not spea[king] shall continue therein.[10] See the Amendment.[11]

XII. If in a Debate there arise more Questions than one and it be controverted which Question shall be first put, the Question first moved and seconded shall be put first unless it be laid aside by general Consent.[12]

XIII. If a Question in a Debate contain more parts than [one] any Member may have the same divided into as many Questions as parts.

XV. No person shall walk in the house while the question is putting, nor shall any one give his vote who was not present when the question was put.[13]

I. The roll of the house shall be called over by the secretary every day within   minutes after the hour to which it was adjourned, and all absentees without leave shall be noted on the roll, and a copy of so much of the said roll as relates to any one colony shall be sent to the Convention or assembly of such colony once in every three months.[14]

Dft (DLC), in various hands. Endorsed: "Report of the Comee on the rules & orders of the House, brought in July 10. 1776 Ordered to lie on the table." The present text represents the Report as submitted by the committee; changes made in Congress are indicated in the textual notes.

On 20 June, TJ, Robert Treat Paine, and Edward Rutledge were appointed a committee to prepare rules for the conduct of Congress (JCC, V, 468). Before 10 July, TJ wrote the following rough notes (DLC: TJ Papers, 2: 270) for the committee, his first jottings on a subject upon which he was to become a world-wide authority — parliamentary procedure.

"No person to read printed papers.

"Every colony present, unless d[ivid]-ed, to be counted.

"No person to vote unless present when question put.

"No person to walk (*or rise from his seat*) while question putting.

"Every person to sit while not speaking.

"Orders of day at 12 o['clock].

"Amendments first proposed to be first put.

"Commrs. or officers to be named before balot.

"Call of the house every morn. Absentees to be noted & retd. to Constity. [returned to Constituency].

"No member to be absent without leave of house or written ord. of conventn. on pain of being retd. to Conventn."

The draft Report printed above is, with the exceptions noted, in the hand of R. T. Paine. On 16 July it was amended, approved, and spread on the Journals as amended (JCC, V, 572-4). The numbering of the paragraphs in the draft was evidently done between its submission and approval; the numbers are in TJ's hand.

1 Preceding six words substituted in TJ's hand for "beg leave to report as their Opinion."

2 Preceding eight words inserted in an unidentified hand.

3 This word added in TJ's hand.

4 Preceding two words substituted in TJ's hand for "Member in the House."

5 Preceding five words substituted in TJ's hand for "give his Voice one way or the other."

6 Preceding five words added in TJ's hand. This and the following paragraph of the Report were deleted by Congress and are roughly crossed out in the MS.

7 Brackets in MS.

8 Preceding five words substituted in TJ's hand for "leave."

9 Preceding five words substituted in TJ's hand for "if by the withdrawing of the said Member he shall break the Representation of the Colony from whence the said Member came."

10 Preceding eight words substituted in TJ's hand for "chair." This paragraph was deleted in Congress.

11 This sentence inserted in Charles Thomson's hand. Article VI was revised before adoption to require members to rise from their seats and address the chair when speaking.

12 This paragraph deleted in Congress.

13 This paragraph is in TJ's hand but was deleted in Congress.

14 This paragraph is in TJ's hand but was deleted in Congress; another paragraph was then added, in John Hancock's hand, reading: "1. That so soon as nine Colonies are present in the House the Congress proceed to Business."

To Francis Eppes

DEAR SIR   Philadelphia, July 15th, 1776.

Yours of the 3d inst. came to hand to-day. I wish I could be better satisfied on the point of Patty's recovery. I had not heard from her at all for two posts before, and no letter from herself now. I wish it were in my power to return by way of the Forest, as you think it will be impracticable for Mrs. Eppes to travel to the mountains. However, it will be late in August before I can get home, and our Convention will call me down early in October. Till that time, therefore, I must defer the hope of seeing Mrs. Eppes and yourself. Admiral Howe is himself arrived at New York, and two or three vessels, supposed to be of his fleet, were coming in. The whole is expected daily.

Washington's numbers are greatly increased, but we do not know them exactly. I imagine he must have from 30 to 35,000 by this time. The enemy the other day ordered two of their men-of-war to hoist anchor and push by our batteries up the Hudson River. Both wind and tide were very fair. They passed all the batteries with ease, and, as far as is known, without receiving material damage; though there was an incessant fire kept up on them. This experiment of theirs, I suppose, is a prelude to the passage of their whole fleet, and seems to indicate an intention of landing above New York. I imagine General Washington, finding he cannot prevent their going up the river, will prepare to amuse them wherever they shall go.

Our army from Canada is now at Crown Point, but still one half down with the smallpox. You ask about Arnold's behavior at the Cedars. It was this. The scoundrel, Major Butterfield, having surrendered three hundred and ninety men, in a fort with twenty or thirty days' provision, and ammunition enough, to about forty regulars, one hundred Canadians, and five hundred Indians, before he had lost a single man—and Maj. Sherburne, who was coming to the relief of the fort with one hundred men, having, after bravely engaging the enemy an hour and forty minutes, killing twenty of them and losing twelve of his own, been surrounded by them, and taken prisoners also—Gen. Arnold appeared on the opposite side of the river and prepared to attack them. His numbers I know not, but believe they were about equal to the enemy. Capt. Foster [Forster], commander of the king's troops, sent over a flag to him, proposing an exchange of prisoners for as many of the king's in our possession, and, moreover, informed Arnold that if he should attack, the Indians would put every man of the prisoners to death. Arnold refused, called a council of war, and, it being now in the night, it was determined to attack next morning. A second flag came over; he again refused, though in an excruciating situation, as he saw the enemy were in earnest about killing the prisoners. His men, too, began to be importunate for the recovery of their fellow-soldiers. A third flag came, the men grew more clamorous, and Arnold, now almost raving with rage and compassion, was obliged to consent to the exchange and six days suspension of hostilities, Foster declaring he had not boats to deliver them in less time. However, he did deliver them so much sooner as that before the six days were expired, himself and party had fled out of all reach. Arnold then retired to Montreal. You have long before this heard of Gen. Thompson's defeat. The truth of that matter has never appeared till lately. You will see it in the public papers. No men on earth ever behaved better than ours did. The enemy behaved dastardly. Col.

Allen (who was in the engagement) assured me this day, that such was the situation of our men, half way up to the thighs in mud for several hours, that five hundred men of spirit must have taken the whole; yet the enemy were repulsed several times, and our people had time to extricate themselves and come off. It is believed the enemy suffered considerably. The above account of Arnold's affair you may rely on, as I was one of a committee appointed to inquire into the whole of that matter, and have it from those who were in the whole transaction, and were taken prisoners.

My sincere affections to Mrs. Eppes, and adieu,

TH. JEFFERSON

MS not located. Text from Randall, *Life*, III, 582-3, where no source is cited. Addressed: "Francis Eppes, Esq. In Charles City."
Eppes' letter to TJ of 3 July has not been found.

Virginia Delegates in Congress to the Executive of Virginia
(Patrick Henry)

[15 July 1776]

We were informed a few weeks ago that 5000 ℔. of lead imported by our colony were landed at Fredsbgh. As it appeared very unlikely it should be wanting in Virga., and the Flying camp forming [in] the Jerseys, in the face of a powerful enemy, are likely to be in distress for this article, we thought we should be wanting to the public cause, which includes that of our own country, had we hesitated to desire it to be brought here. Had the wants of the camp admitted the delay of an application to you we should most certainly have waited an order from you. But their distress is instantaneous. Even this supply is insufficient. The army in Canada, and the army in N. York will want much lead and there seems to be no certain source of supply unless the mines in Virga. can be rendered such. We are therefore by direction of Congress to beg further that you will be pleased to send them what lead can be spared from Wmsburgh., and moreover order 15 or 20 tons to be brought immediately from the mines.

We take the liberty of recommending the lead mines to you as an object of vast importance. We think it impossible they can be worked to too great an extent. Considered as perhaps the sole means of supporting the American cause they are inestimable. As an article of commerce to our colony too they will be valuable: and even the waggonage if done either by the colony or individuals belonging to it will carry to it no trifling sums of money.

We inclose you a resolution of Congress on the subject of the forts and garrisons on the Ohio.[1]

Several vacancies having happened in our battalions, we are unable to have them filled for want of a list of the officers stating their seniority. We must beg the favor of you to furnish us with one. We received from Colo. R. H. Lee a resolution of Convention recommending to us to endeavor that the promotions of the officers be according to seniority without regard to regiments or companies. This is the standing rule of promotion. In one instance indeed the Congress have reserved to themselves a right of departing from seniority; that is where a person either out of the line of command, or in an inferior part of it has displayed eminent talents. Most of the general officers have been promoted in this way. Without this reservation the whole continent must have been supplied with general officers from the Eastern colonies where a large army was formed and officered before any other colony had occasion to raise troops at [all] and a number of experienced, able and valuable officers must have been lost to the public merely from the locality of their situation.

The resolution of our Convention on the subject of salt we shall lay before Congress. The Convention of Pennsylva. did not proceed to business yesterday for want of a quorum. As soon as they do we shall lay before them the proposition from our convention on the differences at Fort Pitt and communicate to you the result. We are Your Excy's.

Dft (DLC). Drafted by TJ for all the Virginia delegates to sign.

Without date or addressee's name, but both are determinable from TJ's letters of 16 July, in conjunction with a resolution of Congress, 14 July, respecting the lead in Virginia (JCC, V, 558). The draft was phrased so that it could be delivered to whoever was executive officer of Virginia; TJ apparently learned next day of Patrick Henry's investiture as governor on 6 July.

[1] This paragraph must have been omitted in the copy sent, for it is the subject of the letter to Henry of 16 July, q.v.

From John Page

MY DEAR JEFFERSON   Wmsburg. July the 15th. 1776.

I have just Time to inclose you a Copy of General Lee's Letter written the Day after the Cannonade of Fort Sullivan. It came to Hand two Days after his other though written 4 Days before it.

This was a glorious affair. Ld. Dunmore has had a most compleat Drubbing. The Fleet left 7 fine Cables and Anchors worth at least £1200, three of their Tenders compleatly furnished fell into our Hands. If we had had only 2 more 18 Pounders and Powder and Ball in plenty we might have taken or utterly destroyed the Dunmore, and all their Tenders. The Fowey did not attempt to assist the Dunmore, the Otter prepared once to fire but received a shot between wind and Water, on which she went off on a Careen. I hope every one here especially of our late Committee will remember how often I insisted on erecting Batteries, and attacking this Fleet. If I could have been listened to, I would have agreed to be hanged if I would not have saved Norfolk and destroyed the Fleet before it— 4-18's and as many 9 Pounders would have done their Business. Our Governour is still so sick that he can not attend to Business. I am presidin[g] Member and am so pestered with Letters and answering them that I have not Time to add, but a few Words more. The N[orth] Carolinians have sent the Clothes which G. Lee wanted for their People. They have also sent a good Stock of Gun powder, and we are sending what can be spared from here to North Carolina to replace what they have lent. For God's Sake set on Foot an Expedition against Detroit. I am yrs, JOHN PAGE

RC (DLC). Enclosure missing.

Dunmore's DRUBBING at Gwyn's Island, 9-10 July, is reported in full in the *Va. Gaz.* (Purdie), 19 July 1776, which also prints GENERAL LEE'S LETTER of 29 June from Charleston, a copy of which was enclosed by Page. EXPE- DITION AGAINST DETROIT: There had been talk in Congress all spring of such an expedition, but it came to nothing (JCC, IV, 301, 318, 324, 373, 395; see also TJ's Memorandum concerning British Forts in the West, printed at the end of this year, below).

From Edmund Pendleton
to the Virginia Delegates in Congress

GENTN. Virga. July 15th. 1776.

I cannot take leave of the duty of writing Official Letters, now transferred to the Governor and Council, without giving you some free thoughts on two Subjects depending before Congress, both of them of importance to this Countrey, I mean the Pensylvania boundary, and the Petition of some factious people on the Ohio to be made a Separate Government. On the first of these You had formerly a Resolution of Convention proposing a temporary boundary to the Pensylvania Assembly, which tho' in fact it permits them to hold land for the present, they have no title to, yet as it curtails much of their claim, may probably meet with some difficulty, and therefore I will communicate some observations On their Charter, which I have been furnished with by Gentlemen who appear acquainted with the Subject.

The bounds are "On the Eastward by the River Delaware so far as it extends Northerly, but if this extension should fall short of the 43d. degree of Latitude, then by the Meridian of the head fountain of Delaware to the 43d. degree of Latitude. On the North it is bounded by the 43d. degree of Latitude. To the Westward as far as 5 degrees West longitude will extend and To the Southward it is bounded by the 40th. degree of Latitude."

The dispute between Pensylvania and Maryland arose from the ambiguity of Expression respecting the Station they were to depart from near New-Castle. It is Supposed that Mr. Penn purchased Ld. Baltimore's consent to the line established, but however that was, a determination or compromise between them, cannot effect Virginia, not party or Privy, and therefore from the Meridian of the head Springs of Potowmack (the determination of the Maryland boundary) we say they are bound by the 40th. degree, at which they are to begin from that Meridian and run out their 5 degrees of Longitude Westward, reckoning from that part of the Delaware where the 40th. degree strikes it; instead of which they set out their Western boundary from 39d. 43m. Latitude, and extended it through our Teritory a great length under pretence that they were to go 5 degrees from every meander of the Dela Ware, so that here seem two manifest errors respecting us, the Coming 17 degrees[1] too far to the Southward to begin the Western boundary and then extending that Western boundary too far; indeed it is further said that this injury was increased by their having made too liberal an Allowance for the difference between common and Horizontal measures on Account of the Mountanous Countrey, but this I suppose to be merely conjectural. I have stated thus much to shew Our pretensions are not merely founded on a Whim of Ld. Dunmore, as they almost made me beleive when at Philad[a.,] but on solid grounds, which however we shall be ready to submit to the Judgment of Impartial Judges as soon as our common Enemy will afford us leisure. In the meantime surely it must be for common Interest to settle a temporary boundary, and that all Jealousies and much more hostilities should subside: Of the Former there appeared too much in Pensylva. on Our Garrisoning Fort Pitt, and in their keeping up yet a number of Troops in that neighbourhood equal to ours; The latter We are told hath been lately repeated, and one of Our Justices confined in their Goal. This does not look like neighbours and freinds united in a most glorious common cause.

As to the Petition from the people on the West of the Alhegany Mountains, I conceive the Congress will not interfere to divide any Government, or rather dismember it without it's own consent, this being one of the Local Subjects only to be discussed by the colonial Legislatures. However, We are informed from Pitsburg that this Plan is set on Foot by a Party there, formed on a junction of the Vandalia, Indiana, and Colo. Croghans Interests, who rather wish to have their claims to lands there settled in a New Government under their joint Influence, than to an Impartial Legislature at Wmsburg.; and that it is by no means the Wish of the people in General: To shew the factious Spirit of the Petitioners, I send you a Copy of a Petition they had just before sent to the Convention to have a New County, and for the Loan of money to support that, which may serve to prove also, their ability to Support a Government. We have it in contemplation that to keep that Countrey, when settled, united with this, will produce none of the Good Purposes of Government, and be exceedingly inconvenient to them. And that therefore they must be a Seperate Government, but this must be Suspended until all Land titles are Adjusted by Us, and the Several Purchases from the Crown or the Indians either confirmed or set aside, to prevent the affairs of the Countrey there in the Infancy of the Government from being distracted by those Various claims: and until the land is settled sufficiently to support Government by Taxes not too burthensome, and to afford discreet Officers of Government. When this is the case, I am persuaded we shall not only consent to their Seperation, but do every thing we can to Nourish and encourage them in their Infant state.

You'l excuse the trouble I have given you on these two Subjects and believe me to be with great regard, Gent. Yr. mo. Obedt. hble Servts.,[2]

EDMD. PENDLETON

A Word in private on the Pensa. boundary not proper for the Public Letter.

It has been ever and yet is beleived that the Pensylvanians for the Sake of engrossing the Indian trade, have constantly done Us Ill Offices with the Indians, and many of our Wars [are] probably imputable to that cause.

You should be on your guard as to one of your brethren in Congress who was an Indian Commissioner last Summer at Fort Pitt, who stands charged by all the Gentlemen then present of directing every Speech and treaty with the Indians to the particular emolument of Pensylva.; and many things unworthy his Public Character. I did expect a Public charge would have been sent to Congress against him by last Convention but it past off I beleive for want of time. I mean not to be his Accuser, Nor do I wish his reputation to be at all effected by this hint, only meant to guard you against Injury to the Countrey, and you'l no doubt avoid mentioning it to any.

RC (DLC). At foot of text of the "Public Letter": "Honble the Delegates in Congress." The private postscript is a fragment of a page, without date, signature, or direction, in DLC: TJ Papers, 234: 41923; it is, however, in Pendleton's hand and is clearly a postscript to this his last letter as president of the committee of safety.

This letter deals with two related matters: the dispute between Virginia and Pennsylvania over the territory west of the Alleghenies, and a current but abortive movement in that region to establish a new state. On the first topic, see the Virginia and Pennsylvania Delegates' Address of 25 July 1775; the Virginia Committee of Safety's letter to the Virginia Delegates, 17 June 1776; and TJ's Memoranda on the Virginia, Pennsylvania, and Maryland Boundaries, printed under the date of 5 Nov. 1776. On the second topic, known as the

"Westsylvania" scheme, initiated in June 1776 by local settlers but believed to have been prompted and supported by the old Croghan, Indiana, and Vandalia interests, see George H. Alden, *New Governments West of the Alleghanies before 1780* (Univ. of Wis., *Bulletin, Historical Ser.*, II, No. 1), Madison, 1897, p. 64-8; F. J. Turner, "Western State-Making in the Revolutionary Era," *Amer. Hist. Rev.*, I (1895-1896), 82-3; Abernethy, *Western Lands*, p. 176-7; Paullin and Wright, *Atlas*, p. 24 and pl. 41C. Frowned on by both Virginia and Pennsylvania authorities and apparently disregarded by Congress, the Westsylvania movement came to nothing. ONE OF YOUR BRETHREN IN CONGRESS: James Wilson; see Thomas Walker to TJ, 13 Sep. 1775.

1 Thus in MS; an error for "17 minutes."
2 Thus in MS.

Virginia Delegates in Congress to the Speaker of the Pennsylvania Convention

SIR   Philada. July 15. 1776.

The honorable the convention of Virga. attending to the inconveniencies which may arise from an unsettled jurisdiction in the neighborhood of fort Pitt, have instructed us to propose to your honorable house to agree on some temporary boundary which may serve for preservation of the peace in that territory until an amicable and final determination may be had before arbiters mutually chosen. Such temporary settlement will from it's nature do prejudice to neither party when at any future day a complete information of facts shall enable them to submit the doubt to a just and final decision. We can assure you that the colony of Virga. does not entertain a wish that one inch should be added to theirs from the territory of a sister colony, and we have perfect confidence that the same just sentiment prevails in your house. Parties thus disposed can scarcely meet with difficulty in adjusting either a temporary or a final settlement. The decision, whatever it be, will not annihilate the lands. They will remain to be occupied by Americans,[1] and whether these be counted in numbers of this or that of the United states will be thought a matter of little moment.[2] We shall be ready to confer on this subject with any gentlemen your house may please to appoint for that purpose and are Sir with every sentiment of respect Your very humble servts.

Dft (DLC). Drafted by TJ for all the delegates to sign.

Written in accordance with the instructions transmitted by Pendleton, president of the committee of safety, to the Virginia delegates, 17 June 1776, q.v. After the instructions had been issued, the Pennsylvania Assembly had been superseded by a revolutionary body, the Convention, which met for the first time this day and elected as president Benjamin Franklin, who was technically, therefore, the recipient of this letter. The letter was read to the Convention the next day, and on the 20th a committee (David Rittenhouse, Thomas Smith, Alexander Lowrey, Owen Biddle, and James Potter) was appointed to confer with the Virginia delegates (Force, *Archives*, 5th ser., II, 1, 3, 5, 7). A copy of the resolution of the Pennsylvania Convention, signed by John Morris, Jr., secretary, was sent to the Virginia delegates and is in DLC, TJ Papers, 2: 273. The two parties may never have sat down together, for in the report of the Pennsylvania committee to its Convention, 14 Sep. 1776, is quoted an undated letter from that committee to the Virginia delegates stating that the committee had found the Virginia Convention's proposed temporary boundary line "very wide from the true limits of *Pennsylvania*, according to the Charter." However, the Pennsylvanians expressed an "earnest desire that a temporary boundary as nearly correspondent to the true one as possible" should be run. Three Virginia delegates, of whom TJ was not one, answered this on 12 Sep., saying that they were limited to discussion of the Virginia proposal but that they would lay the Pennsylvania counter-proposal before the next assembly (Force, *Archives*, 5th ser., II, 40-2). This was accordingly done, and on 5 Nov. 1776 TJ was named first on a committee of the new House of Delegates to make a fresh proposal, for a permanent line (JHD, Oct. 1776, 1828 edn., p. 41). See TJ's Memorandum on the Virginia, Pennsylvania, and Maryland Boundaries, printed under 5 Nov. 1776.

[1] TJ first wrote "the sons of freedom."

[2] "by an American" deleted.

To Patrick Henry

DEAR SIR   [16 July 1776]

The inclosed letter from the President was directed before he knew of your being invested with the office of Governor: you will therefore please to open it. After congratulating you on your appointment and hoping every thing favourable from our new institutions I subscribe myself Dr. Sir Your very humble servt.,

TH: JEFFERSON

RC (The Rosenbach Co., Philadelphia, 1946). Endorsed: "Virginia Delegates July 16. 1776 inclosing a Resolution to take into Continental possesn [th]e Forts at the Mouths of Whealng & the Great Kannaway & the fort at Pittsburg." Enclosure missing.

The enclosure embodied the resolution of Congress of 11 July relative to the Virginia forts and garrisons on the Ohio (JCC, V, 542).

To Fielding Lewis

[S]IR   Philada. July 16. 1776

We were informed a few weeks ago [that 5000 ℔. of]¹ lead imported on account of our colony were landed at Fredsbgh. There appears scarcely a possibility it should be wanting in Virga., more especially when we consider the supplies which may be expected from the mines of that colony. The Flying camp now forming in the Jersies and which will be immediately in the face of a powerful enemy, is likely to be in great want of that article. Did their wants admit the delay of an application to the Governor we should have applied to him, and have not a doubt he would order it hither. But circumstances are too pressing, and we are assured we should incur the censures of our own country were we to permit the publick cause to suffer essentially while the means of preventing it (tho not under our immediate charge) are within our reach. We therefore take the liberty of desiring you to stop so many of the powder waggons now on their way to Wmsburgh as may be necessary and return them immediately with this lead, and whatever more you can collect, sending the powder on by other waggons. But should the lead have been sent to Wmsburgh, the waggons may then proceed on their journey and the governor to whom we have written will take care of the matter.

Dft (DLC). Drafted by TJ for all the Virginia delegates in Congress to sign.

The addressee's name has been established from the resolution of Congress, 14 July, ordering that these instructions be sent express to Lewis, who was superintendent of the state manufactory for small arms at Fredericksburg (JCC, V, 558; see also the Delegates' letter to the Executive of Virginia, 15 July).

¹ Text faded; supplied from letter to the Executive of Virginia, printed under 15 July 1776.

From Richard Stockton

DEAR SIR   Trenton July 19th. 1776.

Upon my arrival at this place I waited upon the New Jersey Convention, and proposed to them their agreeing to furnish 2000 Men for the increase of the flying Camp: they alledged the reasons against the measure which I expected, to wit, their having furnished their full proportion. However, upon my urging the importance of the measure, I was so happy as to be assured that they would, without any regard to their quotas, endeavour to furnish the 2000 Men, and that they should immediatly take the field. They are under the necessity nevertheless of furnishing them from the Militia, which must have a rotation; but their Militia are well disciplined, and the Convention will be careful that this number of 2000 shall be continually in the feild as part of the flying Camp, untill the first of December.

The Convention will forward this immediatly by express. With great respect, I am Dr. Sir, Your most obedt. hb[le. servt.,]

RICHD. STOCKTON

RC (DLC).

Congress on 3 June had organized a "flying camp" to protect the northern Jersey coast (JCC, IV, 412-13). Concerning New Jersey's quota of troops for this unit, see the Proceedings of the New Jersey Provincial Congress, 17 July (Force, *Archives*, 4th ser., VI, 1647, 1653).

From John Page

MY DEAR JEFFERSON   July the 20th. 1776

We are very much at a Loss here for an Engraver to make our Seal. Mr. Wyth and myself have therefore thought it proper to apply to you to assist us in this Business. Can you get the Work done in Philadelphia? If you can, we must get the Favour of you to have it done immediately. The inclosed will be all the Directions you will require. The Workman Engraver[1] may want to know the Size. This you may determine, unless Mr. Wyth should direct the Dimensions. He may also be at a Loss for a Virtus and Libertas, but you may refer him to Spence's Polymetis which must be in some Library in Philadelphia. Pray let us know by the first opportunity whether you can get it done. Before this can reach you, you will have heard of the Glorious News from South-Carolina. Dunmores Fleet was at the Mouth of Potowmack when I heard last from it. It had been at Anchor 16 Hours with a fair Wind up the River and Bay so that it is evident they did not know where to go to. There is no Danger of their returning to the Island unless they get a very considerable Reinforcement and even then we may give them a severe Check and retreat to the Main. They can not enter

Norfolk Harbour without receiving great Dammage for we have Batteries mounting 4, 24, and 5, 18 Pounders besides a number of smaller Cannon. If half these Guns had been mounted in Oct. as I advised, Norfolk would not have been burnt. 2, 18. Pounders at Gwynn's Island almost beat the Dunmore to Pieces, and drove off the whole Fleet. Danny and Chas. Harrison behaved admirably well on that Occasion, so well, that no one seems to regret the Loss of Arundel, who lost his Life by the bursting of a wooden Mortar which was foolishly constructed and he obstinately persisted in his Resolution to fire, though dissuaded from it by every one who saw it. I must refer you to the Papers of this week for the Particulars of the late Cannonade. They were written by Officers and may be depended upon. We have taken a little Tender, since their Flight, which was cruising off the Eastern Shore, in quest of Provisions. Little Jimmy Parker was taken in her. She carried 12 Swivels and 18. Men. We have a fine Brigg mounting 12 4 Pounders under the Command of Captn. Jas. Cocke a brave and experienced Officer now cruising in the Bay and a Row Galley carrying 2 18. Pounders is gone down Jas. River. But I do not like the Galley. She is Clumsey, and I think can not carry the 2 heavy Guns to any Advantage. We expect Lilly will cruise next Week. If we had got our whole Fleet ready before the Attack at Gwynn's Island, we might have taken every Ship the Enemy had except the Roebuck. If they do not get a Reinforcement in 6 Weeks we shall give a good Account of them yet. If General Washington and Howe can but hear of the Affair at Sullivan's Island before they engage, it will go a great Way towards deciding the Dispute. It is impossible it should not animate our Men to the Highest Degree, and dispirit the Enemy. Can not you stop Burgoines Career? I hope you have taken Care of the Lakes. Fort Pitt you know is a Post of the last Importance to Virginia and Pennsylvania. The Indians have murdered a Man within 3 Miles of it. It is an extensive Work much out of Repair, very weekly Garrisoned, by only 100 Men, and is within 4 or 5 Days March of Niagara where our Enemies have Men enough with Savages to spare a Detachment which might come in 24 Hours 100 Miles of their Way, and might take the Fort before it Could be reinforced. This State of things I had from a very sensible Officer who came down last Week as an Express. The Shawne[e] have sent in 4 Hostages to Fort Pitt but then he observes they sent no Interpreter with them. Do consider these Thing[s,] and either reinforce Fort Pitt, or send an Army against Detroit and Niagara. Give my Love to Nelson. Tell him that I have not Time to write another Line being beset with the Governours Business who is still unable to attend to it. Adieu. JOHN PAGE

P.S. I am highly pleased with your Declaration. God preserve the united States. We know the Race is not to the swift nor the Battle to the strong. Do you not think an Angel rides in the Whirlwind and directs this Storm?

I had forgotten to mention till this Moment that there are 2 french gentlemen here, who made their Escape from Ld. Dunmore, when he was under his Confusion, and flying from Gwynns Island. They were taken by a Tender, some Time ago, when they were coming into Norfolk with a Cargo of Arms Powder and Medicine, which when they had disposed of, they intended to have offered their Service to us as Officers in a Troop of Horse, one of them having commanded a Troop in old France, the other had been in the Foot but was willing to serve in the same Corps with his Friend. They say that the Governour of Martineque recommended it to them to come and introduce themselves to us in that Manner. They appear to be Gentlemen. The Council have ordered them to be boarded at Southalls, have given them 20 Pounds a Piece, as they lost all their Clothes with the Enemy and had been plundered by them of their Cash and we promised to write to the Congress to know whether they may expect any Encouragement if they should go to Philadelphia. One of them seems to chuse to return to Martineque, to complain of the ill Treatment he received from Ld. Dunmore. They both lament that their Papers of Credit were taken from them. These may be valuable Men. I for my Part want to detain them here til we can be bet[ter] acquainted with them. The Chevalier De St. Aubin says he is perfectly acquainted with every Maneuv[er] of the Horse. If so, which we may soon know when one or 2 of our Troops come to Town, I hope he m[ay] be appointed Major, but what would you advise [us?] to do? We have advised them to stay here til we can he[ar] from our Delegates. Once more *adieu.* J. P.

RC (DLC). Endorsed: "Page John. July 20. 1776." Enclosure missing.

The Convention's instructions to Page and Wythe respecting a SEAL for the state are in *Conv. Jour.*, May 1776, 1816 edn., p. 85-6, under date of 5 July 1776; see further TJ to Page, 30 July 1776. POLYMETIS: Joseph Spence, *Polymetis: or, an Inquiry concerning the Agreement* between the *Works of the Roman Poets, and the Remains of the Antient Artists,* London, 1747. FRENCH GENTLEMEN: St. Aubin and de Harrincourt, on whom see *Va. Council Jour.*, I, 79-80, 130, 133, 263, 298, and TJ's answer of 30 July.

1 "Engraver" is interlined, but "Workman" is not crossed out.

From Richard Henry Lee

DEAR SIR   Chantilly 21st. July 1776

I thank you much for your favor and its inclosures by this post, and I wish sincerely, as well for the honor of Congress, as for that of the States, that the Manuscript had not been mangled as it is. It is wonderful, and passing pitiful, that the rage of change should be so unhappily applied. However the *Thing* is in its nature so good, that no Cookery can spoil the Dish for the palates of Freemen.

I congratulate you on the great success in South Carolina and we have no reason to be sorry for the disgrace of our African Hero at Qwins [Gwynn's] Island. He is now disturbing us in Potomac having attached himself to St. Georges Island on the North side. But it seems the brave spirit of the Marylanders will not Permit these folks to remain long where they now are. Our friend Mr. Wythe proposes to me by letter that I meet him at Hooes ferry the 3d. of September and I have agreed to do so, unless some pressing call takes me to Congress sooner. Can you have patience so long?

It will always make me happy to hear from you because I am very sincerely your affectionate friend,   RICHARD HENRY LEE

P.S. I will thank you for Dr. Prices pamphlet by next post. How do you like our Government?

RC (DLC). Tr (PPAP). RC addressed and franked: "Thomas Jefferson esquire Member of Congress in Philadelphia Free." Endorsed: "Lee, Rich. Henry." OUR AFRICAN HERO alludes to Lord Dunmore in his capacity as commander of slave troops. PRICES PAMPHLET: Richard Price, *Observations on the Nature of Civil Liberty*, London, 1776; reprinted Phila., 1776.

From Edmund Pendleton

DEAR SIR   Virga. July 22d. 1776.

Ere this reaches you, you'l have been furnished with all Our doings of importance at the last Convention, Our Mode of Government and the several Elections to Offices. I expected you had in the Preamble to our form of Government, exhausted the Subject of complaint against Geo. 3d. and was at a loss to discover what the Congress would do for one to their Declaration of Independence without copying, but find you have acquitted your selves very well on that score; We are now engaged beyond the Power of withdrawing, And I think cannot fail of success in happiness, if we do not defeat our selves by intrigue and Canvassing to be uppermost in Offices of Power and Lucre. I fancy there was much of this in our last Convention, but not being of the party or in the Secret, I cannot speak of it with certainty, but am not otherwise able to Account for the unmerited, cruel degradation of my friend Colo. Harrison, who in my Opinion yields to no member of the Congress in point of Judgment or Integrity, unless he is strangely altered since I left them, and some other unexpected unions of Jarring Elements, which time perhaps may unfold. As to my friend Braxton they have been ever at him, and whatever his own sentiments and conduct may have been, his connections furnished a plausible Foundation for Opposition, and I was not Surprised when he was left out. These things, however intended, may perhaps have their use, as we shall have those Gentlemen here to assist in watching and breaking the Spirit of Party, that bane of all public Councils. I wish you could be here, if you could be Spared from Congress, indeed you must be Spared, to sustain one of the Important Posts in the Judiciary, where I most fear our deficiency, and conceive it to be of the greatest importance in the rearing our Commonwealth. Let but wisdom and Integrity fill those Offices, and we cannot fail of Peace and Security. You are also wanting much in the Revision of our Laws and forming a new body, a necessary work for which few of us have adequate abilities and attention. We are now engaged in the preparitory Steps for choosing Senators next month, to compleat our Legislature against October, when I suppose we shall have a full meeting and long Session. I expect important intelligence from New-York, of which I hope you'l give me a weekly Account; I hear Dunmore is gone into Potowmack and attempting to Land, was repulsed by the Militia, and that Our Cruisers had taken 2 of his tenders. I am Dr. Sr. Yr. Affe. Friend,

EDMD. PENDLETON

If Colo. Harrison is not come away, tell him I expected he would be, or should have wrote him; I hope to se him in his return.

RC (DLC).
The reasons why HARRISON and BRAXTON were not re-elected to Congress are given in Fleming's letter to TJ of 27 July 1776. See also notes to Bill for Regulating the Appointment of Delegates to the Continental Congress, under date of 12 May 1777.

To Francis Eppes

DEAR SIR   Philadelphia, July 23, 1776.

We have nothing new here now but from the southward. The successes there I hope will prove valuable here, by giving new spirit to our people. The ill successes in Canada had depressed the minds of many; when we shall hear the last of them I know not; everybody had supposed Crown Point would be a certain stand for them, but they have retreated from that to Ticonderoga, against everything which in my eye wears the shape of reason. When I wrote you last, we were deceived in General Washington's numbers. By a return which came to hand a day or two after, he then had but 15,000 effective men. His reinforcements have come in pretty well since. The flying camp in the Jerseys under General Mercer begins to form, but not as fast as exigencies require. The Congress have, therefore, been obliged to send for two of our battalions from Virginia. I hope that country is perfectly safe now; and if it is, it seemed hardly right that she should not contribute a man to an army of 40,000, and an army too on which was to depend the decision of all our rights. Lord Howe's fleet has not yet arrived. The first division sailed five days before he did, but report says it was scattered by a storm. This seems probable, as Lord Howe had a long passage. The two other divisions were not sailed when he came away. I do not expect his army will be here and fit for action till the middle or last of August; in the meantime, if Mercer's camp could be formed with the expedition it merits, it might be possible to attack the present force from the Jersey side of Staten Island, and get rid of that beforehand; the militia go in freely, considering they leave their harvest to rot in the field.

I have received no letter this week, which lays me under great anxiety. I shall leave this place about the 11th of next month. Give my love to Mrs. Eppes, and tell her that when both you and Patty fail to write to me, I think I shall not be unreasonable in insisting she shall. I am, dear sir, Yours affectionately, TH. JEFFERSON

MS not located. Text from Randall, *Life*, III, 583, where no source is given. For Virginia's action respecting troops for the "flying camp," see *Va. Council Jour.*, I, 110, under date of 6 Aug.

Memorandum on Testimony concerning Major Hughes

Mr. Foulke.[1] *July 24. 1776.*

Mr. Vernet informed deponent that one of the English officers had applied to Mr. Coignet to serve in the English army instead of the provincial. Vernet wrote his name 'Yousenne' and said he was a major and lodged near Mrs. House's. This it is supposed was 'Hughes' a major, who lodged near there. Coignet applied to Vernet for the same purpose, Vernet refused. Mr. Carmovan gave first notice of this to the deponent before Vernet did. Carmovan and Vernet are both strongly attached to the American cause.

N (DLC).

Nothing further is known of this episode. CARMOVAN is a misspelling for the Chevalier de Kermorvan, a French volunteer who served as an engineer in the Continental army, 1776-1778 (Lasseray,

Les français sous les treize étoiles, under Barazer de Kermorvan).

1 The name partly torn; it may be "Fouché."

From William Fleming

DEAR SIR   Mt. Pleasant 27th. July, 1776.

Our convention having, the 12th. instant, adjourned to the first monday in October, I did not receive yours of the 1st. July 'til I had been a fortnight at home.

I am much concerned at the situation of our affairs in Canada, but am not without hope they may yet be retrieved. A thorough knowledge of the sources of human evils, is, generally speaking, a good step towards pointing out effectual remedies; but I am fearful the procuring hard money, in our present circumstances, will be attended with great difficulty, and it must be very discouraging to young soldiers to meet a formidable enemy in the jaws of a malignant distemper.

The horrid conspiricy at New York affects me exceedingly, and when I reflect that every engine of ministerial tyranny is in motion to effect their diabolical purposes, I cannot suppress my anxiety, lest the seeds of that infernal plot be not totally eradicated. God grant that the authors with all their coadjutors may meet with the justice due to their horrid crime.

I perfectly agree with you in opinion that the severity of our trial is near at hand and perhaps a few weeks will determine the fate of New York, as the enemy in that quarter, if we may believe the public papers, are very formidable; tho' I doubt not they will meet with a very warm reception.

The spirits of our people are, and for some time have been, higher than at any period since the commencement of hostilities; and they are not a little elevated by our late successes at Charles Town, and Gwinn's Island. How a severe reverse of fortune might affect them, I cannot pretend to determine; but those who are much elated with a little success, are generally most dejected in misfortune: however, since the Rubicon is passed, I believe there are few among us, even of the lower class, who have an idea of giving up the cause, happen what will.

With respect to the late nomination of delegates, the reduction of the number to five was on motion of the governor, "first to save expense, and secondly that we might have the assistance of the two supernumeraries in our own government, where gentlemen of abilities are much wanting." It met with little or no opposition. The appointment of Dr. Rickman physician and director general to the continental hospital, when McClurg, a native and regular bred physician had been recommended by the committee of safety, and by Genl. Lee, gave very great offence, and was undoubtedly the cause of Colo. Harrison's being left out, as it was generally supposed Rickmans appointment was through his influence. Mr. Braxton's address on government made him no friends in convention; and many reports were propagated in Wmsburg. (upon what grounds I know not) respecting the extreme imprudent, and inimical conduct of his lady, which, with many people, affected his political character exceedingly, of which Fitzhugh and some other of his friends informed him by letter, before we left town. As to your own case, you may make yourself perfectly easie, for you are as high in the estimation of your countrymen as ever, and the reason you were so late in the nomination was the mention of a letter you had written to Dr. Gilmer, signifying your inclination to resign. He was out of town at the time of the nomination, but desired another gentleman, if the matter came on in his absence, to inform the house he had received such a letter, which he accordingly did, and thereupon arose a debate whether or not your excuse should be admitted. Some were of opinion you were jesting, and some that you were in earnest, and after near half an hours debate, they proceeded to ballot without a question being put, and many of your warmest friends (myself among the rest) erased your name out of their ballots, taking it for granted that your services in congress were to be dispensed with, as the opposition grew faint towards the latter end of the debate. Had it not been for these circumstances, I much doubt whether there would have been three votes against you. Your letter to the president on the same subject appeared the next day, which would have been effectual, had it arrived in time; but as the nomination was over, the house did not seem inclined to a new election; tho' I imagine if your affairs are such as make your longer stay in congress still inconvenient, you will be indulged in October with a recess for the remainder of the year.

Our elections of senators, of whom you have already been informed we are to have twenty four, come on early next month. The districts in our neighbourhood are 1st. Chesterfield, Amelia and Cumberland. 2d. Henrico Goochland and Louisa. 3d. Amherst, Albemarle, and Buckingham. The Candidates are Messrs. Cary and Mayo for the first, (Tabb having lately declined, it is said, in favor of Mayo!), Messrs. T. Mann Randolph and Adams for the second, and Dr. Walker and W. Cabell for the third.

We have a prospect of a fine crop, tho' we begin to suffer with a drought. I was at *Old Con's* last monday, and observed the corn in the Island to be very fine. Our latter wheat is much injured by the rust, and the weavel alredy begin to appear.

I am with great esteem, dear sir, Yr. friend & obed. servt.,

WM. FLEMING

RC (DLC). The CONVENTION had adjourned on the 5th, not the 12th. For the LATE NOMINATION OF DELEGATES, see *Conv. Jour.*, May 1776, 1816 edn., p. 58, under 20 June. BRAXTON'S ADDRESS: Anon., *Address to the Convention of the Colony and Ancient Dominion of Virginia, on the Subject of Government in General, and Recommending a Particular Form to* *Their Consideration*, Phila., 1776 (Sabin 7466, Evans 14669); reprinted in Force, *Archives*, 4th ser., VI, 748-54. Braxton's LADY was the former Elizabeth Corbin; her father (Richard) and her brother (John Tayloe) were loyalists (VMHB, XXX [1922], 82-4, 314-15). TJ'S LETTER . . . TO DR. GILMER: See Edmund Randolph to TJ, 23 June 1776. OLD CON'S: not identified.

From George Wythe

G. W. TO T. J.   Williamsburg, 27 July, 1776

Lord Dunmore, driven from Gwins, retreated to St. George's island in Potowmack, a station we hear he found no less unquiet than what he left, so that he hath gone up that river, distressed, it is imagined for want of water. Ought the precept, 'if thine enemy thirst give him drink,' to be observed towards such a fiend, and in such a war? Our countrymen will probably decide in the negative; and perhaps such casuists as you and I shall not blame them. I had not reached this place before the appointment of delegates. An attempt to alter it as to you was made in vain. When I came here the plan of government had been committed to the whole house. To those who had the chief hand in forming it the one you put into my hands was shewn. Two or three parts of this were, with little alteration, inserted in that: but such was the impatience of sitting long enough to discuss several important points in which they differ, and so many other matters were necessarily to be dispatched before the adjournment that I was persuaded the revision of a subject the members seemed tired of would at that time have been unsuccessfully proposed. The system agreed to in my opinion requires reformation. In October I hope you will effect it. I have directed a carriage to meet me at Hooe's ferry the third of September. So soon as I saw Mr. Bruce I mentioned the copies you wanted. He told me he could not find some of the papers. I propose in a day or two to assist him in searching for them, and wi[ll] desire him to get them ready by the time you will be in Virginia. Farewell.

RC (DLC).

THE ONE YOU PUT INTO MY HANDS: Wythe had carried TJ's Third Draft of a constitution for Virginia to Williamsburg when he left Congress on 13 June; see Virginia Constitution, June 1776, Editorial Note and Document III. MR. BRUCE . . . THE COPIES YOU WANTED: This allusion is unexplained.

To Richard Henry Lee

DEAR SIR   Philadelphia July 29. 1776.

I inclose you Dr. Price's pamphlet. I should have done so sooner but understood your brother was sending many to Virginia and not doubting one would be to you, I laid by the one I had purchased for that purpose. Little new here. Our camps recruit slowly, amazing slowly. God knows in what it will end. The finger of providence has as yet saved us by retarding the arrival of Ld. Howe's recruits. Our army from Canada is now at Tyonderoga, but in a shattered condition. General Sullivan left it and came here to resign on Gates's appointment. His letter of resignation was put in on Friday. It was referred to this morning that a proper rap of the knuckles might be prepared, but on the advice of his friends he asked leave to withdraw it and repair to his duty. The minutiae of the Confederation have hitherto engaged us; the great points of representation, boundaries, taxation &c. being left open. For god's sake, for your country's sake, and for my sake, come. I receive by every post such accounts of the state of Mrs. Jefferson's health, that it will be impossible for me to disappoint her expectation of seeing me at the time I have promised, which supposed my leaving this place on the 11th. of next month. The plan of ——————— is yet untouched. After being read it was privately printed for the consideration of the members and will come on when we shall have got through the Confederation. I am Dr. Sir,

I pray you to come. I am under a sacred obligation to go home.

RC (ViHi). Signature torn or cut away. Addressed and franked: "To Richard Henry Lee esq. at Chantilly in Westmoreland free Th: Jefferson." Twice endorsed.

PRICE'S PAMPHLET: See R. H. Lee to Jefferson, 21 July. SULLIVAN: On Maj. Gen. John Sullivan's threatened resignation, see TJ's Resolution, which follows. The ACCOUNTS OF THE STATE OF MRS.

JEFFERSON'S HEALTH have not survived, presumably because TJ destroyed all letters and references pertaining to her. THE PLAN OF ——— refers to a committee report called "Plan of Treaties," brought in on 18 July and ordered to be printed for the members two days later (JCC, V, 575ff., 594; VI, 1124, No. 121); a copy of the printed text is in DLC: TJ Papers, 2: 279-81.

Resolution on the Case of General Sullivan

[29 July 1776]

Resolved that the former determinations of Congress to pass by rank and seniority on necessary occasions in order to avail their country of superior talents and experience were entered into on mature deliberation as being absolutely requisite for the salvation of these states, the armies of which, tho' large, were embodied on sudden emergencies, and were of necessity in some instances entrusted to the command of persons who, having seen no military duty, could only be appointed from a hope of their fitness: that a scrupulous regard to seniority is condemned by the practice of the wisest republics, in their most virtuous ages; whose citizens, breathing the pure spirit of patriotism, untainted by pride of rank, or avarice of pay, took their post wherever placed, and changed it whenever required, contented to exert their endeavors in any station to save their country.

That the Congress however, tho' they mean to reserve the right of their constituents to pass by seniority when their safety requires it, did not consider themselves as exercising that right in the instance of which General Sullivan complains. That Mr. Gates was appointed Adjutant General with the rank of Brigadier General on the 17th day of June 1774.[1] That on the 22d. day of the same month eight others were appointed Brigadiers General; and being appointed by the same vote, it became necessary to settle their precedence among themselves, for which purpose their names were arranged and numbered in the vote of appointment, and among these Mr. Sullivan was named and numbered as the seventh Brigadier General. That it never was the idea of Congress, by this enumeration, to oust General Gates of that precedence which their previous appointment had meant to give him; and of this they had hoped Genl. Sullivan could not be ignorant, as he was then a member of Congress, was present during the transaction, and contributed by his own vote to place Genl. Gates in a senior station. That therefore, in the late appointment of Genl. Gates to be a Major General, the Congress proceeded and meant to proceed according to Seniority.

That the relinquishment of his command by General Sullivan in the face of an enemy, which[2] he desires may not be imputed to fear, this house does not wish to derive from that motive. They believed him brave, and therefore appointed him.[3]

Resolved that General Sullivan's resignation be accepted.

Dft (DLC). This MS, entirely in TJ's hand, is really five documents or parts thereof, embracing a wide variety of subjects from the description of a horse stall to a fragment of the Declaration of Independence. It consists of three half sheets or six pages, on which are the following: (1) rough draft of the Report on the case of General Sullivan, p. 1 and top of p. 3; (2) fragment of resolutions of Congress on treatment of American prisoners by the British, 17 June 1776, p. 2 (see Report of the Committee on the Cedars Cartel under that date); (3) Fragment of the Composition Draft of the Declaration of Independence (q.v., above), bottom of p. 3; (4) pencilled dimensions and description of a stall in Governor Penn's stable, p. 4 (see Kimball, *Jefferson, Architect*, plate 60—a drawing and notes made from these pencilled memoranda); (5) a fair copy of the Report on General Sullivan, p. 5-6; the last is the text followed here. The date of 29 July is assigned because that is the date on which Jefferson expected to present the Resolution; actually it was never presented, but it was written sometime between 26 and 29 July.

Sullivan, disgruntled because General Gates had been made a major general and had been given command of the Northern Army, presented his letter of resignation to Congress on 26 July 1776, but, on the advice of friends, he withdrew it and TJ therefore did not present this "proper rap of the knuckles" (TJ to R. H. Lee, 29 July 1776). Sullivan's letter is not to be found in the Papers of the Continental Congress, but the Washington Papers contain a copy of his letter to Schuyler, 6 July 1776, outlining his reasons for resigning (see Washington, *Writings*, ed. Fitzpatrick, V, 296-7; Burnett, *Letters of Members*, II, No. 47; JCC, V, 612-13, where references to Sullivan on 26 and 29 July are expunged).

[1] Both in the rough draft and in the fair copy TJ erred in the date; it should be 17 June 1775. The resolution of 22 June appointing Sullivan a brigadier general and naming him seventh on the list was, however, ambiguous: that is, it stipulated that "the number of Brigadier generals be *augmented* to eight" (italics supplied), though eight were named and Gates had already been named (JCC, II, 97, 103).

[2] The words "however unprecedented" are deleted in the fair copy though not in rough draft.

[3] The sentence "He now desires to resign, they therefore accept his resignation" deleted in fair copy, though not in rough draft.

From Edmund Pendleton

DR. SIR   Caroline July 29th. 1776.

I set down to continue my correspondence, tho' have nothing to communicate worthy so much of your time as the reading will require. We have nothing from the Southward, at least that has reached Us, since Genl. Lee's Letter to me. Dunmores Squadron were Pirating up Potowmack last week. I am not informed of any particular damage they did, except to Mr. William Brent of Stafford, in burning his dwelling House and Stable, some Stacks of Hay and wheat. They set fire to every House, but the Matches went Out and they were saved except the two above. I would willingly conceal the shame of some of our Militia on that Occasion, who departed from the Dignity of Men, in Rude behavior to the Enemy 'til they provoked them to come on shore and then in runing away from them. Our third Regiment and a Minute Batallion under your Charles Lewis gone to Potowmack to Watch their Motions, will I doubt not treat them in a different manner if they land in their way. They are retired to their Nest down the River. I forgot to mention that there is a Report of the Creeks and Cherokee Indians having jointly Attacked and killed 30 or 40 of Our people, but in which Countrey I am not told, nor is the Account well authenticated. It is said however that Our freinds had pursued and killed 10 of them, and that one or two on Examination had proved to be white men Painted. The Governor has been Ill ever since his appointment, is on the recovery, and was I hear on Saturday last to go to Hanover to perfect his health. Did you ever transmit me the cost of the Wire you were so kind as to buy for me, if you did, I either did not receive or Mislaid it. Pray let me know the sum in your next, that I may remit it by Mr. Wythe. I am in daily anxious expectation of some important Intelligence from New York, where I think a great Battle must soon be fought. Don't delay, My Dr. Sr., to give me the most early Account of it. I am Yr. Affecte. Friend,

EDMD. PENDLETON

Pray direct my Letters "to be taken out of the Mail at Fredricksburg and given to the New-Castle rider."

RC (DLC). Tr (PPAP).

From Adam Stephen

SIR   Wmburg 29h July 1776

The Commencement of hostilities by the Cherokees, is the only News of general Importance on this Quarter. I hope they will be proceeded against with the Same Rapidity we made use of on the Shawnese Expedition. Then it is probable we may make such an impression upon them as will Strike terror into the most distant Indian Nations. Unsupported by the Country in general, and not assisted by any but those concernd in the Expedition, we Rais'd men, armd, Victual'd and provided them with things absolutly necessary; marchd in to the Enemys Country, about 500 miles distant; and finishd the Expedition in three months: Now the Cherokees are near to the Carolinas; and not so distant from Us as the Shawanese. This is a fine Season for destroying their Corn. General Lee is very easy in his department. The Army of the Enemy grow very discontented, and I am sure will soon become Sickly. It is with dread, and dispondency that I look towards New York. I wish all the Virginia Troops were with Genl. Washington, to give him One Weeks Work and help out the dead lift. I heartily Sympathize with him: there is great difference between a Number of Men, and Soldiers; I hope the Genl. will cripple them so that they cannot penetrate far into our Country; suppose the Issue is not so favourable as we could wish at New York.

The people of that disaffected town should have had twenty Row Galleys, or floating Batteries, lying in the Narrows to Assist the Batteries, and then None of the Enemys ships could have got through with Impunity. Col. Moutrie with his 15 twenty Six pounders did perform Wonders. Such havock has not been before heard of aboard a Ship.

I have got Carriages made for Ten Cannon, from 12 to 24 pounders and have got them Mounted at Portsmouth and windmill point to clear that Harbour.

Norfolk might have been easily Savd. We feel the loss of it daily. Such of the Inhabitants as were our friends would have Expedited our Armd Vessels, fitted our Privateers, and facilitated all our Naval affairs. It was a Magazine of Naval Stores. Lord Dunmores fleet went up Potowmack untill they found the Water fresh enough to drink. Irritated by Some Blackguards of the Stafford Militia, they landed at the House of Mr. William Brent, Situated on Potowmack about ten Miles below Dunfries. The Poltroons, the Militia of Stafford, run, and the Enemy Set fire to the house. They were on their way to burn a fine Mercht. Mill at a Small distance, but 30 of the P. William militia happily arrivd, advancd with good Countenance, and drove him on board.

After this, they went to look for the Runaways, and making briskly up to them, the Stafford men Squatted in thickets, imagind it to be English men, and run them selves almost to death, to avoid falling into the hands of the P. William Militia. Pudet hoc Opprobrium Nobis. I am with Respect Sir Your most Obt hule Sert,

ADAM STEPHEN

P.S. Govr. Henry is in a very low Way, gone to Hanover for his health.

RC (DLC).   DEAD LIFT: "A position or juncture in which one can do no more, an extremity" (OED).

To John Page

DEAR PAGE   Philadelphia, July 30. 1776.

On receipt of your letter we enquired into the probability of getting your seal done here. We find a drawer and an engraver here both of whom we have reason to believe are excellent in their way. They did great seals for Jamaica and Barbadoes both of which are said to have been well done, and a seal for the Philosophical society here which we are told is excellent. But they are expensive, and will require two months to complete it. The drawing the figures for the engraver will cost about 50 dollars, and the engraving will be still more. Nevertheless as it would be long before we could consult you and receive an answer, as we think you have no such hands, and the expence is never to be incurred a second time we shall order it to be done. I like the device of the first side of the seal much. The second I think is too much crouded, nor is the design so striking. But for god's sake what is the 'Deus nobis haec *otia* fecit.' It puzzles every body here; if my country really enjoys that *otium*, it is singular, as every other colony seems to be hard struggling. I think it was agreed on before Dunmore's flight from Gwyn's island so that it can hardly be referred to the temporary *holiday* that has given you. This device is too aenigmatical, since if it puzzles now, it will be absolutely insoluble fifty years hence.

I would not advise that the French gentlemen should come here. We have so many of that country, and have been so much imposed on, that the Congress begins to be sore on that head. Besides there is no prospect of raising horse this way. But if you approve of the Chevalier de St. Aubin, why not appoint him yourselves, as your troops of horse are Colonial not Continental?

The 8th battalion will no doubt be taken into Continental pay from the date you mention. So also will be the two written for lately to come to the Jersies. The 7th. should have been moved in Congress long e'er now, but the muster roll sent us by Mr. Yates was so miserably defective that it would not have been received, and would have exposed him. We therefore desired him to send one more full, still giving it the same date, and I inclosed him a proper form. If he is diligent we may receive it by next post.

The answer to your public letter we have addressed to the governor.

There is nothing new here. Washington's and Mercer's camps recruit with amazing slowness. Had they been reinforced more readily something might have been attempted on Staten island. The enemy there are not more than 8, or 10,000 strong. Ld. Howe has recd. none of his fleet, unless some Highlanders (about 8, or 10 vessels) were of it. Our army at Tyonderoga is getting out of the small pox. We have about 150. carpenters I suppose got there by now. I hope they will out-build the enemy, so as to keep our force on the lake superior to theirs. There is a mystery in the dereliction of Crown-point. The general officers were unanimous in preferring Tyonderoga, and the Feild officers against it. The latter have assigned reasons in their remonstrance which appear unanswerable, yet every one acquainted with the ground pronounce the measure right without answering these reasons.

Having declined serving here the next year, I shall be with you at the first session of our assembly. I purpose to leave this place the 11th. of August, having so advised Mrs. Jefferson by last post, and every letter brings me such an account of the state of her health, that it is with great pain I can stay here till then. But Braxton purposing to leave us the day after tomorrow, the colony would be unrepresented were I to go. Before the 11th. I hope to see Colo. Lee and Mr. Wythe here, tho' the stay of the latter will I hope be short, as he must not be spared from the important department of the law. Adieu, Adieu.

RC (James Parker Smith, Springfield, Mass., 1950). Unsigned. Addressed: "To The honorable John Page esq. Williamsburgh. free Th: Jefferson." Endorsed: "Philada. July 30th. 1776." This letter, which has been printed from the MS only once before, and then in a somewhat unsatisfactory text (*New England Historical and Genealogical Register*, XX [1866], 68-9), was thereafter lost from sight until the present volume was in page proof, when it was located for the editors through the good offices of Miss Alice K. Moore of the Connecticut Valley Historical Museum, Springfield, Mass. YOUR SEAL: See Page to TJ, 20 July.

The history of Virginia seals has been treated at length, with adequate illustrations, by Edward S. Evans in "The Seals of Virginia," published as part of the Virginia State Library *Report* for 1909-1910. THE DRAWER engaged by TJ was Pierre Eugène DuSimitière, a Swiss artist and antiquary living in Philadelphia, on whom see DAB and also a charming account by John Adams in a letter to Mrs. Adams of 14 Aug. 1776 (*Familiar Letters*, p. 210-11). He drew several state seals at this time, and one of his notebooks for 1774-1783, in DLC, contains the following entry, overlooked by Evans:

"August [1776] a drawing in Indian ink for the great Seal of the State of Virginia in two sides of 4½ inches diameter. See Ev. Post July 18." The *Penna. Evening Post* of 18 July 1776 gives a description of the seal as proposed by the Convention.

Furthermore, TJ's Account with the Convention and Commonwealth of Virginia as delegate to Congress in 1776 (Vi) enters two payments of $16 each to Du Simitière for this work, under 9 and 28 Aug. 1776. What happened afterwards is not clear. George Wythe supervised the work in Philadelphia after TJ left Congress (see Wythe's letter to TJ, 18 Nov. 1776), but negotiations to have a seal cut in Europe were carried on for several years thereafter (Evans, p. 35ff.). See also, below, Du Simitière's Design for a Coat of Arms for Virginia, Aug. 1776. The motto objected to by TJ was altered in 1779 to the single word "Perseverando" (Evans, p. 37). THE ANSWER TO YOUR PUBLIC LETTER: Neither letter nor answer has been found.

From Edmund Pendleton

DEAR SIR   Virginia Augt. 3d. 1776.

I have [been] beating my brain about your old Opinion that our Land tenure should be merely Allodial, and a New Opinion frequently mentioned during the last convention, that the unappropriated Lands should all be sold for the benefit of the commonwealth; and it was thrown out, that Congress had some thoughts of taking up this business as a Continental Fund. As to this Last I hope No such Idea has been entertained, Since if the disposition of our Lands be not Local, there can be nothing so, and the reservation to each Colony in the Terms of the Union, of the Sole Power of regulating their internal concerns, will have no force. As to the Sale of the lands, it might have convenience in it respecting our Present Finances, but I fear is against sound Policy. The Charter on which the Colony was founded, intitled every Britain coming to settle to 50 acres of Land, to be held in Soccage by the Payment of an Annual quitrent. This was enlarged afterwards and grants were to be made for 5/ Sterl. in money, and the Laws entitled every man as Far as 400 acres, to gain a title by entry of any Vacant Land with the Surveyor And this has been the Practice for a long term, without complaint; when the Ministry proposed a Sale, we were justly alarmd at the Innovation, and tho' the appropriation of the money now f[or] Public use, would so far mend the Case, yet it appears to me two grand objections would yet remain to such a measure. First we should alter the terms of Our Original Institution in this point and have our people holding Lands on different terms, and Secondly you would throw all the unappropriated Lands into the hands of men of property, in exclusion of the poor, who would not be able to bid against the others, tho' they might raise money to pay the rights for a sufficient quantity to answer their purposes. These reasons I think also operate against your allodial scheme, since at the same time that I would not have the New settlers in a worse condition than the old, It will be the source of murmuring and Injustice, to place them in a better, as they must be, unless you release the old from the payment of Quitrents they have been long accustomed to, against which I think there are Objections of great weight. To hold of the common wealth by the Payment of a certain sum, cannot interfere with the dignity of Freemen, nor can it be thought discouraging to fix the sum at the accustomed one. It upon the whole therefore appears to me best to continue the old mode, transferring rights, former and future quitrents and Escheats to the Common Wealth from the Crown, only confining the grants to small quantities to give the Poor a chance with the Rich of getting some Lands. Pray let me have Your thoughts on this Subject, if [you have] any Liesure from more immediately interesting Objects, for perhaps whilst you are reading this, nay indeed while I am writing, it may be deciding by the sword at New York, whether we shall have any Lands left to dispose of. The event of things there we wait for with anxious expectation. We have a report that Ld. Dunmore's Crew from hence and Clinton's from Charles Town, are gone there, perhaps the papers may inform You, as also that we have had an Engagement with the Cherokees in Fincastle, and worsted them. 15 of their dead came to hand, by the plentiful signs of blood discover'd in the Place they retreated from, it is supposed many more were killed and wounded, whilst our party lost not One, and had only three or 4 slightly wounded. Our party is to be reinforced, and I hope will protect that Countrey from these Savages and their more brutal setters on. My Complts. to Colo. Nelson & all enquiring Acquaintanc[e.] I am Dr. Sr. Yr. Affecte. Friend,   EDMD. PENDLETON

RC (DLC).

For the quit-rent system in colonial Virginia, which Pendleton wished to retain by transferring the crown rights to the state, see B. W. Bond, Jr., *The Quit-* *Rent System in the American Colonies,* New Haven and London, 1919, ch. VIII. See further TJ to Pendleton, 13 Aug., and Pendleton to TJ, 26 Aug. 1776.

To John Page

DEAR PAGE   Philadelphia Aug. 5. 1776.

I am sorry to hear that the Indians have commenced war, but greatly pleased you have been so decisive on that head. Nothing will reduce those wretches so soon as pushing the war into the heart of their country. But I would not stop there. I would never cease pursuing them while one of them remained on this side the Misisippi. So unprovoked an attack and so treacherous a one should never be forgiven while one of them remains near enough to do us injury. The Congress having had reason to suspect the Six nations intended war, instructed their commissioners to declare to them peremptorily that if they chose to go to war with us, they should be at liberty to remove their families out of our settlements, but to remember that they should not only never more return to their dwellings on any terms but that we would never cease pursuing them with war while one remained on the face of the earth: and moreover, to avoid equivocation, to let them know they must recall their young men from Canada, or we should consider them as acting against us nationally. This decisive declaration produced an equally decisive act on their part: they have recalled their young men, and are stirring themselves with anxiety to keep their people in quiet, so that the storm we apprehended to be brewing there it is hoped is blown over. Colo. Lee being unable to attend here till the 20'th inst. I am under the painful necessity of putting off my departure, notwithstanding the unfavorable situation of Mrs. Jefferson's health. We have had hopes till to day of receiving an authentication of the next year's delegation, but are disappointed. I know not who should have sent it, the Governor, or President of Convention: but certainly some body should have done it. What will be the consequence I know not. We cannot be admitted to take our seat on any precedent or the spirit of any precedent yet set. According to the standing rules not only an authentic copy will be required, but it must be entered in the journals verbatim that it may there appear we have right to sit. This seems the more necessary as the quorum is then to be reduced. Some of the newspapers indeed mention that on such a day such and such gentlemen were appointed to serve for the next year, but could newspaper evidence be received, they would not furnish the form of the appointment, nor yet what quorum is to be admitted. Ld. Howe is recruiting fast. Forty odd ships arrived the other day, and others at other times. It is questionable whether our recruits come in so speedily as his. Several valuable West Indian men have been taken and brought in lately, and the spirit of privateering is gaining ground fast. No news from Tionderoga. I inclose you (to amuse your curiosity) the form of the prayer substituted in the room of the prayer for the king by Mr. Duché chaplain to the Congress. I think by making it so general as to take in Conventions, assemblies &c. it might be used instead of that for the parliament. Adieu.

RC (George A. Ball, Muncie, Ind., 1944). Unsigned. Addressed and franked: "To The honorable John Page esq. President of the council of Virginia. free Th: Jefferson." Enclosure missing.

SIX NATIONS: Congress' instructions to the Commissioners do not appear fully in the Journals, but see the resolutions of 14 June (JCC, V, 442) and the correspondence of Gen. Schuyler with Congress as listed in Burnett, *Letters of Members*, II, No. 60, note 2. AUTHENTICATION OF NEXT YEAR'S DELEGATION: Though the terms of the Virginia delegates expired on 11 Aug., the credentials of the new delegation were not presented until 28 Aug. 1776 (JCC, V, 712). Rev. Jacob DUCHE, of Christ Church, Philadelphia, had been appointed chaplain to Congress on 9 July (same, p. 530); his new FORM OF . . . PRAYER is printed in U. of Va., *Chameleon*, I (1831), 21.

To Francis Eppes

DEAR SIR   Philadelphia, Aug. 9th, 1776.

As Col. Harrison was about to have some things packed, I set out upon the execution of your glass commission, and was surprised to find that the whole glass stores of the city could not make out anything like what you desired. I therefore did what I thought would be best, imagining you wanted the number you mentioned at any event, and that not being able to get them of that form, you would take them of any other. I therefore got 4 pint cans, 10s.; 2 quart do. 8s.; and 6 half-pint tumblers, 6s., all of double flint. So that there still remains in my hands £4 16s., Pennsylva. currency.

Your heckle is not yet come. It seems the man who had promised to sell it to the gentleman I employed to get it, now raises some difficulties either to get off others which he calls the set, or to enhance the price. However, the gentleman still expects it, and I am after him every day for it. Our galleys at New York have had a smart engagement with the men-of-war which went up the river; it is believed the enemy suffered a good deal. The galleys are much injured, though we lost but two men. The commander writes us word he retired, that he might go and give them another drubbing, which in plain English meant, I suppose, that he was obliged to retire. Gen. Washington commends the behavior of the men much. They lay pretty close to the enemy, and two of the galleys were exposed to the broadside of their ships almost the whole time. The damage done them proves they were in a warm situation. Madison (of the college) and one Johnson, of Augusta, were coming passengers in the New York packet; they were attacked by one of our armed vessels, and nothing but the intervention of night prevented the packet being taken. She is arrived at New York, and they permitted to come home. In a letter by them, we have intelligence that the French ministry is changed, the pacific men turned out, and those who are for war, with the Duke de Choiseul at their head, are taken in. We have also the king's speech on the prorogation of parliament, declaring he will see it out with us to the bitter end.

The South Carolina army with Clinton Sr., arrived at Staten Island last week, one of their transports, with 5 companies of Highlanders, having first fallen into General Lee's hands. They now make Lord Howe 12,000 strong. With this force he is preparing to attack. He is embarking his cannon; has launched 8 galleys, and formed his men-of-war into line of battle. From these circumstances, it is believed the attack of New York will be within three or four days. They expect with the utmost confidence to carry it, as they consider our army but as a rude undisciplined rabble. I hope they will find it a Bunker's Hill rabble. Notwithstanding these appearances of attack, there are some who believe, and with appearance of reason, that these measures are taken by the enemy to secure themselves and not to attack us. A little time will shew. General Arnold (a fine sailor) has undertaken to command our fleet on the lakes. The enemy are fortifying Oswego, and I believe our army there, when recovered from their sickness, will find they have lost a good campaign, though they have had no battle of moment.

My love to Mrs. Eppes. I hope my letter by last post got there time enough to stay Patty with her awhile longer. Adieu.

TH. JEFFERSON

MS not located. Text from Randall, *Life*, III, 584, where no source is given. Addressed: "Francis Eppes, Esq., At the Forest, By favor of Col. Harrison."

HECKLE: Randall gives this as "teckle," an impossible form. TJ's Account Book has the following entry under 25 Aug. 1776: "Charge F. Eppes a heckle bot of Bringhurst for which I am charged in acct. £9. two boxes for do. 5/." See OED under "hackle." MY LETTER BY LAST POST: Probably missing, since TJ's last known letter to Eppes was dated 23 July 1776.

From Edmund Pendleton

MY DEAR SIR   Caroline Augt. 10. 1776.

Your Esteemed Favor of July 29th. I received with Dr. Price's Judicious Pamphlet which I had before received from my friend Braxton and read with great pleasure, and tho' late, I beleive it will produce benefit to the cause in removing by his clear and explicit reasoning, all scruples which may remain in the minds of Our people. I am also obliged by your Original Declaration of Independance, which I find your brethren have treated as they did your Manifesto last Summer, altered it much for the worse; their hopes of a Reconciliation might restrain them from plain truths then, but what could cramp them now? I am extreamly concerned to hear your disagreable situation is rendered more so, but the indisposition of Mrs. Jefferson; May heaven restore her health and grant you a joyful meeting. I am not able to answer your reasons for not engaging in the Judiciary, not having adopted that kind "That another shall be compelled to serve in an Office that I must be excused from." However I can but lament that it is not agreable and convenient to you, for I do not Assent to your being unqualified, tho' I readily do to your usefulness in the Representative body, where having the Pleasure of Mrs. Jefferson's Company, I hope you'l get cured of your wish to retire so early in life from the memory of man, and exercise Your talents for the nurture of Our new Constitution, which will require all the Attention of it's friends to prune exuberances and Cherish the Plant. I agree our Senate is not on the independant footing I wished, tho' perhaps we should differ as to the proper change. To the mode of Election I should have no Objection, if they were more permanent afterwards, for tho' an advantage is given to the larger Counties in the district, yet it arises from a Superiority of numbers only, and does not seem objectionable. If I remember well, you proposed their Election by the House of Representatives, making them the mere creatures of that body and of course wholly unfit to correct their Errors or Allay casual heats which will at times arise in all large bodies; my principal fear now is that the Delegates will have too much influence in the Senate Elections, as I wish them to be totally independant of each other and to say the truth of the people too, after Election, I mean the Senate holding their Offices for life, unless impeached, and to have been chosen out of the people of great property to secure their Attachment, and to have kept them at the same time pure by not allowing them the Appointment of, or capacity to be appointed to any Lucrative Offices; but this seemed so disagreable to the temper of the times I never mentioned it, and hope the mode Adopted will answer better. Two things become necessary to be considered in fixing the Representation, the right of Suffrage and equality of Representation. In the first I believe we differ, as I think it should be confined to those of fixed Permanent property, who cannot suddenly remove without injury to that property or Substituting another proprietor, and whom alone I consider as having Political Attachment. The persons who when they have produced burthens on the State, may move away and leave them to be born by others, I can by no means think should have the framing of Laws, but may stay, enjoying their benefits and submitting to their Obligations as a kind of Sojourners, so long as they like them and then remove, or may at a very easy rate purchase a right of Suffrage by realizing a very small portion of their property; this however has no relation to Townships being considerable enough for Representation, where residence, apprenticeships or freedom of Companies may justly give a right of voting. As to the equality of Representation, it is an important point and it can't be right for small Counties to have equal weight with large, or 100 to be represented equally with 1000, no more than it is so, that the lower Counties on Delaware, Rhode Island &c. should be on a footing with Virginia in this respect in Congress; but this is a point which admits of alteration, without violating our plan of Government. I don't know how far you may extend your reformation as to Our Criminal System of Laws. That it has hitherto been too Sanguinary, punishing too many crimes with death, I confess, and could wish to se that changed for some other mode of Punishment in most cases, but if you mean to relax all Punishments and rely on Virtue and the Public good as Sufficient to promote Obedience to the Laws, You must find a new race of Men to be the Subjects of it, but this I dare say was not your meaning, however I have heard it insisted on by others.

I suppose I wrote some sad blunder in my Observations about the Pensylvania line, which you laugh at in your Queries. To say the truth they were put into my hands, they appeared to me to be right and I communicated them. However, Ignorant as I realy am in Astronomy and Geography, I surely could never suppose a Degree Was to begin where it should end; but don't let us be amused with foreign Questions from attending to the real merits of the question. May not the 40th. degree begin at the end of the 41st. degree if you are journying towards the Equator as well as at the end of the 39th. if going from it? For Instance if a tra[ct] of Countrey beyond the 40th. was discribed to come to or be bounded by that degree, must not you stop as soon as you are thro' the 41st. or meet that degree (the 40th.)? In this point of View then as the Southern boundary of Pensylvania is "by the 40th. degree," must not they stop when they come to it, or must they take in the belt, and be bounded not by that Degree, but by the 39th? If I was bound to go *to* Phila. must I go *through* the City to accomplish my work, or would it not end when I reach'd it's nearest side. So a tract of Countrey to the North bounded by the Equator, would go to that line, but bounded by the first degree, would stop 60 miles short of it. Hence you discover that I make Pensylvania and not the Equator the Object to reckon from when the bounds of that are to be limited, but I confess I am wading out of my depth and probably giving you more food for Mirth. However I believe you know I hazard my thoughts as they Occur, for the sake of discovering truth tho' often to the disadvantage of my Fame, in betraying my Ignorance. I am glad to hear the new Convention are so well disposed, and hope the matter may be amicably settled some way. I am concerned to find two of Our Regiments are ordered to the Northward at this late Season. I fear their March will occasion sickness in this hot season, that they will arrive too late to be useful and be absent the time wanted here. However if they prove useful there, I shall not regret their departure. I hear Ld. Dunmore and his Fleet are now in Hampton road, waiting I suppose a favourable Opportunity of striking at some prey. I hear nothing of the Indian War since the Accounts in the last Paper. Farewell, I am Yr. Affecte.

EDMD. PENDLETON

RC (DLC). Tr (PPAP).

TJ'S FAVOR OF JULY 29TH to Pendleton giving his reasons for not wishing a judgeship, and discussing the Virginia Constitution and the Pennsylvania-Virginia boundary question is missing. The copy of the Declaration of Independence that TJ made for Pendleton was probably enclosed in TJ's letter of 29 July. That copy has recently been identified by Dr. Bernard Drell, of the University of Chicago, as the one in MHi (reproduced in Boyd, *Declaration of Independence*, 1945, pl. ix). YOUR MANIFESTO: The Declaration of Causes of Taking Up Arms, 6 July 1775, q.v.

To Edmund Pendleton

DEAR SIR   Philadelphia Aug. 13. 1776.

Yours of Aug. 3. came to hand yesterday. Having had no moment to spare since, I am obliged to sit down to answer it at a Committee table while the Committee is collecting. My thoughts therefore on the subject you propose will be merely extempore. The opinion that our lands were allodial possessions is one which I have very long held, and had in my eye during a pretty considerable part of my law reading which I found alwais strengthened it. It was mentioned in a very hasty production, intended to have been put under a course of severe correction, but produced afterwards to the world in a way with which you are acquainted. This opinion I have thought and still think to prove if ever I should have time to look into books again. But this is only meant with respect to the English law as transplanted here. How far our acts of assembly or acceptance of grants may have converted lands which were allodial into feuds I have never considered. This matter is now become a mere speculative point; and we have it in our power to make it what it ought to be for the public good. It may be considered in two points of view 1st. As bringing a revenue into the public treasury. 2. As a tenure. I have only time to suggest hints on each of these heads. 1. Is it consistent with good policy or free government to establish a perpetual revenue? Is it not against the practice of our wise British ancestors? Have not instances in which we have departed from this in Virginia been constantly condemned by the universal voice of our country? Is it safe to make the governing power when once seated in office, independent in it's revenue? Should we not have in contemplation and prepare for an event (however deprecated) which may happen in the possibility of things; I mean a re-acknolegement of the British tyrant as our king, and previously strip him of every prejudicial possession? Remember how universally the people run into the idea of recalling Charles the 2d. after living many years under a republican government.—As to the second was not the separation of the property from the perpetual use of lands a mere fiction? Is not it's history well known, and the purposes for which it was introduced, to wit, the establishment of a military system of defence? Was it not afterwards made an engine of immense oppression? Is it wanting with us for the purpose of military defence? May not it's other legal effects (such of them at least as are valuable) be performed in other more simple ways? Has it not been the practice of all other nations to hold their lands as their personal estate in absolute dominion? Are we not the better for what we have hitherto abolished of the feudal system? Has not every restitution of the antient Saxon laws had happy effects? Is it not better now that we return at once into that happy system of our ancestors, the wisest and most perfect ever yet devised by the wit of man, as it stood before the 8th century?—The idea of Congress selling out[1] unlocated lands has been sometimes dropped, but we have alwais met the hint with such determined opposition that I believe it will never be proposed. I am against selling the lands at all. The people who will migrate to the Westward whether they form part of the old, or of a new colony will be subject to their proportion of the Continental debt then unpaid. They ought not to be subject to more. They will be a people little able to pay taxes. There is no equity in fixing upon them the whole burthen of this war, or any other proportion than we bear ourselves. By selling the lands to them, you will disgust them, and cause an avulsion of them from the common union. They will settle the lands in spite of every body. I am at the same time clear that they should be appropriated in small quantities. It is said wealthy foreigners will come in great numbers, and they ought to pay for the liberty we shall have provided for them. True, but make them pay in settlers. A foreigner who brings a settler for every 100, or 200 acres of land to be granted him pays a better price than if he had put into the public treasury 5/ or 5£. That settler will be worth to the public 20 times as much every year, as on our old plan he would have paid in one paiment only.—I have thrown these loose thoughts together only in obedience to your letter. There is not an atom of them which would not have occurred to you on a moment's contemplation of the subject. Charge yourself therefore with the trouble of reading two pages of[2] such undigested stuff.

By Saturday's post the General wrote us that Ld. Howe had got (I think 100) flat bottomed boats along side, and 30 of them were then loaded with men; by which it was concluded he was preparing to attack. Yet this is Tuesday and we hear nothing further. The General has by his last return, 17000 some odd men, of whom near 4000 are sick and near 3000 at our posts in Long island &c. So you may say he has but 10000 effective men to defend the works of New York. His works, however are good and his men in spirits, which I hope will be equal to an addition of many thousands. He had called for 2000 men from the flying camp which were then embarking to him and would certainly be with him in time even if the attack was immediate. The enemy have (since Clinton and his army joined them) 15,000 men of whom not many are sick. Every influence of Congress has been exerted in vain to double the General's force. It was impossible to prevail on the people to leave their harvest. That is now in, and great numbers are in motion, but they have no chance to be there in time. Should however any disaster befall us at New York they will form a great army on the spot to stop the progress of the enemy. I think there cannot be less than 6 or 8000 men in this city and between it and the flying camp. Our council complain of our calling away two of the Virginia battalions. But is this reasonable. They have no British enemy, and if human reason is of any use to conjecture future events, they will not have one. Their Indian enemy is not to be opposed by their regular battalions. Other colonies of not more than half their military strength have 20 battalions in the feild. Think of these things and endeavor to reconcile them not only to this, but to yeild greater assistance to the common cause if wanted. I wish every battalion we have was now in New York. We yesterday received dispatches from the Commissioners at Fort Pitt. I have not read them, but a gentleman who has, tells me they are favorable. The Shawanese and Delawares are disposed to peace. I believe it, for this reason. We had by different advices information from the Shawanese that they should strike us, that this was against their will, but that they must do what the Senecas bid them. At that time we knew the Senecas meditated war. We directed a declaration to be made to the six nations in general that if they did not take the most decisive measures for the preservation of neutrality we would never cease waging war with them while one was to be found on the face of the earth. They immediately changed their conduct and I doubt not have given corresponding information to the Shawanese and Delawares. I hope the Cherokees will now be driven beyond the Missisipi and that this in future will be declared to the Indians the invariable consequence of their beginning a war. Our contest with Britain is too serious and too great to permit any possibility of avocation from the Indians. This then is the season for driving them off, and our Southern colonies are happily rid of every other enemy and may exert their whole force in that quarter. I hope to leave this place some time this month. I am Dr. Sir Your affectionate friend,   TH: JEFFERSON

P.S. Mr. Madison of the college and Mr. Johnson of Fredsbgh. are arrived in New York. They say nothing material had happened in England. The French ministry was changed.

RC (MeHi). Endorsed: "Thos. Jefferson Esq. Augt. 13th. 76," in Pendleton's hand; "against Selling the publick lands," in another hand.

A VERY HASTY PRODUCTION: TJ's Draft of Instructions to the Virginia Delegates to the Continental Congress (the *Summary View*), July 1774, above.

1 Probably an error for "our."
2 MS: "of of."

Report on a Seal for the United States, with Related Papers

[20 August 1776]

I. FRANKLIN'S PROPOSAL

Moses[1] standing on the Shore, and extending his Hand over the Sea, thereby causing the same to overwhelm Pharoah who is sitting in an open Chariot, a Crown on his Head and a Sword in his Hand. Rays from a Pillar of Fire in the Clouds, reaching to Moses, to express that he acts by Command of the Deity.

Motto, *Rebellion to Tyrants is Obedience to God.*

MS (DLC); in Franklin's hand. For the motto, derived from "Bradshaw's Epitaph," see Appendix II in this volume on that "Epitaph," which was no doubt Franklin's own composition.

1 "in the Dress of a High Priest" inserted and then deleted.

II. JEFFERSON'S PROPOSAL

Pharaoh sitting in an open chariot, a crown on his head and a sword in his hand passing thro' the divided waters of the Red sea in pursuit of the Israelites: rays from a pillar of fire in the cloud, expressive of the divine presence, and command, reaching to Moses who stands on the shore and, extending his hand over the sea, causes it to overwhelm Pharaoh. Motto. Rebellion to tyrants is obedience to god.

MS (DLC).

As set down in this note by TJ, his scheme apparently derives from Franklin's, but this was not TJ's only proposal, and it is not complete. John Adams, writing Mrs. Adams on 14 Aug., reported that

"Mr. Jefferson proposed the children of Israel in the wilderness, led by a cloud by day and a pillar of fire by night; and on the other side, Hengist and Horsa, the Saxon chiefs from whom we claim the honor of being descended, and whose political principles and form of government we have assumed" (*Familiar Letters*, p. 211).

In TJ's Account Book for 1774, but undoubtedly inserted later, appears this suggestion:

"A proper device (instead of arms) for the American states united would be the Father presenting the bundle of rods to his sons.

"The motto 'Insuperabiles si inseparabiles' an answer given in parl. to the H. of Lds. & Comm. 4 Inst. 35. He cites 4. H. 6. nu. 12. parl. rolls, which as I suppose was the time it happd."

The father-and-son story is from Aesop; the motto is adapted from Sir Edward Coke, *The Fourth Part of the Institutes of the Laws of England*, London, 1681, p. 35.

III. DU SIMITIERE'S PROPOSAL

THE COAT OF ARMS OF THE STATES OF AMERICA

The Shield has Six quarters parti one, coupé two; to the first it bears or, a rose ennamelled Gules and argent, for England; to the Second, argent a thistle proper, for Scotland; to the third vert, a harp or, for Ireland; to the fourth azure, a flower de luce or for France; to the fifth or the Imperial Eagle Sable, for Germany; and to the Sixth or, the belgic Lyon Gules, for Holland. (These being the Six principal nations of Europe from whom the Americans have originated.) This Shield within a border gules entoire of thirteen Escutcheons argent linked together by a chain or, each charg'd with initial letters Sable, as follows.

1st NH. 2d MB. 3d RI. 4th C. 5th NY. 6th NJ. 7th, P. 8th, DC. 9th M. 10th, V. 11th. NC. 12th SC. 13th. G. for each of the thirteen Independent States of America.

Supporters, dexter, the Goddess Liberty in a corslet of armour, (alluding to the present times holding in her right hand the Spear and Cap, resting with her left on an anchor emblem of Hope. Senester an American Soldier, compleatly accoutred in his hunting Shirt and trousers, with his tomahawk, powder horn, pouch &c.

holding with [h]is left hand his rifle gun rested, and the Shield of the States with his right.

Crest. The Eye of Providence in a radiant Triangle [whose] Glory extend[s] over the shield and beyond the Supporters.

Motto. E PLURIBUS UNUM.

Legend. Round the whole atchievement. Seal of the[1] united[2] States of America. MDCCLXXVI.

MS (DLC); in DuSimitière's hand, with a small pencil sketch on a separate slip.

Though the committee adopted and recommended DuSimitière's plan for the obverse of the seal almost *in toto*, none of it remained in the Great Seal as finally approved in 1782 except the MOTTO and CREST (reverse). The suggestion for the motto has been attributed to both TJ and Franklin as well as to DuSimitière; but whoever suggested it, its immediate source was undoubtedly the title-page motto on the British *Gentleman's Magazine*, which was familiar to all literate Americans. The pedigree of the phrase has been traced with great learning by M. E. Deutsch, "E Pluribus Unum," *Classical Journal*, XVIII (1922-1923), 387-407. See also Du Simitière's Design for a Coat of Arms for Virginia, Aug. 1776, below. DuSimitière's sketch is reproduced in this volume.

[1] "thirteen" deleted.
[2] "and independent" deleted.

IV. REPORT OF THE COMMITTEE

The great Seal should on one side have the arms of the United States of America which arms should be as follows. The Shield has six Quarters, parti one, coupe two. The 1st. Or, a Rose enammelled gules and argent for England: the 2d Argent, a Thistle proper, for Scotland: the 3d. Verd, a Harp Or, for Ireland: the 4th. Azure a Flower de Luce Or for France: the 5th. Or the Imperial Eagle Sable for Germany: and the 6th. Or the Belgic Lion Gules for Holland, pointing out the Countries from which the States have been peopled. The Shield within a Border Gules entwind of thirteen Scutcheons Argent linked together by a Chain Or, each charged with initial Letters Sable as follows: 1st. NH. 2d M.B. 3d RI. 4th C. 5th NY. 6th NJ. 7th P. 8th DC. 9 M. 10th V. 11th NC. 12th. SC. 13 G. for each of the thirteen independent States of America.

Supporters, dexter the Goddess Liberty in a corselet of Armour alluding to the present Times, holding in her right Hand the Spear and Cap and with her left supporting the Shield of the States; sinister, the Goddess Justice bearing a Sword in her right hand, and in her left a Balance.

Crest. The Eye of Providence in a radiant Triangle whose Glory extends over the Shield and beyond the Figures.

Motto E PLURIBUS UNUM.

Legend round the whole Atchievement. Seal of the United States of America MDCCLXXVI.

On the other side of the said Great Seal should be the following

Device. Pharoah sitting in an open Chariot a Crown on his head and a Sword in his hand passing through the divided Waters of the Red Sea in Pursuit of the Israelites: Rays from a Pillar of Fire in the Cloud, expressive of the divine Presence and Comman[d] beaming on Moses who stands on the Shore and extending his hand over the Sea causes it to overwhe[lm] Pharoah.

Motto Rebellion to Tyrants is Obedience to God.

MS (DLC: PCC, No. 23); copy in hand of James Lovell made in 1780. Endorsed: "No. 1. Copy of a Report made Aug. 10. 1776." (The endorsement date is clearly the copyist's error for "Aug. 20," since the "Rough Journal" of Congress gives the latter date in Charles Thomson's hand, and the committee could not yet have reported when Adams wrote his letter of 14 Aug. concerning his interview with DuSimitière.) The original Report of 20 Aug. 1776 is missing, but from the presence in the Jefferson Papers of the memoranda from which it was compiled there is every reason to suppose that TJ drafted it for the committee.

On 4 July Congress resolved that Franklin, John Adams, and TJ "be a committee, to bring in a device for a seal of the United States of America" (JCC, V, 517-18). The proposals of two of the members and of the artist whom the committee consulted are given above. John Adams' proposal is in his letter to Mrs. Adams of 14 Aug.:

"I proposed the choice of Hercules, as engraved by Gribelin, in some editions of Lord Shaftesbury's works. The hero resting on his club. Virtue pointing to her rugged mountain on one hand, and persuading him to ascend. Sloth, glancing at her flowery paths of pleasure, wantonly reclining on the ground, displaying the charms of both her eloquence and person, to reduce him into vice. But this is too complicated a group for a seal or medal, and it is not original" (Familiar Letters, p. 211; see also Howard P. Arnold, Historic Side-Lights, N.Y. and London, 1899, p. 184ff.).

The Report was brought in on 20 Aug., read, and tabled (JCC, V, 689-91). On 23 Jan. 1777 it was listed in a report on unfinished business, but not until 25 Mch. 1780 was it brought up again, when it was referred to a new committee (same, VII, 58-9; XVI, 287). James Lovell was on the new committee and made the copy from which the text above is printed. The new committee's report was recommitted in its turn, 17 May 1780, and not until 20 June 1782 was a device finally agreed upon; the Great Seal as we have it was largely the creation of Secretary Charles Thomson and William Barton, a private citizen versed in heraldry (same, XVII, 434; XXII, 338-40; Gaillard Hunt, History of the Seal of the United States, Washington, 1909).

To John Page

DEAR PAGE   Philadelphia Aug. 20. 1776.

We have been in hourly expectation of the great decision at New York but it has not yet happened. About three nights ago an attempt was made to burn the two ships which had gone up the river. One of the two fire-rafts prepared for that purpose grappled the Phenix ten minutes but was cleared away at last. A tender however was burnt. The two ships came down on Sunday evening and passed all our batteries again with impunity. Ld. Dunmore is at Staten isld. His sick he sent to Halifax, his effective men he carried to Staten

isld. and the blacks he shipped off to the West Indies. Two gentlemen who had been taken prisoners by the enemy have made their
escape. They say they are now 20,000 and that another division of
5000 foreigners is still expected. They think Ld. Howe will not attack these 10 days, but that he does not wait for his last division,
being confident of victory without. One of these informants was
captain of a continental vessel going for ammunition. The mate and
crew rose and took the vessel. They fell in with the division of the
Hessians which came with the Hessian general and were brought to.
The general learning from the dethroned captain what had happened, immediately threw the piratical mate into irons and had the
captain to dine with him every day till they got to Halifx where he
delivered him, vessel &c. over to the English.—A gentleman who
lived some time in this city, but since last winter has become a resident of St. Eustatia writes that by a Dutch ship from Amsterdam
they have advice that the states of Holland had refused to renew the
prohibition on the exportation of powder to the colonies, or to cede
to the English the Scotch brigade in their service, or to furnish
them with some men of war asked of them by the British court.
This refusal so piqued the ministry that they had been induced to
take several Dutch ships, amongst which he sais were two which
sailed from that island and were carried to London, another to St.
Kitt's. In consequence of this the Dutch have armed 40 ships of
war and ordered 60 more to be built and are raising 20,000 land
forces. The French governor in chief of their W. Indies has not
only refused to permit a captain of a man of war to make prize of our
vessels in their ports but forbidden them to come within gun shot
of the ports. The enemy's men of war being withdrawn from our
whole coast to N. York gives us now fine opportunities of getting
in powder. We see the effect here already.

Two Canadians who had been captains in our Canadian regiment and who General Gates writes us are known in the army to
be worthy of good credit made their escape from St. John's, and
came over to our army from Tyonderoga; and give the following
intelligence. The enemy did not fortify any place we abandoned.
They had 2000 men at Isle aux noix under Genl. Fraser, 2000 at
St. John's under Carleton and some at Montreal. 250 only had been
left at Quebec. It was reported that 4000 English troops which were
to have been a part of that army had perished at sea which gave
great uneasiness. The fleet brot over timber &c. for 50 boats which
they attempted to transport by land from the mouth of Sorel to St.
John's, but could not for want of carriages which had been de-

stroyed. Carleton therefore employed Canadians to build batteaux at St. John's. He has rendered himself very odious to the Canadians by leving contributions on them in general and confiscating the estates of all those who followed our army or who abscond. Great numbers of the Germans desert daily and are anxiously concealed by the inhabitants. 70 Brunswickers disappeared in one day. Their officers are so much afraid of bush-fighting and ambushes that they will not head any parties to pursue the runaways. The men have the same fears, which prevents them from deserting in so great numbers as is supposed they will when once our fleet shall appear cruising on the lake to receive and protect them. Between the 22d. and 24th. July Carleton and the other generals abandoned all their posts on this side Sorel except St. John's with as great precipitation as our poor sick army had done, carrying with them their artillery and provisions. This was occasioned by the arrival and mysterious manoeuvres of a fleet at Quebec supposed French, hoisting different colours and firing at Tenders sent from the town to enquire who they were. 200 men were left at Isle aux noix to send them intelligence of our operations, who they say will go down the river if we return into Canada. For this event the Canadians are offering up prayers at the shrines of all their saints. Carleton sometime ago hearing that we were returning with a considerable reinforcement was so terrified that he would have retired immediately had not some of his spies come in and informed him of the deplorable situation to which the small pox had reduced our army. They are recovering health and spirits. Genl. Gates writes that he had accounts of the roads being crowded with militia coming to his assistance. 600 from New Hampshire came in while he was writing his letter, being the first. His fleet had sailed from Tyonderoga to Crown point. Their number and force as in the margin.

	GUNS		SWIVELS	MEN
1 Schooner	12, 4 ℔rs.		10	50
1 Sloop	12, 4s		10	50
1 Schooner	4, 4s	4, 2s	10	35
1 do.	2, 4s	6, 2s	8	35
2 Gallies, each	1, 12	2, 9s	8	45
2 do. each	3, 9s		8	45
2 do. not quite rigged				

8 more gallies would be ready to join them in a fortnight when they would proceed down the lake. General Arnold (who is said to be a good sailor) had undertaken the command. We have 200 fine ship carpenters (mostly sent from here) at work. I hope a fleet

will soon be exhibited on that lake such as it never bore. The Indians have absolutely refused Carleton in Canada and Butler at Niagara to have any thing to do in this quarrel, and applaud in the highest terms our wisdom and candour for not requiring them to meddle. Some of the most sensible speeches I ever saw of theirs are on this head, not spoken to us, but behind our backs in the councils of our enemies. From very good intelligence the Indians of the middle department will be quiet. That treaty is put off till October. Were it not that it interferes with our Assembly I would go to it, as I think something important might be done there, which could not be so well planned as by going to the spot and seeing it's geography. We have great fear that the sending an agent from Virginia to enlist Indians will have ill consequences. It breaks in upon the plan pursued here, and destroys that uniformity and consistency of counsels which the Indians have noticed and approved in their speeches. Besides they are a useless, expensive, ungovernable ally. I forgot to observe that a captain Mesnard of Canada had come to Genl. Gates after the two abovementioned and confirmed their account in almost every article. One of the German deserters travelled with him to within 20 miles of our camp, when he was obliged to halt through fatigue. He passed 3 others of them. Baron Woedlke is dead. No great loss from his habit of drinking. The infamous Bedel and Butterfeild were ordered by Congress to be tried for their conduct. They have been tried by a Court martial, condemned and broke with infamy. We inclose to you all the Commissions mentioned in the last letter of the delegates, except Innis's to be forwarded to the Eastern shore immediately, and Weedon's and Marshall's who we are informed are on the road hither. Would to god they were in N. York. We wait your recommendations for the 2 vacant majorities. Pray regard military merit alone. The commissions now sent do not fix the officers to any particular battalion so that the commanding officer will dispose of them. Cannot you make use of any interest with Lee or Lewis to call Innis over to the Western shore. He pants for it, and in my opinion has a right to ask it. Adieu, Adieu.

Davis with the 4000 ℔. of gun powder and 90 stand of arms for Virga. got into Eggharbour. We have sent waggons for the powder to bring it here, and shall wait your further order. We were obliged to open Van Bibber & Harrison's letter to the Council of safety of Virga. in order to take out the bill of lading without which it would not be delivered.

RC (MWA). Unsigned. Addressed and franked: "To the Honble. John Page esq. Williamsburgh free Th: Jefferson." Enclosures missing.

All the information in this letter about the military and naval situation in northern New York and Canada was drawn from Gen. Gates' letter, with enclosures, from Ticonderoga, 5 Aug. 1776, read in Congress on 15 Aug. (JCC, V, 659). TJ made extensive notes on Gates' letter; these are in DLC: TJ Papers, 2: 287; the letter and enclosures are printed in Force, *Archives*, 5th ser., I, 795-800, under date of 6 Aug. VAN BIBBER & HARRISON'S LETTER: A letter of 25 July 1776 from this firm of St. Eustatia merchants who furnished the Americans with military and other supplies; letter and invoice printed in VMHB, XVI (1908), 165-6.

Draft of Resolutions on Lord Drummond's Peace Proposals

[22? August 1776]

Resolved that the articles inclosed by Ld. Drummond to Ld. Howe whereby it is proposed 'that it shall be ascertained by calculation what supply towards the general exigency of the state each separate colony shall furnish, to be encreased or lessened in proportion to the growth or decline of such colony, and to be vested in the king by a perpetual grant, in consideration whereof Great Britain should relinquish only her claim to taxation over these colonies' which the said Ld. Drummond suggests 'the colonies were disposed not many months ago to have made the basis of a reconciliation with Gr. Britain' were the unauthorized, officious and groundless suggestions of a person who seems totally unacquainted with either the reasonings or the facts which have attended this great controversey; since from it's first origin to this day there never was a time when these states intimated a disposition to give away in perpetuum their essential right of judging whether they should give or withold their money, for what purposes they should make the gift, and what should be it's continuance.[1]

Resolved that tho' this Congress, during[2] the dependance of these states on the British crown with unwearied supplications sued for peace and just redress, and tho' they still retain a sincere disposition to peace, yet as his Britannic majesty by an obstinate perseverance in injury and a callous indifference to the sufferings and the complaints of these states, has driven them to the necessity of declaring themselves independent, this Congress bound by the voice of their constituents which coincides with their own Sentiments[3] have no power to enter into conference or to receive any propositions on the subject of peace which do not as a preliminary acknowledge these states to be sovereign and independent: and that whenever this shall have been authoritatively admitted on the part of Great Britain they shall at all times and with that earnestness which the love of peace and justice inspires be ready to enter into conference or treaty for the purpose of stopping the effusion of so much kindred blood.

Resolved that the reproof given by Genl. Washington to Ld. Drummond for breach of his parole, and his refusal to give him a pass thro' these states on so idle an errand and after a conduct so dishonorable, be approved by this house and that it be submitted to the General to take such measures as his prudence will[4] suggest to prevent any evil which may happen to these states by Lord Drummond's further continuing a communication with their enemies.

Dft (DLC). Deletions and substitutions in the text, largely omitted here, are included in the text printed in JCC, V, 767, note.

Thomas, styled Lord Drummond, eldest son of the 7th Earl of Perth, was a resident of New York City at the outbreak of the Revolution; a loyalist volunteer, he was captured and then released on parole (Sir J. B. Paul, *The Scots Peerage*, Edinburgh, 1904-1914, VII, 58; W. M. MacBean, *Biographical Register of St. Andrew's Society of New York*, N.Y., 1922, p. 124). Drummond twice approached Gen. Washington in 1776 with peace plans submitted on his own initiative but with the sanction of the British commanders; see Washington's *Writings*, ed. Ford, III, 419-24, IV, 350, and notes there. On 18 Aug. 1776 Washington transmitted to Congress an exchange of correspondence between himself and Drummond, including the latter's sketch of proposals for conciliation, which will be found in Force, *Archives*, 5th ser., I, 1027. These papers were read on 22 Aug. (JCC, V, 696), and a committee must have been appointed to report on the matter. This does not appear in the Journals because, as Hancock informed Washington on 24 Aug., "The Congress having considered the Matter thoroughly, are of Opinion to decline taking any public or farther Notice of his Lordship, or his Letters; and particularly as you have so fully expressed their Sentiments on the subject in your Letter to him. It was the Consideration of this Point that induced Congress to detain the Express till now" (Burnett, *Letters of Members*, II, No. 91).

TJ, with the aid of Adams, must have prepared the present Resolutions as a public answer to Drummond's scheme between 22 and 24 Aug., but Congress then determined to take no notice of it. See also JCC, V, 710, 766.

[1] The following passage was here deleted: "the reservation of which right has been of such distinguished advantage to rights which the people of Gr. Britain and Ireland have been ever too wise to relinquish."
[2] Two preceding words, illegible, supplied from text in JCC.
[3] Preceding six words interlined in John Adams' hand.
[4] One word, illegible, supplied from text in JCC.

From Robert Carter Nicholas

Sir   Williamsburg 24th. Augt. 1776.

I was pleased with the Receipt of your favour Yesterday, being a little apprehensive that Mr. Walton's Note might have miscarried, as I had heard nothing of it. The Amount will stand charged in my Books as so much remitted to our Delegates, as do all the Bills and Money, which I have sent them at different times. I know nothing of the State of the Accounts with the Committee of Safety and Council, which the Gentlemen, no doubt, had their Reasons for opening with them distinct from my Office; all that I have thought necessary for me to do has been to keep within the proper Line of my own Transactions.

Of the Money, which I have remitted, I am very sensible that a large Proportion has been expended in Articles and for Services for this Country. I have repeatedly desired to have an Account of these, distinct from their Accounts of Wages transmitted to me that I might give their Account credit for the Amount and charge the different Articles to the Country in other proper Accounts, according to the Course of my Books, but have not yet been favour'd with it.

I thank you for your Intelligence; a most important Dye seems to be on the Cast, if it is not already thrown. God grant us an happy Issue. I am, with much Esteem, Sir, Yr mo. obt. Servt.,

Ro. C. Nicholas

RC (DLC). TJ's FAVOR acknowledged by Nicholas must have been written about 13 Aug., but is missing.

To Edmund Pendleton

Dear Sir   Philadelphia. Aug. 26. 1776.

Your's of the 10th. inst. came to hand about three days ago, the post having brought no mail with him the last week. You seem to have misapprehended my proposition for the choice of a Senate. I had two things in view: to get the wisest men chosen, and to make them perfectly independent when chosen. I have ever observed that a choice by the people themselves is not generally distinguished for it's wisdom. This first secretion from them is usually crude and heterogeneous. But give to those so chosen by the people a second choice themselves, and they generally will chuse wise men. For this reason it was that I proposed the representatives (and not the people) should chuse the Senate, and thought I had notwithstanding that made the Senators (when chosen) perfectly independent of their electors. However I should have no objection to the mode of election proposed in the printed plan of your committee, to wit, that the people of each county should chuse twelve electors, who should meet those of the other counties in the same district and chuse a senator. I should prefer this too for another reason, that the upper as well as lower house should have an opportunity of superintending and judging of the situation of the whole state and be not all of one neighborhood as our upper house used to be. So much for the wisdom of the Senate. To make them independent, I had proposed that they should hold their places for nine years, and then go out (one third every three years) and be incapable for ever of being re-elected to that house. My idea was that if they might be re-elected, they would be casting their eyes forward to the period of election (however distant) and be currying favor with the electors, and consequently dependent on them. My reason for fixing them in office for a term of years rather than for life, was that they might have in idea that they were at a certain period to return into the mass of the people and become the governed instead of the governors which might still keep alive that regard to the public good that otherwise they might perhaps be induced by their independance to forget. Yet I could submit, tho' not so willingly to an appointment for life, or to any thing rather than a mere creation by and dependance on the people. I think the present mode of election objectionable because the larger county will be able to send and will always send a man (less fit perhaps) of their own county to the exclusion of a fitter who may chance to live in a smaller county. I wish experience may contradict my fears. That the Senate as well as lower [or shall I speak truth and call it upper] house should hold no office of profit I am clear; but not that they should of necessity possess distinguished property. You have lived longer than I have and perhaps may have formed a different judgment on better grounds; but my observations do not enable me to say I think integrity the characteristic of wealth. In general I beleive the decisions of the people, in a body, will be more honest and more disinterested than those of wealthy men: and I can never doubt an attachment to his country in any man who has his family and peculium in it.—Now as to the representative house which ought to be so constructed as to answer that character truly. I was for extending the right of suffrage (or in other words the rights of a citizen) to all who had a permanent intention of living in the country. Take what circumstances you please as evidence of this, either the having resided a certain time, or having a family, or having property, any or all of them. Whoever intends to live in a country must wish that country well, and has a natural right of assisting in the preservation of it. I think you cannot distinguish between such a person

residing in the country and having no fixed property, and one residing in a township whom you say you would admit to a vote.—The
other point of equal representation I think capital and fundamental.
I am glad you think an alteration may be attempted in that matter.
—The fantastical idea of virtue and the public good being a sufficient security to the state against the commission of crimes, which
you say you have heard insisted on by some, I assure you was never
mine. It is only the sanguinary hue of our penal laws which I meant
to object to. Punishments I know are necessary, and I would provide them, strict and inflexible, but proportioned to the crime.
Death might be inflicted for murther and perhaps for treason if you
would take out of the description of treason all crimes which are
not such in their nature. Rape, buggery &c. punish by castration.
All other crimes by working on high roads, rivers, gallies &c. a
certain time proportioned to the offence. But as this would be no
punishment or change of condition to slaves (me miserum!) let
them be sent to other countries. By these means we should be freed
from the wickedness of the latter, and the former would be living
monuments of public vengeance. Laws thus proportionate and mild
should never be dispensed with. Let mercy be the character of the
law-giver, but let the judge be a mere machine. The mercies of the
law will be dispensed equally and impartially to every description
of men; those of the judge, or of the executive power, will be the
eccentric impulses of whimsical, capricious designing man.—I am
indebted to you for a topic to deny to the Pensylvania claim to a
line 39 complete degrees from the equator. As an advocate I shall
certainly insist on it; but I wish they would compromise by an
extension of Mason & Dixon's line. They do not agree to the temporary line proposed by our assembly.

We have assurance (not newspaper, but Official) that the
French governors of the West Indies have received orders not only
to furnish us with what we want but to protect our ships. They
will convoy our vessels, they say, thro' the line of British cruisers.
What you will see in the papers of Capt. Weeks is indubitably true.
The inhabitants of St. Pierre's went out in boats to see the promised
battle, but the British captain chose not to shew. By our last letters
from N. York the enemy had landed 8000 men on Long island.
On Friday a small party, about 40, of them were out maroding and
had got some cattle in a barn. Some riflemen (with whom was our
Jamieson) attacked them, took away the cattle, they retired as far
as the house of Judge Lifford where were their officer's quarters,
they were beaten thence also, and the house burnt by the riflemen.

It is alwais supposed you know that good execution was done. One officer was killed and left with 9 guineas in his pocket, which shews they were in a hurry; the swords and fusees of three other officers were found, the owners supposed to be killed or wounded and carried away. On Saturday about 2000 of them attempted to march to Bedford. Colo. Hans's [Edward Hand's?] battalion of 300 Pennsylvania riflemen having posted themselves in a cornfeild and a wood to advantage attacked them. The enemy had some of their Jagers with them, who it seems are German riflemen used to the woods. General Sullivan (who commands during the illness of Genl. Green) sent some musquetry to support the riflemen. The enemy gave way and were driven half a mile beyond their former station. Among the dead left on the way, were three Jagers. Genl. Washington had sent over 6 battalions to join Sullivan who had before three thousand, some say and rightly I believe 6000; and had posted 5 battalions more on the water side ready to join Sullivan if the enemy should make that the field of trial, or to return to N. York if wanted there. A general embarkation was certainly begun. 13. transports crouded with men had fallen down to the narrows and others loading. So that we expect every hour to hear of this great affair. Washington by his last return had 23,000 men of whom however 5000 were sick. Since this, Colo. Aylett just returned from there, tells us he has received 16 new England battalions, s[o] that we may certainly hope he has 25,000 effective, which is about the strength of the enemy probably, tho' we have never heard certainly that their last 5000, are come, in which case I should think they have but 20,000. Washington discovers a confidence, which he usually does only on very good grounds. He sais his men are high in spirits. Those ordered to Long island went with the eagerness of young men going to a dance. A few more skirmishes would be an excellent preparative for our people. Provisions on Staten island were become so scarce that a cow sold for t[en?] pounds, a sheep for ten dollars. They were barreling up all the horse flesh they could get. Colo. Lee being not yet come I am still here, and suppose I shall not get away till about this day se'nnight. I shall see you in Williamsburgh the morning of the Assembly. Adieu.   TH: J.

RC (MHi: Washburn Papers). Endorsed: "Thomas Jefferson Esqr. Augt. 26. 1776." In another (later?) hand is added: "prefers a Senate for life to one dependent on the people, of whom he wishes them to be quite independent."

The square brackets around the passage in the first paragraph are in the MS.

For commentary on the constitutional views expressed here, see Editorial Note on the Virginia Constitution, above. THE

PRINTED PLAN OF YOUR COMMITTEE: committee (Virginia Constitution, Docu-
George Mason's Plan as laid before the ment IV).

From Edmund Pendleton

DEAR SIR   Virga. Augt. 26th. 1776.

Having been abroad for some time accompanying Mrs. Pendleton on a Visit to a sick Parent, I find my self Indebted for two of
your favors of the 5th and 13th. As to the Allodial System respecting Our Lands, I confess since former conversations with you on
the Subject and your late hint, I have thought a good deal on the
Subject and still think, that the inconveniencies attending any mode
I can Suggest of giving Individuals a title to unappropriated Lands,
without vesting them in the Community and making grants flow
from the Executive Power, greatly overballance those of granting
them on the old terms, which custom has made easy and familiar,
changing the reservations from the Crown to the Community. For
1st. as to a Perpetual revenue, I do not discover the danger of
establishing a Revenue of that sort, provided the quantum be certainly below the unavoidable expence of Government, and the disposition left to the Representatives of the people annually chosen.
The Complaint against our old revenue was founded on the disposition of it being left to the Governor and Council without Account,
a body who from their Constitution were encouraged by those on
whom their existence depended, if not compelled, to thwart rather
than promote the Interest of this people, in the disposal of the Fund.
If tired of the contest, Our people should recal their former Government, it will become immaterial what regulations we make, as in
that case, they will as in that of Chas. 2d. restore the whole without
any stipulations, and all our doings will be Abbrogated. As to the
Tenure, It was the slavish nature of the Feuds which made them
oppressive to the tenant and inconsistent with Freedom, and the
establishment of a Military force independant of the Legislature,
which proved injurious to the Community, but I confess I am not
able to discover disgrace to the tenant or injury to the Society from
their holding of the commonwealth, upon the terms of paying a
small certain annual sum disposeable for common benefit, by their
own representatives: nor what this will retain of the old Feuds?
I highly esteem the old Saxon Laws in General, but cannot Suppose them wholly unalterable for the better after an experience of
so many Centuries. Perhaps they may be better calculated for a

few, Hardy, virtuous men, than for a great Countrey made Opulent by commerce, and therefore in the growth of such a Countrey, it may be wisdom not to draw the Chords too close or refine too much, but to relax in some matters in order to secure those of greater moment. However I will trouble you no further on this Subject as we can discuss it more fully and freely when we meet in October. I am truly sorry to hear Genl. Washington's Forces were so few when you wrote last, and my anxiety is greatly increased by that circumstance, for the event of an Attack, which I fear from Mr. Maddison's Account, would happen before the Arrival of your tardy Reapers, who will have made a glorious Harvest, if in order to Collect their grain into Barns, they shall have lost that and their Countrey. I wish with you all our Batallions to be there in such a case, but my concern is lest that their late call, should render their arrival too late to be of any Service, and bring on them Putrid fevers, much to be Apprehended from so long and Hot Marches in this sickly season. At the same time, I can't agree with you we are free from the danger of their paying Us a Viset this fall with part of their Army. These things I presume influenced our Council to write against Our Regiments being Ordered, And not An Opinion that those Troops ought to remain idle here, or any disinclination to Assist the Common Cause. However they did not, and I am sure will not attempt to interfere with Orders for the March of them or any others you call for. I have not an Article of News, having no Intelligence from the Indians since the last papers. From what you write me, I hope the Ohio Indians will disappoint the Cherokees in their promised Aid. I hear the people in Augusta, Bott. [Botetourt] and Fincastle have avowed they will not now be restrained by Government (if it should so incline) from exterpating that tribe or driving them beyond the Missisippi. This is the last letter I shall address you, as I fear indeed you may be come away ere you get this. I wish you as pleasant a journey as the season will admit and hope you'l find Mrs. Jefferson recovered, as I had the pleasure of hearing in Goochland she was better. Farewell.

EDMD. PENDLETON

I thank you for your Religious present.

RC (DLC). Endorsed: "Pendleton Edmd. Aug. 26. 1776."

YOUR FAVORS: TJ's letter of 5 Aug.

has not been found. YOUR RELIGIOUS PRESENT: Probably Duché's form of prayer, on which see TJ to Page, 5 Aug. 1776.

Report of a Plan to Invite

Foreign Officers in the British Service to Desert

Aug. 27. 1776.

The Congress proceeding to take into further consideration the expediency of inviting from the service of his Britannic majesty such foreigners as by the compulsive authority of their prince may have been engaged therein and sent hither for the purpose of waging war against these states, and expecting that the enlightened minds of the officers having command in those foreign corps will feel more sensibly the cogency of the principles urged in our resolution of the 14th. instant, principles which being derived from the unalterable laws of god and nature cannot be superseded by any human authority or engagement, and willing to tender to them also, as they had before done to the soldiery of their corps a participation of the blessings of peace, liberty, property and mild government, on their relinquishing the disgraceful office on which they have been sent hither Resolved that they will give to all such of the said foreign officers as shall leave the armies of his Britannic majesty in America and chuse to become citizens of these states, unappropriated lands in the following quantities and proportions to them and their heirs in absolute dominion. To a Colonel 1000 acres, to a Lieutenant Colonel 800 as. to a Major 600 as. to a Captain 400 as. to an Ensign 200 as. to every noncommissioned officer 100 as. and to every other officer [or] person employed in the said foreign corps and whose office or emploiment is here specifically named, lands in the like proportion to their rank or pay in the said corps: and moreover that where any officers shall bring with them a number of the said foreign soldiers, this Congress, besides the lands before promised to the said officers and soldiers, will give to such officers further rewards proportioned to the numbers they shall bring over and suited to the nature of their wants. Provided that such foreign officers or soldiers shall come over from the said service before these offers be recalled, [or within after   ].[1]

Dft (DLC).

On 21 May 1776, on the receipt of copies of the treaties between his Britannic Majesty and the German princelings who had agreed to furnish mercenary troops for service in America, Congress appointed a committee "to extract and publish the treaties; . . . and to prepare an address to the foreign mercenaries who are coming to invade America" (JCC, IV, 369). TJ was a member of this committee, but the Journals do not record any action on its part. (There is, however, in DLC: TJ Papers, 1: 146, a draft address in George Wythe's hand probably drawn up at this time and for this purpose; it is printed in JCC, V, 708, note.) On 9 Aug. Congress appointed

James Wilson, TJ, and Richard Stockton a committee "to devise a plan for encouraging the Hessians, and other foreigners, employed by the King of Great Britain . . . to quit that iniquitous service" (JCC, V, 640). The committee brought in a report, in the form of a stirring appeal to both the humane and selfish instincts of the hired troops, on 14 Aug.; this was spread on the Journals and is printed in JCC, V, 653-5, but since no MS survives, its authorship is not determinable. It was probably written by TJ. Franklin was at this time added to the committee, which was instructed to have the appeal translated into German and distributed within the enemy camp (which was on Staten Island). To facilitate their acceptance, Franklin had some of the printed handbills folded and tobacco placed inside them (Franklin to Thomas McKean, 24 Aug., Burnett, *Letters of Members*, II, No. 90). The good effects of the handbills were noticed in the American camp at Amboy, and an officer wrote from there suggesting that a similar appeal be addressed to the German officers (Col. James Wilson to John Hancock, 22 Aug., Force, *Archives*, 5th

ser., I, 1110). Congress thereupon (26 Aug.) appointed TJ, Franklin, and John Adams a committee to prepare such an appeal. TJ drafted the Report (the present document), which was agreed to by Congress next day (JCC, V, 707-8). In the TJ Papers, 2: 299, is a proposed preamble for this Report, in John Adams' hand, which was rejected; it is printed in JCC, V, 655, note, but there wrongly associated with the resolutions of 14 Aug. Franklin, in a letter to Gen. Gates of the 28th (first printed in Force, *Archives*, 5th ser., I, 1193), sent copies of both kinds of handbill (i.e., for privates and for officers), but extensive search has yielded only a single surviving example of either, namely, a copy of the version intended for officers, now in the German State Archives at Marburg, seat of the former Landgraves of Hesse. A fuller account of this early instance of psychological warfare will appear in the *Library Bulletin* of the American Philosophical Society for 1949, by L. H. Butterfield.

[1] Brackets in MS.

DuSimitière's Design
for a Coat of Arms for Virginia

[August 1776]

COAT OF ARMS FOR VIRGINIA AS DEVISED BY MONSR. DE CIMETIERE OF PHILADELPHIA[1]

Field a cross of St. george gules (as a remnant of the ancient coat of arms [showing] the origin of the Virginians to be English) having in the center a sharp pointed knife in pale blade argent handle or, alluding to the name the indians have given to that State.

In the first quarter argent, a tobacco Plant, fleury proper;

in the Second argent two wheat Sheafs in Saltire, proper;

in the third argent a Stalk of indian corn full ripe, proper;

in the fourth vert four fasces waved argent alluding to the four grat rivers of Virginia.

NB the pieces contained in the four above quarters may very well admit of a different disposition from the above if thought necessary and more emblematical or heraldical.

Supporters Dexter a figure dressed as in the time of Queen Elizabeth representing Sir Walter Rawleigh[2] planting with his right hand the standard of liberty with the words MAGNA CHARTA written on it, with his left supporting the sheild. Senester a Virginian rifle man of the present times compleatly accoutr[ed.]

Crest. the crest of the antient arms of Virginia, the bust of a virgin naked and crowned with an antique crown. alluding to the Queen Elizabeth in whose reign the country was discover'd.

Motto. 'Rebellion to Tyrants is Obedience to God,' or 'Rex est qui regem non habet.'[3]

MS, with pencil sketch on verso (DLC); both in DuSimitière's hand, but with additions in the MS by TJ as recorded in the textual notes below.

The relation of the present proposal to DuSimitière's execution of a seal for Virginia (see letter to Page, 30 July 1776) is not clear. The present design no doubt grew out of the conferences between DuSimitière and the members of the Committee of Congress (of which TJ was one) ordered to bring in a device for the seal of the United States; see the

Report of 20 Aug. 1776, above. The "rifle man" and the motto are common features of the two designs. REBELLION TO TYRANTS: See Appendix II in this volume on "Bradshaw's Epitaph." No evidence has been found to show that this proposed coat of arms was executed; the sketch has been reproduced in this volume.

[1] Caption in TJ's hand.
[2] Remainder of sentence in TJ's hand.
[3] Last paragraph in TJ's hand.

Notes for the Report on the Value of Gold and Silver Coins

[2 September 1776]

In Silver. Given the quantity of Standd [Standard] metal, say As 40 : 37 :: qty. Standd metal: qty. of pure silver, or X by .925.

In Gold. Given the quantity of Standd metal, deduct $\frac{1}{12}$ it leaves the qty. of fine gold.

To make a dollar 6/. silver of that alloy must be 4d $\frac{20}{139}$ the pennyweight. I.e. pure silver must be *4d $\frac{7404}{15429}$ the dwt.

*I.e. 7s-5$\frac{3073}{5143}$d or very nearly 7s-5d-6 ye oz.

By Virga. laws 24 grs standard gold = 22 grs pure gold was worth 60d. Therefore 24 grs pure gold was worth 65d$\frac{5}{11}$. 24 grs standard silver = 22.2 grs pure silver was worth 4d. Therefore 24 grs pure silver was worth 4d$\frac{12}{37}$. Therefore the value of pure gold to pure silver was as 15$\frac{3}{22}$: 1.

The English pound Troy contains 12oz.; each ounce 20 dwt.; each dwt. 24 grains; each grain 20 mites.

The English Standard for gold is 22. carats of fine gold + 2. carats alloy. I.e. $\frac{1}{12}$ alloy of silver and copper in equal parts. for silver coin 11oz. 2.dw fine silver + 18.dw. alloy in the pound. I.e. $\frac{3}{40}$ or .075 alloy of fine copper.

	assay	absolute weight	standard metal	value
		dwt grs	dwt grs	d
The Pillar peice of eight	Stand. dwt.	17 9	17 9	53.87
			mi	
The old ecu of France of 60 sols	Worse 1 in the ℔	17 12	17 10 2	54
	car. gr	dwt gr	dw. gr. mi	s d
The old Louis d'or (Fr. milld pistole)	W. 0 ½	4 8	4 7 8	16 9 3
The new Louis d'or (Fr. Gui)	W. 0 1½ in the ℔	5 5⅖	5 3 18	20 0 6
The old Spanish double dubloon	W. 0 0½	17 8	17 5 12	67 1 4
The old Spanish pistole	W. 0 0½	4 8	4 7 8	16 9 3
The double Moeda of Portugal new coind	W. 0 0¼	6 22	6 21 12	26 10 4
The Moeda of Portugal	W. 0 0¼	3 11	3 10 16	13 5 1

French gold seems to be from Worse $\frac{1}{2}$ gr. to W. $1\frac{1}{2}$ gr. Silver from W. 1 dw. to W. $1\frac{1}{2}$ dw.

Spanish   Gold W. $\frac{1}{2}$ gr.   Silver from Eng. Standd to W. $1\frac{1}{2}$ dw.

Portugal Gold W. $\frac{1}{2}$ gr.   Silver 2. dwt.

car. gr.

Dutch   Gold B. 1 2   Silver from W. 44. dw. to B. $4\frac{1}{2}$ dw.

A pound of standard gold is cut into $44\frac{1}{2}$ peices, one of which is put into every guinea.

A pound of standard silver is cut into 62. peices, one of which is put into every shilling.

A pound of *fine* gold is worth £50-19-5 $\frac{5}{11}$ sterl.

A pound of *standard* gold is worth £46-14-6 = $44\frac{1}{2}$ guineas.

A pound of *fine* silver is worth £3-7 $\frac{1}{37}$.

A pound of *standard* silver is worth £3-2 = 62 shillings but at market is from £3-2 to £3-8 and generally £3-6. *standard* silver to *standard* gold legally as 1:15.072 or nearly as $1:15\frac{1}{14}$. but at market as $1:14\frac{1}{6}$

Table of the weight and value of sundry coins as they pass in the United colonies.

	Standard weight	New England lawful money	New York	New Jersey. Pennsylva. Delaware. Maryland.	Virginia Gold: Silver:: 15:1	North Carolina
	dwt gr.	£ s d	£ s d	£	£ s d	£ s d
lish Guineas	5 6	1 8 0	1 17 0	1 14 0	1 6 3	1 17 0
ich Guineas	5 5	1 8 0	1 16	1 13 6	1 6 0½	1 16 0
lish crown	17 6	6 8	8 9	7 6		8 0
lish shilling		1 4	1 6	1 6	1 3	1 8
nish dollar	17 6	6 0	8 0	7 6	5 9	8 0
annes	18 0	4 16 0	6 8	6 0 0	4 10 0	6 8 0
nish pistoles	4 6	1	1 9 0	1 7 0	1 1 3	1 9 0
ich milled						
istole	4 4	1 2	1 8 0	1 6 6	1 0 10	1 8 0
loons of 4.						
istoles	17	4 8	5 16 0	5 8 0	4 5 0	5 16 0
ich crown	17 6	6 8	8 6	7 6	5 9	8 0
d'or	6 18	1 16	2 6 0	2 3 6	1 13 9	2 8 0
nish						
istereen		gold of Jo. to silver of a dollar as 15⅓:1 gold is $\frac{5}{4}$ dwt.	do. here as 15⅓:1	do. here as 15⅓ 1		do. here as 15⅓:1

	Weight & rate in S. Carla. & Georga.	South Carolina	Georgia.	Continental rates Gold:Silver::46:3 15⅓:1	Nominal value made + or − them at present in Virginia.	England Gold:Silver [ ]:1 or 14.76:1
	dwt grs	£ s d	£ s d	Dollars		
glish Guineas		7 7 0	1 3 0	4⅔	+7d	
nch Guineas		7 7 0	1 3 0	4 5/9	+1⅝d	
glish crown	17 6	1 15 0	5 0	11 1/9		
glish shilling	17 12	0 7 0	1 0	2/9	+⅛ d *	
anish dollar	17 12	1 12 6	5 0	1		
annes	18 0	26 0 0	4 0 0	16	+2	
anish pistoles	4 8	6 0 0	18 0			
nch milled						
istole	4 8	6 0 0	18 0	3½	−8½	
bloons of 4.						
istoles	17 0	24 0 0	3 12 0			
nch crown	17 6	1 15 0	5 0	$\frac{1[1]}{9}$ 6	+9d	
i d'or						
anish						
Pistereen		do. here as 15 65/117:1 i.e. nearly as 15⅝:1.	do. here as 15⅓:1.	accordg. to this in an Engl. Guinea Johannes or Moidore 27grs = 1 Dollar Fr. Guin. 27 18/41 grs = 1 Doll. Span. pist. 28 4/11 = 1 Fr. milld pist. .28 4/7 = 1.		

Fine silver, then is to *fine* gold as 1:15.215 or nearly 1:15$\frac{1}{5}$

In Spain and Portugal silver is to gold by law as one to sixteen; but there being at market a premium of 6 pr. Ct. on paiments in silver, it becomes 1:15$\frac{1}{25}$.

In France Silver is to gold by law as 1:14$\frac{1}{2}$ a guinea is there worth 20s-8d-$\frac{1}{2}$.

In Holland [& Hungary][1] gold is lower than in France, a guinea being worth 20s-7-$\frac{1}{2}$.

In Italy, Germany, Poland, Denmark, Sweden, gold is lower than in Holland, a guinea worth from 20/7 to 20/4.

> On the whole Sr. I. Newt. concludes that 'by the course of trade exchange between nation & nation in all Europe fine silver is to fine gold as 1:14$\frac{4}{5}$ or 15. But averaging Engld. Spain Portugal & France it is as 1:14.685 or 1:14$\frac{3}{4}$.[2]

Consequences. Silver is exported from Spain to all Europe.

> From England to all Europe except Spain. being bot at market @ 5/7$\frac{1}{2}$ per oz. or 67/6 per ℔.
> From all Europe to the East Indies where silver is to gold as 1:10 to 12.

History

Silver was to gold antiently as 1:10

On discovery and working of the Plate mines of silver in S. America it rose to 1:16. Spain & Portugal fixed their legal standard then.

The East India trade by Cape of good Hope being opened, this began to bring in gold and take away silver, which lowered [. . . .]

The discovery of the Brasil gold mines has since affected it still more.

Inconveniencies of raising gold to 15$\frac{1}{13}$ instead of 15.

> Occasion exportation of silver; at a loss of $\frac{1}{45}$ which is about 2$\frac{1}{2}$ per Cent.
> Deprive circulation, of silver, nothing but gold left.

A loss upon all the silver in America of $\frac{1}{45}$th. part or 2$\frac{1}{2}$ pr Cent.

This gain, does not [accrue] to a useful merchant, but to a mere money broker, or money jobber.

N (DLC). Written on several sheets and fragments of paper.

These notes were compiled for TJ's revision of the Report on the Value of Gold and Silver Coins (the following document), q.v. Some portions of the original notes have not been printed here because either illegible or repeated in the Report itself.

[1] Brackets in MS.

[2] The quotation from Newton may end here, but there is no closing quotation mark.

Draft Report on the Value of
Gold and Silver Coins

[2 September 1776]

The Committe to whom was recommitted a report from a Committee appointed to ascertain the value of the several species of gold and silver current in these states and the proportion they and each of them bear and ought to bear to Spanish milled dollars have taken the same into consideration and thereupon come to the following resolutions.

Whereas the holders of bills of credit emitted by authority of Congress will be entitled at certain periods, appointed for redemption thereof to receive out of the Treasury of the United states the amount of the said bills in Spanish milled dollars, or the value thereof in gold and silver; and the value of such dollars is different in proportion as they are more or less worn, and the value of other silver, and of gold coins, and also of bullion, when compared with such dollars, is estimated by different rules and proportions in these states, whereby injustice may happen to individuals, to particular states, or to the whole Union as well in paiments into, as out of the Treasury, which ought to be prevented by the declaring the precise weight and fineness of the said Spanish milled dollar now becoming the Money-Unit or common measure of other coins in these states, and by explaining the principles and establishing the rules by which the said common measure shall be applied to other coins and to bullion in order to estimate their comparative value at the said Treasury.

Resolved that it is the opinion of this Committee that all paiments made into or out of the said Treasury ought in good faith to be estimated by the Spanish milled dollar otherwise called the Pillar peice of eight as it comes from the mint, new and unworn; in which state it's weight is 17 dwt 9 grs Troy weight containing sixteen pennyweight, one grain, fourteen and an half mites of fine silver and one pennyweight seven grains, five and an half mites of fine copper, alloy; but that according to the course of merchandize neither the said alloy nor the expences of coinage should be considered as any addition to the value of the said coin.

Resolved that it is the opinion of this Committee that all silver coins or bullion paid into or out of the said treasury ought to be estimated in such paiment according to the quantity of fine silver they contain.

[515]

Resolved that it is the opinion of this Committee that all gold coins or bullion paid into or out of the said treasury ought to be estimated in such paiment according to the quantity of fine gold they contain, and the proportion which the value of fine gold bears to that of fine silver in those foreign markets at which these states will probably carry on commerce; but as the said proportion is different at those markets, it is further the opinion of this committee that the several proportions at the said markets should be averaged and such averaged proportion be observed at the said treasury.

Resolved that it is the opinion of this Committee, after due enquiry made that the several proportions between the value of equal weights of fine silver and of fine gold, at the said markets is at present, when averaged nearly as one to fourteen and one half, and that this proportion should be observed at the said treasury. But as in long tracts of time the proportional values of gold and silver at market are liable to vary, whenever such variation shall have become sensible, this house ought to make a corresponding change in the rates at their treasury.

Resolved that it is the opinion of this committee, after due enquiry made into the fineness of the coins hereafter mentioned, that taking into consideration the quantity of fine gold or silver they contain, and the proportionel value beforementioned between equal weights of fine gold and fine silver, their values expressed by decimal notation in Dollars and parts of a dollar are as follow.

[*Table (see facing page) appears at this point in Dft*]

Resolved that the said coins when of the weight there stated should be [paid] and received at the said treasury for so many Dollars and parts of a dollar as is [there] expressed, and when of a greater or lesser weight should be paid and receiv[ed] for a proportionably greater or lesser number of dollars and parts of a dollar.

Resolved that all silver coins not specially named in the said table, and all silver bullion paid or received at the said treasury be estimated in dollars and parts of a dollar in proportion to the fine silver they respectively contain; and all gold coins not specially named and gold bullion, be estimated in dollars and parts of a dollar in the compound ratios of the quantity of fine gold they contain, and of the aforementioned proportion between the value of equal weights of fine gold and fine silver and that no allowance be made in either case for the value of the alloy nor for the charges of coinage or workmanship.

Resolved that assays should be made as soon as conveniently may be of the fineness of such other coins not stated in the said table as

REPORT ON COINS 1776

Silver Coins.	Proportion of fine Metal	Weight	Fine Metal	Value in Dollars	Weight equivalent to Dollr.	Value of a dwt. in dollars
	oz. dwt.	dwt grs	dwt grs		dwt grs	
e Pillar peice of ight or Spanish illed dollar	11 2 in the ℔ weight	16 1.725	16 1.725	1.	17 9	.057553
e old Ecu of rance, of 60 sols ournois, or rench crown	11 1	17 12	16 2.75	1.002657	17 18.886	.057294
e English Crown	11 2	19 8.5	17 21.675	1.113941	17 9	.057553
e English hilling	11 2	3 20.9	3 13.935	.222788	17 9	.057553
e English ixpence	11 2	1 22.45	1 18.967	.111394	17 9	.057553
Gold Coins	Carats grs.					
e old Spanish)ouble Doubloon	21 23½	17 8	15 20.972	14.321335	1 5.047	0.826230
e old Spanish Pistole	21 23½	4 8	3 23.243	3.580333	1 5.047	.826230
e Double Moeda of Portugal	21 23¼	6 22	6 7.95	5.712035	1 5.061	.825836
e Moeda of Portugal	21 23¼	3 11	3 3.975	2.856017	1 5.061	.824836
e old Louis d'or of France	21 23½	4 8	3 23.243	3.580333	1 5.047	.826230
e new Louis d'or of France	21 22½	5 5.4	4 18.623	4.308871	1 5.102	.824664
e English Guinea of William III	22 0	5 9.438	4 22.651	4.460301	1 5.020	.827014
e English half Guinea of William III	22 0	2 16.719	2 11.325	2.230150	1 5.020	.827014
e Hungary Ducat	23 2	2 5.666	2 3.616	1.940355	1 3.658	.867736
e Ducat of Holland, coined ad legem imperii of Campen in Holland of the bishop of Bamberg of Branden- burgh of Sweden of Denmark	23 2	2 5.5	2 3.456	1.934329	1 3.658	.867736
of Poland	23 2	2 5	2 2.975	1.916251	1 3.658	.867736
of Transylvania	23 1½	2 4.75	2 2.689	1.905493	1 3.683	.866954
of the Duke of Hanover	23 2	2 5.25	2 3.216	1.925288	1 3.658	.867736
e Double Ducat of the Duke of Hanover	23 2	4 10.5	4 6.432	3.850581	1 3.658	.867736
equins of Venice	23 3½	2 5.75	2 3.837	1.948631	1 3.583	.870086

are in circulation within these states, and that they should be inserted in the said table together with their values in Dollars and parts of a dollar in order to render the same more full and adequate to the purposes of public convenience.

And whereas the credit of the said bills as current money [ought] to be supported at the full value therein expressed by the inhabitants of these states, for whose benefit they [are] issued, and who stand bound to redeem the same according to the like value, and the pernicious artifices of [the] enemies of American liberty to impair the credit of the said bills by raising the nominal value of gold and silver ought to be guarded against and prevented.

Resolved that all bills of credit emitted by authority of Congress ought to pass current in all paiments, trade, and dealings in the states, and be deemed equal in value to gold and silver, according to the preceding rates and resolutions; and that whosoever shall offer, de[man]d or rec[eiv]e more in the said bills for any gold or silver coins or bullion than is before rated, or more of the said bills for any lands, houses, goods, ware[s] or merchandise than the nominal sum at which the same might be purchased of the same person with gold or silver, every such person ought to be deemed an enemy to the liberties of these States,[1] and treated accordingly on conviction before such judicature as have been or shall be authorized to hear and determine such offences by the Convention or assembly of the state wherein the offence shall be committed; but where no such judicature is as yet established, Conviction may be had before the committee of inspection of the city, county or district where the said offence shall be committed with liberty of appeal to the Assembly or Convention of such state, until the said Assembly or Convention shall establish such judicature.

Dft (DLC). MS slightly torn and faded in places.

On 19 Apr. 1776 a committee of seven was appointed "to examine and ascertain the value of the several species of gold and silver coins, current in these colonies, and the proportion they ought to bear to Spanish milled dollars" (JCC, IV, 293-4). The report of this committee, largely compiled by George Wythe, was read on 22 May and tabled (same, p. 381-3, where the text is printed). On 24 July, "On motion, *Resolved*, That the report of the committee on gold and silver coins be recommitted: That Mr. Jefferson be added to the said committee" (same, V, 608). TJ's notes for this revised Report are in part printed as the document immediately preceding. The Report itself was brought in, read, and tabled on 2 Sep., the day he left Congress (same, p. 724-8). George Wythe informed him on 11 Nov. 1776 that the Report lay "in the same state of repose as you left it in"; and it was listed among unfinished business on 23 Jan. 1777 (same, VII, 59). This early Report anticipates TJ's repeatedly important role in establishing the money system of the United States. See his Notes on the Establishment of a Money Unit, Apr. 1784, and his Report as secretary of state on establishing uniformity in the currency, weights, and measures of the United States, 4 July 1790.

[1] This word is substituted in a different hand for "colonies," lined out.

From Giovanni Fabbroni

SIR   Paris the 15th Sept 1776

Tis need less to tell You that the present troubles of America postponed the return of Mr. Mazzei's Vessel to Virginia deprived me also of the pleasure of accepting the him [kind?] offers You were so good as to make me. I was not a Little chagrined to find my self all at once bereft (at Least for some time) of the hopes of Seeng that fine Contry the fertility of wich can be equalled by nothings but the magnenimity of its Inhabitants. I hope You will Let me know the particulars of the present War as far as they may relate to Your welfare wit [which] Your Silence and that of my friends in that Country has made me vastly uneasy about. Yet in so good a cause as that of Liberty, their can be no doubt but event will be cround with success. Mr. De Crenis Capt. of Harses who will hand You this is an officier of Some distinction in the Servise of the croun of France. I beg Leave to recommend him to You as a person of merit whose good qualities receive a new Luster from the particular estim he has for the Country he is going to.

I wraite to You at present from Paris where if I can be of any Service to You I hope You will command me. You may direct Your Letters at Paris at racommendetion of *Mr. L'Abbe Niccoli chargé des affaires de La Cour de Toscane au petit Louxembourg at Paris. Vel* at Bordeaux to the House of Messrs. V & P Frenck where I am well informed many vessels arrive from Your place. And if be Your interest to Load for that Market You may depend on the puntuality of these English Gentlemen. I shal remain here till the Month of April 1778 next whom [when?] I will forther inform you may direct to me. Assuring Mrs. Jefferson of my respect I remain very Sincerely Your most obedient humb[le] Servant,   JOHN FABRONI

RC (DLC). Addressed: "To Mre. Jefferson Esqre At Williamsbourg on the James River In Virginia." Endorsed: "Fabroni John." On the cover are notes by TJ concerning his plan to import plantation workers who were skilled in the use of musical instruments; these are evidently notes for his reply to Fabbroni, 8 June 1778, q.v. (Fabbroni spelled his name "Fabroni" in his earliest letters to TJ, but soon altered it to "Fabbroni," the form followed by his family and in this edition.)

TJ's draft acknowledgment (8 June 1778) of the present letter gives it an ambiguous date: 1776 corrected to 1777, or vice versa. Like TJ, we are also in doubt; but the preponderance of evidence indicates that the date as written by Fabbroni is correct. The delay of twenty-one months in TJ's reply may be explained by the delay in the departure for America of DE CRENIS (i.e., Martial-Jean-Antoine Crozat de Crénis; see Lasseray, *Les français sous les treize étoiles*, under Crozat), to whom the letter was entrusted. He did not arrive until just before 17 Aug. 1777, on which date Gen. Washington acknowledged a letter of introduction by him from Benjamin Franklin, written in Paris, 2 Apr. 1777 (Washington, *Writings*, ed. Fitzpatrick, IX, 85-7). De Crénis did not go to Virginia, as expected, and it was evidently some time before he found the means to transmit Fabbroni's letter to TJ. As for Fabbroni, a young Florentine scholar and friend of Philip Mazzei's, the principal reason for his failure to come to America, as he had long wished to do, was that he had come under the patronage of Leopold, Grand Duke of Tuscany, had been sent to observe scientific progress in France and England, and remained abroad for some years (Georges, Baron Cuvier, *Recueil des éloges historiques . . . de l'Institut Royal de France*, Paris, 1819-27, III, 507-8; Mazzei, *Memoirs*, p. 185-6, 199). The intimate tone of the present letter suggests that one or more earlier letters were exchanged, but these have not been found.

From Francis Lightfoot Lee

DEAR SIR   Philadelphia Sepr. 17. 1776

Our affairs at N. York have not much alter'd since your departure, the Militia of the eastern states have mostly left it, and probably improved the Army. The Enemy having by every motion shewn a design to get above our troops, Genl. Washington is busy in removing his stores from the City, and collecting his forces at and about King's bridge, but we fear he has been interrupted by the Enemy, as a very heavy firing was heard there on sunday last.

Genl. Gates in his last Letter says, there was just then heard a heavy cannonade upon the Lake, from whence he judged, our fleet under the command of Genl. Arnold, was engaged with the Enemy, on their way to Crownpoint. We therefore expect every moment to hear of some considerable Actions at both places. All our advices from the Indians, indicate a general war with them. I hope our people will have done the business of the southern Indians, that they may be ready to chastise those of the west.

The week before last Ld. Howe sent Genl. Sullivan to Congress with a message, that he was very sollicitous for peace, that he had great powers, that tho he cou'd not at present acknowlege the Congress, yet he wished to confer with some of the members, as private Gentlemen. This message made a great noise without doors, and it was fear'd wou'd have a bad effect upon our Military operations. The Congress fully apprized of the perfidy and villainous designs of these Ministerial Agents; yet willing to convince our people that they are not averse to peace; sent him in answer That being the representatives of free and independant States, they cou'd not allow their Members to confer with him in their private capacities; but wou'd send a Committee of their body to know his powers and his terms. The Committee met his Lordship last Wednesday on Staten Island, and had the honor to dine upon plate with him, and a three hour's conversation, the substance of which was: that he had waited 2 months in England to prevail with the Ministry to empower him to *confer* and *converse* with some Gentlemen of influence in America. That he was sure of the good intentions of the King and the Ministry; and if we wou'd return to our allegiance, they wou'd revise the late instructions to Governors and Acts of Parliament; and *if* there was any thing in them which appear'd to *them* unreasonable, he did not doubt, but they wou'd make them easy. That he had no power to suspend the operations of war, or to offer any terms. The tories are struck dumb, but I fear it will have a bad effect upon our foreign negotiations; as it will show too great an eagerness in us, to make up with G. B.

This whole transaction will be soon published by Congress, which the next post will bring you, and I hope the Accounts of our glorious Victories. I am Dear Sir Yr. afft. friend & hbl. Servant,

FRANCIS LIGHTFOOT LEE

During the conversation Ld. Howe said it wou'd make him very uneasy to see America plunder'd and laid waste. Doctr. Franklin assured his Ldship we were taking the most effectual measures to save him that uneasiness.

RC (PHi). Addressed and franked: "To Thomas Jefferson esquire To the care of Mr. Charles Dick Fredericksburg Virginia free F. L. Lee." Endorsed: "Lee, Francis Lightfoot."

THE WHOLE TRANSACTION WILL BE SOON PUBLISHED: The report of the committee (Franklin, Adams, and Edward Rutledge) that conferred with Lord Howe on Staten Island, 11 Sep., was on 17 Sep. ordered printed by Congress (JCC, V, 765-6). It was apparently printed only in the newspapers, not separately.

Resolution of Congress
Appointing Franklin, Deane, and Jefferson as Commissioners to France

In Congress Septr. 26th. 1776.

Agreeably to the Order of the Day, Congress proceeded to the Appointment of Commissioners to the Court of France.

Resolved, That three be appointed. The Ballots being taken Mr. Franklin, Mr. Deane, and Mr. Jefferson were elected.

Resolved, That Secrecy shall be observed, until the farther Order of Congress, and that until Permission be obtained from Congress to disclose the Particulars of this Business, no Member be permitted to say any Thing more upon this Subject, than that Congress have taken such Steps as they judge necessary for the Purpose of obtaining foreign Alliance.

Resolved, That an Express be sent to Mr. Jefferson to inform him of his Appointment, and that a Copy of the Resolve for Secrecy be at the same Time transmitted to him; and that he be requested to inform the President at what Time and Place the Vessel shall meet him.

By order of Congress   JOHN HANCOCK
                                                                              Presidt.

MS (MHi). Text in an unidentified hand; signed by John Hancock. Enclosed in Hancock to TJ, 30 Sep. 1776. See notes on letters from Hancock to TJ, 30 Sep., and TJ to Hancock, 11 Oct. 1776.

From Richard Henry Lee

DEAR SIR   Philadelphia 27th Septr. 1776

I should have written to you before now if I had not been uncertain about finding you at home, as the distance was great, and the meeting of our Assembly approaching. All the material events that have happened since you left us are to be found related pretty faithfully in the public papers, which I suppose are regularly conveyed to you.

The plan of foreign treaty is just finished, and yourself, with Doctor Franklin, and Mr. Deane now in France, are the Trustees to execute this all important business. The great abilities and unshaken virtue, necessary for the execution of what the safety of America does so capitally rest upon, has directed the Congress in their choice; and tho ambition may have no influence in this case, yet that distinguished love for your country that has marked your life, will determine you here. In my judgement, the most emminent services that the greatest of her sons can do America will not more essentially serve her and honor themselves, than a successful negotiation with France. With this country, every thing depends upon it, and if we may form a judgement of what is at a distance, the dispositions of that Court are friendly in a high degree, and want only to be properly acted upon, to be wrought into fixt attachment and essential good. We find ourselves greatly endangered by the Armament at present here, but what will be our situation the next campaign, when the present force shall be increas[ed] by the addition of 20 or 30 thousand Russians with a larg[e] body of British and Irish troops? I fear the power of America will fail in the mighty struggle And the barbarous hand of despotism will extirpate libe[rty] and virtue from this our native land; placing in th[eir] stead slavery, vice, ignorance, and ruin. Already these foes of human kind have opened their Courts of Justice (as they call them) on Long Island, and the first frui[ts] of their tender mercies, are confiscation of estates, and condemnation of Whigs to perpetual imprisonment.

The idea of Congress is, that yourself and Dr. Frank[lin] should go in different Ships. The Doctor, I suppose, will sail from hence, and if it is your pleasure, on[e] of our Armed Vessels will meet you in any River in Virginia that you choose.

I am, with singular esteem, dear Sir, your affectionate friend and obedient Servant,   RICHARD HENRY LEE

RC (DLC).

R. H. Lee was one of a committee of four appointed on 26 Sep. 1776 to draft letters of credence to the three newly elected commissioners and to "report the ways and means of providing for their subsistance" (JCC, V, 827). TJ's letter of credence, if sent, has not been found; the form adopted on 28 Sep. will be found in the same, p. 833. PLAN OF TREATY (i.e., Treaties): This had been adopted on 17 Sep. and is printed in the same, p. 768-78.

From John Hancock

SIR   Philadelphia Septr. 30th. 1776.

The Congress having appointed you to fill a most important and honorable Department, it is with particular Pleasure I congratulate you on the Occasion.

By the enclosed Resolves you will percieve, that Doctor Franklin, Mr. Deane, and yourself, are chosen Commissioners at the Court of France, to negotiate such Business as the Congress shall entrust you with. For this Purpose, Letters of Credence, and Instructions will be delivered to Doctor Franklin, and Duplicates forwarded to you and Mr. Deane. You will therefore, be pleased to acquaint me, by the Return of the Express, who brings you this, at what Time and Place it will be most convenient for you to embark, in Order that a Vessel may be sent to take you on Board. A suitable Vessel, will, in the mean Time, be provided here for the Accommodation of Doctor Franklin, it being judged most prudent, that you should sail in different Ships.

As it is fully in your Power, so I am persuaded it is the favorite Wish of your Heart, to promote the Interest and Happiness of your Country; and that you will, in particular, render her the great Services which she so fondly expects from you on this Occasion. With the warmest Wishes for your Health, and a safe and speedy

Passage, I have the Honour to be, with every Sentiment of Esteem, Sir Your most obed. & very hble Servt.,

JOHN HANCOCK, Presidt.

RC (MHi). Endorsed: "Hancock John, Presdt. of Congress. Philada. Sep. 30. 1776. appmt Commr to France with Doctor Franklin & Deane." Enclosure (TJ's Appointment as a Commissioner to France) printed under 26 Sep. 1776.

This letter and its unexpected and important enclosure reached TJ on 8 Oct.

in Williamsburg, where he was attending the House of Delegates (JHD, Oct. 1776, 1828 edn., p. 3; TJ to Hancock, 11 Oct. 1776). Respecting the LETTERS OF CREDENCE, see note on R. H. Lee's letter to TJ, 27 Oct. 1776. The INSTRUCTIONS to the commissioners are printed below under date of 16 Oct. 1776.

To John Hancock

HONORABLE SIR   Williamsburgh Octob. 11. 1776.

Your favor of the 30th. together with the resolutions of Congress of the 26th. Ult. came safe to hand. It would argue great insensibility in me could I receive with indifference so confidential an appointment from your body. My thanks are a poor return for the partiality they have been pleased to entertain for me. No cares for my own person, nor yet for my private affairs would have induced one moment's hesitation to accept the charge. But circumstances very peculiar in the situation of my family, such as neither permit me to leave nor to carry it, compel me to ask leave to decline a service so honorable and at the same time so important to the American cause. The necessity under which I labor, and the conflict I have undergone for three days, during which I could not determine to dismiss your messenger, will I hope plead my pardon with Congress; and I am sure there are too many of that body, to whom they may with better hopes confide this charge, to leave them under a moment's difficulty in making a new choice. I am, Sir, with the most sincere attachment to your honorable body and the great cause they support, their and your most obedient humble servt.,

TH: JEFFERSON

P.S. The bearer Henry Frick being in want of money has a warrant from Genl. Lewis on the paymaster for six dollars with which he must therefore be charged.

RC (DLC: PCC, No. 78, XIII). Dft (DLC). RC addressed: "To the Honble. John Hancock esq. President of the Congress Philadelphia." Endorsed: "Letter from Thos. Jefferson 11 Octr. 1776. read 16. Octr." The postscript is not in the Dft.

This letter was received by Congress on 16 Oct. (JCC, VI, 879). On the 22d:

"Mr. Jefferson having informed Congress that the state of his family will not permit him to accept the honour of going [as] their Commissioner to France, thereupon, *Resolved*, That another be elected in his room. The ballots being taken, Arthur Lee Esqr was elected" (same, p. 897).

Notes and Proceedings
on Discontinuing the Establishment
of the Church of England

[11 October to 9 December 1776]

I. ROUGH DRAFT OF JEFFERSON'S RESOLUTIONS FOR DISESTABLISH-
ING THE CHURCH OF ENGLAND AND FOR REPEALING LAWS IN-
TERFERING WITH FREEDOM OF WORSHIP

II. DRAFT OF BILL FOR EXEMPTING DISSENTERS FROM CONTRIBUT-
ING TO THE SUPPORT OF THE CHURCH

III. JEFFERSON'S OUTLINE OF ARGUMENT IN SUPPORT OF HIS RESO-
LUTION

IV. LIST OF ACTS OF PARLIAMENT AND OF THE VIRGINIA ASSEMBLY,
1661-1759, CONCERNING RELIGION

V. NOTES ON ACTS OF PARLIAMENT AND OF THE VIRGINIA ASSEMBLY
CONCERNING RELIGION

VI. NOTES ON LOCKE AND SHAFTESBURY

VII. NOTES ON EPISCOPACY

VIII. NOTES ON HERESY

IX. MISCELLANEOUS NOTES ON RELIGION

EDITORIAL NOTE

THE importance of Jefferson's legislative activity in 1776 in behalf of
religious tolerance and the confused state of his own documentary
records of this effort, together with the paucity of the legislative record,
make it necessary to present the documents in a different arrangement
and with a more particular comment than has hitherto been attempted.
All of the documents listed above and printed in the same order below
are intimately connected with each other and with the "desperate contests" in which Jefferson engaged in committee and in the House of
Delegates during October and November of 1776. The first of these,
not published heretofore, is a direct forerunner of Jefferson's famous
Bill for Religious Freedom.

Although the growing numbers of dissenters and their increasing
protests against the established Church of England had caused the
legislature to consider the matter from 1769 on, nothing was done
until 1776 (JHB, 1766-1769, p. 205, 252; 1770-1772, p. 186, 249;
Lingley, *Transition in Virginia*, p. 197). In 1774 a petition of Baptists and other dissenters was presented to the House of Burgesses
objecting to the Bill introduced in the Assembly in 1772 extending
the benefits of the Acts of Toleration to dissenters in Virginia. This
petition was referred to the Committee on Religion, of which Jefferson
was a member for the first time, and that committee was directed to
bring in a bill "for allowing a free Toleration to His Majesty's Prot-

estant Subjects in this Colony, who dissent from the Church of England." No further action was taken at this session, but on 11 Nov. 1774 the Presbytery of Hanover drew up another petition protesting against a mere extension of the Acts of Toleration and asking equal liberty, protection, and immunity, including unlimited freedom of speech on religious subjects (JHB, 1773-1776, p. 189; Thomas C. Johnson, *Virginia Presbyterianism and Religious Liberty in Colonial and Revolutionary Times*, Richmond, 1907, p. 64-70; Henry, *Henry*, I, 309-10; a fragmentary copy of the Hanover petition is in DLC: TJ Papers, 235: 42182-90, together with notes pertaining to it; these were perhaps referred to him as a member of the Committee on Religion in 1776). Up to 1776 it was apparent that the legislature was not unwilling to consider toleration in a limited sense—that is, the retention of an established church and the removal of legal disabilities under which dissenters rested—but the adoption of the famous last clause of the Virginia Declaration of Rights in June 1776 provided the impetus for demands for disestablishment of the Church or, at the least, for full equality of rights for dissenters. That clause had declared: "That religion, or the duty which we owe to our Creator, and the manner of discharging it, can be directed only by reason and conviction, not by force or violence, and therefore all men are equally entitled to the free exercise of religion, according to the dictates of conscience; and that it is the mutual duty of all to practice Christian forbearance, love, and charity, towards each other" (*Conv. Jour.*, May 1776, 1816 edn., *Ordinances*, p. 4).

No doubt as a result of this clause in the Declaration of Rights, the legislature in Oct. 1776 was flooded with petitions from dissenting groups. That of Hanover, referred to the Committee on Religion, 24 Oct. 1776 (MS, Vi), for example, petitioned for freedom "from all the incumbrances which a spirit of Domination, prejudice, or bigotry hath interwoven with most other political systems. This we are the more strongly encouraged to expect, by the *Declaration of Rights*, so universally applauded for that dignity, firmness, and precision with which it delineates, and asserts the privileges of society, and the prerogatives of human nature; and which we embrace as the *Magna Charta* of our Common Wealth, that can never be violated without endangering the grand superstructure it was destined to sustain." There was no argument, the petition declared, "in favour of establishing the Christian Religion, but what can be pleaded with equal propriety for establishing the Tenets of Mahomed by those who believe the Alchoran; or if this be not true, it is at least impossible for the Magistrate to adjudge the right of preference among the various Sects that profess the Christian Faith, without erecting a Chair of Infallibility, which would lead us back to the Church of Rome." More, an established church of the State led not only to ambition, arbitrary practices, and "intriguing, seditious spirit" excited by such an establishment, but it also retarded population and interfered with the "progress of the Arts, Sciences, and Manufactories."

This flood of petitions, represented by a mass of MSS in the Virginia State Library, has never been subjected to adequate analysis. Yet it is apparent that the legislature of 1776 viewed the protests of the dissenters as a matter of primary concern, and there can be no doubt that Jefferson was in full accord with the spirit of the dissenters' demand for full equality in the exercise of religious belief and for the disestablishment of the Church. On 11 Oct. 1776 the legislature appointed nineteen members to a Committee on Religion, headed by Braxton and including Jefferson (JHD, 1776, 1828 edn., p. 7). Of the ensuing struggle within the Committee, Jefferson declared in his Autobiography: "These petitions of the dissenters brought on the severest contests in which I have ever been engaged" (Ford, I, 53).

A measure of the "desperate contests in that committee" can be obtained by a comparison of Jefferson's Draft of Resolutions with those reported on 19 Nov. (see Notes to Document I, below; JHD, 1776, 1828 edn., p. 62-3). The former called for the disestablishment of the Church of England, for the repeal of laws granting special privileges to ministers of that church, and for the abolition of levies for the support of the established church. As to the latter, Jefferson declared in his Autobiography, "our opponents carried in the general resolutions of the commee of Nov. 19. a declaration that religious assemblies ought to be regulated, and that provision ought to be made for continuing the succession of the clergy, and superintending their conduct." Thus the movement toward disestablishment was halted in committee, though by 9 Nov. the contests in the Committee on Religion had become so severe that that Committee was discharged of its responsibility to consider the dissenters' petitions, and the important matter was thrown into the Committee of the Whole on the State of the Country (JHD, 1776, 1828 edn., p. 48). The resolutions reported 19 Nov. were referred to a committee of seventeen, including Jefferson and Madison, with directions to bring in a bill.

The fight continued with renewed intensity. The Bill was reported 30 Nov. It has been noted that Jefferson on the preceding day obtained leave of absence for the remainder of the session (same, p. 75; Whitsett, *Caleb Wallace*, p. 53-5). Just prior to the introduction of the Bill on 30 Nov. the House resolved to discharge the Committee appointed on 19 Nov. "except as to so much of the third resolution as relates to exempting the several dissenters from the established church from contributing to its support, so much of the fifth as saves all arrears of salary to incumbents, and empowers vestries to comply with their contracts, excepting also the sixth resolution"; the Committee at the same time were instructed to "make provision for the poor of the several parishes, to regulate the provision made for the clergy, and to empower the several county courts to appoint some of their members to take lists of tithables" where this had not been done (JHD, 1776, 1828 edn., p. 76). Since the Bill was introduced immediately after this resolution was passed, it is clear that these terms had already been agreed upon in committee and the Bill drawn up accordingly (see notes to Document II). The Bill as reported, therefore, did not include that part of Jefferson's original Resolution calling for the repeal of all acts of Parliament oppressive to dissenters. It was debated on 3 Dec. and amended on the following day. On 4 Dec. Jefferson returned to the House, possibly because of the emasculation of the resolutions of 19 Nov. Because of his return, it has been supposed that he was responsible for the amendment restoring the repeal of acts of Parliament (Whitsett, *Caleb Wallace*, p. 53-5; JHD, 1776, 1828 edn., p. 79, 80, 82). This may be so; but the fact is that this particular one of the resolutions of 19 Nov., incorporating part of Jefferson's phraseology, was submitted as an amendment to the Bill in the handwriting of George Mason (see notes to Document II). Thus it is very likely that the repeal of the oppressive acts of Parliament was due in large measure to the author of the Declaration of Rights. Even Mason, however, did not restore Jefferson's Resolution calling for the repeal of the Virginia Act of 1705, and their combined power was not equal to the task of disestablishing the Church of England.

The Act of 1776 for exempting dissenters from contributing to the support of the Church left as a major issue the unresolved question of a general assessment, and another decade elapsed before Jefferson's famous Bill for Religious Freedom became law.

None of the documents in this series is dated. All except Document II and part of Document IX (see below) are embraced in two sequences of MSS or scraps of MSS in DLC: TJ Papers (2: 322-7, embracing Documents VI-VIII; and 234: 41875-81, embracing Documents I, III-V, and part of IX). Both of these sequences are undoubtedly confused, not in the order in which Jefferson must have arranged them originally, and very probably incomplete. Of the first sequence, embracing Documents VI-VIII, Ford (II, 92) wrote in introducing all parts under the general rubric "Notes on Religion": "These are endorsed by Jefferson: 'scraps early in the revolution.' They were probably materials and notes for his speeches in the House of Delegates on the petitions for the disestablishment of the Episcopal Church. Owing to the rebinding it is practically impossible to say if any order was intended." The endorsement "Scraps early in Revolution" is not in Jefferson's hand; hence it cannot serve as a guide to the task of untangling the notes. The division made here is not offered as definitive, but it is made on the basis of paper, handwriting, and subject matter. Document VI is a numbered sequence of four folio pages, written in a narrow column very similar to the single-column pages of Document III, though the handwriting is less formal; this applies also to the two pages of Document VII. Document VIII is written on a smaller sheet with the lines extending across the page. A cursory comparison of the notes in Documents VI-VIII with the outline of Jefferson's arguments in Document III is sufficient to show the extent of his reliance on these notes.

As for the second sequence, embracing Documents I, III, IV, V, and part of IX, it is equally confused. In the present pagination of the MS (234: 41875-81), Jefferson's endorsement, which normally would appear on the verso of the last page, occurs on the recto of that page, and preceding it are two pages (41878 and verso) which clearly belong to a much later date, probably after 1800, and are not printed here.

The endorsement referred to reads as follows: "Notes & proceedings on discontinuing the Establmt of the Church of Engld" (which is the source of the title given to the present sequence of documents), but in view of the fact that the present arrangement of the MS pages and scraps of pages includes more and less than this endorsement implies, that arrangement has been disregarded and the present one settled upon.

A part of Document IX, drawn from elsewhere in the TJ Papers (pencil notes on the verso of TJ's letter to Wythe, 28 Oct. 1776), is obviously related closely to Document III.

In attempting to clarify this situation and to present the various parts of the documentation concerning the move to disestablish the Church, it is very probable that some violence has been done to chronology. It is almost certain that Jefferson compiled his notes from Locke and Shaftesbury, as he assuredly did the lists of acts of Parliament and of the Virginia Assembly, before drafting the Resolution presented below as Document I. For that Resolution specifically includes some of the listed acts that he regarded as obnoxious. It is also certain that the lists of acts were drawn prior to the making of the outline of arguments in Document III. Nevertheless, since an exact chronology for these documents cannot be established, it has seemed preferable for the sake of clarity to arrange them in some logical grouping: (1) the Resolution as originally drafted and the Bill as introduced, which state the object (Documents I-II); (2) the argument advanced in support of this object (Document III); and (3) the materials on which the argument rests (Documents IV-IX). The notes appended to the documents will relate them to each other in a more detailed manner.

On an issue of this importance, for which Jefferson prepared himself with extraordinary thoroughness and into which he threw all his resources of mind and feeling, it has also seemed preferable to depart from general editorial practices and to present the documents as literally as possible. This is particularly desirable in the case of Jefferson's outline of arguments. He was not a ready debater, yet this outline must be the key to one of his most earnest speeches. Its very brevity emphasizes its passionate conviction, and its argument can be closely followed despite difficulties with occasional abbreviations. The following passage at first glance appears puzzling: "Lt. gent. wh hapn of Relign of sta. mke. ca. of oth yn own wt wd b. yr Sensns if n. Secty civl rts bt Modern. of ti. wd b. uneasy till fxd on legal basis. Rts of Conscce mch. mo. tendr." But the argument is clear: "Let gentlemen who happen [to be] of [the] Religion of [the] state make [a] case of other [religion] than [their] own [i.e., assume that some other religion than theirs is the established one]. What would be their Sensations [in such a case] if [there were] no Security [for] civil rights but [the] Moderation of [the spirit of the] times. [They] would be uneasy till [such were] fixed on [a] legal basis. Rights of Conscience [are] much more tender [even than civil rights]."

I. Rough Draft of Jefferson's Resolutions

for Disestablishing the Church of England and for Repealing Laws Interfering with Freedom of Worship

[Before 19 November 1776]

Resolved &c.[1]

That the statutes 1.E.6.c.1. 5 & 6.E.6.c.1. 1.El.c.2. 23.El.c.1. 28.El.c.6. 35.El.c.1. 1.Jac.1.c.4. 3.Jac.1.c.1. 3.Jac.1.c.4. 3.Jac.1.c.21. and the act of ass. 1705.c.6. & so much of all other acts or ⟨ordinances⟩ statutes as ⟨prescribe punishments for the offence of opinions deemed heretical⟩ render criminal the maintaining any opinions in matters of religion or the exercising any mode of worship whatever or as prescribe punishments for the same ⟨; and all acts or statutes⟩ ⟨acts or ordinances made against⟩ ought to be repealed.

Resolved that it is the opn of this Commee that so much of the sd. petitions as prays that the establishment of the Church of England by law in this Commonwealth may be discontinued, and that no pre-eminence may be allowed to any one Religious sect over another, is reasonable; & therefore that the several laws establishing the sd. Church of England, giving peculiar privileges to ⟨the⟩ it's ministers ⟨thereof⟩, & levying for the support thereof ⟨the same⟩ contributions on the people independent of their good will ought to be repealed; saving to such incumbents as are now actually seised of Glebe lands, their rights to such Glebe lands during their lives, & to such parishes as have received private donations for the ⟨use of⟩ support of the sd. Church ⟨of England⟩ the perpetual benefit of such donations.

Dft (DLC). Endorsed in TJ's hand: "Notes & proceedings on discontinuing the Establmt of the Church of Engld." This Rough Draft of Resolutions in TJ's hand is undated; its verso and part of its recto are covered by lists of acts of Parliament and of the House of Burgesses respecting religion and morality (see Notes on Acts of Parliament, &c., Document v, below).

These Resolutions were undoubtedly drafted prior to 19 Nov., for on that date the House adopted the following: "Resolved, . . . that all and every act or statute, either of the parliament of England or of Great Britain, by what-ever title known or distinguished, which renders criminal the maintaining any opinions in matters of religion, forbearing to repair to church, or the exercising any mode of worship whatsoever, or which prescribes punishments for the same, ought to be declared henceforth of no validity or force within this Commonwealth.

"Resolved, That so much of an act of Assembly made in the 4th year of the reign of queen Anne, intituled An act for the effectual suppression of vice, and restraint and punishment of blasphemous, wicked, and dissolute persons, as inflicts certain additional penalties on any person or persons convicted a second time of any of the offences described in the first clause of the said act, ought to be repealed.

"*Resolved*, That so much of the petitions of the several dissenters from the Church established by law within this Commonwealth, as desires an exemption from all taxes and contributions whatever towards supporting the said church and the ministers thereof, or towards the support of their respective religious societies in any other way than themselves shall voluntarily agree, is reasonable.

"*Resolved*, That although the maintaining any matters of religion ought not to be restrained, yet that publick assemblies of societies for divine worship ought to be regulated, and that proper provision should be made for continuing the succession of the clergy, and superintending their conduct.

"*Resolved*, That the several acts of Assembly, making provision for the support of the clergy, ought to be repealed, securing to the present incumbents all arrears of salary, and to the vestries a power of levying for performance of their contracts.

"*Resolved*, That a reservation ought to be made to the use of the said church, in all time coming, of the tracts of glebe lands already purchased, the churches and chapels already built for the use of the several parishes, and of all plate belonging to or appropriated to the use of the said church, and all arrears of money or tobacco arising from former assessments; and that there should be reserved to such parishes as have received private donations, for the support of the said church and its ministers, the perpetual benefit of such donations" (JHD, Oct. 1776, 1828 edn., p. 63).

The first two of the resolutions immediately above were voided by the resolutions of the House of 30 Nov. (same, p. 76); those voided were in substance, of course, TJ's Resolutions. The first was later inserted in the Bill by amendment, but the second was lost for good (see notes to Bill, printed as Document II, below). The Act of 1705 provided extreme penalties for the offense of denying "the being of a God or the holy Trinity or . . . the christian religion to be true, or the holy Scriptures of Old and New Testament to be of divine authority" or asserting that "there are more Gods than one" (Hening, III, 168-9). It is worth noting that, while the sixth of

the resolutions adopted on 19 Nov. includes a part of TJ's phraseology, there is an important difference in the two. Inasmuch as glebe lands and other forms of property were vested in the Church by virtue of public levies, TJ made an exception between glebe lands and private donations; the former were to be enjoyed during life and the latter perpetually. The above resolutions and the Act as adopted protected the Church and its ministers in all forms of property from whatever source "in all time coming." The economic base of a part of these "desperate contests" was also apparent in a petition submitted by members of the established Church and introduced 8 Nov. 1776 (JHD, Oct. 1776, 1828 edn., p. 47).

[1] Among these "Notes & proceedings" is a fragment (TJ Papers, 234: 41880) of a MS which must have been intended by TJ as a preamble to his Resolutions. It reads as follows: "for restoring to the ⟨Inhabitants⟩ Citizens of this Comm'w. the right of maintaining their religious opinions, & of worshipping god in their own way; for releasing them from all legal obligations to frequent churches or other places of worship, ⟨&⟩ for exempting them from contributions for the support of any ⟨church⟩ religious society independant of their good will, ⟨&⟩ for discontinuing the establishment of the church of England by law, & ⟨thereby⟩ taking away the privilege & pre-eminence of one religious sect over another, and thereby ⟨establish [several words illegible] & equal rights among all⟩." Another fragment of what must have been an early draft of these Resolutions on disestablishment is to be found in the MS of TJ's Bill for Establishing a Court of Appeals (TJ Papers, 2: 316 verso). It is heavily crossed out, but the whole is legible. Thus by the fortuitous preservation of the complementary parts of two fragments, it is possible to piece together an important part of the text of TJ's first notable document on the question of the relationship of Church and State. The second of these fragments reads as follows: "⟨for discontinuing the establishment of the English church by law, taking away all privilege & pre-eminence of one religious sect over another; & totally and eternally restraining the civil magistrate from all pretensions of interposing his authority or exercise in matters of religion⟩."

II. Draft of Bill
for Exempting Dissenters from Contributing to the Support of the Church

[30 November 1776]

Whereas[1] it is represented by many of the Inhabitants of this Country who dissent from the Church of England as by Law established that they consider the Assessments and Contributions which they have been hitherto obliged to make towards the support and Maintenance of the said Church and its Ministry as grievous and oppressive, and an Infringement of their religious Freedom. For Remedy whereof[2] and that equal Liberty as well religious as civil may be universally extended to all the good People of this Common Wealth, Be it Enacted by the General Assembly of the Common Wealth of Virginia and it is hereby Enacted by the Authority of the same that all Dissenters of whatever Denomination from the said Church shall from and after the passing this Act be totally free and exempt from all Levies Taxes and Impositions whatever towards supporting and maintaining the said Church as it now is or may hereafter be established and its Ministers.[3] Provided nevertheless and it is hereby farther Enacted by the Authority aforesaid that the Vestries of the several Parishes where the same hath not been already done shall and may and they are hereby authorized and required at such times as they shall appoint to levy and assess on all Tithables within their respective Parishes as well Dissenters as others all such Salaries and Arrears of Salaries as are or may be due to the Ministers or Incumbents of their Parishes for past Services;[4] moreover to make such Assessments on all Tithables as will enable the said Vestries to comply with their legal parochial Engagements already entered into and lastly to continue such future Provision for the poor in their respective Parishes as they have hitherto by Law been accustomed to make. And be it farther Enacted by the Authority aforesaid that there shall in all time coming be saved and reserved to the Use of the Church by Law established the several Tracts of Glebe Land already purchased; the Churches and Chapels already built[5] for the use of the Parishes; all Books Plate & ornaments belonging or appropriated to the use of the said Church and all arrears of Money or Tobacco arising from former Assessments or otherwise and that there shall moreover be saved and reserved to the use of such Parishes as may have received private Donations for the better support of the said Church and its Ministers the perpetual Benefit and enjoyment of all such Donations.

And whereas great Varieties of Opinions have arisen touching the Propriety of a general Assessment or whether every religious society should be left to voluntary Contributions for the support and maintenance of the several Ministers and Teachers of the Gospel who are of different Persuasions and Denominations, and this Difference of Sentiments cannot now be well accommodated, so that it is thought most prudent to defer this matter to the Discussion and final Determination of a future assembly when the Opinions of the Country in General may be better known. To the End therefore that so important a Subject may in no Sort be prejudged, Be it Enacted by the Authority aforesaid that nothing in this Act contained shall be construed to affect or influence the said Question of a general Assessment or voluntary Contribution in any respect whatever.

Provided always that in the mean time the Members of the Established Church shall not in any Parish be subject to the payment of a greater tax for the support of the said Church & its Minister than they would have been, had the Dissenters not been exempted from paying their accustomed proportion, any Law to the contrary notwithstanding.[6]

And whereas it is represented that in some Counties Lists of Tithables have been omitted to be taken, For remedy whereof[7] be it further enacted, that the Courts of the several Counties, where it may be necessary, shall have Power & they are hereby required so soon as may be convenient to appoint some of their own Members to take the Lists of Tithables throughout their respective Counties.

MS (Vi). Two pages in a clerk's hand; one page of amendments in Tazewell's hand; one amendment in George Mason's hand; and one amendment in Robert Carter Nicholas' hand.

It is clear that the Bill as introduced 30 Nov. was drawn up by the committee appointed 19 Nov. not in accord with the six resolutions of the latter date (printed in the note to Document I, above), but in accord with the modification of those resolutions adopted 30 Nov. immediately before the present Bill was introduced. Hence it is plausible to conclude that the Bill as here presented had been agreed upon before TJ left the legislature on 29 Nov. A part

of TJ's Resolutions of 19 Nov. (Document I) was, however, introduced into the Bill by way of amendment.

[1] The page of amendments in Tazewell's hand, referred to above, is headed: "Amendments proposed to the Bill for exempting the different Societies of Dissenters . . . ," and the first amendment listed on this page is prefaced by this remark: "The following to preceed the Preamble of the Bill." Then follows the text of the amendment as enacted into law (Hening, IX, 164). This text is, except for one alteration, the same as that referred to above as being in George Mason's hand. It reads in Mason's text as follows: "Whereas several oppressive

Acts of Parliament respecting Religion have been formerly enacted, and Doubts have arisen and may hereafter arise whether the same are in Force within this Common-Wealth or not, for Prevention whereof Be it enacted by the General Assembly of the Common Wealth of Virginia, and it is hereby enacted by the Authority of the same, That all and every Act or Statute *(either of the Parliament of England, or of Great Britain)* by whatever Title known or distinguished, which renders criminal the maintaining any Opinions in Matters of Religion, forbearing to repair to Church, or the exercising any Mode of worship whatsoever, or which prescribes punishments for the same, shall henceforth be of no Validity or Force within this Common-Wealth." On the Mason amendment are written in Tazewell's hand the following words at the top and bottom respectively: "To stand before the Preamble" and "agreed." The deletion was apparently made before the amendment was offered; for the text as given in Tazewell's list of amendments reads as follows: ". . . all and every Act or Statute by whatever Title known. . . ." After Tazewell had copied the amendment thus, the words "or Statute" were deleted, and the words "of Parliament" substituted therefor; the Act as adopted reads accordingly. It will be noted that this amendment preserves some of the phraseology and much of the substance of TJ's Resolutions of 19 Nov. (Document I, above).

2 Tazewell's list of amendments reads as follows: "Strike out from the Beginning of the Bill to the word *whereof* in the 8th Line and insert And whereas there are within this Commonwealth great Numbers of Dissenters from the Church established by Law, who have been heretofore taxed for it's Support, and it is contrary to the principles of Reason and Justice that any should be compelled to contribute to the Maintenance of a Church with which their Consciences will not permit them to join, and from which they can therefore receive no Benefit; for remedy whereof." This amendment, which reflects more exactly the sentiments and words of the dissenting petitions than does the Bill as introduced, was agreed to and enacted into law (Hening, IX, 165).

3 The words "as it now is or may hereafter be established" are interlined and no doubt represent an amendment, since the number of the line ("17") is written in the margin, a designation occurring only in places where amendments are indicated; however, the amendment is not listed among those detailed by Tazewell. It may have been one offered by the Senate on 9 Dec. (JHD, Oct. 1776, 1828 edn., p. 89).

4 The Act reads: "for services to the first day of January next."

5 The following words are to be found in the Act at this point and may be one of the amendments offered by the Senate: "and such as were begun or contracted for before the passing of this act" (Hening, IX, 165).

6 The foregoing paragraph is underscored in the MS of the Bill and preceded by "2d clause." The Tazewell list of amendments reads as follows: "Page 2. Strike out the second clause & insert And whereas see Treasurer's Amendmt. No. 3." The amendment in Robert Carter Nicholas' hand is headed by the figure "3" and its text coincides with that of the Act at this point: "And Whereas by the Exemptions allowed Dissenters it may be too burthensome in some Parishes to the Members of the established Church if they are still compel'd to support the Clergy by certain fixed Salaries & it is judged best *(for the present)* that this should be done for the present by voluntary *(subscriptions)* Contributions; Be it therefore enacted by the Authority aforesaid that so much of an Act of the General Assembly made in the 22d. Year of the Reign of King George the second entitled 'An Act for the Support of the Clergy & for the regular collecting & paying the Parish Levies or any other Act as provides Salaries for the Ministers & authorizes the Vestries to levy the same, except in the Cases before directed,' shall be & the same is hereby suspended until the End of the next Session of Assembly." The words "or any other Act" are interlined and are in the hand of Tazewell.

7 The words following this point are underscored in the MS and several additional paragraphs substituted therefor in the Act as adopted. These additional paragraphs provide for the method of listing tithables, wheeled carriages subject to tax, and penalties for failure to carry out the terms of the Act (Hening, IX, 166-7). This amendment was probably offered in the House, for the Tazewell amendments read at this point:

"Line 25. Strike out the words as soon as may be convenient & insert at the first or second Court after passing this Act." This minor amendment was, with appropriate changes, probably incorporated in the larger one.

III. Jefferson's Outline of Argument
in Support of His Resolutions

Befre. ent. on Propr. Redress—see wt. is Injury—ye sta. Religs. Lib.

Apostacy. act. 1705.c.6.

    1st. offce. disabld. to hold office.

    2d.   disabled to sue, incapb. of gift or legacy

    3   three years imprismt. however conscients. ye Conversion.

Heresy. ⟨1.El.c.1.⟩ Heretico combura.

    State hs. adoptd. Athanasn. creed.

    Arians therefore Heretics

    eithr. Civl. or Eccles. judge in burn 1.H.P.c.405.

    2. Arians burnt in El. & Jac.

    Socinians.

Recusancy.

    Sacramt. 1.E.6.c.1.

        to deprave it, imprismt. & fine ad libitum

        Quakers.

    Commn. Prayr. 1.El.c.2.

        (a) derogate frm. it—or attend any other Commd. to prison tll. Conform if nt. Confrm. in 3 Months, *abjure.*

        act of ass. addnal. 5/ except on dissentrs.

        wch. is deragn

        Athanasn. creed.

        Commination

        XXXIX Articles

           11th. Faith—Works.

           13. Works sinfl. befre. grace & Inspirn.

           17. Predestination.

           18. No name cn. save bt. Christ.

        Obj. Insultg. & Revilg. offensve. to good men

        ans. so evy. oth transgrn. divne. commd. is yt. sfft. to justify coercn.

        Revilrs. wll. be contemd.—Ministers if Punish, people wll. Pity.

        cool reasg. refutn. compsn. bst. arms fr. Revilrs. to tke. refge. in Fi & Imprmt. seems hd. n. bettr. suppt.

Tenets & Formulars. plannd. by Clergy, yo. stabld. by
civl. hist. Synods, convocns, councils—

 intrig. Cabls. animos. anathem.

 smll. Majorts.—

 cross in baptm. carrd. by 1. in Convocn. El.

 Obj. shll. w. lve. mn. propagte. wt. opns. please?

ans. *Truth* cnt. suffr. by fre. Enquiry—only w. propag.

 Free enquiry enemy only to Error

 if m. forbd. free Argum'—Mahomsm.

 prevnt. Reformn.

(b) No attendg. Chch. whre. Com. Prayr.

 23.El.c.1. 28.El.c.6. 35.El.c.1. 3.Jac.1.c.4.

 20£ a month—or 2/3 of lands:

 10.£ a month for keepg. a person wh. ds. nt. or Im-
prismt & Abjurn.

(d) Attending Conventicles

 same punmts.

 Free govmt. forgets own princ. whn. becmes. intolrt.

4. *Popery.*

5. *Profaneness.* 3.Jac.1.c.21.

 jestingly speakg. name of God, Christ, Ghost, Trinty. £10.
for every offence.

6. *Contribn.*

 is it just?

 yse. peop. p. dble. Contribns.

 ys. is Persecn. in degree

 is it Geners. in Clerg. hire whre. nevr. labord.

Gent. wll. b. surprizd. at detl. yse persecutg. stat.

 mos. men imagne. persecn. unknn. t. our ls.

 legl. sta. Relign. little undstd.

 ye. persecn. gos. nt. t. death bt. in 1. case—Fi. Impr.

 happly. ye. Spirt. of times in favr. of rts. of Conscce.

 if just sch. rts. possd. in Xtnt. wch. lenity of ti. allows
just shd. b. fxd by *law.*

 at ys. ti. of reformn. no laws incompble. left unrepd.

Lt. gent. wh hapn. of Relign. of sta. mke. ca. of oth. yr. own

 wt. wd. b. yr. Sensns. if n. Secty. civl. rts. bt. Modern.
of ti.

 wd. b. uneasy till fxd. on legal basis.

 Rts. of Conscce mch. mo. tendr.

Obj. yse. acts only interrorm.

Ans. acts in terrm. nt. justfble.—m. presme. wll. b. xd.

      leave evy. one at mercy of *Bigot*.

        evy. one shd. kn. undr. wt. law lives

        shd. nt. b. oblgd. recr. to Spirt. of ti. fr. protctn.

           ys. is nt. Secure govmt.—bt. at mercy of events

           Spirt. ti. m. altr.—single Zealt. m. undtke. refrm.

        bad complmt. to law. yt. peop. discrn. iniqty. & nt. xte. it

former attempts at tolern. how have succeeded

      Presbyterian wd. open just wide enough for hms.

      others wd. open it to infidelity, bt. keep out fanaticism

      True mode only for all to concur, & throw open to all.

      ye. prest. chch. too strong for any 1 sect, bt. too weak agt.
        all.[1]

Hs. *State Right* to adopt an Opn. in mattr. Relign.

      whn. mn. ent. Socty. Surrendr. litt. as posble.

      Civl. rts. all yt. r. nec. to Civl. govmt.

      Religs. rts. nt. nec. surrd.

           Individ. cnt. surrdr.—answble. to God

             If is *unalienable right*, [. . .] is Religs.

        God reqres. evy. act acdg. to *Belief*

           yt. Belf. foundd. on Evdce. offd. to his mind.

        as yngs. appr. to hims. nt. to anoth.

Obj. oth. mens Undstgs. *better*.

Ans. hs. own Undstg., wh. mo. or less. judics. only faclty. god

True line betw. Opn. or tendcy. of opn.—& *Overt* act.

        humn. 1. nothg. t. d. wth. Opn. or tendcy.—only Overt acts.

        if magistr. restrn. prins. bec. of tendcy. & h. judge yn.

           Relign. no longer *free*.

        Coercn. exercd. by *fallible men*.

Obj. Belief of *Future State* necess.

Ans. Jewish theocrcy.

        God dd. nt. revl. in *Bible*.

        Sadducees.

⟨*Obj. Religion will decline if not supported*

Ans. Gates of Hell shall not prevail . . .⟩[1]

Is a Relign. of State ⟨*Use*⟩ *Expedt.*

      Purpose mst. be *Uniformty*.

(a) Is *Uniformty. desirble*?

        if evr. cd. b. obtd. wd. be b. suffoctg. free enqry.

           all imprvmts. in Relign. or Philos. hve. bn. frm. settg.

up privte. jdmt. agt. Public—ventrg. dept. Uniformty.

Monksh. imposns.—ignorce.—darknss. suppd. on *ruins* Enqry.

Glorious Reformn. effect of shakg. off Pub. opn.

Mahomsm. supprtd. by stiflg. *free enqry.*

Philos. reformd by *free* enq.

Galileo. Newton

Unifmty. no. mo. nec. in *Relign.* yn. *Philos.*

no consqce. if Newtonn. or Cartesn.

Overt acts all yt. nec.

Diffce. in Religs. opn. supplies place *Censor Morum*

Teachrs. evy. sect inculcte. sa. mor. princ. wh. yn. gve. peculr. priv. to any?

(b) Is *Unifmty. Attainable?*

by *Inquisn.*

by lessr. Punmts.—Burng heretic—Fine. Impr. Abjurn.

Constrt. m. prodce. Hippocr.—nt. prevt. sentimt.

Coercn. mst. b. xrcd. by *fallib.* men—abusd.

Experce. hs. provd. *Unattnb.*

Millns. burnt—tortd.—find.—imprisd. yet men *differ.*

in Romn. Cath. countr. most infidelty.

If Relign. of sta. mst b. stabld. *Is ours right?*

Zealot wll. ans. *yes.*

1/10,000 of men of our Relign.

Obj. all states have *establmt.*

Ans. then all religions have been established[2]

⟨Ans⟩ hve Govng. pwrs. of earth shewn *Infallibilty.* by this?[3]

nevr. pretendd. to it till Xty.

Exam. effects since yt.

hs. God *stampd.* us wth. mark

r. w. whiter—handsmr.—athletc.—wisr.

if n. sch. *Ear-mark* whence ys. *Confidence?*

ans. Reason.

true evy. mn's *Reasn.* judge fr. hms. Presbn. fr.

Presbn.—Episcn. for Episcn.

bt. wh. m. reasn. step int. jdmt. seat of yours?

Advantags. to *Relign.* to put all on footg.

Strengthn. Church.

oblige it's ministers to be *Industrs. Exemplary*

Northern clergy

wh. depdce. or Indepdce. mst. likely to mke. industrs.
Lawyers—Physicns.

Xty. florshd. 300. y. witht. establmt.
soon as establd. *declind*. frm. *Purity*

betrays wnt. confdce. in doctrnes. of chch. to suspct. yt.
reasn. or intrinsck. xcllce. insfft. wtht. seculr. prop.
Gates of hell shall never prevail[2]

Attach People
20,000 beyd. & adjg. Blue ridge.
55,000 in all.
ceding wll. attach.

Obj. *Fixd. Contribn.*
inequalty. of Parishes
no. of dissentrs. difft. in difft. parishs.
Contribn. wll. nt. supprt. Preachrs. in some Chch. min. in
other
Contribn. of sme. yn. wll. be lost or givn. agt. Conscce.
Decln. of rts. is *freedm*. of *Religion*
force mn. to contribte. wn. n. teachr. of sect to recve. is t.
force to supprt. heresy
Quakrs. give no Contribns.
Discorge. fornrs.
N. Engld.

N (DLC). A four-page document written in a long, narrow column. The italicized words (except those in angle brackets) represent words and phrases written by TJ in a hand resembling print. This special hand varies greatly in size and form, so that his several degrees of emphasis can only be approximated in our text.
For the place of this document in TJ's campaign to effect disestablishment, see the general Editorial Note at the beginning of this sequence of documents.

[1] This passage inserted in a different ink.
[2] This line inserted in a different ink.
[3] Two preceding words inserted in a different ink.

IV. List of Acts of Parliament
and of Virginia Assembly, 1661-1759, concerning Religion

1661. c.1. Church to be built or [chap]el of ease.
c.2. Vestries appointed.
c.3. Ministers to be inducted.
c.4. Ministers to provide [reade]rs
c.5. Liturgy to be read.
c.6. Church Catechism

  c.7. Ministers to preach weekly

  c.8. the 30th. of January to be kept a fast.

  c.9. the 29th. of May to be kept holy.

  c.10. Churchwardens to keep the church in repair & provide ornaments[1]

1663. c.1. an act for keeping holy the 13th. of September.

1680. c.4. an act prohibiting unlawful disturbances of divine service.

1705. c.6. an act for the effectual suppression of vice & restraint & punishment of blasphemous, wicked & dissolute persons.[2]

1713. c.1. an act for registring births, christenings, & burials.

1730. c.2. an act for enforcing the act intituled an act for the effectual suppression of vice, & restraint & punishment of blasphemous, wicked & dissolute persons; & for preventing incestuous marriages & copulations.

1744. c.2. an act to explain & amend an act intituled an act for the effectual suppression of vice & restraint & punishment of wicked, blasphemous & dissolute persons.

 ⟨*Stat.2.H.4.c.15.[4.Blackst.45]*[3] *defining heresy & gi* . . . .[4]

  3.H.5.c.7.[4.Bl.47][3] *Lollardy made a heres.* . . .⟩[4]

  1.El.c.1. under which 2 Anabaptists were . . . .[4]

   & 2. Arians in 9. Ja . . . .[4]

  yt. stat. repeald. by 29.Car.2.c.9. but do . . . .[4]

  1.Edw.6.c.1.

  1.Eliz.c.2. 4.Bl.50.

  23.Eliz.c.1.

  3.Jac.1.c.4.

  35.Eliz.c.1.

  27.Eliz.c.2.

  3.Jac.1.c.21.

  33.H.8.c.8.

  1.Jac.1.c.12.

  4.Jac.1.c.5.

  5.Eliz.c.1.

  ⟨*1.Ed.6.c.12.*⟩

1754.c.7. ⟨*act for*⟩ disqualifying dissenters from [. . . .][4]

1756.c.1. act for disarming papists &c.

act.ass.1748.c.2.S.2. 'popish [rec]usants' made incapable of beg. given [. . . .][4]

  1753.pa.300 'po[pish rec]usants convict' incapable of being witness[es in] any cause whatever.

1756.c.1. act for disarm[ing] papists & reputed papists [this act prohibits a papist from keeping horse above £5.][3]

1748.c.26. an act concerning marriages

28. an act for the support of the clergy & for the regular collecting & paying the parish levies

1759.c.7.S.3.4. Dissenter incapable of being Vestryman.

N(DLC). A two-page MS with portions worn or torn away.

This list of Acts of Assembly relating to the colonial church was obviously drawn up before 19 Nov. 1776. See the general Editorial Note at the head of this sequence of documents.

[1] The ten Acts listed above were passed by the Assembly in its session begun 23 Mch. 1661/2, and will be found in Hen-

ing, II, 44-52, where, however, the numbering of the Acts is not the same as TJ's.

[2] This Act is included in TJ's Draft Resolutions (Document I, above) and also in those of 19 Nov. (Document I, note).

[3] Brackets in MS.

[4] MS torn; undetermined number of words missing.

V. Notes on Acts of Parliament
and of the Virginia Assembly concerning Religion

1.E.6.c.1. Rast. 365.a. 'to deprave despise or contemn the sacrament' imprisonmt. & fine ad libitum repd by 1.Mar. parl.1. Sess.2.c.2. but revived by 1.Eli. c.2. and ye. 1.Mar. ws. repd. 1.Jac.

5.6.E.6.c.1. Rast. 365.d. every person to resort to church every Sunday, unless lawful excuse of absence.

Ecclesiasticl. courts to punish offenders.

if any one hear & be present at any form of prayer but 'the book of Common prayer imprisonmt. for 6. months 1st. offnce.—2d. ditto.—3d imprisonmt. for life.

repd. 4.Mar. but this part of it revivd. by 1.El. & ye. whole by 1.Jac. c.25. wch. repd. ye. stat. 1.Mar.

1.El.c.1. Rast. 78.6. heresies defined 'such as have heretofore been determined heresy by the authority of the Canonical scripture, or by the first 4 general councils, or any of them, or by any other general council ⟨wherein⟩ it was declared heresy by the express & plain words of ye. scriptures.

Ecclesiastical Commissrs. to correct. Diocesan may burn the heretic 1.Hale. P. C. 405.

2.Arians burnt under this law in 17.El. & 9.Jac.—repd in Engld. by 29.Car.2. c.9. but not here.

1.El.c.2. Rast. 367.a. if any [minister][1] not beneficed, refuse to use the book of com. prayer or to minister the sacrament in such order & form as set forth in sd. book, or shall use any other rite, ceremonie, order, forme, or manner of celebrating the Lord's supper openly or privily, or use other open prayer than is mentd. in the sd. book; or preach declare or speak any thing in the derogation or depraving of the sd. book or any thing therein contained, he shall be punished by 1 year's imprisonmt. for 1st. offence, & for 2d. offence imprisonmt. for life.

and if any person [layman][1] in any interlude, plays, songs, rimes, or by other open words declare or speak any thing in the derogn., depravg. or despisg. sd. book or any thing therein contained, 1st. offence 100. marks or 6 months imprisonmt. 2d. offence 400. marks or 12 mo. imprisonmt., 3d forfeiture of all his goods and chattels and imprisonmt. for life.

every person to resort to church every Sunday, unless lawful excuse on pain of censures of church & 12d. for every offence.

23.El.c.1. Rast. 82.a. every person absenting himself from church or usual place of the Common prayer to forfeit 20.£ for every month, & give security for good behavior if absent 12. months; persons keeping a schoolmaster who does not go to church 10.£ a month & the Schoolmaster disabled from his profession & be imprisoned a year. Person not [. . .][2] to be committed [. . .][2]

[?]El.c.6. Rast. 8[2?]b. every conveiance [of] lands try[. . .] convicted under [. . .] c.1. void as to the queen. After one conviction [. . .] shall pay half yearly into Exchequer 20.£ a month until they conform without further indictmt. if default in paiment the Queen to seize $\frac{2}{3}$ of lands and keep them.

35.El.c.1. Rast. 85.c. every person absenting from place of the Common prayer one month without lawful excuse, & by printing, writing, or express words or speeches move or persuade any one to deny, withstand & impugn the Queen's supremacy ecclesiastical, or to abstain from church to the service accdg. to law, or to come to or be present at any unlawful assemblies, conventicles or meetings under colour of exercise of religion contrary to the statutes; or if any person obstinately refusing to repair to church or ye. place of Com. prayer, for a month shall join in, or be present at any such assemblies, Conventicles or meetings under colour of exercise of religion, shall be committed to prison till conformity: and if they do not conform in three months & make public recantation, they shall abjure the realm: & if he does not depart, or if he returns, shall suffr. death witht. clergy.

if any person shall relieve, maintain, retain or keep in his house any person (except his father &c.) who shall refuse to go to church for a month shall forfeit £10. a month. 3.Jac.1.c.4. Rast. 89.d. repeals this clause agt. 'relieving &c.' but reenacts it & extends it to keepg. servants & restrains the exception to 'father & mother wantg. other habitation.'

1.Jac.1.c.4. Rast. 86c. confirms the 35.El.

3.Jac.1.c.1. Rast. 368.b. 5th. Nov. (Gunpowdr. plot) every body to go to church.

 c.4. Rast. 87.c.d. &c. against Popish recusants who shall not take the sacrament.

  against all Recusants, protestant or popish, not going to church. gives the k. liberty to refuse the £20. a month given by 23.El. tho' tendered at the day and to take $\frac{2}{3}$ of the lands.

  any person reqd. to take the oath of allegce. & Supremcy. to be imprisd. & incur Premunire.

  every subject going out of the realm to serve foreign prince without havg. previously taken sd. oath, a felon.

3.Jac.1.c.24. Rast. 317.b. if any person in any stage play, interlude, shew, May-game, or Pageant, jestingly & prophanely speak or use the holy name of god, or of Jesus Christ, or the holy ghost, or trinity shall forfeit £10. for every offence.[3]

1661.c.1. directs a church to be built in each parish

 c.2. vestry to be chosen 'by the major part of the parish' to take oaths of allegce. & Supremacy & subscribe to be conformable to doctrine & discipline of ye. Church.

 c.3. no minister to preach unless ordained by some bp. in Engld.

 c.4. parish to provide read[ers.]

 c.5. whole liturgy to be read thoroughly every Sunday

 c.6. the minister not to teach any other than Church Catechism.

 c.7. minister to preach weekly.

 c.8.9. & 1663.c.1. for keepg. holy Jan. 30. May. 9. & Sep. 13.

 c.10. Ch. ward. to keep church in [repair] provide books & ornaments & to collect ministers [. . . .]

[1705]c.6. if [any person] brought up in the Xn. relign. shall by
Arians.   writg. printg. teachg. or speakg. deny the being of a
Jews.   god, or the trinity, or shall assert there are more gods
               than one, or deny the Xn. relign. to be true, or the old &
               new test. to be of divine authority. 1st. offce. disabled
               to hold any office ecclesl. civl. or military. 2d. offence
               disabled to sue, or be capable of gift or legacy & 3.
               years imprisonmt. 1730. c.2. to enforce the foregoing
               act. & 1744.c.2. ditto. this act copd. from 9 & 10
               W.3.c.32.

N (DLC). MS worn; the marginal glosses can no longer be read and are here omitted.
RAST: I.e., William Rastell, *A Collection of Statutes Now in Force*, numerous enlargements and abridgements from 1557 to 1706; TJ's edn. was that of 1611 (*L.C. Cat.*; information from Miss E. M. Sowerby). HALE: Sir Mathew Hale, *Pleas of the Crown*, London, 1678, and later edns.; TJ owned two edns. (*L.C. Cat.*; Library Catalogue, 1815, p. 76).

1 Brackets in MS.
2 Four or five words missing.
3 All of the foregoing is on the verso of TJ Papers, 234: 41881; all that follows is on the recto, along with TJ's Draft Resolutions (Document I, above).

VI. Notes on Locke and Shaftesbury
Locke's works 2d. vol.

Why persecute for diffce. in religs. opinion?
   1. for love to the person.
   2. because of tendency of these opns. to dis[. . . .]
when I see them persecute their nearest connection & acquaintance for gross vices, I shall beleive it may proceed from love. till they do this, I appeal to their own conscences if they will examine, why they do nt. find some other principle. because of tendency. why not then level persecution at the crimes you fear will be introduced? burn or hang the adulterer, cheat &c. or exclude them from offices.

strange should be so zealous against things which tend to produce immorality & yet so indulgent to the immorality when produced. these moral vices all men acknolege to be diametrically against Xty. & obstructive of salvation of souls, but the fantastical points for which we generally persecute are often very questionable as we may be assured by the very different conclusions of people.

our Saviour chose not to propagate his religion by temporal punmts or civil incapacitation, if he had it was in his almighty power. but he chose to ⟨enforce⟩ extend it by it's influence on reason, thereby shewing to others how [they] should proceed.

Commonwealth is 'a society of men constituted for preser[ving]
their *civil ⟨rights⟩ interests.*'

interests are 'life, health, indolency of body, liberty, property.'

the magistrate's jurisdn. extends only to civil rights and from
these considns.:

the magistrate has no power but wt. ye. people gave hm.

the people hv. nt. givn. hm. ⟨powr.⟩ the care of souls bec. y cd. nt.,
y. cd. nt. because no man hs. *right* to abandon ye. care of his
salvation to another.

no man has *power* to let another prescribe his faith. faith is not
faith witht. believing. no man can conform his faith to the dictates of another.

the life & essence of religion consists in the internal persuasion or
belief of the mind. external forms [of wor]ship, when against
our belief, are hypocrisy [and im]piety. Rom.14.23. 'he that
doubteth is damned, if he eat, because he eateth not of faith: for
whatsoever is not of faith is sin.'

if it be said the magistrate may make use of a[rguments] and so
draw the heterodox to truth: I [answer] every man has a commission to admonish, exhort, convince another of error.

[a church] is 'a *voluntary* society of men, joining [themselves]
together of their own accord, in order to the [publick] worshipping of god in such a manner as they judge [accept]able to him
& effectual to the salvation of their souls. [it is] *voluntary* because
no man is *by nature* bound to any church. the hopes of salvation
is the cause of his entering into it. if he find any thing wrong in
it, he [sh]ould be as free to go out as he was to come in.

[w]hat is the power of that church &c.? as it is a society ⟨of volun-
tary⟩ it must have some laws for it's regulation. time & place of
meeting, admitting & excluding members &c. must be regulated.

but as it was a spontaneous joining of members, it follows that it's
laws extend to it's own members only, not to those of any other
voluntary society: for then by the same rule some other voluntary
society might usurp power ⟨of⟩ over them.

Christ has said 'wheresoever 2 or 3 are gatherd. togeth. in his
name he will be in the midst of them.' this is his definition of a
society. he does not make it essential that a bishop or presbyter
govern them. without them it suffices for the salvation of souls.

from the dissensions among sects themselves arises necessarily a
right of chusing & necessity of deliberating to which we will
conform.

but if we chuse for ourselves, we must allow others to chuse also, & so reciprocally. this establishes religious liberty.

why require those things in order to ecclesiastical communion which Christ does not require in order to life eternal? how can that be the church of Christ which excludes such persons from it's communion as he will one day receive into the kingdom of heaven.

the arms of a religious society or church are exhortations admonitions & advice, & ultimately expulsion or excommunication. this last is the utmost limit of power.

how far does the duty of toleration extend? 1. no church is bound by the duty of toleration to retain within her bosom obstinate offenders against her laws. 2. we have no right to prejudice another in his civil enjoiments because he is of another church. if any man err from the right way, it is his own misfortune, no injury to thee, nor therefore art thou to punish him in the things of this life because thou supposest he will be miserable in that which is to come. on the contrary accdg to the spirit of the gospel, charity, bounty, liberality is due to him.

each church being free, no one can have jurisdiction over another; no not even when the civil magistrate joins it. it neither acquires the right of the sword by the magistrate's coming to it, nor does it lose the rights of instruction or excommunication by his going from it. it cannot by the accession of any new member acquire jurisdiction over those who do not accede. he brings only himself, having no power to bring others.

suppose for instance two churches one of Arminians another of ⟨Lutherans⟩ Calvinists in Constantinople. has either any right over the other? will it be said the orthodox one has? every church is to itself orthodox, to others erroneous or heretical.

no man complains of his neighbor for ill management of his affairs, for an error in sowing his land, or marrying his daughter, for consuming his substance in taverns, pulling down, building &c. in all these he has his liberty: but if he do not frequent the church, or there conform to ceremonies, there is an immediate uproar.

the care of every man's soul belongs to himself. but what if he neglect the care of it? well what if he neglect the care of his health or estate, which more nearly relate to the state. will the magistrate make a law that he shall not be poor or sick? laws provide against injury from others; but not from ourselves. God himself will not save men against their wills.

if I be marching on with my utmost vigour in that way which according to the sacred geography leads to Jerusalem streight, why am I beaten & ill used by others because my hair is not of the right cut; because I have not been kept right, bec. I eat flesh on the road, bec. I avoid certain by-ways which seem to lead into briars, bec. among several paths I take that which seems shortest & cleanest, bec. I avoid travellers less grave & keep company with others who are more sour & austere, or bec. I follow a guide crowned with a mitre & cloathed in white. yet these are the frivolous things which keep Xns. at war.

if the magistrate command me to [bring my commodity to a publick store house][1] I bring it because he can indemnify me if he erred & I thereby lose it; but what indemnification can he give me for the kdom. of heaven?

I cannot give up my guidance to the magistrate; because he knows no more of the way to heaven than I do & is less concerned to direct me right than I am to go right. if the jews had followed their kings, amongst so many, what number would have led them to idolatry? consider the vicissitudes among the emperors, Arians, Athans. or among our princes, H.8. E.6. Mary. Elizabeth.

[co]mpulsion in religion is distinguished peculiarly from compulsion in every other thing. I may grow rich by art I am compelled to follow, I may recover health by medicines I am compelled to take agt. my own judgmt., but I cannot be saved by a *worship* I disbelieve & abhor.

whatsoever is lawful in the Commonwealth, or permitted to the subject in the ordinary way, cannot be forbidden to him for religious uses; & whatsoever is prejudicial to the commonwealth in their ordinary uses & therefore prohibited by the laws, ought not to be permitted to churches in their sacred rites. for instance, it is unlawful in the ordinary course of things or in a private house to murder a child. it should not be permitted any sect then to sacrifice children: it is ordinarily lawful (or temporally lawful) to kill calves or lambs. they may therefore be religiously sacrificed. but if the good of the state required a temporary suspension of killing lambs (as during a seige); sacrifices of them may then be rightfully suspended also. this is the true extent of *toleration.*

[tr]uth will do well enough if left to shift for herself. she seldom has received much aid from the power of great men to whom she is rarely known & seldom welcome. she has no need of force to

procure entrance into the minds of men. error indeed has often prevailed by the assistance of power or force.

truth is the proper & sufficient antagonist to error.

[if] any thing pass in a religious meeting seditiously & contrary to the public peace, let it be punished in the same manner & no otherwise than as if it had happened in a fair or market. these meetings ought not to be sanctuaries for faction & flagitiousness.

[Lo]cke denies toleration to those who entertain opns. contrary to those moral rules necessary for the preservation of society; as for instance, that faith is not to be kept with those of another persuasion, that kings excommunicated forfeit their crowns, that dominion is founded in grace, or that obedience is due to some foreign prince, or who will not own & teach the duty of tolerating all men in matters of religion, or who deny the existence of a god. [It was a great thing to go so far (as he himself sais of the parl. who framed the act of tolern.) but where he stopped short, we may go on.]²

[he] sais 'neither Pagan nor Mahamedan nor Jew ought to be excluded from the civil rights of the Commonwealth because of his religion.' shall we suffer a Pagan to deal with us and not suffer him to pray to his god?

[wh]y have Xns. been distinguished above all people who have ever lived for persecutions? is it because it is the genius of their religion? no, it's genius is the reverse. it is the refusing *toleration* to those of a different opn. which has produced all the bustles & wars on account of religion. it was the misfortune of mankind that during the darker centuries the Xn priests following their ambition & avarice & combining with the magistrates to divide the spoils of the people, could establish the notion that schismatics might be ousted of their possessions & destroyed. this notion we have not yet cleared ourselves from. in this case no wonder the oppressed should rebel, & they will continue to rebel & raise disturbance until their civil rights are fully restored to them & all partial distinctions, exclusions & incapacitations removed.

1. Shaftesbury. charact.

as the antients tolerated visionaries & enthusiasts of all kinds so they permitted a free scope to philosophy as a balance. as the Pythagoreans & latter Platonicks joined with the superstition of the times the Epicureans & Academicks were allowed all the use of wit & raillery against it. thus matters were balanced; reason had [full] play & science flourished. these contrarieties produced harmony. superstition & enthusiasm thus let alone never raged to bloodshed persecution &c. but now a new sort of policy, which considers the future lives & happiness of men rather than the present, has taught to distress one another, & raised an antipathy which no temporal interest could ever do, now *uniformity of opn.*, a hopeful project! is looked on as the only remedy agt. this evil & is made the very object of govmt itself. if magistracy should vouchsafe to interpose thus in other sciences we should [have] as bad logic, mathematics & philosophy as we have divinity in countries where the law settles orthodoxy.

[suppose the state should take into head that there should be an uniformity of countenance. men would be obliged to put an artificial bump or swelling here, a patch there &c. but this would be merely hypocritical.]¹ or if the alternative was given of wearing a mask, $\frac{99}{100}$ ths must immediately mask. would this add to the beauty of nature? why otherwise in opinions.]³ [in the middle ages of Xty. opposition to the state opns. was hushed. the consequence was, Xty. became loaded with all the Romish follies. nothing but free argument, raillery, & even ridicule will preserve the purity of religion.]¹

2. Cor. 1. 24. the apostles declare they had no dominion over the faith.⁴

Locke's system of Christianity is this.

Adam was created happy & immortal: but his happiness was to have been *Earthly*, and *earthly* immortality. by *sin* he lost this, so that he became subject to total death (like that of brutes) & to the crosses & unhappinesses of this life. at the intercession however of the son of god this sentence was in part remitted. a life conformable to the law was to restore them again to immortality. and moreover to those who *believed* their *faith* was to be counted for righteousness. not that faith without works was to save them; St. James. c.2. sais expressly the contrary; & all make the fundamental pillars of Xty. to be faith & *repentance*. so that a reformation of life (included under *repentance*) was essential, & defects in this would be made up by their *faith*; i.e. their faith should be counted for righteousness. as to that part of mankind who never had the gospel preached to them, they are 1. Jews. 2. Pagans, or Gentiles. the Jews had the law of works revealed to them. by this therefore they were to be saved: & a *lively* faith in god's promises to send the Messiah would supply small defects. 2. the Gentiles St. Paul sais Rom.2.13. 'the Gentiles have the law written in their hearts' i.e. the law of nature: to which adding a *faith* in God, & his attributes that on their repentance he would pardon them, they also would be justified. this then explains the text 'there is no other *name* under heaven by which a man may be saved.' i.e. the defects in good works shall not be supplied by a faith in Mahomet, Foe,[5] or any other except Christ.

The ⟨essentials⟩ fundamentals of Xty. as found in the gospels are 1. Faith. 2. Repentance. that faith is every[where?] explained to be a beleif that Jesus was the Messiah who had been promised. Repentance was to be proved sincere by good works. the advantages accruing to mankind from our Savior's mission are these: 1. the knolege of one god only. 2. a clear knolege of their duty, or system of morality, delivered on such authority as to give it sanction. 3. the outward forms of religious worship wanted to be purged of that farcical pomp & nonsense with which they were loaded. 4. an inducement to a pious life, by revealing clearly a future existence in bliss, & that it was to be the reward of the virtuous.

The Epistles were written ⟨occasionally⟩ to persons *already Christians*. a person might be a Xn. then before they were written. consequently the ⟨essentials⟩ fundamentals of Xty. were to be found in the preaching of our savior, which is related in the gospels. these fundamentals are to be found in the epistles dropped here & there & promiscuously mixed with other truths. but these other truths are not to be made fundamentals. they serve for edification indeed & explaining to us matters in worship & morality. but being written occasionally it will readily be seen that their explanations are adapted to the notions & customs of the people they were written to. but yet every sentence in them (tho the writers were inspired) must not be taken up & made a fundamental, without assent to which a man is not to be admitted a member of X's church here, or to his kingdom hereafter. the Apostles creed was by them taken to contain all things necessary to salvation, & consequently to a communion.

N (DLC). Four pages closely written in a long narrow column; also two full-size pages, the second of which is blank on the back except for an endorsement in an unidentified hand: "Scraps early in Revolution." The fading of the MS has rendered portions of it semi-legible; the marginal numbers of the paragraphs for the most part cannot be read and are here omitted.

These notes comprise chiefly an abstract of "A Letter concerning Tolera-tion" (1689) in John Locke's *Works*, London, 1714, II, with scattered notes and observations on other religious writings of Locke. The notes on Shaftesbury are a paraphrase, with interpolations, of a passage in section 2 of "A Letter concerning Enthusiasm" (1708) in the 3d Earl of Shaftesbury's *Characteristicks of Men, Manners, Opinions, Times*, London, 1711, I.

[1] Brackets in MS.
[2] Brackets in MS. A footnote by TJ

Design for a seal or coat of arms for the United States. Pencil sketch by P. E. DuSimitière, August 1776.

Design for a coat of arms for Virginia. Pencil sketch by P. E. DuSimitière, August 1776.

follows, reading: "will not his own excellent rule be sufficient here too; to punish these as civil offences. e. gr. to assert that a foreign prince has power within this commonwealth is a misdemeanor. the other opns. may be despised. Perhaps the single thing which may be required to others before toleration to them would be an oath that they would allow toleration to others."

³ This bracket in MS has no mate.

⁴ The foregoing is from TJ Papers, 3: 323-4; the following is from 3: 326-7 and was written at a different sitting.

⁵ Thus clearly in MS, but the reference is enigmatic.

VII. Notes on Episcopacy
Episcopacy.

Gr. Επισκοπος. Lat. Episcopus. Ital. Vescovo.

Fr. Evesque. Saxon. Biscop. Bishop. (overseer)

The epistles of Paul to Timothy & Titus are relied on (together with tradition) for the Apostolic institution of bishops.

As to tradition, if we are protestants we reject all tradition, & rely on the scripture alone, for that is the essence & common principle of all the protestant churches.

As to Scripture. 1.Tim.3.2. 'a bishop must be blameless &c. Επισκοπος.' v. 8. 'likewise must the deacons be grave &c. Διακονος' (ministros) c.5.v.6. he calls Timothy a 'minister' 'Διακονος' c.4.v.14. 'neglect not the gift that is in thee, which was given thee by prophecy with the laying on the hands of the presbytery. πρεσβυτεριον.' c.5. 'rebuke not an elder πρεσβυτερω.'

5.17. 'let the elders that rule well &c. πρεσβυτεροι.'

[5.] 19. 'against an elder (πρεσβυτερου) receive nt. an accusan.'

5.22. 'lay hands suddenly on no man χειρας επιτιθει'

6.11. he calls Timothy 'man of god ανθρωπε του θεου.'

2.Tim.1.6. 'stir up the gift of god which is in thee by the putting on of *my* hands επιθεσεως των χειρων μου.' but ante c.4. v.14. he said it was by the hands of the presbytery. This imposition of hands then was some ceremony or custom frequently repeated, & certainly is as good a proof that Timothy was ordained by the elders (& consequently that they might ordain) as that it was by Paul.

1.11. Paul calls himself 'a preacher' 'an apostle' 'a teacher.' 'κηρυξ και αποστολος και διδασκαλος.' here he designates himself by several synonims as he had before done Timothy. does this prove that every synonim authorizes a different order of ecclesiastics.

4.5. 'do the work of an Evangelist, make full proof of thy ministry εργον ποιησον ευαγγελιστου, την διακονιαν σου πληρο-

φορησον.' Timothy then is called 'επισκοπος, διακονος, ευαγγελ-
ιςτος. ανθρωπος θεου.'

4.11. he tells Tim. to bring Mark with him for 'he is profitable
to me for the ministry διακονια'

Epist. to Titus 1.1. he calls himself 'a servant of god δουλος θεου.'
1.5. 'for this cause left I thee in Crete that thou shouldst set in
order the things that are wanting, and ordain (καταςτησης)
elders in every city, as I had appointed thee. if any be blameless the husband of one wife, having faithful children, not
accused of riot or unruly for a *bishop* must be blameless as the
steward of god &c.' here then it appears that as the elders appointed the bishops, so the bishops appointed the elders. i.e.
they are synonims. again when telling Titus to appoint *elders*
in every city he tells him what kind of men they must be, for
said he a bishop must be &c. so that in the same sentence he
calls elders bishops.

3.10: 'a man that is an heretic after the first & second admonition, reject. αιρετικον.'

Jas.5.14. 'is any sick among you? let him call for the elders
(πρεσβυτερους) of the church, & let them pray over him, anoint-
ing him with oil in the name of the lord.'

another plea for Episcopal governmt. in Religion in England is
it's similarity to the political governmt. by a king. no bishop no
king. this then with us is a plea for governmt. by a presbytery
which resembles republican governmt.

the clergy have ever seen this. the bishops were alwais mere tools
of the crown.

the Presbyterian spirit is known to be so congenial with friendly
liberty, that the patriots after the restoration finding that the
humour of people was running too strongly to exalt the prerogative
of the crown, promoted the dissenting interest as a check and balance, & thus was produced the Toleration act.

St. Peter gave the title of *Clergy* to all god's people till pope Higi-
nus and ye. succeeeding prelates took it from them & appropriated it to priests only. 1.Milt.230.

Origen, being yet a layman, expounded the scriptures publickly &
was therein defended by Alexander of Jerusalem & Theoctistus
of Caesarea producing in his behalf divers examples that the privilege of teaching was antiently permitted to laymen. the first
Nicene council called on the assistance of many learned lay brethren. ib.230.

Bishops were elected by the hands of the whole ch. Ignatius (the most antt. of the extant fathers) writing to the Philadelphians sais 'that it belongs to them as to the church of god to chuse a bishop.' Cambden in his description of Scotld. sais 'that over all the world bps. had no certain diocese till pope Dionysius about the year [26]8 did cut them out, & that the bps of Scotld. exd their function in what place soever they came, indifferently till temp. Malcolm 3. 1070'

Cyprian epist. 68. sais 'the people chefly hath po[wer] either of chusing worthy or refusing unworthy bps.' the council of Nice writing to the African churches exhorts them to chuse orthodox bps. in the pla[ce] of the dead. 1.Milt.254.

Nicephorus Phocas the Greek emperor ann. 1000 first enacted that no bp shd. be chosen without his will. Ignatius in his epistle to those of Tra[. . .] confesseth that the presbyters are his fellow-sellers & fellow benchers, and Cyprian in the 6.41.52. epist. calls the presbyters, 'his Compresbyters,' yet he was a bp.—a modern bp. to be moulded into a primitive one must be elected by the people, undiocest, unrevenued, unlorded, 1.Milt.255.

N (DLC). Two-page MS written in long, narrow column. TJ Papers, 2: 325 recto and verso.

TJ cites two tracts by John MILTON: "The Reason of Church-Government Urg'd against Prelaty" and "Of the Reformation in England," in Milton's *Works*, Amsterdam, 1698, I. The reference to CAMBDEN'S, i.e., William Camden's, account of Scotland (in his *Britannia*, London, 1586, &c.) was drawn from the second tract by Milton. (Both Milton and Camden are entered in TJ's Library Catalogue, 1815.)

VIII. Notes on Heresy

A heretic is an impugner of fundamentals. what are fundamentals? the protestants will say those doctrines which are clearly & precisely delivered in the holy scriptures. Dr. Waterland would say the Trinity. but how far this character [of being clearly delivered?][1] will suit the doctrine of the Trinity I leave others to determine. it is no where expressly declared by any of the earliest fathers, & was never affirmed or taught by the church before the council of Nice [Chillingw. Pref.§18.33.][1] Irenaeus says 'who are the clean? those who go on firmly, believing in the father & in the son.' the fundamental doctrine or the firmness of the Xn. faith in this early age then was to beleive in the *father & son*. —Constantine wrote to Arius & Alexr. treating the question 'as vain foolish & impertinent as a dispute of words without sense which none could explane nor any comprehend &c.' this lre is commended by Eusebius [Vit. Constant. lb.2.c.64 &c.][1] and Socrates [Hist. Eccles. l.1.c.7.][1] as excellent admirable & full of wisdom. 2.Middleton.115. remarks on the story of St. John & [. . . .]

Le saint concil [de Nicée anno 330][1] ayant defini que le fils de dieu est de meme substance que son pere & qu'il est eternel comme lui, composa une Simbole [the Nicene creed][1] où il explique la divinite du *pere & du fils*, et qu'il finit par ces paroles 'dont le regne n'aura point de fin.' car la doctrine qui regarde *le saint esprit* ne fut ajoutée que dans le second concile tenu contre les erreurs de Macedonius, ou ces questions furent agitées. Zonare par Coussin. ann. 330. the second council meant by Zonaras was that of Constantinople ann. 381. D hist. Prim. Xty. pref. XXXVIII. 2d. app. to pref. 49. the Council of Antioch [ann   ][2] expressly affirmed of our saviour ουκ εϛιν ὁμοουϛιος that he was not Consubstantial to the father. the Council of Nice affirmed the direct contrary. D hist. Prim. Xty. Pref. CXXV.[3]

Sabellians. Xn. heretics. that there is but one person in the godhead. That the 'Word' & 'holy spirit' are only virtues, emanations, or functions of the deity.

Socinians. Xn. heretics. that the Father is the one only god; that the Word is no more than an expression of ye. godhead & had not existed from all eternity, that Jes. Christ was god no otherwise than by his superiority above all creatures who were put in subjection to him by the father. that he was not a Mediator, but sent to be a pattern of conduct to men. that the punishmts. of hell are nt. eternl.

Arminians. they think with the Romish church (agt. the Calvinists) that there is an universal grace given to all men, & that man is always *free* & at liberty to receive or reject grace. that god creates men free, that his justice would not permit him to punish men for crimes they are predestinated to commit. they admit the prescience of god, but distinguish between fore-knowing & predestinating. all the fathers, before St. Austin were of this opinion. The church of Engld. founded her article of predestination on his authority.

Arians. Xn. heretics. they avow there was a time when the Son was not, that he was created in time, mutable in nature, & like the Angels liable to sin. they deny the three persons in the trinity to be of the same essence. Erasmus & Grotius were Arians.

Apollinarians. Xn. heretics. they affirm there was but one nature in Christ, that his body as well as soul was impassive & immortal, & that his birth, death & resurrection was only in appearance.

Macedonians. Xn. heretics. they teach that the Holy ghost was a meer creature but superior in excellence to the Angels.

see Broughton. verbo 'Hertics'⁴ an enumeration of 48. sects of Christians pronounced Heretics.

N (DLC). Two pages and part of a third; see below, textual note 3.

The writers quoted and referred to include Daniel WATERLAND (1683-1740), author of numerous theological tracts; William CHILLINGWORTH (1602-1644), author of *The Religion of Protestants a Safe Way to Salvation*, London, 1638, and frequently reprinted; EUSEBIUS, Bishop of Caesarea in Palestine (260?-340?), whose *Vita Constantini* and *Historia Ecclesiastica* are cited; Conyers MIDDLETON (1683-1750), divine and historian, whose *Miscellaneous Works*, London, 1752, are cited; Joannes ZONARAS, 12th century Byzantine historian,

whom TJ cites in a French translation by Louis COUSIN, Paris, 1678; and Thomas BROUGHTON, *A Dictionary of All Religions*, London, 1742; also 1756. (Middleton, Zonaras, and Broughton are entered in TJ's Library Catalogue, 1815.)

¹ Brackets in MS.
² Brackets and blank space in MS.
³ The foregoing, written in a different ink from that which follows, is in TJ Papers, 2: 322; the following part is at 2: 326 recto and verso. All the notes on heretical sects were collected from Broughton's articles thereon.
⁴ Thus in MS.

IX. Miscellaneous Notes on Religion

1662.c.3. Pervis. an act against persons that refuse to have their children baptized.

1663.c.1. Pervis. an act prohibiting the unlawful assembling of quakers.

[1692.c.5. an act encoraging the erecting of a post office in this country.]¹ this was to confirm the establishmt. of that office made in England.

1659.Mar.13. an act for the suppressing the Quakers. I doubt whether the laws of this session are in H. B. office.² the substance is to lay penalty of £100 Sterl. on any captain of ship who shall bring in a Quaker to be levied by an *order* from the Gov. & council or the justices of the county.

that all Quakers already questioned or which shall hereafter arrive shall be apprehended & imprisoned without bail or mainprize till they abjure this country, or give security to depart the colony immediately & not to return.

if they return, to be proceeded against & pursued as contemners of the laws & magistracy:

if they return a second time to be proceeded against as felons.

no person to entertain any [of the Quakers ques]tioned by the Gov. & council or [who shall hereafter be] questd.

no person to [permit] any assembly [of Quakers] in or near his house in pen[alty of £100 sterling.]

no person *at their peril* to dispose [or publish their] books with their tenets & [opinions.]

Justices & [other?] officers at [their peril to take notice of this act to see it] fully [effected and executed.][3]

*4

Impropriety of time—invasion
 nevr. complnd. befre.
 Hierarchy & Monarchy Congenl.
Threatg.
Practice Tolern. nt. Leg.

Stat. of Tolen. Adopted

Propriety of an Estabmt.
 Obj. most states have establmt.
 ans. yn. every Relign. hs. bn. establd.
 ds. ys. Prove Infallibility

Examp. Holland
 Pennsylva. &c.
 [. . . .]
Public Regulns. necessary

1. Open doors
2. Tendcy. of opns.
 Regenern.
 Future state
ys. wd. subjct. Religs. opn.
ys. supportd. Monksh. ignorce.
trust to Ministers
wch. is smallst. inconvce.
3. Ordinatn.
 Leave it to each sect
 yr. own interest lead to it
 Quakers
4. fixed Contributn.
 laborer worthy hire

[. . . .]
while contins. worthy—shd. b. indepdt.
 wll. be afrd. to censure
 ans. The reverse is true
 obj. Rich Philadelphns. refuse

inequalty. of Parishes
    Contribn. wll. nt. suppt.
    Contribn. mst. go to difft. sect or be lost
    Decln. Rts. Freedm. of conscce.
      force to support Error
    Quakers
    Foreigns. discoraged
    Law deft. cts.—Value Xn. Examp.
      Ruin church
[. . . .]
Ye. Stat: justified by hist. times.
    ans. shd. hve. bn. repealed.
All Stat: after 4. [. . .]—Whimsicl.
    Ys. is determin. of law
    obj. Some befre. ys. not in force
    ans. local stat. exceptd.
Obj. act of parl. repeald. mst. be in force here.
    Yn. in repeal Magn. Charta. Stat. of Wills
    Ys. gives up Americn. qu.
Genl. ct. so thought it
Ans. Y dd. nt.

Obj. act. ass. is agt. swearg. Drunkss.—wll. be licence to practice
    [. . . .]
    none but Chst. men obligd. to go to Chch.
Obj. wt. [. . .] Sentimts.
Obj.

*

do not [. . .] inculcate principles of morality.
Why then give peculir. privileges to any.
Romn. Catholics. 4.Bl.54.
Pennsylva.—D. Counts.—N. York—Maryld.
a Romn. Cathol. in Congress—grt. confidce.
Canada
frdly. interchange of Citizens wth. all ye. colonies[5]

[. . . .][6]
Shadford the petner. is appd. by Rankins for Virga.
Westley has written in favr. of ministry
    has been advertzd. in Maryld. gazette as having written agt.
      Junius's lres.
E. of Dartmouth, principl. secretary, a methodist
Shadfd. has signed witht. authority.

Methodsts. in Albem. signd. petns.

Co. L. 11. 260. Hob. 79.

1 Bl. c. 8. 5. Co. 106.

Spelman. Admir. flotsam.

Jacob. beaconage.

2. Shower 232. Comb. 474.

N (DLC). Miscellaneous fragments, described in textual notes below. Partly illegible.

[1] Brackets in MS.

[2] This Act was passed in the session of 1659/60 (Hening, I, 532-3); the parts within brackets, indicating illegible or mutilated portions of the MS, are supplied from the Act itself.

[3] The foregoing is a single-page MS, mutilated, in DLC: TJ Papers, 234: 41879 recto.

[4] The part between asterisks is from a three-page MS (DLC: TJ Papers, 2: 306 verso, 307 recto and verso), in pencil, some parts of which are probably early notes for his Outline of Argument presented above (Document III). There is no means of estimating the number of words missing in the gaps indicated by suspension points.

[5] The foregoing (between the asterisk and this point), in ink, is on the recto of a single mutilated leaf (DLC: TJ Papers, 234: 41880): that which follows is on the verso. The recto also contains part of what must have been intended as the preamble of TJ's Resolution for disestablishing the church (see Document I, note 1).

[6] An entire line is missing.

Bill for the Naturalization of Foreigners

[14 October 1776]

For the encouragement of ⟨Foreign Protestants⟩ foreigners to settle in this Countrey

Be it enacted by the Senate and House of Delegates of Virginia now met in General Assembly That all ⟨Foreign Protestants⟩ ⟨foreigners⟩ ⟨now settled⟩ persons born in other countries and now residing in this ⟨Colony and not naturalized⟩ Commonwealth, and all who may hereafter migrate into the same, who shall go before any Court of Record within the same, and give Satisfactory proof by their own Oath or Affirmation or Otherwise, that they have resided or intend to reside in this Countrey for the space of   years at the least; and who shall take an Oath of Fidelity to the Common Wealth and subscribe to be Obedient to the Laws thereof, shall be considered as Free Citizens of the same and shall be entitled to all the Rights, privileges and immunities civil and religious of this Commonwealth, as if born therein. And the Clerk of the Court shall enter such Oath and Subscription of Record, and give the Person a Certificate thereof, for all which he shall receive the fee of   and no more.

And be it further Enacted that ⟨all Foreign Protestants who⟩

where any foreigners have acquired Lands in the Countrey, and have conveyed the same to others by deed or will, or transmitted them to their children or other Relations; The title of every person now in Actual Possession of such Lands under such conveyance, or transmission, is hereby confirmed in as full and ample manner as if the same had been conveied by natural born ⟨Subjects⟩ citizens of this Commonwealth.

And be it further enacted that there shall be paid by the Treasurer of this ⟨Colony⟩ Commonwealth out of any public money in his hands the sum of 20 dollars to every foreigner who shall come to settle in this Commonwealth for the purpose of defraying his passage hither over sea, and that there shall also be granted to him fifty acres of unappropriated lands wherever he shall chuse the same to be held in ⟨free and absolute⟩ fee simple.

Dft (DLC). In the handwriting of Edmund Pendleton, with alterations by TJ which significantly changed the character of the Bill. Endorsed, as originally written by Pendleton: "Naturalization of Foreign Protestts.," which TJ altered to read: "A Bill for the Naturalization of Foreigners."

This Bill, not printed heretofore, emphasizes another facet of TJ's liberal legislative program and also illuminates the difference between his and Pendleton's points of view. The Bill contains many alterations in TJ's hand throughout the body of the text, the most important of which are: (1) those which were obviously designed to admit Jews to citizenship; and (2) the final paragraph, entirely in TJ's hand, which clearly endeavors to enact by legislation what he had failed to accomplish in his proposed Constitution of Virginia, q.v., though the present Bill goes further than that by offering passage money as well as lands to encourage immigration. A few of these changes are indicated (e.g., the elimination of the words "Foreign Protestants," then the word "foreigners," and finally the substitution of "persons," the former being indicated by italics within angle brackets). On 14 Oct. TJ presented the Bill for the committee appointed for this purpose; on 15 Oct. the Bill was read a second time and referred to a committee of the whole; on 11 Nov. it was debated and amended by the committee of the whole; on 6 Dec. it was postponed to the next meeting of

Assembly and apparently never brought up again (JHD, Oct. 1776, 1828 edn., 12, 14, 51). The naturalization bill of 1779, which was included in *Report of the Committee of Revisors*, 1784, ch. LV, was quite different from the present Bill (Ford, I, 55-6; Hening, X, 129-30). We have no means of knowing what amendments were offered in the committee of the whole on 11 Nov., but the following notes in TJ's hand, endorsed on the back of the Bill, must have been made at the time and suggest the tenor of the debate:

"Physical advantages
   Consumption
   Labor
   Procreation
   [. . . .]
Moral
   Honesty—Veracity
   Religion—is theirs less moral
   Will the amendmt. take ym. better
   all who have not *full rights* are secret
     enem[ies]
Obj. no nation allows them to realize
   Jews advantageous
Ys. wll. narrow ground of formg. act
   Ass."

It is clear from this brief outline of an argument, whose abbreviations suggest that it may have been made during debate, that full rights of citizenship for Jews, Catholics, and other non-Protestant groups were strongly advocated by TJ, who must have been able to convince his colleague Pendleton on the committee, but failed to convince the Assembly.

Bill to Enable Tenants in Fee Tail
to Convey Their Lands in Fee Simple

[14 October 1776]

WHEREAS the perpetuation of property in certain families by means of gifts made to them in fee-tail is contrary to good policy, tends to deceive fair traders who give a credit on the visible possession of such estates, discourages the holder thereof from taking care of[1] and improving the same, and sometimes does injury to the morals of youth by rendering them independent of, and disobedient to, their parents; and whereas the former method of docking such estates tail by special act of assembly formed for every particular case employed very much of the time of the legislature,[2] was burthensome to the public, and also to[3] the individuals[4] who made application for such acts:

Be it therefore enacted by[5] the General Assembly of the Commonwealth of Virginia and it is hereby enacted by authority of the same that any person who now hath, or hereafter may have any estate in feetail general or special in any lands or slaves in possession, or in the use or trust of any lands or slaves in possession, or who now is or hereafter may be entitled to any such estate tail in reversion or remainder after the determination of any estate for life or lives or of any lesser estate, whether such estate tail hath been or shall be[6] created by deed, will, act of assembly, or by any other ways or means, shall[7] have full power to pass, convey, or assure in fee-simple or for any lesser estate the said lands or slaves or use in lands or slaves or such reversion or remainder therein, or any part or parcel thereof, to any person or persons whatsoever by deed or deeds of feoffment, gift, grant, exchange, partition, lease, release, bargain and sale, covenant to stand seised to uses, deed to lead uses, or by his last will and testament, or by any other mode or form of conveiance or assurance by which such lands or slaves, or use in lands or slaves, or such reversion or remainder therein might have been passed conveied or assured had the same been held in fee-simple by the person so passing, conveying or assuring the same: and such deed, will, or other conveiance shall be good and effectual to bar the issue in tail and those in remainder and reverter as to such estate or estates so passed, conveied, or assured by such deed will or other conveiance.

Provided nevertheless that such deed, will, or other conveiance shall be executed, acknoleged, or proved, and recorded in like manner as, and in all cases where, the same should have been done, had the person or persons so conveying or assuring held the said lands or slaves, or use in lands or slaves or such reversion or remainder therein in feesimple.

MS (Vi); in TJ's hand, with amendments partly in TJ's hand and partly in clerk's hand (noted below). Docketed by TJ: "A Bill to enable tenants in feetail to convey their lands in fee-simple"; and by John Tazewell, clerk of the House of Delegates: "1776 Oct: 14. read 1st. Time. 15. read 2d. time & Committed to the Com: of the whole on Thursday. Oct: 17 Com: sat on this Bill & to resolve itself into a Com: thereon again tomorrow.—Oct: 18. Amendments agreed to & to be ingrossed & read a third time."

On 12 Oct. leave was given TJ to bring in such a bill, and Bland, TJ, Starke, and Bullitt were appointed to a committee for the purpose; on 14 Oct. TJ introduced it; on 23 Oct. it was read a third time and passed, TJ carrying it to Senate; on 1 Nov. agreed to by Senate (JHD, Oct. 1776, 1828 edn., p. 10, 12, 13, 17, 18, 23, 36).

This, one of the first bills passed by the legislature after the adoption of the Constitution, was also the first of TJ's great reform bills which he hoped would destroy the foundations of an aristocracy of wealth and "make an opening for the aristocracy of virtue and talent"; in this he was strongly opposed by Pendleton, who offered and, according to TJ, almost succeeded in obtaining an amendment which would have given merely an option to the tenant in tail to convey in fee simple if he so chose to do (Ford, I, 49-50). It is important to note that under Virginia law fee-tail applied to slaves annexed to land as well as land itself. (For a good discussion of the background of TJ's Bill, see Malone, *Jefferson*, I, 251-7; see also Lingley, *Transition in Virginia*, p. 181.)

1 Ford, II, 104, and Hening, IX, 226, omit "of," which may indicate that Ford used another draft (see note 5).

2 Amendment in clerk's hand: "Insert and the same as well as the Method of defeating such estates when of small value"; thus in Hening, IX, 226.

3 Amendment in clerk's hand: "after the Word *to* leave out *the*"; thus in Hening, IX, 226.

4 Amendment in clerk's hand: "Leave out from the Word Individuals to the end of the Clause"; thus in Hening, IX, 226.

5 Ford, II, 104, indicates that the draft in TJ's hand that he used was left blank at this point; in the present text, however, the words "the General Assembly of the Commonwealth of Virginia" were inserted in the handwriting of John Tazewell, clerk of the House. If Ford is correct in describing this as a blank space, he must have seen another copy; yet he includes the amendment in TJ's hand noted below, and this would make it seem unlikely that there were *two* drafts in TJ's hand left in the archives of the House and bearing the same amendment by TJ.

6 TJ originally wrote "shall have been" and then altered it to read "hath been or shall be."

7 The following amendment in TJ's hand changed the character of the Bill from a permissive power to convey in fee simple to an abolition of entails: "line 18. omit 'have &c. to the end of the bill, and insert 'from henceforth, or from the Commencement of such estatetail, stand ipso facto seised, possessed, or entitled of, in, or to, such lands or slaves or use in lands or slaves so held or to be held as aforesaid in possession, reversion, or remainder in full and absolute fee-simple, in like manner as if such deed, will, act of assembly, or other instrument had conveyed the same to him in fee-simple; any words, limitations, or conditions in the said deed, will, act of assembly, or other instrument to the contrary notwithstanding.

"Saving to all and every person and persons, bodies politic and corporate, other than the issue in tail and those in reversion and remainder, all such right, title, interest and estate claim and demand, as they, every, or any of them could or might claim, if this act had never been made: and Saving also to such issue in tail and to those in reversion and remainder any right or title which they may have acquired by their own contract for good and valuable consideration actually and bona fide paid or performed." (This amendment was incorporated in the final Act; Hening, IX,

226-7. Ford, II, 105, includes this amendment, and his text agrees so exactly with the above as to preclude the possibility of his having used another draft of the amendment, though there is a possibility that he may have seen another draft of the Bill itself.)

Both Ford, II, 105, and Malone, *Jefferson*, I, 254, say that TJ himself introduced this amendment; it is most likely that he did so, though the only evidence for it is the fact that it is in his handwriting; none of the amendments carries any indication of the identity of the proposer. It is important to note that TJ's Bill as written merely empowers tenants in tail to convey in fee simple; Malone, *Jefferson*, I, 254, says, therefore, that TJ's original proposal was "much like the one he afterwards attributed to Pendleton" and that, feeling out the opposition, TJ went on to amend his act so as to abolish entirely the system of entails. But, lacking TJ's rough draft of the Bill, we cannot be certain that the text as here given was not written and introduced in order to meet Pendleton's objections, since this Bill carries the same permissive power TJ later associated with Pendleton; certainly the Bill here presented is less in accord with TJ's arguments in behalf of a purely allodial system of land tenure than it is with Pendleton's views (see TJ-Pendleton correspondence May-Aug. 1776), and this amendment agrees both with the preamble to the Bill and with TJ's known principles; Pendleton was not a member of the committee. It is worth noting, however, that in the original MS of his Autobiography TJ first wrote: "I obtained leave to bring in a bill enabling tenants in tail to convey their lands in fee simple." This he altered to read: ". . . to bring in a bill declaring tenants in tail to hold their lands in fee simple"; the statement as first written is correct (JHD, Oct. 1776, 1828 edn., p. 10), but TJ's change in phrasing seems to be a significant indication of his original intent.

Bill for the Revision of the Laws

[15 October 1776]

WHEREAS on the late change which hath of necessity been introduced into the form of government in this country it is become also necessary to make corresponding changes in the laws heretofore in force, many of which are inapplicable to the powers of government as now organised, others are founded on principles heterogeneous to the republican spirit, others which, long before such change, had been oppressive to the people, could yet never be repealed while the regal power continued, and others, having taken their origin while our ancestors remained in Britain, are not so well adapted to our present circumstances of time and place, and it is also necessary to introduce certain other laws, which, though proved by the experience of other states to be friendly to liberty and the rights of mankind, we have not heretofore been permitted to adopt; and whereas a work of such magnitude, labour, and difficulty, may not be effected during the short and busy term of a session of assembly:

Be it therefore enacted by the General Assembly of the commonwealth of Virginia, and it is hereby enacted by the authority of the same, That a committee, to consist of five persons, shall be appointed by joint ballot of both houses (three of whom to be a quorum) who shall have full power and authority to revise, alter, amend, repeal, or introduce all or any of the said laws, to form the same into bills, and report them to the next meeting of the general assembly.

And to prevent any delay which may happen in the proceedings of the said committee, by the death or disability of any member thereof, *Be it farther enacted*, That if either of the said members should die, refuse to act, or be disabled by sickness from proceeding in the said work, it shall be lawful for the remaining members to appoint some other person in his stead and place, which person so appointed is hereby declared a member of the said committee, in like manner as if he had originally been appointed by joint ballot of both houses.

And be it farther enacted, That the said committee shall have power to meet at such times and places as they shall think proper for the purpose of proceeding on the said revisal, to appoint a clerk for their ease and assistance in the work, and to send for any copies of records to the clerk in whose custody they are, which such clerk is hereby directed forthwith to transmit to them.

Provided, That such bills so to be prepared and reported by the committee of revisors shall be of no force or authority until they shall have gone through their several readings in both houses of assembly, and been passed by them in such manner and form as if the same had been originally introduced without the direction of this act.

Text from Hening, IX, 175-7; no MS of the Bill as reported or amended has been located. TJ later said that "Early . . . in the session of 76 . . . I moved and presented a bill for the revision of the laws" (Autobiography, Ford, I, 57-8).

This Act is the basis for the work of the revisal of the laws of Virginia in which TJ was engaged for the next three years (see under 18 June 1779). On 12 Oct. Bland, TJ, and Starke were appointed a committee to bring in a bill for the revision of the laws; Bland reported the Bill 15 Oct.; it passed the House, apparently without amendment, 17 Oct., and TJ carried it to Senate, where five amendments were offered on 24 Oct.; the most important of these increased the number of revisors from three to five, making any three a quorum; all were agreed to by the House

on 25 Oct., save for the fifth amendment, which added these words: "and also to send to any of the United American States for the system of laws in force there, if thought necessary." Senate receded from this amendment and passed the Bill 26 Oct. (JHD, Oct. 1776, 1828 edn., p. 10, 13, 14, 16, 26, 28). On 5 Nov. the House resolved "That Thomas Jefferson, Edmund Pendleton, George Wythe, George Mason, and Thomas Ludwell Lee, esquires, be appointed a committee to revise the laws of this commonwealth." The balloting for these nominees was carried out in accordance with the terms in the Virginia Constitution of 1776 providing for joint ballots: each House exchanged lists of nominees; each voted separately; the ballot box of each was carried to the conference room and there opened by a joint committee. To receive the highest number of ballots in both houses for such an important task and in competition with the names of three of the most distinguished legal minds in America—Pendleton, Wythe, and Mason, all of whom were TJ's seniors—was assuredly a high tribute to his stature as a leader in the reformation of the laws. For the apportionment of the work of revision, the Report at length submitted by the Committee, and TJ's appraisal of the Committee's work, see George Mason's "Plan settled by the committee of Revisors, in Fredericksburg, January, 1777" (partly printed in Rowland, *Mason*, I, 276-7); Report of the Committee of Revisors, 18 June 1779, below; TJ, Autobiography (Ford, I, 58-69); *Notes on Virginia*, Query XIV.

Bills for Dividing Fincastle County

[15 and 26 October 1776]

I. BILL FOR DIVIDING THE COUNTY OF FINCASTLE
INTO TWO DISTINCT COUNTIES

II. BILL FOR DIVIDING THE COUNTY OF FINCASTLE
INTO THREE DISTINCT COUNTIES

EDITORIAL NOTE

THE involved and at times impenetrable legislative history of these two Bills requires special comment. For this was not merely another county division: it was the first great collision between Jefferson and the powerful land speculators. During the two years preceding this session of the Assembly, Jefferson's statements in the *Summary View*, in his correspondence with Pendleton, and in his Drafts of a Constitution had revealed his liberal attitude respecting the uses and potentialities of the vast expanse of fertile lands lying beyond the mountains and within the charter claims of Virginia. To him this was a resource for the development of a country of independent farmers; unappropriated lands would have been, by his Constitution, used for settlers and each person not owning fifty acres of land would have been privileged to appropriate that much; no Indian purchases could have been made without the sanction of the legislature. To others—including many of the most powerful leaders in Virginia and other states—the West offered an unparalleled opportunity for profit. The theme of this great conflict between the aims of statesmanship and the schemes of land-capitalism, together with its impact upon the new institutions being set up, has been explored by many competent scholars, but even those who have dealt with that aspect of the issue involved in the affairs of the Transylvania Company have not explored the intricacies of the history of these Bills to divide Fincastle County. Since Jefferson's liberal statesmanship in behalf of the western settlers triumphed in these Bills over the profit-seeking and proprietary interests of land-capitalism, represented by a relatively few powerful individuals who sought special privileges from the state legislatures and from the Continental Congress and who had influential official connections that ramified in many ways—socially, politically, and economically—, it is important that the struggle over the Fincastle Bills be explored. Indeed, the Bills themselves could not be disentangled without great difficulty unless their legislative history were followed step by step. Once this is done, certain clues to the method by which Jefferson gained his victory may be noted, and the Bills themselves, as documents, may be more accurately presented.

The Transylvania Company, organized by Judge Richard Henderson of North Carolina, based its claim to lands between the Cumberland and Kentucky rivers on an Indian purchase made on 17 March 1775 with the Cherokee. Most of this vast tract of fertile land lay within the charter claims of Virginia, claims that had been first officially stated when the Constitution of 1776 was adopted. Styling themselves the "true and absolute Proprietors of the Colony of Transylvania"— terminology more appropriate to the seventeenth than to the eighteenth century—, Henderson and his associates set about the business of establishing a government for their princely domain. Dispatching an emissary, James Hogg, to the Continental Congress in the autumn of 1775, they endeavoured to have Transylvania admitted to the Union as a fourteenth colony. In Philadelphia Hogg conferred with Jefferson and Wythe. The former informed Hogg that Transylvania's claim lay within the charter limits of Virginia, but also asserted his desire to see new governments established within those limits so long as they were based on liberal principles and properly united with Virginia.

Henderson had been present at Williamsburg with most of the members of his Company during the Convention of 1776 and had presented a petition on 15 June, asserting, with bland disregard for facts, that they had "never entertained thoughts of such an absurdity" as the establishment of a separate government; that neither the Convention nor the Congress had any jurisdiction over the private title to the soil involved in their purchase; that "some interested, artful, and designing persons, by cunning, specious and false suggestions" had raised doubts about the validity of their title; that they were ready to subject themselves "to such government as should be placed by authority over them." The Convention replied to this by its resolution of 24 June 1776 to the effect that no private purchases of land from the Indians should be considered valid until approved by the legislature; the Constitution adopted a few days later, drawing upon Jefferson's Draft, gave this resolution the force of substantive law.

The "interested, artful, and designing persons" complained of by Henderson and his associates had met at Harrodsburg on 8 June as an assembly of anti-Transylvania settlers. Its presiding officer was John Gabriel Jones, nephew of the Gabriel Jones who is said to have been associated with Jefferson in the practice of law and who was the father-in-law of John Harvie. This assembly petitioned Virginia to set off West Fincastle as a separate county and chose as members of the House of Delegates John Gabriel Jones and George Rogers Clark, whom Jefferson had known since boyhood. But Henderson and his associates also had powerful connections. Patrick Henry had flirted with Transylvania in 1775, though now, as governor, he fell in with Clark's plans. There were others in the Virginia legislature interested in Henderson's scheme: Arthur Campbell, for example, who is a key figure in the history of the Fincastle Bills since he was county lieutenant of Fincastle, though at the same time he aspired to be surveyor for Transylvania. Thus with the arrival of Jones and Clark in Williamsburg at the opening of the legislature, and with the ubiquitous Henderson and his associates also present, the issue was joined.

Jones and Clark presented the Harrodsburg petition on 8 Oct., asserting that the "absolute proprietors" of Transylvania intended to erect a "new independent province"; that civil and military officers had been appointed by Henderson and his group, writs of election issued, assemblies convened, a land office opened, and lands sold at exorbitant prices; that the inhabitants of the western part of Fincastle questioned the validity of the Transylvania title, acknowledged themselves within the State of Virginia, and had, after a duly called meeting, elected two delegates who prayed to be admitted to the House. At the same time, Jones and Clark presented a petition asking that the western part of Fincastle be set off as a separate county. On 11 Oct. the House resolved that the delegates could not be admitted, since the inhabitants of western Fincastle were not "allowed by law a distinct representation in the General Assembly." At the same time the Committee on the State of the Country reported the opinion that the inhabitants of the western part of Fincastle "ought to be formed into a distinct county, in order to entitle them to such representation, and other benefits of government." Robert Carter Nicholas, Carter Braxton, and Jefferson were appointed a committee to bring in a Bill for this purpose.

Braxton reported the Bill (No. 1 below) on 15 Oct. The next day it was read the second time and recommitted, this time to a committee composed of Jefferson, who was named first, the members from Augusta (Thomas Lewis and Samuel M'Dowell), and the members for Botetourt (John Bowyer and Patrick Lockhart). Another significant fact occurs from this recommitment: in an issue which involved also the conflicting interests of Tidewater and Piedmont, it is noteworthy that the first committee had included Robert Carter Nicholas and Carter Braxton, both outspoken conservatives from the Tidewater and with land-speculating connections. These were dropped in the recommitment, and, instead of being the minority of a committee dominated by conservatives, Jefferson became the head of one made up of representatives from the western counties. The new committee lost no time in coming to an agreement, reporting their amendments to the Bill the next day, 17 Oct. These were accepted, the Bill passed its second reading, and it was ordered to be engrossed and read a third time. Twice the Bill was postponed and finally, 26 Nov., was defeated. The Bill merely provided for the division of Fincastle into two counties, the western part of Fincastle (embracing most of the Transylvania claim) to be called Kentucky, and the remainder of the parent county of Fincastle to be called Washington.

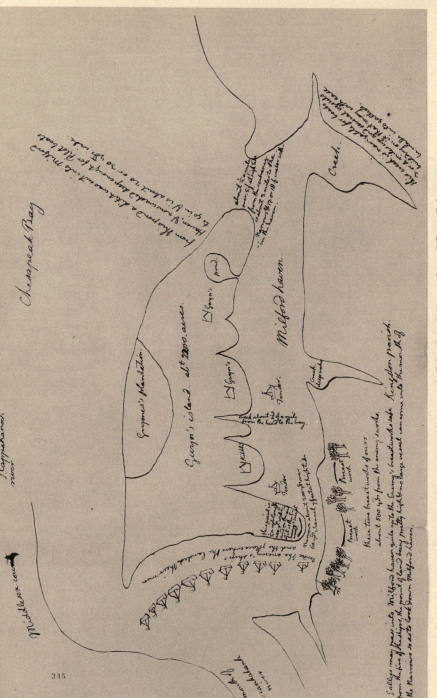

Jefferson's sketch map of Gwynn's Island and the action of June-July 1776.

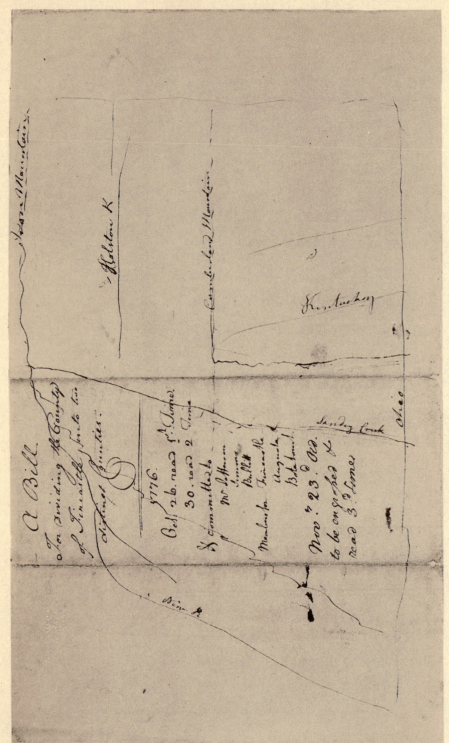

Jefferson's sketch map of the Kentucky region, 1776.

This defeat of the first Bill is puzzling in view of the extraordinary speed with which it and its amendments reached and passed the second reading. But the Committee on Propositions and Grievances—a committee numbering almost half the entire house and including Braxton, Carter, Nicholas and other conservatives—had nevertheless continued to consider the petition from the inhabitants of western Fincastle that had, on 11 Oct., been favorably reported on. The reason for this seems obvious. The shift of the Bill to another committee, Jefferson's emergence as head of this committee having charge of amending the Bill, its introduction on 17 Oct., and its passing the second reading meant that he had clearly been successful in mobilizing western support. With the order to have the Bill engrossed (and it actually was engrossed), Jefferson, no doubt feeling triumphant over his victory for the western settlers against the land speculators, obtained leave from Friday, 18 Oct., until the following Monday. During this week-end Henderson and his associates must have engaged in considerable activity. For, on the same day that Jefferson departed, the final reading of his Bill was postponed until the following Thursday, and on Tuesday, 22 Oct., Braxton reported from the Committee on Propositions and Grievances that the petition of the inhabitants of western Fincastle to be set off in a separate county was reasonable, and his committee was thereupon ordered to bring in a bill for this purpose, surely a strange proceeding in view of the fact that the House had already arrived at this conclusion and had, in fact, twice read and approved the amendments of such a bill. But Braxton and the land speculators and Tidewater planters who were aligned with him took this course because the amendments Jefferson and his followers had made to the Bill introduced by Braxton on 15 Oct. were clearly not to their liking (see notes on Bill No. 1). Such maneuvers no doubt aroused Jefferson to renewed activity, for, two days later, 24 Oct., the House ordered the Committee on Propositions and Grievances to cease its proceedings on the Fincastle petition, though it did not order that committee to refrain from bringing in the bill that it had been directed on 22 Oct. to draw up. But Jefferson also was a member of the Committee on Propositions and Grievances, and the struggle then was transferred to the unrecorded silences of that large and important committee. We can only guess at the intensity of the fight that there took place, but the outcome provides a clue to its course: on Saturday, 26 Oct., it was Jefferson, not Braxton, who reported the new Bill to divide Fincastle. There were now two Fincastle Bills before the House, both bearing the same title, and the one that Jefferson introduced on 26 Oct. was almost identical with that which Braxton had originally brought in on 15 Oct. On 30 Oct. this new Bill passed its second reading and was thereupon referred to a committee which Jefferson headed and which included Charles Simms of West Augusta, Cuthbert Bullitt of Prince William, and the members for Fincastle, Augusta, and Botetourt—all, save Bullitt, representing western counties; Simms, Campbell, and perhaps others of the committee, however, were in one way or another identified with land speculation. Nevertheless, the appointment of this committee on the new Bill is testimony to the quality of Jefferson's leadership on this issue: twice he had displaced Braxton; twice he had become the head of a committee of western representatives; and twice he had assumed charge of bills that had been sponsored by Braxton. The victory was finally won in the Committee on Propositions and Grievances between 24 and 26 Oct. When Jefferson reported the new Bill on the latter date, it was Braxton's Bill (see notes to Bill No. 11), but he and his followers had no intention of allowing it to remain in that state: it was merely more convenient to amend it than to draw a third bill. Jefferson's process of amending was thoroughgoing. When he reported on 23 Nov. that he and his committee had agreed on several amendments, he must have meant several were embraced in one, for the first amendment was to strike out everything following the initial word "Whereas" in Braxton's bill and then to substitute therefor a completely new bill. The "amendments" were read twice and agreed to; two days later the Bill passed its third reading, and Arthur Campbell, one of Henderson's supporters, was designated to carry to the Senate a Bill that symbolized the worst blow that the founder of Transylvania had yet experienced, a blow delivered primarily by Jefferson, though with the support of the western representatives.

Jefferson's "amendment," compared with the bill introduced by Braxton, reveals the force and strength that he threw into the fight. For it provided among other things that Fincastle should be divided into three instead of two counties. If Braxton and the conservatives had left well enough alone and had not endeavored to thwart his amendments to Braxton's first bill, their defeat would not have been so stinging. What they had done was not to frustrate Jefferson, but to arouse and unite his followers so that he was able to give to the western part of the state six instead of four new representatives. More, the Bill included a section which would have made it impossible for surveyors of the great land companies to operate independently of a single official surveyor for each county. Going further, the Bill would have made it impossible for any civil or military officer in Washington and Kentucky counties to hold office if he had taken an oath of office "to the pretended Government of Richard Henderson Gentn. and Company," unless he first made a public renunciation of that government to the Governor and Council. Both of these sections were struck out of the Bill, one probably by the Senate, since the Senate offered three amendments, of which the House accepted one and rejected the others. Both may even have been inserted merely for reasons of political strategy, as an advanced position that Jefferson and his supporters knew they would have to yield, but which would have had bargaining value. The second of these sections especially has the appearance of this, for, once Kentucky and Washington counties were established under Virginia law, "the pretended Government of Richard Henderson Gentn. and Company" could never again be set up without open rebellion against Virginia, and this section of the Bill, therefore, would have little meaning beyond a punitive one.

Jefferson's "amendment" to Braxton's bill not only asserted the sovereignty of Virginia over the Kentucky region claimed by Tran-

sylvania, but it dealt another blow to the conservative Tidewater domi-
nance over political affairs within the state. Arrayed against him in this
struggle were the most powerful forces in Virginia—the plantation
aristocracy of the East and their allies, the land-capitalists, who sought
to exploit the West for profit. Against this powerful combination he
had won a signal victory. There were other results besides these. The
Fincastle Bill was not, in itself, a part of his legislative reform program,
but in seizing upon it because of the great issue involved, he no doubt
created animosities among the leaders of the Tidewater whom he had
defeated, and thus jeopardized parts of his other program, such as the
Court Bills and the Bill for Religious Freedom. Yet, offsetting this, he
had demonstrated his skill as a legislative leader; he had mobilized the
forces of the western part of the state; and in speaking for justice, for
liberal land tenure, and for the use of the West for settlers and not for
exploiters, he laid the foundation of a following that three years later
elevated him to the governorship as the successor to that other leader
of the West, Patrick Henry. Perhaps the greatest significance of the
Fincastle Bills is the conclusive evidence presented to show Jefferson's
skill as a legislative leader and his emergence as an acknowledged
champion of the western settlers.

(On this subject, see C. W. Alvord, *The Mississippi Valley in British
Politics*, Cleveland, 1917; Abernethy, *Western Lands*, p. 123-35, 162-8;
Rudolf Freund, "John Adams and Thomas Jefferson on the Nature of
Landholding in America," *Land Economics*, xxiv [1948], 107-19;
W. S. Lester, *The Transylvania Colony*, Spencer, Ind., 1935; A. M.
Lewis, "Jefferson and Virginia's Pioneers," *Miss. Valley Hist. Rev.*,
xxxiv [1948], 551-88; F. J. Turner, "Western State-Making in the
Revolutionary Era," *Amer. Hist. Rev.*, i [1895], 70-87, 251-69. The
legislative history of these Bills is found in JHD, Oct. 1776, 1828 edn.,
p. 4, 13, 15, 16, 22, 28, 33, 52, 67, 70, 87; the Bill as finally enacted
is in Hening, ix, 257-61.)

I. Bill for Dividing the County of Fincastle into Two Distinct Counties

[15 October 1776]

WHEREAS from the great extent of the County of Fincastle many
inconveniences attend the more distant Inhabitants thereof on
account of[1] their remote situation from the Courthouse of the said
County and many of the said Inhabitants[2] have petitioned this
present General Assembly that the same may be divided, *Be* it
therefore enacted by the General Assembly of the Common Wealth
of Virginia[3] and it is hereby enacted by the authority of the same
that from and after the thirty first day of December next[4] ensuing

the said County of Fincastle be divided into two Counties, that is to say, All that part thereof which lies Westward of the following lines, to wit, beginning at the Mouth of great Sandy Creek, then running up the main branch of the said Creek to Cumberland Mountain, then along the said Mountain South Westerly unto Cumberland Gap, thence by a South line to the boundary of North Carolina, shall be one distinct County and be called and known by the name of Kentucky, and all that part thereof which lies Eastward of the said lines shall be one other distinct County,[5] to be called and known by the name of Washington County.

And for the administration of Justice in the said County of Washington after the same shall take place, *Be* it further enacted by the authority aforesaid that after the said thirty first day of December a Court for the said County of Washington be held by the Justices thereof upon the third Tuesday in every Month in such manner as by the laws of this Colony is provided for other Counties and as[6] shall be by their Commission directed, *Provided* always that nothing herein contained shall be construed to hinder the Sherif or Collector of the said County of Fincastle as the same now Stands entire and undivided from collecting and making distress for any publick dues or Officers fees which shall remain unpaid by the Inhabitants of the said Counties of Washington and Kentucky at the time of its taking place, but such Sherif or Collector shall have the same power to collect and distrain for such dues and fees and shall be answerable for them in the same manner as if this Act had never been made, any Law, Usage or Custom to the contrary thereof in any wise notwithstanding.

And be it further enacted by the authority aforesaid that the court of the said County of Washington shall have jurisdiction of all actions and suits both in Law and Equity which shall be depending before the Court of Fincastle at the time the said division shall take place and shall and may try and determine all such Actions and Suits and issue process and award execution in any such action or Suit in the same manner as the Court of Fincastle might have done if this Act had never been made[7] and the justices of the said County of Fincastle and all Officers of the same shall each and every of them have full power to execute their Offices for the said County of Washington as they might have done for that part of the County of Fincastle had this Act never been made, any Law, usage or custom to the contrary in any wise notwithstanding.

Provided nevertheless that nothing in this Act contained shall be construed to vacate the Seats of the Delegates for the County of

Fincastle who having been chosen by the freemen of that part of the said County of Fincastle to be called by the name of Washington ought of right to retain their Seats as delegates for the County of Washington.

And be it further enacted that every free white man who at the time of elections for delegates or Senators in the said County of Kentucky shall have been for one year preceeding in possession of twenty five acres of land with a house and plantation thereon or one hundred acres of Land without a house or plantation in [either of the said Counties and claiming an estate for life][8] at least in the said land in his own right or in right of his wife shall have a vote or be capable of being chosen at such Election altho' no legal title in the land shall have been conveyed to such possessor and that in all future Elections of Senators the said Counties of Washington and Kentucky together with the County of Botetourt shall form and be one district.

MS (Vi); engrossed copy of Bill. Also another copy (Vi) of the Bill as introduced by Braxton, 15 Oct. The engrossed copy is mutilated and some words have been supplied from the Bill as introduced, as well as from Bill No. II, following. The Bill as introduced is docketed: "A Bill for Dividing the County of Fincastle into two distinct Countys," and also, in hand of John Tazewell: "1776 Oct: 15. read 1st. Time. 16 read 2d. time & committed to Mr. Jefferson & the Members for Augusta & Botetourt. Oct. 17. Amendments reported & agreed to & the Bill with the Amendments to be ingrossed." Paragraph divisions and punctuation, lacking in the engrossed Bill, follow the copy of the Bill as introduced, so far as it goes, and then Bill No. II, so far as it applies.

[1] The words "on account of" in TJ's hand (Bill as introduced).
[2] The words "many of the said inhabitants" in TJ's hand (Bill as introduced).

[3] The enacting clause read, in the Bill as introduced: "by the Senators and Delegates of this present General Assembly."
[4] Places for dates and name of new county were left blank here and below in Bill as introduced.
[5] The remainder of the clause, in the Bill as introduced, read: "and retain the name of Fincastle."
[6] The words "for other counties and as" interlined by TJ in Bill as introduced.
[7] The Bill as introduced ended at this point (save for the phrase "any Law, usage or custom to the contrary in any wise notwithstanding"); the remainder of this Bill must, obviously, have been included in the amendments read by TJ, and agreed to by the House, on 17 Oct.
[8] Words within brackets supplied from Bill No. II, though "either" has been conjectured to replace the inappropriate "any" in that Bill.

II. Bill for Dividing the County of Fincastle into Three Distinct Counties

[26 October 1776]

WHEREAS[1] from the great extent of the County of Fincastle, many inconveniencies attend the more distant inhabitants thereof on account of their remote situation from the Court house of the said

County, and many of the said inhabitants have petitioned this present General Assembly for a division of the same—Be it therefore enacted by the General Assembly of the Commonwealth of Virginia, and it is hereby enacted by the authority of the same, that from and after the last day of December[2] next ensuing the said County of Fincastle shall be divided into three Counties, that is to say, all that part thereof which lies to the South and Westward of a line beginning on the Ohio at the mouth of great Sandy creek and running up the same and the main or north easterly branch thereof to the great Laurel ridge or Cumberland Mountain, thence south westerly along the said Mountain, to the line of North Carolina, shall be one distinct County and called and known by the name of Kentuckey, and all that part of the said county of Fincastle included in the lines beginning at the Cumberland Mountain where the line of Kentucke county intersects the North Carolina line, thence east along the said Carolina line to the top of the Iron Mountain, thence along the same easterly to the source of the south fork of Holstein river, thence northwardly along the highest part of the high lands, ridges and mountains, that divide the waters of the Tennessee from those of the great Kanhawa to the most easterly source of Clinch river, thence Westwardly along the top of the mountains that divide the waters of Clinch river from those of the great Kanhaway and Sandy creek to the line of Kentucke county, thence along the same to the beginning shall be one other distinct county and called and known by the name of Washington, and all the residue of the said county of Fincastle shall be one other distinct county and shall be called and known by the name of Montgomery.

And for the Administration of Justice in the said Counties of Montgomery, Washington and Kentuckey after the same shall take place, Be it further enacted by the authority aforesaid that after the said last day of December a court for every of the said Counties of Montgomery, Washington, and Kentuckey, shall be held by the Justices thereof respectively upon the following days in every Month, to wit, for the County of Montgomery on the first tuesday in every month, for the county of Washington on the last tuesday in every month, and for the county of Kentuckey on the first tuesday in every month in such manner as is by law provided for other counties, and as shall be by their commissions directed.

Provided allways that nothing herein contained shall be construed to hinder the sheriff of the said county of Fincastle as the same now stands intire and undivided from collecting and making distress for any publick dues or officers fees, which shall remain unpaid by the Inhabitants thereof, at the time such division shall take place, but such sheriff shall have the same power to collect and distrain for such dues and fees and shall be accountable for them in the same manner as if this Act had never been made, any law, usage, or custom to the contrary thereof in any wise notwithstanding.

And be it further enacted by the authority aforesaid That the court of said county of Montgomery shall have Jurisdiction of all Actions and Suits in Law and equity which shall be depending before the court of Fincastle county at the time the said division shall take place, and shall and may try and determine all such action and Suits and issue process and award execution in any such Action or Suit and the Justices of the said County of Fincastle who shall reside within the bounds of Montgomery county, after the division and all other Officers of the same shall have power to execute their respective Offices in that part of the said County called Montgomery in as full and Ample a manner as if this Act had never been made, and all the Militia officers of the said County of Fincastle who after the division shall reside in the said county of Washington shall have full power to execute their respective Offices[3] within that part of the said county called Washington until commissions can be issued according to Law.

And be it further enacted that the Justices to be named in the Commission of the peace for the said counties of Montgomery, Washington and Kentucke respectively shall meet for the said county of Kentuckey at Herodsburgh[4] in the said county on the first tuesday in April next, for the said county of Washington at Blacks Fort in the said county on the last Tuesday in January next, and for the said county of Montgomery at Fort Chiswell on the first Tuesday in January next and having taken the oath required by an Ordinance of Convention and Administered the Oath of Office to and taken Bonds according to law of the respective Sheriffs every of the said Courts may proceed to appoint and qualify a Clerk and to fix upon places for holding courts in their respective counties at or as near the centers thereof as the situation and convenience of the respective counties will admit of and shall thence forth proceed to erect the necessary publick Buildings for such Counties at such places respectively and shall also appoint such places for holding Courts untill such Buildings shall be compleated as they shall think fit, provided always that the appointments of the places for holding courts and of Clerks for the several Counties aforesaid shall not be made unless a majority of the Justices for such counties be present where such majority shall have been prevented from attending by bad weather or accidental rise of watercourses, but in all such cases the appointments aforesaid shall be postponed until the then next court days and so on from court day to court day until such obstacles shall be removed.

And be it further enacted that the courts of the said counties shall have power to adjourn themselves to such places as they shall appoint, and after the publick Buildings aforesaid shall be erected for the said counties at the places to be appointed as aforesaid the courts for the said Counties shall be thence forth held at such places.

And be it further enacted that every free white man who at the time of elections of Delegates or Senators for the said several Counties shall have been for one year preceding in possession of twenty five Acres of Land with a house and plantation thereon or One hundred Acres of Land without a house and plantation in any of the said Counties and having right to[5] an estate for life at least in the said land in his own right or in right of his wife, shall have a vote or be capable of being chosen a Representative in the county where his said land shall lie although no legal title in the same shall have been conveyed to such possession and that in all future elections of Senators the said Counties of Montgomery, Washington and Kentucke together with the county of Botetourt shall form and be one district.

And be it further enacted that it shall and may be lawfull for the Governor or in his absence for the President of the Council to appoint a person in every of the said Counties of Montgomery, Washington and Kentuckey to be the first Sheriff thereof respectively, which said Sheriff so appointed shall continue in Office during the term and upon the same conditions as is by law directed for other Sherifs.

And be it further enacted that the Field Officers and Captains of the Militia of Washington County be and they are hereby empowered and required to appoint the Captain and the Ensign and the feild officers and captains of the county of Montgomery to appoint the first and second lieutenants[6] of the Company of regulars directed to be raised in the county of Fincastle as the same stood entire and undivided if the same shall not have been previously appointed by the feild officers and captains of the county of Fincastle[7] agreeable to an Act of this present General Assembly for raising Six Additional Batalions of Infantry on the Continental Establishment.

And whereas great Inconveniences have arisen from the appointment of persons to act as Surveyors in certain counties independant of the county Surveyors, Be it therefore enacted by the Authority aforesaid that there shall be but one principal Surveyor in any of the said counties of who shall keep his office and reside in the county of which he shall be the Surveyor respectively and shall be Subject to the same rules and regulations as is by law provided for other Surveyors. And be it further enacted that all Surveys which shall hereafter be made contrary to this Act and all proceedings thereupon shall be illegal and void, and if any person shall presume to act under any such Appoints in Future they shall for every such Offence forfeit and pay to the Surveyor of the county where the offence shall be committed ten pounds to be recovered by action of Debt or information in any court within this commonwealth.[8]

Provided nevertheless that no person shall be capable of being appointed to or of holding any Office civil or Military within the said Counties of Washington and Kentuckey who hath heretofore taken any Oath of Office to the pretended Government of Richard Henderson Gentn. and Company, until he hath made to the Governor and Council a public renunciation of the Government of the said Henderson & Company.[9]

And whereas from the great extent of the parish of Botetourt the same is become very inconvenient to the Inhabitants thereof, Be it therefore enacted by the Authority aforesaid that from and after the last day of December next the said parish shall be divided into four distinct parishes that is to say all that part of the said parish which lies in the county of Montgomery shall be one distinct parish and be called and known by the name of Montgomery —all that other part of the said parish which lies in the said county of Washington shall be one other distinct parish and be called and known by the name of Washington—all that other part of the said parish which lies in the said county of Kentuckey shall be one other distinct parish and be called and known by the name of Kentuckey—and all that other part of the said parish which lies in the county of Botetourt shall be one other distinct parish and shall retain the name of Botetourt parish.

Provided always that nothing herein contained shall be construed to hinder the Collector of the said parish of Botetourt as the same now stands intire and undivided from collecting and making distress for any dues which shall remain unpaid by the Inhabitants of the said parish at the time of the division's taking place, but such collector shall have the same power to collect or distrain for the said dues and shall be answerable for them in the same manner as if this Act had never been made.

And be it further enacted by the Authority aforesaid that the Vestry of the said parish of Botetourt as the same now stands intire and undivided be and they are hereby disolved.[10]

MS (Vi). In an unidentified hand and docketed: "A Bill for dividing the County of Fincastle into three distinct Counties & the parish of Botetourt into four distinct parishes." Though originally drawn as a separate bill, this document was actually employed as an amendment (though a very sweeping one—see note 1, below) to an earlier bill, MS also in Vi; this is a clerk's copy of the bill introduced from the Committee on Propositions and Grievances, 26 Oct., and is nearly identical with the bill Carter Braxton had first introduced on 15 Oct. (see Editorial Note and notes on Bill No. I, above). This earlier bill has blank spaces left for the names of the counties to be erected and their boundaries and is docketed as follows: "A Bill for Dividing the County of Fincastle into two Distinct Counties," and, in John Tazewell's hand, "1776. Oct. 26. read 1st Time. 30. read 2 Time & committed to Mr. Jefferson Simms Bullitt Members for Fincastle Augusta & Botetourt Novr. 23d. Ord. to be engrossed & read 3d Time." Over this docketing there is a crude map of the Kentucky region showing the principal boundaries named in the bill; the map was drawn by TJ and is reproduced in this volume.

1 "Whereas" is deleted. Above it TJ wrote: "Strike out from the word 'Whereas' to the end of the bill & add"

—then follows the entire text of a new bill offered as an amendment to the Committee on Propositions' Bill described above.

2 All of the blank spaces left for dates and names in the text of the "amendment" are filled in in TJ's hand except where noted; he spelled Kentucky both as "Kentucke" and "Kentuckey."

3 The words "untill recommendations can be made by the County Court and" were deleted, and the following interlined by TJ: "within that part of the said county called Washington until."

4 Two words deleted and "Herodsburgh" interlined by TJ.

5 The word "claiming" deleted and "having right to" interlined by TJ.

6 The words from "and the feild officers" are interlined in TJ's hand.

7 The words from "if the same shall not" are interlined in TJ's hand.

8 This whole paragraph has been crossed out; it was probably deleted before TJ presented the "amendment" to the House on 23 Nov. The Bill as adopted (Hening, IX, 257-61) follows this draft in all respects except for this and two other sections noted below.

9 This paragraph, written in an unidentified hand, may have been the amendment struck out by the Senate.

10 This paragraph has been crossed out in MS, probably before TJ reported his "amendment" on 23 Nov.

Additional Instructions by Congress to Franklin, Deane, and Jefferson

[16 October 1776]

Additional instructions to B F, S D, and T J, commissioners from the united states of America to the king of France.

Whilst you are negotiating the affairs you are charged with at the court of France you will have opportunities of conversing frequen[t]ly with the ministers and agents of other european princes and states residing there.

You shall endeavour, when you find occasion fit and convenient, to obtain from them a recognition of our independency and sovereignty, and to conclude treaties of peace, amity and Commerce between their princes or states and us provided that the same be not incompetent with the treaty you shall make with his most christian majesty; that they do not oblige us to become a party in any war which may happen in consequence thereof, and that the immunities, exemptions, privileges, protection, defense and advantages, or the contrary, ther[e]by stipulated, be equal and reciprocal. If that cannot be effected, you shall, to the utmost of your power, prevent their taking part with Great Britain in the war which his britannic majesty prosecutes against us, or entering into offensive alliances with that king, and protest and present remonstrances against the same, desiring the interposition mediation and good offices on our behalf of his most christian majesty, the king of France, and of any other princes or states whose dispositions are not hostile towards us. In case overtures be made to you by the ministers or agents of any european princes or states for commercial treaties between them and us, you may conclude such treaties accordingly.

Dft (DLC: PCC, No. 25). In the hand of George Wythe, with insertions in another hand. Endorsed by Thomson: "Report of the Commee. on preparing further instructions to the Commissioners postponed. Agreed to Octr. 16. 1776."

No copy of this document has been found among TJ's papers; none may have been sent to him.

Bill for Raising Six Additional Battalions of Infantry

[28 October 1776]

WHEREAS it has been thought necessary by the American Congress that the armies of the United States should be augmented to eighty eight battalions, to be enlisted to serve during the continuance of the present war unless sooner discharged, and that fifteen of the said battalions should be furnished by this Commonwealth; and the said Congress by their resolutions have engaged to give to every non-commissioned officer and private soldier a present bounty of twenty dollars an annual bounty of a suit of clothes to consist for the present year of two linen hunting shirts, two pr. of Overalls, a leathern or woollen waistcoat with sleaves, one pr. of breeches, a hat or leathern cap, 2 shirts, 2 pr. of hose, and 2 pr. of shoes, amounting in the whole to the value of 20 dollars or that sum to be paid to each soldier who shall procure these articles for himself[1] and to provide the following portions of lands to be given at the close of the war, or whensoever discharged to the officers and soldiers who shall engage in the said service, or to their representatives if slain by the enemy, to wit, to every noncommissioned officer or soldier one hundred acres, to every ensign one hundred and fifty acres, to every Lieutenant two hundred acres, to every captain three hundred acres, to every Major four hundred acres, to every Lieutenant Colonel four hundred and fifty acres and to every Colonel five hundred acres:

And whereas there are already in the Continental service eight battalions of regulars raised in this Commonwealth who were enlisted to serve for certain terms only; and one other battalion formerly in the same service and dissolved by the expiration of the time of their enlistment, has been ordered to be reestablished by new levies; which nine battalions are to be taken as part of the fifteen from this commonwealth provided they shall re-enlist for the continuance of the war: and there are also in the service of this Commonwealth [nine companies of marines and][2] five companies of land forces stationed at different posts on the river Ohio whom it may be expedient to engage in the six new battalions now necessary to be raised to complete the said number of fifteen battalions.

Be it therefore enacted by the General assembly of the Commonwealth of Virginia that[3] it shall and may be lawful for the Governor with the advice of his privy council and he and they are hereby required to take such measures as to them shall seem most expedient for engaging the said nine battalions and also so many [of the said marines and][2] of the companies stationed on the Ohio as shall be willing to be of the armies of the United States on the new establishment before recited; and for that purpose to give recruiting powers to the officers commanding the same, or to send special Commissioners if that measure shall appear more effectual, or to adopt any other ways or means most likely to procure their speedy enlistment.

And whereas it will be necessary, in order to augment and form the said marines into one complete battalion, that an additional company or companies should be raised for that purpose, but the numbers which may be wanting of officers and men being now unknown, the appointing and raising the same cannot be precisely directed, be it therefore enacted that it shall and may be lawful for the governor by warrant under his hand to authorize such of the County committees as he shall think proper to appoint such and so many captains and other inferior officers as may be wanting completely to officer the said battalion, who shall immediately proceed to raise their quotas of men: and in case any officer of the Marines engaging in the said service shall fail to raise the quota of men hereafter prescribed for his office before the   day of next it shall be lawful for the governor with the advice of the privy council either to appoint another in his stead or to continue him as shall appear most likely to expedite the raising his said quota.[4]

And be it further enacted that the Committees for the counties of Fincastle, Botetourt, East-Augusta, Hampshire, and   shall each of them appoint one captain, 2 Lieutenants, one Ensign and four Sergeants to be added to the Officers of the five companies stationed on the Ohio or to such of them as shall be willing to engage as aforesaid in the Continental service and shall with them be formed into one battalion; provided that if all or any of the officers of the said five companies stationed on the Ohio shall refuse to enter into the said service it shall be lawful for the Committee of the county from which such officer or officers received his or their appointment to appoint others in their room.[4]

And for raising the said six additional battalions be it further enacted that the Committee for the district of West Augusta[5] shall have power to appoint ten captains twenty Lieutenants and ten Ensigns and the Committees[6] for the other counties in this Commonwealth to appoint the following officers respectively, to wit,[7]

the Commee. for the county of Accomack (1208 militia)
  90 Albemarle (1254 militia) +70 minte. —54 officers = 1270
  82 Amelia (abt. 1150)
  46 Amherst (abt. 650)
142 E. Augusta 1. captain, 2 Lieutenants, & 1 Ensign (abt. 2000)
100 Bedford (abt. 1400)
114 Botetourt 1. Captain, 2 Lieutenants, and 1 Ensign (abt. 1600)
  85 Brunswick (abt. 1200)
  46 Buckingham (600 exclus. officers) +50
  85 Berkeley (abt. 1200. Mr. Wood)

70 Caroline (983)
25 Charles City (350)
58 Charlotte (812 militia)
68 Chesterfeild (abt. 960)
100 Culpeper (abt. 1400)
71 Cumberland (abt. 1000. militia)
50 Dinwiddie (abt. 700. Mr. Tazew.)
57 Dunmore (abt. 800 nt. more yn. 500 besides Menonists &c.)
11 Eliz. City (120) +40
32 Essex (abt. 450)
71 Fairfx (abt. 1000)
78 Fauquier (abt. 1000) +100
90 Frederic (1264 militia)
142 Fincastle 1. Captain, 2 Lieutenants, & 1 Ensign (2000)
64 Gloster (abt. 900)
37 Goochland (520)
71 Halifx (abt. 1000)
50 Hampshire 1. Captain, 2 Lieutenants & 1 Ensign (abt. 700 rank & file)
64 Hanover (abt. 800) +100 min.
35 Henrico (abt. 500)
14 James City (190.)
51 Isle of Wight (abt. 650) +75
32 K. George (abt. 400) +50
42 K & Queen (600)
35 K. Wm. (abt. 500. Mr. Colman. Colo. Brooke)
14 Lancaster (abt. 200)
114 Loudoun (abt. 1600 besides Quakers)
42 Louisa (550. militia abt.) +50 minute men.
42 Lunenburgh (563 militia) +30 minte.
21 Middlesx (abt. 300)
60 Mecklenburgh (850)
57 Nansemd. (abt. 800)
32 N. Kent (448. r. & f.)
71 Norfolk (900) +100
    Northampton
50 Northumbld. (700)
38 Orange (above 500) +50
110 Pittsylva. (1550)
38 Pr. Edwd. (abt. 550 militia)
32 Pr. George (abt. 450)
32 Prss. Anne (abt. 450)

71 Pr. Wm. (917 militia) +75 = 1000.
33 Richmond (abt. 470)
53 Southampton (750)
35 Spotsylva. (500)
35 Stafford (abt. 400) (+100 by Mr. Brent)
25 Surry (abt. 350)
47 Sussex (abt. 660)
 7 Warwick (100)
50 Westmld. (627) +70 = 700
21 York (abt. 260) +40 free negroes
14 Wmsburgh. (200)

———

3352

which several officers so to be appointed shall immediately proceed to enlist the several quotas of men following, that is to say, every Captain shall enlist 28 men, every first Lieutenant 20, every 2d. Lieutenant 16, and every ensign 10 and shall be at liberty to do the same as well within their respective counties as without.[8]

And if any officer shall fail to recruit his quota of men before mention'd on or before the   day of   next[9] the Committee of the county by whom such officer was appointed may either appoint another in his stead, or may continue him if it shall appear to them that the quota of such officer may be sooner completed by his continuance. But if he or the officer appointed in his stead shall further fail to raise the said quota before the   day of next,[10] then the committee of the county who appointed such officer shall make report of the whole matter to the Governor, who with the advice of the privy council shall take such measures thereon as shall seem most likely to expedite the raising the said quota, whether it be by continuing the same officer, or by making a new appointment; and wheresoever any new appointment shall be made on failure of any officer or officers to raise their quota, the men enlisted by such officer or officers so failing shall be delivered over to the officer appointed to succeed him, he refunding to the officer who enlisted the same such recruiting expences as the committee shall judge reasonable.[11]

And be it further enacted that to each of the said six additional battalions 1 Colonel, one Lieutenant Colonel and one Major shall be appointed by joint ballot of both houses of assembly and one chaplain and one Surgeon by the feild officers and captains of each battalion respectively, and that all chaplains and Surgeons as well of the said six battalions as of the nine battalions now in Continental service shall at all times be removeable and others appointed in their stead by the said feild officers and captains of their respective battalions for good reason to them shewn: and the Surgeon's mates shall be appointed by the Surgeon himself with the approbation of the Commanding officer of the battalion and the Adjutant, Regimental Quarter master, Serjeant Major, Quarter master, Serjeant and Drum major by the said Commanding officer of the battalion.

And be it further enacted that the Quotas of men raised by the officers to be appointed by the Committee of *West Augusta*[12] shall be formed into distinct companies by the said Committee which companies shall constitute one of the said six additional battalions: and the Quotas raised by the officers to be appointed by any other Committee shall by the same Committee be formed into one or more companies or parts of a company according to the nature and number of the Quotas: and the said companies and parts of companies shall be formed into battalions of ten companies each by the Governor or in his absence by the President who shall allot to each battalion such of the feild officers to be appointed by the two houses of assembly as he shall judge best suited to the same and shall deliver to the Continental commander in this colony a roll of each battalion as soon as the same shall be so embodied and officered.[13]

And whereas it is apprehended that sufficient care and attention hath not been alwais had by officers to the cleanliness, to the health and to the comfort of the soldiers entrusted to their command be it therefore enacted that so long as any troops from this commonwealth shall be in any service to the Northward thereof it shall and may be lawful for our delegates in Congress and they are hereby required[14] from time to time to enquire into the state and condition of the said troops and the conduct of the officers commanding them and where any troops raised in this Commonwealth are upon duty within the same or any where to the Southward thereof the Governor and council are required to make similar enquiry by such ways or means as shall be in their power; and whensoever it shall be found that any officer appointed by this commonwealth shall have been guilty of negligence or want of fatherly care of the soldiers under his command they are hereby respectively[15] required to report to this assembly the whole truth of the case who hereby reserve to themselves powers of removing such officers:[16] and whenever they shall find that such troops shall have suffered thro' the negligence or inattention of any officer of Continental appointment they are in like manner to make report thereof to this assembly whose duty it will be to represent the same to Congress: and they are further respectively required from time to time to procure and lay before this assembly exact returns of the numbers and condition of such their troops.

Dft (DLC); entirely in TJ's hand. Although much of the text is crossed out and interlined (some parts of which are indicated in notes below), the Bill was apparently in final form and was passed with such alterations as are indicated below. Dft contains marginal headings similar to those in the Act (Hening, IX, 179-84), but these are not given here. A rough draft of the tabulation of troop quotas by counties is in MHi.

On 15 Oct. 1776 TJ was appointed member of committee to draw up Bill; 19 Oct. committee was given instructions as to what numbers of officers and rank and file each battalion was to consist of, and it was stipulated that field officers should be chosen by joint ballot of both houses, and captains and subalterns be appointed by committees of the counties (the last was changed by amendment; see note 6 below); the Bill was presented by TJ and read first time on 28 Oct.; it was amended by committee of the whole on 1 Nov.; it passed the House on 2 Nov.; having been carried to the Senate by TJ, it was agreed to by that body on 7 Nov. (JHD, Oct. 1776, 1828 edn., p. 13, 19, 21, 26, 27, 31, 36, 38, 45).

1 The preceding lines, beginning "an annual bounty of . . . ," are interlined.

2 Brackets are in original. This, together with one of the two paragraphs deleted (see note 4), was undoubtedly thrown out by one of the amendments offered on 1 Nov. For on 25 Oct. the House instructed the committee to insert a clause in the Bill respecting marines. In DLC (TJ Papers, 2:309) there is an undated petition signed by Captains John Allison and John Lee "in behalf of themselves and the other officers of the marine companies" and stating that "they do with great concern find themselves, in their present situation, of very little use to their country, a circumstance the more distressing as they ardently wish to serve effectually the cause they have engaged in. That the

smalness of the vessels, and the manner in which most of them are employd, render their establishment useless at present; and before larger vessels can be ready, the time for which the privates enlisted will be expired. That they find, amongst their men, a general willingness to engage during the war, upon the terms proposed by Congress; and have no doubt, that their companies can speedily be recruited, to the number requisite for a continental Battalion. That the marines are a body of active, robust young fellows, well fitted for the land service, to which they are strongly enclined, whilst at the same time they have withstood all endeavours to engage them in that of the sea. That they have thought it their duty to represent these facts, and with due respect submit to the wisdom of the Assembly, whether such a disposition of them may not be made, as will greatly facilitate the raising the troops required by Congress." On the verso of this petition are two items in TJ's hand: (1) calculations of quotas for the various counties of Virginia with the names of some of the officers; (2) the following Resolution: "That it be an instruction to the Committee appointed to prepare a bill for raising 6 additional battalions to insert in the same a clause or clauses for regimenting and engaging in the Continental service so many of the marine officers and privates in the service of this commonwealth as are willing, and making the same part of one of the said 6 battalions." This resolution was adopted by the House, as an instruction to the committee, on 25 Oct. (JHD, Oct. 1776, 1828 edn., p. 27). Despite this fact, TJ's Bill was amended so as to exclude all reference to the marines.

3 The following was deleted in the Bill, probably before being introduced since it is not bracketed: "a Committee of three persons shall be chosen by joint ballot of both houses to proceed immediately."

4 This entire paragraph is crossed out, probably by amendment of the House.

5 The Bill to divide West Augusta was introduced 29 Oct. (same, p. 32); consequently, the name of West Augusta was afterward deleted from the present Bill and the names of "Yohogania, Monongalia, and Ohio" substituted therefor, so that they occur for the first time not in the Act by which they were created but in the one concerning the six battalions (Hening, IX, 180, 262-6).

6 Despite the instruction given the Committee on 18 Oct. by the House, this was amended to read "and the field officers and captains of the militia, or a major part of them" (same, p. 180).

7 On the verso of the petition referred to in note 2 (TJ Papers, 2: 309) and also in another undated document (DLC: TJ Papers, 2: 308, 309 verso), TJ calculated the various quotas. The draft of the Bill from which the present text derives has, after each county, two additional numbers that have been deleted: thus the entry for Warwick reads as follows: "7 Warwick (100) [8] 7," the last two figures having been crossed out, as was done for almost all other counties. The deleted figures are not represented in the present text, and the two documents noted above are not given because they are merely TJ's progressive calculations for the various quotas. His procedure was as follows: on the basis of the known or estimated militia rolls of each county (the figures given to the right of the name of the county), TJ arrived at a quota of enlistments for each county (the figures given at the left of the name of the county). However, since the instructions given the committee on 18 Oct. designated the number of officers and men of each battalion, the quotas of men here given are not, of course, in the Act; these quotas were in turn used by the House as the basis for determining the number of captains and subalterns to be chosen by the field officers and captains of militia of each county, and the allotment as thus determined is given in the Act (Hening, IX, 180-1). On the recto of the second of the two documents referred to at the beginning of this note, in an unidentified hand, is the following: "Heads of the bill for raising six battalions of infantry on continental account. That the six battalions consist of ten companies each, and each company of sixty eight men rank and file with their proper officers to serve during the continuation of the war, unless sooner discharged by Congress. That each of the battalions be commanded by a colonel a lieutenant colonel, a major, ten captains twenty lieutenants ten ensigns and forty serjeants, and each company to be allowed a drummer and a fifer. The nine companies of marines to be included in the six battalions." This meant that each company of non-commissioned officers and men (68 men plus four sergeants, one drummer and one fifer) totalled 74, or 740 in a battalion. The total number of militia tabulated by TJ on the verso of the document just quoted was 47,255; this figure he divided by 3330 (740 multiplied by 4.5), obtaining the quotient 14; thus one-fourteenth of the militia strength of the county was set as the quota for that county, and this in turn was the figure used in calculating the number of officers to be appointed in each county. TJ arrived at the figure 4.5 by deducting the half-battalion on the Ohio and the whole battalion of West Augusta from the total of six.

8 The Act adds the following at this point: "and be allowed a dollar and one third for each man for recruiting expenses."

9 The Act reads: "first day of January next."

10 The Act reads: "first day of February next."

11 The words "as the committee shall judge reasonable" are not in the Act. At this point the Act includes a paragraph concerning the fixing of places for rendezvous, the reviewing of troops, the issuing of commissions, and the establishing of seniority.

12 See note 5.

13 The remainder of the Bill was deleted by amendment and does not appear in the Act; it is instructive, however, as revealing TJ's concern for the men who were to be furnished by Virginia for the Continental establishment.

14 The following was deleted in the MS: "to send one or more of their body to such encampments."

15 The following was deleted in the MS: "empowered and charged to suspend such officers and." The words are inclosed in square brackets, which would seem to indicate that they were deleted by amendment before the whole passage was struck out by the House.

16 The words following this point are crossed out in the MS.

From George Wythe

Philadelphia 28 Oct 1776

Your letter of the 18th instant, by some accident or other, did not come to hand before it was too late to answer it by this days post. Make use of the house and furniture. I shall be happy if any thing of mine can contribute to make your and Mrs. Jefferson's residence in Williamsburg comfortable. Adieu.

RC (DLC). TJ's LETTER OF THE 18TH INSTANT is missing. It must have contained a request for the use of Wythe's house, a handsome residence still standing on the west side of Palace Street adjacent to Bruton Church in Williamsburg; see *The George Wythe House*, a pamphlet published by Colonial Williamsburg, 1942. Having obtained the permission granted in the present letter, the Jeffersons occupied the Wythe house during November, moving out on 4 Dec. 1776, under which date TJ's Account Book has these entries:
"Pd. for carting furniture to Pinkney's 4/.
"Took two rooms of Pinckney. No rent agreed on. He pays £25. for whole tenement. If I give him half of this it will be a plenty."
Three days later the following entries appear in the Account Book:
"Gave servts. at Mr. Wythe's 14/.
"Left with Mrs. Drummond for Mr. Wythe 30/."

From William Irvin

[Before 1 November 1776]

Being taken sick I had the Opportunity of offering the inclosed Memorial and Petition to but very few. I am perswaded, however, that a large Majority of the two Counties would have signed it, had they had the Opportunity. However, I trust that the reasonableness of the thing in itself, will have more Weight with the Honourable House of Delegates and Senators, than ever so many Names.

Please, Sir, to take it under your Care, and either read it, or have it read in the House, as either Custom, or your own Inclination shall direct, and befriend the Contents, of it, and in so doing you will greatly oblige the greater Part of your Constituants, and many others, and none more than Your cordial Friend and very huml. Servant,   WILLIAM IRVIN

RC (MHi); addressed: "Col. Thomas Jefferson Williamsburg." Address leaf contains faint pencil notes in TJ's hand reading as follows: "Public become security. [Expence?] of Collection nt be refund. y cd collect with less expence. Obj. yt wll gve premium for [paying?] Debts not ye propty of ye Factors." This may refer to the debates on the Act for Sequestering British Property (Hening, IX, 377-80).

The MEMORIAL AND PETITION referred to as being enclosed is undoubtedly the Petition of Dissenters in Albemarle and Amherst counties, introduced on 1 Nov. 1776, q.v. William Irvin was a signer of this petition.

Petition of Dissenters
in Albemarle and Amherst Counties

[Before 1 November 1776]

To the Honourable, the Delegates and Senators, Representatives of the Common Wealth of Virginia, assembled at the City of Williamsburg,

The Memorial and Petition of the Descenters from the Church of England, and others, in the Counties of Abemarle and Amherst, humbly sheweth,

That your Memorialists have never been on an equal footing with the other good People of this Colony, in respect of religious Priviledge, having been obliged, by Law to contribute to the support of the established Church, while at the same Time they were moved from a Principle of Conscience to support that Church of which they called themselves Members: Yet in as much as this was the Mode of Government, established, either when they came into the Colony, or, being Natives, when they became Descenters from the Church of England, for the sake of good Order they have patiently submitted to their Grievances, continuing to be peacable and Loyal Subjects, always ready and willing to stand up with the foremost, in the support of Government and in the Defence of the just Rights and Property of the Subject.

That, when it became necessary, that the Form of Goverment should be new moddeled, in consequence of our having thrown off our Dependance, on the Crown and Parliament of great Britan, Your Memorialists flattered themselves, that, that Form of Goverment, that would secure just and equal Right to the Subject, would be the Choice of every Individual, both from the Consideration of the Justice, and good Policy, that would be contained in it, and also from the Consideration, that, by the Join'd, and strenous Endeavours of every one our Liberty, our all, must be defended against the unjust violators thereof and that therefore all should enjoy equal Priviledge.

That your Memorialists cannot disguise their real Concern to observe that instead hereof, there are many who are still violent for a reestablishment of the Episcopal Church, and to have been informed, that to this End there are sundry Petitions, about to be prefered to the House, sign'd by the Bulk of the People, Nor can they forbear signifying to this Honourable House, their Since [Sense] of the great Iniquity, contained in the Establishing of any one religious Denomination of People worshiping the same God, and all strugling in the same common Cause, in preference to all others, and that all and every other religious Sectary, should be obliged to contribute to the support of that Church, thus established, when it is with the greatest Difficuly that they can support publick Worship in that Way and manner that they rather choose. Your Memorialists judge however, that they may rest quite easy, on refering it to the known Wisdom, Candour and Integrity of this Honourable House, how far such Petitions should be heard and granted, and also how far such a Mode of Goverment should be established.

Your Memorialists conceieve, that to put every religious Denomination on an equal footing, to be supported by themselves independent one of another, would not only be a reasonable and just Mode of Goverment, but, would certainly have an happy Influence, on the greater Purity of the several Churches; on their more free and friendly Intercourse with each other; on suppressing any thing like Feuds, and Animosities amongst the People, and on attaching all, of every Denomination to Goverment.

Such a Form of Goverment is all that your Memorialists Desire, and what they Pray this Honourable House for, nor can they doubt of obtaining this, or any other reasonable Request from a Body so respectable, whom we trust have the equal Happiness of their Constituents in particular, and of the Common Wealth in general, as their highest Motive.

That all propitious Heaven may inspire this Hon. House with Wisdom equal to the Importance of the Business divolved upon them and that this Common Wealth may become the Invy of the Nations and the Glory of the World, shall ever be the ardent Wish of your Memorialists and humble Petitioners!

Charles Lewis	James Norris	John Wallace
Charles Lewis Junr	Bartlet Davies	James Woods
Geo. Gilmor	Masias Jones	David M'Williams
Jno. Coles	John Woods	John Read
John Marks	Wm. M'Cord	Nathan Woods
Bennet Henderson	James Read	David Woods
Charles L. Lewis	David Eperson	Henry Kerr
Phil: Mazzei	Robt. M'Collock	Saml. Karr.
James Kerr	James Black	Josiah Wallace
David Allen	John Morris	Richd. Pilson
Wm. Irvin	Wm. Wallace	Wm. Pilson
Andrew Wallace	John M'Collock	Thomas Wherry
Wm. Shelton	John Alexander	John Jameson

Saml. Jameson	Thos. Evans	Jessey Shelton
Thomas Craig	Edward Nash	Valentine Shelton
John Craig	Presley Dallens	Geo: Shelton
Thos. Jameson	Wm. Huntson	Robert Shelton
Micajah Via	Wm. Pilson	Will: More
John M'Cord	Edwd. Johnson	Jas. Mt:gomery
Saml. M'Cord	Hugh Alexr.	David Mt.gomery
William Woods	Jas: Briget	Wm. Wright
Wm. Tamerlinson	Isaac Harden	Josiah Wood
John Black	Alex. M'Williams	John Wood
John Black	Alexr. Jameson	Richd. Wood
Wm. Ramsey	Wm. Cleveland	John Wood
James Keton	Neal M'Gleester	James Wood
William Norris	Henry Wood	Peter Martain
Chas. Whitlock	William Eads	Geo: Martain
Wm. Fretwell	John Garland	Chas. Martain
Charles Mills	James Burton	Henry Woody
John Wherry	Archle Forbis	Martain Woody
Wm. Norris Senr.	Wm Forbis	John Woody
Gilbert Karr	Thos. Eads	David Woody
John Haggord	Thos. Norval	John Tomson
John Bailey	Wm. Nibbits	Jas. Tomson
David Henderson	William Nibets Junr.	Wm. Tomson
Thos. Anderson	Thomas Nibbets	James Alexr.
James Woodson	Andrew Nibbets	John Alexr.
Thos. Jerman	Chas. Teat	Andrew Wright
Daniel Maupin	William Teat	Bartlet Eads
Saml. Bocock	James Wright	Wm. FizPatrick
Alexr. M'Kenzie	James Right Junr.	Robt. Wright
Bana Burnet	Jacob Wright	Saml. Scot
Zac: Colley	Wm. Shilton	Geo: Blain
Wm. Bannel	Saml. Denney	Will: Loveing
John Rogers	John Denney	Wm. Walton
Jno. Williams	Jason Denney	Jno. Johnston
Jno. Davies	Thos. Forton	Mask Leak
Saml. Stockdon	Zack: Forton	John Wharton
David Graves	John Forton	Beza: Maxwell
John Stockdon	William Bayens	Thos. Maxwell
Alexr. Ramsey	John Bayens	Alexr. Blain
John Dallens	Robt. Bayens	Geo: Blain
John Branhem	John Bird Senr.	Thos. Applin
Ben: Davie	Abner Bird	Jas. Lyon
Barnet Branhem	Bartlet Bird	John Dawson
Joseph Anderson		

MS (Vi). Clerk's copy, with signatures all in the same hand. Endorsed: "Dissenters Petn. 1776 Refd. to Com: of Religion."
This petition was enclosed in the undated letter from William Irvin to

TJ, printed under the present date. It was presented on 1 Nov., probably by TJ since he was a member of the Committee on Religion. This was one of a large number of petitions from dissenters presented shortly after the opening of the Assembly in October. Of these TJ wrote in his Autobiography: "the first republican legislature which met in 76. was crowded with petitions to abolish this spiritual tyranny. These brought on the severest contests in which I have ever been engaged. Our great opponents were Mr. Pendleton and Robert Carter Nicholas, honest men, but zealous churchmen. The petitions were referred to the committee of the whole house on the state of the country; and after desperate contests in that committee, almost daily from the 11th of Octob. to the 5th of December, we prevailed so far only as to repeal the laws which rendered criminal the maintenance of any religious opinions, the forbearance of repairing to church, or the exercise of any mode of worship" (Ford, I, 53). In the passage that follows, TJ points out that the petitions were invariably referred to the Committee on Religion, which was appointed 11 Oct. and consisted of 19 members, including TJ; on 9 Nov. that committee was relieved of this question and it was referred to the Committee of the Whole on the State of the Country. The petitions were the result of a concerted purpose: many of them were identical in phraseology (see notes to Notes and Proceedings, 11 Oct. to 9 Dec. 1776). Copies of three of these petitions, drawn from a very large number in the Virginia State Archives, are in the TJ Editorial Files. These are: (1) a petition from Albemarle, Amherst, and Buckingham counties, which was referred to the Committee on Religion, 22 Oct. 1776, and again referred to the Committee on the State of the Country on 9 Nov.; it is signed by 77 persons, including TJ's neighbor and friend Philip Mazzei, as well as several other signers of the above petition; (2) a petition from Albemarle, Amherst, and Botetourt counties, also presented and referred to the Committee on Religion on 22 Oct., containing signatures of 73 persons; (3) a petition from the Presbytery of Hanover County, referred to the Committee on Religion, 24 Oct. 1776, signed by John Todd, Moderator, and Caleb Wallace, Clerk.

From Richard Henry Lee

DEAR SIR   Philadelphia 3d. Novr. 1776

As I have received no answer to the letter I wrote you by the Express from Congress I conclude it has miscarried. I heared with much regret that you had declined both the voyage, and your seat in Congress. No Man feels more deeply than I do, the love of, and the loss of, private enjoyments; but let attention to these be universal, and we are gone, beyond redemption lost in the deep perdition of slavery. By every account from lake Champlain we had reason to think ourselves in no danger on that water for this Campaign. Nor did Gen. Arnold seem to apprehend any until he was defeated by an enemy four times as strong as himself. This Officer, fiery, hot and impetuous, but without discretion, never thought of informing himself how the enemy went on, and he had no idea of retiring when he saw them coming, tho so much superior to his force! Since his defeat, our people evacuated Crown point, and joined their whole strength at Ticonderoga. We do not hear the enemy have thought proper to visit them there, and the Season must now stop operations on the Lake. On the [borders of] the Sound it has been a war of skirmishes, in which I [think we] have gained 5 out of 6.

Never was a Ship more mauled [than] a Frigate that lately attempted Fort Washington, she had [26] eighteen pounders thro her and most of the guns double s[hotted.] At the same time an attack on the same place by land w[as] repelled, but the day following the enemy gained an emine[nce] from our people near the white plains, on the sound, about 10 miles above Kingsbridge. The loss on our part in killed, wounded, and Missing, between 3 and 400, the enemies loss considerable but numbers not fixt. Our troops fought well and retired in order before a much superior force. This was McDougals brigade consisting of York, Maryland, and I believe some Eastern Troops. In a skirmish the next day We learn the enemy were defeated. By London papers middle of August it seems quite probable that the quarrel between Spain and Portugal with the manoeuvres of the Russian fleet, will produce events in Europe of great importance to our cause.

I have been informed that very malignant and very scandalous hints and innuendo's concerning me have been uttered in the house. From the justice of the House I should expect they would not suffer the character of an absent perso[n] (and one in their service) to be reviled by any slande[rous] tongue whatever. When I am present, I shall be perfect[ly] satisfied with the justice I am able to do myself. From your candor Sir, and knowledge of my political mo[ve]ments I hope such mistatings as may happen in y[our] presence will be rectified.

Among the various difficulties that press our Country, I know of none greater than the want of Ships and Seamen. Perhaps a good basis for remedying the latter might be an alteration of the Act of Assembly for binding out Orphan and poor Children, and direct that, for some time at least, the whole of such children should be bound to the Sea. Without safe Ports to build ships in, and give protection to foreign Vessels, our trade must long lang[uish.] Would it not be proper therefore, to make Portsmouth and Norfolk immediately as strong as Cannon can render them, by adding to the guns already [there] as many from York as will answer the purpo[ses. Gen.] Stephen tells me that the works he laid out at [Ports]mouth will put (if properly gunned) that [pla]ce in a state of security from any Seaforce [tha]t can come against it. The Cannon are of no use at York, experience proving incontestibly, that Ships will pass any fort or Battery with ease, when favored by wind and tide. The quantity of seasoned timber said to be in the neighborhood of Norfolk would furn[ish] a number of fine Vessels, whether for fighting or for commerce. I think the large Sea gallies that carry such a number of men for war and for the navigatio[n] part of the Vessel, are well contrived for the defence of our bay and for raising seamen quickly. I sent our Navy board a draught of the large gallies building here by order of Congress. It seems to me, that for the different purposes of battery and Ships our Country could well employ a thousand Cannon. How very important is it that the Cannon foundery on James river should be pushed on with all possible vigor and attention. I understand Mr. Ballantine manages some part of these works, if so, my fears are that very little may be expected. He will talk amazingly, promise most fairly, but do nothing to purpose. This I fancy has been the case with a variety of that Gentlemans undertakings, but such conduct, in the Cannon business, will ruin us. I am very uneasy, I own, on this account. Let us have Cannon, Small Arms, gun powder, and industry; we shall be secure—But it is in vain to have good systems of Government and good Laws, if we are exposed to the ravage of the Sword, without means of resisting. This winter will be an age to us if rightly employed. Let us get strong in Vessels, Troops, and proper fortifications in proper places. Let us import plenty of military stores, soldiers, cloathing, and Sail cloth for tents, shipping &c. I do not think our armed Vessels can be so well [em]ployed in any other business as in m[aking] two or three trips to the French and Dutch Islands for these necessaries, carrying Tobacco and fine flour to purchase them.

I am with much esteem dear Sir, affectionately yours,

RICHARD HENRY LEE

P.S. Let every method be essayed to get the valuable old papers that Colo. Richard Bland was possessed of. R. H. L.

RC (DLC). Tr (PPAP). RC addressed: "Thomas Jefferson esquire at Williamsburg in Virginia Free R. H. Lee." Endorsed: "Lee, Rich. Henry." RC torn in margins; missing words have been supplied in square brackets from Tr.

R. H. Lee's LETTER . . . BY THE EXPRESS is that of 27 Sep. 1776, above. The HINTS AND INNUENDO'S, said by Lee to be circulating against him in the House of Delegates, were probably the accusation that Lee had, in writing, demanded rentals of his tenants in tobacco or in gold or silver specie, fearing paper money would depreciate; see Bland Papers, I, 57; Burk, Hist. of Va., IV, 225-6; notes to Bill for Regulating the Appointment of Delegates to the Continental Congress, 12 May 1777; and R. H. Lee to TJ, 3 May 1779. The OLD PAPERS belonging to Col. Richard Bland, "the Virginian Antiquarian," who had died on 26 Oct., were in part acquired by TJ; see Kingsbury, Records of the Virginia Company, I, 41-8.

Bill to Establish the Places

of Holding Courts in the Counties of
Pittsylvania and Henry

[4 November 1776]

For fixing the places of holding courts for the counties of Pittsylvania and Henry Be it enacted by the General assembly of the Commonwealth of Virginia that it shall and may be lawful for the freeholders of the said county of Pittsylvania qualified by law to vote for representatives in general assembly, and they are hereby required to meet at the house of Richard Farthing in the said county on   the   day of   next, then and there to chuse the most convenient place (having due regard as well to the extent of the said county as to the populousness of it's several parts) for holding courts for the said county in future.

And be it further enacted that notice of the said time and place of election shall be given to the freeholders of the said county of Pittsylvania by the Sheriff, ministers and readers, in the same manner and under the like penalties as are directed for giving notice of an election of representatives to serve in General assembly, and that the election shall be held by the said sheriff in the same manner as such election of representatives to serve in General Assembly, writing down the names of the places voted for, every one in a separate column of his poll, and the names of every freeholder voting under the place for which he votes: and the place for which the most votes shall be given shall thenceforth be the place for holding courts for the said county: and after the election shall be made the sheriff shall return the original poll, attested by himself, to the clerk's office of the said county, by whom the same shall be recorded.

And be it further enacted that the same rules and proceedings shall be observed in every article relating to the said election, and all persons failing to do their respective duties shall incur the same penalties and be subject to the same actions as are prescribed by law in case of an election of representatives to serve in General assembly.

And be it further enacted that it shall and may be lawful for the freeholders of the said county of Henry qualified by law to vote for representatives to serve in General assembly, and they are hereby required, at the time and place of meeting to make their first choice of representatives (which place is hereby declared to be the plantation of John Rolands[1]) to make choice also of the most convenient place for holding courts for the said county of Henry in future having due regard as well to the extent of the said county as to the populousness of it's several parts, which election shall be notified and held, and in all circumstances be conducted by the same rules and proceedings, and all persons failing to do their respective duties shall incur the like penalties and be subject to the same action as before directed for the county of Pittsylvania.

Provided that if the freeholders of either of the said counties of Pittsylvania or Henry shall be prevented by rain snow or accidental rise of watercourses from assembling at the places of election on either of the days beforementioned that then it shall and may be lawful for the sheriff and he is hereby required to postpone the election so prevented, until that day week, and so in like manner from week to week so often as the case shall happen.

And whereas by the usual course of the law sheriffs cannot be qualified for their offices but by the justices of the peace in open court at the courthouse of their counties; and no court can be held for the qualification of a sheriff for the said county of Henry until a place for holding the same is fixed on as before directed; be it therefore enacted that the sheriff for the county of Pittsylvania[2] shall have authority and power and he is hereby required to notify and hold the said election for the county of Henry as well of a place for holding courts as aforesaid as for making their first choice of Representatives to serve in General assembly, in like manner and subject to the same penalties and actions as are before prescribed in the case of the election for the county of Pittsylvania.[2]

MS (Vi). Endorsed by TJ: "A Bill to establish the places of holding Courts in the Counties of Pittsylvania & Henry. Nov 4 read 1st Time Nov 5th 2d time & com to whole." Endorsed by clerk: "A Bill to establish the places of holding Courts in the Counties of Pittsylvania & Henry. Novr. 4th. read 1st. Time Novr. 6th Committed Novr. 21st. Mr. Talbot Jefferson Terry & Members of Pittsylvania & Mr. Fleming."

On 25 Oct. TJ was appointed to a committee to bring in Bill (see clerk's endorsement for legislative course to 21 Nov.); on 2 Dec. a new committee reported amendments which were read twice and agreed to; on 5 Dec. read third time, passed, TJ carrying Bill to Senate; on 9 Dec. agreed to by Senate with amendments, in which House concurred (JHD, Oct. 1776, 1828 edn., p. 27, 40, 44, 65, 78, 83, 90). This involved course reveals a story which can best be appreciated by comparing TJ's draft with the Bill as adopted 9 Dec. (Hening, IX, 242-3). What TJ obviously fought for was the right of the people to determine the seat of their most important unit of local government and for that seat to be placed most conveniently for all and nearest the center of population; what the legislature adopted was an Act giving the justices of the peace the right to qualify sheriffs, to erect public buildings in the two counties, and to place the county seats with reference to geography—"at or as near the centre . . . as the situation and convenience of the respective counties will admit of." After this conflict between TJ's regard for the rights and convenience of the people and the legislature's concern for a simpler procedure and geographic equality, almost nothing was left of TJ's original Bill when the amending process had been completed (but see Ford, II, 116).

1 In the MS the name of another person, probably Edward Lewis, was first written by TJ. "John Rolands" was substituted in another hand. This appears as "John Rowlands" in Hening.
2 TJ first wrote "Fincastle" and then struck it out.

Memoranda

on the Virginia, Pennsylvania, and Maryland Boundaries

[5 November 1776]

If the Monongahela is the line it will throw 300. Virginia families into Pennsylva. Most of these live between the Yohiogany and Monongahela. Not one third of that number of Pennsylvanians would be thrown on the Virginia side.

If the Laurel hill is the boundary it will place on the Virginia side all the Virginia settlers, and about 200. families of Pennsylvania settlers.

A middle line is thought to be just.

Braddock's old road crosses the Yohiogany in the Allegany mountain. Then turns along by the head of Redstone on the West side the Yohiogany and crosses the Laurel hill about 6. miles from Stewart's (or Hart's) crossing, then crosses the river at Stewart's crossing, Jacob's creek 4. mi. above mouth, Swiglie 5. mi. above mouth, then goes down to the Monongahela about 2 mi. below the mouth of Yohiagany then recrosses it within a mile, and there stopped. A line then run from the mouth of Turtle creek to the mouth of the first creek that empties into the Allegany above Croghan's. This would give tolerable satisfaction to Virginia, would throw about 150 Pennsylvas. into Virga. and about 20. or 30 Virginians into Pennsylva. The 150. Pennsylvas. live in such manner dispersed on the Yohiogany and Monongahela that no line will throw them into Pennsylva.

If Braddock's road cannot be established, the Laurel hill and Yohiogany might do without great uneasiness, and so from mouth of Turtle as before.

'All that tract or part of land in America, with the islands therein contained, as the same is bounded on the East by Delaware river, from twelve miles distance Northwards of Newcastle town unto the three and fortieth degree of Northern latitude, if the said river doth extend so far Northward; but if the said river shall not extend so far Northward, then by the said river so far as it doth extend; and from the head of the said river, the Eastern bounds are to be determined by a Meridian line, to be drawn from the head of the said river unto the said forty third degree. The said land to extend Westward five degrees in Longitude, to be computed from the said Eastern bounds; and the said lands to be bounded on the North by the beginning of the three and fortieth degree of Northern latitude, and on the South by a circle drawn at twelve miles distance from Newcastle Northward and Westward unto the beginning of the fortieth degree of Northern Latitude, and then by a straight line Westwards to the limits of longitude, abovementioned.'

Most Southern point of Philadelphia is in Longitude from Greenwich 5H-0'-35" West. Latitude 39°-56'-29",2

The length of a degree of latitude as measured by Mason and Dixon is 68.896 statute miles.

The boundary between Maryland and Pennsylvania was agreed by Ld. Baltimore and Penn to be a line of Latitude 15. miles South of Philadelphia, from the intersection of that line with the Meridian tangent of the circle drawn round Newcastle by a 12 miles radius. This process therefore will determine the latitude of that line.

> Miles   Miles
> As 68.899 :: 1° :: 15 : 13'-3". 7 difference between
> Latitude of Philadelphia and the boundary line.
> Therefore from 39°-56'-29".2 the Latitude of Philadelphia
> Deduct   13- 3 .7 the difference of Latitude
> leaves   39°-43'-25".5 the latitude of the line.

Therefore Pennsylvania is to run down 43'-25".5 Southwardly.

Maryland charter dated 8. Car. 1. June 20.
to Cecilius Calvert Baron of Baltimore in Ireland.

'All that part of a peninsula lying in the parts of America between the ocean on the east and the bay of Chesepeak on the West and divided from the other part thereof by a right line drawn from the promontory or cape of land called Watkins point (situate in the aforesaid bay near the river Wigheo) on the west unto the main ocean on the East, and between that bound on the South unto the part of delaware bay on the North which lieth under the fortieth degree of Northerly latitude from the Equinoctial where New-England ends: and all the tract of land between the bounds aforesaid, that is to say, passing from the aforesaid bay called Delaware bay in a right line by the degree aforesaid unto the true meridian of the first fountain of the river Puttowmack, and from thence tending toward the South unto the further bank of the aforesaid river and following the West and South side thereof unto a certain place called Cinquack, situate near the mouth of the said river where it falls into the bay of Cheseapeack and from thence by a streight line unto the aforesaid promontory and place called Watkin's point (so that all that tract of land divided by the line aforesaid drawn between the main ocean and Watkin's point unto the promontory called cape Charles and all it's appurtenances do remain entirely excepted to us our heirs and successors for ever.)'

The above is extracted from a book of Col. Byrd's bound in Vellum lettered 'Antient Records' which contains most of the colony charters, together with copies of public papers of various kinds which seem to be extracted principally from the Records, they come down as low as Apr. 28. 1722.

1663. c. 2. Pervis: an act concerning the bounds of this Collonie on the Easterne shoare.

Arguments

Common acceptation of location of degree. Maryland charter proves it. Qu. 1. Vezey. 444.

It is nearer to end of 40°.

Mistake in latitude

End of 39°. strikes ocean, not Delaware.

Penn gave Baltimore £5000 to run the line where it is. This is the compromise enforced in Vezey. Why not confine him to begin somewhere in the circle, which is one of the specific parts of description.

The grant of the Northern neck 1. Car. 2. being 32 years before the grant of Pennsylva. to Penn effectually excludes so much of their Southern claim as comes within Ld. Fairfax's territory.

N (DLC). This is a collection of notes written on three sheets of paper of different dimensions and with different watermarks.

These memoranda were set down at several different times, doubtless over a period of years, for the handwriting and ink vary markedly from one group of notes to another, and sometimes from one part of the same sheet of paper to another part. The several sections are here indicated by rules between them, but attempts to date the different sections have proved inconclusive. They are printed all together because they are

so gathered in Jefferson's papers, and under this date because on 5 Nov. 1776 TJ was named at the head of a committee of the House of Delegates to make a fresh proposal for a permanent line between Virginia and Pennsylvania (JHD, Oct. 1776, 1828 edn., p. 41; see letter of Virginia Delegates to Pennsylvania Convention, 15 July 1776). The committee did not report until 17 Dec., three days after TJ had left Williamsburg; it is therefore impossible to determine TJ's share in the new proposal. Brought in by George Mason and adopted by the House, the report yielded the Forks of the Ohio to Pennsylvania, following precisely the western (but not the southern) line claimed by Gov. Penn in 1774 (JHD, Oct. 1776, 1828 edn., p. 101; Paullin and Wright, *Atlas*, pl. 97G). The dispute by no means ended here, but during the national struggle of the next two years it was quiescent, and TJ was not concerned with it again until he became governor. PERVIS: John Purvis, comp., *A Complete Collection of All the Laws of Virginia Now in Force*, London [1684?]. VEZEY: Francis Vesey, the elder, comp., *Cases Argued and Determined in . . . Chancery, . . . from . . . 1746-7 to 1755*, London, 1771. Both these works were owned by TJ (Library Catalogue, 1815, p. 73, 72).

Bill for Altering the Rates of Copper Coin in Virginia

[7 November 1776]

For rendering the halfpenny peices of Copper coin of this Commonwealth of more convenient value and by that means introducing them into more general circulation; be it enacted by the General assembly of the Commonwealth of Virginia that from and after the passing of this act the said peices of Copper coin shall pass in all paiments for one penny each of current money of Virginia.

Provided nevertheless as was heretofore provided by the laws that no person shall be obliged to take above one shilling of the said copper coin in any one paiment of twenty shillings or under, nor more than two shillings and six pence of the said coin in any one paiment of a greater sum than twenty shillings.

MS (Vi). Docketed by TJ: "A Bill for altering the rates of the Copper coin of this Commonwealth." Endorsed in at least two other hands: "1776 Nov. 7. Read the first Time. Novr. 8th. read 2d. Time and Committed to whole. November 21st. rejected."

TJ was appointed to a committee, 7 Nov., to bring in this Bill, and he reported it the same day (JHD, Oct. 1776, 1828 edn., p. 45, 46, 65).

From George Wythe

GW TO T.J.   11 Nov. 1776

The resolutions describing treasons are inclosed. The report for ascertaining the value of coins, &c. remains in the same state of repose as you left it in, among several others that are, as the president says, not acted upon. I gave Col. Harrison an extract of that part of your letter which related to him, and asked him what answer I should make? He told me he would do what you desired so soon as he could. The enemy's army we are credibly informed have left their camp at Whiteplains and retreated towards New-york. I just now hear that Carleton, on the 28th of last month evacuated Crown point, and is retiring to Quebec. Tell the speaker I will endeavour soon to discharge my arrears to him. Adieu.

RC (DLC). Enclosure missing.

RESOLUTIONS DESCRIBING TREASONS: Presumably the resolutions adopted by Congress on 24 June 1776, one of which recommended that the several colonial legislatures pass laws for punishing treasons (JCC, V, 475). TJ had on 28 Oct. been appointed to a committee of the

House of Delegates to prepare a bill declaring what shall be treason (JHD, Oct. 1776, 1828 edn., p. 30). TJ's Report on VALUE OF COINS is printed above under 2 Sep. 1776. The letter in which TJ mentions COL. HARRISON is missing. THE SPEAKER: Edmund Pendleton, elected without opposition, 7 Oct. (same, p. 3).

Bill for the Removal
of the Seat of Government of Virginia

[11 November 1776]

WHEREAS great numbers of the Inhabitants of this Commonwealth must frequently, and of necessity resort to the seat of Government, where General assemblys are convened, Superior Courts are held and the Governor and Council usually transact the executive business of Government, and the equal rights of all the said Inhabitants require that such seat of Government should be as nearly central to all, as may be, having regard only to Navigation the benefits of which are necessary for encouraging the growth of a Town. *And Whereas* it has been found by the experience of some of our Sister States a very distressing circumstance, in times of war, that their seats of Government were so situated as to be exposed to the insults, and injuries of the publick enemy, which ⟨dangers may be avoided⟩ distresses may be prevented in this Commonwealth and equal Justice done to all ⟨the⟩ it's Citizens of this Commonwealth by removing ⟨the⟩ it's seat of Government to the town of   in the County of   which is more safe and central than any other Town situated on navigable water.

Be it therefore enacted, by the General Assembly of the Commonwealth of Virginia, that six whole squares of ground, surrounded each of them by four streets, and containing all the ground within such streets situate   in the said Town of   and on an open and airy part thereof shall be appropriated to the use and purpose of public buildings.

And be it further enacted that on one of the said squares shall be erected one house for the use of the General assembly to be called the Capitol which said Capitol shall contain two rooms or apartments for the use of the Senate and their Clerk, and two others for the use of the House of Delegates and their Clerk, and others for the purposes of Conferences, Committees, and a Lobby, of such forms and dimensions as shall be adapted to their respective purposes. *And* on one other of the said squares shall be erected another building to be called the General Courthouse which shall contain two rooms or apartments for the use of the Court of Appeals and its Clerk, two others for the use of the High Court of Chancery and its Clerk, two others for the use of the General Court and its Clerk, two others for the use of the Court of Admiralty and its Clerk, two others for the use of the Privy Council and its Clerk and others for the uses of Grand and petty juries of such forms and dimensions as shall be adapted to their respective purposes, which said houses shall be built in a handsome manner with walls of Brick, and Porticos, where the same may be convenient or Ornamental: on one other of the said Squares, shall be built a house with three apartments for the Ordinary use of the Clerks of the High Court of Chancery, General Court, and Court of Admiralty; each of them to have one of the said apartments: one other house with three apartments, to be used as a land office: and one other for a publick jail with few apartments for the present, but so planned as to admit of addition in future: two other of the said Squares shall be appropriated to the use of the Governor of the Commonwealth for the time being, to be built on hereafter, and one other square shall be appropriated to the use of a publick Market.

And be it further enacted that five persons shall be appointed by joint Ballot of both houses of Assembly to be called the Directors of the publick buildings who, or any three of them, shall be and are hereby empowered to make choice of such squares of ground situate as before directed as shall be most proper and convenient for the said publick purposes; to agree on plans for the said buildings; to employ proper workmen to erect the same; to procure necessary materials for them; and to draw on the Treasurer of this Commonwealth from time to time as the same shall be wanting for any sums of money not exceeding six thousand pounds in the whole; which draughts he is hereby authorized to answer out of any public money which shall be in his hands at the time: and in case of the death of any of the said Directors, or their refusal to act, the Governor[1] is hereby authorized to appoint others in their stead who shall have the same powers as if they had been ⟨*chosen*⟩ appointed by joint Ballot of both houses as before directed.

And to the end that reasonable satisfaction may be paid and allowed for all such Lotts of ground as by virtue of this Act may be taken and appropriated to the uses aforesaid, *Be it further enacted* that the Clerk of the County of is hereby empowered and required at the desire of the said Directors to issue a writ[2] directed to the Sheriff of the said County, commanding him to summon and impannel twelve able and discreet Freeholders, no ways concerned in interest in the said Lotts of land, nor in any ways related to the Owners or Proprietors thereof to meet[3] at the said Town of on a certain day to be named in the said writ, not under five nor more than ten days from the date thereof who shall be sworn by the said Sheriff,[4] and shall upon their Oaths value and appraise the said Lots of ground in so many several and distinct parcels as shall be owned by several and distinct owners, and according to their respective interests and Estates therein; and if the said valuation can not be completed in one day then the said Sheriff shall adjourn the said Jurors from day to day until the same be completed, and after such valuation and appraisement so made, the said Sheriff shall forthwith return the same under the hands and Seals of the said Jurors to the Clerks office of the said County. And the right and property of the said Owners ⟨of⟩ in the said lots of land shall be immediately divested and be transferred to this Commonwealth in full and absolute dominion, any want of consent or disability to consent in the said owners notwithstanding.

And be it further Enacted, that the Costs and charges of the purchase of the said Lotts of land shall be paid and satisfied by the publick at the next Session of Assembly to the several and respective proprietors or owners thereof according to the valuation made as aforesaid.

And be it further Enacted that it shall and may be lawful for the[5] said Directors and they are hereby required to rent at the publick expence for the use of the Governor such Houses and Lotts of land as may be necessary for his accomodation until buildings for that purpose may with convenience be erected by the Publick.

And Whereas it may be expedient to enlarge the said Town of by laying off an additional number of Lotts to be added thereto and it may also happen that some of the Lands adjacent to the said Town, not yet laid off into Lotts, may be more convenient for the publick uses, *Be it therefore enacted* that it shall and may be lawful for the of the said town of and they are hereby required to cause two hundred additional lots or half acres of land to be laid off adjacent to such parts of the said Town of   as to them shall seem most convenient for the use of those who may⁶ chuse to settle in the said Town.⁷ *And* the said Directors shall be at Liberty to appropriate the six squares aforesaid either from among the Lotts now in the said town, or those to be laid off as before directed, or may have the said Six Squares laid off in any place adjacent to the said Town, and the said Six squares and two hundred Lotts shall thenceforth be added to and be a part of the said town of   saving always to the proprietors of the Land so to be laid off into lotts their full right to the said lotts (other than the Six squares aforesaid) when the same shall be laid off.

And Be it further Enacted that from and after the 25th day of December which shall be in the Year of our Lord 1777. the said Court of Appeals, High Court of Chancery, General Court and Court of Admiralty shall thenceforth hold their Sessions in the said General Courthouse: that the first meeting of General Assembly after the same 25th day of December shall in like manner be in the said Capitol, and the Clerks of the two houses of Assembly and of the said several Courts are hereby authorized and required, at some convenient time before hand, to remove, at the publick expence, their several records to the said Offices to be provided and appropriated to them respectively by the said Directors.

MS (Vi). Fair copy made by a clerk but corrected by TJ at five places; the corrections are here incorporated in the text, and the matter rejected is enclosed in angle brackets. Endorsed by TJ: "A Bill for the removal of the seat of Government," and docketed by the clerk: "1776 Nov. 11. Read first time & Rejected." Also Dft (DLC); in TJ's hand and endorsed by him: "A Bill for the removal of the seat of governm't. Notes & draughts rough." Actually, as happened with others of TJ's papers at this period, the rough draft of this Bill is also a rough draft of a Bill he prepared in 1779 for the same purpose. The rough draft as it stood in 1776, from which the copy was made, was in 1779 revised again for the Bill introduced 29 May 1779, q.v. (From this 1779 revision of the draft, TJ made a fair copy, though with many alterations; this fair copy Ford, II, 106-109, assigns erroneously to 1776.) The draft includes additions and deletions both in its 1776 state and in its 1779 overlay. The distinction between the deletions in the rough draft as it stood in

1776 and those made in 1779 is made possible by the fact that fair copies of each of these states is available for comparison. Only the significant deletions made in the draft in 1776 are indicated in the textual notes below.

This Bill, preceded by similarly unsuccessful attempts to remove the seat of government from Williamsburg in 1761 and 1772 (Ford, I, 55), exhibits four aspects of TJ's far-reaching legislative program: (1) his endeavor to equalize advantages and opportunities as between the Piedmont and the Tidewater regions; (2) his concern with defense measures; (3) his interest in capitol-planning, foreshadowing his later work on the plans of the national capitol; and (4) the close relationship between his political and his architectural concepts (on which see especially Fiske Kimball, "Jefferson and the Public Buildings of Virginia, II: Richmond, 1779-1780," *Huntington Libr. Quart.*, XII [1948-1949], 303-10). Other states at this period were concerned with the problem of removing capitols from the coastal plain to the interior, but it is doubtful if the draftsman of any similar act of legislation embraced such a combination of varied interests and purposes. On 14 Oct. 1776 TJ was appointed to a committee to bring in such a bill; it was reported on 11 Nov., when it was defeated by a vote of 61 to 38 (JHD, Oct. 1776, 1828 edn., p. 11, 51; *Va. Gaz.* [D & H], 15 Nov. 1776; see Ford, II, 106).

1 Draft originally read: "the survivors are empowered"; this was changed to: "the Speakers of the two houses of legislature"; this in turn was altered to: "the Governor is hereby authorized"; but in 1779 TJ again changed this to read: "by joint ballot of both houses of assembly." Finally, in the Bill as adopted in 1779, the contingency-appointment clause was omitted altogether, as was the matter of a specific sum of money.

2 Deleted from the draft in 1776: "in the nature of a writ of Ad quod damnum"; in 1779 the phrase was restored and the Bill as then adopted includes it.

3 Deleted from the draft in 1776: "at such time or times as."

4 Deleted from the draft in 1776: "sworn by any justice of the peace."

5 Deleted from the draft in 1776: "Governor."

6 Deleted from the draft in 1776: "purchase the same from the owners thereof."

7 Deleted from the draft in 1776: "and to cause also the said six squares of land of 2 acres each for public use as aforesaid to be laid off in such places as the directors shall appoint if to the said directors it shall." This, incidentally, is the only mention in any of the drafts of the 1776 or 1779 Bills specifying the size of the lots.

Notes concerning the Bill for the Removal of the Seat of Government of Virginia

[11 November 1776?]

1. Central

    Rts. of Western pe. eql. to Eastrn. of Memb. of Legisl.

    Expedt.

        Invasn. of Uplds.

           disordrs.

        Criminls. Expens

        Executve. shd. b. Centrl

           Heart — Sun —

           Chch. — Ct. house.

2. Safe

    Inconvs. Bostn. — N.Y.

    Expce. of defce. — treasy. Magazn.

    Wmsb. indefensble. — if li. [line] abve. — below, one sit [sitting?] cost 50,000£ a year

    nt. necess. to defd. if govmt. remvd. only defnd. harbrs.

3. Navigble. Water nec. to grt. town

    advge. of grt. town to Manfters. trde. husbdry.

Wmsbgh. nevr. cn. b. grt. — 100 y. xprce. [experience]
addn. of 500. men dbld. price
   Native prodns. of earth.
shews cnt. feed grt. city
4. Health
   no chdr. [children?] raised
5. Expce — 2500 + 2500 + 1000 = 6000
   Wmsb. 1000£ week = 6000 in 6 weeks
   wth. all ys. nt. safe [with all this not safe]

N (DLC). These memoranda are written on the last page of the draft Bill for the Removal of the Seat of Government, introduced 11 Nov. 1776, q.v. It is not possible to say whether these notes, which obviously pertain to the Removal Bill, were made in 1776 or 1779; the cost figures would indicate the latter, but in that year the arguments in favor of removal (as indicated by the speedy adoption of the Bill) were so compelling that TJ must not have needed to make such elaborate memoranda for debate. There is another column of notes on the MS, parallel to this, but faded so much as to be illegible, save for occasional words and phrases, such as "obj. Expce. low calculd. good Capitol," &c., proving that these notes are to the same purpose. The MS contains a third set of notes, which may possibly refer to the Virginia Constitution (though they can scarcely apply to it unless this Bill had been drawn up as early as May 1776, which is very unlikely); possibly these notes refer to the work of the Revisors of the Laws: "1. Legislative. 2. Executive. 3. Judiciary Property 4 Liberty 5 Crimes 6 health 7 Morality 8 Officers 9 Proceedings."

These notes, never previously published, are among TJ's most engaging papers. Never a debater or ready speaker, TJ reveals here for the first time something of his method as a legislator. Obviously he was no rival to the eloquent persuasiveness of Patrick Henry: to begin with the argument that "Rights of Western people [are] equal to Eastern" must have appealed to the delegates of the Piedmont, but to say that a century of experience had shown that "Wmsbgh. nevr. cn. b. grt." [Williamsburg never can be great] or that, in case of invasion, that city could not be defended, was scarcely calculated to win over the Tidewater aristocrats who still held disproportionate power in the legislature. This, too, is TJ's first articulate vision of a great capital city, in which advantages would be held forth to manufactures, trade, and husbandry—a vision of considerable interest in view of his later attitude toward cities.

From George Wythe

GW TO TJ   Philadelphia, 18 November. 1776.

Whenever you and the speaker think I should return to Virginia to engage in the part which shall be assigned to me in revising the laws, I shall attend you. As to the time and place of meeting and my share in this work, I can accommodate myself to the appointment, and be content with the allotment my colleagues shall make. In the mean time, I purpose to abide here, if the enemy do not drive me away; an event some think not improbable. What to think of it myself I know not: especially if a report we heard today, 'that the garrison in fort Washington, consisting of 2,000 men, surrendered themselves prisoners, at the first summons,' be confirmed. Are the judges in chancery, whilst they are on the circuits, to hear cases in equity? If not, are forty days in the year sufficient for that business? I suppose not. I will inquire tomorrow by whom the regimental paymasters are to be appointed; and if I have time before the departure of the post, will let you know: if by congress your recommendation of Mr. Moore shall be remember[ed.] The journals shall also be sent to you, if they can be procured. The conveniency of my house servants and furniture to you and Mrs. Jefferson adds not a little to their value in my estimation. Our best respects to the lady. Be so kind as let me know if our general assembly hath agreed to give any additional bounty to the non-commissioned officers and soldiers of the new levies more than what congress had offered. The eastern states, or some of them, by doing a thing of that kind, have much embarrassed us. I understood by the person employed to draw the figures for our great seal that you intended to propose an alteration in those on the reverse. I wish you would propose it; for though I had something to do in designing them, I do not like them. Let me know of the alteration, if any; and send a neat impression made by the old seal. It will be useful to the workman. Adieu.

My compliments to Mr. Page. I wrote to him several weeks since, and desired him to send me an impression made by the old seal—that I received no answer I attribute to his ill health. I wish it better.

This morning (19 Nov.) we hear fort Washington was not taken last Sunday morning the day after the garrison was supposed to have surrendered by the report mentioned above; but it seems it is invested.

RC (DLC). REVISING THE LAWS: Wythe was appointed to the Committee of Revisal on 5 Nov. (JHD, Oct. 1776, 1828 edn., p. 41). Nothing else is known of the MR. MOORE recommended by TJ in an evidently missing letter. OUR GREAT SEAL: See TJ to Page, 30 July 1776.

Drafts of Bills Establishing Courts of Justice

[25 November to 4 December 1776]

I. BILL FOR ESTABLISHING A COURT OF APPEALS

II. BILL FOR ESTABLISHING A HIGH COURT OF CHANCERY

III. BILL FOR ESTABLISHING A GENERAL COURT

IV. BILL FOR ESTABLISHING A COURT OF ADMIRALTY

V. BILL FOR BETTER REGULATING THE PROCEEDINGS
IN THE COUNTY COURTS

EDITORIAL NOTE

THE remodeling of the judiciary was among Jefferson's first objects as he embarked in Oct. 1776 on one of the most far-reaching legislative reforms ever undertaken by a single person. His ideas concerning an independent judiciary for the new commonwealth had been set forth in his proposed Constitution. Though the principal elements of his judicial system had at least been recognized in the Constitution adopted by the Convention, legislation was necessary to establish the various courts. The full impact of Jefferson's creative reforms with respect to the judiciary has not been fully realized, perhaps because his various Bills suffered differing fates, one being delayed for over two years before adoption and one failing of enactment altogether. The opposition that these judicial reforms encountered has, as a result, received relatively more attention than the system that he endeavored to establish. This opposition was, as Jefferson himself fully realized, a strenuous one, and it was grounded not only upon the conservative antipathies that most of his reform program had to encounter but also upon the fear of many of Virginia's planters that they would be exposed to ruin if courts were opened and British creditors enabled to sue for the payment of long-overdue debts (Malone, *Jefferson*, I, 250, 259-60; I. S. Harrell, *Loyalism in Virginia*, Durham, N.C., 1926, 154ff.; TJ's Autobiography, Ford, I, 48). Nevertheless, the important fact to be noted here is that all of the Judiciary Bills introduced in 1776 were drawn by him, all reflected the ideas set forth in his Constitution, and all were, in his view, intended to harmonize with the republican principles that he endeavored to introduce in all branches of Virginia's polity. The varying fates that his Bills experienced should not be allowed to minimize the creative achievement that he attempted in the autumn of 1776. Hence, for the first time, all of his Judiciary Bills are brought together in one sequence and presented both in the form as originally written and, through notes appended to each, in the form as finally enacted. In the light of these Bills, though some were long delayed in enactment, it is not too much to recognize him as the preeminent architect of Virginia's judiciary under the new Constitution.

On this important subject, however, Jefferson's later statement was in error: "On the 11th. I moved for leave to bring in a bill for the establishmt of courts of justice, the organization of which was of importance; I drew the bill. It was approved by the commee, reported and passed after going thro' it's due course" (Autobiography, Ford, I, 48). This remembered statement is quite different from the actual history of his judicial reform. On 11 Oct. 1776, the House of Delegates granted leave to bring in a Bill "for the establishment of courts of justice within this Commonwealth," and for the purpose appointed the following committee, in the order named: Jefferson, Smith, Bullitt, Fleming, Watts, Williams, Gray, Bland, Braxton, and Curle. On 1 Nov., possibly as a result of the committee's request, the House of Delegates instructed the committee to "divide the subject . . . into five distinct bills, under the following titles: *A bill for establishing a Court of Appeals, A bill for establishing a High Court of Chancery, A bill for establishing a General Court, A bill for establishing a Court of Admiralty,* and *A bill for regulating the proceedings of County Courts*" (JHD, 1776, 1828 edn., p. 9, 35). This judicial structure conforms to that advocated by Jefferson in his Constitution.

The first three of these Bills were introduced by Jefferson for the committee on 25 Nov. and immediately encountered determined resistance, if indeed they had not already experienced opposition in committee from such conservatives as Braxton. The remaining two Bills were presented on 4 Dec.

The Bill for establishing a Court of Admiralty passed almost at once. Virginia was a maritime state, and the establishment of a court having jurisdiction over prizes and other objects of maritime law was therefore a matter of first importance. The other four Bills, however, were opposed strongly. Jefferson endeavored to allay the fears of debt-ridden planters by introducing a Bill for suspending executions for debts in order, as the preamble to this Bill stated, to make it possible to establish and open the courts. But this device was unsuccessful. The Bill for creating a Court of Appeals did not become law until 15 Dec. 1778; those for establishing a High Court of Chancery and a General Court were not adopted by the legislature until 9 and 19 Jan. 1778, respectively.

As for the Bill for regulating the proceedings in the County Courts, introduced 4 Dec. 1776, no action was ever taken on it. This fact is illuminating. It indicates that opposition to Jefferson's judiciary program was not solely that of fear of exposure to judgment for debt, a reason that was undoubtedly present but has probably been exaggerated. In the first place, the county courts were already open. This most important of all local governmental units remained virtually unchanged by the Revolution and indeed continued so, in most respects, until the Constitution of 1867 (A. O. Porter, *County Government in Virginia,* N.Y., 1947, p. 100-54). Almost exempt from local control, violating the universally accepted principle of the separation of powers by embracing judicial, legislative, and administrative authority, and having the key office of sheriff under its domination, these courts were the bulwark of the old order, and little had been done by the Constitution of 1776 to change the system. Jefferson had assaulted this stronghold of political power in his proposed Constitution by providing, among other things, that sheriffs should be popularly elected and should hold office for limited terms, but his proposal had had little if any chance of being adopted. In the second place, the fear of executions for debts could scarcely apply to the Bill for regulating the proceedings of County Courts, since the jurisdiction of these courts was limited to civil suits involving not more than £10. Their continuance, therefore, did not frighten the planters who labored under mountainous debts to British creditors, and few British debt cases, if any, came into these courts since the debts were almost always for larger amounts (James Monroe to TJ, 1 May 1792). For these reasons, it seems clear that the failure of the legislature to adopt the Bill for regulating proceedings in the County Courts must have been due to some other cause or combination of causes. Among these, undoubtedly, is the fact that Jefferson's Bill intended to regularize proceedings; to elevate the character of the judicial process (for example, his provision for the purchase of law books); to require the courts to be more attentive to their local constituency by receiving at all times, instead of one stated time, such propositions and grievances as the people of the county might care to submit; and to repeal the authority given by the law of 1748 to county courts to grant commissions for the examination of witnesses.

Though it is obvious that Jefferson's judicial reforms were far less radical than those he attempted in other areas affecting the legal, political, and economic structure of society in Virginia, it is equally obvious that any attempt to remold an institution so surrounded by tradition and custom as the judiciary would meet with opposition on the part of those attached to accustomed ways. Fear of executions for debt explains some but by no means all of the opposition that Jefferson's judiciary Bills encountered.

I. Bill for Establishing a Court of Appeals

[25 November 1776]

For establishing a court of Appeals for finally determining all suits and controversies, be it enacted by the General assembly that at such place as shall be appointed by act of General assembly there shall be holden a court of Appeals, (*to consist of the Judges of the High court of Chancery, the Judges of the General court, and the Judges of the court of Admiralty, any nine of them to be a court, to have precedence in the said court according to seniority.*)[1]

Every such judge before he enters upon the duties of his office in the said court shall in open court take and subscribe the oath of fidelity to the Commonwealth, and take the following oath of office, to wit, 'You shall swear that you will well and truly serve this Commonwealth in the office of a judge of the court of Appeals, and that you will do equal right to all manner of people, great and small, high and low, rich and poor, without respect of persons: you shall not take by yourself or by any other any gift, fee, or reward of gold, silver or any other thing directly or indirectly of any person or persons great or small for any matter done or to be done by virtue of your office, except such fees or salary as shall be by law appointed: you shall not maintain by yourself or any other, privily or openly, any plea or quarrel, depending in the courts of this Commonwealth: you shall not delay any person of right for the letters or request of any person, nor for any other cause; and if any letter or request come to you contrary to the law, you shall nothing do for such letter or request, but you shall proceed to do the law, any such letter or request notwithstanding: and finally in all things belonging to your said office, during your continuance therein, you shall faithfully justly and truly, according to the best of your skill and judgment, do equal and impartial justice without fraud, favor, affection or partiality.'[2]

There shall be two sessions of the said court in every year, to wit, one to begin on the 29th. day of March if not Sunday and then on the next day, the other to begin on the 29th. day of August if not Sunday, and then on the next day, to continue each of them six days, Sunday excluded, unless the business depending before them shall be finished in less time; in which case the Judges may adjourn to the next succeeding court.

The said court shall have power to hear and finally determine all suits and controversies whatsoever which shall be brought before them by appeal from the High court of chancery, the General court, or Court of Admiralty, or by writ of error sued out to any decree, judgment, or sentence of either of the said courts: or which shall be adjourned thither from either of the said courts on account of difficulty: but no suit whatsoever shall be originally commenced in the said court of Appeals.[3] If the said court shall at any time be equally divided in opinion on any question coming before them by appeal, the decree, judgment or sentence of the court below on such question shall stand confirmed.

Provided that no appeal shall be allowed to the said court, or writ of error sued thereout, unless the matter in dispute, exclusive of costs, shall be of the value of fifty pounds, or that some Franchise be in question: and that upon all such appeals or writs of error the party prosecuting the same shall give bond and security in the same manner, and shall be liable to the like damages upon the affirmance of the decree, judgment, or sentence, as is provided and directed upon Appeals to, or writs of error sued out of the General court.

The said court of Appeals shall have power to appoint a tip-staff and Cryer, and also a clerk, who shall issue writs of error, upon bond and security given to him, in all cases where the same are hereby allowed to be issued, and shall receive and carefully preserve transcripts of the records upon all such writs, and on Appeals, which shall be transmitted to him by the clerks of the High court of Chancery, the General court and court of Admiralty respectively, entering the names of the parties in a docket in the order he shall receive them, that the suits may be heard in a regular course, without preference to suitors, unless the court for good cause to them shewn, shall order any cause to be heard out of it's turn: the said clerk shall also attend the court during their several sittings, and make due entries of their proceedings; and shall certify their affirmance or reversal of the decree judgment or sentence in each case, with the costs of the party prevailing, to the court where the said decree, judgment or sentence was given; which court shall enter up the same, and execution shall issue thereupon as well for the costs expended in the court of appeals, as the other matters recovered by the decree, judgment or sentence.

No appeal shall be allowed to the said court or writ of error issued until a final judgment be given in the court from whence the appeal is, or to which the writ of error is directed.

Previous to the hearing of each cause in the said court, a clear and concise state of the case of each party, with the points intended to be insisted on, shall be drawn up and signed by the party's counsel and printed copies thereof delivered to each of the Judges for their perusal and consideration, the expence whereof shall be taxed in the bill of costs.[4]

Dft (DLC). Docketed by TJ: "A Bill for establishing a Court of Appeals." Also docketed in the hand of John Tazewell: "1776 Nov. 25. Read the first Time. 27. Read 2d. time & committed to Com: of whole. Decr. 9th. The above was put off til next session." Just below this TJ wrote: "31.E.3.c.12" and "27.El. c.8."

On 30 Oct. 1777 TJ was appointed to a committee to bring in a Bill on this subject, but no further action was taken during this session. On 4 Dec. 1778 the matter was taken up again; on 8 Dec. the Bill was introduced; on 12 Dec. it was passed as amended by the House; and on 15 Dec. 1778 it was agreed to by the Senate (JHD, Oct. 1777, 1827 edn., p. 7; Oct. 1778, p. 99, 102, 106, 109, 111, 113).

[1] The part within angle brackets was struck out by TJ and the following inter-

lined: "which in causes &c. see other paper." The other paper referred to is a draft of an amendment in TJ's hand reading: "pa. 1. line 4. leave out 'to consist &c.' to the end of the clause & insert 'which in causes removed after decision from the High court of Chancery shall consist of the Judges of the General court and court of Admiralty; in those from the General court shall consist of the Judges of the High-court of Chancery and court of Admiralty; in those from the court of Admiralty shall consist of the Judges of the High-court of Chancery and General court; and in those adjourned into the said court from either of the others before decision on account of difficulty, shall consist of the judges of all the said courts: who shall have precedence in the said court according to seniority. Three fourths of the members who are to be of the said court in any case shall be sufficient to proceed to business. The judges also of that court from which the cause is removed after decision, shall attend in their places at the hearing thereof and shall deliver the reasons of their judgments.' " The law as enacted made several modifications in this amendment: causes appealed after decision from Chancery were to be tried by judges of the General Court and three assistant judges chosen by joint ballot of both houses of the legislature; those from the General Court to be tried by judges of the High Court of Chancery and the assistant judges; those from Admiralty and those removed before decision from Chancery and the General Court to be tried by all of the judges, those of Chancery to have first precedence and those of the General Court next (Hening, IX, 522).

2 This oath is taken, with appropriate omissions of references to the king and the royal authority, almost literally from the oath administered to judges of the General Court in its common law jurisdiction prior to the Revolution (see Act for Establishing the General Court, 1748; Hening, V, 468).

3 At this point there is another amendment in TJ's hand, on a separate slip of paper: "pa. 2. at end of 2d. clause add 'nor shall any judgment of the General court be reversed therein unless the Chancellors sitting in the cause ⟨be unanimous in⟩ concur in the opinion for reversal, with so many others of the judges as shall make a majority of the said court: but where such concurrence is wanting and in all other cases where the said court shall be equally divided in opinion the former judgment decree or sentence shall stand confirmed.' " TJ later struck out this amendment and interlined instead the sentence which follows in the text. In this clause the denial of original jurisdiction to the Court of Appeals was omitted in the Act as adopted (Hening, IX, 523-4).

4 At this point TJ added: "Any person who had &c. see another paper." The other paper is missing, but the Act as adopted includes a final paragraph providing that any person who had entered an appeal from the General Court to the King's Privy Council (the judiciary committee of which was the court of last resort for appeals from the colonies) and had not had such an appeal affirmed, reversed, or dismissed, could have the appeal transferred to the Court of Appeals (Hening, IX, 525). This and the two amendments noted above (notes 1 and 3) were in all probability made in 1776, and all three were probably made by TJ. If so, there appear to have been no substantial modifications of the Bill as he wrote it originally.

II. Bill for Establishing a High Court of Chancery

[25 November 1776]

FOR establishing a Court of general Jurisdiction in Chancery, Be it enacted by the General Assembly of the commonwealth of Virginia,[1] That at some certain place[2] to be appointed by Act of General Assembly and at the times hereinafter directed shall be held a principal Court of Judicature for this commonwealth which shall be called the High Court of Chancery and shall consist of three judges to be chosen from time to time, by the joint ballot of both houses of Assembly and commissioned by the Governor, to hold their office so long as they shall respectively demean themselves well therein any two of them to be a court.[3]

Every person so commissioned before he enters upon the duties of his office, shall, in open Court, take and subscribe the oath of fidelity to this commonwealth and take the following oath of office to wit "You shall swear that well and truly you will serve this Commonwealth in the office of Judge of the High Court of Chancery and that you will do equal right to all manner of people great and small, high and low, rich and poor, according to Equity and good conscience and the laws and usages of Virginia without respect of persons, you shall not take by yourself, or by any other, any gift, fee, or reward of gold, silver or any other thing directly or indirectly of any person or persons great or small for any matter done[4] by virtue of your office; except such fees, or salary as shall be by law appointed, you shall not maintain by yourself or any other privily or openly any plea or quarrel depending in the Courts of this Commonwealth, you shall not delay any person of right for the letters or request of any person nor for any other cause, and if any letter or request come to you contrary to law, you shall nothing do for such letter or request but you shall proceed to do the law any such letter or request notwithstanding, and finally in all things belonging to your said office during your continuance therein, you shall faithfully, justly, and truly according to the best of your skill and judgment do equal and impartial justice without fraud, favour, affection or partiality. *So help you God*," and if any person shall presume to execute the said office without having taken the said oaths he shall forfeit and pay the sum of five hundred pounds for his said offence.

The said Court shall have general jurisdiction over all persons and in all causes in Chancery, whether brought before them by original process, appeal from any inferior Court, Certiorari, or other legal means, but no person shall commence an original suit in the said Court in a matter of less value than ten pounds except it be against the justices of any County, or other inferior Court or the Vestry of any Parish on pain of having the same dismissed with Costs.

There shall be two Sessions of the said Court in every year, to wit, one to begin on the fifth day of April, if not Sunday, and then on the next day, the other on the fifth day of September[5] if not Sunday, and then on the next day, to continue each of them eighteen days, Sundays excluded, if they shall so long have business to require their attendance, if not they may when the business is dispatched adjourn to the next Court. The said Court shall however be considered as always open so as to grant injunctions, Writs of ne exeat or other process heretofore allowed by the laws to be issued in time of Vacation by the Clerk of the General Court in Chancery.

The said Court shall have power from time to time to appoint a Clerk who shall hold his office during good behaviour and be entitled to such fees or Salary as shall be established by the legislature.

All original process to bring any person to answer any bill, petition, or information in the said Court and all subsequent process thereupon shall be issued and signed by the Clerk in the name of the Commonwealth and bear teste by the first Commissioner[6] of the said Court; shall be returnable to the first or seventeenth day of the Term which shall be next after the suing out such process and may be executed at any time before the return day thereof. And if any process shall be executed so late that the Sheriff hath not reasonable time to return the same before the day of appearance and thereupon any subsequent process shall be awarded the Sheriff shall not execute such subsequent process but shall return the first process by him executed on which there shall be the same proceedings, as if it had been returned in due time, and all Appeals from decrees in Chancery obtained in any inferior Court shall be made to the third day of the next term.

In all Suits in the said Court the following rules and methods shall be observed that is to say—

The Complainant shall file his Bill within one Calendar month after the day of appearance, or may be ruled on the requisition of the defendant to file such Bill and if he fails to do so within one Calendar month after such rule the suit shall be dismissed with costs and upon the Complainants dismissing his Bill, or the defendants dismissing the same for want of prosecution the Complainant shall pay costs to be taxed by the Clerk of the Court: for which costs a subpoena or other process of contempt may issue returnable on any return day.

The Complainant may amend his Bill before the defendant or his Attorney hath taken out a copy thereof, or in a small matter afterwards without paying costs, but if he amend in a material point after such copy obtained, he shall pay the defendant all costs occasioned thereby.

If the defendant shall not appear on the day of appearance (which in all cases shall be the second day after the term to which the subpoena is returnable) an attachment shall be awarded and issued against him returnable to the next term, which being returned executed, if the defendant doth not appear or being brought into Court upon any such process shall obstinately refuse to answer, the Complainants Bill shall be taken pro: confesso[7] and the matter thereof decreed accordingly.

The defendant within three calendar months after his appearance and Bill filed shall put in his answer to be filed with the Clerk in the office, at the expiration of which time, if no answer be filed the Clerk upon request shall issue an Attachment returnable to the next court, and if no answer be filed upon the return of such Attachment executed, the Complainants Bill shall be taken as confessed and the matter thereof decreed and if the Attachment be returned not executed, an Attachment with proclamations, and such subsequent process of contempt may issue as was heretofore issued out of the General Court sitting in Chancery in like cases.

No process of contempt shall issue unless the subpena be returned served by a sworn officer or affidavit be made of the service thereof.

Every defendant may swear to his answer before any judges of this or of the General Court or any justice of the peace.

When a cross Bill shall be preferred,[8] the defendant or defendants to the first Bill shall answer thereto, before the defendant or defendants to the cross Bill shall be compellable to answer such cross bill.

The Complainant shall reply or file exceptions within two Calendar months after the answer shall have been put in. If he fails so to do the defendant may give a rule to reply with the Clerk of the Court which being expired, and no replication or exceptions filed the suit shall be dismissed with costs, but the Court may order the same to be retained if they see cause on payment of costs.

If the Complainant's Attorney shall except against any answer as insufficient he may file his exceptions and give rule with the Clerk to make a better answer within two Calendar months, and if within that time the defendant shall put in a sufficient answer the same shall be received without costs, but if any defendant insist on the sufficiency of his answer, or neglect, or refuse to put in a sufficient answer, or shall put in another insufficient answer, the Plaintiff may set down his exceptions to be argued the next term in Court and after the expiration of such rule, or any second insufficient answer put in no further or other answer shall be received, but upon payment of costs.

If upon argument the Complainants exceptions shall be over ruled or the defendants answer adjudged insufficient, the Complainant shall pay to the defendant or the defendant to the Complainant such costs as shall be allowed by the Court.

Upon a second answer adjudged insufficient costs shall be doubled. If a defendant shall put in a third insufficient answer which shall be so adjudged[9] the Complainant may go on with the subsequent process of contempt as if no answer had been put in.

Rules to plead, answer, reply, rejoin or other proceedings not before particularly mentioned, when necessary, shall be given from month to month with the Clerk in his office, and shall be entered in a rule book for the information of all Parties, Attornies or Solicitors concerned therein.

No defendant shall be admitted to put in a rejoinder unless it be filed on or before the expiration of the rule to rejoin, but the Complainant may proceed to the examination of witnesses.[10]

After an Attachment with proclamation returned, no plea or demurrer shall be received, unless by order of Court upon motion.

If the Complainant conceives any plea or demurrer to be naught, either for the matter or manner of it he may set it down with the Clerk to be argued. Or if he thinks the plea good but not true he may take issue upon it and proceed to trial by jury as hath been heretofore used in other causes in Chancery where trial hath been by jury. And if thereupon the plea shall be found false the Complainant shall have the same advantages as if it had been so found by verdict at common Law.

If a plea or demurrer be over ruled, no other plea or demurrer shall be thereafter received but the defendant shall answer the allegations of the Bill.

If the Complainant shall not proceed to reply to, or set for hearing as before mentioned any plea or demurrer before the second Court after filing the same, the Bill may be dismissed of course with costs.

Upon a plea or demurrer, argued, and over ruled, costs shall be paid, as where an answer is judged insufficient, and the defendant shall answer within two Calendar months after, but if adjudged good the defendant shall have his costs.

If any defendant shall obstinately insist on a demurrer after the same hath been over ruled by the Court, and shall refuse to answer, the Bill shall be taken as confessed and the matter thereof decreed.[11]

After any Bill filed and before the defendant hath answered, upon oath made that any of the Complainants witnesses are aged or infirm or going out of the country, the Clerk may issue a commission for taking the examination of such witnesses de bene esse the party praying such commission giving reasonable notice to the adverse party of the time and place of taking the depositions.

All matters of fact material to the determination of the cause which in the course of the proceedings shall be affirmed by the one party and denied by the other, shall be tried[12] by Jury, for which purpose an issue or issues shall be made up by declaration and plea as hath heretofore been used in Chancery when issues have been specially directed to be made up and tried by Jury.

And for rendering the said trials more convenient to parties and witnesses, a venue shall be laid in the Declaration a transcript of the record deliverd to the Clerk of Assise where the said venue is laid and a trial be had before the judge of the same assise in every case in such manner as is directed by law in actions at the common law, saving to the Defendant the same benefit of evidence by his own answer as hath been heretofore allowed in trials before the Court of Chancery. Nevertheless the judges for good cause to them shewn, may direct the venue to be changed in any cause or may order any trial to be had at their bar and not at the Assises.

The judge of Assise shall certifie under his seal upon or with each record transmitted, the verdict which shall be given therein, together with such demurrers, or exceptions to evidence, or to the opinion of the Court as he shall be desired by either party to certifie, which verdict and other certificates the Clerk of Assise shall return in convenient time to the office of the Clerk in Chancery.

When the Postea shall be return'd if the Complainant shall not within one Calendar month thereafter set down the cause for hearing with the Clerk, the Defendant may have the same set down at his request.[13]

The Court in their sittings may regulate all proceedings in the Office and for good cause shewn may set aside any dismissions and reinstate the suits, on such terms as shall appear equitable.

For prevention of errors in entering up the decrees and orders of the court the proceedings of every day shall be drawn up at large by the clerk and read in open court the next day (except those of the last day of each term, which shall be drawn up, read and corrected the same day) and any necessary corrections made therein, when they shall be signed by the presiding judge of the court and preserved among the records.

And for the more entire and better preservation of the records of the court, when any cause shall be finally determined, the clerk shall enter all the pleadings therein and other matters relating thereto, together in a book to be kept for that purpose, so that an entire and perfect record may be made thereof, and those wherein the title to lands is determined shall be entered in separate books to be kept for that purpose only.[14]

The Court in their Sessions or any two of the Judges in vacation may grant writs of Certiorari for removing before them the proceedings on any suit in Chancery depending in any county or other inferior Court, writs of ne exeat to prevent the departure of any defendant out of the Country, until security be given for performing the decree, and writs of Injunction to stay Execution of Judgments obtained in any of the Courts of common Law subject nevertheless to the rules following That is to say

No writ of Certiorari shall be granted to remove any suit unless the matter in dispute be of value sufficient to intitle the High Court of Chancery to original jurisdiction therein: nor unless ten days notice of the motion be given to the adverse party: nor in Vacation but upon such petition and affidavit as are by law directed for writs of Certiorari to be granted by the General Court and in all cases bond and security shall be given for performing the decree of the said High Court of Chancery before the issuing of the Certiorari. Writs of ne exeat shall not be granted but upon a bill filed and affidavits made to the truth of its allegations, which being produced to the Court in term time or to two judges in Vacation they may grant or refuse such writ as to them shall seem just, and if granted, they shall direct to be indorsed thereon in what penalty bond and security shall be required of the defendant.

If the Defendant shall by answer satisfie the Court there is no reason for his restraint; or give sufficient security to perform the Decree the writ may be discharged.

No Injunction shall be granted to stay proceedings in any suit at law, unless the matter in dispute be of value sufficient to admit of original jurisdiction in the said High Court of Chancery, nor unless the Court in Term time or two judges thereof in Vacation shall be satisfied of the Plaintiffs equity either by affidavit certified at the foot of the Bill that the allegations thereof are true, or by other means, and shall order the same, in which case the Complainant shall enter into bond with sufficient security[15] for paying all money and tobacco and costs due or to become due to the Plaintiff in the action at Law, and also all such costs as shall be awarded against him or her in case the Injunction shall be dissolved.

The said High Court of Chancery shall take cognizance of and hear and determine all suits in Chancery which were depending in the General Court at its last adjournment[16] in the same manner as if the said Suits had been originally commenced in or appeals enterd to the said High Court of Chancery.

If any suit shall be depending or hereafter commenced against any Defendant or Defendants who are out of this country and others within the same having in their hands effects of or otherwise indebted to such absent defendant or defendants and the appearances of such absentees be not entered and security given to the satisfaction of the Court for performing the decrees upon affidavit that such Defendant or defendants are out of the Country, or that upon enquiry at his her or their usual place of abode, he she or they could not be found so as to be served with process, in all such cases the said High Court of Chancery may make any order and require surety if it shall appear necessary to restrain the defendants in this Country from paying, conveying away or secreting the debts by them owing to, or the effects in their hands of such absent defendant or defendants and for that purpose may order such debts to be paid and effects delivered to the said Plaintiff or Plaintiffs upon their giving sufficient security for the return thereof to such persons and in such manner as the Court shall direct. The Court shall also appoint some day in the succeeding term for the absent defendant or defendants to enter his or their appearance to the suit and give security for performing the decree, a copy of which order shall be forthwith published in the Virginia gazette and continued for two months successively and shall also be published on some Sunday immediately after divine service in such Parish Church or Churches as the Complainant[17] shall direct; and another copy shall be Posted at the front doors of the said Court.

If such absent defendant or defendants shall not appear and give such security within the time limited or such further time as the Court may allow them for good cause shewn, the Court may proceed to take such proof as the Complainant shall offer, and if they shall thereupon be satisfied of the Justice of the demand they may order the Bill to be taken as confessed and make such order and decree therein as shall appear just, and may inforce due performance and execution thereof by such ways and means as hath heretofore been used for inforcing other decrees, requiring the Plaintiff or Plaintiffs to give security as the Court shall approve, for abiding such future order as may be made for restoring the estate or effects to the absent defendant or defendants upon his or their appearance and answering the Bill: and if the Plaintiff or Plaintiffs shall refuse to give, or not be able to procure such security the effects shall remain under the direction of the Court in the hands of a receiver or otherwise for so long time, and shall then be finally disposed of in such manner as to the Court shall seem just.

If any defendant or defendants shall be in custody upon any process of contempt, and be brought into Court by virtue of a writ of Habeas corpus or other process, and shall refuse or neglect to enter his or her appearance according to the rules of the Court or appoint an Attorney of the Court to do the same for him, The Court in such case may direct an Attorney to enter an appearance for the Defendant or defendants, and thereupon such proceedings may be had as if he or they had actually entered an appearance; but if such defendant or defendants shall be in custody at the time a decree shall be made, upon Refusal or neglect to enter an appearance or to appoint an Attorney as aforesaid, or shall be forthcoming so as to be served with a copy of the Decree then such defendant or defendants shall be served with such copy before any process shall be taken out to compel the performance thereof. And if such defendant or defendants shall die in custody before such service, then his Heir, if any real estate be sequestered or affected by such decree, or if only personal estate, his Executor or Administrator shall be served with a copy in a reasonable time after such death shall be known to the Plaintiff and who is such Heir Executor, or Administrator.

If any person or persons who shall be out of the Country[18] at the time any decree is pronounced as aforesaid, shall within seven years from the passing such decree return to this country and appear openly or in case of his or her death if his or her Heir Executor or Administrator shall within the said seven years be and appear openly within this country,[18] the Plaintiff or Plaintiffs their Executors or Administrators shall serve such person or persons so returning or appearing with a copy of the decree within a reasonable time after such return or appearance shall be known to the Plaintiff or Plaintiffs and thereupon such defendants or their representatives may within twelve months after such service, or those defendants not served with a copy, or their representatives, may within seven years after the decree pronounced appear in Court and petition to have the case reheard. And upon their paying down or giving security for payment of such costs, as the Court shall think reasonable, they shall be admitted to answer the Bill, and issue may be joined, and witnesses on both sides examined, and such other proceedings, decree and execution had, as if there had been no former decree in the cause. But if the several defendants or their representatives, upon whom the decree shall be so served shall not within twelve months after such service and the other defendants or their representatives upon whom no such service is made shall not within seven years from the time of the decree pronounced appear and petition to have the cause reheard as aforesaid, and pay or secure to be paid such costs as the Court may think reasonable as aforesaid, All and every decree to be made in pursuance of this Act against any defendant or defendants so failing, shall stand absolutely confirmed against him, her, or them, his, her, or their heirs, Executors and Administrators and all persons claiming under him, her, or them by virtue of any act or conveyance, done or made subsequent to the commencement of the suit. And at the end of such term, the Court may make such further order for quieting the Plaintiff or Plaintiffs in any such suits, in their possession of and title to the Estate and effects so sequestered or made liable, as to them shall seem reasonable.[19]

MS (Vi); in clerk's hand, with alterations in TJ's hand and two paragraphs written by him on an inserted slip. Endorsed by TJ: "for establishing a High court of Chancery"; amendments by House in clerk's hand, all of which are indicated in notes below. Another MS (Vi); in clerk's hand, with some minor alterations in TJ's hand; docketed by clerk: "A Bill For establishing a high Court of Chancery. 1777 Nov. 7th. Read the first time. Novr. 8th. Read 2d. time & committed"; amendments noted below and the two drafts distinguished by being referred to as 1776 Bill and 1777 Bill. Except for TJ's alterations and amendments in 1776 and 1777, both texts are almost identical with each other and with the law as enacted; hence the whole legislative history of the Bill is traced here.

There can be little doubt that TJ was the author of this Bill in 1776. The best account of his purpose in advocating such a court is set forth in his letter to Mazzei of 28 Nov. 1785, where he regards chancery jurisdiction ideally as making "the administration of justice progressive almost in equal pace with the progress of commerce and refinement of morality"; he also notes that, "to guard . . . effectually against the dangers apprehended from a court of Chancery, the legislature of Virginia . . . very wisely introduced into it the trial by jury for all matters of fact." This Bill was introduced by TJ, 25 Nov., when it was read the first time; 29 Nov., it was read a second time and referred to Committee of the Whole; 3 Dec., considered by House and amendments agreed to; 13 Dec., it was postponed to next session (JHD, Oct. 1776, 1828 edn., p. 69, 75, 80, 96). (These amendments, noted below, aid in proving that this is the 1776 draft; some were incorporated in 1777 Bill and some were disregarded in that Bill. Notes below also indicate priority of this text; since the Senate at no time offered amendments in 1776 or 1777 Bills, the amendments to this text can only have been those made by the House in 1776.) On 30 Oct. 1777 TJ was appointed to committee to bring in Bill on this subject; Bill introduced by Nicholas, 7 Nov.; read second time, 8 Nov., and referred to Committee of Whole; 2 Jan. 1778, amended by Committee of Whole; 3 Jan., read third time and passed, Prentis carrying Bill to Senate; 9 Jan., agreed to by Senate (JHD, Oct. 1778, 1827 edn., p. 8, 15, 17, 96, 99, 108; Hening, IX, 389-99).

1 The words "of the commonwealth of Virginia" struck out in 1777 Bill, one of the indications of priority of the present text.

2 Williamsburg was designated as the place in 1778, and Richmond in 1779 (Hening, IX, 434; X, 89).

3 TJ interlined a change in the 1777 Bill to cause it to read "two of whom may hold a Court," which is the reading of the Act (Hening, IX, 389), a change proving the present text to be the earlier.

4 Amendment to 1777 Bill: "After 'done' insert 'or to be done' agd."; Act of 1778 reads thus.

5 Amendment to 1776 Bill altered this to 1 March and 1 September; amendment in 1777 Bill: "Leave out from the Word April to the Word then and insert 'or if that be Sunday' agd." Act of 1778 agrees with amendment to 1777 Bill.

6 Amendment to 1776 Bill: "Strike out the word Commissioner and insert Judge"; so written in 1777 Bill and in Act of 1778.

7 Amendment to 1776 Bill: "Strike out the words pro confesso and insert as confessed"; so written in 1777 Bill and in Act of 1778.

8 Amendment to 1776 Bill: "Strike out the word preferred and insert exhibited"; so written in 1777 Bill and in Act of 1778.

9 Amendment to 1776 Bill: "After the word adjudged insert he or she may be examined upon Interrogatories and committed until he or she shall answer them and pay Costs, if the defendant after process of Contempt, put in an insufficient answer which shall be so adjudged." The 1777 Bill and Act of 1778 incorporate this amendment.

10 Amendment to 1777 Bill: "Leave out from the word 'proceed' to the word 'after' . . . and insert 'to set his Cause down for hearing' agd." Act of 1778 incorporates this amendment.

11 Amendment to 1777 Bill deleted words "shall obstinately insist . . . by the Court, and," and inserted: "After a Demurrer shall have been over ruled"; thus in Act of 1778.

12 Amendment to 1776 Bill: "At the word tried insert 'upon Evidence given vivâ voce in open Court, and where witnesses are absent through Sickness or other unavoidable Cause, upon their Depositions taken as the Laws direct' " and also: "after the Word Jury insert 'if either party shall desire it, or the Court shall think proper to direct the same.' " This amendment was thus copied (except that "open Court" was changed to "said Court") into the 1777 Bill, but an amendment to 1777 Bill at this point deleted the second part of 1776 Bill amendment; it was reconsidered, but struck out again, and is not in Act of 1778. This proves TJ right on a point heretofore challenged (Ford, I, 51).

13 All but one sentence of the preceding three paragraphs were deleted in the 1776 Bill. The list of amendments reads as follows: "Strike out 28, 29 and 30th Clauses, except the words of the 28th Clause Saving to the Defendant the same Benefit of Evidence by his own answer as hath been heretofore allowed in Trials before the Court of Chancery." They were not included in the 1777 Bill, but a draft of an amendment in TJ's hand (DLC: TJ Papers, 233: 41701) covering these paragraphs precisely was evidently offered in 1777. His efforts to restore the whole of these deleted paragraphs failed; however, two amendments adopted at this point in the 1777 Bill cause the 1777 Bill to read as in Act of 1778 (Hening, IX, 394, sect. xxvi and xxvii, the latter of which substantially enacts the last of the three deleted paragraphs from 1776 Bill).

14 This and the preceding paragraph were written by TJ on a slip of paper inserted at this point; these paragraphs were copied in this order in 1777 Bill and in Act of 1778.

15 Amendment to 1777 Bill: "Insert to be approved by the said Court or Judges"; thus in Act of 1778.

16 The 1777 Bill inserts at this point, though not recorded as an amendment, the words "or have been commenced therein since such adjournment"; thus in Act of 1778.

17 "Complainant" struck out in 1777 Bill and "Court" interlined in TJ's hand; thus in Act of 1778.

18 Changed to "Commonwealth" in 1777 Bill and in Act of 1778.

19 Act of 1778 adds a paragraph not in 1776 or 1777 Bills, giving each of the Chancery judges a salary of £500 and stating taxes on processes.

III. Bill for Establishing a General Court

[25 November 1776]

FOR establishing a Court of Common Law of general jurisdiction for the more speedy and easy administration of Justice in this Commonwealth and for regulating the proceedings therein.

Be it enacted That, at some certain place to be appointed by act of general assembly, and at the Times herein after directed, there shall be held one principal Court of Judicature for this Commonwealth; which shall be stiled the General Court of Virginia; and, shall consist of five Judges to be chosen by joint ballot of both houses of the General Assembly, and Commissioned by the Governor for the Time being to hold their offices so long as they shall respectively demean themselves well therein; any three of them to be a Court; and the said Judges shall have precedence in Court, as they may stand in nomination on the ballot, and the person first named shall be called chief Justice of such Court.[1] Every person so Commissioned, before he enters upon the duties of his office, shall in Open Court take and subscribe the Oath of fidelity to the Commonwealth, and take the following Oath of office, to wit, "You shall swear that well and truly you will serve this Commonwealth in the office of a Judge of the General Court, and that you will do equal right to all manner of people great and small high and low, rich and poor according to Law, without respect of persons. You shall not take by yourself or by any other privily or openly any Gift, fee or reward of Gold, Silver or any other thing directly or indirectly of any person or persons, great or small for any matter done or to be done by virtue of your office; except such Fees or salary, as shall be by Law appointed. You shall not maintain by yourself or any other privily or openly any plea or Quarrel depending in the Courts of this Commonwealth. You shall not deny or delay any person of common right for the letters or request of any person, nor for any other cause, and, if any letter or request come to you contrary to the law, you shall nothing do for such letter or request, but you shall proceed to do the Law, any such Letter or request notwithstanding; And finally, in all things belonging to your said office during your continuance therein, you shall faithfully, justly and truly, according to the best of your skill and Judgment, do equal and impartial Justice, without fraud, favour, affection or partiallity," So help you God; which Oaths shall be administerd by the

Governor or other presiding chief Majistrate in presence of the
Council of State[2] and, if any person shall presume to sit in Court or
execute the said office without having taken the said Oaths, he shall,
for such offence, forfeit the sum of five hundred pounds. The jurisdiction of the said Court shall be general over all persons and in
all causes, matters or things at common Law, whether brought
before them by Original process, by appeal from any inferior Court
Habeas Corpus, Certiorari, Writ of Error, supersedeas, mandamus
or by any other legal ways or means provided always that no person
shall sue out Original process for the trial of any matter or thing
in the General Court of less value than ten pounds or two thousand
pounds of Tobacco, except it be against the Justices of a County
or other inferior Court, or the Vestry of a Parish, on Penalty of
being nonsuited and having his suit dismissed with Costs.[3] There
shall be two sessions of the said Court in every Year, to wit one to
begin on the first day of March, if not Sunday, and then on the
Monday thereafter; and the other to begin on the first day of August,[4] if not Sunday, and then, on the Monday following; to continue each of them twenty four natural days, Sunday's exclusive,
unless the Business depending before them shall be finished in less
Time; in which case the Judges may adjourn to the next succeeding
Court; and if it should so happen that a sufficient number of Judges
should not attend on the day appointed, any one of the said Judges
may adjourn the Court from day to day for six day's successively;
and, if a sufficient number of Judges should not be able to attend
at the end of such adjournments, all suits, depending in such Court,
shall stand continued over to the next succeeding Court.[5] The said
Court shall have power, from time to time to appoint a Clerk, one
or more assistant Clerks, a Crier and Tipstaff, who shall hold their
offices respectively, during good behaviour, and be intitled to such
fees or salaries, as shall be established by Law, and the Sherif or
so many of the under sheriffs, as shall be thought necessary, of the
County where such Court may be held, shall attend the said Court,
during their sessions.[6]

All original process to bring any person or persons to answer
in any Action or Suit, Information, Bill or plaint in the said Court,
and all subsequent process thereon, all attachments or other Writs
of what nature soever, awarded by the said Court, shall be Issued
and signed by the Clerk of the said Court in the name of the Commonwealth, shall bear Teste by the chief Justice of the Court and
be returnable on the respective days of the next succeeding Court,
as followeth; that is to say, all process for the Commonwealth on

Criminal Prosecutions to the sixth day; all appeals, Writs of Error, Supersedeas, Certiorari, Mandamus, prohibition, and all other writs and process, except subpoenas for Witnesses to the eighth or twenty third day of the said Court; and all such process may be executed at any Time before the return day, except in such cases wherein it is otherwise directed by Law. And, if any Writ or process shall be executed so late that the Sherif or other officer hath not reasonable Time to return the same before the day of appearance thereto, and an Alias, Pluries, Attachment or other Process be awarded thereupon, the sherif shall not execute such subsequent Process, but shall return the first process by him executed, on which there shall be the same proceedings, as if it had been returned in due time.

In all actions or suits, which may be commenced against the Governor of this Commonwealth, any member of the privy Council or the sherif of any County, during his continuance in office, instead of the Ordinary process, a summons shall Issue to the sherif or other proper officer, reciting the cause of Action and summoning such Defendant to appear and answer the same on the proper return day in the next General Court; and, if such Defendant being summoned or a Copy left at his house ten days, before the return day, shall not appear to Answer the same on Attachment shall be awarded against his Estate, and thereafter, the proceedings in the suit shall be in like manner, as is directed in case of an Attachment awarded upon the Sherifs returning Non est Inventus on Ordinary process.

In all actions to recover the penalty for breach of any penal Law, not particularly directing special Bail to be given in Actions of Slander, Trespass, Assault and Battery, Actions on the Case for Trover or other wrongs, and all other personal actions, except such as shall be hereinafter particularly mentioned, the Plaintiff or his Attorney shall, on pain of having his suit Dismissed with Costs, indorse on the Original Writ or subsequent Process the true species of Action, that the sherif, to whom the same is directed, may be thereby informed whether Bail is to be demanded on the execution thereof; and, in the cases before mentioned, the sheriff may take the Engagement of any Attorney practising in the General Court indorsed upon the Writ that he will appear for the Defendant or Defendants, and such appearance shall be entered with the Clerk in the office on the second day after the end of the Court to which such process is returnable; which is hereby declared to be the appearance day in all process returnable to any day of the Court next preceding. And every Attorney, failing to enter an appearance according to such engagement, shall forfeit to the Plaintiff fifty shillings for which Judgment shall be immediately entered and Execution may Issue thereupon. Provided always that any Judge of the said Court, in Actions of Trespass, Assault and Battery, Trover and Conversion, and, in actions on the case, where, upon proper affidavit or affirmation, as the case may be, it shall appear to him proper that the Defendant or Defendants should give appearance Bail, may, and he is hereby authorised to direct such Bail to be taken by indorsement on the Original Writ or subsequent process, and every sherif shall Govern himself accordingly.[7]

In all actions of Debt, founded on any Writing Obligatory, Bill or note in Writing for the Payment of Money or Tobacco, all actions of Covenant or Detinue,[8] in which cases the true species of action shall be endorsed on the Writ, as before directed, appearance Bail is to be required, the sheriff shall return on the Writ the name of the Bail by him taken, and a Copy of the Bail Bond to the Clerks office, before the day of appearance; and, if the Defendant shall fail to appear accordingly, or shall not give special Bail, being ruled thereto by the Court, the Bail for appearance may defend the suit and shall be subject to the same Judgment and recovery as the Defendant might or would be subject to, if he had appeared and given special Bail. And if the sherif shall not return Bail, and a Copy of the Bail Bond, or the Bail returned shall be judged insufficient by the Court and the Defendant shall fail to appear or give special Bail, if ruled thereto, in such case the sherif may have the like liberty of defence and shall be subject to the same recovery, as is provided in the case of appearance Bail; and, if the sherif depart this life before Judgment be confirmed against him, in such case, the Judgment may be Confirmed against his Executors or Administrators, or, if there shall not be a Certificate of Probat or Administration granted, then it may be confirmed against his Estate, and a Writ of Fieri Facias may, in either case, be Issued. But the Plaintiff shall object to the sufficiency of the Bail, during the sitting of the Court, to which the writ is returnable, or in the office at the first or second rule day after that Court and, at no time thereafter. And all questions concerning the sufficiency of Bail so objected to in the office shall be determined by the Court on the eighth day of the succeeding Court and, in all cases where the Bail shall be Adjudged insufficient and Judgment entered against the sherif he shall have the same remedy against the Estate of the Bail as against the Estate of the Defendant. Also that every Judgment entered in the office

against a Defendant and Bail or against a Defendant and Sherif
shall be set aside, if the Defendant upon the eighth day of the succeeding Court shall be allowed to appear without Bail, put in good
Bail, being ruled so to do, or surrender himself in Custody and shall
Plead to Issue immediately; on which eighth day the Court shall
also regulate all other Proceedings in the office, during the preceding Vacation and rectify any mistakes or errors, which may have
happened therein.

In every case, where Judgment shall be confirmed against any
Defendant or Defendants, and his Bail or the Sherif, his Executors,
Administrators or Estate, as aforesaid; the Court, upon a Motion
of such Bail or of such Sherif, his Executors or Administrators, or
any other person on behalf of his Estate may Order an Attachment
against the Estate of such Defendant or Defendants returnable to
the next succeeding Court and, upon the execution and return of
such attachment the Court shall order the Estate seised or so much
thereof as will be sufficient to satisfy the Judgment and Costs and
all Costs, accruing on the Attachment, to be Sold, as Goods taken
in execution upon a fieri facias and out of the money such Judgment and all Costs shall be satisfied, and the surplus, if any restored
to the Defendant or Defendants when required.

Any Judge of the said Court, when the Court is not sitting, or
any Justice of the peace authorized for that purpose by the said
Court, may take a recognizance of Special Bail, in any Action
therein depending, which shall be taken de bene esse and shall be
transmitted by the person taking the same, before the next succeeding General Court to the Clerk of the said Court to be filed with the
Papers in such Action, and if the Plaintiff or his Attorney shall
except to the sufficiency of Bail so taken, notice of such exception
shall be given to the Defendant or his Attorney at least ten days
previous to the day on which such exception shall be taken. And if
such Bail shall be judged insufficient by the Court the Recognizance
thereof shall be discharged and such proceedings shall be had as if
no such Bail had been taken. Every Special Bail[9] may surrender the
Principal before the Court where the suit hath been or shall be depending at any time either before or after Judgment shall be given;
and thereupon the Bail shall be discharged and the Defendant or
Defendants shall be Committed to the Custody of the Sherif or
Gaoler attending such Court, if the Plaintif or his Attorney shall
desire the same; or such special Bail may discharge himself or herself by surrendering the principal or principals to the Sherif of the
County, where the Original Writ was served, and such sherif shall

receive such Defendant or Defendants and Commit him, her or them to the Gaol of his County, and shall give a receipt for the Body or Bodies of such Defendant or Defendants, which shall be by the Bail forthwith transmitted to the Clerk of the Court, where the suit is or was depending. When such render, after Judgment, shall be to the sherif, he shall keep such Defendant or Defendants in his Custody in the same manner and subject to the like Rules, as are provided for Debtors committed in Execution, during the space of twenty days; unless the Creditor, his Attorney, or Agent, shall sooner consent to his, her or their Discharge; the Bail shall give immediate notice of such render to the Creditor his Attorney or Agent; and if within the said twenty days, such Creditor his Attorney or Agent shall not, in Writing, charge the Debtor or Debtors in Execution, he, she or they shall be forthwith discharged out of Custody, but the Plaintif or Plaintifs may nevertheless afterwards sue out an Execution either against the Bodies or Estates of such Debtor or Debtors.

When the Sherif or other proper officer shall return on any Original or mesne process that he hath taken the Body of any Defendant and committed him to Prison for want of Appearance Bail, the Plaintif may proceed, and the Defendant make his defence, in like manner, as if his appearance had been entered and accepted, but such Defendant shall not be discharged out of Custody until he shall put in good Bail or the Plaintif shall be ruled by Court to accept an appearance without Bail, and, where any Defendant, after appearance entered, shall be confined in prison, the Plaintif may file his Declaration, give a Rule to plead and deliver Copies of such Declaration and rule to the Defendant or his attorney; and, if the Defendant shall fail to enter his plea within two months after receiving such Declaration and Notice, the Plaintif may have Judgment by Default as in other cases.

Where the Sherif or other proper officer shall return on any Writ of Capias to answer in any civil Action, that the Defendant is not found within his Bailiwick, the Plaintif may either sue out an alias or a Pluries Capias until the Defendant be arrested or a Testatum Capias, where he shall be removed into another County, or may, at his Election, sue out an Attachment against the Estate of the Defendant to force an appearance. And, if the Sherif or other officer shall return that he hath Attached any Goods, and the Defendant shall not appear and replevy the same by entering his appearance and giving Special Bail, in case he shall be ruled so to do, the Plaintif shall file his Declaration and be entitled to a Judgment for his Debt or Damages & Costs, which Judgment shall be final in all Actions of Debt founded on any Specialty, Bill or Note in Writing ascertaining the Demand; and, in other cases, the Damages shall be settled by a Jury sworn to enquire thereof; the Goods Attached shall remain in the hands of the officer, till such final Judgment be entered, and then be Sold in the same manner, as Goods taken upon a Fieri Facias; and, if the Judgment shall not be thereby satisfied, the Plaintif may sue out Execution for the residue; and, in case more Goods be attached, than will satisfie the Judgment, the surplus shall be returned to the Defendant. On the Return of a Pluries Capias that the Defendant is not to be found the Court, instead of the Process to outlawry formerly used, may Order a Proclamation to be Issued, warning the Defendant to appear at a certain day therein to be named or that Judgment will be rendered against him, which Proclamation shall be Published on three successive Court days at the Door of the Court-house of the County, to which the last process was directed and also three Times in the Virginia Gazette; and, if the Defendant fails to appear, pursuant to such Proclamation, the same proceedings shall be had and the same Judgment given, as in other cases of Default.[10] In the prosecution of all suits in the General Court the following rules shall be observed.

The Plaintif shall file his Declaration in the Clerk's office at the succeeding rule day after the Defendant shall have entered his appearance, or the Defendant may then enter a Rule for the Plaintif to declare; and, if he shall fail or neglect so to do at the succeeding Rule day, or shall at any Time fail to prosecute his suit, he shall be nonsuited and pay to the Defendant or Tenant, besides his Costs, One hundred and fifty pounds of Tobacco, where his place of abode is at the distance of twenty Miles or under from the place of holding the General Court; and, where it is more, five pounds of Tobacco for every mile above twenty. One month, after the Plaintiff hath filed his Declaration, he may give a Rule to plead with the Clerk, and, if the Defendant shall not plead accordingly, at the expiration of such Rule, the Plaintiff may enter Judgment by default for his Debt or Damages and Costs.

All Rules to declare, plead, reply, rejoin or for other proceedings, shall be given regularly, from Month to Month, shall be entered in a Book to be kept by the Clerk for that purpose and shall be out on the succeeding Rule day.[11]

All Judgments by Default, for want of an Appearance, Special Bail or pleas as aforesaid, and Nonsuits or Dismissions obtained in the office and not set aside on the eighth day of the succeeding General Court, shall be entered by the Clerk as of that day, which Judgment shall be final in Actions of Debt founded on any Specialty Bill or Note in Writing ascertaining the Demand, and, in all other cases the Damages shall be ascertained by a Jury to be impanel'd and sworn to enquire thereof as is hereinafter directed.

In all such cases and other Judgments for Plaintiff or Defendant, the Clerk shall allow a Lawyer's Fee in the Bill of Costs, if the party employed one, which fee, in real, personal or mixed actions, where the Title or Bounds of Land shall or may come in question, shall be five pounds or one thousand pounds of Tobacco, and, in all other Cases fifty shillings or five hundred pounds of Tobacco, at the election of the party Paying.

No Plea in abatement or of Non est factum shall be admitted or received unless the party offering the same shall prove the truth thereof by affidavit or affirmation[12] as the case may be; and where a plea in Abatement shall upon argument be Judged insufficient, the Plaintif shall recover full Costs to the Time of overruling such plea, a Lawyers fee only excepted. The Plaintif, in Replevin and the Defendant in all other actions may plead as many several matters whether of Law or Fact as he shall think necessary for his defence.

In all Cases, where a Fine is laid on the Justices of any County Court or the Vestry of a Parish, one Action may be brought against all the Members jointly.

Immediately, after the end of each General Court, the Clerk shall make a Transcript of the Record in each and every suit depending in the said Court, wherein an Issue is to be Tried or enquiry of Damages to be made and transmit the same to the Clerks of the respective Assizes where such Suits are to be tried according to the regulations hereafter mentioned.[13]

For trial of Issues and enquiry of Damages, upon the Records so transmitted, there shall, in every Year, be holden a Court of Assize at the places and Times following. At Accomack Courthouse on the thirtieth day of April and thirtieth day of september; at Nansemond Sussex, Powhatan and Fairfax Courthouses on the tenth day of May and tenth day of October; at the Capitol, in the City of Williamsburg, at Charlotte, Culpeper and Frederick Courthouses on the twenty fifth day of May and twenty fifth day of October; at Essex, Bedford, Albemarle, and Monongalia Courthouses on the fifth day of June and fifth day of November. At Spotsylvania, Montgomerie, Augusta and Yohogania Courthouses on the fifteenth day of June and fifteenth day of November; or, if any of the said several days shall happen to be Sundays, the said Courts shall begin respectively on the next day and shall continue to sit till they have finished all the Business depending before them, or so much thereof, as can be done before it is necessary for the Judge to proceed to the next Assize.[13]

In all actions or suits at Common Law, whether real, personal or mixed, which were depending in the General Court at the Time of it's last Adjournment or have been since commenced therein, or, which shall be hereafter instituted in this Court, wherein the Venue is or shall be laid in the Declaration in either of the Counties of Accomack or Northampton, the Issue shall be tried or enquiry of Damages made at the said Court of Assize to be held at Accomack Courthouse; If the Venue is or shall be laid in either of the Counties of Princess Anne, Norfolk, Nansemond or Isle of Wight or South-ampton the Issues shall be tried or enquiry of Damages made at the said Court of Assize to be held at Nansemond Courthouse; If the Venue is or shall be laid in either of the Counties of Elizabeth City, Warwick, York, James City, Charles City, New Kent, King William or Gloucester, the Issues shall be tried or enquiry of Damages be made at the said Court of Assize to be held at the Capitol in the City of Williamsburg; If the Venue is or shall be laid in either of the Counties of Lancaster, Northumberland, Richmond, Westmorland, Essex, Middlesex or King and Queen the Issues shall be tried or enquiry of Damages be made at the said Court of Assize to be held at Essex Courthouse; If the Venue is or shall be laid in either of the Counties of Hanover, Caroline, Spotsylvania, Stafford or King George, the Issues shall be tried or enquiry of Damages be made at the said Court of Assize to be held at Spotsylvania Courthouse: If the Venue is or shall be laid in either of the Counties of Surry, Sussex, Brunswick, Dinwiddie or Prince George, the Issues shall be tried or enquiry of Damages be made at the said Court of Assize to be held at Sussex Courthouse: If the Venue is or shall be laid in either of the Counties of Mecklenburg, Lunenburg, Charlotte, Hali-fax, or Prince Edward, the Issues shall be tried and enquiry of Damages be made at the said Court of Assize, to be held at Char-lotte Courthouse: If the Venue is or shall be laid in either of the Counties of Pittsylvania, Henry, Bedford, or Buckingham, the Issues shall be tried or enquiry of Damages be made at the said Court of Assize to be held at Bedford Courthouse. If the Venue is or shall be laid in either of the Counties of Bottetourt, Montgomerie, Washington or Kentucky, the Issues shall be tried or enquiry of Damages be made at the said Court of Assize to be held at Montgomerie Courthouse: If the Venue is or shall be laid in either of the Counties of Henrico, Chesterfield, Powhatan, Cumberland or Amelia the Issues shall be tried or enquiry of Damages be made at the said Court of Assize, to be held at Powhatan Courthouse; if the Venue is, or shall be laid in either of the Counties of Orange, Culpeper or Fauquier, the issues shall be tried or enquiry of damages be made at the said Court of Assize to be held at Culpeper Courthouse; If the venue is or shall be laid in either of the Counties of Louisa, Goochland, Fluvanna, Albemarle or Amherst the issues shall be tried or enquiry of damages be made at the said Court of Assize to be held at Albemarle Courthouse; if the venue is or shall be laid in either of the Counties of Augusta or Dunmore, the issues shall be tried or enquiry of damages be made at the said Court of Assize, to be held at Augusta Courthouse; If the venue is or shall be laid in either of the Counties of Prince William, Fairfax or Loudon, the issues shall be tried or enquiry of damages be made at the said Court of Assize, to be held at Fairfax Courthouse; If the venue is or shall be laid in either of the Counties of Berkeley, Frederick or Hampshire, the issues shall be tried or enquiry of damages be made at the said Court of Assize, to be held at Frederick Courthouse; If the venue is or shall be laid in either of the Counties of Monongalia or Ohio, the issues shall be tried or enquiry of damages be made at the said Court of Assize, to be held at Monongalia Courthouse; and, if the venue is or shall be laid in the County of Yohogania the issues shall be tried or enquiry of damages be made at the Court of Assize, to be held at Yohogania Courthouse.[13]

To avoid improper trials by the management of a Plaintiff or his Attorney, the venue, in transitory actions, shall be laid in the County where the defendant is arrested, or an Attachment to force his appearance levied, but may be changed by direction of the Court for good cause shewn.[13]

At some convenient time, previous to the holding of each Court of Assize, the Judges of the General Court shall allot and regulate, among themselves, the Court or Courts, at which each of them shall attend; and, if by sickness or other disability, any one or more of them shall be unable to go to the Circuit so allotted to him or them, The Governor with the consent of the Council may appoint some other fit and able person to perform the said duty in the room of each Judge so unable, and give him a Commission accordingly; who, having before the Governor or Council taken an Oath of Fidelity to the Commonwealth and the Oath herein before appointed to be taken by the Judges mutatis mutandis, shall have the same power to sit and hold the Court of Assize to which he is appointed, as if he was a Judge of the General Court; each of the said Judges shall have power to try all issues, and enquire of damages by a Jury, upon all Records so to be transmitted to him, and therein to determine all questions about the legality of Evidence and other matters of Law which may arise; For which trials he is to cause the Sheriff of the County wherein his Sitting is (which Sheriff shall attend him during his whole Session) to impannel and return Jurors of the Bystanders, qualified as the Law directs to be sworn of Jurys; he shall certifie under his Seal upon or with each Record transmitted, the Verdict, which shall be given therein, together with such Demurrers or exceptions to evidence or to the Opinion of the Court, as he shall be desired by either party to certifie; which Verdict and other Certificates the Clerk of the Assize shall in convenient time, before the succeeding Court, return to the Clerk's Office.[13]

Every person summoned to attend as a Juror and failing so to do, shall be fined by the said Court, at their discretion, not exceeding four hundred pounds of Tobacco, to the use of this Commonwealth; to be levied by the Sheriff and paid to the Publick Treasurer, subject to the disposition of the General Assembly.[13]

On the return of the Postea or certificate aforesaid to the Clerk's Office, in all such cases where a general Verdict shall be given for either Party, and there be no exceptions certified, as aforesaid, and where no reasons are filed to stay Judgment, within fourteen days after the Postea returned, the General Court next succeeding the Trial shall enter up Judgment and Execution may issue thereupon; and, in all causes, wherein a special Verdict shall be given, exceptions certified or reasons filed in arrest of Judgment, the Clerk shall put them on the Dockett for argument at the following General Court.[13]

The Judges of the General Court, for good cause to them shewn, shall nevertheless have power to order any Action or suit depending before them or enquiry of damages to be made to be tried at their Barr.[13]

The Judges of the General Court shall have power, from time to time, to appoint a Clerk of each Assize, who shall continue during good behaviour, shall keep his Office in the County, where the Assize is to be held, attend the Judges, during their sittings, and make due entries and certificates of all matters and things, as he shall be directed by the said Judges; he shall issue Subpoenas for witnesses for either party, upon the Records sent him and do all other things, which the duty of his Office may require, for which he shall be allowed such fees, as may be established by Law and none other.[13]

Before every General Court, the Clerk shall enter in a particular Dockett all such causes and those only, in which an Issue is to be tried, or enquiry of Damages to be made or a Special Verdict, Case agreed, Demurrer, Appeal or other matter of Law to be argued in the same order as they stand in the course of proceeding, setting, as near as may be, an equal number of causes to each day, and the Clerk of each Assize Court shall, in like manner, prepare a Dockett of all the causes to be tried at such Court, setting them down in the same order also, as they stand in the course of the proceedings.[14]

When any cause shall be finally determined, the Clerk of the General Court shall enter all the Pleadings and Papers filed as evidence therein and the Judgment thereupon, so as to make a complete record thereof; and those wherein the title to Lands is determined, shall be entered in separate Books to be kept for that purpose.

For prevention of Errors in entering up the Judgments of the said Court, the proceedings of every day shall be drawn at large by the Clerk against the next sitting of the Court, when the same shall be read in open Court and such corrections, as are necessary being made therein, they shall be signed by the Presiding Judge and carefully preserved among the Records.[15]

In all cases, where Witnesses are required to attend at the General Court a summons shall be issued by the Clerk expressing the day and place, they are to appear, the names of the Party to the suit and in whose behalf they are summoned.

When any witness shall be about to depart the Country or by Age, Sickness or otherwise shall be unable to attend the Court, upon Affidavit thereof or on a certificate from any Justice of the Peace, the Court, when they are sitting, or any Judge thereof in vacation may, on request of either Party, award a Commission for taking the Deposition of such Witness, de bene esse, to be read as evidence at the trial, in case the Witness shall then be unable to attend; but the Party obtaining such Commission shall give reasonable notice to the other Party of the time and place of taking the Deposition; otherwise the same shall be void and all Depositions so taken in any Cause sent to be tried at the Assize shall be transmitted with the Record in such suit.

If any Party in a suit at common Law shall make Oath that he verily believes his claim or defence, as the case may be or a material point thereof depends on the testimony of a single Witness, the Court or Judges, as aforesaid may award a Commission to take the Deposition of such Witness, de bene esse, although he or she be not about to depart the Country, nor under any disability the Party in such case giving ten days notice of the time and place of taking such Deposition to the adverse Party.

If any person summoned as a Witness and attending the Court, Judges of Assize or the Commissioners appointed to take his or her Deposition, as aforesaid, shall refuse to give evidence upon Oath or Affirmation,[16] as the case may be, to the best of his or her knowledge, every person so refusing shall be committed to Prison either by the Court or Commissioners, there to remain without Bail or Mainprize,[17] until he or she shall give such evidence.

No person convicted of Perjury shall be capable of being a Witness in any case, nor shall any Negroe, Mulattoe or Indian be admitted to give evidence but against or between Negroes, Mulattoes or Indians.

If any person, summoned as a Witness to attend the General Court or any Court of Assize, shall fail to attend accordingly the Court or Judges of Assize shall fine such person five Pounds, or one thousand pounds of Tobacco, at the option of the Payer, to the use of the Party, for whom such Witness was summoned; and the Witness, so failing, shall farther be liable to the Action of the Party for all damages sustained by the non-attendance of such Witness; but, if sufficient cause of his or her inability to attend be shewn to the Court or Judges of Assize, as the case may be, at the time he or she ought to have appeared or at the next succeeding Court or Assize then no fine or Action shall be incurred by such failure.

Witnesses shall be privileged from Arrests in Civil cases, during their attendance at the General Court or Courts of Assize, coming to and returning from thence, allowing one day for every twenty miles from their places of abode, and all such Arrests shall be void.[18]

Every Witness, summoned and attending the General Court or Courts of Assize, shall be paid by the Party, at whose suit the summons issues, two pounds of Tobacco or four pence per Mile[19] for travelling to the place of attendance and the same for returning, besides Ferriages, and sixty Pounds of Tobacco or ten shillings per day for his attendance; which allowance shall be entered by the Clerk, of course, except where disputes arise concerning the same, and then such disputes shall be determined by the General Court or Court of Assize respectively, and such allowance, together with the fees accruing to the Clerk and Sheriff in each suit in the Court of Assize, shall be certified by the Clerk with the Record and returned to the Clerk of the General Court to be allowed in the Bill of Costs.

There shall not be allowed in the Bill of Costs the charge of more than three Witnesses for the proof of any one particular fact.

Where any person or persons Body Politic or Corporate shall think themselves aggrieved by the Judgment or Sentence of any County Court or Court of Hustings,[20] in any Action Suit or contest whatever, where the Debt or Damages or other thing recovered or Claimed in such Suit, exclusive of the Costs, shall be of the Value of Ten pounds or two thousand pounds of Tobacco, or, where the Title or Bounds of Land shall be drawn in Question, or the contest shall be concerning Mills, Roads, the Probat of Wills, or Certificates for obtaining Administration, such person or persons, Body Politic or Corporate, may enter an Appeal to the General Court, from such Judgment or Sentence.[21]

Where the Defendant in any personal Action, Appeals, if the Judgment be affirmed, the Damages, besides Costs, shall be ten Per Centum Per annum upon the principal sum and Costs recovered in the Inferior Court, in satisfaction of all Damages or Interest.[22] In real or mixed actions, the Damages shall be Ten pounds or two thousand pounds of Tobacco, besides Costs; and, where the Plaintif appeals in any Action, if the Judgment be affirmed, and, in all Controversies about Mills, Roads, Probat of Wills, or Certificates for Administration, if the sentence of the Inferior Court be affirmed the party appealing shall pay to the other five pounds or One thousand pounds of Tobacco, besides all Costs.

No appeal, Writ of Error or Supersedeas shall be granted in any Cause, until a final Judgment shall be given in the County or other inferior Court.

The party praying[23] a Writ of Supersedeas shall petition the Judges of the General Court for the same, pointing out the Errors he means to assign in the proceedings, and procure some attorney practising in the General Court, to Certify that, in his Opinion, there is sufficient matter of Error for reversing the Judgment. Whereupon the Court in their sessions, or any two Judges, in vacation, may Order such writ to be Issued or reject the Petition, as to them shall seem just; but no supersedeas shall be Issued in any case, except such, as in respect to it's value or nature, would have admitted of an appeal.

Writs of Error shall not be sued out of the General Court to Judgments of Inferior Courts, but with leave of the Court, upon

Motion of the party desiring the same; and ten days previous Notice thereof given, in Writing, to the adverse party.

Before granting any Appeal or Issuing a Writ of Error or Supersedeas the party praying the same shall enter into Bond with sufficient Security in a reasonable Penalty, with Condition to satisfy and pay the Amount of the recovery in the County or other inferior Court and all Costs and Damages awarded by the General Court, in case the Judgment or sentence be Affirmed.

If, upon hearing any Appeal, Writ of Error or supersedeas, the Judgment of the inferior Court shall be reversed, the General Court shall enter such Judgment thereupon, as ought to have been entered in the inferior Court.

If any Person or Persons shall desire to remove any Suit depending in an inferior Court into the General Court, Provided the same be Originally Cognizable therein, a Certiorari for such removal may be granted by the General Court for good cause shewn upon motion and ten days notice thereof given in Writing to the Adverse party; or, in Vacation, the party desiring such Writ shall by Petition to the Judges of the General Court set forth his or her reasons and make Oath before a Magistrate to the truth of the Allegations of such petition; whereupon any two Judges of the said Court may under their hands Order the Certiorari to Issue and direct the penalty of the Bond to be taken Previous thereto or may reject such Petition, as to them shall seem just; Provided that ten days previous Notice of the Time and place of applying for such Writ be given in Writing to the Adverse party; upon which Order of the Judges, the Clerk shall Issue the Certiorari; Provided that the party shall enter into Bond with sufficient security in the Penalty so directed, with Condition for satisfying all money or Tobacco and Costs, which shall be recovered against the party in such suit; but, if any suit so removed by Writ of Certiorari shall be remanded to the inferior Court by Writ of Procedendo or otherwise, such Cause shall not afterwards be removed into the General Court, before Judgment shall be given therein in the inferior Court.

The Clerk of the General Court shall carefully preserve all such petitions for Writs of Certiorari with the affidavits thereto in the office; and, if any person in such affidavit shall take a false Oath and be thereof Convicted upon a prosecution commenced within twelve months after the offence committed, such offender shall suffer the pains and penalties directed for wilful and Corrupt Purgery.[24]

Where any Person shall be committed in any Civil Action to

the Gaol of any County or Corporation for a Cause or matter Cognizable in the General Court, it shall be lawful for the Clerk of the General Court and he is hereby required upon the application of such person and a Certificate of his or her being Actually in Goal, to Issue a Writ of Habeas Corpus cum causa to remove the Body of such prisoner into the public Prison for Debtors, and the cause of his Commitment into the General Court returnable on the first day of the succeeding General Court if Issued in Vacation, or to the last day of the Term if Sued out whilst the Court are sitting.

If any person Committed for Treason or Felony, specially expressed in the Warrant of Commitment, shall apply to the General Court the first Week of the Term, if the Trial is to be at Bar, or to the Judge of the Assize, where the Trial is to be on the first day of his session and desire to be brought to Trial, and shall not be Indicted and Tried sometime in that Term or session, the Judges shall set such prisoner at Liberty upon Bail for his appearance to answer the offence at the next succeeding Term or session; unless it appears by affidavit that the Witnesses for the Commonwealth could not be produced at such Term or session. And, if any such prisoner shall not be Indicted and tried the second Term or session after commitment, he shall be discharged from his Imprisonment in manner aforesaid. Provided this shall not extend to discharge any person in Custody of the sherif for any other Cause.[25]

All Writs of Habeas Corpus sued out during the Sessions of Assize shall be returnable before the Judge proceeding on the Circuit in which the prisoner is detained.[13]

The Courts of Assize at their several sittings to be held, as aforesaid, shall have full power to hear and determine all Treasons, Murders, Felonies and other Crimes and Misdeameanors, which shall be brought before them in their respective Circuits.[26] When any person not being a slave shall be charged, before a Justice of the Peace with any Criminal offence, which in the Opinion of such Justice ought to be examined into by the County Court, the said Justice shall take the Recognizance of all material Witnesses to appear before such Court and immediately by his Warrant Commit the person so Charged to the County Gaol, and moreover shall Issue his Warrant to the Sherif of the County requiring him to summon the Justices of the County to meet at their Court-house on a certain day, not less than five or more than Ten day's after the date thereof, to hold a Court for examination of the Fact, which Court shall consider whether, as the case may appear to them, the prisoner may be discharged from further prosecution, may be Tried in the County or must be tried in the General Court or Court of Assize; if they shall be of Opinion that the Fact may be tried in the County the prisoner shall be bound over to the next Grand Jury Court to be held for that County for Trial, or, upon refusing to give sufficient Bail, shall be remanded to the County Gaol, there to remain until such Court, or until he or she shall be Bailed. But if they shall be of Opinion that the Prisoner ought to be Tried in the General Court or Court of Assize they shall take the Depositions of the Witnesses and bind such as they shall think proper by recognizances to appear and give Evidence against such Criminal at his Trial; and, having remanded the Prisoner to Gaol, any two of the Justices, one being of the Quorum, by warrant under their hands and seals, shall direct the sherif or his Deputy to remove the prisoner and commit him to the Gaol of that assize Court, at which the Issues in civil cases for the County from whence he is removed are herein directed to be Tried, there to be safely kept until he or she be discharged by due course of Law. By virtue of which Warrant the sherif, as soon as may be, shall remove the Prisoner and deliver him or her with the Warrant to the keeper of the Assize Gaol, who shall receive and safely keep him or her accordingly.[27]

And for Enabling the Sherif safely to Convey and deliver such Prisoner the said two Justices by their Warrant shall empower him, as well within his County as without, to impress such and so many Men, Horses and Boats, as shall be necessary for the Guard and safe Conveyance of the Prisoner, proceeding therein as the Laws may direct in Cases of Impressing on other Occasions, and all persons are to pay due Obedience to such Warrant.[28]

Provided that, if such person shall in the Opinion of the Court be Bailable by Law, he or she shall not be removed within twenty days after the examining Court, but shall and may be admitted to Bail before any Justice of the same County within that Time or at any Time afterwards before any Judge of the General Court.

When any person shall be so removed to be Tried for Treason or Felony, the Clerk of the County, from whence the Prisoner is removed, shall immediately after the Court held for his or her examination Issue a Writ of venire Facias to the Sherif of the County commanding him to summon twelve good and lawful Men, being Freeholders of the County, residing as near as may be to the place, where the Fact is alledged to have been Committed, to come before the Court of Assize, where the Prisoner is to be Tried at it's next session, and return a pannel of their names, which Freeholders or so many of them, as shall appear, not being challenged, together with so many other good and lawful Freeholders of the bystanders, as will make up the number twelve, shall be a lawful Jury for the Trial of such Prisoner.

Every Venire man summoned and attending such Court of Assize shall have the same allowance for travelling and attendance as is herein before provided for Witnesses, to be paid by the Public.

If any Person summoned as a Venire Man shall fail to attend accordingly, not having a reasonable excuse to be made at the time he should have appeared or at the next General Court or Court of Assize for that District, the Court of Assize may fine every such person not exceeding forty shillings or four hundred pounds of Tobacco for the use of the Commonwealth.

If a Prisoner shall desire any Witnesses to be summoned for him or her to appear, either at the examining Court or on the Trial at the Assizes, the Clerk of the Assize or of the County Court, as the case may be, shall Issue Subpoena for such Witnesses, who being summoned and attending, shall have the like allowance for travelling and attendance and be subject to the same Penalty for failing to attend, as is provided for Witnesses in Civil Causes.

The keepers of the respective Assize Gaols, by Order of any two Justices of the same County, may impress Guards for the safe keeping of all Prisoners in their Custody to be paid by the Public.

The fee to the Sherif of the County and to the Assize Gaoler for keeping and Dieting any such Prisoner shall be one shilling per day and no more.

Where the Criminal shall be Convicted and hath Estate sufficient to pay the Charges of Prosecution, the whole shall be paid out of such Estate, and the Public only made Chargeable where there is no such Estate or not sufficient to be found.

The Sherif of each of the Counties of Accomack, Nansemond, York, Essex, Spotsylvania, Sussex, Charlotte, Bedford, Montgomerie, Powhatan, Culpeper, Albemarle, Augusta, Fairfax, Frederick, and Monongalia, Yohogania, for the Time being, shall before every meeting of the Court of assize in their respective Counties summon Twenty four Freeholders of the Counties Assigned to each Assize, qualified as the Laws require, for Grand Jurors to appear at the succeeding Court of Assize, which twenty four Men or any sixteen of them, shall be a Grand Jury and shall enquire of and present all Treasons, Murders, Felonies or other Misdemeanors whatever which shall have been committed or done in any of the Counties within the Jurisdiction of such assize Courts respectively. And, upon any Indictment for a Capital offence being found by a Grand Jury to be true against any person or persons, the Judges shall cause such person or persons to be immediately arraigned and tried by a Petit Jury, summoned as herein before directed and he or they being found Guilty, pass such Judgment, as the Laws direct, and thereupon award Execution; and, if the Prisoner shall be found not Guilty, to acquit him or her of the Charge.

Provided that in all Trials the Defendant shall, on petition be allowed Counsel, and that when sentence of Death shall be passed upon any Prisoner, there shall be one Calender Month at least between the Judgment and Execution.

The Judges of the General Court may also on other Occasions upon good Cause shewn, order any Prisoner committed for a Capital offence to be removed by Habeas Corpus or otherwise to the Public Gaol, in order to be tried at the Bar of the General Court, and thereupon a venire facias shall Issue to summon a Jury of the vicinage for his trial at Bar; and, as well for the enquiry into such offences, as all others committed within this Commonwealth, except only where the penalty inflicted by Law, is less than twenty shillings, or two hundred pounds of Tobacco, a Grand Jury shall be summoned and sworn in the General Court on the sixth day of each Term. But no Grand Jury shall make any presentments of their own knowledge upon the Information of fewer than two of their own Body.[29]

Every person summoned to appear on a Grand Jury and failing to attend not having a reasonable excuse shall be fined by the Judge, not exceeding four hundred pounds of Tobacco to the use of the Commonwealth.[30]

Upon Presentment made by the Grand Jury at any Court of Assize of an offence not Capital, the Judge shall order the Clerk to Issue a summons or other proper process against the person or persons presented, to appear and answer such Presentment at the next Court of Assize and thereupon hear and determine the same according to Law.

The Attorney General of the Commonwealth or some other person, to be appointed by the Judges of the General Court and Commissioned by the Governor, to continue in office during good behaviour, shall attend each of the said Assize Courts in behalf of the Commonwealth.[13]

The Clerk of Assize of each Court shall in a Book by him kept for that purpose enter the names of all Venire Men and Witnesses, who attend for the Trial of Criminals at such Court, the number of Days each shall attend, the Ferries they shall have Crossed and the Distances they shall have travelled on that occasion, and transmit the same, after every Court, to the Clerk of the General Court, who shall make the like Entries of all Venire Men and Witnesses, who attend the Trial of Criminals at the Bar of the General Court, and shall, before every Session of General Assembly, deliver all such Books to the Clerk of the house of Delegates, that the allowance may be made to such Venire men and Witnesses.[31]

The Gaoler in every County, where any Assize is held, shall constantly attend the said Court of Assize and execute the Command of the Judges from Time to Time, and take or receive into his Custody all persons by the Court to him Committed on Original or mesne Process or in Execution in any Civil Suit or for any contempt of the Court, and him or them safely keep, until thence discharged by due course of Law, and may demand and receive of every such Prisoner the legal fees for diet and care; but where such Prisoner is so poor as not to be able to subsist him or herself in Prison, the Goaler shall be allowed by the Public one shilling per day for the maintainance of every such poor Prisoner and no security shall be demanded of him or her, nor shall he or she be detained for such Prison Fees; and every Gaoler, during his continuance in office, shall be exempted from serving in the Militia and on Jury's and shall have such allowance over and above the Fees, as by the General Assembly shall be thought reasonable.[32]

All the Penalties hereby inflicted and not otherwise appropriated shall be one Moiety to the use of the Commonwealth and disposed of, as the General Assembly shall direct and the other Moiety to the informer, and be recovered by action of Debt or Information in any Court of Record, where the same is Cognizable, and where Fines shall be laid by the Courts of Assize on any person or persons for not attending as Jury men, the Clerks of Assize shall Certify the names of the Persons the fines severally imposed upon them and the County in which they reside to the Clerk of the General Court, who shall annually, before the last of January, transmit to the Sherif of each County a list of all such Fines, and all others imposed to the use of the Commonwealth by the General Court on persons residing in the County, and such Sherif shall collect and Levy the same in like manner, as is provided for County Levys; and account for and pay the Money, deducting five Percentum for Commission, and also Insolvents to the Treasurer of this Commonwealth on or before the first day of September; or the said Treasurer may recover the same with Costs by Motion in the General Court on ten days previous Notice given in Writing of such Motion; and the Clerk of the General Court shall deliver Copies of all lists so sent to the Sherifs to the Treasurer, to Enable him to call such Sherifs to Account.

This Act shall commence and be in force from and after the first day of   next, and all other Acts so far as they relate to any matter or thing contained or within the Perview of this Act are hereby repealed.[33]

MS (Vi). Clerk's copy, 40 numbered pages, docketed: "An Act for establishing a General Court. Oct. 1777." Another copy in clerk's hand, MS (Vi), 13 pages numbered in fours, docketed: "An Act for establishing a General Court Oct 1777." These are not identical. Each differs from the other and from the Act as finally adopted (Hening, IX, 401-19). The text used here differs from the second MS text principally in its provision for an elaborate system of assize courts. Since assize courts were embraced in the Bill as reported in 1776 and were eliminated by amendment at the Oct. 1777 session, the text employed here may be regarded as substantially if not precisely the same as that drawn up and reported in 1776. Hence for the sake of clarity the text used here is referred to as the 1776 Bill, and the second MS text is referred to as the 1777 Bill. Both were under discussion during the Oct. 1777 session of the Assembly, but the second is probably the later text, since it incorporates no provisions for assize courts, though in phraseology and other details it differs from the Act as adopted more than does the 1776 Bill, as the textual notes indicate. Accompanying these MSS is a single sheet headed: "Amendments to the Bill for establishing a General Court & Courts of Assize." These amendments are in part the same as the 52 amendments made in the Bill by the Senate on 17 Jan. 1778, the most important of which delete all provisions for assize courts (JHD, Oct. 1777, 1827 edn., p. 117-18). However, the page and line references in this list of amendments are not correlated either with the MS of the 1776 Bill or with that of the 1777 Bill; hence they must refer to another MS of the former, not now known to be extant.

On 25 Nov. 1776 TJ presented a Bill for a General Court according to a direction of the House of 1 Nov. That direction had been for the establishment of a General Court. It is to be noted, however, that, as introduced, the Bill was "A Bill for establishing a General Court *and Courts of Assize.*" On 27-29 Nov. the Bill was discussed in committee of the whole; on 5 Dec. it was amended and ordered to be engrossed and read the third time. On 13 Dec., however, it was postponed until next session of Assembly (JDH, Oct. 1776, 1828 edn., p. 35, 69, 71, 72, 75, 83, 96). On 10 May 1777 a committee, of which TJ was a member, was given leave to bring in a Bill for establishing "a General Court and Courts of Assize." On 30 Oct. 1777 this direction was again given to a committee of which TJ was head. The Bill reported 7 Nov., was passed by the House, after amendment, on 3 Jan. 1778, and was amended by the Senate on 17 Jan. (JHD, Oct. 1777, 1827 edn. (p. 7, 15, 17, 95, 98-9, 116, 117-19, 120).

[1] The 1777 Bill does not include the provision concerning precedence and the designation of the chief justice, though the Act as finally adopted does (sect. ii).
[2] The 1777 Bill does not include the requirement that oaths be administered by the governor in presence of the council of state, though the Act as finally adopted does (sect. ii).
[3] The Act as adopted includes at this point a clause authorizing the transfer of suits depending before the old General Court to the new (sect. iv).
[4] The 1777 Bill provides for sessions on 1 Apr. and 1 Oct. and the Act as adopted calls for sessions on 1 Mch. and 10 Oct. (sect. v).
[5] The 1777 Bill does not include the clauses providing for day-to-day adjournment because of lack of quorum, but the

Act as adopted does (sect. v).

6 The 1777 Bill does not provide for the appointment of "one or more assistant Clerks, or Crier and Tipstaff or for attendance of sheriff and under sheriffs," though the Act as adopted does (sect. vi).

7 The proviso authorizing any judge of the court to direct a defendant to give bail is not in the 1777 Bill, though it is in the Act as adopted (sect. xii).

8 The 1777 Bill contains, but the Act as adopted does not, the following at this point: "and all actions on the case for the recovery of Money due on a Mutuatus, quantum meruit, Emisset or Indebitatus assumpsit for Goods sold, or for work and labour done and performed. . . ."

9 The Act as adopted includes (sect. xix-xx) the provisions concerning special bail as here given, but the 1777 Bill did not permit any but judges of the General Court to take a recognizance of special bail, did not require it to be transmitted by the person taking it to the clerk of the court before the next succeeding General Court, and did include the following reenactment of earlier procedures concerning special bail: "but if such Bail shall be judged sufficient or be not excepted to within the time aforesaid the same shall stand and the Bail be chargeable in the same manner as if the Recognizance had been taken in Court. Or such Recognizance of Bail may be taken and returned and have the effect as directed by an Act of Assembly Intituled 'An Act for taking special Bail in the Country upon Actions and Suits in the General Court.' And every person becoming special Bail for any Defendant or Defendants either in Court or in manner aforesaid shall be liable for the Judgment given against the Principle in the same manner and upon the like proceedings as have been heretofore used in England and this State, unless he render the Body of the Principle in his discharge according to the Rules of those proceedings or according to an Act of Assembly intituled 'An Act for amending and declaring the Law concerning the escape of Debtors out of the Prison Rules and for other purposes therein mentioned.' "

10 The Act as adopted agrees with the text of the 1776 Bill concerning a warning proclamation "instead of the process to outlawry formerly used" (sect. xxii-xxiii), but the 1777 Bill continues the earlier method, as set forth in the following: "And where an appearance cannot otherwise be inforced in any civil action, or the defendant cannot be taken upon an Execution against his Body, the Plaintif on the return of a Pluries Capias or Capias ad satisfaciendum that the defendant is not to be found, may sue out an Exigent and Proclamation in order that the defendant may be outlawed thereupon."

11 The Act as adopted (sect. xxv) agrees with the text here given, but the 1777 Bill differs from it in the following: "All rules to declare, plead, reply, rejoin, or for other proceedings shall be given regularly from Month to Month and shall be out in one Calendar month, and shall be entered in a Book kept by the Clerk for that purpose to the intent that all attornies and others by inspecting the Book may be certainly and readily informed what proceedings have been or are to be in the Causes depending, and no Rule shall be given between one Rule day and another."

12 The Act as adopted agrees with the text here given (sect. xxviii), but the 1777 Bill does not provide for proof by affirmation and also provides that the plaintiff in replevin and the defendant in all other actions "be not admitted to plead and demur to the whole."

13 This paragraph is not in the 1777 Bill or in the Act as adopted. Only the text as here given includes provisions respecting assize courts. References to assize courts occurring at various places in the text of the 1776 Bill and later deleted by amendment are not indicated except, as here, where whole paragraphs are involved.

14 The Act as adopted (sect. xxxi) and the 1777 Bill agree in the last part of this paragraph, reading as follows: ". . . setting, as near as may be, an equal number of causes to each day."

15 The Act as adopted (sect. xxxiii) agrees with the text here given, but the 1777 Bill provides that proceedings recorded by the clerk shall be read in open court the next day, except those of the last day of the term, which are required to be drawn up, read, and corrected the same day.

16 The Act as adopted (sect. xxxvii) agrees with the text as here given, but the 1777 Bill reads: "(or being one of the people called Quakers, upon his or her solemn affirmation)."

17 The Act as adopted (sect. xxxvii) agrees with the text as here given, but

the 1777 Bill omits "or Mainprize."

18 The Act as adopted (sect. xl) agrees with the text here given, but the 1777 Bill provides that *all* witnesses "shall be privileged from the service of any writ or process or other distress whatsoever."

19 The Act as adopted (sect. xl) agrees with the text here given, but the 1777 Bill provided for "one pound and an half of Tobacco, or three pence per mile."

20 The Act as adopted (sect. xlii) agrees with the text here given, but the 1777 Bill reads: "of any County or other inferior court."

21 The 1777 Bill contains, but the 1776 Bill and the Act as adopted do not, the following provisions for the manner of assigning error: "in any personal action or suit where the Judgment shall not exceed twenty pounds, or four thousand pounds of Tobacco, the Appellant shall assign error in matter of right only, and if upon the hearing in the General Court, the Judgment shall appear to be according to the right of the Cause, the same shall be affirmed, notwithstanding any mispleading or error in matter of form; where the Judgment shall be for more than those sums and shall not exceed fifty pounds or ten thousand pounds of Tobacco, the Appellant may assign errors in matter of right and such errors in the form or manner of proceedings, as were insisted on in the inferior Court and none other: And in all suits of greater value than the sums last mentioned, in suits concerning the titles or bounds of Land and in all other controversies above mentioned, the Appellant may assign any errors of form or substance."

22 The Act as adopted (sect. xliii) agrees with the text here given, but the 1777 Bill provides the same damages and costs in "any personal or mixed action appeals" and "In Ejectments and real Actions" the damages were to be £5 or 1000 pounds of tobacco. The 1777 Bill differs also in providing that the appellant should pay "fifty shillings or 500 ℔s of Tobacco besides all costs" if the sentence of the inferior court should be affirmed.

23 The 1777 Bill agrees with the text here given but the Act as adopted and the MS from which it was printed by Hening (sect. xlvi) reads, erroneously, "paying."

24 Thus in MS.

25 The proviso in the last sentence of this paragraph is in the Act as finally adopted (sect. lv), but not in the 1777 Bill, which has the following: "Provided that if any person discharged from his imprisonment for criminal cause either by Habeas Corpus, or for want of prosecution as aforesaid, shall at the time be charged in debt or other action or with Process in a civil cause, he shall be kept in custody according to Law for such other suit."

26 The Act as adopted (sect. lvi) and the 1777 Bill agree with the text as here given except in applying the jurisdiction to the General Court. The 1777 Bill also has the following, not included in either the present text or the Act as adopted: "The General Court in their Sessions shall have Jurisdiction of all Treasons, Murders, Felonies or other crimes and misdemeanors committed or done within this Commonwealth, and shall proceed to the trial of all Persons committed to Gaol for Capital offences, in like manner and subject to such Regulations as by an Act of Assembly made in the year 1748 intituled 'An Act directing the method of trial of criminals for Capital Offences, and for other purposes therein mentioned,' are prescribed and directed; and give Judgment according to Law against all such as shall be convicted; and Award Execution thereupon, Saving to the Governor his right of granting Pardons according to the Constitution of Government.

"The said Judges shall also have Power to proceed upon all Indictments and Punishments for Offences not Capital which shall be formed or made before them by Grand Juries to be summoned and sworn on the sixth day of each term in like manner and for the purposes as mentioned in an Act of Assembly made in the year last mentioned, intituled 'An Act concerning Juries.' And shall issue process and proceed to trial and Judgment upon all such Indictments and Presentments according to Law and the practice heretofore used in the General Court.

"The said Judges or any three of them shall moreover have full power and are hereby required to meet at the place appointed for holding the General Court on the second Tuesday in June and on the second Tuesday in December in every year then and there to hold a Court of Oyer and Terminer and Gaol Delivery for the trial of all such Capital Offenders as may then be in the Public

Gaol; they may adjourn from day to day until all such Criminals according to Law and in the manner prescribed by the said Act directing the method of trial of Criminals for Capital Offences and for other purposes therein mentioned. . . ."

27 Except for the provision concerning the jurisdiction of the General Court (see note 26), the 1777 Bill does not contain any of the matter in this paragraph concerning an examining court, though the Act as adopted does (sect. lvii).

28 This and the succeeding ten paragraphs are not in the 1777 Bill, though they are in the Act as adopted (sect. lvii-lxvi), except for the elimination or alteration of references to assize courts, clerks of assize, assize jails, &c.

29 This paragraph is not in the 1777 Bill, though it is in the Act as adopted (sect. lviii) except for the provision concerning removal of capital offenders for trial before a jury of the vicinage. However, sect. xl of the Act as adopted empowers the General Court to try all causes before it and to cause the sheriff to "empannel and return jurors of the byestanders."

30 This and the succeeding paragraphs are not in the 1777 Bill, though they are in the Act as adopted (sect. lxix-lxx).

31 This and the succeeding paragraphs are not in the 1777 Bill, though they are in the Act as adopted (sect. lxxi).

32 At this point the Act as adopted contains two sections (sect. lxxiii-lxxiv) not in the 1776 Bill or the 1777 Bill. These sections provide for salaries of judges and for a tax on process.

33 This paragraph is not in MS of 1777 Bill. That Bill, however, includes at different places the following interesting sections which are not in the 1776 Bill or the Act as adopted:

"And for prevention of delay by arresting Judgments and vexatious Appeals, the several Acts of the British Parliament commonly called the Statutes of Jeofails and amendments shall be and are hereby adopted in this Commonwealth. . . .

"And for effectually securing the personal liberty of the Citizens of this Commonwealth Be it hereby enacted that the several Acts of the British Parliament commonly called and known by the name of the Habeas Corpus Acts shall be and are hereby adopted in this Commonwealth. . . ."

There is an even more important draft of a memorandum in TJ's hand respecting writs of habeas corpus that may have been intended for insertion in the 1776 Bill (DLC: TJ Papers, 232: 42062). This draft reads as follows: "⟨And forasmuch as it will happen that many counties of this commonwealth will be so remote from the General court in term time and from the judges thereof in vacation that the inhabitants may be long deprived of their liberty and sometimes be altogether removed before they shall be able to apply for and obtain a writ of Habeas corpus from the said court or any of it's judges: be it therefore enacted that⟩ the said General court shall from time to time assign in every county some one of the most able learned and fit of the justices of the said county who (no judge of the said court being in the said county at the time) shall receive applications for ⟨writs of Habeas corpus from any persons restrained of their liberty as aforesaid and thereupon to order in the cases before directed, which shall⟩ issue and direct to any person within his county writs of Habeas corpus in the same manner as the court or one of the judges thereof may do returnable before the said General court in term time or any judge thereof in vacation, on which writs the same proceedings shall lie as if they had been issued by the said court or a judge thereof." It is possible that TJ drafted this as a separate bill; but the deletion of the preamble in the MS makes it more plausible to assume that he had intended it as an addition to the General Court Bill.

IV. Bill for Establishing
a Court of Admiralty

[4 December 1776]

For establishing a court of Admiralty, Be it enacted by the General assembly of the Commonwealth of Virginia that at some certain[1] place to be appointed by act of General assembly there shall be held as often as there may be occasion a court of Admiralty to consist of three judges to be chosen by joint ballot of both houses of assembly and commissioned by the Governor any two of them to make a court, and to hold their offices for so long time as they shall demean themselves well therein.

Every person so commissioned before he enters upon the duties of his office shall in open court take and subscribe the oath of fidelity to the Commonwealth, and take the following oath of office to wit. 'You shall swear that well and truly you will serve this Commonwealth in the office of a judge of the court of Admiralty: that you will do equal right to all manner of people great and small, high and low, rich and poor, of what country or nation soever they be, without respect of persons. You shall not take by yourself or by any other any gift, fee, or reward of gold, silver, or any other thing directly or indirectly of any person or persons, great or small for any matter done or to be done by virtue of your office except such fees or salary as shall be by law appointed. You shall not maintain by yourself or by any other privily or openly any plea or quarrel depending in the said court. You shall not delay any person of right for the letters or request of any one, nor for any other cause; and if any letter or request come to you contrary to the law you shall nothing do for such letter or request. But you shall proceed to do the law, any such letter or request notwithstanding. And finally, in all things belonging to your said office, during your continuance therein you shall faithfully, justly and truly according to the best of your skill and judgment, do equal and impartial justice, without fraud, favor, affection, or partiality.'[2] And if any person shall presume to execute the said office without having taken the said oaths, he shall forfeit and pay the sum of 500£ for his said offence, one moiety to the use of this Commonwealth and the other to the informer, to be recovered with costs by action of debt in any court of record.

The said court shall have cognisance[3] of all causes heretofore of Admiralty jurisdiction in this country, and shall be governed in their proceedings and decisions by[4] the regulations of the Continental Congress, acts of general Assembly, English statutes prior to the fourth year of the reign of king James the first, and[5] the laws of Oleron, the Rhodian and Imperial laws so far as the same have been heretofore observed in the English courts of admiralty, save only in the instances hereafter provided for.

If in any case the Regulations of the American[6] Congress shall differ from those established by act of the General assembly of this Commonwealth,[7] if such case relate to a capture from any public enemy with whom the United states of America are or may be at war the said regulations of the Congress shall[8] be observed; in all other cases, the supremacy of the laws of this Commonwealth within the same shall prevail.

To prevent all doubts which may arise, it is declared that the said court shall have jurisdiction in no case whatever of any capital offence.[9]

The said judges shall have power to appoint[10] a register and marshall each of whom, before he enters upon the execution of his office shall take the oath of fidelity to the Commonwealth, and[11] shall give bond with sufficient security to be approved by the court, payable to the Governor and his successors, the said Register in the penalty of[12]   pounds, and the Marshall in the penalty of[13]   pounds with condition for their true and faithful performance of the duty of their respective offices, and accounting for and paying all money which may come to their hands by virtue thereof: which bonds may severally be put in suit and prosecuted by and at the costs of any party grieved, and shall not become void on the first recovery, but may from time to time be again put in suit by parties injured and at their costs, until the whole penalty shall be recovered thereupon.

The said court shall administer the oath of fidelity to the Commonwealth to all proctors before they shall be allowed to practice in the said court.

The said court shall have power to direct sale to be made at any time of perishable goods, taking sufficient caution that the proceeds of such sale be secured to the person to whom the same shall be decreed.

Every person commencing a suit in the said court shall file his libel, setting forth the ground of his claim with the register, who shall thereupon issue a citation directed to the Marshall commanding him to serve the same on any ship or vessel with their cargoes, rigging, Apparel, and furniture, which may be claimed, or against which satisfaction for any demand[14] may be required by the libel, as also to summon the master or owner of such ship or vessel, if to be found, to appear on a certain day and at the place therein mentioned to shew cause, if any he or they can, why the claim of the libellant should not be allowed, and the Marshall shall return the truth of the case upon every such citation, and if the same shall be returned served upon such master or owner, and no person shall appear on the court day to which the same is returnable to gainsay the proceeding, the libel shall be taken for confessed, and the court shall proceed to pronounce such sentence thereupon as shall be agreeable to law; but if the master or owner, or any other person in his or their behalf shall appear and enter into a defence of the suit, in such case[15] the court shall proceed to trial, sentence and execution. And if the marshal shall return on the citation that the master or owner of any such ship or vessel is not to be found, then the court shall cause proclamation to be published in the Virginia gazette for three weeks successively, requiring any persons interested to appear and defend the claim of the libellant: and if no person shall appear to make a defence at or before the expiration of the third week of proclamation, the libel shall be taken for confessed and the court shall proceed to judgment and execution thereupon, taking cautionary security of the libellant to have the effects forthcoming subject to the future decree of the court:[16] and the court shall direct a copy of the decree to be published for[17] weeks in the Virginia gazette: and if within[18]   after pronouncing such decree the master or owner or others in their behalf shall apply to the court, desire to be admitted to a defence of the suit and give sufficient security for paiment of such costs as shall be awarded against him or them if cast therein, in that case such defence shall be admitted and the court shall proceed to trial in like manner as if such appearance had been made at the return of the Citation.

In all cases of claim to any ship or vessel, their cargoes or appurtenances, after a final or Conditional judgment, the court shall have power, if they see cause, to require security for costs.

The court shall and may award costs in all such cases as appear reasonable, and executions for such costs may be issued by the Register against the body or estate of the person adjudged to pay the same, directed to any sheriff of the Commonwealth who shall execute the same in like manner, and for the same fees, and be subject to the like penalties and forfeitures for the non-execution or undue execution thereof and to the same remedy for not paying the money levied thereupon or which ought to have been levied as is directed by law in the case of such executions sued out of the courts of Common law.

Provided always that in all cases of condemnation of vessels their cargoes and appurtenances, the costs shall be paid out of the sales of the said vessels cargoes and appurtenances, and not be levied on the master or owner defending the same.

All matters of fact put in issue shall be tried by jury, unless in cases of captures from an enemy which shall be tried by the court but if such capture be from an enemy with whom the United states of America are or may be at war, then such trial shall be by court or jury as the American Congress shall direct.

Where any person or persons bodies politic or corporate shall think himself or themselves aggrieved by the final sentence of the said court in any case of capture from an enemy with whom the United states of America are at war, such Appeal shall be allowed as directed by the American Congress; and in all other cases, if of greater value than   besides the costs,[19] he or they may be allowed an appeal from such sentence to the court of Appeals, or may sue out a writ of error to such sentence returneable in the court of Appeals, the party appealing or suing out such writ, entering into bond with sufficient security paiable to the other party, with condition for prosecuting the appeal or writ of error and paying all such costs and damages as shall be awarded in case the sentence be affirmed and thereupon the register of the Admiralty shall transmit a copy of the record and proceedings, and the Appeal or writ of error shall be heard thereupon in like manner and the damages on affirmance shall be the same as is directed by law in the case of Appeals from the High court of Chancery.

The fees of the register shall be such as shall be settled by the General assembly;[20] and those of the Marshal for any services shall be such as are allowed by law to sheriffs for the like services[21] save only where the amount of the sales upon any execution would be so great as that the marshal's fees would exceed the sum of £50.[22] in which case the marshall shall be entitled to the said sum of £50[22] only as a full fee for his services in levying the said execution.

Provided alwais and be it enacted that in all cases of Condemnation of vessels with their cargoes and appurtenances, as lawful prize taken from the enemy by a private ship or vessel of war wherein neither the Continent in General, or this Commonwealth in particular are interested, if the Libellant or his Agent shall desire it, the court shall have power to order the sale of the vessel, cargo and appurtenances, to be made by such libellant or his agent and an account of sales to be returned to court by him or them without any fee or reward to be given or paid to the Marshall for such sale.

And whereas by the expiration of the ordinance constituting judges to hear and determine causes maritime the several suits depending before the said judges are discontinued be it therefore enacted that the said suits shall be again reinstated in the condition in which they stood at the time of discontinuance and transferred, together with all the records of the said judges, into the court of Admiralty established by this act by which such sentence and other proceedings shall be had in the said suits as if the same had been originally commenced in the said court of Admiralty.

Dft (DLC). This rough draft is endorsed by TJ: "A Bill For establishing a court of Admiralty." Reported by TJ 4 Dec.; read second time 9 Dec. and amended by committee of the whole; read third time and passed 14 Dec.; approved by Senate 16 Dec. (JHD, Oct. 1776, 1828 edn., p. 82, 89, 97, 98).

The speed and unanimity with which this Bill was passed indicates the importance of the subject to a maritime commonwealth. TJ's Bill proceeded from this rough draft to final enactment with fewer amendments than almost any other legislation from his pen, most of the changes made by the legislature being necessary to supply blank spaces in TJ's draft (Hening, IX, 202-206). This Bill is important also in showing (see below) that TJ must have occasionally submitted his drafts to one or more colleagues for criticism.

1 The Act omits "certain."

2 This oath is substantially the same as that required of judges of the courts established by the three preceding Bills.

3 Draft deletes: "jurisdiction in."

4 Draft deletes: "such rules, laws, customs, and usages as."

5 Draft deletes: "such other rules, laws, customs, and usages as."

6 Draft deletes: "Continental."

7 Draft deletes: "the said regulations of Congress shall prevail in all cases relating to captures."

8 Draft deletes: "prevail."

9 Interlined in draft in another hand and then struck out: "but the said offences shall be tried in the General Court by a Jury of Bystanders, &c."

10 Act reads "an advocate" at this point; this and the changes made in the Act, noted above and below, are the only differences between the draft and the law.

11 Act reads at this point: "and the said register and marshall shall each."

12 Act reads: "one thousand pounds."

13 Act reads: "ten thousand pounds."

14 Draft deletes: "of wages, building, or otherwise may be claimed."

15 Draft deletes: "an issue shall be made up and tried by a jury of the by-standers to be summoned by the Marshall or his deputy and judgment shall be entered for the libellant or defendant, according to the verdict of such jury, and the court shall direct a proper execution thereof."

16 Interlined query in draft in another hand: "Wouldn't it be better to allow the Libellant sell perishable goods and return the money." This was struck out.

17 Act reads: "three."

18 Act reads: "one year."

19 The words "if of greater . . . besides the costs" were struck out by amendment (Hening, IX, 205).

20 Act reads: "and until such regulation shall be made the said fees shall be settled and adjusted by the said court."

21 Interlined in draft in another hand: "Except in cases where his fees shall not exceed"; this was struck out, but the proviso following this point (written in the margin of the draft) shows that TJ accepted the suggestion.

22 An amendment to the Bill altered this to read "one hundred pounds" (Hening, IX, 206).

V. Bill for Better Regulating the Proceedings in the County Courts

[4 December 1776]

For amendment of the act of General assembly passed in the year 1748 intituled 'an act for establishing county courts, and for regulating and settling the proceedings therein' be it enacted by the General assembly of the Commonwealth of Virginia[1] that instead of the oaths of[2] allegiance and supremacy, the oath of abjuration and subscription to the test by the said act directed and the oath directed to be taken by an ordinance passed this present year[3] to enable the then magistrates and officers to continue the administration of justice, every justice[4] shall take and subscribe the oath of fidelity to this commonwealth, and instead of the oath of a justice of the county court in Chancery directed by the same act, he shall take the following oath, to wit 'you shall swear that well and truly you will serve the Commonwealth of Virginia in the office of a justice in the County court of   in Chancery, and that you will do equal right to all manner of people, great and small, high and low, rich and poor, according to equity and good conscience and the laws and usages of this Commonwealth, without favour affection, or partiality. So help you God.'[5]

The said County courts shall also have jurisdiction and power to try all persons charged before them with being inimical to, or assisting the enemies of America, as the Ordinances in that case direct, instead of the Commissioners formerly appointed for such trials, whose power and jurisdiction shall cease from and after the[6] passing of this Act.

The said County courts shall cause Grand juries to be summoned to appear in the months of February, May, August, and November annually in the same manner, for the same purposes and under the like penalties as directed to be done for the months of May and November by an act intituled 'an act concerning juries.'

And instead of the court for receiving and certifying propositions and grievances and publick claims directed to be held before every session of assembly by an act passed in the year 1705 intituled 'an Act for regulating the election of burgesses, for settling their privileges and for ascertaining their allowances' and of the court for proof of public claims directed to be held in like manner before every session of assembly, by one other act passed in the same year 1705 and intituled 'an act concerning public claims' the said county courts shall in future at all times during their sessions, when required, receive and certify propositions and grievances and receive proofs of public claims, in like manner as is directed to be done by the said acts, and the said special courts for receiving and certifying propositions, grievances and public claims, and for proof of public claims shall henceforth be discontinued.

To give full time for executing process issuing from such courts in the larger counties of this Commonwealth, it shall and may be lawful for the clerk of any county court at the request of the party to make such process returnable to the first or second court after the same shall be issued.

All process against the Governor or any member of the Privy council, or the sheriff of any county, and the proceedings thereupon, shall be after the same manner in the county court as directed for the General court in an act of this present General assembly.

Upon executing any process whereupon bail shall be requirable, the sheriff shall return therewith the names of the bail by him taken; and if he shall not return bail, or the bail returned shall be judged insufficient by the court, or the defendant shall fail to appear or to give special bail, when ruled thereto by the court, such sheriff or bail shall be subject to the same judgment and recovery, and shall have the same liberty of defence, relief and remedy as in like cases is provided by the said act of this present session of assembly in suits depending in the General court.

All matters of fact material to the determination of the cause which in the course of the proceedings in any suit in chancery in the said county courts shall be affirmed[7] by the one party and denied by the other shall be tried by jury[8] upon evidence given vivâ voce in open court, and where witnesses are absent through sickness or other unavoidable cause, upon their depositions taken as the laws direct,[9] for which purpose an issue or issues shall be made up by declaration and plea as hath been heretofore used in Chancery when issues have been specially directed to be made up and tried by jury, saving to the defendant the same benefit of evidence by his own answer as hath been heretofore allowed in trials before the court of Chancery. And so much of the said act for establishing County courts as directs that Commissions to examine witnesses may be awarded by the court[10] after replication filed shall henceforth be repealed.

If the complainant shall not at the next court after such trial where trial[11] is necessary, or after issue joined where no such trial is necessary, set down the cause for hearing, the defendant may have it set down at his request.

For assisting the said County courts in their adjudications, it shall and may be lawful for them to levy annually the sum of ten pounds[12] to be by them disposed of in purchasing approved law books for the use of the said courts while in session.

Dft (DLC). Endorsed by TJ: "A Bill for better regulating the proceedings of the County courts"; at bottom of p. 4 TJ added a more formal title: "Title 'a bill to amend an act intituled "an act for establishing county courts & for regulating & settling the proceedings therein." '" Also MS (Vi), in a clerk's hand, amended as noted below by TJ; this bears TJ's formal title, which he struck out, causing it to read as first stated above; it is also endorsed by the clerk: "Decr. 4. 1776 Read the first Time Decr. 13th. 2d. Reading put off til next Session." The MS also has a page headed "Amendments to the Bill for better Regulating the Proceedings in the County Courts"; these amendments are noted below.

This effort to reform the county court proceedings met with failure, for no evidence has been found that the Bill ever came up for a second reading, though TJ was appointed 10 May 1777 to a committee having the same purposes as this Bill (JHD, May 1777, 1827 edn., p. 6; A. O. Porter, County Government in Virginia, N.Y., 1947, especially p. 100-54.)

[1] Amendment: "strike out the words Common Wealth of Virginia."

[2] Deleted in draft: "a justice of the county court in Chancery."

[3] Amendment: "Strike out the words *this present year* and insert *last Session of Assembly*." This oath (Hening, IX, 126) stands in contrast to TJ's explicit words, merely requiring the justices to "do equal right and justice to all men, to the best of my judgement, and according to law."

[4] TJ inserted in the clerk's copy: "hereafter to be commissioned."

[5] Amendment: "At the end of the first clause insert *which oaths shall be administered to the presiding Magistrate by any two of the others and by him to the rest.*"

[6] Deleted in draft: "31st day of Decemb."

[7] TJ changed clerk's copy to read: "are affirmed."

[8] Amendment: "Strike out the words *by Jury.*"

[9] Amendment: "After the word *direct* insert By a Jury if either party shall desire it, or the Court shall think proper to direct the same."

[10] Clerk's copy omits: "by the Court."

[11] Clerk's copy omits: "where trial."

[12] Amendment: "Leave a Blank for the Sum of Money."

Report on the Petition
of Arthur Upshur

[28 November 1776]

The Committee of Privileges and Elections have, according to Order, had under their consideration the Petition of Arthur Upshur to them referred and have agreed to the following report.[1] Your Committee find that the said Arthur Upshur, having several Vessels on the Stocks, cleared one of them out for the British West Indies on the 20th. day of July 1775; but that the said Vessel was not launched until the 26th. day of August:

That on the 2d. day of September when the Storm happened, the said Vessel had no part of her loading on board. That the said Vessel sailed after the 10th. day of September, to one of the foreign

West India Islands with a load of Indian Corn. That on the 2d. day of October following the Committee of the County of Accomack proceeded to enquire into the matter and on such enquiry declared the said Upshur had violated the Continental Association by sending out the said Vessel, and Ordered his Case to be published in the Virginia Gazette. That after the return of the said Vessel, the said Upshaw[2] (as appears by the Minutes of the said Committee) denying that he had intentionally violated the said Association, voluntarily submitted the matter again to the determination of the Committee, who, at a Session held on the 8th. day of January 1776, upon further enquiry were of Opinion that he had violated the said Association ignorantly; but that having behaved obstinately and ill afterwards, he ought to be fined and they accordingly fined him £100. which sum the said Upshur deposited with a Member of the Committee.

Your Committee further find that the said Petitioner hath, both before and since the said transaction, conducted himself as a friend to the American Cause.

Whereupon the Committee have come to the following Resolutions.

Resolved, that it is the Opinion of this Committee, that tho' the Committee of Accomack were actuated by the best of Motives, yet they erred in proceeding to impose a fine upon the Petitioner, and that therefore the said fine ought to be restored to the said Petitioner by the person with whom it was deposited.

Resolved, as the Opinion of this Committee, that the Petitioner, having violated the said Association through ignorance and having in other respects conducted himself as a friend to the American Cause, ought to be restored to the rights of dealing and intercourse with his Country.

MS (Vi). Clerk's copy; docketed: "1776 Decr. 2. agreed to. John Tazewell C. H. D." and "Dec. 4. 1776. agreed to by Senate   J. Pendleton C.S." Upshur's petition was presented 6 Nov. and referred to the committee on privileges and elections; TJ reported for the committee 28 Nov. (JHD, Oct. 1776, 1828 edn., p. 42, 73). On the Upshur case see VMHB, XV (1907-1908), 158-9.

[1] The words "and have agreed to the following report" are interlined in TJ's hand.
[2] The Report was printed in *Va. Gaz.* (Purdie), 13 Dec. 1776, where the spelling Upshaw has been corrected to read Upshur.

Bill to Establish
Auditors of Public Accounts

[5 December 1776]

For the regular settlement of all Publick accounts, *Be it enacted* by the general Assembly of the commonwealth of Virginia, and it is hereby enacted by the authority of the same; that an *Auditor General* of accounts shall henceforth be established to be appointed by the Governor with the advice and consent of the privy council and continued in office during good behaviour[1] and it shall be the business of the said auditors to examine, state and settle all publick accounts of Sheriffs and other Collectors, according to the Laws of this commonwealth and to certifie the same to the Treasurer, to examine and settle all claims against the country for Sallarys of the necessary officers of Government and other accounts as established by Law, and issue his warrant on the Treasurer for the payment of the same to be countersign'd by the Governor. And he shall receive and examine all accounts of the Navy board, and of the commissioners of the Army, which shall come certified to him and issue his warrants as before on the Treasurer for the payment of the same specifying in each warrant the nature and amount of the account for which it is issued and the said Auditor shall keep regular accounts of the expenditure of all sums of money for the different departments, which together with his vouchers for the same shall be laid before the General Assembly or the Governor and Council when thereunto required.[2]

And whereas in time of War the multiplicity of business and urgency of frequent demands, makes it more especially necessary to adopt some further and more adequate mode of expediting the publick business and the time limited by ordinance for the appointment of Commissioners for that purpose being nearly expired, *Be it* therefore enacted by the authority aforesaid that two Commissioners of the Army shall be appointed in manner aforesaid, whose duty it shall be to examine, state, and certifie all accounts relative to the Army to the Auditor General. And the said Commissioners shall have power to administer oaths for the proof of accounts referred to them and[3] shall keep regular books of accounts to be laid before the General Assembly or the Governor and Council when required, and the said auditor and[4] each of the said Commissioners shall receive the sum of fifteen shillings[5] ℔ day during his continuance in office for his service therein.

And be it further enacted that the Governor with the advice and consent of the Privy council, shall have full power and authority to suspend the said Auditor or Commissioners for neglect of duty, misbehaviour in office or for any other cause to them appearing and certifie the cause of such suspension to the next succeeding General Assembly.[6]

Dft (Vi). Clerk's copy, with interlineations by TJ and two other unidentified hands. Docketed: "A Bill to Establish Auditors of Publick accounts" and, in the hand of John Tazewell, "1776 Decr. 5. read the first time. Decr. 9. Committed to Com. of the whole."

TJ was appointed 15 Oct. to committee to bring in Bill; 5 Dec., Bill reported; 14 Dec., debated by House and amended; 16 Dec., passed by House; and 17 Dec., approved by Senate (JHD, Oct. 1776, 1828 edn., p. 14, 84, 90, 97, 98, 99). Bill as enacted was quite different from draft reported by the committee: it provided for three commissioners or auditors, who were to be appointed by joint ballot of both houses, were to take an oath of fidelity and an oath of office, and were to receive £200 per annum; nothing was said in the Act about their holding office during good behavior or during pleasure; and if any died, refused, or was unable to serve, the governor could appoint a substitute until the next session of the legislature (Hening, IX, 245-7).

[1] The words "his pleasure" are deleted in MS, and "good behaviour" interlined.

[2] The following is deleted in MS: "*And* be it further enacted that the Auditor so appointed shall receive the sum of   per annum for his services."

[3] The preceding fifteen words are interlined in TJ's hand.

[4] The preceding four words are interlined in TJ's hand.

[5] The preceding two words are filled in in TJ's hand.

[6] This clause is more consonant with tenure during pleasure, as first written in MS, than with tenure during good behavior; the incongruity disappeared, however, when all reference to tenure was deleted by amendment.

Bill for the Trial of Offenses Committed out of Virginia

[5 December 1776]

For the punishment of Treasons, misprisions of treasons or concealments of treason, felonies, robberies, murthers and confederacies hereafter to be committed out of this Commonwealth:

Be it enacted by the General assembly of the Commonwealth of Virginia that all treasons, misprisions of treasons, concealments of treasons, felonies, robberies, murthers, and confederacies hereafter to be committed in or upon the sea, or in any haven, river, creek or other place by land or by water not being within the body of any county of this Commonwealth, shall be enquired, tried, heard, determined and judged in such counties and places in this Commonwealth as shall be limited by the Governor's commission or commissions to be directed for the same in like form and condition as if any such offence or offences had been committed or done in or upon the land: and such commission shall be had under the seal of the Commonwealth directed to any three or more of the judges of the General court, from time to time and as oft as need shall require to hear and determine such offences after the common course of the laws of this Commonwealth, used for treasons, misprisions of treasons, concealments of treasons, felonies murthers, robberies, and confederacies of the same, done and committed upon the land within this Commonwealth.

And be it enacted by the authority aforesaid that such persons to whom such commission or commissions shall be directed, or two of them at the least, shall have full power and authority to enquire of such offences and of every of them, by the oaths of twelve good and lawful inhabitants in the county limited in their commission in such like manner and form, as if such offences had been committed upon the land within the same county; and that every indictment found and presented before such Commissioners, of any treasons, misprisions of treasons, Concealments of treasons, felonies, robberies murthers, manslaughters, or such other offences, being committed or done in and upon the seas, or in or upon any haven river, creek or other place by land or by water not being within the body of any county of this commonwealth, shall be good and effectual in the law; and if any person or persons happen to be indicted for any such offence done or hereafter to be done upon the seas, or in any other place above limited, that then such order, process, judgment, and execution shall be used, had, done and made, to and against every such person and persons so being indicted, as against Traytors, felons, murtherers, and other offenders aforesaid for treason, misprision of treason, concealment of treason, felony robbery, murther, or other such offences done upon the land, as by the laws of this Commonwealth is accustomed; and that the trial of such offence or offences if it be denied by the offender or offenders, shall be had by twelve lawful men inhabited in the county limited within such commission, which shall be directed as is aforesaid, and no challenge or challenges to be had for the county; and such as shall be convict of any such offence or offences by verdict, confession, or process, by authority of any such commission, shall have and suffer such pains of death, losses of lands, goods and chattels, as if they had been attainted and convicted of any treasons, misprisions of treasons, concealment of treasons, felonies, robberies, or other the said offences done upon the lands.

And be it enacted by authority aforesaid, that for treasons, misprisions of treasons, concealments of treasons, robberies, felonies, murthers, and confederacies done upon the sea or seas, or in or upon any haven, river or creek not being within the body of any county of this Commonwealth, the offenders shall not be admitted to have the benefit of his or their clergy, but be utterly excluded thereof and from the same.

Provided alway, that this act extend not to be prejudicial or hurtful to any person or persons, for taking any victual, cables, ropes, anchors, or sails, which any such person or persons (compelled by necessity) taketh of or in any ship which may conveniently spare the same, so the same person or persons pay out of hand for the same victual, cables, ropes, anchors, or sails, money or money-worth, to the value of the thing so taken, or do deliver for the same a sufficient bill obligatory to be paid within months next ensuing the making of such bills, and that the makers of such bills well and truly pay the same debt at the day to be limited within the said bills.

Dft (Vi). Docketed by TJ: "A Bill for the trial of offences committed out of this Commonwealth," and by a clerk: "Decr. 5th. 1776 read the first time."

There is no evidence that the Bill was read a second time. However, TJ included a bill for the same purpose in the Report of the Committee of Revisors (see under 18 June 1779, ch. LXVI), revised again in 1786 (Hening, XII, 330-1).

Bill for Suspending Executions for Debts

[6 December 1776]

Whereas by the expiration of the act for the regulating and collecting certain officers fees, and by the troubles which have since subsisted in this country the administration of justice hath been in a great measure suspended; and altho' it is thought proper to revive and establish the courts of justice for the purpose of securing and preserving internal peace and good order, of determining disputed rights and titles, and of ascertaining and securing just debts and unsettled demands which might otherwise be lost by the death of witnesses or insolvency of debtors; yet nevertheless it may produce great oppression and ruin to debtors to suffer executions to be levied or decrees to be inforced, during the present limited and uncertain state of our trade, for debts heretofore contracted: Be it therefore enacted by the General assembly of the Commonwealth of Virginia that when judgment shall be entered or decree passed in any court of record for the recovery of money due from the defendant or defendants before the passing of this act, if such defendant or defendants shall *give to the said court good and sufficient security*[1] for paiment *of the money*[1] whensoever by a restoration of trade or from other circumstances it shall appear proper to the General assembly to pass an act for levying executions or enforcing decrees for money then such court shall order execution of the said judgment or process for enforcing the said decree to be stayed, *entering of record the recognisance of such security,*[1] so that if the money be not paid when directed by such future act of assembly, a Scire facias may issue thereon[2] without the necessity of commencing a new suit.

Dft (Vi). Docketed in TJ's hand: "A Bill for suspending executions for Debts" and, in a clerk's hand: "Decr. 6th Read 1st. Time Decr. 9th Read 2d. & committed to Com: of the whole Decr. 13 Order put off til next session."

TJ was appointed to the committee to bring in the Bill, 5 Dec., and Mason introduced it on 6 Dec. This compromise measure, intended to relieve the fear that with the opening of the courts debtors would be ruined by executions, failed, but see under 14 Jan. 1778, "An act to open the courts of justice and to revive and amend an act for better regulating and collecting certain officers

fees," and also the Act of the same session for sequestering British Property and enabling British debts to be paid into the loan office (JHD, Oct. 1776, 1828 edn., p. 83, 85, 89, 96; Malone, *Jefferson*, I, 259; Hening, IX, 368-9, 377-80; JHD, Oct. 1777, 1827 edn., p. 114).

[1] Evidently the words underscored were the object of some amendments offered in the committee of the whole, but there is no means of ascertaining what changes were intended.

[2] A caret inserted here suggests that TJ intended to designate another amendment at this point.

From Patrick Henry

SIR   Decr. 19th. 1776

In Pursuance of a Resolution of the Legislature, I am to appoint a fit Person in every County to collect from the Inhabitants of this Commonwealth all the BLANKETS and RUGS they are willing to spare for the Use of the Soldiery. I have to beg of you, Sir, to accept of that Appointment for your County, and to draw upon me for the Amount of the Purchase. When it is considered that those who are defending our Country are in the extremest Want of Blankets, and that our Army cannot take the Field without a Supply of that Article, I have Hopes that our worthy Countrymen will spare from their Beds a Part of that Covering which the exposed Situation of the Soldier teaches him to expect from the Humanity of those for whom he is to fight. From your Zeal for the publick Service, I have the Pleasure to hope for your Exertion to forward this important Business, and send what Blankets you get to me.

I am, Sir, Your most obedient humble Servant, P. HENRY JR.

Printed letter, with autograph signature and date added (MeHi). Endorsed by TJ: "rec'd. Jan. 28. 1777." The resolution for appointing a person in each county to collect blankets for the troops was agreed to on 6 Dec. 1776 (JHD, Oct. 1776, 1828 edn., p. 84).

From Adam Stephen

Camp on Delawar 30 miles from Philadelphia
[ca. 20] Dec. 1776

SIR

The Enemy like locusts Sweep the Jerseys with the Besom of destruction. They to the disgrace of a Civilisd Nation Ravish the fair Sex, from the Age of Ten to Seventy. The Tories are Baneful in pointing out the friends to the American Cause, and giving Notice of every Motion we make.

The Enemy have made greater progress than they themselves expected owing to the Weakness of our Counsels and our Attempt to mantain The Forts Washington and Lee.

Our Salvation under Heaven, depends on our Raising an Army Speedily. Every lover of Liberty should with Spirit promote the Recruiting Service.

Genl. Lee had the misfortune to be taken prisoner to the 13th Inst. He had Saunterd about three miles and a half from his Army —lodged the night before at a house recommended to him by a Colo. Vanhorn, a person in the Enemys Service, who is appointed to Sign pardons on the peoples Submission; and Stayd at the place untill ten O'Clock on the 13th, when 50 light horsemen Supposd to be detachd by Advice of Vanhorn, came to the house and carryd him off. He had thirteen men of a Guard but they were Stragling and Absent except three.

By accounts from Old France of Octob 1st. That Nation is on the Eve of a War with England.

I expect that we shall have hot Work as soon as the Delawar is frozen over.

If we lose Philadelphia and let it Stand, it will go near to Ruin us. They will open the port, give great prices for Wheat and flour and Seduce the Body of the People.

Three of Mr. Allens Sons, and Jo. Galloway are with the Enemy in Trenton. A Frigate went in pursuit of the Reprisal Capt. Wicks with Franklin on Board; Must they not have had Intelligence from a member of Congress? Would it not be adviseable to open the doors of Congress and have the Debates in publick?

Let the Secret Business be done, by a Committee, or the Boards of Admiralty and War; after the plan has been Settled by Committees of the Whole house in Secret. We Should then have a better Chance of distinguishd [distinguishing] the Spirited from the Languid Members— I wish you the Compliments of the Season & am Sr your hble St.,   ADAM STEPHEN

RC (DLC). Endorsed: "General Stevens Dec. 1776."

This letter must have been written between 15 Dec., when Washington received word of the capture of Charles Lee at Basking Ridge, N.J. (Washington, *Writings*, ed. Fitzpatrick, VI, 375-6), and 25 Dec., when the Americans attacked Trenton.

Declaration
of the Virginia Association of Baptists

[25 December 1776]

THE SENTIMENTS of the BAPTISTS with regard to a GENERAL ASSESMENT on the People of Virginia for the support of Preachers of the Gospel; collected and agreed to, in an Association of Ministers and Deligates from the Churches of that Perswasion, met at Dover in Goochland, the 25th. of December 1776.

That "it is contrary to the Principles of *Reason and Justice* that any should be compelled to contribute to the Maintenance of a Church with which their Consciences will not permit them to join, and from which they can therefore recieve no Benefit";[1] is not merely the Opinion of the Dissenters (whose hardships on that Score have *feelingly convinced* them of the Truth of it; but is the Declaration of the Hon. the General Assembly of Virginia. And we are happy to find the Progress of Liberty so far advanced that the Legislature has passed "an Act for exempting the different Societies of Dissenters, from contributing to the support and maintenance of the Church as by Law established, and its Ministers."

There is yet one undetermined Point "touching the propriety of a General Assesment, or whether every religious Society should be left to voluntary Contributions for the support and maintenance of the several Ministers and Teachers of the Gospel who are of different Perswasions and Denominations."[1] And as our Representatives have "thought most prudent to refer this Matter to the discussion and final Determination of a future Assembly when the Opinions of the Country in general may be better known";[1] we look upon it to be not only an Apology for, but a *Call* to us to publish our Sentiments with relation thereunto.

We believe that Preachers should be supported only by *voluntary Contributions* from the People, and that a general Assesment (however harmless, yea useful some may concieve it to be) is pregnant with various Evils destructive to the Rights and Priveleges of religious Society.

"No Man or set of Men are entituled to exclusive or seperate Emoluments or Priveleges from the Community but in consideration of public Services."[2] If, therefore, the State provides a Support for Preachers of the Gospel, and they receive it in Consideration of their Services, they must certainly when they Preach act as Officers of the State, and ought to be Accountable thereto for their Conduct, not only as Members of civil Society, but also *as Preachers.* The Consequence of this is, that those whom the State employs in its Service, it has a Right to *regulate* and *dictate to*; it may judge and determine *who* shall preach; *when* and *where* they shall preach; and *what* they must preach. The *mutual Obligations* between Preachers and the Societies they belong to, should this be the Case, must be evidently weakened — Yea, farewel to the last Article of the Bill of Rights! Farewel to "the free exercise of Religion,"[2] if civil Rulers go so far out of their Sphere as to take the Care and Management of *religious Affairs* upon them!

Sorry should we be to see the *Seeds of Oppression* sown by the Hand of Power amongst us, and as we think it our Duty, to our utmost *in a legal Way*, to retard, or if possible, to prevent the luxuriant Growth of a Plant that has always brought forth the most *bitter and baneful Fruit* wherever it has been cultivated, should a general Assesment take place, the Preachers of our Communion, unitedly agree (and we doubt not but the Conduct of *every dissenting Minister in the Commonwealth* will be *uniform* on such an Occasion) to give *Discharges in full* to every Person who shall direct the Payment of his Quota of the Assesment to them, leaving all such with respect to Contributions, to the *Freedom* of their own Will.

MS (DLC). In an unknown hand; unsigned; apparently a copy transmitted to TJ.

[1] Quoted from the Act for Exempting Dissenters (Hening, IX, 164-7).
[2] Quoted from the Virginia Declaration of Rights.

Memorandum
concerning Military Service of Baptists

[1776]

Baptist Officers that we can recollect are Capt. Joseph Spencer, Ensign Samuel French, and Ensign Thomas Bush from Orange Capt. Ambrose Dudley from Spotsylvania and Capt. Thos. Berry from Frederick.

Baptists enlisted near Elijah Craig are Charles Green in Colonel Baylor's Regiment of light Horse Wm. Tomlinson in Col. Gibson's Regiment. Baptist's Sons, James Dearing, Edward Dearing, John Land, and Lewis Land. There is but one Young man who is a Baptist and in a single State in the Neighbourhood that has not enlisted.

Baptists enlisted near Jeremiah Walker are, John Thornton, Edmund Anyar, James Berkley, John Collicot, Stephen Pace and James Mitchell. Baptist's Sons, John Walton 1st. Lieutenant, John Fowlkes, Wm. Berkley and Alexr. Berkley. There is but one Young Man in the Neighbourhood who is a Baptist and in a single State, that has not enlisted, and he is so much an Invalid that he is not on the Militia List.

Had the Baptists been backward as is alledged, no doubt but they would have smarted for it, by the late Act for pitching upon Men to fill up the last 6 Regiments, but there were no Baptists nor Baptist's Sons pitched upon in the Counties of Amelia and Orange, where we reside, nor for ought we know any thing else.

MS (DLC). In an unidentified hand. Endorsed by TJ: "Baptists."
The presence of this document among TJ's papers is doubtless explained by his fight in support of religious liberty

(see W. T. Thom, "The Struggle for Religious Freedom in Virginia: the Baptists," *Johns Hopkins Univ. Studies in Hist. and Pol. Sci.*, ser. XVIII [1900], p. 48-9.

Memorandum
concerning British Forts in the West

[1776]

there is a bar off Presque isle which prevents large vessels coming near the shore.

distance from Pittsbgh to Cayahoga by land 150 miles. There are some morasses on the road, but may be made good for carriages.

cayahoga is a deep creek at the dryest season. But the mouth is barred as Presque isle is.

in a hard winter they travel on the ice from Cayahoga to Sandusky & Detroit, & slays might go from Pittsburgh were the roads clear of fallen timber. the want of provender is the only objection to a winter campaign by land, admitting the Indians sit still.

during the winter the king's armed vessels are laid by & frozen up in a narrow creek a few miles below fort Detroit.

from Sandusky to Roche de bout & from thence to Detroit is very swampy ground. but from Pittsbgh. to Sandusky a good road may be made even for carriages.

armed vessels of the enemy on the lake badly manned, mostly with impressed Canadians who also do duty in the fort, which they are strengthening as much as possible.

the inhabitants distressed. near 50. families gone to Roche de bout, Kickayuga, and Port Vincent.

the garrison at Niagara consisted in May 1776. of four complete companies.

one of the armed vessels of enemy on Lake Erie mounted 24 guns, the other 16. guns.

get every necessary article at Fort Pitt before mention purpose.

the men to be raised in mean time and kept within frontiers, mending roads to Pittsburgh & bridges.

then call 6 nations, & inform them, ask leave.

a French decln to inhabitts. abt. Detroit.

all heavy carriages to Pittsburgh must be before middle Novemb.

every thing under 100 ℔ should be packed in bundles or boxes, because carried best & cheapest on horses from Carlile or Connigocheague.

2500 ℔. has been carried in a waggon to Pittsbgh. when roads & bridges in repair.

1800 ℔ is the common load.

Edwd. Morton near Carlisle was Waggon master to the king on this road, and is now most experienced in that business.

waggons have 40/ pr. C. or 20/ pr. day to Fort Pitt. 6/ pr. C. to Carlisle. Pack horses have 20/ per C. from Carlisle.

for navigation on Allegany boats must be built. 2 men (if the stuff is provided) will build one boat in 10 days to carry a ton.

portage between French cr. and Presque isle is almost a continued swamp, and in it's present state is impassable with heavy burthens.

the Allegany is navigable with canoes to Le boeuf, but not so for large boats when the waters are low.

N (DLC). The date is problematical, though certainly after May 1776.

This document, which possibly is an incomplete MS, may indeed refer to a later plan for a campaign against British strongholds in the West, such as that outlined by TJ in 1780 (see TJ to George Rogers Clark, 25 Dec. 1780, and Malone, *Jefferson*, I, 334-5), though it is scarcely likely that at that date he would have thought it worth while to note the size of the Niagara garrison in May 1776. The subject was much dis-

cussed in Congress in the spring of 1776 before TJ arrived in Philadelphia, and during the summer Page raised the question of a western campaign with TJ (see Page to TJ, 15 and 20 July 1776; A. M. Lewis, "Jefferson and Virginia's Pioneers," *Miss. Valley Hist. Rev.*, XXXIV [1948], 568-70; see also TJ's abstract of a letter from Zeisberger to ———, 23 Sep. 1777, DLC: TJ Papers, 3: 394). It seems likely, therefore, that the Memorandum may have been made around 1776-1777.

Militia Return as County Lieutenant

[1776]

Capt Orl[ando] Jones's company		Jeremiah Nichols	Clear
		Ice-and Snow[2]	Clear
Joshua Fry	Clear		15.
William Gaines	Clear		
Alexander Gordon	Clear	Capt. Wallace's co.	
Mesheck Hitchcock	Clear	Thomas Anderson	Clear
Henley Hamner	Clear	John Black senr.	Clear
Richard Harper	Clear	Alexander Black	Clear
Christopher Hudson	Service	John Black junr.	Clear
William Tompkins	Clear	William Black	Clear
Travis Tucker	Clear	John Davies	Clear
Thomas Wingfeild	Clear	Benjamin Davies	Clear
Charles Catlet[1]	Clear	Francis Davies	Clear
		Adam Kerr	Clear
	11.	William Kerr	Clear
		Gilbert Kerr	Clear
Capt. Wm. Sims's co.		Hugh McWilliams	Clear
William Allen	Clear	John McWilliams	Clear
James Barlow	Clear	Saml. McCord	Clear
Major Dowell	Clear	John McCue	Clear
David Dalton junr.	Clear	John Massie	Clear
Robert Douglass. quaker.	Clear	John Moore	Clear
Gravit Edwards	Service	Robert Pilson	Clear
Nehemiah Grinning	Service	Davies Stockdon	Clear
John Grinning	Clear	Thomas Stockdon	Clear
John Hamock	Clear	William Tomlinson	Clear
Abraham Monday	Service	James Woods	Clear
Jonathan Monday	Clear	John Wheary	Service
George Mansfeild	Service	William Davis[3]	Clear
Campbell McCauley	Clear		24.

CAPT. DAVIES'S CO.

Henry Burke	Clear
Bartlet Davies	Clear
Thompson Epperson	Clear
John Innis	Service
James Keaton	Clear
Samuel McCulloch	Service
John McDaniel	Clear
Uriah McDaniel	Clear
David Owen	Service
John Shifflet	Clear
Richard Snow	Service
Roger Thompson	Clear
Evan Thos. Watson[4]	Clear

13.

CAPT. ROB. HARRIS'S CO.

David Blackwell	Clear
Bernis Brown Wm. Cave	Service
John Brown	Clear
William Craig	Clear
Benjamin Clarke	Clear
George Webb Jones	Clear
Lewis Jones	Service
William Jones	Service
Daniel Maupin (son of John)	Clear
Daniel Maupin (son of Daniel)	Clear
Cornelius Maupin (son of John)	Clear
Cornelius Maupin (son of Daniel)	Clear
Thomas Maupin	Clear
William Maupin junr.	Clear
Harris Massey	Clear
Thomas Massey	Clear
Joseph Marshall	Clear
William Norris	Clear
Robert Rhodes	Service
John Thurmond	Clear
Benjamin Thurmond	Service
Thomas Wherry[5]	Clear

22.

CAPT. DALTON'S CO.

Samuel Barksdale	Clear
Martin Consolver	Clear

Samuel Davies	Clear
Isaac Davies	Clear
Thomas Davies	Clear
William Davies	Clear
James Granford	Clear
James Herring	Clear
George Herring	Service
Christopher Herring	Clear
David Mills	Clear
Zachariah Mills	Clear
John McRae	Clear
Alexander McCulloch	Service
John Ozby	Clear
James Rippetoe	Clear
Simon Ramsay	Clear
William Ramsay	Clear
Achilles Rogers	Clear
John Spradling	Clear
William Simpson	Clear
Samuel Twyman	Clear
William Watts	Clear
Joseph Ward[6]	Clear

24.

CAPT. JOHN JONES'S CO.

Lodowick Cook	Clear
Randolph Cartee	Clear
John Eubanks	Clear
William Eubanks	Service
William Leak	Service
Jesse Melton	Service
Benjamin Melton	Clear
William Statham	Clear
David Statham	Clear
Charles Statham	Clear
Geo. Wilbleduf	Service
Chas. Bowyer[7]	Clear

11.

CAPT. SMITH'S CO.

Bradley Carter	Clear
James Consolver	Clear
Micajah Chiles	Clear
John Grayson	Clear
William Gragg	Clear
Michael Harlow	Clear
William Hayes	Clear

John Mills	Clear	**CAPT. LEWIS'S CO.**	
Menan Mills	Clear	James Beck	Clear
Charles Mitchel	Clear	James Carver	Clear
Charles Pettus	Clear	Richard Carver	Clear
Thomas Smith (fifer)	Service	Christopher Clarke junr	Clear
Solomon Wood	Clear	Bowler Clarke	Clear
James Wilson[8]	Clear	James Clarke	Clear
14		William Cambden	Clear
		Peter Hall	Clear
CAPT. MARTIN'S CO.		John Mickie. Lieutt.	Clear
Thomas Apling	Clear	James Olverson	Clear
David Apling	Clear	Chiles Terril	Clear
Samuel Blaine	Clear	Alexandr. White	Clear
John Blaine	Clear	Jas. Robinson	Service
James Blaine	Clear	Martin Bunch[11]	Clear
James Barrett	Clear	14	
Richard Baker	Service		
Elijah Baker	Clear	**CAPT. CHARLES SIMS'S CO.**	
John Douglass	Clear		
John Garland	Clear	Green Clay	Clear
John Herd	Clear	Charles Denton	Service
Samuel Murril	Clear	David Grymes	Clear
George Murril	Clear	William Moon	Clear
George Martin	Clear	John Sorrow	Clear
Stephen Moore	Clear	Henry Wood	Clear
Joshua Tadlock	Service	Samuel Wood[12]	Clear
John Thurmond	Clear	7	
Joso. Toms[9]	Clear		
18		**CAPT. BENJ. HARRIS'S CO.**	
CAPT. WINGFEILD'S CO.			
John Bailey	Clear	Capt. Benj. Harriss	Service
Edward Butler	Service	Wm. Jordan	Clear
William Calvert	Clear	Benj. Jordan	Clear
William Fosset	Clear	Chas. Irving	Clear
Humphrey Gaines	Clear	Thos. Upton	Clear
Stephen Hughes	Clear	Robt. Davis	Clear
Randolph Jefferson	Clear	Benj. Miles	Clear
Isaac Jackson	Clear	Wm. Miles	Clear
John Jouett jr.	Clear	Richd. Miles	Clear
William Leak	Clear	John Cheatham[13]	Service
Hastings Marks	Clear	10	
George Manly	Clear		
Joseph Neilson	Clear	**CAPT. WHEELER'S CO.**	
Thomas West	Clear		
William Wingfeild[10]	Clear	John Britt	Service
15.		Jeremiah Collins	Clear

Bartlet Dednam	Clear	William Henderson	
Thomas Green	Clear	Robert Priddy	
Rowland Horseley	Clear	Joseph Roberts	
Charles Lewis	Clear	James Taylor	
Henry McMannus	Clear	Roger Tandy	
Andrew Ray	Clear	William Tandy[15]	
Micajah Wheeler junr.	Clear		
John Wheeler	Clear	14	
Richard Wood	Clear		
Alexr. McKinzie[14]	Service	CAPT. HENDERSON'S CO.	

13.

LIEUT. MEDLIN'S CO.

		Thomas Adams	Clear
		Anderson Bryan	Clear
		John Collins	Service
		Richard Gaines	Clear
George Beaver	Clear	Daniel Harvie	Service
John Beaver	Service	Richard Harvie	Service
Edmond Burnett		Henry Kirbie	Clear
John Clarkson		Isham Lewis	Clear
Micajah Carr		Richard Sharpe	Clear
William Carter		David Whipple[16]	Clear
Jesse Gooch			
John Hammock		10.	

A roll of the Volunteers, draughts and substitutes for the county of Albemarle.[17]

1. William Lewis Benge.
2. Alexander McCullock (marches with Louisa men.)
3. Stanhope Johnson for Gravit Edwards.
4. Nehemiah Grinning   deserted
5. Abraham Monday. [. . .]ty Continentl. officer
6. George Mansfeild.
7. John Innis. v. ⟨deserted⟩ James Keaton
8. Uriah McDaniel for Saml. McCulloch.
9. David Owen
10. John McDaniel for Richard Snow.
11. Lewis Williams for Bernis Brown.
12. Lewis Jones. Discharged
13. William Jones
14. Richard Garbutt for Robert Rhodes
15. Sabert King for Benjamin Thurmond.
16. William Eubanks. ⟨deserted⟩
17. William Leak.   Appeared
18. Jesse Melton. deserted ⟨I expect will appear⟩
19. George Wilbleduff.   deserted
20. Richard Gully for George Herring.
21. John Willis for Thomas Smith ⟨deserted⟩
22. Richard Baker.   deserted
23. Joshua Tadlock.
24. James Robertson

25. Edward Butler. on furlow to meet at Alexa. Apl. 1st
26. David Denton for Charles Denton.
27. Benjamin Harris. On Furlow 'till 26th. Jn.
28. John Cheatham. Sick
29. Alexander Mckenzie. detained by an arrest.
30. John Collins
31. Peter Howard for Daniel Harvie.
32. Richard Harvie
33. John Beaver   deserted
34. John Carver for Christopher Hudson
35. Nicholas Burger for John Wherry
36. John Britt.

Certified by

TH: JEFFERSON CY. LT.

Tabular MS (DLC). Names in TJ's hand (with a few exceptions) and notations in several other hands. A second tabular MS (DLC), referred to below in note 17, is a fair copy by TJ of the final part of the Return relating to "Volunteers, draughts and substitutes."

The date of these papers is uncertain but can certainly be confined to late 1776 or early 1777.

[1] In Capt. Jones' company the name of Richardson Hamner is deleted.

[2] In Capt. Sims' company the names of the following are struck out: Edward Broddie, Philip Bush, Thomas Barlow, John Calton, Bradley Dalton, James Grinning, John Smith, John Stockdon, Elijah Watts.

[3] In Capt. Wallace's company the names of the following are struck out: William Cleaveland, David Henderson, James Isbell, William Pilson.

[4] In Capt. Davies' company the names of the following are struck out: William Ballard, M. Lewis Benge, James Dunn, William Keaton "(son of John)," Sabert King, Joseph Mills, Joseph Watson.

[5] In Capt. Harris' company the names of the following are struck out: David Clarke, Joel Harris, Thomas Jones, "Daniel Maupin (son of Gabriel)," David Maupin.

[6] In Capt. Dalton's company the names of the following are struck out: "William Ballard (son of Bland)," Micajah Consolver, John Carver, Samuel Dalton, Henry Fowler, Samuel Fowler, David Herring, Augustine Smith, David Wood.

[7] In Capt. Jones' company the names of the following are struck out: Charles Denton, John Langford.

[8] In Capt. Smith's company the names of Presley Dollins and Robert Ware are struck out.

[9] In Capt. Martin's company the names of George Maxwell and Joshua Moran are struck out.

[10] In Capt. Wingfeild's company the following name is struck out: "John Grier over age."

[11] In Capt. Lewis' company the names of the following are struck out: Zachariah Defoe, Achilles Denton, Laurence Ferguson, Richard Hill, "John Sutton junr."

[12] In Capt. Sims' company the names of the following are struck out: Richard Goolsby, Chesley Kinney, Richard Moon, Littlebury Moon, Richard Wood, William Battersby Watkins.

[13] The list of this company is not in TJ's hand.

[14] In Capt. Wheeler's company the names of the following are struck out: Philip Gooch, Horsely Goodman, Laurence Shifflet, Waddy Thompson, Tarlton Woodson, Michael Wallace, Samuel Bunch.

[15] In Lt. Medlins' company the name of George Taylor is struck out.

[16] In Capt. Henderson's company the names of Francis Gaines, William Reynolds, and John Sneade are struck out.

[17] The second tabular MS (DLC: TJ Papers, 6: 1063), mentioned in the descriptive note above, is used as the text of this document from this point on. It is actually a fair copy of the final portion of the MS which has provided the text up to this point. The earlier MS (or draft) has, however, some comments not in the fair copy, such as "John McDaniel, send letter to Dan. Ferguson," "Lewis Jones said to be unfit," "Sabert King. lives with Henry Austin," "John Carver. stays with Alexr. McCulloch," &c. The name "Benge" is spelled "Bang" in the draft.

Appendix I

Historical and Bibliographical Notes on
A Summary View of the Rights of British America

TJ left more than one account of the composition, publication, and effects of his Draft of Instructions to the Virginia Delegates in Congress, printed above under the date of July 1774. The best known of these accounts is in his Autobiography, following a review of public events in Virginia during May-June 1774. Here TJ summarizes the line of reasoning he pursued in his paper and differentiates his position from that of "Our other patriots"; tells of his being kept from attending the Convention by an attack of dysentery, and of how the draft was rejected by the Convention but published by his friends; and, finally, gives details of the alleged steps taken in England to proscribe him along with other American leaders.[1]

Another account by TJ is in a separate, undated memorandum he drew up between 1809 (when the first edition of Botta's *Storia della guerra dell' independenza degli Stati Uniti d'America* was published at Paris) and 1821 (when TJ prepared his Autobiography). This two-page MS (DLC: TJ Papers, 1:111) was printed by Randolph in 1829 at the beginning of "Note C" to the Autobiography, as an introduction to the Draft of Instructions, the text of which follows without separate caption.[2] As the last (deleted) sentence in the memorandum indicates (see below), TJ clearly intended the paper to serve as such an introduction at the time he drew it up; but the editors who have so used it have been remiss in failing to note, either in their lists of contents or in their indexes, where the paper best known to the world as *A Summary View*, &c., may be found. Here follows the text of the memorandum:

[1] Ford, I, 12-14. For incidental mentions by TJ of the *Summary View*, see letters to Meriwether Jones, 19 Oct. 1804; to John W. Campbell, 3 Sep. 1809; and to William Plumer, 31 Jan. 1815. Though these add no material facts, a letter *from* Meriwether Jones, 15 Oct. 1804 (DLC), explains why TJ sent his own copy of *A Summary View* to Jones at this time. In the preceding June, Jones had defended TJ in the columns of the Richmond *Enquirer* against the charge that "shortly before the declaration of Independence, you had drafted and signed an humble and adulatory address to the King of England. In the defence alluded to, I mentioned, that at that crisis of American affairs, you were always considered foremost of your cotemporaries; and in support of my assertion I instanced a string of Resolutions of which you were the author, and which were forwarded to the Moderator of the Convention at Williamsburg in 1774. These Resolutions, Mr. Edmd. Randolph informed me, were considered a day or two in advance of the spirit of the times, but that himself, and some other young patriots were so captivated with their point and elegance, that they procured their publication by subscription: he told me too, that he had a copy of the Resolutions which were at my command. Upon this information, I promised the readers of the Enquirer, to prove, by showing them the resolutions in question, that you foresaw very early in the progress of our revolution, that independence and liberty were inseparable." However, searches by both Randolph and Jones had failed to produce a copy, and Jones asked the loan of TJ's copy, which was duly forwarded. *A Summary View* was reprinted in the Richmond *Enquirer* in two installments, 3 and 7 Nov. 1804.

[2] TJR, I, 100-2. The same arrangement was followed by H. A. Washington and by Lipscomb & Bergh (HAW, I, 122-4; L & B, I, 181-4).

APPENDIX I

"ON THE INSTRUCTIONS GIVEN TO THE 1ST DELEGATION OF VIRGINIA TO CONGRESS IN AUGUST 1774.

"The legislature of Virginia happened to be in session in Williamsburg when news was recieved of the passage, by the British parliament, of the Boston port bill. This was to take effect on the 1st. day of June then ensuing. The House of Burgesses thereupon past a resolution recommending to their fellow-citizens that that day should be set apart for fasting and prayer to the supreme being, imploring him to avert the calamities then threatening us, and to give us one heart and one mind to oppose every invasion of our liberties. The next day, May 20.[3] 1774. the Governor dissolved us. We immediately repaired to a room in the Raleigh tavern, about 100. paces distant from the Capitol, formed ourselves into a Meeting, Peyton Randolph in the chair, and came to resolutions declaring that an attack on one colony to enforce arbitrary acts, ought to be considered as an attack on all, and to be opposed by the united wisdom of all. They therefore appointed a committee of correspondence to address letters to the Speakers of the several Houses of Representatives of the Colonies, proposing the appointment of deputies from each to meet *annually in a General Congress*, to deliberate on their common interests, and on the measures to be pursued in common. The members then separated to their several homes, except those of the Committee, who met the next day, prepared letters according to instruction, and dispatched them by messengers express to their several destinations. It had been agreed also by the Meeting that the Burgesses who should be elected under the writs then issuing should be requested to meet in Convention on a certain day in August to learn the result of these letters, and to appoint delegates to a Congress, should that measure be approved by the other colonies.

"At the election, the people re-elected every man of the former assembly as a proof of their approbation of what they had done. Before I left home to attend the Convention, I prepared what I thought might be given in instruction to the Delegates who should be appointed to attend the General Congress proposed. They were drawn in haste with a number of blanks, with some uncertainties and inaccuracies of historical facts, which I neglected at the moment, knowing they could be readily corrected at the meeting. I set out on my journey, but was taken sick on the road, and unable to proceed. I therefore sent on by express two copies, one under cover to Patrick Henry, the other to Peyton Randolph, who I knew would be in the chair of the Convention. Of the former no more was ever heard or known. Mr. Henry probably thought it too bold as a first measure,[4] as the majority of the members did. On the other copy being laid on the table of the Convention by Peyton Randolph, as the proposition of a member who was prevented from attendance by

[3] Error for May 26; see the Fast-Day Resolution, 24 May 1774, above, and note there. Some other inaccuracies in TJ's narrative may be corrected by reference to the documents, with their accompanying notes, for May-July 1774.

[4] "Whether Mr. Henry disapproved the ground taken, or was too lazy to read it (for he was the laziest man in reading I ever knew) I never learned: but he communicated it to nobody." TJ's Autobiography, Ford, I, 13.

NOTES ON THE SUMMARY VIEW

sickness on the road, tamer sentiments were preferred, and I believe, wisely preferred; the leap I proposed being too long as yet for the mass of our citizens. The distance between these, and the instructions actually adopted is of some curiosity however, as it shews the inequality of pace with which we moved, and the prudence required to keep front and rear together. My creed had been formed on unsheathing the sword at Lexington. They printed the paper however, and gave it the title of 'a Summary view of the rights of British America.' In this form it got to London, where the opposition took it up, shaped it to Opposition views, and in that form it ran rapidly thro' several editions.[5]

"Mr. Marshall, in his history of Genl. Washington c. 3. speaking of this proposition for committees of correspondence and for a General Congress says 'this measure had already been proposed in town meeting in Boston,' and some pages before he had said that 'at a session of the General court of Massachusets in Sep. 1770. that court, in pursuance of a favorite idea of uniting all the colonies in one system of measures elected a committee of correspondence to communicate with such committees as might be appointed by the other *colonies*.'[6] This is an error. The committees of correspondence elected by Massachusets were expressly for a correspondence among the several *towns* of that province only. Beside[s] the text of their proceedings, his own Note X. proves this. The 1st. proposition for a general correspondence between the several states, and for a General Congress was made by this meeting of Aug. 1774. Botta copying Marshall has repeated his error and so it will be handed on from copyist to copyist ad infinitum. Here follow my proposition, and the more prudent one which was adopted."[7]

Edmund Randolph told of the effect of TJ's proposed Instructions upon the members of the Convention when they were read privately:

"I distinctly recollect the applause bestowed on the most of them, when they were read to a large company at the house of Peyton Randolph, to whom they were addressed. Of all, the approbation was not equal. From the celebrated letters of the Pennsylvania Farmer (John Dickinson) we had been instructed to bow to the external taxation of parliament, as resulting from our migration, and a necessary dependence on the mother country. But this composition of Mr. Jefferson, shook this conceded principle, although it had been confirmed by a still more celebrated pamphlet, written by Daniel Dulany of Maryland, and cited by Lord Chatham, as a text book of American rights. The young ascended with Mr. Jefferson to the source of those rights; the old required time for consideration, before they could tread this lofty ground, which, if it had not been abandoned, at least had not been fully occupied, throughout America. From what cause it happened,

[5] See the bibliographical notes below.

[6] John Marshall, *The Life of George Washington*, Phila., 1804-1807, II, 163, 149.

[7] The final sentence was at some later time struck out by TJ, but was printed by T. J. Randolph and by the other edi-

tors who have followed his lead. The *actual* Instructions to the Virginia Delegates follow in TJR and the other editions as "Note D" to the Autobiography. These are printed in the present edition under the date of Aug. 1774, above.

that the resolutions were not printed by the order of the convention does not appear; but as they were not adopted several of the author's admirers subscribed to their publication. When the time of writing is remembered, a range of inquiry not then very frequent, and marching far beyond the politicks of the day, will surely be allowed to them."[8]

As TJ pointed out in his letter to Meriwether Jones of 19 Oct. 1804, "the title, the motto and the preface" of the Williamsburg pamphlet "were of the editors." The title-page of this, the *editio princeps* (Sabin 35918, Evans 13350, Clayton-Torrence 418), is reproduced in the present volume from TJ's own copy in the Library of Congress. The motto, printed on the verso of the title-page, was drawn from Cicero's *De Officiis*, I, xxxiv, and was thus translated: "It is the indispensable duty of the supreme magistrate to consider himself as acting for the whole community, and obliged to support its dignity, and assign to the people, with justice, their various rights, as he would be faithful to the great trust reposed in him." The Preface reads:

"THE following piece was intended to convey to the late meeting of DELEGATES the sentiments of one of their body, whose personal attendance was prevented by an accidental illness. In it the sources of our present unhappy differences are traced with such faithful accuracy, and the opinions entertained by every free American expressed with such a manly firmness, that it must be pleasing to the present, and may be useful to future ages. It will evince to the world the moderation of our late convention, who have only touched with tenderness many of the claims insisted on in this pamphlet, though every heart acknowledged their justice. Without the knowledge of the author, we have ventured to communicate his sentiments to the public; who have certainly a right to know what the best and wisest of their members have thought on a subject in which they are so deeply interested."

The corrections made by TJ in both text and notes of his own copy of the Williamsburg imprint will be found in the textual notes on the Draft Instructions as printed above under the date of July 1774.

The precise date of the publication of *A Summary View* has not been established. No announcement by the printer (Mrs. Rind) has been found. George Washington entered the sum of 3s. 9d. in his accounts, "By Mr. Jeffersons Bill of Rights," on 6 Aug. 1774, the last day of the Convention.[9] This sum seems too small for a contribution toward printing costs; it probably represents the cost of three copies of *A Summary View* then being, or about to be, printed. Proof positive of publication by the end of August appears in a letter from Thomas Walker to William Preston, 4 Sep. 1774, which contains this paragraph: "The Inclosed Piece wrote by Mr. Thos. Jefferson, the perusal of which I expect will give you satisfaction, your care of it I can depend on as I have no other copy."[10]

Patrick Henry evidently took copies of *A Summary View* with him to Philadelphia when he attended the first Continental Congress, 5

---

8 Randolph, "Essay," VMHB, XLIII (1935), 216.

9 *Diaries*, II, 159, note.

10 WHi: Preston Papers.

Sep.,[11] and doubtless other members of the Virginia delegation did so likewise. Hence Jefferson's proposed Instructions served more than the purpose for which they were originally intended, for *A Summary View* was shortly reprinted in Philadelphia, by John Dunlap (Sabin 35918, Evans 13351), and thus got into continental circulation. There is unconfirmed evidence that reprints were also issued at New York, Boston, and Norfolk.[12]

Copies were also sent to England, where the pamphlet was twice reprinted before the end of the year by the London bookseller G. Kearsly (Sabin 35918, Clayton-Torrence 419). Titles and texts of all the editions are the same as those of the Williamsburg edition, but a dedicatory address "To the King," very free in its language, was prefixed to the London reprints.[13] Ford (i, 423) states that this address

[11] See Professor Abernethy's edition of *A Summary View*, Scholars' Facsimiles and Reprints, N.Y., 1943, p. viii-ix; also his *Western Lands*, p. 114-15.

[12] For the Boston and New York edns., see the extract from Dixon & Hunter's *Va. Gaz.*, 14 Jan. 1775, below. Evans 13352 enters a Norfolk edn., "Printed by William Duncan and Co., [1774]." Evans records no copy, and his MS notes do not disclose the source of his information, which was presumably a newspaper advertisement (private communication from Clifford K. Shipton, Librarian, American Antiquarian Society). Duncan and Co. published a Norfolk *Virginia Gazette*, 1774-1775.

[13] This dedicatory address is here quoted in full:

SIR,

THERE is not a man of thought, in the whole nation, who does not espouse bad measures from bad principles, but is justly alarmed, and seriously anxious, for the common good. Affairs of such magnitude now employ the public attention, as seem to involve in them the *fate* of EMPIRE. The times are big with great events. What will be the consequence, it is not in human sagacity to foretel. But if the same system be pursued, which for a long time hath employed the attention of your Majesty's ministers, they ought to tremble for their heads.

The present contentions with America, if not soon happily terminated, must end in such scenes of trouble, bloodshed, and devastation, which, in contemplation alone, shock us with horror. But little time remains for deliberation, or choice: a blow will lead on to the decisive scene; and the sword must end what tyranny began. This æra of your Majesty's reign is likely to be marked with the most important characters. It is impossible for subjects to stand by idle, unaffected spectators, when they see their Sovereign, and themselves, nearly involved in distresses, which, for ought he can foresee, may end in the ruin of both: you, Sir! may lose your sovereignty and honour; we, our liberties, fortunes, and lives.

The charge of presumption upon individuals, for speaking freely upon these important things, is at once taken off, by the evidence of the things themselves, and the transcendant interest that every man has in them. Of the *modes* of carrying on the weighty affairs of state; of the artifice, cunning, address, and subtilty of courts, it is the general lot to be ignorant: but of the *great principles* of government, especially of this free state, of those laws, and proceedings, that are either subversive, or corroborative of the system, many are as able to judge as any minister employed in your Majesty's service. These, with the first laws of nature, the prerogatives of man in human society, with the sacred and immutable laws of justice, equity, moderation, and wisdom, men fully understand, who were never tutored, or well received at court; where indeed, for the most part, men are more likely to lose than gain, accurate ideas of these things. They are not among the arcana imperii: we can judge of them; and have a fair, undoubted, constitutional right, as free subjects, who claim liberty by birth-right, and enjoy it by the laws, to apply these principles to the present conduct of your Majesty's ministers. And, in justice bound to our country, and ourselves, and that fidelity we owe, Sir, to you, as our Sovereign, we openly declare, that the whole proceedings against our brethren in America, who are entitled, in common "was written by Arthur Lee." This is altogether likely, since Lee (who was in London) was very actively engaged in propaganda efforts in behalf of America at this time, but no conclusive evidence of his authorship has been found, and TJ himself never knew who wrote this address. The address was also published separately, for under "London

with ourselves, to the privileges of men, and the liberties, franchises, and protection of Englishmen, are in open violation of the natural laws of equity and justice; and unparalleled infractions upon the principles, and promulgated laws of this free state: not to say, that every idea of good policy is sacrificed to maintain and inforce the most vicious and dangerous system that ever infatuated despots pursued.

Fruitless were the hopes that these few pages will effect, what the sagest counsels, the most consummate wisdom, and plainest remonstrances, of some of the wisest, and best men, of the present age, have not been able to accomplish. But if the perusal, either by your Majesty, or your ministers, should, for a moment, suspend the fatal counsels, or designs which are now taking, or seem systematically planned to overturn AMERICAN LIBERTY, I shall think my labours well rewarded. God is my witness, that I write not these things to excite sedition, or stir up rebellion: I should deem my life well disposed of, if, by the sacrifice, your Majesty could learn the wisdom of righteous government, and your ministers be taught to counsel good things. Happy should I be to convince your Majesty, where legal authority ends, and tyranny begins; and that your dignity alone consists in the happiness of your subjects; and that when virtue and justice forsake your councils, error and ruin must inevitably ensue. With your Majesty's ministers we can keep no longer. If at any time we pitied their innocent infirmities, that pity has long ago been converted into abhorrence from the wickedness of their counsels, and the injustice of their deeds. By their breaches upon your prerogative, Sir! they have broken down the legal barriers of the constitution, and destroyed the distinctions of government; they have changed, or attempted to change lawful possession into arbitrary dominion: and, in the mad career, they may endeavour to make their Sovereign dispense with every thing that entitles him to obedience; and, by this means, convert the first duty of subjects

into an opposition, which the great, and primary law of nature, self-defence, makes necessary. Those cruel, in-expedient, tyrannical measures, which first they adopted, respecting America, notwithstanding the perilous circumstances into which they have brought both the colonies, and our own country, they carry violently on; as if they could persuade us that perseverance was integrity; and open oppression, state necessity. Their system is not only manifestly repugnant to the laws of this state; but it runs counter to the whole stream of authority, and examples derived from the various histories of the several states of the world. From them, they ought to have learned that confidence is the first, and strongest principle of obedience; and, which once lost, is seldom recovered; and that almost all struggles for liberty, against violence, and oppression, have been crowned with success; and, without impiety, whatever doctrines concerning Providence may prevail at court, we attribute such success to the interposition of Heaven: and to Heaven the Americans now appeal. And, would to God that any accommodations could soften those rigours which your Majesty's ministers seemed determined to pursue. But it seems that no equivalent but *Liberty*, will be deemed a *sufficient satisfaction* for the affronts which the honest struggles for freedom have given: under the pretence of law, natural justice and equity fall defeated; and the constitution is wounded under the semblance of a temporary cure. Your ministers, Sir! are total strangers to those nice temperaments and allays to mitigate the evils and maladies of the state, in which much of the wisdom of government consists. They strain, where they ought to relax; and think to accomplish by exertion, what they want abilities to effect by lenient measures. They do not see these happy mediums, so necessary in the adjustments of great affairs; by which authority is preserved on the one hand, and allegiance secured on the other. These impracticable men renounce all

News" in Dixon & Hunter's *Va. Gaz.*, 14 Jan. 1775, appears an item dated 5 Nov. reading: "Such Gentlemen as have received, from their correspondents in the colonies, copies of the New York, Philadelphia, Boston, or Williamsburg editions, of the *Summary View of the Rights of British America*, may have the dedication to the King, printed with the London edition, gratis, by applying to the publisher, at No. 46 in Fleet Street."

---

expedients but power. They have recourse to arms, when they should seek only counsel. They attempt that by oppression, which justice, well administered, would more effectually accomplish. They talk of enforcing the laws, when they are violating the constitution: and urge the necessities of state, when they themselves are the authors of the very necessities of which they complain. They are for doing that in a free state, which the most despotic, in like circumstances, if wise, would carefully avoid. What is there, Sir! to countenance so great a hazard of ruining America, and distressing ourselves? of exciting them to arms, and ourselves to the slaughter of our own sons? have your ministers, Sir! discovered mines of inexhaustible riches in America, which they wish to plunder, to discharge our enormous national debt? Alas! they will find no other riches but what a strenuous industry has gained; virtue, which the love of Liberty has inspired; and a race of men not degenerate enough to part with Freedom without a noble struggle. Before their charters were violated, their laws infringed, their trade oppressed, one of their chief cities, and its inhabitants, proscribed, and military expeditions sent to awe and intimidate them, their lives and fortunes were at our disposal: can subjects offer, can they give more? I will be bold to declare to your Majesty, that before these fatal proceedings, no nation in the known history of the world, considering the growing strength, grandeur, and extent of that mighty empire, tho' dependent, could ever boast such confidence and obedience, as Great Britain did in her Colonies. These are *now* in danger of being irrecoverably lost, not by their defection, but our own unaccountable folly. *Quos Deus vult perdere, eos prius dementat.*

Your ministers, Sir! as tyrants ever do, justify their oppressions, by the resistance they have met with: and perhaps have imposed upon their Prince, by talking of the satisfaction which the honour and dignity of the crown should receive upon their supposed violation. Satisfy, Sir! the dignity and honour of the crown; but let your ministers beware that they do not sacrifice your crown to the vain, and impracticable schemes of satisfying its honour, and maintaining its dignity. I will boldly affirm, Sir, that if the dignity and honour of the crown are to be purchased at the rate your ministers seem to estimate them, that the price will be held too dear by every good, and virtuous man in the nation.

And here, Sir! pause—disappoint your ministers, and gratify millions of your subjects. The Americans have not as yet revolted. They have not thrown off their allegiance. Their submission is so *habitual*, that it cannot easily be dispensed with. Do them but *justice*, and they will esteem it an act of *Grace*. They will call that a *favour now*, which *hereafter* they will claim as their *right*. What they *now* demand, the following pages, which, with all due submission, I offer to your Majesty, will declare—hitherto they have kept themselves within proper limits; and have extended their requests no farther than they were countenanced by the laws, and that friendly protection, which, from our country, they had reason to expect. But further oppressions, Sir, may probably change their *mode* of suit. Allegiance will sometimes relax its submission. Wisdom itself does not intermeddle in the regulation of extremities; and what can moderate the conduct of despair? When dangers surround men they are not very nice in the *method* of salvation. And the *only* means of extricating themselves, will appear the *right*. When our friends rise up to oppress us, it is pardonable, and justifiable, to throw ourselves into the arms, even of an enemy, for protection.

I am,
With all due submission,
and allegiance,
Your Majesty's faithful subject,
TRIBUNUS.

At least three British periodicals noticed the appearance of *A Summary View* in their Nov. 1774 issues, but the only significant notice is that in the *Monthly Review* which was written by Edward Bancroft; this is reprinted by Ford.[14] The report that TJ's authorship of *A Summary View* led to his being added to a list of persons named in a bill of attainder passed by the House of Lords but then dropped, was always believed by TJ himself, who had his information from good sources; but it cannot be authenticated and was probably only a rumor.[15] His belief that the London editions were "shaped . . . to Opposition views" by interpolation may be explained by the fact that the preface to the London editions (whether or not written by Arthur Lee) embodies the views of the radical opposition in England. (TJ may never have seen the London pamphlet.)

In America, of course, the authorship of this patriotic and popular tract greatly enhanced TJ's reputation. He was a marked man when he arrived in Congress the following June. Samuel Ward, a Rhode Island delegate, wrote Henry Ward on 22 June 1775: "Yesterday the famous Mr. Jefferson a Delegate from Virginia in the Room of Mr. Randolph arrived, I have not been in Company with him yet, he looks like a very sensible, spirited, fine Fellow and by the Pamphlet which he wrote last Summer he certainly is one."[16] John Adams said in his "Autobiography" that TJ's appointment to the committee to draft a Declaration of Independence was in part directly owing to the repute of *A Summary View*: "Mr. Jefferson had the reputation of a masterly pen; he had been chosen a delegate in Virginia, in consequence of a very handsome public paper which he had written for the House of Burgesses, which had given him the character of a fine writer."[17] Though Adams' statement is inaccurate in details, his main point is correct: the Congress as a whole and the members of the committee individually looked with confidence to the author of *A Summary View* for a masterly declaration on the great topic assigned.

The ideas in *A Summary View* have been analyzed by TJ's biographers and by numerous students of American political thought in the age of the Revolution. A recent article by Anthony M. Lewis, "Jefferson's Summary View as a Chart of Political Union" (wmq, 3d ser., v [1948], 34-51), emphasizes the constructive features of TJ's thinking at this time and provides convenient references to previous discussions.

---

[14] I, 423. See *Monthly Review*, LI, 393; *Critical Review*, XXXVIII, 391; *London Magazine*, XLIII, 555.

[15] See TJ's Autobiography (Ford, I, 13-14), and Burk-Girardin, *Hist. of Va.*, IV, App. XII, note.

[16] Early transcript (RHi) from an unlocated original.

[17] Adams, *Works*, II, 511. For a very different appraisal of *A Summary View* by John Adams' son, see John Quincy Adams' *Memoirs*, under the dates of 15- 16 Jan. 1831 (VIII, 277-80). Adams had been reading TJ's writings in the Randolph edn. and was shocked by the apparent levity of TJ's account of "cooking up" the Fast-Day Resolution in May 1774. His strictures on TJ's proposed Instructions to the Virginia Delegates were likewise severe, for he believed neither the facts nor the reasoning in that paper to be sound, while its language was "far more insulting . . . than the famous letter of 'Junius.' "

Appendix II

"Bradshaw's Epitaph": The Source of "Rebellion to tyrants is obedience to God."

In 1828 Nicholas P. Trist, who had studied law with TJ and who in 1824 had married Virginia Jefferson Randolph, granddaughter of the President, explored the contents of an old trunk full of papers that he found in the study at Monticello. In one of the bundles, Trist came upon "the epitaph on John Bradshaw; and, in its company, copies of several letters bearing date years before the earliest of those contained among his [TJ's] papers as arranged by himself, which, to the best of my recollection, began in 1779." Trist's account of this matter, in a memorandum furnished to H. S. Randall many years later, is printed by Randall partly at I, 231-2, and partly at III, 585-6 (Appendix IV). It continues:

"The epitaph on Bradshaw, written on a narrow slip of thin paper, was a fine specimen. This has gone to France, through Gen. La Fayette, for M. De Syon,[1] a young friend of his who accompanied him on his triumphal visit to our country, and was with him at Monticello. De Syon (who afterwards did his part in the 'three days') having expressed an earnest desire to possess a piece of Mr. J.'s MS, I had promised to make his wish known at some suitable moment. But, having postponed doing so until too late, and being struck with the appropriateness of this epitaph as a present for a pupil of La Fayette (and, through him, to the mind of 'Young France'), I asked and obtained Mr. Randolph's consent to its receiving that destination.

" 'Tis evident, that the motto which we find on one of Mr. J.'s seals was taken from this epitaph, which, as we see from the note appended thereto, was supposed to be one of Dr. Franklin's *spirit-stirring* inspirations."

Then follows Trist's transcript of TJ's holograph copy of the "Epitaph," which TJ headed merely with the year when he saw and copied it. Randall's repunctuated text is reproduced below, but corrections (as indicated in the footnotes) have been made from the holograph, privately owned and not now (1949) available for publication.

1776.

The following inscription was made out, three years ago, on the cannon, near which the ashes of President Bradshaw were lodged, on the top of a high hill near Martha Bray,[2] in Jamaica, to avoid the rage against the Regicides exhibited at the Restoration:

[1] Randall erroneously prints this name as "De Lyon." Lafayette had introduced M. de Syon to TJ in a letter from New York, 13 July 1825 (*Lafayette-Jefferson Letters*, p. 434).

[2] Randall gives "Bay," a false correction by him or by Trist. Marthabrea or Martha Brae is a village with harbor in Trelawny parish, Cornwall co., northeastern Jamaica. "Bray" is the form found in the newspaper printing, 14 Dec. 1775, mentioned later in the present Appendix.

Stranger!

Ere thou pass, contemplate this cannon, nor regardless be told

That near its base lies deposited

the Dust of

JOHN BRADSHAW:

Who, nobly superior to all selfish regards,

Despising alike the pageantry of courtly splendour,

The blast of calumny, and the terrors of royal vengeance,

presided in the illustrious band

of Heroes and Patriots

who fairly and openly adjudged

CHARLES STEWART[3]

Tyrant of England,

To a public and exemplary death:

Thereby presenting to the amazed world,

And transmitting down through applauding ages,

The most glorious example

Of unshaken virtue, love of freedom, and impartial justice,

Ever exhibited in the blood-stained theatre of human actions.

Oh Reader!

Pass not on, till thou hast blest his memory,

And never—never forget,

That REBELLION TO TYRANTS IS OBEDIENCE TO GOD.

From many circumstances, there is reason to believe there does not exist any such inscription as the above, and that it was written by Dr. Franklin, in whose hands[4] it was first seen. [This note was evidently a remark by Mr. J. himself.]

Here ends Trist's memorandum. The earliest known printed text of the "Epitaph" is in Towne's *Pennsylvania Evening Post*, 14 Dec. 1775. This printing was apparently first given scholarly attention by Howard Payson Arnold, who in his *Historic Side-Lights*, N.Y. and London, 1899, p. 237-78, argued with great force and learning that the "Epitaph" was composed at this time out of whole cloth by Benjamin Franklin for propaganda purposes. Arnold's discovery was overlooked by Franklin authorities until recently, but Carl Van Doren has accepted his arguments and prints the "Epitaph" in *Benjamin Franklin's Autobiographical Writings*, N.Y., 1945, p. 412-13. Indeed, once Franklin's authorship has been suggested, it seems the most likely thing in the world. John Bradshaw (1602-1659), president of the commission that sentenced Charles I, had been praised by Milton and was in American

[3] This is TJ's spelling in the MS. The newspaper text and Randall both print "STUART."

[4] MS probably, but not certainly, reads "hand."

eyes one of the principal victims of Stuart tyranny. The evidence is incontrovertible that his body, with those of Cromwell and Ireton, was exhumed and dishonored in Jan. 1661, and there is nothing to connect him with Jamaica prior to 1775. (See DNB, which does not mention the Jamaica tradition.)

Franklin's invention, which is of a piece with numerous others he contrived, succeeded perhaps better than any of the rest, and he never divulged his authorship. The "Epitaph" was probably circulated as a broadside, for in the Appendix to the *Memoirs of Thomas Hollis*, London, 1780, II, 789, it is printed with this headnote:

"The following Epitaph is often seen pasted up in the houses in North America. It throws some light upon the principles of the people, and may in some measure account for the asperity of the war carrying on against them. The original is engraved upon a cannon at the summit of a steep hill near Martha Bray in Jamaica."

Ezra Stiles, who knew Franklin, swallowed the hoax without much qualification, for he not only copied the "Epitaph" in Jan. 1776, but quoted it in a work published in 1794, mentioning at the same time the "secret tradition" that Bradshaw was reburied in Jamaica (Stiles, *Literary Diary*, I, 649; Arnold, *Historic Side-Lights*, p. 275). Later on, one historian of Jamaica, lacking evidence for the tradition, invented some, or had some foisted on him. Arnold prints from George W. Bridges' *Annals of Jamaica* (1826) a letter giving full particulars of the reburial of Bradshaw and the cannon monument on a hill near Martha Brae. The letter is supposed to have been written by Bryan Edwards in Jan. 1775. But Bryan Edwards (1743-1800), long-time resident of Jamaica and its most trustworthy historian, had written in his *History, Civil and Commercial, of the British West Indies*, 3d edn., London, 1801, I, 213, note:

"It is reported also, that the remains of President Bradshaw were interred in Jamaica; and I observe in a splendid book, entitled *Memoirs of Thomas Hollis*, an epitaph which is said to have been inscribed on a cannon that was placed on the President's grave; but it is, to my own knowledge, a modern composition."

It is evident that TJ was much struck by the concluding line of the "Epitaph." Besides copying the whole text in 1776, he suggested "Rebellion to Tyrants . . ." as an alternative motto for the Virginia Coat of Arms (see DuSimitière's Design therefor, Aug. 1776, above); he subsequently placed the phrase upon the seal he used on his own letters (see reproduction in Randall, *Life*, II, facing frontispiece); and in a letter to Edward Everett, 24 Feb. 1823, he quoted the same phrase to justify occasional violation of syntax: "Correct it's syntax, 'Rebellion *against* tyrants is obedience to God,' it has lost all the strength and beauty of the antithesis." The ambiguity of one word in TJ's note on the "Epitaph" as he copied it in 1776 leaves us in the dark as to how TJ first encountered it. Was it in Franklin's "hand" or in his "hands"? Clearly Franklin did not admit his authorship, but just as clearly TJ considered the "Epitaph" to be Franklin's creation.

Preliminary indexes will be issued periodically for groups of volumes. A comprehensive index of persons, places, subjects, etc., arranged in a single consolidated sequence, will be issued at the conclusion of the series.

THE PAPERS OF THOMAS JEFFERSON is composed in Monticello, a type specially designed by the Mergenthaler Linotype Company for this series. Monticello is based on a type design originally developed by Binny & Ronaldson, the first successful typefounding company in America. It is considered historically appropriate here because it was used extensively in American printing during the last thirty years of Jefferson's life, 1796 to 1826; and because Jefferson himself expressed cordial approval of Binny & Ronaldson types.

Composed and printed by Princeton University Press. Illustrations are reproduced in collotype by Meriden Gravure Company, Meriden, Connecticut. Paper for the series is made by W. C. Hamilton & Sons, at Miquon, Pennsylvania; cloth for the series is made by Holliston Mills, Inc., Norwood, Massachusetts. Bound by the J. C. Valentine Company, New York.

DESIGNED BY P. J. CONKWRIGHT